THE OXFORD BIBLE READER'S DICTIONARY & CONCORDANCE

(CYCLOPEDIC CONCORDANCE)

OXFORD UNIVERSITY PRESS

Oxford University Press, Walton Street, Oxford OX2 6DP
London Glasgow New York Toronto
Delhi Bombay Calcutta Madras Karachi
Kuala Lumpur Singapore Hong Kong Tokyo
Nairobi Dar es Salaam Cape Town
Melbourne Auckland
and associates in
Beirut Berlin Ibadan Mexico City Nicosia

Printed in Great Britain
at the University Press, Oxford
by Eric Buckley
Printer to the University

NOTE

THE OXFORD BIBLE READER'S DICTIONARY & CONCORDANCE contains a selection of the *Oxford Helps to the Study of the Bible*, thoroughly revised so as to embody the results of the most recent researches. For the greater convenience of teacher and student the information given in the forty-seven alphabetical lists of the *Helps* has been rearranged in a single alphabetical order, so that any subject about which information is required may be instantly found in its proper alphabetical place, without the necessity of reference to an index, or of search in a table of contents.

But though the arrangement is that of a Dictionary the BIBLE READER'S DICTIONARY & CONCORDANCE is much more than a word-book, for many of the cyclopedic articles of the *Helps* are included, each in its alphabetical place, and wherever it is necessary cross references to these are given under the more special entries. For instance, each weight, measure, and coin is entered in its own place in the general alphabetical order, and under each entry a reference is given to the general articles, such as Weights, Measures, or Coins, in which further information will be found.

In this edition the text and maps remain as before, but a new and improved set of illustrations has been included, selected from various sources with the assistance of Mr. John Stirling, to whom the publishers express their gratitude.

KEY TO PRONUNCIATION

THE syllable on which the accent falls is followed by the sign. The other signs have the following meanings:

ä *as in* ah, arm, father
ă „ abet, hat, dilemma
ā „ tame
â „ fare
ĕ „ met, her, second
ē „ mete
ë „ tame
e *unmarked is mute as in* site
ī *as in* fine
ĭ „ him, fir, plentiful
ï „ machine
ị „ peculiar
ō „ alone
ŏ „ on, protect
ô „ nor
ọ „ son
ū „ tune
û „ rude
ŭ „ us
ü „ turner

ȳ *as in* lyre
y̆ „ typical, fully
a̅a̅ = ă *of* am
a͡a = â (as in fare)
a̅e̅ *as in* mediaeval
æ *(unmarked) similar but unaccented*
a͡i *as in* aisle
ai „ hail
a̅o̅ = o *of* alone
a͡u *as in* maul
e͡e „ heed
e͡i = i *of* fine
e͡u *as in* neuter
e̅w̅ „ few
o͡i „ oil
ç „ celestial
ch „ character
ġ „ giant
ṡ „ his
s̅i̅ „ Asia

SUMMARY OF CONTENTS

LIST OF ILLUSTRATIONS

THE OXFORD BIBLE READER'S DICTIONARY AND CONCORDANCE (CYCLOPEDIC CONCORDANCE)

Aaron, ȃa′-ron, BROTHER of MOSES, the FIRST HIGH PRIEST, cometh forth to meet Moses; can speak well.
appointed by God to be Moses' spokesman. Ex. 4. 14–16, 27. [Ex. 5. 1, 4.
with Moses appeals to Pharaoh; chided by him.
his rod becomes a serpent. Ex. 7. 10.
changes the waters into blood. Ex. 7. 20.
causes the plagues of frogs, lice, flies. Ex. 8. 5, 17, 24.
with Moses—the plague of boils. Ex. 9. 10.
with Hur holds up Moses' hands. Ex. 17. 12.
set apart for priest's office. Ex. 28.
makes the golden calf. Ex. 32. 4; God's anger thereat. Ex. 32. 7; Deu. 9. 20.
his excuse to Moses. Ex. 32. 22.
consecration. Ex. 29.; Lev. 8.
offers sacrifice. Lev. 9.
his sons (Nadab and Abihu) offer strange fire, and die. Lev. 10. 1; Num. 3. 4.
his sons (Eleazar and Ithamar) censured by Moses. Lev. 10. 16.
not to drink wine when going into the tabernacle. Lev. 10. 8.
speaks against Moses. Num. 12.
rebuked by God. Num. 12. 9.
spoken against by Korah. Num. 16. 3.
makes atonement, and the plague is stayed. Num. 16. 46–48.
his rod buds, and is kept in ark for a token. Num. 17. 8
for unbelief excluded from the promised land. Num. 20. 12.
dies on mount Hor. Num. 20. 28.
chosen by God. Ps. 105. 26; Heb. 5. 4.
his line. 1 Chr. 6. 49.

Aaronites, ȃa′-ron-ītes, descendants of Aaron. 1 Chr. 12. 27.

Ab, the fifth month of the Jewish sacred year, = August. Ez. 7. 9. *See* MONTHS.

Abaddon, ă-băd′-dŏn, 'destruction;' angel of the bottomless pit. Rev. 9. 11.

Abagtha, ă-băg′-thă, 'given by fortune.' Esth. 1. 10.

Abana, ăb′-ă-nă, same as AMANA; river of Damascus. 2 Kn. 5. 12. R. V. Abanah.

Abarim, ăb′-ă-rĭm, 'regions beyond.' Num. 27. 12. mountains of, including Nebo, Pisgah, Hor. Num. 33. 47, 48; Deu. 32. 49.

Abase. Ezek. 21. 26, and *a.* him that is high.
Dan. 4. 37, walk in pride, he is able to *a.*
Mat. 23. 12; Lu. 14. 11; 18. 14, whosoever exalteth himself shall be *a.* R. V. humbled.
Phil. 4. 12, I know how to be *a.*
See Job 40. 11; Isa. 31. 4; 2 Cor. 11. 7. [8. 3.

Abated. Gen. 8. 3; Lev. 27. 18; Deu. 34. 7; Jud.

Abba, ăb′-bă, 'father.' Mk. 14. 36; Rom. 8. 15; Gal. 4. 6. [11. 17.

Abda, ăb′-dă, 'servant.' (1) 1 Kn. 4. 6. (2) Neh.

Abdeel, ăb′-deel, same as ABDIEL. Jer. 36. 26.

Abdi, ăb′-dī, 'my servant.' (1) 1 Chr. 6. 44. (2) 2 Chr. 29. 12. (3) Ez. 10. 26.

Abdiel, ăb′-dĭ-ĕl, '*s.* of God.' 1 Chr. 5. 15.

Abdon, ăb′-dŏn, 'servile.' (1) A judge. Jud. 12. 13. (2) 1 Chr. 8. 30. (3) 2 Chr. 34. 20. (4) 1 Chr. 8. 23. [1. 7.

Abed-nego, ă-bĕd′-nĕ-gō, 'servant of Nebo.' Dan. saved in fiery furnace. Dan. 3. *See* Isa. 43. 2.

Abel, ā′-bĕl. (1) 'a son,' or, 'vanity;' second son of Adam. Gen. 4. 2.
his offering accepted. Gen. 4. 4.
slain by Cain. Gen. 4. 8.
righteous. Mat. 23. 35; 1 John 3. 12.
blood of. Lu. 11, 51; Heb. 12. 24.
faith of. Heb. 11. 4.
(2) A meadow. 2 Sam. 20. 14.

Abel-beth-maachah, ā′-bĕl-bĕth-mā′-ă-chăh, 'meadow of the house of Maachah.' 1 Kn. 15. 20; 2 Kn. 15. 29.

Abel-maim, ā′-bĕl-mā′-ĭm, 'meadow of the waters.' 2 Chr. 16. 4.

Abel-meholah, ā′-bĕl-mĕ-hō′-lăh, '*m.* of dancing.' Jud. 7. 22; 1 Kn. 4. 12; 19. 16.

Abel-mizraim, ā′-bĕl-mĭz′-rā-ĭm, '*m.* of Egypt;' mourning of the Egyptians. Gen. 50. 11.

Abel-shittim, ā′-bĕl-shĭt′-tĭm, '*m.* of acacias.' Num. 33. 49.

Abez, ā′-bĕz. Jos. 19. 20. R. V. Ebez.

Abhor. Ex. 5. 21, made our savour to be *a.*
Job 19. 19, my inward friends *a.*
Ps. 78. 59, God wroth, and *a.* Israel.
89. 38, thou hast cast off and *a.* R. V. rejected.
107. 18, soul *a.* all manner of meat.
119. 163, I hate and *a.* lying.
Prov. 22. 14. *a.* of the Lord shall fall therein.
Isa. 7. 16, land thou *a.* shall be forsaken.
66. 24, they shall be an *a.* unto all flesh.
Ezek. 16. 25, beauty to be *a.* R. V. an abomination.
Am. 6. 8, I *a.* the excellency of Jacob.
See Lev. 26. 11; Job 42. 6; Rom. 12. 9.

Abi, ā′-bī, shortened form of ABIAH. 2 Kn. 18. 2.

Abia, ă-bī′-ă, Greek form of following. Mat. 1. 7.

Abiah, ă-bī′-ăh. (1) same as ABIJAH. 2 Kn. 18. 2. (2) 1 Chr. 2. 24.

Abi-albon, ā′-bī-ăl′-bŏn. 2 Sam. 23. 31.

Abiasaph, ă-bī′-ă-săph, 'my father has gathered.' Ex. 6. 24.

Abiathar, ă-bī′-ă-thăr, 'the Great One is father.' 1 Sam. 22. 20.

Abib, ā′-bĭb, 'an ear of corn,' or 'green ear;' the first month of the Jewish sacred year = April. Ex. 12. 2; 13. 4. *See* MONTHS.
the Hebrew passover month. Ex. 23. 15; 34. 18.

Abida, ă-bī′-dă, the same as ABIDAH. 1 Chr. 1. 33.

Abidah, ă-bī′-dăh, 'my father took knowledge.' Gen. 25. 4.

Abidan, ă-bī′-dăn, 'my *f.* is judge.' Num. 1. 11.

Abide. (1) *trans.* await, wait for.
Joel 2. 11, day very terrible, who can *a.* it.
Acts 20. 23, bonds and afflictions *a.* me.
(2) *intr.* dwell, remain.
Gen. 44. 33, let servant *a.* instead of lad.
Ex. 16. 29, *a.* every man in his place. [ing.
Num. 24. 2, he saw Israel *a.* in tents. R. V. dwell-
31. 19, *a.* without camp seven days. R. V. encamp.

1 Sam. 5. 7, ark of God not *a*. with us.
Job 24. 13, nor *a*. in the paths thereof.
Ps. 15. 1, Lord who shall *a*. in thy tabernacle. R. V. sojourn.
91. 1, shall *a*. under the shadow.
Prov. 15. 31, ear that heareth reproof *a*. among wise.
Eccl. 1. 4, the earth *a*. for ever.
Jer. 42. 10, if ye will still *a*. in this land. [dwell.
49. 18, 33; 50. 40, there shall no man *a*. R. V.
Hos. 3. 3, thou shalt *a*. many days.
Mat. 10. 11; Mk. 6. 10; Lu. 9. 4, there *a*. till ye go.
Lu. 2. 8, shepherds *a*. in field.
19. 5. to-day I must *a*. at thy house.
24. 29, *a*. with us, it is toward evening.
John 3. 36, wrath of God *a*. on him.
5. 38, not his word *a*. in you.
14. 16, another Comforter that he may *a*.
15. 4, *a*. in me.
5, he that *a*. in me bringeth.
10, *a*. in my love.
Acts 16. 15, come to my house and *a*.
1 Cor. 3. 14, if any man's work *a*.
13. 13, now *a*. faith, hope, charity.
2 Tim. 2. 13, if we believe not he *a*.
See Gen. 29. 19; Num. 35. 25; Eccl. 8. 15.

Abiel, ā-bī'-ĕl, 'God is my *f*.' (1) 1 Sam. 9. 1; 1 Chr. 8. 33. (2) 1 Chr. 11. 32. R. V. Abi-Albon.

Abiezer, ā-bī-ē'-zĕr, 'my *f*. is help.' (1) ancestor of Gideon. Jos. 17. 2; Jud. 6. (2) 2 Sam. 23. 27.

Abiezrite, ā'-bī-ĕz'-rīte, a descendant of ABIEZER. Jud. 6. 11.

Abigail, ăb'-ĭ-gail, 'my father is joy.' (1) wife of Nabal, and afterwards of David. 1 Sam. 25. 14, 39.
mother of Chileab, according to 2 Sam. 3. 3, or Daniel, according to 1 Chr. 3. 1.
(2) 1 Chr. 2. 16; 2 Sam. 17. 25. [3. 35.

Abihail, ăb'-ĭ-hail, 'my father is strength.' Num.

Abihu, ā-bī'-hū, 'He (*i. e.* God) is father;' son of Aaron. Ex. 6. 23.
offers strange fire, and dies. Lev. 10. 2.

Abihud, ā-bī'-hŭd, 'my father is majesty.' 1 Chr. 8. 3.

Abijah, ā-bī'-jăh, 'Jehovah is my *f*.' (1) king of Judah, walked in the sins of his *f*. 1 Kn. 15. 3.
makes war against Israel. 2 Chr. 13.
(2) son of Jeroboam, his death foretold by Ahijah the prophet. 1 Kn. 14. 1-12. [Kn. 14. 31.

Abijam, ā-bī'-jăm, another spelling of ABIJAH. 1

Abilene, ăb-ĭ-lē'-nē, 'a grassy place' (?). Lu. 3. 1.

Ability. Ez. 2. 69, they gave after their *a*.
Dan. 1. 4, had *a*. to stand in the palace.
Mat. 25. 15, to each according to *a*.
1 Pet. 4. 11, the *a*. God giveth. R. V. strength.
See Lev. 27. 8; Neh. 5. 8; Acts 11. 29. [10. 28.

Abimael, ā-bĭm'-ā-ĕl, 'a father is God' (?). Gen.

Abimelech, ā-bĭm'-ĕ-lĕch, 'Melech is *f*.' Gen. 20. 2.
(1) king of Gerar; reproved by God about Abraham's wife. Gen. 20. 3. [9, 14.
rebukes Abraham and restores Sarah. Gen. 20.
healed at Abraham's prayer. Gen. 20. 17.
(2) another; Isaac rebuked by, for denying his wife. Gen. 26. 10.
covenants with Isaac. Gen. 26. 28. [Jud. 8. 31.
(3) king at Shechem; son of the judge Gideon.
murders his brethren. Jud. 9. 5.
his death. Jud. 9. 54.

Abinadab, ā-bĭn'-ā-dăb, 'my father is noble.' (1) 1 Sam. 7. 1.
receives the ark from Philistines. 2 Sam. 6. 3.
(2) 1 Sam. 16. 8. (3) 1 Sam. 31. 2. (4) 1 Kn. 4. 11.

Abiner, ăb'-ĭ-nĕr, same as ABNER. 1 Sam. 14. 50 (marg.). [Jud. 4. 6.

Abinoam, ā-bĭn'-ō-ăm, 'my father is delight.'

Abiram, ā-bī'-răm, 'the High One is my *f*.' or, 'my *f*. is lofty.' (1) Num. 16. 1. [Num. 16.
with Korah and Dathan, rebels against Moses.
his punishment. Num. 16. 31; 26. 10.
(2) 1 Kn. 16. 34.

Abishag, ăb'-ĭ-shăg, 'my father is a wanderer;' the Shunammite, ministers to David. 1 Kn. 1. 3.
cause of breach between Solomon and Adonijah. 1 Kn. 2. 22.

Abishai, ăb'-ĭ-shâi, 'my father is Jesse;' brother of Joab. 1 Sam. 26. 6; 1 Chr. 2. 16. [6-9.
with David carries off Saul's spear. 1 Sam. 26.
slays three hundred men. 2 Sam. 23. 18. *See also* 1 Chr. 11. 20; 18. 12. [1 Kn. 15. 2.

Abishalom, ā-bī'-shā-lŏm, 'my father is peace.'

Abishua, ā-bī'-shū-ā, 'my *f*. is wealth.' (1) 1 Chr. 6. 4. (2) 1 Chr. 8. 4. [28.

Abishur, ā-bī'-shûr, 'my *f*. is a wall.' 1 Chr. 2.

Abital, ā-bī'-tăl, 'my *f*. is the dew.' 2 Sam. 3. 4.

Abitub, ā-bī'-tŭb, 'my *f*. is goodness.' 1 Chr. 8. 11. [13.

Abiud, ā-bī'-ŭd, Greek form of ABIHUD. Mat. 1.

Abjects, outcasts, despised persons. Ps. 35. 15, the *a*. gathered themselves together. R. V. smiters.

Able. Ex. 18. 21, provide able men.
Deu. 16. 17, every man give as he is *a*.
Jos. 23. 9, no man *a*. to stand before you. R. V. hath stood.
1 Sam. 6. 20, who is *a*. to stand before God.
1 Kn. 3. 9, who is *a*. to judge.
2 Chr. 2. 6, who is *a*. to build.
Prov. 27. 4, who is *a*. to stand before envy.
Am. 7. 10, land not *a*. to bear his words.
Mat. 3. 9, God is *a*. of these stones.
9. 28, believe ye that I am *a*.
20. 22, are ye *a*. to drink of cup.
Lu. 12. 26, not *a*. to do least.
Acts 6. 10, not *a*. to resist wisdom.
Rom. 4. 21, what he had promised he was *a*.
8. 39, *a*. to separate us from love of God.
1 Cor. 10. 13, tempted above that ye are *a*.
2 Cor. 3. 6, *a*. ministers of new testament. R. V. sufficient as.
Eph. 3. 18, *a*. to comprehend with all saints. R. V. strong.
Phil. 3. 21, *a*. to subdue all things.
Heb. 2. 18, *a*. to succour tempted.
Jas. 4. 12, *a*. to save and destroy.
Jude 24, *a*. to keep you from falling.
Rev. 5. 3, no man *a*. to open book.
6. 17, who shall be *a*. to stand.

Abner, ăb'-nĕr, 'my father is Ner;' cousin of Saul, commander of his army. 1 Sam. 14. 50.
reproved by David. 1 Sam. 26. 5, 14.
makes Ish-bosheth king. 2 Sam. 2. 8.
goes over to David. 2 Sam. 3. 8.
slain by Joab. 2 Sam. 3. 27.
mourned by David. 2 Sam. 3. 31.

Aboard. Acts 21. 2. [our *a*.

Abode. (1) *n*. John 14. 23, we will come and make
See 2 Kn. 19. 27; Isa. 37. 28.
(2) *v*. Gen. 49. 24, his bow *a*. in strength.
Ex. 24. 16, glory of the Lord *a*. on Sinai. [sat.
Jud. 21. 2, the people *a*. there before God. R. V.
Ez. 8. 15, *a*. we in tents. R. V. encamped.
Lu. 1. 56, Mary *a*. with her three months.
John 1. 32, the Spirit, and it *a*. on him.
39, they came and *a*. with him. [stood.
8. 44, a murderer, and *a*. not in truth. R. V.
Acts 14. 3, long time *a*., speaking boldly. R. V. tarried.
18. 3, Paul *a*. with them and wrought.

Abolish. 2 Cor. 3. 13, the end of that which is *a*. R. V. was passing away.
Eph. 2. 15, *a*. in his flesh the enmity.
2 Tim. 1. 10, Christ, who hath *a*. death.
See Isa. 2. 18; 51. 6; Ezek. 6. 6. [idols.

Abominable. 1 Kn. 21. 26, Ahab *a*. in following
Job. 15. 16, how much more *a*. is man.
Ps. 14. 1; 53. 1, they have done *a*. works.
Isa. 14. 19, cast out like *a*. branch.
65. 4; Jer. 16. 18, broth of *a*. things.
Jer. 44. 4, this *a*. thing that I hate.
Tit. 1. 16, in works they deny him, being *a*.
1 Pet. 4. 3, walked in *a*. idolatries.

Abomination, a hateful thing, hence, often, an idol, object of worship (Ex. 8. 26).
Gen. 43. 32; 46. 34, *a*. to Egyptians.
Lev. 18. 26, shall not commit any *a*.

Deu. 7. 26, nor bring *a.* into house.
18. 9, after the *a.* of nations.
12, because of *a.* the Lord doth drive.
25. 16, do unrighteously are *a.* to God.
1 Sam. 13. 4, Israel had in *a.* with Philistines.
Prov. 3. 32; 11. 20, froward *a.* to the Lord.
8. 7, wickedness an *a.* to my lips.
15. 8, 9, 26; 21. 27, sacrifice, etc. of wicked are *a.*
28. 9, even his prayer shall be *a.*
Isa. 44. 19, residue thereof an *a.*
Jer. 4. 1, put away thine *a.* out of sight.
6. 15; 8. 12, ashamed when committed *a.*
Ezek. 5. 9, the like, because of all thine *a.*
33. 29, land desolate because of *a.* [tion.
Dan. 11. 31; Mat. 24. 15; Mk. 13. 14, *a.* of desola-
Lu. 16. 15, esteemed among men *a.* with God.
Rev. 21. 27, in no wise enter that worketh *a.*

Abomination, of desolation. Dan. 9. 27; 11. 31; 12. 11; Mat. 24. 15; Mk. 13. 14.
national. Deu. 18. 9, 12; Ezek. 5. 11; 7.; 8. 6; 11. 18; 16. 22; Hos. 6. 10.
of offerings. Lev. 7. 18; Deu. 17. 1; 23. 18; Prov. 15. 8; Isa. 1. 13.
prayer of the wicked. Prov. 28. 9.
impurity. Lev. 18. 22; 20. 13.
defilement. Lev. 11. 43; Deu. 24. 4; 1 Kn. 11. 5; Prov. 16. 12; Isa. 66. 17; Ezek. 16; Rev. 21. 8, 27.
falsity. Prov. 11. 1; 17. 15; 20. 10, 23.
idolatry. Deu. 7. 25, 26; 27. 15; 2 Kn. 23. 13; Jer. 2. 7; Ezek. 18. 12; Mal. 2. 11.
pride. Prov. 6. 16; 16. 5.
froward. Prov. 3. 32; 11. 20. R. V. perverse.

Abound. Prov. 28. 20, faithful shall *a.* with blessings.
Rom. 15. 13, that ye may *a.* in hope.
1 Cor. 15. 58, always *a.* in work.
2 Cor. 1. 5, as sufferings *a.* so consolation *a.*
See Rom. 3. 7; 5. 15; Phil. 4. 12.

Above. Deu. 28. 13, *a.* only and not beneath.
Job 31. 2, portion of God from *a.* [upward.
Prov. 15. 24, way of life *a.* to wise. R. V. goeth
Mat. 10. 24; Lu. 6. 40, disciple not *a.* master.
John 3. 31, cometh from *a.* is *a.* all.
8. 23, I am from *a.*
Rom. 14. 5, one day *a.* another.
1 Cor. 4. 6, *a.* that which is written. R. V. beyond.
Gal. 4. 26, Jerusalem *a.* is free.
See Gen. 48. 22; Ps. 138. 2; Jas. 1. 17.

Abraham, ā'-bră-hăm, 'father of a multitude.' Gen. 17. 5.
(Abram) begotten by Terah. Gen. 11. 27.
blessed by God, and sent to Canaan. Gen. 12. 5.
goes down to Egypt. Gen. 12. 10. [20. 2.
causes his wife to pass as his sister. Gen. 12. 13;
strife between him and Lot. Gen. 13. 7.
separates from Lot. Gen. 13. 11. [16.
his seed to be as the dust of the earth. Gen. 13.
delivers Lot from captivity, and refuses the spoil. Gen. 14. 16. [19; Heb. 7. 4.
blessed by Melchizedek, king of Salem. Gen. 14.
his faith counted for righteousness. Gen. 15. 6.
God's covenant with. Gen. 15. 18; Ps. 105. 9.
he and house circumcised. Gen. 17.
entertains angels. Gen. 18.
pleads for Sodom. Gen. 18. 23.
sends away Hagar and Ishmael. Gen. 21. 14.
his faith in offering Isaac. Gen. 22.
buys Machpelah of Ephron the Hittite for a burying-place. Gen. 23.
sends for a wife for his son. Gen. 24.
gives his goods to Isaac. Gen. 25. 5.
dies (in a good old age). Gen. 25. 8.
his faith and works. Isa. 41. 8; 51. 2; John 8. 33; Acts 7. 2; Rom. 4.; Gal. 3. 6; Heb. 11. 8; Jas. 2. 21.
his posterity. Gen. 25. 1.

Abram, ā'-brăm, 'a lofty father.' Gen. 11. 26.

Absalom, ăb'-să-lom, 'my *f.* is peace;' David's son. 2 Sam. 3. 3.
slays Amnon. 2 Sam. 13. 28.
conspires against David. 2 Sam. 15.
David flies from. 2 Sam. 15. 17.
caught by head in an oak. 2 Sam. 18. 9.
slain by Joab. 2 Sam. 18. 14.
wept by David. 2 Sam. 18. 33; 19. 1.

Absent. 1 Cor. 5. 3; Col. 2. 5, *a.* in body.
2 Cor. 5. 6, *a.* from Lord.
See Gen. 31. 49; 2 Cor. 10. 1. [idols.

Abstain. Acts 15. 20, 29, *a.* from pollutions of
1 Thes. 5. 22, *a.* from all appearance of evil.
1 Pet. 2. 11, *a.* from fleshly lusts.
See 1 Thes. 4. 3; 1 Tim. 4. 3.

Abstinence. Acts. 27. 21, after long *a.* Paul stood forth. R. V. long without food. [plaint.

Abundance. 1 Sam. 1. 16, out of *a.* of my com-
1 Kn. 18. 41, sound of *a.* of rain.
1 Chr. 29. 21, offered sacrifices in *a.*
Ps. 52. 7, trusted in *a.* of riches.
72. 7; Jer. 33. 6. *a.* of peace.
Eccl. 5. 10, loveth *a.* with increase.
5. 12, *a.* of rich not suffer to sleep. R. V. fulness.
Mat. 12. 34, out of *a.* of heart.
13. 12; 25. 29, he shall have more *a.*
Lu. 12. 15, life consisteth not in *a.*
Lu. 21. 4, of their *a.* R. V. superfluity.
2 Cor. 8. 2, of affliction the *a.* of their joy.
12. 7, through *a.* of revelations. R. V. exceeding greatness.
See Job 36. 31; Rom. 5. 17; Rev. 18. 3.

Abundant. Job 36. 28, clouds drop and distil *a.*
Ps. 145. 7, *a.* utter the memory. R. V. omits.
Isa. 56. 12, as this day and more *a.* R. V. great beyond measure. [all.
1 Cor. 15. 10; 2 Cor. 11. 23, laboured more *a.* than
1 Tim. 1. 14, grace was exceeding *a.*
Tit. 3. 6, shed *a.* through Jesus Christ. R. V. richly. [richly.
2 Pet. 1. 11, entrance administered *a.* R. V.
See Ex. 34. 6; Isa. 55. 7; 1 Pet. 1. 3.

Abuse. 1 Cor. 7. 31, use world as not *a.* R. V. (marg.) using it to the full.
9. 18, that I *a.* not my power. R. V. so as not to use it to the full.
See Jud. 19. 25; 1 Sam. 31. 4; 1 Chr. 10. 4.

Accad, ăc'-căd. Gen. 10. 10.

Accept. Gen. 4. 7, shalt thou not be *a.* [ing.
Lev. 10. 19, *a.* before the Lord. R. V. well pleas-
Deu. 33. 11, *a.* the work of his hands.
1 Sam. 18. 5, *a.* in sight of all people. R. V. good.
2 Sam. 24. 23, the Lord thy God *a.* thee.
Esth. 10. 3, *a.* of his brethren. [respect.
Job. 13. 8; 32. 21, will ye *a.* his person. R. V.
42. 8, 9, him will I *a.*
Prov. 18. 5, not good to *a.* wicked.
Jer. 14. 12; Am. 5. 22, I will not *a.* them.
37. 20; 42. 2, supplication be *a.*
Ezek. 20. 40; 43. 27, I will *a.*
Mal. 1. 13, should I *a.* this.
Lu. 4. 24, no prophet is *a.*
Acts 10. 35, he that worketh righteousness is *a.*
Rom. 15. 31, service *a.* of saints.
2 Cor. 5. 9, present or absent we may be *a.* R. V. well pleasing.
See Ps. 119. 108; Eccl. 12. 10; Mal. 1. 8.

Access to God by faith. Rom. 5. 2; Eph. 2. 18; 3. 12; Heb. 7. 19; 10. 19. *See* Isa. 55. 6; Hos. 14. 2; Joel 2. 12; John 14. 6; Jas. 4. 8. [31. 6.
its blessedness, Ps. 65. 4; 73. 28; Isa. 2. 3; Jer.

Accho, ăc'-chō, 'hot sand;' later Gr. name, Ptolemais (Acts 21. 7). A seaport north of Mt. Carmel, Jud. 1. 31.

Accomplish. Job 14. 6, *a.* as an hireling.
Ps. 64. 6, they *a.* diligent search.
Prov. 13. 19, desire *a.* is sweet.
Isa. 40. 2, her warfare is *a.*
Lu. 12. 50, straitened till it be *a.*
1 Pet. 5. 9, afflictions are *a.* in brethren.
See Isa. 55. 11; Lu. 18. 31; 22. 37.

Accord. Acts 1. 14; 4. 24; 8. 6; Phil. 2. 2.
Acts 2. 1, with one *a.* R. V. together.

According. Ex. 12. 25, *a.* as he hath promised.
Deu. 16. 10, *a.* as God hath blessed thee.
Job. 34. 11; Jer. 17. 10; 32. 19, *a.* to ways.
Jer. 26. 14; Mat. 16. 27; Rom. 2. 6; 2 Tim. 4. 14, *a.* to works.
John 7. 24, *a.* to the appearance.

Acts, Chronology of; with the Pauline Epistles.

Dates according to recent schemes.

A. D. Lewin.	Events.	Contemporary History, A. D.	Hastings' B. D.	Ramsay.	Lightfoot.	Blass.	Harnack.	Encyc. Biblica.	Weizsäcker.
30	The Pentecost of Acts 2	Tiberius, Emperor, 14–37. *Pontius Pilate, Procurator*, 26.	29–30	30	30	29	29–30	30	30
31	Spread of the Gospel at Jerusalem	}	30–35						
35	Preaching of Stephen	}							
36	Martyrdom of Stephen	Deposition of Pilate, 36	36	33	34	30 ?	30	31–35	35
37	Conversion of Saul of Tarsus	Death of Tiberius, 16 March, A. D. 37. Accession of Caligula.	36	33	34	30 ?	30	31–35	35
38	His retirement to Arabia (Gal. 1. 17)	Release of Herod Agrippa I.							
	Philip converts the Samaritans and the Ethiopian eunuch (Acts 8.).								
39	Herod Antipas banished to Gaul. His dominions given to Herod Agrippa I.	Caligula orders his statue to be set up at Jerusalem.							
40	Circuit of St. Peter	Seneca, 4 B. C.–65 A. D.							
	Conversion of Cornelius.								
41	Herod Agrippa I., King (Acts 12. 1) of Judæa and Samaria	Claudius becomes emperor, 24 Jan., 41; continues till 13 Oct., 54.							
42	Spread of the Church to Antioch.								
	The disciples first called Christians *at Antioch* (Acts 11. 26).	Seneca in exile, 41–49.							
44	Persecution by Herod Agrippa	Romans in Britain, 43.							
	Martyrdom of St. James.								
	Imprisonment of St. Peter.								
	Death of Herod Agrippa (Acts 12. 23)	*Cuspius Fadus, Procurator*	44	44	44	44	44	44	44
45	*First Missionary Journey of Saul and Barnabas* (Acts 13., 14.)	London founded, 57.	47	47	48	45	45		
46	Their return to Antioch	*Tiberius Alexander, Procurator*	49	50	51	46	47		
48	The Judaisers at Antioch	*Ventidius Cumanus, Procurator.*							
	Council at Jerusalem (Lewin)	Expulsion of the Jews from Rome, 48 ?	49	50	51	47	47	45 or 49	52
49	*St. Paul's Second Missionary Journey with Silas* (Acts 16.–18.)	....	49	50	....	48	46		
51	He comes to Macedonia.								
52	St. Paul at Corinth	*Felix, Procurator*, 52–59	late in 50	late in 51	late in 52	......	late in 48	summer, 47–49 or 49–53	
	The Epistles to the Thessalonians.								
53	St. Paul leaves Corinth and sails to Ephesus	Gallio, proconsul of Achaia.							
	At Jerusalem at the Feast of Tabernacles.	....	52	53	....	50	49	53	
54	Return to Antioch	Claudius dies. Accession of Nero, 54.							
	St. Paul's Third Missionary Journey	....	52	53	....	50	49		
54–57	At Ephesus	Birth of Tacitus, 55.							
57	*First Epistle to the Corinthians.*								

	Riot at Ephesus.								
	Leaves for Troas, comes to Macedonia....	....	55	56	57	......	53		
	Second Epistle to the Corinthians.								
	Reaches Corinth and stays three months.								
58	*Epistle to the Galatians.*								
	Epistle to the Romans.								
	Leaves Corinth for Jerusalem....	....	56	57	58	54	53	54 or 58	
	Arrest in the Temple.								
	Sent to Cæsarea (Acts 23. 23).								
59	Interview with Felix (Acts 24.)..........	Nero murders Agrippina.							
60	St. Paul before Festus and Agrippa.......	Recall of Felix. *Porcius Festus, Procurator*, 59.							
	Appeals to Cæsar (Acts 25. 11).								
	Sails for Rome (Acts 27.).								
	Shipwreck at Malta.								
61	St. Paul reaches Rome, and lives in his own hired house (Acts 28.)	Rebellion of Boadicea in Britain.....	59	60	61	56	57	57 or 61	61
62	Writes his Epistles to *the Philippians, the*								
63	*Colossians, Philemon, and the Ephesians*	Great earthquake at Pompeii........	61	62	63	......	59	59 or 63	
	St. Paul is heard, and released..........	*Albinus, Procurator.*							
	Epistle to the Hebrews (?).								
	Goes to Asia by way of Macedonia.								
64	Sails with Titus to Crete, and returns to Ephesus.	*Great Fire of Rome, ascribed by Nero to the Christians*, 19 July, 64.							
	Leaving Timothy there, he goes by Philippi to Corinth............................	*Gessius Florus, Procurator.*							
	First Epistle to Timothy.								
	Epistle to Titus.								
	Winters at Nicopolis.								
65	Journey to Dalmatia (?), and through Macedonia to Troas.								
	Apprehension. Sent to Rome.								
66	First Trial before the Emperor	The Jewish War begins.							
	Second Epistle to Timothy..............	Massacre by Florus at Jerusalem.							
	Martyrdom of St. Paul..................	Repulse of Cestius Gallus..........	64, 65	66, 67	67	67, 68	64	July or Aug. 64	
70	Destruction of Jerusalem.								

NOTE. — The dates in the left-hand column are from Lewin. Those in the first right-hand column are very nearly in accord with those of Mr. C. H. Turner in Dr. Hastings' *Dictionary of the Bible*, and not far from the average of the leading authorities. Dates are also given from a number of leading scholars to show the variation of opinions, usually within narrow limits, and that we must be "content with what Harnack describes as relative rather than absolute chronology." The dates of secular events are derived originally from Tacitus, Josephus, and Eusebius. These do not in all cases agree, although there are considerations, such as the different times of beginning the year, which may bring them closer together. But the dates are abundantly accurate for all practical purposes.

ACT

Rom. 8. 28, called *a.* to his purpose.
Rom. 12. 6, gifts differing *a.* to grace.
2 Cor. 8. 12, *a.* to that a man hath.
See Mat. 9. 29; Tit. 3. 5.
Account. Mat. 12. 36, give *a.* in day of judgment.
Lu. 16. 2, give *a.* of stewardship.
20. 35, *a.* worthy to obtain.
Rom. 14. 12, every one give *a.* to God.
Gal. 3. 6, *a.* to him for righteousness. R. V. reckoned.
Heb. 13. 17, watch as they that give *a.*
See Job 33. 13; Ps. 144. 3; 1 Pet. 4. 5.
Accursed. Jos. 6. 18; 7. 1; 22. 20; 1 Chr. 2. 7, *a.* thing. R. V. devoted.
Rom. 9. 3, wish myself *a.* from Christ.
1 Cor. 12. 3, no man calleth Jesus *a.*
Gal. 1. 8, 9, preach other gospel, let him be *a.* R. V. anathema, in N. T.
Accursed, what so called. Deu. 21. 23; Jos. 6. 17; 7. 1; 1 Chr. 2. 7; Isa. 65. 20; Gal. 1. 8.
Accusation. Lu. 19. 8, any thing by false *a.* R. V. wrongfully.
1 Tim. 5. 19, against elder receive not *a.*
2 Pet. 2. 11; Jude 9, railing *a.* R. V. judgement.
See Mat. 27. 37; Mk. 15. 26; Lu. 6. 7.
Accuse. Prov. 30. 10, *a.* not servant to his master. R. V. slander.
Mat. 27. 12, when *a.* he answered nothing.
Lu. 16. 1, was *a.* that he had wasted.
John 5. 45, I will *a.* you to the Father.
Tit. 1. 6, not *a.* of riot or unruly.
See Mat. 12. 10; Mk. 3. 2; Lu. 11. 54; Rev. 12. 10.
Accuser. Job 1. 6; Zech 3. 1; 2 Tim. 3. 3.
Aceldama, ă-çĕl'-dă-mă, 'field of blood.' Mat. 27. 8; Acts 1. 19.
Achaia, ă-chā'-ă, Greece (without Thessaly). [Acts 18. 12.
Paul in. Acts 18.
contribution for poor by. Rom. 15. 26; 2 Cor. [9. 2.
See 1 Cor. 16. 15; 2 Cor. 11. 10.
Achaicus, ă-chā'-ĭ-cŭs, 'belonging to Achaia.' 1 Cor. 16. 17.
Achan, or **Achar,** ā'-chăn, ā'-chär, 'he troubled.' takes the accursed thing; is stoned. Jos. 7.; 22. 20; 1 Chr. 2. 7.
Achaz, ā'-chăz, Greek form of AHAZ. Mat. 1. 9.
Achbor, ăch'-bôr, 'a mouse.' Gen. 36. 38.
Achim, ā'-chĭm, short form of JACHIN. Mat. 1. 14.
Achish, ā'-chĭsh, 'angry' (?); king of Gath, succours David. 1 Sam. 21. 10; 27. 2; 28. 1; 29. 6. *See* 1 Kn. 2. 39.
Achmetha, ăch-mē'-thă. Ez. 6. 2.
Achor, ā'-chôr, 'trouble;' valley of, Achan slain there. Jos. 7. 26. *See* Hos. 2. 15.
Achsa, ăch'-să, same as following. 1 Chr. 2. 49.
Achsah, ăch'-săh, 'anklet;' Caleb's daughter, won in marriage by Othniel. Jos. 15. 16; Jud. 1. 13.
asks her father's blessing. Jud. 1. 15.
Achshaph, ăch'-shăph, 'enchantment' (?). Jos. [11. 1.
Achzib, ăch'-zĭb, 'deceit.' Jos. 15. 44.
Acknowledge. Ps. 32. 5; 51. 3, I *a.* my sin.
Prov. 3. 6, in all thy ways *a.* him.
Isa. 63. 16, though Israel *a.* us not.
1 John 2. 23, he that *a.* the Son. R. V. confesseth.
See Dan. 11. 39; Hos. 5. 15.
Acquaint. Job 22. 21; Ps. 139. 3; Isa. 53. 3.
Eccl. 2. 3, *a.* mine heart. R. V. guiding me.
Acquaintance. Job 19. 13; Ps. 31. 11; 55. 13.
Acquit. Job 10. 14; Nah. 1. 3.
Actions. 1 Sam. 2. 3.
Activity. Gen. 47. 6, men of *a.* R. V. able.
Acts, Chronology of. *See* pages 4 and 5.
Adadah, ă-dā'-dăh, 'festival' (?). Jos. 15. 22.
Adah, ā'-dăh, 'ornament.' Gen. 4. 19.
Adaiah, ă-dâi'-ăh, 'Jehovah hath adorned.' 2 [Kn. 22. 1.
Adalia, ă-dā'-lĭ-ă. Esth. 9. 8.
Adam, ăd'-ăm, 'man.' Gen. 2. 19. R. V. the man. (1) created. Gen. 1.
called the son of God. Lu. 3. 38.
blessed. Gen. 1. 28.
placed in Eden. Gen. 2. 8.
first called Adam. Gen. 2. 19.
creatures named by. Gen. 2. 19.
calls his wife Eve. Gen. 3. 20.
his fall and punishment. Gen. 3.
hides from God. Gen. 3. 8.
ground cursed for his sake. Gen. 3. 17.
his death. Gen. 5. 5.
his transgression. Job 31. 33; Rom. 5. 1
first Adam. 1 Cor. 15. 45; 1 Tim. 2. 13.
in, all die. 1 Cor. 15. 22.
the last. 1 Cor. 15. 45.
(2) a place. Jos. 3. 16.
Adamah, ăd'-ă-măh, 'earth.' Jos. 19. 36.
Adamant (Ezek. 3. 9). Heb. *Shâmir:* Gk. πέτρα. The corundum, a stone which is next to the diamond in hardness. (*See* Jos. Ant. iii. 7, § 5.)
Adami, ăd'-ă-mī. Jos. 19. 33.
Adar, ā'-där. The twelfth month of the Sacred Year=March. Esth. 3. 7; 9. 21. *See* MONTHS.
Adbeel, ăd'-bĕēl. Gen. 25. 13. [59.
Addan, ăd'-dăn; a city of the captivity. Ez. 2.
Addar, ăd'-där, 'great' (?). 1 Chr. 8. 3.
Adder, the translation of four Hebrew words.
(1) (Ps. 58. 4; 91. 13.) Heb. *Péthen:* Gk. ἀσπίς: Zoölogical Species, *Cobra.*
(2) (Gen. 49. 17.) Heb. *Shĕphîphôn:* Gk. ὄφις: Zoöl. S. *Cerastes Hasselquistii:* R. V. marg. horned snake; A. V. marg. arrowsnake.
(3) (Ps. 140. 3.) Heb. *'Ahshûb:* Gk. βασιλίσκος: Zoöl. S. *Vipera Euphratica.*
(4) (Prov. 23. 32; Job 20. 14, 16.) Heb. *Tziph'ônî:* Gk. ἀσπίς: Zoöl. S. *Daboia xanthina.*
Addi, ăd'-dī, 'ornament' (?). Lu. 3. 28.
Addicted themselves, devoted, or dedicated, themselves. 1 Cor. 16. 15. R. V. set.
Additions. 1 Kn. 7. 29, 30, 36. R. V. wreaths.
Addon, ăd'-dŏn, same as ADDAN. Neh. 7. 61.
Ader, ā'-dĕr, 'flock.' 1 Chr. 8. 15. R. V. Eder.
Adiel, ăd'-ĭ-ĕl, 'ornament of God.' 1 Chr. 4. 36.
Adin, ā'-dĭn, 'delicate.' Ez. 2. 15.
Adina, ăd'-ĭ-nă, same as preceding. 1 Chr. 11. 42.
Adino, ăd'-ĭ-nō. 2 Sam. 23. 8.
Adithaim, ăd-ī-thā'-ĭm, 'twofold booty.' Jos. 15. 36.
Adjure, charge solemnly, conjure. Jos. 6. 26; 1 Sam. 14. 24; 1 Kn. 22. 16; 2 Chr. 18. 15; Mat. 26. 63; Mk. 5. 7; Acts 19. 13.
Adlai, ăd-lā'-ī, 'my righteousness.' 1 Chr. 27. 29.
Admah, ăd'-măh, same as ADAMAH, city of the plain, near Sodom. Gen. 10. 19.
Admatha, ăd-mā'-thă, 'unrestrained.' Esth. 1. 14.
Administer, R. V. minister. 1 Cor. 12. 5; 2 Cor. 8. 19, 20; 9. 12.
Admiration, wonder, astonishment. Rev. 17. 6.
Admire. 2 Thes. 1. 10, to be *a.* in all. R. V. marvelled at.
Jude 16, persons in *a.* R. V. showing respect of.
Admonish. Acts 27. 9, Paul *a.* them.
Rom. 15. 14; Col. 3. 16, *a.* one another.
1 Thes. 5. 12, over you in Lord and *a.* you.
2 Thes. 3. 15, *a.* him as a brother.
Heb. 8. 5, Moses was *a.* of God. R. V. is warned.
See Eccl. 4. 13; 12. 12; Jer. 42. 19.
Admonition. 1 Cor. 10. 11; Eph. 6. 4; Tit. 3. 10.
Adna, ăd'-nă, 'pleasure.' Ez. 10. 30.
Adnah, ăd'-năh. (1) same as preceding. 2 Chr. 17. 14; (2) 1 Chr. 12. 20.
Ado, stir, tumult, commotion. Mk. 5. 39.
Adoni-bezek, ăd'-ō-nī-bē'-zĕk, 'lord of Bezek.' Jud. 1. 5.
Adonijah, ăd-ō-nī'-jăh, 'Jehovah is my Lord;' fourth son of David. 2 Sam. 3. 4.
usurps the kingdom. 1 Kn. 1. 5, 11, 25.
is pardoned by Solomon. 1 Kn. 1. 53. [25.
seeking to obtain Abishag, is slain. 1 Kn. 2. 17–
Adonikam, ăd-ō-nī'-kăm, 'my lord has arisen.' Ez. 2. 13. [1 Kn. 4. 6.
Adoniram, ăd-ō-nī'-răm, 'my lord is exalted.'
Adoni-zedec, ăd'-ō-nī-zē'-dĕc, 'lord of righteousness;' king of Jerusalem, resists Joshua. Jos. 10. 1.
his death. Jos. 10. 26.
Adoption of the children of God. John 1. 12; 20.

17; Rom. 8. 14; 2 Cor. 6. 18; Gal. 4.; Eph. 1. 5; Heb. 2. 10; 12. 5; Jas. 1. 18; 1 John 3. 1.
of Israel. Ex. 4. 22; Hos. 11. 1; Rom. 9. 4.
of the Gentiles. Isa. 66. 19; Hos. 2. 23; Acts 15. 3; Rom. 8. 15, 23; 9. 24; Gal. 4. 5; Eph. 1. 5; 2.; 3.; Col. 1. 27.

Adoraim, ăd-ō-rā′-ĭm, 'two chiefs' (?). 2 Chr. 11. 9.

Adoram, ăd-ŏr′-ăm, contracted from ADONIRAM. 2 Sam. 20. 24.

Adorn. Isa. 61. 10; Rev. 21. 2, bride *a.* herself.
1 Tim. 2. 9; 1 Pet. 3. 3, 5, women *a.*
Tit. 2. 10, *a.* doctrine of God.
See Jer. 31. 4; Lu. 21. 5.

Adrammelech, ă-drăm′-mĕ-lĕch, 'Adar is king.' [2 Kn. 17. 31.

Adramyttium, ăd-ră-mўt′-tĭ-ŭm. Acts 27. 2.

Adria, ā′-drĭ-ă. Acts 27. 27. R. V. the sea of Adria.

Adriel, ā′-drĭ-ĕl, 'flock of God.' 1 Sam. 18. 19.

Adullam, ă-dŭl′-lăm. Jos. 12. 15.
cave of. 1 Sam. 22. 1; 1 Chr. 11. 15.

Adullamite, ă-dŭl′-lăm-īte, a native of Adullam. Gen. 38. 1.

Adultery, of Tamar. Gen. 38. 24.
of David. 2 Sam. 11. 2.
of Herod. Mk. 6. 17.
woman taken in. John 8. 3.
in what it consists. Mat. 5. 28; 15. 19; 19. 9; Mk. [7. 21; 10. 11.
forbidden. Ex. 20. 14; Deu. 5. 18; Mat. 19. 18; Rom. 13. 9; Gal. 5. 19.
penalty of. Lev. 20. 10; Mal. 3. 5; 1 Cor. 6. 9; Heb. 13. 4.
spiritual. Jer. 3.; 13. 27; Ezek. 16.; 26.; Hos. 1.; 2.; Rev. 2. 22.

Adummim, ă-dŭm′-mĭm, 'the red' (men ?). Jos. 15. 7.

Advanced. Esth. 3. 1; 5. 11; 10. 2.
1 Sam. 12. 6, *a.* Moses. R. V. appointed.

Advantage. Lu. 9. 25, what is a man *a.* R. V. profited.
1 Cor. 15. 32, what *a.* R. V. profit.
2 Cor. 2. 11, lest Satan get *a.*
See Job 35. 3; Rom. 3. 1; Jude 16.

Adventure, venture; '*a.* himself' = venture (to go). Acts 19. 31.
So Deu. 28. 56; Jud. 9. 17.

Adversary. Deu. 32. 43; Ps. 89. 42; Isa. 59. 18; Jer. 46. 10; Nah. 1. 2; Lu. 13. 17, his *a.*
Ex. 23. 22, I will be *a.* to thy *a.*
Num. 22. 22, angel stood for *a.*
1 Kn. 5. 4, neither *a.* nor evil.
11. 14, 23, Lord stirred up *a.*
Job 31. 35, that mine *a.* had written.
Ps. 38. 20; 69. 19; 109. 4. 20, 29; Isa. 1. 24, mine *a.*
74. 10, how long shall *a.* reproach.
Isa. 50. 8, who is mine *a.*
64. 2; Jer. 30. 16; Mic. 5. 9, thine *a.*
Am. 3. 11, *a.* shall be round the land.
Mat. 5. 25, agree with thine *a.*
Lu. 12. 58, when thou goest with thine *a.*
1 Cor. 16. 9, there are many *a.*
Phil. 1. 28, terrified by your *a.*
1 Tim. 5. 14, give no occasion to *a.*
Heb. 10. 27, indignation shall devour *a.*
1 Pet. 5. 8, because your *a.* the devil.
See 1 Sam. 2. 10; Isa. 9. 11; 11. 13.

Adversity. 1 Sam. 10. 19; 2 Sam. 4. 9; 2 Chr. 15. 6, all *a.* R. V. calamity (in 1 Sam.).
Ps. 10. 6, I shall never be in *a.*
94. 13; Prov. 24. 10; Eccl. 7. 14, day of *a.*
Prov. 17. 17, brother is born for *a.*
Isa. 30. 20, bread of *a.*
Heb. 13. 3, remember them which suffer *a.* R. V. are evil entreated.
See Ps. 31. 7; 35. 15.

Advertise, to give notice, inform. Num. 24. 14; Ruth 4. 4. R. V. disclose (in Ruth).

Advice. 1 Sam. 25. 33, blessed be thy *a.* R. V. wisdom.
2 Sam. 19. 43, that our *a.* should not be first.
2 Chr. 10. 9, 14, what *a.* give ye. R. V. counsel.
Prov. 20. 18, with good *a.* make war. R. V. guidance.
2 Cor. 8. 10, herein I give my *a.* R. V. judgement.
See Jud. 19. 30; 20. 7; 2 Chr. 25. 17.

Advise. 1 Kn. 12. 6, how do ye *a.* R. V. counsel.
Prov. 13. 10, with the well *a.* is wisdom.
Acts 27. 12, the more part *a.* to depart.

Advise thyself, consider. 1 Chr. 21. 12. *See* also 2 Sam. 24. 13.

Advisement, consideration. 1 Chr. 12. 19.

Advocate. 1 John 2. 1, an *a.* with the Father.

Æneas, æ-nē′-ăs, healing of. Acts 9. 33. Also spelt Eneas.

Ænon, æ′-nŏn, 'springs;' John baptises at. John 3. 23.

Afar off. Jer. 23. 23, a God *a.*
30. 10; 46. 27, I will save them from *a.*
Mat. 26. 58; Mk. 14. 54; Lu. 22. 54, followed *a.*
Acts 2. 39, promise to all *a.*
Eph. 2. 17, preached to you *a.* R. V. far off.
Heb. 11. 13, seen the promises *a.* R. V. from afar.
See Gen. 22. 4; Ez. 3. 13.

Affairs. 1 Chr. 26. 32, pertaining to God and *a.* of king.
2 Tim. 2. 4, entangleth himself with *a.*
See Dan. 2. 49; 3. 12; Eph. 6. 21, 22.

Affect, to seek after, pay court to. Gal. 4. 17.

Affected. Acts 14. 2, minds evil *a.* against brethren.

Affecteth. Lam. 3. 51, mine eye *a.* my heart.

Affection. 1 Chr. 29. 3, have set *a.* to house of God.
Rom. 1. 31; 2 Tim. 3. 3, without natural *a.*
Col. 3. 2, set your *a.* on things above. R. V. mind.
3. 5, inordinate *a.* R. V. passion.

Affection to God's house. 1 Chr. 29. 3; Ps. 26. 8; [84. 2, 10.
to God (panting for). Ps. 42. 1; 119.
set on things above. Col. 3. 2.
fleshly affections to be crucified. Gal. 5. 16, 24; [2 Pet. 2. 10.

Affectioned, affected, disposed. Rom. 12. 10, be kindly *a.* one to another.

Affections, desires, passions. Rom. 1. 26; Gal. 5. 24.

Affinity. 1 Kn. 3. 1; 2 Chr. 18. 1; Ez. 9. 14.

Affirm. Acts 25. 19. Jesus, whom Paul *a.* to be alive.
See Rom. 3. 8; 1 Tim. 1. 7; Tit. 3. 8.

Afflict. Lev. 16. 29, 31; Num. 29. 7; Isa. 58. 3, 5, *a.* your souls.
Num. 11. 11, wherefore hast thou *a.* R. V. evil entreated (dealt ill with).
Ru. 1. 21, Almighty hath *a.* me.
1 Kn. 8. 35; 2 Chr. 6. 26, turn when thou dost *a.*
11. 39, I will *a.* seed of David.
Job 6. 14, to *a.* pity should be shewed. R. V. ready to faint.
Ps. 44. 2, how thou didst *a.* people.
55. 19, God shall hear and *a.* R. V. answer.
82. 3, do justice to the *a.*
90. 15, the days wherein thou hast *a.*
119. 67, before I was *a.*
140. 12, maintain cause of *a.*
Prov. 15. 15, days of the *a.* evil.
22. 22, neither oppress the *a.*
31. 5, pervert judgment of *a.*
Isa. 51. 21, hear thou *a.* and drunken.
53. 7, oppressed and *a.* R. V. humbled himself.
54. 11, thou *a.* tossed with tempest.
63. 9, in all their *a.* he was *a.*
Lam. 1. 5, 12, the Lord hath *a.*
Nah. 1. 12, I will *a.* no more.
Zep. 3. 12, I will leave an *a.* people.
2 Cor. 1. 6, *a.* it is for consolation.
1 Tim. 5. 10, if she have relieved the *a.*
Heb. 11. 37, destitute, *a.*, tormented.
Jas. 4. 9, be *a.* and mourn and weep.
5. 13, is any *a.*, let him pray. R. V. suffering.

Afflicted, duty towards. Job 6. 14; Ps. 82. 3; Prov. 22. 22; 1 Tim. 5. 10; Jas. 1. 27; 5. 13.

Affliction. Gen. 29. 32; Deu. 26. 7; Ps. 25. 18, looked on *a.*
Ex. 3. 7; Acts 7. 34, have seen *a.* of people.
Deu. 16. 3; 1 Kn. 22. 27; 2 Chr. 18. 26, bread of *a.*
2 Chr. 20. 9, cry to thee in *a.*

132. 1, remember David and all his *a.*
119. 50, this my comfort in *a.*
Ps. 34. 19, many are *a.* of righteous.
36. 8, cords of *a.*
30. 16, 27, days of *a.*
Job 5. 6, *a.* cometh not forth of the dust.
33. 12, in *a.* besought the Lord. R. V. distress.
Isa. 30. 20, water of *a.*
48. 10, furnace of *a.*
Jer. 16. 19, refuge in day of *a.*
Lam. 3. 1, man that hath seen *a.*
Hos. 5. 15, in their *a.* they will seek.
Mk. 4. 17, *a.* ariseth for the word's sake. R. V. tribulation.
Acts 20. 23, bonds and *a.* abide me.
2 Cor. 2. 4, out of much *a.* I wrote.
4. 17, light *a.* for moment.
8. 2, great trial of *a.*
Phil. 1. 16, add *a.* to bonds.
Heb. 10. 32, great fight of *a.* R. V. sufferings.
11. 25, suffer *a.* with people. R. V. be evil entreated.
Jas. 1. 27, visit fatherless in *a.*

Affliction the result of sin. 2 Sam. 12. 14; Ps. 90. 7; Ezek. 6. 13.
foretold. Gen. 15. 13; Isa. 10. 12, Jer. 29. 17; 42. 16; Ezek. 20. 37.
man born to. Job 5. 6, 7.
comes from God. Gen. 15. 13; Num. 14. 33; 2 Kn. 6. 33; Job 10. 15; Ps. 66. 11; Isa. 9. 1.
sent in mercy. Gen. 50. 20; Ex. 1. 12; Deu. 8. 16; Ps. 106. 43; Ezek. 20. 37; Nah. 1. 12; Mat. 24. 9; Acts 20. 23; Rom. 8. 18; Heb. 12. 6; Jas. 5. 10; Rev. 7. 14.
promises of support under. Ps. 46. 5; Isa. 25. 4; 43. 2; Jer. 16. 19; 39. 17; Nah. 1. 7; Mat. 11. 28; John 14.; Acts 14. 22; Heb. 2. 18; Rev. 3. 10.
resignation under. Ps. 119. 75.
comfort under. Ps. 27. 5; Isa. 49. 13; 61. 2; Jer. 31. 13; Mat. 5. 4; Lu. 7. 13; John 16. 20, 33; 2 Cor. 1. 4; 7. 6; 1 Pet. 4. 13.
object of. 1 Cor. 11. 32; 1 Pet. 5. 10.
effects of. 2 Cor. 4. 17. [Rev. 3. 19.
proof of God's love. Prov. 3. 12; Heb. 12. 6;
endurance of. 1 Sam. 3. 18; 2 Sam. 12. 16; Neh. 9. 3; Job 1. 21; 2. 10; 5. 17; 13. 15; 34. 31; Ps. 18. 6; 27. 4; 39. 9; 50. 15; 55. 16, 22; 56. 3; 71. 14; Jer. 50. 4; Lam. 3. 39; Lu. 21. 19; Rom. 12. 12; 2 Cor. 1. 9; 1 Thes. 4. 13; 2 Thes. 1. 4; Heb. 12. 1; Jas. 1. 4; 5. 10; 1 Pet. 2. 20.
supplication under. Jud. 4. 3; 1 Sam. 1. 10; 2 Sam. 24. 10; 2 Kn. 19. 16; 20. 1, 2; 2 Chr. 14. 11; 20. 6; Ez. 9. 6; Neh. 9. 32; Job 10. 2; 13. 23; 33. 26; Ps. 66. 13; Jer. 17. 13; 31. 18; Lam. 5. 1; Dan. 9. 3; Hab. 3. 2; Mat. 26. 39; 2 Cor. 12. 8; Jas. 5. 13.
exhortation under. Deu. 8. 3; Neh. 1. 18; Prov. 3. 11; John 5. 14.
confession of sin under. Num. 21. 7; Job 7. 20; Ps. 32. 5; Isa. 64. 5, 6; Jer. 31. 18; Mic. 7. 9.
repentance under. Job 34. 31; Ps. 78. 34; Hos. 6. 1; Lu. 15. 17.
support under. Deu. 4. 30, 31; 2 Chr. 7. 13, 14; Job 33. 26; Ps. 73. 26; Isa. 10. 20.
deliverances from. Ps. 34. 4, 19; 40. 2; 126. 2, 3; Prov. 12. 13; Isa. 63. 9; Jon. 2. 1, 2; 2 Tim. 3. 11; 4. 17, 18.
benefits of. Job 23. 10; 36. 8; Ps. 66. 10; 119. 67, 71; Eccl. 7. 2; Isa. 1. 25; 26. 9; 48. 10; Lam. 3. 27, 39, Ezek. 14. 11; Hos. 2. 6; 5. 15; Mic. 6. 9; Zec. 13. 9; John 15. 2; Acts 14. 22; Rom. 5. 3; 2 Cor. 4. 8; 12. 7; Phil. 1. 12; Heb. 12. 10; 1 Pet. 2. 20.

Affright. Isa. 21. 4, fearfulness *a.* me.
Mk. 16. 5, they were *a.* R. V. amazed.
16. 6, be not *a.*, ye seek Jesus. R. V. amazed.
See Deu. 7. 21; 2 Chr. 32. 18; Jer. 51. 32.

Afoot. Mk. 6. 33; Acts 20. 13.

Afore, beforehand. Rom. 9. 23.

Aforetime. Dan. 6. 10, prayed as *a.*
Rom. 15. 4, things were written *a.*
See Isa. 52. 4; Jer. 30. 20. [20, be not *a.*

Afraid. Mat. 14. 27; Mk. 5. 36; 6. 50; John 6. Gen. 20. 8; Ex. 14. 10; Mk. 9. 6; Lu. 2. 9, sore *a.* Lev. 26. 6; Job 11. 19; Isa. 17. 2; Ezek. 34. 28; Mic. 4. 4; Zep. 3. 13, none make *a.*
Jud. 7, 3, whosoever is fearful and *a.* R. V. trembling.
1 Sam. 18. 29, Saul yet the more *a.*
Neh. 6. 9, they all made us *a.*
Job 3. 25, that I was *a.* of is come.
9. 28, I am *a.* of sorrows.
Ps. 27. 1, of whom shall I be *a.*
56. 3, what time I am *a.*
65. 8, *a.* at thy tokens.
91. 5, *a.* for terror by night.
112. 7, *a.* of evil tidings.
Isa. 51. 12, be *a.* of a man that shall die.
Mk. 9. 32; 10. 32, *a.* to ask him.
John 19. 8, Pilate was more *a.*
Gal. 4. 11, I am *a.* of you.
Heb. 11. 23, not *a.* of commandment.
See Deu. 1. 17; Ps. 3. 6; 56. 11.

Afresh. Heb. 6. 6.

Afternoon. Jud. 19. 8. R. V. the day declineth.

Afterwards. 1 Sam. 24. 5, *a.* David's heart smote him.
Ps. 73. 24, *a.* receive me to glory.
Prov. 20. 17, deceit sweet, but *a.*
24. 27, prepare work and *a.* build. [stilleth it.
29. 11, wise man keepeth till *a.* R. V. back and
John 13. 36, thou shalt follow me *a.*
1 Cor. 15. 23, *a.* they that are Christ's. R. V. then.
See Ex. 11. 1; Mat. 21. 32; Gal. 3. 23.

Agabus, ăg′-ă-bŭs, probably Greek form of Hagab; famine and Paul's sufferings foretold by. Acts 11. 28; 21. 10.

Agag, ā′-găg, 'violent' (?); king of Amalek. (1) spoken of by Balaam. Num. 24. 7.
(2) spared by Saul, slain by Samuel. 1 Sam. 15.

Agagite, ăg′-ă-gīte. Esth. 3. 1.

Against. Lu. 2. 34; Acts 19. 36; 28. 22, spoken *a.*
See Gen. 16. 12; Mat. 12. 30; Lu. 11. 23.

Agar, ā′-găr, same as HAGAR. Gal. 4. 24.

Agate (Ex. 28. 19). Heb. *Shĕbô*: Gk. ἀχάτης. Agate is said to derive its name from the river Achates, in Sicily. In Isa. 54. 12, it is spoken of as a material for windows, but may then refer to mica. R. V. rubies.
Ex. 39. 12, an *a.*
Ezek. 27. 16, and *a.*

Aged. 2 Sam. 19. 32; Job 15. 10; Tit. 2. 2, *a.* men.
Philem. 9, Paul the *a.* R. V. (marg.) ambassador.
See Job 12. 20; 29. 8; 32. 9.

Agee, ā′-ġee, 'fugitive' (?). 2 Sam. 23. 11.

Ages. Eph. 2. 7; 3. 5, 21; Col. 1. 26.

Agone, the old form of 'ago.' 1 Sam. 30. 13.

Agony, Christ's, in the garden. Mat. 26. 36; Lu. 22. 44, etc.

Agree. Am. 3. 3, except they be *a.* R. V. (marg.) have made an appointment.
Mat. 5. 25, *a.* with adversary.
18. 19, two of you shall *a.*
Mk. 14. 56, 59, witness *a.* not.
Acts 15. 15, to this *a.* words of the prophets.
1 John 5. 8, these three *a.* in one.
See Mat. 20. 2; Lu. 5. 36; Acts 5. 9; Rev. 17. 17.

Agreement. Isa. 28. 15; 2 Cor. 6. 16.

Agrippa, ă-grĭp′-pă, 'a wild olive.' (1) Acts 12. 1–4, 23.
(2) Paul's defence before. Acts 25. 22; 26.
almost persuaded. Acts 26. 28.

Aground. Acts 27. 41.

Agur, ā′-gur, hireling' (?); prophecy. Prov. 30.

Aha. Ps. 35. 21; 40. 15; 70. 3; Isa. 44. 16; Ezek. 25. 3; 26. 2; 36. 2.

Ahab, ā′-hăb, 'uncle.' (1) king of Israel. 1 Kn. 16. 29.
marries Jezebel; his idolatry. 1 Kn. 16. 31.
meets Elijah. 1 Kn. 18. 17.
defeats the Syrians. 1 Kn. 20.
punished for sparing Ben-hadad. 1 Kn. 20. 42.
takes Naboth's vineyard. 1 Kn. 21. 16.
his repentance. 1 Kn. 21. 27.
trusts false prophets, and is mortally wounded at Ramoth-gilead. 1 Kn. 22. 6, 34; 2 Chr. 18.

(2) (son of Kolaiah), and Zedekiah, lying prophets. Jer. 29. 21.
Aharah, ă-hâr'-ăh. 1 Chr. 8. 1.
Aharhel, ă-här'-hĕl. 1 Chr. 4. 8.
Ahasai, ă-hā'-sâl, 'Jehovah hath grasped;' called also JAHZERAH. Neh. 11. 13.
Ahasbai, ă-hăs'-bâl. 2 Sam. 23. 34.
Ahasuerus, ă-hă-sū-ē'-rŭs, 'mighty man' (?); reigns from India to Ethiopia. Esth. 1. 1.
Vashti's disobedience to, and divorce. Esth. 1. 12; 2. 4.
makes Esther queen. Esth. 2. 17.
advances Haman. Esth. 3. 1.
his decree to destroy the Jews. Esth. 3. 12.
rewards Mordecai's loyalty. Esth. 6.
hangs Haman. Esth. 7. 9; 8. 7.
advances Mordecai. Esth. 9. 4; 10.
Ahava, ă-hā'-vă. Ez. 8. 15.
Ahaz, ā'-hăz, 'he hath seized;' king of Judah. 2 Kn. 15. 38; 16.
spoils the temple. 2 Kn. 16. 17.
his idolatry. 2 Chr. 28. 2.
afflicted by Syrians. 2 Chr. 28. 5.
comforted by Isaiah. Isa. 7.
will not ask a sign. Isa. 7. 12.
Ahaziah, ā-hă-zī'-ăh, 'Jehovah hath seized;' (1) king of Israel. 1 Kn. 22. 40, 49.
his sickness and idolatry. 2 Kn. 1.
his judgment by Elijah. 2 Kn. 1.
(2) king of Judah, his wicked reign. 2 Kn. 8. 25.
goes with Joram to meet Jehu. 2 Kn. 9. 21.
smitten by Jehu. 2 Kn. 9. 27; 2 Chr. 22. 9.
Ahban, äh'-băn, 'brother of a wise man.' 1 Chr. 2. 29.
Aher, ā'-hĕr, 'another.' 1 Chr. 7. 12.
Ahi, ā'-hī, 'brother of Jehovah.' 1 Chr. 5. 15.
Ahiah, ă-hī'-ăh, '*b.* of Jehovah.' (1) 1 Sam. 14. 3. (2) 1 Kn. 4. 3.
Ahiam, ă-hī'-ăm. 2 Sam. 23. 33.
Ahian, ă-hī'-ăn, 'brotherly.' 1 Chr. 7. 19.
Ahiezer, ā-hī-ē'-zĕr, 'my brother is help.' Num. 1. 12.
Ahihud, ă-hī'-hŭd, '*b.* of majesty.' Num. 34. 27.
Ahijah, ă-hī'-jăh, same as AHIAH; prophesies to Jeroboam against Solomon. 1 Kn. 11. 31.
against Jeroboam, and foretells his son's death. 1 Kn. 14. 7.
Ahikam, ă-hī'-kăm, 'my *b.* has arisen.' 2 Kn. 22. 12.
protects Jeremiah. Jer. 26. 24.
Ahilud, ă-hī'-lŭd, 'child's *b.*' 2 Sam. 8. 16.
Ahimaaz, ă-hī'-mă-ăz, 'my *b.* is anger;' son of Zadok, serves David. 2 Sam. 15. 27; 17. 17; 18. 19.
Ahiman, ă-hī'-măn, 'my *b.* is a gift' (?). Num. 13. 22.
Ahimelech, ă-hĭm'-ĕ-lĕch, '*b.* of the king.' 1 Sam. 21. 1.
slain by Saul's order, for assisting David. 1 Sam. 22. 18.
Ahimoth, ă-hī'-mōth, 'my *b.* is death.' 1 Chr. 6. 25.
Ahinadab, ă-hĭn'-ă-dăb, 'my *b.* is noble.' 1 Kn. 4. 14.
Ahinoam, ă-hĭn'-ō-ăm, 'my *b.* is grace.' 1 Sam. 14. 50.
Ahio, ă-hī'-ō, 'brotherly.' 2 Sam. 6. 3.
Ahira, ă-hī'-ră, 'my *b.* is wicked.' Num. 1. 15.
Ahiram, ă-hī'-răm, 'my *b.* is lofty.' Num. 26. 38.
Ahiramites, ă-hī'-răm-ītes, descendants of Ahiram. Num. 26. 38.
Ahisamach, ă-hĭs'-ă-măch, 'my *b.* has supported.' Ex. 31. 6.
Ahishahar, ă-hī'-shā-här, 'brother of the dawn.' 1 Chr. 7. 10.
Ahishar, ă-hī'-shär, 'my *b.* has sung.' 1 Kn. 4. 6.
Ahithophel, ă-hĭth'-ō-phĕl, 'my *b.* is folly' (?); his treachery. 2 Sam. 15. 12, 31; 16. 20.
disgrace, and suicide. 2 Sam. 17. 1, 23. *See* Ps. 41. 9; 55. 12; 109.
Ahitub, ă-hī'-tŭb, 'my *b.* is goodness.' 1 Sam. 14. 3.
Ahlab, äh'-lăb, 'fertility' (?). Jud. 1. 31.
Ahlai, äh'-lā-ī, 'O! would that' (?). 1 Chr. 2. 31.
Ahoah, ă-hō'-ăh, same as AHIJAH (?). 1 Chr. 8. 4.
Ahohite, ă-hō'-hīte, a descendant of Ahoah. 2 Sam. 23. 9.
Aholah, ă-hō'-lăh, '(she who has) her own tent;' (Samaria), and Aholibah (Jerusalem), their adulteries. Ezek. 23. 4.
Aholiab, ă-hō'-lĭ-ăb, 'father's tent;' inspired to construct the tabernacle. Ex. 31. 6; 35. 34; 36. &c.
Aholibah, ă-hŏl'-ĭ-băh, 'my tent is in her.' Ezek. 23. 4.
Aholibamah, ă-hŏl-ĭ-bā'-măh, 'tent of the high place.' Gen. 36. 2.
Ahumai, ă-hū'-mâl. 1 Chr. 4. 2.
Ahuzam, ă-hū'-zăm, 'possessor.' 1 Chr. 4. 6.
Ahuzzath, ă-hŭz'-zăth, 'possession.' Gen. 26. 26.
Ai, ā'-ī, 'a heap of ruins;' men of, contend with Israel. Jos. 7. 2, 5.
Aiah, âl'-ăh, 'hawk.' 2 Sam. 3. 7.
Aiath, âl'-ăth, 'ruins.' Isa. 10. 28.
Aija, âl'-jă, same as AI. Neh. 11. 31.
Aijalon, âl'-jă-lŏn, 'place of gazelles.' Jos. 21. 24.
Aijeleth Shahar, âl'-jĕ-lĕth shā'-här, 'morning hind.' Ps. 22. title.
Aileth. Gen. 21. 17; Jud. 18. 23; 1 Sam. 11. 5; 2 Sam. 14. 5; Ps. 114. 5; Isa. 22. 1.
Ain, ā'-ĭn, 'an eye,' or 'fountain.' Num. 34. 11.
Air. Job 41. 16, no *a.* can come between.
1 Cor. 9. 26, as one that beateth the *a.*
14. 9, ye shall speak into *a.*
1 Thes. 4. 17, meet Lord in *a.*
See 2 Sam. 21. 10; Eccl. 10. 20; Acts 22. 23; Rev. 9. 2.
Ajah, ā'-jăh, same as AIAH. Gen. 36. 24.
Ajalon, ăj'-ă-lŏn, same as AIJALON. Jos. 19. 42.
Akan, ā'-kăn. Gen. 36. 27.
Akkub, ăk'-kŭb, 'insidious.' 1 Chr. 3. 24.
Akrabbim, ăk-răb'-bĭm, 'scorpions.' Num. 34. 4.
Alabaster, the oriental alabaster, a stalagmite carbonate of lime, used in making vases or vessels for unguents. Mat. 26. 7; Mk. 14. 3; Lu. 7. 37, where the Gr. ἀλάβαστρον refers to an alabaster box or vase.
Alameth, ăl'-ă-mĕth, 'covering.' 1 Chr. 7. 8.
Alammelech, ă-lăm'-mĕ-lĕch, 'king's oak' (?). Jos. 19. 26.
Alamoth, Upon, al'-ă-mōth, (Heb. ă-lă'-mōth). Ps. 46., title. 'After the manner of maidens,' that is 'for soprano voices.'
Alarm (how sounded). Num. 10. 5, when ye blow an *a.*
Jer. 4. 19; 49. 2, *a.* of war.
Joel 2. 1, sound *a.* in holy mountain.
See 2 Chr. 13. 12; Zep. 1. 16.
Alas. 2 Kn. 6. 5, 15, *a.* my master.
Ezek. 6. 11, stamp, and say *a.*
See Num. 24. 23; Jer. 30. 7; Rev. 18. 10.
Albeit, although it be so. Ezek. 13. 7; Philem. 19.
Alemeth, ăl'-ĕ-mĕth. (1) same as ALAMETH. 1 Chr. 8. 36. (2) 1 Chr. 6. 60.
Alexander, ăl-ĕx-ăn'-dĕr, 'defending men.'
(1) Mk. 15. 21.
(2) a member of the Sanhedrin. Acts 4. 6.
(3) an Ephesian Jew. Acts 19. 33.
(4) the coppersmith. 1 Tim. 1. 20; 2 Tim. 4. 14.
Alexandria, ăl-ĕx-ăn'-drĭ-ă, the city on the north coast of Egypt named after Alexander. Acts 18. 24. *See* under EGYPT.
Alexandrians, ăl-ĕx-ăn'-drĭ-ăns. Acts 6. 9.
Algum, or **Almug** (1 Kn. 10. 11, 12; 2 Chr. 2. 8; 9. 10, 11), Gk. ξύλα πελεκητά and ξύλα πεύκινα. There were two kinds of this timber: (1) from Lebanon, (2) from Ophir. Both were used in building the Temple. For musical instruments, the latter was used, and was probably *Pterocarpus santalinus*, or red sandalwood of India.
Aliah, ăl'-ĭ-ăh, same as ALVAH. 1 Chr. 1. 51.
Alian, ăl'-ĭ-ăn, same as ALVAN. 1 Chr. 40.
Alien. Deu. 14. 21, sell it to an *a.* R. V. a foreigner.
Ps. 69. 8, an *a.* unto my mother's children.
Eph. 2. 12, *a.* from commonwealth. R. V. alienated.
Heb. 11. 34, armies of the *a.*
See Ex. 18. 3; Job 19. 15; Isa. 61. 5; Lam. 5. 2.

Alienated. Ezek. 23. 17; Eph. 4. 18; Co. 1. 21.

Alike. Job 21. 26, lie down *a.* in dust.
Ps. 33. 15, fashioneth hearts *a.* R. V. of them all.
Eccl. 9, 2, things cometh *a.* to all.
See Ps. 139. 12; Eccl. 11. 6; Rom. 14. 5.

Alive. Lev. 16. 10, scapegoat presented *a.*
Num. 16. 33, went down *a.* into pit.
Deu. 4. 4, are *a.* every one of you.
32. 39; 1 Sam. 2. 6, I kill and I make *a.*
Ezek. 13. 18; 18. 27, save soul *a.*
Mk. 16. 11, heard that he was *a.*
Lu. 15. 24, 32, son was dead and is *a.*
24. 23, angels who said he was *a.*
Acts 1. 3, showed himself *a.*
Rom. 6. 11, *a.* to God.
1 Cor. 15. 22, all be made *a.*
1 Thes. 4. 15, we who are *a.* and remain.
Rev. 1. 18, I am *a.* for evermore.
See 2 Kn. 5. 7; Dan. 5. 19; Rev. 2. 8; 19. 20.

Alleging, setting forth by arguments, bringing evidence for. Acts 17. 3.

Allegory. Gal. 4. 24, which things are an *a.*

Alleluia, ăl-lē-lū'-jă, 'praise ye the Lord.' Rev. 19. 1.

Allon, ăl'-lŏn, 'an oak.' (1) Jos. 19. 33. R. V. oak. (2) 1 Chr. 4. 37.

Allon-bachuth, ăl'-lŏn-bā'-chŭth, 'oak of weeping.' Gen. 35. 8.

Allow, to approve of. (Old French; from Lat. *allaudare.*) Lu. 11. 48; Acts 24. 15; Rom. 7. 15 (R. V. know); 14. 22.

Allowance. 2 Kn. 25. 30.

All things. 1 Cor. 6. 12, *a.* are lawful but not expedient.

All to brake, broke all to pieces. *To-brake* is the past tense of the old verb *to-breken,* to break in pieces. (Often treated as if *all-to*=altogether. Jud. 9. 53. R. V. omits.)

Allure. Hos. 2. 14; 2 Pet. 2. 18.

Almighty. Ex. 6. 3, by the name of God *A.*
Job 11. 7, canst thou find out the *A.*
29. 5, when *A.* was yet with me.
Ezek. 1. 24; 10. 5, heard as voice of *A.*
Rev. 1. 8; 4. 8; 11. 17, *A.* who was, and is.

Almighty (God). Gen. 17. 1; Num. 24. 4; Ru. 1. 20; Job 5. 17; Ps. 91. 1; Isa. 13. 6.

Almodad, ăl-mō'-dăd, 'God is loved' (?). Gen. 10. 26.

Almon, ăl'-mŏn, 'hiding.' Jos. 21. 18.

Almond, Heb. *Shâked:* Gk. καρυίνη [βακτηρία]; ἀμύγδαλον: Bot. N. *Amygdalus communis.* The almond blossoms before the leaves come out, hence its Hebrew name *shâked,* 'hasten' or 'watch.' (*See* the play on the word, Jer. 1. 11, 12, 'a rod of *shâked* tree . . . for I will *hasten* (*shâked*).') *See* Hazel.
Num. 17. 8, and yielded *a.*
Eccl. 12. 5, *a.* tree shall flourish.

Almon-diblathaim, ăl'-mŏn-dĭb-lă-thā'-ĭm, 'hiding of the two cakes' (?). Num. 33. 46.

Alms (*sing. num.*), a charitable gift. Lu. 11. 41; 12. 33; Acts 3. 3; 10. 2.
Mat. 6. 1, do not your *a.* R. V. righteousness.

Almsgiving. Mat. 6. 1; Lu. 11. 41; 12. 33.
examples of. Acts 3. 2; 10. 2; 24. 17.

Almug. *See* Algum.

Aloes, or **Lign-Aloes.** (Num. 24. 6.) Heb. (1) *Ahâlim,* (2) *Ahâloth:* Gk. στακτή, σκηναί, ἀλοή: Bot. N. *Aquilaria agallocha.* (1) A spice. (2) A vigorous native tree used by Balaam as a figure of the prosperity of Israel. The aloes of medicine differs from both.
Ps. 45. 8, smell of . . . and *a.*
S. of S. 4. 14, *a.,* with all the chief spices.
John 19. 39, a mixture of myrrh and *a.*

Alone. Num. 11. 14; Deu. 1. 9, bear all these people *a.*
1 Kn. 11. 29, they two *a.* in field.
Job 1. 15, escaped *a.* to tell.
Ps. 136. 4, *a.* doeth great wonders.
Mat. 4. 4; Lu. 4. 4, not live by bread *a.*
Lu. 9. 18, 36; John 6. 15, Jesus was *a.*
13. 8, let *a.* this year also.
See Gen. 2. 18; Mat. 18. 15; Jas. 2. 17.

Aloof, intentionally afar off, at a distance. Ps. 38. 11.

Aloth, ā'-lŏth. 1 Kn. 4. 16. R. V. Bealoth.

Alpha (A). The first letter of the Greek alphabet, of which Omĕga (long O) is the last. Alpha and Omega are used to signify 'the first and the last' (Rev. 1. 8, 11). Rev. 21. 6; 22. 13.

Alphæus, ăl-phæ'-ŭs, 'successor.' (1) Mat. 10. 3. (2) Mk. 2. 14.

Already. Eccl. 1. 10, is named *a.*
See Mal. 2. 2; John 3. 18; Phil. 3. 16.

Altar. Mat. 5. 23, bring gift to *a.*
23. 18, swear by *a.*
1 Cor. 9. 13, wait at *a.*
10. 18, partakers of the *a.*
Heb. 13. 10, we have an *a.*

Altar, built by Noah, Gen. 8. 20. Abram, Gen. 12. 7, 8; 13. 4, 18; 22. 9. Isaac, Gen. 26. 25. Jacob, Gen. 33. 20; 35. 7. Moses, Ex. 17. 15. Balaam, Num. 23. 1. Reubenites, &c., Jos. 22. 10. Saul, 1 Sam. 14. 35. Elijah, 1 Kn. 18. 30, 32. Solomon, [2 Chr. 4. 1.
of Damascus. 2 Kn. 16. 10.
commanded. Gen. 35. 1.
how built, of earth. Ex. 20. 24.
of stone. Ex. 20. 25.
of wood. Ex. 27. 1.
of incense. Ex. 30. 1; 37. 25.
golden. Rev. 8. 3; 9. 13.
gift brought to. Mat. 5. 23.
we have an. Heb. 13. 10.

Al-taschith, ăl-tăs'-chĭth. Ps. 57.–59., titles. 'Destroy not,' the first words of some well-known song. *See* Isa. 65. 8, where the words, 'Destroy it not; for a blessing is in it,' are probably the first line of a vintage song.

Alter. Ps. 89. 34, nor *a.* thing gone out of my lips.
Lu. 9. 29, fashion of countenance *a.*
See Lev. 27. 10; Dan. 6. 8.

Altogether. Ps. 14. 3; 53. 3, *a.* become filthy. R. V. together.
50. 21, *a.* such an one as thyself.
S. of S. 5. 16, he is *a.* lovely.
See Ps. 19. 9; 39. 5; 139. 4.

Alush, ā'-lŭsh. Num. 33. 13.

Alvah, ăl'-văh. Gen. 36. 40.

Alvan, ăl'-văn, 'tall.' Gen. 36. 23.

Always. Job 7. 16, I would not live *a.*
Ps. 103. 9, not *a.* chide.
Mat. 28. 20, I am with you *a.* R. V. (marg). all the days.
Mk. 14. 7; John 12. 8, me ye have not *a.*
Phil. 4. 4, rejoice in Lord *a.*
See Ps. 16. 8; Isa. 57. 16; John 11. 42.

Amad, ā'-măd. Jos. 19. 26.

Amal, ā'-măl, 'labour,' 'sorrow.' 1 Chr. 7. 35.

Amalek, ăm'-ă-lĕk. Gen. 36. 12.
fights with Israel in Rephidim, and is defeated. Ex. 17. 8, 13.
perpetual war declared against. Ex. 17. 16; Deu. 25. 17.
smitten by Gideon. Jud. 7. 12.
by Saul. 1 Sam. 14. 48; 15. 8.
by David. 1 Sam. 27. 9; 30. 17.

Amalekite, ă-măl'-ĕk-īte, self-accused of killing Saul; slain by David. 2 Sam. 1. 10, 15.

Amalekites, ă-măl'-ĕk-ītes, descendants of Amalek, dwelling in Sinai and the desert south of Palestine. Gen. 14. 7.

Amam, ā'-măm, 'metropolis' (?). Jos. 15. 26.

Amana, ă-mā'-nă, 'fixed' (?). S. of S. 4. 8.

Amariah, ăm-ă-rī'-ăh, 'Jehovah has promised.' 1 Chr. 6. 7.

Amasa, ă-mā'-să, 'burden;' captain of the host of Absalom. 2 Sam. 17. 25.
slain by Joab. 2 Sam. 20. 9, 10; 1 Kn. 2. 5.

Amasai, ă-mā'-săi, 'burdensome.' (1) 1 Chr. 6. 25. (2) 1 Chr. 12. 18.

Amashai, ă-măsh'-ăi. Neh. 11. 13.

Amasiah, ăm-ă-sī'-ăh, 'Jehovah is bearer.' 2 Chr. 17. 16.

Amazed. Mat. 19. 25, disciples exceedingly *a.*
Mk. 2. 12; Lu. 5. 26, *a.,* and glorified God.
14. 33, he began to be sore *a.*
Lu. 9. 43, *a.* at mighty power of God.
See Ezek. 32. 10; Acts 3. 10.

Amazement, confusion, terror, bewilderment. 1 Pet. 3. 6. R. V. terror.
Amaziah, ăm-ă-zī'-ăh, 'Jehovah has been mighty.' (1) king of Judah, his good reign. 2 Kn. 14. 1; 2 Chr. 25. 1.
defeats Edom. 2 Chr. 25. 11.
defeated by Joash king of Israel. 2 Chr. 25. 21.
slain at Lachish. 2 Kn. 14. 19.
(2) priest of Beth-el. Am. 7. 10.
Ambassadors. 2 Chr. 32. 31, the business of the [a.
2 Cor. 5. 20, we are *a*. for Christ.
See Prov. 13. 17; Isa. 18. 2; 33. 7; Jer. 49. 14; Obad. 1.; Eph. 6. 20.
Ambassage, embassy. Lu. 14. 32.
Amber (Ezek. 1. 4, 27; 8. 2). Heb. *Ḥashmal*: Gk. ἤλεκτρον. The name 'amber' is applied only to the fossil resin.
Ambition reproved. Mat. 18. 1; 20. 25; 23. 8; Lu. 22. 24.
punishment of. Prov. 17. 19; Isa. 14. 12; Ezek. 31. 10.
of Babel. Gen. 11. 4.
Aaron and Miriam. Num. 12. 2.
Korah, Dathan, and Abiram. Num. 16. 3.
Absalom. 2 Sam. 15. 10.
Adonijah. 1 Kn. 1. 5.
Babylon. Jer. 51. 53.
James and John. Mat. 20. 21.
man of sin. 2 Thes. 2. 3.
Diotrephes. 3 John 9.
Ambush. Jos. 8. 4; Jud. 20. 29; 2 Chr. 20. 22.
Ambushment, ambuscade, men lying in wait. 2 Chr. 13. 13.
Amen, ä'-mĕn, a Hebrew word meaning literally *firm*, *sure*, *faithful* (Rev. 3. 14); (tantamount to an oath). Num. 5. 22, the woman shall say *A*.
Deu. 27. 15-26, the people shall say *A*.
Ps. 41. 13; 72. 19; 89. 52, *A*. and *A*.
106. 48, let all the people say, *A*.
Mat. 6. 13; Rom. 16. 27, glory for ever, *A*.
1 Cor. 14. 16, of the unlearned say, *A*.
2 Cor. 1. 20, and in him, *A*.
Rev. 3. 14, these things saith the *A*.
See Rev. 22. 20.
Amend. Jer. 7. 3; 26. 13; 35. 15; John 4. 52.
Lev. 5. 16, make *a*. R. V. restitution.
Amerce, to punish by a fine, to fine. Deu. 22. 19; 2 Chr. 36. 3 (in R. V.).
Amethyst (Ex. 28. 19; Rev. 21. 20). Heb. *Aḥlâmah* (dream-stone): Gk. ἀμέθυστος. A variety of quartz of a purple color.
Ami, ā'-mī, probably same as AMON. Ez. 2. 57.
Amiable, lovely. Ps. 84. 1. [Mat. 1. 4.
Aminadab, ă-mĭn'-ă-dăb, same as AMMINADAB.
Amiss. 2 Chr. 6. 37; Dan. 3. 29; Lu. 23. 41; Jas. 4. 3.
Amittai, ă-mĭt'-tāī, 'true.' 2 Kn. 14. 25.
Ammah, ăm'-măh. 2 Sam. 2. 24.
Ammi, ăm'-mī, 'my people.' Hos. 2. 1.
Ammiel, ăm'-mĭ-ĕl, 'people of God.' (1) Num. 13. 12. (2) 2 Sam. 9. 4. (3) 1 Chr. 3. 5. (4) 1 Chr. 26. 5.
Ammihud, ăm'-mĭ-hŭd, 'my *p*. is majesty.' Num. 1. 10.
Amminadab, ăm-mĭn'-ă-dăb, 'my *p*. is noble.' Ex. 6. 23.
Amminadib, ăm'-mĭ-nă-dĭb, same as preceding. S. of S. 6. 12. R. V. my princely people.
Ammishaddai, ăm-mĭ-shăd'-dāī, '*p*. of the Almighty.' Num. 1. 12.
Ammizabad, ăm-mĭ'-ză-băd, 'my *p*. hath granted.' 1 Chr. 27. 6.
Ammon, ăm'-mon, 'son of my *p*.' (?) : son of Lot, Gen. 19. 38. children of, Gen. 19. 38.
not to be meddled with. Deu. 2. 19.
not to enter the congregation. Deu. 23. 3.
make war on Israel, and are conquered by Jephthah. Jud. 11. 4, 33.
slain by Saul. 1 Sam. 11. 11.
outrage David's servants. 2 Sam. 10.
tortured by David. 2 Sam. 12. 26.
prophecies concerning. Jer. 25. 21; 49. 1; Ezek. 21. 28; 25. 2, 3; Am. 1. 13; Zep. 2. 8.

Ammonites, ăm'-mon-ītes, a tribe descended from Ammon. Deu. 2. 20.
Ammonitess, ăm-mon-ī'-tĕss, feminine of preceding. 2 Chr. 12. 13.
Amnon, ăm'-nŏn, 'faithful;' son of David. 2 Sam. 3. 2.
outrages Tamar. 2 Sam. 13.
slain by Absalom. 2 Sam. 13. 28.
Amok, ā'-mŏk, deep. Neh. 12. 7. [18.
Amon, ā'-mŏn. (1) 'master workman.' 2 Kn. 21.
king of Judah. 2 Kn. 21. 19; 2 Chr. 33. 20.
his idolatry. 2 Kn. 21. 21; 2 Chr. 33. 23.
killed by his servants. 2 Kn. 21. 23.
(2) a god, 'the secret one.' Nah. 3. 8 (marg.).
Amorite, ăm'-ō-rīte, 'mountaineer.' Gen. 10. 16.
Amorites, ăm'-ō-rītes, their iniquities. Gen. 15. 16; Deu. 20. 17; Jos. 3. 10.
Amos, ā'-mŏs, 'bearer of a burden.' One of the minor prophets, a native of Judah but prophesying in Israel.
declares God's judgment upon the nations. Am. 1. 1, 2.
and upon Israel. Am. 3. 1, &c.
his call. Am. 7. 14, 15.
foretells Israel's restoration. Am. 9. 11.
Amoz, ā'-mŏz, strong. Isa. 1. 1.
Amphipolis, ăm-phĭp'-ŏ-lĭs, named from the river Strymon flowing *round the city*. Acts 17. 1.
Amplias, ăm'-plĭ-ăs, short form of Ampliatus, 'enlarged.' Rom. 16. 8.
Amram, ăm'-răm, 'the people is high.' Ex. 6. 18.
Amramites, ăm'-răm-ītes, the descendants of Amram. Num. 3. 27.
Amraphel, ăm-rā'-phĕl. Gen. 14. 1.
Amzi, ăm'-zī, strong. 1 Chr. 6. 46.
Anab, ā'-năb, 'place of grapes.' Jos. 11. 21.
Anah, ā'-năh. Gen. 36. 2.
Anaharath, ă-nā'-hă-răth. Jos. 19. 19.
Anaiah, ă-nāī'-ăh, 'Jehovah has answered.' Neh. 8. 4.
Anak, ā'-năk, 'long-necked' (?). Num. 13. 22, 33.
Anakims, ăn'-ă-kĭms, a tribe near Hebron, called after Anak. Num. 13. 22; Deu. 1. 28; Deu. 9. 2.
cut off by Joshua. Jos. 11. 21.
Anamim, ăn'-ă-mĭm. Gen. 10. 13.
Anammelech, ă-năm'-mĕ-lĕch. 2 Kn. 17. 31.
Anan, ā'-năn, 'a cloud.' Neh. 10. 26.
Anani, ă-nā'-nī, shortened form of ANANIAH. 1 Chr. 3. 24.
Ananiah, ăn-ă-nī'-ăh, 'Jehovah meets.' Neh. 3. 23.
Ananias, ăn-ă-nī'-ăs, Greek form of HANANIAH.
(1) (and Sapphira), their lie and death. Acts 5. 1.
(2) (disciple), sent to Paul at Damascus. Acts 9. 10; 22. 12.
(3) (high priest), Paul brought before. Acts 22. 30.
Paul smitten by order of. Acts 23. 2.
rebuked by Paul. Acts 23. 3.
Anath, ā'-năth. Jud. 3. 31.
Anathema, ă-năth'-ĕ-mă (1 Cor. 12. 3), a Greek word denoting a thing or person devoted to God, and hence, as animals so devoted were put to death, 'doomed to destruction,' 'accursed.' In 1 Cor. 16. 22, it is not to be joined in one expression with Maran-atha (which see).
Anathoth, ăn'-ă-thŏth. Jos. 21. 18.
men of, condemned for persecuting Jeremiah. Jer. 11. 21. *See* 1 Kn. 2. 26.
Anchor. Heb. 6. 19, have as an *a*. of the soul.
Ancient of days. Dan. 7. 22, until the *a*. came.
Ancients, elders (*sub. plur.*). Isa. 3. 14, &c.
And, if. (A peculiar use of the word.) Gen. 44. 30; Num. 5. 30.
And if, if. (Literally, if-if; *see* above.) Mat. 24. 48.
Andrew, ăn'-drew, 'manly;' the Apostle. Mat. 4. 18; Mk. 1. 29; 13. 3; John 1. 40; 6. 8; 12. 22; Acts 1. 13.
Andronicus, ăn-drŏ-nī'-cŭs, disciple at Rome. Rom. 16. 7.
Anem, ā'-nĕm, same as EN-GANNIM (?). 1 Chr. 6. 73.

Aner, ā'-nĕr. (1) Gen. 14. 13. (2) 1 Chr. 6. 70.
Anethothite, ăn-ĕ-thō'-thīte, or **Anetotbite**, ăn-ĕ-tō'-thīte, a man of Anathoth. 2 Sam. 23. 27.
Angel is the Greek word for a 'messenger,' and is used generally of the 'ministering spirits' sent out as messengers of God; less frequently of men so sent.
Gen. 48. 16, the *A.* who redeemed me.
Ps. 8. 5, lower than the *a.* R. V. God.
34. 7, *a.* of Lord encampeth. [mighty.
78. 25, man did eat *a.* food. R. V. food of the
Eccl. 5. 6, nor say before *a.* it was error.
Isa. 63. 9, *a.* of his presence saved them.
Hos. 12. 4, he had power over *a.*
Mat. 13. 39, reapers are the *a.*
Mk. 12. 25; Lu. 20. 36, are as *a.* in heaven.
Lu. 22. 43, an *a.* strengthening him.
John 5. 4, *a.* went down at a certain season.
Acts 12. 15, it is his *a.*
1 Cor. 6. 3, we shall judge *a.*
2 Cor. 11. 14, transformed into *a.* of light.
Heb. 2. 2, word spoken by *a.*
2. 16, not nature of *a.*
13. 2, entertained *a.* unawares.
1 Pet. 1. 12, *a.* desire to look into.
Angels, nature, office, duties, and characteristics of. 2 Sam. 14. 20; 1 Kn. 19. 5; Neh. 9. 6; Job 25. 3; 38. 7; Ps. 68. 17; 91. 11; 103. 20; 104. 4; 148. 2; Isa. 6. 2; Dan. 6. 22; Mat. 13. 39; 16. 27; 18. 10; 24. 31; 25. 31; Mk. 8. 38; Lu. 15. 7; 16. 22; Acts 7. 53; 12. 7; 27. 23; Eph. 1. 21; Phil. 2. 10; Col. 1. 16; 2. 10; 1 Thes. 4. 16; 2 Thes. 1. 7; 1 Tim. 3. 16; 5. 21; Heb. 1. 6; 2. 2; 12. 22; 1 Pet. 1. 12; 3. 22; 2 Pet. 2. 11; Jude 9; Rev. 5. 2; 7.; 11.; 12. 7; 14. 6; 17.
announce the nativity. Lu. 2. 13.
minister to Christ. Mat. 4. 11; 26. 53; Lu. 22. 43; John 1. 51.
saints shall judge. 1 Cor. 6. 3.
not to be worshipped. Col. 2. 18; Rev. 19. 10; 22. 9.
rebellious. 2 Pet. 2. 4; Jude 6.
Angel of the Lord appears to Hagar, Gen. 16. 7; 21. 17. Abraham, Gen. 18, &c. Lot, Gen. 19. Moses, Ex. 3. 2. Balaam, Num. 22. 23. Israelites, Jud. 2. Gideon, Jud. 6. 11. Manoah's wife, Jud. 13. 3. Manoah, Jud. 13. 11. David, 2 Sam. 24. 17; 1 Chr. 21. 16. Elijah, 1 Kn. 19. 7. Daniel, Dan. 8. 16; 9. 21; 10. 11; 12. Joseph, Mat. 1. 20. Mary Magdalene, Mat. 28. 2-7. Zacharias, Lu. 1. 11. Mary, Lu. 1. 26. The Shepherds, Lu. 2. 8-12. Peter, Acts 5. 19; 12. 7. Philip, Acts 8. 26. Cornelius, Acts 10. 3. Paul, Acts 27. 23. *See* Ps. 34. 7; 35. 5; Zec. 1. 11.
Angels of the Churches. Rev. 1. 20; 2.; 3., &c.
Anger. Gen. 49. 7, cursed be their *a.*
Neh. 9. 17, slow to *a.*
Ps. 6. 1; Jer. 10. 24, rebuke me not in *a.*
30. 5, *a.* endureth but a moment.
Prov. 15. 1, grievous words stir up *a.*
19. 11, discretion deferreth *a.*
Eccl. 7. 9, *a.* resteth in bosom of fools.
Mk. 3. 5, he looked on them with *a.*
Col. 3. 8, put off *a.*, wrath, malice.
Anger, nature and effects of. Gen. 27. 45; 44. 18; 49. 7; Ex. 32. 19; Ps. 37. 8; 69. 24; Prov. 15. 18; 16. 32; 19. 11; 21. 19; 29. 22; Eccl. 7. 9; Isa. 13. 9; 30. 27; Jer. 44. 6; Mat. 5. 22; Tit. 1. 7. *See* WRATH.
remedy for. Prov. 15. 1; 21. 14.
to be put away. Eph. 4. 26, 31; Col. 3. 8.
Anger (DIVINE). Gen. 3. 14; 4.; 18. 30; Deu. 29. 20; 32. 19; Jos. 23. 16; 2 Kn. 22. 13; Ez. 8. 22; Job 9. 13; Ps. 7. 11; 21. 8; 78. 21, 58; 89. 30; 90. 7; 99. 8; 103. 9; 106. 40; Prov. 1. 30; Isa. 1.; 3. 8; 9. 13; 13. 9; 47. 6; Jer. 2. 35; 3. 5; 7. 19; 44. 3; Nah. 1. 2; Mk. 3. 5; 10. 14; John 3. 36; Rom. 1. 18; 3. 5; 1 Cor. 10. 22; Eph. 5. 6; Col. 3. 6; 1 Thes. 2. 16; Heb. 3. 18; 10. 26; Rev. 21. 8; 22.
kindled. Ex. 4. 14; Num. 11. 1; 12. 9, &c.; Jos. 7. 1; 2 Sam. 6. 7; 24. 1; 2 Kn. 13. 3; Jer. 17. 4; Hos. 8. 5; Zec. 10. 3.
slow. Ps. 103. 8; Jon. 4. 2; Nah. 1. 3.
deferred. Isa. 48. 9.
instances of. Gen. 19.; Ex. 14. 24; Job 9. 13; 14. 13; Ps. 76. 6; 78. 49; 90. 7; Isa. 9. 19; Jer. 7. 20; 10. 10; Lam. 1.; Ezek. 7.; 9.; Nah. 1.
treasured up for the wicked. Rom. 2. 5; 2 Pet. 3. 7.
prayed against. Ex. 32. 11; 2 Sam. 24. 17; Ps. 2. 12; 6.; 27. 9; 30. 8; 38.; 39. 10; 74.; 76. 7; 79. 5; 80. 4; 85. 4; 90. 11; Isa. 64. 9; Jer. 4. 8; Lam. 3. 39; Dan. 9. 16; Mic. 7. 9; Hab. 3. 2; Zep. 2. 2; 3. 8; Mat. 10. 28; Lu. 18. 13.
propitiation of, by Christ. Rom. 3. 25; 5. 9; 2 Cor. 5. 18; Eph. 2. 14; Col. 1. 20; 1 Thes. 1. 10; 1 John 2. 2.
turned away by repentance. 1 Kn. 21. 29; Job 33. 27, 28; Ps. 106. 45; 107. 13, 19; Jer. 3. 12; 18. 8; 31. 18; Hos. 14. 4; Joel 2. 14; Jon. 3. 9, 10; Lu. 15. 18.
Angle, the implement for angling, a fishing-rod, with line and hook. Isa. 19. 8.
Angry. Ps. 7. 11, God is *a.* with the wicked.
Prov. 14. 17, he that is soon *a.*
22. 24, make no friendship with *a.* man. R. V. man that is given to anger.
25. 23, so doth an *a.* countenance.
Jon. 4. 4, doest thou well to be *a.*?
Mat. 5. 22, whosoever is *a.* with brother.
John 7. 23, are ye *a.* at me.
Eph. 4. 26, be *a.* and sin not.
Tit. 1. 7, bishop not soon *a.*
Anguish. Ex. 6. 9, hearkened not for *a.*
Job 7. 11, I will speak in *a.* of spirit.
Rom. 2. 9, tribulation and *a.* on every soul.
2 Cor. 2. 4, out of much *a.* of heart.
See Gen. 42. 21; Isa. 8. 22; John 16. 21.
Aniam, ă-nī'ăm, 'lament of people.' 1 Chr. 7. 19.
Anim, ā'-nĭm, 'fountains.' Jos. 15. 50.
Animals of the Bible (AQUATIC).
Jonah's Fish (Shark?). Jon. 1. 17. Heb. *Dâg gâdôl:* Gk. κῆτος. A great fish, a sea-monster. So in the Greek of Mat. 12. 40. A. V. 'whale.'
Tobit's Fish (Sheat-fish? *Siluridæ*), Gk. ἰχθύς. Possibly a crocodile.
Onycha (Wing-shell, *Strombus*), Ex. 30. 34; Ecclus. 24. 15. Heb. *Schĕchéleth:* Gk. ὄνυξ, onyx, a claw or nail, the small shell on the foot of many molluscs, with which the larger shell is closed, from which one of the ingredients of 'frankincense' was obtained.
Pearls (Pearl oyster, *Avicula Margaritifera*), Job 28. 18. Heb. *Gâbîsh:* Gk. μαργαρῖται: R. V. 'crystal.'
Purple [Shell fish] (Purple fish, *Murex brandaris; M. trunculus*), Heb. *Argaman.* From this the purple dye was obtained.
Whale (1) (some *land*-monster: *Dragon*, or *Serpent?*), Ex. 7. 9; Deu. 32. 33; Ps. 91. 13; Jer. 51. 34. Heb. *Tannîn:* Gk. κῆτος.
(2) (some *sea*-monster: *Crocodilus?*), Job 7. 12; Ps. 74. 13; Isa. 27. 1; Ezek. 29. 3; 32. 2.
See LEVIATHAN.

Animals of the Bible (Mammalia).

In its physical characteristics Palestine is unique, combining the most opposite physical features: *e. g.*, maritime and inland, mountain and plain, luxuriance and desert, cold and tropical, glacial and volcanic, pastoral and arable. Some species of animals, formerly abundant, have disappeared, *e. g.*, the lion, wild bull, rhinoceros, bison; but eighty species of mammalia still exist there.

Grounded on the Rev. W. Houghton's Paper ("Transactions of Society of Biblical Archæology").

Animal Denoted.	English Translation.	Hebrew Original.	Septuagint Translation.	Assyrian Inscriptions.	Remarks.	Zoölogical Genus or Species.
Antelope	Pygarg	Dîshôn	πύγαργος	Da-as-su	....	Addax.
Antelope	Wild ox	Têo	ἔλαφος	Burkhiïs	....	Oryx leucoryx.
Ape	Ape	Kôph	πίθηκος	Udumu	....	Presbytes entellus.
Ass (tame)	Ass	Hămôr	ὄνος	Imiru	....	Asinus vulgaris.
Ass (wild)	Wild ass	Pére	ἥμιππος	Tseri	....	Asinus hemippus.
Bear	Bear	Dôb	ἄρκτος	Dabuu	....	Ursus Syriacus.
Bull (domestic)	Cattle, oxen	Aleph	κτήνη	Alap	....	Bos Taurus.
Bull (wild ox)	Unicorn	Rĕêm	μονοκέρως	Ri-i-mu	....	Bos primigenius.
Camel	Camel	Gâmâl	κάμηλος	Gammalu	....	{ Camelus Arabicus. Camelus Bactrianus.
Cat	Cat	None	αἴλουρος	None	....	Felis domestica.
Coney (rock-rabbit)	Coney	Shâphân	δασύπους	....	....	Hyrax Syriacus.
Deer (roebuck)	Fallow deer	Yaḥmûr	βούβαλος	....	....	Alcephalus bubalis.
Dog	Dog	Késleb	κύων	Kalbu	....	Canis familiaris.
Dolphin	....	....	....	Nakhiru	*Syr.* Nakhira	Delphinus.
Fallow deer	Hart, hind	Ayyâl	ἔλαφος	Ailu	....	Cervus Mesopotamicus.
Gazelle	Roe, roebuck	Tsĕbî	δορκάς	Tsabiï	....	Gazella gutturosa.
Goat (he)	He-goat	'Attûd	τράγος	Atudu	....	Capra hircus.
Goat (he)	He-goat	Tsâphîr	τράγος	Tsapparu	The Paseng	Capra ægagrus.
Goat (wild)	Chamois	Zémer	καμηλοπάρδαλις	Ditanu	....	Rupicapra tragus.
Goat (wild)	Wild goat	Yâ'êl	....	....	....	Ibex Bedeanus, or Capra Sinaitica.
Greyhound (war-horse?)	Greyhound	Zarzir	ἀλέκτωρ	None	Figured on Assyrian dish.	Doubtful.
Hare	Hare	Arnébeth	χοιρογρύλλιος	} Annabu.	....	{ Lepus Sinaiticus. Lepus Caspius.
Horse	Horse	Sûs	ἵππος	Susu	....	Equus caballus.
Hippopotamus	Behemoth	Bĕhêmôth	θηρία	....	*Coptic* P-ehemout.	
Hyæna	Doleful creatures	[Ôaḥ, *pl.* Ôḥim]	None	Akhu	....	Hyæna striata.
Jackal	Fox	Shûâl	ἀλώπηξ	Asi (?)	....	Canis vulpes.
Leopard	Leopard	Nâmêr	πάρδαλις	Niïmru	....	Leopardus varius.
Lion	Lion	Aryeh	λέων	Ne-essu	....	Felis leo.
Mole-rat (chameleon)	Mole	Tinshémeth	ἀσπάλαξ	....	....	Spalax typhlus.
Mouse	Mouse	'Akhbar	μῦς	....	....	Dipus, and Alactaga.
Mule	Mule	Péred	ἡμίονος	Parie.		
Ox	Young bull	Shôr	μόσχος	....	*Chald.* Thôr	Bos Taurus.
Ox	Oxen	Bâkâr	ταῦρος	Buchal rimi.		
Ram	Ram	Ayïl	κριός	Ailur	....	Ovis aries.
Rhinoceros	....	....	....	Alap nahr.	....	Rhinoceros unicornis.
Sheep	Sheep	Tsôn	πρόβατα	Tsieni	....	Ovis laticaudatus.
Sheep (wild) *See* Wild Goat.	....	....	....	Arnu	*Syr.* Arno	Capra ægagrus.
Swine	Swine, Boar	Ḥâzîr	σῦς, ὗς	....	....	Suidæ.
Unicorn. *See* Ox.						
Weasel or Pole-cat	Weasel	Ḥôled	γαλῆ	....	....	Putorius of the Mustelidæ.
Wolf	Wolf	Zĕêb	....	Ziïbu	Zebu	} Canis lupus.
Wolf	....	....	λύκος	Aciluv	....	

Anise, Gk. ἄνηθον: Bot. N. *Anethum graveolens.* *See* Dill. Mat. 23. 23.
Anna, ăn′-nă, 'grace.' A prophetess. Lu. 2. 36.
Annas, ăn′-năs, Greek form of Hananiah; high priest. Lu. 3. 2.
Christ brought to. John 18. 13, 24.
Peter and John before. Acts 4. 6.
Anoint. Deu. 28. 40; 2 Sam. 14. 2, *a.* not thyself.
Isa. 21. 5, arise and *a.* shield.
61. 1; Lu. 4. 18, *a.* to preach.
Mk. 14. 8, *a.* my body to burying.
Lu. 7. 46, my head thou didst not *a.*
John 9. 6, *a.* eyes of blind man.
12. 3, Mary *a.* feet of Jesus.
2 Cor. 1. 21, he which *a.* us is God.
1 John 2. 27, the same *a.* teacheth.
Rev. 3. 18, *a.* thine eyes with eyesalve.
See Jud. 9. 8; Jas. 5. 14.
Anointed, the (Christ). Ps. 2. 2; Isa. 61. 1; Lu. 4. 18; Acts 4. 27; 10. 38.
the Lord's. 1 Sam. 24. 10; 26. 9; Ps. 84. 9; Ps. 132. 10.
mine. 1 Sam. 2. 35; 1 Chr. 16. 22.
Anointing of Aaron and his sons as priests, Lev. 6. 20; 8. 10; 10. 7. Saul as king, 1 Sam. 10. 1. David, 1 Sam. 16. 13. Solomon, 1 Kn. 1. 39. Elisha, 1 Kn. 19. 16. Jehu, 2 Kn. 9. 6. Joash, 2 Kn. 11. 12. Christ by Mary, Mat. 26. 6; Mk. 14. 3; John 12. 3; by a woman that was a sinner, Lu. 7. 37.
of the Spirit. 2 Cor. 1. 21; 1 John 2. 20.
Anointing Oil. Ex. 30. 25, it shall be an holy *a.*
37. 29, he made the holy *a.*
Anon, i. e., *in one* (instant) immediately. Mat. 13. 20; Mk. 1. 30.
Another. Prov. 27. 2, let *a.* praise thee.
2 Cor. 11. 4; Gal. 1. 6, 7, *a.* gospel. R. V. a different.
Jas. 5. 16, pray one for *a.*
See 1 Sam. 10. 6; Job 19. 27; Isa. 42. 8; 48. 11.
Answer (*n.*). Job 19. 16; 32. 3; S. of S. 5. 6; Mic. 3. 7; John 19. 9, no *a.*
Prov. 15. 1, a soft *a.* turneth.
Prov. 16. 1, *a.* of tongue from the Lord.
1 Pet. 3. 15, be ready to give *a.*
3. 21, *a.* of good conscience.
See Job. 35. 12; Lu. 2. 47; 2 Tim. 4. 16.
Answer (*v.*). Job 11. 2, multitude of words be *a.*
Ps. 65. 5, by terrible things wilt thou *a.*
Prov. 1. 28, I will not *a.*
18. 13, *a.* a matter before he heareth.
26. 4, 5, *a.* not a fool.
Eccl. 10. 19, money *a.* all things.
Lu. 21. 14, meditate not what to *a.*
2 Cor. 5. 12, somewhat to *a.*
Col. 4. 6, how ye ought to *a.*
Tit. 2. 9, not *a.* again.
See 1 Kn. 18. 29; Ps. 138. 3; Isa. 65. 12, 24.
Ant (Prov. 6. 6-8; 30. 25). Heb. *Nĕmâlah:* Gk. μύρμηξ: Zoöl. S. *Formica* or *Myrmica;* abundant in Palestine.
Antelope. (1) (Deu. 14. 5). Heb. *teō.* A. V. 'wild ox,' but correctly 'antelope' in R. V.
(2) Heb. *Dîshôn*, the pygarg.
Antichrist, ăn′-tĭ-christ, 'adversary to Christ.' 1 John 2. 18, 22; 2 John 7. *See* 2 Thes. 2. 9; 1 Tim. 4. 1.
Antioch, ăn′-tĭ-ŏch, named in honor of Antiochus. (1) capital of Syria; starting point of Paul's first missionary journey. Acts 6. 5.
disciples first called Christians at. Acts 11. 26.
Barnabas and Saul called to apostleship at. Acts 13. 1.
Paul withstands Peter at. Gal. 2. 11.
(2) (Pisidia) Paul's first address at. Acts 13. 16.
Paul and Barnabas persecuted at. Acts 13. 50.
Antipas, ăn′-tĭ-păs, contraction of Antipater. Martyr. Rev. 2. 13.
Antipatris, ăn-tĭp′-ă-trĭs, from the foregoing. Acts 23. 31.
Antiquity. Isa. 23. 7.
Antothijah, ăn-tō-thī′-jăh, 'prayers answered by Jehovah' (?). 1 Chr. 8. 24.
Antothite, ăn′-tō-thīte, a man of Anathoth. 1 Chr. 11. 28.
Anub, ā′-nŭb, 'bound together' (?). 1 Chr. 4. 8.
Any thing, as to anything. Acts 25. 8.
Apart. Mat. 14. 13, desert place *a.*
14. 23; 17. 1, mountain *a.*
Mk. 6. 31, come ye yourselves *a.*
See Ps. 4. 3; Zec. 12. 12; Jas. 1. 21.
Ape, 1 Kn. 10. 22. Heb. *Kôph:* Gk. πίθηκος. None are now found in Palestine.
Apelles, ă-pĕl′-lēs. Saluted by Paul. Rom. 16. 10.
Apharsachites, ă-phär′-să-chītes. Ez. 5. 6.
Apharsathchites, ă-phär-săth′-chītes. Ez. 4. 9.
Apharsites, ă-phär′-sītes. Ez. 4. 9.
Aphek, ā′-phĕk, 'fortress' (?). Jos. 12. 18.
defeat of Saul at. 1 Sam. 29. 1. *See* Jos. 13. 4; 1 Sam. 4. 1; 1 Kn. 20. 26.
Aphekah, ă-phē′-kăh, same as preceding. Jos. 15. 53.
Aphiah, ă-phī′-ăh. 1 Sam. 9. 1.
Aphik, ā′-phĭk, same as Aphek. Jud. 1. 31.
Aphrah, ăph′-răh, 'dust.' Mic. 1. 10. R. V. Beth-le-Aphrah.
Aphses, ăph′-sēs, 'dispersion.' 1 Chr. 24. 15. R. V. Happizzeh.
Apocrypha. Non-canonical Books.
Apollonia, ăp-ŏl-lō′-nĭ-ă. Acts 17. 1.
Apollos, ă-pŏl′-lŏs, another form of Apollonius; eloquent and mighty in the Scriptures. Acts 18. 24; 19. 1; 1 Cor. 1. 12; 3. 4.
Apollyon, ă-pŏl′-lў-on, 'one that exterminates.' Rev. 9. 11.
Apostates. Deu. 13. 13; Mat. 24. 10; Lu. 8. 13; John 6. 66; 1 Tim. 4. 1; Heb. 3. 12; 6. 4; 10. 25; 2 Pet. 3. 17; 1 John 2.
their doom. Zep. 1. 4; 2 Thes. 2. 8; 2 Pet. 2. 17.
Apostle is from the Greek, meaning 'one who is sent forth, a delegate.' The word is used specially of 'the twelve' (also of St. Paul, Rom. 1. 1; 1 Cor. 9. 1, 2), but also in a wider sense, in which it is applied to such men as Matthias, James the Lord's brother, Barnabas, Andronicus and Junias. The first qualification was 'to have seen the Lord,' i. e., to be a witness of the Resurrection: the second, effectual missionary work (the signs of an apostle, 2 Cor. 12. 12: but divine appointment and commission was also necessary (1 Cor. 12. 28; Eph. 4. 11).
Apostles, calling of the. Mat. 4. 18, 21; 9. 9; Mk. 1. 16; Lu. 5. 10; John 1. 38.
their appointment and powers. Mat. 10.; 16. 19; 18. 18; 28. 19; Mk. 3. 13; 16. 15; Lu. 6. 13; 9.; 12. 11; 24. 47; John 20. 23; Acts 9. 15, 27; 20. 24; 1 Cor. 5. 3; 2 Thes. 3. 6; 2 Tim. 1. 11.
witnesses of Christ. Lu. 1. 2; 24. 33, 48; Acts 1. 2, 22; 10. 41; 1 Cor. 9. 1; 15. 5; 2 Pet. 1. 16; 1 John 1. 1.
their sufferings. Mat. 10. 16; Lu. 21. 16; John 15. 20; 16. 2, 33; Acts 4., &c.; 1 Cor. 4. 9, 2 Cor. 1. 4; 4. 8; 11. 23, &c.; Rev. 1. 9, &c.
their names written in heaven, Rev. 21. 14.
false, condemned, 2 Cor. 11. 13.

Apostles, The Twelve.

No.	Name.	Surname.	Parents.	Home.	Business.	Writings.	Work.	Death.
1	SIMON.	Peter = *Rock.* Cephas = *Rock.*	Jonah.	Early life in Bethsaida, afterwards at Capernaum.	Fisherman.	1 Peter, 2 Peter, (Mark?)	Miss'nary to Jews far as Rome. Babylon, 1 Pet. 5. 13, prob. = Rome.	Crucified head downward, at Rome. *Tradition.*
2	ANDREW.		Jonah.		Fisherman.		Preached in Scythia, Greece, and Asia Minor. *Tradition.*	Crucified on St. Andrew's cross (X). *Tradition.*
3	JAMES, the elder.	Boanerges or *Sons of Thunder.*	Zebedee and Salome.	Bethsaida and afterwards in Jerusalem.	Fisherman.		Preached in Jerusalem and Judea.	Beheaded by Herod A. D. 44, at Jerusalem.
4	JOHN, the beloved disciple.				Fisherman.	Gospel. 3 Epistles. Revelation.	Labored among the churches of Asia Minor, especially Ephesus.	Banished to Patmos, A. D. 95. Recalled. Died a natural death. *Tradition.*
5	JAMES, the less or younger.		Alphæus or Cleophas and Mary.	Galilee.		(Epistle of James?)	Preached in Palestine and Egypt. (Bishop of Jerusalem?)	Crucified in Egypt (*tradition*), or thrown from a pinnacle in Jerusalem. *The Ch. Historian, Hegesippus.*
6	JUDE.	Same as Thaddæus and Lebbæus.		Galilee.		Epistle of Jude.	Preached in Assyria and Persia. *Tradition.*	Martyred in Persia. *Tradition.*
7	PHILIP.			Bethsaida.			Preached in Phrygia.	Died at Hierapolis in Phrygia. *Early Ephesian tradition.*
8	BARTHOLOMEW.	Nathaniel.		Cana of Galilee.				Flayed to death. *Tradition.*

Apostles, The Twelve—(*Continued*)

No.	Name.	Surname.	Parents.	Home.	Business.	Writings.	Work.	Death.
9	Matthew.	Levi.	Alphæus.	Capernaum.	Tax collector. Publican.	Gospel.		Died a martyr in Ethiopia. *Tradition.*
10	Thomas.	Didymus.		Galilee.			Claimed by the Syrian Christians as founder of their church; perhaps also in Persia and India.	Martyred. Shot by a shower of arrows while at prayer. *Tradition.*
11	Simon.	The Cananæan, or *Zelotes.*		Galilee.				Crucified. *Tradition.*
12	Judas.	Iscariot.		Kerioth of Judea.				Suicide.

Apothecary. R. V. perfumer, Ex. 30. 25; Eccl. 10. 1.
Appaim, ăp'-pā-ĭm, 'the nostrils.' 1 Chr. 2. 30.
Apparel, exhortations concerning. Deu. 22. 5; 1 Tim. 2. 9; 1 Pet. 3. 3.
of Jewish women described. Isa. 3. 16.
Apparelled, dressed. Lu. 7. 25.
Apparently, plainly, openly. Num. 12. 8.
Appear. Col. 3. 4; 1 Tim. 6. 14; 2 Tim. 1. 10; 4. 8; Tit. 2. 13; Heb. 9. 28, *a.* of Christ. (In Col. R. V. manifested.)
1 Sam. 16. 7, man looketh on the outward *a.*
Ps. 42. 2, when shall I *a.* before God.
90. 16, let thy work *a.*
S. of S. 2. 12, flowers *a.* on earth.
Mat. 6. 16, *a.* to men to fast. R. V. be seen of.
23. 28, outwardly *a.* righteous.
Rom. 7. 13, that it might *a.* sin. R. V. be shewn to be.
2 Cor. 5. 10, we must all *a.* R. V. be made manifest.
5. 12, glory in *a.*
1 Thes. 5. 22, *a.* of evil. R. V. every form.
1 Tim. 4. 15, profiting may *a.* R. V. be made manifest.
1 Pet. 1. 7, *a.* of Christ. R. V. revelation.
See Ex. 23. 15; Mat. 24. 30; Lu. 19. 11.
Appease. Gen. 32. 20; Prov. 15. 18; Acts 19. 35.
Appertain. Num. 16. 30; Jer. 10. 7. [29. 8.
Appetite. Job 38. 39; Prov. 23. 2; Eccl. 6. 7; Isa.
Apphia, ăpph'-ĭ-ă. Philem. 2.
Appii forum, ăp'-pĭ-ī fôr'-ŭm, 'forum,' or 'market-place of Appius.' Forty miles south of Rome. Acts 28. 15.
Apple (Prov. 25. 11; S. of S. 2. 3; Joel 1. 12). Heb. *Tappûaḥ:* Gk. μῆλον. The apricot is probably the fruit intended.
Apple of the eye, the eye-ball. Deu. 32. 10; Prov. 7. 2.
Apply. Ps. 90. 12; Prov. 2. 2; 22. 17; 23. 12; Eccl. 7. 25.
Appoint. Job 7. 3, wearisome nights are *a.*
14. 5, thou hast *a.* bounds.
30. 23, house *a.* for all living.
Ps. 79. 11; 102. 20, preserve those *a.* to die.
Mat. 24. 51; Lu. 12. 46, *a.* him his portion.
Acts 6. 3, seven men whom we may *a.*
1 Thes. 5. 9, not *a.* to wrath.
See Job 14. 13; Ps. 104. 19; Acts 17. 31. [11.
Appointed, armed, equipped, provided. Jud. 18.
Apprehend, take into custody, arrest. Acts 12. 4; 2 Cor. 11. 32.
Apprehend. Phil. 3. 12. 'The passage throughout has reference to the Grecian games; *apprehend* in the first part of the sentence meaning to lay hold of the goal, and so receive the prize; in the second part, meaning to take hold of by the hand and introduce to the course, as was customary.'
Approach. Isa. 58. 2, take delight in *a.* God.
Lu. 12. 33, where no thief *a.*
1 Tim. 6. 16, light no man can *a.*
Heb. 10. 25, as ye see the day *a.*
See Deu. 31. 14; Job 40. 19; Ps. 65. 4.
Approve. (1) Ps. 49. 13, posterity *a.* sayings.
Rom. 16. 10, *a.* in Christ.
Phil. 1. 10, *a.* things that are excellent.
2 Tim. 2. 15, show thyself *a.*
(2) to prove, attest. Acts 2. 22.
(3) to test, try. Rom. 2. 18.
Apt. 2 Kn. 24. 16; 1 Tim. 3. 2; 2 Tim. 2. 24.
Aquila, ă-quĭl'-ă, an eagle; (and Priscilla) go with Paul from Corinth to Ephesus. Acts 18. 2, 19.
their constancy. Rom. 16. 3; 1 Cor. 16. 19.
Apollos instructed by. Acts 18. 26.
Ar, ăr, 'city.' Num. 21. 15.
Ara, âr'-ă, 'lion' (?). 1 Chr. 7. 38.
Arab, âr'-ăb, 'ambush.' Jos. 15. 52.
Arabah, ăr'-ă-băh, the deep valley extending from Mt. Hor to the eastern arm of the Red Sea. Used in many passages of the R. V., but rendered 'plain' in the A. V. except in Jos. 18. 18.
Arabia, ă-rā'-bĭ-ă. Ps. 72. 10, 15; Isa. 21. 13; Jer. 25. 24; Gal. 1. 17.
kings of, pay tribute. 2 Chr. 9. 14; 17. 11; 26. 7.
Arabian, ă-rā'-bĭ-ăn, a person from Arabia. Neh. 2. 19; Isa. 13. 20; Acts 2. 11.
Arad, âr'-ăd, 'wild ass' (?). (1) Num. 21. 1.
(2) Jos. 12. 14; 1 Chr. 8. 15.
Arah, âr'-ăh, 'traveller.' 1 Chr. 7. 39.

Aram, âr'-ăm, a name of certain districts in Syria and Mesopotamia. Gen. 10. 22.
Aramæan language; Syriac, the language of Syria (= Aram) and Palestine in the time of Christ.
Aramæans, Syrians.
Aramitess, ăr-ăm-ī'-tĕss, a female inhabitant of Aram. 1 Chr. 7. 14.
Aram-naharaim, ăr'-ăm-nā-hă-rā'-ĭm, 'Aram of the two rivers;' Mesopotamia. Ps. 60. title.
Aram-zobah, âr'-ăm-zō'bah. Ps. 60. title.
Aran, ăr'-ăn, 'wild' goat. Gen. 36. 28.
Ararat, ăr'-ă-răt, a mountainous country north of Assyria. Mt. Ararat is a mountain 17,260 ft. high, halfway between the Black Sea and the Caspian.
ark rested on. Gen. 8. 4. *See* Jer. 51. 27.
Araunah, ă-raŭ'-năh, 'calf' (?); (Ornan), Jebusite, sells to David site for temple. 2 Sam. 24. 16; 1 Chr. 21. 15, 18; 22. 1.
Arba, or **Arbah**, är'-bă, är'-băh. Gen. 35. 27.
Arbathite, är'-bă-thīte. 1 Chr. 11. 32. [35.
Arbite, är'bīte, an inhabitant of Arab. 2 Sam. 23.
Archangel. 1 Thes. 4. 16, voice of *a*.
Jude 9, Michael the *a*. contending.
Archelaus, är-chĕ-lā'-ŭs, prince, king of Judæa, feared by Joseph. Mat. 2. 22.
Archers. Gen. 21. 20, and became an *a*.
49. 23, the *a*. have sorely grieved him.
1 Sam. 31. 3, and the *a*. hit him.
2 Chr. 35. 23, and the *a*. shot at king Josiah.
Job 16. 13, his *a*. compass me.
Archevites, är'-chĕ-vītes, the men of Erech, *q. v.* Ez. 4. 9.
Archi, är'-chī, an inhabitant of Erech. Jos. 16. 2. R. V. Archites.
Archippus, är-chĭp'-pŭs, 'master of the horse' (?). Col. 4. 17.
Archite, är'-chīte, a native of Erech. 2 Sam. 15. 32.
Arcturus, ärc-tū'-rŭs, 'bear-guard,' probably the constellations known as the Great Bear. Job 9. 9; 38. 32.
Ard, ärd. Gen. 46. 21. [40.
Ardites, ärd'-ītes, descendants of Ard. Num. 26.
Ardon, är'-dŏn. 1 Chr. 2. 18.
Areli, ă-rē'-lī, 'heroic' (?). Gen. 46. 16.
Arelites, ă-rē'-lītes, a family descended from Areli. Num. 26. 17.
Areopagite, ăr-ē-ŏp'-ă-gīte, 'belonging to the Council held on Areopagus.' Acts 17. 34.
Areopagus, ăr-ē-ŏp'-ă-gŭs, 'hill of Ares or Mars,' at Athens; Paul preaches on. Acts 17. 19.
Aretas, ăr'-ē-tăs. 2 Cor. 11. 32.
Argob, är'-gŏb. (1) a rocky district. Deu. 3. 4. (2) 2 Kn. 15. 25.
Arguing. Job 6. 25.
Arguments. Job 23. 4.
Argurion. Another name for the stater. A. V. 'a piece of money,' Mat. 26. 15; = tetradrachm, the 'piece of money,' Mat. 17. 27; = the shekel, = about 2 shillings, 9 pence = 65 cents. *See* Money.
Aridai, ăr'-ĭ-dâi, 'desire of Hari' (Vishna). Esth. 9. 9.
Aridatha, ăr-ĭ-dā'-thă, 'given by Hari.' Esth. 9. 8.
Arieh, ăr'-ĭ-ĕh, 'lion.' 2 Kn. 15. 25.
Ariel, âr'-ĭ-ĕl, 'lion,' or 'hearth of God.' Ez. 8. 16.
Aright. Ps. 50. 23; 78. 8; Prov. 15. 2.
Prov. 23. 31, moveth *a*. R. V. smoothly.
Arimathæa, ăr-ĭm-ă-thæ'-ă, the same as Ramah. Mat. 27. 57.
Arioch, ăr'-ĭ-ŏch. Gen. 14. 1.
Arisai, ăr'-ĭ-sâi. Esth. 9. 9.
Arise. 1 Kn. 18. 44, there *a*. a little cloud.
Neh. 2. 20, *a*. and build.
Ps. 68. 1, let God *a*.
88. 10, dead *a*. and praise thee.
112. 4, to upright *a*. light.
Mal. 4. 2, Sun of righteousness *a*.
Mk. 2. 11; Lu. 7. 14; 8. 54; Acts 9. 40, I say *a*.
Lu. 15. 18, I will *a*. and go.
Eph. 5. 14, *a*. from the dead.
2 Pet. 1. 19, till daystar *a*.
See Isa. 26. 19; Jer. 2. 27.
Aristarchus, ăr-ĭs-tär'-chŭs, 'best ruling;' fellow-prisoner of Paul. Acts 19. 29; 20. 4; 27. 2; Col. 4. 10; Philem. 24.
Aristobulus, ă-rĭs-tō-bū'-lŭs, 'best counsellor;' his household greeted by Paul. Rom. 16. 10.
Ark. The word means a covered chest, or box. Three important arks are mentioned, viz.:—
(1) Noah's ark (Heb. *Têbhâh*).
ordered, Gen. 6. 14; 1 Pet. 3. 20.
dimensions, &c., Gen. 6. 15, &c.
Noah's faith in making, Heb. 11. 7; 1 Pet. 3. 20.
(2) That in which the infant Moses was hidden by his mother (Heb. *Têbhâh*). Ex. 2. 3. It is not an uncommon thing at this day to see an Egyptian mother twist papyrus stalks into such a wicker cradle, smear it with pitch, cover it with a lid of wicker-work, place her infant in it, and swim across the Nile, pushing the ark in front of her. The Hebrew word *Têbhâh* is connected with the Egyptian word *teb*, a box, reed-boat, or sarcophagus.
(3) The Ark of the Covenant (Heb. *Arôn*). This sacred object was a chest made of acacia wood overlaid with gold, the lid of which constituted the 'mercy-seat' (Ex. 25. 17), or place of propitiation, over which two cherubim extended their wings.
directions for making. Ex. 25. 10; 37. 1.
passes Jordan. Jos. 3. 15; 4. 11.
compasses Jericho. Jos. 6. 11.
captured by Philistines. 1 Sam. 4. 11.
restored. 1 Sam. 6. [13.; 15.; 16.
taken to Jerusalem. 2 Sam. 6.; 15. 24, 29; 1 Chr.
brought into the temple by Solomon. 1 Kn. 8. 3; 2 Chr. 5. *See* Heb. 9. 4.
Ark in heaven. Rev. 11. 19.
Arkite, är'-kīte, 'fugitive' (?). Gen. 10. 17.
Arm of God. Ex. 15. 16; Deu. 33. 27; Job 40. 9; Ps. 77. 15; 89. 13; 98. 1; Isa. 33. 2; 51. 5; 52. 10; 53. 1; Jer. 27. 5; Lu. 1. 51; Acts 13. 17.
Armageddon, är-mă-gĕd'-dŏn, 'height of Megiddo.'
Rev. 16. 16. R. V. Har-Magedon.
Armenia, är-mē' nĭ-ă, 'land of Aram.' 2 Kn. 19. 37. R. V. land of Ararat.
Armoni, är-mō'-nī, 'belonging to a palace.' 2 Sam. 21. 8.
Armour. The arms mentioned in the Bible may be divided into two classes. (1) *offensive*, the sword, spears of several kinds, bow and arrows, sling. (*q. v.*)
(2) *defensive*, breastplate, helmet, greaves, shield. (*q. v.*)
1 Sam. 17. 54, but he put his *a*. in his tent.
1 Kn. 22. 38, and they washed his *a*. R. V. harlots washed themselves there.
Isa. 22. 8, didst look in that day to *a*.
Lu. 11. 22, his *a*. wherein he trusted.
Rom. 13. 12, let us put on *a*. of light.
2 Cor. 6. 7, approving by *a*. of righteousness.
Eph. 6. 11, 13, put on the *a*. of God.
Armour, Goliath's. 1 Sam. 17. 5, 54.
of God. Rom. 13. 12; 2 Cor. 6. 7; 10. 4; Eph. 6. 13; 1 Thes. 5. 8. [ing *a*.
Arms. Deu. 33. 27, underneath are the everlast-
See Gen. 49. 24; Job 22. 9; Ps. 37. 17; Mk. 10. 16.
Army. 1 Sam. 17. 10, I defy the *a*. of Israel.
Job 25. 3, is there any number of his *a*.
Lu. 21. 20, Jerusalem compassed with *a*.
Acts 23. 27, then came I with an *a*. R. V. soldiers.
Heb. 11. 34, *a*. of the aliens.
See S. of S. 6. 4; Ezek. 37. 10.
Arnan, är'-năn, 'active.' 1 Chr. 3. 21.
Arnon, är'-nŏn, 'swift,' or 'noisy;' a river flowing into the Jordan from the east. Num. 21. 13.
Arod, âr'-ŏd, 'wild ass' (?). Num. 26. 17.
Arodi, ă-rō'-dī, same as preceding. Gen. 46. 16.

Arodites, ăr'-ō-dītes, descendants of Arod. Num. 26. 17.
Aroer, ă-rō'-ĕr, 'ruins' (?), or, 'juniper' (?). (1) Deu. 2. 36.
built by children of Gad. Num. 32. 34.
boundary of Reuben. Jos. 13. 16.
(2) a city of Simeon. 1 Sam. 30. 28. [44.
Aroerite, ă-rō'-ĕr-īte, a man of Aroer. 1 Chr. 11.
Arpad, är'-păd. 2 Kn. 18. 34.
Arphad, är'-phăd, same as preceding. Isa. 36. 19.
Arphaxad, är-phăx'-ăd. Gen. 10. 22. R. V. Arpachshad.
Array (*n.*). Jud. 20. 20, put in *a.*
1 Tim. 2. 9 (clothing, dress), not with costly *a.*
Array (*v.*). To dress or clothe.
Job 40. 10, *a.* thyself with glory.
Jer. 43. 12, shall *a.* himself with land.
Mat. 6. 29, *a.* like one of these.
Rev. 7. 13, *a.* in white robes.
17. 4, woman was *a.*
19. 8, *a.* in fine linen.
Arrived. Lu. 8. 26, *a.* at the country.
Acts 20. 15, we *a.* at Samos. R. V. touched.
Arrogancy. 1 Sam. 2. 3; Prov. 8. 13; Isa. 13. 11.
Jer. 48. 29.
Arrow. Num. 24. 8, pierce through with *a.*
Ps. 38. 2, thine *a.* stick fast.
76. 3, brake the *a.* of the bow.
91. 5, *a.* that flieth by day.
Prov. 25. 18, false witness sharp *a.*
26. 18, casteth *a.* and death.
Ezek. 5. 16, evil *a.* of famine.
See Deu. 32. 23; 2 Sam. 22. 15; Job 6. 4; 41. 28.
Artaxerxes, är-tă-xĕrx'-ēs, 'honoured king' (?).
(1) (king of Persia), oppresses the Jews. Ez. 4.
(2) (Longimanus), permits Ezra to restore the temple, Ez. 7; and Nehemiah to rebuild Jerusalem, Neh. 2.
Artemas, är'-tĕ-măs, shortened form of Artemidorus (?). Tit. 3. 12.
Artificer. Gen. 4. 22, *a.* in brass. R. V. cutting instruments of.
2 Chr. 34. 11, *a.* and builders. R. V. carpenters.
See 1 Chr. 29. 5; Isa. 3. 3.
Artillery, weapons as in R. V. here = bow and arrows. 1 Sam. 20. 40.
Aruboth, ă-rū'-bōth, 'windows.' 1 Kn. 4. 10.
Arumah, ă-rū'-măh. Jud. 9. 41.
Arvad, är'-văd. Ezek. 27. 8. [10. 18.
Arvadite, är'-vă-dīte, inhabitant of Arvad. Gen.
Arza, är'-ză, 'earth.' 1 Kn. 16. 9.
As, a Roman bronze coin = the Greek Assarion = half-penny = 1 cent. *See* Money.
Asa, ā'-să, 'physician;' his good reign. 1 Kn. 15. 8.
wars with Baasha. 1 Kn. 15. 16.
his prayer against the Ethiopians. 2 Chr. 14. 11.
his zeal. 2 Chr. 15.
seeks aid of the Syrians. 2 Chr. 16.
reproved by Hanani the seer. 2 Chr. 16. 7.
reigns forty years, and dies much honoured. 2 Chr. 16. 13.
Asahel, ăs'-ă-hĕl, 'God hath made;' his rashness; slain by Abner in self-defence. 2 Sam. 2. 18; 3. 27; 23. 24; 1 Chr. 11. 26.
Asahiah, ăs-ă-hī'-ăh, 'Jehovah hath made.' 2 Kn. 22. 12.
Asaiah, ă-sāi'-ăh, 'Jehovah hath made.' 1 Chr. 4. 36.
Asaph, ā'-săph, 'collector.' (1) a Levite, musical composer, and leader of David's choir. 1 Chr. 6. 39; 2 Chr. 5. 12; 29. 30; 35. 15; Neh. 12. 46; Psalms 50 and 73 to 83 ascribed to him.
(2) 2 Kn. 18. 18. [4. 16.
Asareel, ăs'-ă-rēel, 'God has bound' (?). 1 Chr.
Asarelah, ăs-ă-rē'-lăh, same as Jesharelah. 1 Chr. 25. 2.
Ascend. Ps. 68. 18; Rom. 10. 6; Eph. 4. 8, *a.* on high.
John 1. 51, angels of God *a.*
3. 13, no man hath *a.* to heaven.
20. 17, I am not yet *a.*
Rev. 8. 4, smoke of incense *a.*
Rev. 11. 12, they *a.* up to heaven.
See Ps. 24. 3; 139. 8.
Ascension of Christ (from Olivet). Lu. 24. 50; John 14. 2; 16. 7; Acts 1. 9; 2. 33; Rom. 8. 34; Eph. 4. 8; 1 Pet. 3. 22.
typified. Lev. 16. 15; Heb. 6. 20; 9. 7-12. Enoch, Gen. 5. 24. Joseph, Gen. 41. 43. Moses, Ex. 19, 3. Aaron, Lev. 16. 3. Elijah, 2 Kn. 2. 11.
Ascent. This word is used of a viaduct built by Solomon to connect his palace with the Temple on Moriah. For 'ascent of Akrabbim,' *see* Num. 34. 4; Jos. 15. 3 (R. V.); Jud. 1. 36; and for 'ascent of Ziz,' *see* 2 Chr. 20. 16 (marg. and R. V.).
Ascribe. Deu. 32. 3; Job 36. 3; Ps. 68. 34.
Asenath, ăs'-ĕ-năth, 'belonging to Neith' (a goddess of the Egyptians) (?). Gen. 41. 45.
wife of Joseph. Gen. 41. 45; 46. 20.
Aser, ā'-sĕr, same as Asher. Lu. 2. 36.
Ash (Isa. 44. 14). Heb. *Oren:* Gk. πίτυς: Bot. N. *Pinus halepensis,* — the Aleppo pine. R. V. 'fir tree.' Not the common ash.
Ashamed. Job 11. 3, shall no man make *a.*
Ps. 25. 3, let none that wait be *a.*
31. 1, let me never be *a.*
34. 5, their faces were not *a.* R. V. shall never be confounded.
Isa. 45. 17, not *a.* world without end.
65. 13, ye shall be *a.*
Jer. 2. 26, as a thief is *a.*
6. 15; 8. 12, were they *a.*
12. 13, *a.* of your revenues.
14. 4, plowmen were *a.*
Lu. 16. 3, to beg I am *a.*
Rom. 1. 16, not *a.* of Gospel.
5. 5, hope maketh not *a.* [to shame.
9. 33; 10. 11, believeth shall not be *a.* R. V. put
2 Tim. 1. 8, not *a.* of testimony.
2. 15, workman that needeth not to be *a.*
Heb. 2. 11, not *a.* to call them brethren.
11. 16, not *a.* to be called their God. R. V. *a.* of them.
1 Pet. 4. 16, suffer as Christian, not be *a.*
See Gen. 2. 25; 2 Tim. 1. 12.
Ashan, ăsh'-ăn, 'smoke.' Jos. 15. 42.
Ashbea, ăsh-bē'-ă, 'I conjure.' 1 Chr. 4. 21.
Ashbel, ăsh'-bĕl. Gen. 46. 21.
Ashbelites, ăsh'-bĕl-ītes, the descendants of Ashbel. Num. 26. 38.
Ashchenaz, ăsh-chē'-năz, same as Ashkenaz. 1 Chr. 1. 6.
Ashdod, ăsh'-dŏd, 'a strong place' (?). Jos. 15. 46.
city of Philistines; the ark carried there; men of, smitten. 1 Sam. 5.
reduced by Uzziah. 2 Chr. 26. 6.
predictions concerning. Jer. 25. 20; Am. 1. 8; Zep. 2. 4; Zec. 9. 6.
Ashdodites, ăsh'-dō-dītes, the inhabitants of Ashdod. Neh. 4. 7.
Ashdoth-pisgah, ăsh'-dōth-pĭs'-găh, 'slopes,' or, 'springs' of Pisgah. Jos. 12. 3.
Ashdothites, ăsh'-dŏ-thītes, same as Ashdodites. Jos. 13. 3.
Asher, ăsh'-ĕr, 'fortunate,' 'happy.' (1) son of Jacob. Gen. 30. 13.
his descendants. Num. 1. 40; 26. 44; 1 Chr. 7. 30; their inheritance. Jos. 19. 24; Jud. 5. 17.
See Ezek. 48. 34; Rev. 7. 6.
Anna, prophetess, descended from. Lu. 2. 36.
(2) a town. Jos. 17. 7.
Asherah, ăsh-ĕr'-ăh, a sacred tree, pole, or pillar, connected with the worship of Ashteroth, Baal and other deities, probably representing the tree of life. Rendered *grove* in the A. V. Deu. 16. 21; Jud. 6. 26; 2 Kn. 17. 10.
Asherites, ăsh'-ĕr-ītes, descendants of Asher. Jud. 1. 32.
Ashes. Gen. 18. 27, which am but dust and *a.*
Job 2. 8, and he sat down among the *a.*
13. 12, remembrances are like unto *a.*
30. 19, and become like dust and *a.*
42. 6, and repent in dust and *a.*
Ps. 102. 9, I have eaten *a.* like bread.

Isa. 44. 20, he feedeth on *a*.
Jon. 3. 6, king sat in *a*.
Heb. 9. 13, if the *a*. of an heifer. [21.
See 2 Sam. 13. 19; Esth. 4. 1; Isa. 58. 5; Mat. 11.
Ashima, ă-shī′-mă. 2 Kn. 17. 30.
Ashkelon, ăsh′-kĕ-lon (Askelon). Jud. 1. 18; 14. 19; 1 Sam. 6. 17; 2 Sam. 1. 20.
prophecies concerning. Jer. 25. 20; 47. 5; Am. 1. 8; Zep. 2. 4; Zec. 9. 5.
Ashkenaz, ăsh-kē′-năz. Gen. 10. 3.
Ashnah, ăsh′-năh, 'strong' (?). Jos. 15. 33.
Ashpenaz, ăsh′-pē-năz. Dan. 1. 3.
Ashriel, ăsh′-rĭ-ĕl, same as Asriel. 1 Chr. 7. 14.
Ashtaroth, ăsh′-tă-rōth. (1) plural of Ashtoreth, were figures of the Babylonian goddess Ishtar, the Astarte or Aphrodite of the Greeks. Jos. 9. 10.
idolatrous worship of. by Israel, Jud. 2. 13; 1 Sam. 12. 10. by Solomon, 1 Kn. 11. 5, 33.
(2) capital of Og. Deu. 1. 4; Jos. 9. 10.
Ashterathite, ăsh-tē′-ră-thite, a native of Ashtaroth. 1 Chr. 11. 44.
Ashteroth Karnaim, ăsh′-tĕ-rōth kär-nā′-ĭm, 'Ashtaroth of the two horns.' Gen. 14. 5.
Ashtoreth, ăsh′-tō-rĕth. 1 Kn. 11. 5.
Ashur, ăsh′-ŭr. 1 Chr. 2. 24.
Ashurites, ăsh′-ū-rītes. 2 Sam. 2. 9.
Ashvath, ăsh′-văth. 1 Chr. 7. 33.
Asia, ā′-siă, in the N. T. not the continent, but a Roman province in the western part of Asia Minor, including Ephesus, Smyrna, Pergamos, Thyatira, Sardis, Philadelphia, and Laodicea. (Rev. 2.; 3.) Acts 2. 9.
Aside. 2 Kn. 4. 4; Mk. 7. 33; Heb. 12. 1.
Asiel, ăs′-ĭ-ĕl, 'created by God.' 1 Chr. 4. 35.
Ask. Ps. 2. 8; Isa. 45. 11, *a*. of me.
Isa. 65. 1, sought of them that *a*. not.
Mat. 7. 7; Lu. 11. 9, *a*. and it shall be given.
21. 22, whatsoever ye *a*.
Mk. 6. 22, *a*. what thou wilt.
John 14. 13; 15. 16, *a*. in my name.
Jas. 1. 5, let him *a*. of God.
1 Pet. 3. 15, *a*. reason of hope.
1 John 3. 22; 5. 14, whatsoever we *a*.
See Deu. 32. 7; John 4. 9, 10; 1 Cor. 14. 35.
Ask at=ask of. Dan. 2. 10.
Askelon, ăs′-kĕ-lon. *See* Ashkelon. Jud. 1. 18.
Asleep. S. of S. 7. 9, those that are *a*.
Mat. 8. 24; Mk. 4. 38, but he was *a*.
26. 40; Mk. 14. 40, disciples *a*.
1 Cor. 15. 6, some are fallen *a*.
1 Thes. 4. 13, 15, them that are *a*.
2 Pet. 3. 4, since fathers fell *a*.
Asnah, ăs′-năh, 'bramble.' Ez. 2. 50.
Asnapper, ăs-năp′-pĕr, same as Assur-bani-pal, 'Assur has formed a son.' Ez. 4. 10. R. V. Osnapper.
Asp. Heb. *Péthen*: Gk. ἀσπίς: Zoöl. S. *Egyptian cobra* (*Naja haje*). Rare in Palestine.
Deu. 32. 33, the cruel venom of *a*.
Job 20. 14, 16, it is the gall of *a*.
Isa. 11. 8, play on the hole of the *a*.
Rom. 3. 13, the poison of *a*.
Aspatha, ăs-pā′-thă. Esth. 9. 7.
Asriel, ăs′-rĭ-ĕl, 'the bound of God.' Num. 26. 31.
Asrielites, ăs-rĭ-ē′-lītes, 'the family of Asriel.' Num. 26. 31.
Ass. (1) (*domestic*) (Jud. 5. 10.) (*Equus asinus*) Heb. *Hămôr*: Gk. ὄνος.
(2) (*wild*). Heb. (a) (*Arôd*, only in Job 39. 5-8).
(b) *Pérĕ*. Gk. ὄναγρος. *Equus hemionus*, Jer. 2. 24; 14. 6.
Gen. 49. 14, Issachar is a strong *a*. couching.
Num. 22. 30, am not I thine *a*.
Prov. 26. 3, bridle for *a*.
Isa. 1. 3, *a*. his master's crib.
Jer. 22. 19, burial of an *a*.
Zec. 9. 9; Mat. 21. 5, riding on *a*.
Lu. 14. 5, *a*. fallen into pit.
2 Pet. 2. 16, dumb *a*. speaking. [16.
Ass, Balaam rebuked by. Num. 22. 28; 2 Pet. 2.
laws concerning. Ex. 13. 13; 23. 4; Deu. 22. 10.
Christ rides on one (Zec. 9. 9). Mat. 21.; John 12. 14, &c.
(wild) described. Job 39. 5; Hos. 8. 9.
Assarion, a bronze coin (A. V. *farthing* Mat. 10. 29) = the Roman As or $\frac{1}{16}$ of the denarius (originally $\frac{1}{10}$), about a half-penny = 1 cent. *See* Money.
Assassins (Acts 21. 38, R. V.). This is a better rendering of the word σικάριοι—the Greek form of the Latin word *sicarii*, from *sica*, 'a short sword or dagger'—than the 'murderers' of the A. V. A secret society of political assassins.
Assault. Esth. 8. 11; Acts 14. 5; 17. 5. [ciples.
Assay (attempt). Acts 9. 26, Saul *a*. to join dis-
Acts 16. 7, they *a*. to go to Bithynia.
Heb. 11. 29, Egyptians *a*. to do.
See Deu. 4. 34; 1 Sam. 17. 39; Job 4. 2.
Assembling for worship. Lev. 23.; Deu. 16. 8; Heb. 10. 25. David's love for, Ps. 27. 4; 42.; 43.; 65.; 84.; 87.; 118. 26; 122.; 134.; 135. *See* Isa. 4. 5.; Mal. 3. 16; Mat. 18. 20.
instances of. 1 Kn. 8.; 2 Chr. 5.; 29.; 30.; Neh. 8.; Lu. 4. 16; John 20. 19; Acts 1. 13; 2. 1; 3. 1; 13. 2; 16. 13; 20. 7.
Assent. 2 Chr. 18. 12, with one *a*. R. V. mouth.
Acts 24. 9, Jews also *a*. R. V. joined in the charge.
Asshur, ăssh′-ŭr, 'the gracious One' (?). Gen. 10. 22.
Asshurim, ăssh-ū′-rĭm. Gen. 25. 3.
Assigned. Gen. 47. 22; Jos. 20. 8; 2 Sam. 11. 16.
Assir, ăs′-sĭr, 'captive.' Ex. 6. 24.
Assist. Rom. 16. 2. [an uproar.
Associate. Isa. 8. 9, *a*. yourselves. R. V. make
Assos, ăs′-sŏs, seaport of Mysia. Acts 20. 13.
Assur, ăs′-sŭr, same as Asshur. Ez. 4. 2. R. V. Assyria.
Assurance. Isa. 32. 17, effect of righteousness *a*. R. V. confidence.
Col. 2. 2, full *a*. of understanding.
1 Thes. 1. 5, gospel came in much *a*. R. V. (marg.) fulness.
Heb. 6. 11; 10. 22, full *a*. R. V. fulness.
Assurance of faith and hope, Isa. 32. 17; Col. 2. 2; 1 Thes. 1. 5; 2 Tim. 1. 12; Heb. 6. 11; 10. 22.
confirmed by love, 1 John 3. 14, 19; 4. 18.
Assure, to convince, persuade. 2 Tim. 3. 14; 1 John 3. 19.
Asswage, assuage, subside. Gen. 8. 1; Job 16. 5.
Assyria, ăs-sÿr′-ĭ-ă, was the name given to that part of Mesopotamia which lies to the north of Babylon; so named from Asshur. *See* under Babylonia. Gen. 2. 14.
Israel carried captive to. 2 Kn. 15. 29; 17.
army of, miraculously destroyed. 2 Kn. 19. 35; Isa. 37. 36.
prophecies concerning. Isa. 8.; 10. 5; 14. 24; 30. 31; 31. 8; Mic. 5. 6; Zep. 2. 13.
its glory. Ezek. 31. 3.
Assyrians, ăs-sÿr′-ĭ-ăns, pure Semites; i. e., descendants of Shem; inhabitants of Assyria. Gen. 10. 22; Isa. 10. 5.
Astaroth, ăs′-tă-rōth, same as Ashtaroth. Deu. 1. 4.
Astonied, old form of 'astonished.' Ez. 9. 3; Job 17. 8; Dan. 3. 24; 4. 19.
Astonished. Mat. 7. 28; 22. 33; Mk. 1. 22; 6. 2; 11. 18.
Lu. 4. 32, *a*. at his doctrine.
2. 47, *a*. at his understanding. R. V. amazed.
5. 9, *a*. at draught of fishes. R. V. amazed.
24. 22, women made us *a*. R. V. amazed.
Acts 9. 6, Saul trembling and *a*.
12. 16, saw Peter, they were *a*. R. V. amazed.
13. 12, deputy believed, being *a*.
See Job 26. 11. Jer. 2. 12.
Astonishment. 2 Chr. 29. 8; Jer. 25. 9, *a*. and hissing.
Ps. 60. 3, made us drink wine of *a*. R. V. stag-
Jer. 8. 21, *a*. hath taken hold. [gering.
See Deu. 28. 28, 37; Ezek. 5. 15.

Astrologers. Isa. 47. 13, let now the *a.*
Dan. 2. 2; 4. 7; 5. 7, the *a.* R. V. enchanters.
Asuppim, ă-sŭp′-pĭm, 'stores.' 1 Chr. 26. 15. R. V. the storehouse.
Asyncritus, ă-sȳn′-crĭ-tŭs, 'incomparable;' a disciple. Rom. 16. 14.
Atad, ā′-tăd, 'buckthorn.' Gen. 50. 10.
Atarah, ăt′-ă-răh, 'a crown.' 1 Chr. 2. 26.
Ataroth, ăt′-ă-rōth, 'crowns.' Num. 32. 3.
Ataroth-adar, Ataroth-addar, ăt′-ă-rōth-ā′-dār, ăt′-ă-rōth-ăd′-dār, name of a place. Jos. 16. 5; 18. 13.
Ater, ā′-tĕr, 'binder' (?). Ez. 2. 16.
Athach, ā′-thăch. 1 Sam. 30. 30.
Athaiah, ă-thāi′-ăh. Neh. 11. 4.
Athaliah, ăth-ă-lī′-ăh, 'whom Jehovah has afflicted;' daughter of Ahab, mother of Ahaziah. 2 Kn. 8. 26.
slays the seed royal, Joash only saved. 2 Kn. 11. 1; 2 Chr. 22. 10.
slain by order of Jehoiada. 2 Kn. 11. 16; 2 Chr. 23. 15.
Athenians, ă-thē′-nĭ-ăns, people of Athens. Acts 17. 21.
Athens, ăth′-ĕns, 'under the protection of Athene;' capital of Greece, the most famous literary centre of the world. Paul argues with philosophers in the market-place, and defends himself before the Court of Areopagus. Acts 17. 16–31; 1 Thes. 3. 1.
Athirst. Mat. 25. 44; Rev. 21. 6; 22. 17.
Athlai, ăth-lā′-ī, shortened form of Athaliah. Ez. 10. 28.
At one, set, (would have) reconciled (them). Acts 7. 26. Hence the verb 'atone' = at one (to reconcile), and 'atonement' = at-one-ment.
Atonement. Lev. 23. 28; 25. 9, a day of *a.*
2 Sam. 21. 3, wherewith shall I make *a.*
Rom. 5. 11, by whom we received *a.* R. V. reconciliation.
Atonement under the law. Ex. 29. 36; 30.; Lev. 1.; 4. 20, &c. Num. 8. 21.
made by Aaron for the plague. Num. 16. 46.
made by Christ. Rom. 3. 24; 5. 6; 2 Cor. 5. 18; Gal. 1. 4; 3. 13; Tit. 2. 14; Heb. 9. 28; 1 Pet. 1. 19; 2. 24; 3. 18; 1 John 2. 2; Rev. 1. 5; 13. 8, &c.
prophecies concerning. Isa. 53.; Dan. 9. 24; Zec. 13. 1, 7; John 11. 50.
commemorated in the Lord's supper. Mat. 26. 26; 1 Cor. 11. 23.
Atonement, Day of. This fast was observed on the 10th of the month Tisri (October) as the great day of national humiliation, and expiation of the sins both of the priests and the people. The ritual is prescribed in Lev. 16.; 23. 26-32; Num. 29. 7-11. This is the 'fast' of Acts 27. 9, after which navigation was dangerous.
Atroth, ăt′-rōth, same as Ataroth. Num. 32. 35.
Attai, ăt′-tā-ī, 'opportune.' 1 Chr. 2. 35.
Attain. Ps. 139. 6, I cannot *a.* to it.
2 Sam. 23. 19; 1 Chr. 11. 25, he *a.* not to first [three.
Rom. 9. 30, Gentiles *a.* to righteousness.
Phil. 3. 11, 16, that I might *a.*
See Gen. 47. 9; Prov. 1. 5; Ezek. 46. 7; 1 Tim. [4. 6.
Attalia, ăt-tă-lī′-ă, so called from Attalus, the royal founder of the city, seaport on the coast of Pamphylia. Acts 14. 25.
Attend. Ps. 17. 1; 61. 1; 142. 6, *a.* to my cry.
Prov. 4. 20, my son, *a.* to my words.
See Ps. 55. 2; 86. 6.
Attendance. (1) Heb. 7. 13. (2) attention. 1 Tim. 4. 13. R. V. heed.
Attent, attentive. 2 Chr. 6. 40; 7. 15.
Attentive. Neh. 1. 6; Job 37. 2; Ps. 130. 2; Lu. 19. 48.
Attire. Lev. 16. 4; Jer. 2. 32; Ezek. 23. 15.
Audience, a hearing, not a company of hearers.
1 Chr. 28. 8, in *a.* of our God.
Lu. 7. 1; 20. 45, in *a.* of people.
Acts 13. 16, ye that fear God give *a.*
See Ex. 24. 7; Acts 15. 12.
Augment. Num. 32. 14.
Augustus, âu-gŭs′-tŭs, 'venerable.' Lu. 2. 1.

Austere. Lu. 19. 21.
Author. 1 Cor. 14. 33; Heb. 5. 9; 12. 2.
Authority. Mat. 7. 29; Mk. 1. 22, as one having *a.*
8. 9; Lu. 7. 8, I am a man under *a.*
21. 23; by what *a.*
Lu. 4. 36; 9. 1, power and *a.* over devils.
19. 17, have *a.* over ten cities.
John 5. 27, *a.* to execute judgment.
1 Cor. 15. 24, put down all *a.*
1 Tim. 2. 2, kings and all in *a.*
2. 12, suffer not a woman to usurp *a.* R. V. have dominion.
Tit. 2. 15, rebuke with all *a.*
1 Pet. 3, 22, angels and *a.* subject.
See Prov. 29. 2; 2 Cor. 10. 8; Rev. 13. 2.
Ava, ā′-vă. 2 Kn. 17. 24.
Availeth. Esth. 5. 13; Gal. 5. 6; Jas. 5. 16.
Aven, ā′-vĕn, 'idolatry.' Ezek. 30. 17.
Avenge. Deu. 32. 43, he will *a.* blood.
Jos. 10. 13, sun stayed till people *a.*
1 Sam. 24. 12, the Lord judge and *a.*
2 Sam. 22. 48; Ps. 18. 47, it is God that *a.* me. R. V. executeth vengeance for.
Esth. 8. 13, Jews *a.* themselves.
Isa. 1. 24, I will *a.* me of mine enemies.
Lu. 18. 3, *a.* me of my adversary.
See Gen. 4. 24; Lev. 19. 18; Jer. 5. 9; 9. 9.
Avenger. 'Whoso sheddeth man's blood, by man shall his blood be shed,' was, and still is, the universal law of the Semitic race, and its execution primarily devolved (with other duties, Lev. 25.) upon the nearest kinsman of the deceased, but extended also to the whole tribe. The Hebrew code restricted this law by providing 'Cities of Refuge,' to which the manslayer might flee in cases of 'manslaughter.' (Num. 35. 10–15.) *See* Refuge, Cities of.
Ps. 8. 2; 44. 16, enemy and *a.*
1 Thes. 4. 6, the Lord is the *a.*
See Deu. 19. 6; Jos. 20. 5.
Averse. Mic. 2. 8.
Avim, ā′-vĭm, 'ruins' (?) in the Philistine country. Deu. 2. 23; Jos. 13. 3; 18. 23. R. V. Avvim.
Avims, Avites, ā′-vĭms, ā′-vītes. Deu. 2. 23; Jos. 13. 3.
Avith, ā′-vĭth. Gen. 36. 35.
Avoid. (1) Prov. 4. 15, *a.* it, pass not by it.
1 Tim. 6. 20; 2 Tim. 2. 23; Tit. 3. 9, *a.* babblings.
(2) to retire, escape, withdraw. 1 Sam. 18. 11.
See Rom. 16. 17; 2 Cor. 8. 20.
Avouched, avowed, declared (to be). Deu. 26. 17, 18.
Awake. Ps. 17. 15, when I *a.*, with thy likeness.
73. 20, as a dream when one *a.*
Prov. 23. 35, *a.* I will seek it again.
Isa. 51. 9, *a.*, *a.*, put on strength.
Joel 1. 5, *a.* ye drunkards.
Zec. 13. 7, *a.* O sword.
Lu. 9. 32, when *a.* they saw his glory.
Rom. 13. 11, high time to *a.*
1 Cor. 15. 34, *a.* to righteousness.
Eph. 5. 14, *a.* thou that sleepest.
See Jer. 51. 57; John 11. 11.
Aware. S. of S. 6. 12; Jer. 50. 24; Lu. 11. 44.
Away with, 'put up with,' endure, tolerate. Isa. 1. 13.
Awe. Ps. 4. 4; 33. 8; 119. 161.
Awl. Ex. 21. 6; Deu. 15. 17.
Axe. Ps. 74. 5, famous as he had lifted up *a.*
Isa. 10. 15, shall the *a.* boast.
Mat. 3. 10; Lu. 3. 9, the *a.* is laid to root.
See 1 Sam. 13. 20; 1 Kn. 6. 7; 2 Kn. 6. 5.
Azal, ā′-zăl. Zec. 14. 5. R. V. Azel.
Azaliah, ăz-ă-lī′-ăh, 'Jehovah has reserved.' 2 Kn. 22. 3.
Azaniah, ăz-ă-nī′-ăh, 'Jehovah hath heard.' Neh. 10. 9.
Azarael, ăz-ă-rā′-ĕl, 'God hath helped.' Neh. 12. 36.
Azareel, ăz′-ă-rēel, same as preceding. 1 Chr. 12. 6.
Azariah, ăz-ă-rī′-ăh, 'Jehovah hath helped.' (1) 2 Chr. 22. 6.

(2) (Uzziah) king of Judah, his good reign. 2 Kn. 14. 21; 2 Chr. 26.
his wars. 2 Chr. 26.
invades the priest's office. 2 Chr. 26. 16.
struck with leprosy. 2 Kn. 15. 5; 2 Chr. 26. 20.
(3) prophet, exhorts Asa. 2 Chr. 15.

Azaz, ā'-zăz, 'strong.' 1 Chr. 5. 8.

Azazel, ăz'-ă-zĕl. Lev. 16. 8 (marg. & R. V.). A. V. scapegoat.

Azaziah, ăz-ă-zī'-ăh, 'Jehovah hath strengthened.' 1 Chr. 15. 21.

Azbuk, ăz'-bŭk. Neh. 3. 16.

Azekah, ă-zē'-kăh, 'dug over.' Jos. 10. 10.

Azel, ā'-zĕl, 'noble' (?). 1 Chr. 8. 37.

Azem, ā'-zĕm, 'strength,' 'bone.' Jos. 15. 29.

Azgad, ăz'-găd, 'Gad is strong.' Ez. 2. 12. [20.

Aziel, ā'-zĭ-ĕl, 'God is my strength.' 1 Chr. 15.

Aziza, ă-zī'-ză, 'strong.' Ez. 10. 27.

Azmaveth, ăz-mā'-vĕth, 'death is strong' (?). (1) 2 Sam. 23. 31. (2) Ez. 2. 24.

Azmon, ăz'-mŏn. Num. 34. 4.

Aznoth-tabor, ăz'-nōth-tā'-bôr, 'ears (i. e., summits) of Tabor.' Jos. 19. 34.

Azor, ā'-zôr, 'helper.' Mat. 1. 13. [Acts 8. 40.

Azotus, ă-zō'-tŭs, the Greek form of ASHDOD.

Azriel, ăz'-rĭ-ĕl, 'God is my help.' 1 Chr. 5. 24.

Azrikam, ăz-rī'-kăm, 'my help has arisen.' 1 Chr. 3. 23.

Azubah, ă-zū'-băh, forsaken. (1) 1 Chr. 2. 18. (2) 1 Kn. 22. 12.

Azur, ā'-zûr, same as AZOR. Jer. 28. 1.

Azzah, ăz'-zăh, 'strong,' 'fortified,' same as Gaza. Deu. 2. 23.

Azzan, ăz'-zăn, 'strong.' Num. 34. 26.

Azzur, ăz'-zûr, same as AZOR. Neh. 10. 17.

Baal, bā'-ăl, Heb. Băăl, plural Bā'-ăl-ĭm, 'lord,' 'master,' 'possessor,' 'owner.' (1) The Baals were local deities of the Canaanites, worshipped chiefly at the high places and on housetops. Jos. 13. 17; 1 Kn. 16. 31; 18. 18, 19, 20, 22.
worshipped. Num. 22. 41; Jud. 2. 13; 8. 33; 1 Kn. 16. 32; 18. 26; 2 Kn. 17. 16; 19. 18; 21. 3; Jer. 2. 8; 7. 9; 12. 16; 19. 5; 23. 13; Hos. 2. 8; 13. 1, &c.
his altars and priests destroyed by Gideon, Jud. 6. 25. by Elijah, 1 Kn. 18. 40. by Jehu, 2 Kn. 10. 18. by Jehoiada, 2 Kn. 11. 18. by Josiah, 2 Kn. 23. 4; 2 Chr. 34. 4.
(2) a place. 1 Chr. 4. 33.
(3) a person. 1 Chr. 5. 5.

Baalah, bā'-ă-lăh, 'mistress.' Jos. 15. 10. [44.

Baalath, bā'-ă-lăth, same as preceding. Jos. 19.

Baalath-beer, bā'-ă-lăth-bēer, 'mistress of a well.' Jos. 19. 8.

Baal-berith, bā'-ăl-bē'-rĭth, 'lord of covenant.' Jud. 8. 33.

Baale, bā'-ă-lē, plural of Baal. 2 Sam. 6. 2. [17.

Baal-gad, bā'ăl-găd, 'lord of fortune.' Jos. 11.

Baal-hamon, bā'-ăl-hā'-mŏn, 'lord of a multitude.' S. of S. 8. 11.

Baal-hanan, bā'-ăl-hā'-năn, 'Baal is gracious.' Gen. 36. 38.

Baal-hazor, bā'-ăl-hā'-zôr, 'lord of a village.' 2 Sam. 13. 23.

Baal-hermon, bā'-ăl-hĕr'-mon, 'lord of Hermon.' Jud. 3. 3.

Baali, bā'-ă-lī, 'my lord.' Hos. 2. 16. [2.

Baalim, bā'-ă-lĭm, 'lords.' Jud. 2. 11; 2 Chr. 28.

Baalis, bā'-ă-lĭs, 'son of delight' (?). Jer. 40. 14.

Baalism, the worship of Baal, everywhere present when Israel entered Canaan.

Baal-meon, bā'-ăl-mē'-on, 'lord of habitation.' Num. 32. 38.

Baal-peor, bā'-ăl-pē'-ôr, 'lord of Peor.' Num. 25. 3.
the trespass of Israel concerning. Num. 25.; Deu. 4. 3; Ps. 106. 28; Hos. 9. 10.

Baal-perazim, bā'-ăl-pĕ-rā'-zĭm, 'lord of breaches.' David's victory over Philistines at. 2 Sam. 5. 20. R. V. (marg.) place of breaking faith.

Baal-shalisha, bā'-ăl-shăl'-ĭ-shă, 'lord of Shalisha.' 2 Kn. 4. 42.

Baal-tamar, bā'-ăl-tā'-măr, 'possessor of palm trees.' Jud. 20. 33.

Baal-zebub, bā'-ăl-zē'-bŭb, 'lord of flies;' false god of Ekron. Ahaziah rebuked for sending to inquire of. 2 Kn. 1. 2.

Baal-zephon, bā'-ăl-zē'-phŏn, 'lord of Zephon.' Ex. 14. 2.

Baana, bā'-ă-nă, 'son of distress' (?). 1 Kn. 4. 12.

Baanah, bā'-ă-năh (same as BAANA), and Rechab. for murdering Ish-bosheth, slain by David. 2 Sam. 4. 2.

Baara, bā'-ă-ră, 'foolish.' 1 Chr. 8. 8.

Baaseiah, bā'-ă-sei'-ăh, 'work of Jehovah.' 1 Chr. 6. 40.

Baasha, bā-ăsh'-ă, king of Israel, destroys the house of Jeroboam. 1 Kn. 15. 16, 27.
Jehu's prophecy concerning him. 1 Kn. 16. 1.

Babbler. Eccl. 10. 11; Acts 17. 18.

Babbling. Prov. 23. 29; 1 Tim. 6. 20; 2 Tim. 2. 16.

Babe. Ps. 8. 2; Mat. 21. 16, out of mouth of *b.*
17. 14, leave their substance to *b.*
Isa. 3. 4, *b.* shall rule over them.
Mat. 11. 25; Lu. 10. 21, revealed to *b.*
Rom. 2. 20, teacher of *b.*
1 Cor. 3. 1, *b.* in Christ.
1 Pet. 2. 2, newborn *b.*
See Ex. 2. 6; Lu. 2. 12, 16; Heb. 5. 13.

Babel, bā'-bĕl, connected by a play on the word with a root meaning 'he confounded.' *See* Gen. 11. 9: compare under BABYLON.
Nimrod king of. Gen. 10. 10. [14. 9.
confusion of tongues at the building of. Gen.

Babylon, băb'-ў-lon, Greek form of Bab-ilu, 'the gate of God.' (1) The metropolis of Chaldea, on the site of the tower of Babel. Gen. 10. 10; 2 Kn. 17. 30; 20. 12.
ambassadors from, to Hezekiah. 2 Kn. 20. 12; 2 Chr. 32. 31; Isa. 39.
Jewish captivity there. 2 Kn. 25.; 2 Chr. 36.; Jer. 39.; 52.
return from. Ez. 1.; Neh. 2.
greatness of. Dan. 4. 30.
taken by the Medes. Dan. 5. 30.
fall of. Isa. 13. 14; 21. 2; 47.; 48.; Jer. 25. 12; 50.; 51.
church in. 1 Pet. 5. 13.
(2) the Great. Rev. 14. 8; 17.; 18.

Babylonia and Assyria.

By *Babylonia* (the plain of Shinar, Gen. 10. 10) is meant the great alluvial district of the lower Euphrates and Tigris, which extends from about 30° to 33° N. lat. Owing probably to the great fertility of its soil, it was from prehistoric times a populous region, and it is now known to have been, with its great capital Babylon, the cradle of the civilization of western Asia. *Assyria* lies further to the north, to the east of the Tigris, from about 35° to 37° N. lat., above the confluence of the Tigris and its tributary, the river Zab. In Gen. 10. 8, it is said that Nimrod the Babylonian built the Assyrian capital Nineveh: and modern researches do at least show that the civilization of the northern was derived from that of the southern district. The language of both these regions was *Semitic:* i. e., the races inhabiting them belonged to the same division of the human race as the Hebrews: but the monuments prove that Babylonia was at a remote period peopled by a non-Semitic race (the *Sumerian*), from which the cuneiform (wedge-shaped) writing of the extant monuments was derived.

During the nineteenth century a world of new knowledge was opened up by the excavation of ancient sites in Assyria and Babylonia, and by the almost miraculous decipherment of the vast stores of cuneiform documents there discovered. One single site, that of Nippur, excavated by the expedition of the University of Pennsylvania, yielded over 20,000 inscriptions and some 25,000 clay tablets.

The cuneiform literature, notably the tablets found in the library of Assurbanipal at Nineveh, throws a remarkable light on the early chapters of Genesis. The Babylonian mythology, we learn, contained an account of creation which, like that of the Hebrews, was divided into seven stages; it contained also the story of a deluge from which one family was saved by an ark, which they did not leave until a dove, a swallow, and a raven had been sent out to see whether they could find dry land. These Babylonian legends contain many rude polytheistic elements, and their moral tone contrasts markedly with that of the narratives in Genesis; but there can be little doubt that in them we have the sources from which the Hebrew cosmogony was derived. (For a detailed account see Sayce, *Fresh Light from the Ancient Monuments*, or Ryle, *Early Narratives of Genesis.*)

The oldest *historical* record by which the cuneiform literature illustrates the Old Testament history is that relating to the Babylonian king Chammu-rabi (perhaps about 1900 B. C.), who consolidated North and South Babylonia into one kingdom, by overcoming Eri-aku of Larsa. Some scholars identify these rulers with Amraphel of Shinar and Arioch of Ellasar (Gen. 14. 1-16), who with Chedorlaomer of Elam and Tidal of Goiim were overthrown by Abraham on their return from an expedition against the cities of the Dead Sea; but the identification is not undisputed.

Assyria and Israel. The rise of the Assyrian Empire belongs to the fifteenth and following centuries B. C. Before that time Babylonia had been of relatively greater importance: but a remarkable series of tablets unearthed at Tell-el-Amarna in Egypt proves that by about 1430 B. C. Assyria had become so predominant that the Assyro-Babylonian language and writing were used even in Egypt as the medium of diplomatic correspondence.

In the twelfth century the sway of the Assyrian Tiglath-Pileser I. extended as far west as the Phœnician coast: during the two following centuries internal weakness hindered the expansion of the Assyrian Empire, and room was left for the growth of the Syrian kingdom and of that of Israel. But in the ninth century the Assyrians began to move southward: it is even possible that Omri, king of Israel, was made tributary to them. Certainly in 854 B. C. Shalmaneser II. overthrew a coalition in which Syria and Israel took a part, and in 842 the same king took tribute from Jehu. From this time onward the policy of Assyria was a continual menace to Israel and Judah, to whom the intermediate state of Syria proved an ineffectual bulwark. A revolt of Syria and Israel in 734 B. C. only led to the fall of Damascus, the deportation of the people of Gilead and Naphtali and the subjection of Judah to Assyria. Israel now began to look toward Egypt for help, but in vain. Samaria, besieged in 725 by Shalmaneser IV., was taken in 722 by Sargon, who also defeated an Egyptian army at Raphia in 720. The northern kingdom now disappeared from history, and the time of Judah was short. A revolt of the Babylonian Merodach-Baladan against Assyria (721-710) led Hezekiah to hope for deliverance from that quarter: the prophet Isaiah, however, succeeded in proving to the king the folly of attempting to revolt, and of seeking help from Egypt. But in 702 Hezekiah, with other Palestinian kings, refused to pay tribute: and when Sennacherib came south for vengeance, only a sudden catastrophe averted from Jerusalem a doom that seemed inevitable (701).

From this point the Assyrians begin to disappear from Biblical history. They conquered Egypt at the beginning of the seventh century, but soon lost it again: and at the end of that century the Medes and Babylonians overthrew their empire and destroyed Nineveh (607). The Syrian and Palestinian part of the Assyrian Empire was not left to the Babylonians in undisputed possession. Pharaoh Necho of Egypt marched northward to claim it, but after having overcome the ineffectual resistance of Josiah at Megiddo was defeated at Carchemish by Nebuchadnezzar the Chaldæan (605). Josiah's successor Jehoiakim wavered between the Chaldæans and the Egyptians: but in 597 Jerusalem was taken by Nebuchadnezzar: Jehoiakim's son and successor Jehoiachin was carried off to Babylon with nearly the whole population of the city.

The new Babylonian empire was of short duration. Nebuchadnezzar had time to make Babylon one of the world's wonders, but his successors achieved nothing: and in 538 Cyrus the Elamite, who had already overthrown the Medes and created an empire extending from the Caspian to the Persian Gulf, and from the Indus to the Mediterranean, entered Babylon as a conqueror, and the ancient Semitic empire gave place to that of Persia.

Babylonians, băb-ȳ-lō'-nī-ăns, people of Babylon. Ezek. 23. 15.

Babylonish, băb-ȳ-lō'-nĭsh, of, or belonging to, Babylon. Jos. 7. 21.

Baca, bā'-că, 'weeping,' or, 'balsam-tree;' valley of misery. Ps. 84. 6.

Bachrites, băch'-rītes, the family of Becher. Num. 26. 35.

Back. Jos. 8. 26, drew not his hand *b.*
1 Sam. 10. 9, he turned his *b.*
Neh. 9. 26, cast law behind *b.*
Ps. 129. 3, plowers plow on my *b.*
Prov. 10. 13; 19. 29; 26. 3, rod for *b.*
Isa. 38. 17, cast sins behind *b.*
50. 6, gave *b.* to smiters.
See Num. 24. 11; 2 Sam. 19. 10; Job 26. 9.

Backbiting, slandering, forbidden. Ps. 15. 3; Prov. 25. 23; Rom. 1. 30; 2 Cor. 12. 20.

Backside, the back part, rear. Ex. 3. 1.

Backsliding. Prov. 14. 14, *b.* in heart filled with his own ways.
Jer. 3. 6, 8, 11, 12, *b.* Israel.
8. 5, perpetual *b.*
14. 7, our *b.* are many.
Hos. 4. 16, as a *b.* heifer. R. V. stubborn.
11. 7, bent to *b.* from me.
14. 4, will heal their *b.*

Backsliding (turning from God). 1 Kn. 11. 9; Mat. 18. 6; 2 Cor. 11. 3; Gal. 3. 1; 5. 4. Israel, Ex. 32.; Isa. 1.; Jer. 2. 19; 3. 6, 11; 12.; 14.; 22.; Hos. 4. 16; 11. 7. Saul, 1 Sam. 15. 11. Solomon, 1 Kn. 11. 3, 4. Peter, Mat. 26. 70-74; Gal. 2. 14.
God's displeasure at. Ps. 78. 57, 58, 59.
punishment of. Prov. 14. 14; Jer. 2. 19; 5. 6.
pardon for, promised. 2 Chr. 7. 14; Jer. 3. 12; 31. 20; 36. 3, &c.; Hos. 14. 4.
restoration from. Ps. 80. 3; 85. 4; Lam. 5. 21.
healing of. Jer. 3. 22; Hos. 14. 4; 5. 15.

Backward. 2 Kn. 20. 10; Isa. 38. 8, let shadow return *b.*
Job 23. 8, *b.*, but I cannot perceive.
Ps. 40. 14; 70. 2, driven *b.*
Isa. 59. 14, judgment is turned *b.*
Jer. 7. 24, they went *b.* and not forward.
See Gen. 9. 23; 49. 17; John 18. 6.

Bad. Gen. 24. 50; 31. 24, 29; Lev. 27. 12, 14, 33; Num. 13. 19; 24. 13; 2 Sam. 13. 22; 14. 17; 1 Kn. 3. 9; Mat. 22. 10; 2 Cor. 5. 10, good or *b.*
See Lev. 27. 10; Ez. 4. 12; Jer. 24. 2; Mat. 13. 48.

Badger (Ex. 26. 14; Ezek. 16. 10). Heb. (Taḥash): Gk. ὑάκινθος. R. V. seal; marg. porpoise. *Taḥash* seems a generic word for 'dolphins,' 'seals,' &c., and in Ezek. 16. 10 appears to mean sealskin.

Badgers' skins. Badger is used only of the skin from which the outer covering for the tabernacle, &c., was made. Ex. 25. 5. R. V. sealskins.

Badness. Gen. 41. 19.

Bag. Deu. 25. 13; Prov. 16. 11; Mic. 6. 11, *b.* of weights.
Job 14. 17, transgression sealed in *b.*
Isa. 46. 6, lavish gold out of *b.*
Hag. 1. 6, *b.* with holes.
Lu. 12. 33, *b.* that wax not old. R. V. purses.

ASSYRIAN FISH-GOD

From a bas-relief on the palace of Assur-nasir-pal, king of Assyria about 885–860 B.C., now in the British Museum. (*Picture Post Library*)

ASSYRIAN KING RECEIVING TRIBUTE

From a bas-relief on the Black Obelisk set up by Shalmaneser III, king of Assyria 859–824 B.C., now in the British Museum. The winged disc is the symbol of the god Ashur, and the kneeling figure is 'Jehu, son of Omri', king of Israel.

John 12. 6; 13. 29, a thief, and had the *b*.
See 1 Sam. 17. 40; 2 Kn. 5. 23; Prov. 7. 20.

Baharumite, bă-hă-rū'-mite, an inhabitant of Bahurim. 1 Chr. 11. 33.

Bahurim, bă-hū'-rĭm, '(village of) young men.' 2 Sam. 16. 5.

Bajith, bā'-jĭth (same as BETH), 'house.' Isa. 15. 2.

Bakbakkar, băk-băk'-kär. 1 Chr. 9. 15.

Bakbuk, băk'-bŭk, 'a flask.' Ez. 2. 51.

Bakbukiah, băk-bū-kī'-ăh, 'emptying (i. e., wasting) of Jehovah' (?). Neh. 11. 17.

Bake. Gen. 19. 3; Lev. 26. 26; 1 Sam. 28. 24; Isa. 44. 15, *b*. bread.
Ex. 12. 39; Lev. 24. 5, *b*. cakes.
See Gen. 40. 17; Ex. 16. 23; Lev. 2. 4; Num. 11. 8.

Baker. Gen. 40. 1; 41. 10; 1 Sam. 8. 13; Jer. 37. 21; Hos. 7. 4.

Balaam, bā'-lăam, requested by Balak to curse Israel, is forbidden. Num. 22. 5, 13.
his anger. Num. 22. 27.
blesses Israel. Num. 23. 19; 24.
his prophecies. Num. 23. 9, 24; 24. 17.
his wicked counsel. Num. 31. 16; Deu. 23. 4.
See Jos. 24. 9; Jud. 11. 25; Mic. 6. 5; 2 Pet. 2. 15; Jude 11; Rev. 2. 14.
slain. Num. 31. 8; Jos. 13. 22.

Balac, bā'-lăc, same as BALAK. Rev. 2. 14.

Baladan, băl'-ă-dăn, 'He has given a son.' 2 Kn. 20. 12.

Balah, bā'-lăh. Jos. 19. 3.

Balak, bā'-lăk, 'devastator.' Num. 22. 2.

Balance. Lev. 19. 36; Prov. 16. 11; Ezek. 45. 10, just *b*.
Job 37. 16, the *b*. of clouds.
Ps. 62. 9, laid in *b*., lighter than vanity.
Prov. 11. 1; 20. 23; Hos. 12. 7; Am. 8. 5; Mic. 6. 11, false *b*.
Isa. 40. 12, 15, weighed hills in *b*.
46. 6, weigh silver in the *b*.
Rev. 6. 5, a pair of *b*.
See Job 6. 2; 31. 6; Jer. 32. 10.

Bald. 2 Kn. 2. 23, go up, thou *b*. head.
Jer. 48. 37; Ezek. 29. 18, every head *b*.
See Lev. 13. 40; Jer. 16. 6; Ezek. 27. 31.

Baldness. Isa. 3. 24, instead of well set hair *b*.
22. 12, call to weeping and *b*.
Mic. 1. 16, enlarge thy *b*. as eagle.
See Lev. 21. 5; Deu. 14. 1; Ezek. 7. 18; Am. 8. 10.

Ball. Isa. 22. 18.

Balm, or Balsam. Heb. *Tzŏrî*: Gk. ῥητίνη: Bot. N. *Balsamodendron Gileadense*. There is little doubt that the balm of Scripture was the aromatic resin which flows from the trunks of the species of Balsamodendron which grow in southern Syria and northeast Africa.
Jer. 8. 22; 46. 11, *b*. in Gilead.
See Gen. 37. 25; 43. 11; Jer. 51. 8; Ezek. 27. 17.

Bamah, bā'-măh, 'high place.' Ezek. 20. 29.

Bamoth, bā'-mōth, 'high places.' Num. 21. 19.

Bamoth-baal, bā'-mōth-bā'-ăl, '*h. p.* of Baal.' Jos. 13. 17.

Band of soldiers. This was the Roman cohort, the tenth part of a legion. It consisted nominally of six hundred men under the command of six centurions. Usually it numbered from 400 to 600. The Augustan band, Acts 27. 1; the Italian band, Acts 10. 1 = a cohort raised in Italy for service abroad.

Bands. Ps. 2. 3; 107. 14, break their *b*. asunder.
73. 4, there are no *b*. in their death.
Hos. 11. 4, drew them with *b*. of love.
Zec. 11. 7, two staves, Beauty and *B*.
Mat. 27. 27; Mk. 15. 16, gathered to him whole *b*.
See Job 38. 31; Eccl. 7. 26; Lu. 8. 29; Col. 2. 19.

Bani, bā'-nī, 'built.' 2 Sam. 23. 36.

Banished. 2 Sam. 14. 13; Ez. 7. 26; Lam. 2. 14.

Bank. (1) Gen. 41. 17; Ezek. 47. 7, *b*. of the river.
(2) Lu. 19. 23, gavest not money into *b*.
(3) A mound, for besieging a city. 2 Sam. 20. 15. R. V. mount.

Banner. Ps. 20. 5, in name of God set up *b*.
See Ps. 60. 4; S. of S. 2. 4; 6. 4; Isa. 13. 2.

Banquet. (1) in the Hebrew, 'to drink,' 'banquet' formerly meaning only 'dessert.' Esth. 5. 4; 7. 1; S. of S. 2. 4; Dan. 5.; Am. 6. 7.
(2) Job 41. 6, make a *b*. of him. R. V. traffic.

Baptism. (Gk. βάπτισμα.) A sacrament or symbolic rite of universal obligation, instituted by our Lord as a means of admission into the Christian Church; practised by John the Baptist as a sign of repentance. Metaphorically (Mk. 10. 38; Lu. 12. 50) of an overwhelming by sorrow.
Mat. 20. 22; Mk. 10. 38; Lu. 12. 50, to be baptized with *b*.
21. 25; Mk. 11. 30; Lu. 7. 29; 20. 4; Acts 1. 22; 18. 25; 19. 3, *b*. of John.
Mk. 1. 4; Lu. 3. 3; Acts 13. 24; 19. 4, *b*. of repentance.
Rom. 6. 4; Col. 2. 12, buried with him by *b*.
Eph. 4. 5, one Lord, one faith, one *b*.
Heb. 6. 2, doctrine of *b*.

Baptism of John. Mat. 3. 6; Mk. 1. 4; Lu. 3.; John 1. 19, 25, 28, 31; Acts 19. 4.
by disciples, not by Christ. John 4. 2.
form of. Mat. 28. 19.
Pharisees' answer concerning John's. Mat. 21. 25; Mk. 11. 31; Lu. 20. 4.
appointed by Christ. Mat. 28. 19; Mk. 16. 16; John 3. 22; 4. 1.
its signification. Acts 2. 38; 19. 4; 22. 16; Rom. 6. 3; 1 Cor. 10. 2; 12. 13; 15. 29; Gal. 3. 27; Col. 2. 12; Tit. 3. 5; 1 Pet. 3. 21.
instances of. Acts 8. 12, 38; 9. 18; 10. 48; 16. 15, 33; 1 Cor. 1. 16.
Crispus and Gaius baptized by Paul. 1 Cor. 1. 14.
one baptism. Eph. 4. 5.

Baptize. Mat. 3. 11; Mk. 1. 8; Lu. 3. 16, *b*. with Holy Ghost.
3. 14, I have need to be *b*.
3. 16, Jesus when *b*. went up.
Mk. 16. 16, he that believeth and is *b*.
Lu. 3. 7, multitude came to be *b*.
3. 12; 7. 29, publicans to be *b*.
3. 21, Jesus being *b*., and praying.
7. 30, Pharisees and lawyers being not *b*.
John 1. 33, he that sent me to *b*.
3. 22, 23, tarried with them and *b*.
4. 1, 2, Jesus made and *b*. more.
Acts 2. 38, repent and be *b*.
2. 41, gladly received word were *b*.
8. 12, *b*. both men and women.
8. 16, *b*. in name of Jesus.
8. 36, what doth hinder to be *b*.
9. 18, Saul arose and was *b*.
10. 47, can any forbid *b*.
16. 15, 33, *b*. and household.
18. 8, many believed and were *b*.
22. 16, be *b*. and wash away thy sins.
Rom. 6. 3; Gal. 3. 27, were *b*. into Jesus.
1 Cor. 1. 13, were ye *b*. in name of Paul.
10. 2, were all *b*. in cloud.
12. 13, all *b*. into one body.
15. 29, *b*. for the dead.

Barabbas, bär-ăb'-băs, 'son of Abba or father;' a robber, released instead of Jesus. Mat. 27. 16; Mk. 15. 6, 7; Lu. 23. 18; John 18. 40.

Barachel, bă-rā'-chĕl, 'God hath blessed.' Job 32. 6.

Barachias, băr-ă-chī'-ăs, 'Jehovah hath blessed.' Mat. 23. 35.

Barak, bâr'-ăk, 'lightning;' delivers Israel from Sisera. Jud. 4. 5, 6; Heb. 11. 32.

Barbarians, foreigners, those not Greeks. Acts 28. 4; Rom. 1. 14; 1 Cor. 14. 11.

Barbarous, foreign. Acts 28. 2.

Barbed, furnished with projecting points. Job 41. 7.

Barber. Ezek. 5. 1.

Bare (*v*.). Ex. 19. 4; Deu. 1. 31; Isa. 53. 12; 63. 9; Mat. 8. 17; 1 Pet. 2. 24.

Bare (*ad*.). Isa. 52. 10; 1 Cor. 15. 37.

Barefoot. 2 Sam. 15. 30; Isa. 20. 2, 3.

Barhumite, bär-hū'-mīte, same as BAHARUMITE. 2 Sam. 23. 31.

Bariah, bă-rī′-ăh, 'a fugitive.' 1 Chr. 3. 22.
Bar-jesus, bär-jē′-sŭs, 'son of Jesus;' (Elymas) smitten with blindness by Paul. Acts 13. 6.
Bar-jona, bär-jō′-nă, 'son of Jona' (Simon). Mat. 16. 17.
Barked. Joel 1. 7.
Barkos, bär′-kŏs. Ez. 2. 53.
Barley. Heb. *Sĕôrah:* Gk. κριθαί: Bot. N. *Hordeum distichum*, and other varieties. The common food in Palestine of men, horses, asses, and draught oxen.
Ex. 9. 31, *b.* was in the ear.
Deu. 8. 8, a land of wheat and *b.*
Ru. 1. 22, beginning of *b.* harvest.
John 6. 9, five *b.* loaves.
Rev. 6. 6, three measures of *b.*
Barn. The ancient granaries of Palestine were caves in the limestone rock. Jud. 6. 11. Such subterranean caves may still be seen in use on the hill of Jezreel. The barns which existed in Palestine in the time of our Saviour (Lu. 12. 18) were solid edifices.
Job 39. 12, gather thy seed into *b.* R. V. threshing-floor.
Mat. 6. 26; Lu. 12. 24, nor gather into *b.*
13. 30, gather wheat into *b.*
Lu. 12. 18, pull down my *b.*
See 2 Kn. 6. 27; Joel 1. 17; Hag. 2. 19.
Barnabas, bär′-nă-băs, 'son of exhortation,' or, 'consolation;' Levite of Cyprus, sells his lands. Acts 4. 36.
preaches at Antioch. Acts 11. 22.
accompanies Paul. Acts 11. 30; 12. 25; 13.; 14.; 15.; 1 Cor. 9. 6.
disagrees with Paul about John Mark. Acts 15. 36.
is misled at Antioch by Judaizing emissaries from Jerusalem. Gal. 2. 13.
Barrel. 1 Kn. 17. 12, 14; 18. 33.
Barren. 2 Kn. 2. 19, water naught and ground *b.*
Ps. 107. 34, fruitful land into *b.* R. V. salt desert.
Isa. 54. 1, sing, O *b.*, thou that didst not bear.
2 Pet. 1. 8, neither *b.* nor unfruitful. R. V. idle.
See Ex. 23. 26; Job 24. 21; Lu. 23. 29.
Barrenness: of Sarah, Gen. 11. 30; 16. 1; 18. 1; 21. Rebekah, 25. 21. Rachel, 29. 31; 30. 1. Manoah's wife, Jud. 13. Hannah, 1 Sam. 1. Shunammite, 2 Kn. 4. 14. Elisabeth, Lu. 1. *See* Ps. 113. 9; Isa. 54. 1; Gal. 4. 27.
Bars. Job 17. 16, down to the *b.* of the pit.
Ezek. 38. 11, having neither *b.* nor gates.
See 1 Sam. 23. 7; Job 38. 10; Ps. 107. 16; Isa. 45. 2.
Barsabas, bär′-să-băs, 'son of Seba.' (1) Acts 1. 23. (2) Acts 15. 22.
Bartholomew, bär-thŏl′-ŏ-mew̄, '*s.* of Talmai;' the apostle. Mat. 10. 3; Mk. 3. 18; Lu. 6. 14; Acts 1. 13.
Bartimæus, bär-tī-mæ̆′-ŭs, '*s.* of Timæus;' blindness cured near Jericho. Mk. 10. 46.
Baruch, băr′-ŭch, 'blessed;' receives Jeremiah's evidence. Jer. 32. 12, 13; 36.
discredited by Azariah, and carried into Egypt. Jer. 43. 6.
God's message to. Jer. 45.
Barzillai, bär-zĭl-lă′-ī, 'man of iron;' loyalty to David. 2 Sam. 17. 27.
David's recognition of. 2 Sam. 19. 31; 1 Kn. 2. 7.
Base (*a.*). lowly, humble. Job 30. 8, children of *b.* men. Mal. 2. 9, I have made you *b.*
1 Cor. 1. 28, *b.* things of the world.
2 Cor. 10. 1, in presence am *b.*
See 2 Sam. 6. 22; Isa. 3. 5; Ezek. 17. 14; Dan. 4. [17.
Base (*n.*). 1 Kn. 7. 27, &c. Ten *b.* of brass.
Baser sort, lower orders (without the idea of wickedness). Acts 17. 5.
Bashan, bā′-shăn, 'soft rich soil.' A broad fertile plateau east of the Jordan; conquered. Num. 21. 33; Deu. 3. 1; Ps. 68. 15, 22; 135. 11; 136. 20.
Bashan-havoth-jair, bā′-shăn-hā′-vōth-jā′-ĭr, 'Bashan of the villages of Jair.' Deu. 3. 14.
Bashemath, băsh′-ĕ-măth, 'perfume' (?). Gen. 26. 34.
Basket. Baskets were of various kinds and sizes: (1) The Κόφινος, *Cophinus*, reticule, or hand-basket, usually carried on the arm (cf. Juvenal, Sat. iii. l. 14); the basket used after the feeding of the five thousand (Mat. 14. 20; Mk. 6. 43; Lu. 9. 17; John 6. 13). (2) A light open wicker basket, used for carrying food upon the head. This Pharaoh's chief baker carried (Gen. 40. 17). (3) A market-basket, such as that in which the lad was hawking the barley loaves and fishes. (4) A larger kind (σπυρίς), or store-basket used after the feeding of the four thousand (Mat. 15. 37; Mk. 8. 8). (5) A larger and stronger kind (σαργάνη), used for hoisting supplies up to the battlements of a besieged city. It was in one of these that Paul was lowered down from the walls of Damascus (2 Cor. 11. 33).
Deu. 28. 5, 17, blessed be thy *b.*
Am. 8. 1, *b.* of summer fruit.
Mat. 16. 9; Mk. 8. 19, how many *b.*
See Ex. 29. 23; Jud. 6. 19; Jer. 24. 2.
Basmath, băs′-măth, same as BASHEMATH. 1 Kn. [4. 15.
Bason. John 13. 5, poureth water into a *b.*
See Ex. 12. 22; 24. 6; 1 Chr. 28. 17; Jer. 52. 19.
Bastard. Deu. 23. 2, a *b.* shall not enter.
Zec. 9. 6, *b.* shall dwell in Ashdod.
Heb. 12. 8, *b.* and not sons.
Bat (Lev. 11. 19; Deu. 14. 18; Isa. 2. 20). Heb. *Atallêph:* Gk. νυκτερίς. There are bats innumerable now in Palestine. Bats are included in the Bible among 'birds,' and also among 'creepers on all fours.'
Bath, the unit of Liquid Measures, as Ephah is of the Dry = Ephah = Greek Metretes = about 9 gallons (8 gal. 5.12 pts.) = the 'firkin' of John 2. 6. *See* MEASURES.
1 Kn. 7. 26, it contained two thousand *b.*
2 Chr. 2. 10, twenty thousand *b.* of wine.
Ez. 7. 22, an hundred *b.* of wine.
Isa. 5. 10, shall yield one *b.*
Bath. Among the Hebrews bathing was practised as a religious rite for the removal of ceremonial pollution (Lev. 15. 5, 16–28; 17. 16; Num. 19. 7; Ru. 3. 3; 2 Sam. 12. 20). The high priest bathed at his inauguration (Lev. 8. 6), and on the Day of Atonement (Lev. 16. 4, 24).
Bath-rabbim, băth-răb′-bĭm, 'daughter of many.' S. of S. 7. 4.
Bath-sheba, băth′-shĕ-bă, '*d.* of the oath.' 2 Sam. 11. 3.
wife of Uriah, taken by David. 2 Sam. 11.; 12.
appeals to David for Solomon against Adonijah. 1 Kn. 1. 15.
intercedes with Solomon for Adonijah. 1 Kn. 2. 19.
Bath-shua, băth′-shŭ-ă, 'daughter of plenty.' 1 Chr. 3. 5.
Battle. 1 Sam. 17. 20, host shouted for *b.*
17. 47; 2 Chr. 20. 15, the *b.* is the Lord's.
1 Chr. 5. 20, they cried to God in *b.*
Ps. 18. 39, strength to *b.*
55. 18, delivered my soul from *b.*
Eccl. 9. 11, nor *b.* to strong.
Jer. 50. 22, sound of *b.* in land.
See Job 39. 25; 41. 8; Ps. 76. 3; 140. 7.
Battle, a body of troops. 1 Chr. 19. 9.
Battle, directions about. Deu. 20. 1.
exemptions from. Deu. 20. 5, 6, 7.
of great day of God. Rev. 16. 14.
Battlements. Deu. 22. 8, make a *b.*
Jer. 5. 10, take away her *b.* R. V. branches.
Battles of Israelites, &c. Gen. 14.; Ex. 17.; Num. 31.; Jos. 8.; 10.; Jud. 4.; 7.; 8.; 11.; 20.; 1 Sam. 4.; 11.; 14.; 17.; 31.; 2 Sam. 2.; 10.; 18.; 21. 15; 1 Kn. 20.; 22.; 2 Kn. 3.; 1 Chr. 18.; 19.; 20.; 2 Chr. 13.; 14. 9; 20.; 25.
Bavai, bă-vā′-ī. Neh. 3. 18.
Bay Tree (Ps. 37. 35). Heb. *Ezrah*, native: Gk. κέδρος τοῦ Λιβάνου: R. V. 'green tree in its native soil;' not any particular tree.
Bazlith, băz′-lĭth, 'a making naked' (?). Neh. 7. 54.

Bazluth, băz'-lŭth, same as BAZLITH. Ez. 2. 52.
Bdellium (Gen. 2. 12). Heb. *Bĕdôlaḥ:* Gk. ἄνθραξ. Some suppose it to be the gum of a Balsamodendron (*see* BALM); others a precious stone.
Beacon. Isa. 30. 17.
Bealiah, bē-ă-lī'-ăh, 'Jehovah is lord.' 1 Chr. [12. 5.
Bealoth, bĕ-ā'-lŏth, plural of BAALAH. Jos. 15. 24.
Beam. (1) Ps. 104. 3, who layeth *b.* in waters.
(2) a piece of wood. Mat. 7. 3; Lu. 6. 42.
See Jud. 16. 14; 2 Kn. 6. 2; Hab. 2. 11.
Bean (2 Sam. 17. 28; Ezek. 4. 9). Heb. *Pôl:* Gk. κύαμος: Bot. N. *vicia faba.*
Bear (*n.*). Heb. *Dôb:* Gk. ἄρκτος.
Isa. 11. 7, cow and *b.* shall feed.
59. 11, roar like *b.*
Hos. 13. 8, as a *b.* bereaved.
Am. 5. 19, a *b.* met him.
See 1 Sam. 17. 34; 2 Sam. 17. 8; 2 Kn. 2. 24; [Prov. 17. 12.
Bear (*v.*). Gen. 4. 13, greater than I can *b.*
13. 6; 36. 7, land not able to *b.*
43. 9; 44. 32, let me *b.* blame.
Ex. 20. 16; 1 Kn. 21. 10; Lu. 11. 48; John 1. 7; 5. 31; 8. 18; 15. 27; Acts 23. 11; Rom. 8. 16; 1 John 1. 2; 5. 8, *b.* witness.
28. 12, Aaron *b.* names before Lord.
Lev. 24. 15; Ezek. 23. 49; Heb. 9. 28, *b.* sin.
Num. 11. 14; Deu. 1. 9, not able to *b.* people.
Esth. 1. 22; Jer. 5. 31; Dan. 2. 39, *b.* rule.
Ps. 91. 12; Mat. 4. 6; Lu. 4. 11, they shall *b.* thee [up.
Prov. 18. 14, wounded spirit who can *b.*
Isa. 52. 11, clean that *b.* vessels.
Jer. 31. 19, *b.* reproach of youth.
Lam. 3. 27, good to *b.* yoke in youth.
Mat. 3. 11, not worthy to *b.*
27. 32; Mk. 15. 21; Lu. 23. 26, *b.* cross.
John 16. 12, cannot *b.* them now.
Rom. 13. 4, *b.* not sword in vain.
15. 1, *b.* infirmities of the weak. [covereth.
1 Cor. 13. 7, charity *b.* all things. R. V. (marg.)
15. 49, *b.* image of the heavenly.
Gal. 6. 2, 5, *b.* burdens.
6. 17, *b.* in my body.
See Ex. 28. 38; Deu. 1. 31; Prov. 12. 24. [grown.
Beard. 2 Sam. 10. 5; 1 Chr. 19. 5, till *b.* be
Ps. 133. 2, even Aaron's *b.*
Ezek. 5. 1, cause razor to pass on *b.* [41. 5.
See Lev. 13. 29; 1 Sam. 21. 13; 2 Sam. 20. 9; Jer.
Beards, laws concerning. Lev. 19. 27; 21. 5.
Bearing. Ps. 126. 6, *b.* precious seed.
John 19. 17, *b.* cross.
Rom. 2. 15; 9. 1, conscience *b.* witness.
2 Cor. 4. 10, *b.* about in body dying of Jesus.
Heb. 13. 13, *b.* his reproach.
See Gen. 1. 29; Num. 10. 17; Mk. 14. 13.
Beast. Job 12. 7, ask *b.*, they shall teach.
18. 3, counted as *b.*
Ps. 49. 12, like *b.* that perish.
73. 22, as *b.* before thee.
Prov. 12. 10, regardeth life of *b.*
Eccl. 3. 19, no pre-eminence above *b.*
1 Cor. 15. 32, fought with *b.*
Jas. 3. 7, every kind of *b.* is tamed.
2 Pet. 2. 12, as natural brute *b.*
Beasts, creation of. Gen. 1. 24.
power over, given to man. Gen. 1. 26, 28; Ps. 8. 7.
named by Adam. Gen. 2. 20.
saved from the flood. Gen. 7. 2.
ordinance concerning. Ex. 22. 19. [12.
clean and unclean. Lev. 11.; Deu. 14. 4; Acts 10.
set apart for God. Ex. 13. 12; Lev. 27. 9.
subjects of God's care. Ps. 36. 6; 104. 10, 11; 147. 9.
Daniel's vision of. Dan. 7.
John's vision. Rev. 4. 7; 13. &c.
Beat. Isa. 2. 4; Mic. 4. 3, *b.* swords.
Lu. 12. 47, *b.* with many stripes.
1 Cor. 9. 26, as one that *b.* the air. [5; 13. 9.
See Prov. 23. 14; Joel 3. 10; Mic. 4. 13; Mk. 12.
Beautiful. Ps. 48. 2, *b.* for situation is Zion.
Eccl. 3. 11, every thing *b.* in his time.
S. of S. 6. 4, thou art *b.*, O my love.
Isa. 4. 2, the branch of the Lord be *b.*
52. 1, O Zion, put on thy *b.* garments.
52. 7; Rom. 10. 15, how *b.* are the feet.
64. 11, *b.* house is burnt up.
Jer. 13. 20, where is thy *b.* flock?
Mat. 23. 27, sepulchres which appear *b.*
Beautiful gate of temple. Acts 3. 2, 10.
Beautiful women, instances: Rachel, Gen. 29. 17. Abigail, 1 Sam. 25. 3. Bath-sheba, 2 Sam. 11. 3. Esther, Esth. 2. 7.
Beauty. Ez. 7. 27, to *b.* the Lord's house.
Ps. 27. 4; 90. 17; Zec. 9. 17, *b.* of the Lord.
39. 11, *b.* to consume away.
50. 2, perfection of *b.*
Prov. 31. 30, *b.* is vain. [Isa. 3. 24.
Beauty, vanity of. Ps. 39. 11; Prov. 6. 25; 31. 30;
danger of. Gen. 12. 11; 26. 7; 34.; 2 Sam. 11.;
consumeth away. Ps. 39. 11; 49. 14. [13. &c.
Beauty and Bands. Zec. 11. 7, two staves, *b.*
Beauty of holiness, 1 Chr. 16. 29; 2 Chr. 20. 21; Ps. 29. 2; 96. 9; 110. 3.
Bebai, bē-bā'-ī. Ez. 8. 11.
Because, in order that. Mat. 20. 31.
Becher, bē'-chĕr, 'a young camel.' Gen. 46. 21.
Bechorath, bĕ-chō'-răth, 'firstborn.' 1 Sam. 9. 1.
Beckon. Lu. 1. 22; John 13. 24; Acts 12. 17; 21. 40.
Becometh. Ps. 93. 5, holiness *b.* thy house.
Rom. 16. 2; Eph. 5. 3, as *b.* saints.
Phil. 1. 27; 1 Tim. 2. 10; Tit. 2. 3, as *b.* gospel.
See Prov. 17. 7; Mat. 3. 15.
Bed. The word bed, wherever used in the Bible, must be understood to refer only to the mattress on which people slept. It resembled a very thick quilt. It was one of these little mattresses which our Lord bade the palsied man roll up and carry to his home. (Mat. 9. 6; Mk. 2. 9; John 5. 11.) Bedsteads are still generally unknown in the East.
Job 7. 13, when I say my *b.* shall comfort.
33. 15, in slumberings upon *b.*
Ps. 63. 6, when I remember thee upon my *b.*
See 2 Kn. 4. 10; Isa. 28. 20; Mk. 4. 21; Lu. 8. 16.
Bedad, bē'-dăd. Gen. 36. 35.
Bedan, bē'-dăn. 1 Sam. 12. 11. [10. 35.
Bedeiah, bĕ-dēī'-ăh, 'servant of Jehovah' (?). Ez.
Bedstead. Deu. 3. 11, was a *b.* of iron.
Bee (Deu. 1. 44; Jud. 14. 8; 1 Sam. 14. 25; Ps. 118. 12; Isa. 7. 18). Heb. *Dĕbôrah:* Gk. μέλισσα: Zoöl. S. *Apis mellifica, Apis Ligustica.* Various species are numerous in Palestine.
Frequent reference is made in O. T. and N. T. to wild bees: their honey (Deu. 32. 13; Jud. 14. 8; 1 Sam. 14. 25; Ps. 81. 16, &c.; Mk. 1. 6.), and their ferocity (Ps. 118. 12, and metaphorically, Isa. 7. 13).
Beeliada, bēē-lī'-ă-dā, 'Baal has known.' 1 Chr. 14. 7.
Beelzebub, or, more correctly, *Beelzebul.* In the N. T. apparently a contemptuous designation of Satan. Mat. 10. 25. The R. V. in all passages keeps Beelzebub in the text with Beelzebul in margin.
prince of devils. Mat. 12. 24; Mk. 3. 22; Lu. 11. 15.
Christ's miracles ascribed to. Mat. 12. 24, &c.
Beer, bēēr, 'a well.' Num. 21. 16.
Beera, bēēr'-ă, same as BEER. 1 Chr. 7. 37.
Beerah, bēēr'-ăh, same as BEER. 1 Chr. 5. 6. [8.
Beer-elim, bēēr-ē'-lĭm, 'well of heroes.' Isa. 15.
Beeri, bēēr'-ī, 'my *w.*' Gen. 26. 34.
Beer-lahai-roi, bēēr-lā'-hāī-rōī, '*w.* of the living One who seeth me.' Gen. 16. 14.
Beeroth, bēēr'-ōth, 'wells.' Jos. 9. 17.
Beerothite, bēēr'-ō-thīte, a person of Beeroth. 2 Sam. 23. 37.
Beer-sheba, bēēr-shē'-bă, 'well of the oath,' lay on the border of the Southern Desert, twenty-seven miles southwest of Hebron.
Abraham dwells at. Gen. 21. 31; 22. 19; 28. 10.
Hagar relieved at. Gen. 21. 14.

Jacob comforted at. Gen. 46. 1.
Elijah flees to. 1 Kn. 19. 3.
Beesh-terah, bē-ĕsh'-tĕ-răh, 'house, or, temple of Ashtoreth' (?). Jos. 21. 27.
Beetle. (1) (Lev. 11. 21, 22) Heb. *Ḥargôl:* Gk. ὀφιομάχη: R. V. cricket; marg. a kind of locust or grasshopper. (2) (Hab. 2. 11) Heb. *Ḥâphîs*: Gk. κάνθαρος. Bochart renders it 'scarabæus,' or sacred beetle of Egypt. Gesenius and others agree with the A. V., and translate it 'beam.' So R. V. More than 400 species of beetles have been found in Palestine.
Beeves, *plur.* of 'beef;' used of oxen. Lev. 22. 19, 21; Num. 31. 28, 38.
Befall. Gen. 42. 4; 44. 29, mischief befall him.
Gen. 49. 1; Deu. 31. 29; Dan. 10. 14, *b.* in last days.
Jud. 6. 13, why is all this *b.* us?
Ps. 91. 10, no evil *b* thee.
Eccl. 3. 19, *b.* men, *b.* beasts, one thing *b.*
See Lev. 10. 19; Deu. 31. 17; Acts 20. 19.
Beg. Ps. 37. 25; 109. 10; Prov. 20. 4; Lu. 16. 3.
Beggar. 1 Sam. 2. 8; Lu. 16. 20, 22.
Beggarly, worthless. Gal. 4. 9.
Begin. Ezek. 9. 6, *b.* at my sanctuary.
1 Pet. 4. 17, judgment *b.* at house of God.
See 1 Sam. 3. 12; 2 Cor. 3. 1.
Beginning. Gen. 1. 1, in the *b.* God created heaven.
Job 8. 7, though thy *b.* was small.
Ps. 111. 10; Prov. 1. 7; 9. 10, *b.* of wisdom.
119. 160, word true from *b.*
Eccl. 7. 8, better end than *b.*
Mat. 19. 8, from *b.* not so.
Lu. 24. 47, *b.* at Jerusalem.
John 1. 1, in the *b.* was the Word.
2. 11, this *b.* of miracles.
Heb. 3. 14, hold *b.* of confidence.
Rev. 1. 8; 21. 6; 22. 13, I am the *b.*
See 1 Chr. 17. 9; Prov. 8. 22, 23; Col. 1. 18.
Begotten. Ps. 2. 7; Acts 13. 33; Heb. 1. 5; 5. 5, this day have I *b.* thee.
1 Pet. 1. 3, *b.* to a lively hope.
See Job 38. 28; 1 Cor. 4. 15; Philem. 10.
Beguile. Gen. 29. 25; Jos. 9. 22, wherefore hast thou *b.* me.
2 Pet. 2. 14, *b.* unstable souls.
See Num. 25. 18; 2 Cor. 11. 3.
Begun. Gal. 3. 3, having *b.* in Spirit.
Phil. 1. 6, hath *b.* good work.
See Deu. 3. 24; 2 Cor. 8. 6; 1 Tim. 5. 11.
Behalf. Job 36. 2, speak on God's *b.*
Phil. 1. 29, in *b.* of Christ.
1 Pet. 4. 16, glorify God on this *b.* R. V. in this name.
See 2 Chr. 16. 9; 2 Cor. 1. 11; 5. 12.
Behave. 1 Sam. 18. 5, 14, 15, 30, David *b.* wisely.
1 Chr. 19. 13, *b.* ourselves valiantly.
Ps. 101. 2, I will *b.* wisely.
Isa. 3. 5, child shall *b.* proudly.
1 Thes. 2. 10, how unblameably we *b.*
1 Tim. 3. 2, bishop of good *b.*
See Ps. 131. 2; 1 Cor. 13. 5; Tit. 2. 3.
Beheaded. Mat. 14. 10; Mk. 6. 16; Lu. 9. 9; Rev. 20. 4.
Behemoth, bē'-hĕ-mŏth, the hippopotamus. Job 40. 15.
Behind. Ex. 10. 26, not hoof be left *b.*
Phil. 3. 13, things which are *b.*
Col. 1. 24, fill up what is *b.*
See 1 Kn. 14. 9; Neh. 9. 26; 2 Cor. 11. 5.
Behold. Ps. 37. 37, *b.* the upright.
Mat. 18. 10, their angels always *b.*
John 17. 24, that they may *b.* glory.
2 Cor. 3. 18, *b.* as in a glass. R. V. reflecting.
See Num. 24. 17; Ps. 91. 8; 119. 37.
Behoved. Lu. 24. 46; Heb. 2. 17.
Bekah, bē'-kăh, ½ shekel in weight = 112 gs. Ex. 38. 26. *See* Weights.
Bel, bĕl, another form of Baal, an idol. Isa. 46. 1; Jer. 50. 2.
Bela, bē'-lă, 'destruction.' Gen. 14. 2.
Belah, bē'-lăh, same as Bela. Gen. 46. 21.

Belaites, bē'-lă-ītes, descendants of Bela. Num. 26. 38.
Belial, bē'-lĭ-ăl, 'worthless;' children of, wicked men so called. Deu. 13. 13; Jud. 19. 22; 1 Sam. 10. 27.
Belief. 2 Thes. 2. 13.
Believe. Num. 14. 11, how long ere they *b.* me.
2 Chr. 20. 20, *b.* Lord, *b.* prophets.
Ps. 78. 22, they *b.* not in God.
Prov. 14. 15, simple *b.* every word.
Mat. 8. 13, as thou hast *b.*, so be it.
9. 28, *b.* ye that I am able.
21. 25; Mk. 11. 31, why then did ye not *b.*
27. 42, come down and we will *b.*
Mk. 5. 36; Lu. 8. 50, only *b.*
9. 23, canst *b.* all things possible.
11. 24, *b.* that ye receive.
16. 13, neither *b.* they them.
Lu. 1. 1, things most surely *b.* R. V. which have been fulfilled.
8. 13, which for a while *b.*
24. 25, slow of heart to *b.*
24. 41, *b.* not for joy.
John 1. 7. all through him might *b.*
2. 22, they *b.* the scripture.
3. 12, *b.* heavenly things.
5. 44, how can ye *b.* which receive honour.
5. 47, how shall ye *b.* my words.
6. 36, seen me and *b.* not.
7. 5, neither did his brethren *b.*
7. 48, have any of the rulers *b.*?
10. 38, *b.* the works.
11. 15, to intent ye may *b.*
11. 26, never die, *b.* thou this?
11. 48, all men will *b.*
John 12. 36, *b.* in the light.
17. 21, the world may *b.*
20. 25, I will not *b.*
20. 29, have not seen yet have *b.*
Acts 4. 32, multitude of them that *b.*
13. 39, all that *b.* are justified.
13. 48, ordained to eternal life *b.*
16. 34, *b.* with all his house.
Rom. 4. 11, father of all that *b.*
4. 18, against hope *b.* in hope.
9. 33, *b.* not ashamed.
10. 34, how shall they *b.*
1 Cor. 7. 12, wife that *b.* not.
2 Cor. 4. 13, we *b.* and therefore speak.
Gal. 3. 22, promise to them that *b.*
2 Thes. 1. 10, admired in all that *b.*
Heb. 10. 39, *b.* to saving of soul.
11. 6, must *b.* that he is.
Jas. 2. 19, devils *b.* and tremble.
1 Pet. 2. 6, he that *b.* shall not be confounded.
See Ex. 4. 5; 19. 9; Isa. 43. 10; Mat. 21. 22; John 8. 24; 10. 37; Acts 9. 26.
Bells (Zec. 14. 20). Heb. *Mĕtzillôth:* Gk. χαλινός: A. V. marg. bridles. Probably metal cups suspended to bridles either for ornament, or for tinkling purposes.
upon the priest's ephod. Ex. 28. 33; 39. 25.
Belly. Gen. 3. 14; Job 15. 2; Mat. 15. 17; Mk. 7. 19; John 7. 38; Rom. 16. 18; Phil. 3. 19; Tit. 1. 12.
Belongeth. Deu. 32. 35; Ps. 94. 1; Heb. 10. 30.
Beloved. Deu. 33. 12, *b.* dwell in safety.
Ps. 127. 2, giveth his *b.* sleep.
Dan. 9. 23; 10. 11, 19, greatly *b.*
Mat. 3. 17; 17. 5; Mk. 1. 11; 9. 7; Lu. 3. 22; 2 Pet. 1. 17, *b.* son.
Lu. 9. 35, my *b.* son. R. V. my chosen.
Rom. 11. 28, *b.* for fathers' sakes.
Eph. 1. 6, accepted in the *b.*
Col. 4. 9; Philem. 16, *b.* brother.
See Neh. 13. 26; S. of S. 2. 16; Rom. 16. 9.
Belshazzar, bĕl-shăz'-zär, is the Babylonian name *Bêl-shar-usur*, and means 'Bel protect the king!' (Dan. 5. 22; 7. 1.)
his profane feast, warning, and death. Dan. 5.
Belteshazzar, bĕl-tē-shăz'-zär, 'preserve his life' (?).
Daniel so named. Dan. 1. 7; 4. 8, &c.

Bemoan. Job 42. 11; Jer. 15. 5; Nah. 3. 7.
Ben, bĕn, 'son.' 1 Chr. 15. 18.
Benaiah, bĕ-nāī'-ăh, 'Jehovah has built.' 2 Sam. 8. 18.
valiant acts of. 2 Sam. 23. 20; 1 Chr. 11. 22; 27. 5.
proclaims Solomon king. 1 Kn. 1. 32.
slays Adonijah, Joab, and Shimei. 1 Kn. 2. 25-46.
Ben-ammi, bĕn-ăm'-mī, 'son of my people.' Gen. 19. 38.
Bend. Ps. 11. 2; Isa. 60. 14; Ezek. 17. 7.
Beneath. Prov. 15. 24, depart from hell *b.*
Isa. 14. 9, hell from *b.* is moved.
John 8. 23, ye are from *b.*
See Deu. 4. 39; Jer. 31. 37.
Bene-berak, bĕn'-ĕ-bē'-răk, 'sons of Barak,' or 'of lightning.' Jos. 19. 45.
Benefactors. Lu. 22. 25.
Benefit. Ps. 68. 19, loadeth us with *b.* R. V. beareth our burden.
1 Tim. 6. 2, partakers of the *b.*
See 2 Chr. 32. 25; Ps. 103. 2; 2 Cor. 1. 15; Philem. 14.
Bene-jaakan, bĕn'-ĕ-jā'-ă-kăn, 'sons of Jaakan.' Num. 33. 31.
Benevolence. 1 Cor. 7. 3, wife due *b.* R. V. her due.
Ben-hadad, bĕn-hā'-dăd, 'son of Hadad.' Kings of Syria.
(1) league with Asa against Baasha. 1 Kn. 15. 18.
(2) wars with Ahab. 1 Kn. 20.
baffled by Elisha. 2 Kn. 6. 8.
besieges Samaria. 2 Kn. 6. 24; 7.
slain by Hazael. 2 Kn. 8. 7.
(3) son of Hazael, wars with Israel. 2 Kn. 13. 3, 25.
See Jer. 49. 27; Am. 1. 4.
Ben-hail, bĕn'-hāīl, 'son of might.' 2 Chr. 17. 7.
Ben-hanan, bĕn-hā'-năn, '*s.* of one who is gracious.' 1 Chr. 4. 20.
Beninu, bĕ-nī'-nū, 'our *s.*' Neh. 10. 13.
Benjamin, bĕn'-jă-mĭn, '*s.* of the right hand,' i. e., 'fortunate;' (first named Ben-oni, '*s.* of my sorrow'), patriarch, youngest son of Jacob, his birth at Bethlehem. Gen. 35. 16, 18.
goes into Egypt. Gen. 43. 15.
Joseph's stratagem to detain. Gen. 44.
Jacob's prophecy concerning. Gen. 49. 27.
his descendants. Gen. 46. 21; 1 Chr. 7. 6.
twice numbered. Num. 1. 36; 26. 38.
blessed by Moses. Deu. 33. 12.
their inheritance. Jos. 18. 11.
their wickedness chastised. Jud. 20.; 21.
the first king chosen from. 1 Sam. 9.; 10.
support the house of Saul. 2 Sam. 2. 9.
afterwards adhere to that of David. 1 Kn. 12. 21; 1 Chr. 11.
the tribe of Paul. Phil. 3. 5. *See* Ps. 68. 27; Ezek. 48. 32; Rev. 7. 8.
Benjamite, bĕn'-jă-mīte, a man of the tribe of Benjamin. Jud. 20. 35.
Beno, bē'-nō, 'his son.' 1 Chr. 24. 26.
Ben-oni, bĕn-ō'-nī, '*s.* of my sorrow.' Gen. 35. 18.
Ben-zoheth, bĕn-zō'-hĕth, '*s.* of Zoheth.' 1 Chr. 4. 20.
Beon, bē'-ŏn, contracted from BAAL-MEON. Num. 32. 3.
Beor, bē'-ôr, 'burning.' (1) Gen. 36. 32. (2) Num. 22. 5.
Bera, bē'-ră. Gen. 14. 2.
Berachah, bĕ-rā'-chăh, 'blessing.' (1) 1 Chr. 12. 3.
(2) valley of, why so named. 2 Chr. 20. 26.
Berachiah, bĕr-ă-chī'-ăh, 'Jehovah hath blessed.' 1 Chr. 6. 39.
Beraiah, bĕ-rāī'-ăh, 'Jehovah hath created.' 1 Chr. 8. 21.
Berea, bĕ-rē'-ă. *See* BERŒA.
Bereave. Gen. 42. 36; 43. 14, *b.* of children.
Eccl. 4. 8, *b.* my soul of good.
Jer. 15. 7; 18. 21, I will *b.* them.
See Ezek. 5. 17; 36. 12; Hos. 13. 8.
Berechiah, bĕr-ĕ-chī'-ăh, same as BERACHIAH.
(1) 1 Chr. 9. 16. (2) 2 Chr. 28. 12. (3) 1 Chr. 3. 20.
(4) Zec. 1. 1.
Bered, bē'-rĕd, 'hail.' Gen. 16. 14.
Beri, bē'-rī, 'my well.' 1 Chr. 7. 36.
Beriah, bĕ-rī'-ăh. Gen. 46. 17. Num. 26. 44.
Beriites, bĕ-rī'-ītes, 'descendants of Beriah.'
Berites, bē'-rītes. 2 Sam. 20. 14.
Berith, bē'-rĭth, 'a covenant.' Jud. 9. 46.
Bernice, bĕr-nī'-çē, 'Victoria.' Acts 25. 13.
Berodach-baladan, bĕr-ō'-dăch-băl'-ă-dăn, 'Berodach (same as MERODACH) has given a son.' 2 Kn. 20. 12.
Berœa, Bĕ-rē'-ă, a city of Macedonia, 60 miles S. W. of Thessalonica. Paul preaches at. Acts 17. 10.
Jews more noble than those of Thessalonica. Acts 17. 11.
Berothah, bĕ-rō'-thăh, 'wells.' Ezek. 47. 16.
Berothai, bĕ-rō'-thāī, 'my wells.' 2 Sam. 8. 8.
Berothite, bē'-rō-thīte, same as BEEROTHITE. 1 Chr. 11. 39.
Beryl (Gen. 2. 12; Ex. 28. 20). Heb. *Shôham:* Gk. *βηρύλλιον*: A. V. and R. V. onyx; R. V. marg. beryl. By some *shôham* is thought to be the onyx; by others, the aquamarine, turquoise, or also amazon-stone (a kind of felspar). For the stone translated 'beryl' in Exodus, see CHRYSOLITE.
Besai, bē'-sāī. Ez. 2. 49.
Beseech. Job 42. 4, hear, I *b.* thee.
Mat. 8. 5; Lu. 7. 3, centurion *b.* him.
Lu. 9. 38, I *b.* thee look on my son.
2 Cor. 5. 20, as though God did *b.* you.
Eph. 4. 1, *b.* you to walk.
Philem. 9, for love's sake *b.* thee.
See Ex. 33. 18; Jon. 1. 14; Rom. 12. 1.
Beset. Ps. 22. 12; 139. 5; Hos. 7. 2; Heb. 12. 1.
Beside. Mk. 3. 21; Acts 26. 24; 2 Cor. 5. 13.
Besiege. Deu. 28. 52; Eccl. 9. 14; Isa. 1. 8.
Besodeiah, bĕs-ō-dēī'-ăh, 'in the secret of Jehovah.' Neh. 3. 6.
Besom, a broom. Isa. 14. 23.
Besor, bē'-sôr, cool (?). 1 Sam. 30. 9.
Besought. Ex. 32. 11; Deu. 3. 23; 1 Kn. 13. 6; 2 Chr. 33. 12; Jer. 26. 19, *b.* the Lord.
Mat. 8. 31; Mk. 5. 10; Lu. 8. 31, devils *b.* him.
8. 34; Lu. 8. 37, *b.* him to depart.
John 4. 40, *b.* that he would tarry.
2 Cor. 12. 8, I *b.* the Lord thrice.
See Gen. 42. 21; Esth. 8. 3.
Best. 1 Sam. 15. 9, 15, spared *b.* of sheep.
Ps. 39. 5, at *b.* state vanity.
Lu. 15. 22, *b.* robe.
1 Cor. 12. 31, *b.* gifts. R. V. greater.
See Gen. 43. 11; Deu. 23. 16; 2 Sam. 18. 4.
Bestead, beset (with difficulties). Isa. 8. 21.
Bestir. 2 Sam. 5. 24.
Bestow. (1) stow away. Lu. 12. 17, no room to *b.* my fruits.
(2) give away. 1 Cor. 13. 3.
1 Cor. 15. 10, grace *b.* on me not in vain.
Gal. 4. 11, lest I have *b.* labour in vain.
1 John 3. 1, manner of love Father *b.*
See 1 Chr. 29. 25; Isa. 63. 7; John 4. 38.
Betah, bē'-tăh, 'confidence.' 2 Sam. 8. 8.
Beten, bē'-tĕn, 'valley' (?). Jos. 19. 25.
Bethabara, bĕth-ăb'-ă-ră, 'house of passage;' place where John baptized. John 1. 28. R. V. Bethany.
Beth-anath, bĕth'-ă-năth, 'temple of Anat.' Jos. 19. 38.
Beth-anoth, bĕth'-ă-nōth, same as BETH-ANATH. Jos. 15. 59.
Bethany, bĕth'-ă-nȳ, 'house of unripe dates' (?); lies on the eastern shoulder of the Mount of Olives, little more than a mile east of Jerusalem.
visited by Christ. Mat. 21. 17; 26. 6; Mk. 11. 1; Lu. 19. 29; John 12. 1.
raising of Lazarus at. John 11. 18.
ascension of Christ at. Lu. 24. 50.
Beth-arabah, bĕth-ăr'-ă-băh, '*h.* of the desert' (?). Jos. 15. 6.
Beth-aram, bĕth-âr'-ăm. Jos. 13. 27.
Beth-arbel, bĕth-är'-bĕl. Hos. 10. 14.

Beth-aven, bĕth-ā'-vĕn, '*h.* of vanity' (i. e., of idols). Jos. 7. 2.
Beth-azmaveth, bĕth-ăz-mā'-vĕth, '*h.* of the strength of death.' Neh. 7. 28.
Beth-baal-meon, bĕth-bā'-ăl-mē'-on, '*h.* of Baal-meon.' Jos. 13. 17.
Beth-barah, bĕth-bâr'-ăh, same as BETHABARA. Jud. 7. 24.
Beth-birei, bĕth-bĭr'-ĕ-ī. 1 Chr. 4. 31.
Beth-car, bĕth'-cär, '*h.* of a lamb.' 1 Sam. 7. 11.
Beth-dagon, bĕth-dā'-gŏn, '*h.* of Dagon.' Jos. 15. 41.
Beth-diblathaim, bĕth-dĭb-lă-thā'-ĭm, '*h.* of the two cakes,' i. e., of figs. Jer. 48. 22.
Beth-eden, bĕth-ē'-dĕn, '*h.* of Eden.' Am. 1. 5 (marg.).
Beth-el, bĕth'-ĕl, Beitin, city of Palestine, formerly Luz, named Beth-el by Jacob. Gen. 28. 19; 31. 13; eight miles north of Jerusalem.
altar built by Jacob at. Gen. 35. 1.
occupied by the house of Joseph. Jud. 1. 22.
sons of prophets resident there. 2 Kn. 2. 2, 3; 17. 28.
the king's chapel. Am. 7. 13.
idolatry of Jeroboam at. 1 Kn. 12. 28; 13. 1.
reformation by Josiah at. 2 Kn. 23. 15.
Beth-elite, bĕth'-ĕl-īte, an inhabitant of Beth-el. 1 Kn. 16. 34.
Beth-emek, bĕth-ē'-mĕk, 'house of the valley.' Jos. 19. 27.
Bether, bē'-thĕr, 'separation.' S. of S. 2. 17.
Bethesda, bĕth-ĕs'-dă, 'house of mercy;' pool of, at Jerusalem, almost certainly identified with a twin-pool discovered in 1888, about 160 yards north-west of St. Stephen's Gate.
miracles wrought at. John 5. 2.
Beth-ezel, bĕth-ē'-zĕl. Mic. 1. 11.
Beth-gader, bĕth-gā'-dĕr, '*h.* of the wall.' 1 Chr. 2. 51.
Beth-gamul, bĕth-găm'-ŭl, '*h.* of the weaned,' or, 'recompense.' Jer. 48. 23.
Beth-haccerem, bĕth-hăc'-cĕ-rĕm, '*h.* of the vineyard.' Neh. 3. 14.
Beth-haran, bĕth-hâr'-ăn. Num. 32. 36.
Beth-hogla, bĕth-hŏg'-lă, the same as following. Jos. 15. 6.
Beth-hoglah, bĕth-hŏg'-lăh, '*h.* of the partridge.' Jos. 18. 19.
Beth-horon, bĕth-hôr'-ŏn, '*h.* of the hollow or cave.' Jos. 10. 10; 1 Sam. 13. 18.
Bethink. 1 Kn. 8. 47; 2 Chr. 6. 37.
Beth-jeshimoth, bĕth-jĕsh'-ĭ-mōth, the same as following. Jos. 12. 3.
Beth-jesimoth, bĕth-jĕs'-ĭ-mōth, '*h.* of the deserts.' Num. 33. 49.
Beth-lebaoth, bĕth-lĕ-bā'-ōth, '*h.* of lionesses.' Jos. 19. 6.
Bethlehem, bĕth'-lĕ-hĕm, 'house of bread,' is about five miles south of Jerusalem. Gen. 35. 19. It is also called Ephrath and Ephratah, ĕph'-rā-tăh (Mic. 5. 2), *B.* the fruitful (?), to distinguish it from the northern city of the same name (Jos. 19. 15).
(originally Ephratah). Naomi and Ruth return to. Ru. 1.-4.
David anointed at. 1 Sam. 16. 13; 20. 6.
well of. 2 Sam. 23. 15; 1 Chr. 11. 17.
Christ's birth at. Mat. 2. 1; Lu. 2. 4; John 7. 42; predicted. Mic. 5. 2 (Ps. 132. 5, 6).
babes of, slain. Mat. 2. 16.
Beth-lehemite, bĕth'-lĕ-hĕm-īte, a man of Bethlehem. 1 Sam. 16. 1.
Beth-lehem-judah, bĕth'-lĕ-hĕm-jū'-dăh, '*B.* of Judah.' Jud. 17. 7.
Beth-maachah, bĕth-mā'-ă-c͟hăh, 'house of Maachah.' 2 Sam. 20. 14.
Beth-marcaboth, bĕth-mär'-că-bōth, '*h.* of chariots.' Jos. 19. 5.
Beth-meon, bĕth-mē'-ŏn, '*h.* of habitation.' Jer. 48. 23.
Beth-nimrah, bĕth-nĭm'-răh, '*h.* of a leopard.' Num. 32. 36.

Beth-palet, bĕth-pā'-lĕt, '*h.* of escape,' or 'of Pelet.' Jos. 15. 27.
Beth-pazzez, bĕth-păz'-zĕz, '*h.* of dispersion.' Jos. 19. 21.
Beth-peor, bĕth-pē'-ôr, 'temple of Peor.' Deu. 3. 29.
Bethphage, bĕth'-phă-ġē, 'house of unripe figs.' Mat. 21. 1.
Beth-phelet, bĕth'-phĕ-lĕt, same as BETH-PALET. Neh. 11. 26.
Beth-rapha, bĕth-rā'-phă, 'house of Rapha.' 1 Chr. 4. 12.
Beth-rehob, bĕth-rē'-hŏb, '*h.* of Rehob' (i. e., the street). Jud. 18. 28.
Bethsaida, bĕth-sā'-ĭ-dă, '*h.* of fishing.' Two towns were probably so called, situated near the head of the Sea of Galilee, deriving their name from the great shoals of fish attracted thither by the hot springs. They were probably separated only by the river Jordan.
native place of Philip, Peter, and Andrew. Mk. 6. 45; John 1. 44; 12. 21.
blind man cured at. Mk. 8. 22.
condemned for unbelief. Mat. 11. 21.
Christ feeds the five thousand at. Lu. 9. 10-17.
Beth-shan, bĕth'-shăn, 'house of rest.' 1 Sam. 31. 10.
Beth-shean, bĕth-shē'-ăn, same as BETH-SHAN. Jos. 17. 11.
Beth-shemesh, bĕth-shē'-mĕsh, 'temple of the sun.' (1) Jos. 15. 10.
men of, punished for looking into the ark. 1 Sam. 6. 19.
great battle at. 2 Kn. 14. 11.
(2) Jos. 19. 38.
(3) = On (Heliopolis, 'house of the sun'), Jer. 43. 13.
Beth-shemite, bĕth-shē'-mīte, a native of Beth-shemesh. 1 Sam. 6. 14.
Beth-shittah, bĕth-shĭt'-tăh, 'house of acacias.' Jud. 7. 22.
Beth-tappuah, bĕth-tăp'-pū-ăh, '*h.* of apples.' Jos. 15. 53.
Bethuel, bĕ-thū'-ĕl, 'man of God' (?). Gen. 22. 22.
Bethul, bĕth'-ŭl, same as BETHEL (?). Jos. 19. 4.
Beth-zur, bĕth'-zûr, 'house of rock.' Jos. 15. 58.
Betimes, early. Gen. 26. 31; 2 Chr. 36. 15; Job 8. 5; Prov. 13. 24.
Betonim, bĕt'-ō-nĭm, 'pistachio nuts.' Jos. 13. 26.
Betray. Mat. 26. 16; Mk. 14. 11, opportunity to *b.* 27. 4, I *b.* innocent blood.
1 Cor. 11. 23, same night he was *b.*
See Mat. 24. 10; Mk. 14. 18; Lu. 22. 21, 22; John 6. 64; 21. 20.
Betroth. Hos. 2. 19, 20.
Betrothal, laws concerning. Ex. 21. 8; Lev. 19. 20; Deu. 20. 7.
Better. 1 Sam. 15. 22, to obey *b.* than sacrifice.
1 Kn. 19. 4, I am not *b.* than my fathers.
Ps. 63. 3, lovingkindness *b.* than life.
Eccl. 4. 9, two are *b.* than one.
7. 10, former days *b.* than these.
Mat. 12. 12, man *b.* than a sheep. R. V. of more value.
Lu. 5. 39, he saith the old is *b.*
Phil. 2. 3, each esteem other *b.* than himself.
Heb. 1. 4, much *b.* than angels.
11. 16, a *b.* country.
2 Pet. 2. 21, *b.* not have known the way.
See Eccl. 2. 24; S. of S. 1. 2; Jon. 4. 3.
Beulah, bēū'-lăh, 'married.' Isa. 62. 4.
Bewail. Lu. 8. 52, all wept and *b.* her.
Lu. 23. 27, of women which also *b.*
2 Cor. 12. 21, *b.* many who have sinned.
See Deu. 21. 13; Jud. 11. 37; Rev. 18. 9.
Beware. Jud. 13. 4, *b.* and drink not wine.
Job 36. 18, *b.* lest he take thee away.
Mat. 16. 6; Mk. 8. 15; Lu. 12. 1, *b.* of leaven.
Mk. 12. 38; Lu. 20. 46, *b.* of scribes.
Lu. 12. 15, *b.* of covetousness. R. V. keep from.
Phil. 3. 2, *b.* of dogs, *b.* of evil workers.
See Deu. 6. 12; 8. 11; 15. 9.
Bewitched. Acts 8. 9, *b.* the people. R. V. amazed.
Gal. 3. 1, who hath *b.* you.

Bewray, to reveal, disclose. Prov. 29. 24; Isa. 16. 3; Mat. 26. 73.
Bewrayer, an informer. 2 Macc. 4. 1.
Beyond. Num. 22. 18; 2 Cor. 8. 3; Gal. 1. 13; 1 Thes. 4. 6.
Bezai, bē-zā'-ī. Ez. 2. 17.
Bezaleel, bĕz'-ă-lēel, 'in the shadow of God;' constructs the tabernacle. Ex. 31. 2; 35. 30; 36.–38.
Bezek, bē'-zĕk, 'lightning' (?). Jud. 1. 4.
Bezer, bē'-zĕr, 'fortress.' (1) Deu. 4. 43. (2) 1 Chr. 7. 37.

Bible, Names of.

1. *The Bible.* '*Biblos*' was the name given to the inner bark of the papyrus, which was used as we now use writing-paper. Hence the papyrus when written upon came to be called *Biblos*, and from the word *Biblion*, a papyrus roll, comes our word *Bible*.

2. *The Scriptures.* The term simply means '*The Writings*,' from the Latin *scribere*, to write.

3. *The Law* and *The Law and the Prophets.* The first name expresses the fact that the Bible contains God's law to man, and the second that conjoined with the law were prophecies concerning times to come.

4. *The Oracles.* The word signifies *things spoken*, from the Latin *orare*, to speak. Many things in the Bible have a 'Thus saith the Lord,' before them.

5. *The Old and New Testaments.* 'Covenants' would better express the meaning. The two great divisions of the Bible contain God's *covenants* with man.

6. *God's Word.* So called because the Bible expresses God's thought toward man.

7. *The Canon.* 'Canon' means a rule or standard, and was in early Christian times applied to the Creed: it also meant a *list*, and the 'canonical' books were those included in the recognized list of the Church's books.

Bible, Facts concerning.

The first complete translation of the whole Bible into English was made by John Wycliffe, A. D. 1380–1382.

The first book ever printed was the Bible. The first Bible was printed between the years 1450 and 1455, at Mentz, by Guttenberg, the reputed inventor of printing.

First New Testament printed in English was that of William Tyndale, A. D. 1525–1526.

First Bible printed in English was Miles Coverdale's, A. D. 1535.

The Old Testament was divided into *chapters*, as they now stand, by Cardinal Hugo, in the middle of the thirteenth century. These chapters were divided into verses, as we now have them, by Rabbi Nathan, and adopted by Robert Stephens, a French printer, in his edition of the Vulgate, in 1555, and transferred to the Authorized Version in 1611.

The Authorized Version of the Bible was 'set forth' in the year 1611.

The Revised Version of the English Bible was begun in England June 22, 1870, and in America October 4, 1872.

The Revised New Testament was published in May, 1881; the Revised Old Testament in May, 1885.

Bible, Statistics of the.

	Old Testament.	New Testament.	Whole Bible.
Number of books	39	27	66
Number of chapters	929	260	1,189
Number of verses	23,214	7,959	31,173
Number of words	592,439	181,253	773,692
Number of letters	2,728,100	838,380	3,566,480
Middle book	Proverbs.	2 Thessalonians.	Micah and Nahum.
Middle chapter	Job 29.	Romans 13 and 14.	Psalm 117.
Middle verse	2 Chronicles 20. 17.	Acts 17. 17.	Psalm 118. 8.
Least book	Obadiah.	3 John.	3 John.
Least verse	1 Chronicles 1. 1.	John 11. 35.	John 11. 35.

These facts were ascertained by a gentleman in 1718; also by an English gentleman, at Amsterdam, in 1772; and the investigation is said to have taken each gentleman three years.

Bichri, bĭch'-rī, 'young.' 2 Sam. 20. 1.
Bid, to invite; 'bidden' = invited. Mat. 22. 9.
Bidkar, bĭd'-kär, 'son of piercing' (?). 2 Kn. 9. 25.
Bier. 2 Sam. 3. 31; Lu. 7. 14.
Bigtha, bĭg'-thă. Esth. 1. 10.
Bigthan, bĭg'-thăn, 'gift of God' (?); and Teresh, their conspiracy against Ahasuerus. Esth. 2. 21.
Bigthana, bĭg-thā'-nă, same as Bigthan. Esth. 6. 2.
Bigvai, bĭg-vā'-ī, 'happy' (?). Ez. 2. 2.
Bildad, bĭl'-dăd, 'Bel has loved.' Job 2. 11; his answers to Job. Job 8.; 18.; 25.
Bileam, bĭ'-lē-ăm, same as Ibleam (?). 1 Chr. 6. 70.
Bilgah, bĭl'-găh, 'cheerfulness.' 1 Chr. 24. 14.
Bilgai, bĭl-gā'-ī, same as Bilgah. Neh. 10. 8.
Bilhah, bĭl'-häh. Gen. 29. 29.
Jacob's children by. Gen. 30. 5.
Bilhan, bĭl'-hăn. Gen. 36. 27.
Billows. Ps. 42. 7; Jon. 2. 3.
Bilshan, bĭl'-shăn, 'seeker' (?). Ez. 2. 2.
Bimhal, bĭm'-hăl, 'son of circumcision' (?). 1 Chr. 7. 33.
Bind. (1) to imprison, or confine closely. Job 26. 8; Acts 9. 14.
(2) Prov. 6. 21, *b.* them continually upon heart.
Isa. 61. 1, *b.* up brokenhearted.
Mat. 12. 29; Mk. 3. 27, *b.* strong man.
16. 19; 18. 18, *b.* on earth.
See Num. 30. 2; Job 26. 8; 38. 31.
Binea, bĭ'-nē-ă. 1 Chr. 8. 37.
Binnui, bĭn'-nū-ī, 'a building' (?). Ez. 8. 33.
Bird. 2 Sam. 21. 10, suffered not *b.* to rest.
S. of S. 2. 12, time of the singing of *b.*
Jer. 12. 9, heritage like a speckled *b.* R. V. *b.* of prey.
Mat. 8. 20; Lu. 9. 58, *b.* of air have nests.
Birds. Ps. 11. 1; 104. 17; 124. 7; Prov. 1. 17; 6. 5, &c.; Eccl. 10. 20; Jer. 12. 9; Am. 3. 5; Mat. 8. 20; Rev. 18. 2.
what to be used in sacrifices. Gen. 15. 9; Lev. 14. 4; Lu. 2. 24.
what are abomination. Lev. 11. 13; Deu. 14. 12.
nests of. Deu. 22. 6. *See* Fowls.

Birds found in Palestine.

REFERENCES TO THOSE NAMED IN SCRIPTURE UNDER EACH NAME.

There are about 350 kinds of birds to be found in Palestine. The following are some of the most interesting:—

Bat.	Hawk.	Peacock.
Bee-eater.	Hawk, Night.	Pelican.
Bittern.	Hen.	Pigeon.
Blackbird.	Heron.	Plover.
Blackcap.	Hoopoe.	Quail.
Blue Jay.	Jay.	Raven.
Bulbul.	Kestrel.	Redstart.
Chat.	Kingfisher.	Robin.
Cock.	Kite.	Sand-grouse.
Cormorant.	Lapwing.	Sandpiper.
Corn-Bunting.	Lark.	Shrike.
Crane.	Magpie.	Sparrow.
Crow.	Nightingale.	Starling.
Cuckoo.	Nightjar.	Stork.
Dove.	Nuthatch.	Sunbird.
Ducks.	Osprey.	Swallow.
Dunlin.	Ossifrage.	Swan.
Eagle.	Ostrich.	Swift.
Fowl, Fatted.	Owl.	Thrush.
Gier-Eagle.	Owl, Great.	Tit, Great.
Glede.	Owl, Little.	Turtledove.
Goldfinch.	Owl of Desert.	Vulture.
Grakle.	Owl, Screech.	Wagtail.
Grouse.	Partridge.	Water-rail.
Harrier.		

Birsha, bĭr′-shă. Gen. 14. 2.
Birth. John 9. 1, blind from *b.*
Gal. 4. 19, of whom I travail in *b.*
See Eccl. 7. 1; Isa. 66. 9; Lu. 1. 14.
Birthday. Gen. 40. 20, which was Pharaoh's *b.*
Mat. 14. 6; Mk. 6. 21, when Herod's *b.* was kept.
Birthright, law concerning. Deu. 21. 15.
despised by Esau, and obtained by Jacob. Gen. 25. 31; 27. 36; Heb. 12. 16.
lost by Reuben. 1 Chr. 5. 1.
Births foretold:—
of Ishmael. Gen. 16. 11.
of Isaac. Gen. 18. 10.
of Samson. Jud. 13. 3.
of Samuel. 1 Sam. 1. 11, 17.
of Josiah. 1 Kn. 13. 2.
of Shunammite's son. 2 Kn. 4. 16.
of John the Baptist. Lu. 1. 13.
of Messias. Gen. 3. 15; Isa. 7. 14; Mic. 5. Lu. 1. [31.
Birzavith, bĭr-ză′-vĭth, 'apparent' (?). 1 Chr. 7. 31.
Bishlam, bĭsh′-lăm, 'son of peace' (?). Ez. 4. 7.
Bishop, Gr. ἐπίσκοπος = an overseer, a secular term of Greek administration. It is used in a general sense in Acts 20. 28, but in Phil. 1. 1. and the Pastoral Epistles has a technical meaning as the title of the second grade of Church official — under the Apostles but over the Deacons. It is in N. T. synonymous with πρεσβύτερος or elder. *See* Tit. 1. 5 & 7.
qualifications of. 1 Tim. 3. 1, if a man desire office of *b.*
Tit. 1. 7, *b.* must be blameless.
1 Pet. 2. 25, Shepherd and *B.* of your souls.
See Acts 1. 20.
Bit. Ps. 32. 9; Jas. 3. 3.
Bite. Prov. 23. 32, at last it *b.* like serpent.
Mic. 3. 5, prophets that *b.* with teeth.
Gal. 5. 15, if ye *b.* and devour one another.
See Eccl. 10. 8; Am. 5. 19; 9. 3.
Bithiah, bĭth′-ĭ-ăh, 'daughter (i. e., worshipper) of Jehovah.' 1 Chr. 4. 18.
Bithron, bĭth′-rŏn, 'a ravine.' 2 Sam. 2. 29.
Bithynia, bĭ-thy̆n′-ĭă. Acts 16. 7.
Bitter. Ex. 12. 8; Num. 9. 11, with *b.* herbs.
Deu. 32. 24, devoured with *b.* destruction.
Job 13. 26, writest *b.* things.
Isa. 5. 20, that put *b.* for sweet.
Isa. 24. 9, drink *b.* to them that drink it.
Jer. 2. 19, an evil thing and *b.*
Mat. 26. 75; Lu. 22. 62, Peter wept *b.*
Col. 3. 19, be not *b.* against them.
See Ex. 1. 14; 15. 23; 2 Kn. 14. 26.
Bittern. Heb. *Kippôd:* Gk. ἐχῖνος. (Specimens, *Botaurus stellaris.* So called from the bellowing noise made by the male bird in springtime. *Ardeola minuta*, bought at Jerusalem.) Isa. 14. 23; 34. 11; Zep. 2. 14. The context seems to demand the idea of some marsh-loving bird, fond of waste and solitary places. Hence not the 'porcupine' of the R. V.
Bitterness. Job 10. 1; 21. 25; Isa. 38. 15, in *b.* of soul.
Prov. 14. 10, heart knoweth own *b.*
Acts 8. 23, in the gall of *b.*
Eph. 4. 31, let all *b.* be put away.
Heb. 12. 15, lest any root of *b.*
See 1 Sam. 15. 32; Prov. 17. 25; Rom. 3. 14.
Bitumen (Gen. 11. 3). Heb. *Ḥêmâr:* Gk. ἄσφαλτος. A kind of asphalt. A. V. 'slime.' R. V. marg. 'bitumen.'
Bizjothjah, bĭz-jŏth′-jăh. Jos. 15. 28.
Biztha, bĭz′-thă, 'a eunuch' (?). Esth. 1. 10.
Black. Mat. 5. 36; Jude 13; Rev. 6. 5.
Blade. Jud. 3. 22; Mat. 13. 26; Mk. 4. 28.
Blains, pustules, swellings, bubbles of matter. Ex. 9. 9.
Blame. 2 Cor. 6. 3; 8. 20; Gal. 2. 11; Eph. 1. 4.
Blameless. 1 Cor. 1. 8, be *b.* in day of the Lord.
Phil. 2. 15, that ye may be *b.*
See Mat. 12. 5; Phil. 3. 6; Tit. 1. 6, 7.
Blaspheme, originally means simply 'to speak insultingly,' but is also technically applied in O. T. and N. T. to the special sin of serious profanity.
2 Sam. 12. 14, occasion to enemies to *b.*
Ps. 74. 10, 18; enemies *b.*
Isa. 52. 5, my name continually is *b.*
Mat. 9. 3, scribes said, this man *b.*
Mk. 3. 29, *b.* against Holy Ghost.
Acts 26. 11, I compelled them to *b.*
Rom. 2. 24, name of God is *b.* through you.
Jas. 2. 7, *b.* that worthy name.
Blasphemy. Mat. 12. 31, all manner of *b.*
26. 65; Mk. 14. 64, he hath spoken *b.*
Lu. 5. 21, who is this which speaketh *b.*?
See Ex. 20. 7; Ps. 74. 18; Isa. 52. 5; Ezek. 20. 27; 35. 12; Mat. 15. 19; Lu. 22. 65; Col. 3. 8; Rev. 2. 9; 13. 5, 6; 16. 9.
Blasphemy, punishment of, death. Lev. 24. 16; 1 Kn. 21. 10.
mercy for. 1 Tim. 1. 13.
Christ accused of. Mat. 9. 3; 26. 65; Mk. 2. 7; Lu. 5. 21; John 10. 33.
others falsely accused of, and stoned: Naboth, 1 Kn. 21. 13. Stephen, Acts 6. 13; 7. 54.
occasion to blaspheme given by David. 2 Sam. 12. 14.
See also 1 Tim. 5. 14; 6. 1.
against Holy Ghost. Mat. 12. 31; Mk. 3. 28; Lu. 12. 10; 1 John 5. 16.
Blasted, blighted. Gen. 41. 6.
Blasting, blight. Deu. 28. 22; 1 Kn. 8. 37.
Blastus, blăs′-tŭs, 'a shoot.' Chamberlain of Herod Agrippa. Acts 12. 20.
Blaze abroad, to blazon, proclaim everywhere. Mk. 1. 45.
Bleating. Jud. 5. 16; 1 Sam. 15. 14.
Blemish. 2 Sam. 14. 25, no *b.* in him.
Dan. 1. 4, children in whom was no *b.*
Eph. 5. 27, holy and without *b.*
1 Pet. 1. 19, a lamb without *b.* and spot.
Blemish, priests to be without. Lev. 21. 17.
offerings free from. Ex. 12. 5, &c.; Lev. 1. 3, &c.; Deu. 15. 21; 17. 1, &c.
the church to be without. Eph. 5. 27.
Lamb without, Christ compared to. 1 Pet. 1. 19.
Bless. 1 Chr. 4. 10, O that thou wouldest *b.* me.
Isa. 65. 16, *b.* himself in God of truth. [curse.
Mat. 5. 44; Lu. 6. 28; Rom. 12. 14, *b.* them that

Blessed. Deu. 28. 3, *b.* in city, *b.* in field.
Prov. 10. 7, memory of just is *b.*
Isa. 32. 20, *b.* are ye that sow.
Acts 20. 35, more *b.* to give than receive.
2 Cor. 11. 31, *b.* for evermore.
Tit. 2. 13, looking for that *b.* hope.
See Gen. 12. 3; 39. 5; Ps. 1. 1; 65. 4; 84. 4, 5; 112. 1; Isa. 30. 18; Mat. 5. 3-11; 25. 34; Lu. 6. 21; 12. 37; 14. 15; Rom. 4. 6, 9.

Blessed, those chosen, called, chastened by God. Ps. 65. 4; Eph. 1. 3, 4.—Isa. 51. 2; Rev. 19. 9.—Ps. 94. 12.
who trust, fear, delight in God. Ps. 2. 12; 34. 8; 40. 4; 84. 12; Jer. 17. 7.—Ps. 128. 1, 4.—Ps. 112. 1.
who hear and obey. Ps. 119. 2; Mat. 13. 16; Lu. 11. 28; Jas. 1. 25; Rev. 1. 3; 22. 7, 14.
who know, believe, and suffer for Christ. Mat. 16. 16, 17.—Mat. 11. 6; Lu. 1. 45; Gal. 3. 9.—Lu. 6. 22.
who endure temptation, Jas. 1. 12; watch against sin, Rev. 16. 15; rebuke sinners, Prov. 24. 25; die in the Lord, Rev. 14. 13.
the undefiled, pure, just, children of the just, righteous, upright, faithful, poor in spirit, meek, merciful, peacemakers. Ps. 119. 1.—Mat. 5. 8.—Ps. 106. 3; Prov. 10. 6.—Prov. 20. 7.—Ps. 5. 12.—Ps. 112. 2.—Prov. 28. 20.—Mat. 5. 3.—Mat. 5. 5.—Mat. 5. 7.—Mat. 5. 9.
the bountiful. Deu. 15. 10; Ps. 41. 1; Prov. 22. 9; Lu. 14. 13, 14.
sins forgiven. Ps. 32. 1, 2; Rom. 4. 7.
persons blessed: Abraham by God, Gen. 12. 2; 22. 17. Jacob by Isaac, Gen. 27. 27. Jacob by God, Gen. 48. 3. Joseph and his sons by Jacob, Gen. 48. 9, 14; the twelve tribes by Moses, Deu. 33.

Blessedness. Rom. 4. 6, 9; Gal. 4. 15.

Blessing. Deu. 23. 5; Neh. 13. 2, turned curse into *b.*
Job 29. 13, *b.* of him that was ready to perish.
Prov. 10. 22, *b.* of Lord maketh rich.
28. 20, faithful man shall abound with *b.*
Isa. 65. 8, destroy it not, a *b.* is in it.
Mal. 2. 2, I will curse your *b.*
3. 10, pour you out a *b.*
Rom. 15. 29, fulness of *b.* of Gospel.
1 Cor. 10. 16, cup of *b.* which we bless.
Jas. 3. 10, proceed *b.* and cursing.
Rev. 5. 12, worthy to receive honour and *b.*

Blessing and cursing the people, form of. Num. 6. 22; Deu. 11. 26; 27. 15, &c.
and glory. Rev. 5. 12, 13; 7. 12.

Blessing of Jacob. A poetical and prophetic description of the characteristics and history of the twelve tribes. Gen. 49. 1-27.

Blessing of Moses. A poetical review of the twelve tribes put into the mouth of Moses, in which the tribes of Joseph (Ephraim and Manasseh) are glorified and Judah regarded as separatist. Deu. 33.

Blind (*n.*), laws concerning the. Lev. 19. 14; Deu. 27. 18.

Blind (*v.*). Ex. 23. 8; Deu. 16. 19, the gift *b.* the wise.
1 Sam. 12. 3, bribe to *b.* mine eyes.
2 Cor. 3. 14; 4. 4, their minds were *b.* R. V. hardened.
1 John 2. 11, darkness hath *b.*

Blindness. Eph. 4. 18, because of *b.* of their heart. R. V. hardening.

Blindness inflicted on the men of Sodom. Gen. 19. 11.
on the Syrian army. 2 Kn. 6. 18.
on Saul of Tarsus. Acts 9. 8.
on Elymas at Paphos. Acts 13. 11.
healed by Christ. Mat. 9. 27; 12. 22; 20. 30; Mk. 8. 22; 10. 46; Lu. 7. 21; John 9. (Isa. 35. 5).
SPIRITUAL. Ps. 82. 5; Isa. 56. 10; 59. 9; Mat. 6. 23; 15. 14; 23. 16; John 1. 5; 3. 19; 9. 39; 1 Cor. 2. 14; 2 Pet. 1. 9; 1 John 2. 9; Rev. 3. 17.
judicially inflicted. Deu. 28. 28; Ps. 69. 23; Isa. 6. 9; 44. 18; Zec. 12. 4; Mat. 13. 13; John 12. 40; Acts 28. 26; Rom. 11. 7; 2 Cor. 3. 14; 4. 4.
prayer for deliverance from. Ps. 13. 3; 119. 18.
removed by Christ. Isa. 9. 2; 42. 7; Lu. 4. 18; John 8. 12; 9. 39; 2 Cor. 3. 14; 4. 6; Eph. 5. 8; Col. 1. 13; 1 Thes. 5. 4; 1 Pet. 2. 9.

Blood. Gen. 9. 6, whoso sheddeth man's *b.*
Jos. 2. 19; 1 Kn. 2. 32, *b.* on head.
Ps. 51. 14, deliver me from *b.*-guiltiness.
72. 14, precious shall *b.* be in his sight.
Prov. 29. 10, the *b.*-thirsty hate upright.
Isa. 9. 5, garments rolled in *b.*
Jer. 2. 34, the *b.* of poor innocents.
Ezek. 9. 9, land is full of *b.*
18. 13; 33. 5, his *b.* be upon him.
Hab. 2. 12, buildeth a town with *b.*
Mat. 9. 20; Mk. 5. 25; Lu. 8. 43, issue of *b.*
16. 17, flesh and *b.* hath not revealed.
27. 4, I have betrayed innocent *b.*
27. 25, his *b.* be on us and our children.
Mk. 14. 24; Lu. 22. 20, my *b.* shed.
Lu. 22. 20; 1 Cor. 11. 25, new testament in my *b.*
22. 44, sweat as drops of *b.* falling.
John 1. 13, born not of b.
6. 54, 55, 56, drinketh my *b.*
Acts 15. 20; 21. 25, abstain from *b.*
17. 26, made of one *b.*
20. 28, church purchased with his *b.*
Rom. 3. 25, through faith in his *b.*
5. 9, justified by his *b.*
1 Cor. 10. 16, communion of *b.* of Christ.
11. 27, guilty of body and *b.* of the Lord.
15. 50, flesh and *b.* cannot inherit.
Eph. 1. 7; Col. 1. 14, redemption through his *b.*
Heb. 9. 22, without shedding of *b.*
10. 29; 13. 20, *b.* of the covenant.
1 Pet. 1. 19, with precious *b.* of Christ.
Rev. 7. 14; 12. 11, in the *b.* of the Lamb.
See Ps. 55. 23; Rev. 16. 6; 17. 6.

Blood, eating of, forbidden to:—
man after the flood. Gen. 9. 4.
the Israelites under the law. Lev. 3. 17; 17. 10, 12, 13; Deu. 12. 16, 24; 1 Sam. 14. 32, 33.
the Gentile Christians. Acts 15. 20, 29.
water turned into: as a sign, Ex. 4. 30, with ver. 9. as a judgment, Ex. 7. 17; Rev. 8. 8; 11. 6.
law respecting. Lev. 7. 26; 19. 26; Deu. 12. 16; Ezek. 33. 25; Acts 15. 29. enforced by Saul, 1 Sam. 14. 32.
shedding of human, forbidden. Gen. 9. 5, 6; Deu. 21. 1-9; Ps. 106. 38; Prov. 6. 16, 17; Isa. 59. 3; Jer. 22. 17; Ezek. 22. 4; Mat. 27. 6.
of legal sacrifices. Ex. 23. 18; 29. 12; 30. 10; 34. 25; Lev. 4. 7; 17. 11; Heb. 9. 13, 19-22; 10. 4.
of the covenant. Ex. 24. 8; Zec. 9. 11; Heb. 10. 29; 13. 20.
OF CHRIST. 1 Cor. 10. 16; Eph. 2. 13; Heb. 9. 14; 1 Pet. 1. 19; 1 John 1. 7.
salvation by. Heb. 9. 12; 13. 12; Rev. 1. 5. *See* Heb. 9. 22.
in the LORD's Supper. Mat. 26. 28; Mk. 14. 24; Lu. 22. 20; 1 Cor. 11. 25.
redemption by. Eph. 1. 7; Col. 1. 20; Heb. 10. 19; 12. 24; 1 Pet. 1. 2; 1 John 1. 7; Rev. 1. 5; 5. 9; 12. 11.
typified,—under the law. Ex. 12. 13; 29. 16; 30. 10; Lev. 1. 5; 4.; 16. 15; Heb. 9. 7, &c.

Blossom. Isa. 35. 1, desert shall *b.* as the rose.
Hab. 3. 17, fig tree shall not *b.*
See Gen. 40. 10; Num. 17. 5; Isa. 27. 6.

Blot. Ex. 32. 32; Ps. 69. 28; Rev. 3. 5, *b.* out of book.
Isa. 44. 22, *b.* out as thick cloud.
Acts 3. 19, repent that sins may be *b.* out.
Col. 2. 14, *b.* out handwriting.
See Deu. 9. 14; 2 Kn. 14. 27; Jer. 18. 23.

Blush. Ez. 9. 6; Jer. 6. 15; 8. 12.

Boanerges, bō-ăn-ĕr'-ġēs, 'sons of thunder;' James and John surnamed by Christ. Mk. 3. 17.

Boast (*n.*). Ps. 34. 2; Rom. 2. 17, 23; 3. 27.

Boast (*v.*). 1 Kn. 20. 11, not *b.* as he that putteth it off.
Ps. 49. 6; 94. 4, *b.* themselves.
Prov. 27. 1, *b.* not of to-morrow.
2 Cor. 11. 16, that I may *b.* myself a little.

Eph. 2. 9, lest any man should *b.*
Jas. 3. 5, tongue *b.* great things.
Boasting deprecated. 1 Kn. 20. 11; Ps. 49. 6; 52. 1; 94. 4; Prov. 20. 14; 25. 14; 27. 1; Isa. 10. 15; Rom. 1. 30; 11. 18; 2 Cor. 10.; Jas. 3. 5; 4. 16.
of Paul. 2 Cor. 7. 14; 8. 24; 9. 3, 4; 11. 10.
excluded under the gospel. Rom. 3. 27; Eph. 2. 9.
Boats. John 6. 22; Acts 27. 16, 30.
Boaz, bō'-ăz, 'fleetness.' (1) Ru. 2. 1.
his conduct towards Ruth. Ru. 2.; 3.; 4.
ancestor of David and Christ. Ru. 4. 17, 22; Mat. 1. 5; Lu. 3. 23, 32.
(2) and JACHIN (strength and stability), pillars of the temple. 2 Chr. 3. 17.
Bocheru, bō'-chĕ-rū, 'firstborn' (?). 1 Chr. 8. 38.
Bochim, bō'-chĭm, 'weepers;' Israel rebuked by an angel at. Jud. 2. 1-3.
Israel repent at. Jud. 2. 4, 5.
Bodily. Lu. 3. 22; 2 Cor. 10. 10; Col. 2. 9; 1 Tim. 4. 8.
Body. Job 19. 26, worms destroy this *b.* R. V. my skin . . . destroyed.
Prov. 5. 11, when thy flesh and *b.* are consumed.
Mat. 5. 29, *b.* cast into hell.
6. 22; Lu. 11. 34, *b.* full of light.
6. 25; Lu. 12. 22, take no thought for *b.*
Mk. 5. 29, felt in *b.* that she was healed.
Lu. 17. 37, wheresoever the *b.* is.
John 2. 21, the temple of his *b.*
Acts 19. 12, from his *b.* were brought.
Rom. 6. 6, *b.* of sin destroyed.
7. 24, *b.* of this death.
12. 1, present your *b.* a living sacrifice.
12. 4; 1 Cor. 12. 14, many members, one *b.*
1 Cor. 9. 27, I keep under my *b.*
13. 3, though I give my *b.* to be burned.
2 Cor. 5. 8, absent from the *b.*
12. 2, whether in *b.* or out of the *b.*
Gal. 6. 17, I bear in *b.* marks.
Phil. 3. 21, like to his glorious *b.*
1 Pet. 2. 24, in his own *b.* on tree.
Body (human), not to be dishonoured. Lev. 19. 28; 21. 5; Deu. 14. 1.
to be pure. Rom. 12. 1; 1 Cor. 6. 13; 1 Thes. 4. 4.
of a Christian, the temple of the Holy Ghost. 1 Cor. 3. 16; 6. 19; 2 Cor. 6. 16.
dead, laws concerning. Lev. 21. 11; Num. 5. 2; 9. 6; 19. 11; Deu. 21. 23; Hag. 2. 13.
will be raised again. Mat. 22. 30; 1 Cor. 15. 12; Phil. 3. 21. *See* RESURRECTION.
BODY OF CHRIST (Heb. 10. 5). pierced by soldiers, John 19. 34. buried by Joseph, Mat. 27. 60; Mk. 15. 46; Lu. 23. 53; John 19. 42.
the Church so called. Rom. 12. 5; 1 Cor. 10. 17; 12. 12; Eph. 1. 22; 4. 12; 5. 23; Col. 1. 18; 2. 19; 3. 15.
Bohan, bō'-hăn, 'thumb' (?). Jos. 15. 6.
Boils and blains, the plague of. Ex. 9. 10; Rev. 16. 2.
See 2 Kn. 20. 7; Job 2. 7.
Bold. Eccl. 8. 1, the *b.* of face changed. R. V. hardness.
John 7. 26, he speaketh *b.* R. V. openly.
2 Cor. 10. 2, I may not be *b.*
Eph. 3. 12, we have *b.* and access.
Heb. 4. 16, let us come *b.* to throne.
1 John 4. 17, have *b.* in day of judgment.
Boldness through faith. Prov. 28. 1; Isa. 50. 7; Acts 5. 29; Eph. 3. 12; Heb. 10. 19; 1 John 4. 17.
exhortations to. Jos. 1. 7; 2 Chr. 19. 11; Jer. 1. 8; Ezek. 3. 9; Heb. 4. 16.
of Peter and John, Acts 4. 13; 5. 29. Stephen, Acts 7. 51. Paul, Acts 9. 27; 13. 46; 19. 8; 2 Cor. 7. 4; Gal. 2. 11. Apollos, Acts 18. 26.
Bolled, formed into round seed-vessels; podded for seed. Ex. 9. 31.
Bond. Acts 8. 23, in *b.* of iniquity.
Eph. 4. 3, *b.* of peace.
Col. 3. 14, *b.* of perfectness.
See Num. 30. 2; Ezek. 20. 37; Lu. 13. 16.
Bondage of Israel in Egypt. Ex. 1.-12.; Ps. 105. 25; Acts 7. 6.
in Babylon. 2 Kn. 25.; Ez. 1.; 9. 7; Neh. 1.; Esth. 3.; Dan. 1.
SPIRITUAL. John 8. 33, 34; Acts 8. 23; Rom. 6. 16; 7. 23; 8. 2; Gal. 2. 4; 4. 3; 5. 1; 1 Tim. 3. 7; 2 Tim. 2. 26; Heb. 2. 14, 15; 2 Pet. 2. 19.
deliverance by Christ. Isa. 61. 1; Lu. 4. 18; John 8. 36; Rom. 8. 2; Gal. 3. 13.
Bondmaid, a female slave. Lev. 19. 20, a woman that is a *b.*
25. 44, and thy *b.*
Gal. 4. 22, the one by a *b.* R. V. handmaid.
Bondman, a slave. Deu. 15. 15; 16. 12; 24. 18.
Bondmen. Gen. 43. 18; Lev. 25. 44.
Bondwoman. Gen. 21. 10; Gal. 4. 30.
Bone. Ex. 12. 46; Num. 9. 12, neither shall ye break a *b.* thereof.
Job 20. 11, *b.* full of sin.
40. 18, *b.* as pieces of brass.
Ps. 51. 8, the *b.* broken may rejoice.
Prov. 12. 4, as rottenness in his *b.*
Mat. 23. 27, full of dead men's *b.*
Lu. 24. 39, spirit hath not flesh and *b.*
Bones, first mentioned. Gen. 2. 23.
Joseph's. Gen. 50. 25; Ex. 13. 19; Heb. 11. 22.
scattered as a judgment. 2 Kn. 23. 14; Ps. 53. 5; 141. 7; Jer. 8. 1; Ezek. 6. 5.
of the paschal lamb not broken. Ex. 12. 46; also Christ's, John 19. 36.
vision of the dry bones. Ezek. 37.
Bonnets of the priests, directions for making. Ex. 28. 40; 29. 9; 39. 28; Ezek. 44. 18. *See* MITRE.
Book. Job 19. 23, printed in a *b.*
31. 35, adversary had written a *b.*
Isa. 34. 16, seek out of the *b.* of the Lord.
Mal. 3. 16, *b.* of remembrance.
Lu. 4. 17, when he had opened *b.*
John 21. 25, world could not contain *b.*
Phil. 4. 3; Rev. 3. 5; 13. 8; 17. 8; 20. 12; 21. 27; 22. 19, *b.* of life.
Rev. 22. 19, take away from words of *b.*
Book of Life. Ex. 32. 32; Ps. 69. 28; Dan. 12. 1; Phil. 4. 3; Rev. 3. 5; 13. 8; 17. 8; 21. 27; 22. 19.
opened, Rev. 20. 12.
of the Law. Deu. 28. 61; 29. 27, &c.; Gal. 3. 10.
found and read. 2 Kn. 22. 8; 23. 2; Neh. 8. 8.
of Jasher (the upright). Jos. 10. 13; 2 Sam. 1. 18.
Books. The ancient Babylonian books were clay cylinders or tablets. The Egyptians wrote on papyrus. Hebrew books were anciently written upon prepared skins of sheep, goats, &c., attached to a roller, upon which they were rolled tightly. The N. T. books were undoubtedly written on papyrus rolls. (St. Paul's 'parchments' may have been rough notes, 2 Tim. 4. 13.) In the 4th century A. D. parchment books were taking the place of papyrus rolls.
See Ex. 17. 14; 1 Sam. 10. 25; Eccl. 12. 12; Dan. 9. 2; John 21. 25; 2 Tim. 4. 13.
of various persons. 1 Chr. 29. 29; 2 Chr. 9. 29; 12. 15; 20. 34.
of Solomon. 1 Kn. 4. 32; 11. 41.
of judgment. Dan. 7. 10; Rev. 20. 12.
burned at Ephesus. Acts 19. 19.
Booth. Job 27. 18; Jon. 4. 5.
Booths. Lev. 23. 42, ye shall dwell in *b.*
Neh. 8. 14, Israel shall dwell in *b.*
Booty. Num. 31. 32; Jer. 49. 32; Hab. 2. 7; Zep. 1. 13.
Booz, bō'-ŏz, same as BOAZ. Mat. 1. 5.
Borders of the land determined. Num. 34.; Jos. 1. 4; Ezek. 47. 13.
Boring of the ear. Ex. 21. 6.
Born. Job 5. 7, man *b.* to trouble.
14. 1; 15. 14; 25. 4; Mat. 11. 11, *b.* of a woman.
Ps. 87. 4, this man was *b.* there.
Isa. 9. 6, unto us a child is *b.*
66. 8, shall a nation be *b.* at once.
John 3. 3; 1 Pet. 1. 23, *b.* again.
6. 8, *b.* of Spirit.
1 Cor. 15. 8, as one *b.* out of due time.
1 Pet. 2. 2, as new-*b.* babes.
John 1. 13; 1 John 4. 7; 5. 1, 4, 18, *b.* of God.
See Job 3. 3; Prov. 17. 17; Eccl. 3. 2.
Borne. Ps. 55. 12, an enemy, then I could have *b.* it.
Isa. 53. 4, *b.* our griefs, carried our sorrows.

Mat. 23. 4; Lu. 11. 46, grievous to be *b.*
See Job 34. 31; Lam. 5. 7; Mat. 20. 12.

Borrow. Deu. 15. 6; 28. 12, lend but not *b.*
Ps. 37. 21, wicked *b.* and payeth not.
Prov. 22. 7, the *b.* is servant.
Mat. 5. 42, him that would *b.* of thee.

Borrowing. Ex. 22. 14; Deu. 15. 1, &c.; 2 Kn. 6. 5.
its evils. Prov. 22. 7.
of Israel from the Egyptians. Ex. 3. 22; 11. 2; 12. 35. R. V. ask.

Boscath, bŏs′-căth, stony, elevated ground. 2 Kn. 22. 1. R. V. Bozkath.

Bosom. Ps. 35. 13, prayer returned into own *b.*
Prov. 6. 27, take fire in his *b.*
Isa. 40. 11, carry lambs in *b.*
Lu. 16. 22, carried into Abraham's *b.*
John 1. 18, in the *b.* of the Father.
13. 23, leaning on Jesus' *b.*
See Ex. 4. 6; Deu. 13. 6; Job 31. 33.

Bosor, bō′-sŏr. Greek and Aramaic form of Beor. 2 Pet. 2. 15. R. V. Beor.

Bosses, large knobs, projecting ornaments. Job 15. 26.

Botany of the Bible.

A noted scientist says of Palestine, 'There is not another spot on earth where so much of nature is focussed as in this little corner. You have Alpine cold and torrid heat. Here are all the animals, birds, insects, plants, shells, rocks of all zones.'

The plants mentioned in the Bible are as follows. See each under its own name.

N. B. — The *names* to which an asterisk (*) is prefixed do not occur in the A. V., but the trees, plants, &c., are supposed to be indicated by the original text.

Almond.	Fir.	Oak.
Algum, Almug.	Fitches.	Oil tree.
Aloes.	Flag.	Olive.
Anise.	Flax.	Onions.
Apple.	Frankincense.	Palm tree.
Ash.	Galbanum.	Pannag.
Balm, Balsam.	Gall.	Pine tree.
Barley.	Garlick.	Pomegranate.
Bay tree.	Gopher.	Poplar.
Bdellium.	Gourd.	Pulse.
Bean.	Grass.	Reed.
Box.	Grove.	Rose.
Bramble.	Hay.	Rue.
Brier.	Hazel.	Rush.
Bulrush.	Heath.	Rye.
Bush, Burning.	Hemlock.	Saffron.
Calamus.	Herb.	Seaweed.
Camphire.	Husks.	Shittah tree.
Cane, Sweet.	Hyssop.	Shittim wood.
Caper.	Juniper.	Soap.
Cassia.	*Ladanum.	Sodom, Vine of.
Cedar.	Leeks.	Spelt.
Chesnut.	Lentiles.	Spicery.
Cinnamon.	Lily.	Spikenard.
*Citron.	Mallow.	Stacte.
Cockle.	Mandrake.	Sycamine.
Coriander.	Manna.	Sycomore.
Corn.	*Mastick tree.	Tares.
*Cotton.	Melons.	Teil.
Cucumber.	Millet.	Thick trees.
Cummin.	Mint.	Thistle.
Cypress.	Mulberry.	Thorn.
Desire.	Mustard.	Thyine wood.
*Dill.	Myrrh.	Vine.
Dove's Dung.	Myrtle.	Wheat.
Ebony.	Nard.	Willow.
Elm.	Nettles.	With.
Fig tree.	Nuts.	Wormwood.

Botch, eruption of the skin, a boil. Deu. 28. 27.

Bottle. Various words are rendered in the A. V. of the O. T. by 'bottle.' In the New the only one so rendered is ἀσκός (Mat. 9. 17; Mk. 2. 22) = the Latin *uter*, a skin-bottle. The larger bottles were made of the skin of a he-goat, the smaller of a kid's skin.
Jud. 4. 19, a *b.* of milk.
1 Sam. 1. 24; 10. 3; 16. 20; 2 Sam. 16. 1, a *b.* of [wine.
Ps. 56. 8, put thou my tears into thy *b.*
119. 83, like a *b.* in the smoke.
See Gen. 21. 14, 15; Hab. 2. 15.

Bottles. Jos. 9. 13, these *b.* of wine. R. V. wine- [skins.
1 Sam. 25. 18, and two *b.* of wine.
Job 32. 19, ready to burst like new *b.*
Hos. 7. 5, sick with *b.* of wine. R. V. heat.
Mat. 9. 17; Mk. 2. 22; Lu. 5. 37, new wine in old *b.*

Bottom. (1) valley. Zec. 1. 8.
(2) Ex. 15. 5; Lev. 4. 25; Job 36. 30; Mat. 27. 51.

Bottomless. Rev. 9. 1; 11. 7; 17. 8; 20. 1, 2, the *b.* pit.

Bough. Gen. 49. 22; Deu. 24. 20; Jud. 9. 48; Job 14. 9; Ps. 80. 10; Ezek. 31. 3.

Bought. Lu. 14. 18; 1 Cor. 6. 20; 7. 23; 2 Pet. 2. 1.

Bound. Ps. 107. 10, being *b.* in affliction.
Prov. 22. 15, foolishness *b.* in heart of child.
Acts 20. 22, *b.* in spirit to Jerusalem.
1 Cor. 7. 27, art thou *b.* to a wife.
2 Tim. 2. 9, word of God is not *b.*
Heb. 13. 3, in bonds as *b.* with them.
See Gen. 44. 30; Mat. 16. 19; Mk. 5. 4.

Bountiful. Prov. 22. 9, a *b.* eye shall be blessed.
Isa. 32. 5, nor churl said to be *b.*
See Ps. 13. 6; 116. 7; 119. 17; 2 Cor. 9. 6.

Bounty. 1 Kn. 10. 13; 2 Cor. 9. 5.

Bow in the cloud, sign of God's mercy. Gen. 9. 13, &c.; Ezek. 1. 28.

Bow (*v.*). Gen. 27. 29; Ex. 12. 27; 20. 5; 1 Sam. 24. 8; Isa. 45. 23; Mk. 15. 19; Eph. 3. 14.

Bow and arrows. The bow was used both for hunting and war. The tribe of Benjamin was especially noted for its archers. The arrows were made of cane or polished wood, with heads of iron, copper, or stone.
Gen. 48. 22; Jos. 24. 12; 1 Sam. 18. 4; 2 Sam. 1. 18, 22; 1 Kn. 22. 34; 2 Kn. 9. 24; 1 Chr. 5. 18; Job 6. 4; Ps. 44. 6; 78. 57; Jer. 49. 35; Hos. 7. 16; Rev. 6. 2.

Bowels, compassionate feelings, affections. Gen. 43. 30, his *b.* did yearn.
Isa. 63. 15, where is sounding of thy *b.*
2 Cor. 6. 12, straitened in *b.*
Phil. 1. 8, after you in *b.* of Christ.
2. 1, if there be any *b.*
Col. 3. 12, *b.* of mercies.
1 John 3. 17, *b.* of compassion.
See Acts 1. 18; Philem. 12.

Bowl. Num. 7. 25, one silver *b.*
Eccl. 12. 6, golden *b.* be broken.
Am. 6. 6, that drink wine in *b.*
Zec. 4. 2, with a *b.* upon the top of it.

Box (Isa. 41. 19; 60. 13). Heb. *Têasshûr:* Gk. πύξος: Bot. N. (1) *Buxus longifolia.* (2) *Juniperus Phœnicea:* R. V. marg. 'cypress.' The Palestine box resembles ours, but is larger (20 feet high).

Bozez, bō-zĕz, 'shining' (?). 1 Sam. 14. 4.

Bozkath, bŏz′-kăth, same as Boscath. Jos. 15. 39.

Bozrah, bŏz′-răh, 'sheepfold,' or 'fortress.' (1) Gen. 36. 33.
prophecies concerning. Isa. 34. 6; 63. 1; Jer. 49. 13; Am. 1. 12.
(2) Jer. 48. 24.

Bracelet. Gen. 24. 30; Ex. 35. 22; Isa. 3. 19. R. V. brooches, in Ex.

Brake. 2 Kn. 23. 14; 2 Chr. 34. 4, Josiah *b.* images.
Mat. 14. 19; 15. 36; 26. 26; Mk. 6. 41; 8. 6; 14. 22; Lu. 9. 16; 22. 19; 24. 30; 1 Cor. 11. 24, blessed and *b.*
See Ex. 32. 19; 1 Sam. 4. 18; Lu. 5. 6; John 19. 32.

Bramble, Brier, Thistle, Thorn. (Jud. 9. 14) Heb. *Atâd:* Gk. ῥάμνος. (Prov. 15. 19; Mic. 7. 4). Heb. *Hedek:* Gk. ἄκανθα. (Isa. 34. 13; Job. 31. 40) Heb. *Hôäch:* Gk. κνίδη and ἄκανθα. (Gen. 3. 18) Heb. *Dardar:* Gk. τρίβολος. (Gen. 3. 18) Heb. *Kôtz:* Gk. ἄκανθα. (Isa. 55. 13) Heb. *Naatzûz:* Gk. στοιβή. (Isa. 7. 23, 25) Heb. *Shâmîr:*

Gk. ἄκανθα. (Ezek. 2. 6; 28. 24) Heb. *Sillôn:* Gk. ἄκανθα ὀδύνης. (Prov. 22. 5) Heb. *Tsînîm:* Gk. τρίβολος. (Mat. 7. 16) Gk. ἄκανθα. (Lu. 6. 44) Gk. βάτος. (Mat. 7. 16) Gk. τρίβολος. These Hebrew and Greek words are not the names of particular species of plants, but general terms applied to spine-bearing plants. The Heb. word *Barkonim* (Jud. 8. 7, 16), translated 'briers,' was probably a sharp-toothed threshing instrument, or a plant used as such.

Branch. Job 14. 7, tender *b.* not cease. [leaf.
Prov. 11. 28, righteous flourish as *b.* R. V. green
Jer. 23. 5, will raise a righteous *B.*
Mat. 13. 32; Lu. 13. 19, birds lodge in *b.*
21. 8; Mk. 11. 8; John 12. 13, cut down *b.*

Branch (of the Lord), prophecies concerning. Isa. 4. 2; Jer. 23. 5; Zec. 3. 8; 6. 12; John 15. 5; Rom. 11. 16.

Brand. Jud. 15. 5, set the *b.* on fire.
Zec. 3. 2, as a fire *b.* plucked out.

Brass. (1) metal. The Heb. *Nechôsheth* is used for (*a*) pure copper, Deu. 8. 9; (*b*) bronze (copper and zinc); (*c*) brass (copper and tin).
(2) copper money, Mat. 10. 9.

Brass used in the tabernacle and temple. Ex. 25. 3; 26. 11; 1 Kn. 7. 14.
altar of. Ex. 39. 39; 2 Kn. 16. 14.
mentioned. Lev. 26. 19; Deu. 28. 23; Job 6. 12; 1 Cor. 13. 1; Rev. 1. 15.

Bravely, finely, gaudily. Judith 10. 4.

Bravery, finery, showy dress. Isa. 3. 18.

Brawler. Prov. 25. 24; 1 Tim. 3. 3; Tit. 3. 2.

Bray. (1) Job 6. 5; 30. 7.
(2) to pound, or bruise. Prov. 27. 22.

Breach. Isa. 58. 12, the repairer of the *b.*
Lam. 2. 13, thy *b.* is great like the sea.
See Lev. 24. 20; Ps. 106. 23; Am. 4. 3; 6. 11.

Breaches, creeks, harbours. Jud. 5. 17.

Bread was principally in the form of thin cakes, baked upon the hearth or in the oven; those eaten by the poor were made of barley meal, with oil instead of butter. They were leavened or unleavened, and kneaded in a trough.
Deu. 8. 3; Mat. 4. 4; Lu. 4. 4, not live by *b.* alone.
Ru. 1. 6, visited people in giving them *b.*
1 Kn. 17. 6, ravens brought *b.* and flesh.
Job 22. 7, withholden *b.* from hungry.
33. 20, life abhorreth *b.*
Ps. 132. 15, satisfy poor with *b.*
Prov. 9. 17, *b.* eaten in secret.
12. 11; 20. 13; 28. 19, satisfied with *b.*
31. 27, eateth not *b.* of idleness.
Eccl. 11. 1, cast *b.* on waters.
Isa. 33. 16, *b.* given and waters sure.
55. 2, money for that which is not *b.*
55. 10, seed to sower, *b.* to eater.
Mat. 4. 3; Lu. 4. 3, stones made *b.*
6. 11; Lu. 11. 3, give us daily *b.*
15. 26; Mk. 7. 27, take children's *b.*
Lu. 24. 35, known in breaking *b.*
Acts 2. 42; 20. 7; 27. 35, breaking *b.*
2 Thes. 3. 8, eat any man's *b.* for nought.

Bread, Adam's curse. Gen. 3. 19.
rained from heaven (manna). Ex. 16. 4.
miraculously supplied. 2 Kn. 4. 42; John 6. &c.
a type of Christ. John 6. 31; 1 Cor. 10. 16.
offered before the Lord. Ex. 25. 30; Lev. 8. 26; 24. 5.
hallowed, David obtains from Ahimelech. 1 Sam. 21. 4.
used in the Lord's Supper. Lu. 22. 19; 24. 30; Acts 2. 42; 20. 7; 1 Cor. 10. 16; 11. 23.
unleavened. Gen. 19. 3; Ex. 12. 8; 1 Sam. 28. 24; 2 Kn. 23. 9. figuratively used, 1 Cor. 5. 8.

Break. S. of S. 2. 17; 4. 6, day *b.* and shadows flee. R. V. be cool.
Isa. 42. 3; Mat. 12. 20, bruised reed shall he not *b.*
Jer. 4. 3; Hos. 10. 12, *b.* up fallow ground.
Acts 21. 13, to weep and *b.* my heart.
See Ps. 2. 3; Mat. 5. 19; 9. 17; 1 Cor. 10. 16.

Breastplate, defensive armour. (Heb. *Shiryôn*) = the θώραξ of the Greeks and the *lorica* of the Romans, first mentioned in the description of the arms of Goliath (1 Sam. 17. 5), covering the most vulnerable parts of the body. *See* 1 Kn. 22. 34; Isa. 59. 17; Eph. 6. 14.

Breastplate of the high priest (set in gold) **R. V.** Ex. 28. 17-20. The names are taken from the text and margin of the R. V. of Exodus. The figures show the order of the stones as given in Exodus.

3 Emerald.	2 Topaz.	1 Ruby, or Sardius.
6 Sardonyx. (Diamond, A. V.)	5 Sapphire.	4 Carbuncle.
9 Amethyst.	8 Agate.	7 Amber, or Jacinth.
12 Jasper.	11 Beryl.	10 Chalcedony, or Chrysolite.

Breastplate of the high priest described. Ex. 28. 15; 39. 8.
of righteousness. Eph. 6. 14.
of faith and love. 1 Thes. 5. 8.

Breath. Gen. 2. 7; 6. 17; 7. 15, *b.* of life.
Isa. 2. 22, cease from man whose *b.*
Ezek. 37. 5, 10, I will cause *b.* to enter.
Acts 17. 25, he giveth to all life and *b.*
See Ps. 146. 4; 150. 6.

Breath (life) dependent upon God. Gen. 2. 7; 6. 17; Job 12. 10; 33. 4; Ps. 104. 29; Ezek. 37. 5; Dan. 5. 23; Acts 17. 25.
of God, its power. 2 Sam. 22. 16; Job 4. 9; Ps. 33. 6; Isa. 11. 4; 30. 28.

Breathe. Ps. 27. 12; Ezek. 37. 9; John 20. 22.

Breeches. Ex. 28. 42; Lev. 6. 10; 16. 4; Ezek. 44. 18.

Brethren. Mat. 23. 8, all ye are *b.*
Mk. 10. 29; Lu. 18. 29, no man left house or *b.*
Col. 1. 2, faithful *b.* in Christ.
1 John 3. 14, because we love the *b.*
See Gen. 42. 8; Prov. 19. 7; John 7. 5.

Brethren, duty of, towards each other. Gen. 13. 8; Deu. 15. 7; 24. 14; Ps. 133.; Mat. 5. 22; 18. 15, 21; 25. 40; John 13. 34; 15. 12, &c.; Rom. 12. 10; 1 Cor. 6.; 8. 13; Gal. 6. 1; 1 Thes. 4. 9; 2 Thes. 3. 15; Heb. 13. 1; 1 Pet. 1. 22; 3. 8; 2 Pet. 1. 7; 1 John 2. 9; 3. 17.

Bribe. 1 Sam. 12. 3, have I received any *b.* R. V. ransom.
Ps. 26. 10, right hand is full of *b.*

Bribery forbidden. Ex. 23. 2, 6; Deu. 16. 19.
denounced. Job 15. 34; Prov. 17. 23; 29. 4; Eccl. 7. 7; Isa. 5. 23; 33. 15; Ezek. 13. 19; Am. 2. 6.
of Delilah. Jud. 16. 5.
of Samuel's sons. 1 Sam. 8. 3.
of Judas. Mat. 26. 14.
of the soldiers. Mat. 28. 12.
punished. Job 15. 34.

Brickle, easily broken, brittle. Wisd. 15. 13.

Brickmaking, as described in Exodus, may still be seen in Egypt. In the Fourth Egyptian Room of the British Museum are exhibited a number of bricks made of clay mixed with straw, sand, and broken pottery. Some are stamped with the names of Thothmes I. B. C. 1633; Thothmes III., B. C. 1600; Amenophis III., B. C. 1500; and Rameses II., B. C. 1333. Babylonian bricks stamped with the name of Nebuchadnezzar II., mentioned in the Book of Daniel, measure 13×13×3 in.
See Gen. 11. 3; Ex. 1. 14; 5. 7, 10; Isa. 9. 10; 65. 3.

Bride. Isa. 61. 10; Jer. 2. 32; Rev. 21. 2; 22. 17.
Bridegroom. Mat. 25. 1. to meet the *b.*
John 3. 29, because of *b.* voice.
See Ps. 19. 5; Isa. 62. 5; Mat. 9. 15.
Bridle. Prov. 26. 3, a *b.* for the ass.
Jas. 1. 26, *b.* not his tongue.
3. 2, able to *b.* whole body.
See 2 Kn. 19. 28; Ps. 39. 1; Isa. 37. 29.
Brier, see BRAMBLE.
Brigandine, a light coat of scale-armour. Jer. 46. 4; 51. 3.
Bright. Job 37. 21, *b.* light in the clouds.
Isa. 60. 3, to *b.* of thy rising.
62. 1, righteousness go forth as *b.*
Mat. 17. 5, *b.* cloud overshadowed.
2 Thes. 2. 8, *b.* of his coming. R. V. manifestation.
Heb. 1. 3, the *b.* of his glory. R. V. effulgence.
Rev. 22. 16, the *b.* and morning star.
See Lev. 13. 2; Jer. 51. 11; Zec. 10. 1.
Brim. 1 Kn. 7. 26; Jos. 3. 15; John 2. 7.
Brimstone. Gen. 19. 24, rained upon Sodom and Gomorrah *b.*
Isa. 30. 33, like a stream of *b.*
Rev. 9. 17, issued fire and *b.*
14. 10, tormented with fire and *b.*
19. 20, a lake of fire and *b.*
Brink. Gen. 41. 3; Ex. 2. 3; 7. 15; Jos. 3. 8.
Broad. Ps. 119. 96; Mat. 7. 13; 23. 5.
Broided, braided, plaited. 1 Tim. 2. 9.
Broidered, embroidered. Ex. 28. 4; Ezek. 16. 10, 13; 27. 7, 16, 24, *b.* work.
Broiled. Lu. 24. 42.
Broken. Ps. 34. 18; 51. 17; 69. 20, *b.* heart.
John 10. 35, scripture cannot be *b.*
19. 36, bone shall not be *b.*
Eph. 2. 14, *b.* down middle wall.
See Job 17. 11; Prov. 25. 19; Jer. 2. 13.
Brood. Lu. 13. 34.
Brook. 1 Sam. 17. 40; Ps. 42. 1; 110. 7.
Broth. Jud. 6. 19; Isa. 65. 4.
Brother. Prov. 17. 17, *b.* born for adversity.
18. 9, slothful *b.* to waster.
18. 19, *b.* offended harder to be won.
18. 24, friend closer than *b.*
Eccl. 4. 8, neither child nor *b.*
Mat. 10. 21, *b.* shall deliver up *b.*
1 Cor. 6. 6, *b.* goeth to law with *b.*
2 Thes. 3. 15, admonish as *b.*
See Gen. 4. 9; Mat. 5. 23; 12. 50; Mk. 3. 35.
Brotherly. Rom. 12. 10; 1 Thes. 4. 9; Heb. 13. 1, *b.* love.
See Am. 1. 9; 2 Pet. 1. 7.
Brow. Isa. 48. 4; Lu. 4. 29.
Bruise (*n.*). Isa. 1. 6; Jer. 30. 12; Nah. 3. 19.
Bruise (*v.*). 2 Kn. 18. 21, staff of this *b.* reed.
Isa. 42. 3; Mat. 12. 20, *b.* reed shall he not break.
53. 5, *b.* for our iniquities.
See Gen. 3. 15; Isa. 53. 10; Rom. 16. 20.
Bruit, report, rumour. (Fr. *bruit*, noise.) Jer. 10. 22; Nah. 3. 19.
Brutish. Ps. 92. 6, a *b.* man knoweth not.
Prov. 30. 2, I am more *b.* than any.
Jer. 10. 21, pastors are become *b.*
See Ps. 49. 10; Jer. 10. 8; Ezek. 21. 31.
Bucket. Num. 24. 7; Isa. 40. 15.
Buckler, a small round shield. 2 Sam. 22. 31; Job 15. 26; Ps. 18. 2; 91. 4; Prov. 2. 7.
Bud. Num. 17. 8; Isa. 18. 5; 61. 11; Hos. 8. 7.
Buffet, to strike, beat with the hands. Mat. 26. 67; 1 Cor. 4. 11; 2 Cor. 12. 7; 1 Pet. 2. 20.
Build. Ps. 127. 1, labour in vain that *b.*
Eccl. 3. 3, a time to *b.* up.
Isa. 58. 12, *b.* old waste places.
Mat. 7. 24; Lu. 6. 48, wise man *b.* on rock.
Lu. 14. 30, began to *b.*, not able to finish.
Acts 20. 32, able to *b.* you up.
Rom. 15. 20, lest I *b.* on another.
1 Cor. 3. 12, if any *b.* on this foundation.
Eph. 2. 22, in whom ye are *b.* together.
See 1 Chr. 17. 12; 2 Chr. 6. 9; Eccl. 2. 4.
Builder. Ps. 118. 22; Mat. 21. 42; Mk. 12. 10; Lu. 20. 17; Acts 4. 11; 1 Pet. 2. 7, *b.* refused.
1 Cor. 3. 10, as a wise master-*b.*
Heb. 11. 10, whose *b.* and maker is God.
See 1 Kn. 5. 18; Ez. 3. 10.
Building. 1 Cor. 3. 9; 2 Cor. 5. 1; Eph. 2. 21; Col. 2. 7.
Bukki, bŭk'-kī, 'proved of Jehovah.' Num. 34. 22.
Bukkiah, bŭk-kī'-ăh, same as BUKKI. 1 Chr. 25. 4.
Bul, bûl, eighth month in the Jewish sacred year = Nov. 1 Kn. 6. 38. *See* MONTHS.
Bull. Gen. 32. 15; Ps. 22. 12; Jer. 52. 20; Heb. 9. 13. *See* UNICORN, OX, and DEER.
Bulrush. Six Hebrew words are used of rushes, and are translated somewhat indiscriminately.
(1) Heb. *Gômé*: Gk. θίβη, πάπυρος βίβλινος and ἕλος: Bot. N. *Cyperus papyrus*: A. V. bulrush and rush, R. V. marg. papyrus. The material of Moses' ark, which grew in miry places. The famous papyrus. It has a triangular stem, eight to ten feet high, ending in a bushy top of slender leaves, among which the seeds are produced.
(2) (Isa. 19. 7). Heb. *'Arôth*: Gk. τὸ ἄχι τὸ χλωρόν: R. V. meadows.
(3) (Job 8. 11; Gen. 41. 2). Heb. *Ahû*: Gk. ἄχι βούτομον: R. V. reed-grass.
(4) (Ex. 2. 3, 5; Jon. 2. 5). Heb. *Sûph*: Gk. τὸ ἕλος. A general term for water-weeds, whether growing in the sea or in the river.
(5) (Isa. 9. 14; 19. 15). Heb. *Agmôn* (paraphrased in LXX.): Gk. κάλαμος: Bot. N. *Arundo phragmites*. Probably the common reed of Egypt and Palestine, a tall thin cane, twelve feet high, with a bushy blossom, bending before the wind and rising again,—the 'reed shaken with the wind' (Mat. 11. 7).
(6) (Gen. 41. 5, 22). Heb. *Kâneh*: Gk. κάλαμος. The general term for a 'stem;' whether the 'stalk' of wheat, the stem, or 'shaft,' of a candlestick (Ex. 25. 31), a measuring rod, or 'reed' (Ezek. 40. 5).
Bulwark, a fortification. Isa. 26. 1, salvation for walls and *b.*
See Deu. 20. 20; Ps. 48. 13; Eccl. 9. 14.
Bunah, bū'-năh, prudence. 1 Chr. 2. 25.
Bunch, a (camel's) hump. Isa. 30. 6.
Bundle. Gen. 42. 35; 1 Sam. 25. 29; Mat. 13. 30; Acts 28. 3.
Bunni, bŭn'-nī, 'built.' Neh. 9. 4.
Burden. Num. 11. 11, the *b.* of all this people.
Eccl. 12. 5, grasshopper shall be a *b.*
Mat. 11. 30, my *b.* is light.
20. 12, borne *b.* and heat of day.
23. 4; Lu. 11. 46, bind heavy *b.*
Gal. 6. 2, 5, bear his own *b.*
2 Cor. 12. 16, I did not *b.* you.
Burden, signifying prophecy. 2 Kn. 9. 25; Isa. 13.; 15.; 17.; 19.; 21.; 22.; 23.; Nah. 1. 1.
cast on the Lord. Ps. 55. 22.
of affliction. Isa. 58. 6; 2 Cor. 5. 4.
of iniquities. Ps. 38. 4.
of Christ, light. Mat. 11. 30.—Acts 15. 28; Rev. 2. 24.
borne for others. Gal. 6. 2.
Burdensome. Zec. 12. 3; 2 Cor. 11. 9; 1 Thes. 2. 6.
Burial, want of, a calamity. Deu. 28. 26; Ps. 79. 2; Eccl. 6. 3; Isa. 14. 19; Jer. 7. 33; 16. 4; 25. 33; 34. 20.
of Sarah, Gen. 23. 19. Abraham, Gen. 25. 9. Isaac, Gen. 35. 29. Jacob, Gen. 50. Abner, 2 Sam. 3. 31, 32. Christ, Mat. 27. 57; Lu. 23. 50. Stephen, Acts 8. 2.
Burn. Ps. 39. 3, musing the fire *b.* R. V. kindled.
Prov. 26. 23, *b.* lips and wicked heart. R. V. fervent.
Isa. 9. 18, wickedness *b.* as fire.
33. 14, dwell with everlasting *b.*
Mal. 4. 1, day that shall *b.* as oven.
Mat. 13. 30, bind tares to *b.* them.
Lu. 3. 17, chaff *b.* with fire unquenchable.

Lu. 12. 35, loins girded and lights *b.*
24. 32, did not our heart *b.*
John 5. 35, he was a *b.* and shining light.
1 Cor. 13. 3, give my body to be *b.*
Heb. 6. 8, whose end is to be *b.*
Rev. 4. 5, lamps *b.* before throne.
19. 20, into a lake *b.*
See Gen. 44. 18; Ex. 3. 2; 21. 25.

Burning Bush. Heb. *Seneh:* Gk. βάτος: Bot. N. *Acacia Nilotica.* Only used of the 'burning bush,' the thorny acacia of the Arabian peninsula, the *sûnt* of Egypt, akin to the shittah tree and senna.
the Lord appears to Moses in, Ex. 3. 2; Mk. 12. 26; Lu. 20. 37; Acts 7. 35.

Burnt offering. Ps. 40. 6, *b.* thou hast not required.
Isa. 61. 8, I hate robbery for *b.* R. V. with iniquity.
Jer. 6. 20, your *b.* not acceptable.
Hos. 6. 6, knowledge more than *b.*
Mk. 12. 33, love neighbour more than *b.* [6. 8.

Burnt offerings, law concerning. Lev. 1.; illustrations of. Gen. 8. 20; 22. 13; Ex. 18. 12; 1 Sam. 7. 9; Ez. 3. 4; Job 1. 5. *See* Ps. 40. 6; 51. 19; Isa. 40. 16; Heb. 10.
the continual. Ex. 29. 38; Num. 28. 3; 1 Chr. 16. 40; 2 Chr. 13. 11.

Burst. Job 32. 19; Prov. 3. 10; Mk. 2. 22; Lu. 5. 37.

Bury. Mat. 8. 21; Lu. 9. 59, suffer me to *b.* my father.
Mat. 8. 22; Lu. 9. 60, let dead *b.* dead.
John 19. 40, manner of the Jews is to *b.*
Rom. 6. 4; Col. 2. 12, *b.* with him by baptism.
1 Cor. 15. 4, he was *b.* and rose again.
See Gen. 23. 4; 47. 29; Mat. 14. 12.

Bushel. Mat. 5. 15; Mk. 4. 21; Lu. 11. 33 = Roman Modius = nearly a peck.

Business. 1 Sam. 21. 8, king's *b.* requireth haste.
Ps. 107. 23, do *b.* in great waters.
Prov. 22. 29, diligent in *b.*
Lu. 2. 49, about my Father's *b.* R. V. house.
Rom. 12. 11, not slothful in *b.*
1 Thes. 4. 11, study to do your own *b.*
See Jos. 2. 14; Jud. 18. 7; Neh. 13. 30.

Busybodies. 2 Thes. 3. 11, but are *b.*
1 Tim. 5. 13, tattlers also and *b.*
1 Pet. 4. 15, *b.* in other men's matters.
See Prov. 20. 3; 26. 17; 1 Thes. 4. 11.

Butler, or Cup-bearer (botler) one who offers wines and drinks at the meals of the rich. A responsible officer in royal households (Gen. 40. 1-21; 41. 9; Neh. 1. 11).

Butter. The Hebrews were ignorant of the art of *churning* butter; but they made a kind of clotted cream by subjecting new milk to fermentation, which imparted to it a pleasant acid flavour somewhat resembling that of lemon cream. This was probably the 'butter in a lordly dish' which Jael brought to Sisera, when she had 'opened a bottle of milk.' Jud. 4. 19; 5. 25.
Isa. 7. 15, 22, *b.* and honey shall he eat.
See Job 29. 6; Ps. 55. 21; Prov. 30. 33.

Buy. Lev. 22. 11, *b.* any soul with money.
Prov. 23. 23, *b.* the truth.
Isa. 55. 1, *b.* and eat, *b.* wine and milk.
Mat. 25. 9, go to them that sell and *b.*
John 4. 8, disciples were gone to *b.* meat.
Jas. 4. 13, we will *b.* and sell and get gain.
Rev. 3. 18, *b.* of me gold tried.
13. 17, no man *b.* save he that had mark.
18. 11, no man *b.* her merchandise.
See Gen. 42. 2; 47. 19; Ru. 4. 4; Mat. 13. 44.

Buyer. Prov. 20. 14; Isa. 24. 2; Ezek. 7. 12.

Buz, bŭz, 'contempt.' Gen. 22. 21. [1. 3.

Buzi, bū'-zī, 'descended from Buz' (?). Ezek.

Buzite, bū'-zīte, 'a descendant of Buz.' Job 32. 2.

By, against, in 1 Cor. 4. 4.

By and by, immediately. Hence, 'not by and by' = not at once. Mat. 13. 21; Mk. 6. 25; Lu. 17. 7; 21. 9.

Byways. Jud. 5. 6.

Byword, a proverb. Job 17. 6; 30. 9, a *b.* of the people.
Ps. 44. 14, a *b.* among the heathen.
See Deu. 28. 37; 1 Kn. 9. 7; 2 Chr. 7. 20.

Cab, căb. 2 Kn. 6. 25. A measure, = one eighteenth of an ephah = 2.16 litres = nearly two quarts (1.92).
See Measures.

Cabbon, căb'-bŏn. Jos. 15. 40.

Cabin, a cell, dark cellar. Jer. 37. 16.

Cabul, cā'-bŭl, like naught (?). (1) Jos. 19. 27. (2) 1 Kn. 9. 13.

Caesar, çæ'-sär. Mat. 22. 17.
Augustus. Lu. 2. 1.
Tiberius. Lu. 3. 1.
Claudius, time of dearth. Acts 11. 28.
Paul appeals to. Acts 25. 11.
household of. Phil. 4. 22.

Cæsarea, çæ-să-rē'-ă, named after Augustus Cæsar. Acts 8. 40.
Peter sent there. Acts 10.
Paul visits. Acts 21. 8. [Acts 23. 23.
Paul sent to Felix there and detained two years.

Cæsarea Philippi, çæ-să-rē'ă phĭ-lĭp'-pī, named after Philip the tetrarch; visited by Christ. Mat. 16. 13; Mk. 8. 27.

Cage. Jer. 5. 27; Rev. 18. 2.

Caiaphas, cā'-ă-phăs, high priest, prophesies concerning Christ. John 11. 49.
his counsel. Mat. 26. 3. [22. 71.
he condemns Him. Mat. 26. 65; Mk. 14. 63; Lu.

Cain, cain, 'possession' (?) (1) Gen. 4. 1.
his anger. Gen. 4. 5.
murders Abel. Gen. 4. 8; 1 John 3. 12.
his punishment. Gen. 4. 11; Jude 11.
(2) Jos. 15. 57.

Cainan, cā-ī'-năn, a smith (?). Gen. 5. 9.

Cake. 2 Sam. 6. 19, to every man a *c.* of bread.
1 Kn. 17. 13, make me a little *c.* first.
See Jud. 7. 13; Jer. 7. 18; 44. 19; Hos. 7. 8.

Calah, cā'-läh. Gen. 10. 11. [day of *c.*

Calamity. Deu. 32. 35; 2 Sam. 22. 19; Ps. 18. 18,
Ps. 57. 1, until *c.* be overpast.
Prov. 1. 26, I will laugh at your *c.*
17. 5, he that is glad at *c.*
19. 13, foolish son *c.* of father.
27. 10, brother's house in day of *c.*
See Job 6. 2; Prov. 24. 22.

Calamus (Ex. 30. 23; Ezek. 27. 19). Heb. *Kâneh bosem:* Gk. κάλαμος εὐώδης, *sweet cane.* Some aromatic cane or grass, probably one of the lemon-grasses of India, such as *Andropogon schœnanthus.*

Calcol, căl'-col, 'sustenance.' 1 Chr. 2. 6.

Caldron. 1 Sam. 2. 14; Jer. 52. 18, 19; Ezek. 11. 3.

Caleb, cā'-lĕb, 'a dog' (?). (1) faith of. Num. 13. 30; 14. 6; permitted to enter Canaan, Num. 26. 65; 32. 12; Deu. 1. 36.
his request. Jos. 14. 6.
his possessions. Jos. 15. 13.
gives his daughter to Othniel to wife. Jud. 1. 13.
(2) 1 Chr. 2. 18. (3) 1 Chr. 2. 50.

Caleb-ephratah, cā'-lĕb-ĕph'-ră-tăh, '*C.* the fruitful.' 1 Chr. 2. 24.

Calendar, Jewish. *See* Months.

Calf. Isa. 11. 6; Lu. 15. 23.

Calf, golden, Aaron's transgression in making. Ex. 32.; Acts 7. 40.
of Samaria. Hos. 8. 5, 6.

Calkers, men who stop the seams of ships with tow. Ezek. 27. 9, 27.

Call of God to repentance and salvation. Ps. 49.; 50., &c.; Prov. 1. 20; 2.-8.; Isa. 1.; 45. 20; 55.; Jer. 35. 15; Hos. 6.; 14.; Joel 2.; Jon. 3.; Mat. 3.; 11. 28; John 7. 37; 12. 44; Rom. 8. 28; 9.; 10.; 11.; 2 Cor. 5. 20; Rev. 2. 5; 3. 3, 19; 22. 17.
danger of rejecting. Ps. 50. 17; Prov. 1. 24; 29. 1; Isa. 6. 9; 66. 4; Jer. 6. 19; 26. 4; 35. 17; Mat. 22.

3; John 12. 48; Acts 13. 46; 18. 6; 28. 24; Rom. 11. 8; 2 Thes. 2. 10; Heb. 2. 1; 12. 25; Rev. 2. 5.

Call of Noah, Gen. 6. 13. Abraham, Gen. 12. Jacob, Gen. 28. 12. Moses, Ex. 3. Gideon, Jud. 6. 11. Samuel, 1 Sam. 3. Elijah, 1 Kn. 17. Elisha, 1 Kn. 19. 16, 19. Isaiah, Isa. 6. Jeremiah, Jer. 1. Ezekiel, Ezek. 1. Hosea, Hos. 1.
of Amos. Am. 1.; 7. 14. *See* Mic. 1. 1; Zep. 1. 1; Hag. 1. 1; Zec. 1. 1.
of Jonah. Jon. 1. [1. 39.
of Peter, &c. Mat. 4. 18; Mk. 1. 16; Lu. 5.; John
of Paul. Acts 9.; Rom. 1. 1; Gal. 1. 1, 12; 1 Tim. 1.

Calling. Acts 7. 59; 22. 16, *c.* on name of the Lord.
Rom. 11. 29, *c.* of God without repentance.
1 Cor. 7. 20, abide in same *c.*
Eph. 1. 18, the hope of his *c.*
Phil. 3. 14, prize of high *c.*
2 Thes. 1. 11, worthy of this *c.*
2 Tim. 1. 9, called us with holy *c.*
Heb. 3. 1, partakers of heavenly *c.*
2 Pet. 1. 10, make *c.* and election sure.

Calling or vocation of the gospel. Rom. 11. 29; 1 Cor. 1. 26; Eph. 1. 18; 4. 1; Phil. 3. 14; 2 Thes. 1. 11; 2 Tim. 1. 9; Heb. 3. 1; 1 Pet. 2. 9; 2 Pet. 1. 10; Rev. 19. 9.

Calm. Ps. 107. 29; Jon. 1. 11; Mat. 8. 26; Mk. 4. 39; Lu. 8. 24.

Calneh, căl′-nĕh. Gen. 10. 10.

Calno, căl′-nō, same as Calneh. Isa. 10. 9.

Calvary, căl′-vă-rȳ, 'skull.' Lu. 23. 33.

Calves. 1 Kn. 12. 28, made two *c.* of gold.
See Hos. 14. 2; Mal. 4. 2.

Camel. (1) (Job 1. 3). Heb. *Gâmâl:* Gk. *κάμηλος*: the generic name for camel. including both the Arabian one-humped (*Camelus dromedarius*) and Bactrian two-humped species (*Camelus Bactrianus*); but the latter was rare.
(2) (Isa. 60. 6). Heb. *Béker*, a young camel or dromedary.
Isa. 60. 6, the multitude of *c.* shall cover thee.
Mat. 19. 24, it is easier for a *c.*
23. 24, strain at a gnat, swallow a *c.*
See Gen. 24, 64; Ex. 9. 3; Lev. 11. 4; Deu. 14. 7; 1 Chr. 5. 21; Job 1. 3.

Camel's hair. Raiment of camel's hair (Mat. 3. 4) was not a skin, but a coat of cloth, woven from the hair of the camel. Such is the ordinary outer garment of the Bedawîn of to-day.

Camon, cā′-mŏn, 'stability' (?). Jud. 10. 5.

Camp (*n.*). Ex. 14. 19, angel went before *c.*
16. 13, quails covered the *c.*
Num. 1. 52, every man by his own *c.*
Deu. 23. 14, Lord walketh in midst of *c.*
See 1 Sam. 4. 6, 7; Heb. 13. 13.

Camp (*v.*). Isa. 29. 3; Jer. 50. 29; Nah. 3. 17.

Camp of Israelites. Ex. 14. 19; Num. 1. 52; 2.; 24. 5.
to be kept holy. Lev. 6. 11; 13. 46; Num. 5. 2; Deu. 23. 10; Heb. 13. 11.

Camphire (S. of S. 1. 14; 4. 13). Heb. *Côpher:* Gk. *κύπρος*: Bot. N. *Lawsonia alba.* R. V. 'henna-flowers.' A small shrub, with dark bark, leaves pale green like a lilac, and bearing clusters of white and yellow blossoms, very fragrant; from which is obtained the henna dye with which the Arabs dye their nails, palms, etc.

Cana, cā′-nă, Christ turns water into wine at. John 2.
nobleman visits Christ at. John 4. 46, 47.

Canaan, cā′-nă-ăn, 'low region.' (1) land of. Ex. 23. 31; Jos. 1. 4; Zep. 2. 5.
promised to Abraham. Gen. 12. 7; 13. 14; 17. 8.
inhabitants of. Ex. 15. 15.
their wickedness at Sodom and Gomorrah. Gen. 13. 13; 19.
Israelites not to walk in the ways of. Lev. 18. 3, 24, 30; 20. 23.
daughters of. Gen. 28. 1, 6, 8.
language of. Isa. 19. 18.
kingdoms of. Ps. 135. 11.
king of. Jud. 4. 2, 23, 24; 5. 19.
wars of. Jud. 3. 1.
dwelling of Abraham in, Gen. 12. 6. Isaac and Jacob, Gen. 28. Esau, Gen. 36. Joseph, Gen. 37.
allotted to children of Israel. Jos. 14.
the spies visit, and their report. Num. 13.
Moses sees, from Pisgah. Num. 27. 12; Deu. 3. 27; 34. 1.
(2) a son of Ham, grandson of Noah, cursed on account of his father's mockery of Noah. Gen. 9. 18, 25.

Canaanite, cā′-nă-ăn-īte, 'a zealot.' Mk. 3. 18. R. V. Cananæan. *See* Zealots.

Canaanites, cā′-nă-ăn-ītes, 'inhabitants of Canaan,' especially those of Hamitic blood. Jud. 1. 1.

Canaanitess, cā-nă-ăn-ī′-tĕss, 'feminine of preceding.' 1 Chr. 2. 3.

Canaanitish, cā-nă-ăn-ī′-tĭsh. Gen. 46. 10.

Candace, căn′-dă-çē, Queen of Ethiopia. Acts 8. 27.

Candle. Heb. *nêr:* Gk. *λύχνος*. Wherever the word occurs in the A. V. the R. V. more correctly substitutes *lamp* (with the single exception of Jer. 25. 10). The lamps were earthenware, shaped like a butter-boat.
Job 29. 3, when his *c.* shined upon my head.
Ps. 18. 28, thou wilt light my *c.*
Prov. 20. 27, spirit of man *c.* of the Lord.
Zep. 1. 12, search Jerusalem with c.
Mat. 5. 15; Mk. 4. 21; Lu. 8. 16; 11. 33, lighted a *c.*
Rev. 18. 23, *c.* shine no more in thee.
22. 5, need no *c.* nor light.
See Job 18. 6; 21. 17; Prov. 24. 20.

Candlestick, a lamp-stand. Mat. 5. 15; Mk. 4. 21. In Dan. 9. 5, a candelabrum.
2 Kn. 4. 10, let us set for him a *c.*
See Heb. 9. 2; Rev. 2. 5.

Candlestick in the tabernacle. Ex. 25. 31; 37. 17; Lev. 24. 4; Num. 8. 2-4.
in visions. Zec. 4. 2; Rev. 1. 12.

Cane, Sweet (Isa. 43. 24; Jer. 6. 20). Heb. *Kâneh hattôb:* Gk. *κιννάμωμον*; *cinnamon.* Probably the same as Calamus, *q. v.* R. V. marg. calamus.

Canker (an old spelling of 'cancer'). 2 Tim. 2. 17. R. V. gangrene.

Cankered, corroded, rusted. Jas. 5. 3.

Cankerworm, locust, in some of its forms. Ps. 105. 34; Joel 1. 4.

Canneh, căn′-nĕh, probably same as Calneh. Ezek. 27. 23.

Canticles = 'songs,' one of the titles of the 'Song of Solomon.'

Caper-berry (Eccl. 12. 5, R. V.). Heb. *ăbîyyônâh.* A. V. desire. The fruit of the *Capparis spinosa.* The ripe berry is 2 to 2½ inches in length. The young berries are pungent and stimulating to the appetite. 'The caper-berry shall fail,' R. V., may mean that in old age it fails to act as a stimulant. The expression in R. V. margin, 'the caper-berry shall burst,' refers to the bursting of the seed pods, as an emblem of death.

Capernaum, că-pĕr′-nă-ŭm, 'village of Nahum' or 'of consolation,' on the north-west shore of the sea of Galilee; Christ dwells at. Mat. 4. 13; John 2. 12.
preaches at. Mat. 4. 17; Mk. 1. 21.
miracles at. Mat. 8. 5; 17. 24; John 4. 46; 6. 17.
parables at. Mat. 13. 18, 24; Mk. 4.
condemned for impenitence. Mat. 11. 23; Lu. 10. 15.

Caphthorim, căph′-thō-rĭm, same as Caphtorim. 1 Chr. 1. 12.

Caphtor, căph′-tŏr, 'Crete' (?). Deu. 2. 23; Am. 9. 7.

Caphtorim, Caphtorims. căph′-tō-rĭm, căph′-tō-rĭms, 'inhabitants of Caphtor.' Gen. 10. 14.

Cappadocia, căp-pă-dō′-çĭ-ă. Acts 2. 9; 1 Pet. 1. 1.

Captive. Ex. 12. 29, firstborn of *c.* in dungeon.

Isa. 51. 14, *c.* exile hasteneth.
52. 2, O *c.* daughter of Zion.
2 Tim. 2. 26, taken *c.* at his will.
3. 6, lead *c.* silly women.
See 2 Kn. 5. 2; Isa. 14. 2; 61. 1; Lu. 4. 18.
Captivity. Rom. 7. 23, into *c.* to law of sin.
2 Cor. 10. 5, bringing into *c.* every thought.
See Job 42. 10; Ps. 14. 7; 85. 1.
Captivity of Israelites foretold. Lev. 26. 33; Deu. 28. 36.
of ten tribes. Am. 3.; 4.; 7. 11; fulfilled, 2 Kn. 17.; 1 Chr. 5. 26.
of Judah foretold. Isa. 39. 6; Jer. 13. 19; 20. 4; 25. 11; 32. 28; fulfilled, 2 Kn. 25.; 2 Chr. 36.; Esth. 2.; Ps. 137.; Jer. 39.; 52.; Dan. 1.
return from. Ez. 1.; Neh. 2.; Ps. 126.
Carbuncle (Ex. 28. 17; R. V. marg. emerald). Heb. *Bâreketh:* Gk. σμάραγδος. A mistranslation in Ex. 28. for 'emerald,' the only *green* stone 'flashing light,' which is the meaning of the Hebrew. It is likened to a rainbow in Rev. 4. 3.
Carcas, cär′-căs. Esth. 1. 10.
Carcase. Isa. 66. 24; Mat. 24. 28; Heb. 3. 17.
Carchemish, cär-chē′-mĭsh. On the upper Euphrates: scene of the defeat of Pharaoh-Necho by Nebuchadnezzar. Jer. 46. 2.
Care (*n.*). Jer. 49. 31, nation that dwelleth without *c.*
Mat. 13. 22; Mk. 4. 19, *c.* of this world.
Lu. 8. 14; 21. 34, choked with *c.*
1 Cor. 9. 9, doth God take *c.* for oxen.
12. 25, have same *c.* one for another.
2 Cor. 11. 28, the *c.* of all the churches. R. V. anxiety.
1 Pet. 5. 7, casting all your *c.* on him. R. V. anxiety.
Care (*v.*). 2 Sam. 18. 3, they will not *c.* for us.
Ps. 142. 4, no man *c.* for my soul.
John 12. 6, not that he *c.* for poor.
Acts 18. 17, Gallio *c.* for none of those things.
Phil. 2. 20, naturally *c.* for your state.
Care, worldly, deprecated. Mat. 6. 25; Lu. 8. 14; 12. 22; John 6. 27; 1 Cor. 7. 32; Phil. 4. 6; 1 Tim. 6. 8; 2 Tim. 2. 4; Heb. 13. 5.
Martha reproved for. Lu. 10. 41.
(loving) of the Samaritan. Lu. 10. 34.
of Christ for His mother. John 19. 26.
of Paul for the Corinthians. 2 Cor. 7. 12; 11. 28.
of Titus for the Corinthians. 2 Cor. 8. 16.
for Paul by Philippians. Phil. 4. 10.
to be cast on God. 1 Pet. 5. 7.
of thoughts. Ps. 39. 1.
Careah, că-rē′-ăh, 'bald.' 2 Kn. 25. 23.
Careful, very anxious. Jer. 17. 8, not be *c.* in year of drought.
Dan. 3. 16, we are not *c.* to answer.
Lu. 10. 41, thou art *c.* about many things.
Phil. 4. 6, be *c.* for nothing.
Heb. 12. 17, he sought it *c.* with tears.
See 2 Kn. 4. 13; Phil. 4. 10; Tit. 3. 8.
Carefulness, great anxiety. Ezek. 12. 18; 1 Cor. 7. 32; 2 Cor. 7. 11.
Careless, free from care. Jud. 18. 7; Isa. 32. 9; 47. 8; Ezek. 39. 6.
Carmel, cär′-mĕl, 'the park,' or 'the garden-land.' (1) city of, in the tribe of Zebulun, below the eastern end of Mt. Carmel. Jos. 12. 22; 1 Sam. 25.
(2) Mount, Elijah and the prophets of Baal. 1 Kn. 18.
the Shunammite woman goes to Elisha at. 2 Kn. 4. 25.
her child restored to life by Elisha. 2 Kn. 4. 34.
Carmelite, cär′-mĕl-īte, 'an inhabitant of Carmel.' 1 Sam. 30. 5.
Carmelitess, cär-mĕl-ī′-tĕss, feminine of preceding. 1 Sam. 27. 3.
Carmi, cär′-mī, 'a vine-dresser.' (1) Gen. 46. 9. (2) 1 Chr. 4. 1; 2. 18. (3) Jos. 7. 1.
Carmites, cär′-mītes, descendants of Carmi. Num. 26. 6.

Carnal. Rom. 7. 14, *c.*, sold under sin.
8. 7, *c.* mind is enmity.
1 Cor. 3. 1, not speak but as to *c.*
2 Cor. 10. 4, weapons of our warfare not *c.*
See 1 Cor. 9. 11; Col. 2. 18; Heb. 7. 16; 9. 10.
Carpenters. 2 Sam. 5. 11, and cedar trees and *c.*
Zec. 1. 20, and the Lord shewed me four *c.* R. V. smiths.
Carpenter's son. Mat. 13. 55; Mk. 6. 3, is not this the *c.*?
Carpus, cär′-pŭs, 'fruit' (?). 2 Tim. 4. 13.
Carriage, that which is carried; baggage. Jud. 18. 21; 1 Sam. 17. 22; Isa. 10. 28; 46. 1; Acts 21. 15.
Carry. 1 Kn. 18. 12, Spirit of the Lord shall *c.* thee.
Isa. 40. 11, *c.* lambs in his bosom.
53. 4, *c.* our sorrows.
63. 9, *c.* them all days of old.
Ezek. 22. 9, men *c.* tales to shed blood. R. V. slanderous men.
Mk. 6. 55, began to *c.* about in beds.
John 5. 10, not lawful to *c.* thy bed. R. V. take up.
21. 18, and *c.* thee whither thou wouldest not.
Eph. 4. 14, *c.* about with every wind.
1 Tim. 6. 7, we can *c.* nothing out.
Heb. 13. 9, not *c.* about with divers.
2 Pet. 2. 17, clouds *c.* with a tempest. R. V. driven.
Jude 12, clouds *c.* about of winds.
See Ex. 33. 15; Num. 11. 12; Deu. 14. 24.
Carshena, cär-shē′-nă. Esth. 1. 14.
Cart. Isa. 5. 18, draw sin as with a *c.* rope.
Am. 2. 13, *c.* full of sheaves.
See 1 Sam. 6. 7; 2 Sam. 6. 3; 1 Chr. 13. 7; Isa. 28. 28.
Case. Ps. 144. 15, happy people in such a *c.*
Mat. 5. 20, in no *c.* enter heaven. R. V. wise.
John 5. 6, long time in that *c.*
See Ex. 5. 19; Deu. 19. 4; 24. 13.
Casement. Prov. 7. 6. R. V. lattice.
Casiphia, căs-ĭ-phī′-ă, 'silver' (?). Ez. 8. 17.
Casluhim, căs-lū′-hĭm. Gen. 10. 14.
Cassia. (1) (Ex. 30. 24). Heb. *Kiddah:* Gk. ἶρις: R. V. costus. One of the ingredients in the anointing oil. In Ezek. 27. 19, an article of merchandise.
(2) (Ps. 45. 8). Heb. *Ketzîôth:* Gk. κασία.
Both words probably refer to some *Cassia lignea*, the product of *Cinnamomum cassia*, cassia buds, and cassia bark, i. e., the bark of other kinds of *Cinnamomum* than that which yields true cinnamon.
Cast. (1) Prov. 16. 33, lot is *c.* into lap.
Mat. 5. 29; Mk. 9. 45, whole body *c.* into hell.
Mk. 9. 38; Lu. 9. 49, one *c.* out devils.
Lu. 21. 1, *c.* gifts into treasury.
John 8. 7, first *c.* stone at her.
2 Cor. 10. 5, *c.* down imaginations.
1 Pet. 5. 7, *c.* all care upon him.
1 John 4. 18, love *c.* out fear.
(2) considered. Lu. 1. 29, *c.* in her mind.
(3) cast-off. Jer. 38. 11, *c.* clouts.
See Ps. 76. 6; Prov. 26. 18; 3 John 10.
Cast about, turned round, came back again. Jer. 41. 14.
Castaway, outcast. 1 Cor. 9. 27, lest I be a *c.*
Castle. Num. 31. 10; Prov. 18. 19; Acts 21. 34.
Castor, căs′-tôr; and Pollux, Paul's ship. Acts 28. 11.
Cat (Baruch 6. 22). Gk. αἴλουρος. Not mentioned in the Canonical books.
Catch. Ps. 10. 9, to *c.* the poor.
Mat. 13. 19, devil *c.* away. R. V. snatcheth.
Lu. 5. 10, from henceforth thou shalt *c.* men.
John 10. 12, wolf *c.* sheep. R. V. snatcheth.
See 2 Kn. 7. 12; Ezek. 19. 3; Mk. 12. 13.
Caterpiller. Joel 1. 4, the palmerworm of A. V. Heb. *Gâzâm:* Gk. κάμπη. *Œdipoda migratoria*, the larvæ of locusts, butterflies, moths, and any lava destroying buds of plants.
Cattle (Ps. 50. 10). Heb. *Aleph:* Gk. κτήνη. There were two kinds, long- and short-horned, the former more numerous. *See* Ox.

Gen. 46. 32, their trade to feed *c.*
Ex. 10. 26, our *c.* shall go with us. [for prey.
Deu. 2. 35; 3. 7; Jos. 8. 2, the *c.* ye shall take
Ps. 50. 10, *c.* upon a thousand hills.
See Gen. 1. 25; Jon. 4. 11.

Cattle of Jacob increased. Gen. 30. 43.
regulations respecting. Ex. 20. 10; 21. 28; 22. 1; 23. 4; Deu. 5. 14; 22. 1; 25. 4; (1 Cor. 9. 9; 1 Tim. 5. 18).
of Israelites in Egypt saved. Ex. 9. 4.
an example of obedience. Isa. 1. 3.
referred to by Christ. Mat. 12. 11; Lu. 13. 15; 14. 5.

Cauda, R. V.; same as CLAUDA.

Caught. Gen. 22. 13, ram *c.* by horns.
John 21. 3, that night they *c.* nothing.
2 Cor. 12. 2, *c.* up to third heaven.
12. 16, I *c.* you with guile.
1 Thes. 4. 17, be *c.* up together with them.
See 2 Sam. 18. 9; Prov. 7. 13; Rev. 12. 5.

Caul. (1) a net for the hair. Isa. 3. 18. (2) the membrane that surrounds the heart. Hos. 13. 8.

Cause (*n.*). Mat. 19. 5; Mk. 10. 7; Eph. 5. 31, for this *c.* shall a man leave.
1 Cor. 11. 30, for this *c.* many are sickly.
1 Tim. 1. 16, for this *c.* I obtained mercy.
See Prov. 18. 17; 2 Cor. 4. 16; 5. 13.

Cause (*v.*). Ez. 6. 12, God *c.* his name to dwell.
Ps. 67. 1; 80. 3, *c.* his face to shine.
Rom. 16. 17, them who *c.* divisions.
See Deu. 1. 38; 12. 11; Job 6. 24.

Causeless. 1 Sam. 25. 31; Prov. 26. 2.

Caves. 1 Kn. 18. 4, Obadiah hid them by fifty in *c.*
19. 9, and he came thither unto a *c.*
Isa. 2. 19, go into a *c.* for fear of the Lord.
See Gen. 19. 30; 23. 19; 49. 29; Jos. 10. 16; 1 Sam. 13. 6; 22. 1; 24. 10.

Cease. Deu. 15. 11, poor never *c.* out of land.
Job 3. 17, the wicked *c.* from troubling.
Ps. 46. 9, he maketh wars to *c.*
Prov. 26. 20, strife *c.*
Eccl. 12. 3, grinders *c.* because few.
Acts 20. 31, I *c.* not to warn.
1 Cor. 13. 8, tongues they shall *c.*
1 Thes. 5. 17, pray without *c.*
1 Pet. 4. 1, hath *c.* from sin.
See Gen. 8. 22; Isa. 1. 16; 2. 22.

Cedar (Lev. 14. 4; Ps. 104. 16; Ezek. 31. 3-9). Heb. *Erez*: Gk. κέδρος: Bot. N. *Cedrus Libani.* Cedar is used in Scripture generically of the whole pine-tree family, and specially of the cedar of Lebanon.
Jud. 9. 15, devour the *c.* of Lebanon.
1 Kn. 5. 6, they hew me *c.* trees out of Lebanon.
6. 15, with boards of *c.*
Job 40. 17, he moveth his tail like a *c.*
Ps. 92. 12, grow like a *c.* in Lebanon.
Isa. 2. 13, upon all the *c.* of Lebanon.
See Ps. 104. 16; 148. 9; S. of S. 5. 15; Ezek. 17. 3.

Cedron, çē'-drŏn, same as KIDRON. John 18. 1.

Celebrate. Lev. 23. 32; Isa. 38. 18.

Celestial. 1 Cor. 15. 40.

Cenchrea, çĕn'-chré-ă, 'millet;' Paul shaves his head at. Acts 18. 18.
seaport of Corinth, church there. Rom. 16. 1.

Censer. Ezek. 8. 11, every man his *c.*
Heb. 9. 4, holiest had the golden *c.*
Rev. 8. 3, angel having a golden *c.*
8. 5, angel took the *c.* and filled.
See Lev. 10. 1; 16. 12; Num. 16. 17; 1 Kn. 7. 50.

Centurion. (1) servant of, healed. Mat. 8.; Lu. 7.
(2) at crucifixion acknowledges Christ. Mat. 27. 54; Mk. 15. 39; Lu. 23. 47.
(3) (Cornelius) Acts 10. 1.
(4) in charge of Paul. Acts 27. 43.

Cephas, çē'-phăs; (Peter) a stone. John 1. 42; 1 Cor. 1. 12; 3. 22; 9. 5; 15. 5; Gal. 2. 9. *See* PETER.

Ceremonies. Num. 9. 3. R. V. ordinances.

Certain. Ex. 3. 12, *c.* I will be with thee.
1 Cor. 4. 11, no *c.* dwellingplace.
Heb. 10. 27, a *c.* looking for of judgment.
See Deu. 13. 14; 1 Kn. 2. 37; Dan. 2. 45.

Certify. 2 Sam. 15. 28; Gal. 1. 11.

Chafed, heated, exasperated, angry. 2 Sam. 17. 8.

Chaff. Mat. 3. 12; Lu. 3. 17, burn up *c.* with fire.
See Jer. 23. 28; Hos. 13. 3; Zep. 2. 2.

Chain. Mk. 5. 3, no, not with *c.*
Acts 12. 7, Peter's *c.* fell off.
2 Tim. 1. 16, not ashamed of my *c.*
2 Pet. 2. 4, into *c.* of darkness. R. V. pits.
Jude 6, everlasting *c.* under darkness.
See Ps. 73. 6; Lam. 3. 7; Isa. 40. 19.

Chalcedony (Rev. 21. 19). Gk. χαλκηδών. The name chalcedony is now applied to a transparent or translucent indistinctly crystallized variety of quartz, usually to the white or gray variety.

Chalcol, chăl'-cŏl, same as CALCOL. 1 Kn. 4. 31.

Chaldæans, Chaldeans, chăl-dæ'-ăns, chăl-dē'-ăns, inhabitants of Chaldea; afflict Job. Job 1. 17.
besiege Jerusalem. 2 Kn. 24. 2; 25. 4; Jer. 37.-39.
wise men of, preserved by Daniel. Dan. 2. 24.
prophecies concerning. Isa. 23. 13; 43. 14; 47. 1; 48. 14; Hab. 1. 5.

Chaldea, chăl-dē'-ă. Jer. 50. 10.

Chaldees, chăl'-dēēs, same as CHALDÆANS. Gen. 11. 28.

Chalk-stones. Isa. 27. 9, altar as *c.*

Challengeth, claimeth. Ex. 22. 9.

Chamber is the general term for any room in a house. It is only in the houses of kings and nobles that it means a 'bed-room,' since the majority of houses were only one story high.
2 Kn. 4. 10, little *c.* on wall.
Ps. 19. 5, as bridegroom coming out of *c.*
Isa. 26. 20, enter into thy *c.*
Ezek. 8. 12, *c.* of imagery.
Mat. 24. 26, in secret *c.*
Acts 9. 37; 20. 8, in upper *c.*
See Prov. 7. 27; Dan. 6. 10; Joel 2. 16.

Chambering, wanton living, sensuality. Rom. 13. 13.

Chamberlain. 2 Kn. 23. 11; Esth. 1. 10; 6. 2; Acts 12. 20; Rom. 16. 23.

Chameleon. (1) (Lev. 11. 30). Heb. *Côăh*: Gk. χαμαιλέων: Zoöl. S. *Psammosaurus scincus.* T.: *Hydrosaurus Niloticus.* T.: R. V. land-crocodile, or monitor lizard.
(2) (Lev. 11. 30). Heb. *Tinshémeth*: Gk. ἀσπάλαξ: Zoöl. S. *Chameleo vulgaris.* T.: R. V. chameleon. A. V. mole.

Chamois (Deu. 14. 5). Heb. *Zémer*, springing or leaping; Gk. καμηλοπάρδαλις, camelopard. Not our chamois, nor the camelopard, but the wild goat, or the mountain sheep with its curving horns two feet in length.

Champaign, plain, level country. Deu. 11. 30; R. V. Arabah.

Champion. 1 Sam. 17. 4, 51.

Chanaan, chā'-nă-ăn, another form of 'Canaan.' Acts 7. 11.

Chance. 1 Sam. 6. 9; 2 Sam. 1. 6; Eccl. 9. 11; Lu. 10. 31.

Change (*n.*). Job 14. 14, till my *c.* come. R. V. release.
Prov. 24. 21, meddle not with them given to *c.*
See Jud. 14. 12; Zec. 3. 4; Heb. 7. 12.

Change (*v.*). Ps. 15. 4, sweareth and *c.* not.
102. 26, as vesture shalt thou *c.* them.
Lam. 4. 1, fine gold *c.*
Mal. 3. 6, I the Lord *c.* not.
Rom. 1. 23, *c.* glory of uncorruptible God.
1 Cor. 15. 51, we shall all be *c.*
2 Cor. 3. 18, *c.* from glory to glory.
See Job 17. 12; Jer. 2. 36; 13. 23.

Channel. Ps. 18. 15; Isa. 27. 12.

Chanoch, chăn'-ŏch, same as ENOCH. Gen. 4. 17 (marg.).

Chant. Am. 6. 5. R. V. sing idle songs.

Chapel. Am. 7. 13, for it is the king's *c.*

Chapiter, *capital* of a pillar or column. Ex. 36. 38.

Chapmen, merchants, dealers. 2 Chr. 9. 14.

Chapt, cracked, through heat and drought. Jer. 14. 4.
Charashim, chā-rā'-shĭm, 'craftsmen.' 1 Chr. 4. 14.
Charchemish, chär-chē'-mĭsh, same as CARCHEMISH. 2 Chr. 35. 20.
Charge. Job 1. 22, nor *c.* God foolishly.
4. 18, angels he *c.* with folly.
Mat. 9. 30; Mk. 5. 43; Lu. 9. 21, Jesus *c.* them.
Acts 7. 60; 2 Tim. 4. 16, lay not sin to their *c.*
Rom. 8. 33, who shall lay any thing to *c.*
1 Cor. 9. 18, gospel without *c.*
1 Tim. 1. 3, *c.* that they teach no other.
5. 21; 2 Tim. 4. 1, I *c.* thee before God.
6. 17, *c.* them that are rich.
See Ps. 35. 11; 91. 11; Mk. 9. 25.
Charge of God to Moses and Aaron. Ex. 6. 13.
of Moses to Joshua. Deu. 31. 7.
of David to Solomon. 1 Kn. 2. 1; 1 Chr. 22. 6.
of Jehoshaphat to the judges. 2 Chr. 19. 6.
of Paul to the elders of the church at Ephesus. Acts 20. 17.
of Paul to Timothy. 1 Tim. 5. 21; 2 Tim. 4. [2. 9.
of Peter to the elders. 1 Pet. 5.
Chargeable. 2 Sam. 13. 25; 2 Cor. 11. 9; 1 Thes.
Charged, burdened, put to expense. 1 Tim. 5. 16.
Charger, a large dish. (So called from carrying a *charge* or burden.) Mat. 14. 8; Mk. 6. 25.
Charges be at, to discharge the cost, or pay expenses. Acts 21. 24.
Chariots. Ex. 14. 6, he made ready his *c.*
1 Sam. 13. 5, Philistines gathered 30,000 *c.*
2 Sam. 10. 18, David slew the men of 700 *c.*
2 Kn. 2. 11, there appeared a *c.* of fire.
Ps. 20. 7, some trust in *c.*
Nah. 3. 2, and of the jumping *c.*
See 2 Kn. 6. 14, 17; Ps. 68. 17.
Charity. Rom. 14. 15, now walkest not *c.*
Col. 3. 14, put on *c.*
2 Thes. 1. 3, *c.* aboundeth.
1 Tim. 1. 5, end of commandment is *c.*
2 Tim. 2. 22, follow faith, *c.*, peace.
Tit. 2. 2, sound in faith, in *c.*
1 Pet. 4. 8, *c.* cover sins.
2 Pet. 1. 7, to brotherly kindness *c.*
Jude 12, spots in feasts of *c.*
Charity (love to our neighbour). Mk. 12. 33; Rom. 13. 8, 9, 10; 1 Cor. 13. 1-8, 13; 1 Thes. 1. 3; 3. 6; 4. 9; 1 Tim. 1. 5; 4. 12; 2 Tim. 3. 10; Heb. 6. 10; Jas. 2. 8; 1 Pet. 1. 22; 1 John 2. 10; 3. 14; 4. 11; Rev. 2. 19.
commanded. Lev. 19. 18; Deu. 10. 19; Mat. 5. 44; 22. 39; 1 Cor. 14. 1; 16. 14; Gal. 5. 14; 6. 10; Eph. 4. 2; 1 John 3. 23; 4. 7, 21; 2 John 5.
its signs and effects. 1 Cor. 8. 1; 13.; Gal. 5. 6, 13, 22; Eph. 3. 17; 4. 16; 5. 2; Col. 3. 14.
evidences of. Lev. 19. 11; 25. 35; Isa. 58. 7; Mat. 18. 15; 25. 35; John 13. 35; Rom. 12. 15; 1 Cor. 12. 26; Eph. 4. 32; 1 Thes. 5. 14; Heb. 6. 10; 1 Pet. 4. 8; 1 John 3. 10, 14; 4. 20.
exemplified by Christ. John 13. 34; 15. 12; Eph. 5. 2, 25; Rev. 1. 5.
(almsgiving). Prov. 19. 17; Mat. 19. 21; Lu. 11. 41; 12. 33; 18. 22; Acts 10. 2, 4; 2 Cor. 9.; 3 John 6.
Charmer. Deu. 18. 11; Ps. 58. 5; Jer. 8. 17.
Charran, chăr'-răn, same as HARAN. Acts 7. 2.
Chase. Lev. 26. 8, five *c.* hundred.
Deu. 32. 30; Jos. 23. 10, one *c.* thousand.
See Job 18. 18; Ps. 35. 5; Lam. 3. 52.
Chaste. 2 Cor. 11. 2; Tit. 2. 5; 1 Pet. 3. 2.
Chasten. Deu. 8. 5, as a man *c.* son.
Ps. 6. 1; 38. 1, nor *c.* me in displeasure.
94. 12, blessed is the man whom thou *c.*
Prov. 19. 18, *c.* thy son while there is hope.
2 Cor. 6. 9, as *c.* and not killed. [he *c.*
Heb. 12. 6; Rev. 3. 19, whom the Lord loveth
Heb. 12. 11, no *c.* seemeth to be joyous.
See Ps. 69. 10; 73. 14; 118. 18.
Chastisement. Deu. 11. 2; Job 34. 31; Isa. 55. 5.
Chatter. Isa. 38. 14.
Chavah, chăv'-ăh, same as EVE. Gen. 3. 20 (marg.).

Chebar, chē'-bär, 'great' (?), a Babylonian river, modern Nahr or Naru; Ezekiel's visions at. Ezek. 1.; 3. 15; 10. 15.
Check, reproof, rebuke. Job 20. 3.
Chedorlaomer, chĕd-ŏr-lā-ō'-mĕr, 'servant of Laomer' (?); king of Elam, takes Lot prisoner, but subdued by Abram. Gen. 14.
Cheek. Mat. 5. 39; Lu. 6. 29, smiteth on right *c.*
See Job 16. 10; Isa. 50. 6; Lam. 3. 30.
Cheek teeth, molar teeth. Joel 1. 6. R. V. jaw.
Cheer. Prov. 15. 13, maketh a *c.* countenance.
Zec. 9. 17, corn make young men *c.* R. V. flourish.
John 16. 33, be of good *c.*, I have overcome.
Acts 23. 11; 27. 22, 25, be of good *c.*
Rom. 12. 8, he that sheweth mercy with *c.*
2 Cor. 9. 7, God loveth a *c.* giver.
See Jud. 9. 13; Mat. 9. 2; 14. 27; Mk. 6. 50.
Chelal, chē'-lăl, 'completion' (?). Ez. 10. 30.
Chelluh, chĕl'-lŭh. Ez. 10. 35.
Chelub, chē'-lŭb, 'bird-trap' (?). (1) 1 Chr. 4. 11. (2) 1 Chr. 27. 26.
Chelubai, chĕ-lū'băi, same as CALEB (3). 1 Chr. 2. 9.
Chemarims, chĕm'-ă-rĭms, 'priests dressed in black attire.' Zep. 1. 4.
Chemosh, chē'-mŏsh; god of Moab. Num. 21. 29; Jud. 11. 24; Jer. 48. 7, 13, 46.
worshipped by Solomon. 1 Kn. 11. 7.
Chenaanah, chĕ-nā'-ă-năh, fem. of Canaan (?) (1) 1 Kn. 22. 11. (2) 1 Chr. 7. 10.
Chenani, chĕ-nā'-nī, probably same as CHENANIAH. Neh. 9. 4.
Chenaniah, chĕn-ă-nī'-ăh, 'Jehovah is firm.' 1 Chr. 15. 22.
Chephar-haammonai, chē'-phär-hă-ăm'-mō-năi, 'village of the Ammonites.' Jos. 18. 24.
Chephirah, chĕ-phī'-răh, 'village.' Jos. 9. 17.
Cheran, chē'-răn. Gen. 36. 26.
Cherethims, chĕr'-ĕ-thĭms, 'Cretans' (?). Ezek. 25. 16.
Cherethites, chĕr'-ĕ-thītes, same as preceding. 2 Sam. 8. 18.
(and Pelethites), David's guard. 2 Sam. 15. 18.
Cherisheth. Eph. 5. 29; 1 Thes. 2. 7.
Cherith, chē'-rĭth, 'gorge' (?); a brook 'before,' i. e., east of Jordan, probably in Gilead. Elijah fed by ravens. 1 Kn. 17. 5.
Cherub, chē'-rub, a place. Ez. 2. 59.
Cherubims, chĕr'-ū-bĭms, properly Cherubim, plural of Cherub. Ex. 25. 19.
in garden of Eden. Gen. 3. 24.
for the mercy seat and the temple. Ex. 25. 18; 37. 7; 1 Kn. 6. 23; 2 Chr. 3. 10; Ps. 80. 1; Ezek. 41. 18.
Ezekiel's visions of. Ezek. 1.; 10.
Chesalon, chĕs'-ă-lŏn. 'confidence.' Jos. 15. 10.
Chesed, chĕs'-ĕd. Gen. 22. 22.
Chesil, chĕs'-ĭl, 'a fool.' Jos. 15. 30.
Chesnut (Gen. 30. 37). Heb. *'Armôn:* Gk. *πλάτανος*: Bot. N. *Platanus orientalis:* R. V. plane tree, which is undoubtedly correct. It grows by watercourses, and is one of the finest trees in the country, growing sometimes to be 100 feet high.
Chesulloth, chĕ-sŭl'-lŏth, 'flanks.' Jos. 19. 18.
Chezib, chē'-zĭb, 'false.' Gen. 38. 5.
Chickens. Mat. 23. 37.
Chide. Ex. 17. 2; Jud. 8. 1; Ps. 103. 9.
Chidon, chī'-dŏn, 'javelin.' 1 Chr. 13. 9.
Chiefest. S. of S. 5. 10; Mk. 10. 44; 2 Cor. 11. 5.
Chief Priests consulted by Herod. Mat. 2. 4.
their persecution of Christ. Mat. 16. 21; Mk. 14. 1; 15. 31; John 7. 32.
Child. Gen. 42. 22, do not sin against the *c.*
Ps. 131. 2, quieted myself as a weaned *c.*
Prov. 20. 11, a *c.* is known by his doings.
22. 6, train up a *c.* in way.
15, foolishness in heart of *c.*

Isa. 9. 6, to us a *c.* is born.
65. 20, *c.* shall die an hundred years old.
Lu. 1. 66, what manner of *c.*
John 4. 49, come ere my *c.* die.
1 Cor. 13. 11, when I was a *c.*
2 Tim. 3. 15, from a *c.* hast known.
See Ex. 2. 2; Eccl. 4. 13; 10. 16; Heb. 11. 23.

Children. 1 Sam. 16. 11, are here all thy *c.*
Ps. 34. 11, come, ye *c.*, hearken to me.
45. 16, instead of fathers all be *c.*
Ps. 128. 3, thy *c.* like olive plants.
Isa. 8. 18; Heb. 2. 13, I and *c.* given me.
30. 9, lying *c.*, *c.* that will not hear.
63. 8, *c.* that will not lie.
Jer. 31. 15; Mat. 2. 18, Rachel weeping for her *c.*
Ezek. 18. 2, *c.* teeth on edge.
Mat. 15. 26; Mk. 7. 27, not take *c.* bread.
17. 26, then are the *c.* free. R. V. sons.
19. 14; Mk. 10. 14; Lu. 18. 16, suffer little *c.*
Lu. 16. 8, *c.* of this world wiser than *c.* of light. R. V. sons.
20. 36, *c.* of God and the resurrection. R. V. sons.
John 12. 36; Eph. 5. 8; 1 Thes. 5. 5, *c.* of light.
Rom. 8. 16; Gal. 3. 26; 1 John 3. 10, witness that we are the *c.* of God. R. V. sons (in Rom. & Gal.).
Eph. 4. 14, be henceforth no more *c.*
5. 6; Col. 3. 6, *c.* of disobedience. R. V. sons.
6. 1; Col. 3. 20, *c.*, obey your parents.
1 Tim. 3. 4, having his *c.* in subjection.
See Num. 16. 27; Esth. 3. 13; Mat. 14. 21. [128.

Children the gift of God. Gen. 33. 5; Ps. 127.;
a blessing. Prov. 10. 1; 15. 20; 17. 6; 23. 24; 27. 11; 29. 3.
duty of. Ex. 20. 12; Lev. 19. 3, 32; Deu. 5. 16; 30. 2; Prov. 1. 8; 6. 20; 13. 1; 15. 5; 19. 27; 23. 22; 24. 21; 28. 7, 24; Eccl. 12. 1; Eph. 6. 1; Col. 3. 20; 1 Tim. 5. 4; Heb. 12. 9; 1 Pet. 5. 5.
slain by she-bears. 2 Kn. 2. 23. [31. 15).
of Bethlehem, slain by Herod. Mat. 2. 16 (Jer.
blessed by Christ. Mat. 19. 13; Mk. 10. 13; Lu. 18. 15.
of God. Eph. 5. 1; Heb. 12. 5; 1 Pet. 1. 14.
of light. Lu. 16. 8; John 12. 36; Eph. 5. 8; 1 Thes. 5. 5.
OBEDIENT: —
CHRIST. Lu. 2. 51.
Isaac. Gen. 22. 6.
Jephthah's daughter. Jud. 11. 36.
Samuel. 1 Sam. 2. 26.
WICKED. 1 Sam. 2. 12, 25; Prov. 15. 5; 17. 21; 19. 13, 26; 28. 7, 24; 30. 11; Isa. 3. 5; Ezek. 22. 7.
their punishment. Ex. 21. 15; Deu. 21. 18; 27. 16; 2 Kn. 2. 23; Prov. 30. 17; Mk. 7. 10.
of the devil. Acts 13. 10.

Chileab, chī'-lĕ-ăb. 2 Sam. 3. 3.

Chilion, chī'-lĭ-ŏn, 'wasting away.' Ru. 1. 2.

Chilmad, chĭl'-măd. Ezek. 27. 23.

Chimham, chĭm'-hăm, 'longing.' 2 Sam. 19. 37.

Chinnereth, chĭn'-nĕ-rĕth, 'a lyre.' Num. 13. 11; Jos. 19. 35; or **Chinneroth**, chĭn'-nĕ-rŏth, Jos. 11. 2; one of the early names of the Sea of Galilee, from a city of that name whose site is unknown.

Chios, chī'-ŏs. Acts 20. 15.

Chisleu, chĭs'-leū, the ninth month of the Jewish sacred year = December. Neh. 1. 1. *See* MONTHS.

Chislon, chĭs'-lŏn, 'confidence.' Num. 34. 21.

Chisloth-tabor, chĭs'-lŏth-tā'-bŏr, 'flanks of Tabor.' Jos. 19. 12.

Chittim, chĭt'-tĭm, probably Cyprus; prophecies of. Num. 24. 24; Isa. 23. 1, 12; Dan. 11. 30.

Chiun, chī'-ŭn, 'pedestal,' or name of a god (i. e., Saturn). Am. 5. 26.

Chloe, chlō'-ē, 'grass.' 1 Cor. 1. 11. [20. 3.

Chode, did chide, disputed. Gen. 31. 36; Num.

Choice. 1 Sam. 9. 2, Saul a *c.* young man.
Acts 15. 7, God made *c.* among us.
See Gen. 23. 6; 2 Sam. 10. 9; Prov. 8. 10.

Choke. Mat. 13. 22; Mk. 4. 19; Lu. 8. 14.

Choler, anger. Dan. 8. 7; 11. 11.

Chor-ashan, chôr-ăsh'-ăn, 'smoking furnace.' 1 Sam. 30. 30; or for BOR-ASHAN, 'smoking pit.'

Chorazin, chō-rā'-zĭn, a town near Capernaum, inland from the Sea of Galilee. Mat. 11. 21.

Chose. Ps. 33. 12, people *c.* for his inheritance.
89. 19, exalted one *c.* out of people.
Prov. 16. 16; 22. 1, rather to be *c.*
Jer. 8. 3, death *c.* rather than life.
Mat. 20. 16; 22. 14, many called, few *c.*
Lu. 10. 42, hath *c.* that good part.
14. 7, they *c.* the chief rooms.
John 15. 16, ye have not *c.* me.
Acts 9. 15, he is a *c.* vessel.
Rom. 16. 13, *c.* in the Lord.
1 Cor. 1. 27, 28, God hath *c.* foolish things.
Eph. 1. 4, according as he hath *c.* us.
1 Pet. 2. 4, *c.* of God and precious.
2. 9, a *c.* generation.
See Ex. 18. 25; 2 Sam. 6. 21; 1 Chr. 16. 13.

Chozeba, chō-zē'-bă, 'deceiver.' 1 Chr. 4. 22.

Christ. Mat. 16. 16, thou art the *C.*
24. 5, many shall come saying, I am *C.*
John 4. 25, the Messias which is called *C.*
4. 29, is not this the *C.*
6. 69, we are sure that thou art that *C.*
Phil. 1. 15, 16, some preach *C.* of contention.
1 Pet. 1. 11, the Spirit of *C.* did signify.
1 John 2. 22, denieth that Jesus is the *C.*
5. 1, whoso believeth Jesus is the *C.*
Rev. 20. 4, they reigned with *C.* a thousand years.
20. 6, priests of God and *C.*

Christ, the 'anointed,' Greek for MESSIAH. Mat. 1. 1.
LORD JESUS. Mat. 1. 21; Lu. 2. 11; John 1. 41; 4. 42; Acts 5. 31; 11. 17; 13. 23; 15. 11; 16. 31; 20. 21; Rom. 5. 1, 11; 6. 23; 7. 25; 13. 14; 15. 6, 30; 16. 18; 1 Cor. 1. 2, 3, 7, 10; 5. 4; Eph. 5. 20; Phil. 3. 20; 1 Tim. 1. 1, 12; 3. 13; 4. 6; 5. 21; 2 Tim. 1. 10; Tit. 1. 4; 2. 13; 3. 6; Philem. 3, 5, 25; Heb. 13. 8, 21; Jas. 1. 1; 1 Pet. 1. 3; 2 Pet. 1. 1, 11; 2. 20; 3. 2, 18; 1 John 4. 10; Jude 1, 4, 17, 21; Rev. 22. 21.
CHARACTER OF: —
holy. Lu. 1. 35; Acts 4. 27; Rev. 3. 7.
righteous. Isa. 53. 11; Heb. 1. 9.
faithful. Isa. 11. 5; 1 Thes. 5. 24.
true. John 1. 14; 7. 18; 1 John 5. 20.
just. Zec. 9. 9; John 5. 30; Acts 22. 14.
guileless. Isa. 53. 9; 1 Pet. 2. 22.
sinless. John 8. 46; 2 Cor. 5. 21.
spotless. 1 Pet. 1. 19.
innocent. Mat. 27. 4.
harmless. Heb. 7. 26.
resisting temptation. Mat. 4. 1-10. [34; 15. 10.
obedient to God the Father. Ps. 40. 8; John 4.
subject to His parents. Lu. 2. 51.
zealous. Lu. 2. 49; John 2. 17; 8. 29.
meek. Isa. 53. 7; Zec. 9. 9; Mat. 11. 29.
lowly in heart. Mat. 11. 29.
merciful. Heb. 2. 17.
patient. Isa. 53. 7; Mat. 27. 14.
long-suffering. 1 Tim. 1. 16. [13; 19. 41.
compassionate. Isa. 40. 11; Mat. 15. 32; Lu. 7.
benevolent. Mat. 4. 23, 24; 9. 35; Acts 10. 38.
loving. John 13. 1; 15. 13.
self-denying. Mat. 8. 20; 2 Cor. 8. 9.
humble. Lu. 22. 27; Phil. 2. 8.
resigned. Lu. 22. 42.
forgiving. Lu. 23. 34.
saints to be conformed to. Rom. 8. 29.
COMPASSION OF: — [verse 7.
necessary to His priestly office. Heb. 5. 2, with
manifested for the
weary and heavy laden. Mat. 11. 28-30.
weak in faith. Isa. 40. 11; 42. 3, with Mat. 12. 20.
tempted. Heb. 2. 18.
afflicted. Lu. 7. 13; John 11. 33.
diseased. Mat. 14. 14; Mk. 1. 41.
poor. Mk. 8. 2. [3. 16.
perishing sinners. Mat. 9. 36; Lu. 19. 41; John
an encouragement to prayer. Heb. 4. 15.

Christ, Date of the Birth of.

It is very perplexing to many to find that Jesus was actually born four years before the time from which we count his birth. The simple reason is that no one calculated dates from the birth of Christ till centuries after He was born, and then Dionysius Exiguus, the monk who published the calculations in A. D. 526, made a mistake of four years. He placed the birth of Christ in the year of Rome (A. U. C.) 754. But Herod the Great, who slew the innocents of Bethlehem, died in April of the year of Rome 750; so that Christ must have been born several months before, or not later than the last of 749. The following table will help to make the matter clear: —

Year of Rome (*Anno Urbis Conditæ* = A. U. C.)	749	750	751	752	753	754	755	756
Year of Our Lord (*Anno Domini* = A. D.).....	5	4	3	2	1	1	2	3
Age of Jesus..............................	birth	1st year	2nd	3rd	4th	5th	6th	7th

It should be carefully noted that the numbers are *ordinal*, standing for *first*, *second*, etc.

Jesus was probably born at the very close of B. C. 5, which would be only *four* years before our era, for in a week after the 25th of December, B. C. 5, it was January, B. C. 4.

Since it is impossible to rectify the dates in all books and records over the world, we simply apply the true dates to the life of Christ. He was five years old at the close of A. D. 1.

DIVINE NATURE OF: —
as Jehovah. Col. 1. 16; Isa. 6. 1-3, with John 12. 41; Isa. 8. 13, 14, with 1 Pet. 2. 8; Isa. 40. 3, with Mat. 3. 3; Isa. 40. 11; 44. 6, with Rev. 1. 17; Isa. 48. 12-16, with Rev. 22. 13; Jer. 23. 5, 6, with 1 Cor. 1. 30; Joel 2. 32, with Acts 2. 21, and 1 Cor. 1. 2; Mal. 3. 1, with Mk. 1. 2, and Lu. 2. 27; Heb. 13. 20; Jas. 2. 1.
The Eternal God and Creator, Judge and Saviour. Ps. 45. 6, 7; 102. 24-27, with Heb. 1. 8, 10-12; Isa. 9. 6; Eccl. 12. 14, with 1 Cor. 4. 5; Jer. 10. 10, with John 15. 20; Hos. 1. 7, with Tit. 2. 13; John 1. 1; Rom. 9. 5; 2 Cor. 5. 10; 2 Tim. 4. 1.
fellow and equal to God. Zec. 13. 7; John 5. 17, 23; 16. 15; Phil. 2. 6; 1 Thes. 3. 11; 2 Thes. 2. 16, 17.
as the Lord from heaven, Lord of the sabbath, and Lord of all. Gen. 2. 3, with Mat. 12. 8; Acts 10. 36; Rom. 10. 11-13; 1 Cor. 15. 47.
Son of God. Mat. 26. 63-67; John 1. 14, 18; 3. 16, 18; 1 John 4. 9.
one with the Father. John 10. 30, 38; 12. 45; 14. 7-10; 17. 10.
sending the Spirit, equally with the Father. John 14. 16, with John 15. 26.
Creator, Supporter, and Preserver of all things. John 1. 3; Col. 1. 16, 17; Heb. 1. 2, 3.
possessed of the fulness of the Godhead. Col. 2. 9; Heb. 1. 3.
raising the dead. John 5. 21; 6. 40, 54.
raising Himself from the dead. John 2. 19, 21; 10. 18.
Eternal, Omnipresent, Omnipotent, and Omniscient. Ps. 45. 3; Isa. 9. 6; Mic. 5. 2; Mat. 18. 20; 28. 20; John 1. 1; 3. 13; 16. 30; 21. 17; Phil. 3. 21; Col. 1. 17; Heb. 1. 8-10; Rev. 1. 8.
God. He redeems, purifies, and presents the Church unto Himself. Eph. 5. 27, with Jude 24, 25; Rev. 5. 9, with Tit. 2. 14.
acknowledged by voice from heaven. Mat. 3. 17; 17. 5; John 12. 28.
His blood the blood of God. Acts 20. 28.
object of divine worship. Acts 7. 59; 2 Cor. 12. 8, 9; Heb. 1. 6; Rev. 5. 12.
object of faith. Ps. 2. 12, with 1 Pet. 2. 6; Jer. 17. 5, 7, with John 14. 1.
saints live unto Him as God. Rom. 6. 11, and Gal. 2. 19, with 2 Cor. 5. 15.
acknowledged by Thomas. John 20. 28.

CHRIST, GLORY OF: —
as divine. John 1. 1-5; Phil. 2. 6, 9, 10.
God the Son. Mat. 3. 17; Heb. 1. 6, 8.
equal to the Father. John 10. 30, 38.
the Firstborn. Col. 1. 15, 18.
the Firstbegotten. Heb. 1. 6.
Lord of lords, &c. Rev. 17. 14.
the image of God. Col. 1. 15; Heb. 1. 3.
Creator. John 1. 3; Col. 1. 16; Heb. 1. 2.
the Blessed of God. Ps. 45. 2.
Mediator. 1 Tim. 2. 5; Heb. 8. 6.
Prophet. Deu. 18. 15, 16, with Acts 3. 22.
Priest. Ps. 110. 4; Heb. 4. 15.
King. Isa. 6. 1-5, with John 12. 41.
Judge. Mat. 16. 27; 25. 31, 33. [14.
Shepherd. Isa. 40. 10, 11; Ezek. 34.; John 10. 11,
Head of the Church. Eph. 1. 22.
the true Light. Lu. 1. 78, 79; John 1. 4, 9.
the foundation of the Church. Isa. 28. 16.
the Way. John 14. 6; Heb. 10. 19, 20.
the Truth. 1 John 5. 20; Rev. 3. 7.
the Life. John 11. 25; Col. 3. 4; 1 John 5. 11.
Incarnate. John 1. 14.
in His words. Lu. 4. 22; John 7. 46.
His works. Mat. 13. 54; John 2. 11.
his sinless perfection. Heb. 7. 26-28.
the fulness of His grace and truth. Ps. 45. 2, with John 1. 14.
His transfiguration. Mat. 17. 2, with 2 Pet. 1. 16-18.
His exaltation. Acts 7. 55, 56; Eph. 1. 21. [12.
celebrated by the redeemed. Rev. 5. 8-14; 7. 9-
revealed in the gospel. Isa. 40. 5.
saints shall rejoice at the revelation of. 1 Pet. 4. 13.
saints shall behold, in heaven. John 17. 24.

THE HEAD OF THE CHURCH: —
appointed by God. Eph. 1. 22. [21. 42.
declared by Himself head of the corner. Mat.
declared by St. Paul. Eph. 4. 12, 15; 5. 23.
as such has pre-eminence in all things. 1 Cor. 11. 3; Eph. 1. 22; Col. 1. 18.
commissioned His apostles. Mat. 10. 1, 7; 28. 19; John 20. 21.
instituted the sacraments. Mat. 28. 19; Lu. 22. 19, 20.
imparted gifts. Ps. 68. 18, with Eph. 4. 8.
saints complete in. Col. 2. 10.

HARMONY OF THE LIFE OF. *See* pages 44-52.

HUMAN NATURE OF, PROVED BY HIS
conception. Mat. 1. 18; Lu. 1. 31.
birth. Mat. 1. 16, 25; 2. 2, 4; Lu. 2. 7, 11.
partaking of our flesh and blood. John 1. 14; Heb. 2. 14.
having a human soul. Mat. 26. 38; Lu. 23. 46; Acts 2. 31.
circumcision. Lu. 2. 21.
increase in wisdom and stature. Lu. 2 52.
weeping. Lu. 19. 41; John 11. 35.
hungering. Mat. 4. 2; 21. 18.
thirsting. John 4. 7; 19. 28.
sleeping. Mat. 8. 24; Mk. 4. 38.
weariness. John 4. 6. [11. 33; 12. 27.
man of sorrows. Isa. 53. 3, 4; Lu. 22. 44; John

buffeted. Mat. 26. 67; Lu. 22. 64.
enduring indignities. Lu. 23. 11.
scourged. Mat. 27. 26; John 19. 1.
nailed to the cross. Lu. 23. 33, with Ps. 22. 16.
death. John 19. 30.
pierced side. John 19. 34.
burial. Mat. 27. 59, 60; Mk. 15. 46.
resurrection. Acts 3. 15; 2 Tim. 2. 8.
being called like us in all things except sin. Acts 3. 22; Phil. 2. 7, 8; Heb. 2. 17; without sin, John 8. 46; 18. 38; Heb. 4. 15; 7. 26, 28; 1 Pet. 2. 22; 1 John 3. 5.
evidence of the senses appealed to. John 20. 27; 1 John 1. 1, 2.
necessary to His mediatorial office. Rom. 6. 15, 19; 1 Cor. 15. 21; Gal. 4. 4, 5; 1 Tim. 2. 5; Heb. 2. 17.

WAS OF THE SEED OF
the woman. Gen. 3. 15; Isa. 7. 14; Jer. 31. 22; Lu. 1. 31; Gal. 4. 4.
Abraham. Gen. 22. 18, with Gal. 3. 16; Heb. 2. 16.
David. 2 Sam. 7. 12, 16; Ps. 89. 35, 36; Jer. 23. 5; Mat. 22. 42; Mk. 10. 47; Acts 2. 30; 13. 23; Rom. 1. 3.
genealogies of. Mat. 1. 1; Lu. 3. 23.
attested by Himself. Mat. 8. 20; 16. 13.
confession of, a test of belonging to God. 1 John 4. 2.
acknowledged by men. Mk. 6. 3; John 7. 27; 19. 5; Acts 2. 22.
denied by Antichrist. 1 John 4. 3; 2 John 7.

NAMES, TITLES, AND OFFICES OF. (The R. V. rendering is given in parenthesis.)
Adam, the second. 1 Cor. 15. 45, 47.
Advocate, an. 1 John 2. 1.
(The) Alpha and (the) Omega. Rev. 1. 8; 21. 6; 22. 13.
Amen. Rev. 3. 14.
Author and Finisher (Perfecter) of our faith. Heb. 12. 2.
Author of eternal salvation. Heb. 5. 9.

Beginning of the creation of God. Rev. 3. 14.
Blessed and only Potentate. 1 Tim. 6. 15.
Branch. Zec. 3. 8; 6. 12.
Bread of God. John 6. 33.
Bread of Life. John 6. 35.

Captain (Author) of Salvation. Heb. 2. 10.
Child (Servant), Holy. Acts 4. 27.
Child, Little. Isa. 11. 6.
Christ, the. Mat. 16. 16; Mk. 8. 29; Lu. 9. 20; John 6. 69.
Corner-stone. Eph. 2. 20; 1 Pet. 2. 6.
Counsellor. Isa. 9. 6.

David. Jer. 30. 9; Ezek. 34. 23; 37. 24; Hos. 3. 5.
David, Son of. Mat. 9. 27; 21. 9.
Day-spring. Lu. 1. 78.
Day-star. 2 Pet. 1. 19.
Deliverer. Rom. 11. 26.
Desire of all nations. Hag. 2. 7.

Emmanuel. Isa. 7. 14; 8. 8; Mat. 1. 23.
Everlasting Father. Isa. 9. 6.

Faithful witness. Rev. 1. 5; 3. 14.
Fellow, my. Zec. 13. 7.
First and Last. Rev. 1. 17.
Firstbegotten (Firstborn). Heb. 1. 6; Rev. 1. 5.

God. Isa. 40. 9; John 20. 28; 1 John 5. 20.
God blessed for ever. Rom. 9. 5.
Governor. Mat. 2. 6.

Head over all things. Eph. 1. 22.
Heir of all things. Heb. 1. 2.
High Priest. Heb. 4. 14; 5. 10.
Holy, the most. Dan. 9. 24.
Holy One. Lu. 4. 34; Acts 3. 14 (and righteous); Rev. 3. 7 (he that is holy).
Horn of Salvation. Lu. 1. 69.

I AM. Ex. 3. 14, with John 8. 58.
Image of God. 2 Cor. 4. 4.

Jehovah. Isa. 26. 4.
Jesus. Mat. 1. 21; 1 Thes. 1. 10.
Just (Righteous) One. Acts 3. 14; 7. 52; 22. 14.

King of Israel. John 1. 49.
King of the Jews. Mat. 2. 2.
King of kings. 1 Tim. 6. 15; Rev. 17. 14; 19. 16.

Lamb of God. John 1. 29, 36; Rev. 5. 6; 6. 1, 16; 12. 11; 13. 8; 15. 3; 19. 7; 22. 1, 3.
Lawgiver. Isa. 33. 22, with Jas. 4. 12.
Life, the. John 14. 6.
Life, Bread of. John 6. 35.
Light of the World. John 8. 12; 9. 5.
Light, True. John 1. 9; 12. 35.
Lion of the tribe of Judah. Rev. 5. 5.
Living stone. 1 Pet. 2. 4.
Lord. Zec. 14. 3; Mat. 3. 3; Mk. 11. 3.
Lord God: Almighty, Rev. 15. 3. of the holy Prophets (of the spirits of the Prophets), 22. 6.
Lord of all. Acts 10. 36.
Lord of Glory. 1 Cor. 2. 8; Jas. 2. 1.
Lord of lords. 1 Tim. 6. 15; Rev. 17. 14; 19. 16.
Lord our Righteousness. Jer. 23. 6; 33. 16; Mal. 4. 2; Acts 17. 31; Rom. 5. 18; Phil. 1. 11; Heb. 7. 2; 2 Pet. 1. 1.

Maker and Preserver of all things. John 1. 3, 10; 1 Cor. 8. 6; Col. 1. 16; Heb. 1. 2, 10; Rev. 4. 11.
Man, the. 1 Tim. 2. 5.
Man, the second. 1 Cor. 15. 47.
Mediator. Gal. 3. 19; 1 Tim. 2. 5; Heb. 2. 17; 7. 25; 8. 6; 9. 15; 10. 10; 12. 2, 24; 13. 15.
Messiah. Dan. 9. 25; John 1. 41.
Mighty God. Isa. 9. 6.
Mighty One of Jacob. Isa. 60. 16.
Morning star. Rev. 22. 16.

Nazarene. Mat. 2. 23.

Passover, our. 1 Cor. 5. 7.
Priest for ever. Heb. 5. 6.
Prince. Acts 5. 31.
Prince of Life. Acts 3. 15.
Prince of Peace. Isa. 9. 6.
Prince (Ruler) of the kings of the earth. Rev. 1. 5.
Prophet, Priest, and King. Deu. 18. 15; Isa. 49.; 50.; 51.; 52.; Nah. 1. 15; Mat. 2. 2; 23. 36; 24. 4; 25. 34; Lu. 4. 1, 15, 16, 18, 24; 5. 3, 17, 32; 19. 41; 21. 10, 25; 22. 34; 23. 2, 27; 24. 19; John 18. 37; 19. 14, 19; Acts 17. 7; 1 Tim. 1. 17; 6. 15; Heb. 1. 8; 2. 17; 3. 1; Rev. 1. 5; 11. 15; 15. 3; 17. 14; 19. 16.
Propitiation. Rom. 3. 25; 1 John 2. 2.

Redeemer. Job 19. 25; Isa. 59. 20.
Righteous, the. 1 John 2. 1.
Root and offspring of David. Rev. 5. 5; 22. 16.
Ruler in Israel. Mic. 5. 2.

Same yesterday, to-day, and for ever. Heb. 13. 8.
Saviour. Lu. 2. 11; John 4. 42; Acts 5. 31; 13. 23; Eph. 5. 23; 2 Pet. 1. 1; 3. 2; 1 John 4. 14; Jude 25.
Servant, my. Isa. 52. 13.
Shepherd and Bishop of souls. 1 Pet. 2. 25.
Shepherd in the land. Zec. 11. 16; 13. 7.
Shepherd of the sheep, Great. Heb. 13. 20.
Shepherd, the chief. 1 Pet. 5. 4.
Shepherd, the good. John 10. 11.
Shiloh. Gen. 49. 10.
Son, a. Heb. 3. 6.
Son, the. Ps. 2. 12; Heb. 1. 8.
Son, my beloved. Mat. 3. 17; 17. 5; Lu. 9. 35 (chosen).
Son, only-begotten. John 1. 14, 18; 3. 16, 18.
Son of David. Mat. 9. 27; 21. 9.

Christ, Harmony of the Life of.

The order of events is in general according to Andrews' "Life of Christ."

PERIOD.	OUTLINE.	EVENTS.	PLACE.	DATE.	MAT.	MARK.	LUKE.	JOHN.	JOHN THE BAPTIST.
	INTRODUCTION.	Preëxistence						1 : 1–14	
		Genealogies			1 : 1–17		3 : 23-38		
PREPARATIONS.	CHILDHOOD B. C. 5 to A. D. 26. AND YOUTH.	Annunciation to Mary	Nazareth	March B. C. 5.			1 : 26–38		B. C. 5.
		Birth of John the Baptist	Judea	June "			1 : 57–80		Childhood and youth.
		Birth of Jesus	Bethlehem	Dec. "	1 : 18–25		2 : 1–7		
		Song of the angels	"	" "			2 : 8–20		
		Visit of the wise men	"	Jan. B. C. 4	2 : 1–12				
		Flight into Egypt	Egypt	Feb. "	2 : 13–23				
		Childhood and youth at Nazareth.	Nazareth	B. C. 2–26	2 : 23		2 : 39, 40, 51, 52		
		First Passover at Jerusalem, when 12 years old.	Jerusalem	April A. D. 8			2 : 41–50		
	PREPARATIONS. A. D. 26.	Ministry of John the Baptist, six months before, and a year and three months parallel with Jesus' ministry.	Wilderness of Judea	From summer of A. D. 26 to Mar. A. D. 28.	3 : 1–12	1 : 1–8	3 : 1–18		A. D. 26. Summer.
		Baptism of Jesus	Jordan	January 27	3 : 13–17	1 : 9–11	3 : 21–23		
		Temptation of Jesus	Wilderness of Judea.	Jan.–Feb. 27	4 : 1–11	1 : 12, 13	4 : 1–13		
A. D. 27. Feb. JUDEAN MINISTRY (about one year). Dec.	FIRST YEAR OF JESUS' MINISTRY. A. D. 27. YEAR OF BEGINNINGS.	First disciples	Bethabara	A. D. 27. February				1 : 15–51	PUBLIC MINISTRY OF JOHN.
		First miracle. Wedding at Cana.	Cana	"				2 : 1–12	
		First cleansing of the temple.	Jerusalem	April 11–17				2 : 13–25	
		First recorded discourse, — to Nicodemus.	"	" "				3 : 1–21	
		First great ministry in Judea.	Judea	Summer and autumn.				3 : 22–36	
		Departure for Galilee		December				4 : 1–3	
		First converts in Samaria at Jacob's well.	Sychar	"				4 : 4–42	
		Healing of the nobleman's son.	Capernaum	"				4 : 43–54	
		A few weeks spent by Jesus in retirement, or unrecorded.		A. D. 28. Jan.–Mar.					

STREET IN BETHLEHEM
A photograph taken about 1918. (*John Stirling*)

BETHANY

From the Olivet footpath leading to Jerusalem. (*L. A. Fereday*)

April A. D. 28. — **The Great Galilean Ministry** (one year and nine months).

Second Year. **A. D. 28.**

Passover............	Jerusalem ..	Mar. 30–Apr. 5	....	....	....	**5** : 1
Healing at the pool of Bethesda and discourses.	"	" "	....	....	....	**5** : 2–47
Imprisonment of John the Baptist.	Macherus...	March	**14** : 3–5	**6** : 17, 18	**3** : 19, 20	....
Returns to Galilee. Beginning of *Great Galilean Ministry*.	Galilee	April..........	**4** : 12	**1** : 14, 15	**4** : 14, 15	....
Jesus rejected at Nazareth.	Nazareth ...	"	....	....	**4** : 16–30	....
Takes up his abode at Capernaum.	Capernaum.	"	**4** : 13–17	....	**4** : 31	....
Calling disciples to be fishers of men.	Sea of Galilee.	April, May...	**4** : 18–22	**1** : 16–20	**5** : 1–11	....
Many miracles..........	Capernaum .	" "	**8** : 14–17	**1** : 21–34	**4** : 31–41	....
First circuit of Galilee..	Galilee	" "	**4** : 23, 24	**1** : 35–39	**4** : 42–44	....
Healing of a leper......	"	May..........	**8** : 2–4	**1** : 40–45	**5** : 12–16	....
Healing a paralytic.....	Capernaum..	May, June	**9** : 2–8	**2** : 1–12	**5** : 17–26	....
The call of Matthew....	"	" "	**9** : 9	**2** : 13, 14	**5** : 27, 28	....
Discourse on the Sabbath	"	" "	**12** : 1–8	**2** : 23–28	**6** : 1–5	....
The man with the withered hand healed on the Sabbath.	"	" "	**12** : 9–14	**3** : 1–6	**6** : 6–11	....
Calling of the twelve...	Horns of Hattin.	Midsummer...	**10** : 2–4	**3** : 13–19	**6** : 12–19	....
Sermon on the Mount ..	"	"	chapters **5**, **6**, **7**	....	**6** : 20–49	....
Healing of the centurion's servant..........	Capernaum..	"	**8** : 5–13	....	**7** : 1–10	....
Raising of the widow's son.	Nain.......	"	....	....	**7** : 11–17	....
John the Baptist sends to Jesus.	Galilee	"	**11** : 2–19	....	**7** : 18–35	....
Warnings and invitations (here or at the beginning of the Perean ministry).	"	....	**11** : 20–30	....	....	....
The woman, a sinner. The two debtors. At Pharisee's house.	....	Midsummer...	....	....	**7** : 36–50	....
Another tour of Galilee.	Galilee	Autumn	....	....	**8** : 1–3	....
Healing of a blind and dumb demoniac and discourses thereon.	Capernaum..	"	**12** : 22–45	**3** : 22–30	(**11** : 14–23)	....
Visit of his mother and brethren.	"	"	**12** : 46–50	**3** : 31–35	**8** : 19–21	....

Imprisoned, March A. D. 28. — John the Baptist in prison at Macherus one year.

Christ, Harmony of the Life of — (*Continued*).

Period.	Outline.	Events.	Place.	Date.	Mat.	Mark.	Luke.	John.	John the Baptist.
The Great Galilean Ministry — (*continued*).	Year of Fundamental Principles.	Eight parables by the seaside.	By Sea of Galilee.	"	**13** : 1–53	**4** : 1–34	**8** : 4–18	....	
		Stilling of the tempest..	On Sea of Galilee.	"	**8** : 18–27	**4** : 35–41	**8** : 22–25	....	
		Restoration of the demoniac.	Gergesa	"	**8** : 28–34	**5** : 1–20	**8** : 26–39	....	
		Matthew's feast........	Capernaum..	"	**9** : 10–17	**2** : 15–22	**5** : 29–39	....	
		Jairus' daughter raised to life; woman cured.	"	"	**9** : 18–26	**5** : 21–43	**8** : 40–56	....	
		Cure of two blind men and a dumb possessed.	"	"	**9** : 27–34	....	....	....	Martyred March A. D. 29.
	Third Year.	Second rejection at Nazareth.	Nazareth....	**A. D. 29.** Winter........	**13** : 53–58	**6** : 1–6	....	....	
		The twelve sent forth ..	Galilee	"	**9** : 35 to **11** : 1	**6** : 6–13	**9** : 1–6	....	
		Death of John the Baptist.	Macherus...	March........	**14** : 1–12	**6** : 14–29	**9** : 7–9	....	
		Feeding of the five thousand.	Bethsaida...	April	**14** : 13–21	**6** : 30–46	**9** : 10–17	**6** : 1–15	
		Jesus walks upon the water.	Sea of Galilee.	"	**14** : 22–33	**6** : 47–52	....	**6** : 16–21	
		Heals many that are sick.	Gennesaret..	"	**14** : 34, 35	**6** : 53–56	....	....	
		Discourse on the bread of life.	Capernaum..	"	....	....	....	**6** : 22–71	
		Discourse on eating with unwashen hands.	"	"	**15** : 1–20	**7** : 1–23	....	....	
		Journey toward Sidon. Heals daughter of Syrophenician woman.	Region of Tyre and Sidon.	Summer......	**15** : 21–28	**7** : 24–30	....	....	
		Return through Decapolis, and miracles of healing.	Decapolis...	"	**15** : 29–31	**7** : 31–37	....	....	
		Feeding the four thousand.	"	"	**15** : 32–39	**8** : 1–10	....	....	
		Demanding a sign from heaven and the warning.	Capernaum.. Sea of Galilee	"	**16** : 1–12	**8** : 11–21	....	....	
	A. D. 29.	Blind man healed	Bethsaida...	"	....	**8** : 22–26	....	....	

	YEAR OF DEVELOPMENT.	Peter's confession of faith.	Near Cesarea Philippi.	"	16 : 13–20	8 : 27–30	9 : 18–21	....
		Jesus for the first time foretells his death and resurrection.	"	"	16 : 21–23	8 : 31 to 9 : 1	9 : 22–27	....
		The transfiguration	"	"	17 : 1–13	9 : 2–13	9 : 28–36	....
		Healing of demoniac boy	Philippi	Summer	17 : 14–21	9 : 14–29	9 : 37–43	....
		Jesus again foretells his death and resurrection	Galilee	"	17 : 22, 23	9 : 30–32	9 : 43–45	....
		Jesus and the children..	Capernaum.	"	18 : 1–14	9 : 33–50	9 : 46–50	....
		Discourse and parable on forgiving.	"	Summer	18 : 15–35	....	....	....
	GREAT DEEDS AMID GREAT OPPOSITION.	At the Feast of Tabernacles.	Jerusalem ..	Autumn	....	....	....	7 : 1 to 10 : 21
		Discourses on the water of life.	"	October 11–18.	....	....	....	7 : 32–44
		On light and freedom...	"	" "	....	....	....	8 : 12–59
		On one born blind......	"	" "	....	....	....	9 : 1–39
		The Good Shepherd	"	" "	....	....	....	10 : 1–21
		Returns to Galilee.........	....	Autumn.......				....
Dec. A. D. 29. PEREAN MINISTRY (four or five months).		Final departure from Galilee.	Galilee......	Nov., Dec.....	19 : 1	10 : 1	9 : 51	....
		Mission of the seventy..	Perea.......	" "	....	....	10 : 1–24	....
		Parable of Good Samaritan.	"	" "	....	....	10 : 25–37	....
		Discourse on prayer....	"	" "	....	....	11 : 1–13	....
		Answers attacks of the Pharisees.	"	" "	....	....	11 : 14–54	....
		Discourse on great moral truths. The rich fool.	"	" "	....	....	12 : 1–59	....
		Discourses. Galileans slain by Pilate. Barren fig tree. Healing on the Sabbath. Parables of mustard seed and leaven. The strait gate. Lament over Jerusalem.	"	" "	....	....	13 : 1–35	....
		Jesus the guest of Mary and Martha.	Bethany....	" "	....	....	10 : 38–42	....
		Feast of dedication. Discourses.	Jerusalem...	December 20–27.	....	....	....	10 : 22–39
				A. D. 30.				
		Jesus retires beyond Jordan.	Perea.......	January......	....	....	....	10 : 40–42
		Dines with a Pharisee. Discussions.	"	"	....	....	14 : 1–14	....

INCREASING OPPOSITION.

Christ, Harmony of the Life of — (*Continued*).

INCREASING OPPOSITION — (*Continued*).

PERIOD.	OUTLINE.	EVENTS.	PLACE.	DATE.	MAT.	MARK.	LUKE.	JOHN.
PEREAN MINISTRY — (*Continued*).		Parable of the great supper.	Perea	January	....	....	**14** : 15–24	....
		Counting the cost of being a disciple.	"	"	....	....	**14** : 25–35	....
	A. D. 30.	Parables of lost sheep and lost piece of silver.	"	"	....	....	**15** : 1–10	....
	THREE MONTHS.	Parable of prodigal son.	"	"	....	....	**15** : 11–32	....
		Parable of unjust steward.	"	"	....	....	**16** : 1–13	....
		Parable of rich man and Lazarus.	"	"	....	....	**16** : 14–31	....
		Instruction on forgiveness and faith.	"	"	....	....	**17** : 1–10	....
		Raising of Lazarus	Bethany	February	....	....	....	**11** : 1–46
		Jesus retires to Ephraim in northern Judea till near the time for the Passover.	Ephraim	February, March.	....	....	....	**11** : 47–57
	CULMINATION OF MIRACLES AND TEACHING.	The healing of the ten lepers.	On borders of Samaria.	March	....	....	**17** : 11–19	....
		The sudden coming of the kingdom.	Perea	"	....	....	**17** : 20–37	....
		The importunate widow. The Pharisee and the publican.	"	"	....	....	**18** : 1–14	....
		Discourse about divorce.	"	"	**19** : 2–12	**10** : 2–12	....	....
		Christ blesses little children.	"	"	**19** : 13–15	**10** : 13–16	**18** : 15–17	....
		The rich young ruler	"	"	**19** : 16–30	**10** : 17–31	**18** : 18–30	....
		Parable of the laborers in the vineyard.	"	"	**20** : 1–16	....	....	....
March A. D. 30.		Our Lord makes a third prediction of his death and resurrection.	"	"	**20** : 17–19	**10** : 32–34	**18** : 31–34	....
		Ambitious request of James and John.	"	"	**20** : 20–28	**10** : 35–45	....	....
		Healing of two blind men (Bartimeus) near Jericho.	Jericho	"	**20** : 29–34	**10** : 46–52	**18** : 35–43	....

		Events.	Place.	Time.	Mat.	Mark.	Luke.	John.
Friday, Mar. 31.		Visit to Zaccheus the publican.	"	"			19 : 1-10	
		Parable of the pounds (Minæ).	"	"			19 : 11-28	
The Last Week.		Jesus arrives at Bethany from Jericho.	Bethany	Fri., Mar. 31				12 : 1
		Anointing by Mary	"	Sat., April 1	26 : 6-13	14 : 3-9		12 : 2-11
		Triumphal entry. Visit to temple. Return to Bethany.	Jerusalem	Sun., April 2	21 : 1-11	11 : 1-11	19 : 29-44	12 : 12-19
		Cursing of the barren fig tree.	Mt. of Olives.	Mon., April 3	21 : 18, 19	11 : 12-14		
		Cleansing of the temple. Return to Bethany.	Jerusalem	" "	21 : 12-17	11 : 15-19	19 : 45-48 21 : 37, 38	
	Last Day of Public Teaching.	The fig tree withered. Lesson on faith.	Mt. of Olives.	Tues., April 4	21 : 20-22	11 : 20-26		
		Christ's authority questioned.	Temple at Jerusalem.	" "	21 : 23-27	11 : 27-33	20 : 1-8	
		Parable of the two sons.	"	" "	21 : 28-32			
		Parable of the wicked husbandmen.	"	" "	21 : 33-46	12 : 1-12	20 : 9-19	
		Parable of the marriage of the king's son.	"	" "	22 : 1-14			
		Pharisees question Jesus about tribute.	"	" "	22 : 15-22	12 : 13-17	20 : 20-26	
		Sadducees question about resurrection.	"	" "	22 : 23-33	12 : 18-27	20 : 27-40	
		Lawyer questions about the great commandment.	"	" "	22 : 34-40	12 : 28-34		
		Jesus asks, "What think ye of Christ?"	"	" "	22 : 41-46	12 : 35-37	20 : 41-44	
		Woes against the scribes and Pharisees.	"	" "	23 : 1-36	12 : 38-40	20 : 45-47	
		Lamentation over Jerusalem.	"	" "	23 : 37-39			
		The widow's mite	"	" "		12 : 41-44	21 : 1-4	
		Greeks seek Jesus. Discourse.	"	" "				12 : 20-50

Christ, Harmony of the Life of — (*Continued*).

Period.	Outline.	Events.	Place.	Time.	Mat.	Mark.	Luke.	John.
The Last Week — (*Continued*).	**A. D. 30.**	Prophecy of overthrow of the temple and end of the world.	Mt. of Olives.	Tues., April 4..	**24** : 1–51......	**13** : 1–37....	**21** : 5–36....	....
		Parable of the ten virgins	" "	" "	**25** : 1–13......	....	....	....
		Parable of the talents...	" "	" "	**25** : 14–30......	....	....	....
		The last judgment......	" "	" "	**25** : 31–46......	....	....	....
		Plotting of rulers. Bargain of Judas	Jerusalem .	" "	**26** : 1–5..... **26** : 14–16....	**14** : 1, 2... **14** : 10, 11..	**22** : 1–6.....	....
		Jesus in retirement.....	Bethany.....	Wed., April 5..	....	....	....	....
	The Last Supper.	Preparation for the Passover.	Jerusalem ...	Thurs., April 6.	**26** : 17–19.....	**14** : 12–16....	**22** : 7–13.....	....
		Arrival at upper room..	"	" "	**26** : 20.........	**14** : 17.......	**22** : 14.......	....
		Strife for precedence...	"	" "	....	....	**22** : 24–30....	....
		Jesus washes the feet of his disciples.	"	" "	....	....	....	**13** : 1–20.....
		The paschal supper	"	" "	....	....	**22** : 15–18....	....
		Jesus declares the betrayer. Judas goes out.	"	" "	**26** : 21–25.....	**14** : 18–21....	**22** : 21–23....	**13** : 21–35....
		Institution of the Lord's Supper.	"	" "	**26** : 26–29.....	**14** : 22–25....	**22** : 19–20..	(1 Cor. **11** : 23–25) .....
		Jesus foretells the fall of Peter.	"	" "	....	....	**22** : 31–38....	**13** : 36–38....
		Farewell discourse of Jesus.	"	" "	....	....	....	chaps. **14**–**16** ....
		Prayer of Jesus for his disciples.	"	" "	....	....	....	**17** : 1–26.....
		Jesus goes forth. Peter's confidence.	"	" "	**26** : 30–35.....	**14** : 26–31....	**22** : 39.......	**18** : 1–3......
		The agony in the garden of Gethsemane.	Mt. of Olives.	" "	**26** : 36–46.....	**14** : 32–42....	**22** : 40–46....	....
		The betrayal..........	"	" "	**26** : 47–50.....	**14** : 43–45....	**22** : 47, 48 ...	**18** : 4–9......
		The arrest	"	Midnight	**26** : 50–56.....	**14** : 46–52....	**22** : 49–53....	**18** : 10–12....
	The Jewish Trial.	Jesus led to Annas, then to Caiaphas.	Jerusalem..	Fri., April 7, 1–5 A. M.	....	....	....	**18** : 13–15....
		Jesus before Caiaphas ..	"	"	**26** : 57, 58	**14** : 53, 54 ...	**22** : 54, 55 ...	**18** : 19–24....
		Jesus before the Sanhedrim.	"	"	**26** : 59–66.....	**14** : 55–64....	....	....
		Denials of Peter.......	"	"	**26** : 69–75.....	**14** : 66–72....	**22** : 56–62....	**18** : 15–18 .. **18** : 25–27 ..

CHR

Jerusalem and Vicinity. Friday, Apr. 7.		Jesus mocked by his enemies.	"	"	26 : 67, 68	14 : 65	22 : 63–65	
		Meeting of the Sanhedrim. Jesus condemned for blasphemy.	"	5–6 A. M.	27 : 1, 2	15 : 1	22 : 66–71 23 : 1	
	The Roman Trial.	Death of Judas	"	"	27 : 3–10	Acts 1 : 18, 19		
		Jesus before Pilate; on three charges.	"	"	27 : 11–14	15 : 2–5	23 : 2–5	18 : 28–38
		Jesus sent to Herod	"	"			23 : 6–12	
		Pilate seeks to release Jesus. Jews demand Barabbas.	"	"	27 : 15–23	15 : 6–14	23 : 13–23	18 : 38–40
		Jesus is condemned, scourged, and mocked by soldiers.	"	"	27 : 26–30	15 : 15–19	23 : 24, 25	19 : 1–3
		Pilate again seeks to release Jesus.	"	"	27 : 24, 25			19 : 4–16
		Jesus is led away to be crucified.	"	9 A. M.	27 : 31–34 27 : 38	15 : 20, 23 15 : 25, 27, 28	23 : 26–32	19 : 16–18
	The Crucifixion.	The superscription	Jerusalem	9 A. M.	27 : 37	15 : 26	23 : 38	19 : 19–22
		First word from the cross ("Father, forgive them").	"	"			23 : 33, 34	
		Soldiers cast lots for his garments.	"	"	27 : 35, 36	15 : 24	23 : 34	19 : 23, 24
		Jews mock at Jesus on the cross.	"	"	27 : 39–44	15 : 29–32	23 : 35–37	
		Second word (the penitent thief).	"	"			23 : 39–43	
		Third word ("Woman, behold thy son").	"	"				19 : 25–27
		Darkness covers the land	"	12 M.	27 : 45	15 : 33	23 : 44, 45	
		Fourth word (cry of distress to God).	"	"	27 : 46, 47	15 : 34, 35		
		Fifth word ("I thirst")	"	"	27 : 48, 49	15 : 36		19 : 28, 29
		Sixth word ("It is finished").	"	"				19 : 30
		Seventh word ("Into thy hands," etc.).	"	"			23 : 46	
		Jesus dies. Veil rent. Earthquake.	"	3 P. M.	27 : 50–56	15 : 37–41	23 : 45, 46–49	19 : 30
		Jesus is pierced with a spear in the side.	"	"				19 : 31–37
		The burial. The watch at the sepulchre.	"	3–6 P. M.	27 : 57–66	15 : 42–47	23 : 50–56	19 : 38–42
		The morning of the resurrection.	Jerusalem	Sun., April 9.	28 : 2–4			

CHR

Christ, Harmony of the Life of — (*Continued*).

PERIOD.	OUTLINE.	EVENTS.	PLACE.	TIME.	MAT.	MARK.	LUKE.	JOHN.
RESURRECTION DAYS.	THE RESURRECTION.	Women come to the sepulchre.	Jerusalem	Sun., April 9	**28** : 1	**16** : 1-4	**24** : 1, 2	**20** : 1
		Mary Magdalene calls Peter and John.	"	" "				**20** : 2
		The women at sepulchre.	"	" "	**28** : 5-8	**16** : 5-8	**24** : 3-8	
		Peter and John go to the sepulchre.	"	" "			**24** : 12	**20** : 3-10
		Jesus appears to Mary Magdalene.	"	" "		**16** : 9-11		**20** : 11-18
		He appears to the women.	"	" "	**28** : 9, 10		**24** : 9-11	
		The guard report to the priests.	"	" "	**28** : 11-15			
		Jesus appears to two on the way to Emmaus.	Emmaus	" "		**16** : 12, 13	**24** : 13-35	
		He appears to Peter	Jerusalem	" "		(1 Cor. **15** : 5)		
		He appears to the apostles except Thomas.	"	" "	(1 Cor. **15** : 5)	**16** : 14	**24** : 36-48	**20** : 19-23
		He appears to all the apostles including Thomas.	Jerusalem	Sun., April 16				**20** : 24-29
		He appears to seven in Galilee.	Sea of Galilee	April				**21** : 1-23
		He appears to a multitude, more than 500.	Galilee	April, May	**28** : 16-20	**16** : 15-18	(1 Cor. **15** : 6)	
		He appears to James	"		(1 Cor. **15** : 7)			
	THE ASCENSION.	He appears to all the apostles.	Jerusalem		(Acts **1** : 1-8)		**24** : 49	
		The ascension	Bethany	Thur., May 18	(Acts **1** : 9-12)	**16** : 19	**24** : 50-53	
		Conclusions of Mark and John.				**16** : 20		**20** : 30, 31; **21** : 24, 25
	CONTINUED LIFE.	Holy spirit given. Pentecost.	Jerusalem	Sun., May 28	(Acts **2** : 1-11)			
		Jesus appears to Paul	Damascus	A. D. 37	(Acts **22** : 6-16)			
		Jesus appears to John	Patmos	A. D. 68 or 96	(Rev. **1** : 9-20)			
		Jesus our high priest in heaven.			(Heb. **9** : 11-28)			
		New heaven and earth, where Jesus reigns.			(Rev. **21** : 1-27)			

CHR

Son of God. Mat. 2. 15; 3. 17; 4. 3, 6; Lu. 1. 32, 35; 3. 22; 4. 3, 9; 4. 34. 41; John 1. 34, 49; 3. 16, 18, 35, 36; 5. 22, 23; 6. 40, 69; 12. 26; 13. 3; 14. 13; 15. 23; 16. 27, 30; 17. 1; 19. 7; Rom. 1. 9; 5. 10; 8. 3, 29, 32; 1 Cor. 1. 9; Gal. 1. 16; 4. 4, 6; Col. 1. 13; 1 Thes. 1. 10; Heb. 1. 2, 5, 8; 3. 6; 4. 14; 5. 5, 8; 6. 6; 7. 3; 1 John 4. 1, 3, 7; 3. 23; 4. 9, 10; 5. 9.
Son of Man. Ezek. 2. 1; Mat. 8. 20; 9. 6; 10. 23; 11. 19; 12. 8, 32, 40; 13. 37, 41; 16. 13; 17. 9, 22; 24. 27, 30, 44; 25. 31; 26. 2, 24, 45; Mk. 8. 38; 9. 12, 31; 13. 26; Lu. 5. 24; 6. 22; 9. 22, 26; 11. 30; 12. 8; 17. 22; 18. 8; 19. 10; 21. 36; 22. 48; John 1. 51; 3. 13; 5. 27; 6. 27, 53, 62; 8. 28; 12. 23, 34; 13. 31; Acts 7. 56; Rev. 1. 13.
Son of the Highest (Most High). Lu. 1. 32.
Star. Num. 24. 17.
Star, the bright and (the) morning. Rev. 22. 16.
Sun of Righteousness. Mal. 4. 2.

Truth, the. John 14. 6.

Vine, the. John 15. 1, 5.

Way, the. John 14. 6.
Witness, faithful and true. Rev. 3. 14.
Wonderful. Isa. 9. 6.
Word. John 1. 1; Acts 10. 36; 1 John 5. 7.
Word of God. Rev. 19. 13.

PROPHECIES RELATING TO —

1. His First Advent.
The fact. Gen. 3. 15; Deu. 18. 15; Ps. 89. 20; Isa. 2. 2; 28. 16; 32. 1; 35. 4; 42. 6; 49. 1; 55. 4; Ezek. 34. 24; Dan. 2. 44; Mic. 4. 1; Zec. 3. 8.
The time. Gen. 49. 10; Num. 24. 17; Dan. 9. 24; Mal. 3. 1.
His Divinity. Ps. 2. 7, 11; 45. 6, 7, 11; 72. 8; 89. 26, 27; 102. 24-27; 110. 1; Isa. 9. 6; 25. 9; 40. 10; Jer. 23. 6; Mic. 5. 2; Mal. 3. 1.
Human Generation. Gen. 12. 3; 18. 18; 21. 12; 22. 18; 26. 4; 28. 14; 49. 10; 2 Sam. 7. 14; Ps. 18. 4-6, 50; 22. 22, 23; 89. 4, 20, 36; 132. 11; Isa. 11. 1; Jer. 23. 5; 33. 15.

2. His Forerunner.
Isa. 40. 3; Mal. 3. 1; 4. 5.

3. His Nativity and Early Years.
The fact. Gen. 3. 15; Isa. 7. 14; Jer. 31. 22.
The place. Num. 24. 17, 19; Mic. 5. 2.
Adoration by Magi. Ps. 72. 10, 15; Isa. 60. 3, 6.
Descent into Egypt. Hos. 11. 1.
Massacre of Innocents. Jer. 31. 15.

4. His Mission and Office.
Mission. Gen. 12. 3; 49. 10; Num. 24. 19; Deu. 18. 18; Ps. 21. 1; Isa. 59. 20; Jer. 33. 16.
Priest like Melchizedek. Ps. 110. 4.
Prophet like Moses. Deu. 18. 15.
Conversion of Gentiles. Isa. 11. 10; Deu. 32. 43; Ps. 18. 49; 19. 4; 117. 1; Isa. 42. 1; 45. 23; 49. 6; 65. 1; Hos. 1. 10; 2. 23; Joel 2. 32.
Galilee, ministry in. Isa. 9. 1, 2.
Miracles. Isa. 35. 5, 6; 42. 7; 53. 4.
Spiritual graces. Ps. 45. 7; Isa. 11. 2; 42. 1; 53. 9; 61. 1, 2.
Preaching. Ps. 2. 7; 78. 2; Isa. 2. 3; 61. 1; Mic. 4. 2.
Purification of Temple. Ps. 69. 9.

5. His Passion.
Rejection by Jews and Gentiles. Ps. 2. 1; 22. 12; 41. 5; 56. 5; 69. 8; 118. 22, 23; Isa. 6. 9, 10; 8. 14; 29. 13; 53. 1; 65. 2.
Persecution. Ps. 22. 6; 35. 7, 12; 56. 5; 71. 10; 109. 2; Isa. 49. 7; 53. 3.
Triumphal entry into Jerusalem. Ps. 8. 2; 118. 25, 26; Zec. 9. 9.
Betrayal by own friend. Ps. 41. 9; 55. 13; Zec. 13. 6.
Betrayal for thirty pieces. Zec. 11. 12.
Betrayer's death. Ps. 55. 15, 23; 109. 17.
Purchase of potter's field. Zec. 11. 13.
Desertion by disciples. Zec. 13. 7.
False accusation. Ps. 27. 12; 35. 11; 109. 2; Ps. [2. 1, 2.
Silence under accusation. Ps. 38. 13; Isa. 53. 7.
Mocking. Ps. 22. 7, 8, 16; 109. 25.
Insult, buffeting, spitting, scourging. Ps. 35. 15, 21; Isa. 50. 6.
Patience under suffering. Isa. 53. 7-9.
Crucifixion. Ps. 22. 14, 17.
Gall and vinegar, offer of. Ps. 69. 21.
Prayer for enemies. Ps. 109. 4.
Cries upon the cross. Ps. 22. 1; 31. 5.
Death in prime of life. Ps. 89. 45; 102. 24.
Death with malefactors. Isa. 53. 9, 12.
Death attested by convulsions of nature. Am. 5. 20; Zec. 14. 4, 6.
Casting lots for vesture. Ps. 22. 18.
Bones not to be broken. Ps. 34. 20.
Piercing. Ps. 22. 16; Zec. 12. 10; 13. 6.
Voluntary death. Ps. 40. 6-8.
Vicarious suffering. Isa. 53. 4-6, 12; Dan. 9. 26.
Burial with the rich. Isa. 53. 9.

6. His Resurrection.
Ps. 16. 8-10; 30. 3; 41. 10; 110. 1-7; Hos. 6. 2.

7. His Ascension.
Ps. 16. 11; 24. 7; 68. 18; 110. 1; 118. 19.
Dominion universal and everlasting. 1 Chr. 17. 11-14; Ps. 72. 8; Isa. 9. 7; Dan. 7. 14; Ps. 2. 6-8; 8. 6; 110. 1-3; 45. 6. 7.

8. His Second Advent.
Ps. 50. 3-6; Isa. 9. 6, 7; 66. 18; Dan. 7. 13, 14; Zec. 12. 10; 14. 4-8.
See also PROPHECIES AND THEIR FULFILMENT.

Christian, chrĭs'-tĭan, a follower of Christ. Acts 11. 26; 26. 28; 1 Pet. 4. 16.

Christs, false, and prophets, warnings against. Mat. 7. 15; 24. 4, 5, 11, 24; Mk. 13. 22; Acts 20. 29; 2 Thes. 2. 8; 1 Tim. 4. 1; 2 Pet. 2. 1; Rev. 13.

Chronicles. The First and Second Chronicles form one work in the Hebrew, and are entitled, *The Acts or Annals of the Days*, from which our title, 'Chronicles,' arises. They give a history parallel to that of The Kings, but from a different standpoint.

Chronology of the Acts. *See* ACTS, CHRONOLOGY OF.

Chronology of the Old Testament.

I. CREATION OF MAN TO THE DELUGE.

USSHER FROM THE HEBREW.	EVENTS.	HALES FROM THE SEPTUAGINT.	EUSEBIUS.
B. C.		B. C.	B. C.
	THE CREATION (in the beginning)............		
4004............	Adam and Eve created............	5411	
"	The Fall............	"	
	Birth of Cain............	"	
	Birth of Abel............	"	
3875............	Murder of Abel............		
"	Banishment of Cain............		

I. Creation of Man to the Deluge—(*Continued*).

Ussher from the Hebrew.	Events.	Hales from the Septuagint.	Eusebius.
B. C.		B. C.	B. C.
3874	Birth of Seth	5181	
3074	Death of Adam	4481	
3017	Translation of Enoch	3914	
2948	Birth of Noah	3755	
2348	The Deluge	**3155**	2959
1656 years.	Period.	2256 years.	

Remarks.

The Chronology of the Old Testament, as given in the Hebrew text, is represented with much accuracy by the marginal dates inserted in many editions of the Authorized English Version. These dates, reduced to system by Archbishop Ussher (*Annales Veteris Testamenti*, 1650), were first added to the English Bible by Bishop Lloyd, in the great edition of 1701.

The dates of Archbishop Ussher for this period are convenient for keeping the succession of events, but are not authoritative, as is agreed by the most conservative scholars. They are only one of several possible arrangements. Opinions of chronologers as to the 'era of Creation' vary indeed by many centuries.

(Ussher 4004 B. C.
Hales (Sept.) 5411 "
Jewish reckoning 3760 B. C.
Alexandrian 5503 ").

The question is, in fact, insoluble.

II. The Deluge to the Exodus.

Ussher.			
2348	The Deluge	?	
2347–8	The Covenant with Noah	Armenia.	
2247	Confusion of tongues	Babylonia.	
1998	Death of Noah	Arabia.	
1996	Birth of Abram at Ur	Chaldea.	
1926	Abram moves from Ur to Haran	Mesopotamia.	
1921	The call of Abram	"	B. C. 1921.
1921	Abram and Lot move to Canaan	Canaan.	
1918	Abram and Lot separate		215 + 215 = **430** years of Ex. 12: 40. The sojourn in a strange land.
"	Lot goes to Sodom	Sodom.	
"	Abram settles in Hebron	Hebron.	
1913	Lot carried away captive by Chedorlaomer	Sodom.	
"	Lot rescued by Abram	Near Damascus.	
1912	The covenant with Abram	Hebron.	
1910	The birth of Ishmael	"	
1897	The covenant renewed	"	
"	Abram's name changed to Abraham	"	
"	Sarai's name changed to Sarah	"	
"	Abraham entertains three angels	"	
"	Abraham intercedes for Sodom	"	
"	The escape of Lot	Sodom.	
"	The destruction of Sodom	"	
1896	The birth of Isaac	Moab.	
1894	Hagar and Ishmael sent away	"	
1871	The sacrifice of Isaac	Moriah in Jerusalem.	
1860	The death of Sarah	Hebron.	
1857	Marriage of Isaac and Rebekah	Lahai Roi.	
1837	Birth of Jacob and Esau	Beersheba.	
1822	Death of Abraham	"	
1804	Esau sells his birthright	Lahai Roi.	
"	Isaac's prosperity	Gerar.	
"	The covenant confirmed	Beersheba.	
1760	Jacob steals Esau's blessing	"	
"	Starts for Padan-aram	Bethel.	
"	Jacob's vision at Bethel	"	
1753	**Jacob marries Leah and Rachel**	**Padan-aram.**	

II. The Deluge to the Exodus — (*Continued*).

Ussher.			215 + 216 = 430 years of Ex. 12: 40. The sojourn in a strange land.
1752 to 1739	Jacob's children (except Benjamin) born.	Padan-aram.	
1739	Jacob returns to Canaan..........................		
"	Wrestles with the angel	Penuel.	
"	Jacob's name changed to Israel...........	"	
1729	Birth of Benjamin.....	Bethlehem.	
"	Death of Rachel....................................	"	
"	Joseph's dreams....................................	Hebron.	
"	Joseph sold into Egypt...........................	Dothan.	
1728	Joseph a slave of Potiphar.....................	Egypt.	
1718	Is thrown into prison.............................	"	
1716	Death of Isaac	Hebron.	
"	Joseph interprets Pharaoh's dreams.....	Egypt.	
"	Is made ruler over Egypt	"	
"	The seven years of plenty begin...........	"	
"	Birth of Ephraim and Manasseh.............	"	
1709	The seven years of famine begin............	"	
1707	Joseph made known to his brethren.......	"	1706.
1706	Jacob moves to Egypt	"	
"	He and his family settle in Goshen........	"	
1689	Jacob's death	"	The 430 years according to others.
1635	Joseph's death..	"	
1571	Birth of Moses..	"	
1531	The exile of Moses	Arabia.	1491 B. C.
1491	The Exodus...	Red Sea.	

					Brugsch.	Mahler.	Price.
2348 —	**The Period, 857 years**	—	**to 1491**				
or 2348 —	The Period, 1048 years	—	to 1300	1300	1300	1335	1280

Remarks.

The two principal points on which there is a marked difference of opinion in relation to this period are: 1. The date of the Exodus: 2. The period over which the 430 years of Ex. 12. 40 and Gal. 3. 17 extends.

"The sojourning of the children of Israel, which they sojourned in Egypt, was 430 years." The Sept. says "in Egypt and in the land of Canaan." That is, the 430 years covers the whole period from Abraham's entrance into Canaan to the Exodus, with which agrees Paul's statement in Gal. 3. 17, that from the covenant with (or call of) Abraham to the giving of the law (less than a year after the Exodus) was 430 years. In Gen. 15. 13, 14, it is said that they should be strangers in a strange land, and be afflicted 400 years, nearly the same as Ex. 12. 40. But, in very truth, the children of Israel were strangers in a strange land from the time that Abraham left his home for the promised land, and during that whole period of 430 years to the Exodus, they were nowhere rulers in the land.

Another reason in favour of this view is the difficulty of arranging any other system of chronology that will agree with the Biblical statements. In 1 Kn. 6. 1, it is stated that there were 480 years from the Exodus to the building of the Temple.

Starting with B. C. 1012 as the date of the Temple, which cannot be more than a few years out of the way (not more than thirty-seven years according to the Eponym Canon), we obtain the following dates: —

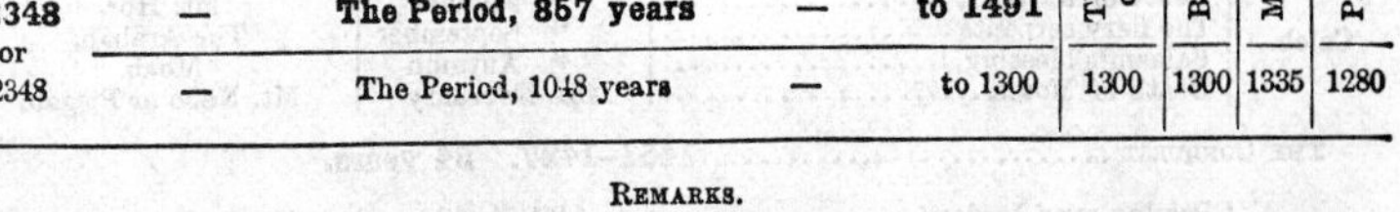

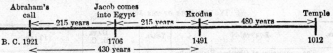

If the 430 years were wholly spent in Egypt, the dating would be somewhat in this manner: —

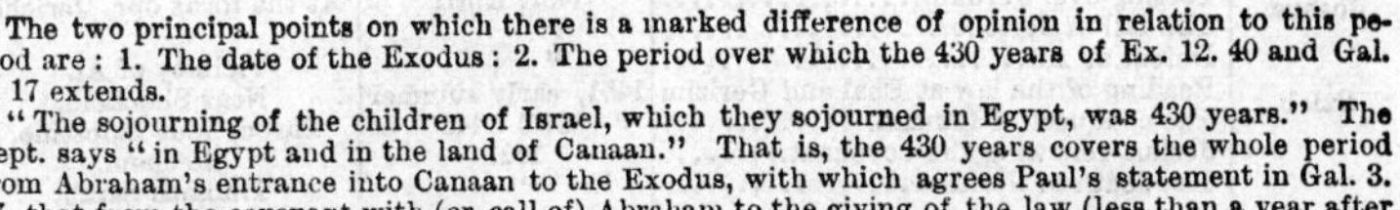

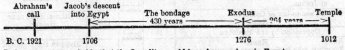

It does not seem probable that the Israelites could have been so long in Egypt.

The present tendency of modern scholarship is to accept the late date of about 1300 B. C. for the Exodus, Rameses II. as the Pharaoh of the oppression, and his son Menephtah (Merenptah) as the Pharaoh

of the Exodus. Prof. Edward L. Curtis, in Hastings' *Bible Dictionary*, says that 'the Exodus can in no case be placed earlier than after the reign of Rameses II.; ' but adds in a note that since that statement was in type (1898), the new inscription of King Merenptah may require the assignment of the Exodus to an earlier period. And Prof. James Orr, in *The Expositor* for March, 1897, argues stoutly for Thothmes and against Rameses.

It is impossible as yet to obtain certainty as to these early dates. Prof. Karl Marti, in Prof. Cheyne's *Encyclopedia Biblica*, states that the earliest date certain beyond doubt in the Chronology of the Old Testament is the year 854 B. C., the date of the battle of Karkar, when Ahab was defeated by Shalmaneser II.

III. From the Exodus to the Conquest.

Persons.	Events.	Date B. C. (Ussher).	Place.
	Exodus	April, 1491.	
Training in the Wilderness ....1491–1451. 40 years.			
	Giving of the manna	1491, May	East of Gulf of Suez, the
Moses.	The pillar of fire	" "	western branch of Red Sea.
	The Ten Commandments given	" "	Sinai, a high mountain in
	The golden calf	" July	Arabia.
	The tabernacle set up	1490, March	
Aaron.	The ceremonial law given	April, May	Wilderness of Arabia be-
	Nadab and Abihu		tween the two branches of
	The wanderings in the wilderness	1491–1451	the Red Sea.
Joshua.	New start for Canaan	1452, April	Kadesh.
	Waters from the rock	" "	Meribah.
	Death of Aaron	" summer	Mt. Hor.
Caleb.	The fiery serpents	" September	The Arabah.
	Balaam's blessing	" Autumn	Moab.
	Death of Moses	1451, February	Mt. Nebo or Pisgah.
The Conquest ....1451–1427. 24 years.			
Joshua.	Passing over Jordan	1451, April	At the fords opp. Jericho.
	The fall of Jericho	"	
	Defeat at Ai	"	Vicinity of Ai.
Caleb.	Reading of the law at Ebal and Gerizim	1451, early summer	Near Shechem.
	The conquest of Canaan	1451–1443	Throughout Palestine.
	Joshua renewing the covenant	1427	Shechem.
	The death of Joshua	"	Timnath Serah.
1491 — The Period, 64 years — to 1427			

Remarks.

The exact chronology is very uncertain during this whole period. There is a wide difference of opinion among scholars, and the latest Bible Dictionaries are unwilling to furnish even conjectural dates for most of the events. It seems, therefore, more helpful to the practical study of this period to give the dates in the margins of our Bibles, with the understanding that they are not authoritative, but give the general order and arrangement of events, and are as good as any that can be obtained.

IV. The Rule of the Judges.

Judges.	Events.	Years.		Date B. C.	Place.
	The oppression of Chushan-Rishathaim, from Mesopotamia, during the last years of Joshua.	8		1427	Palestine.
1 *Othniel*, son-in-law of Caleb.	**Rest.**	40		1387	Othniel lived near Hebron.
	Oppression by the Moabites.	18			
2 *Ehud*.	**Rest.**	80		1289	Ehud in the region of Jericho. Shamgar in the south-west.
3 *Shamgar*, who in these years by irregular acts, like those of Samson, saved the people from the Philistines.					

IV. The Rule of the Judges — (*Continued*).

Judges.	Events.	Years.		Date B. C.	Place.
	Oppression by Jabin, King of Canaan, with 900 chariots of iron.	20			
4 *Barak*, with *Deborah*.	**Rest.**	40		1229	Kadesh of Naphtali in the north; west of Lake Merom.
	Oppression by Midianites.	7			
5 *Gideon*. Ruth.	**Rest.**	40		1182	Moreh in the plain of Jezreel, southern part of Galilee.
6 *Abimelech*.		3			Shechem.
7 *Tola*.	**Rest.**	23		1156	Mount Ephraim.
8 *Jair*.	**Rest.**	22		1134	Gilead, east of Jordan.
	East Israel. Oppression of Amorites.	18	40 years of oppression by the Philistines.		West Israel. 12 *Eli*. 1154–1114. 13 Abdon.
9 *Jephthah*. Gilead.	**Rest.**	6			So. West Israel. 14 *Samson*. 1116–1096.
10 *Ibzan*. Bethlehem.	**Rest.**	7			15 *Samuel*. 1114–1094.
11 *Elon*. Zebulon.	**Rest.**	10		1094	Partial **Rest.**
1427	— **The Period, 332 years** —				**to 1095.**

Remarks.

The Period of the Judges. According to 1 Kn. 6. 1, there were 480 years between the Exodus and the commencement of the Temple in the fourth year of Solomon's reign. Deducting from this the 40 years in the wilderness, 25 years of Joshua in Canaan, and 20 or 40 for Saul's reign, 40 for David's reign, and 3 years of Solomon's reign, the period of the Judges would be 480 — 148 = 332 years (or 480 — 128 = 352 years) including the judgeships of Eli and Samuel up to the beginning of the reign of Saul. Of this about 280 years belong to the book of Judges. But if we add together the numbers given in Judges, they amount to 410 years. For this and other reasons it is entirely probable that 'the oppressions and deliverances were not successive, but, in part, synchronous. They were, in fact, without exception, local struggles; and it is not only conceivable, but highly probable, that while one part of the land was enjoying security under its judge, other tribes were groaning under the foreign yoke.' — *Professor Moore.* While several of the events were thus occurring at the same time in different parts of the land, in other cases the judges ruled practically over the whole. 'The judges formed temporary heads in particular centres, or over particular groups of tribes, — Barak, in the north of Israel, Gideon, in the centre, Jephthah, on the east of Jordan, Samson, in the extreme southwest.' — *Professor Driver.*

V. The United Kingdom.

The Kingdom of Saul. 40 years.	Ussher B. C.	Revised from Assyrian records.	Place.	Remarks.
Saul the first king	**1095**	**1057**	Gibeah of Saul.	
David born	1085		Bethlehem.	
Saul rejected	1079			
David anointed	1065		Bethlehem.	
David and Goliath	1063		Valley of Elah, in Judah.	
David's marriage to Michal	1062			
David's flight from Saul	"		Gibeah, Nob, Gath.	
David's exile	"			Tyre flourishes under Hiram.
David collects 400 followers	"		Cave of Adullam.	Gad the prophet.
David spares Saul	1060		Engedi.	
David and Nabal	1059		Carmel, in mountains of Judah.	

V. The United Kingdom — (*Continued*).

The Kingdom of David. 40 years.	Ussher. B. C.	Revised from Assyrian records.	Place.	Remarks.
David among the Philistines	1057		Ziklag.	
Death of Saul and Jonathan	1055		Mt. Gilboa.	
David made king..........	1055	1017	Hebron.	
David king over Judah....	1055–1048		Capital at Hebron.	
David made king over all Israel..................	1048		Capital at Jerusalem.	
The ark brought to Zion...	1042		Kirjath-jearim and Jerusalem.	
David's sin and repentance	1034		Jerusalem.	Nathan the prophet.
Absalom's rebellion.......	1023		Hebron, Jerusalem.	
Death of David...........	1015		Jerusalem.	Tyre a flourishing commercial kingdom.
The Kingdom of Solomon. 40 yrs.				
Solomon made king.......	1015	977	Jerusalem.	The beginning of exact chronology.
The temple foundations laid	1012		"	Shishak king of Egypt.
The temple dedicated......	1004		"	
Visit of the Queen of Sheba	995		"	Syrian kingdom of Damascus founded by Rezin.
Solomon's death..........	**975**	**937**	"	

1095	–	**Period, 120 years**	–	**975**
1057				**937**

VI. The Divided Kingdom, Judah and Israel.

Kings of Judah.	Dates B. C. Ussher.	Dates B. C. Revised from Assyrian records.	Kings of Israel.	Prophets.	Contemporary History.	Dates B. C.	Dates fixed by the Assyrian Eponym Canon.	Mahler's astronomical chronology.
Disruption of the Kingdom	**975**	**937**						
Rehoboam : 17 years.	975	937	Jeroboam I. : 22 years		Expedition of Shishak (E.) against Jerusalem.			Rehoboam 945
Abijah : 3 years	957	920	18th year		Assyrian Eponym Canon begins.	900		
Asa : 40 years	955	917	20th "					Asa 925
2nd year	954	915	Nadab : 2 years.					
3rd "	953	914	Baasha : 24, or 12.					
14th " about					Expedition of Zerah against Jerusalem.			
26th "	930	891	Elah : 2 years.					
27th "	929	889	Zimri — Tibni : 4 years.					
31st "	929	885	Omri : 6 years (or 12)					Omri 892
38th "	918	876	Ahab : 22 years.					
Jehoshaphat : 25 yrs.	917	875						Jehoshaphat 883
					Year of the 'Moabite stone' (about)	860		
				Elijah	Assur-nasir-pal (A.) conquers as far as Lebanon.			
					Attack on Ramoth-Gilead (S.). Ahab slain.			
17th year	897	854	Ahaziah : 2 years					
(Jehoram, regent) 18th year	......	853	Jehoram : 12 years		Alliance of the two kingdoms with Edom against Moab.			
Jehoram : 8 years	893	851			Siege of Samaria by Ben-hadad I. (S.).			
Ahaziah : 1 year	885	843	12th year					
Athaliah : 6 years	884	842	Jehu : 28 years		War with Hazael (S.).			
Joash : 40 years	878	836	7th year		Accession of Shalmaneser II.	850		Jehu 852
				Elisha	Assyrian war with Ben-hadad II. and Jehu (?). (Some read the name as Ahab.) Battle at Karkar.		Battle of Karkar 854	Joash 845

CHR

VI. The Divided Kingdom, Judah and Israel — (*Continued*).

Kings of Judah.	Dates B. C. Ussher.	Dates B. C. Revised from Assyrian records.	Kings of Israel.	Prophets.	Contemporary History.	Dates B. C.	Dates fixed by the Assyrian Eponym Canon.	Mahler's astronomical chronology.
					Renewed war with Syria, now under Hazael. Damascus taken. Tribute of Jehu, called 'son of Omri.'	836 814	Tribute of Jehu 842	
23rd year	856	815	Jehoahaz : 17 years		Black Obelisk.			
37th "	842	798	Jehoash : 16 years					
Amaziah : 29 years ..	840	796	2nd year		....	....	....	Jehoash 807
					Ramman-nirari III.	812		
15th year	......	782	Jeroboam II. : 41 years ..	....	Conquests by Israel of Syrian territory.			
(Uzziah, regent)	811	789 767						
Uzziah (sole)			27th year	....	Shalmaneser III., king of Assyria.	783		
			....	Amos	The first Olympiad, B. C. 776. Greek exact chronology begins.	776		
					Total eclipse of sun (June 15), visible at Nineveh. The basis of the Assyrian dates.	763		
			....					
(Uzziah) 38th year ...	773	741	Zachariah : ½ year		Pul (generally identified with Tiglath-pileser III.) advances against Israel.	745	Tribute of Menahem 738	
39th " ..	772	741	Shallum : 1 month					
39th " ..	772	741	Menahem : 10 years	Hosea				
(Jotham, regent)	......	753						
(Uzziah) 50th year ..	761	737	Pekahiah : 2 years		First (Assyrian) Captivity of Israel.	....	....	Uzziah 777
52nd year	759	736	Pekah : 20 years					
Jotham (sole), to ...	742	....	2nd year		Accession of Tiglath-pileser III. He plunders Damascus.	731		
Ahaz : 16 years	742	735	17th year (? 7th year) ..		Rezin (S.) harasses Judah. Ahaz seeks Assyrian aid.	735	Tribute of Ahaz 734	
12th year	730	729	Hoshea : 9 years					
Hezekiah : 29 years	726	726 715	....		Accession of Shalmaneser IV.	727		
			....		....	....	....	Hezekiah 693
6th year	722 721	722, *or* '1	**Fall of Samaria**		Shalmaneser begins the siege of Samaria.		Fall of Samaria 721	
				Isaiah	Sargon, the usurper, successor to Shalmaneser.			
			....		Second (Assyrian) captivity of Israel.			

				Micah	Merodach-baladan (B.) sends embassy to Jerusalem.			
					Sargon's campaign against Egypt. He defeats Sabaco (So).			
					Sargon defeats Merodach-baladan, and becomes King of Babylon.			
					Sennacherib (son of Sargon) succeeds to sole dominion.	705		
					Invasion of Judah by Sennacherib. His army destroyed.	701	Invasion of Sennacherib 701	
Manasseh : 55 years.	697	{ 697 686	....					
					Accession of Esar-haddon. He attacks Manasseh. Carries him to Babylon.	671		
			....	Nahum	Accession of Assur-bani-pal. Defeat of Tirhakah.	668		
Amon : 2 years.....	642	641	....		Assyrian Eponym Canon ends.			
Josiah : 31 years	640	639	....	Zephaniah	....	....	....	Josiah 609
			....		Accession of Nabopolassar. Nebuchadnezzar, his son and general.	625		
			....	Habakkuk	Pharaoh-necho (E.) attacks Assyria. Josiah, drawn into the conflict, falls.			
Jehoahaz : 3 months	609	608						
Jehoiakim : 11 years	609	608	....		The Fall of Nineveh	606	1st year of Nebuchadnezzar 604	
Beginning of Captivity	606	{ 606 604	Jerusalem taken by Nebuchadnezzar		Nebuchadnezzar makes Judah tributary.	606		
			Daniel and other princes carried to Babylon					
			10,000 leading citizens carried to Babylon, among them *Ezekiel*, and the great grandfather of *Mordecai*, uncle of Esther	Jeremiah	Nebuchadnezzar's sole reign....	604		
Jehoiachin : 3 months	598	597						
Zedekiah : 11 years..	598	597			Pharaoh-hophra. See Jer. 44. 30.	....	....	Zedekiah 568
Fall of Jerusalem.	{ 588 586	586	Temple destroyed } 832 carried captive }		....	586	{ Fall of Jerusalem 586	
	975 or 937	—		Period	389 or 351 years	—	586	

NOTE 1. The data for this period are the explicit chronological statements of Scripture, chiefly in the books of Kings and Chronicles. These assign to each reign its duration; and, after the division of the kingdom, give cross references to the times of the contemporary kings. The difficulty is that the

VI. The Divided Kingdom, Judah and Israel — (*Continued*).

lists of Israel and Judah do not agree. From the accession of Rehoboam to the sixth year of Hezekiah, the year of the destruction of Samaria, 255 years appear to be enumerated in the line of Judah, 241 in that of Israel. Some unknown fact would very possibly place the lists in harmony; and it is probable either (1) that there were in the Israelite line intervals of interregnum, so *lengthening* the period; or (2) that in the line of David there were times of associated sovereignty, — father with son, — the years in the annals being counted to both, so *shortening* the period. The former explanation is generally adopted in the older chronologies, but the latter appears the more satisfactory. There can be little doubt that Jotham, for instance, reigned for several years conjointly with his father Uzziah, who himself had previously been associated with Amaziah. It must be remembered that the Hebrews counted the unfinished years of a reign as complete. Thus a reign beginning a little before the end of one year, and ending a little after the close of the next, would be reckoned as of three years, although really hardly more than one. It follows that the same year will be often reckoned twice, as belonging to two different reigns.

Note 2. The dates given in the first column are those arranged by Archbishop Ussher, and placed in the margins of our Bibles. They vary but from one to forty years from the revised chronology, and whichever one we accept as correct, it is necessary to record the Ussher chronology for the sake of comparison. The dates in the revised chronology are those of Hastings' *Bible Dictionary*, closely compared with those of Prof. George Adam Smith in his *Book of the Twelve Prophets*, and Prof. Cheyne's *Encyclopedia Biblica*.

Note 3. The most important extra-Biblical source of the chronology of this period is found in the Assyrian inscriptions. In 1862 Sir Henry Rawlinson discovered among the records of the stone libraries of Nineveh, on certain slabs, important historical documents, called the Assyrian Eponym Canon, by which we have the Assyrian record of chronology during a large part of the history of the kingdom of Israel.

The *Eponyms* were annually elected Assyrian officers, like the Roman consuls, and, like them, events were commonly dated by reference to their term of office. An accurate register was kept, with notes of important events and the succession of kings. These constitute the Canon. Its dates harmonize with the Bible in their order and general accuracy, and are exact as to 722 B. C. for the fall of Samaria, and 586 B. C. for the destruction of Jerusalem, and are thus a marvellous confirmation of the Bible. But in details the Assyrian dates vary from those Ussher has derived from the Bible numbers, from seven to forty years. The records are complete from 897 to 666 B. C., as well as for shorter periods before and after. There are several copies, all of which closely agree. They contain notices of the succession of kings and the most important events in their respective years. From the mention of a total eclipse in 763 is determined the date of all the remaining years. The persons and events in next to the last column of the preceding table are mentioned in the Eponym Canon.

Note 4. The dates in the last column of the above table are from the remarkable astronomical calculations of the astronomer Mahler, based on the Biblical notices of such possible events, taken from the *Encyclopedia Biblica*.

VII. The Captivity and Return to the Close of the Canon.

The seventy years of Exile. { Beginning at different points and ending at equi-different points.

First Captivity. 606 or 604 — 70 years. — **First Return.** 536

580 The golden idol and the fiery furnace.
571 Last of Ezekiel's prophecies.
Daniel's visions.
538 The den of lions.
536 Cyrus' Decree for the Return.

The later prophecies of the book of Isaiah belong to the last part of the exile.

Nebuchadnezzar becomes king of Babylon... 605
The seven wise men flourish in Greece......
First World-Kingdom, Babylonia, 605–538.
Rise of *Cyrus*. Capture of Babylon by Cyrus. 538
Darius the Mede, king of Babylon two years. 538–536
Pythagoras, the philosopher who invented the multiplication table.................. 570
Second World-Kingdom, Medo-Persian, 538–333.
Cyrus sole ruler of Babylon and the empire.
Tarquinius Superbus at Rome............... 534–509
Pisistratus founded first public library at Athens.................................. 544

Final Captivity. 586 — 70 years. — **Completion of Temple.** 516
Destruction of city and temple.

The Return from Exile, and Restoration of the Nation.

B. C.	Jews.	Prophets.	Scriptures.	Contemporary History.	B. C.
536	First return, under Zerubbabel, with a company of 50,000 exiles.	Daniel still living. Haggai and Zechariah urge the completion of the temple, 520.	Book of Ezra. Prophecies of Haggai. Prophecies of Zechariah.	The Cyrus Cylinder.	
				Solon the Wise died	558
535	The foundations of the temple laid.			Confucius, the Chinese philosopher, flourished	559–476
520	The second temple, work upon.			*Darius Hystaspes*........................	521–486
Mch. 515	The second temple completed.			Battle of Marathon........................	490
				Xerxes	486–465
483	Xerxes' (Ahasuerus') Feast.			His great invasion of Greece with an army of 5,000,000........................	483–480
479	Esther becomes queen.			Defeats at Thermopylæ and Salamis.......	480
473	She saves her countrymen from destruction.			Herodotus	484–424
458	Second return, under Ezra, from Babylon.		Revision of the Scriptures.	Socrates	470–399
445	Nehemiah, at Susa, hears from Jerusalem.	Fifth book of the Psalms, 107–150.		Plato	427–347

CHR

The Return from Exile, and Restoration of the Nation — (*Continued*).

B. C.	Jews.	Prophets.	Scriptures.	Contemporary History.	B. C.
444	Nehemiah builds the wall of Jerusalem.		Nehemiah.	*Artaxerxes Longimanus*	465–425
433	Nehemiah recalled to Susa.				
427	Returns to Jerusalem. Reforms.			Pericles..................................	444
397–317	Aided, or soon followed, by Malachi.	Prophecies of Malachi.	Malachi.	First Peloponnesian War..................	431
				Conquest of Persian Empire by Alexander the Great........................	332

586. — Period, 189 years — 397.

VIII. Period between the Old and New Testaments.

B. C.	Jews in Palestine and Egypt.	Contemporary Events.
350	Jaddua, High Priest.	Egypt a Persian province.
336	....	Darius Codomannus, King of Persia: era of Alexander the Great.
334	....	Alexander invades Persia. Victory at the Granicus.
333	....	Battle of Issus.
332	Alexander visits Jerusalem ..	Foundation of Alexandria.
331	Settlement of Jews at Alexandria..........	Battle of Arbela.
330	Onias I., High Priest	Death of Darius: end of the Persian Empire.
323	....	Death of Alexander. The Ptolemies take the Egyptian kingdom; the Seleucidæ the Syrian.
320	Ptolemy Soter captures Jerusalem. Palestine subject to Egypt.	Colonies of Jews in Egypt and Cyrene.

B. C.	Jews in Palestine and Egypt.	Contemporary Events.
314	Palestine subject to Syria.	
310	Simon the Just, High Priest.	
301	Palestine reverts to Egypt...	Battle of Ipsus.
284	Beginning of the LXX. translation of the Old Testament.	Ptolemy Philadelphus.
264	....	First Punic War.
219	....	Second Punic War.
201	....	Colonies of Jews from Babylon transplanted to Asia Minor.
198	Antiochus the Great becomes master of Palestine.	
170	Tyranny of Antiochus Epiphanes.	
168	Revolt of Mattathias.	
167	Rise of the Maccabees.	
166	Judas Maccabæus.	
165	Battles of Beth-horon and Emmaus.	

VIII. Period between the Old and New Testaments — (*Continued*).

B. C.	Jews in Palestine and Egypt.	Contemporary Events.
165	Re-dedication of the Temple.	
161	Judas killed in battle at Eleasa: Jonathan succeeds him. Asmonæan line of priestly rulers established.	
149	....	Third Punic War.
146	....	Fall of Carthage and Corinth.
		Greece a Roman province.
144	Murder of Jonathan Maccabæus.	
141	Simon Maccabæus completes the deliverance of Palestine.	
135	Murder of Simon Maccabæus: John Hyrcanus succeeds him.	
130	Hyrcanus destroys the temple on Mount Gerizim.	
109	First mention of Pharisees and Sadducees.	
107	Accession of Aristobulus, under the title of 'king.'	
106	Alexander Jannæus.	
	First mention of the Essenes.	
79	Alexandra, queen.	
69	Aristobulus II.	
63	Pompey subjugates Judæa...	Conspiracy of Catiline.
60	....	The first triumvirate.
58	....	Cæsar in Gaul.
54	The temple plundered by Crassus.	
48	....	Battle of Pharsalia: death of Pompey.

B. C.	Jews in Palestine and Egypt.	Contemporary Events.
48	Hyrcanus II. restored.	
47	Antipater the Idumæan appointed by Cæsar procurator of Judæa.	
	Herod made governor of Galilee.	
44	....	Assassination of Cæsar.
43	Death of Antipater.	
40	Hyrcanus banished; Antigonus succeeds: last of the Asmonæan priestly line.	
	Herod at Rome.	
	Herod appointed king of Judæa.	
37	Herod captures Jerusalem.	
31	....	Battle of Actium.
30	....	Egypt conquered by Cæsar. Line of the Ptolemies ends.
29	....	Temple of Janus closed.
27	....	Augustus made emperor.
19	Herod begins to rebuild the temple.	
16	Herod goes to meet Agrippa and invites him to Judæa.	Agrippa sent to settle the affairs of Syria.
15	Agrippa visits Judæa.	
14	He confirms the privileges of the Jews.	
11	The outer temple finished.	
4	Herod dies at Jericho soon after the Nativity of our Lord.	

IX. The New Testament Period.

(For fuller details see **Christ**, Harmony of Life of; and **Acts**, Chronology of.)

	Christian History.	Contemporary History.
Dec. B. C. 5	Birth of Christ.	Death of Herod the Great.
A. D. 30	Crucifixion.	Augustus Cæsar, 30 B. C. to 19th Aug. A. D. 14. Tiberius emp. 14 A. D.–16th Mch. A. D. 37.
" 30	Pentecost.	Pontius Pilate, 26 A. D.–early A. D. 36.
" 36	Conversion of Paul.	Caligula emp. 16th Mch. 37–24th Jan. 41.
" 44	Death of Herod.	Herod Agrippa I. made king, A. D. 37.
" 45	1st Missionary Journey.	Claudius emp. 24th Jan. 41–13th Oct. 54.
" 50	Council at Jerusalem.	
" 50	2nd Missionary Journey.	
" 54	3rd " "	Nero emp. 13th Oct. 54–9th June, 68.
" 60	Paul at Rome.	
" 62	Close of the Acts.	Burning of Rome 19th July, 64.
" 66	Martyrdom of Paul.	Outbreak of Jewish War, 66.
		Galba, Otho, and Vitellius, emps. 9th June, 68–20th Dec. 69.
" 70	Destruction of Jerusalem.	Vespasian emp. 1st July, 69.

Chrysolite (Rev. 21. 20). Gk. χρυσόλιθος, gold stone. A silicate of magnesium and iron, commonly of a bright yellow or green color, and varying from transparent to translucent; the oriental topaz, something like the Scotch cairngorm.

Chrysoprase, or Chrysoprasus (Rev. 21. 20). Gk. χρυσόπρασος, gold-leek. A variety of chalcedony, commonly apple-green in color, and often extremely beautiful. But probably the chrysoprase of Rev. 21. 20 is a greenish shade of beryl.

Chub, chŭb. Ezek. 30. 5.

Chun. chŭn, 'upright.' 1 Chr. 18. 8.

Church. Mat. 18, 17, tell it to the *c*.
Acts 2. 47, added to *c*. daily.
7. 38, the *c*. in the wilderness.
19. 37, neither robbers of *c*.
20. 28, feed the *c*. of God.
Rom. 16. 5; 1 Cor. 16. 19; Philem. 2, *c*. in house.
1 Cor. 14. 28, 34, keep silence in the *c*.
Eph. 5. 24, the *c*. is subject to Christ.
5. 25, as Christ loved the *c*.
Col. 1. 18, 24, head of the body the *c*.
Heb. 12. 23, the *c*. of the firstborn.

Church of God. Acts 20. 28; 1 Cor. 1. 2; 10. 32; 11. 22; 15. 9; Gal. 1. 13; 1 Tim. 3. 5.
foundation and increase of. Mat. 16. 18; Acts 2. 47; Col. 1. 18.
authority and teaching of. Mat. 18. 17; Acts 11. 26, 27; 1 Cor. 5. 4; 12. 28.
organization of. Acts 14. 23; 1 Cor. 4. 17; 14. 4, 5.
persecuted. Acts 8. 3; 12. 1; 15. 9; Gal. 1. 13; Phil. 3. 6.
saluted. Acts 18. 22; Rom. 16. 5; 10. 16; 1 Cor. 16. 19.
loved of Christ. Eph. 5. 25, 29.
edification of. 1 Cor. 14. 4, 19, 28, 34.

Churches, the seven, in Asia. Rev. 1. 4, 11, 20; 2. 7, 11, 17, 29; 3. 6, 13, 22; 22. 16.

Churlish. 1 Sam. 25. 3, but the man was *c*.

Chushan-rishathaim, chū'-shăn-rĭsh-ă-thā'-ĭm. Oppresses Israel. Jud. 3. 8, 9, 10.

Chuza, chū'-ză. Lu. 8. 3.

Ciel, to cover the interior upper surface, wainscot. 2 Chr. 3. 5; Jer. 22. 14, &c.

Cilicia, çĭ-lĭç'-ĭ-ă, disciples there. Acts 15. 23, 41.
the country of Paul. Acts 21. 39; Gal. 1. 21.
Paul born at Tarsus in. Acts 22. 3.

Cinnamon (Ex. 30. 23; Prov. 7. 17). Heb. *Kinnemôn*: Gk. κιννάμωμον: Bot. N. *Cinnamomum Zeylanicum*. The tree is a native of Ceylon, belongs to the laurel family, growing thirty feet high, and is cultivated chiefly for its bark.

Cinneroth, çĭn'-nĕ-rŏth, same as Chinneroth. 1 Kn. 15. 20.

Circle. Isa. 40. 22.

Circuit. 1 Sam. 7. 16; Job 22. 14; Ps. 19. 6; Eccl. 1. 6.

Circumcise. Rom. 4. 11, though not *c*.
Gal. 5. 2, if ye be *c*. Christ shall profit nothing.
Phil. 3. 5, *c*. the eighth day.

Circumcision. Rom. 3. 1, what profit is there of *c*.
15. 8, Jesus Christ minister of *c*.
Gal. 5. 6; 6. 15, in Christ neither *c*. availeth.
Phil. 3. 3, the *c*. which worship God.
Col. 2. 11, *c*. without hands.
3. 11, neither *c*. nor uncircumcision.

Circumcision, the covenant of. Gen. 17. 10, 23-25; John 7. 22; Acts 7. 8.
Shechemites submit to. Gen. 34. 24.
Zipporah resents it. Ex. 4. 25.
incumbent on strangers sojourning. Ex. 12. 48.
renewed by Joshua. Jos. 5. 2.
of John. Lu. 1. 59.
of Jesus. Lu. 2. 21.
of Timothy. Acts 16. 3.
superseded by the Gospel. Acts 15.; Gal. 5. 2.
of heart. Deu. 10. 16; 30. 6.
spiritual. Phil. 3. 3; Col. 2. 11.
when profitable, and how. Rom. 2. 25; 3. 30; 4. 9; 1 Cor. 7. 19; Gal. 5. 6; 6. 15.

Circumspect. Ex. 23. 13; Eph. 5. 15.

Cis, çĭs. Acts 13. 21, same as Kish.

Cistern. Eccl. 12. 6, the wheel broken at the *c*.
Jer. 2. 13, hewed out *c*., broken *c*.
See 2 Kn. 18. 31; Prov. 5. 15; Isa. 36. 16.

Cithern, a stringed instrument; the word has now become 'guitar.' (Lat. *cithara*.) 1 Macc. 4. 54.

Cities, spared or besieged. Deu. 20. 10.
to be destroyed. Deu. 20. 16.

Cities of refuge. Num. 35. 6, Deu. 19.; Jos. 20. Hebron (in *Judah*), Shechem (in *Ephraim*), Kedesh (in *Naphtali*), Bezer (in *Reuben*), Golan (in *Manasseh*), Ramoth (in *Gad*).

Citizen. Lu. 15. 15; 19. 14; Acts 21. 39; Eph. 2. 19.

Citron (Lev. 23. 40). Heb. *'Etz hâdâr*: Gk. καρπὸς ξύλον· Bot. N. *Citrus Medica*. A. V. and R. V. goodly trees. Probably the citron, a native of India, the most common of the orange tribe in Palestine.

City. 2 Sam. 19. 37, I may die in mine own *c*.
Ps. 46. 4, make glad the *c*. of God.

Ps. 107. 4, found no *c.* to dwell in.
127. 1, except Lord build *c.*
Prov. 8. 3, wisdom crieth in *c.*
16. 32, than he that taketh a *c.*
Eccl. 9. 14, a little *c.* and few men.
Isa. 33. 20, *c.* of solemnities.
Zec. 8. 3, a *c.* of truth.
Mat. 5. 14, *c.* set on a hill.
21. 10, all the *c.* was moved.
Lu. 24. 49, tarry in the *c.*
Acts 8. 8, great joy in that *c.*
Heb. 11. 10, a *c.* that hath foundations.
12. 22, the *c.* of living God.
Heb. 13. 14, no continuing *c.*
Rev. 16. 19, the *c.* of the nations fell.
20. 9, compassed the beloved *c.*
See Gen. 4. 17 : 11. 4 ; Jon. 1. 2 ; Rev. 14. 8 ; 21. 10.

Clad. 1 Kn. 11. 29; Isa. 59. 17.

Clamour. Prov 9. 13; Eph. 4. 31.

Clap. Ps. 47. 1, *c.* your hands, all ye people.
98. 8, let the floods *c.* their hands.
Isa. 55. 12, the trees shall *c.* their hands.
Lam. 2. 15, all that pass by *c.* their hands.
See 2 Kn. 11. 12 ; Job 27. 23 ; 34. 37.

Clauda, clau'-dă, an island S. W. of Crete. Acts 27. 16. R. V. Cauda.

Claudia, clau'-dĭ-ă. 2 Tim. 4. 21.

Claudius, clau'-dĭ-ŭs. Acts 11. 28.

Claudius Lysias, clau'-dĭ-ŭs lȳs'-ĭ-ăs, chief captain, rescues Paul. Acts 21. 31 ; 22. 24 ; 23. 1. sends him to Felix. Acts 23. 26.

Clave. (1) did split. Gen. 22. 3; Num. 16. 31; 1 Sam. 6. 14.
(2) did cling. Ru. 1. 14, Ruth *c.* to her mother-in-law.
2 Sam. 23. 10, his hand *c.* to the sword.
Neh. 10. 29, they *c.* to their brethren.
Acts 17. 34, certain men *c.* to Paul.

Claws. Deu. 14. 6; Dan. 4. 33; Zec. 11. 16. R. V. (in Zec.) hoofs.

Clay. (1) (Isa. 29. 16; 45. 9; 64. 8; Jer. 18. 4) Heb. *Hômer :* Gk. πηλός. A tenacious earth, like that so called by us, used for making bricks and earthenware. It was less cohesive than ours, and accordingly for the former purpose was bound together by an admixture of straw before being baked, and for building purposes was mixed with sand.
(2) (Isa. 41. 25). Heb. *Tîț:* Gk. πηλός. *Tîț* (*lit.* dirt) was, and still is, the common building material of the mud-houses of the peasantry of Palestine.
Job 10. 9, thou hast made me as *c.*
13. 12, bodies like to bodies of *c.*
33. 6, I also am formed out of *c.*
Ps. 40. 2, out of the miry *c.*
Dan. 2. 33, part of iron, part of *c.*
John 9. 6, made *c.* and anointed.
Rom. 9. 21, power over the *c.*

Clean. (1) 2 Kn. 5. 12, may I not wash and be *c.*
Job 14. 4, who can bring *c.* out of unclean.
15. 15, heavens not *c.* in his sight.
Ps. 24. 4, he that hath *c.* hands.
51. 10, create in me *c.* heart.
Prov. 16. 2, *c.* in his own eyes.
Isa. 1. 16, wash you, make you *c.*
52. 11, be *c.* that bear vessels of the Lord.
Ezek. 36. 25, then will I sprinkle *c.* water.
Mat. 8. 2 ; Mk. 1. 40 ; Lu. 5. 12, thou canst make me *c.*
23. 25 ; Lu. 11. 39, make *c.* the outside.
Lu. 11. 41, all things *c.* unto you.
John 13. 11, ye are not all *c.*
15. 3, *c.* through word I have spoken.
Acts 18. 6, I am *c.*
Rev. 19. 8, arrayed in fine linen *c.* and white.
(2) entirely, completely. Lev. 23. 22; Jos. 3. 17; Ps. 77. 8.

Cleanness. 2 Sam. 22. 21 ; Ps. 18. 20 ; Am. 4. 6.

Cleanse. Ps. 19. 12, *c.* me from secret faults.
73. 13, I have *c.* my heart in vain.
Prov. 20. 30, blueness of wound *c.* evil.
Mat. 8. 3, immediately his leprosy was *c.*
10. 8 ; 11. 5 ; Lu. 7. 22, *c.* lepers.
23. 26, *c.* first that which is within.
Lu. 4. 27, none was *c.* saving Naaman.
17. 17, were not ten *c.*
Acts 10. 15 ; 11. 9, what God hath *c.*
2 Cor. 7. 1, let us *c.* ourselves.
Jas. 4. 8, *c.* your hands, ye sinners.
1 John 1. 7, 9, *c.* us from all sin.
See Ezek. 36. 25 ; Mk. 1. 44.

Clear. Gen. 44. 16, now shall we *c.* ourselves.
Ex. 34. 7, by no means *c.* the guilty.
2 Sam. 23. 4, *c.* shining after rain.
Job 11. 17, age shall be *c.* than noonday.
Ps. 51. 4, be *c.* when thou judgest.
Mat. 7. 5 ; Lu. 6. 42, see *c.* to pull out mote.
Mk. 8. 25, saw every man *c.*
Rom. 1. 20, things from creation *c.* seen.
Rev. 21. 11 ; 22. 1, light *c.* as crystal.
See Gen. 24. 8 ; S. of S. 6. 10 ; Zec. 14. 6.

Cleave. (1) adhere. 2 Kn. 5. 27, leprosy shall *c.* to thee.
Job 29. 10 ; Ps. 137. 6; Ezek. 3. 26, *c.* to roof of mouth.
Ps. 119. 25, my soul *c.* to dust.
(2) remain faithful. Gen. 2. 24; Jos. 23. 8; Mat. 19. 5; Mk. 10. 7 ; Acts 11. 23 ; Rom. 12. 9.
(3) split. Eccl. 10. 9, he that *c.* wood shall be endangered.

Clefts. S. of S. 2. 14; Isa. 2. 21; Jer. 49. 16; Am. 6. 11; Obad. 3.

Clemency. Acts 24. 4.

Clement, clĕm'-ĕnt, 'kind ;' fellowlabourer of Paul. Phil. 4. 3.

Cleopas, clē'-ŏ-păs, either a shortened form of Cleopatros, or a Greek form of Alphæus ; a disciple. Lu. 24. 18. *See* EMMAUS.

Cleophas, clē'-ŏ-phăs, probably same as preceding. John 19. 25.

Clerk. Acts 19. 35.

Climb. John 10. 1, but *c.* up some other way.
See 1 Sam. 14. 13 ; Am. 9. 2; Lu. 19. 4.

Clods. Job 21. 33, the *c.* of the valley shall be [sweet.
See Job 7. 5 ; Isa. 28. 24 ; Hos. 10. 11; Joel 1. 17.

Cloke. Mat. 5. 40; Lu. 6. 29, let him have thy *c.* also.
1 Thes. 2. 5, a *c.* of covetousness.
1 Pet. 2. 16, a *c.* of maliciousness.

Close (*v.*). Gen. 2. 21 ; Isa. 29. 10 ; Mat. 13. 15.

Close. (1) Prov. 18. 24, sticketh *c.* than a brother.
(2) secret, unrevealed. Lu. 9. 36, they kept it close.
See Num. 5. 13 ; 1 Chr. 12. 1 ; Job 28. 21.

Closet, a private room, bedroom. Mat. 6. 6 ; Lu. [12. 3.

Cloth was woven, dyed, and fulled with soap, by the Hebrews, and was made from flax, silk, and wool. Tent cloth was made from the hair of camel or goat. 1 Sam. 19. 13 ; 21. 9 ; Mat. 9. 16 ; Mk. 2. 21.

Clothe. Ps. 65. 13, pastures *c.* with flocks.
109. 18, c. himself with cursing.
132. 9, *c.* with righteousness.
132. 16, *c.* with salvation.
Prov. 23. 21, drowsiness shall *c.* a man.
31. 21, household *c.* with scarlet.
Isa. 50. 3, *c.* heavens with blackness.
61. 10, *c.* with garments of salvation.
Mat. 6. 30 ; Lu. 12. 28, *c.* grass of field.
6. 31, wherewithal shall we be *c.*
11. 8 ; Lu. 7. 25, man *c.* in soft raiment.
25. 36, 43, naked and ye *c.* me.
Mk. 1. 6, *c.* with camel's hair.
5. 15 ; Lu. 8. 35, *c.* and in right mind.
15. 17, *c.* Jesus with purple.
Lu. 16. 19, *c.* in purple and fine linen.
2 Cor. 5. 2, desiring to be *c.* upon.
1 Pet. 5. 5, be *c.* with humility.
Rev. 3. 18, that thou mayest be *c.*
12. 1, woman *c.* with the sun.
19. 13, *c.* with a vesture dipped in blood.
See Ex. 40. 14 ; Esth. 4. 4.

Clothes. Deu. 29. 5 ; Neh. 9. 21, *c.* not waxen old.
Mk. 5. 28, if I touch but his *c.*

Lu. 2. 7, in swaddling *c.*
8. 27, a man that ware no *c.*
19. 36, spread *c.* in the way.
24. 12; John 20. 5, linen *c.* laid.
John 11. 44, bound with grave-*c.*
Acts 7. 58, laid down *c.* at Saul's feet.
22. 23, cried out and cast off *c.*
See Gen. 49. 11; 1 Sam. 19. 24; Neh. 4. 23.

Clothing. Ps. 45. 13, her *c.* of wrought gold.
Prov. 27. 26, lambs are for thy *c.*
31. 22, her *c.* is silk and purple.
31. 25, strength and honour are her *c.*
Isa. 3. 7, in my house is neither bread nor *c.*
23. 18, merchandise for durable *c.*
59. 17, garments of vengeance for *c.*
Mat. 7. 15, in sheep's *c.*
Mk. 12. 38, love to go in long *c.* R. V. robes.
Acts 10. 30, a man in bright *c.*
Jas. 2. 3, to him that weareth gay *c.*
See Job 22. 6; 24. 7; 31. 19; Ps. 35. 13.

Clothing, coats of skins the first. Gen. 3. 21.
rending of. Gen. 37. 29, 34; Num. 14. 6; Jud. 11. 35; Acts 14. 14.
washing of, ordered. Ex. 19. 10; Lev. 11. 25; Num. 19. 7.

Cloud. Ex. 13. 21; 14. 24; Neh. 9. 19, a pillar of *c.*
1 Kn. 18. 44, 45, a little *c.*
Ps. 36, 5, faithfulness reacheth to *c.* R. V. skies.
97. 2, *c.* and darkness round about him.
99. 7, spake in *c.* pillar.
Prov. 3. 20, *c.* dropped down dew.
Eccl. 11. 4, regardeth the *c.* not reap.
12. 2, nor *c.* return after rain.
Isa. 5. 6, command *c.* rain not.
44. 22, blotted out as thick *c.*
60. 8, fly as a *c.*
Dan. 7. 13; Lu. 21. 27, Son of man with *c.*
Hos. 6. 4; 13. 3, goodness as morning *c.*
Mat. 17. 5; Mk. 9. 7; Lu. 9. 34, *c.* overshadowed.
24. 30; 26. 64; Mk. 13. 26; 14. 62, in *c.* with power.
1 Cor. 10. 1, fathers under *c.*
1 Thes. 4. 17, caught up in *c.* [mists.
2 Pet. 2. 17, *c.* carried with tempest. R. V.
Jude 12, *c.* without water.
Rev. 1. 7, he cometh with *c.*
14. 14-16, white *c.*

Cloud, pillar of, children of Israel guided by. Ex. 13. 21; 14. 19; Neh. 9. 19; Ps. 78. 14; 105. 39; 1 Cor. 10. 1.
appearance of the Lord in. Ex. 24. 15; 34. 5; 40. 34; Lev. 16. 2; Num. 11. 25; 12. 5; 1 Kn. 8. 10; Ezek. 10. 4; Mat. 17. 5; Lu. 21. 27; Rev. 14. 14.

Clouted, patched. Jos. 9. 5.

Clouts, rags, pieces of cloth. Jer. 38. 11.

Cloven. Lev. 11. 3; Deu. 14. 7; Acts 2. 3.

Cluster. Isa. 65. 8, new wine in *c.*
See Num. 13. 23; S. of S. 1. 14; Rev. 14. 18.

Cnidus, cnī'-dŭs, 'nettle' (?). Acts 27. 7.

Coal. Prov. 6. 28, hot *c.* and not be burned.
25. 22; Rom. 12. 20, heap *c.* of fire.
John 18. 18; 21. 9, fire of *c.*
See Job 41. 21; Ps. 18. 8; Isa. 6. 6.

Coast, Lat. *costa*, a rib, or side: the border of a region or country. 1 Chr. 4. 10; Mat. 8. 34; Mk. 5. 17.

Coat. Mat. 5. 40, take away thy *c.*
10. 10; Mk. 6. 9, neither provide two *c.*
Lu. 6. 29, thy *c.* also.
John 19. 23, *c.* without seam.
21. 7, fisher's *c.*
Acts 9. 39, the *c.* which Dorcas made.
See Gen. 3. 21; 37. 3; 1 Sam. 2. 19.

Cochineal (Isa. 1. 18). Heb. *Tôla'*: Gk. κόκκινος: Zool. S. *Coccus ilicis*. R. V. and A. V. crimson. Lit. crimson worm, an insect attaching itself to the holm-oak. The dye is found in the wingless female. It is dark red, of the size of the kernel of a cherry, but when dried, smaller than a wheat grain. It is very abundant in Palestine.

Cock, Gk. ἀλέκτωρ. Mat. 26. 34; Mk. 13. 35; 14. 30; Lu. 22. 34.

Cockatrice (Isa. 11. 8; 14. 29; 59. 5). Heb. *Tzeph'a, Tziph'ôni*: Gk. ἀσπίς: Zool. S. *Daboia xanthina*; R. V. basilisk; marg. adder.

Cocker, to spoil, or pamper, a child. Ecclus. 30. 9.

Cockle (Job 31. 40). Heb. *Boshah*: Gk. βάτος: R. V. marg. 'or, noisome weeds;' occurs only once in A. V., but the same Hebrew word is translated 'wild grapes' in Isa. 5. 2, 4. The root of the Hebrew suggests a 'noisome weed,' or plant of intolerable stench.

Coffer. 1 Sam. 6. 8, 11, 15.

Coffin. Gen. 50. 26.

Cogitations. Dan. 7. 28. R. V. thoughts.

Cold. Prov. 20. 4, by reason of *c.* R. V. winter.
25. 13, *c.* of snow in harvest.
25. 20, garment in *c.* weather.
25. 25, *c.* waters to thirsty soul.
Mat. 10. 42, cup of *c.* water.
24. 12, love of many wax *c.*
2 Cor. 11. 27, in *c.* and nakedness.
Rev. 3. 15, neither *c.* nor hot.
See Gen. 8. 22; Job 24. 7; 37. 9; Ps. 147. 17.

Col-hozeh, cŏl-hō'-zĕh, 'every one that seeth.' Neh. 3. 15.

Collar. Jud. 8. 26 (R. V. pendants); Job 30. 18.

Collection. 2 Chr. 24. 6; Acts 11. 29; Rom. 15. 26; 1 Cor. 16. 1.

College. 2 Kn. 22. 14; 2 Chr. 34. 22. R. V. second quarter.

Collops, slices, or flakes, of meat or fat. Job 15. 27.

Colony, not a modern colony, but one 'settled with freedmen and soldiers, and organized as to government, laws, and social customs on the model of imperial Rome.' Acts 16. 12.

Colosse, cŏ-lŏs'-sē, a city in the valley of the Lycus, in Asia Minor.

Colossians, cŏ-lŏs'-sĭăns, 'people of Colosse.' encouraged and warned. Col. 1.; 2.
exhorted to holiness. Col. 3.; 4.

Colour. (1) Gen. 37. 3, coat of many *c.*
Prov. 23. 31, *c.* in the cup.
See Ezek. 1. 4; Dan. 10. 6.
(2) pretext, pretence. Acts 27. 30.

Colt. Zec. 9. 9; Mat. 21. 2; John 12. 15.

Come by, to get possession of. Acts 27. 16. R. V. secure.

Comely. Ps. 33. 1, praise is *c.* [seemly.
1 Cor. 11. 13, is it *c.* that a woman. R. V.
See 1 Sam. 16. 18; Prov. 30. 29; Isa. 53. 2. R. V. in Prov. stately.

Comfort (*n.*). Mat. 9. 22; Mk. 10. 49; Lu. 8. 48;
2 Cor. 13. 11, be of good *c.*
Acts 9. 31, *c.* of Holy Ghost.
Rom. 15. 4, patience and *c.* of scriptures.
2 Cor. 1. 3, God of all *c.*
7. 13, were comforted in your *c.*
Phil. 2. 1, if any *c.* of love.
See Job 10. 20; Ps. 94. 19; 119. 50; Isa. 57. 6.

Comfort (*v.*). Gen. 37. 35; Ps. 77. 2; Jer. 31. 15, refused to be *c.*
Ps. 23. 4, rod and staff *c.*
Isa. 40. 1, *c.* ye, *c.* ye, my people.
49. 13; 52. 9, God hath *c.* his people.
61. 2, *c.* all that mourn.
66. 13, as one whom his mother *c.*
Mat. 5. 4, they shall be *c.*
Lu. 16. 25, he is *c.*, and thou art tormented.
John 11. 19, to *c.* concerning their brother.
2 Cor. 1. 4, able to *c.* them.
1 Thes. 4. 18, *c.* one another with these words.
5. 11, wherefore *c.* yourselves together.
5. 14, *c.* the feebleminded.
See Gen. 5. 29; 18. 5; 37. 35.

Comfortable. Isa. 40. 2; Hos. 2. 14; Zec. 1. 13.

Comforter. Job 16. 2, miserable *c.* are ye all.
Ps. 69. 20, looked for *c.* but I found none.
John 14. 16, give you another *C.*
15. 26, when the *C.* is come.

John 16. 7, *C.* will not come.
See 2 Sam. 10. 3; 1 Chr. 19. 3.
Comfortless. John 14. 18.
Command. Ps. 33. 9, he *c.* and it stood fast.
Lu. 8. 25, he *c.* even the winds.
9. 54, *c.* fire from heaven.
John 15. 14, if ye do what I *c.* you.
Acts 17. 30, *c.* all men everywhere.
See Gen. 18. 19; Deu. 28. 8.
Command of God to Adam. Gen. 2. 16.
to Moses. Ex. 3. 14.
to Joshua. Jos. 1. 9.
of Moses to the sons of Levi. Deu. 31. 10.
of Christ to the twelve. Mat. 10. 5; Mk. 16. 15.
to Peter. John 21. 15.
Commander. Isa. 55. 4.
Commandment. Ps. 119. 86, *c.* are faithful.
119. 96, *c.* exceeding broad.
119. 127, I love thy *c.*
119. 143, thy *c.* are my delight. [R. V. precepts.
Mat. 15. 9; Mk. 7. 7; Col. 2. 22, the *c.* of men.
Lu. 23. 56, rested according to *c.*
John 13. 34; 1 John 2. 7; 2 John 5, a new *c.*
Rom. 7. 12, *c.* is holy, just, and good.
1 Cor. 7. 6; 2 Cor. 8. 8, by permission not by *c.*
Eph. 6. 2, first *c.* with promise. [charge.
1 Tim. 1. 5, end of the *c.* is charity. R. V.
Commandments (Ten) delivered. Ex. 20.; 31. 18; Deu. 5. 6.
two tables of, broken. Ex. 32. 19.
renewed. Ex. 34. 1; Deu. 10. 1.
fulfilled by Christ. Mat. 5. 17; 19. 17; 22. 35; Mk. 10. 17; Lu. 10. 25; 18. 18.
Commend. (1) to bring commendation upon, enhance. Lu. 16. 8, *c.* unjust steward.
Rom. 3. 5, unrighteousness *c.* righteousness of God. R. V. enhance.
5. 8, God *c.* his love toward us.
1 Cor. 8. 8, meat *c.* us not.
2 Cor. 3. 1; 5. 12, *c.* ourselves.
4. 2, *c.* to every man's conscience.
10. 18, not he that *c.* himself is approved.
See Prov. 12. 8; Eccl. 8. 15.
(2) to commit to one's charge. Lu. 23. 46, into thy hands I *c.*
See Acts 14. 23; 20. 32.
Commission. Ez. 8. 36; Acts 26. 12.
Commit. Ps. 37. 5, *c.* thy way to the Lord.
Jer. 2. 13, have *c.* two evils. [R. V. trust.
John 2. 24, Jesus did not *c.* himself to them.
5. 22, hath *c.* judgment to Son. R. V. given.
Rom. 3. 2, were *c.* oracles of God. R. V. intrusted with.
2 Cor. 5. 19, had *c.* to us word of reconciliation.
1 Tim. 6. 20, keep what is *c.* to thee.
2 Tim. 2. 2, *c.* thou to faithful men.
1 Pet. 2. 23, *c.* himself to him that judgeth.
See Job 5. 8; Ps. 31. 5; 1 Cor. 9. 17.
Commodious. Acts 27. 12.
Common. (1) shared in by all men alike. Eccl. 6. 1, evil. and it is *c.* among men. R. V. heavy upon.
Mk. 12. 37, the *c.* people heard him gladly.
Acts 2. 44; 4. 32, all things *c.* [bear.
1 Cor. 10. 13, temptation *c.* to men. R. V. can
Eph. 2. 12, aliens from *c.* wealth.
See Lev. 4. 27; Num. 16. 29; 1 Sam. 21. 4. [all).
(2) profane, unclean to a Jew (because used by
Acts 10. 14; 11. 8, never eaten any thing *c.*
10. 15; 11. 9, call not thou *c.*
Commotion. Jer. 10. 22; Lu. 21. 9.
Commune. Job 4. 2, if we *c.* with thee.
Ps. 4. 4; 77. 6; Eccl. 1. 16, *c.* with own heart.
Zec. 1. 14, angel that *c.* with me. R. V. talked.
See Ex. 25. 22; 1 Sam. 19. 3; Lu. 6. 11; 22. 4.
Communicate, to impart. Gal. 6. 6, let him that is taught *c.*
1 Tim. 6. 18, be willing to *c.*
Heb. 13. 16, do good and *c.*
See Gal. 2. 2; Phil. 4. 14, 15.
Communication, conversation, talk. Mat. 5. 37, let your *c.* be yea.
Lu. 24. 17, what manner of *c.*
1 Cor. 15. 33, evil *c.* corrupt good manners. R. V. company.
Eph. 4. 29, let no corrupt *c.* proceed.
See 2 Kn. 9. 11; Philem. 6.
Communion, joint partaking, partaking in common. 2 Cor. 6. 14; 13. 14.
Communion of the Body and Blood of Christ. 1 Cor. 10. 16.
Lord's Supper instituted. Mat. 26. 26; Mk. 14. 22; Lu. 22. 19; 1 Cor. 11. 23.
self-examination for. Acts 2. 42; 20. 7; 1 Cor. 10. 21; 11. 28.
unworthily partaken. 1 Cor. 11. 27.
Communion of Saints. *See* FELLOWSHIP.
Compact, firmly united, strongly built. Ps. 122. 3; Eph. 4. 16.
Companion. Job 30. 29, a *c.* to owls.
Ps. 119. 63, a *c.* to them that fear thee.
Prov. 13. 20, *c.* of fools shall be destroyed.
28. 7, *c.* of riotous men.
28. 24, the *c.* of a destroyer.
Acts 19. 29, Paul's *c.* in travel.
Phil. 2. 25; Rev. 1. 9, brother and *c.* in labour.
See Ex. 32. 27; Jud. 11. 38; 14. 20.
Company. 1 Sam. 10. 5; 19. 20, a *c.* of prophets.
Ps. 55. 14, walked to house of God in *c.* R. V. with the throng.
68. 11, great was the *c.* of those. R. V. the women . . . are a great host.
Mk. 6. 39; Lu. 9. 14, sit down by *c.*
2 Thes. 3. 14, have no *c.* with him. [hosts.
Heb. 12. 22, innumerable *c.* of angels. R. V.
See Num. 16. 6; Jud. 9. 37; 18. 23.
Company, evil, to be avoided. Ps. 1. 1; 26. 4; Prov. 1. 10; 2. 12; 4. 14; 12. 11; 13. 20; 14. 7; 22. 24; 24. 19; 29. 3, 24; Rom. 1. 32; 1 Cor. 5. 9; 15. 33; Eph. 5. 7.
Compare. Prov. 3. 15; 8. 11, not to be *c.* to wisdom.
Isa. 40. 18, what likeness will ye *c.* to him?
46. 5, to whom will ye *c.* me.
Lam. 4. 2, *c.* to fine gold.
Rom. 8. 18, not worthy to be *c.* with glory.
1 Cor. 2. 13, *c.* spiritual things with spiritual.
See Ps. 89. 6; 2 Cor. 10. 12.
Comparison. Jud. 8. 2; Hag. 2. 3; Mk. 4. 30.
Compass (*n.*). Isa. 44. 13, marketh it with a *c.*
Compass (*v.*), encircle, encompass, make a circuit of.
Ps. 5. 12, with favour *c.* as with a shield.
32. 7, *c.* with songs of deliverance.
32. 10, mercy shall *c.* him about. [gird.
Isa. 50. 11, *c.* yourselves with sparks. R. V.
Mat. 23. 15, *c.* sea and land.
Lu. 21. 20, Jerusalem *c.* with armies.
Heb. 5. 2, he also is *c.* with infirmity.
12. 1, *c.* about with cloud of witnesses.
See Jos. 6. 3; Job 16. 13; Jer. 31. 22.
Compass, fetch a, to make a circuit. 2 Sam. 5. 23; 2 Kn. 3. 9; Acts 28. 13.
Compassion. Ps. 78. 38; 86. 15; 111. 4; 112. 4, full of *c.*
Isa. 49. 15, that she should not have *c.*
Lam. 3. 22, his *c.* fail not.
3. 32; Mic. 7. 19, yet will he have *c.* [with *c.*
Mat. 9. 36; 14. 14; Mk. 1. 41; 6. 34, Jesus moved
18. 33, *c.* on thy fellowservant. R. V. mercy.
20. 34, had *c.* on them and touched.
Mk. 5. 19, the Lord hath had *c.* R. V. mercy.
9. 22, have *c.*, and help us.
Lu. 10. 33, the Samaritan had *c.*
15. 20, father had *c.*, and ran.
Rom. 9. 15, I will have *c.* on whom I will.
Heb. 5. 2, have *c.* on ignorant. R. V. bear gently with.
1 Pet. 3. 8, of one mind, having *c.*
1 John 3. 17, shutteth up bowels of *c.*
Jude 22, of some have *c.*, making a difference. R. V. mercy.
Compassion. Job 6. 14; Ps. 35. 13; Zec. 7. 9; Rom. 12. 15; 2 Cor. 11. 29; Gal. 6. 2; Col. 3. 12; Heb. 13. 3; Jas. 1. 27; 1 Pet. 3. 8.

Christ's, Mat. 15. 32; 20. 34; Lu. 7. 13, 21; Heb. 2. 17; 4. 15; 5. 2.
Compel. Mat. 5. 41, *c.* thee to go a mile.
27. 32; Mk. 15. 21, *c.* to bear cross.
Lu. 14. 23, *c.* to come in. [strove to make.
Acts 26. 11, I *c.* them to blaspheme. R. V.
See Lev. 25. 39; 2 Cor. 12. 11; Gal. 2. 3.
Complain. Ps. 144. 14, no *c.* in our streets. R. V. outcry.
Lam. 3. 39, wherefore doth a living man *c.*
Jude 16, these are murmurers, *c.*
See Num. 11. 1; Jud. 21. 22; Job 7. 11.
Complaint. Job 23. 2, to day is my *c.* bitter.
Ps. 142. 2, I poured out my *c.* before him.
See 1 Sam. 1. 16; Job 7. 13; 9. 27; 10. 1.
Complete. Lev. 23. 15; Col. 2. 10; 4. 12. [3. 18.
Comprehend. (1) understand. Job 37. 5; Eph.
(2) to comprise, include, contain. Isa. 40. 12; Rom. 13. 9.
(3) to overcome (John 1. 5). R. V. margin.
Conaniah, cō-nă-nī'-ăh. 2 Chr. 35. 9, same as CONONIAH.
Conceal. Prov. 12. 23, prudent man *c.* knowledge.
25. 2, glory of God to *c.* a thing.
Jer. 50. 2, publish and *c.* not.
See Gen. 37. 26; Deu. 13. 8.
Conceit, estimation, opinion. Rom. 11. 25; 12. 16, wise in your own *c.*
Conceit (reproved). Prov. 3. 7; 12. 15; 18. 11; 20. 5; 28. 11; Isa. 5. 21.
Conceive. Ps. 7. 14, *c.* mischief brought forth falsehood.
51. 5, in sin did my mother *c.* me.
Acts 5. 4, why hast thou *c.* this thing.
Jas. 1. 15, when lust *c.*, it bringeth forth.
See Job 15. 35; Isa. 7. 14; 59. 4.
Concern. Lu. 24. 27, things *c.* himself.
Rom. 9. 5, as *c.* the flesh Christ came.
16. 19, simple *c.* evil.
Phil. 4. 15, *c.* giving and receiving.
1 Tim. 6. 21, have erred *c.* the faith.
1 Pet. 4. 12, *c.* fiery trial.
See Lev. 6. 3; Num. 10. 29; Ps. 90. 13; 135. 14.
Concision, a cutting off, hence a schism, a faction. Phil. 3. 2. [28.
Conclude. (1) to decide. Acts 21. 25; Rom. 3.
(2) to include, class together. Rom. 11. 32; Gal. 3. 22.
Conclusion. Eccl. 12. 13. R. V. end.
Concord. 2 Cor. 6. 15.
Concupiscence, evil desire, lust. Col. 3. 5; 1 Thes. 4. 5, mortify evil *c.* [*c.* me.
Condemn. Job 10. 2, I will say to God, do not
Am. 2. 8, drink wine of the *c.* R. V. such as have been fined.
Mat. 12. 7, ye would not have *c.* the guiltless.
12. 37, by thy words shalt be *c.*
12. 42; Lu. 11. 31, rise in judgment and *c.*
20. 18, shall *c.* him to death.
27. 3, Judas when he saw he was *c.*
Mk. 14. 64, all *c.* him to be guilty.
Lu. 6. 37, *c.* not and ye shall not be *c.*
John 3. 17, God sent not his Son to *c.* R. V. judge.
3. 18, believe not is *c.* R. V. judged.
8. 10, hath no man *c.* thee?
8. 11, neither do I *c.* thee.
Rom. 2. 1, thou *c.* thyself.
8. 3, *c.* sin in the flesh.
8. 34, who is he that *c.*?
14. 22, that *c.* not himself. R. V. judgeth.
Tit. 2. 8, sound speech that cannot be *c.*
Jas. 5. 6, ye *c.* and killed the just.
5. 9, grudge not lest ye be *c.* R. V. judged.
1 John 3. 21, if our heart *c.* us not.
See Job 9. 20; 15. 6; Mat. 12. 41.
Condemnation. John 3. 19, this is the *c.*, that light. R. V. judgement.
2 Cor. 3. 9, the ministration of *c.*
1 Tim. 3. 6, the *c.* of the devil.
Jas. 5. 12, lest ye fall into *c.* R. V. judgement.
Jude 4, of old ordained to this *c.*
Condemnation for sin, universal. Ps. 14. 3; 53. 3; Rom. 3. 12, 19; 5. 12, 16; 6. 23.
for unbelief. John 3. 18.
by the law. 2 Cor. 3. 6, 9. [23. 14.
by impenitence and hypocrisy. Mat. 11. 20;
according to our deeds. 2 Cor. 11. 15.
of false teachers. 2 Pet. 2. 1; Jude 4.
deliverance from, by Christ. John 3. 18; 5. 24; Rom. 8. 1, 33.
final. Mat. 25. 46; Rev. 20. 15.
Condescend. Rom. 12. 16.
Condition. 1 Sam. 11. 2; Lu. 14. 32.
Conduit. 2 Kn. 18. 17; 20. 20; Isa. 7. 3; 36. 2. Heb. *teâlâh:* Gk. ὑδραγωγός: Lat. *aquæductus:* a channel for the conveyance of water. Solomon supplied water for Jerusalem through a conduit from a reservoir 2½ miles south-west of Bethlehem. A conduit, hewn out of the solid rock, 1,750 feet in length, unites the Pool of Siloam with the 'Virgin's Fountain.'
Coney (Lev. 11. 5; Ps. 104. 18; Prov. 30. 26). Heb. *Shâphân:* Gk. δασύπους. R. V. marg. correctly, '*Hyrax Syriacus*, or rock-badger,' an animal somewhat like a rabbit in size and habits.
Confection, compound of various spices. Ex. 30. 35. R. V. perfume.
Confectionaries, those who make or sell confections, as sweetmeats, or spices. 1 Sam. 8. 13.
Confederate. Gen. 14. 13; Isa. 7. 2; 8. 12; Obad. 7.
Conference. Gal. 2. 6, somewhat in *c.* R. V. in repute.
Conferred. Gal. 1. 16.
Confess. Prov. 28. 13, whoso *c.* and forsaketh.
Mat. 10. 32; Lu. 12. 8, *c.* me before men.
John 9. 22, if any man did *c.*
12. 42, rulers did not *c.* him.
Acts 23. 8, Pharisees *c.* both.
Rom. 10. 9, shall *c.* with thy mouth.
14. 11; Phil. 2. 11, every tongue *c.*
Heb. 11. 13, *c.* they were strangers.
Jas. 5. 16, *c.* your faults one to another.
1 John 1. 9, if we *c.* our sins.
4. 2, every spirit that *c.* Christ.
4. 15, whoso shall *c.* that Jesus is the Christ.
Rev. 3. 5, I will *c.* his name before my Father.
See 1 Kn. 8. 33; 2 Chr. 6. 24.
Confession. 1 Tim. 6. 13.
Confession of Christ unto salvation. Mat. 10. 32; Mk. 8. 35; John 12. 42; Rom. 10. 9; 2 Tim. 2. 12; 1 John 2. 23; 4. 2.
of sin. Lev. 5. 5; 16. 21; Jos. 7. 19; Dan. 9. 20; 1 John 1. 9.
examples of. Num. 12. 11; 21. 7; Jos. 7. 20; 1 Sam. 7.; 15. 24; Ez. 9. 6; Neh. 1. 6; 9.; Ps. 51.; Dan. 9. 4; Lu. 23. 41.
at the offering of first fruits. Deu. 26. 1.
one to another. Jas. 5. 16. [of the earth.
Confidence. (1) Ps. 65. 5, the *c.* of all the ends
118. 8, 9, than to put *c.* in man.
Prov. 3. 26, the Lord shall be thy *c.*
14. 26, in fear of the Lord is strong *c.*
Isa. 30. 15, in *c.* shall be your strength.
Jer. 2. 37, hath rejected thy *c.*
Eph. 3. 12, access with *c.* by the faith of him.
Phil. 3. 3, 4, no *c.* in flesh.
(2) R. V. boldness. Heb. 3. 6, 14, hold fast *c.*
10. 35, cast not away *c.*
1 John 2. 28, we may have *c.*
3. 21, we have *c.* toward God.
5. 14, this is the *c.* we have in him.
See Job 4. 6; 18. 14; 31. 24; Prov. 25. 19.
Confident. Ps. 27. 3; Prov. 14. 16; 2 Cor. 5. 6; Phil. 1. 6.
Confirm. Isa. 35. 3, *c.* the feeble knees.
Mk. 16. 20, *c.* the word with signs.
Acts 14. 22, *c.* the souls of the disciples.
15. 32, 41, exhorted brethren, and *c.* them.
Rom. 15. 8, *c.* the promises made to fathers.
See 2 Kn. 15. 19.
Confirmation. Phil. 1. 7; Heb. 6. 16.
Confiscation. Ez. 7. 26.
Conflict. Phil. 1. 30; Col. 2. 1.
Conform. Rom. 8. 29; 12. 2; Phil. 3. 10.

Confound, to put to confusion, destroy. Ps. 22. 5, fathers trusted and were not *c.*
40. 14; 70. 2, ashamed and *c.*
Acts 2. 6, multitude were *c.*
9. 22, Saul *c.* the Jews.
See Gen. 11. 7; Ps. 71. 13; 129. 5; Jer. 1. 17.
Confused. Isa. 9. 5; Acts 19. 32.
Confusion. (1) ruin, destruction. Ps. 70. 2; 71. 1; 109. 29; Isa. 24. 10.
(2) Dan. 9. 7, to us belongeth *c.* of faces.
Acts 19. 29, city was filled with *c.*
1 Cor. 14. 33, God not author of *c.*
Congealed. Ex. 15. 8.
Congratulate. 1 Chr. 18. 10. R. V. bless.
Congregation. Num. 14. 10, all the *c.* bade stone them.
Neh. 5. 13, all the *c.* said Amen.
Ps. 1. 5, nor sinners in the *c.* of the righteous.
26. 12, in the *c.* will I bless the Lord.
Prov. 21. 16, in the *c.* of the dead.
Joel 2. 16, sanctify the *c.*
Acts 13. 43, when the *c.* was broken up.
See Ex. 16. 2; 39. 32.
Congregation (of Israel), all to keep the passover. Ex. 12, &c.
sin offering for. Lev. 4. 13; 16. 17. [15. 35.
to stone offenders. Lev. 24. 14; Num. 14. 10;
who not to enter. Deu. 23. 1.
Coniah, cō-nī′-ăh, contracted from Jeconiah. Jer. 22. 24.
Cononiah, cō-nō-nī′-ăh, 'Jehovah has set up.' 2 Chr. 31. 12.
Conquerors. Rom. 8. 37; Rev. 6. 2.
Conscience. (1) Acts 24. 16, *c.* void of offence.
Rom. 2. 15; 9. 1; 2 Cor. 1. 12, *c.* bearing witness.
13. 5; 1 Cor. 10. 25, 27, 28, for *c.* sake.
1 Cor. 8. 10, 12, weak *c.*
1 Tim. 1. 5, 19; Heb. 13. 18; 1 Pet. 3. 16, a good *c.*
3. 9, mystery of faith in pure *c.*
4. 2, *c.* seared with hot iron.
Heb. 9. 14, purge *c.* from dead works.
10. 22, hearts sprinkled from evil *c.* [10. 2.
(2) consciousness, knowledge. 1 Cor. 8. 7; Heb.
Conscience convicts of sin. Gen. 3. 10; 4. 13; 42. 21; 1 Sam. 24. 5; Prov. 20. 27; Mat. 27. 3; Lu. 9. 7; John 8. 9; Rom. 2. 15.
purified by faith. 1 Tim. 1. 19; 3. 9; 2 Tim. 1. 3.
purified by blood of Christ. Heb. 9. 14; 10. 2, 22.
a good. Acts 23. 1; Heb. 13. 18; 1 Pet. 3. 16.
effects of a good. Acts 24. 16; Rom. 13. 5; 14. 22; 2 Cor. 1. 12; 1 Pet. 2. 19.
of others to be respected. Rom. 14. 21; 1 Cor. 8.; 10. 28.
seared. 1 Tim. 4. 2; defiled, Tit. 1. 15.
ignorant. Acts 26. 9; Rom. 10. 2. [Lord.
Consecrate. 1 Chr. 29. 5, to *c.* his service to the
Mic. 4. 13, I will *c.*
Heb. 7. 28, who is *c.* forevermore. R. V. perfected.
10. 20, living way which he hath *c.* R. V. dedicated.
Consecration of priests. Ex. 28. 3; 29.; Lev. 8.
of the Levites. Ex. 32. 29; Num. 8. 5.
of Christ. Heb. 7.; 8.; 10. 20.
Consent. Ps. 50. 18, a thief, thou *c.* with him.
Prov. 1. 10, if sinners entice thee, *c.* not.
Zep. 3. 9, to serve with one *c.*
Lu. 14. 18, with one *c.* began to make excuse.
See Deu. 13. 8; Acts 8. 1; Rom. 7. 16.
Consider. Ps. 8. 3, when I *c.* the heavens.
41. 1, blessed is he that *c.* the poor.
48. 13, *c.* her palaces.
Ps. 50. 22, *c.* this, ye that forget God.
Prov. 6. 6, *c.* her ways and be wise.
23. 1, *c.* diligently what is before thee.
24. 12, doth not he *c.* it. [eth.
Prov. 28. 22, and *c.* not that poverty. R. V. know-
Eccl. 5. 1, they *c.* not that they do evil. R. V. know.
7. 14, in day of adversity *c.*
Isa. 1. 3, my people doth not *c.* [understand.
Jer. 23. 20; 30. 24, in latter days ye shall *c.* R. V.
Ezek. 12. 3, it may be they will *c.*
Hag. 1. 5, 7, *c.* your ways.
Mat. 6. 28; Lu. 12. 27, *c.* lilies of the field.
7. 3, *c.* not the beam.
Lu. 12. 24, *c.* the ravens.
Gal. 6. 1, *c.* thyself lest thou also be tempted.
Heb. 3. 1, *c.* the Apostle and High Priest.
7. 4, now *c.* how great this man was.
10. 24, *c.* one another to provoke.
12. 3, *c.* him that endured.
13. 7, *c.* the end of their conversation.
Consideration, exhortations to. Deu. 4. 39; 32. 29; Jud. 18. 14; 1 Sam. 12. 24; Job 23. 15; 37. 14; Ps. 8. 3; 50. 22; Prov. 6. 6; Eccl. 4. 1; 5. 1; 7. 13; Hag. 1. 5; Mat. 6. 28; 2 Tim. 2. 7; Heb. 3. 1; 7. 4; 10. 24; 12. 3.
Consist. (1) Lu. 12. 15. (2) subsist, remain unchanged. Col. 1. 17.
Consolation. Job 15. 11, are the *c.* of God small.
Lu. 6. 24, ye have received your *c.*
Rom. 15. 5, the God of *c.* R. V. comfort.
Phil. 2. 1, if there be any *c.* in Christ.
2 Thes. 2. 16, everlasting *c.* R. V. comfort.
Heb. 6. 18, strong *c.* R. V. encouragement.
See Jer. 16. 7; Lu. 2. 25; Acts 4. 36.
Consolation under affliction. Deu. 33. 27; Job 19. 25; Ps. 10. 14; 23.; 34. 6; 41. 3; 42. 5; 51. 17; 55. 22; 69. 29; 71. 9, 18; 73. 26; 94. 19; 119. 50; 126.; Eccl. 7. 3; Isa. 1. 18; 12. 1; Lam. 3. 22; Ezek. 14. 22; Hos. 2. 14; Mic. 7. 18; Zec. 1. 17; Mat. 11. 28; Lu. 4. 18; 15.; John 14.; 15.; 16.; Rom. 15. 4; 16. 20; 1 Cor. 10. 13; 14. 3; 2 Cor. 1. 3; 5. 1; 7. 6; 12. 9; Col. 1. 11; 1 Thes. 4. 14; 5. 11; 2 Thes. 2. 16; Heb. 4. 9; 6. 18; 12.; Jas. 1. 12; 4. 7; 2 Pet. 2. 9; Rev. 2. 10; 7. 14; 14. 13.
Consort, associate with. Acts 17. 4.
Conspiracy of Absalom. 2 Sam. 15. 2.
against Christ. Mat. 26. 3; Mk. 3. 6; 14. 1; Lu. 22. 2; John 11. 55; 13. 18.
against Paul. Acts 23. 12.
Conspirators. 2 Sam. 15. 31.
Constancy. Rom. 16. 4.
of Ruth. Ru. 1. 14.
Constantly, without varying, confidently. 1 Chr. 28. 7.
Prov. 21. 28; Acts 12. 15; Tit. 3. 8.
Constrain. Job 32. 18; Lu. 24. 29; 2 Cor. 5. 14. 1 Pet. 5. 2.
Consult. Ps. 83. 3; Mk. 15. 1; Lu. 14. 31; John 12. 10.
Consume. Ex. 3. 2, bush was not *c.*
Deu. 4. 24; 9. 3; Heb. 12. 29, a *c.* fire.
1 Kn. 18. 38; 2 Chr. 7. 1, fire fell and *c.* the sacrifice.
Job 20. 26, fire not blown shall *c.* him.
Ps. 39. 11, *c.* away like a moth.
Mal. 3. 6, therefore ye are not *c.*
Lu. 9. 54, *c.* them as Elias did.
Gal. 5. 15, take heed that ye be not *c.*
Jas. 4. 3, that ye may *c.* it on your lusts.
See Ex. 32. 10; 33. 3; Deu. 5. 25; Jos. 24. 20.
Consummation. Dan. 9. 27.
Consumption. Lev. 26. 16; Deu. 28. 22; Isa. 10. 22. R. V. in Isa. consummation.
Contain. (1) 1 Kn. 8. 27; 2 Chr. 2. 6; 6. 18. (2) to remain continent, restrain themselves. 1 Cor. 7. 9.
Contemn. Ps. 10. 13; 15. 4; 107. 11; Ezek. 21. 10.
Contempt. Prov. 18. 3, wicked cometh, then cometh *c.*
Dan. 12. 2, awake to everlasting *c.*
See Esth. 1. 18; Job 31. 34; Ps. 119. 22.
Contemptible. Mal. 1. 7, 12; 2. 9; 2 Cor. 10. 10.
Contend. Isa. 49. 25, I will *c.* with him that *c.*
50. 8, who will *c.* with me.
Jer. 12. 5, how canst thou *c.* with horses.
See Job 10. 2; 13. 8; Eccl. 6. 10; Jude 3, 9.
Content. Mk. 15. 15, willing to *c.* the people.
Lu. 3. 14, be *c.* with your wages.
Phil. 4. 11, I have learned to be *c.*
1 Tim. 6. 6, godliness with *c.* is great gain.
6. 8, having food let us be *c.*
Heb. 13. 5, be *c.* with such things as ye have.
See Gen. 37. 27; Jos. 7. 7; Job 6. 28; Prov. 6. 35.

Contention. Prov. 18. 18, the lot causeth *c.* to cease.
19. 13, *c.* of a wife.
23. 29, who hath *c.*
Acts 15. 39, the *c.* was sharp.
1 Cor. 1. 11, there are *c.* among you.
Phil. 1. 16, preach Christ of *c.* R. V. faction.
1 Thes. 2. 2, to speak with much *c.* R. V. conflict.
Tit. 3. 9, avoid *c.* and strivings.
See Prov. 13. 10; 17. 14; 18. 6; 22. 10.
Contentious. Prov. 21. 19; 26. 21; 27. 15; Rom. 2. 8; 1 Cor. 11. 16.
Contentment, godliness with, great gain. Ps. 37. 16; Prov. 30. 8; 1 Tim. 6. 6.
exhortations to. Ps. 37. 1; Lu. 3. 14; 1 Cor. 7. 20; 1 Tim. 6. 8; Heb. 13. 5.
Continual. Ps. 34. 1; 71. 6, praise *c.* in my mouth.
40. 11, let thy truth *c.* preserve me.
73. 23, I am *c.* with thee.
Prov 6. 21, bind them *c.* on thine heart.
15. 15, merry heart hath a *c.* feast.
Isa. 14. 6, smote with a *c.* stroke.
52. 5, my name is *c.* blasphemed.
Lu. 18. 5, lest by her *c.* coming.
24. 53, were *c.* in the temple.
Acts 6. 4, give ourselves *c.* to prayer.
Rom. 9. 2, I have *c.* sorrow in my heart.
Heb. 7. 3, abideth a priest *c.*
See Ex. 29. 42; Num. 4. 7; Job 1. 5.
Continuance. Deu. 28. 59; Ps. 139. 16; Isa. 64. 5; Rom. 2. 7.
Continue. Job 14. 2, as a shadow and *c.* not.
Ps. 72. 17, name shall *c.* as long as the sun.
Isa. 5. 11, *c.* till wine inflame them.
Jer. 32. 14, evidences may *c.* many days.
Lu. 6. 12, he *c.* all night in prayer.
22. 28, that *c.* with me in my temptation.
John 8. 31, if ye *c.* in my word.
15. 9, *c.* ye in my love.
Acts 1. 14; 2. 46, *c.* with one accord.
12. 16, Peter *c.* knocking.
13. 43, to *c.* in grace of God.
14. 22, exhorting them to *c.* in faith.
26. 22, I *c.* unto this day.
Rom. 6. 1, shall we *c.* in sin.
12. 12; Col. 4. 2, *c.* in prayer.
Gal. 3. 10, that *c.* not in all things.
Col. 1. 23; 1 Tim. 2. 15, if ye *c.* in the faith.
1 Tim. 4. 16; 2 Tim. 3. 14, *c.* in them.
Heb. 7. 23, not suffered to *c.* by reason.
7. 24, this man *c.* ever.
13. 1, let brotherly love *c.*
13. 14, here have we no *c.* city.
Jas. 4. 13, and *c.* there a year.
2 Pet. 3. 4, all things *c.* as they were.
1 John 2. 19, no doubt have *c.* with us.
See 1 Sam. 12. 14; 13. 14; 2 Sam. 7. 29.
Contradiction. Heb. 7. 7; 12. 3.
Contrariwise. 2 Cor. 2. 7; Gal. 2. 7; 1 Pet. 3. 9.
Contrary. Acts 18. 13, *c.* to the law.
26. 9, many things *c.* to name of Jesus.
Gal. 5. 17, *c.* the one to the other.
1 Thes. 2. 15, *c.* to all men.
1 Tim. 1. 10, *c.* to sound doctrine.
Tit. 2. 8, he of the *c.* part may be ashamed.
See Lev. 26. 21; Esth. 9. 1; Mat. 14. 24; Acts 17. 7.
Contribution for saints. Acts 20. 35; Rom. 15. 26; 2 Cor. 8.
Contrite, ground to powder; hence, humbled, penitent, sorrowful. (Lat. *contritus.*) Ps. 34. 18; 51. 17; Isa. 57. 15; 66. 2.
Controversy. Jer. 25. 31, a *c.* with the nations.
Mic. 6. 2, hath a *c.* with his people.
1 Tim. 3. 16, without *c.* great is the mystery.
See Deu. 17. 8; 19. 17; 21. 5; 25. 1.
Convenient, becoming, fitting, suitable. Prov. 30. 8, feed me with food *c.* R. V. needful.
Acts 24. 25, when I have a *c.* season.
Rom. 1. 28, things which are not *c.*
Eph. 5. 4, talking, jesting, are not *c.*
See Jer. 40. 4; Mk. 6. 21; 1 Cor. 16. 12.
Conversant. Jos. 8. 35; 1 Sam. 25. 15.

Conversation. (1) citizenship. Eph. 2. 3; Phil. 3. 20.
(2) behaviour, manner of life. Ps. 37. 14, such as be of upright *c.*
50. 23, that ordereth his *c.* aright.
Phil. 1. 27, *c.* as becometh the gospel.
1 Tim. 4. 12, an example in *c.*
Heb. 13. 7, considering end of their *c.*
1 Pet. 1. 15; 2 Pet. 3. 11, holy *c.*
1. 18, redeemed from vain *c.*
2. 12, your *c.* honest among Gentiles.
3. 1, won by *c.* of wives.
2 Pet. 2. 7, vexed with filthy *c.*
Conversation (*conduct*), upright. Ps. 37. 14; 50. 23; Phil. 3. 20; 1 Tim. 4. 12; Heb. 13. 5; Jas. 3. 13; 1 Pet. 2. 12; 2 Pet. 3. 11.
as becometh the gospel. 2 Cor. 1. 12; Eph. 4. 1; Phil. 1. 27; 1 Pet. 1. 15; 2. 12.
(*speech*): of the Lord with Moses, Ex. 33. 9. Jesus with Nicodemus, John 3. with the woman of Samaria, John 4. 7-27. on the walk to Emmaus, Lu. 24. 13. of Peter with Cornelius, Acts 10. 27. of Festus and Agrippa, Acts 26. 31. *See* Col. 4. 6.
Conversion of sinners proceeds from God. 1 Kn. 18. 37; Ps. 19. 7; 78. 34; Prov. 1. 23; Jer. 31. 18; John 6. 44; Acts 3. 26; 11. 21. *See* Ps. 51. 13; Isa. 1. 16; 6. 10; Ezek. 18. 23; 36. 25; Joel 2. 13; 2 Cor. 5. 17; 1 Thes. 1. 9.
call to. Isa. 1. 16; Mat. 3. 2; 4. 17; 10. 7; Acts 2. 38; 17. 30; Jas. 4. 8.
prayer for. Ps. 80. 7; 85. 4; Lam. 5. 21.
instruments of, blessed. Dan. 12. 3; 1 Tim. 4. 16; Jas. 5. 19.
of the Jews. Acts 2. 41; 4. 32, 6. 7.
of Paul. Acts 9.; 22.; 26.
of the Gentiles, foretold, Isa. 2. 2; 11. 10; 60. 5; 66. 12. fulfilled, Acts 8. 26; 10.; 15. 3; Rom. 10.; 11.; 1 Cor. 1.;. Eph. 2.; 3.; 1 Thes. 1.
Convert. Ps. 19. 7, perfect, *c.* the soul. R. V. restoring.
Isa. 6. 10; Mat. 13. 15; Mk. 4. 12; John 12. 40; Acts 28. 27, lest they *c.* R. V. turn again.
Mat. 18. 3, except ye be *c.* R. V. turn.
Lu. 22. 32, when *c.* strengthen thy brethren.
Acts 3. 19, repent and be *c.* R. V turn again.
Jas. 5. 19, 20, and one *c.* him.
See Ps. 51. 13; Isa. 1. 27.
Convicted. John 8. 9.
Convince. (1) to refute. Job 32. 12, none of you that *c.* Job.
Tit. 1. 9, able to *c.* gainsayers.
(2) to convict. John 8. 46, which of you *c.* me of [sin.
See Acts 18. 28; 1 Cor. 14. 24.
Convocation. Ex. 12. 16; Lev. 23. 2; Num. 28. [26.
Cook. 1 Sam. 8. 13; 9. 23, 24.
Cool. Gen. 3. 8; Lu. 16. 24.
Coos, cō′-ŏs, an island generally called Cos. Paul sails to. Acts 21. 1.
Copper, Brass (Ex. 38. 8; 2 Kn. 25. 13; Ez. 8. 27). Heb. *Neḥôsheth:* Gk. χαλκός. Brass, R. V. The Hebrew term is used indifferently for pure copper, and its alloys, bronze (copper and zinc) and brass (copper and tin).
Coppersmith. 2 Tim. 4. 14.
Copy. Deu. 17. 18; Jos. 8. 32; Prov. 25. 1.
Cor, the same as Homer, *q. v.* Ezek. 45. 14. *See* Measures.
Corban (Heb. *Korbān*, an offering). The word is used in the O. T. of anything offered or vowed to God. *See* Mk. 7. 11.
Cord. Prov. 5. 22, holden with the *c.* of sins.
Eccl. 4. 12, a threefold *c.*
12. 6, silver *c.* loosed.
Isa. 5. 18, draw iniquity with *c.*
54. 2, lengthen *c.*
Hos. 11. 4, the *c.* of a man.
John 2. 15, scourge of small *c.*
See Jud. 15. 13; Ps. 2. 3; 118. 27; Jer. 38. 6.
Core, cōr′-ē, Greek form of Korah. Jude 11.
Coriander (Ex. 16. 31). Heb. *Gad:* Gk. κόριον: Bot. N. *Coriandrum sativum.* Only once mentioned, when manna is compared to it. It is an

umbelliferous plant, with white blossoms and globular aromatic fruits.

Corinth, cŏr′-ĭnth, one of the chief commercial cities of Greece, on the isthmus connecting its two parts. Paul and Apollos at. Acts 18.; 19. 1.

Corinthians, cŏ-rĭn′-thĭ-ăns, inhabitants of Corinth.
their divisions, &c., censured. 1 Cor. 1.; 5.; 11. 18.
their faith and graces. 2 Cor. 3.
instructed concerning spiritual gifts. 1 Cor. 14.; and the resurrection. 1 Cor. 15.
exhorted to charity, &c. 1 Cor. 13.; 14. 1; 2 Cor. 8.; 9.
their false teachers exposed. 2 Cor. 11. 3, 4, 13.
Paul commends himself to. 2 Cor. 11.; 12.

Cormorant. (1) (Lev. 11. 17). Heb. *Shâlâk:* Gk. καταράκτης. (Specimen, *Phalacrocorax carbo.*) The common cormorant which frequents the coast, and is found on the Sea of Galilee and on the Jordan.
(2) (Isa. 34. 11). Heb. *Kâath:* Gk. πελεκᾶς: R. V. and A. V. marg. pelican. The true rendering.

Corn, a general name for any kind of grain, as wheat, barley, millet, spelt. Eleven different Hebrew words are used for corn in its different states.
(1) (Num. 18. 27). Heb. *Dâgân:* Gk. σῖτος: grain in general.
(2) (Jud. 15. 5). Heb. *Kâmah:* Gk. στάχυς: standing corn.
(3) (Gen. 41. 49). Heb. *Bar:* Gk. σῖτος: winnowed corn or grain.
(4) (Ruth 2. 2). Heb. *Shibbôleth:* Gk. στάχυς: ears of corn.
(5) (Lev. 2. 14). Heb. *Karmel:* Gk. χῖδρον: R. V. corn in the ear.
(6) (Jos. 5. 11). Heb. *'Abûr:* Gk. σῖτος: old corn.
(7) (Jos. 5. 11). Heb. *Kâli:* (omitted in LXX.) parched corn.
(8) (Lev. 2. 16). Heb. *Géres:* Gk. χῖδρον: R. V. bruised corn.
(9) (Ruth 2. 7). Heb. *'Omer:* Gk. δράγμα: sheaves.
(10) (Job 24. 6). Heb. *Belîl:* provender as in R. V.
(11) Gen. 42. 1, 2, 3). Heb. *Shéber:* Gk. πράως σῖτος: grain in general.
Gen. 42. 2; Acts 7. 12, *c.* in Egypt.
Job 5. 26, like as a shock of *c.*
Ps. 4. 7, in time their *c.* increased.
65. 9, prepared them *c.*
65. 13, valleys covered over with *c.*
72. 16, handful of *c.* in the earth.
Prov. 11. 26, he that withholdeth *c.*
Zec. 9. 17, *c.* shall make men cheerful.
Mat. 12. 1; Mk. 2. 23; Lu. 6. 1, pluck *c.*
Mk. 4. 28, full *c.* in the ear. [grain.
John 12. 24, a *c.* of wheat fall into ground. R. V.
See Gen. 27. 28; 41. 57; Deu. 33. 28; Isa. 36. 17.

Corn (treading out). The unthreshed wheat is laid upon the ground in a circle, and a yoke of oxen driven round and round over it, dragging after them a heavy log of wood, on the under surface of which are inserted rows of thin flint stones, about two inches apart, and projecting half an inch from the surface. Deu. 25. 4; 1 Cor. 9. 9; 1 Tim. 5. 18.

Cornelius, côr-nē′-lĭ-ŭs, devout centurion. Acts 10. 1.
his prayer answered, Acts 10. 3. sends for Peter, 10. 9. baptized, 10. 48.

Corner. Ps. 118. 22; Eph. 2. 20, head stone of *c.*
144. 12, daughters as *c.* stones.
Isa. 28. 16; 1 Pet. 2. 6, a precious *c.* stone.
Mat. 6. 5, pray in *c.* of the streets.
Rev. 7. 1, on four *c.* of the earth.
See Job 1. 19; Prov. 7. 8; 21. 9.

Cornet. (1) (Dan. 3. 5, 7, 10, 15). Heb. *Kéren:* Gk. σάλπιγξ. The primitive trumpet of ram's horn.
(2) (1 Chr. 15. 28; 2 Chr. 15. 14; Ps. 98. 6; Hos. 5. 8).
Heb. *Shôphâr:* Gk. σωφέρ, σάλπιγξ, κερατίνη. A long horn turned up at the end, the national trumpet for rallying the people.
(3) (2 Sam. 6. 5). Heb. *Mĕna' an' im:* Gk. αὐλοί· R. V. castanets; marg. 'sistra,' a rattle (very common in the East), consisting of an oval hoop with a handle, having cross-bars of metal rods, on which loose rings were threaded, jingling when shaken, like the plates of a timbrel.

Corpse. 2 Kn. 19. 35; Isa. 37. 36; Nah. 3. 3; Mk. 6. 29.

Correct. Prov. 3. 12, whom the Lord loveth he *c.* R. V. reproveth.
29. 17, *c.* thy son.
29. 19, servant will not be *c.* by words.
Jer. 10. 24, *c.* me, but with judgment.
30. 11; 46. 28, I will *c.* thee in measure.
Heb. 12. 9, we have had fathers which *c.* us.
See Job 5. 17; Ps. 39. 11; 94. 10.

Correction. Prov. 22. 15, rod of *c.* shall drive it.
Jer. 2. 30; 5. 3; 7. 28; Zep. 3. 2, receive *c.*
2 Tim. 3. 16, scripture profitable for *c.*
See Job 37. 13; Prov. 3. 11; 7. 22; 15. 10.

Corrupt. Deu. 4. 16, take heed lest ye *c.*
31. 29, after my death ye will *c.*
Mat. 6. 19, moth *c.* R. V. consume.
7. 17; 12. 33; Lu. 6. 43, a *c.* tree.
1 Cor. 15. 33, evil communications *c.*
2 Cor. 2. 17, not as many, which *c.* the word.
7. 2, we have *c.* no man.
11. 3, lest your minds be *c.*
Eph. 4. 22, put off old man which is *c.*
4. 29, let no *c.* communication.
1 Tim. 6. 5; 2 Tim. 3. 8, men of *c.* minds.
Jas. 5. 2, your riches are *c.*
See Gen. 6. 11; Job 17. 1; Prov. 25. 26.

Corrupters. Isa. 1. 4; Jer. 6. 28.

Corruptible. Rom. 1. 23; 1 Cor. 9. 25; 15. 53; 1 Pet. 1. 18; 3. 4.

Corruption. Ps. 16. 10; 49. 9; Acts 2. 27; 13. 35, not see *c.*
Jon. 2. 6, brought up life from *c.* R. V. the pit.
Rom. 8. 21, from bondage of *c.*
1 Cor. 15. 42, 50, sown in *c.*
Gal. 6. 8, of flesh reap *c.*
2 Pet. 1. 4, the *c.* that is in world.
2. 12, perish in their own *c.* R. V. destroying.
See Lev. 22. 25; Job 17. 14; Isa. 38. 17.

Corruptly. 2 Chr. 27. 2; Neh. 1. 7.

Cosam, cō′-săm. Lu. 3. 28.

Cost. 2 Sam. 24. 24; 1 Chr. 21. 24, offer of that which *c.* nothing.
Lu. 14. 28, sitteth down and counteth *c.* [2. 9.
See 2 Sam. 19. 42; 1 Kn. 5. 17; John 12. 3; 1 Tim.

Cotes, huts, sheds (for sheep, &c.). 2 Chr. 32. 28.

Cottage. Isa. 1. 8; 24. 20; Zep. 2. 6.

Cotton (Esth. 1. 6). A. V. and R. V. hangings. Heb. *Carpas:* Gk. κάρπασος: Bot. N. *Gossypium herbaceum.* The description should be rendered 'white and violet-coloured cotton.' 'Green' is rendered 'cotton' in R. V. margin. Cotton was then unknown in Palestine, though now abundant. As Ahasuerus reigned from India to Ethiopia, no doubt the brightly coloured cotton cloth of India would form part of the furnishings of his magnificent palace.

Couch. Lu. 5. 19, let him down with *c.*
5. 24, take up thy *c.*
Acts 5. 15, laid sick on *c.* [6. 4.
See Gen. 49. 4; Job 7. 13; 38. 40; Ps. 6. 6; Am.

Coucheth, lies, lies flat. Deu. 33. 13.

Could. Isa. 5. 4; Mk. 6. 19; 9. 18; 14. 8.

Coulter. 1 Sam. 13. 20, 21.

Council. Mat. 5. 22; 10. 17; Acts 6. 12.

Council of the Jews. Mat. 26. 3, 59; Mk. 15. 1.
the apostles arraigned before. Acts 4.; 5. 27.
Paul's discourse before. Acts 23.

Counsel. Neh. 4. 15, brought their *c.* to nought.
Job 38. 2; 42. 3, darkeneth *c.* by words.
Ps. 1. 1, *c.* of the ungodly.
33. 11; Prov. 19. 21, *c.* of Lord standeth.
55. 14, took sweet *c.* together.
73. 24, guide me with thy *c.*
Prov. 1. 25, 30, set at nought all my *c.*
11. 14, where no *c.* is, people fall R. V. wise guidance.
15. 22, without *c.* purposes are disappointed.
21. 30, there is no *c.* against the Lord.
Eccl. 8. 2, I *c.* thee keep king's commandment.
Isa. 28. 29, wonderful in *c.*
30. 1, that take *c.*. but not of me.
40. 14, with whom took he *c.*
46. 10, my *c.* shall stand.
Jer. 32. 19, great in *c.*, mighty in working.
Hos. 10. 6, ashamed of his own *c.*
Mk. 3. 6; John 11. 53, took *c.* against Jesus.
Acts 2. 23, determinate *c.* of God.
4. 28, what thy *c.* determined before.
5. 38, if this *c* be of men.
20. 27, declare all *c.* of God.
1 Cor. 4. 5, make manifest *c.* of the heart.
Eph. 1. 11, after the *c.* of his own will.
Heb. 6. 17, the immutability of his *c.*
Rev. 3. 18, I *c.* thee to buy gold tried in fire.
See Ex. 18. 19; Jos. 9. 14; 2 Sam. 15. 31.

Counsel, advantage of good. Prov. 12. 15; 13. 10; 20. 18; 27. 9.
of God, asked by Israel. Jud. 20. 18.
by Saul. 1 Sam. 14. 37.
by David. 1 Sam. 23. 2, 10; 30. 8; 1 Chr. 14. 10.
See Ps. 16. 7; 33. 11; 73. 24; Prov. 8. 14; Rev. 3. 18.
danger of rejecting. 2 Chr. 25. 16; Prov. 1. 25, 26; Jer. 23. 18-22; Lu. 7. 30.
of the wicked, condemned. Job 5. 13; 10. 3; 21. 16; Ps. 1. 1; 5. 10; 33. 10; 64. 2-7; 81. 12; 106. 43; Isa. 7. 5; Hos. 11. 6; Mic. 6. 16.

Counsellor. Prov. 11. 14; 15. 22; 24. 6, in multitude of *c.*
12. 20, to *c.* of peace is joy.
Mic. 4. 9, is thy *c.* perished? [councillor.
Mk. 15. 43; Lu. 23. 50, an honourable *c.* R. V.
Rom. 11. 34, who hath been his *c.*
See 2 Chr. 22. 3; Job 3. 14; 12. 17.

Count (*n.*), a reckoning, account. Ex. 12. 4.

Count (*v.*). Gen. 15. 6; Ps. 106. 31; Rom. 4. 3; Gal. 3. 6, *c.* for righteousness.
Ps. 44. 22, *c.* as sheep for the slaughter.
Prov. 17. 28, even a fool is *c.* wise.
Isa. 32. 15, field be *c.* for a forest.
Mat. 14. 5; Mk. 11. 32, they *c.* him as a prophet.
Acts 5. 41; 2 Thes. 1. 5, 11; 1 Tim. 5. 17, *c.* worthy.
20. 24, neither *c.* I my life dear.
Phil. 3. 7, 8, I *c.* loss for Christ.
3. 13, I *c.* not myself to have apprehended.
Heb. 10. 29, *c.* blood an unholy thing.
Jas. 1. 2, *c.* it all joy.
2 Pet. 3. 9, as some men *c.* slackness.
See Num. 23. 10; Job 31. 4; Ps. 139. 18, 22.

Countenance. 1 Sam. 16. 7, look not on his *c.* or stature.
16. 12; 17. 42, David of beautiful *c.*
Neh. 2. 2, why is thy *c.* sad?
Job 14. 20, thou changest his *c.*
Ps. 4. 6; 44. 3; 89. 15; 90. 8, light of thy *c.*
Prov. 15. 13, merry heart maketh cheerful *c.*
27. 17, sharpeneth *c.* of his friend.
Eccl. 7. 3, by sadness of *c.* heart made better.
Isa. 3. 9, their *c.* doth witness against them.
Mat. 6. 16, hypocrites of a sad *c.*
28. 3; Lu. 9. 29, *c.* like lightning.
Rev. 1. 16, his *c.* as the sun shineth.
See Gen. 4. 5; Num. 6. 26; Jud. 13. 6.

Countervail, to compensate for. Esth. 7. 4.

Country. Prov. 25. 25, good news from a far *c.*
Mat. 13. 57; Mk. 6. 4; Lu. 4. 24; John 4. 44, in his own *c.*
21. 33; 25. 14; Mk. 12. 1, went to far *c.*
Lu. 4. 23, do also here in thy *c.*
Acts 12. 20, their *c.* nourished by king's *c.*
Heb. 11. 9, sojourned as in strange *c.*
11. 16, desire a better *c.*
See Gen. 12. 1; 24. 4; Jos. 9. 6; Lu. 15. 13.

Countrymen. 2 Cor. 11. 26; 1 Thes. 2. 14.

Coupled. 1 Pet. 3. 2.

Courage. Deu. 31. 6; 7. 23; Jos. 10. 25; Ps. 27. 14; 31. 24, be of good *c.*
Acts 28. 15, thanked God and took *c.*

Courage, exhortations to. Num. 13. 20; Deu. 31. 6; Jos. 1. 6; 10. 25; 2 Sam. 10. 12; 13. 28; 2 Chr. 19. 11; Ez. 10. 4; Ps. 27. 14; 31. 24; Isa. 41. 6; 1 Cor. 16. 13; Eph. 6. 10.
through faith: Abraham, Heb. 11. 8, 17. Moses, Heb. 11. 25. Israelites, Heb. 11. 29. Barak, Jud. 4. 16. Gideon, Jud. 7. 1. Jephthah, Jud. 11. 29. Samson, Jud. 16. 28. Jonathan, 1 Sam. 14. 6. Daniel, Dan. 6. 10, 23. Jonah, Jon. 3. 3.
See Boldness, Confidence.

Course. Acts 20. 24; 2 Tim. 4. 7, finished my *c.*
2 Thes. 3. 1, may have free *c.* R. V. run.
Jas. 3. 6, setteth on fire the *c.* of nature. R. V. wheel.
See Jud. 5. 20; Ps. 82. 5; Acts 13. 25.

Course, by, in due order. 1 Cor. 14. 27.

Courses of the Levites established by David. 1 Chr. 23.; 24. *See* Lu. 1. 5.
of the singers. 1 Chr. 25.
of the porters. 1 Chr. 26.
of the captains. 1 Chr. 27. [tabernacle.

Court. Ex. 27. 9, thou shalt make the *c.* of the
38. 9, and he made the *c.*
Ps. 65. 4, that he may dwell in thy *c.*
84. 2, fainteth for the *c.* of the Lord.
92. 13, flourish in the *c.* of our God.
100. 4, enter into his *c.* with praise.
Isa. 1. 12, who required this to tread my *c.*?
Lu. 7. 25, live delicately are in kings' *c.*
See Isa. 34. 13; Jer. 19. 14; Ezek. 9. 7.

Courtesy, exhortation to. Col. 4. 6; Jas. 3. 17; 1 Pet. 3. 8.
examples of. Acts 27. 3; 28. 7.

Cousin, a kinsman or kinswoman, more remote than a brother or sister. Lu. 1. 36, 58.

Covenant. Num. 18. 19; 2 Chr. 13. 5, *c.* of salt.
25. 12, my *c.* of peace.
Ps. 105. 8; 106. 45, he remembereth his *c.* for ever.
111. 5, ever mindful of his *c.*
Isa. 28. 18, your *c.* with death disannulled.
Mat. 26. 15, they *c.* with him. R. V. weighed unto him.
Acts 3. 25, children of the *c.*
Rom. 9. 4, to whom pertaineth the *c.*
Eph. 2. 12, strangers from *c.* of promise.
Heb. 8. 6, mediator of a better *c.*
12. 24, mediator of the new *c.*
13. 20, blood of the everlasting *c.*

Covenant of God:—
with Noah. Gen. 6. 18; 9. 8.
with Abraham. Gen. 15. 7, 18; 17. 2 (Lu. 1. 72; Acts 3. 25; Gal. 3. 16, 17).
with Isaac. Gen. 17. 19; 26. 3. [16. 16).
with Jacob. Gen. 28. 13 (Ex. 2. 24; 6. 4; 1 Chr.
with the Israelites. Ex. 6. 4; 19. 5; 24.; 34. 27; Lev. 26. 9; Deu. 5. 2; 9. 9; 26. 16; 29.; Jud. 2. 1; Jer. 11.; 31. 33; 50. 5; Acts 3. 25.
with Phinehas. Num. 25. 13. [Ps. 25. 14.
with David. 2 Sam. 23. 5; Ps. 89. 3, 28, 34. *See*
God mindful of. Deu. 7. 9; 1 Kn. 8. 23; Ps. 105. 8; 111. 5, &c.
danger of despising. Deu. 28. 15; Jer. 11. 2; Heb. 10. 29.

Covenant, signs of:—salt, Lev. 2. 13; Num. 18. 19; 2 Chr. 13. 5. the sabbath, Ex. 31. 12.
book of the. Ex. 24. 7; 2 Kn. 23. 2; Heb. 9. 19.
between Abraham and Abimelech. Gen. 21. 27.
Joshua and Israelites. Jos. 24. 25.
David and Jonathan. 1 Sam. 18. 3; 20. 16; 23. 18.

New Covenant. Jer. 31. 31; Rom. 11. 27; Heb. 8. 8.
ratified by Christ (Mal. 3. 1). Lu. 1. 68-80; Gal. 3. 17; Heb. 8. 6; 9. 15; 12. 24.
a covenant of peace. Isa. 54. 10; Ezek. 34. 25; 37. 26.

unchangeable. Ps. 89. 34; Isa. 54. 10; 59. 21.
everlasting. Gen. 9. 16; 17. 13; Lev. 24. 8; Isa. 55. 3; 61. 8; Ezek. 16. 60, 62; 37. 26; Heb. 13. 20.

Cover. Ex. 15. 5, depths *c.* them, sank as stone.
33. 22, I will *c.* them.
1 Sam. 28. 14, an old man *c.* with a mantle.
Esth. 7. 8, they *c.* Haman's face.
Ps. 32. 1; Rom. 4. 7, blessed whose sin is *c.*
73. 6, violence *c.* them as a garment.
91. 4, he shall *c.* thee with his feathers.
104. 6, thou *c.* it with the deep.
Prov. 10. 6, 11, violence *c.* mouth of the wicked.
10. 12, love *c.* all sins.
12. 16, a prudent man *c.* shame. R. V. concealeth.
17. 9, he that *c.* transgression seeketh love.
28. 13, he that *c.* sins shall not prosper.
Isa. 26. 21, earth no more *c.* her slain.
Mat. 8. 24, ship *c.* with waves.
10. 26; Lu. 12. 2, there is nothing *c.*
1 Cor. 11. 4, having his head *c.*
11. 6, if women be not *c.* R. V. veiled.
11. 7, a man ought not to *c.* his head. R. V. head veiled.
1 Pet. 4. 8, charity shall *c.* multitude of sins.
See Gen. 7. 19; Ex. 8. 6; 21. 33; Lev. 16. 13.

Covering. Job 22. 14, thick clouds are a *c.* to him.
24. 7, naked have no *c.* in the cold.
26. 6, destruction hath no *c.*
31. 19, if I have seen any poor without *c.*
Isa. 28. 20, *c.* narrower than he can wrap.
See Gen. 8. 13; Lev. 13. 45; 2 Sam. 17. 19.

Covert, shelter, hiding-place. 1 Sam. 25. 20; Ps. 61. 4; Isa. 4. 6; 16. 4; 32. 2.

Covet. Prov. 21. 26, he *c.* greedily all the day.
Hab. 2. 9, *c.* an evil covetousness. R. V. getteth
Acts 20. 33, I have *c.* no man's silver.
1 Cor. 12. 31, *c.* earnestly the best gifts. R. V. desire.
1 Tim. 6. 10, while some *c.* after, they erred. R. V. reaching after.

Covetous. Prov. 28. 16, he that hateth *c.* shall prolong.
Ezek. 33. 31, their heart goeth after *c.* R. V. gain.
Mk. 7. 22, out of heart proceedeth *c.*
Rom. 1. 29, filled with all *c.*
1 Cor. 6. 10; Eph. 5. 5, nor *c.* inherit kingdom.
Eph. 5. 3, but *c.*, let it not be named.
2 Tim. 3. 2, men shall be *c.* R. V. lovers of money.
Heb. 13. 5, conversation without *c.* R. V. be ye free from the love of money.
2 Pet. 2. 3, through *c.* make merchandise.
2. 14, exercised with *c.* practices.

Covetousness described. Ps. 10. 3; Prov. 21. 26; Eccl. 4. 8; 5. 10; Ezek. 33. 31; Hab. 2.; Mk. 7. 22; Eph. 5. 5; 1 Tim. 6. 10; 2 Pet. 2. 14.
forbidden. Ex. 20. 17; Deu. 5. 21; Lu. 12. 15; Rom. 13. 9.
its evil consequences. Prov. 1. 18; 15. 27; 28. 20; Ezek. 22. 13; 1 Tim. 6. 9.
its punishment. Job 20. 15; Isa. 5. 8; 57. 17; Jer. 6. 12; 22. 17; Mic. 2. 1; Hab. 2. 9; 1 Cor. 5. 10; 6. 10; Eph. 5. 5; Col. 3. 5.
of Laban. Gen. 31. 41.
of Balaam. Num. 22. 21 (2 Pet. 2. 15; Jude 11).
of Achan. Jos. 7. 21.
of Saul. Sam. 15. 9.
of Ahab. 1 Kn. 21.
of Gehazi. 2 Kn. 5. 20.
of Judas. Mat. 26. 14.
of Ananias and Sapphira. Acts 5.
of Felix. Acts 24. 26.

Cow. Lev. 22. 28; Job 21. 10; Isa. 11. 7.

Coz, cŏz, 'thorn.' 1 Chr. 4. 8.

Cozbi, cŏz'-bī, 'deceitful,' slain by Phinehas. Num. 25. 15.

Crackling. Eccl. 7. 6.

Cracknels, crisp cakes or biscuits. 1 Kn. 14. 3.

Craft. (1) occupation, trade. Acts 18. 3, of the same *c.*
Acts 19. 25, by this *c.* we have our wealth.
19. 27, our *c.* is in danger.
(2) Job 5. 13; 1 Cor. 3. 19, taketh wise in their *c.*
Lu. 20. 23, he perceived their *c.*
2 Cor. 4. 2, not walking in *c.*
12. 16, being *c.* I caught you.
Eph. 4. 14, carried away with cunning *c.*
See Dan. 8. 25; Rev. 18. 22.

Craftsman, a skilled workman. Acts 19. 24.

Crag. Job 39. 28.

Crane (Isa. 38. 14; Jer. 8. 7). Heb. *Âgûr*, twitterer: Gk. χελιδών: A. V. crane; R. V. swallow. (Specimen, *Grus cinerea.* T.) 'A crane or a swallow' in Isa. 38. 14, should be 'a twittering swallow' or 'a swallow and a twitterer' (another kind of swallow). *Dr. Post.*

Crashing. Zep. 1. 10.

Crave. Prov. 16. 26; Mk. 15. 43.

Create. Isa. 40. 26, who hath *c.* these things?
43. 7, *c.* him for my glory.
65. 17, I *c.* new heavens and new earth.
Jer. 31. 22, the Lord hath *c.* a new thing.
Am. 4. 13; he that *c.* wind.
Mal. 2. 10, hath not one God *c.* us?
1 Cor. 11. 9, neither was man *c.* for woman.
Eph. 2. 10, *c.* in Christ Jesus.
4. 24, after God is *c.* in righteousness.
Col. 1. 16, by him were all things *c.*
1 Tim. 4. 3, which God *c.* to be received.
See Gen. 1. 1; 6. 7; Deu. 4. 32; Ps. 51. 10.

Creation. Mk. 10. 6; 13. 19; Rom. 1. 20; 8. 22; 2 Pet. 3. 4.

Creator. Eccl. 12. 1; Isa. 40. 28; Rom. 1. 25; 1 Pet. 4. 19.

Creature. (1) created thing. Mk. 16. 15; Col. 1. 23, preach to every *c.*
2 Cor. 5. 17; Gal. 6. 15, new *c.*
Col. 1. 15, firstborn of every *c.*
1 Tim. 4. 4, every *c.* of God is good.
See Gen. 1. 20; 2. 19; Isa. 13. 21; Ezek. 1. 20.
(2) the creation. Rom. 8. 19-22.

Creatures. Ezek. 1. 5, came the likeness of four living *c.*

Creditor. Deu. 15. 2; 2 Kn. 4. 1; Isa. 50. 1; Mat. 18. 23; Lu. 7. 41.

Creek. Acts 27. 39. R. V. bay.

Creep. Ps. 104. 20, beasts of the forest *c.* forth.
104. 25, in sea are *c.* things.
Ezek. 8. 10, form of *c.* things portrayed.
Acts 10. 12; 11. 6, Peter saw *c.* things.
2 Tim. 3. 6, they *c.* into houses.
Jude 4, certain men *c.* in unawares.
See Gen. 1. 25; 7. 8; Lev. 11. 41; Deu. 4. 18.

Crescens, crĕs'-çĕns, 'growing;' goes to Dalmatia. 2 Tim. 4. 10.

Crete, crēte, visited by Paul. Acts 27. 7.

Cretes or **Cretians**, crētes, crē'-tĭ-ăns, 'inhabitants of Crete.' Acts 2. 11; Tit. 1. 12.

Crew. Mat. 26. 74; Mk. 14. 68; Lu. 22. 60.

Crib. Job 39. 9; Prov. 14. 4; Isa. 1. 3.

Crime. Job 31. 11; Acts 25. 16.

Crimson. 2 Chr. 2. 7; Isa. 1. 18; Jer. 4. 30.

Cripple. Acts 14. 8.

Crisping pins, not our crimping pins, but an ornamental bag or satchel. Isa. 3. 22. R. V. satchels.

Crispus, crĭs'-pŭs, 'curled;' baptized by Paul. Acts 18. 8; 1 Cor. 1. 14.

Crocodile (Lev. 11. 29). Gk. κροκόδειλος: R. V. great lizard. A. V. tortoise. The crocodile is probably the animal called LEVIATHAN, *q. v.*

Crooked. Eccl. 1. 15; 7. 13, *c.* cannot be made straight.
Isa. 40. 4; 42. 16; Lu. 3. 5, *c.* shall be made straight.
45. 2, make the *c.* places straight.
59. 8; Lam. 3. 9, *c.* paths.
Phil. 2. 15, in midst of a *c.* nation.
See Lev. 21. 20; Deu. 32. 5; Job 26. 13.

Crops. Lev. 1. 16; Ezek. 17. 22.

Cross. Mat. 16. 24; Mk. 8. 34; 10. 21; Lu. 9. 23, [take up *c.*
27. 32; Mk. 15. 21; Lu. 23. 26, compelled to bear *c.*
27. 40; Mk. 15. 30, come down from *c.*

John 19. 25, there stood by *c.*
1 Cor. 1. 17; Gal. 6. 12; Phil. 3. 18, *c.* of Christ.
1. 18, preaching of the *c.*
Gal. 5. 11, offence of the *c.*
6. 14, glory save in the *c.*
Eph. 2. 16, reconcile both by the *c.*
Phil. 2. 8, the death of the *c.*
Col. 1. 20, peace through blood of the *c.*
2. 14, nailing it to his *c.*
Heb. 12. 2, for joy endured the *c.*

Cross, Christ dies upon the. Mat. 27. 32; Phil. 2. 8; Heb. 12. 2.
preaching of. 1 Cor. 1. 18.
to be taken up, self-denial. Mat. 10. 38; 16. 24.
offence of the, Gal. 5. 11. persecution for, Gal. 6. 12.

Crouch. 1 Sam. 2. 36; Ps. 10. 10.

Crow (Prov. 30. 17). Heb. *'Oreb:* Gk. *κόραξ*: A. V. and R. V. ravens. (Specimen, *Corvus umbrinus.*) The term includes the whole tribe of crows, e. g., ravens, rooks, jackdaws, &c.

Crown. (1) The Greek *στέφανος*, a garland, wreath, chaplet. It formed the prize at the Greek games, and was worn by feasters. Hence it became a symbol of victory or joy. This was the 'crown' of thorns placed in mockery on the Saviour's head.
(2) *διάδημα*, diadem (so rendered in R. V.), occurs only in Rev. 12. 3; 13. 1; 19. 12. It was originally the Persian badge of royalty, a ribbon of blue and white worn round the turban: thus the word means a crown as the sign and symbol of kingship.

Crown. Job 19. 9, taken the *c.* from my head.
Ps. 8. 5; Heb. 2. 7, 9, *c.* with glory and honour.
65. 11, thou *c.* the year.
103. 4, *c.* thee with lovingkindness.
Prov. 4. 9, a *c.* of glory shall she deliver.
12. 4, virtuous woman is a *c.*
14. 18, prudent *c.* with knowledge.
16. 31, hoary head a *c.* of glory.
17. 6, children's children are the *c.* of old men.
Isa. 28. 1, woe to the *c.* of pride.
Mat. 27. 29; Mk. 15. 17; John 19. 2, a *c.* of thorns.
1 Cor. 9. 25, to obtain a corruptible *c.*
Phil. 4. 1, my joy and *c.*
1 Thes. 2. 19, a *c.* of rejoicing.
2 Tim. 2. 5, not *c.* except he strive.
4. 8, a *c.* of righteousness.
Jas. 1. 12; Rev. 2. 10, *c.* of life.
1 Pet. 5. 4, a *c.* of glory.
Rev. 3. 11, hold fast, that no man take thy *c.*
4. 10, cast *c.* before throne.
19. 12, on head were many *c.*
See Ex. 25. 25; Job 31. 36. [30; Lev. 8. 9.

Crown (and mitre), high priest's. Ex. 29. 6; 39. 30; Lev. 8. 9.
of thorns. John 19. 5.
of righteousness. 2 Tim. 4. 8.
of life. Jas. 1. 12; Rev. 2. 10.
of glory. 1 Pet. 5. 4.
incorruptible. 1 Cor. 9. 25. *See* Rev. 4. 4; 9. 7.

Crucifixion was unknown to the Jews, until introduced by the Romans, who used it only for the punishment of slaves and the lowest malefactors. But persons were hanged on a tree after they were slain as far back as the days of Joshua (8. 29).

Crucify. Mat. 27. 22, all said, Let him be *c.*
Mk. 15. 13; Lu. 23. 21; John 19. 6, 15, *c.* him.
Acts 2. 23, by wicked hands ye have *c.*
Rom. 6. 6, old man is *c.* with him.
1 Cor. 1. 13, was Paul *c.* for you.
1. 23, we preach Christ *c.*
2. 2, save Jesus Christ and him *c.*
2 Cor. 13. 4, though he was *c.* through weakness.
Gal. 2. 20, I am *c.* with Christ.
3. 1, Christ set forth *c.*
5. 24, have *c.* the flesh.
6. 14, the world is *c.* unto me.
Heb. 6. 6, *c.* to themselves afresh.
See Mat. 20. 19; 23. 34; 27. 31; Mk. 15. 20.

Cruel. Ps. 25. 19, with *c.* hatred.
Ps. 27. 12, breathe out *c.*
74. 20, full of the habitations of *c.*
Prov. 5. 9, give thy years to the *c.*
11. 17, *c.* troubleth his own flesh.
12. 10, tender mercies of the wicked are *c.*
27. 4, wrath is *c.*
S. of S. 8. 6, jealousy is *c.*
Heb. 11. 36, trials of *c.* mockings.

Cruelty condemned. Ex. 23. 5; Ps. 27. 12; Prov. 11. 17; 12. 10; Ezek. 18. 18.
of Simeon and Levi. Gen. 34. 25; 49. 5, 7.
of Pharaoh. Ex. 1. 8; 6. 9.
of Adoni-bezek. Jud. 1. 7. [15. 16).
of Herod. Mat. 2. 16 (Jud. 9. 5; 2 Kn. 3. 27; 10.; 15. 16).

Crumbs. Mat. 15. 27; Mk. 7. 28; Lu. 16. 21.

Cruse, small cup or vessel for holding liquids. 1 Sam. 26. 11; 1 Kn. 14. 3; 17. 12; 19. 6; 2 Kn. 2. 20.

Crush. Job 5. 4, children are *c.* in the gate.
39. 15, forgetteth that the foot may *c.* them.
See Lev. 22. 24; Num. 22. 25; Deu. 28. 33.

Cry (*n.*). 1 Sam. 5. 12, *c.* of the city went up to heaven.
Job 34. 28, he heareth the *c.* of the afflicted.
Ps. 9. 12, forgetteth not *c.* of the humble.
34. 15, ears are open to their *c.*
Prov. 21. 13, stoppeth his ears at the *c.* of the poor.
Mat. 25. 6, at midnight there was a *c.* made.
See Gen. 18. 20; Ex. 2. 23; Num. 16. 34.

Cry (*v.*). Ex. 14. 15, wherefore *c.* thou unto me?
Lev. 13. 45, cover his lip, and *c.* unclean.
Job 29. 12, I delivered poor that *c.*
Ps. 147. 9, food to young ravens which *c.*
Prov. 8. 1, doth not wisdom *c.*
Isa. 58. 1, *c.* aloud, spare not.
Mat. 12. 19, he shall not strive nor *c.*
20. 31; Mk. 10. 48; Lu. 18. 39, they *c.* the more.
Lu. 18. 7, elect who *c.* day and night.
John 7. 37, Jesus *c.* if any man thirst.
Acts 19. 32; 21. 34, some *c.* one thing and some another.
See Ex. 5. 8; 32. 18; 2 Kn. 8. 3. [Rev. 21. 4.

Crying. Prov. 19. 18; Isa. 65. 19; Heb. 5. 7; Rev. 21. 4.

Crystal. Job 28. 17; Ezek. 1. 22; Rev. 4. 6; 21. 11; 22. 1.

Cubit. Heb. *ammah:* Gk. *πῆχυς*. The ordinary unit of length among the Hebrews; originally the length from the elbow to the tip of the fingers (Deu. 3. 11), i. e., six hand-breadths.
The primitive cubit, from the Siloam inscription, 8th century B. C., was 17.6 in. 2 Chr. 3. 3.
Under the Roman empire the ordinary Jewish cubit was 21.6 in. Mat. 6. 27; John 21. 8.
Greek cubit, 18 in. *See* MEASURES.

Cuckoo (Lev. 11. 16). Heb. *Shaḥaph:* Gk. *λάρος*. R. V. 'seamew,' a gull. (Specimens, *Cuculus canorus*, found in the Jordan Valley; *Oxylophus glandarius*, found at Ain Fasail.)

Cucumber. (1) (Num. 11. 5). Heb. *Kisshuîm:* Gk. *σίκυοι*: Bot. N. *Cucumis sativus.*
(2) (Isa. 1. 8). Heb. *Mikshah:* Gk. *σικυήρατον*; Bot. N. *Cucumis chate.* A staple article of diet for the poor in summer.

Cumber, encumber, occupy unprofitably. Deu. 1. 12; Lu. 10. 40; 13. 7.

Cumi, cū'-mi, 'arise.' Mk. 5. 41.

Cummin (Isa. 28. 25, 27). Heb. *Cammôn:* Gk. *κύμινον*: Bot. N. *Cuminum cyminum.* An umbelliferous plant, whose seeds were used as spice in bread and stewed meats, and as a medicine. They resemble caraways, but are larger and lighter in colour.

Cunning. (1) skill, knowledge. 1 Kn. 7. 14, *c.* to work.
Ps. 137. 5, let my hand forget her cunning.
(2) knowing, skilful. Gen. 25. 27, a *c.* hunter.
Jer. 9. 17, send for *c.* women.
Eph. 4. 14, carried about by *c.* craftiness.
2 Pet. 1. 16, not follow *c.* devised fables.
See Ex. 38. 23; 1 Sam. 16. 16; Dan. 1. 4.
(3) wrought with peculiar skill. Ex. 31. 4.

Cup. Ps. 116. 13, take *c.* of salvation.
Mat. 10. 42; Mk. 9. 41, *c.* of cold water.
20. 22; Mk. 10. 39, drink of my *c.*
23. 25, make clean outside of *c.* [took *c.*
26. 27; Mk. 14. 23; Lu. 22. 17; 1 Cor. 11. 25,
26. 39; Mk. 14. 36; Lu. 22. 42, let this *c.* pass.
Lu. 22. 20; 1 Cor. 11. 25, this *c.* is new testament.
John 18. 11, *c.* which my father hath given.
1 Cor. 10. 16, *c.* of blessing we bless.
11. 26, as often as ye drink this *c.*
11. 27, drink this *c.* unworthily.
See Gen. 40. 11; 44. 2; Prov. 23. 31.
Curdled. Job 10. 10.
Cure. Lu. 7. 21, in that hour he *c.* many.
9. 1, power to *c.* diseases.
13. 32, I do *c.* to-day.
See Jer. 33. 6; 46. 11; Hos. 5. 13; Mat. 17. 16.
Curious. (1) carefully or artfully wrought. Ex. 28. 8; Ps. 139. 15.
(2) magical. Acts 19. 19.
Current. Gen. 23. 16. [and *c.*
Curse (*n.*). Deu. 11. 26, I set before you blessing
23. 5, turned *c.* into blessing.
Mal. 3. 9, ye are cursed with a *c.*
Gal. 3. 10, are under the *c.*
Rev. 22. 3, no more *c.*
See Gen. 27. 12; Num. 5. 18.
Curse (*v.*). Lev. 19. 14, not *c.* the deaf.
Num. 23. 8, how shall I *c.* whom God hath not.
Jud. 5. 23, *c.* ye Meroz, *c.* ye bitterly.
Job 2. 9, *c.* God and die. R. V. renounce.
Ps. 62. 4, they bless, but *c.* inwardly.
Mal. 2. 2, I will *c.* your blessings.
Mat. 5. 44; Lu. 6. 28; Rom. 12. 14, bless them that *c.* you.
26. 74; Mk. 14. 71, he began to *c.*
Mk. 11. 21, fig tree thou *c.*
John 7. 49, knoweth not the law are *c.*
Gal. 3. 10, *c.* is every one that continueth not.
Jas. 3. 9, therewith *c.* we men.
See Gen. 12. 3; Num. 22. 6.
Curse upon the earth in consequence of the fall. Gen. 3. 17; 8. 21.
upon Cain. Gen. 4. 11.
on Canaan. Gen. 9. 25. [Jer. 20. 14.
by Job on his birth, Job 3. 1. also by Jeremiah,
upon the breakers of the law. Lev. 26. 14; Deu. 11. 26; 27. 13; 28. 15; 29. 19; Jos. 8. 34; Prov. 3. 33.
Christ redeems from. Rom. 3.; Gal. 3. 1.
Cursed, who so called. Deu. 27. 15; Prov. 11. 26; 27. 14; Jer. 11. 3; 17. 5; Lam. 3. 65; Zec. 5. 3; Mal. 1. 14; Mat. 25. 41; Gal. 3. 10; 2 Pet. 2. 14.
of God to be cut off. Ps. 37. 22.
Cursing forbidden. Ex. 21. 17; Ps. 109. 17; Prov. 30. 11; Jas. 3. 10.
to return blessing for. Mat. 5. 44; Rom. 12. 14.
Curtain. Ex. 26. 36, the length of one *c.*
Cush, cŭsh. (1) Ham's eldest son, Gen. 10. 6. (2) Ps. 7. (title). (3) country, Ethiopia, Gen. 2. 13.
Cushan, cū'-shăn, same meaning as Cush. Hab. 3. 7.
Cushi, cū'-shī, 'Ethiopian.' (1) announces Absalom's death, 2 Sam. 18. 21. R. V. the Cushite. (2) Zep. 1. 1. (3) Jer. 36. 14.
Custom. (1) Lu. 4. 16, as his *c.* was, went into synagogue.
John 18. 39, ye have a *c.*
Acts 16. 21, teach *c.* which are not lawful.
1 Cor. 11. 16, we have no such *c.*
See Gen. 31. 35; Jud. 11. 39; Jer. 10. 3.
(2) a tribute, tax, toll. Mat. 9. 9; Mk. 2. 14; Lu. 5. 27, receipt of *c.*
Mat. 17. 25, of whom do kings take *c.*
Rom. 13. 7, *c.* to whom *c.*
Cuth, cŭth. 2 Kn. 17. 30.
Cuthah, cū'-thăh, same as Cuth. 2 Kn. 17. 24.
Cutting. Ex. 31. 5; 35. 33; Isa. 38. 10; Mk. 5. 5.
Cutting the flesh forbidden. Lev. 19. 28; Deu. 14. 1.
practised by prophets of Baal. 1 Kn. 18. 28.
Cymbals. (1) (1 Chr. 15. 16, 19, 28; 16. 5, 42; 25. 6; 2 Chr. 5. 13; 29. 25; Ez. 3. 10; Neh. 12. 27). Heb. *Metziltaim:* Gk. κύμβαλα, one form of cymbals.
(2) (2 Sam. 6. 5; Ps. 150. 5; 1 Cor. 13. 1). Heb. *Tziltzĕlîm:* Gk. κύμβαλα. A generic term for cymbals.
(3) (1 Sam. 18. 6). Heb. *Shâlîshîm:* Gk. κύμβαλα: R. V. marg. triangles or three-stringed instruments.
Cypress (Isa. 44. 14). Heb. *Tirzah* (omitted in LXX.): Bot. N. *Cupressus sempervirens:* R. V. 'holm tree,' or oak, *Quercus ilex.*
Cyprus, çȳ'-prŭs, 'copper.' Acts 4. 36.
disciples there. Acts 11. 19.
Paul and Barnabas preach there. Acts 13. 4.
Barnabas and Mark go there. Acts 15. 39. [21.
Cyrene, çȳ-rē'-nē, Simon of. Mat. 27. 32; Mk. 15.
disciples of. Acts 11. 20; 13. 1.
Cyrenian, çȳ-rē'-nĭ-ăn, a native of Cyrene. Acts 6. 9.
Cyrenius, çȳ-rē'-nĭ-ŭs, Greek form of the Roman name Quirinius, governor of Syria. Lu. 2. 2.
Cyrus, çȳ'-rŭs. 2 Chr. 36. 22.
king of Persia, prophecies concerning. Isa. 44. 28; 45. 1. *See* Dan. 6. 28; 10. 1.
his proclamation for rebuilding the temple. 2 Chr. 36. 22; Ez. 1.

Dabareh, dăb'-ă-rĕh, pasture. Jos. 21. 28.
Dabba (Lev. 11. 29). Heb. *Tzâb:* Gk. κροκόδειλος χερσαῖος: Zool. S. *Uromastix spinipes* (tortoise of A. V.), a large species of lizard, common in the sands of Arabia, well known in Judæa.
Dabbasheth, dăb'-bă-shĕth, 'hump of a camel.' Jos. 19. 11.
Daberath, dăb'-ĕ-răth. Jos. 19. 12, same as Dabareh.
Dagger. Jud. 3. 16, 21, 22. R. V. sword.
Dagon, dā'-gŏn, national idol-god of the Philistines, sacrificed to. Jud. 16. 23.
smitten down in temple at Ashdod. 1 Sam. 5. 3, 4.
Saul's head fastened in house of. 1 Chr. 10. 10.
Daily. Ps. 13. 2, sorrow in my heart *d.* R. V. all the day.
68. 19, *d.* loadeth us.
Prov. 8. 30, I was *d.* his delight.
Dan. 8. 11; 11. 31; 12. 11, *d.* sacrifice taken away. R. V. continual.
Mat. 6. 11; Lu. 11. 3, our *d.* bread.
Lu. 9. 23, take up cross *d.*
Acts 2. 47, added to church *d.*
6. 1, the *d.* ministration.
16. 5, churches increased *d.*
17. 11, searched the scriptures *d.*
1 Cor. 15. 31, I die *d.*
Jas. 2. 15, destitute of *d.* food.
See Num. 4. 16; 28. 24; Neh. 5. 18; Dan. 1. 5.
Dainty. Ps. 141. 4, let me not eat of their *d.*
Prov. 23. 3, be not desirous of his *d.*
See Gen. 49. 20; Job 33. 20; Rev. 18. 14.
Dalaiah, dă-lāī'-ăh, 'Jehovah hath drawn.' 1 Chr. 3. 24.
Dale. Gen. 14. 17; 2 Sam. 18. 18. R. V. vale.
Dalmanutha, dăl-mă-nū'-thă. Mk. 8. 10.
Dalmatia, dăl-mā'-tiă. 2 Tim. 4. 10.
Dalphon, dăl'-phŏn. Esth. 9. 7.
Dam. Ex. 22. 30; Lev. 22. 27; Deu. 22. 6.
Damage. Prov. 26. 6, drinketh *d.* [loss.
Acts 27. 10, voyage will be with much *d.* R. V.
2 Cor. 7. 9, receive *d.* by us in nothing. R. V. loss.
See Ez. 4. 22; Esth. 7. 4; Dan. 6. 2.
Damaris, dăm'-ă-rĭs, 'a young girl' (?). Cleaves to Paul. Acts 17. 34.
Damascenes, dăm'-ăs-çēnes, 'people of Damascus.' 2 Cor. 11. 32.
Damascus, dă-măs'-cŭs. The capital of Syria, and the most ancient city in the world.
first mentioned. Gen. 14. 15.
subjugated by David. 2 Sam. 8. 6; 1 Chr. 18. 6.
Elisha's prophecy there. 2 Kn. 8. 7.

taken by Tiglath-pileser, king of Assyria. 2 Kn. 16. 9.
restored to Israel by Jeroboam. 2 Kn. 14. 28.
king Ahaz copies an altar there. 2 Kn. 16. 10.
Paul's journey to. Acts 9.; 22. 6.
Paul restored to sight, and baptized there. Acts 9. 17, 18.
prophecies concerning. Isa. 7. 8; 8. 4; 17. 1; Jer. 49. 23; Am. 1. 3.

Damn, to judge, condemn. Mk. 16. 16; Rom. 14. 23; 2 Thes. 2. 12.

Damnable, destructive. 2 Pet. 2. 1.

Damnation, or **Condemnation.** These words were used as equivalent terms when the A. V. was issued; sometimes with a graver, sometimes with a lighter meaning. In 1 Cor. 11. 29, the reference is to self-judgment.
Mat. 23. 33, can ye escape the *d.* of hell? R. V. judgement.
Mk. 3. 29, in danger of eternal *d.* R. V. sin.
John 5. 29, the resurrection of *d.* R. V. judgement.
Rom. 13. 2, receive to themselves *d.* R. V. judgement.
1 Cor. 11. 29, eateth and drinketh *d.* R. V. judgement.
2 Pet. 2. 3, their *d.* slumbereth not. R. V. destruction.
See Mat. 23. 14; Mk. 12. 40; 16. 16; Lu. 20. 47; John 5. 29; Rom. 3. 8; 13. 2; 2 Thes. 2. 12; 1 Tim. 5. 12; 2 Pet. 2. 3.

Damsel. Ps. 68. 25, among them were the *d.* playing.
Mat. 14. 11; Mk. 6. 28, given to the *d.* [maid.
26. 69; John 18. 17, *d.* came to Peter. R. V.
Mk. 5. 39, the *d.* is not dead. R. V. child.
Acts 12. 13, a *d.* came to hearken. R. V. maid.
16. 16, *d.* possessed with a spirit. R. V. maid.
See Gen. 24. 55; 34. 3; Jud. 5. 30; Ru. 2. 5.

Dan, dăn, judge. (1) son of Jacob, by Rachel's handmaid. Gen. 30. 6.
(2) tribe of, numbered. Num. 1. 38; 26. 42.
their inheritance. Jos. 19. 40.
blessed by Jacob. Gen. 49. 16.
blessed by Moses. Deu. 33. 22.
win Laish, and call it Dan. Jud. 18. 29.
set up idolatry. Jud. 18. 30; 1 Kn. 12. 29.

Dance. Ex. 32. 19, he saw the calf, and *d.*
1 Sam. 18. 6, came out singing and *d.*
2 Sam. 6. 14, David *d.* before the Lord.
Job 21. 11, their children *d.*
Ps. 30. 11, turned my mourning into *d.*
149. 3; 150. 4, praise him in the *d.*
Eccl. 3. 4, a time to *d.*
Mat. 11. 17; Lu. 7. 32, piped, and ye have not *d.*
14. 6; Mk. 6. 22, daughter of Herodias *d.*

Dancing as a mark of rejoicing. Ex. 15. 20; 32. 19; Jud. 11. 34; 21. 21; 1 Sam. 21. 11; 2 Sam. 6. 14; Eccl. 3. 4; Jer. 31. 13; Lam. 5. 15.
of Herodias' daughter pleases Herod. Mat. 14. 6; Mk. 6. 22.

Dandled. Isa. 66. 12.

Danger, in, liable (to); i. e., liable to be condemned. Mat. 5. 21, 22; Mk. 3. 29 (R. V. guilty). Acts 19. 27; 27. 9.

Daniel, dăn'-jel, 'God is my judge.' (1) (Belteshazzar), with other captives, taken from Jerusalem to Babylon. Dan. 1. 3, 6.
taught the learning of the Chaldeans. Dan. 1. 4.
will not take the king's meat or drink. Dan. 1. 8.
has understanding in dreams. Dan. 1. 17.
interprets the royal dreams. Dan. 2.; 4. and handwriting on wall, Dan. 5. 17.
made chief president by Darius. Dan. 6. 2.
conspired against by the princes. Dan. 6. 4.
idolatrous decree against, issued, Dan. 6. 9. breach thereof, Dan. 6. 10.
cast into the lion's den, Dan. 6. 16. preservation in, Dan. 6. 22.
his vision of the four beasts, Dan. 7. 12. ram and he-goat, Dan. 8. 3.
his prayer. Dan. 9. 3. [10. 10; 12. 13.
promise of return from captivity. Dan. 9. 20; name mentioned. Ezek. 14. 14, 20; 28. 3.
(2) others. 1 Chr. 3. 1; Ez. 8. 2.
(3) book of, belongs to the time of the Exile, is partly historical and partly prophetical, and may be divided into two portions of six chapters each.

Danites, dăn'-ītes, descendants of Dan. Jud. 13. 2.

Dan-jaan, dăn-jā'-ăn, Dan. 2 Sam. 24. 6.

Dannah, dăn'-năh. Jos. 15. 49.

Dara, dâr'-ă, probably contracted from the next word. 1 Chr. 2. 6.

Darda, där'-dă. 1 Kn. 4. 31.

Dare. Rom. 5. 7, some would even *d.* to die.
See Job 41. 10; Rom. 15. 18; 1 Cor. 6. 1; 2 Cor. 10. 12.

Darius, dă-rī'-ŭs, 'king' (?). (1) (the Median) takes Babylon, Dan. 5. 31. his decree to fear the God of Daniel, Dan. 6. 25.
(2) Ez. 4. 5.
decree concerning the rebuilding of the temple. Ez. 6.
(3) Neh. 12. 22.

Dark. Job 12. 25, they grope in the *d.*
22. 13, can he judge through *d.* cloud? R. V. thick darkness.
24. 16, in the *d.* they dig.
38. 2, that *d.* counsel by words.
Ps. 49. 4; Prov. 1. 6, *d.* sayings.
69. 23; Rom. 11. 10, let their eyes be *d.*
88. 12, wonders be known in the *d.*
Eccl. 12. 2, stars be not *d.*
12. 3, look out of windows be *d.*
Zec. 14. 6, shall not be clear nor *d.*
Mat. 24. 29; Mk. 13. 24, sun be *d.*
Lu. 23. 45, sun *d.* and vail rent.
John 20. 1, early, when it was yet *d.*
Rom. 1. 21, foolish heart was *d.*
Eph. 4. 18, understanding *d.* [10.
See Gen. 15. 17; Ex. 10. 15; Num. 12. 8; Joel 2.

Darkness. Deu. 5. 22, spake out of thick *d.*
28. 29, grope as the blind in *d.*
1 Sam. 2. 9, wicked shall be silent in *d.*
2 Sam. 22. 10; Ps. 18. 9, *d.* under his feet.
22. 29; Ps. 18. 28, Lord will enlighten my *d.*
1 Kn. 8. 12; 2 Chr. 6. 1, dwell in thick *d.*
Job 3. 5; Ps. 10. 10, *d.* and shadow of death.
10. 22, land where the light is as *d.*
30. 26, waited for light there came *d.*
Ps. 91. 6, pestilence that walketh in *d.*
97. 2, clouds and *d.* are round about him.
112. 4, to upright ariseth light in *d.*
139. 12, *d.* and light alike to thee.
Prov. 20. 20, lamp be put out in *d.*
Eccl. 2. 13, as far as light excelleth *d.*
2. 14, fool walketh in *d.*
Isa. 58. 10, thy *d.* as noon day.
60. 2, *d.* cover the earth, gross *d.*
Joel 2. 2, day of clouds and thick *d.*
Mat. 6. 23; Lu. 11. 34, body full of *d.*
8. 12; 22. 13; 25. 30, outer *d.*
10. 27; Lu. 12. 3, what I tell in *d.* speak.
Lu. 1. 79; Rom. 2. 19, light to them that sit in *d.*
22. 53; Col. 1. 13, the power of *d.*
23. 44, *d.* over all the earth.
John 1. 5, *d.* comprehended it not.
3. 19, loved *d.* rather than light.
12. 35, walk while ye have light, lest *d.*
Acts 26. 18, turn from *d.* to light.
Rom. 13. 12; Eph. 5. 11, works of *d.*
1 Cor. 4. 5, hidden things of *d.*
2 Cor. 4. 6, light to shine out of *d.*
6. 14, what communion hath light with *d.*?
Eph. 6. 12, rulers of the *d.* of this world.
1 Thes. 5. 5, not of the night nor of *d.*
Heb. 12. 18, to blackness and *d.*
1 Pet. 2. 9, out of *d.* into marvellous light.
2 Pet. 2. 4, into chains of *d.*
1 John 1. 5, in him is no *d.* at all.
1. 6, and walk in *d.*, we lie.
2. 8, the *d.* is past.
2. 9, hateth his brother, is in *d.*
2. 11, *d.* hath blinded his eyes.

JERUSALEM FROM THE NORTH-EAST
The 'Dome of the Rock' (left centre) now occupies the site of the Temple. (*John Stirling*)

STREET IN JERUSALEM

The traditional 'Via Dolorosa' (Way of Sorrows) along which Christ passed to Calvary.
(*John Stirling*)

Rev. 16. 10, kingdom full of *d.*
See Gen. 1. 2; Ex. 20. 21.
Darkness divided from light. Gen. 1. 18.
created by God. Isa. 45. 7.
supernatural. Gen. 15. 12; Ex. 10. 21; 14. 20; Jos. 24. 7; Rev. 8. 12; 9. 2; 16. 10.
at the crucifixion. Mat. 27. 45; Mk. 15. 33; Lu. 23. 44.
figurative of punishment. Mat. 8. 12; 22. 13; 2 Pet. 2. 4, 17; Jude 6.
of the mind. Job 37. 19; Prov. 2. 13; Eccl. 2. 14; Isa. 9. 2; 42. 7; John 1. 5; 3. 19; 8. 12; 12. 35; Rom. 13. 12; 1 Cor. 4. 5; 2 Cor. 4. 6; 6. 14; Eph. 5. 8; 1 Thes. 5. 4; 1 Pet. 2. 9; 1 John 1. 5; 2. 9.
powers of. Lu. 22. 53; Eph. 6. 12; Col. 1. 13.
Darkon, där'-kŏn, 'rapid walker' (?). Ez. 2. 56.
Darling. Ps. 22. 20; 35, 17.
Dart. A weapon like a large arrow or small spear. 2 Sam. 18. 14; 2 Chr. 32. 5. Sometimes darts were wrapped in a burning material. Eph. 6. 16; Job 41. 26; Prov. 7. 23; Eph. 6. 16.
Dash. Ps. 2. 9; Isa. 13. 16; Hos. 13. 16, *d.* in pieces.
91. 12; Mat. 4. 6; Lu. 4. 11, *d.* thy foot.
137. 9, that *d.* thy little ones.
See Ex. 15. 6; 2 Kn. 8. 12; Jer. 13. 14.
Dathan, dā'-thăn. Num. 16. 1.
Daub. Ex. 2. 3; Ezek. 13. 10; 22. 28. [art thou?
Daughter. Gen. 24. 23, 47; Jud. 11. 34, whose *d.*
27. 46, weary of life because of *d.* of Heth.
Deu. 28. 53, eat flesh of sons and *d.*
2 Sam. 1. 20, lest *d.* of Philistines rejoice.
12. 3, lamb was unto him as a *d.*
Ps. 45. 9, kings' *d.* among honourable women.
144. 12, our *d.* as corner stones.
Prov. 30. 15, horseleech hath two *d.*
31. 29, many *d.* have done virtuously.
Eccl. 12. 4, the *d.* of music. [of the *d.*
Isa. 22. 4; Jer. 9. 1; Lam. 2. 11; 3. 48, spoiling
Jer. 6. 14, healed hurt of *d.* of my people.
8. 21, for hurt of *d.* am I hurt.
9. 1, weep for slain of *d.* of my people.
Mic. 7. 6; Mat. 10. 35; Lu. 12. 53, *d.* riseth against mother.
Mat. 15. 28, her *d.* was made whole.
Lu. 8. 42, one only *d.*, about twelve years of age.
13. 16, this woman *d.* of Abraham.
Heb. 11. 24, refused to be son of Pharaoh's *d.*
See Gen. 6. 1; Ex. 1. 16; 21. 7; Num. 27. 8.
Daughters, their inheritance determined. Num. 27. 6; 36.
David, dā'-vĭd, 'beloved' (?). King, son of Jesse. Ru. 4. 22; 1 Chr. 2.; Mat. 1.
anointed by Samuel. 1 Sam. 16. 8.
plays the harp before Saul. 1 Sam. 16. 19.
his zeal and faith. 1 Sam. 17. 26, 34.
kills Goliath of Gath. 1 Sam. 17. 49.
at first honoured by Saul. 1 Sam. 18.
Saul, jealous of, tries to kill. 1 Sam. 18. 8, 12.
afterwards persecuted by him. 1 Sam. 19.; 20.
loved by Jonathan, 1 Sam. 18. 1; 19. 2; 20.; 123. 16. and by Michal, 1 Sam. 18. 28; 19. 11.
overcomes the Philistines. 1 Sam. 18. 27; 19. 8.
flees to Naioth. 1 Sam. 19. 18.
eats of the shewbread. 1 Sam. 21.; Ps. 52.; Mat. 12. 4.
flees to Gath, and feigns madness. 1 Sam. 21. 10, 13; Ps. 34.; 56.
dwells in the cave of Adullam. 1 Sam. 22.; Ps. 63.; 142.
escapes Saul's pursuit. 1 Sam. 23.; Ps. 57.
twice spares Saul's life. 1 Sam. 24. 4; 26. 5.
his wrath against Nabal appeased by Abigail. 1 Sam. 25. 23.
dwells at Ziklag. 1 Sam. 27.
dismissed from the army by Achish. 1 Sam. 29. 9.
chastises the Amalekites, and rescues the captives. 1 Sam. 30. 16.
kills messenger who brings news of Saul's death. 2 Sam. 1. 15.
laments the death of Saul and Jonathan. 2 Sam. 1. 17.
becomes king of Judah. 2 Sam. 2. 4.
forms a league with Abner. 2 Sam. 3. 13.
laments Abner's death. 2 Sam. 3. 31.
avenges the murder of Ish-bosheth. 2 Sam. 4. 9.
becomes king of all Israel. 2 Sam. 5. 3; 1 Chr. 11.
his victories. 2 Sam. 2.; 5.; 8.; 10.; 12. 29; 21. 15; 1 Chr. 18.-20.; Ps. 60.
brings the ark to Zion. 2 Sam. 6.; 1 Chr. 13.; 15.
his psalms of thanksgiving. 2 Sam. 22.; 1 Chr. 16. 7; Ps. 18.; 103.; 105.
Michal despises him for dancing before the ark. 2 Sam. 6. 20.
reproves her. 2 Sam. 6. 21.
desires to build God a house, 2 Sam. 7. 2. and is forbidden by Nathan, 1 Chr. 17. 4.
God's promises to him. 2 Sam. 7. 11; 1 Chr. 17. 10.
his prayer and thanksgiving. 2 Sam. 7. 18; 1 Chr. 17. 16.
his consideration for Mephibosheth. 2 Sam. 9.
his sin concerning Bath-sheba and Uriah. 2 Sam. 11.; 12.
repents at Nathan's parable of the ewe lamb. 2 Sam. 12.; Ps. 51.
Absalom conspires against. 2 Sam. 15.; Ps. 3.
Ahithophel's treachery against. 2 Sam. 15. 31; 16.; 17.
Shimei curses. 2 Sam. 16. 5; Ps. 7.
Barzillai's loyalty. 2 Sam. 17. 27.
grieves over Absalom's death. 2 Sam. 18. 33; 19. 1.
returns to Jerusalem. 2 Sam. 19. 15.
pardons Shimei. 2 Sam. 19. 16.
Sheba's conspiracy against. 2 Sam. 20.
atones for the Gibeonites. 2 Sam. 21.
his mighty men. 2 Sam. 23. 8; 1 Chr. 11. 10.
tempted by Satan, numbers the people. 2 Sam. 24.; 1 Chr. 21.
regulates the service of the tabernacle. 1 Chr. 23.-26.
exhorts the congregation to fear God. 1 Chr. 28.
appoints Solomon his successor. 1 Kn. 1.; Ps. 72.
his charge to Solomon, 1 Kn. 2; 1 Chr. 28. 9. to build a house for the sanctuary, 1 Chr. 22. 6; 28. 10.
his last words. 2 Sam. 23.
his death. 1 Kn. 2.; 1 Chr. 29. 26.
the progenitor of Christ. Mat. 1. 1; 9. 27; 21. 9; comp. Ps. 110. with Mat. 22. 41; Lu. 1. 32; John 7. 42; Acts 2. 25; 13. 22; 15. 15; Rom. 1. 3; 2 Tim. 2. 8; Rev. 5. 5; 22. 16.
prophecies concerning. Ps. 89.; 132.; Isa. 9. 7; 22. 22; 55. 3; Jer. 30. 9; Hos. 3. 5; Am. 9. 11.
Dawn. Ps. 119. 147, I prevented the *d.* of the morning.
2 Pet. 1. 19, till the day *d.*
See Jos. 6. 15; Jud. 19. 26; Job 3. 9; 7. 4.
Day.
The *Natural* Day was from sunrise to sunset.
The *Natural* Night was from sunset to sunrise.
The *Civil* Day was from sunset one evening to sunset the next; for, 'the Evening and the Morning were the first day.'

NIGHT (*Ancient*).

First Watch (Lam. 2. 19) till midnight.
Middle Watch (Jud. 7. 19) till 3 A. M.
Morning Watch (Ex. 14. 24) till 6 A. M.

DAY (*Ancient*).

Morning till about 10 A. M.
Heat of day till about 2 P. M.
Cool of day till about 6 P. M.

NIGHT (*New Testament*).

First Watch, *evening* = 6 to 9 P. M.
Second Watch, *midnight* = 9 to 12 P. M.
Third Watch, *cock-crow* = 12 to 3 A. M.
Fourth Watch, *morning* = 3 to 6 A. M.

DAY (*New Testament*).

Third hour = 6 to 9 A. M.
Sixth hour = 9 to 12 midday.
Ninth hour = 12 to 3 P. M.
Twelfth hour = 3 to 6 P. M.

For number of days in each month, *see* MONTHS, the Jewish Calendar.
Gen. 41. 9, I do remember my faults this *d.*
Deu. 4. 32, ask of the *d.* that are past.
1 Sam. 25. 8, come in a good *d.*
2 Kn. 7. 9, this *d.* is a *d.* of good tidings.
1 Chr. 23. 1 ; 29. 28 ; 2 Chr. 24. 15, full of *d.*
29. 15 ; Job 8. 9, our *d.* as a shadow.
Neh. 4. 2, will they make an end in a *d.*
Job 7. 1, *d.* like the *d.* of an hireling.
14. 6, till he accomplish his *d.*
19. 25, stand at latter *d.* upon the earth.
21. 30, reserved to *d.* of destruction.
32. 7, I said, *d.* should speak.
Ps. 2. 7 ; Acts 13. 33 ; Heb. 1. 5, this *d.* have I begotten thee.
19. 2, *d.* unto *d.* uttereth speech.
84. 10, a *d.* in thy courts.
Prov. 3. 2, 16, length of *d.*
4. 18, more and more to perfect *d.*
27. 1, what a *d.* may bring forth.
Eccl. 7. 1, *d.* of death better than *d.* of birth.
12. 1, while the evil *d.* come not.
Isa. 2. 12 ; 13. 6, 9 ; Joel 1. 15 ; 2. 1 ; Zep. 1. 7 ; Zec. 14. 1, *d.* of the Lord.
10. 3, in the *d.* of visitation.
27. 3, the Lord will keep it night and *d.*
58. 5, acceptable *d.* to the Lord.
65. 20, an infant of *d.*
Joel 2. 11, 31 ; Zep. 1. 14 ; Mal. 4. 5 ; Acts 2. 20, great *d.* of the Lord.
Zec. 4. 10, despised *d.* of small things.
Mal. 3. 2, who may abide *d.* of his coming.
Mat. 7. 22, many will say in that *d.*
Mat. 24. 36 ; Mk. 13. 32, that *d.* knoweth no man.
24. 50 ; Lu. 12. 46, in a *d.* looked not for.
25. 13, ye know not the *d.* nor the hour.
Lu. 21. 34, that *d.* come unawares.
23. 43, to *d.* shalt thou be with me.
John 6. 39, raise it again at last *d.*
8. 56, Abraham rejoiced to see my *d.*
9. 4, I must work while it is *d.*
Acts 17. 31, he hath appointed a *d.*
Rom. 2. 5, wrath against *d.* of wrath.
14. 5, esteemeth every *d.* alike.
2 Cor. 6. 2, the *d.* of salvation.
Phil. 1. 6, perform it until *d.* of Christ.
1 Thes. 5. 2 ; 2 Pet. 3. 10, *d.* cometh as a thief.
5. 5, children of the *d.*
Heb. 13. 8, Jesus Christ same to *d.* and for ever.
2 Pet. 3. 8, one *d.* as a thousand years.
See Gen. 1. 5 ; 27. 2 ; Job 1. 4 ; Ps. 77. 5 ; 118. 24 ; John 11. 24 ; 12. 48 ; 1 Cor. 3. 13 ; Rev. 6. 17 ; 16. 14 ; 20. 10.

Days (last). Isa. 2. 2, it shall come to pass in the last *d.*
See Mic. 4. 1 ; Acts 2. 17 ; 2 Tim. 3. 1 ; Heb. 1. 2 ; Jas. 5. 3 ; 2 Pet. 3. 3.

Daysman. A man who appoints a day for hearing a cause, hence an umpire, arbitrator. Job 9. 33.

Dayspring. Job 38. 12, *d.* to know his place.
Lu. 1. 78, *d.* from on high hath visited us.

Daystar. 2 Pet. 1. 19, *d.* arise in your hearts.

Deacons appointed. Acts 6. ; Phil. 1. 1.
their qualifications. Acts 6. 3 ; 1 Tim. 3. 8.

Dead. Lev. 19. 28, cuttings for the *d.*
Ru. 1. 8, as ye have dealt with *d.*
1 Sam. 24. 14 ; 2 Sam. 9. 8 ; 16. 9, *d.* dog.
Ps. 31. 12, forgotten as a *d.* man.
115. 17, *d.* praise not the Lord.
Prov. 9. 18, knoweth not that the *d.* are there.
Eccl. 4. 2, the *d.* which are already *d.*
9. 4, living dog better than *d.* lion.
9. 5, *d.* know not any thing.
10. 1, *d.* flies cause ointment.
Isa. 26. 19, thy *d.* men shall live.
Jer. 22. 10, weep not for the *d.*
Mat. 8. 22, let the *d.* bury their *d.*
Mat. 9. 24 ; Mk. 5. 39 ; Lu. 8. 52, not *d.* but sleepeth.
11. 5 ; Lu. 7. 22, deaf hear, *d.* raised.
Mat. 22. 32, not God of the *d.*
23. 27, full of *d.* men's bones.
Mk. 9. 10, rising from *d.* should mean.
Lu. 15. 24, 32 ; Rev. 1. 18, *d.* and is alive again.
16. 31, though one rose from the *d.*
John 5. 25, *d.* shall hear.
6. 49, did eat manna, and are *d.*
11. 25, though *d.*, yet shall he live.
11. 44, he that was *d.* came forth.
Acts 10. 42 ; 2 Tim. 4. 1, judge of quick and *d.*
26. 23, first that should rise from *d.*
Rom. 6. 2, 11 ; 1 Pet. 2. 24, *d.* to sin.
7. 4 ; Gal. 2. 19, *d.* to the law.
14. 9, Lord both of *d.* and living.
1 Cor. 15. 15, if the *d.* rise not.
15. 35, how are the *d.* raised.
2 Cor. 1. 9, trust in God who raiseth *d.*
5. 14, then were all *d.*
Eph. 2. 1 ; Col. 2. 13, *d.* in trespasses and sins.
5. 14, arise from the *d.*
Col. 1. 18, firstborn from the *d.*
2. 20 ; 2 Tim. 2. 11, *d.* with Christ.
1 Thes. 4. 16, *d.* in Christ shall rise first.
1 Tim. 5. 6, *d.* while she liveth.
Heb. 6. 1 ; 9. 14, from *d.* works.
11. 4, being *d.*, yet speaketh.
13. 20, brought again from the *d.*
Jas. 2. 17, 20, 26, faith *d.* R. V. barren.
1 Pet. 4. 6, preached to them that are *d.*
Jude 12, twice *d.*
Rev. 1. 5, first-begotten of the *d.*
3. 1, a name that thou livest and art *d.*
14. 13, blessed are the *d.*
20. 5, rest of *d.* lived not again.
20. 12, the *d.* small and great.
20. 13, sea gave up *d.*

Dead, the. Job 3. 18 ; 14. 12 ; Ps. 6. 5 ; 88. 10 ; 115. 17 ; 146. 4 ; Eccl. 9. 5 ; 12. 7 ; Isa. 38. 18.
resurrection of. Job 19. 26 ; Ps. 49. 15 ; Isa. 26. 19 ; Dan. 12. 2, 13 ; John 5. 25 ; 1 Cor. 15. 12.
raised by Elijah, 1 Kn. 17. 17. by Elisha, 2 Kn. 4. 32 ; 13. 21. by CHRIST, Mat. 9. 24 ; Mk. 5. 41 ; Lu. 7. 12 ; 8. 54 ; John 11. by Peter, Acts 9. 40. by Paul, Acts 20. 10.
sleep in Jesus. 1 Thes. 4. 13.

Deadly. Mk. 16. 18, drink any *d.* thing.
Jas. 3. 8, tongue full of *d.* poison.
See 1 Sam. 5. 11 ; Ps. 17. 9 ; Ezek. 30. 24.

Deaf. Ps. 58. 4, like *d.* adder that stoppeth.
Isa. 29. 18, shall the *d.* hear the words.
Mat. 11. 5 ; Lu. 7. 22, the *d.* hear.
Mk. 7. 37, he maketh the *d.* to hear.
9. 25, thou *d.* spirit, come out.
See Ex. 4. 11 ; Lev. 19. 14 ; Isa. 42. 18 ; 43. 8.

Deal (a measure). Ex. 29. 40, with the one lamb, a tenth *d.* of flour.
Lev. 14. 10, three tenth *d.* of fine flour for a meat offering.

Deal. (1) to act. Gen. 24. 49, *d.* kindly.
Lev. 19. 11, nor *d.* falsely.
Job 42. 8, *d.* with you after folly.
Ps. 75. 4, *d.* not foolishly.
Prov. 12. 22, they that *d.* truly his delight.
Isa. 21. 2 ; 24. 16, treacherous dealer *d.* treacherously.
26. 10, in land of uprightness *d.* unjustly.
Jer. 6. 13 ; 8. 10, every one *d.* falsely.
Hos. 5. 7, have *d.* treacherously against the Lord.
Zec. 1. 6, as Lord thought, so hath he *d.*
Lu. 2. 48, why hast thou thus *d.* with us ?
Rom. 12. 3, according as God hath *d.*
See Gen. 32. 9 ; Ex. 1. 10 ; Deu. 7. 5 ; 2 Chr. 2. 3.
(2) to distribute. Isa. 58. 7.

Dealing. 1 Sam. 2. 23 ; Ps. 7. 16 ; John 4. 9.

Dear. (1) Jer. 31. 20, is Ephraim my *d.* son.
Rom. 12. 19 ; 1 Cor. 10. 14 ; 2 Cor. 7. 1 ; 12. 19 ; Phil. 4. 1 ; 2 Tim. 1. 2 ; 1 Pet. 2. 11, *d.* beloved.
Eph. 5. 1, followers of God as *d.* children.
Col. 1. 13, into kingdom of his *d.* Son.
1 Thes. 2. 8, because ye were *d.* unto us.
(2) precious, of value. Acts 20. 24.
See Jer. 12. 7 ; Lu. 7. 2 ; Philem. 1.

Dearth. 2 Chr. 6. 28, if there be a *d.* in the land.
Neh. 5. 3, buy corn because of *d.*
Acts 11. 28, Agabus signified a great *d.*
See Gen. 41. 54; 2 Kn. 4. 38; Jer. 14. 1; Acts 7. 11.
Death. Num. 16. 29, if these men die common *d.*
23. 10, let me die *d.* of righteous.
Jud. 5. 18, jeoparded lives to the *d.*
16. 16, soul was vexed to *d.*
16. 30, which he slew at his *d.* were more.
Ru. 1. 17, if aught but *d.* part thee and me.
1 Sam. 15. 32, the bitterness of *d.* past.
20. 3, but a step between me and *d.*
2 Sam. 1. 23, in *d.* not divided.
22. 5; Ps. 18. 4; 116. 3, waves of *d.* compassed.
Job 3. 21, long for *d.*, but it cometh not.
7. 15, my soul chooseth *d.*
30. 23, thou wilt bring me to *d.*
Ps. 6. 5, in *d.* no remembrance.
13. 3, lest I sleep the sleep of *d.*
23. 4, valley of shadow of *d.*
48. 14, our guide even unto *d.*
68. 20, the issues from *d.*
89. 48, what man shall not see *d.*?
102. 20, loose those appointed to *d.*
107. 10, in darkness and shadow of *d.*
116. 15, precious is *d.* of his saints.
Prov. 7. 27, to chambers of *d.*
8. 36, that hate me love *d.*
14. 32, righteous hath hope in his *d.*
24. 11, deliver them drawn to *d.*
S. of S. 8. 6, love is strong as *d.*
Isa. 9. 2; Jer. 2. 6, land of the shadow of *d.*
25. 8; 1 Cor. 15. 54, swallow up *d.* in victory.
38. 18, for *d.* cannot celebrate thee.
Jer. 8. 3, *d.* chosen rather than life.
9. 21, *d.* come up to our windows.
Ezek. 18. 32; 33. 11, no pleasure in *d.*
Hos. 13. 14, O *d.*, I will be thy plagues.
Mat. 15. 4; Mk. 7. 10, let him die the *d.*
16. 28; Mk. 9. 1; Lu. 9. 27, not taste of *d.*
26. 38; Mk. 14. 34, my soul is sorrowful to *d.*
Mk. 5. 23; John 4. 47, lieth at point of *d.*
Lu. 2. 26, should not see *d.* before.
22. 33, will go to prison and *d.*
John 5. 24; 1 John 3. 14, passed from *d.* to life.
8. 51, 52, keep my saying, shall never see *d.*
11. 4, sickness not unto *d.*
12. 33; 18. 32; 21. 19, signifying what *d.*
Acts 2. 24, having loosed pains of *d.*
Rom. 1. 32, such things are worthy of *d.*
5. 10; Col. 1. 21, 22, reconciled by the *d.*
5. 12, *d.* by sin and so *d.* passed on all.
5. 14, 17, *d.* reigned from Adam to Moses.
6. 5, planted in likeness of his *d.*
6. 21, end of those things is *d.*
6. 23, wages of sin is *d.*
8. 2, law of sin and *d.*
1 Cor. 3. 22, life or *d.* all are yours.
11. 26, shew the Lord's *d.* till he come.
15. 21, by man came *d.*
15. 55, 56, O *d.*, where is thy sting?
2 Cor. 1. 9, sentence of *d.* in ourselves.
2. 16, savour of *d.* unto *d.*
4. 12, *d.* worketh in us.
11. 23, in *d.* oft.
Phil. 2. 8, *d.*, even *d.* of the cross.
Heb. 2. 9, taste *d.* for every man.
2. 15, through fear of *d.* were.
Jas. 1. 15, sin bringeth forth *d.*
1 John 5. 16, a sin unto *d.*
Rev. 1. 18, keys of hell and of *d.*
2. 10, be faithful unto *d.*
2. 11; 20. 6, 14, second *d.*
6. 8, his name that sat on him was *d.*
9. 6, seek *d.* and *d.* shall flee.
20. 13, *d.* and hell delivered up.
21. 4, no more *d.*
Death the consequence of Adam's sin. Gen. 2. 17; 3. 19; Rom. 5. 12; 6. 23; 1 Cor. 15. 21.
universal. Job 1. 21; 3. 17; 14. 1, 10; 21. 13; Ps. 49. 19; 89. 48; Eccl. 5. 15; 8. 8; 9. 5, 10; 11. 8; Heb. 9. 27.
threatened. Rom. 1. 32.
characterized. Gen. 3. 19; Deu. 31. 16 (John 11. 11); Job 1. 21; 3. 13; 10. 21; 12. 22; 14. 2; 16. 22; 24. 17; Ps. 16. 10; 23. 4; 104. 29; Eccl. 9. 10; Hab. 2. 5; Lu. 12. 20; 2 Cor. 5. 1, 8; Phil. 1. 23; 1 Tim. 6. 7; 2 Pet. 1. 14.
as a punishment. Gen. 9. 6; Ex. 12. 29, 30; 21. 12; 22. 18; 31. 14; 35. 2; Lev. 20. 2; 21. 9; 1 Kn. 21. 10; Mat. 15. 4.
vanquished by Christ. Rom. 6. 9; 1 Cor. 15. 26 (Hos. 13. 14); 2 Tim. 1. 10; Heb. 2. 15; Rev. 1. 18.
prayers and exhortations concerning. 2 Kn. 20. 1; Ps. 39.; 90.; Eccl. 9. 10; John 9. 4; 1 Pet. 1. 24.
unknown in heaven. Lu. 20. 36; Rev. 21. 4.
persons exempted from:—Enoch, Gen. 5. 24; Heb. 11. 5. Elijah, 2 Kn. 2. 11. *See* 1 Cor. 15. 51; 1 Thes. 4. 17.
SPIRITUAL. Isa. 9. 2; Mat. 4. 16; 8. 22; Lu. 1. 79; John 6. 53; Rom. 5. 15; 6. 13; 8. 6; Eph. 2. 1; 4. 18; Col. 2. 13; 1 Tim. 5. 6; Heb. 6. 1; 9. 14; 1 John 3. 14; Rev. 3. 1.
deliverance from, by Christ. John 5. 24; Rom. 6. 11; Eph. 2. 5; 5. 14; 1 John 5. 12.
ETERNAL. Prov. 14. 12; Dan. 12. 2; Mat. 7. 13; 10. 28, 23. 33; 25. 30, 41; Mk. 9. 44; John 5. 29; Rom. 1. 32; 2. 8; 6. 23; 9. 22; 2 Thes. 1. 7; Jas. 4. 12; 2 Pet. 2. 17.
(the second death). Rev. 2. 11; 19. 20; 20. 14; 21. 8.
salvation from, by Christ. John 3. 16; 8. 51.
by conversion from sin. Jas. 5. 20.
of CHRIST, foretold. Isa. 53.; Dan. 9. 26; Zec. 13. 7.
See Mat. 26. 31 (Deu. 21. 23; Gal. 3. 13); Heb. 2. 9; 12. 2; 1 Pet. 1. 11.
voluntary. Lu. 12. 50; John 10. 11, 18; Heb. 10. 7.
its object. Isa. 53.; Dan. 9. 26; Mat. 20. 28; Rom. 5. 6; 6. 10; 1 Cor. 5. 7; 1 Tim. 2. 6; Tit. 2. 14; Heb. 9. 26; 1 Pet. 1. 18; Rev. 1. 5.
of SAINTS. Num. 23. 10; 2 Kn. 22. 20; Ps. 23. 4; 48. 14; 116. 15; Prov. 14. 32; Isa. 26. 19; 57. 1; Dan. 12. 2; Lu. 16. 25; John 11. 11; 2 Cor. 5. 8; Phil. 1. 21; 2 Tim. 4. 8; Heb. 11. 13; Rev. 2. 10.
of Abraham, Gen. 25. 8. Isaac, Gen. 35. 29. Jacob, Gen. 49. Aaron, Num. 20. 23. Moses, Deu. 34. 5. Joshua, Jos. 24. 29. David, 1 Kn. 2. Elisha, 2 Kn. 13. 14. Stephen, Acts 7. 54. Dorcas, Acts 9. 37.
OF THE WICKED. Job 18. 11; 21. 13; 27. 19; Ps. 34. 16; 49. 14; 73. 19; Prov. 10. 7; 11. 7; 14. 32; 29. 1; Isa. 14. 9; Ezek. 3. 19; 18. 23; Dan. 12. 2; Lu. 12. 20; 16. 22; John 8. 21; Acts 1. 25.
of Nadab and Abihu, Lev. 10. 1, 2; Num. 3. 4. Korah, &c., Num. 16. 32. Hophni and Phinehas, 1 Sam. 4. 11. Absalom, 2 Sam. 18. 9. Ahab, 1 Kn. 22. 34. Jezebel, 2 Kn. 9. 33. Athaliah, 2 Chr. 23. 15. Haman, Esth. 7. 10. Judas, Mat. 27. 5; Acts 1. 18. Ananias, &c., Acts 5. 5. Herod, Acts 12. 23.
Debase. Isa. 57. 9.
Debate. (1) strife, contention. Isa. 58. 4; Rom. 1. 29; 2 Cor. 12. 20.
(2) Prov. 25. 9, *d.* thy cause.
Debir, dē'-bĭr, 'sanctuary,' or 'innermost room of a temple.' (1) king of Eglon, Jos. 10. 3. (2) cities, Jos. 15. 7; 15. 49. (3) district, Jos. 13. 26.
Deborah, dĕb'-ō-răh, 'bee.' (1) Rebekah's nurse, death of. Gen. 35. 8.
(2) the prophetess judges and delivers Israel, Jud. 4. her song, Jud. 5.
Debt. 2 Kn. 4. 7, go, pay thy *d.* and live.
Neh. 10. 31, leave the exaction of every *d.*
Prov. 22. 26, be not sureties for *d.*
Mat. 18. 27, forgave him the *d.*
See 1 Sam. 22. 2; Mat. 6. 12; Rom. 4. 4.
Debt censured. Ps. 37. 21; Prov. 3. 27; Lu. 16. 5; Rom. 13. 8.
Debtor. Mat. 6. 12, as we forgive our *d.*
Lu. 7. 41, creditor which had two *d.*
Rom. 1. 14, I am *d.* to the Greeks.

8. 12, we are *d.*, not to the flesh.
15. 27, their *d.* they are.
Gal. 5. 3, *d.* to do the whole law.
See Ezek. 18. 7; Mat. 18. 21; 23. 16; Lu. 16. 5.
Decapolis, dĕ-căp'-ō-lĭs, 'ten cities.' A district east of the Jordan. Mat. 4. 25.
Decay. Lev. 25. 35; Neh. 4. 10; Heb. 8. 13.
Decease. Isa. 26. 14; Mat. 22. 25; Lu. 9. 31; 2 Pet. 1. 15.
Deceit. Ps. 10. 7, mouth full of *d.* and fraud.
36. 3, words are iniquity and *d.*
55. 23, *d.* men shall not live half their days.
Prov. 12. 5, counsels of wicked are *d.*
20. 17, bread of *d.* is sweet.
27. 6, kisses of an enemy are *d.*
31. 30, favour is *d.* and beauty vain.
Jer. 14. 14; 23. 26, prophesy the *d.* of their heart.
17. 9, heart is *d.* above all things.
48. 10, that doeth work of the Lord *d.*
Hos. 11. 12, compasseth me with *d.*
Am. 8. 5, falsifying balances by *d.*
Zep. 1. 9, fill their masters' houses with *d.*
Mat. 13. 22; Mk. 4. 19, the *d.* of riches.
Mk. 7. 22, out of heart proceed *d.*
Rom. 3. 13, they have used *d.*
2 Cor. 4. 2, handling word of God *d.*
11. 13, false apostles, *d.* workers.
Eph. 4. 22, according to *d.* lusts.
Col. 2. 8, vain *d.*, after tradition.
See Ps. 50. 19; Jer. 5. 27; Mic. 6. 11.
Deceit proceeds from the heart. Prov. 12. 20; Jer. 17. 9.
by false prophets. 1 Kn. 22.
(and lying), work of the devil. John 8. 44; Acts 5. 3.
Some Memorable Instances of:—
the serpent and Eve. Gen. 3.
Abram and his wife. Gen. 12. 14.
Isaac and his wife. Gen. 26. 10.
Jacob and Esau. Gen. 27.
Jael and Sisera. Jud. 4. 20.
the old prophet. 1 Kn. 13. 18.
Rahab and spies at Jericho. Jos. 2. 1, 4, 5.
Gehazi and Naaman. 2 Kn. 5. 20.
Herod and the wise men. Mat. 2. 7, 8.
Ananias and Sapphira. Acts 5. 1. *See* Lying.
Deceive. Deu. 11. 16, take heed that your heart be not *d.*
2 Kn. 19. 10; Isa. 37. 10; let not thy God *d.* thee.
Job 12. 16, the *d.* and the *d.* are his.
Jer. 20. 7, thou hast *d.* me and I was *d.*
37. 9, *d.* not yourselves.
Obad. 3, pride of heart hath *d.* thee.
Mat. 24. 24, if possible *d.* the very elect.
27. 63, remember that *d.* said.
John 7. 12, nay, but he *d.* the people. R. V. leadeth astray.
7. 47, are ye also *d.*? R. V. led astray.
1 Cor. 6. 9; 15. 33; Gal. 6. 4, be not *d.*
2 Cor. 6. 8, as *d.*, and yet true.
Eph. 4. 14, whereby they lie in wait to *d.*
5. 6; 2 Thes. 2. 3; 1 John 3. 7, let no man *d.* you.
1 Tim. 2. 14, Adam was not *d.*
2 Tim. 3. 13, worse and worse, *d.* and being *d.*
1 John 1. 8, no sin, we *d.* ourselves. R. V. lead astray.
2 John 7, many *d.* entered into world.
See Gen. 31. 7; Isa. 44. 20; Ezek. 14. 9; Rev. 12. 9; 19. 20.
Decently, in a becoming manner. 1 Cor. 14. 40.
Decision. Joel 3. 14, valley of *d.*
Decision, how manifested. Ex. 32. 26; Num. 14. 24; Deu. 6. 5; Jos. 1. 7; 24. 15; 1 Kn. 18. 21; 2 Chr. 15. 12; Isa. 56. 6; Lu. 9. 62; 1 Cor. 15. 58; Heb. 3. 6, 14; Jas. 1. 8; 4. 7.
opposed to wavering. Deu. 5. 32; 1 Kn. 18. 21; Ps. 78. 8; Mat. 6. 24; Jas. 1. 8.
of Moses. Ex. 32. 26.
of Caleb. Num. 13. 30.
of Joshua. Jos. 24. 15.
of Ruth. Ru. 1. 16.
of Paul. Acts 21. 13; Gal. 1. 16.
Deck. Job 40. 10, *d.* thyself with majesty.
Isa. 61. 10, as a bridegroom *d.* himself.
Jer. 4. 30, though thou *d.* thee with ornaments.
10. 4, they *d.* it with silver.
See Prov. 7. 16; Ezek. 16. 11; Rev. 17. 4; 18. 16.
Declaration. Esth. 10. 2; Job 13. 17; Lu. 1. 1; 2 Cor. 8. 19.
Declare, to make clear or manifest. Gen. 41. 24, none could *d.* it.
1 Chr. 16. 24; Ps. 96. 3, *d.* glory among heathen.
Job 21. 31, who shall *d.* his way to his face.
31. 37, I would *d.* number of my steps.
Ps. 2. 7, I will *d.* decree.
9. 11, *d.* among the people his doings.
19. 1, heavens *d.* glory of God.
30. 9, shall dust *d.* thy truth.
40. 10, I have *d.* thy faithfulness.
66. 16, I will *d.* what he hath done.
75. 9, I will *d.* for ever.
118. 17, live and *d.* the works of the Lord.
145. 4, one generation shall *d.* thy mighty acts.
Isa. 3. 9, they *d.* their sin as Sodom.
41. 26; 45. 21, who hath *d.* from beginning.
45. 19, I *d.* things that are right.
46. 10, *d.* end from the beginning.
53. 8; Acts 8. 33, who shall *d.* his generation.
66. 19, *d.* my glory among Gentiles.
John 17. 26, have *d.* thy name and will *d.* it.
Acts 13. 32, we *d.* to you glad tidings.
17. 23, him *d.* I unto you.
20. 27, *d.* the counsel of God.
Rom. 1. 4, *d.* to be Son of God with power.
1 Cor. 3. 13, day shall *d.* it.
See Jos. 20. 4; John 1. 18; Heb. 11. 14; 1 John 1. 3.
Decline. (1) to turn aside. Deu. 17. 11, thou shalt not *d.* from sentence.
2 Chr. 34. 2, *d.* neither to right nor left.
(2) to sink to a lower level. Ps. 102. 11.
109. 23, days like a shadow that *d.*
119. 51, 157, not *d.* from thy law.
See Ex. 23. 2; Job 23. 11; Prov. 4. 5; 7. 25.
Decrease. Gen. 8. 5; Ps. 107. 38; John 3. 30.
Decree. Job 22. 28, thou shalt *d.* a thing and it shall be.
28. 26, made a *d.* for the rain.
Ps. 148. 6, a *d.* which shall not pass.
Prov. 8. 15, by me princess *d.* justice.
8. 29, he gave to the sea his *d.* R. V. its bounds.
Isa. 10. 1, that *d.* unrighteous *d.*
Acts 16. 4, delivered the *d.* to keep.
See Dan. 2. 9; 6. 8; Acts 17. 7; 1 Cor. 7. 37.
Dedan, dē'-dăn. Gen. 10. 7.
Dedanim, dē'-dă-nĭm, inhabitants of Dedan. Isa. 21. 13.
Dedicate. Deu. 20. 5, lest he die and another *d.* it.
Jud. 17. 3, wholly *d.* silver to the Lord.
1 Chr. 26. 27, of spoil they did *d.* [R. V. devoted.
Ezek. 44. 29, every *d.* thing shall be theirs.
See 1 Kn. 7. 51; 8. 63; 15. 15; 1 Chr. 18. 11; Heb. 9. 18.
Dedication, Feast of. John 10. 22. This feast was instituted to commemorate the cleansing of the temple after its defilement by Antiochus Epiphanes (Dan. 11. 31). 1 Macc. 4. 52-59. It was kept on the 25th of the winter month *Chisleu*, December, and lasted eight days.
Dedication of tabernacle. Ex. 40.; Lev. 8.; Num. 7.
of temple. 1 Kn. 8.; 2 Chr. 5. 6.
of wall of Jerusalem. Neh. 12. 27.
Deed. Ex. 9. 16; 1 Sam. 25. 34; 26. 4, in very *d.*
2 Sam. 12. 14, by this *d.* hast given occasion.
Ez. 9. 13, come upon us for our evil *d.*
Neh. 13. 14, wipe not out my good *d.*
Ps. 28. 4; Isa. 59. 18; Jer. 25. 14; Rom. 2. 6, according to their *d.*
Lu. 11. 48, ye allow the *d.* of your fathers.
23. 41, due reward of our *d.*
24. 19, a prophet mighty in *d.*
John 3. 19, because their *d.* were evil.
8. 41, ye do the *d.* of your father.
Acts 7. 22, Moses, mighty in word and *d.*
Rom. 3. 20, by *d.* of law no flesh justified.
3. 28, justified without *d.* of the law.
Col. 3. 9, put off old man with his *d.*

Col. 3. 17, whatsoever ye do in word or *d.*
Jas. 1. 25, shall be blessed in his *d.*
1 John 3. 18, not love in word, but in *d.*
See Gen. 44. 15; Lu. 23. 51; Acts 19. 18.
Deeds of the body mortified. Rom. 8. 13; 13. 14; 1 Cor. 9. 27. denounced, 2 Pet. 2. 10.
Deemed. Acts 27. 27. R. V. surmised.
Deep. Gen. 7. 11; 8. 2, fountains of *d.*
Deu. 33. 13, the *d.* that coucheth beneath.
Job 38. 30, face of *d.* is frozen.
41. 31, maketh the *d.* boil like a pot.
Ps. 36. 6, thy judgments are a great *d.*
42. 7, *d.* calleth to *d.*
95. 4, in his hand are the *d.* places.
107. 24, see his wonders in the *d.*
Prov. 22. 14; 23. 27, strange women *d.* pit.
Isa. 63. 13, led them through *d.*
Mat. 13. 5, no *d.* of earth.
Lu. 5. 4, launch into *d.*
6. 48. digged *d.* and laid foundations.
8. 31, command to go into the *d.*
John 4. 11, the well is *d.*
1 Cor. 2. 10, searcheth *d.* things of God.
See Job 4. 13; 33. 15; Prov. 19. 15; Rom. 10. 7.
Deer. (1) (Deu. 12. 15). Heb. *Tsĕbî:* Gk. δορκάς: R. V. gazelle. There are four Hebrew words probably denoting deer or antelopes: (1) *Tsĕbî* ('roe,' or 'roe-buck,' A. V.), the gazelle. 2 Sam. 2. 18; Isa. 13. 14; Acts 9. 36, Tabitha.
(2) (Deu. 14. 5; Isa. 51. 20). Heb. *Tô*, or *teô:* Gk. ἔλαφος ('wild ox,' and 'wild bull,' A. V.), the antelope.
(3) (Deu. 14. 5). Heb. *Dîshôn:* Gk. πύγαργος (the 'pygarg,' A. V.), probably the Mendes antelope (*Addax nasomaculatus*).
(4) (Deu. 14. 5; 1 Kn. 4. 23). Heb. *Yaḥmûr:* Gk. βούβαλος (fallow deer, A. V.), the *Alcephalus bubalis*, still called 'yachmur' by Arabs.
Defame. Jer. 20. 10; 1 Cor. 4. 13.
Defeat. 2 Sam. 15. 34; 17. 14.
Defence. Job 22. 25, the Almighty shall be thy *d.* R. V. treasure.
Ps. 7. 10, my *d.* is of God. R. V. shield.
59. 9, 17; 62. 2, for God is my *d.* R. V. high tower.
89. 18; 94. 22, Lord is *d.*
Eccl. 7. 12, wisdom a *d.*, money a *d.*
Isa. 33. 16, place of *d.* munitions of rocks.
Phil. 1. 7, 17, in *d.* of the gospel.
See Num. 14. 9; Acts 19. 33; 22. 1. [36. 1.
Defenced, fenced, defended by fortifications. Isa.
Defend. Ps. 5. 11, shout for joy, because thou *d.* them.
82. 3, *d.* the poor and fatherless.
Zec. 9. 15, Lord of hosts shall *d.* them.
Acts 7. 24, *d.* him and avenged the oppressed.
See Ps. 20. 1; 59. 1; Isa. 31. 5.
Defile. Ex. 31. 14, that *d.* sabbath be put to death. R. V. profaneth.
Num. 35. 33, blood *d.* the land. R. V. polluteth.
2 Kn. 23. 13, high places did king *d.*
Neh. 13. 29, they have *d.* the priesthood.
Ps. 74. 7, *d.* dwelling place of thy name. R. V. profaned.
106. 39, *d.* with their own works.
Isa. 59. 3, your hands are *d.* with blood.
Jer. 2. 7; 16. 18, ye *d.* my land.
Ezek. 4. 13, eat their *d.* bread. R. V. unclean.
23. 38, they have *d.* my sanctuary.
36. 17, they *d.* it by their own ways.
Dan. 1. 8, would not *d.* himself with meat.
Mat. 15. 11, 18, 20; Mk. 7. 15, 20, 23, *d.* a man.
John 18. 28, lest they should be *d.*
1 Cor. 3. 17, if any man *d.* temple of God. R. V. destroyeth.
8. 7, conscience being weak is *d.*
1 Tim. 1. 10, *d.* themselves. R. V. abusers of.
Tit. 1. 15, to *d.* nothing pure, even conscience *d.*
Heb. 12. 15, thereby many be *d.*
Jude 8, filthy dreamers *d.* flesh.
Rev. 3. 4, few not *d.* their garments.
See Ex. 31. 41; Lev. 21. 4; Jas. 3. 6; Rev. 21. 27.

Defraud. 1 Sam. 12. 3, 4, whom have I *d.*?
Mk. 10. 19; 1 Cor. 7. 5, *d.* not.
1 Cor. 6. 7, rather suffer to be *d.*
6. 8, do wrong and *d.* your brethren.
2 Cor. 7. 2, we have *d.* no man.
See Lev. 19. 13. R. V. oppress. 1 Thes. 4. 6. R. V. wrong.
Degenerate. Jer. 2. 21.
Degree, rank, station, position. Ps. 62. 9, men of low *d.*, high *d.*
1 Tim. 3. 13, purchase to themselves good *d.*
Jas. 1. 9, brother of low *d.* rejoice.
See 1 Chr. 17. 17; Lu. 1. 52.
Dehavites, dĕ-hā′-vītes. Ez. 4. 9.
Dehort, to dissuade. 1 Mac. 9. 9. [Bendekar.
Dekar, dē′-kär, 'piercing.' 1 Kn. 4. 9. R. V.
Delaiah, dĕl-âī′-ăh, 'Jehovah has drawn.' 1 Chr. 24. 18. [ing. R. V. tarrieth.
Delay. Mat. 24. 48; Lu. 12. 45, my lord *d.* his com-
Acts 9. 38, that he would not *d.* to come.
See Ex. 22. 29; 32. 1; Acts 25. 17.
Delectable. Isa. 44. 9.
Delicacy. Rev. 18. 3. R. V. wantonness.
Delicate. (1) Prov. 29. 21, *d.* bringeth up servant.
Isa. 47. 1, no more called tender and *d.*
Lam. 4. 5, that did feed *d.* are desolate.
Lu. 7. 25, that lived *d.* are in kings' courts.
See Deu. 28. 54, 56; Jer. 6. 2; Mic. 1. 16.
Delicately, daintily, effeminately. 1 Sam. 15. 32. R. V. cheerfully.
Deliciously, luxuriously. Rev. 18. 7. R. V. wanton.
Delight (*n.*). Deu. 10. 15, the Lord had a *d.* in thy fathers.
1 Sam. 15. 22, hath Lord as great *d.* in offerings.
2 Sam. 15. 26, I have no *d.* in thee.
Job 22. 26, shalt thou have *d.* in the Almighty.
Ps. 1. 2, his *d.* is in law of Lord.
16. 3, to excellent in whom is my *d.*
119. 24, testimonies my *d.* and counsel.
119. 77, 92, 174, thy law is my *d.*
119. 143, thy commandments are my *d.*
Prov. 8. 30, I was daily his *d.*
8. 31, my *d.* were with sons of men.
18. 2, fool hath no *d.* in understanding.
19. 10, *d.* not seemly for a fool. R. V. delicate living.
S. of S. 2. 3, under his shadow with great *d.*
Isa. 58. 13, call sabbath a *d.*
See Prov. 11. 1; 12. 22; 15. 8; 16. 13.
Delight (*v.*). Job 27. 10, will he *d.* himself in the Almighty?
Ps. 37. 4, *d.* also in the Lord.
37. 11, meek shall *d.* in abundance of peace.
51. 16, thou *d.* not in burnt offering.
94. 19, thy comforts *d.* my soul.
Isa. 42. 1, elect in whom my soul *d.*
55. 2, soul *d.* itself in fatness.
62. 4, the Lord *d.* in thee.
Mic. 7. 18, he *d.* in mercy.
Rom. 7. 22, I *d.* after the inward man.
See Num. 14. 8; Prov. 1. 22; 2. 14; Mal. 3. 1.
Delightsome, delightful. Mal. 3. 12.
Delilah, dĕ-lī′-lăh, delicate. Jud. 16. 4.
Deliver. Ex. 3. 8; Acts 7. 34, I am come down to *d.* them.
Num. 35. 25, congregation shall *d.* slayer.
Deu. 32. 39; Isa. 43. 13, any *d.* out of my hand.
2 Chr. 32. 13, were gods able to *d.* their lands.
Job 5. 19, shall *d.* thee in six troubles.
36. 18, great ransom cannot *d.* R. V. turn thee aside.
Ps. 33. 17, nor *d.* any by great strength.
56. 13, *d.* my feet from falling.
144. 10, *d.* David from hurtful sword.
Prov. 24. 11, forbear to *d.* them.
Eccl. 9. 15, by wisdom *d.* city.
Isa. 50. 2, have I no power to *d.*?
Jer. 1. 8, I am with thee to *d.* thee.
39. 17, I will *d.* in that day.
Dan. 3. 17, for God is able to *d.*, and will *d.*
6. 14, king set heart on Daniel to *d.*
Am. 2. 14, neither shall mighty *d.*

Am. 9. 1, he that escapeth shall not be *d.*
Mal. 3. 15, they that tempt God are *d.*
Mat. 6. 13; Lu. 11. 4, *d.* us from evil.
11. 27; Lu. 10. 22, all things *d.* to me of my Father.
26. 15, I will *d.* him to you.
Acts 2. 23, being *d.* by the counsel of God.
Rom. 4. 25, was *d.* for our offences.
7. 6, we are *d.* from the law.
8. 21, creature shall be *d.*
2 Cor. 4. 11, *d.* to death for Jesus' sake.
2 Tim. 4. 18, *d.* me from every evil work.
Jude 3, faith once *d.* to saints.
See Rom. 8. 32; 2 Cor. 1. 10; Gal. 1. 4; 2 Pet. 2. 7.

Deliverance. 2 Kn. 5. 1, by him had given *d.* to Syria.
1 Chr. 11. 14, saved by great *d.* R. V. victory.
Ps. 32. 7, compass me with songs of *d.*
Lu. 4. 18, preach *d.* to the captives.
Heb. 11. 35, not accepting *d.*
See Gen. 45. 7; Joel 2. 32; Obad. 17.

Deliverances: Lot, Gen. 14.; 19. Moses, Ex. 2. Israel, Ex. 14.; Jud. 4.; 7.; 15.; 1 Sam. 7.; 14.; 17.; 2 Kn. 19.; 2 Chr. 14.; 20. Daniel, Shadrach, Meshach, and Abed-nego, Dan. 3. 19; 6. 22. The Apostles, Acts 5. 19; 12. 7; 16. 26; 28. 1; 2 Tim. 4. 17.

Deliverer. Jud. 3. 9; Ps. 18. 2; 40. 17; 70. 5; 144. 2; Acts 7. 35; Rom. 11. 26.

Delusion. Isa. 66. 4; 2 Thes. 2. 11.

Demand. Dan. 4. 17; Mat. 2. 4; Lu. 3. 14.

Demas, dē'-măs, probably same as following. Col. 4. 14.

Demetrius, dē-mē'-trĭ-ŭs, 'belonging to Demeter.' (1) silversmith. Acts 19. 24. (2) disciple. 3 John 12.

Demonstration. 1 Cor. 2. 4.

Den. Job 37. 8, then the beasts go into *d.*
Isa. 11. 8, put hand on cockatrice *d.*
Jer. 7. 11, is this house a *d.* of robbers.
Mat. 21. 13; Mk. 11. 17, a *d.* of thieves.
Heb. 11. 38, in deserts and in *d.* R. V. caves.
See Jud. 6. 2; Dan. 6. 7; Am. 3. 4.

Denarius, or **Denarion,** 'ten asses,' a silver coin. (A. V. Penny. Mat. 18. 28, &c.) The Roman Imperial denarius, 60 grs. = 8½d., or 16 cents. *See* more exactly under MONEY.

Denial of Christ deprecated. 2 Tim. 1. 8; Tit. 1. 16; 2 Pet. 2. 1; Jude 4.
its punishment. Mat. 10. 33; 2 Tim. 2. 12; 2 Pet. 2. 1; Jude 4, 15.
by Peter. Mat. 26. 69.
by the Jews. John 18. 40; 19. 15; Acts 3. 13.

Denier of Christ, liar and antichrist. 1 John 2. 22; 4. 3.
will be denied by Him. Mat. 10. 33; Mk. 8. 38; 2 Tim. 2. 12.
brought to swift destruction. 2 Pet. 2. 1; Jude 4, 15.

Denounce. Deu. 30. 18.

Deny. Jos. 24. 27, lest ye *d.* your God.
Prov. 30. 9, lest I be full and *d.* thee.
Lu. 20. 27, which *d.* resurrection.
2 Tim. 2. 13, he cannot *d.* himself.
Tit. 1. 16, in works they *d.* him.
See 1 Tim. 5. 8; 2 Tim. 3. 5; Tit. 2. 12.

Depart. Gen. 49. 10, sceptre not *d.* from Judah.
2 Sam. 22. 22; Ps. 18. 21, have not *d.* from my God.
Job 21. 14; 22. 17, they say to God, *d.*
28. 28, to *d.* from evil is understanding.
Ps. 6. 8; Mat. 7. 23; Lu. 13. 27, *d.*, ye workers of iniquity.
34. 14; 37. 27, *d.* from evil, and do good.
105. 38, Egypt was glad when they *d.*
Prov. 15. 24, he may *d.* from hell beneath.
Prov. 22. 6, when old he will not *d.* from it.
27. 22, yet will not foolishness *d.*
Mat. 14. 16, they need not *d.*
25. 41, *d.* from me, ye cursed.
Lu. 2. 29, lettest thou thy servant *d.* in peace.
4. 13, devil *d.* for a season.
21. 21, let them in midst *d.*
John 13. 1, when Jesus knew he should *d.*
2 Cor. 12. 8, besought that it might *d.* from me.
Phil. 1. 23, desire to *d.*
1 Tim. 4. 1, some shall *d.* from the faith.
2 Tim. 2. 19, nameth Christ *d.* from iniquity.
See Isa. 54. 10; Mic. 2. 10; 2 Tim. 4. 6; Heb. 3. 12.

Deposed. Dan. 5. 20.

Deprived. Gen. 27. 45; Job 39. 17; Isa. 38. 10.

Depth. Job 28. 14, *d.* saith, it is not in me.
Ps. 33. 7, he layeth up *d.* in storehouses.
77. 16, waters afraid, *d.* troubled.
106. 9, led through *d.* as through wilderness.
107. 26, they go down again to *d.*
Prov. 8. 24, when no *d.* I was brought forth.
25. 3, heaven for height, earth for *d.*
Mat. 18. 6, better drowned in *d.* of sea.
Mk. 4. 5, no *d.* of earth.
Rom. 11. 33, the *d.* of the riches.
See Isa. 7. 11; Mic. 7. 19; Rom. 8. 39.

Deputed. 2 Sam. 15. 3.

Deputy. 1 Kn. 22. 47; Esth. 8. 9; 9. 3. R. V. governors. Acts 13. 7; 18. 12; 19. 38. R. V. proconsul (governor of a province).

Derbe, dĕr'-bē, 'juniper' (?). A city of Lycaonia, in Asia Minor. Acts 14. 6.

Deride. Hab. 1. 10; Lu. 16. 14; 23. 35.

Derision. Job 30. 1, younger than I have me in *d.*
Ps. 2. 4, the Lord shall have them in *d.*
44. 13; 79. 4, a *d.* to them round us.
Jer. 20. 7, 8, in *d.* daily.
Lam. 3. 14, I was a *d.* to my people.
See Ps. 119. 51; Ezek. 23. 32; 36. 4; Hos. 7. 16.

Descend. Ezek. 26. 20; 31. 16, with them that *d.* into pit.
Mat. 7. 25, 27, rain *d.* and floods came.
Mk. 1. 10; John 1. 32, 33, Spirit *d.*
15. 32, let Christ now *d.* from cross.
Rom. 10. 7, who shall *d.* into the deep?
Eph. 4. 10, he that *d.* is same that ascended.
Jas. 3. 15, this wisdom *d.* not.
Rev. 21. 10, great city *d.* out of heaven.
See Gen. 28. 12; Ps. 49. 17; 133. 3; Prov. 30. 4.

Descent. Lu. 19. 37; Heb. 7. 3, 6.

Describe. (1) to mark out. Jos. 18. 4, 6.
(2) Jud. 8. 14; Rom. 4. 6; 10. 5.

Descry, to spy out, reconnoitre. Jud. 1. 23.

Desert. Ps. 78. 40, oft did they grieve him in *d.*
102. 6, like an owl of the *d.*
Isa. 35. 1, the *d.* shall rejoice.
35. 6; 43. 19, streams in the *d.*
40. 3, in *d.* a highway for our God.
Jer. 2. 6, led us through land of *d.*
17. 6, like the heath in the *d.*
25. 24, people that dwell in *d.* shall drink.
Mat. 24. 26, say, behold, he is in the *d.*
Lu. 1. 80, John in *d.* till his showing.
9. 10, aside privately into *d.* place.
John 6. 31, did eat manna in *d.*
See Ex. 5. 3; 19. 2; Isa. 51. 3; Mk. 6. 31.

Deserts. Ps. 28. 4; Ezek. 7. 27.

Deserve. Jud. 9. 16; Ez. 9. 13; Job 11. 6.

Desirable. Ezek. 23. 6, 12, 23.

Desire (*n.*) 2 Chr. 15. 15, sought him with their whole *d.*
Job 34. 36, my *d.* is that Job may be tried.
Ps. 10. 3; 21. 2; Rom. 10. 1, heart's *d.*
37. 4, he shall give thee the *d.* of thine heart.
54. 7; 59. 10; 92. 11; 112. 8, *d.* on enemies.
92. 11; 112. 10; 140. 8, *d.* of the wicked.
145. 16, the *d.* of every living thing.
Prov. 10. 24; 11. 23, the *d.* of righteous.
13. 12, when *d.* cometh, it is a tree of life.
19. 22, the *d.* of a man is his kindness.
21. 25, the *d.* of slothful killeth him.
Ezek. 24. 16, 21, 25, the *d.* of thine eyes.
Mic. 7. 3, great man uttereth mischievous *d.* R. V. mischief of his soul.
Hab. 2. 5, enlargeth *d.* as hell.
Hag. 2. 7, the *d.* of all nations.
Lu. 22. 15, with *d.* I have *d.* to eat.
Eph. 2. 3, fulfilling *d.* of flesh and mind.
Phil. 1. 23, having a *d.* to depart.
See Gen. 3. 16; Job 14. 15; 31. 16.

Desire (Eccl. 12. 5). Heb. *Abiggônah:* **Gk.** **κάππαρις:** **Bot. N.** ***Capparis Ægyptiaca:*** **R. V.**

caper-berry (marg. 'or, desire'). Eaten as a stimulant to the appetite. *See* Caper.
Desire (*v.*). Deu. 14. 26, whatsoever thy soul *d.*
1 Sam. 2. 16, take as much as thy soul *d.*
12. 13, behold the king whom ye *d.*
Neh. 1. 11, servants who *d.* to fear thy name. R. V. delight.
Job 13. 3, I *d.* to reason with God.
Ps. 19. 10, more to be *d.* than gold.
27. 4, one thing I *d.* of the Lord.
34. 12, that *d.* life and loveth many days.
40. 6, sacrifice and offering thou didst not *d.*
45. 11, king greatly *d.* thy beauty.
73. 25, none on earth I *d.* beside thee.
107. 30, to their *d.* haven. [pared.
Prov. 3. 15; 8. 11, all thou canst *d.* not to be com-
13. 4, soul of sluggard *d.*, and hath not.
Eccl. 2. 10, what my eyes *d.* I kept not.
Isa. 53. 2, no beauty that we should *d.*
Hos. 6. 6, I *d.* mercy and not sacrifice.
Mic. 7. 1, soul *d.* firstripe fruit. [shame.
Zep. 2. 1, O nation not *d.* R. V. that hath no
Mat. 12. 46; Lu. 8. 20, his brethren *d.*
13. 17, have *d.* to see those things.
20. 20, *d.* a certain thing of him.
Mk. 9. 35, if any *d.* to be first.
10. 35, do for us whatsoever we *d.*
11. 24, what things ye *d.* when ye pray.
15. 6; Lu. 23. 25, prisoner whom they *d.*
Lu. 9. 9, who is this, and he *d.* to see him.
10. 24, kings have *d.* to see.
16. 21, *d.* to be fed with crumbs.
20. 46, scribes *d.* to walk in long robes.
22. 15, have *d.* to eat this passover.
22. 31, Satan hath *d.* to have you.
Acts 3. 14, *d.* a murderer to be granted.
1 Cor. 14. 1, and *d.* spiritual gifts.
2 Cor. 5. 2, *d.* to be clothed upon.
Gal. 4. 9, ye *d.* again to be in bondage.
4. 21, ye that *d.* to be under the law.
6. 12, many *d.* to make shew in the flesh.
Eph. 3. 13, I *d.* that ye faint not.
Phil. 4. 17, not because I *d.* a gift; I *d.* fruit.
1 Tim. 3. 1, he *d.* a good work.
Heb. 11. 16, they *d.* a better country.
Jas. 4. 2, ye *d.* to have, and cannot obtain.
1 Pet. 1. 12, the angels *d.* to look into.
2. 2, as babes *d.* sincere milk of word.
1 John 5. 15, we have petitions we *d.*
See Gen. 3. 6; Job 7. 2; Ps. 51. 6; Lu. 5. 39.
Desired, longed-for, missed, regretted. (From Lat. *desiderare.*) 2 Chr. 21. 20.
Desirous. Prov. 23. 3; Lu. 23. 8; John 16. 19; Gal. 5. 26.
Desolate. Ps. 25. 16, have mercy, for I am *d.*
40. 15, let them be *d.* for reward.
143. 4, my heart within me is *d.*
Isa. 54. 1; Gal. 4. 27, more are children of *d.*
62. 4, nor shall thy land any more be termed *d.*
Jer. 2. 12, be ye very *d.*, saith the Lord.
32. 43; 33. 12, *d.* without man or beast.
Ezek. 6. 6, your altars may be made *d.*
Dan. 11. 31; 12. 11, abomination that maketh *d.*
Mal. 1. 4, return and build the *d.* places. R. V. waste.
Mat. 23. 38; Lu. 13. 35, house left to you *d.*
Acts 1. 20, let his habitation be *d.*
1 Tim. 5. 5, widow indeed, and *d.*
Rev. 18. 19, in one hour is she made *d.*
See Ps. 34. 22; Jer. 12. 10; Joel 2. 3; Zec. 7. 14.
Desolation. 2 Kn. 22. 19, they should become a *d.* and a curse.
Ps. 46. 8, what *d.* he hath made in the earth.
74. 3; Jer. 25. 9; Ezek. 35. 9, perpetual *d.*
Prov. 1. 27, when your fear cometh as *d.* R. V. a storm.
3. 25, the *d.* of the wicked. [generations.
Isa. 61. 4, raise up former *d.*, the *d.* of many
Dan. 9. 26, to end of war *d.* are determined.
Zep. 1. 15, a day of wrath, wasting, and *d.* [*d.*
Mat. 12. 25; Lu. 11. 17, house divided brought to
Lu. 21. 20, then know *d.* is nigh.
See Lev. 26. 31; Jos. 8. 28; Job 30. 14.

Despair. 1 Sam. 27. 1; Eccl. 2. 20.
Despair deprecated. Deu. 20. 3; Ps. 27. 13; 31. 24; 37. 1; 42. 11; Prov. 24. 10; Isa. 40. 30; Lu. 18. 1; 2 Cor. 4. 8; Gal. 6. 9; 2 Thes. 3. 13; Heb. 12. 3.
Desperate. Job 6. 26; Isa. 17. 11; Jer. 17. 9.
Despise. Num. 11. 20, ye have *d.* the Lord. R. V. rejected.
15. 31; Prov. 13. 13; Isa. 5. 24; 30. 12, *d.* the word.
1 Sam. 2. 30, that *d.* me shall be lightly esteemed.
Neh. 4. 4, hear, O God, for we are *d.*
Esth. 1. 17, so that they *d.* their husbands. [ing.
Job 5. 17; Prov. 3. 11; Heb. 12. 5, *d.* not chasten-
19. 18, young children *d.* me.
36. 5, God is mighty and *d.* not any.
Ps. 51. 17, contrite heart thou wilt not *d.*
53. 5, put to shame, because God *d.* them. R. V. rejected.
73. 20, thou shalt *d.* their image.
102. 17, he will not *d.* their prayer.
Prov. 1. 7, fools *d.* wisdom.
1. 30; 5. 12, *d.* reproof.
6. 30, men do not *d.* a thief.
15. 5, fool *d.* father's instruction.
15. 20, foolish man *d.* his mother.
15. 32, refuseth instruction *d.* own soul.
19. 16, he that *d.* his ways shall die. R. V. careless of.
Prov. 30. 17, *d.* to obey his mother, ravens shall.
Eccl. 9. 16, poor man's wisdom is *d.*
Isa. 33. 15, he that *d.* gain of oppressions.
49. 7, saith Lord to him whom man *d.*
Jer. 49. 15, I will make thee small and *d.*
Ezek. 20. 13, 16, they *d.* my judgments. R. V. rejected.
22. 8, thou hast *d.* holy things. [jected.
Am. 2. 4, they *d.* the law of the Lord. R. V. re-
Zec. 4. 10, who hath *d.* day of small things.
Mal. 1. 6, wherein have we *d.* thy name?
Mat. 6. 24; Lu. 16. 13, hold to one, *d.* the other.
18. 10, *d.* not one of these little ones.
Lu. 10. 16, *d.* you, *d.* me; *d.* him that sent me.
18. 9, righteous, and *d.* others.
Rom. 2. 4, *d.* thou the riches of his goodness.
1 Cor. 1. 28, things *d.* God hath chosen.
4. 10, ye are honourable, but we are *d.*
11. 22, *d.* ye the church of God.
16. 11, let no man therefore *d.* him. [eth.
1 Thes. 4. 8, *d.* not man, but God. R. V. reject-
5. 20, *d.* not prophesyings.
1 Tim. 4. 12, let no man *d.* thy youth.
6. 2, not *d.* because brethren.
Tit. 2. 15, let no man *d.* thee.
Heb. 12. 2, endured cross, *d.* the shame.
Jas. 2. 6, ye have *d.* the poor. R. V. dishonoured.
See Gen. 16. 4; 25. 34; 2 Sam. 6. 16; Rom. 14. 3.
Despisers. Acts 13. 41; 2 Tim. 3. 3.
Despite, contempt, contumely. Ezek. 25. 6; Heb. 10. 29.
Despiteful. Ezek. 25. 15; 36. 5; Rom. 1. 30.
Despitefully, spitefully, maliciously. Mat. 5. 44; Lu. 6. 28; Acts 14. 5. R. V. shamefully.
Destitute. Ps. 102. 17, will regard prayer of *d.*
Prov. 15. 21, folly is joy to him that is *d.* of wisdom. R. V. void.
1 Tim. 6. 5, *d.* of the truth. R. V. bereft.
Heb. 11. 37, being *d.*, afflicted, tormented.
See Gen. 24. 27; Ezek. 32. 15; Jas. 2. 15.
Destroy. Gen. 18. 23, *d.* righteous with the wicked. R. V. consume.
Ex. 22. 20, he shall be utterly *d.*
Deu. 9. 14, let me alone that I may *d.* them.
1 Sam. 15. 6, depart, lest I *d.* you with them.
2 Sam. 1. 14, *d.* Lord's anointed.
Job 2. 3, movedst me to *d.* without cause.
10. 8, made me, yet thou dost *d.* me.
19. 10, he hath *d.* me on every side. R. V. broken down.
19. 26, though worms *d.* this body.
Ps. 40. 14; 63. 9, seek my soul to *d.* it.
145. 20, all the wicked will he *d.*
Prov. 1. 32, prosperity of fools shall *d.* them.
13. 23, is *d.* for want of judgment.

Prov. 31. 3, that which *d.* kings.
Eccl. 9. 18, one sinner *d.* much good.
Isa. 10. 7, it is in his heart to *d.*
11. 9; 65. 25, *d.* in holy mountain.
19. 3, I will *d.* the counsel thereof.
28. 2, as a *d.* storm.
Jer. 13. 14, I will not spare but *d.* them.
17. 18, *d.* them with double destruction.
23. 1, woe to pastors that *d.* the sheep.
Ezek. 9. 1, with *d.* weapon in his hand.
22. 27, *d.* souls to get dishonest gain.
Dan. 8. 24, he shall *d.* wonderfully.
Hos. 13. 9, thou hast *d.* thyself.
Mat. 5. 17, not to *d.* but to fulfil.
10. 28, fear him that is able to *d.*
12. 14; Mk. 3. 6; 11. 18, they might *d.* him.
21. 41, he will miserably *d.* those.
22. 7, and *d.* those murderers.
27. 20, ask Barabbas and *d.* Jesus.
Mk. 1. 24; Lu. 4. 34, art thou come to *d.*
12. 9; Lu. 20. 16, *d.* the husbandmen.
14. 58, say, I will *d.* this temple.
15. 29, thou that *d.* the temple.
Lu. 6. 9, is it lawful to save life or *d.*
9. 56, is not come to *d.* men's lives.
17. 27, flood came and *d.* them all.
John 2. 19, Jesus said, *d.* this temple.
Rom. 14. 15, *d.* not him with thy meat.
1 Cor. 6. 13, God shall *d.* both it and them.
Gal. 1. 23, preacheth the faith he once *d.*
2. 18, if I build the things which I *d.*
2 Thes. 2. 8, *d.* with brightness of his coming.
Heb. 2. 14, *d.* him that had the power.
Jas. 4. 12, able to save and to *d.*
1 John 3. 8, *d.* the works of the devil.
See Gen. 6. 17; Isa. 65. 8; Rom. 6. 6; 2 Pet. 2. 12; Jude 5.

Destroyer. Ex. 12. 23, not suffer *d.* to come.
Jud. 16. 24, delivered the *d.* of our country.
Job 15. 21, in prosperity the *d.* shall come.
Ps. 17. 4, kept from paths of the *d.* R. V. violent.
Prov. 28. 24, the companion of a *d.*
See Job 33. 22; Isa. 49. 17; Jer. 22. 7; 50. 11.

Destruction. 2 Chr. 22. 4, his counsellors to his *d.*
26. 16, heart lifted up to *d.* R. V. so that he did corruptly.
Esth. 8. 6, endure to see *d.* of my kindred.
Job 5. 21, neither be afraid of *d.*
21. 17, how oft cometh *d.* R. V. calamity.
26. 6, *d.* hath no covering. R. V. Abaddon.
31. 3, is not *d.* to the wicked. R. V. calamity.
Ps. 9. 6, *d.* are come to a perpetual end.
35. 8, into that very *d.* let him fall.
73. 18, thou castest them down to *d.*
90. 3, turnest man to *d.*
91. 6, the *d.* that wasteth at noonday.
103. 4, redeemeth thy life from *d.*
Prov. 1. 27, *d.* cometh as a whirlwind. R. V. calamity.
10. 14, mouth of foolish near *d.*
10. 15, *d.* of poor is their poverty.
14. 28, want of people *d.* of the prince.
16. 18, pride goeth before *d.*
17. 19, exalteth gate seeketh *d.*
18. 7, fool's mouth is his *d.*
27. 20, hell and *d.* never full. R. V. Abaddon.
31. 8, such as are appointed to *d.* R. V. left desolate.
Isa. 14. 23, the besom of *d.*
19. 18, the city of *d.*
59. 7, wasting and *d.* in their paths.
60. 18, *d.* be no more heard.
Jer. 17. 18, destroy with double *d.*
46. 20, *d.* cometh out of north.
50. 22, sound of great *d.* in the land.
Lam. 2. 11; 3. 48; 4. 10, *d.* of the daughter of my people.
Hos. 13. 14, O grave, I will be thy *d.*
Mat. 7. 13, broad way leadeth to *d.*
Rom. 3. 16, *d.* and misery in their ways.
9. 22, vessels fitted to *d.*
Phil. 3. 18, 19, many walk whose end is *d.*
1 Thes. 5. 3, then sudden *d.* cometh.
2 Thes. 1. 9, punished with everlasting *d.*
1 Tim. 6. 9, lusts drown men in *d.*
2 Pet. 2. 1, bring on themselves swift *d.*
3. 16, wrest to their own *d.*
See Job 21: 20; 31. 23; Prov. 10. 29; 21. 15.

Detain. Jud. 13. 15, 16; 1 Sam. 21. 7.

Determinate, determined upon, fixed. Acts 2. 23.

Determination. Zep. 3. 8.

Determine. Ex. 21. 22, pay as the judges *d.*
1 Sam. 20. 7, be sure evil is *d.* by him.
Job 14. 5, seeing his days are *d.*
Dan. 11. 36, that that is *d.* shall be done.
Lu. 22. 22, Son of man goeth as it was *d.*
Acts 3. 13, Pilate was *d.* to let him go.
17. 26, hath *d.* the times appointed.
1 Cor. 2. 2, I *d.* not to know anything.
See 2 Chr. 2. 1; 25. 16; Isa. 19. 17; Dan. 9. 24.

Detest. Deu. 7. 26.

Detestable. Jer. 16. 18; Ezek. 5. 11; 7. 20; 11. 18; 37. 23.

Deuel, deū′-ĕl, the same as Reuel (?). Num. 1. 14.

Deuteronomy, deū-tĕ-rŏn′-ŏ-mȳ, a recapitulation of the law, name of the fifth book of the Pentateuch.

Device. Esth. 9. 25, *d.* return on his own head.
Ps. 10. 2, let them be taken in the *d.*
33. 10, maketh *d.* of the people of none effect.
37. 7, bringeth wicked *d.* to pass.
Prov. 1. 31, be filled with their own *d.*
12. 2, man of wicked *d.* will he condemn.
19. 21, many *d.* in a man's heart.
Eccl. 9. 10, no work nor *d.* in grave.
Jer. 18. 12, will walk after our own *d.*
Dan. 11. 24, 25, he shall forecast *d.*
Acts 17. 29, like stone graven by man's *d.*
2 Cor. 2. 11, not ignorant of his *d.*
See 2 Chr. 2. 14; Esth. 8. 3; Job 5. 12.

Devil. The word is a contracted form of *Diabolus*, the Greek διάβολος. This word properly means a malicious accuser, and is used in the Greek Testament and LXX. as an equivalent of the Hebrew word Satan, which means an adversary. Job 1.
(Abaddon, Apollyon, Beelzebub, Belial, Satan), the adversary of God and man. 1 Pet 5. 8.
prince of the devils. Mat. 12. 24.
of powers of the air. Eph. 2. 2.
of this world. John 14. 30.
sinner from the beginning. 1 John 3. 8.
cast out of heaven. Lu. 10. 18.
cast down to hell. 2 Pet. 2. 4; Jude 6.
as serpent, causes the fall of man. Gen. 3. 1.
lies to Eve. Gen. 3. 4.
cursed by God. Gen. 3. 14.
appears before God. Job 1. 6; 2. 1.
called Abaddon and Apollyon. Rev. 9. 11.
Beelzebub. Mat. 12. 24.
Belial. 2 Cor. 6. 15.
Satan. Lu. 10. 18.
tempted Christ. Mat. 4. 3-10; Mk. 1. 13; Lu. 4. 2.
Eve. Gen. 3.
David. 1 Chr. 21. 1.
Job. Job 2. 7.
desired to have the apostles. Lu. 22. 31.
resists Joshua (figuratively). Zec. 3.
repulsed by Christ. Mat. 4. 10; Lu. 4. 8, 12.
enters into Judas Iscariot. Lu. 22. 3; John 13. 2.
into Ananias. Acts 5. 3.
As Prince and God of this World, he
perverts the scriptures. Mat. 4. 6.
opposes God's work. Zec. 3. 1; 1 Thes. 2. 18.
hinders the gospel. Mat. 13. 19; 2 Cor. 4. 4.
works lying wonders. 2 Thes. 2. 9; Rev. 16. 14.
appears as an angel of light. 2 Cor. 11. 14.
is the father of lies. John 8. 44; 1 Kn. 22. 22.
Vanquished by Christ: —
by resisting him. Mat. 4. 11.
by casting out devils. Mat. 4. 24; 8. 31; Mk. 1. 23; 5. 2; Lu. 9. 42; 11. 20; 13. 32.
by giving power to exorcise. Mat. 10. 1; Mk. 16. 17; Lu. 9. 1; Acts 16. 18; 19. 12.
by destroying the works of. 1 John 3. 8.
in His death. Col. 2. 15; Heb. 2. 14.

DAMASCUS: 'ST. PAUL'S WALL'

According to tradition the place where St. Paul was let down in a basket and escaped from the City (Acts ix. 25, 2 Cor. xi. 32–33). (*Picture Post Library*)

TEMPLE OF 'DIANA OF THE EPHESIANS'

An artist's reconstruction of the chief temple of the city of Ephesus (Acts xix. 34–35).
(Picture Post Library)

by BELIEVERS to be resisted. Rom. 16. 20; 2 Cor. 2. 11; 11. 3; Eph. 4. 27; 6. 16; 2 Tim. 2. 26; Jas. 4. 7; 1 Pet. 5. 9; 1 John 2. 13; Rev. 12. 11.
CHARACTER OF: —
presumptuous. Job 1. 6; Mat. 4. 5, 6.
proud. 1 Tim. 3. 6.
powerful. Eph. 2. 2; 6. 12.
wicked. 1 John 2. 13.
malignant. Job 1. 9; 2. 4.
subtle. Gen. 3. 1, with 2 Cor. 11. 3.
deceitful. 2 Cor. 11. 14; Eph. 6. 11.
fierce and cruel. Lu. 8. 29; 9. 39, 42; 1 Pet. 5. 8.
Apostasy is of the. 2 Thes. 2. 9; 1 Tim. 4. 1.
shall be condemned at the judgment. Jude 6; Rev. 20. 10.
everlasting fire is prepared for. Mat. 25. 41.
COMPARED TO: — a fowler, Ps. 91. 3. fowls, Mat. 13. 4. a sower of tares, Mat. 13. 25, 28. a wolf, John 10. 12. a roaring lion, 1 Pet. 5. 8. a serpent, Rev. 12. 9; 20. 2.
THE WICKED: —
are the children of. Mat. 13. 38; Acts 13. 10; 1 John 3. 10.
turn aside after. 1 Tim. 5. 15.
do the lusts of. John 8. 44.
are possessed by. Lu. 22. 3; Acts 5. 3; Eph. 2. 2.
blinded by. 2 Cor. 4. 4.
deceived by. 1 Kn. 22. 21, 22; Rev. 20. 7, 8.
ensnared by. 1 Tim. 3. 7; 2 Tim. 2. 26.
troubled by. 1 Sam. 16. 14.
punished together with. Mat. 25. 41.

Devilish. Jas. 3. 15.

Devils, demons, confess Jesus to be Christ. Mat. 8. 29; Mk. 1. 24; 3. 11; 5. 7; Lu. 4. 34, 41; Acts 19. 15; Jas. 2. 19.
sacrifices offered to. 1 Cor. 10. 20; Rev. 9. 20. R. V. he-goats, Lev. 17. 7; 2 Chr. 11. 15. R. V. demons. Deu. 32. 17; Ps. 106. 37.

Devise. Ex. 31. 4; 35. 32, 35, *d.* works in gold.
Ps. 35. 4, to confusion that *d.* my hurt.
36. 4, he *d.* mischief on his bed.
41. 7, against me do they *d.* my hurt.
Prov. 3. 29, *d.* not evil against thy neighbour.
6. 14, he *d.* mischief continually.
6. 18, a heart that *d.* wicked imaginations.
14. 22, err that *d.* evil, *d.* good.
16. 9, man's heart *d.* his way.
Isa. 32. 7, *d.* wicked devices to destroy poor.
32. 8, the liberal *d.* liberal things.
2 Pet. 1. 16, cunningly *d.* fables.
See 2 Sam. 14. 14; Jer. 51. 12; Lam. 2. 17; Mic. 2. 1.

Devote. Lev. 27. 21, 28; Num. 18. 14; Ps. 119. 38.

Devotions. Acts 17. 23.

Devour. Gen. 37. 20, evil beast hath *d.* him.
41. 7, 24, seven thin *d.* the seven rank.
Ex. 24. 17; Isa. 29. 6; 30. 27, 30; 33. 14, *d.* fire.
Lev. 10. 2, fire from Lord *d.* them.
Deu. 32. 24, *d.* with burning heat.
2 Sam. 11. 25, sword *d.* one as well as another.
18. 8, wood *d.* more than sword *d.*
2 Sam. 22. 9; Ps. 18. 8, fire out of his mouth *d.*
Job 18. 13, death shall *d.* his strength.
Ps. 80. 13, beasts of field *d.* it.
Prov. 20. 25, man who *d.* that which is holy.
30. 14, jaw teeth as knives to *d.*
Isa. 1. 7, strangers *d.* it in your presence.
1. 20, if ye rebel, be *d.* with sword.
Jer. 2. 30, your sword hath *d.* prophets.
3. 24, shame *d.* labour of our fathers.
30. 16, that *d.* thee shall be *d.*
Ezek. 15. 7, fire shall *d.* them.
23. 37, pass through fire to *d.* them.
Hos. 8. 14; Am. 1. 14; 2. 2, it shall *d.* palaces.
Joel 2. 3, a fire *d.* before them.
Am. 4. 9, fig trees, palmerworm *d.* them.
Hab. 1. 13, wicked *d.* man that is more righteous.
Zep. 1. 18; 3. 8, *d.* by fire of jealousy.
Mal. 3. 11, will rebuke the *d.* for your sakes.
Mat. 13. 4; Mk. 4. 4; Lu. 8. 5, fowls *d.* them.
23. 14; Mk. 12. 40, Lu. 20. 47, *d.* widows' houses.
Lu. 15. 30, thy son hath *d.* thy living.
2 Cor. 11. 20, if a man *d.* you.
Gal. 5. 15, ye bite and *d.* one another.
Heb. 10. 27, which shall *d.* adversaries.
1 Pet. 5. 8, seeking whom he may *d.*
See Gen. 31. 15; 2 Sam. 2. 26; Ps. 50. 3; 52. 4.

Devout. Lu. 2. 25, Simeon was just and *d.*
Acts 2. 5; 8. 2, *d.* men.
See Acts 10. 2; 13. 50; 17. 4, 17; 22. 12.

Dew. Gen. 27. 28, God give thee the *d.* of heaven.
Deu. 32. 2, my speech shall distil as the *d.*
33. 13, for the *d.*, and for the deep.
Jud. 6. 37, if the *d.* be on the fleece only.
2 Sam. 1. 21, let there be no *d.*
17. 12, we will light on him as *d.* falleth.
1 Kn. 17. 1, there shall not be *d.* nor rain,
Job 38. 28, who hath begotten drops of *d.*
Prov. 3. 20, clouds drop down *d.*
Isa. 18. 4, like *d.* in heat of harvest.
Dan. 4. 15, 23, 25, 33, wet with *d.* of heaven.
Hos. 6. 4; 13. 3, goodness as early *d.*
Hag. 1. 10, heaven is stayed from *d.*
See Ex. 16. 13; Num. 11. 9; Job 29. 19; Ps. 110. 3; 133. 3; Prov. 19. 12; Isa. 26. 19; Hos. 14. 5.

Diadem. Job 29. 14; Isa. 28. 5; 62. 3; Ezek. 21. 26.

Dial. 2 Kn. 20. 11; Isa. 38. 8, gone down in the *d.* of Ahaz.

Diamond (Ex. 28. 18; 39. 11). Heb. *Yahălom* (omitted in LXX.); R. V. marg. sardonyx. The diamond was unknown to the early Hebrews, and could not have been used in the 'breastplate,' because the Hebrews knew of no means of engraving a name upon it. *Yahălom* is variously conjectured to be the onyx, or alabaster, or jasper.
See Jer. 17. 1; Ezek. 28. 13.

Diana, dī-ăn'-ă, same as Greek Artemis. Of Ephesians, tumult concerning. Acts 19. 24.

Diblaim, dĭb-lā'-ĭm, 'two cakes of figs.' Hos. 1. 3.

Diblath, dĭb'-lăth, supposed to be the same as RIBLAH. Ezek. 6. 14.

Diblathaim, dĭb-lă-thā'-ĭm, same as DIBLAIM (?). Num. 33. 46. *See* ALMON-DIBLATHAIM.

Dibon, dī'-bŏn. (1) Num. 21. 30. (2) Neh. 11. 25.

Dibon-gad, dī'-bŏn-găd, 'Dibon of Gad.' Num. 33. 45.

Dibri, dĭb'-rī, 'eloquent.' Lev. 24. 11.

Did. Mat. 13. 58, he *d.* not many mighty works.
John 4. 29, all things that ever I *d.*
9. 26, what *d.* he to thee?
15. 24, works which none other man *d.*
See Gen. 6. 22; 1 Sam. 1. 7; Job 1. 5; 1 Pet. 2. 22.

Didrachmon. (A. V. Tribute money, Mat. 17. 24). The 'double drachmé,' a silver coin = two drachms of Antioch, about 112 grs., equivalent to a Jewish half-shekel, about 1s. 5d., or 32 cents. *See* MONEY.

Didymus, dĭd'-ў-mŭs, twin (Thomas). John 11. 16; 20. 24.

Die. Gen. 2. 17; 20. 7; 1 Sam. 14. 44; 22. 16; 1 Kn. 2. 37, 42; Jer. 26. 8; Ezek. 3. 18; 33. 8, 14, surely *d.*
Gen. 3. 3; Lev. 10. 6; Num. 18. 32, lest ye *d.*
27. 4; 45. 28; Prov. 30. 7, before I *d.*
Ex. 21. 12, smiteth a man that he *d.*
Lev. 7. 24; 22. 8; Deu. 14. 21; Ezek. 4. 14, that *d.* of itself.
Num. 16. 29, if these *d.* common death.
23. 10, let me *d.* death of righteous.
Deu. 31. 14, days approach that thou must *d.*
Ru. 1. 17, where thou *d.* will I *d.*
2 Sam. 3. 33, *d.* Abner as a fool *d.*?
2 Kn. 20. 1; Isa. 38. 1, shalt *d.* and not live.
2 Chr. 25. 4; Jer. 31. 30, every man *d.* for own sin.
Job 2. 9, his wife said, Curse God and *d.*
3. 11, why *d.* I not from the womb?
12. 2, wisdom shall *d.* with you.
14. 14, if a man *d.*, shall he live again?
21. 23, one *d.* in full strength.
21. 25, another *d.* in bitterness of soul.
29. 18, I shall *d.* in my nest.
Ps. 41. 5, when shall he *d.* and name perish?
49. 10, wise men *d.*, likewise the fool.
49. 17, when he *d.* carry nothing away.
Prov. 5. 23, he shall *d.* without instruction.
10. 21, fools *d.* for want of wisdom.

Prov. 11. 7, *d.* his expectation perish.
Eccl. 2. 16, how *d.* the wise man?
7. 17, why shouldest thou *d.* before thy time?
9. 5, living know they shall *d.*
Isa. 66. 24; Mk. 9. 44, worm shall not *d.*
Jer. 27. 13; Ezek. 18. 31; 33. 11, why will ye *d.*?
28. 16, this year thou shalt *d.*
34. 5, thou shalt *d.* in peace.
Ezek. 18. 4, 20, soul that sinneth shall *d.*
18. 32, no pleasure in death of him that *d.*
33. 8, wicked man shall *d.* in iniquity.
Am. 6. 9, if ten men in house they shall *d.*
9. 10, sinners of my people shall *d.*
Jon. 4. 3, 8, it is better to *d.* than live.
Mat. 15. 4; Mk. 7. 10, let him *d.* the death.
22. 27; Mk. 12. 22; Lu. 20. 32, woman *d.* also.
26. 35; Mk. 14. 31, though I *d.* with thee.
Lu. 7. 2, servant was ready to *d.*
16. 22, beggar *d.*, rich man also *d.*
20. 36, nor can they *d.* any more.
John 4. 49, come down ere my child *d.*
11. 21, 32, my brother had not *d.*
11. 37, that even this man should not have *d.*
11. 50; 18. 14, that one man *d.* for people.
11. 51, that Jesus should *d.* for nation.
12. 24, except a corn of wheat *d.*
19. 7, by our law he ought to *d.*
Acts 9. 37, Dorcas was sick and *d.*
21. 13, ready also to *d.* at Jerusalem.
25. 11, I refuse not to *d.*
Rom. 5. 7, for righteous man will one *d.*
7. 9, sin revived and I *d.*
8. 34, it is Christ that *d.*
14. 7, no man *d.* to himself.
14. 9, Christ both *d.*, rose, and revived.
14. 15; 1 Cor. 8. 11, for whom Christ *d.*
1 Cor. 15. 3, Christ *d.* for our sins.
15. 22, as in Adam all *d.*
15. 31, I *d.* daily.
15. 36, not quickened except it *d.*
2 Cor. 5. 14, if one *d.* for all.
Phil. 1. 21, to *d.* is gain.
1 Thes. 4. 14, we believe that Jesus *d.*
5. 10, who *d.* for us that we should live.
Heb. 7. 8, here men that *d.* receive tithes.
9. 27, appointed unto men once to *d.*
11. 13, these all *d.* in faith.
Rev. 3. 2, things that are ready to *d.*
9. 6, men shall desire to *d.*
14. 13, the dead that *d.* in the Lord.

Diet. Jer. 52. 34. R. V. allowance.

Differ. Rom. 12. 6; 1 Cor. 4. 7; 15. 41; Gal. 4. 1.

Difference. Lev. 10. 10; Ezek. 44. 23, a *d.* between holy and unholy.
11. 47; 20. 25, *d.* between clean and unclean.
Ezek. 22. 26, they have put no *d.* between.
Acts 15. 9, put no *d.* between us.
Rom. 3. 22; 10. 12, for there is no *d.*
See Ex. 11. 7; 1 Cor. 12. 5; Jude 22.

Dig. Ex. 21. 33, *d.* a pit and not cover it.
Deu. 6. 11; Neh. 9. 25, wells *d.* which thou *d.* not.
8. 9, out of hills mayest *d.* brass.
Job 6. 27, ye *d.* a pit for your friend. R. V. make merchandise of.
24. 16, in the dark they *d.*
Ps. 7. 15; 57. 6, *d.* a pit and is fallen.
Isa. 51. 1, hole of pit whence ye are *d.*
Mat. 21. 33, and *d.* a winepress.
25. 18, *d.* in the earth and hid.
Lu. 13. 8, till I *d.* about it.
16. 3, I cannot *d.*, to beg I am ashamed.
See Job 3. 21; Ezek. 8. 8; 12. 5; Lu. 6. 48.

Digit, i. e., finger-breadth (Jer. 52. 21) = 0.023 metres or 0.91 inches. *See* MEASURES.

Dignity. Eccl. 10. 6, folly set in great *d.*
2 Pet. 2. 10; Jude 8, speak evil of *d.*
See Gen. 49. 3; Esth. 6. 3; Hab. 1. 7.

Diklah, dĭk′-lăh, 'a palm tree.' Gen. 10. 27.

Dilean, dĭ′-lĕ-ăn. Jos. 15. 38.

Diligence. 2 Tim. 4. 9; Jude 3.

Diligence, exhortations to, in the service of God, &c. Ex. 15. 26; Deu. 4. 9; 6. 7; 13. 14; 24. 8; Jos. 1. 7; Ez. 7. 23; Ps. 37. 10; 112. 1; Prov. 2. 3.; 4.; 7.; 8.; Isa. 55. 2; Jer. 12. 16; Zec. 6. 15; Lu. 12. 58; Rom. 12. 8; 2 Cor. 8. 7; 1 Tim. 5. 10; Heb. 6. 11; 11. 6; 12. 15; 1 Pet. 1. 10; 2 Pet. 3. 14.
in worldly business. Prov. 10. 4; 12. 24; 13. 4; 21. 5; 22. 29; 27. 23; Rom. 12. 11; 2 Thes. 3. 11.

Diligent. Jos. 22. 5, take *d.* heed to commandment.
Ps. 64. 6, accomplish a *d.* search.
Lu. 15. 8, seek *d.* till she find it.
Acts 18. 25, taught *d.* the things of the Lord. R. V. carefully.
2 Tim. 1. 17, in Rome sought me *d.*
Heb. 12. 15, looking *d.* lest any man fail.
See Deu. 19. 18; Prov. 11. 27; 23. 1; Mat. 2. 7.

Dill (Mat. 23. 23). A. V. anise. Gk. ἄνηθον: Bot. N. *Anethum graveolens:* R. V. marg. dill. A little umbelliferous plant, grown for its aromatic fruits, which are used in medicine and for seasoning.

Dim. Deu. 34. 7, eye not *d.* nor force abated.
Job 17. 7, eye also *d.* by reason of sorrow.
Lam. 4. 1, gold become *d.*
See Gen. 27. 1; 48. 10; 1 Sam. 3. 2; Isa. 8. 22.

Diminish. Deu. 4. 2; 12. 32, nor *d.* aught from it.
Prov. 13. 11, gotten by vanity shall be *d.*
Rom. 11. 12, *d.* of them be riches of Gentiles.
See Ex. 5. 8; Lev. 25. 16; Jer. 26. 2; Ezek. 16. 27.

Dimnah, dĭm′-năh, 'dunghill.' Jos. 21. 35.

Dimness. Isa. 8. 22; 9. 1.

Dimon, dī′-mŏn, same as DIBON (2). Isa. 15. 9.

Dimonah, dī-mō′-năh, probably same as preceding. Jos. 15. 22.

Dinah, dī′-năh, 'vindicated.' Jacob's daughter, Gen. 30. 21. outraged by Shechem, Gen. 34. 2. avenged by Simeon and Levi, Gen. 34. 25.

Dinaites, dī′-nā-ītes. Ez. 4. 9.

Dine. Gen. 43. 16; Lu. 11. 37; John 21. 12, 15.

Dinhabah, dĭn′-hă-băh. Gen. 36. 32.

Dinner. Prov. 15. 17; Mat. 22. 4; Lu. 11. 38; 14. 12.

Dionysius, dī-ō-nȳs′-ĭ-ŭs, 'belonging to Dionysus;' the Areopagite, believes. Acts 17. 34.

Diotrephes, dī-ŏt′-rĕ-phēs, 'nourished by Zeus, loveth preeminence.' 3 John 9.

Dip. Lev. 4. 6; 9. 9; 17. 14, priest shall *d.* his finger.
Ru. 2. 14, *d.* morsel in vinegar.
1 Sam. 14. 27, *d.* rod in honeycomb.
2 Kn. 5. 14, Naaman *d.* in Jordan.
Mat. 26. 23; Mk. 14. 20, *d.* hand in dish.
John 13. 26, when he had *d.* the sop.
Rev. 19. 13, a vesture *d.* in blood. R. V. sprinkled.
See Gen. 37. 31; Jos. 3. 15; Lu. 16. 24.

Direct. Job 32. 14, he hath not *d.* his words.
37. 3, he *d.* it under the whole heaven. R. V. sendeth.
Ps. 5. 3, in morning will I *d.* my prayer. R. V. order.
119. 5, O that my ways were *d.* to keep. R. V. established.
Prov. 3. 6, he shall *d.* thy paths.
11. 5, righteousness shall *d.* his way
16. 9, the Lord *d.* his steps.
21. 29, as for upright he *d.* his way.
Eccl. 10. 10, wisdom profitable to *d.*
Isa. 40. 13, who hath *d.* Spirit of the Lord.
Jer. 10. 23, not in man to *d.* his steps.
2 Thes. 3. 5, *d.* your hearts into love of God.
See Gen. 46. 28; Isa. 45. 13; 61. 8; 1 Thes. 3. 11.

Direction. Num. 21. 18. R. V. sceptre.

Directly. Num. 19. 4; Ezek. 42. 12.

Dirt. Jud. 3. 22; Ps. 18. 42; Isa. 57. 20.

Disallowed. (1) Num. 30. 5, 8, 11.
(2) 1 Pet. 2. 4, 7. R. V. rejected.

Disannul, to annul entirely. Isa. 14. 27, Lord purposed, who shall *d.* it?
28. 18, your covenant with death shall be *d.*
Gal. 3. 15, 17, covenant no man *d.*
See Job 40. 8; Heb. 7. 18.

Disappoint. Job 5. 12; Ps. 17. 13; Prov. 15. 22.

Discern. 2 Sam. 19. 35; 1 Kn. 3. 9, *d.* between good and bad.
Ez. 3. 13, could not *d.* noise of joy.

Job 4. 16, could not *d.* form thereof.
6. 30, cannot my taste *d.* perverse things.
Prov. 7. 7, I *d.* among the youths.
Eccl. 8. 5, wise man's heart *d.* time.
Jon. 4. 11, cannot *d.* between right and left.
Mal. 3. 18, *d.* between righteous and wicked.
Mat. 16. 3; Lu. 12. 56, *d.* face of sky.
1 Cor. 2. 14, they are spiritually *d.*
11. 29, not *d.* the Lord's body.
12. 10, to another is given *d.* of spirits.
Heb. 4. 12, the word is a *d.* of the thoughts.
5. 14, exercised to *d.* good and evil.
See Gen. 27. 23; 31. 32; 38. 25; 2 Sam. 14. 17.

Discharge. 1 Kn. 5. 9; Eccl. 8. 8.

Disciple. Isa. 8. 16, seal law among my *d.*
Mat. 10. 1; Lu. 6. 13, called his twelve *d.*
10. 24; Lu. 6. 40, *d.* not above his master.
10. 42, give cup of water in the name of a *d.*
12. 2, thy *d.* do that which is not lawful.
15. 2, why do *d.* transgress tradition.
17. 16, brought to thy *d.*, and they could not cure.
19. 13; Mk. 10. 13, the *d.* rebuked them.
20. 17, Jesus took *d.* apart.
22. 16, Pharisees sent their *d.*
26. 18; Mk. 14. 14; Lu. 22. 11, keep passover with [*d.*
26. 35, likewise also said the *d.*
26. 56, all the *d.* forsook him and fled.
28. 7, tell his *d.* he is risen.
28. 13, say ye, his *d.* came by night.
Mk. 2. 18; Lu. 5. 33, why do *d.* of John fast?
4. 34, he expounded all things to *d.*
7. 2, *d.* eat with unwashen hands.
7. 5, why walk not *d.* according to tradition?
Lu. 5. 30, Pharisees murmured against *d.*
6. 20, lifted up eyes on *d.*
11. 1, as John taught his *d.*
14. 26, 27, 33, cannot be my *d.*
19. 37, *d.* began to rejoice and praise God.
19. 39, Master, rebuke thy *d.*
John 2. 11, his *d.* believed on him.
4. 2, Jesus baptized not, but his *d.*
6. 22, his *d.* were gone away alone.
6. 66, many of his *d.* went back.
7. 3, that thy *d.* may see works.
8. 31; 13. 35, then are ye my *d.* indeed.
9. 27, will ye also be his *d.*?
9. 28, thou art his *d.*, we are Moses' *d.*
13. 5, began to wash *d.* feet.
15. 8, so shall ye be my *d.*
18. 15, 16, that *d.* was known.
18. 17, 25, art not thou one of his *d.*?
19. 26; 20. 2; 21. 7, 20, *d.* whom Jesus loved.
19. 38, a *d.* of Jesus, but secretly for fear.
20. 18, told *d.* she had seen the Lord.
21. 23, that that *d.* should not die.
21. 24, this is the *d.* which testifieth.
Acts 9. 1, slaughter against *d.*
9. 26, essayed to join himself to *d.*
11. 26, *d.* called Christians first.
20. 7, *d.* came together to break bread.
20. 30, to draw away *d.* after them.
21. 16, an old *d.* with whom we should lodge.

Disciples of Christ. Mat. 11. 1; John 18. 1, 2; 20. 26; etc.
the seventy sent out to work miracles and preach. Lu. 10.
their names written in heaven. Lu. 10. 20.
three thousand added to the church. Acts 2. 41.
five thousand believers. Acts 4. 4.
called Christians at Antioch. Acts 11. 26.
of JOHN enquire of Christ. Mat. 9. 14; 11. 2.
follow Christ. John 1. 37.
dispute about purifying. John 3. 25.
baptized by Paul, and receive the Holy Ghost. Acts 19. 1.

Discipline. Job 36. 10. R. V. instruction.

Disclose. Isa. 26. 21.

Discomfited. Jud. 4. 15, Lord *d.* Sisera.
8. 12, Gideon *d.* all the host.
2 Sam. 22. 15; Ps. 18. 14, lightnings, and *d.* them.
Isa. 31. 8, his young men shall be *d.* R. V. tributary.
See Ex. 17. 13; Num. 14. 45; Jos. 10. 10.

Discomfiture. 1 Sam. 14. 20.

Discontented. 1 Sam. 22. 2.

Discontinue. Jer. 17. 4.

Discord censured. Prov. 6. 14, 19; 16. 29; 17. 9; 18. 8; 26. 20; Rom. 1. 29; 2 Cor. 12. 20.

Discourage. Num. 32. 7, wherefore *d.* the heart of the children of Israel.
Deu. 1. 21, fear not, nor be *d.* R. V. dismayed.
1. 28, our brethren have *d.* our heart.
Col. 3. 21, your children, lest they be *d.*
See Num. 21. 4; 32. 9; Isa. 42. 4.

Discover, to uncover, lay bare. 2 Sam. 22. 16; Ps. 18. 15, foundations of the world *d.*
Job 12. 22, he *d.* deep things.
41. 13, who can *d.* face of his garment?
Ezek. 21. 24, your transgressions are *d.*
See Ps. 29. 9; Isa. 22. 8; Hos. 7. 1; Hab. 3. 13.
1 Sam. 14. 8, 11, we will *d.* ourselves to them.
Prov. 25. 9, *d.* not a secret to another. R. V. disclose.

Discreet. Gen. 41. 33, 39; Mk. 12. 34; Tit. 2. 5.

Discretion. Ps. 112. 5; Prov. 11. 22; Isa. 28. 26; Jer. 10. 12.
commended. Ps. 34. 12; Prov. 1. 4; 2. 11; 3. 21; 5. 2; 19. 11.

Disdained. 1 Sam. 17. 42; Job 30. 1.

Disease. Ex. 15. 26; Deu. 7. 15, none of these *d.* on you.
Deu. 28. 60, bring on thee all *d.* of Egypt.
2 Kn. 1. 2; 8. 8, 9, recover of *d.*
2 Chr. 16. 12, in *d.* sought not the Lord.
Job 30. 18, by force of my *d.*
Ps. 103. 3, who healeth all thy *d.*
Eccl. 6. 2, vanity, and it is an evil *d.*
Ezek. 34. 4, *d.* have ye not strengthened.
34. 21, have pushed *d.* with your horns.

Diseases sent by God. Ex. 9.; 15. 26; Num. 12. 10; Deu. 28. 60; 2 Kn. 1. 4; 5. 27; 2 Chr. 21. 18; 26. 21; Job 2. 6, 7.
cured by Christ. Mat. 4. 23; 9. 20; John 5. 8.
power given to His disciples to cure, Lu. 9. 1; Acts 28. 8. exercised, Acts 3. 1; 9. 34; 28. 8, 9.

Disfigure. Mat. 6. 16.

Disgrace. Jer. 14. 21.

Disguises resorted to. 1 Sam. 28. 8; 1 Kn. 14. 2; 20. 38; 22. 30; 2 Chr. 18. 29; 35. 22.
disfiguring of face for the dead forbidden. Lev. 19. 28; Deu. 14. 1.

Dish. Jud. 5. 25; 2 Kn. 21. 13; Mat. 26. 23; Mk. 14. 20.

Dishan, dī'-shăn, 'antelope' (?). Gen. 36. 28.

Dishon, dī'-shŏn, same as preceding. Gen. 36. 21.

Dishonesty. 2 Cor. 4. 2. R. V. shame.

Dishonour. Ps. 35. 26; 71. 13, clothed with shame and *d.*
Prov. 6. 33, a wound and *d.* shall he get.
Mic. 7. 6, son *d.* father.
John 8. 49, I honour my Father, ye *d.* me.
Rom. 9. 21, one vessel to honour, another to *d.*
1 Cor. 15. 43, sown in *d.*
2 Cor. 6. 8, by honour and *d.*
2 Tim. 2. 20, some to honour, some to *d.*
See Ez. 4. 14; Rom. 1. 24; 2. 23; 1 Cor. 11. 4, 5.

Disinherit. Num. 14. 12.

Dismayed. Deu. 31. 8; Jos. 1. 9; 8. 1; 10. 25; 1 Chr. 22. 13; 28. 20; 2 Chr. 20. 15, 17; 32. 7; Isa. 41. 10; Jer. 1. 17; 10. 2; 23. 4; 30. 10; 46. 27; Ezek. 2. 6; 3. 9, fear not nor be *d.*
Jer. 17. 18, let them be *d.*, let not me be *d.*
See 1 Sam. 17. 11; Jer. 8. 9; 46. 5; Obad. 9.

Dismissed. 2 Chr. 23. 8; Acts 15. 30; 19. 41.

Disobedience. Eph. 2. 2, children of *d.*

Disobedience, and its results. Lev. 26. 14; Deu. 8. 11; 27.; 28. 15; Jos. 5. 6; 1 Sam. 2. 30; 12. 15; Neh. 9. 26; Ps. 78. 10; Isa. 3. 8; 42. 24; Jer. 9. 13; 18. 10; 22. 21; 35. 14; Rom. 5. 19; Eph. 5. 6; Tit. 1. 16; 3. 3; Heb. 2. 2.
See Adam and Eve, Gen. 3. Pharaoh, Ex. 5. 2. Achan, Jos. 7. Saul, 1 Sam. 13. 9; 15. Man of God, 1 Kn. 13. 21, 26. Jonah, Jon. 1.; 2.

Disobedient. Lu. 1. 17, turn *d.* to wisdom of just.
Acts 26. 19, not *d.* to heavenly vision.

Rom. 1. 30; 2 Tim. 3. 2, *d.* to parents.
10. 21, a *d.* and gainsaying people.
1 Tim. 1. 9, law for lawless and *d.* R. V. unruly.
Tit. 3. 3, we ourselves were sometime *d.*
1 Pet. 2. 7, to them which be *d.* R. V. disbelieve.
3. 20, spirits, which sometime were *d.*

Disorderly. 1 Thes. 5. 14; 2 Thes. 3. 6, 7, 11.

Dispensation. 1 Cor. 9. 17, a *d.* of the gospel is committed me. R. V. stewardship.
Eph. 1. 10, in the *d.* of the fulness of times.
3. 2, the *d.* of the grace of God.
Col. 1. 25, according to the *d.* of God.

Dispersed. Esth. 3. 8, and *d.* among the people.
Prov. 15. 7, lips of wise *d.* knowledge.
Isa. 11. 12, the *d.* of Judah.
John 7. 35, go unto the *d.* among the Gentiles.

Dispersed (prophecies concerning). Jer. 25. 34; Ezek. 12. 15; 20. 23; 36. 19; Zep. 3. 10.

Displayed. Ps. 60. 4.

Displease. Num. 11. 1, *d.* the Lord. R. V. speaking evil in the ears of.
22. 34, if it *d.* thee, I will get me back.
2 Sam. 11. 27, thing David had done *d.* the Lord.
1 Kn. 1. 6, father had not *d.* him at any time.
Ps. 60. 1, thou hast been *d.* R. V. angry.
Prov. 24. 18, lest the Lord see it, and it *d.* him.
Isa. 59. 15, it *d.* him there was no judgment.
Jon. 4. 1, it *d.* Jonah exceedingly.
Mat. 21. 15, scribes saw it, they were *d.*
Mk. 10. 14, Jesus was much *d.*
10. 41, much *d.* with James and John.
See Gen. 48. 17; 1 Sam. 8. 6; 18. 8; Zec. 1. 2.

Displeasure. Deu. 9. 19; Jud. 15. 3; Ps. 2. 5; 6. 1; 38. 1.

Dispose. Job 34. 13; 37. 15; Prov. 16. 33; 1 Cor. 10. 27.

Disposition. Acts 7. 53. R. V. as it was ordained (by angels).

Dispossess. Num. 33. 53; Deu. 7. 17; Jud. 11. 23.

Disputation. Acts 15. 2; Rom. 14. 1.

Dispute. Job 23. 7, the righteous might *d.* with him. R. V. reason.
Mk. 9. 33, what was it ye *d.* of by the way?
1 Cor. 1. 20, where is the *d.* of this world?
Phil. 2. 14, do all things without *d.*
1 Tim. 6. 5, perverse *d.* R. V. wranglings.
Jude 9. Michael the archangel when he *d.*

Disputing, with God, forbidden, Rom. 9. 20; 1 Cor. 1. 20. with men, Mk. 9. 33; Acts 9. 29; 15. 7; 17. 17; Rom. 14. 1; Phil. 2. 14; 1 Tim. 1. 4; 4. 7; 6. 20; 2 Tim. 2. 14; Tit. 3. 9.

Disquiet. 1 Sam. 28. 15, why *d.* to bring me up?
Ps. 42. 5, 11; 43. 5, why art thou *d.* within me?
See Ps. 38. 8; 39. 6; Jer. 50. 34.

Dissemble. Jos. 7. 11; Ps. 26. 4; Prov. 26. 24; Jer. 42. 20; Gal. 2. 13.

Dissension. Acts 15. 2; 23. 7, 10.

Dissimulation. Rom. 12. 9; Gal. 2. 13.

Dissolved. (1) Isa. 34. 4, host of heaven shall be *d.*
2 Cor. 5. 1, house of tabernacle *d.*
2 Pet. 3. 11, all these things shall be *d.*
3. 12, heavens being on fire shall be *d.*
(2) Dan. 5. 16, *d.* doubts.
See Job 30. 22; Ps. 75. 3; Isa. 14. 31; 24. 19; Dan. 5. 12; Nah. 2. 6.

Distaff. Prov. 31. 19.

Distil. Deu. 32. 2; Job 36. 28.

Distinction. 1 Cor. 14. 7.

Distinctly. Neh. 8. 8.

Distract. Ps. 88. 15; 1 Cor. 7. 35.

Distress. Gen. 42. 21, therefore is this *d.* come upon us.
Jud. 11. 7, why are ye come when ye are in *d.*?
1 Sam. 22. 2, every one in *d.* came to David.
2 Sam. 22. 7; Ps. 18. 6; 118. 5; 120. 1, in *d.* I called.
1 Kn. 1. 29, redeemed my soul out of all *d.*
2 Chr. 28. 22, in *d.* Ahaz trespassed more.
Neh. 2. 17, ye see the *d.* we are in. R. V. evil case.
Ps. 25. 17; 107. 6, 13, 19, 28, out of *d.*
Prov. 1. 27, mock when *d.* cometh.
Isa. 25. 4, a strength to needy in *d.*
Obad. 12, 14; Zep. 1. 15, day of *d.*
Lu. 21. 23, shall be great *d.* in the land.
21. 25, on earth *d.* of nations.
Rom. 8. 35, shall *d.* separate us? R. V. anguish.
1 Cor. 7. 26, good for present *d.*
2 Cor. 6. 4, approving ourselves in *d.*
12. 10, take pleasure in *d.*
See Gen. 35. 3; Neh. 9. 37; 2 Cor. 4. 8; 1 Thes. 3. 7.

Distribute. Neh. 13. 13, office was to *d.* to brethren.
Job 21. 17, God *d.* sorrows in his anger.
Lu. 18. 22, sell and *d.* to poor.
John 6. 11, given thanks, he *d.*
Rom. 12. 13, *d.* to necessity of saints.
1 Cor. 7. 17, as God hath *d.* to every man.
2 Cor. 9. 13, your liberal *d.* R. V. contribution.
See Jos. 13. 32; Acts 4. 35; 2 Cor. 10. 13; 1 Tim. 6. 18.

Ditch. Ps. 7. 15, fallen into *d.* he made.
Mat. 15. 14; Lu. 6. 39, both fall into *d.* R. V. pit.
See 2 Kn. 3. 16; Job 9. 31; Prov. 23. 27; Isa. 22. 11.

Divers. Deu. 22. 9, sow vineyard with *d.* kinds.
22. 11, garment of *d.* sorts. R. V. mingled stuff.
25. 13, not have in bag *d.* weights.
25. 14, *d.* measures, great and small.
Prov. 20. 10, 23, *d.* weights and measures abomination.
Mat. 4. 24; Mk. 1. 34; Lu. 4. 40, *d.* diseases.
24. 7; Mk. 13. 8; Lu. 21. 11, in *d.* places.
Mk. 8. 3, for *d.* of them came from far. R. V. some.
1 Cor. 12. 10, to another *d.* kinds of tongues.
2 Tim. 3. 6; Tit. 3. 3, led away with *d.* lusts.
Jas. 1. 2, joy in *d.* temptations. R. V. manifold.
See Eccl. 5. 7; Heb. 1. 1; 2. 4; 9. 10; 13. 9.

Diverse. Esth. 3. 8, laws *d.* from all people.
1 Cor. 12. 6, *d.* of operations, but same God.
See Esth. 1. 7; 1 Cor. 12. 4, 28.

Divide. Lev. 11. 4-7, 26; Deu. 14. 7, not eat these of them that *d.* the hoof.
Jos. 19. 49, an end of *d.* the land.
1 Kn. 3. 25, *d.* living child in two.
Job 27. 17, innocent shall *d.* silver.
Ps. 68. 12; Prov. 16. 19; Isa. 9. 3; 53. 12, *d.* spoil.
Am. 7. 17, thy land shall be *d.* by line.
Mat. 12. 25; Mk. 3. 24; Lu. 11. 17, kingdom or house *d.*
12. 26; Mk. 3. 26; Lu. 11. 18, *d.* against himself.
Lu. 12. 13, that he *d.* inheritance with me.
12. 14, who made me a *d.*?
12. 52, five in one house *d.*
12. 53, father *d.* against son.
15. 12, he *d.* unto them his living.
Acts 14. 4; 23. 7, multitude *d.*
1 Cor. 1. 13, is Christ *d.*?
12. 11, *d.* to every man severally as he will.
2 Tim. 2. 15, rightly *d.* word of truth. R. V. handling.
Heb. 4. 12, piercing to *d.* asunder.
See Dan. 7. 25; Hos. 10. 2; Mat. 25. 32; Lu. 22. 17.

Divination, Magic, Witchcraft, &c.
There are various Hebrew words by which these traffickers in superstitious rites were described. They may be classified thus:—

(*a*) **Diviners** professed to see visions or to obtain information by gazing into a cup (Gen. 44. 5), by means of arrows, by the inspection of livers of victims, and by teraphim, a kind of image (Ezek. 21. 21). Compare the divination amongst the Midianites (Num. 22. 7) and the Philistines (1 Sam. 6. 2).

(*b*) **Wizards, Witches** or **Sorcerers,** literally knowing ones, thought-readers (Lev. 19. 31; Deu. 18. 11).

(*c*) **Necromancers** (Deu. 18. 11), supposed to be possessed with **familiar spirits,** e. g., the witch of En-dor, who was professedly a 'medium' between the living and the dead.

(*d*) **Soothsayers, Monthly Prognosticators,** and **Observers of Times** were astrologers, who would draw horoscopes and foretell events by examining the conjunctions and oppositions of the heavenly bodies (Isa. 2. 6; 47. 13, &c.).

(*e*) **Magicians** or 'engravers' (Ex. 32. 4) were perhaps originally a literary caste. Compare the case of the magi or wise men who came from the East to worship Christ.

(*f*) **Enchanters** were serpent charmers, and another class were probably conjurers, gifted with sleight of hand. Probably amongst their hidden arts there may be reckoned quickness of wit, the power of a strong will over a weak one, the possession of secret information, the strange gift called 'clairvoyance,' the modern hypnotism or 'second sight,' the use of drugs and mechanical devices.

See also Isa. 8. 19-21; Acts 19. 19.

Divination. Num. 23. 23, neither is any *d.* against Israel.
Acts 16. 16, damsel with a spirit of *d.*
See 2 Kn. 17. 17; Ezek. 13. 23.

Divine (*v.*). Gen. 44. 15, wot ye not that I can *d.*?
1 Sam. 28. 8, *d.* unto me by the familiar spirit.
Ezek. 13. 9, prophets that *d.* lies.
21. 29, they *d.* lies unto thee.
Mic. 3. 11, prophets *d.* for money.
See Gen. 44. 5; Ezek. 22. 28; Mic. 3. 6. [3, 4.

Divine (*ad.*). Prov. 16. 10; Heb. 9. 1; 2 Pet. 1.

Diviner. *See* DIVINATION.

Division. Ex. 8. 23, will put a *d.* between my people.
Jud. 5. 15, for *d.* of Reuben. R. V. watercourses.
Lu. 12. 51, I tell you nay, but rather *d.*
John 7. 43; 9. 16; 10. 19, *d.* because of him.
Rom. 16. 17, mark them which cause *d.*
See 1 Cor. 1. 10; 3. 3; 11. 18.

Divorce, when permitted. Deu. 24. 1; Mat. 5. 32. condemned by Christ. Mk. 10. 4.

Dizahab, dī'-ză-hăb, 'abounding in gold.' Deu. 1. 1.

Do. Ru. 3. 5, all thou sayest I will *d.*
Eccl. 3 12, for a man to *d.* good.
Isa. 46. 11, I will also *d.* it.
Hos. 6. 4, what shall I *d.* unto thee?
Mat. 7. 12, men should *d.* to you, *d.* ye even so.
23. 3, they say, and *d.* not.
Lu. 10. 28, this *d.*, and thou shalt live.
22. 19; 1 Cor. 11. 24, this *d.* in remembrance.
John 15. 5, without me ye can *d.* nothing.
Rom. 7. 15, what I would, that *d.* I not.
2 Cor. 11. 12, what I *d.*, that I will *d.*
Gal. 5. 17, ye cannot *d.* the things ye would.
Phil. 4. 13, I can *d.* all things through Christ.
Heb. 4. 13, with whom we have to *d.*
Jas. 1. 23, a hearer, not a *d.* of the word.
See John 6. 38; 10. 37; Rev. 19. 10; 22. 9.

Do to wit, to make to know. 2 Cor. 8. 1.

Doctor, teacher. Lu. 2. 46, sitting in the midst of the *d.*
5. 17, *d.* of the law sitting by.
Acts 5. 34, Gamaliel, a *d.* of the law.

Doctrine. Prov. 4. 2, I give you good *d.* [sage.
Isa. 28. 9, made to understand *d.* R. V. the mes-
Jer. 10. 8, the stock is a *d.* of vanities. R. V. instruction of idols.
Mat. 15. 9; Mk. 7. 7, teaching for *d.* commandments of men.
16. 12, the *d.* of the Pharisees.
Mk. 1. 27; Acts 17. 19, what new *d.* is this? R. V. teaching.
John 7. 17, do his will shall know of the *d.* R. V. teaching.
Acts 2. 42, continued in apostles' *d.* R. V. teaching.
5. 28, filled Jerusalem with your *d.* R. V. teaching.
Rom. 6. 17, obeyed that form of *d.* R. V. teaching.
16. 17, contrary to the *d.* R. V. teaching.
1 Cor. 14. 26, every one hath a *d.* R. V. teaching.
Eph. 4. 14, every wind of *d.*
1 Tim. 1. 10, contrary to sound *d.*
4. 6, nourished in words of good *d.*
4. 13, give attendance to *d.* [ing.
4. 16, take heed to thyself and *d.* R. V. teach-
2 Tim. 3. 10, hast fully known my *d.* R. V. teaching.
3. 16, scripture profitable for *d.* R. V. teaching.
2 Tim. 4. 2, with all longsuffering and *d.* R. V. teaching.
Tit. 1. 9, by sound *d.* to exhort and convince.
2. 1, things which become sound *d.*
2. 7, in *d.* showing uncorruptness.
2. 10, adorn the *d.* of God our Saviour.
Heb. 6. 1, principles of the *d.*
6. 2, the *d.* of baptisms. R. V. teaching.
13. 9, not carried about with strange *d.* R. V. teachings.
2 John 9, abideth in *d.* of Christ. R. V. teaching.
See Deu. 32. 2; Job 11. 4; 1 Tim. 5. 17.

Doctrine of CHRIST. Mat. 7. 28, 29; Mk. 4. 2; John 7. 16; Acts 2. 42; 1 Tim. 4. 16; 6. 3; 2 Tim. 3. 16; Tit. 1. 1; 2. 1; Heb. 6. 1; 2 John 9.
obedience to. Rom. 6. 17.
not to be blasphemed. 1 Tim. 6. 1, 3; Tit. 2. 7, 10; 2 John 10.
no other to be taught. 1 Tim. 1. 3; 4. 6, 13.

Doctrines, false. Jer. 10. 8; Mat. 15. 9; 16. 12; Eph. 4. 14; 2 Thes. 2. 11; 1 Tim. 4. 1; 2 Tim. 4. 3; Heb. 13. 9; Rev. 2. 14.
to be avoided. Jer. 23. 16; 29. 8; Col. 2. 8; 1 Tim. 1. 4; 6. 20.

Dodai, dō'-dâi, 'beloved.' 1 Chr. 27. 4. [10. 4.

Dodanim, dō'-dă-nĭm, same as RODANIM. Gen.

Dodavah, dō'-dă-văh, 'beloved of Jehovah.' 2 Chr. 20. 37.

Dodo, dō'-dō, his beloved, same as DODAI. 2 Sam. 23. 9.

Doeg, dō'-ĕg, 'anxious,' the Edomite. 1 Sam. 21. 7.
slays the priests. 1 Sam. 22. 9.

Dog. Heb. *Kéleb:* Gk. *κύων.* Three kinds of dogs are now found in Palestine; (1) The pariah dog of towns and villages, the scavenger of the East; (2) the Syrian sheep-dog, like a Scotch collie; (3) the Persian greyhound. *See* GREYHOUND.
Ex. 11. 7, against Israel not a *d.* move.
Deu. 23. 18, not bring price of *d.* into house.
Jud. 7. 5, that lappeth as *d.* lappeth.
1 Sam. 17. 43; 24. 14; 2 Sam 3. 8, am I a *d.*?
2 Sam. 9. 8, upon such a dead *d.* as I am.
2 Kn. 8. 13, what, is thy servant a *d.*?
Job 30. 1, disdained to set with *d.*
Ps. 22. 20, darling from power of the *d.*
59. 6, they make noise like a *d.*
Prov. 26. 11; 2 Pet. 2. 22, as a *d.* returneth.
26. 17, like one that taketh a *d.* by ears.
Eccl. 9. 4, living *d.* better than dead lion.
Isa. 56. 10, they are all dumb *d.*
66. 3, as if he cut off a *d.* neck.
Mat. 7. 6, give not that which is holy to *d.*
15. 27; Mk. 7. 28, the *d.* eat of crumbs.
Phil. 3. 2, beware of *d.*
Rev. 22. 15, without are *d.*
See Ex. 22. 31; 1 Kn. 14. 11; 21. 23; 22. 28.

Doing. Ex. 15. 11, fearful in praises, *d.* wonders.
Jud. 2. 19, ceased not from their own *d.*
1 Sam. 25. 3, churlish and evil in his *d.*
1 Chr. 22. 16, arise, and be *d.*
Neh. 6. 3, I am *d.* a great work.
Ps. 9. 11; Isa. 12. 4, declare his *d.*
66. 5, terrible in *d.* toward children of men.
77. 12, I will talk of thy *d.*
118. 23; Mat. 21. 42; Mk. 12. 11, the Lord's *d.*
Mic. 2. 7, are these his *d.*?
Mat. 24. 46; Lu. 12. 43, shall find so *d.*
Acts 10. 38, went about *d.* good.
Rom. 2. 7, patient continuance in well *d.*
2 Cor. 8. 11, perform the *d.* of it.
Gal. 6. 9; 2 Thes. 3. 13, weary in well *d.*
Eph. 6. 6, *d.* will of God from heart.
1 Pet. 2. 15, with well *d.* put to silence.
3. 17, suffer for well *d.*
4. 19, commit souls in well *d.*
See Lev. 18. 3; Prov. 20. 11; Isa. 1. 16; Jer. 4. 4.

Doleful. Isa. 13. 21; Mic. 2. 4.

Dominion. Gen. 27. 40, when thou shalt have *d.* R. V. break loose.
37. 8, shalt thou have *d.* over us?

Num. 24. 19, come he that shall have *d.*
Job 25. 2, *d.* and fear are with him.
38. 33, canst thou set the *d.* thereof?
Ps. 8. 6, *d.* over works of thy hands.
19. 13; 119. 133, let them not have *d.* over me.
72. 8; Zec. 9. 10, *d.* from sea to sea.
Isa. 26. 13, other lords have had *d.* over us.
Dan. 4. 34; 7. 14, *d.* is an everlasting *d.*
Mat. 20. 25, princes of Gentiles exercise *d.*
Rom. 6. 9, death hath no more *d.*
6. 14, sin shall not have *d.*
7. 1, law hath *d.* over a man.
2 Cor. 1. 24, not *d.* over your faith.
Eph. 1. 21, above all *d.*
Col. 1. 16, whether they be thrones or *d.*
See Dan. 6. 26; 1 Pet. 4. 11; Jude 25; Rev. 1. 6.

Door. Gen. 4. 7, sin lieth at the *d.*
Ex. 12. 7, strike blood on *d.* posts.
33. 8; Num. 11. 10, every man at tent *d.*
Jud. 16. 3, Samson took *d.* of the gate.
Job 31. 9, laid wait at neighbour's *d.*
31. 32, I opened my *d.* to the travellers.
38. 17, the *d.* of the shadow of death.
41. 14, who can open *d.* of his face?
Ps. 24. 7, ye everlasting *d.*
78. 23, opened the *d.* of heaven.
84. 10, rather be *d.*-keeper.
141. 3, keep the *d.* of my lips.
Prov. 5. 8, come not nigh *d.* of her house.
8. 3, wisdom crieth at *d.*
26. 14, as *d.* turneth on hinges.
Eccl. 12. 4, *d.* shall be shut in the streets.
Isa. 6. 4, posts of the *d.* moved.
26. 20, enter, and shut thy *d.* about thee.
Hos. 2. 15, for a *d.* of hope.
Mal. 1. 10, who would shut the *d.* for nought?
Mat. 6. 6, when thou hast shut thy *d.*
24. 33; Mk. 13. 29, near, even at the *d.*
25. 10, and the *d.* was shut.
27. 60; 28. 2; Mk. 15. 46, *d.* of sepulchre.
Mk. 1. 33, city gathered at the *d.*
2. 2, not so much as about the *d.*
Lu. 13. 25, master hath shut to the *d.*
John 10. 1, 2, entereth not by *d.*
10. 7, 9, I am the *d.*
18. 16, Peter stood at the *d.* without.
18. 17, damsel that kept the *d.*
20. 19, 26, when *d.* were shut, Jesus came.
Acts 5. 9, feet at the *d.* to carry thee out.
14. 27, opened the *d.* of faith.
1 Cor. 16. 9, great *d.* and effectual.
2 Cor. 2. 12, *d.* opened to me of the Lord.
Col. 4. 3, open a *d.* of utterance.
Jas. 5. 9, judge standeth before the *d.*
Rev. 3. 8, set before thee an open *d.*
3. 20, I stand at *d.* and knock.
4. 1, behold, a *d.* opened in heaven. [16. 26.
See Ex. 21. 6; Deu. 11. 20; Isa. 57. 8; Acts 5. 19;

Dophkah, dŏph'-kăh. Num. 33. 12.

Dor, dôr, 'dwelling.' Jos. 11. 2.

Dorcas, dôr'-căs, 'gazelle.' Gk. for Tabitha. raised from death by Peter. Acts 9. 36, 40.

Dote. Jer. 50. 36; Ezek. 23. 5; 1 Tim. 6. 4.

Dothan, dō'-thăn, two wells or cisterns (?). Gen. 37. 17.

Double. Gen. 43. 12, 15, take *d.* money in hand.
Ex. 22. 4, 7, 9, he shall restore *d.*
Deu. 15. 18, worth a *d.* hired servant.
2 Kn. 2. 9, a *d.* portion of thy spirit.
1 Chr. 12. 33; Ps. 12. 2, a *d.* heart.
Isa. 40. 2, received *d.* for all her sins.
Jer. 16. 18, recompense their sin *d.*
1 Tim. 3. 8, deacons not *d.* tongued.
5. 17, worthy of *d.* honour.
Jas. 1. 8, a *d.* minded man unstable.
4. 8, purify your hearts, ye *d.* minded. [18. 6.
See Gen. 41. 32; Isa. 61. 7; Ezek. 21. 14; Rev.

Doubt. (1) Deu. 28. 66, thy life shall hang in *d.*
Job 12. 2, no *d.* ye are the people.
Ps. 126. 6, shall *d.* come again, rejoicing.
Dan. 5. 12, 16, dissolving of *d.*
Mat. 14. 31, wherefore didst thou *d.*?
21. 21, if ye have faith, and *d.* not.
Mk. 11. 23, shall not *d.* in his heart. [then.
Lu. 11. 20, no *d.* kingdom of God is come. R. V.
John 10. 24, how long dost thou make us to *d.*? R. V. hold us in suspense.
Acts 5. 24, they *d.* whereunto this would grow.
28. 4, no *d.* this man is a murderer.
Rom. 14. 23, he that *d.* is damned if he eat.
Gal. 4. 20, I stand in *d.* of you. R. V. perplexed about.
1 Tim. 2. 8, pray without wrath and *d.* R. V. disputing.
1 John 2. 19, would no *d.* have continued.
(2) to fear, be afraid of. Ecclus. 9. 13.
See Lu. 12. 29; Acts 2. 12; Phil. 3. 8.

Dough. Num. 15. 20, a cake of the first of your *d.*
Neh. 10. 37, the firstfruits of our *d.*
Ezek. 44. 30, give unto the priest the first of your *d.*

Dove (Isa. 38. 14). Heb. *Yônah:* Gk. περιστερά, a species of pigeon.
Ps. 55. 6, that I had wings like a *d.*
Isa. 38. 14; 59. 11, mourn like *d.*
60. 8, flee as *d.* to their windows.
Mat. 10. 16, be harmless as *d.*
21. 12; Mk. 11. 15; John 2. 14, them that sold *d.*
See Jer. 48. 28; Hos. 7. 11.

Dove. Noah's. Gen. 8. 8.
sacrificial. Gen. 15. 9; Lev. 12. 6; 14. 22.
figurative. Ps. 68. 13; 74. 19; S. of S. 1. 15; 2. 14.
Holy Spirit in form of. Mat. 3. 16; Mk. 1. 10; Lu. 3. 22; John 1. 32.

Dove's Dung (2 Kn. 6. 25). Heb. *Ḥiryônim:* Gk. κόπρος περιστερῶν: probably not a nauseous plant, but to be literally interpreted.

Down. 2 Sam. 3. 35, if I taste ought till sun be *d.*
2 Kn. 19. 30; Isa. 37. 31, again take root *d.*
Ps. 59. 15, let them wander up and *d.*
109. 23, I am tossed up and *d.*
Eccl. 3. 21, spirit of the beast that goeth *d.*
Zec. 10. 12, walk up and *d.* in his name.
See Jos. 8. 29; Ps. 139. 2; Ezek. 38. 14. [18. 25.

Dowry. Gen. 30. 20; 34. 12; Ex. 22. 17; 1 Sam.

Drachme, or **Drachma** (A. V. piece of silver, Lu. 15. 8) = a drachm of Antioch = 8½ pence = 16 cents, equivalent to a Roman denarius. *See* Money.

Drag. Hab. 1. 15, 16; John 21. 8.

Dragon. (1) Isa. 34. 13; Jer. 9. 11. Heb. *Tan.* A. V. 'dragon,' and 'sea monster' in Lam. 4. 3. R. V. jackal, *q. v.*
(2) Heb. *Tannîn,* 'a long animal,' land serpent. Ex. 7. 9; Ps. 91. 13; a sea monster, Gen. 1. 21. A. V. whales.
Ps. 74. 13 (margin); dragon, Ezek. 29. 3.

Dragon. Deu. 32. 33, their wine is the poison of *d.*
Neh. 2. 13, before the *d.* well.
Job 30. 29, I am a brother to *d.* R. V. jackals.
Ps. 148. 7, praise the Lord, ye *d.*
Isa. 43. 20, the *d.* and owls shall honour me.
Rev. 20. 2, the *d.*, that old serpent.
See Rev. 12. 3; 13. 2, 11; 16. 13.

Drank. 1 Sam. 30. 12, nor *d.* water three days and nights.
2 Sam. 12. 3, and *d.* of his own cup.
1 Kn. 17. 6, and he *d.* of the brook.
Dan. 1. 5, appointed of the wine he *d.*
5. 4, they *d.* wine, and praised the gods.
Mk. 14. 23, and they all *d.* of it.
Lu. 17. 27, 28, they *d.*, they married.
John 4. 12, than our father, who *d.* thereof.
1 Cor. 10. 4, for they *d.* of that spiritual Rock.
See Gen. 9. 21; 24. 46; 27. 25; Num. 20. 11.

Draught or **Draught house,** a privy. 2 Kn. 10. 27; Mat. 15. 17; Mk. 7. 19.

Draught (of fishes). Lu. 5. 4, 9; John 21. 6, 11.

Drave. Ex. 14. 25; Jos. 24. 12; Jud. 6. 9.

Draw. Job 40. 23, trusteth he can *d.* up Jordan.
41. 1, canst thou *d.* out leviathan?
Ps. 28. 3, *d.* me not away with wicked.
37. 14, wicked have *d.* out sword.
55. 21, yet were they *d.* swords.
88. 3, my life *d.* nigh unto the grave.

Eccl. 12. 1, nor years *d.* nigh.
S. of S. 1. 4, *d.* me, we will run after thee.
Isa. 5. 18, *d.* iniquity with cords.
12. 3, *d.* water from wells of salvation.
Jer. 31. 3, with lovingkindness have I *d.* thee.
Mat. 15. 8, people *d.* nigh me with their mouth.
Lu. 21. 8, the time *d.* near.
21. 28, your redemption *d.* nigh.
John 4. 11, thou hast nothing to *d.* with.
4. 15, thirst not, neither come hither to *d.*
6. 44, except the Father *d.* him.
12. 32, if lifted up, will *d.* all men.
Heb. 10. 22, *d.* near with true heart.
10. 38, 39, if any *d.* back.
Jas. 4. 8, *d.* nigh to God, he will *d.*
See Acts 11. 10; 20. 30; Heb. 7. 19; Jas. 2. 6.

Drawer. Deu. 29. 11; Jos. 9. 21.

Dread. Gen. 28. 17, how *d.* is this place!
Deu. 2. 25; 11. 25, begin to put *d.* of thee.
Isa. 8. 13, let him be your *d.*
Mal. 4. 5, the great and *d.* day. R. V. terrible.
See Gen. 9. 2; Ex. 15. 16; Dan. 9. 4.

Dream. Job 20. 8, shall fly away as a *d.*
33. 15, 16, in a *d.* he openeth the ears.
Ps. 73. 20, as a *d.* when one awaketh.
126. 1, we were like them that *d.*
Eccl. 5. 3, a *d.* cometh through much business.
Jer. 23. 28, prophet that hath a *d.*
Joel 2. 28; Acts 2. 17, old men *d. d.*
Jude 8, filthy *d.* defile the flesh.

Dreams, vanity of. Job 20. 8; Ps. 73. 20; Isa. 29. 8; Jer. 23. 28; 27. 9; Zec. 10. 2.
from God. Job 33. 15; Joel 2. 28.
of Abimelech, Gen. 20. 3. Jacob, Gen. 28. 12; 31. 10. Laban, Gen. 31. 24. Joseph, Gen. 37. 5. Pharaoh's servants, Gen. 40. 5. Pharaoh, Gen. 41. Midianite, Jud. 7. 13. Solomon, 1 Kn. 3. 5. Nebuchadnezzar, Dan. 2.; 4. Joseph, Mat. 1. 20; 2. 13. Wise men, Mat. 2. 12. Pilate's wife, Mat. 27. 19.

Dregs. Ps. 75. 8; Isa. 51. 17.

Dress. (1) till, prune, cultivate. Gen. 2. 15, put man in garden to *d.* it.
Deu. 28. 39, plant vineyards and *d.* them.
(2) 2 Sam. 12. 4, poor man's lamb, and *d.* it.
See Ex. 30. 7; Lu. 13. 7; Heb. 6. 7.

Drew. Gen. 47. 29, time *d.* nigh that Israel must die.
Ex. 2. 10, because I *d.* him out of the water.
Jos. 8. 26, Joshua *d.* not his hand back.
1 Kn. 22. 34; 2 Chr. 18. 33, man *d.* a bow.
2 Kn. 9. 24, Jehu *d.* bow with full strength.
Hos. 11. 4, *d.* them with cords of a man.
Zep. 3. 2, she *d.* not near to her God.
Mat. 21. 34, when time of fruit *d.* near.
Lu. 24. 15, Jesus himself *d.* near.
Acts 5. 37, and *d.* away much people.
See Esth. 5. 2; Lam. 3. 57; Acts 7. 17.

Drink (*n.*). Lev. 10. 9, do not drink strong *d.* when ye go.
Num. 6. 3, separate himself from strong *d.*
Deu. 14. 26, bestow money for strong *d.*
29. 6, strong *d.* these forty years.
Prov. 20. 1, strong *d.* is raging.
31. 4, not for princes to drink strong *d.*
31. 6, give strong *d.* to him that is ready to perish.
Isa. 24. 9, strong *d.* shall be bitter.
28. 7, erred through strong *d.*
Mic. 2. 11, prophesy of wine and strong *d.*
Hab. 2. 15, that giveth his neighbour *d.*
Hag. 1. 6, ye are not filled with *d.*
Mat. 25. 35, 37, 42, thirsty, and ye gave me *d.*
John 4. 9, a Jew, askest *d.* of me.
6. 55, my blood is *d.* indeed.
Rom. 12. 20, if thine enemy thirst, give him *d.*
14. 17, the kingdom of God is not meat and *d.* R. V. eating and drinking
1 Cor. 10. 4, same spiritual *d.*
Col. 2. 16, judge you in meat or in *d.*
See Gen. 21. 19; Isa. 5. 11, 22; 32. 6; 43. 20; Lu. 1. 15; 1 Tim. 5. 23.

Drink (*v.*). Ex. 15. 24, what shall we *d.*?
17. 1, no water for people to *d.*
2 Sam. 23. 16; 1 Chr. 11. 18, David would not *d.*
Ps. 36. 8, *d.* of the river of thy pleasures.
60. 3, *d.* the wine of astonishment.
80. 5, gavest them tears to *d.*
110. 7, he shall *d.* of the brook in the way.
Prov. 5. 15, *d.* waters of thine own cistern.
31. 5, lest they *d.*, and forget the law.
31. 7, let him *d.*, and forget his poverty.
Eccl. 9. 7, *d.* wine with merry heart.
S. of S. 5. 1, *d.*, yea, *d.* abundantly.
Isa. 5. 22, mighty to *d.* wine.
65. 13, my servants shall *d.*, but ye.
Jer. 35. 2, give Rechabites wine to *d.*
35. 6, we will *d.* no wine.
35. 14, to this day they *d.* none.
Ezek. 4. 11, thou shalt *d.* water by measure.
Am. 2. 8, *d.* the wine of the condemned.
Zec. 9. 15, they shall *d.*, and make a noise.
Mat. 10. 42, whoso shall give to *d.*
20. 22; Mk. 10. 38, are ye able to *d.*?
26. 27, saying, *d.* ye all of it.
26. 29; Mk. 14. 25; Lu. 22. 18, when I *d.* it new.
26. 42, may not pass except I *d.*
Mk. 9. 41, shall give you cup of water to *d.*
16. 18, if they *d.* any deadly thing.
John 4. 10, give me to *d.*
7. 37, let him come to me and *d.*
18. 11, cup given me, shall I not *d.* it?
Rom. 14. 21, not good to *d.* wine.
1 Cor. 10. 4, did all *d.* same spiritual drink.
11. 25, as oft as ye *d.* it.
12. 13, made to *d.* into one Spirit.
See Mk. 2. 16; Lu. 7. 33; 10. 7.

Drink offerings. Ex. 29. 40; Lev. 23. 13; Num. 6. 17; 15. 5 (Gen. 35. 14).
to idols. Isa. 57. 6; Jer. 7. 18; 44. 17; Ezek. 20. 28.

Drive. Gen. 4. 14, thou hast *d.* me out.
Ex. 23. 28, hornets shall *d.* out Hivite.
Deu. 4. 19, lest thou be *d.* to worship them. R. V. drawn away.
Job 24. 3, they *d.* away ass of the fatherless.
30. 5, they were *d.* forth from among men.
Prov. 14. 32, wicked *d.* away in his wickedness.
22. 15, rod shall *d.* it away.
25. 23, north wind *d.* away rain. R. V. bringeth forth.
Jer. 46. 15, stood not, because Lord did *d.* them.
Dan. 4. 25; 5. 21, they shall *d.* thee from men.
Hos. 13. 3, as chaff *d.* with whirlwind.
Lu. 8. 29, he was *d.* of the devil.
Jas. 1. 6, wave *d.* with the wind.
See 2 Kn. 9. 20; Jer. 8. 3; Ezek. 31. 11.

Dromedary (Jer. 2. 23). Heb. *Béker, bikrah.* *See* Camel.
1 Kn. 4. 28, straw for the horses and *d.* R. V. swift steeds.
Esth. 8. 10, and young *d.*
Isa. 60. 6, the *d.* of Midian and Ephah.
Jer. 2. 23, thou art a swift *d.* traversing her ways.

Drop (*n.*). Job 36. 27, maketh small the *d.* of water.
Isa. 40. 15, as the *d.* of a bucket.
See Job 38. 28; S. of S. 5. 2; Lu. 22. 44.

Drop (*v.*). Deu. 32. 2, doctrine shall *d.* as the rain.
Job 29. 22, my speech *d.* upon them.
Ps. 65. 11, paths *d.* fatness.
68. 8, heavens *d.* at presence of God.
Eccl. 10. 18, through idleness house *d.* through. R. V. leaketh.
Isa. 45. 8, *d.* down, ye heavens.
Ezek. 20. 46, *d.* thy word toward the south.
See 2 Sam. 21. 10; Joel 3. 18; Am. 9. 13.

Dropsy. Lu. 14. 2, a man which had the *d.*

Dross. Ps. 119. 119; Prov. 25. 4; 26. 23; Isa. 1. 22, 25; Ezek. 22. 18.

Drought. Deu. 28. 24; 1 Kn. 17.; Isa. 58. 11; Jer. 17. 8; Hos. 13. 5; Hag. 1. 11.

Drove. Gen. 3. 24; 15. 11; 32. 16; 33. 8; John 2. 15.

Drown. S. of S. 8, 7, neither can floods *d.* it.
1 Tim. 6. 9, that *d.* men in perdition.
See Ex. 15. 4; Mat. 18. 6; Heb. 11. 29.

Drowsiness. Prov. 23. 21.

Drunk. 2 Sam. 11. 13, David made Uriah *d.*
1 Kn. 20. 16, was drinking himself *d.*
Job 12. 25; Ps. 107. 27, stagger like a *d.* man.
Jer. 23. 9, I am like a *d.* man.
Lam. 5. 4, we have *d.* water for money.
Hab. 2. 15, makest him *d.* also.
Mat. 24. 49; Lu. 12. 45, drink with the *d.*
Acts 2. 15, these are not *d.*
1 Cor. 11. 21, one is hungry, and another *d.*
1 Thes. 5. 7, they that be *d.* are *d.* in the night.
See Lu. 5. 39; John 2. 10; Eph. 5. 18; Rev. 17. 6.

Drunkard. Deu. 21. 20, our son is a glutton and a *d.*
Prov. 23. 21, *d.* and glutton come to poverty.
26. 9, as a thorn goeth into hand of *d.*
1 Cor. 6. 10, nor *d.* shall inherit.
See Ps. 69. 12; Isa. 24. 20; Nah. 1. 10.

Drunkards, woe to. Isa. 5. 11; 28. 1; Joel 1. 5; Lu. 21. 34; Rom. 13. 13; 1 Cor. 5. 11; Gal. 5. 21. *See also* 1 Thes. 5. 7; 1 Pet. 4. 3. *See* WINE.
punished. Deu. 21. 20; Am. 6. 7; Nah. 1. 10; Mat. 24. 49; Lu. 12. 45; 1 Cor. 6. 10; Gal. 5. 21.

Drunkenness. Deu. 29. 19, to add *d.* to thirst. R. V. destroy the moist with the dry.
Eccl. 10. 17, eat for strength, not for *d.*
Ezek. 23. 33, shalt be filled with *d.*
See Lu. 21. 34; Rom. 13. 13; Gal. 5. 21.

Drunkenness: of Noah, Gen. 9. 21. Lot, Gen. 19. 33. Nabal, 1 Sam. 25. 36. Elah, 1 Kn. 16. 9. Ben-hadad, 1 Kn. 20. 16. Belshazzar, Dan. 5. 4. The Corinthians, 1 Cor. 11. 21.

Drusilla, drū-sĭl'-lă. Acts 24. 24.

Dry. Prov. 17. 22, a broken spirit *d.* the bones.
Isa. 44. 3, pour floods on *d.* ground.
Mat. 12. 43; Lu. 11. 24, through *d.* places.
Mk. 5. 29, fountain of blood *d.* up.
See Ps. 107. 33, 35; Isa. 53. 2; Mk. 11. 20.

Due. Lev. 10. 13, 14, it is thy *d.*, and thy sons' *d.*
26. 4; Deu. 11. 14, rain in *d.* season.
Ps. 104. 27; 145. 15; Mat. 24. 45; Lu. 14. 42, meat in *d.* season.
Prov. 15. 23, word spoken in *d.* season.
Mat. 18. 34, pay all that was *d.*
Lu. 23. 41, the *d.* reward of our deeds.
Rom. 5. 6, in *d.* time Christ died.
Gal. 6. 9, in *d.* season we shall reap.
See Prov. 3. 27; 1 Cor. 15. 8; Tit. 1. 3; 1 Pet. 5. 6.

Duke, a leader, commander, chief. Gen. 36. 15.

Dulcimer (Dan. 3. 5, 10, 15). Chald. *Sumphônyah:* Gk. συμφωνία: R. V. marg. 'bagpipe,' probably correct. The real dulcimer is the *Psantêrîn* (translated 'psaltery' in A. V.), an instrument formed of strings tightly stretched, by fixed pins and turning screws, over a rectangular sounding-board or box; and was played by hammers struck with the hand against the strings. It is the germ of the piano.

Dull. Mat. 13. 15; Acts 28. 27; Heb. 5. 11.

Dumah, dū'-măh, 'silence.' Gen. 25. 14.

Dumb. Ex. 4. 11, who maketh the *d.*?
Prov. 31. 8, open thy mouth for the *d.*
Isa. 35. 6, the tongue of the *d.* shall sing.
53. 7; Acts 8. 32, as sheep before shearers is *d.*
56. 10, they are all *d.* dogs.
Ezek. 3. 26, be *d.*, and shalt not be a reprover.
Hab. 2. 19, woe to him that saith to *d.* stone.
Mat. 9. 32; 12. 22; 15. 30; Mk. 7. 37; 9. 17, *d.* man.
See Ps. 39. 2; Dan. 10. 15; Lu. 1. 20; 11. 14; 2 Pet. 2. 16.

Dung. 1 Sam. 2. 8; Ps. 113. 7, lifteth beggar from *d.*-hill.
Lu. 13. 8, till I dig about it, and *d.* it.
14. 35, neither fit for land nor *d.*-hill.
Phil. 3. 8, count all things but *d.*
See Neh. 2. 13; Lam. 4. 5; Mal. 2. 3.

Dungeon. Gen. 40. 15; 41. 14; Ex. 12. 29; Jer. 38. 6; Lam. 3. 53.

Dura, dū'-ră, plain of, golden image set up. Dan. 3. 1.

Durable. Prov. 8. 18; Isa. 23. 18.

Dureth. Mat. 13. 21. R. V. endureth.

Durst. Mat. 22. 46; Mk. 12. 34; Lu. 20. 40, nor *d.* ask questions.
John 21. 12, none of disciples *d.* ask.
See Esth. 7. 5; Job 32. 6; Acts 5. 13; Jude 9.

Dust. Gen. 2. 7, Lord God formed man of *d*
3. 14, *d.* shalt thou eat.
3. 19, *d.* thou art.
18. 27, who am but *d.* and ashes.
Job 10. 9, wilt thou bring me into *d.* again?
22. 24; 27. 16, lay up gold as *d.*
34. 15, man shall turn again to *d.*
42. 6, I repent in *d.* and ashes.
Ps. 30. 9, shall the *d.* praise thee?
102. 14, servants favour *d.* thereof.
103. 14, remembereth that we are *d.*
104. 29, they die and return to their *d.*
Eccl. 3. 20, all are of the *d.*, and turn to *d.* again.
12. 7, then shall the *d.* return to the earth.
Isa. 40. 12, comprehended *d.* of the earth.
65. 25, *d.* shall be serpent's meat.
Lam. 3. 29, he putteth his mouth in the *d.*
Dan. 12. 2, many that sleep in *d.* shall awake.
Mic. 7. 17, lick the *d.* like a serpent. [from feet.
Mat. 10. 14; Mk. 6. 11; Lu. 9. 5, shake off *d.*
Lu. 10. 11, even *d.* of your city.
Acts 22. 23, as they threw *d.* into the air.
See Ex. 8. 16; Num. 23. 10; Deu. 9. 21; Jos. 7. 6; Job 2. 12; 39. 14; Lam. 2. 10.

Duty. Eccl. 12. 13, the whole *d.* of man.
Lu. 17. 10, that which was our *d.* to do.
Rom. 15. 27, their *d.* is to minister.
See Ex. 21. 10; Deu. 25. 5; 2 Chr. 8. 14; Ez. 3. 4.

Dwarfs not to minister. Lev. 21. 20.

Dwell. Deu. 12. 11, cause his name to *d.* there.
1 Sam. 4. 4; 2 Sam. 6. 2; 1 Chr. 13. 6, *d.* between the cherubims. R. V. sitteth upon.
1 Kn. 8. 30; 2 Chr. 6. 21, heaven thy *d.* place.
Ps. 23. 6, will *d.* in house of the Lord.
37. 3, so shalt thou *d.* in the land.
84. 10, than to *d.* in tents of wickedness.
132. 14, here will I *d.*
133. 1, good for brethren to *d.* together.
Isa. 33. 14, who shall *d.* with devouring fire?
33. 16, he shall *d.* on high.
57. 15, I *d.* in the high and holy place.
John 6. 56, *d.* in me and I in him. R. V. abideth.
14. 10, the Father that *d.* in me. R. V. abiding.
14. 17, for he *d.* with you, and shall be in you. R. V. abideth.
Rom. 7. 17, sin that *d.* in me.
Col. 2. 9, in him *d.* fulness of Godhead.
3. 16, word of Christ *d.* in you richly.
1 Tim. 6. 16, *d.* in the light.
2 Pet. 3. 13, wherein *d.* righteousness.
1 John 3. 17, how *d.* the love of God in him? R. V. abide.
4. 12, God *d.* in us. R. V. abideth.
See Rom. 8. 9; 2 Cor. 6. 16; Jas. 4. 5.

Dyed. Ex. 25. 5; Isa. 63. 1; Ezek. 23. 15.

Dying. 2 Cor. 4. 10, the *d.* of Lord Jesus.
6. 9, as *d.* and behold we live.
See Num. 17. 13; Lu. 8. 42; Heb. 11. 21.

Each. Isa. 57. 2, *e.* one walking in his uprightness.
Ezek. 4. 6, *e.* day for a year.
Acts 2. 3, cloven tongues sat on *e.*
Phil. 2. 3, let *e.* esteem other.
See Ex. 18. 7; Ps. 85. 10; 2 Thes. 1. 3.

Eagle. (1) (Deu. 32. 11). Heb. *Nésher:* Gk. ἀετός. (Specimens, *Circætus Gallicus; Gyps fulvus.* T. Found at Yebua.) The word is used by the Arabs for the true eagles, of which there are eight species in the Holy Land, and for the vulture, of which there are four species.
(2) Gier (Lev. 11. 18). Heb. *Raḥam:* Gk. πορφυρίων: R. V. vulture. (Specimen, *Neophron percnopterus.*) The 'Egyptian vulture' or 'Pharaoh's hen,' common in Asia and all parts of Africa.

Eagle. Ex. 19. 4, how I bare you on *e.* wings.
2 Sam. 1. 23, were swifter than *e.*
Job 9. 26, *e.* that hasteth to prey.
39. 27, doth the *e.* mount up?
Ps. 103. 5, youth renewed like *e.*
Isa. 40. 31, mount up with wings as *e.*

Ezek. 1. 10, they four also had the face of an *e.*
17. 3, a great *e.* with great wings.
Obad. 4, thou shalt exalt thyself as the *e.*
Mat. 24. 28; Lu. 17. 37, *e.* be gathered.
Rev. 4. 7, the fourth beast was like a flying *e.*
See Dan. 4. 33; Rev. 12. 14.

Ear (*n.*). Neh. 1. 6, let thine *e.* be attentive.
Job 12. 11; 34. 3, doth not *e.* try words?
29. 11, when the *e.* heard me, it blessed me.
42. 5, heard of thee by the hearing of the *e.*
Ps. 45. 10, and incline thine *e.*
58. 4, like the deaf adder that stoppeth her *e.*
78. 1, give *e.*, O my people.
94. 9, he that planted the *e.*, shall he not hear?
Prov. 15. 31, the *e.* that heareth the reproof.
17. 4, liar giveth *e.* to naughty tongue.
18. 15, *e.* of wise seeketh knowledge.
20. 12, hearing *e.*, seeing eye, Lord made.
22. 17, bow down thine *e.*
25. 12, wise reprover on obedient *e.*
Eccl. 1. 8, nor the *e.* filled with hearing.
Isa. 48. 8, from that time thine *e.* not opened.
50. 4, he wakeneth my *e.* to hear.
55. 3, incline your *e.*, and come unto me.
59. 1, neither his *e.* heavy, that it cannot.
Jer. 9. 20, let your *e.* receive word of the Lord.
Amos 3. 12, out of mouth of lion piece of an *e.*
Mat. 10. 27, what ye hear in *e.*, preach.
26. 51; Mk. 14. 27, smote off his *e.*
1 Cor. 2. 9, nor *e.* heard.
12. 16, if *e.* say, because I am not the eye.
Rev. 2. 7, he that hath an *e.* let him hear.

Ear (*v.*), to plough, till the ground. (Chaucer has 'to ere;' from A. S. *erian*, to plough.) Deu. 21. 4; 1 Sam. 8. 12; Isa. 30. 24.

Earing, ploughing. Gen. 45. 6; Ex. 34. 21.

Early. Ps. 46. 5, and that right *e.*
63. 1, *e.* will I seek thee.
90. 14, satisfy us *e.* with thy mercy.
Prov. 1. 28; 8. 17, seek me *e.* shall find me. R. V. diligently.
S. of S. 7. 12, get up *e.* to vineyards.
Hos. 6. 4; 13. 3, as *e.* dew.
Jas. 5. 7, the *e.* and latter rain.
See Jud. 7. 3; Lu. 24. 22.

Early rising. Gen. 19. 27; 26. 31; 28. 18; Jos. 3. 1; Jud. 6. 38; 1 Sam. 9. 26; 15. 12; 17. 20; Mk. 1. 35; 16. 2; John 8. 2; 20. 1; Acts 5. 21.

Earnest. Job 7. 2, as servant *e.* desireth shadow.
Jer. 31. 20, I do *e.* remember him still.
Mic. 7. 3, do evil with both hands *e.* R. V. diligently.
Lu. 22. 44, in agony he prayed more *e.*
Rom. 8. 19, the *e.* expectation of the creature.
1 Cor. 12. 31, covet *e.* best gifts.
2 Cor. 5. 2, *e.* desiring to be clothed.
Phil. 1. 20, to my *e.* expectation and hope.
Jude 3, *e.* contend for the faith.
See Acts 3. 12; Heb. 2. 1; Jas. 5. 17.

Earnest, a pledge, security. 2 Cor. 1. 22; 5. 5, the *e.* of the spirit.
Eph. 1. 14, the *e.* of our inheritance.

Earneth. Hag. 1. 6.

Earring. Gen. 35. 4; Ex. 32. 2; Jud. 8. 25; Prov. 25. 12 (nose ring); Ezek. 16. 12.

Ears. Ex. 10. 2, tell it in *e.* of thy son.
1 Sam. 3. 11; 2 Kn. 21. 12; Jer. 19. 3, at which *e.* shall tingle.
2 Sam. 7. 22, we have heard with our *e.*
Job 15. 21, dreadful sound is in his *e.*
28. 22, heard fame with our *e.*
Ps. 18. 6, my cry came even into his *e.*
34. 15, his *e.* are open unto their cry.
Ps. 115. 6; 135. 17, they have *e.*, but hear not.
Prov. 21. 13, stoppeth *e.* at cry of the poor.
23. 9, speak not in *e.* of a fool. R. V. hearing.
26. 17, one that taketh dog by the *e.*
Isa. 6. 10; Mat. 13. 15; Acts 28. 27, make *e.* heavy.
Mat. 13. 16, blessed are your *e.*
Mk. 7. 33, put his fingers into *e.*
8. 18, having *e.*, hear ye not?
Acts 7. 51, uncircumcised in heart and *e.*
17. 20, strange things to our *e.*
2 Tim. 4. 3, having itching *e.*
Jas. 5. 4, entered into *e.* of the Lord.
1 Pet. 3. 12, his *e.* are open to prayer.

Ears (*of corn*). Deu. 23. 25; Mat. 12. 1.

Ears, he that hath, to hear. Mat. 11. 15; 13. 16; Mk. 4. 9, 23; 7. 16; Rev. 2. 7, &c.
have, but hear not. Ps. 115. 6; Isa. 42. 20; Ezek. 12. 2; Mat. 13. 12; Mk. 8. 18; Rom. 11. 8.
the Lord's, open to prayer. 2 Sam. 22. 7; Ps. 18. 6; 34. 15; Jas. 5. 4; 1 Pet. 3. 12.
opened by God. Job 33. 16; 36. 15; Ps. 40. 6; Mk. 7. 35.

Earth. Three Hebrew words are translated earth:
(1) Gen. 50. 22. Heb. *Eretz:* Gk. ἡ γῆ, the earth, or globe generally.
(2) Gen. 9. 20). Heb. *Adâmah:* Gk. γῆ, red earth.
(3) (Gen. 3. 14; Isa. 47. 1). Heb. '*Aphar:* Gk. γῆ, dry earth, or dust.
Gen. 8. 22, while *e.* remaineth.
10. 25, in his days was *e.* divided.
18. 25, shall not Judge of all the *e.* do right?
Num. 14. 21, all *e.* filled with glory.
16. 30, if the *e.* open her mouth. R. V. ground.
Deu. 32. 1, O *e.*, hear the words of my mouth.
Jos. 3. 11; Zec. 6. 5, Lord of all the *e.*
23. 14, going way of all the *e.*
1 Kn. 8. 27; 2 Chr. 6. 18, will God dwell on the *e.*?
2 Kn. 5. 17, two mules' burden of *e.*
Job 7. 1, appointed time to man upon *e.*
9. 24, *e.* given into hand of wicked.
19. 25, stand at latter day upon *e.*
26. 7, hangeth *e.* upon nothing.
38. 4, when I laid foundations of the *e.*
41. 33, on *e.* there is not his like.
Ps. 2. 8, uttermost parts of *e.*
8. 1, excellent is thy name in *e.*
16. 3, to saints that are in the *e.*
25. 13, his seed shall inherit the *e.* R. V. land.
33. 5, the *e.* is full of the goodness.
34. 16, cut off remembrance from the *e.*
37. 9, 11, 22, wait on Lord shall inherit *e.*
41. 2, shall be blessed upon the *e.*
46. 2, not fear, though the *e.* be removed.
46. 6, uttered voice, the *e.* melted.
46. 8, desolations made in the *e.*
46. 10, will be exalted in the *e.*
47. 9, shields of the *e.* belong to God.
48. 2, joy of the whole *e.*
50. 4, call to *e.*, that he may judge.
57. 5; 108. 5, glory above all the *e.*
58. 11, a God that judgeth in the *e.*
60. 2, made the *e.* to tremble.
63. 9, lower parts of the *e.*
65. 8, dwell in uttermost parts of *e.*
65. 9, visitest *e.*, and waterest it.
67. 6; Ezek. 34. 27, *e.* yield increase.
68. 8, *e.* shook, heavens dropped.
71. 20, bring me up from depths of the *e.*
72. 6, showers that water the *e.*
72. 16, handful of corn in the *e.*
73. 9, tongue walketh through *e.*
73. 25, none on *e.* I desire beside thee.
75. 3; Isa. 24. 19, *e.* dissolved.
83. 18; 97. 9, most high over all *e.*
90. 2, or ever thou hadst formed the *e.*
97. 1, Lord reigneth, let *e.* rejoice.
99. 1, Lord reigneth, let *e.* be moved.
102. 25; 104. 5; Prov. 8. 29; Isa. 48. 13, laid foundation of *e.*
104. 13, the *e.* is satisfied.
104. 24, the *e.* is full of thy riches.
112. 2, seed mighty upon *e.*
115. 16, *e.* given to children of men.
119. 19, stranger in the *e.*
119. 64, the *e.* full of thy mercy.
119. 90, established the *e.*, it abideth.
146. 4, he returneth to the *e.*
147. 8, prepareth rain for the *e.*
148. 13, glory above *e.* and heaven.
Prov. 3. 19; Isa. 24. 1, Lord founded the *e.*
8. 23, set up from everlasting, or ever *e.* was.
8. 26, he had not yet made *e.*, nor fields.

Prov. 11. 31, righteous recompensed in *e.*
25. 3, the *e.* for depth.
30. 14, teeth as knives to devour poor from *e.*
30. 16, the *e.* not filled with water.
30. 21, for three things *e.* is disquieted.
30. 24, four things little upon *e.*
Eccl. 1. 4, the *e.* abideth for ever.
3. 21, spirit of beast goeth to *e.*
5. 9, profit of the *e.* for all.
12. 7, dust return to *e.*
Isa. 4. 2, fruit of *e.* excellent.
11. 9, *e.* full of knowledge of the Lord.
13. 13, *e.* shall remove out of her place.
14. 16, is this the man that made *e.* tremble?
26. 9, when thy judgments are in the *e.*
26. 21, *e.* shall disclose her blood.
34. 1, let the *e.* hear.
40. 22, sitteth on circle of the *e.*
40. 28, Creator of ends of *e.* fainteth not.
44. 24, spreadeth abroad *e.* by myself.
45. 22, be saved, all ends of the *e.*
49. 13, be joyful, O *e.*
51. 6, the *e.* shall wax old.
66. 1, the *e.* is my footstool.
66. 8, shall *e.* bring forth in one day?
Jer. 15. 10, man of contention to whole *e.*
22. 29; Mic. 1. 2, O *e.*, *e.*, hear word of Lord.
31. 22, hath created new thing in *e.*
51. 15, made the *e.* by his power.
Ezek. 9. 9, the Lord hath forsaken the *e.*
43. 2, the *e.* shined with his glory.
Hos. 2. 22, the *e.* shall hear the corn.
Am. 3. 5, bird fall in snare on *e.*
8. 9, darken *e.* in the clear day.
9. 9, least grain fall upon the *e.*
Jon. 2. 6, *e.* with bars about me.
Mic. 6. 2, ye strong foundations of the *e.*
7. 2, good man perished out of the *e.*
7. 17, move like worms of the *e.*
Nah. 1. 5, *e.* burnt up at his presence.
Hab. 2. 14, *e.* filled with knowledge.
3. 3, the *e.* full of his praise.
Hag. 1. 10, *e.* stayed from her fruit.
Zec. 4. 10, eyes of Lord run through *e.*
Mal. 4. 6, lest I smite *e.* with a curse.
Mat. 5. 5, meek shall inherit *e.*
5. 35, swear not by the *e.*
6. 19, treasures upon *e.*
9. 6; Mk. 2. 10; Lu. 5. 24, power on *e.* to forgive.
10. 34, to send peace on *e.*
13. 5; Mk. 4. 5, not much *e.*
16. 19; 18. 18, shalt bind on *e.*
18. 19, shall agree on *e.*
23. 9, call no man father on *e.*
25. 18, 25, digged in the *e.*
Mk. 4. 28, *e.* bringeth forth fruit of herself.
4. 31, less than all seeds in the *e.*
9. 3, no fuller on *e.* can white them.
Lu. 2. 14, on *e.* peace.
23. 44, darkness over all *e.* R. V. the whole land.
John 3. 12, I have told you *e.* things.
3. 31, of *e.* is *e.*, and speaketh of the *e.*
12. 32, lifted up from the *e.*
17. 4, I have glorified thee on the *e.*
Acts 8. 33, life taken from the *e.*
9. 4, 8; 26. 14, Saul fell to the *e.*
22. 22, away with such a fellow from *e.*
Rom. 10. 18, sound went into all *e.*
1 Cor. 15. 47, first man is of the *e.*, *e.*
15. 48, as is the *e.*, such are they that are *e.*
15. 49, the image of the *e.*
2 Cor. 4. 7, treasure in *e.* vessels.
Col. 3. 2, affection not on things on *e.*
Phil. 3. 19, who mind *e.* things.
Heb. 6. 7, *e.* drinketh in the rain.
8. 4, if he were on *e.*
11. 13, strangers on the *e.*
12. 25, refused him that spake on *e.*
12. 26, voice then shook the *e.*
Jas. 3. 15, this wisdom is *e.*
5. 5, lived in pleasure on *e.*
5. 7, the precious fruit of the *e.*
5. 18, and the *e.* brought forth her fruit.
2 Pet. 3. 10, the *e.* shall be burnt up.
Rev. 5. 10, we shall reign on the *e.*
7. 3, hurt not the *e.*
18. 1, *e.* lightened with his glory.
20. 11, from whose face the *e.* fled.
21. 1, a new *e.*
See Gen. 1. 1, 11; 3. 17; 7. 10; Ex. 9. 29; Job 12. 8; Ps. 24. 1; Isa. 65. 16; Mic. 1. 4; Zep. 3. 8; 2 Pet. 3. 7, 13; Rev. 20. 9.

Earthquake. 1 Kn. 19. 11; Isa. 29. 6; Am. 1. 1; Zec. 14. 5; Mat. 24. 7; 27. 54; Acts 16. 26; Rev. 6. 12; 8. 5; 11. 13; 16. 18.

Ease. Ex. 18. 22, so shall it be *e.* for thyself.
Deu. 28. 65, among nations find no *e.*
Job 12. 5, thought of him that is at *e.*
16. 6, though I forbear, what am I *e.*
21. 23, dieth, being wholly at *e.*
Ps. 25. 13, his soul shall dwell at *e.*
Prov. 14. 6, knowledge is *e.* unto him that understandeth.
Isa. 32. 9, 11, women that are at *e.*
Am. 6. 1, woe to them that are at *e.*
Mat. 9. 5; Mk. 2. 9; Lu. 5. 23, is *e.* to say.
11. 30, my yoke is *e.*
19. 24; Mk. 10. 25; Lu. 18. 25, *e.* for camel.
1 Cor. 13. 5, not *e.* provoked.
14. 9, words *e.* to be understood.
Heb. 12. 1, sin which doth so *e.* beset.
Jas. 3. 17, *e.* to be intreated.
See Jer. 46. 27; Zec. 1. 15; Lu. 12. 19.

East. Gen. 41. 6; 23. 27, blasted with *e.* wind.
Ex. 10. 13, Lord brought an *e.* wind.
Job 1. 3, greatest of all men of the *e.*
15. 2, fill his belly with *e.* wind.
27. 21, *e.* wind carrieth him away.
38. 24, scattereth *e.* wind on the earth.
Ps. 48. 7, breakest ships with *e.* wind.
75. 6, promotion cometh not from *e.*
103. 12, as far as *e.* from west.
Isa. 27. 8, stayeth rough wind in day of *e.* wind.
Ezek. 19. 12, the *e.* wind drieth up her fruit.
43. 2, glory of God of Israel came from way of *e.*
47. 1, house stood toward the *e.*
Hos. 12. 1, Ephraim followeth *e.* wind.
13. 15, though fruitful, an *e.* wind shall come.
See Jon. 4. 5, 8; Mat. 2. 1; 8. 11; 24. 27.

Easter. Acts 12. 4, intending after *E.* to bring him forth. R. V. the Passover.

Eat. Gen. 2. 17, in day thou *e.* thou shalt die.
9. 4; Lev. 19. 26; Deu. 12. 16, blood not *e.*
24. 33, not *e.* till I have told.
43. 32, Egyptians might not *e.* with Hebrews.
Ex. 12. 16, no work save that which man must *e.*
23. 11, that the poor may *e.*
29. 34, shall not be *e.*, because holy.
Lev. 25. 20, what shall we *e.* seventh year?
Num. 13. 32, a land that *e.* up inhabitants.
Jos. 5. 11, 12, *e.* of old corn of the land.
1 Sam. 14. 30, if haply people had *e.* freely.
28. 20, had *e.* no bread all day.
28. 22, *e.*, that thou mayest have strength.
2 Sam. 19. 42, have we *e.* at all of the king's cost?
1 Kn. 19. 5; Acts 10. 13; 11. 7, angel said, Arise and *e.*
2 Kn. 4. 43, 44, they shall *e.*, and leave thereof.
6. 28, give thy son, that we may *e.* him.
Neh. 5. 2, corn that we may *e.*, and live.
Job 3. 24, my sighing cometh before I *e.*
5. 5, whose harvest the hungry *e.* up.
6. 6, *e.* without salt.
21. 25, another never *e.* with pleasure.
31. 17, have *e.* my morsel alone.
Ps. 22. 26, meek shall *e.* and be satisfied.
69. 9; John 2. 17, zeal hath *e.* me up.
102. 9, have *e.* ashes like bread.
Prov. 1. 31; Isa. 3. 10, *e.* fruit of their own way.
13. 25, *e.* to satisfying of soul.
18. 21, they that love it shall *e.* the fruit.
23. 1, sittest to *e.* with ruler.
24. 13, *e.* honey, because it is good.
25. 27, not good to *e.* much honey.
Eccl. 2. 25, who can *e.* more than I?
4. 5, fool *e.* his own flesh.
5. 11, goods increase, they increased that *e.*

Eccl. 5. 12, sleep be sweet, whether he *e.* little or much.
5. 17, all his days also he *e.* in darkness.
5. 19; 6. 2, not power to *e.* thereof.
10. 16, thy princes *e.* in the morning.
10. 17, blessed when princes *e.* in due season.
Isa. 4. 1, we will *e.* our own bread.
7. 15, 22, butter and honey shall he *e.*
11. 7; 65. 25, lion *e.* straw like ox.
29. 8, he *e.*, awaketh, and is hungry.
51. 8, worm shall *e.* them like wool.
55. 1, come ye, buy and *e.*
55. 2, *e.* ye that which is good.
55. 10, give bread to the *e.*
65. 13, my servants shall *e.*, but ye shall be.
Jer. 5. 17, they shall *e.* up thine harvest.
15. 16, words were found, and I did *e.* them.
24. 2; 29. 17, figs could not be *e.* [grapes.
31. 29; Ezek. 18. 2, the fathers have *e.* sour
Ezek. 3. 1-3, *e.* this roll.
4. 10, *e.* by weight.
Dan. 4. 33, *e.* grass as oxen. [enough.
Hos. 4. 10; Mic. 6. 14; Hag. 1. 6, *e.*, and not have
10. 13, have *e.* the fruit of lies.
Mic. 7. 1, there is no cluster to *e.*
Mat. 6. 25; Lu. 12. 22, what ye shall *e.* [cans?
9. 11; Mk. 2. 16; Lu. 15. 2, why *e.* with publi-
12. 1, ears of corn, and *e.*
12. 4, *e.* shewbread, which was not lawful to *e.*
14. 16; Mk. 6. 37; Lu. 9. 13, give ye them to *e.*
15. 20, to *e.* with unwashen hands.
15. 27; Mk. 7. 28, dogs *e.* of crumbs.
15. 32; Mk. 8. 1, multitude have nothing to *e.*
24. 49, to *e.* and drink with the drunken.
Mk. 2. 16, when they saw him *e.* with.
6. 31, no leisure so much as to *e.*
11. 14, no man *e.* fruit of thee.
Lu. 5. 33, but thy disciples *e.* and drink.
10. 8, *e.* such things as are set before you.
12. 19, take thine ease, *e.*, drink.
13. 26, we have *e.* and drunk in thy presence.
15. 23, let us *e.* and be merry.
22. 30, that ye may *e.* at my table.
24. 43, he took it, and did *e.* before them.
John 4. 31, Master, *e.*
4. 32, meat to *e.* ye know not of.
6. 26, because ye did *e.* of loaves.
6. 52, can this man give us his flesh to *e.*?
6. 53, except ye *e.* the flesh.
Acts 2. 46, did *e.* their meat with gladness.
9. 9, Saul did neither *e.* nor drink.
11. 3, thou didst *e.* with them. [R. V. taste.
23. 14, will *e.* nothing until we have slain Paul.
Rom. 14. 2, one believeth he may *e.* all things; weak *e.* herbs.
14. 6, *e.* to the Lord.
14. 20, who *e.* with offence.
14. 21, neither to *e.* flesh nor drink wine.
1 Cor. 5. 11, with such an one no not to *e.*
8. 7, *e.* it as a thing offered to idol.
8. 8, neither if we *e.* are we better.
8. 13, I will *e.* no flesh while world.
9. 4, have we not power to *e.*?
10. 3, all *e.* same spiritual meat.
10. 27, *e.*, asking no question.
10. 31, whether ye *e.* or drink.
11. 29, he that *e.* unworthily.
2 Thes. 3. 10, work not, neither should he *e.*
Heb. 13. 10, whereof they have no right to *e.*
Rev. 2. 7, *e.* of the tree of life.
2. 17, will give to *e.* of hidden manna.
19. 18, *e.* flesh of kings.
See Jud. 14. 14; Prov. 31. 27; Isa. 1. 19; 65. 4.

Ebal, ē'-băl, stony (?). (1) Gen. 36. 23.
(2) A mountain of Samaria, opposite Mt. Gerizim on the south. Between these was the ancient Shechem. It is 3077 feet high. Deu. 27. 4.
mount, curses delivered from. Deu. 27. 13; Jos. 8. 33.

Ebed, ē'-bĕd, servant. (1) Jud. 9. 26. (2) Ez. 8. 6.

Ebed-melech, ē'-bĕd-mĕl'-ĕch, 'servant of the king.' Ethiopian eunuch, intercedes with king Zedekiah for Jeremiah. Jer. 38. 7; 39. 16.

Eben-ezer, ĕb'-ĕn-ē'-zĕr, 'stone of help.' Israelites smitten by Philistines at. 1 Sam. 4. 1.
'hitherto hath the Lord helped us' (stone raised by Samuel in memory of defeat of the Philistines). 1 Sam. 7. 12.

Eber, ē'-bĕr, 'the region beyond.' Gen. 10. 21.

Ebiasaph, ē-bī'-ă-săph, same as ABIASAPH. 1 Chr. 6. 23.

Ebony (Ezek. 27. 15). Heb. *Hobnim* (omitted in LXX.): Bot. N. *Diospyros ebenum*. It is the heart-wood of the date-plum tree, which grows in Ceylon and south India.

Ebronah, ĕb-rō'-năh, 'passage' (?). Num. 33. 34. R. V. Abronah.

Ecbatana, ĕc-băt'-ă-nă. Ez. 6. 2 (marg.).

Ecclesiastes, ĕc-clē-sĭ-ăs'-tēs, 'the preacher;' the title of a book written by an unknown author, representing the experience of Solomon.

Ed, ĕd, 'witness.' Jos. 22. 34.

Edar, ē'-där, 'flock.' Gen. 35. 21. R. V. Eder.

Eden, ē'-dĕn, 'pleasantness.' (1) Garden of. Gen. 2. 8.
Adam driven from. Gen. 3. 24.
mentioned. Isa. 51. 3; Ezek. 28. 13; 31. 9; 36. 35; Joel 2. 3.
(2) 2 Kn. 19. 12. (3) 2 Chr. 29. 12. (4) Am. 1. 5.

Eder, ē'-dĕr, 'flock,' same as EDAR. 1 Chr. 23. 23.

Edge. Prov. 5. 4; Heb. 4. 12; Eccl. 10. 10.

Edification. Rom. 15. 2; 2 Cor. 10. 8; 13. 10.

Edify, to build; also, to build up. Rom. 14. 19, wherewith one may *e.*
15. 2, please his neighbour to *e.*
1 Cor. 8. 1, charity *e.*
10. 23, all things lawful, but *e.* not.
14. 3, he that prophesieth speaketh to *e.*
14. 4, *e.* himself, *e.* the church.
Eph. 4. 12, for *e.* of the body of Christ.
See Acts 9. 31; 2 Cor. 10. 8; 13. 10; 1 Tim. 1. 4.

Edom, ē'-dom, 'red.' (1) Esau. Gen. 25. 30.
(2) (Idumea) the land of Esau. Gen. 32. 3; Isa. 63. 1.
prophecies concerning. Isa. 34.; Jer. 25. 21; 49. 7; Ezek. 25. 13; 35.; Am. 1. 11; Obad. 1.

Edomites, ē'-dom-ītes, 'inhabitants of Edom,' the descendants of Esau. Gen. 36.
deny Moses passage through Edom. Num. 20. 18.
their possessions. Deu. 2. 5; Jos. 24. 4.
not to be abhorred. Deu. 23. 7.
subdued by David. 2 Sam. 8. 14.
revolt. 2 Kn. 8. 20; 2 Chr. 21. 8.
subdued by Amaziah. 2 Kn. 14. 7; 2 Chr. 11. 25.

Edrei, ĕd'-rĕ-ī, 'strong.' Num. 21. 33.

Effect. Num. 30. 8, make vow of none *e.*
2 Chr. 7. 11, Solomon prosperously *e.* all.
Ps. 33. 10, devices of the people of none *e.*
Isa. 32. 17, the *e.* of righteousness quietness.
Mat. 15. 6; Mk. 7. 13, commandment of God of none *e.*
1 Cor. 1. 17, lest cross be of none *e.*
Gal. 5. 4, Christ is become of none *e.*
See Rom. 3. 3; 4. 14; 9. 6; Gal. 3. 17. [opened.

Effectual. 1 Cor. 16. 9, a great door and *e.* is
Eph. 3. 7; 4. 16, the *e.* working.
Jas. 5. 16, *e.* prayer of righteous man.
See 2 Cor. 1. 6; Gal. 2. 8; 1 Thes. 2. 13.

Effeminate. 1 Cor. 6. 9.

Egg. Job 6. 6, taste in the white of an *e.*
39. 14, ostrich leaveth *e.* in earth.
Lu. 11. 12, if he ask an *e.*
See Deu. 22. 6; Isa. 10. 14; 59. 5; Jer. 17. 11.

Eglah, ĕg'-lăh, 'heifer.' 2 Sam. 3. 5.

Eglaim, ĕg'-la-ĭm. Isa. 15. 8.

Eglon. (1) Moabite king: oppresses Israel, Jud. 3. 12, 14; slain by Ehud, Jud. 3. 21.
(2) city. Jos. 10. 3. [Gen. 12. 10.

Egypt, ē'-ġўpt, 'black.' Abram goes down into.
Joseph sold into, Gen. 37. 36. his advancement, fall, imprisonment, and restoration there, Gen. 39.; 40.; 41.
Jacob's sons go to buy corn in. Gen. 42.
Jacob and all his seed go there. Gen. 46. 6.

children of Israel wax mighty there, Ex. 1. 7.
afflicted, and build treasure cities, Ex. 1. 11.
plagued on account of Israelites. Ex. 7.-11.
children of Israel depart from. Ex. 13. 17. [14.
army of, pursue and perish in the Red sea. Ex.
kings of, harass Judah. 1 Kn. 14. 25; 2 Kn. 23. 29; 2 Chr. 12. 2; 35. 20; 36. 3; Jer. 37. 5.
the 'remnant of Judah' go there. Jer. 43. 7.
Jesus taken to. Mat. 2. 13.
prophecies concerning. Gen. 15. 13; Isa. 11. 11; 19.; 20.; 27. 12; 30. 1; Jer. 9. 26; 25. 19; 43. 8; 44. 28; 46.; Ezek. 29.-32.; Dan. 11. 8; Hos. 9. 3; 11.; Joel 3. 19; Zec. 10. 10; 14. 18.

Egypt, the Israelites in; the oppression and Exodus. It is strange that as yet no clear corroboration of the Biblical narrative from the age of Joseph to that of Moses has been afforded by the decipherment of Egyptian monuments. It is a generally accepted *conjecture* that the career of Joseph belongs to the epoch of the Hyksos or Shepherd kings, a non-Egyptian dynasty who are said to have governed Egypt from about 2000 to 1600 B. C.; but beyond the fact that under non-Egyptian kings a foreigner might easily rise to eminence, there is no positive evidence to support this view. The Pharaoh of the oppression is generally identified with Rameses II. (between 1300 and 1200 B. C.), and not without reason. The site of Pithom, one of the 'treasure-cities' built by the Israelites for their oppressor, has been discovered. It was a brick-walled town with great store-chambers of brick, and inscriptions found on the spot shew that it was founded by Rameses II. The Exodus is then placed under Rameses II.'s successor Menephtah (Merenptah). It is in an inscription of this monarch that the first clear allusion to the Israelites is found. This document records a general restoration of peace after a victory over Libyan invaders; and among the enemies whose downfall is recalled, the name *Ysiraal* occurs; 'Ysiraal is desolated, its seed (*or* fruit) is not.' It can hardly be said that this allusion makes it easier to place the Exodus under Menephtah. The name of Israel occurs together with Palestinian names such as Ashkelon and Canaan, and this suggests that the Israelites had already reached and settled in Palestine; at the same time it is conceivable that the 'desolation' of the Israelites is a courtly exaggeration for their disappearance from Egypt.

Of the actual sojourn of the Hebrews in Egypt the monuments tell us nothing; yet they provide many illustrations of the manners and customs alluded to in Genesis and Exodus. Thus we find officials in positions analogous to that of Joseph, cupbearers, and royal bakers; and we read of the hoarding of corn in years of plenty and its distribution in time of famine.

Egypt and the Jews under the monarchy. During the age of the judges and that of the first kings Egypt had little to do with the Hebrews. Solomon, among other foreign alliances, 'made affinity' with an Egyptian king and married his daughter; but in the time of Rehoboam, Shishak, king of Egypt, to whom the rebel Jeroboam had previously gone for refuge, invaded Judah (2 Kn. 14. 25) and devastated it. This invasion is also recorded in an Egyptian relief at Karnak, from which it appears that it did not leave the northern kingdom untouched.

In the 8th century B. C. the Palestinian peoples, who were beginning to feel the pressure of Assyria from the north, began also to look southward to Egypt for help. Thus about 725 B. C. Hoshea of Israel was persuaded by So or Sabako, an Egyptian officer who afterwards founded the 25th dynasty, to revolt from Assyria. The policy of Sabako was doubtless to make Samaria and Syria a barrier between Assyria and Egypt, it resulted, however, in the destruction of the northern kingdom. The politicians of Judah attempted even after this to persuade their kings to trust in Egypt, and one of the great tasks of the prophet Isaiah was to combat this futile policy. Tirhakah of Egypt marched against Sennacherib in the first years of the 7th century; but Esar-haddon in 671 struck the power of Egypt to the ground, and was able to style himself 'king of Upper and Lower Egypt and of Ethiopia.' His successor Assurbanipal was much engaged in suppressing rebellion in Egypt; an Egyptian inscription gives a graphic picture of his successful attack on No (Thebes), to the fall of which Nahum alludes (Nahum 3. 8) in his warning to Nineveh.

But the power of Assyria had now begun to wane, and in the time of Psammitichus I. (663-610) Egypt regained its independence. His successor Necho formed aggressive plans against Assyria. Josiah of Judah, vainly attempting to stay his advance, was killed at Megiddo. Necho himself failed in his enterprise, being routed by Nebuchadnezzar at Carchemish. Yet he and his country continued to be the bane of Judæan politics. His intrigues were the ruin of Jehoiakim; and Zedekiah's reliance on the Egyptian Hophra was the cause of the final siege and fall of Jerusalem (586). After the murder of the governor Gedaliah, a remnant that remained in Judah fled to Egypt, and settled to the east of the Delta; thither Jeremiah accompanied them, and in the place of their refuge Tahpanes prophesied the coming of Nebuchadnezzar and the ruin of Egypt. Discoveries at this place make it clear that this prophecy was subsequently fulfilled.

In 525 B. C., with the conquests of Cambyses, began a period in which Egypt was subject to Persia; this subjection came to an end in 404, but Egypt had no settled government till the coming of Alexander the Great (332). The rule of a series of Macedonian kings (the Ptolemies) came to an end only with the incorporation of Egypt in the Roman Empire (B. C. 31).

Egypt and the Jews after the Exile. The stream of commerce drew many Jews to Egypt in the 3rd century B. C., and especially to Alexandria, where they had been granted special privileges by Alexander himself. In the 2nd century the Egyptian Jews possessed a separate temple at Leontopolis; by the time of our Lord the Alexandrian Jews were the most cultured and wealthiest Jewish community in the world; and long before then they had been a large and prosperous body, occupying two of the five city wards, and governed by a separate official. Here the great Greek translation of the Old Testament was made, during the 3rd and 2nd centuries B. C. This version was called the Septuagint from a legend which assigned its composition to the miraculously unanimous work of seventy (or seventy-two) independent translators. Alexandria became also the home of a special type of Jewish philosophical theology, best represented by Philo (a contemporary of St. Paul), the great allegorical interpreter of the Bible. From here came the learned Apollos (Acts 18. 24), and it has been held that the Epistle to the Hebrews is the work of an Alexandrian writer.

Early Christian tradition connected the founding of the Alexandrian Church with St. Mark; but little is known of it before about 190 A. D., when it appears as the most learned and liberal church of the age, and a great centre of Christian education.

Egypt, River of. Num. 34. 5. The south-west boundary of the Promised Land. The modern Wady El-'Arîsh, flowing into the Mediterranean midway between Gaza and Pelusium. 1 Kn. 8. 65; Isa. 27. 12.

Egyptian, ē-gȳp'-tiăn, a native of Egypt. 1 Sam. 30. 11.

EGYPTIAN GODS

Court and west pylon of the Temple of Horus at Edfu, showing figures of Egyptian gods.
(*Donald McLeish*)

EGYPTIAN GOD AND PHARAOH

Part of temple at Karnak: on the left the god Osiris and the Pharaoh Thothmes III (1501–1447 B.C.): on the right the same Pharaoh. (*Donald McLeish*)

Egyptians, Religion of the Ancient.

(1) *Egyptian beliefs about the future life.* There were in Egypt several entirely different beliefs about the future life; but in one form or another the immortality of the soul was taken as an axiom.

(A) The simplest and most natural belief was that the soul hovered about the cemetery, under the form of a human-headed bird (see plate); and required food and drink, without which it would be reduced to feeding on refuse. To keep it in the grave, and satisfy it, jars of food and water were placed with the body. These were afterward commuted to models and then to painted figures of the food, and also of the servants and the occupations which the soul might desire.

(B) When a god of the dead was accepted, the dead were easily supposed to belong to him, and to form part of his kingdom, ruled over like that of an earthly king. The blessed fields of Aalu were the kingdom of Osiris; and the soul, after being tried and accepted by Osiris, entered into the labours and the joys of the unseen world, where the soul is seen plowing, reaping, and threshing amid the canals in the fields of Aalu.

(C) The prominence of sun-worship brought everything into connection with Ra, the sun. As the sun floated over the earth on the celestial ocean, or passed into the terrors of the hours of darkness, so the soul was supposed to join the sun, and share in its joy by day or its divine strength to oppose the demons of the night.

(D) The belief that the body was essential to some future condition of happiness led to its elaborate preservation by embalming, so fitting it for union with the soul in another life; though none of the other three theories seem to require this. This last is the only belief which implies the dogma of a resurrection.

The origins of these doctrines all lie in the prehistoric age. The theory A certainly belongs to the oldest burials that we know, in which a food vessel is always placed with the dead. Later are found the tools and weapons which imply the theory B, of the kingdom of Osiris like this earth; and the multitude of slave figures found in later times are intended to work for the dead in that state. Probably later than this is the less material theory C, of accompanying the sun in its course, and the complex geography of the hours of the night. Last of all was the theory D, which involves mummification, and which did not come into common use until the early historical times. The multitude of amulets of later date belong to this view.

(2) *Various sources of Egyptian religion.* Just as there were different beliefs about the soul, derived from different races who came into the country, so each race and tribe brought in its own worship. The earliest state that we can trace points to each divinity having been at first the sole god of one tribe or family; and the whole of the complication of polytheism in Egypt arose from the amalgamation of religions, which always takes place in mixed races.

It seems most probable that different classes of gods belong to different sources along with the different beliefs concerning the soul. There are about forty important divinities, beside some four hundred minor varieties of these and spirits of Hades. The principal deities may be classed in four main types. (A) The animal gods. (B) The human gods, as Osiris, Isis, Horus, and others. (C) The cosmic gods, such as Ra the sun, Harakhti, Seb, Nut, Shu, &c. (D) The abstract gods of principles, Ptah, Maat, Min, Hathor, &c. These classes probably correspond in origin to the four beliefs about the soul, similarly lettered. A probably belongs to the negro element; B to the Libyan or North African European race; C to the Mesopotamian influence; D to the last great invasion which founded the dynasties of Egyptian history.

In later times arose innumerable complications of combined gods, such as Ptah-Sokar-Osiris-Khentamenti; and the habit of attributing the nature of several gods to one who was most prominent. In this way arose the later monotheism, which was only a fused polytheism.

One very remarkable outburst of a scientific monotheism of sun-worship is without parallel. About 1400 B. C. Amenhotep III. introduced, and his son Akhenaten ('The glory of the Disc') enforced, the worship of the radiant energy of the sun, in the same terms that a modern religious materialist might use. This idea came from Mesopotamia with the foreign queens, and gives a valuable hint of religious thought there at a time before the Exodus.

Some of the later Egyptian ideas and phraseology of Greek times may possibly have had an indirect influence on Christian thought. The book of Wisdom, which is Alexandrian in origin, is the nursery of St. Paul's thought and phrases; and in funeral inscriptions of that age we find that such an one 'went to Osiris in his fortieth year,' as in Christian epitaphs.

The late Egyptian religion was marked by the special prominence of Isis and Horus, and the transference of their worship to Italy, where Isis was widely worshipped during the early centuries of the Roman Empire.

Ehi, ē'-hī, shortened from AHIRAM. Gen. 46. 21.

Ehud, ē'-hŭd. (1) judge, delivers Israel. Jud. 3. 15.
(2) 1 Chr. 7. 10.

Either. Gen. 31. 24, speak not *e.* good or bad.
Eccl. 11. 6, prosper *e.* this or that.
Mat. 6. 24; Lu. 16. 13, *e.* hate the one.
John 19. 18, on *e.* side one.
Rev. 22. 2, on *e.* side the river.
See Deu. 17. 3; 28. 51; Isa. 7. 11; Mat. 12. 33.

Eker, ē'-kĕr, same as ACHAR. 1 Chr. 2. 27.

Ekron, ĕk'-rŏn, 'eradication.' Jos. 13. 3.
taken. Jud. 1. 18.
men of, smitten with emerods. 1 Sam. 5. 12.
their trespass offering for recovery. 1 Sam. 6. 17.
prophecies concerning. Am. 1. 8; Zep. 2. 4; Zec. 9. 5.

Ekronites, ĕk'-rŏn-ītes, 'inhabitants of Ekron.' Jos. 13. 3.

Eladah, ĕl'-ă-dăh, 'God has adorned.' 1 Chr. 7. 20. R. V. Eleadah.

Elah, ē'-lăh, 'terebinth.' (1) Gen. 36. 41.
(2) king of Israel. 1 Kn. 16. 8, 10.
(3) valley of, Saul sets the battle in array against the Philistines. 1 Sam. 17. 2.
David slays Goliath there. 1 Sam. 17. 49.

Elam, ē'-lăm, 'Highlands.' (1) Son of Shem. Gen. 10. 22.
(2) A region beyond the Tigris, east of Babylonia, the seat of an ancient empire whose capital was Susa or Shushan.
Chedorlaomer, king of. Gen. 14.

Elamites, ē'-lăm-ītes, 'inhabitants of Elam.' Ez. 4. 9; Acts 2. 9.

Elasah, ĕl-ā'-săh, 'God has made.' Ez. 10. 22.

Elath, ē'-lăth, 'lofty trees. Deu. 2. 8.

El-beth-el, ĕl-bĕth'-ĕl, 'God of the house of God.' Gen. 35. 7.

Eldaah, ĕl-dā'-ăh, 'God has called.' Gen. 25. 4.

Eldad, ĕl'-dăd, 'God has loved.' Num. 11. 26.

Elder. 1 Sam. 15. 30, honour me before *e.* of people.
Job 15. 10, aged men, much *e.* than thy father.
32. 4, waited, because they were *e.* than he.
Prov. 31. 23, husband known among *e.*
Mat. 15. 2; Mk. 7. 3, tradition of the *e.*
1 Tim. 5. 17, let *e.* that rule be worthy.
Tit. 1. 5, ordain *e.* in every city.
Heb. 11. 2, the *e.* obtained good report.
Jas. 5. 14, call for *e.* of the church.
1 Pet. 5. 1, the *e.* I exhort, who am an *e.*
5. 5, younger submit to the *e.*
See John 8. 9; 1 Tim. 5. 2.

Elders, seventy. Ex. 24. 1; Num. 11. 16.
of ISRAEL. Lev. 4. 15; Deu. 21. 19; 1 Sam. 16. 4
Ez. 5. 5; Ps. 107. 32; Ezek. 8. 1.

of EGYPT. Gen. 50. 7.
of the CHURCH. Acts 14. 23; 15. 4, 6, 23; 16. 4; 20. 17; Tit. 1. 5; Jas. 5. 14; 1 Pet. 5. 1; 2 John 1.; 3 John 1.
Paul's charge to. Acts 20. 17.
Peter's charge to. 1 Pet. 5.
the TWENTY-FOUR. Rev. 4. 4; 7. 11; 14. 3.

Elead, ĕl'-ĕ-ăd, 'God has testified.' 1 Chr. 7. 21.

Elealeh, ĕl-ĕ-ā'-lĕh, 'God ascends.' Num. 32. 3.

Eleasah, ĕl-ē-ā'-săh, same as ELASAH. 1 Chr. 2. 39.

Eleazar, ĕl-ē-ā'-zär, 'God has aided.' (1) son of Aaron, and chief priest. Ex. 6. 23; 28.; 29.; Lev. 8.; Num. 3. 2; 4. 16; 16. 36; 20. 26, 28; 27. 22; 31. 13; 34. 17; Jos. 17. 4; 24. 33.
(2) son of Abinadab, keeps the ark. 1 Sam. 7. 1.
(3) one of David's captains. 2 Sam. 23. 9; 1 Chr. 11. 12.

Elect. Isa. 42. 1, mine *e.*, in whom my soul delighteth. R. V. chosen.
45. 4, mine *e.* I have called by name. R. V. chosen.
65. 9, 22, mine *e.* shall inherit. R. V. chosen.
Mat. 24. 22; Mk. 13. 20, for *e.* sake days shortened.
24. 24; Mk. 13. 22, deceive very *e.*
24. 31; Mk. 13. 27, gather together his *e.*
Lu. 18. 7, avenge his own *e.*
Rom. 8. 33, to charge of God's *e.*
Col. 3. 12, put on as the *e.* of God.
1 Tim. 5. 21, charge thee before *e.* angels.
1 Pet. 1. 2, *e.* according to foreknowledge.
2. 6, corner stone *e.*, precious.
See 2 Tim. 2. 10; 1 Pet. 5. 13; 2 John 1. 13.

Election, of God. 1 Thes. 1. 4; Tit. 1. 1.
its privileges and duties. Mk. 13. 20; Lu. 18. 7; Rom. 8. 29; 11. 5; 1 Cor. 1. 27; 2 Pet. 1. 10.

El-elohe-Israel, ĕl-ĕl'-ō-hĕ-ĭs'-rā-ĕl, 'God, the God of Israel;' the altar erected by Jacob at Shalem. Gen. 33. 20.

Elements, rudiments. Gal. 4. 3, 9.
component or constituent parts. 2 Pet. 3. 10.

Eleph, ē'-lĕph, 'ox' (?). Jos. 18. 28.

Elephant (1 Kn. 10. 22, 'ivory'). Heb. *Shen habbim*, lit. 'teeth of elephants,' as in A. V. marg. The word *habbim* prob. of Tamil origin. Gk. ὀδόντες ἐλεφάντινοι.

Eleven. Gen. 32. 22, Jacob took his *e.* sons.
37. 9, and *e.* stars made obeisance.
Acts 1. 26, he was numbered with the *e.*
See Mat. 28. 16; Mk. 16. 14; Lu. 24. 9.

Elhanan, ĕl-hā'-năn, 'God has been gracious,' one of David's warriors. 2 Sam. 21. 19; 23. 24; 1 Chr. 11. 26; 20. 5.

Eli, ē'-lī, 'my God.' Eli, Eli, lama sabachthani? Mat. 27. 46; Mk. 15. 34.

Eli, ē'-lī, 'height;' high priest and judge, blesses Hannah, who bears Samuel. 1 Sam. 1. 17, 20.
Samuel brought to. 1 Sam. 1. 25.
wickedness of his sons. 1 Sam. 2. 22.
rebuked by man of God. 1 Sam. 2. 27.
ruin of his house shewed to Samuel by God. 1 Sam. 3. 11.
his sons slain. 1 Sam. 4. 10.
his death. 1 Sam. 4. 18.

Eliab, ē-lī'-ăb, 'God is father.' Num. 1. 9.

Eliada, Eliadah, ē-lī'-ă-dă, ē-lī'-ă-dăh, 'God knows.' 2 Sam. 5. 16.

Eliah, ē-lī'-ăh, same name as ELIJAH. 1 Chr. 8. 27.

Eliahba, ē-lī-ăh'-bă, 'God hides.' 2 Sam. 23. 32.

Eliakim, ē-lī'-ă-kĭm, 'God establishes:' (1) chief minister of Hezekiah; his conference with Rabshakeh's ambassadors; mission to Isaiah. 2 Kn. 18.; 19.
prefigures kingdom of Christ. Isa. 22. 20–25.
(2) son of Josiah, made king by Pharaoh, and named Jehoiakim. 2 Kn. 23. 34; 2 Chr. 36. 4.

Eliam, ē-lī'-ăm, 'people's God.' 2 Sam. 11. 3.

Elias, ē-lī'-ăs, same as ELIJAH. Mat. 27. 47, 49; Mk. 15. 35, 36; John 1. 21. *See* ELIJAH.

Eliasaph, ē-lī'-ă-săph, 'God had added.' Num. 1. 14.

Eliashib, ē-lī-ăsh'-ĭb, 'God restores;' high priest, builds the wall. Neh. 3. 1.
allied unto Tobiah. Neh. 13. 4.

Eliathah, ē-lī'-ă-thăh, 'God has come.' 1 Chr. [25. 4.

Elidad, ē-lī'-dăd, 'God has loved.' Num. 34. 21.

Eliel, ē-lī'-ĕl, 'my God is God.' 1 Chr. 5. 24.

Elienai, ĕl-ĭ-ē'-nāi, 'unto Jehovah are mine eyes.' 1 Chr. 8. 20.

Eliezer, ĕl-ĭ-ē'-zĕr, 'God is help.' (1) Abraham's steward. Gen. 15. 2.
(2) son of Moses. Ex. 18. 4; 1 Chr. 23. 15.
(3) prophet. 2 Chr. 20. 37.

Elihoenai, ĕl-ĭ-hō-ē'-nāi, same as ELIOENAI. Ez. [8. 4.

Elihoreph, ē-lī-hôr'-ĕph. 1 Kn. 4. 3.

Elihu, ē-lī'-hū, 'He is my God.' 1 Sam. 1. 1.
reproves Job's friends, Job 32. and Job's impatience, Job 33. 8. and self-righteousness, Job 34. 5.
declares God's justice, Job 33. 12; 34. 10; 35. 13; 36. power, Job 33.–37. and mercy, Job 33. 23; 34. 28.

Elijah, ē-lī'-jăh, 'Jehovah is God.' (1) the Tishbite, prophet, predicts great drought. 1 Kn. 17. 1; Lu. 4. 25; Jas. 5. 17.
hides at the brook Cherith, and is fed by ravens. 1 Kn. 17. 5 (19. 5).
raises the widow's son. 1 Kn. 17. 21.
his sacrifice at Carmel. 1 Kn. 18. 38.
slays the prophets of Baal at the brook Kishon. 1 Kn. 18. 40.
flees from Jezebel into the wilderness of Beersheba. 1 Kn. 19.; Rom. 11. 2.
anoints Elisha. 1 Kn. 19. 19.
by God's command denounces Ahab in Naboth's vineyard. 1 Kn. 21. 17.
his prediction fulfilled. 1 Kn. 22. 38; 2 Kn. 9. 36; 10. 10.
condemns Ahaziah for enquiring of Baal-zebub. 2 Kn. 1. 3, 16.
two companies sent to take him burnt with fire from heaven. 2 Kn. 1. 10; Lu. 9. 54.
divides Jordan. 2 Kn. 2. 8.
taken up by chariot of fire. 2 Kn. 2. 11.
his mantle taken by Elisha. 2 Kn. 2. 13.
appears at Christ's transfiguration. Mat. 17. 3; Mk. 9. 4; Lu. 9. 30.
precursor of John the Baptist. Mal. 4. 5; Mat. 11. 14; 16. 14; Lu. 1. 17; 9. 8, 19; John 1. 21.
(2) 1 Chr. 8. 27.

Elika, ē-lī'-kă. 2 Sam. 23. 25.

Elim, ē'-lĭm, 'terebinths.' Ex. 15. 27.

Elimelech, ē-lĭm'-ĕ-lĕch, 'God is king.' Ru. 1. 2.

Elioenai, ĕl-ĭ-ō-ē'-nāi, 'unto Jehovah are mine eyes.' 1 Chr. 3. 23.

Eliphal, ē-lī'-phăl, 'God has judged.' 1 Chr. 11. 35.

Eliphalet, ē-lĭph'-ă-lĕt, 'God is deliverance.' 2 Sam. 5. 16.

Eliphaz, ē-lī'-phăz, 'God is fine gold' (?). Gen. 36. 4.
reproves Job. Job 4.; 5.; 15.; 22.
God's wrath against him, Job 42. 7. he offers a burnt offering, and Job prays for him, Job 42. 8.

Elipheleh, ē-lĭph'-ĕ-lĕh, 'may God distinguish him.' 1 Chr. 15. 18.

Eliphelet, ē-lĭph'-ĕ-lĕt, same as ELIPHALET. 1 Chr. 3. 8.

Elisabeth, ē-lĭs'-ă-bĕth, same as ELISHEBA, cousin of Virgin Mary, and mother of John the Baptist. Lu. 1. 5.
angel promises her a son. Lu. 1. 13.
her salutation to Mary. Lu. 1. 42.

Eliseus, ĕl-ĭ-sē'-ŭs, Greek form of ELISHA. Lu. [4. 27.

Elisha, ē-lī'-shă, 'God is salvation.' (1) succeeds Elijah. 1 Kn. 19. 16.
receives his mantle, and divides Jordan. 2 Kn. 2. 13.
heals the waters with salt. 2 Kn. 2. 22.
bears destroy the children who mock him. 2 Kn. [2. 24.
his miracles: water, 2 Kn. 3. 16. oil, 4. 4. Shunammite's son, 4. 32. death in the pot, 4. 40. feeds a hundred men with twenty loaves, 4. 44. Naaman's leprosy, 5. 14. iron swims, 6. 5. Syrians struck blind, 6. 18.

prophesies plenty in Samaria when besieged. 2 Kn. 7. 1.
sends to anoint Jehu. 2 Kn. 9. 1.
his death. 2 Kn. 13. 20.
miracle wrought by his bones. 2 Kn. 13. 21.
Elishah, ē-lī′-shăh. (1) Gen. 10. 4. (2) Ezek. 27. 7.
Elishama, ē-lī′-shă-mă, 'God has heard.' Num. 1. 10.
Elishaphat, ē-lī-shā′-phăt, 'God has judged.' 2 Chr. 23. 1.
Elisheba, ē-lī′-shĕ-bă, 'God is an oath.' Ex. 6. 23.
Elishua, ē-lī′-shū-ă, same as Elisha. 2 Sam. 5. 15.
Eliud, ē-lī′-ŭd, 'God of Judah.' Mat. 1. 14.
Elizaphan, ē-lī-zā′-phăn, 'God has protected.' Num. 3. 30.
Elizur, ē-lī′-zŭr, 'God is a Rock.' Num. 1. 5.
Elkanah, ĕl-kā′-năh, 'God has possessed.' Ex. 6. 24.
Samuel's father. 1 Sam. 1.
Elkoshite, ĕl′-kŏ-shīte, 'inhabitant of Elkosh.' Nah. 1. 1.
Ellasar, ĕl-lā′-sär. Gen. 14. 1.
Elm (Hos. 4. 13). Heb. *Elah* (omitted in LXX.): Bot. N. *Pistacia terebinthus:* R. V. terebinth. 'Elm' occurs only once in the A. V., but *elah*, of which it is a translation, occurs often. It is the terebinth which has the general appearance of the oak, only smaller, usually translated 'oak' in R. V. with 'terebinth' in the margin. *See* Teil tree.
Elmodam, ĕl-mō′-dăm, same as Almodad. Lu. 3. 28.
Elnaam, ĕl-nā′-ăm, 'God is pleasantness.' 1 Chr. 11. 46.
Elnathan, ĕl-nā′-thăn, 'God has given.' 2 Kn. 24. 8.
Eloi, ē′-lō-ī, 'my God.' Mk. 15. 34.
Elon, ē′-lŏn, 'terebinth.' (1) Gen. 26. 34. (2) judges Israel. Jud. 12. 11.
Elon-beth-hanan, ē′-lŏn-bĕth-hā′-năn, 'oak of the house of grace.' 1 Kn. 4. 9.
Elonites, ē′-lŏn-ītes, 'descendants of Elon.' Num. 26. 26.
Eloquent. Ex. 4. 10; Isa. 3. 3; Acts 18. 24.
Eloth, ē′-lōth, same as Elath. 1 Kn. 9. 26.
Elpaal, ĕl-pā′-ăl, God 'of doing' (?). 1 Chr. 8. 11.
Elpalet, ĕl′-pă-lĕt, same as Eliphalet. 1 Chr. 14. 5.
El-paran, ĕl-pâr′-ăn, 'terebinth of Paran.' Gen. 14. 6.
Eltekeh, ĕl′-tĕ-kĕh. Jos. 19. 44.
Eltekon, ĕl′-tĕ-kŏn. Jos. 15. 59.
Eltolad, ĕl-tō′-lăd. Jos. 15. 30.
Elul, ē′-lŭl. Neh. 6. 15. The sixth month of the sacred year = Sept. *See* Months.
Eluzai, ē-lū′-zāi, 'God is my strength.' 1 Chr. 12. 5.
Elymas, ĕl′-ȳ-măs, 'a wise man,' or, 'an Elamite' (Bar-jesus). Acts 13. 6, 8.
Elzabad, ĕl-zā′-băd, 'God has given.' 1 Chr. 12. 12.
Elzaphan, ĕl-zā′-phăn, 'God has protected.' Ex. 6. 22.
Embalmed. Gen. 50. 2, the days of those which are *e.*
50. 26, and they *e.* him.
See John 19. 39.
Embalming. Gen. 50. 2. The process of preserving the human body by gums, spices, bitumen, &c. The body so preserved is called a 'mummy' from the Arabic *Mûmîâ*, bitumen.
Embolden. Job 16. 3; 1 Cor. 8. 10.
Embrace. Job 24. 8, *e.* rock for want of shelter.
Eccl. 3. 5, a time to *e.*
Heb. 11. 13, seen and *e.* promises. R. V. greeted.
See Prov. 4. 8; 5. 20; Lam. 4. 5; Acts 20. 1.
Embroider. Ex. 28. 39; 35. 35; 38. 23.
Emerald (Ex. 28. 18; 39. 11; Rev. 4. 3; 21. 19). Heb. *Nôphek:* Gk. ἄνθραξ: R. V. marg. carbuncle; 'Carbuncle' is supposed to be a more correct version: the name is used for several bright red stones.
Emerods, hemorrhoids, the piles. Deu. 28. 27, and with *e.*
1 Sam. 5. 6, and smote them with *e.*
Emims, ē′-mĭms, 'terrible men,' 'giants.' Gen. 14. 5; Deu. 2. 10. R. V. Emim.
Eminent, high, lofty. Ezek. 16. 24, 31, 39; 17. 22.
Emmanuel, ĕm-măn′-ū-ĕl, same as Immanuel, 'God with us.' Isa. 7. 14; 8. 8; Mat. 1. 23.
Emmaus, ĕm-mā′-ŭs, 'hot springs' (?). Lu. 24. 13. Christ talks with Cleopas and another on the way to. Lu. 24. 15.
Emmor, ĕm′-mŏr, same as Hamor. Acts 7. 16.
Empire. Esth. 1. 20. R. V. kingdom.
Employ. Deu. 20. 19; 1 Chr. 9. 3; Ez. 10. 15; Ezek. 39. 14.
Empty. Gen. 31. 42; Mk. 12. 3; Lu. 1. 53; 20. 10, sent *e.* away.
Ex. 3. 21, ye shall not go *e.*
23. 15; 34. 20; Deu. 16. 16, appear before me *e.*
Deu. 15. 13, not let him go away *e.*
Job 22. 9, thou hast sent widows away *e.*
Eccl. 11. 3, clouds *e.* themselves on the earth.
Isa. 29. 8, awaketh, and his soul is *e.*
Jer. 48. 11, Moab *e.* from vessel to vessel.
Nah. 2. 2, the emptiers have *e.* them out.
Mat. 12. 44, come, he findeth it *e.*
See 2 Sam. 1. 22; 2 Kn. 4. 3; Hos. 10. 1.
Emulation. Rom. 11. 14; Gal. 5. 20. R. V. jealousy.
Enabled. 1 Tim. 1. 12. [(marg.).
Enajim, ĕn′-ă-jĭm, same as Enam. Gen. 38. 14
Enam, ē′-năm, 'two fountains.' Jos. 15. 34.
Enan, ē′-năn. Num. 1. 15.
Encamp. Ps. 27. 3, though host *e.* against me.
34. 7, angel of Lord *e.* round.
See Num. 10. 31; Job 19. 12; Ps. 53. 5.
Enchanters were serpent charmers, and another class were probably conjurers, gifted with sleight of hand. Deu. 18. 10; Jer. 27. 9.
Enchantments forbidden. Lev. 19. 26; Deu. 18. 9; Isa. 47. 9.
Encountered. Acts 17. 18. [him.
Encourage. Deu. 1. 38; 3. 28; 2 Sam. 11. 25, *e.*
Ps. 64. 5, they *e.* themselves in an evil matter.
See 1 Sam. 30. 6; 2 Chr. 31. 4; 35. 2; Isa. 41. 7.
End. Gen. 6. 13, the *e.* of all flesh before me.
Ex. 23. 16; Deu. 11. 12, in the *e.* of the year.
Num. 23. 10, let my last *e.* be like his.
Deu. 8. 16, do thee good at thy latter *e.*
32. 29, consider their latter *e.*
Job 6. 11, what is mine *e.*, that I should prolong?
8. 7; 42. 12, thy latter *e.* shall increase.
16. 3, shall vain words have an *e.*?
26. 10, till day and night come to an *e.* R. V. confines of.
Ps. 7. 9, wickedness of wicked come to an *e.*
9. 6, destructions come to perpetual *e.*
37. 37, the *e.* of that man is peace.
39. 4, make me to know my *e.*
73. 17, then understood I their *e.*
102. 27, the same, thy years have no *e.*
107. 27, are at their wit's *e.*
119. 96, an *e.* of all perfection.
Prov. 14. 12, the *e.* thereof are ways of death.
17. 24, eyes of fool in *e.* of earth.
19. 20, be wise in thy latter *e.*
25. 8, lest thou know not what to do in *e.*
Eccl. 3. 11, find out from beginning to the *e.*
4. 8, no *e.* of all his labour.
4. 16, no *e.* of all the people.
7. 2, that is the *e.* of all men.
7. 8, better the *e.* of a thing.
10. 13, the *e.* of his talk is madness.
12. 12, of making books there is no *e.*
Isa. 9. 7, of his government shall be no *e.*
46. 10, declaring *e.* from beginning.
Jer. 5. 31, what will ye do in *e.* thereof?
8. 20, harvest past, summer *e.*
17. 11, at his *e.* shall be a fool.
29. 11, to give you an expected *e.*
31. 17, there is hope in thine *e.*

Lam. 1. 9, remembereth not her last *e.*
4. 18; Ezek. 7. 2, our *e* is near, *e.* is come.
Ezek. 21. 25; 35. 5, iniquity shall have an *e.*
Dan. 8. 17, 19; 11. 27, at the time of *e.*
11. 45, he shall come to his *e.*, and none shall help him.
12. 8, what shall be the *e.*?
12. 13, go thy way till the *e.* be.
Hab. 2. 3, at the *e.* it shall speak.
Mat. 10. 22; 24. 13; Mk. 13. 13, endureth to *e.*
13. 39, harvest is *e.* of the world.
24. 3, what sign of the *e.* of the world?
24. 6; Mk. 13. 7; Lu. 21. 9, the *e.* is not yet.
24. 14, then shall the *e.* come.
24. 31, gather from one *e.* of heaven.
26. 58, Peter sat to see the *e.*
28. 20, I am with you, even unto the *e.*
Mk. 3. 26, cannot stand, but hath an *e.*
Lu. 1. 33, of his kingdom there shall be no *e.*
22. 37, things concerning me have an *e.*
John 13. 1, he loved them unto the *e.*
18. 37, to this *e.* was I born.
Rom. 6. 21, the *e.* of these things is death.
6. 22, the *e.* everlasting life.
10. 4, the *e.* of the law for righteousness.
1 Cor. 10. 11, on whom *e.* of world are come.
Phil. 3. 19, whose *e.* is destruction.
1 Tim. 1. 5, the *e.* of the commandment.
Heb. 6. 8, whose *e.* is to be burned.
6. 16, an oath an *e.* of strife.
7. 3, neither beginning nor *e.* of life.
9. 26, once in the *e.* hath he appeared.
13. 7, considering *e.* of their conversation.
Jas. 5. 11, ye have seen *e.* of the Lord.
1 Pet. 1. 9, receiving the *e.* of your faith.
1. 13, be sober, and hope to the *e.*
4. 7, the *e.* of all things is at hand.
4. 17, what shall the *e.* be of them that obey not?
Rev. 2. 26, keepeth my works unto *e.*
21. 6; 22. 13, the beginning and the *e.*
See Ps. 19. 6; 65. 5; Isa. 45. 22; 52. 10; Jer. 4. 27.

Endamage, to injure, damage. Ez. 4. 13.

Endanger. Eccl. 10. 9; Dan. 1. 10.

Endeavour. Ps. 28. 4; Eph. 4. 3; 2 Pet. 1. 15.

Endless. 1 Tim. 1. 4; Heb. 7. 16.

En-dor, ĕn′-dôr, 'fountain of Dor.' Jos. 17. 11.
witch of. 1 Sam. 28. 7.

Endue, to endow, furnish with. Gen. 30. 20; 2 Chr. 2. 12; Lu. 24. 49; Jas. 3. 13.

Endure. Gen. 33. 14, as the children be able to *e.*
Esth. 8. 6, how can I *e.* to see evil?
Job 8. 15, hold it fast, but it shall not *e.*
31. 23, I could not *e.* R. V. could do nothing.
Ps. 9. 7; 102. 12; 104. 31, Lord shall *e.* for ever.
30. 5, anger *e.* a moment, weeping *e.* for a night.
52. 1, goodness of God *e.* continually.
72. 5, as long as sun and moon *e.*
72. 17, his name shall *e.* for ever.
100. 5, his truth *e.* to all generations.
106. 1; 107. 1; 118. 1; 136. 1; 138. 8; Jer. 33. 11, his mercy *e.* for ever.
111. 3; 112. 3, 9, his righteousness *e.* for ever.
119. 160, every one of thy judgments *e.*
135. 13, thy name, O Lord, *e.* for ever.
145. 13, thy dominion *e.*
Prov. 27. 24, doth *e.* to every generation.
Ezek. 22. 14, can thy heart *e.*?
Mat. 10. 22; 24. 13; Mk. 13. 13, *e.* to the end.
Mk. 4. 17, so *e.* but for a time.
John 6. 27, meat that *e.* unto life.
Rom. 9. 22, God *e.* with much longsuffering.
1 Cor. 13. 7, charity *e.* all things.
2 Tim. 2. 3, *e.* hardness as good soldier.
4. 3, they will not *e.* sound doctrine.
4. 5, watch, *e.* afflictions.
Heb. 10. 34, in heaven a better and *e.* substance.
12. 7, if ye *e.* chastening.
Jas. 1. 12, blessed is man that *e.* temptation.
5. 11, we count them happy which *e.*
1 Pet. 1. 25, the word of the Lord *e.* for ever.
2. 19, if a man for conscience *e.* grief.
See Heb. 10. 32; 11. 27; 12. 2, 3.

En-eglaim, ĕn-ĕg′-lā-ĭm, 'fountain of two calves.' Ezek. 47. 10.

Enemies, treatment of. Ex. 23. 4; 1 Sam. 24. 10; Job 31. 29; Prov. 24. 17; 25. 21; Mat. 5. 44; Lu. 6. 35.
David and Saul. 1 Sam. 24. 10; 26. 9.
God delivers out of the hand of. 1 Sam. 12. 11; Ez. 8. 31; Ps. 18. 48; 59.; 61. 3; 110. 1; Isa. 62. 8.
of God, their punishment. Ex. 15. 6; Deu. 32. 41; Jud. 5. 31; Esth. 7.; 8.; Ps. 68. 1; 92. 9; Isa. 1. 24; 37. 36; 2 Thes. 1. 8; Heb. 10. 13; Rev. 21. 8.

Enemy. Ex. 23. 22, I will be *e.* to thine *e.*
Deu. 32. 31, our *e.* themselves being judges.
Jos. 7. 12, Israel turned backs before *e.*
Jud. 5. 31, so let all thy *e.* perish.
1 Sam. 24. 19, if man find *e.*, will he let him go?
1 Kn. 21. 20, hast thou found me, O mine *e.*?
Job 13. 24, wherefore holdest thou me for *e.*?
Ps. 8. 2, still the *e.* and avenger.
23. 5, in presence of mine *e.*
38. 19, mine *e.* are lively.
61. 3, a strong tower from the *e.*
72. 9, his *e.* shall lick the dust.
119. 98, wiser than mine *e.*
127. 5, speak with *e.* in the gate.
139. 22, I count them mine *e.*
Prov. 16. 7, maketh his *e.* at peace.
24. 17, rejoice not when *e.* falleth.
25. 21; Rom. 12. 20, if *e.* hunger, give bread.
27. 6, kisses of *e.* deceitful.
Isa. 9. 11, Lord shall join *e.* together.
59. 19, when *e.* shall come in like a flood.
63. 10, he was turned to be their *e.*
Jer. 15. 11, will cause *e.* to entreat thee well.
30. 14, wounded thee with wound of *e.*
Mic. 7. 6, man's *e.* men of his own house.
Mat. 5. 43, said, thou shalt hate thine *e.*
5. 44; Lu. 6. 27, 35, I say, love your *e.*
13. 25, 28, 39, his *e.* sowed tares.
Lu. 19. 43, thine *e.* shall cast a trench.
Acts 13. 10, thou *e.* of all righteousness.
Rom. 5. 10, if when *e.* we were reconciled.
11. 28, concerning the gospel they are *e.*
Gal. 4. 16, am I become your *e.*?
Phil. 3. 18, the *e.* of the cross.
Col. 1. 21, were *e.* in your mind.
2 Thes. 3. 15, count him not as an *e.*
Jas. 4. 4, friend of the world is the *e.* of God.

Engaged. Jer. 30. 21.

En-gannim, ĕn-găn′-nĭm, 'fountain of gardens.' Jos. 15. 34.

En-gedi, ĕn-gē′-dī, 'fountain of the kid.' City of Judah, Jos. 15. 62.
David dwells there. 1 Sam. 23. 29; 24. 1.

Engines. 2 Chr. 26. 15, and he made in Jerusalem *e.*
Ezek. 26. 9, and he shall set *e.* of war.

Engrafted. Jas. 1. 21.

Engrave. Ex. 28. 11; 35. 35; 38. 23; Zec. 3. 9; 2 Cor. 3. 7.

En-haddah, ĕn-hăd′-dăh, 'fountain of sharpness,' i. e., swift fountain. Jos. 19. 21.

En-hakkore, ĕn-hăk-kôr′-ē, 'fountain of him that calleth.' Jud. 15. 19.

En-hazor, ĕn-hā′-zôr, 'fountain of the village.' Jos. 19. 37.

Enjoin. Job 36. 23; Philem. 8.; Heb. 9. 20.

Enjoy. Lev. 26. 34; 2 Chr. 36. 21, land shall *e.* her sabbaths.
Eccl. 2. 1, *e.* pleasure, this also is vanity.
2. 24; 3. 13; 5. 18, soul *e.* good.
1 Tim. 6. 17, giveth us all things to *e.*
See Num. 36. 8; Isa. 65. 22; Heb. 11. 25.

Enlarge. (1) Deu. 12. 20, when the Lord shall *e.* thy border.
Ps. 25. 17, troubles of heart *e.*
119. 32, when thou shalt *e.* my heart.
Isa. 5. 14, hell hath *e.* herself.
2 Cor. 6. 11, 13; 10. 15, our heart is *e.*
(2) to set at liberty. Ps. 4. 1, thou hast *e.* me in distress.
See Isa. 54. 2; Hab. 2. 5; Mat. 23. 5.

Enlighten. Ps. 19. 8; Eph. 1. 18; Heb. 6. 4.
En-mishpat, ĕn-mĭsh'-păt, 'fountain of judgment.' Gen. 14. 7.
Enmity. Rom. 8. 7, carnal mind is *e.*
Eph. 2. 15, 16, having abolished the *e.*
Jas. 4. 4, friendship of world *e.* with God.
See Gen. 3. 15; Num. 35. 21; Lu. 23. 12.
Enoch, ē'-nŏch, dedication. Gen. 4. 17.
his faith, Heb. 11. 5. prophecy, Jude 14. translation, Gen. 5. 24.
Enos, ē'-nŏs, 'man.' Gen. 4. 26.
Enosh, ē'-nŏsh, same as Enos. 1 Chr. 1. 1.
Enough. Gen. 33. 9, 11, I have *e.*, my brother.
45. 28, it is *e.*, Joseph is alive.
Ex. 36. 5, people bring more than *e.*
2 Sam. 24. 16; 1 Kn. 19. 4; 1 Chr. 21. 15; Mk. 14. 41; Lu. 22. 38, it is *e.*, stay thine hand.
Prov. 28. 19, shall have poverty *e.*
30. 15, four things say not, it is *e.*
30. 16, fire saith not, it is *e.*
Isa. 56. 11, dogs which can never have *e.*
Jer. 49. 9, will destroy till they have *e.*
Hos. 4. 10, eat, and not have *e.*
Obad. 5, stolen till they had *e.*
Mal. 3. 10, room *e.* to receive it.
Mat. 10. 25, *e.* for disciple.
25. 9, lest there be not *e.*
See Deu. 1. 6; 2 Chr. 31. 10; Hag. 1. 6; Lu. 15. 17.
Enquire. Ex. 18. 15, people come to me to *e.* of God.
2 Sam. 16. 23, as if a man had *e.* of oracle.
2 Kn. 3. 11, is there not a prophet to *e.*?
Ps. 78. 34, returned and *e.* early after God.
Ezek. 14. 3, should I be *e.* of at all by them?
20. 3, 31, I will not be *e.*
36. 37, I will yet for this be *e.* of.
Zep. 1. 6, those that have not *e.* for.
Mat. 10. 11, *e.* who in it is worthy. R. V. search out.
1 Pet. 1. 10, which salvation the prophets *e.* R. V. sought.
See Deu. 12. 30; Isa. 21. 12; John 4. 52.
Enrich. 1 Sam. 17. 25; Ps. 65. 9; Ezek. 27. 33; 1 Cor. 1. 5; 2 Cor. 9. 11.
En-rimmon, ĕn-rĭm'-mon, 'fountain of the pomegranate.' Neh. 11. 29.
En-rogel, ĕn-rō'-gĕl, 'fountain of the fuller.' Jos. 15. 7; 18. 16; 2 Sam. 17. 17; 1 Kn. 1. 9.
Ensample, example. 1 Cor. 10. 11, happened to them for *e.*
Phil. 3. 17, as ye have us for an *e.*
2 Thes. 3. 9, to make ourselves an *e.*
See 1 Thes. 1. 7; 1 Pet. 5. 3; 2 Pet. 2. 6.
En-shemesh, ĕn-shē'-mĕsh, 'fountain of the sun.' Jos. 15. 7.
Ensign. (1) flag, banner. Num. 2. 2; Isa. 5. 26; 18. 3; 30. 17. (2) Ps. 74. 4; Isa. 11. 10; Zec. 9. 16.
Ensnared. Job 34. 30.
Ensue, to pursue, follow after. 1 Pet. 3. 11.
Entangle. Ex. 14. 3; Mat. 22. 15; Gal. 5. 1.
En-tappuah, ĕn-tăp'-pū-ăh, 'fountain of the apple tree.' Jos. 17. 7.
Enter. Ps. 100. 4, *e.* his gates with thanksgiving.
119. 130, the *e.* of thy word giveth light. R. V. opening.
Isa. 26. 2, righteous nation may *e.* in.
26. 20, *e.* thou into thy chambers.
Ezek. 44. 5, mark well *e.* in of the house.
Mat. 6. 6, prayest, *e.* into thy closet.
7. 13; Lu. 13. 24, *e.* in at strait gate.
10. 11; Lu. 10. 8, 10, what city ye *e.*
Mat. 18. 8; Mk. 9. 43, better to *e.* into life.
19. 17, if thou wilt *e.* into life, keep.
25. 21, well done, *e.* into joy.
Mk. 5. 12; Lu. 8. 32, we may *e.* into swine.
14. 38; Lu. 22. 46, lest ye *e.* into temptation.
Lu. 9. 34, feared as they *e.* cloud.
13. 24, many will seek to *e.*
John 3. 4, can he *e.*?
4. 38, ye are *e.* into their labours.
10. 1, 2, *e.* not by the door.
Rom. 5. 12, sin *e.* into world.
1 Cor. 2. 9, neither have *e.* into heart of man.
Heb. 3. 11, 18, shall not *e.* into rest.
Heb. 4. 10, he that is *e.* into rest.
6. 20, forerunner is for us *e.*
2 Pet. 1. 11, so an *e.* shall be ministered.
See Ps. 143. 2; Prov. 17. 10; Mat. 15. 17.
Entice. Jud. 14. 15; 16. 5, *e.* husband that he may declare.
2 Chr. 18. 19, Lord said, who shall *e.* Ahab?
Prov. 1. 10, if sinners *e.* thee.
1 Cor. 2. 4; Col. 2. 4, with *e.* words. R. V. persuasive.
See Job 31. 27; Prov. 16. 29; Jas. 1. 14.
Enticers to idolatry to be stoned. Deu. 13. 10.
Entreat, to treat, deal with. Mat. 22. 6; Lu. 18. 32, *e.* them spitefully.
Entry. 1 Chr. 9. 19; Prov. 8. 3; Ezek. 8. 5; 40. 38.
Environ. Jos. 7. 9.
Envy. Job 5. 2, *e.* slayeth the silly one. R. V. jealousy.
Ps. 73. 3, I was *e.* at the foolish.
Prov. 3. 31, *e.* not the oppressor.
14. 30, *e.* is rottenness of the bones.
23. 17, let not heart *e.* sinners.
24. 1, 19, be not *e.* against evil men.
27. 4, who is able to stand before *e.*? R. V. jealousy.
Eccl. 4. 4, for this a man is *e.*
9. 6, their love, hatred, and *e.* is perished.
Mat. 27. 18; Mk. 15. 10, for *e.* they delivered.
Acts 7. 9, patriarchs moved with *e.*
13. 45; 17. 5, Jews filled with *e.* R. V. jealousy.
Rom. 1. 29, full of *e.*, murder.
13. 13, walk honestly, not in *e.* R. V. jealousy.
1 Cor. 3. 3, among you *e.* and strife. R. V. jealousy.
13. 4, charity *e.* not.
2 Cor. 12. 20, I fear lest there be e.
Gal. 5. 21, works of flesh are *e.*, murders.
5. 26, *e.* one another.
Phil. 1. 15, preach Christ even of *e.*
1 Tim. 6. 4, whereof cometh *e.*
Tit. 3. 3, living in malice and *e.*
Jas. 4. 5, spirit in us lusteth to *e.*
Envy. Prov. 14. 30; 27. 4; Eccles. 4. 4; Ezek. 31. 9; 35. 9; Mat. 27. 18; Acts 7. 9; Rom. 1. 29; 1 Cor. 3. 3; 2 Cor. 12. 20; Gal. 5. 21; 1 Tim. 6. 4; Tit. 3. 3; Jas. 4. 5.
forbidden. Ps. 37. 1; Prov. 3. 31; 24. 1, 19; Rom. 13. 13; 1 Pet. 2. 1.
its evil consequences. Job 5. 2; Ps. 106. 16, 17; Prov. 14. 30; Isa. 26. 11; Jas. 3. 16.
Joseph sold for. Gen. 37. 11; Acts 7. 9.
Epænetus, ĕp-æ'-nĕ-tŭs, 'laudable.' Rom. 16. 5.
Epaphras, ĕp'-ă-phrăs, contracted from the next word (?). commended, Col. 1. 7; 4. 12.
Epaphroditus, ĕp-ăph-rō-dī'-tŭs, 'lovely.' Paul's joy at his recovery, Phil. 2. 25; his kindness, Phil. 4. 18.
Epenetus, ĕp-ē'-nĕ-tŭs, same as Epænetus. Rom. 16. 5.
Ephah, ē'-phah, a son of Midian. Gen. 25. 4.
Ephah, a dry measure, the unit of measurement = 38.88 litres = about a bushel (1.08) according to Josephus. *See* Measures.
Lev. 19. 36; Ezek. 45. 10, a just *e.*
Zec. 5. 6, this is an *e.* that goeth forth.
Ephai, ē'-phăi, 'languishing' (?). Jer. 40. 8.
Epher, ē'-phĕr, 'calf.' Gen. 25. 4.
Ephes-dammim, ē'-phĕs-dăm'-mĭm, 'boundary of blood.' 1 Sam. 17. 1.
Ephesians, ĕph-ē'-siăns, inhabitants of Ephesus. Acts 19. 28.
election. Eph. 1. 4.
adoption of grace. Eph. 1. 6.
dead in sin quickened. Eph. 2. 1, 5.
Gentiles made nigh. Eph. 2. 13.
unity and kindness enjoined. Eph. 4.-6.
Ephesus, ĕph'-ĕ-sŭs. An important commercial city of Asia Minor, and capital of the Roman province of Asia. Celebrated for a splendid temple of Diana (Acts 19. 24). It became the Christian centre of Asia through the preaching of Paul and his subsequent sojourn there of nearly three years (Acts 19. 10). It was the home of Timothy and the apostle John.
visited by Paul. Acts 18. 19; 19. 1.

miracles there. Acts 19. 11.
tumult there. Acts 19. 24.
Paul's address at Miletus to the elders of. Acts 20. 17.
Paul fights with beasts there. 1 Cor. 15. 32.
tarries there. 1 Cor. 16. 8.
Ephlal, ĕph'-lăl, judgment (?). 1 Chr. 2. 37.
Ephod. (1) father of Hanniel. Num. 34. 23.
(2) This word has two senses in O. T.: (1) a priestly garment. (2) An image or object of idolatrous worship. Jud. 17. 5; 2 Sam. 6. 14, &c.
Ex. 28. 6, they shall make the *e.* of gold.
39. 2, and he made the *e.* of gold.
Jud. 8. 27, and Gideon made an *e.* thereof.
17. 5, and made an *e.*
Ephphatha, ĕph'-phă-thă, 'be opened.' Mk. 7. 34.
Ephraim, ē'-phră-ĭm, 'fruitful;' younger son of Joseph. Gen. 41. 52.
Jacob blesses Ephraim and Manasseh. Gen. 48. 14.
his descendants numbered. Num. 1. 10, 32; 2. 18; 26. 35; 1 Chr. 7. 20.
their possessions. Jos. 16. 5; 17. 14; Jud. 1. 29.
chastise the Midianites. Jud. 7. 24.
quarrel with Gideon, Jud. 8. 1. and Jephthah, Jud. 12.
revolt from the house of David. 1 Kn. 12. 25.
chastise Ahaz and Judah. 2 Chr. 28. 6, 7.
release their prisoners. 2 Chr. 28. 12.
carried into captivity. 2 Kn. 17. 5; Ps. 78. 9, 67; Jer. 7. 15.
repenting, called God's son. Jer. 31. 20.
prophecies concerning. Isa. 7.; 9. 9; 11. 13; 28. 1; Hos. 5.-14; Zec. 9. 10; 10. 7.
Ephraimites, ē'-phră-ĭm-ītes, 'inhabitants of Ephraim.' Jud. 12. 4.
Ephrain, ē'-phră-ĭn, same as EPHRON. 2 Chr. 13. 19.
Ephratah, or **Ephrath**, ĕph'-ră-tăh, ē'-phrăth, 'fruitful' (?). (1) 1 Chr. 2. 50.
(2) (Beth-lehem). Gen. 35. 16; Ps. 132. 6; Mic. 5. 2.
Ephrathites, ĕph'-ră-thītes, inhabitants of Ephrath. Ru. 1. 2.
Ephron, ē'-phrŏn, 'of or belonging to a calf.' Gen. 23. 8.
the Hittite, sells Machpelah to Abraham. Gen. 23. 10.
Epicureans, ĕp-ĭ-cū-rē'-ăns, 'followers of Epicurus.'
philosophers, encounter Paul at Athens. Acts 17. 18.
Epistle. 2 Cor. 3. 1, nor need *e.* of commendation.
3. 2, ye are our *e.*
3. 3, to be the *e.* of Christ.
2 Thes. 2. 15; 3. 14, by word or *e.*
2 Pet. 3. 16, as also in all his *e.*
See Acts 15. 30; 23. 33; 2 Cor. 7. 8; 2 Thes. 3. 17.
Equal. (1) 55. 13, a man mine *e.*, my guide.
Prov. 26. 7, legs of lame not *e.* R. V. hang loose.
Isa. 40. 25; 46. 5, to whom shall I be *e.*?
Mat. 20. 12, hast made them *e.* to us.
Lu. 20. 36, are *e.* to angels.
John 5. 18; Phil. 2. 6, *e.* with God.
See Ex. 36. 22; 2 Cor. 8. 14; Gal. 1. 14.
(2) just, right. Ps. 17. 2, eyes behold things that are *e.* R. V. equity.
Ezek. 18. 25, 29; 33. 17, 20, is not my way *e.*?
Col. 4. 1, give servants what is *e.*
Equity. Ps. 98. 9, judge the people with *e.*
Prov. 1. 3, receive instruction of *e.*
2. 9, understand judgment and *e.*
17. 26, not good to strike princes for *e.* R. V. uprightness.
Eccl. 2. 21, a man whose labour is in *e.* R. V. skilfulness.
See Isa. 11. 4; 59. 14; Mic. 3. 9; Mal. 2. 6.
Er, ĕr, 'watchful.' Gen. 38. 3.
Eran, ē'-răn. Num. 26. 36.
Eranites, ē'-răn-ītes, posterity of Eran. Num. 26. 36.
Erastus, ē-răs'-tŭs, 'beloved;' ministers to Paul. Acts 19. 22; Rom. 16. 23; 2 Tim. 4. 20.
Erech, ĕr'-ĕch. Gen. 10. 10.
Erected. Gen. 33. 20.
Eri, ē'-rī, same as ER. Gen. 46. 16.
Erites, ē'-rītes, descendants of Eri. Num. 26. 16.
Err. Ps. 95. 10, people that do *e.* in their heart.
119. 21, do *e.* from thy commandments. R. V. wander.
Isa. 3. 12; 9. 16, lead thee cause to *e.*
28. 7, they *e.* in vision.
35. 8, wayfaring men shall not *e.*
Mat. 22. 29; Mk. 12. 24, *e.*, not knowing scriptures.
1 Tim. 6. 10, have *e.* from the faith. R. V. been led astray.
6. 21, have *e.* concerning the faith.
Jas. 1. 16, do not *e.*, beloved brethren. R. V. be not deceived.
5. 19, if any do *e.* from truth.
See Isa. 28. 7; 29. 24; Ezek. 45. 20.
Errand. Gen. 24. 33; Jud. 3. 19; 2 Kn. 9. 5.
Error. Ps. 19. 12, who can understand his *e.*?
Eccl. 5. 6, neither say thou, it was an *e.*
10. 5, evil which I have seen as an *e.*
Mat. 27. 64, last *e.* worse than first.
Jas. 5. 20, converteth sinner from *e.*
2 Pet. 3. 17, led away with *e.* of wicked.
1 John 4. 6, the spirit of *e.*
See Job 19. 4; Rom. 1. 27; Heb. 9. 7; Jude 11.
Esaias, ē-sāi'-ăs, same as ISAIAH. Mat. 3. 3.
Esar-haddon, ē'-săr-hăd'-dọn, 'Assur hath given a brother;' powerful king of Assyria. 2 Kn. 19. 37; Ez. 4. 2; Isa. 37. 38.
Esau, ē'-sâu, 'hairy;' son of Isaac. Gen. 25. 25 (Mal. 1. 2; Rom. 9. 13).
sells his birthright. Gen. 25. 29 (Heb. 12. 16).
deprived of the blessing. Gen. 27. 38.
his anger against Jacob, Gen. 27. 41. and reconciliation, Gen. 33.
his riches and descendants. Gen. 36.; 1 Chr. 1. 35.
Escape. Gen. 19. 17, *e.* for thy life, *e.* to mountain.
1 Kn. 18. 40; 2 Kn. 9. 15, let none of them *e.*
Esth. 4. 13, think not thou shalt *e.* in king's house.
Job 11. 20, wicked shall not *e.*
19. 20, *e.* with skin of my teeth.
Ps. 55. 8, I would hasten my *e.*
Prov. 19. 5, speaketh lies shall not *e.*
Eccl. 7. 26, whoso pleaseth God shall *e.*
Isa. 20. 6; Heb. 2. 3, how shall we *e.*?
Ezek. 33. 21, one that had *e.* came to me.
Am. 9. 1, he that *e.* shall not be delivered.
Mat. 23. 33, how can ye *e.* damnation?
Lu. 21. 36, worthy to *e.*
John 10. 39, he *e.* out of their hands. R. V. went forth.
Acts 27. 44, they *e.* all safe to land.
28. 4, he *e.* sea, yet vengeance.
Heb. 11. 34, through faith *e.* edge of sword.
12. 25, if they *e.* not who refused.
2 Pet. 1. 4, *e.* corruption in the world.
1. 20, after they *e.* pollutions.
See Deu. 23. 15; Ps. 124. 7; 1 Cor. 10. 13.
Eschew, to avoid, shun. Job 1. 1; 2. 3; 1 Pet. 3. 11.
Esdraëlon (known also as the VALLEY OF MEGIDDO), the great battle-field of Palestine, is by far the most important of its inland plains. In shape it is an irregular triangle, bounded on the north by the Galilæan hills, on the east by the mountains of Gilboa and the hill of Moreh, and on the south and west by the hills of Samaria and the range of Carmel.
Esek, ē'-sĕk, 'strife.' Gen. 26. 20.
Esh-baal, ĕsh-bā'-ăl, 'man of Baal.' 1 Chr. 8. 33.
Eshban, ĕsh'-băn. Gen. 36. 26.
Eshcol, ĕsh'-cŏl, 'cluster.' Gen. 14. 13.
grapes of. Num. 13. 23.
Eshean, ĕsh'-ĕ-ăn, 'support' (?). Jos. 15. 52.
Eshek, ē'-shĕk, 'oppression.' 1 Chr. 8. 39.
Eshkalonites, ĕsh'-kă-lọn-ītes, men of Ashkelon. Jos. 13. 3.
Eshtaol, ĕsh'-tā-ŏl. Jos. 15. 33.
Eshtaulites, ĕsh-tā-ū'-lītes, inhabitants of Eshtaol. 1 Chr. 2. 53. R. V. Eshtaolites.
Eshtemoa, ĕsh-tĕ-mō'-ă, 'obedience.' Jos. 21. 14.

Eshtemoh, ĕsh′-tĕ-mōh, same as Eshtemoa. Jos. 15. 50.
Eshton, ĕsh′-tŏn, 'effeminate.' 1 Chr. 4. 11.
Esli, ĕs′-lī, same as Azaliah (?). Lu. 3. 25.
Especially. Gal. 6. 10; 1 Tim. 4. 10; 5. 8; Philem. 16.
Espouse. S. of S. 3. 11; Jer. 2. 2; 2 Cor. 11. 2.
Espy. Gen. 42. 27; Jos. 14. 7; Jer. 48. 19; Ezek. 20. 6.
Esrom, ĕs′-rŏm, same as Hezron. Mat. 1. 3.
Essenes, ĕs-sēnz′, Gr. Ἐσσηνοι, not mentioned in Scripture, but described by Josephus as one of the 'three philosophical sects among the Jews,' the other two being of course the Pharisees and the Sadducees. The origin of their name is unknown. Philo calls them Essæi, because of their saintliness; for *hosioi* (=saintly) is the same word as Essæi. They were a sort of monastic society, bound together by oaths to piety, justice, obedience, honesty, and secrecy. Their three rules were 'the love of God, the love of virtue, the love of man.' They were ascetics, and generally celibates. Our Lord never pronounced woes against them as He did against the Sadducees and Pharisees. Josephus gives their number as 4000.
Establish. Ps. 40. 2, and *e.* my goings.
90. 17, *e.* work of our hands.
Prov. 4. 26, let thy ways be *e.*
12. 19, lip of truth *e.* for ever.
16. 12, throne *e.* by righteousness.
20. 18, every purpose *e.* by counsel.
24. 3, by understanding is house *e.*
29. 4, king by judgment *e.* the land.
Isa. 7. 9, if ye will not believe, ye shall not be *e.*
16. 5, in mercy shall the throne be *e.*
Jer. 10. 12; 51. 15, he *e.* world by wisdom.
Mat. 18. 16, two witnesses every word *e.*
Rom. 3. 31, yea, we *e.* the law.
10. 3, to *e.* their own righteousness.
Heb. 13. 9, the heart be *e.* with grace.
2 Pet. 1. 12, be *e.* in the present truth.
See Am. 5. 15; Hab. 2. 12; Acts 16. 5.
Estate. Ps. 136. 23, remembered us in low *e.*
Eccl. 1. 16, lo, I am come to great *e.*
Rom. 12. 16, condescend to men of low *e.* R. V. things that are lowly.
Jude 6, angels kept not first *e.* R. V. own principality.
See Ezek. 36. 11; Dan. 11. 7; Lu. 1. 48.
Estates, men of rank or high station. Mk. 6. 21.
Esteem. Deu. 32. 15, lightly *e.* rock of salvation.
1 Sam. 2. 30, despise me shall be lightly *e.*
18. 23, I am a poor man, and lightly *e.*
Job 23. 12, I have *e.* the words of his mouth.
36. 19, will he *e.* thy riches?
41. 27, he *e.* iron as straw.
Ps. 119. 128, I *e.* all thy precepts.
Isa. 53. 4, did *e.* him smitten.
Lam. 4. 2, *e.* as earthen pitchers.
Lu. 16. 15, highly *e.* among men.
Rom. 14. 5, one man *e.* one day above another.
14. 14, that *e.* any thing unclean.
Phil. 2. 3, let each *e.* other better.
1 Thes. 5. 13, *e.* highly for work's sake.
Heb. 11. 26, *e.* reproach greater riches.
See Prov. 17. 28; Isa. 29. 17; 1 Cor. 6. 4.
Esther, ĕs′-thĕr, 'the planet Venus.' Esth. 2. 7. (Hadassah) made queen in the place of Vashti. Esth. 2. 17.
pleads for her people. Esth. 7. 3, 4.
Estimation. Lev. 27. 2–8, 15–19. [Ezek. 14. 5.
Estranged. Job 19. 13; Ps. 78. 30; Jer. 19. 4;
Etam, ē′-tăm, 'a place of ravenous creatures' (?). Jud. 15. 8.
Eternal. Deu. 33. 27, the *e.* God is thy refuge.
Isa. 60. 15, will make thee an *e.* excellency.
Mat. 19. 16, Mk. 10. 17; Lu. 10. 25; 18. 18, what shall I do that I may have *e.* life?
25. 46, righteous into life *e.*
Mk. 3. 29, is in danger of *e.* damnation.
10. 30, receive in world to come *e.* life.
John 3. 15, believeth in him have *e.* life.
4. 36, gathereth fruit unto life *e.*
5. 39, scriptures, in them *e.* life.
6. 54, drinketh my blood hath *e.* life.
6. 68, thou hast words of *e.* life.
10. 28, give sheep *e.* life.
12. 25, hateth life, shall keep it to life *e.*
17. 2, give *e.* life to as many.
17. 3, this is life *e.*, that they might know thee.
Acts 13. 48, many as were ordained to *e.* life.
Rom. 2. 7, who seek for glory, *e.* life.
5. 21, grace reign to *e.* life.
6. 23, gift of God is *e.* life.
2 Cor. 4. 17, an *e.* weight of glory.
4. 18, things not seen are *e.*
5. 1, house *e.* in the heavens.
Eph. 3. 11, according to *e.* purpose.
1 Tim. 6. 12, 19, lay hold on *e.* life.
Tit. 1. 2; 3. 7, in hope of *e.* life.
Heb. 5. 9, author of *e.* salvation.
6. 2, doctrine of *e.* judgment.
9. 15, promise of *e.* inheritance.
1 Pet. 5. 10, called to *e.* glory by Christ.
1 John 1. 2, *e.* life, which was with the Father.
2. 25, this is the promise, even *e.* life.
3. 15, no murderer hath *e.* life.
5. 11, record, that God hath given to us *e.* life.
5. 13, know that ye have *e.* life.
5. 20, this is true God, and *e.* life.
Jud. 7, vengeance of *e.* fire.
See Rom. 1. 20; 1 Tim. 1. 17; 2 Tim. 2. 10; Jude 21.
Eternity. Isa. 57. 15.
Etham, ē′-thăm. Ex. 13. 20.
Ethan, ē′-thăn, 'firm.' 1 Kn. 4. 31.
Ethanim, ĕth′-ă-nĭm, 'gifts' (?). 1 Kn. 8. 2. The same as Tisri, the seventh month of the sacred year = Oct. *See* Months.
Ethbaal, ĕth-bā′-ăl, 'with Baal.' 1 Kn. 16. 31.
Ether, ē′-thĕr, 'plenty.' Jos. 15. 42.
Ethiopia, ē-thĭ-ō′-pĭ-ă, (region of) 'burnt faces' (?). Gen. 2. 13. R. V. Cush.
Ethiopian, ē-thĭ-ō′-pĭ-ăn, a native of Ethiopia. Jer. 13. 23.
Ethiopians, ē-thĭ-ō′-pĭ-ăns, invading Judah, subdued by Asa. 2 Chr. 14. 9. *See* Num. 12. 1; 2 Kn. 19. 9; Esth. 1. 1; Job 28. 19.
prophecies concerning. Ps. 68. 31; 87. 4; Isa. 18.; 20.; 43. 3; 45. 14; Jer. 46. 9; Ezek. 30. 4; 38. 5; Nah. 3. 9; Zep. 3. 10.
Ethnan, ĕth′-năn, 'a gift.' 1 Chr. 4. 7.
Ethni, ĕth′-nī, 'bountiful.' 1 Chr. 6. 41.
Eubulus, eû-bū′-lŭs, 'prudent.' 2 Tim. 4. 21.
Eunice, eû-nī′-çē, commended (Acts 16. 1); 2 Tim. 1. 5. [the *e.*
Eunuchs. Isa. 56. 4, for thus saith the Lord to
Mat. 19. 12, for there are some *e.*
Acts 8. 27, an *e.* of great authority.
See Isa. 56. 3.
Euodia, eû-ō′-dĭ-ă, 'success.' Phil. 4. 2.
Euphrates, eû-phrā′-tēs, the river, the western boundary of Mesopotamia (= the land between the rivers); the river on which Babylon was built; called in R. V. 'the river' (1 Kn. 4. 21); N. E. boundary of Solomon's dominions; one of the rivers of Eden. Gen. 2. 14; 15. 18; Deu. 11. 24; Jos. 1. 4; 2 Sam. 8. 3; Jer. 13. 4; 46. 2; 51. 63.
typical. Rev. 9. 14; 16. 12.
Euroclydon, eû-rŏc′-lȳ-dŏn, 'storm from the east.' Acts 27. 14. R. V. Euraquilo.
Eutychus, eû′-tȳ-chŭs, fortunate, restored. Acts 20. 9, 12.
Evangelists, 'Ministers of the Church, who assisted the Apostles in spreading the Gospel, or Evangel, of our Lord Jesus Christ.' Acts 21. 8; Eph. 4. 11; 2 Tim. 4. 5.
Eve, ēve, 'life.' Gen. 3. 20.
created. Gen. 1. 27; 2. 18.
her fall and fate. Gen. 3. *See* Adam.
Evening. 1 Sam. 14. 24, cursed that eateth till *e.*
1 Kn. 17. 6, brought bread morning and *e.*
Ps. 90. 6, in *e.* cut down and withereth.
104. 23, goeth to his labour until the *e.*

Ps. 141. 2, prayer as the *e.* sacrifice.
Eccl. 11. 6, in *e.* withhold not thine hand.
Jer. 6. 4, shadows of *e.* stretched out.
Hab. 1. 8; Zep. 3. 3, *e.* wolves.
Zec. 14. 7, at *e.* time shall be light.
Mat. 14. 23, when *e.* was come, he was there alone.
Lu. 24. 29, abide, for it is toward *e.*
See Gen. 30. 16; Ps. 65. 8; Mat. 16. 2; Mk. 14. 17.

Event. Eccl. 2. 14; 9. 2, 3.

Ever. Gen. 3. 22, lest he eat, and live for *e.*
Gen. 43. 9; 44. 32, let me bear blame for *e.*
Ex. 14. 13, ye shall see them no more for *e.*
Lev. 6. 13, fire *e.* burning on altar. R. V. continually.
Deu. 5. 29; 12. 28, be well with them for *e.*
13. 16, a heap for *e.*
32. 40, lift up hand and say, I live for *e.*
Job 4. 7, who *e.* perished?
Ps. 9. 7, Lord shall endure for *e.*
12. 7, thou wilt preserve them for *e.*
22. 26, your heart shall live for *e.*
23. 6, dwell in house of the Lord for *e.*
29. 10, Lord sitteth king for *e.*
33. 11, counsel of Lord standeth for *e.*
37. 26, he is *e.* merciful, and lendeth. R. V. all the day long.
48. 14, our God for *e.* and *e.*
49. 9, that he should still live for *e.*
51. 3, my sin is *e.* before me.
52. 8, trust in mercy of God for *e.* and *e.*
61. 4, will abide in tabernacle for *e.*
73. 26, my strength and portion for *e.*
74. 19, forget not congregation of poor for *e.*
81. 15, their time should have endured for *e.*
92. 7, they shall be destroyed for *e.*
93. 5, holiness becometh thine house for *e.*
102. 12, thou shalt endure for *e.*
103. 9, not keep his anger for *e.*
105. 8, remember his covenant for *e.*
119. 89, for *e.* thy word is settled.
132. 14, this is my rest for *e.*
146. 6, Lord keepeth truth for *e.*
146. 10, Lord shall reign for *e.*
Prov. 27. 24, riches not for *e.*
Eccl. 3. 14, whatsoever God doeth shall be for *e.*
Isa. 26. 4, trust in Lord for *e.*
32. 17, assurance for *e.*
34. 10; Rev. 14. 11; 19. 3, smoke shall go up for *e.*
40. 8, word of God shall stand for *e.*
57. 16, will not contend for *e.*
Lam. 3. 31, Lord will not cast off for *e.*
Mat. 6. 13, thine is the glory for *e.*
21. 19; Mk. 11. 14, no fruit grow on thee for *e.*
John 8. 35, servant abideth not for *e.*
12. 34, heard that Christ abideth for *e.*
14. 16, Comforter abide for *e.*
Rom. 9. 5, God blessed for *e.*
1 Thes. 4. 17, so shall we *e.* be with the Lord.
5. 15, *e.* follow good.
2 Tim. 3. 7, *e.* learning.
Heb. 7. 25, he *e.* liveth to make.
13. 8, same yesterday, to day, and for *e.*
See Mat. 24. 21; Lu. 15. 31; John 10. 8.

Everlasting. Ex. 40. 15; Num. 25. 13, an *e.* priesthood.
Ps. 90. 2, from *e.* to *e.* thou art God.
139. 24, lead me in way *e.*
Prov. 8. 23, I was set up from *e.*
10. 25, righteous is an *e.* foundation.
Isa. 9. 6, called the *e.* Father.
26. 4, in the Lord is *e.* strength.
33. 14, with *e.* burnings.
35. 10; 51. 11; 61. 7, *e.* joy.
45. 17, with *e.* salvation.
54. 8, with *e.* kindness.
55. 13, for an *e.* sign.
56. 5; 63. 12, an *e.* name.
60. 19, 20, an *e.* light.
Jer. 31. 3, with an *e.* love.
Hab. 3. 6, the *e.* mountains. R. V. eternal.
Mat. 18. 8; 25. 41, into *e.* fire. R. V. eternal.
19. 29, inherit *e.* life. R. V. eternal.
25. 46, into *e.* punishment.
Lu. 16. 9, into *e.* habitations. R. V. eternal.
18. 30, in world to come *e.* life. R. V. eternal.
John 3. 16, 36, believeth shall have *e.* life.
4. 14, water springing up into *e.* life. R. V. eternal.
5. 24, heareth my word hath *e.* life.
6. 27, meat which endureth to *e.* life.
6. 40, seeth Son may have *e.* life.
12. 50, his commandment is life *e.*
Acts 13. 46, unworthy of *e.* life. R. V. eternal.
Rom. 6. 22, free from sin, the end *e.* life.
Gal. 6. 8, of Spirit reap life *e.* R. V. eternal.
2 Thes. 1. 9, punished with *e.* destruction.
2. 16, given us *e.* consolation.
Jude 6, reserved in *e.* chains.
Rev. 14. 6, having the *e.* gospel. R. V. eternal.
See Dan. 4. 3; 7. 27; 2 Pet. 1. 11.

Evermore. Ps. 16. 11, pleasures for *e.*
37. 27, do good and dwell for *e.*
121. 8, preserve thy going out for *e.*
133. 3, the blessing, life for *e.*
John 6. 34, *e.* give us this bread.
1 Thes. 5. 16, rejoice *e.*
Heb. 7. 28, consecrated for *e.*
Rev. 1. 18, I am alive for *e.*
See 2 Kn. 17. 37; Ps. 77. 8; 106. 31.

Every. Gen. 4. 14, *e.* one that findeth me shall slay me. R. V. whosoever.
6. 5, *e.* imagination of heart evil.
Lev. 19. 10, neither shall gather *e.* grape. R. V. [the fallen.
Deu. 4. 4, alive *e.* one of you this day.
2 Kn. 18. 31, eat *e.* one of his fig tree.
2 Chr. 30. 18, pardon *e.* one.
Ps. 29. 9, *e.* one doth speak of glory.
32. 6, for this shall *e.* one that is godly.
68. 30, till *e.* one submit himself.
119. 101, refrained from *e.* evil way.
Prov. 2. 9, *e.* good path.
7. 12, in *e.* corner.
14. 15, simple believeth *e.* word.
20. 3, *e.* fool will be meddling.
30. 5, *e.* word of God is pure.
Eccl. 10. 3, saith to *e.* one he is a fool.
Jer. 51. 29, *e.* purpose of the Lord.
Mat. 4. 4, by *e.* word that proceedeth.
7. 8; Lu. 11. 10, *e.* one that asketh.
Mk. 1. 45, came from *e.* quarter.
Lu. 19. 26, to *e.* one which hath shall be given.
Rom. 14. 11, *e.* knee bow, *e.* tongue confess.
2 Cor. 10. 5, *e.* thought.
Eph. 1. 21; Phil. 2. 9, far above *e.* name.
1 Tim. 4. 4, *e.* creature of God.
2 Tim. 2. 19, *e.* one that nameth.
2. 21, *e.* good work.
Heb. 12. 1, *e.* weight.
Jas. 1. 17, *e.* good and perfect gift.
1 Pet. 2. 13, *e.* ordinance of man.
1 John 4. 1, believe not *e.* spirit.
4. 7, *e.* one that loveth.
Rev. 6. 11, robes given to *e.* one.
See Gen. 27. 29; Acts 2. 38; 17. 27; 20. 31.

Evi, ē'-vī, 'desire.' Num. 31. 8.

Evidence. Jer. 32. 10; Heb. 11. 1.

Evident. Gal. 3. 1, Christ hath been *e.* set forth. R. V. openly.
3. 11, that no man is justified is *e.*
Phil. 1. 28, an *e.* token of perdition.
See Job 6. 28; Heb. 7. 14, 15. [R. V. openly.

Evidently, clearly, plainly, visibly. Acts 10. 3.

Evil. Gen. 6. 5; 8. 21, thoughts of heart only *e.*
47. 9, few and *e.* have the days.
Ex. 32. 14; 2 Sam. 24. 16; 1 Chr. 21. 15, repented of the *e.*
Deu. 28. 54, eye *e.* towards his brother.
28. 56, her eye *e.* towards husband.
Job 2. 10, receive good, and not *e.*
30. 26, looked for good, then *e.* came.
Ps. 34. 14; 37. 27; Prov. 3. 7, depart from *e.*
35. 12; 109. 5, they rewarded me *e.*
40. 12, innumerable *e.* have compassed.
Prov. 14. 19, *e.* bow before the good.
15. 3, beholding the *e.* and good.
17. 13, whoso rewardeth *e.* for good.

Isa. 1. 4, a seed of *e.*-doers.
5. 20, that call *e.* good, and good *e.*
7. 15, 16, refuse the *e.* and choose the good.
Jer. 2. 13, have committed two *e.*
2. 19, know it is an *e.* thing and bitter.
24. 3; 29. 17, *e.* figs, very *e.* R. V. bad.
42. 6, whether good or *e.*, we will obey.
Mat. 5. 45, rise on *e.* and good.
6. 34, sufficient unto the day is the *e.* thereof.
7. 11; Lu. 11. 13, if ye, being *e.*
7. 18, good tree cannot bring forth *e.*
9. 4, wherefore think *e.* in your hearts?
Mk. 9. 39, lightly speak *e.* of me.
Lu. 6. 22, cast out your name as *e.*
6. 35, he is kind to the *e.*
6. 45, *e.* man bringeth forth *e.*
John 3. 20, doeth *e.* hateth light.
18. 23, if I have spoken *e.*
Acts 23. 5, not speak *e.* of ruler.
Rom. 7. 19, the *e.* I would not.
12. 9, abhor that which is *e.*
12. 17, recompense to no man *e.* for *e.*
12. 21, overcome *e.* with good.
1 Thes. 5. 22, appearance of *e.*
1 Tim. 6. 10, the root of all *e.*
2 Tim. 4. 18; Jas. 3. 16, every *e.* work.
Tit. 3. 2, speak *e.* of no man.
Jas. 3. 8, tongue an unruly *e.*
1 Pet. 3. 9, not rendering *e.* for *e.*
See Prov. 13. 21; Isa. 45. 7; Eccl. 12. 1; Eph. 5. 16; 6. 13.

Evilfavouredness, ugliness, deformity. Deu. 17. 1.

Evil-merodach, ē'-vĭl-mĕr'-ō-dăch, 'man of Merodach.'
king of Babylon, restores Jehoiachin. 2 Kn. 25. 27; Jer. 52. 31.

Exact. Deu. 15. 2, shall not *e.* it of neighbour.
Neh. 5. 7, 10, 11, you *e.* usury.
10. 31, leave the *e.* of every debt.
Job 11. 6, God *e.* of thee less.
Lu. 3. 13, *e.* no more than what is.
See Ps. 89. 22; Isa. 58. 3; 60. 17.

Exaction (usury, &c.), forbidden. Lev. 25. 35; Deu. 15. 2; Prov. 28. 8; Ezek. 22. 12; 45. 9; Lu. 3. 13; 1 Cor. 5. 10.
disclaimed, Neh. 5. 1; 10. 31.

Exalt. 1 Chr. 29. 11, *e.* as head above all.
Ps. 12. 8, when vilest men are *e.*
34. 3, let us *e.* his name together.
92. 10, my horn shalt thou *e.*
97. 9, *e.* far above all gods.
Prov. 4. 8, *e.* her, and she shall promote thee.
11. 11, by blessing of upright the city is *e.*
14. 29, he that is hasty of spirit *e.* folly.
14. 34, righteousness *e.* a nation.
17. 19, he that *e.* his gate. R. V. raised high.
Isa. 2. 2; Mic. 4. 1, mountain of Lord's house *e.*
40. 4, every valley shall be *e.*
Ezek. 21. 26, *e.* him that is low.
Mat. 11. 23; Lu. 10. 15, *e.* to heaven. [abased.
23. 12; Lu. 14. 11; 18. 14, *e.* himself shall be
2 Cor. 11. 20, if a man *e.* himself.
12. 7, *e.* above measure.
Phil. 2. 9, God hath highly *e.* him.
2 Thes. 2. 4, *e.* himself above all that is called.
1 Pet. 5. 6, he may *e.* in due time.
See Ex. 15. 2; Job 24. 24; Lu. 1. 52; Jas. 1. 9.

Examine. Ps. 26. 2, *e.* me, O Lord.
Acts 4. 9, if we this day be *e.*
22. 24, 29, *e.* by scourging.
1 Cor. 11. 28, let a man *e.* himself. R. V. prove.
2 Cor. 13. 5, *e.* yourselves. R. V. try.
See Ez. 10. 16; Acts 24. 8; 25. 26; 1 Cor. 9. 3.

Example. John 13. 15, I have given you an *e.*
1 Tim. 4. 12, be thou an *e.* of believers.
1 Pet. 2. 21, Christ suffered, leaving an *e.*
Jude 7, an *e.*, suffering vengeance.
See Mat. 1. 19; 1 Cor. 10. 6; Heb. 4. 11; 8. 5.

Example of Christ. Mat. 11. 29; John 13. 15; Rom. 15. 3, 5; Phil. 2. 5; 1 Pet. 2. 21.
prophets. Heb. 6. 12; Jas. 5. 10. [Thes. 1. 6.
apostles. 1 Cor. 4. 16; 11. 1; Phil. 3. 17; 4. 9; 1

Exceed. Mat. 5. 20, except righteousness *e.*
2 Cor. 3. 9, ministration doth *e.* in glory.
See 1 Sam. 20. 41; 2 Chr. 9. 6; Job 36. 9.

Exceeding. Gen. 15. 1, thy *e.* great reward.
27. 34, an *e.* bitter cry.
Num. 14. 7, land is *e.* good.
1 Sam. 2. 3, so *e.* proud.
Ps. 21. 6, *e.* glad with thy countenance.
43. 4, God my *e.* joy.
119. 96, commandment *e.* broad.
Prov. 30. 24, four things *e.* wise.
Jon. 1. 16, men feared the Lord *e.*
4. 6, *e.* glad of the gourd.
Mat. 2. 10, with *e.* great joy.
4. 8, an *e.* high mountain.
5. 12, rejoice and be *e.* glad.
8. 28, possessed with devils, *e.* fierce.
17. 23; 26. 22, they were *e.* sorry.
19. 25, they were *e.* amazed.
26. 38; Mk. 14. 34, my soul is *e.* sorrowful.
Mk. 6. 26, king *e.* sorry.
9. 3, raiment *e.* white.
Lu. 23. 8, Herod was *e.* glad.
Acts 7. 20, Moses was *e.* fair.
26. 11, being *e.* mad against them.
Rom. 7. 13, sin might become *e.* sinful.
2 Cor. 4. 17, *e.* weight of glory.
7. 4, *e.* joyful in our tribulation.
Gal. 1. 14, *e.* zealous of traditions.
Eph. 1. 19, the *e.* greatness of his power.
2. 7, the *e.* riches of his grace.
3. 20, able to do *e.* abundantly.
2 Thes. 1. 3, your faith groweth *e.*
2 Pet. 1. 4, *e.* great and precious promises.
Jude 24, present you faultless with *e.* joy.
See 1 Sam. 26. 21; Jon. 3. 3; Heb. 12. 21.

Excel. Gen. 49. 4, thou shalt not *e.*
Prov. 31. 29, thou *e.* them all.
Eccl. 2. 13, wisdom *e.* folly.
2 Cor. 3. 10, the glory that *e.* R. V. surpasseth.
See Ps. 103. 20; 1 Cor. 14. 12.

Excellency. Ex. 15. 7, the greatness of thine *e.*
Job 4. 21, doth not their *e.* go away? R. V. is not their tent-cord plucked up within them?
13. 11, shall not his *e.* make you afraid?
Isa. 60. 15, will make thee an eternal *e.*
1 Cor. 2. 1, not with *e.* of speech.
2 Cor. 4. 7, that the *e.* of the power. R. V. exceeding greatness.
Phil. 3. 8, loss for the *e.* of Christ.
See Gen. 49. 3; Ex. 15. 7; Eccl. 7. 12; Ezek. 24. 21.

Excellent. Job 37. 23, *e.* in power.
Ps. 8. 1, 9, how *e.* is thy name!
16. 3, to the *e.*, in whom is my delight.
36. 7, how *e.* thy lovingkindness!
Prov. 8. 6; 22. 20, I will speak of *e.* things.
12. 26, righteous more *e.* than neighbour. R. V. a guide to.
17. 7, *e.* speech becometh not a fool.
17. 27, of an *e.* spirit. R. V. cool.
Isa. 12. 5, he hath done *e.* things.
28. 29, is *e.* in working.
Dan. 5. 12; 6. 3, *e.* spirit found in Daniel.
Rom. 2. 18; Phil. 1. 10, things more *e.*
1 Cor. 12. 31, a more *e.* way.
2 Pet. 1. 17, voice from the *e.* glory.
See S. of S. 5. 15; Lu. 1. 3; Heb. 1. 4; 8. 6; 11. 4.

Except. Gen. 32. 26, *e.* thou bless me.
Deu. 32. 30, *e.* their Rock had sold them.
Ps. 127. 1, *e.* Lord build house.
Am. 3. 3, *e.* they be agreed.
Mat. 5. 20, *e.* your righteousness exceed.
18. 3, *e.* ye be converted.
24. 22; Mk. 13. 20, *e.* days be shortened.
Mk. 7. 3, Pharisees *e.* they wash oft.
Lu. 13. 3; Rev. 2. 5, 22, *e.* ye repent.
John 3. 2, *e.* God be with him.
3. 5, *e.* a man be born.
4. 48, *e.* ye see signs and wonders.
20. 25, *e.* I see print of nails.
Acts 26. 29, *e.* these bonds.
Rom. 10. 15, how preach, *e.* they be sent?
1 Cor. 15. 36, *e.* it die.

2 Tim. 2. 5, *e.* he strive lawfully.
See Rom. 7. 7; 1 Cor. 14. 5; 15. 27; 2 Thes. 2. 3.
Excess. Mat. 23. 25; Eph. 5. 18; 1 Pet. 4. 3, 4.
Exchange. Mat. 16. 26; Mk. 8. 37, in *e.* for his soul.
See Gen. 47. 17; Lev. 27. 10; Ezek. 48. 14.
Exchanger, money-changer, banker. Mat. 25. 27.
Exclude. Rom. 3. 27; Gal. 4. 17.
Excommunication. Exclusion from communion or fellowship, generally of the church. An instance of Jewish excommunication is found in John 9. 34; *see* also Lu. 6. 22.
For Christian excommunication *see* our Lord's rule in Mat. 18. 15–18. For the Apostolic practice *see* especially 1 Tim. 1. 20; 1 Cor. 5. 11; 2 Cor. 2.
Excuse. Lu. 14. 18; Rom. 1. 20; 2. 15; 2 Cor. 12. 19.
Execration. Jer. 42. 18; 44. 12.
Execute. Deu. 33. 21, he *e.* the justice of the [Lord.
1 Chr. 6. 10; 24. 2; Lu. 1. 8, *e.* priest's office.
Ps. 9. 16, Lord known by the judgment he *e.*
103. 6, Lord *e.* righteousness and judgment.
Jer. 5. 1, if any *e.* judgment, I will pardon.
John 5. 27, authority to *e.* judgment.
Rom. 13. 4, minister of God to *e.* wrath.
See Hos. 11. 9; Mic. 5. 15; Joel 2. 11.
Exercise. Ps. 131. 1, *e.* myself in things too high.
Jer. 9. 24, *e.* lovingkindness.
Mat. 20. 25; Mk. 10. 42; Lu. 22. 25, *e.* dominion.
Acts 24. 16, I *e.* myself, to have a conscience.
1 Tim. 4. 7, *e.* thyself unto godliness.
Heb. 5. 14, *e.* to discern good and evil.
12. 11, to them which are *e.* thereby.
See Eccl. 1. 13; 3. 10; Ezek. 22. 29; Rev. 13. 12.
Exercised, practised in, made familiar with. 2 Pet. 2. 14.
Exhort. Lu. 3. 18, many things in his *e.*
Acts 13. 15, any words of *e.*
Rom. 12. 8, he that *e.*, on *e.*
1 Tim. 6. 2, these things *e.* and teach.
Tit. 1. 9, may be able to *e.*
2. 15, *e.* and rebuke with authority.
Heb. 3. 13; 10. 25, *e.* one another daily.
13. 22, suffer word of *e.*
See Acts 11. 23; 2 Cor. 9. 5; Tit. 2. 6, 9.
Exile. 2 Sam. 15. 19; Isa. 51. 14.
Exodus, ĕx'-ŏ-dŭs, 'departure.' (1) the name given to the departure of the Israelites from Egypt.
(2) The name of the second book of the Pentateuch.
Exorcists (Acts 19. 13). 'The original meaning of the word *exorcise* was to *adjure*, as in Mat. 26. 63. Hence exorcists were those who pretended to cast out devils by commanding them in the Divine Name to come forth.'
See under DIVINATION.
Expect, to await, wait. Heb. 10. 13.
Expectation. Ps. 9. 18, the *e.* of the poor.
62. 5, my *e.* is from him.
Prov. 10. 28; 11. 7, 23, *e.* of the wicked.
Isa. 20. 5, ashamed of their *e.*
20. 6, such is our *e.*
Rom. 8. 19, the *e.* of the creature.
Phil. 1. 20, my earnest *e.* and hope.
See Jer. 29. 11; Acts 3. 5; Heb. 10. 13.
Expedient. John 11. 50; 16. 7; 18. 14; 1 Cor. 6. 12.
Expel. Jos. 23. 5; Jud. 11. 7; 2 Sam. 14. 14.
Expenses. Ez. 6. 4, 8.
Experience. Gen. 30. 27; Eccl. 1. 16; Rom. 5. 4.
Expert. 1 Chr. 12. 33; Jer. 50. 9; Acts 26. 3.
Expired. 1 Chr. 17. 11; Acts 7. 30; Rev. 20. 7.
Exploits. Dan. 11. 28, 32. R. V. his pleasure.
Expound. Jud. 14. 14, 19, could not *e.* riddle.
Mk. 4. 34, when they were alone, he *e.* all things.
Lu. 24. 27, *e.* the scriptures. R. V. interpreted.
See Acts 11. 4; 18. 26; 28. 23.
Express, exact, very. Heb. 1. 3.
Expressly. 1 Sam. 20. 21; Ezek. 1. 3; 1 Tim. 4. 1.
Extend. Ps. 16. 2; 109. 12; Isa. 66. 12.
Extinct. Job 17. 1; Isa. 43. 17.
Extol. Ps. 30. 1; 145. 1, I will *e.* thee.
Ps. 68. 4, *e.* him that rideth. R. V. cast up a highway for.
See Ps. 66. 17; Isa. 52. 13; Dan. 4. 37.
Extortion. Ezek. 22. 12; Mat. 23. 25.
Extortioner. Ps. 109. 11, let *e.* catch all he hath.
Isa. 16. 4, the *e.* is at an end.
1 Cor. 5. 11, if any man be an *e.*
See Lu. 18. 11; 1 Cor. 5. 10; 6. 10.
Extreme. Deu. 28. 22; Job 35. 15.
Eye. Gen. 3. 6, pleasant to the *e.*
3. 7, *e.* of both were opened.
27. 1, his *e.* were dim.
49. 12, his *e.* shall be red with wine.
Num. 10. 31, be to us instead of *e.*
16. 14, wilt thou put out *e.*?
24. 3, 15, man whose *e.* are open said.
Deu. 3. 27, lift up *e.*, behold with thine *e.*
12. 8; Jud. 17. 6; 21. 25, right in own *e.*
16. 19, gift blind *e.* of wise.
28. 32, *e.* look, and fail with longing.
32. 10, kept him as apple of *e.*
34. 7, his *e.* was not dim.
1 Kn. 1. 20, *e.* of all Israel upon thee.
8. 29, 52; 2 Chr. 6. 20, 40, *e.* open towards this [house.
20. 6, whatsoever is pleasant in thine *e.*
2 Kn. 6. 17, Lord opened *e.* of young man.
6. 20, open the *e.* of these men.
2 Chr. 16. 9; Zec. 4. 10, *e.* of Lord run to and fro.
34. 28, nor thine *e.* see all the evil.
Job 7. 8; 20. 9, *e.* that hath seen me.
11. 20, the *e.* of wicked shall fail.
15. 12, what do thine *e.* wink at?
19. 27, mine *e.* shall behold, and not another.
28. 7, path vulture's *e.* hath not seen.
28. 10, his *e.* seeth every precious thing.
29. 11, when the *e.* saw me.
29. 15, I was *e.* to the blind.
31. 16, caused *e.* of widow to fail.
Ps. 11. 4, his *e.* try children of men.
15. 4, in whose *e.* a vile person.
19. 8, enlightening the *e.*
33. 18, *e.* of Lord on them that fear him.
34. 15; 1 Pet. 3. 12, *e.* of Lord on the righteous.
36. 1, no fear of God before his *e.*
69. 3; 119. 82, 123; Lam. 2. 11, mine *e.* fail.
77. 4, holdest mine *e.* waking.
116. 8, delivered mine *e.* from tears.
119. 18, open mine *e.*
132. 4, not give sleep to mine *e.*
Prov. 10. 26, as smoke to the *e.*
20. 12, the seeing *e.*
22. 9, a bountiful *e.*
23. 29, redness of *e.*
27. 20, the *e.* of man never satisfied.
30. 17, the *e.* that mocketh.
Eccl. 1. 8, *e.* is not satisfied with seeing.
2. 14, wise man's *e.* are in his head.
6. 9, better sight of *e.* than wandering of desire.
11. 7, for the *e.* to behold the sun.
Isa. 1. 15, I will hide mine *e.* from you.
29. 10, the Lord hath closed *e.*
33. 17, thine *e.* shall see the king in his beauty.
40. 26; Jer. 13. 20, lift up your *e.* on high.
Jer. 5. 21; Ezek. 12. 2, have *e.* and see not.
9. 1, mine *e.* a fountain of tears.
13. 17, mine *e.* shall weep sore.
14. 17, let mine *e.* run down with tears.
24. 6, set mine *e.* upon them for good.
Lam. 2. 18, let not apple of *e.* cease.
Ezek. 24. 16, 25, the desire of thine *e.*
Hab. 1. 13, of purer *e.* than to behold evil.
Mat. 5. 29, if right *e.* offend thee.
13. 16, blessed are your *e.*
18. 9; Mk. 9. 47, to enter with one *e.*
Mk. 8. 18, having *e.*, see ye not?
Lu. 1. 2, from beginning were *e.* witnesses.
24. 16, their *e.* were holden.
John 11. 37, could not this man, which opened *e.*
Gal. 4. 15, have plucked out your *e.*
Eph. 1. 18, the *e.* of your understanding.
2 Pet. 2. 14, having *e.* full of adultery.
1 John 2. 16, the lust of the *e.*
See Deu. 11. 12; Ez. 5. 5; Ps. 32. 8; Prov. 3. 7; 12.

15; 15. 3; 16. 2; 21. 2; Mat. 20. 33; John 10. 21; 1 Pet. 3. 12.
Eyeservice, service performed only when under supervision. Eph. 6. 6; Col. 3. 22, not with *e.* as menpleasers.
Ezar, ē'-zăr, 'treasure'(?). 1 Chr. 1. 38. R. V. Ezer.
Ezbai, ĕz'-băi. 1 Chr. 11. 37.
Ezbon, ĕz'-bŏn. Gen. 46. 16.
Ezekias, ĕz-ē-kī'-ăs, same as HEZEKIAH. Mat. 1. 9.
Ezekiel, ē-zēk'-ĭĕl, 'God will strengthen.' Ezek. 1. 3.
sent to house of Israel. Ezek. 2.; 3.; 33. 7.
his visions of God's glory. Ezek. 1.; 8.; 10.; 11. 22.
of the Jews' abominations, &c. Ezek. 8. 5.
their punishment. Ezek. 9.; 11.
of the resurrection of dry bones. Ezek. 37.
his vision of the measuring of the temple. Ezek. 40.
intercedes for Israel. Ezek. 9. 8; 11. 13.
his dumbness. Ezek. 3. 26; 24. 26; 33. 22.
his parables. Ezek. 15.; 16.; 17.; 19.; 23.; 24.
exhorts Israel against idols. Ezek. 14. 1; 20. 1.; 33. 30.
rehearses Israel's rebellions, Ezek. 20. and the sins of the rulers and people of Jerusalem, 22.; 23.; 24.
predicts Israel's and the nations' doom. Ezek. 21.; 25.
Ezel, ē'-zĕl, 'departure'(?). 1 Sam. 20. 19.
Ezem, ē'-zĕm, 'bone.' 1 Chr. 4. 29.
Ezer, ē'-zĕr. (1) 'treasure.' Gen. 36. 21.
(2) 'help.' 1 Chr. 4. 4.
Ezion-gaber, *or* **Ezion-geber**, ē'-zĭ-ŏn-gā'-bĕr, ē'-zĭ-ŏn-gē'-bĕr, 'the backbone of a giant,' on the Red Sea. Num. 33. 35; 1 Kn. 9. 26.
Eznite, ĕz'-nīte. 2 Sam. 23. 8.
Ezra, ĕz'-ră, 'help.' (1) scribe, goes up from Babylon to Jerusalem. Ez. 7. 1; 8. 1.
his commission from Artaxerxes to rebuild the temple. Ez. 7. 11.
fast ordered by. Ez. 8. 21.
reproves the people. Ez. 10. 9.
reads the book of the law. Neh. 8.
reforms corruptions. Ez. 10.; Neh. 13.
(2) 1 Chr. 4. 17.
Ezrahite, ĕz'-ră-hīte, a descendant of Zerah. 1 Kn. 4. 31.
Ezri, ĕz'-rī, 'my help.' 1 Chr. 27. 26.

Fables. 1 Tim. 1. 4; 4. 7; 2 Tim. 4. 4; Tit. 1. 14; 2 Pet. 1. 16.
Face. Gen. 4. 14, from thy *f.* shall I be hid.
32. 30, I have seen God *f.* to *f.*
Ex. 33. 11, Lord spake to Moses *f.* to *f.*
34. 29, skin of *f.* shone.
34. 33; 2 Cor. 3. 13, put vail on *f.*
Lev. 19. 32, shall honour the *f.* of the old man.
Deu. 25. 9, spit in his *f.*, saying.
1 Sam. 5. 3, Dagon was fallen on his *f.*
2 Kn. 4. 29, 31, lay staff on *f.* of child.
14. 8, let us look one another in *f.*
Ez. 9. 7; Dan. 9. 8, confusion of *f.*
Neh. 8. 6, worshipped with *f.* to ground.
Job 1. 11; 2. 5, curse thee to thy *f.*
4. 15, spirit passed before my *f.*
13. 24; Ps. 44. 24; 88. 14, wherefore hidest thou thy *f.*?
Ps. 13. 1, how long wilt thou hide thy *f.*
27. 9; 69. 17; 102. 2; 143. 7, hide not thy *f.*
34. 5, *f.* not ashamed.
84. 9, look upon *f.* of anointed.
Prov. 27. 19, in water *f.* answereth to *f.*
Eccl. 8. 1, wisdom maketh *f.* to shine.
Isa. 3. 15, ye grind *f.* of the poor.
25. 8, wipe tears from off all *f.*
50. 7, set my *f.* like flint.
59. 2, sins have hid his *f.* from you.
Jer. 2. 27, turned their back, and not *f.*
5. 3, their *f.* harder than a rock.
30. 6, all *f.* turned into paleness.
Dan. 10. 6, *f.* as appearance of lightning.
Hos. 5. 5, testifieth to his *f.*
Mat. 6. 17, wash thy *f.*
Mat. 11. 10; Mk. 1. 2; Lu. 7. 27, messenger before *f.*
16. 3; Lu. 12. 56, discern *f.* of sky.
17. 2, his *f.* did shine as sun.
18. 10, angels behold *f.* of my Father.
Lu. 2. 31, before *f.* of all people.
9. 51, 53, set his *f.* to Jerusalem.
22. 64, struck him on *f.*
1 Cor. 13. 12, then *f.* to *f.*
2 Cor. 3. 18, all, with open *f.*
Gal. 1. 22, I was unknown by *f.*
2. 11, withstood him to the *f.*
Jas. 1. 23, beholding *f.* in glass.
Rev. 20. 11, from whose *f.* earth fled away.
See 1 Kn. 19. 13; Dan. 1. 10; Acts 6. 15; 20. 25.
Face of GOD hidden from them that do evil. Ps. 34. 16; Isa. 59. 2; Ezek. 39. 23.
to be sought. 2 Chr. 7. 14; Ps. 31. 16; 80. 3; Dan. 9. 17.
seen by Jacob. Gen. 32. 30.
Fade. Isa. 1. 30, whose leaf *f.*
24. 4, earth mourneth and *f.*, the world *f.*
40. 7, the flower *f.*
64. 6, all *f.* as a leaf.
Jer. 8. 13, and the leaf shall *f.*
Ezek. 47. 12, whose leaf shall not *f.* R. V. wither.
Jas. 1. 11, rich man shall *f.* away.
1 Pet. 1. 4; 5. 4, inheritance that *f.* not away.
See 2 Sam. 22. 46; Ps. 18. 45; Isa. 28. 1.
Fail. Gen. 47. 16, if money *f.*
Deu. 28. 32, thine eyes shall *f.* with longing.
Jos. 21. 45; 23. 14; 1 Kn. 8. 56, there *f.* not any good thing.
1 Sam. 17. 32, let no man's heart *f.* him.
1 Kn. 2. 4; 8. 25, shall not *f.* a man on throne.
17. 14, neither shall cruse of oil *f.*
Ez. 4. 22, take heed that ye *f.* not. R. V. be not slack.
Job 14. 11, as waters *f.* from sea.
19. 14, my kinsfolk have *f.*
Ps. 12. 1, the faithful *f.* among men.
31. 10; 38. 10, my strength *f.* me.
77. 8, doth his promise *f.*
89. 33, nor suffer my faithfulness to *f.*
142. 4, refuge *f.* me.
Eccl. 10. 3, his wisdom *f.* him.
12. 5, desire shall *f.*
Isa. 15. 6, the grass *f.*
19. 5, waters shall *f.*
31. 3, they shall all *f.* together.
32. 6, cause drink of thirsty to *f.*
32. 10, the vintage shall *f.*
34. 16, no one of these shall *f.* R. V. be missing.
38. 14, eyes *f.* with looking upward.
41. 17, tongue *f.* for thirst.
59. 15, truth *f.*
Jer. 14. 6, their eyes did *f.*
15. 18, as waters that *f.*
48. 33, I caused wine to *f.* R. V. cease.
Lam. 3. 22, his compassions *f.* not.
4. 17, our eyes as yet *f.*
Ezek. 12. 22, every vision *f.*
Am. 8. 4, make poor of land to *f.*
Hab. 3. 17, labour of olive shall *f.*
Lu. 12. 33, treasure that *f.* not.
16. 9, when ye *f.* they may receive you.
16. 17, one tittle of law *f.* R. V. fall.
21. 26, hearts *f.* them for fear. R. V. men fainting.
22. 32, that thy faith *f.* not.
1 Cor. 13. 8, charity never *f.* R. V. be done away.
Heb. 1. 12, thy years shall not *f.*
11. 32, time would *f.* me to tell.
12. 15, lest any man *f.* of grace of God. R. V. falleth short.
See Deu. 31. 6; Ps. 40. 12; 143. 7; Isa. 44. 12.
Fain (*a.*), glad. 1 Mac. 6. 54.
Fain (*adv.*), gladly, with longing. Job 27. 22; Lu. 15. 16.
Faint. Gen. 25. 29, 30, came from field, and he was *f.*
45. 26, Jacob's heart *f.*
Jud. 8. 4, *f.* yet pursuing.
Job 4. 5, now it is come, and thou *f.*
Ps. 27. 13, I had *f.*, unless I had believed.
107. 5, their soul *f.* in them.
Prov. 24. 10, if thou *f.* in day of adversity.
Isa. 1. 5, whole heart *f.*
10. 18, as when a standardbearer *f.*

Isa. 40. 28, Creator of earth *f.* not.
40. 29, giveth power to the *f.*
40. 30; Am. 8. 13, even youths shall *f.*
40. 31, walk, and not *f.*
44. 12, he drinketh no water, and is *f.*
Jer. 8. 18; Lam. 1. 22; 5. 17, my heart is *f.*
Mat. 15. 32; Mk. 8. 3, lest they *f.* by the way.
Lu. 18. 1, pray, and not to *f.* [not.
2 Cor. 4. 1, 16, as we have received mercy, we *f.*
Gal. 6. 9, reap, if we *f.* not.
Heb. 12. 3, wearied and *f.* in your minds.
12. 5, nor *f.* when thou art rebuked.
See Deu. 20. 8; Ps. 84. 2; 119. 81; Mat. 9. 36.

Fair. Job 37. 22, *f.* weather out of the north. R. V. golden splendour.
Ps. 45. 2, *f.* than children of men.
Prov. 11. 22, a *f.* woman without discretion.
26. 25, when he speaketh *f.*, believe not.
S. of S. 1. 8; 5. 9; 6. 1, thou *f.* among women.
6. 10, *f.* as the moon.
Isa. 5. 9, houses great and *f.*
Jer. 4. 30, in vain shalt thou make thyself *f.*
12. 6, though they speak *f.* words.
Dan. 1. 15, their countenances appeared *f.*
Mat. 16. 2, it will be *f.* weather.
Acts 7. 20, Moses was exceeding *f.*
Rom. 16. 18, by *f.* speeches deceive.
See Gen. 6. 2; Isa. 54. 11; Ezek. 27. 12.

Fair Havens, a harbour on the S. coast of Crete. One of the stations on Paul's journey to Rome. Acts 27. 8.

Faith. Deu. 32. 20, children in whom is no *f.*
Mat. 6. 30; 8. 26; 14. 31; 16. 8; Lu. 12. 28, ye of little *f.*
8. 10; Lu. 7. 9, so great *f.*
9. 2; Mk. 2. 5; Lu. 5. 20, seeing their *f.*
9. 22; Mk. 5. 34; 10. 52; Lu. 8. 48; 17. 19, thy *f.* hath made thee whole.
9. 29, according to your *f.*
15. 28, great is thy *f.*
17. 20, *f.* as a grain of mustard seed.
21. 21, if ye have *f.*, ye shall not only do this.
23. 23, omitted judgment, mercy, and *f.*
Mk. 4. 40, how is it ye have no *f.*?
11. 22, have *f.* in God.
Lu. 7. 50, thy *f.* hath saved thee.
8. 25, where is your *f.*?
17. 5, increase our *f.*
18. 8, shall he find *f.* on the earth?
22. 32, that thy *f.* fail not.
Acts 3. 16, the *f.* which is by him.
6. 5; 11. 24, a man full of *f.*
14. 9, perceiving he had *f.* to be healed.
14. 27, opened the door of *f.*
15. 9, purifying their hearts by *f.*
16. 5, established in the *f.*
26. 18, sanctified by *f.*
Rom. 1. 5, grace for obedience to *f.*
1. 17, revealed from *f.* to *f.*
3. 27, boasting excluded by *f.*
3. 28; 5. 1; Gal. 2. 16; 3. 24, justified by *f.*
4. 5, *f.* counted for righteousness.
4. 16, it is of *f.*, which is of the *f.* of Abraham.
19. 20, being not weak in *f.*
5. 2, we have access by *f.*
10. 8, the word of *f.*, which we preach.
10. 17, *f.* cometh by hearing.
12. 3, the measure of *f.*
12. 6, prophesy according to proportion of *f.*
14. 1, weak in *f.* receive ye.
14. 22, hast thou *f.*?
14. 23, what is not of *f.* is sin.
1 Cor. 2. 5, your *f.* should not stand in wisdom.
13. 2, though I have all *f.*
13. 13, now abideth *f.*
15. 14, and your *f.* is also vain.
16. 13, stand fast in the *f.*
2 Cor. 1. 24, not have dominion over *f.*
4. 13, same spirit of *f.*
5. 7, we walk by *f.*
13. 5, examine whether ye be in the *f.*
Gal. 2. 20, I live by the *f.* of Son of God.
3. 2, by the hearing of *f.*
3. 12, law is not of *f.*
3. 23, before *f.* came.
5. 6, *f.* which worketh by love.
6. 10, the household of *f.*
Eph. 3. 12, access by *f.* of him.
3. 17, dwell in your hearts by *f.*
4. 5, one Lord, one *f.*
4. 13, in the unity of the *f.*
6. 16, the shield of *f.*
Phil. 1. 27, striving together for the *f.* of the gospel.
Col. 1. 23, if ye continue in the *f.*
2. 5, the stedfastness of your *f.*
1 Thes. 1. 3; 2 Thes. 1. 11, your work of *f.*
5. 8, the breastplate of *f.*
2 Thes. 3. 2, all men have not *f.*
1 Tim. 1. 2; Tit. 1. 4, my own son in the *f.*
1. 5; 2 Tim. 1. 5, *f.* unfeigned.
2. 15, if they continue in *f.*
3. 13, great boldness in the *f.*
4. 1, shall depart from the *f.*
5. 8, he hath denied the *f.*
6. 10, 21, erred from the *f.*
6. 12, fight the good fight of *f.*
2 Tim. 3. 8, reprobate concerning the *f.*
4. 7, I have kept the *f.*
Tit. 1. 1, the *f.* of God's elect.
Heb. 4. 2, not being mixed with *f.*
6. 1, not laying again the foundation of *f.*
6. 12, through *f.* inherit the promises.
10. 22, in full assurance of *f.*
11. 1, *f.* is substance of things hoped for.
11. 4, 5, 7-9, &c., by *f.* Abel, &c.
11. 6, without *f.* it is impossible.
11. 13, these all died in *f.*
11. 33, through *f.* subdued kingdoms.
11. 39, a good report through *f.*
12. 2, author and finisher of our *f.*
13. 7, whose *f.* follow.
Jas. 1. 3; 1 Pet. 1. 7, the trying of your *f.*
1. 6, let them ask in *f.*
2. 1, have not *f.* with respect of persons.
2. 5, rich in *f.*
2. 14, man say he hath *f.*, can *f.* save him?
2. 17, *f.* without works is dead.
2. 18, thou hast *f.*, and I have works.
2. 22, *f.* wrought with his works.
5. 15, the prayer of *f.* shall save.
1 Pet. 1. 9, the end of your *f.*
5. 9, resist stedfast in the *f.*
2 Pet. 1. 1, like precious *f.*
1. 5, add to your *f.* virtue.
1 John 5. 4, overcometh the world, even our *f.*
Jude 3, earnestly contend for the *f.*
20, your most holy *f.*
Rev. 2. 13, hast not denied my *f.*
2. 19, I know thy works and *f.*
13. 10, patience and *f.* of the saints.
14. 12, they that keep the *f.* of Jesus.

Faith, Heb. 11. justification by, Rom. 3. 28; 5. 1, 16; Gal. 2. 16. Purification by, Acts 15. 9. Sanctification by, Acts 26. 18.
object of, Father, Son, and Holy Ghost. Mk. 11. 22; John 6. 29; 14. 1; 20. 31; Acts 20. 21; 2 Cor. 13. 14.
given by the Spirit. 1 Cor. 2. 5; 12. 9.
in Christ. Acts 8. 12; 2 Tim. 3. 15.
unity of. Eph. 4. 5, 13; Jude 3.
leads to salvation, &c. Mk. 16. 16; John 1. 12; 3. 16, 36; 6. 40, 47; Acts 16. 31; Gal. 3. 11; Eph. 2. 8; Heb. 11. 6; 1 Pet. 1. 9; 1 John 5. 10.
works by love. 1 Cor. 13.; Gal. 5. 6; Col. 1. 4; 1 Thes. 1. 3; 1 Tim. 1. 5; Philem. 5; Heb. 10. 23; 1 Pet. 1. 22; 1 John 3. 14, 23.
without works is dead. Jas. 2. 17, 20.
produces peace, joy, hope in believing. Rom. 5. 1; 15. 13; 2 Cor. 4. 13; 1 Pet. 1. 8.
excludes boasting, &c. Rom. 3. 27; 4. 2; 1 Cor. 1. 29; Eph. 2. 9.
blessings received through. Mk. 16. 16; John 6. 40; 12. 36; 20. 31; Acts 10. 43; 16. 31; 26. 18; Rom. 1. 17 (Hab. 2. 4); Rom. 3. 21; 4. 16; 5. 1; 2 Cor. 5. 7; Gal. 2. 16; 3. 14, 26; Eph. 1. 13; 3. 12,

17; 1 Tim. 1. 4; Heb. 4. 3; 6. 12; 10. 38; 1 Pet. 1. 5; Jude 20.
miracles performed through. Mat. 9. 22; Lu. 8. 50; Acts 3. 16.
power of. Mat. 17. 20; Mk. 9. 23; 11. 23; Lu. 17. 6.
trial of. 2 Thes. 1. 4; Heb. 11. 17; Jas. 1. 3, 12; 1 Pet. 1. 7.
overcometh the world. 1 John 5. 4.
shield of the Christian. Eph. 6. 16; 1 Thes. 5. 8.
contend earnestly for the. Jude 3.
exhortations to continue in. 1 Cor. 16. 13; 2 Cor. 13. 5; Eph. 6. 16; Phil. 1. 27; Col. 1. 23; 2. 7; 1 Thes. 5. 8; 1 Tim. 1. 19; 4. 12; 6. 11; 2 Tim. 2. 22; Tit. 1. 13; Heb. 10. 22.
examples of: Caleb, Num. 13. 30. Shadrach, Meshach, and Abed-nego, Dan. 3. 17. Daniel, Dan. 6. 10. Ninevites, Jon. 3. 5. Peter, Mat. 16. 16. Nathanael, John 1. 49. Martha, John 11. 27. Stephen, Acts 6. 5. Ethiopian eunuch, Acts 8. 37. Barnabas, Acts 11. 24.

Faithful. 2 Sam. 20. 19, one of them that are *f.* in Israel.
Neh. 7. 2, a *f.* man, and feared God.
9. 8, his heart *f.* before thee.
13. 13, counted *f.* to distribute.
Ps. 12. 1, the *f.* fail among men.
89. 37, a *f.* witness in heaven.
101. 6, the *f.* of the land.
119. 86, commandments *f.*
119. 138, testimonies *f.* R. V. faithfulness.
Prov. 11. 13, *f.* spirit concealeth.
13. 17, *f.* ambassador is health.
14. 5; Isa. 8. 2; Jer. 42. 5, a *f.* witness.
20. 6, a *f.* man who can find?
25. 13, as snow in harvest, so is a *f.* messenger.
27. 6, *f.* are wounds of a friend.
28. 20, *f.* man shall abound.
Isa. 1. 21, 26, *f.* city.
Mat. 24. 45; Lu. 12. 42, who is a *f.* and wise servant?
25. 21, good and *f.* servant.
25. 23; Lu. 19. 17, *f.* in a few things.
Lu. 16. 10, *f.* in least *f.* in much.
Acts 16. 15, if ye have judged me *f.*
1 Cor. 4. 2, required in stewards that a man be *f.*
4. 17, Timothy *f.* in the Lord.
Gal. 3. 9, blessed with *f.* Abraham.
Eph. 6. 21; Col. 1. 7; 4. 7, a *f.* minister.
1 Thes. 5. 24, *f.* is he that calleth you.
2 Thes. 3. 3, Lord is *f.*, who shall stablish you.
1 Tim. 1. 15; 4. 9; 2 Tim. 2. 11; Tit. 3. 8, a *f.* saying.
3. 11, wives *f.* in all things.
2 Tim. 2. 2, commit to *f.* men.
2. 13, yet he abideth *f.*
Heb. 2. 17, a *f.* high priest.
3. 2, *f.* to him that appointed him.
10. 23; 11. 11, he is *f.* that promised.
1 Pet. 4. 19, as unto a *f.* Creator.
1 John 1. 9, he is *f.* and just to forgive.
Rev. 1. 5; 3. 14, the *f.* witness.
2. 10, be thou *f.* unto death.
2. 13, my *f.* martyr.
17. 14, called, and chosen, and *f.*
21. 5; 22. 6, these words are true and *f.*

Faithfully. 2 Chr. 19. 9; 34. 12; Jer. 23. 28; 3 John 5.

Faithfulness. Ps. 5. 9, no *f.* in their mouths.
36. 5, thy *f.* reacheth unto the clouds.
40. 10; 88. 11, declared thy *f.*
89. 33, nor suffer my *f.* to fail.
92. 2, shew forth thy *f.* every night.
Isa. 11. 5, *f.* the girdle of his reins.
Lam. 3. 23, great is thy *f.*

Faithfulness commended in the service of God. 2 Kn. 12. 15; 2 Chr. 31. 12; Mat. 24. 45; 2 Cor. 2. 17; 4. 2; 3 John 5.
towards men. Deu. 1. 16; 1 Sam. 26. 23; Ps. 141. 5; Prov. 11. 13; 13. 17; 14. 5; 20. 6; 25. 13; 27. 6; 28. 20; Lu. 16. 10; 1 Cor. 4. 2; 1 Tim. 3. 11; 6. 2; Tit. 2. 10.
of Abraham. Gen. 22.; Gal. 3. 9.
of Joseph. Gen. 39. 4, 22.
of Moses. Num. 12. 7; Heb. 3. 5.
of David. 1 Sam. 22. 14.
of Daniel. Dan. 6. 4.
of Paul. Acts 20. 20.
of Timothy. 1 Cor. 4. 17.
of God. Deu. 7. 9; Ps. 36. 5; 40. 10; 88. 11; 89. 1; 92. 2; 119. 75; 143. 1; Isa. 25. 1; Lam. 3. 23.

Faithless. Mat. 17. 17; Mk. 9. 19; Lu. 9. 41; John 20. 27.

Fall (*n.*). Prov. 16. 18, haughty spirit before a *f.*
Mat. 7. 27, great was the *f.* of it.
Lu. 2. 34, set for the rise and *f.* of many.
Rom. 11. 12, if the *f.* of them be the riches.
See Jer. 49. 21; Ezek. 26. 15; 31. 16; 32. 10.

Fall (*v.*). Gen. 45. 24, see ye *f.* not out by the way.
Lev. 25. 35, thy brother be *f.* in decay. R. V. his hand fail.
1 Sam. 3. 19, let none of his words *f.*
2 Sam. 1. 19, 25, 27, how are the mighty *f.*
3. 38, great man *f.* this day.
24. 14; 1 Chr. 21. 13, *f.* into hands of God.
2 Kn. 14. 10, why meddle that thou shouldest *f.*?
Job 4. 13; 33. 15, deep sleep *f.* on men.
Ps. 5. 10, let them *f.* by their own counsels.
7. 15, is *f.* into ditch.
16. 6, lines *f.* in pleasant places.
37. 24, though he *f.*, not utterly cast down.
56. 13; 116. 8, deliver my feet from *f.*
72. 11, kings shall *f.* down before him.
91. 7, a thousand shall *f.* at thy side.
Prov. 10. 8, 10, a prating fool shall *f.*
11. 14, where no counsel is, the people *f.*
11. 28, he that trusteth in riches shall *f.*
13. 17; 17. 20, *f.* into mischief.
24. 16, just man *f.* seven times.
24. 17, rejoice not when thine enemy *f.*
26. 27; Eccl. 10. 8, diggeth a pit shall *f.* therein.
Eccl. 4. 10, woe to him that is alone when he *f.*
11. 3, where the tree *f.*, there it shall be.
Isa. 14. 12, how art thou *f.*!
34. 4, as the leaf *f.* from the vine. R. V. fadeth.
40. 30, the young men shall utterly *f.*
Jer. 49. 26; 50. 30, young men *f.* in her streets.
Ezek. 24. 6, let no lot *f.* on it.
Dan. 3. 5; 11. 26; Mat. 4. 9, *f.* down and worship.
Hos. 10. 8; Lu. 23. 30; Rev. 6. 16, say to hills, *f.* on us.
Mic. 7. 8, when I *f.*
Zec. 11. 2, the cedar is *f.*
Mat. 10. 29, sparrow *f.* on ground.
12. 11, *f.* into pit on sabbath day.
15. 14; Lu. 6. 39, both *f.* into the ditch.
21. 44; Lu. 20. 18, *f.* on this stone.
24. 29; Mk. 13. 25, stars *f.* from heaven.
Lu. 8. 13, in time of temptation *f.* away.
10. 18, Satan as lightning *f.* from heaven.
Rom. 14. 4, to his master he standeth or *f.*
14. 13, occasion to *f.*
1 Cor. 10. 12, take heed lest he *f.*
15. 6, 18, some are *f.* asleep.
Gal. 5. 4, ye are *f.* from grace.
1 Tim. 3. 6, *f.* into the condemnation.
3. 7, lest he *f.* into reproach.
6. 9, rich *f.* into temptation.
Heb. 4. 11, lest any *f.* after same example.
6. 6, if they *f.* away.
10. 31, to *f.* into hands of living God.
Jas. 1. 2, joy when ye *f.* into temptation.
1. 11; 1 Pet. 1. 24, flower thereof *f.*
5. 12, lest ye *f.* into condemnation.
2 Pet. 1. 10, ye shall never *f.* R. V. stumble.
3. 17, lest ye *f.* from stedfastness.
See Isa. 21. 9; Lam. 5. 16; Rev. 14. 8; 18. 2.

Fall of Adam and Eve. Gen. 3. *See* Adam.
sin and death caused by. Gen. 3. 19; Rom. 5. 12; 1 Cor. 15. 21.

Falling. Job 4. 4; 2 Thes. 2. 3; Jude 24.

Fallow. Jer. 4. 3; Hos. 10. 12.

False. Ex. 20. 16; Deu. 5. 20; Mat. 19. 18, shalt not bear *f.* witness.
23. 1, shalt not raise a *f.* report.
2 Kn. 9. 12, it is *f.*, tell us now.

Ps. 119. 104, 128, I hate every *f.* way.
120. 3, thou *f.* tongue. R. V. deceitful.
Prov. 6. 19; 12. 17; 14. 5; 19. 5; 21. 28; 25. 18, a *f.* witness.
11. 1; 20. 23, a *f.* balance.
Mat. 15. 19, out of heart proceed *f.* witness.
24. 24; Mk. 13. 22, *f.* Christs and *f.* prophets.
26. 59, 60; Mk. 14. 56, 57, *f.* witness against Christ.
Mk. 13. 22, *f.* prophets shall rise.
Lu. 19. 8, any thing by *f.* accusation. R. V. wrongfully.
1 Cor. 15. 15; found *f.* witnesses of God.
2 Cor. 11. 13, such are *f.* apostles.
11. 26, perils among *f.* brethren.
2 Tim. 3. 3; Tit. 2. 3, *f.* accusers.
See Gal. 2. 4; 2 Pet. 2. 1; 1 John 4. 1.

Falsehood. Job 21. 34. in answers remaineth *f.*
Ps. 7. 14, hath brought forth *f.*
144. 8, 11, right hand of *f.*
Isa. 28. 15, under *f.* have we hid ourselves.
57. 4, a seed of *f.*
59. 13, words of *f.*
Mic. 2. 11, walking in the spirit and *f.*
See 2 Sam. 18. 13; Jer. 13. 25; Hos. 7. 1.

Falsely. Lev. 6. 3, 5; 19. 12; Jer. 5. 2; 7. 9; Zec. 5. 4, swear *f.*
Jer. 5. 31; 29. 9, prophets prophesy *f.*
Mat. 5. 11, evil *f.*, for my sake.
1 Tim. 6. 20, science *f.* so called.
See Jer. 43. 2; Lu. 3. 14; 1 Pet. 3. 16.

False witnesses condemned. *See* WITNESSES.

Fame. Jos. 9. 9, we heard the *f.* of God.
1 Kn. 10. 1; 2 Chr. 9. 1, *f.* of Solomon.
Zep. 3. 19, get them *f.* in every land. R. V. a name.
Mat. 4. 24; Mk. 1. 28; Lu. 4. 14, 37; 5. 15, *f.* of Jesus.
9. 31, spread abroad his *f.*
14. 1, Herod heard of the *f.*
See Gen. 45. 16; Num. 14. 15; Job 28. 22; Isa. 66. 19.

Familiar. Job 19. 14; Ps. 41. 9; Jer. 20. 10.

Familiar spirits, possessors of, to die. Lev. 20. 27.
not to be sought after. Lev. 19. 31; Isa. 8. 19.
Saul destroys, 1 Sam. 28. 3. in his distress enquires of one remaining, 1 Sam. 28. 7. his punishment, 1 Chr. 10. 13, 14.
Manasseh deals with. 2 Kn. 21. 6.
Paul casts out. Acts 16.

Family. Gen. 12. 3; 28. 14, in thee all *f.* be blessed.
Lev. 25. 10, return every man to his *f.*
Deu. 29. 18, lest a *f.* turn away from God.
1 Sam. 9. 21, my *f.* the least.
18. 18, what is my father's *f.*?
1 Chr. 4. 38, princes in their *f.*
Ps. 68. 6, setteth the solitary in *f.*
Jer. 3. 14, one of a city, and two of a *f.*
10. 25, on *f.* that call not.
31. 1, God of all the *f.* of Israel.
Zec. 12. 12, every *f.* apart.
Eph. 3. 15, whole *f.* in heaven and earth.
See Num. 27. 4; Jud. 1. 25; Am. 3. 2.

Famine. 2 Sam. 21. 1, a *f.* in days of David.
1 Kn. 8. 37; 2 Chr. 20. 9, if there be *f.*
18. 2; 2 Kn. 6. 25, sore *f.* in Samaria.
2 Kn. 8. 1, the Lord hath called for a *f.*
Job 5. 20, in *f.* he shall redeem thee.
5. 22, at *f.* thou shalt laugh.
Ps. 33. 19, to keep them alive in *f.*
37. 19, in the days of *f.* shall be satisfied.
Jer. 24. 10; 29. 17, will send *f.* among them.
42. 16, *f.* shall follow close.
Lam. 5. 10, black because of *f.*
Ezek. 5. 16, evil arrows of *f.*
36. 29, I will lay no *f.* upon you.
Am. 8. 11, a *f.*, not of bread.
Mat. 24. 7; Mk. 13. 8; Lu. 21. 11, *f.* in divers places.
See Lu. 15. 14; Rom. 8. 35.

Famine threatened. Jer. 14. 15; 15. 2; Ezek. 5. 12; 6. 11; Mat. 24. 7; Acts 11. 28.
described. Jer. 14.; Lam. 4.; Joel 1.
occurs in Canaan, Gen. 12. Egypt, Gen. 41.; 47. 13. Israel, Ru. 1. 1; 2 Sam. 21. 1; 1 Kn. 18. 2; 2 Kn. 6. 25; 7.; Lu. 4. 25.
Shunammite forewarned of. 2 Kn. 8. 1.
king of Egypt warned of, by Joseph. Gen. 40.
(of God's word). Am. 8. 11.

Famish. Gen. 41. 55; Prov. 10. 3; Isa. 5. 13; Zep. 2. 11.

Famous. Ru. 4. 11, 14; 1 Chr. 5. 24; Ps. 74. 5; Ezek. 23. 10.

Fan, a winnowing-fan. Isa. 30. 24; Jer. 15. 7; 51. 2; Mat. 3. 12.

Fanners, winnowers. Jer. 51. 2.

Far. Gen. 18. 25; 1 Sam. 20. 9, that be *f.* from thee.
Deu. 12. 21; 14. 24, if place too *f.* from thee.
Jud. 19. 11; Mk. 6. 35; Lu. 24. 29, day *f.* spent.
1 Sam. 2. 30; 22. 15; 2 Sam. 20. 20; 23. 17, be it *f.* from me.
Job 5. 4, children *f.* from safety.
11. 14; 22. 23, put iniquity *f.* away.
19. 13, put my brethren *f.* from me.
34. 10, *f.* be it from God to do wickedness.
Ps. 10. 5, thy judgments are *f.* out of sight.
22. 11; 35. 22; 38. 21; 71. 12, be not *f.* from me.
97. 9, *f.* above all gods.
103. 12, *f.* as east from west.
Prov. 31. 10, *f.* above rubies.
Isa. 43. 6; 60. 4, 9, sons from *f.*
46. 12, *f.* from righteousness.
57. 19, peace to him that is *f.* off.
Am. 6. 3, put *f.* away evil day.
Mat. 16. 22, be it *f.* from thee, Lord.
Mk. 12. 34, not *f.* from the kingdom.
13. 34, as a man taking a *f.* journey. R. V. sojourning in another country.
John 21. 8, they were not *f.* from land.
Acts 17. 27, not *f.* from every one of us.
Rom. 13. 12, the night is *f.* spent.
2 Cor. 4. 17, a *f.* more exceeding. R. V. more and more exceedingly.
Eph. 1. 21, *f.* above all principality.
2. 13, *f.* off made nigh.
4. 10, *f.* above all heavens.
Phil. 1. 23, which is *f.* better.
Heb. 7. 15, it is yet *f.* more evident. R. V. more abundantly.
See Isa. 33. 17; Mat. 15. 8; Mk. 8. 3.

Fare. 1 Sam. 17. 18; Jon. 1. 3; Lu. 16. 19.

Farewell. Lu. 9. 61; Acts 18. 21; 2 Cor. 13. 11.

Farm. Mat. 22. 5.

Farthing. (1) Lat. *quadrans:* Gk. *kodrantes* = ¼ farthing = ½ cent. Mat. 5. 26; Mk. 12. 42.
(2) Gk. *assarion* = ¼ penny = 1 cent. Mat. 10. 29; Lu. 12. 6. *See* MONEY.

Fashion. Job 10. 8; Ps. 119. 73, thine hands have *f.* me.
31. 15, did not one *f.* us?
Ps. 33. 15, he *f.* hearts alike.
139. 16, in continuance were *f.*
Isa. 45. 9, say to him that *f.* it.
Mk. 2. 12, never saw it on this *f.*
Lu. 9. 29, the *f.* of his countenance.
1 Cor. 7. 31, the *f.* of this world passeth.
Phil. 2. 8, found in *f.* as a man.
See Gen. 6. 15; Ex. 32. 4; Ezek. 42. 11; Jas. 1. 11.

Fast. (1) 2 Sam. 12. 23, he is dead, wherefore should I *f.*?
Isa. 58. 3, why have we *f.*, and thou seest not?
58. 4, ye *f.* for strife.
58. 5, wilt thou call this a *f.*?
58. 6, is not this the *f.* that I have chosen?
Joel 1. 14, sanctify a *f.*
Zec. 7. 5, did ye at all *f.* unto me?
Mat. 6. 16, when ye *f.*, be not.
6. 18, appear not to *f.*
Mk. 2. 19, can children of bridechamber *f.*?
Lu. 18. 12, I *f.* twice in the week.
(2) Ps. 33. 9, he commanded, and it stood *f.*
65. 6, setteth *f.* the mountains.
(3) close, near. Ru. 2. 8, abide here *f.* by.

Fast proclaimed. Lev. 23. 27, 29; 2 Chr. 20. 3; Ez. 8. 21; Neh. 9.; Esth. 4. 16; Joel 2. 15; Jon. 3. 5.
season of, referred to. Acts 27. 9.
the true and the false. Isa. 58.; Zec. 7.; Mat. 6. 16.

Fasten. Eccl. 12. 11, as nails *f.* by the masters.
Isa. 22. 23, 25, I will *f.* him as a nail.
Lu. 4. 20, eyes of all were *f.* on him.
Acts 11. 6, when I had *f.* mine eyes.
See 1 Sam. 31. 10; Job 38. 6; Acts 3. 4; 28. 3.
Fasting. Ps. 35. 13, I humbled myself with *f.*
109. 24, knees weak through *f.*
Jer. 36. 6, upon the *f.* day.
Mk. 8. 3, send them away *f.*
1 Cor. 7. 5, give yourselves to *f.* and prayer.
2 Cor. 6. 5, in stripes, in *f.*
11. 27, in *f.* oft.
Fasting turned into gladness. Zec. 8. 19.
Christ excuses his disciples for not. Mat. 9. 14; Mk. 2. 18; Lu. 5. 33.
of Moses (twice) for forty days. Ex. 24. 18; 34. 28; Deu. 9. 9, 18.
of David. 2 Sam. 12. 16.
of Elijah. 1 Kn. 19. 8.
other examples. Dan. 6. 18; 9. 3.
of Christ. Mat. 4. 2, &c.
of early Christians. Acts 13. 2; 14. 23.
recommended. 1 Cor. 7. 5.
Fasts. The only fast appointed by the Law was the Day of Atonement on the 10th of Tisri (Lev. 16.), but during the Captivity four annual fasts were observed by the Jews: In the New Testament we have reference to (1) 'the fast,' i. e., the 'Day of Atonement' (Acts 27. 9); (2) the weekly fasts (Mat. 9. 14; Mk. 2. 18; Lu. 5. 33; 18. 12; Acts 10. 30). They seem to have been introduced some time after the Captivity, and were observed not as obligatory but as meritorious acts, especially by Pharisees, on the second and fifth days of the week. The fasts of forty days by Moses (Ex. 24. 18; 34. 28) and by Elijah (1 Kn. 19. 8) are shadows of the great fast of our Lord (Mat. 4. 2; Mk. 1. 12, 13; Lu. 4. 2).
Fat. Gen. 45. 18, shall eat the *f.* of the land.
Gen. 49. 20, his bread shall be *f.*
Deu. 32. 15, Jeshurun waxed *f.*, and kicked.
Neh. 8. 10, eat the *f.*, and drink the sweet.
9. 25, 35, took a *f.* land, and became *f.*
Ps. 17. 10, inclosed in their own *f.*
92. 14, shall be *f.* and flourishing. R. V. full of sap.
119. 70, heart *f.* as grease.
Prov. 11. 25, liberal soul made *f.*
13. 4, soul of diligent made *f.*
15. 30, good report maketh the bones *f.*
Isa. 10. 16, among his *f.* ones leanness.
25. 6, feast of *f.* things.
Hab. 1. 16, by them their portion is *f.*
See Gen. 41. 2; Ex. 29. 13; Lev. 3. 3, 17; 7. 22; Num. 13. 20; Jud. 3. 17.
Fat, vessel for liquor; same as 'vat.' Joel 2. 24.
Father. Gen. 15. 15, go to thy *f.* in peace.
17. 4; Rom. 4. 17, a *f.* of nations.
Ex. 15. 2, he is my *f.* God, I will exalt him.
20. 5; Num. 14. 18, iniquity of *f.* upon children.
21. 15, he that smiteth his *f.*
21. 17; Lev. 20. 9, he that curseth his *f.*
Jud. 17. 10; 18. 19, be to me a *f.* and a priest.
1 Sam. 10. 12, who is their *f.*?
2 Sam. 10. 2; 1 Chr. 19. 2, as his *f.* shewed kindness.
1 Kn. 19. 4, no better than my *f.*
2 Kn. 2. 12; 13. 14, Elisha cried, my *f.*, my *f.*
6. 21, my *f.*, shall I smite them?
1 Chr. 28. 9, know thou the God of thy *f.*
2 Chr. 32. 13, what I and my *f.* have done.
Ez. 7. 27, blessed be the Lord God of our *f.*
Job 29. 16, I was a *f.* to the poor.
31. 18, brought up with me as with a *f.*
38. 28, hath the rain a *f.*
Ps. 27. 10, when my *f.* and mother forsake me.
39. 12, as all my *f.* were.
68. 5, *f.* of fatherless.
95. 9; Heb. 3. 9, your *f.* tempted me.
103. 13, as a *f.* pitieth his children.
Prov. 4. 1, the instruction of a *f.*
4. 3, I was my *f.* son.
10. 1; 15. 20, wise son maketh a glad *f.*
17. 21, the *f.* of a fool hath no joy.
17. 25; 19. 13, foolish son grief to his *f.*
Isa. 9. 6, the everlasting *F.*
49. 23, kings shall be thy nursing *f.*
63. 16; 64. 8, doubtless thou art our *f.*
Jer. 3. 4, wilt thou not cry, my *f.*?
31. 9, I am a *f.* to Israel.
31. 29; Ezek. 18. 2, *f.* have eaten sour grapes.
Ezek. 18. 4, as the soul of the *f.*
22. 7, set light by *f.* and mother.
Mal. 1. 6, if I be a *f.*, where is mine honour?
2. 10, have we not all one *f.*?
Mat. 5. 16, 45, 48, your *F.* in heaven.
6. 8, 32; Lu. 12. 30, your *F.* knoweth.
6. 9; Lu. 11. 2, our *F.* which art in heaven.
7. 21; 12. 50, the will of my *F.*
8. 21; Lu. 9. 59, to go and bury my *f.*
10. 21, *f.* deliver up the child.
10. 37, he that loveth *f.* or mother.
18. 10, behold the face of my *F.*
18. 14, not the will of your *F.*
23. 9, call no man *f.* on earth.
25. 34, ye blessed of my *F.*
Mk. 14. 36; Rom. 8. 15; Gal. 4. 6, Abba, *F.*
Lu. 2. 49, about my *F.* business.
6. 36, as your *F.* is merciful.
11. 11, of any that is a *f.*
12. 32, it is your *F.* good pleasure.
15. 21, *f.*, I have sinned.
16. 27, send him to my *f.* house.
22. 42, *F.*, if thou be willing.
23. 34, *F.*, forgive them.
23. 46, *F.*, into thy hands.
John 1. 14, as of the only begotten of the *F.*
5. 21, as the *F.* raiseth up the dead.
5. 22, the *F.* judgeth no man.
5. 23, even as they honour the *F.*
5. 37; 8. 16; 12. 49; 14. 24, the *F.* which hath sent me.
6. 37, all the *F.* giveth me.
6. 46; 14. 8, 9, hath seen the *F.*
8. 41, we have one *F.*, even God.
8. 44, devil is a liar, and the *f.* of it.
8. 49, I honour my *F.*
10. 15, as the *F.* knoweth me.
10. 29, my *F.* is greater than all.
12. 27, *F.*, save me from this hour.
12. 28, *F.*, glorify thy name.
13. 1, should depart unto the *F.*
14. 6, no man cometh to the *F.*, but by me.
14. 16; 16. 26, I will pray the *F.*
14. 28, I am come from the *F.*
15. 1, my *F.* is the husbandman.
15. 16, whatsoever ye ask of the *F.*
16. 16, because I go to the *F.*
16. 32, the *F.* is with me.
17. 1, *F.*, the hour is come.
20. 17, I ascend to my *F.* and your *F.*
Acts 24. 14, so worship I the God of my *f.*
Rom. 4. 11, the *f.* of all that believe.
1 Cor. 4. 15, yet have ye not many *f.*
2 Cor. 1. 3, *F.* of mercies, God of all comfort.
Gal. 1. 14, zealous of the traditions of my *f.*
4. 2, the time appointed of the *f.*
Eph. 4. 6, one God and *F.* of all.
6. 4, *f.*, provoke not your children.
Phil. 2. 11, to the glory of the *F.*
2. 22, as a son with the *f.*
Col. 1. 19, it pleased the *F.* that in him.
1 Tim. 5. 1, entreat him as a *f.*
Heb. 1. 5, I will be to him a *F.*
7. 3, without *f.*, without mother.
12. 9, the *F.* of spirits.
Jas. 1. 17, the *F.* of lights.
2 Pet. 3. 4, since the *f.* fell asleep.
1 John 1. 3, fellowship with the *F.*
2. 1, an advocate with the *F.*
2. 13, I write unto you, *f.*
2. 15, the love of the *F.* is not in him.
2. 23, hath not the *F.*
3. 1, what manner of love the *F.* hath.
5. 7, the *F.*, the Word, and Holy Ghost.
See 1 Chr. 29. 10; John 5. 26; Acts 1. 4; 15. 10.
Fatherless. Ps. 10. 14, the helper of the *f.*
Prov. 23. 10, the fields of the *f.*

Isa. 1. 23, they judge not the *f.*
10. 2, that they may rob the *f.*
Jer. 49. 11, leave thy *f.* children.
Hos. 14. 3, in thee the *f.* findeth mercy.
Mal. 3. 5, against those that oppress *f.*
Jas. 1. 27, to visit the *f.* and widows.
Fatherless, GOD the God of. Ps. 146. 9; Jer. 49. 11; Hos. 14. 3.
God the helper of. Deu. 10. 18; Ps. 10. 14; 146. 9; father of, Ps. 68. 5.
duty towards. Ex. 22. 22; Deu. 14. 29; 24. 17; Job 31. 17; Prov. 23. 10; Isa. 1. 17; Jer. 7. 6; Jas. 1. 27.
the wicked oppress. Job 6. 27; 22. 9; Ps. 94. 6; Isa. 1. 23; 10. 2; Jer. 5. 28; Ezek. 22. 7.
Fathers, duty of. Deu. 21. 18; Prov. 3. 12; 13. 24; 19. 18; 22. 6, 15; 23. 13; 29. 15, 17; Lu. 11. 11; Eph. 6. 4; Col. 3. 21; Heb. 12. 9.
children to obey. Ex. 20. 12; Prov. 6. 20; Eph. 6. 1; Col. 3. 20.
Fathoms. Acts 27. 28.
Fatlings. 2 Sam. 6. 13; Isa. 11. 6; Mat. 22. 4.
Fatness. Ps. 36. 8, the *f.* of thine house.
63. 5, as with marrow and *f.*
65. 11, thy paths drop *f.*
73. 7, eyes stand out with *f.*
Isa. 55. 2, soul delight itself in *f.*
See Gen. 27. 28; Jud. 9. 9; Rom. 11. 17.
Fauchion = falchion, a curved sword. Judith 13. 6.
Fault. Gen. 41. 9, I remember my *f.* this day.
Ps. 19. 12, cleanse me from secret *f.*
Dan. 6. 4, find none occasion nor *f.* in him.
Mat. 18. 15, tell him his *f.*
Lu. 23. 4; John 18. 38; 19. 4, 6, I find no *f.* R. V. crime.
Rom. 9. 19, why doth he yet find *f.*?
Gal. 6. 1, overtaken in a *f.*
Jas. 5. 16, confess your *f.* R. V. sins.
Rev. 14. 5, are without *f.* before throne. R. V. blemish.
See Deu. 25. 2; 1 Sam. 29. 3; 2 Sam. 3. 8.
Faultless. Heb. 8. 7; Jude 24.
Faulty. 2 Sam. 14. 13; Hos. 10. 2.
Favour. Gen. 39. 21, *f.* in the sight of the keeper.
Ex. 3. 21; 11. 3; 12. 36, *f.* in sight of Egyptians.
Deu. 33. 23, satisfied with *f.*
Ps. 5. 12, with *f.* wilt thou compass him.
30. 5, his *f.* is life.
102. 13, the set time to *f.* her. R. V. have pity upon.
102. 14, *f.* the dust thereof. R. V. have pity on.
112. 5, a good man sheweth *f.*
Prov. 13. 15, good understanding giveth *f.*
14. 35; 19. 12, the king's *f.*
18. 22, obtaineth *f.* of the Lord.
31. 30, *f.* is deceitful.
Lu. 2. 52, increased in *f.* with God and man.
Acts 2. 47, having *f.* with all people.
See Eccl. 9. 11; Dan. 1. 9.
Favour of GOD bestowed on CHRIST. Mat. 3. 16; 17. 5; Lu. 2. 52; John 11. 41; 12. 28.
on the righteous. Job 33. 26; Ps. 5. 12; Prov. 3. 4; 8. 35; 12. 2.
on Job, Job 42. 10. Abraham, Gen. 18. 17. the Israelites, Ps. 44. 3; 85. 1. the Virgin Mary, Lu. 1. 30. David, Acts 7. 46.
Favourable. Jud. 21. 22; Job 33. 26; Ps. 77. 7; 85. 1.
Fear (*n.*). (1) Gen. 9. 2, the *f.* of you on every beast.
20. 11, *f.* of God not in this place.
Deu. 2. 25; 11. 25; 1 Chr. 14. 17, *f.* of thee on nations.
Job 4. 6, is not this thy *f.*?
15. 4, thou castest off *f.*
39. 22, he mocketh at *f.*
Ps. 5. 7, in thy *f.* will I worship.
14. 5, there were they in great *f.*
19. 9, *f.* of the Lord is clean.
34. 11, I will teach you the *f.* of the Lord.
36. 1; Rom. 3. 18, no *f.* of God before his eyes.
53. 5, in *f.* where no *f.* was.
111. 10; Prov. 1. 7; 9. 10, *f.* beginning of wisdom.
Prov. 1. 26, 27, mock when your *f.* cometh.
3. 25, not afraid of sudden *f.*
10. 27, *f.* of Lord prolongeth days.
Prov. 14. 26, in *f.* of Lord is strong confidence.
14. 27, *f.* of Lord a fountain of life.
15. 16, better little with *f.* of Lord.
19. 23, *f.* of Lord tendeth to life.
23. 17, be thou in *f.* of the Lord all the day long.
29. 25, *f.* of man bringeth a snare.
Eccl. 12. 5, when *f.* shall be in the way. R. V. terrors.
Isa. 8. 12, neither fear ye their *f.*
14. 3, Lord give thee rest from *f.*
29. 13, *f.* toward me taught by men.
Jer. 30. 5, a voice of *f.*, not of peace.
32. 40, I will put my *f.* in their hearts.
Mal. 1. 6, where is my *f.*?
Mat. 14. 26, disciples cried for *f.*
Lu. 21. 26, hearts failing them for *f.*
John 7. 13; 19. 38; 20. 19, for *f.* of the Jews.
1 Cor. 2. 3, with you in weakness and *f.*
2 Cor. 7. 5, without were *f.*
7. 11, what *f.*, what desire.
7. 15; Eph. 6. 5; Phil. 2. 12, with *f.* and trembling.
Heb. 2. 15, *f.* of death.
11. 7, Noah moved with *f.*
12. 28, with reverence and godly *f.* R. V. awe.
Jude 12, feeding themselves without *f.*
23, others save with *f.*
(2) an object of fear. Gen. 31. 42. R. V. fear.
Fear (*v.*). Gen. 22. 12, I know that thou *f.* God.
42. 18, this do, and live, for I *f.* God.
Ex. 1. 21, because they *f.* God.
14. 13, *f.* not, stand still, and see.
18. 21, able men, such as *f.* God,
20. 20, *f.* not, God is come to prove.
Deu. 4. 10, that they may learn to *f.*
5. 29, O that they would *f.* me.
28. 58, *f.* this glorious name.
28. 66, thou shalt *f.* day and night.
1 Kn. 18. 12, I thy servant *f.* the Lord.
1 Chr. 16. 30; Ps. 96. 9, *f.* before him all earth. R. V. tremble.
Neh. 7. 2, he *f.* God above many.
Job 1. 9, doth Job *f.* God for nought?
11. 15, put iniquity away, thou shalt not *f.*
Ps. 27. 1, whom shall I *f.*?
27. 3, my heart shall not *f.*
31. 19, laid up for them that *f.* thee.
34. 9, *f.* the Lord, ye his saints.
56. 4; 118. 6, will not *f.* what flesh can do.
66. 16, come, all ye that *f.* God.
76. 7, thou art to be *f.*
86. 11, unite my heart to *f.* thy name.
115. 11, ye that *f.* the Lord, trust.
119. 74, they that *f.* thee will be glad.
Prov. 3. 7; 24. 21, *f.* the Lord, and depart.
28. 14, happy is the man that *f.* always.
31. 30, woman that *f.* the Lord.
Eccl. 3. 14, that men should *f.* before him.
5. 7, but *f.* thou God.
9. 2, as he that *f.* an oath.
12. 13, *f.* God, and keep his commandments.
Isa. 8. 12, neither *f.* ye their fear.
35. 4, to them of fearful heart, *f.* not.
41. 10; 43. 5, *f.* thou not, I am with thee.
41. 14, *f.* not, thou worm Jacob.
Jer. 5. 24, neither say they, let us *f.* the Lord.
10. 7, who would not *f.* thee, King of nations?
33. 9, they shall *f.* and tremble.
Dan. 6. 26, that men *f.* before the God of Daniel.
Zep. 3. 7, I said, surely thou wilt *f.* me.
Mal. 3. 16, they that *f.* the Lord spake.
4. 2, to you that *f.* my name.
Mat. 1. 20, *f.* not to take to thee.
10. 28; Lu. 12. 5, *f.* him who is able.
14. 5; 21. 46, Herod *f.* the multitude.
21. 26; Mk. 11. 32; Lu. 20. 19, we *f.* the people.
Mk. 4. 41, they *f.* exceedingly.
5. 33, woman *f.* and trembling came.
11. 18, scribes *f.* Jesus.
Lu. 9. 34, *f.* as they entered cloud.
12. 32, *f.* not, little flock.
18. 2, judge which *f.* not God.
19. 21, I *f.* thee, because thou art.
23. 40, dost not thou *f.* God?

John 9. 22, because they *f.* the Jews.
Acts 10. 22, just, and one that *f.* God.
10. 35, he that *f.* is accepted.
13. 26, whosoever among you *f.* God.
Rom. 8. 15, bondage again to *f.*
11. 20, not highminded, but *f.*
2 Cor. 11. 3; 12. 20, I *f.* lest.
1 Tim. 5. 20, rebuke, that others may *f.*
Heb. 5. 7, heard in that he *f.*
13. 6, I will not *f.* what man.
1 John 4. 18, that *f.* not perfect in love.

Fear of God. Job 28. 28; Ps. 19. 9; Prov. 1. 7; 8. 13; 9. 10; 14. 27; 15. 33.
advantages of. Ps. 15. 4; 25. 14; 31. 19; 33. 18; 60. 4; 61. 5; 85. 9; 103. 11; 111. 5; 112. 1; 145. 19; 147. 11; Prov. 10. 27; 14. 26; 15. 33; 19. 23; 22. 4; Eccl. 8. 12; Mal. 3. 16; 4. 2; Lu. 1. 50; 2 Cor. 7. 1; Rev. 11. 18.
commanded. Lev. 19. 14; Deu. 4. 10; 6. 2; 28. 58; Jos. 24. 14; 1 Sam. 12. 14; 2 Kn. 17. 38; 1 Chr. 16. 30; Ps. 2. 11; 33. 8; Prov. 3. 7, 23. 17; 24. 21; Isa. 8. 13; Eccl. 5. 7, 8. 12; 12. 13; Rom. 11. 20; Eph. 6. 5; Phil. 2. 12; Col. 3. 22; Heb. 4. 1; 1 Pet. 2. 17; Rev. 14. 17.
enjoined. Deu. 10. 12; Jos. 4. 24; Job 13. 11; Ps. 2. 11; 76. 7; 130. 4; Jer. 10. 7; Mat. 10. 28; Lu. 12. 5; Heb. 12. 28; Rev. 14. 7; 15. 4.
of punishment, causing torment. Gen. 3. 8; 4. 14; Prov. 28. 1; Isa. 2. 19; 33. 14; Lu. 19. 21; Acts 24. 25; Rom. 8. 15; Heb. 10. 27; 1 John 4. 18; Rev. 6. 16; 21. 8.

Fearful. (1) impressing, awe. Ex. 15. 11, *f.* in praises.
Ps. 139. 14, *f.* and wonderfully made.
Lu. 21. 11, *f.* sights. R. V. terrors.
Heb. 10. 31, *f.* thing to fall into the hands.
(2) timid, afraid. Isa. 35. 4, to them of a *f.* heart.
Mat. 8. 26; Mk. 4. 40, why are ye *f.*?
Heb. 10. 27, *f.* looking for of judgment.
See Deu. 20. 8; Jud. 7. 3; Rev. 21. 8.

Fearfulness. Ps. 55. 5; Isa. 21. 4; 33. 14.

Feast. Job 1. 4, his sons went and *f.* in their houses.
Ps. 35. 16, hypocritical mockers in *f.*
Prov. 15. 15, merry heart continual *f.*
Eccl. 7. 2; Jer. 16. 8, the house of *f.*
10. 19, *f.* is made for laughter.
Isa. 1. 14, your appointed *f.* my soul hateth.
Am. 5. 21, I despise your *f.* days.
8. 10, turn your *f.* into mourning.
Mat. 23. 6; Mk. 12. 39; Lu. 20. 46, uppermost rooms at *f.*
26. 5; Mk. 14. 2, not on the *f.* day.
Lu. 2. 42, after the custom of the *f.*
14. 13, when thou makest a *f.*
John 7. 8, go ye up to this *f.*
7. 14, about the midst of the *f.*
7. 37, that great day of the *f.*
13. 29, buy what we need against the *f.*
Acts 18. 21, I must by all means keep this *f.*
1 Cor. 5. 8, let us keep the *f.*
10. 27, if any bid you to a *f.*
See Jud. 14. 10; Mal. 2. 3.

Feasts, examples of.
Solomon's. 1 Kn. 8. 1; 2 Chr. 7. 9.
of Ahasuerus. Esth. 1.
of Purim. Esth. 9. 20.
of Job's children. Job 1. 4.
of Belshazzar. Dan. 5.
of Herod. Mk. 6. 21, &c.
given by Levi. Mat. 9. 10; Lu. 5. 29.
of charity. 1 Cor. 11. 22; 2 Pet. 2. 13; Jude 12.

Feasts, Jewish.
A. *Lunar Feasts.* I. The Sabbath. The law of one day's rest in seven is in Ex. 20. 8 connected with the day of God's rest after creation, and in Deu. 5. 12-15 with the deliverance from Egypt. This observance belongs to a whole class of Jewish feasts regulated by the cycle of the phases of the moon, and would seem akin to practices far older than Moses. Thus the ancient Assyrians kept the 7th, 14th, 21st, and 28th of each month as days of rest. On the Sabbath the daily sacrifices were doubled, and all work was prohibited. The details of this prohibition became in post-exilic times both burdensome and unreal, and called forth strong protests from our Lord.

The Christian Lord's Day, or Sunday, has no original connection with the Sabbath. Primitive Jewish Christians would keep both Sabbath and Sunday: but Christians were not to be judged 'in respect of a Sabbath' (Col. 2. 16). The tendency to base the obligation of Lord's Day observance on the Decalogue is not older than the 4th century A. D.

II. The New Moon. The legal codes prescribed numerous burnt-offerings on the recurrence of each new moon, with a special sin-offering. We hear of these days also as specially used for consulting prophets (2 Kn. 4. 23), for special sacrificial meals in family life (1 Sam. 20.), and for days of rest (Am. 8. 5). Special sacrifices were ordered for the new moon of the seventh, or sabbatical, month, which was called the 'feast of trumpets.'

III. The Sabbatical Year. The significance given by the lunar cycle to the number seven was extended also to years. Every seventh year was an agricultural Sabbath, and the land was left untilled. Slaves were released, or offered release (Ex. 21. 2-6), and debtors set free (Deu. 15. 1-6). The fruit of the land in this year belonged to the poor.

IV. The Year of Jubilee was a further extension of the principle exemplified in III. In every fiftieth year (the year after seven times seven years) mortgaged property was returned to its original owner, and Hebrew slaves were set free. *See* Lev. 25. 8-16 & 23-35, 27. 16-25.

B. *Annual Historical Feasts.* I. The Passover, and the Feast of Unleavened Bread. Later Judaism reckoned these two feasts as one, but originally they were distinct. *Passover* was connected by the Jews with the tenth of the plagues; the sprinkling of the blood of the Paschal lamb being a remembrance of the sign by which the Hebrews were separated from the Egyptians. This feast was kept on the 14th day of the first month (Abib or Nisan), by a common sacrificial meal, in which a lamb was eaten (as in peace-offerings), its blood sprinkled (as in the ritual of atonement), and the flesh and bones wholly consumed (as in burnt-offerings). It appears that in the Passover the historical association was grafted upon an older usage, i. e., that of offering the firstlings of the flock to God. Similarly the feast of *unleavened bread*, or *Mazzōth*, was in origin agricultural, and signified the offering of the firstfruits of the field. It began on the 15th day of Abib or Nisan, and lasted seven days; on the second day a sheaf of the new corn was offered (with a lamb of the first year). The exclusion of leaven from all Jewish houses during these days had historical associations with the haste of the Exodus (Ex. 12. 34); but the connection of leaven with ceremonial pollution appears to be much older (Ex. 23. 18), and the root idea of Mazzōth would seem to be the separation of the fruit of the new year from the leaven of the old.

II. Pentecost, or the Feast of Weeks. This was a festival of the completed wheat-harvest, and was kept fifty days after the offering of the firstling sheaf. On the fiftieth day sacrifices like those of the days of unleavened bread were offered; but the central feature was the offering of two loaves of the new wheat. *See* Ex. 34. 22; 23. 16; Lev. 23. 15-21; Deu. 16. 9-12.

III. Tabernacles. This feast was kept from the 15th to the 22nd day of the seventh month, or Tisri. Its historical associations were connected with the wanderings of the Israelites in the wilderness, which were commemorated by the usage of living in tents or booths during these days (Lev. 23. 39-43). The origin of the feast is indicated by its other name, 'feast of ingathering' (Ex. 23. 16); it was the festival of the end of the harvest of fruit, oil, and wine. In Num. 29. 12-40 very numerous sacrifices are prescribed for it; and in later times many further ceremonies were added, which made it the most joyful of all feasts; e. g., the fetching of water from Siloam to the altar, the lighting of many lights, a daily procession round the altar, and the singing of many Psalms, notably the 'Hallel' (Ps. 113.-118.).

C. *The Minor Feasts.* I. PURIM. The feast of *Purim* (or 'lots') was historically connected with the deliverance of the Jews from Haman (Esth. 3. 7; 9. 15-32); its days were the 14th and 15th of the twelfth month, Adar. The book of Esther was read on the night of the 13th amid loud imprecations against Haman and his house: the whole feast was one of boisterous mirth.

II. The ENCÆNIA, or DEDICATION. The temple was re-consecrated for the worship of Jehovah, after its pollution by Antiochus Epiphanes, in 164 B. C. In remembrance of this re-dedication Judas Maccabæus instituted a festival of eight days, beginning on the 25th of the ninth month, Chisleu. From the joyful illumination of every house at this feast it was also called the 'feast of lights.' It is referred to in John 10. 29 as a winter festival.

Feathers. Job 39. 13; Ps. 91. 4; Dan. 4. 33.

Fed. Gen. 48. 15, who *f.* me all my life long.
Ps. 37. 3, verily thou shalt be *f.*
Ezek. 34. 8, shepherds *f.* themselves, not flock.
Mat. 25. 37, hungred, and *f.* thee.
1 Cor. 3. 2, I have *f.* you with milk.
See Deu. 8. 3; Ps. 78. 72; 81. 16; Lu. 16. 21.

Feeble. Neh. 4. 2, what do these *f.* Jews?
Job 4. 4; Isa. 35. 3; Heb. 12. 12, strengthened the *f.* knees.
Ps. 105. 37, not one *f.* person.
Prov. 30. 26, conies a *f.* folk.
Ezek. 7. 17; 21. 7, all hands shall be *f.*
1 Thes. 5. 14, comfort the *f.*-minded. R. V. faint-hearted.
See Gen. 30. 42; Jer. 47. 3; 1 Cor. 12. 22.

Feed. Gen. 46. 32, trade hath been to *f.* cattle.
1 Kn. 17. 4, commanded ravens to *f.* thee.
22. 27, *f.* him with bread of affliction.
Ps. 28. 9, *f.* them, and lift them up for ever.
Prov. 15. 14, mouth *f.* on foolishness.
30. 8, *f.* me with food convenient.
Isa. 5. 17, lambs shall *f.* after their manner.
11. 7; 27. 10, cow and bear shall *f.*
44. 20, he *f.* on ashes.
61. 5, strangers shall *f.* your flocks.
65. 25, the wolf and lamb shall *f.*
Jer. 3. 15, pastors *f.* you with knowledge.
6. 3, *f.* every one in his place.
Hos. 12. 1, Ephraim *f.* on wind.
Zec. 11. 4, *f.* the flock of the slaughter.
Mat. 6. 26, your heavenly Father *f.* them.
Lu. 12. 24, sow not, yet God *f.* them.
John 21. 15-17, *f.* my lambs.
Rom. 12. 20, if enemy hunger, *f.* him.
1 Pet. 5. 2, *f.* the flock of God.
See S. of S. 1. 7; Acts 20. 28; Rev. 7. 17.

Feel. Gen. 27. 12, 21, my father will *f.* me.
Acts 17. 27, if haply they might *f.* after.
See Jud. 16. 26; Job 20. 20; Eccl. 8. 5.

Feeling. Eph. 4. 19, being past *f.*
Heb. 4. 15, touched with *f.* of infirmities.

Feet. Gen. 49. 10, lawgiver from between his *f.*
Deu. 2. 28, I will pass through on my *f.*
Jos. 3. 15, *f.* of priests dipped in Jordan.
14. 9, land whereon *f.* have trodden.
Ru. 3. 14, she lay at his *f.*
1 Sam. 2. 9, keep *f.* of his saints.
2 Sam. 22. 37; Ps. 18. 36, my *f.* did not slip.
2 Kn. 6. 32, sound of his master's *f.*
13. 21, dead man stood on his *f.*
Neh. 9. 21, their *f.* swelled not.
Job 29. 15, *f.* was I to the lame.
Ps. 8. 6; 1 Cor. 15. 27; Eph. 1. 22, all things under his *f.*
22. 16, pierced my hands and my *f.*
31. 8, set my *f.* in a large room.
40. 2, my *f.* on a rock.
56. 13; 116. 8, deliver my *f.* from falling.
Ps. 66. 9, suffered not our *f.* to be moved.
73. 2, my *f.* were almost gone.
115. 7, *f.* have they, but walk not.
119. 105, a lamp to my *f.*
122. 2, our *f.* shall stand within thy gates.
Prov. 1. 16; 6. 18; Isa. 59. 7, *f.* run to evil.
4. 26, ponder path of thy *f.*
5. 5, her *f.* go down to death.
6. 13, speaketh with his *f.*
6. 28, and his *f.* not be burnt.
7. 11, her *f.* abide not in house.
19. 2, he that hasteth with his *f.*
S. of S. 5. 3, washed my *f.*, how shall I defile?
7. 1; Isa. 52. 7, how beautiful are *f.*
Isa. 3. 16, tinkling with *f.*
6. 2, with twain he covered his *f.*
23. 7, her own *f.* shall carry her.
26. 6, the *f.* of the poor. [51, dust of *f.*
49. 23; Mat. 10. 14; Mk. 6. 11; Lu. 9. 5; Acts 13.
52. 7; Nah. 1. 15, the *f.* of him that bringeth.
60. 13, place of my *f.* glorious.
Lam. 3. 34, crush under *f.* prisoners.
Ezek. 2. 1, 2; 3. 24, stand upon thy *f.*
24. 17, 23, shoes upon thy *f.*
25. 6, stamped with thy *f.*
32. 2, troublest waters with thy *f.*
34. 18, 19, foul residue with *f.*
Dan. 2. 33, 42, *f.* part iron and part clay.
10. 6; Rev. 1. 15; 2. 18, *f.* like polished brass.
Nah. 1. 3, clouds are the dust of his *f.*
Zec. 14. 4, *f.* shall stand on Zion.
Mat. 7. 6, trample them under *f.*
18. 8, rather than having two *f.*
28. 9, they held him by the *f.*
Lu. 1. 79, guide our *f.* into way of peace.
7. 38, she kissed his *f.* and anointed them.
8. 35, sitting at the *f.* of Jesus.
10. 39, Mary sat at Jesus' *f.*
24. 39, 40, behold my hands and my *f.*
John 11. 2; 12. 3, wiped *f.* with her hair.
12. 3, anointed the *f.* of Jesus.
13. 5, began to wash disciples' *f.*
13. 6, dost thou wash my *f.*?
13. 8, thou shalt never wash my *f.*
13. 10, needeth not save to wash his *f.*
20. 12, one angel at head, other at *f.*
Acts 3. 7, his *f.* received strength.
4. 35, 37; 5. 2, laid at apostles' *f.*
5. 9, *f.* of them that buried thy husband.
14. 8, a man impotent in his *f.*
21. 11, Agabus bound his own hands and *f.*
22. 3, at *f.* of Gamaliel.
Rom. 3. 15, *f.* swift to shed blood.
10. 15, the *f.* of them that preach.
16. 20, bruise Satan under your *f.*
1 Cor. 12. 21, nor head to the *f.*, I have no need.
Eph. 6. 15, your *f.* shod with preparation.
Rev. 1. 17, I fell at his *f.* as dead.
13. 2, *f.* as *f.* of a bear.
19. 10; 22. 8, at his *f.* to worship.
See 2 Sam. 4. 4; 2 Kn. 9. 35; 1 Tim. 5. 10.

Feign. 1 Sam. 21. 13, David *f.* himself mad.
Ps. 17. 1, prayer not out of *f.* lips.
Jer. 3. 10, turned to me *f.*
Lu. 20. 20, *f.* themselves just men.
See 2 Sam. 14. 2; 1 Kn. 14. 5, 6; Neh. 6. 8.

Felix, fē'-lĭx, 'happy;' governor of Judæa. Paul sent to. Acts 23. 24.
Paul's defence before him. Acts 24. 10.
trembles at Paul's preaching, but leaves him bound. Acts 24. 25.

Fell. Gen. 4. 5, his countenance *f.*
Jos. 6. 20, the wall *f.* flat.
1 Kn. 18. 38, fire of Lord *f.*, and consumed.
2 Kn. 6. 5, as one was *f.* a beam.
Dan. 4. 31, then *f.* a voice from heaven.
Jon. 1. 7, lot *f.* on Jonah.
Mat. 7. 25; Lu. 6. 49, house *f.* not
Lu. 8. 23, Jesus *f.* asleep.
10. 30, 36, *f.* among thieves.
13. 4, upon whom tower *f.*
Acts 1. 25, from which Judas *f.*
1. 26, lot *f.* on Matthias.

Acts 13. 36, f. on sleep.
2 Pet. 3. 4, since fathers f. asleep.
Rev. 16. 19, cities of the nations f.
See Mat. 13. 4; Acts 10. 44; 19. 35; 20. 9.
Felloes, the pieces making up the rim of a wheel. 1 Kn. 7. 33.
Fellow. Ex. 2. 13, wherefore smitest thou thy f.?
1 Sam. 21. 15, this f. to play the madman.
2 Sam. 6. 20, as one of the vain f.
2 Kn. 9. 11, wherefore came this mad f.?
Ps. 45. 7; Heb. 1. 9, oil of gladness above thy f.
Eccl. 4. 10, one shall lift up his f.
Zec. 13. 7, the man that is my f.
Mat. 11. 16, like children calling to their f.
24. 49, begin to smite his f.-servants. [man.
26. 61, this f. said, I am able to destroy. R. V.
26. 71; Lu. 22. 59, this f. was also with Jesus. R. V. man.
Lu. 23. 2, found this f. perverting. R. V. man.
John 9. 29, as for this f. R. V. man.
Acts 17. 5, lewd f. of the baser sort.
22. 22, away with such a f.
24. 5, this man a pestilent f.
Eph. 2. 19, f.-citizens with the saints.
3. 6, Gentiles f.-heirs.
Phil. 4. 3; 1 Thes. 3. 2; Philem. 24, f.-labourers.
3 John 8, f.-helpers to the truth.
See Col. 4. 11; Philem. 2; Rev. 19. 10; 22. 9.
Fellowship. Lev. 6. 2, delivered in f. R. V. bargain.
Acts 2. 42, in doctrine and f.
1 Cor. 1. 9, called to the f. of his Son.
10. 20, not have f. with devils. R. V. communion.
2 Cor. 6. 14, what f. hath righteousness?
Eph. 3. 9, the f. of mystery. R. V. dispensation.
5. 11, have no f. with.
Phil. 1. 5, your f. in the gospel.
2. 1, if any f. of the Spirit.
3. 10, the f. of his sufferings.
1 John 1. 3, our f. is with the Father.
1. 7, we have f. one with another.
Fellowship of Christ. 1 Cor. 1. 9; 12. 27; 2 Cor. 4. 11; Phil. 3. 10. *See* 1 Cor. 10. 16.
of the Spirit. Phil. 2. 1.
of the saints. Acts 2. 42; 2 Cor. 8. 4; Gal. 2. 9; Phil. 1. 5; 1 John 1. 3.
with evil, forbidden. Ps. 94. 20; 1 Cor. 10. 20; 2 Cor. 6. 14; Eph. 5. 11.
Felt. Ex. 10. 21; Prov. 23. 35; Mk. 5. 29; Acts 28. 5.
Female. Mat. 19. 4; Mk. 10. 6, made them male and f.
Gal. 3. 28, in Christ neither male nor f.
See Gen. 7. 16; Lev. 3. 1; 27. 4; Deu. 4. 16.
Fence. Job 10. 11; 19. 8; Ps. 62. 3; Isa. 5. 2.
Ferret (Lev. 11. 30). Heb. *Anâkah*: Gk. μυγαλῆ: R. V. gecko. An unclean 'creeping thing,' probably the gecko, 'the most repulsive of the lizards of Palestine,' which frequents rocks, ruins, and houses.
Fervent. (1) burning. 2 Pet. 3. 10, 12.
(2) ardent, glowing, fervid. Acts 18. 25; Rom. 12. 11, f. in spirit.
Jas. 5. 16, f. prayer availeth much.
1 Pet. 1. 22, with a pure heart f.
See 2 Cor. 7. 7; Col. 4. 12; 1 Pet. 4. 8. [24. 27.
Festus, fĕs'-tŭs, joyful; governor of Judæa. Acts
Paul brought before him. Acts 25.
Paul's defence before. Acts 25. 8; 26.
acquits Paul. Acts 25. 14; 26. 31.
Fetch. Num. 20. 10, must we f. water?
Job 36. 3, I will f. my knowledge from far.
Isa. 56. 12, I will f. wine. [bring.
Acts 16. 37, come themselves and f. us out. R. V.
See Deu. 19. 5; 2 Sam. 14. 3; Acts 28. 13.
Fetters. Jud. 16. 21; Ps. 105. 18; 149. 8; Mk. 5. 4; Lu. 8. 29.
Fever. Deu. 28. 22, the Lord shall smite thee with a f.
Mat. 8. 14; Mk. 1. 30, Simon's wife's mother lay sick of a f.
John 4. 52, at the seventh hour the f. left him.
Few. Gen. 29. 20, they seemed but a f. days.
Gen. 47. 9, f. and evil have the days of my life.
1 Sam. 14. 6, to save by many or f.
17. 28, with whom left those f. sheep?
2 Kn. 4. 3, borrow not a f.
Neh. 7. 4, city large, people f.
Job 14. 1, man is of f. days.
16. 22, when a f. years are come.
Eccl. 5. 2, let thy words be f.
Mat. 7. 14, f. there be that find it.
9. 37; Lu. 10. 2, the labourers are f.
15. 34; Mk. 8. 7, a f. little fishes.
20. 16; 22. 14, many called, f. chosen.
25. 21, faithful in a f. things.
Mk. 6. 5, laid hands on a f. sick folk.
Lu. 12. 48, beaten with f. stripes.
13. 23, are there f. that be saved?
Rev. 3. 4; a f. names even in Sardis.
See Deu. 7. 7; Ps. 109. 8; Heb. 12. 10.
Fidelity. Tit. 2. 10, shewing good f.
Field. Deu. 21. 1, if one be found slain in f.
1 Sam. 22. 7, will he give every one of you f.?
Prov. 24. 30, the f. of the slothful.
Isa. 5. 8, that lay f. to f.
Mat. 13. 38, the f. is the world.
13. 44, treasure hid in a f.
John 4. 35, look on the f.
Jas. 5. 4, labourers which reaped your f.
See Mat. 6. 28; 27. 7; Acts 1. 19.
Fierce. Gen. 49. 7, anger, for it was f.
Deu. 28. 50, a nation of a f. countenance.
Mat. 8. 28, exceeding f.
Lu. 23. 5, and they were more f. R. V. urgent.
2 Tim. 3. 3, men shall be incontinent, f.
Jas. 3. 4, driven of f. winds. R. V. rough.
See 2 Sam. 19. 43; Isa. 33. 19; Dan. 8. 23.
Fiery. Deu. 33. 2, a f. law for them.
Dan. 3. 6, a f. furnace.
Eph. 6. 16, the f. darts of the wicked.
Heb. 10. 27, judgment and f. indignation. R. V. a fierceness of fire.
1 Pet. 4. 12, concerning the f. trial.
See Num. 21. 6; Deu. 8. 15; Isa. 14. 29.
Fig. 2 Kn. 20. 7; Isa. 38. 21, take a lump of f.
Jer. 24. 1, two baskets of f. were set before the temple.
Mat. 7. 16; Lu. 6. 44, do men gather f. of thistles?
Rev. 6. 13, casteth untimely f.
See Jer. 8. 13. [for you.
Fight. Ex. 14. 14; Deu. 1. 30; 3. 22; 20. 4, Lord f.
Jos. 23. 10, he it is that f. for you.
1 Sam. 25. 28, f. the battles of the Lord.
2 Kn. 10. 3, f. for your master's house.
Neh. 4. 14, f. for your brethren, sons, and wives.
Ps. 144. 1, teacheth my fingers to f.
John 18. 36, then would my servants f.
Acts 5. 39; 23. 9, f. against God.
1 Cor. 9. 26, so f. I.
2 Cor. 7. 5, without were f.
1 Tim. 6. 12; 2 Tim. 4. 7, the good f.
Heb. 10. 32, great f. of afflictions.
11. 34, valiant in f. R. V. war.
Jas. 4. 1, wars and f. among you.
4. 2, ye f. and war. R. V. make war.
See Zec. 10. 5; 14. 14; Rev. 2. 16.
Fig tree. The fig is the earliest named tree in the Bible. There are four Heb. words for it.
(1) (Gen. 3. 7; Deu. 8. 8). The name of the tree. Heb. *Tĕĕnah*: Gk. συκῆ: Bot. N. *Ficus carica*. The other three denote different stages or conditions of the fruit.
(2) (S. of S. 2. 13). Heb. *Pag*: Gk. ὄλυνθος: the 'green fig,' or unripened fruit remaining on the trees through the winter. (Bethphage is the 'house of *green figs*,' a sunless ravine.)
(3) (Hos. 9. 10). Heb. *Bikkûrah*: Gk. σκοπός: 'first-ripe.'
(4) (1 Sam. 25. 18). Heb. *Dĕbêlah*: Gk. παλάθη: 'cakes of figs.'
1 Kn. 4. 25; Mic. 4. 4, dwelt under his f.
2 Kn. 18. 31; Isa. 36. 16, eat every one of his f.
Hab. 3. 17, although f. shall not blossom.
Mat. 21. 19, presently the f. withered away.

Mk. 11. 13, seeing a *f.* afar off.
Lu. 21. 29, behold the *f.*
Jas. 3. 12, can the *f.* bear olive berries?
See Jud. 9. 10; Lu. 13. 6; John 1. 48.

Fig tree (parable of). Mat. 24. 32; Lu. 21. 29.

Figure. Deu. 4. 16; Rom. 5. 14; 1 Cor. 4. 6; Heb. 9. 9; 1 Pet. 3. 21.

Fill. Num. 14. 21; Ps. 72. 19; Hab. 2. 14, earth *f.* with glory.
Job 23. 4, *f.* my mouth with arguments.
Ps. 81. 10, open mouth, I will *f.* it.
104. 28, they are *f.* with good. R. V. satisfied.
Prov. 3. 10, barns *f.* with plenty.
14. 14, *f.* with his own ways.
30. 22, a fool when *f.* with meat.
Isa. 65. 20, who hath not *f.* his days.
Mat. 5. 6; Lu. 6. 21, they shall be *f.*
Mk. 7. 27, let the children first be *f.* [Ghost.
Lu. 1. 15; Acts 4. 8; 9. 17; 13. 9, *f.* with Holy
14. 23, that my house may be *f.*
John 16. 6, sorrow hath *f.* your heart. [trine.
Acts 5. 28, ye have *f.* Jerusalem with your doc-
14. 17, *f.* our hearts with food and gladness.
Rom. 1. 29, *f.* with all unrighteousness.
15. 14, *f.* with all knowledge.
Eph. 1. 23, him that *f.* all in all.
3. 19, *f.* with fulness of God.
5. 18, be *f.* with the Spirit.
Phil. 1. 11, *f.* with fruits of righteousness.
Col. 1. 24, *f.* up what is behind.
Jas. 2. 16, be ye warned and *f.* [finished.
Rev. 15. 1, in them is *f.* up wrath of God. R. V.
See Dan. 2. 35; Lu. 2. 40; 15. 16; John 2. 7.

Filth. Isa. 4. 4, washed away the *f.* of Zion.
1 Cor. 4. 13, as the *f.* of the world.

Filthiness. 2 Cor. 7. 1, cleanse from all *f.* of flesh. R V. defilement.
Eph. 5. 4, nor let *f* be named.
Jas. 1. 21, lay apart all *f.*

Filthiness, figurative of sin. Job 15. 16; Ps. 14. 3; Isa. 1. 6; 64. 6; Ezek. 24. 13.
purification from, Isa. 4. 4; Ezek. 22. 15; 36. 25; Zec. 3. 3; 13. 1; 1 Cor. 6. 11; 2 Cor. 7. 1.

Filthy. Job 15. 16, how much more *f.* is man?
Ps. 14. 3; 53. 3, altogether become *f.*
Isa. 64. 6, as *f.* rags. R. V. a polluted garment.
Zec. 3. 3, clothed with *f.* garments.
Col. 3. 8, put off *f.* communication. R. V shameful speaking.
1 Tim. 3. 3; Tit. 1. 7; 1 Pet. 5. 2, *f.* lucre. R. V. money.
2 Pet. 2. 7, vexed with *f.* conversation. R. V. lascivious.
Jude 8, *f.* dreamers. R. V. in their dreamings.
Rev. 22. 11, he that is *f.*, let him be *f.*

Finally. 2 Cor. 13. 11; Eph. 6. 10; Phil. 3. 1; 4. 8; 2 Thes. 3. 1; 1 Pet. 3. 8.

Find. Num. 32. 23, be sure your sin will *f.* you out.
Job 9. 10; Rom. 11. 33, things past *f.* out.
23. 3, where I might *f.* him.
Prov. 4. 22, life to those that *f.* them.
8. 17; Jer. 29. 13, seek me early shall *f.* me.
8. 35, whoso *f.* me, *f.* life.
18. 22, *f.* a wife, *f.* a good thing.
Eccl. 9. 10, thy hand *f.* to do, do it.
11. 1, *f.* it after many days.
Isa. 58. 13, *f.* thine own pleasure.
Jer. 6. 16; Mat. 11. 29, *f.* rest to your souls.
Mat. 7. 7; Lu. 11. 9, seek, and ye shall *f.*
7. 14, few there be that *f.* it.
10. 39, loseth his life shall *f.* it.
22. 9, as many as ye shall *f.*
Mk. 11. 13, he might *f.* any thing thereon.
13. 36, he *f.* you sleeping.
Lu. 15. 4, 8, till he *f.* it.
18. 8, shall he *f.* faith on earth?
John 1. 41, first *f.* his brother.
Rom. 7. 21, I *f.* a law that when I would.
Heb. 4. 16, *f.* grace to help.
See John 7. 34; 2 Tim. 1. 18; Rev. 9. 6. [gold.

Fine (*n.*). Ps. 19. 10, more to be desired than *f.*
81. 16; 147. 14, the *f.* of the wheat.
Prov. 25. 12, as an ornament of *f.* gold. [pure.
Lam. 4. 1, how is the *f.* gold changed! R. V.
Mk. 15. 46, Joseph brought *f.* linen.
See Job 28. 17; Lu. 16. 19; Rev. 18. 12; 19. 8.

Fine (*v.*). to refine (gold, &c.). Job 28. 1.

Finger. Ex. 8. 19, this is the *f.* of God.
31. 18; Deu. 9. 10, written with the *f.* of God.
1 Kn. 12. 10; 2 Chr. 10. 10, little *f.* thicker.
Prov. 7. 3, bind them on thy *f.*
Isa. 58. 9, the putting forth of the *f.*
Dan. 5. 5, the *f.* of a man's hand.
Mat. 23. 4; Lu. 11. 46, not move with *f.*
Lu. 16. 24, the tip of his *f.*
John 8. 6, with his *f.* wrote on ground.
20. 25, put my *f.* into print of nails.
20. 27, reach hither thy *f.* [11. 20.
See Ps. 8. 3; Prov. 6. 13; Isa. 2. 8; 59. 3; Lu.

Finish. 1 Chr. 28. 20, till thou hast *f.*
Neh. 6. 15, so the wall was *f.*
Lu. 14. 28–30, whether sufficient to *f.*
John 4. 34, to do his will and *f.* his work.
5. 36, which the Father hath given me to *f.*
17. 4, I have *f.* the work. R. V. accomplished.
19. 30, it is *f.*
Acts 20. 24; 2 Tim. 4. 7, that I might *f.* my course.
2 Cor. 8. 6, *f.* in you the same grace. R. V. complete.
Heb. 12. 2, Jesus, author and *f.* of our faith. R. V. perfecter.
Jas. 1. 15, sin when it is *f.* R. V. fullgrown.
See Dan. 9. 24; Rev. 10. 7; 11. 7; 20. 5.

Fir (Isa. 37. 24; S. of S. 1. 17). Heb. *Bĕrôsh; Bĕrôth:* Gk. κυπάρισσος: Bot. N. *Pinus halepensis; Pinus pinea; Pinus pyrenaica:* R. V. marg. cypress. The Heb. Bĕrōsh probably included pine, cypress, and juniper.
Isa. 41. 19, I will set in the desert the *f.*-tree.
55. 13, instead of the thorn shall come up the *f.*-tree.
60. 13, the *f.*-tree.
Hos. 14. 8, I am like a green *f.*-tree.

Fire. Gen. 22. 7, behold the *f.* and the wood.
Ex. 3. 2, bush burned with *f.*
22. 6, he that kindled *f.* shall make restitution.
Lev. 10. 2, *f.* from the Lord.
18. 21; Deu. 18. 10; 2 Kn. 17. 17; 23. 10, pass through *f.*
Jud. 15. 5, brands on *f.*, and burnt corn.
1 Kn. 18. 24, that answereth by *f.*
19. 12, the Lord was not in the *f.*
1 Chr. 21. 26, Lord answered him by *f.*
Ps. 39. 3, musing, the *f.* burned.
74. 7, they have cast *f.* into thy sanctuary.
Prov. 6. 27, can a man take *f.*?
26. 18, mad man who casteth *f.*-brands.
26. 20, no wood, the *f.* goeth out.
26. 21, as wood is to *f.*, so is a contentious man.
Isa. 9. 19, as the fuel of the *f.*
24. 15, glorify the Lord in the *f.* R. V. east.
43. 2, walkest through *f.* not be burned.
44. 16, I have seen the *f.*
64. 2, the melting *f.* burneth.
66. 15, the Lord will come with *f.*
66. 16, by *f.* will the Lord plead.
66. 24; Mk. 9. 44, neither their *f.* quenched.
Jer. 20. 9, word as a *f.* in my bones.
Ezek. 36. 5, in the *f.* of my jealousy.
Dan. 3. 27, the *f.* had no power.
Am. 4. 11, as a *f.*-brand plucked out.
Nah. 1. 6, fury poured out like *f.*
Zec. 2. 5, a wall of *f.* round about.
3. 2, a brand plucked out of the *f.*
Mal. 3. 2, like a refiner's *f.* [into *f.*
Mat. 3. 10; 7. 19; Lu. 3. 9; John 15. 6, tree cast
3. 11; Lu. 3. 16, baptize with *f.*
13. 42, cast them into furnace of *f.*
18. 8; 25. 41; Mk. 9. 43, 46, everlasting *f.*
Lu. 9. 54, wilt thou that we command *f.*?
12. 49, come to send *f.* on earth.
17. 29, same day it rained *f.* and brimstone.
Acts 2. 3, cloven tongues like as of *f.*
1 Cor. 3. 13, revealed by *f.*, and the *f.* shall try.
3. 15, saved, yet so as by *f.*

2 Thes. 1. 8, in flaming *f.* taking vengeance.
Heb. 1. 7, his ministers a flame of *f.*
11. 34, quenched violence of *f.*
Jas. 3. 5, a little *f.* kindleth.
3. 6, the tongue is a *f.*
1 Pet. 1. 7, gold tried with *f.*
2 Pet. 3. 7, reserved unto *f.*
3. 12, heavens being on *f.*
Jude 7, vengeance of eternal *f.*
23, pulling them out of the *f.*
Rev. 3. 18, buy gold tried in the *f.*
20. 9, *f.* came down from God.
20. 10, devil cast into lake of *f.*
20. 14, death and hell cast into *f.*
21. 8, the lake that burneth with *f.*

Fire, pillar of. Ex. 13. 21; Neh. 9. 12.
God appears by. Ex. 3. 2; 13. 21; 19. 18; Deu. 4. 12; 2 Sam. 22. 13; Isa. 6. 4; Ezek. 1. 4; Dan. 7. 10; Mal. 3. 2; Mat. 3. 11; Rev. 1. 14; 4. 5.
for consuming sacrifices. Gen. 15. 17; Lev. 9. 24; Jud. 13. 20; 1 Kn. 18. 38; 2 Chr. 7. 1.
not to be kindled on the sabbath. Ex. 35. 3.
emblem of God's word. Jer. 23. 29; Acts 2. 3.
instrument of judgment. Gen. 19. 24; Ex. 9. 23; Lev. 10.; Num. 11. 1; 16. 35; 2 Kn. 1. 10; Am. 7. 4; 2 Thes. 1. 8; Rev. 8. 8.
everlasting. Deu. 32. 22; Isa. 33. 14; 66. 24; Mk. 9. 44; Jude 7; Rev. 20. 10.
God is a consuming. Heb. 12. 29.

Firkin. John 2. 6. Gk. *metretes* = bath = nearly 9 gallons. *See* MEASURES.

Firm. Jos. 3. 17; Job 41. 24; Ps. 73. 4; Heb. 3. 6.

Firmament. Gen. 1. 6, let there be a *f.*
Ps. 19. 1, the *f.* sheweth his handywork.
Ezek. 1. 22, the likeness of the *f.*
Dan. 12. 3, shine as the brightness of the *f.*

First. 1 Kn. 17. 13, make a little cake *f.*
Ez. 3. 12; Hag. 2. 3, the glory of the *f.* house.
Job 15. 7, art thou the *f.* man born?
Prov. 3. 9, honour the Lord with *f.*-fruits.
18. 17, *f.* in his own cause.
Isa. 43. 27, thy *f.* father hath sinned.
Mat. 5. 24, *f.* be reconciled.
6. 33, seek ye *f.* the kingdom.
7. 5, *f.* cast out the beam.
12. 29; Mk. 3. 27, except he *f.* bind strong man.
12. 45, last state of that man worse than *f.*
17. 10, 11; Mk. 9. 12, Elias must *f.* come.
20. 10, when the *f.* came, they supposed.
22. 38; Mk. 12. 28–30, the *f.* commandment.
Mk. 4. 28, *f.* the blade.
9. 35, if any desire to be *f.*, same shall be last.
13. 10, gospel must *f.* be published.
Lu. 14. 28, sitteth not down *f.*
17. 25, but *f.* must he suffer many things.
John 1. 41, *f.* findeth his brother Simon.
5. 4, whosoever *f.* stepped in.
8. 7, let him *f.* cast a stone.
Acts 11. 26, called Christians *f.* at Antioch.
Rom. 2. 9, 10, of the Jew *f.*
8. 23, the *f.*-fruits of the Spirit.
8. 29, *f.*-born among many brethren.
11. 16, if the *f.*-fruit be holy.
1 Cor. 12. 28, *f.* apostles, secondarily prophets.
14. 30, let the *f.* hold peace.
15. 20, 23, Christ the *f.*-fruits.
15. 45, the *f.* man was made a living soul.
15. 46, not *f.* which is spiritual.
15. 47, *f.* man is of the earth.
2 Cor. 8. 5, *f.* gave their own selves.
8. 12, if there be *f.* a willing mind.
Eph. 6. 2, the *f.* commandment with promise.
Col. 1. 15, 18, the *f.*-born of every creature.
1 Thes. 4. 16, dead in Christ shall rise *f.*
2 Thes. 2. 3, a falling away *f.*
1 Tim. 1. 16, that in me *f.* R. V. as chief.
2. 13, Adam was *f.* formed.
3. 10, let these *f.* be proved.
5. 4, learn *f.* to shew piety at home.
5. 12, cast off their *f.* faith.
2 Tim. 4. 16, at my *f.* answer no man.
Tit. 3. 10, after *f.* and second admonition.
Heb. 5. 12, which be the *f.* principles.
Heb. 7. 27, *f.* for his own sins.
10. 9, taketh away the *f.*
Jas. 3. 17, *f.* pure, then peaceable.
1 Pet. 4. 17, if judgment *f.* begin at us.
1 John 4. 19, because he *f.* loved us.
Jude 6, kept not their *f.* estate. R. V. own principality.
Rev. 2. 4, left thy *f.* love.
2. 5, do thy *f.* works.
20. 5, this is the *f.* resurrection.
21. 1, *f.* heaven and *f.* earth passed away.

Firstborn, claims of the. Gen. 43. 33; Deu. 21. 15; 2 Chr. 21. 3; Col. 1. 15 (Heb. 12. 23).
dedicated to God. Ex. 13. 2, 12; 22. 29; 34. 19; Deu. 15. 19.
how redeemed. Ex. 34. 20; Num. 3. 41; 8. 18.
in Egypt killed. Ex. 11. 4; 12. 29.

Firstfruits, laws relating to. Ex. 22. 29; 23. 16; 34. 26; Lev. 23. 9; Num. 18. 12, 13; 28. 26.
form of dedicating. Deu. 26. 5.
the priests' portion of. Num. 18. 12; Deu. 18. 4.

Fish. Eccl. 9. 12, *f.* taken in an evil net.
Hab. 1. 14, men as the *f.* of the sea.
Mat. 7. 10, if he ask a *f.*
14. 17; Mk. 6. 38; Lu. 9. 13, five loaves and two *f.*
John 21. 3, Peter saith, I go a *f.*
1 Cor. 15. 39, one flesh of beasts, another of *f.*
See Jer. 16. 16; Lu. 24. 42.

Fish, the waters bring forth. Gen. 1. 20.
of Egypt destroyed. Ex. 7. 21.
prepared for Jonah. Jon. 1. 17.
caught for tribute. Mat. 17. 27.
miraculous draughts of. Lu. 5. 6; John 21. 6.
on fire of coals. John 21. 9.

Fisheries, Table of. *See* p. 120.

Fishers. Mat. 4. 18; Mk. 1. 16, for they were *f.*
4. 19; Mk. 1. 17, *f.* of men.
John 21. 7, he girt his *f.* coat unto him.

Fit. Job 34. 18, is it *f.* to say to a king?
Lu. 9. 62, is *f.* for the kingdom.
14. 35, it is not *f.* for the dunghill.
Col. 3. 18, submit, as it is *f.* in the Lord. R. V. fitting.
See Lev. 16. 21; Prov. 24. 27; Ezek. 15. 5; Rom. 9. 22.

Fitches. Two Hebrew words are translated 'fitches.' (1) (Isa. 28. 25, 27). Heb. *Ketzaḥ*: Gk. μελάνθιον: Bot. N. *Nigella sativa*: R. V. marg. 'black cummin, *Nigella sativa*.' It is the fennel, cultivated for its pungent black seeds. (2) Ezek. 4. 9; Heb. *Cussémeth*, 'spelt;' elsewhere translated 'rye,' *q. v.*

Fitly. Prov. 25. 11; Eph. 2. 21; 4. 16.

Fixed. Ps. 57. 7; 108. 1; 112. 7; Lu. 16. 26.

Flag. *See* BULRUSH.

Flagon, a large bottle or flask. 2 Sam. 6. 19. R. V. a cake (of raisins).

Flame. Gen. 3. 24, at garden of Eden a *f.* sword.
Jud. 13. 20, angel ascended in *f.*
Isa. 5. 24, as the *f.* consumeth chaff.
29. 6, a *f.* of devouring fire.
43. 2, neither shall *f.* kindle.
66. 15, rebuke with *f.* of fire.
Ezek. 20. 47, the *f. f.* shall not be quenched.
Lu. 16. 24, tormented in this *f.*
See Ps. 29. 7; Heb. 1. 7; Rev. 1. 14; 2. 18.

Flatter. Job 17. 5, he speaketh *f.* to his friends. R. V. denounceth for a prey.
32. 21, 22, give *f.* titles to man.
Ps. 5. 9, they *f.* with their tongue.
12. 2, *f.* lips and double heart.
Prov. 20. 19, meddle not with him that *f.* R. V. openeth wide.
26. 28, a *f.* mouth worketh ruin.
1 Thes. 2. 5, neither used we *f.* words.
See Ps. 78. 36; Prov. 2. 16; 24. 24; 28. 23; 29. 5; Dan. 11. 21, 32, 34.

Flax was the earliest material known to have been cultivated and manufactured for clothing purposes.
(1) (Ex. 9. 31; Isa. 19. 9). Heb. *Pishtah*: Gk. λίνον: Bot. N. *Linum usitatissimum*.
(2) (Gen. 41. 42). Heb. *Shêsh*: Gk. βύσσος: R. V. 'fine linen;' marg. 'cotton;' A. V. 'fine linen;' marg. 'silk;' perhaps the yarn.

Fisheries of Palestine, with their Products.

N. B. — T. = *Tristram*; H. = *Houghton*.

Waters.	English Name.	Ichthyological Species.	Remarks.
Gennesaret, L. ...	Bream.	Chromis Niloticus. H.	
	Sheat-fish.	Clarias macracanthus. T.	The *Siluroids* are unfit for food, and are the 'bad fish cast away' by the fishermen (Mat. 13. 47, 48).
		Coracinus. T.	
		Hemichromis. T.	Found by Livingstone in S. E Africa.
	Carp.		
	Perch.		
	Dog-fish.	Labeo barbus canis. H.	
Jabbok, R.	Barbel.	Barbus longiceps.	The Jabbok swarms with fish, swimming in a continuous line, coming and going. T.
Jordan............	Minnow.	Cyprinodon Hammonis. H.	These all die on reaching the Dead sea, where they are devoured by the birds waiting for them. (*Cf.* Ezek. 47. 10.)
	Barbel.		
	Bream.		
Kishon, R.	Blenny.	Blennius lupulus.	Fewer fish in the streams flowing westward than in those flowing eastward.

(3) (Lev. 6. 10). Heb. *Bad:* Gk. λίνον: 'linen;' perhaps the cloth.
(4) (Esth. 8. 15). Heb. *Bûtz:* Gk. βύσσος: 'fine linen;' sometimes worth its weight in gold.
(5) (Jud. 14. 12). Heb. *Sâdin:* Gk. σινδών: A. V. 'sheets:' R. V. 'linen garments.'
(6) (Prov. 7. 16). Heb. *Etûn* (omitted in LXX.): R. V. 'yarn of Egypt.' The corresponding Greek word (ὀθόνη) is the 'great sheet' in Peter's vision, and the gravecloth of Jesus (John 19. 40).
(7) (1 Kn. 10. 28). Heb. *Mikveh* (omitted in LXX.): A. V. 'linen yarn:' R. V. 'drove.' Its signification is doubtful.

Flea (1 Sam. 24. 14; 26. 20). Heb. *Par'ôsh:* Gk. ψύλλος: Zoöl. S. *Pulex irritans.* Only twice mentioned, as an illustration of the most insignificant of creatures. Fleas swarm in the very sand of Egypt, and in the dust of all parts of Palestine, — the greatest pests of man and beast.

Flee. Lev. 26. 17, 36, ye shall *f.* when none pursueth.
Num. 10. 35, them that hate thee *f.* before thee.
Neh. 6. 11, should such a man as I *f.*?
Job 14. 2, he *f.* as a shadow.
Ps. 139. 7, whither shall I *f.*?
Prov. 28. 1, the wicked *f.* when no man pursueth.
28. 17, he shall *f.* to the pit.
S. of S. 2. 17; 4. 6, till shadows *f.* away.
Isa. 35. 10; 51. 11, sighing shall *f.* away.
Mat. 3. 7; Lu. 3. 7, to *f.* from wrath to come.
10. 23, in one city, *f.* to another.
24. 16; Mk. 13. 14; Lu. 21. 21, *f.* to mountains.
26. 56; Mk. 14. 50, forsook him and *f.*
John 10. 5, not follow, but will *f.* from him.
10. 13, the hireling *f.*
1 Tim. 6. 11, *f.* these things.
2 Tim. 2. 22, *f.* youthful lusts.
Jas. 4. 7, he will *f.* from you.
See 1 Cor. 6. 18; 10. 14; Rev. 12. 6, 14.

Fleece. Jud. 6. 37, I will put a *f.* of wool in the floor.

Flesh. Gen. 2. 24; Mat. 19. 5; Mk. 10. 8; 1 Cor. 6. 16; Eph. 5. 31, one *f.*
6. 12, all *f.* had corrupted his way.
6. 13, end of all *f.* is come.
Gen. 7. 21, all *f.* died.
Ex. 16. 3, when we sat by the *f.* pots.
Lev. 17. 14, the life of all *f.* is the blood.
19. 28, cuttings in your *f.*
Num. 11. 33, while *f.* was between their teeth.
16. 22; 27. 16, God of spirits of all *f.*
1 Kn. 17. 6, bread and *f.* in morning and evening.
2 Chr. 32. 8, with him is an arm of *f.*
Neh. 5. 5, our *f.* is as the *f.* of our brethren.
Job 19. 26, in my *f.* shall I see God.
33. 21, his *f.* is consumed away.
Ps. 16. 9; Acts 2. 26, my *f.* shall rest in hope.
65. 2, to thee shall all *f.* come.
78. 20, can he provide *f.*?
Prov. 5. 11, mourn, when *f.* consumed.
11. 17, the cruel troubleth his own *f.*
23. 20, among riotous eaters of *f.*
Eccl. 4. 5, the fool eateth his own *f.*
12. 12, weariness of the *f.*
Isa. 40. 5, all *f.* shall see it.
40. 6; 1 Pet. 1. 24, all *f.* is grass.
Ezek. 11. 19; 36. 26, a heart of *f.*
Joel 2. 28; Acts 2. 17, pour Spirit on all *f.*
Mat. 16. 17, *f.* and blood hath not revealed it.
24. 22; Mk. 13. 20, there should no *f.* be saved.
26. 41; Mk. 14. 38, spirit willing, *f.* weak.
Lu. 24. 39, spirit hath not *f.* and bones.
John 1. 14, Word made *f.*, and dwelt.
6. 51, 54, 55, bread I give is my *f.*
6. 52, can this man give us his *f.*?
John 6. 63, the *f.* profiteth nothing.
8. 15, ye judge after the *f.*
17. 2, power over all *f.*
Rom. 6. 19, because of the infirmity of your *f.*
8. 3, condemned sin in the *f.*
8. 8, they that are in *f.* cannot please God.
8. 9, not in the *f.*, but the Spirit.
12. 13, to live after the *f.*
9. 3, kinsmen according to the *f.*
9. 5, of whom as concerning the *f.*
13. 14, make not provision for the *f.*
1 Cor. 1. 29, that no *f.* should glory.
15. 39, all *f.* not the same *f.*
15. 50, *f.* and blood cannot inherit.
2 Cor. 12. 7, a thorn in the *f.*
Gal. 1. 16, I conferred not with *f.* and blood.

FISHERMEN ON THE LAKE OF GALILEE

A photograph, with Tiberias in the background, taken before modern developments in the area. (*Picture Post Library*)

RIVER JORDAN
Photograph of a landscape that has probably changed little since Biblical times. (*John Stirling*)

Gal. 2. 20, life I now live in the *f.*
5. 17, *f.* lusteth against the Spirit.
Eph. 2. 3, lusts of *f.*, desires of *f.*
Phil. 3. 3, 4, no confidence in the *f.*
1 Tim. 3. 16, manifest in the *f.*
1 Pet. 3. 18, Christ put to death in *f.* [in *f.*
1 John 4. 2; 2 John 7, denieth that Christ is come
Jude 8, dreamers defile the *f.*
23, hating garment spotted by *f.*

Flesh allowed to be eaten. Gen. 9. 3.
contrasted with spirit. John 1. 13; 3. 6; Rom. 7. 5; 8. 1; Gal. 3. 3; 5. 17; 6. 8.
lusts of the, to be mortified. 2 Cor. 7. 1; Gal. 5. 16-19; 6. 8; Col. 2. 11; 1 Pet. 4. 2; 1 John 2. 16.
God manifest in the. John 1. 14; 1 Tim. 3. 16; Heb. 2. 14; 1 Pet. 3. 18; 4. 1. to be acknowledged, 1 John 4. 2; 2 John 7.

Fleshly. 2 Cor. 1. 12; 3. 3; Col. 2. 18; 1 Pet. 2. 11.

Flies. Ex. 8. 21, 31, I will send swarms of *f.* upon thee.
Ps. 78. 45, he sent divers sorts of *f.* among them.
105. 31, he spake, and there came divers sorts of *f.*

Flight. Isa. 52. 12; Am. 2. 14; Mat. 24. 20; Heb. 11. 34.

Flint. Num. 20. 11; Deu. 8. 15; 32. 13; Ps. 114. 8; Isa. 5. 28; 50. 7; Ezek. 3. 9; 1 Cor. 10. 4.

Flock. Jer. 13. 20, where is the *f.*, thy beautiful *f.*? [sheep.
Ezek. 34. 31, the *f.* of my pasture are men. R. V.
Zec. 11. 7, the poor of the *f.*
Lu. 12. 32, fear not, little *f.*
Acts 20. 28, take heed to the *f.*
20. 29, not sparing the *f.*
1 Pet. 5. 2, feed the *f.* of God.
5. 3, being ensamples to the *f.*
See Ezek. 36. 37; Mal. 1. 14; Mat. 26. 31.

Flood. Jos. 24. 2, on other side of the *f.* R. V. beyond the River.
Job 28. 11, he bindeth *f.* from overflowing.
Ps. 32. 6, in *f.* of great waters.
S. of S. 8. 7, neither can *f.* drown love.
Isa. 44. 3, *f.* upon the dry ground. R. V. streams.
59. 19, enemy come in like a *f.* R. V. rushing stream.
Mat. 7. 25, the *f.* came, and the winds blew.
24. 38, in days before the *f.*
24. 39; Lu. 17. 27, knew not till *f.* came.
See Gen. 6. 17; 7. 11; 8.; 9. 11; Ps. 90. 5; 2 Pet. 2. 5; Rev. 12. 15.

Floor, threshingfloor. 1 Sam. 23. 1, they rob the threshing-*f.*
2 Sam. 24. 21, to buy the threshing-*f.* of thee.
Hos. 9. 1, loved a reward on every corn-*f.*
Mic. 4. 12, gather as sheaves into the *f.*
Mat. 3. 12; Lu. 3. 17, purge his *f.*
See Deu. 15. 14; Dan. 2. 35; Joel 2. 24. [them.

Flour. Ex. 29. 2, of wheaten *f.* shalt thou make
Lev. 2. 2, take thereout his handful of the *f.*

Flourish. Ps. 72. 7, in his days shall the righteous *f.*
90. 6, in the morning it *f.*
92. 12, righteous shall *f.* like a palm tree.
103. 15, as flower so he *f.*
Prov. 11. 28, righteous shall *f.* as branch.
14. 11, tabernacle of upright *f.* [blossom.
Eccl. 12. 5, when the almond tree shall *f.* R. V.
S. of S. 6. 11; 7. 12, whether the vine *f.* R. V. hath budded.
Ezek. 17. 24, have made dry tree to *f.* [vived.
Phil. 4. 10, your care of me hath *f.* R. V. re-
See Ps. 92. 14; Dan. 4. 4.

Flow. Ps. 147. 18, wind to blow, and waters *f.*
S. of S. 4. 16, that the spices may *f.* out.
Isa. 2. 2, all nations shall *f.* unto it.
64. 1, 3, mountains *f.* at thy presence.
Jer. 31. 12, shall *f.* to the goodness of the Lord.
John 7. 38, shall *f.* living water.
See Job 20. 28; Isa. 60. 5; Joel 3. 18; Mic. 4. 1.

Flower. 1 Sam. 2. 33, shall die in *f.* of age.
Job 14. 2, cometh forth as a *f.*
S. of S. 2. 12, the *f.* appear on earth.
Isa. 28. 1, 4, glorious beauty is a fading *f.*
Isa. 40. 6, as the *f.* of the field.
40. 7; Nah. 1. 4; Jas. 1. 10; 1 Pet. 1. 24, *f.* fadeth.
See Job 15. 33; Isa. 18. 5; 1 Cor. 7. 36.

Flute (Dan. 3. 5, 7, 10, 15). Chald. *Mashrôkîtha:* Gk. σῦριγξ. Probably the Syrinx, or Pan's pipes, an ancient musical instrument consisting of a series of tubes, the tone being produced by blowing with the breath across the upper ends. Flute-like instruments of different kinds date from the earliest times.

Flux, a flowing, effusion; a 'bloody *f.*' = dysentery. Acts 28. 8.

Fly (*n.*). (1) (Ex. 8. 21; Ps. 78. 45) Heb. *Arôb*, or *Oreb:* Gk. κυνόμυια: Zoöl. S. *Musca*, or *Culex*. The word means 'swarms' or 'divers sorts.' It is probably here generic, including in the 'plague of swarms' flies, sand-flies, gnats, mosquitoes, &c.
(2) (Eccl. 10. 1). Heb. *Zebûb:* Gk. μυῖα, only twice mentioned; once here, referring to the common fly, whose swarms would corrupt any unguent or savoury compote in a few minutes. (In Isa. 7. 18) (Zoöl. S. *Hippobosca*, or *Œstrus*), a gadfly tormenting the horses on the banks of the Nile, where 'probably the poisonous *Tsetse*, described by Livingstone, is meant.'

Fly (*v.*). Job 5. 7, as sparks *f.* upward.
Ps. 55. 6, then would I *f.* away.
90. 10, and we *f.* away.
Prov. 23. 5, riches *f.* away.
Isa. 60. 8, that *f.* as a cloud.
See Dan. 9. 21; Rev. 14. 6; 19. 17.

Foal. Gen. 49. 11; Zec. 9. 9; Mat. 21. 5.

Foam. Hos. 10. 7; Mk. 9. 18; Lu. 9. 39; Jude 13.

Foes. Ps. 27. 2; 30. 1; 89. 23; Mat. 10. 36; Acts 2. 35.

Fold. Prov. 6. 10; 24. 33, *f.* of the hands to sleep.
Eccl. 4. 5, fool *f.* his hands and eateth.
Hab. 3. 17, flock cut off from the *f.*
John 10. 16, one *f.*, and one shepherd.
See Isa. 13. 20; 65. 10; Nah. 1. 10.

Folk. Prov. 30. 26; Jer. 51. 58; Mk. 6. 5; John 5. 3.

Follow. Num. 14. 24, Caleb hath *f.* me fully.
1 Kn. 18. 21, God, *f.* him.
Ps. 23. 6, goodness and mercy shall *f.* me.
63. 8, my soul *f.* hard after thee.
68. 25, the players *f.* after.
Prov. 12. 11; 28. 19, that *f.* vain persons.
Isa. 5. 11, that they may *f.* strong drink.
Hos. 6. 3, if we *f.* on to know the Lord.
Am. 7. 15, took me as I *f.* the flock.
Mat. 4. 19; 8. 22; 9. 9; 16. 24; 19. 21; Mk. 2. 14; 8. 34; 10. 21; Lu. 5. 27; 9. 23, 59; John 1. 43; 21. 22, Jesus said, *f.* me.
8. 19; Lu. 9. 57, 61, Master, I will *f.* thee.
Mk. 10. 28; Lu. 18. 28, we left all, and *f.* thee.
10. 32, as they *f.*, they were afraid.
Lu. 22. 54, Peter *f.* afar off.
John 10. 27, my sheep hear my voice, and *f.* me.
13. 36, thou canst not *f.* me now.
Rom. 14. 19, *f.* things that make for peace.
1 Cor. 10. 4, the rock that *f.* them.
14. 1, *f.* after charity.
Phil. 3. 12, I *f.* after. R. V. press on.
1 Thes. 5. 15, ever *f.* that which is good.
1 Tim. 5. 24, some men they *f.* after.
6. 11; 2 Tim. 2. 22, *f.* righteousness.
Heb. 12. 14, *f.* peace with all men.
13. 7, whose faith *f.* R. V. imitate.
1 Pet. 1. 11, the glory that should *f.*
2. 21, that ye should *f.* his steps.
2 Pet. 2. 15, *f.* the way of Balaam.
Rev. 14. 4, they that *f.* the Lamb.
14. 13, their works do *f.* them.
See Mk. 9. 38; 1 Pet. 3. 13; 2 Pet. 1. 16; Rev. 6. 8.

Followers. Eph. 5. 1, *f.* of God, as dear children.
Heb. 6. 12, *f.* of them who through faith.

Folly. 1 Sam. 25. 25, and *f.* is with him.
Job 4. 18, his angels he charged with *f.*
24. 12, yet God layeth not *f.* to them.
42. 8, lest I deal with you after your *f.*
Ps. 49. 13, this their way is their *f.*
85. 8, let them not turn again to *f.*

Prov. 13. 16, a fool layeth open his *f.*
14. 8, the *f.* of fools is deceit.
14. 18, the simple inherit *f.*
16. 22, instruction of fools is *f.*
17. 12, rather than a fool in his *f.*
26. 4, answer not a fool according to his *f.*
26. 5, answer fool according to his *f.*
Eccl. 1. 17, to know wisdom and *f.*
2. 13, wisdom excelleth *f.*
7. 25, the wickedness of *f.*
10. 6, *f.* is set in great dignity.
2 Cor. 11. 1, bear with me a little in my *f.*
2 Tim. 3. 9, their *f.* shall be manifest.
See Jos. 7. 15; Prov. 14. 24; Isa. 9. 17.

Food. Gen. 3. 6, tree good for *f.*
Ex. 21. 10, her *f.* shall not be diminished.
Deu. 10. 18, in giving him *f.* and raiment.
Job 23. 12, more than my necessary *f.*
24. 5, wilderness yieldeth *f.* [mighty.
Ps. 78. 25, did eat angels' *f.* R. V. bread of the
104. 14, bring forth *f.* out of the earth.
136. 25, giveth *f.* to all flesh.
Prov. 6. 8, gathereth her *f.* in harvest.
13. 23, much *f.* in tillage of poor.
30. 8, with *f.* convenient for me.
31. 14, she bringeth her *f.* from far.
2 Cor. 9. 10, minister bread for your *f.*
1 Tim. 6. 8, having *f.* and raiment.
Jas. 2. 15, destitute of daily *f.*
See Gen. 1. 29; 2. 9; 6. 21; 9. 3; 41. 35; Lev. 22. 7; Ps. 145. 16; 147. 9.

Fool. 2 Sam. 3. 33, died Abner as a *f.* dieth?
Ps. 14. 1; 53. 1, *f.* said in his heart.
75. 4, to *f.*, deal not foolishly.
Prov. 1. 7, *f.* despise wisdom. R. V. the foolish.
3. 35, shame the promotion of *f.*
10. 8, 10, a prating *f.* shall fall.
10. 21, *f.* die for want of wisdom.
10. 23, sport to a *f.* to do mischief. [V. foolish.
11. 29, the *f.* shall be servant to the wise. R.
12. 15, way of *f.* right in own eyes. R. V. the foolish.
12. 16, *f.* wrath presently known.
13. 16, *f.* layeth open his folly.
13. 20, companion of *f.* shall be destroyed.
14. 8, folly of *f.* is deceit.
14. 9, *f.* make a mock at sin.
14. 16, the *f.* rageth, and is confident.
15. 2, mouth of *f.* poureth out foolishness.
15. 5, a *f.* despiseth his father's instruction.
16. 22, the instruction of *f.* is folly. [wise.
17. 28, a *f.*, when he holdeth his peace, counted
20. 3, every *f.* will be meddling.
29. 11, a *f.* uttereth all his mind.
Eccl. 2. 14, *f.* walketh in darkness.
2. 16, how dieth wise man? as the *f.*
2. 19, who knoweth whether wise or a *f.*?
5. 3, a *f.* voice is known by multitude of words.
10. 14, a *f.* is full of words.
Isa. 35. 8, wayfaring men, though *f.*
Jer. 17. 11, at his end he shall be a *f.*
Hos. 9. 7, the prophet is a *f.*
Mat. 5. 22, shall say, thou *f.*
23. 17, ye *f.* and blind.
Lu. 12. 20, thou *f.*, this night. R. V. foolish one.
24. 25, O *f.*, and slow of heart.
1 Cor. 3. 18, let him become a *f.*
2 Cor. 11. 16, let no man think me a *f.* [ish.
12. 11, I am a *f.* in glorying. R. V. become fool-
Eph. 5. 15, walk not as *f.*, but as wise. R. V. unwise.

Foolish. Deu. 32. 6, O *f.* people.
2 Sam. 24. 10; 1 Chr. 21. 8, I have done very *f.*
Job 2. 10, as one of the *f.* women.
Ps. 73. 3, I was envious at the *f.* [ple ones.
Prov. 9. 6, forsake the *f.*, and live. R. V. sim-
9. 13, a *f.* woman is clamorous.
14. 1, the *f.* plucketh it down.
17. 25; 19. 13, a *f.* son is grief.
Eccl. 7. 17, neither be thou *f.*
Jer. 4. 22, my people are *f.*
Mat. 7. 26, unto a *f.* man. [senseless.
Rom. 1. 21, their *f.* heart was darkened. R. V.
1 Cor. 1. 20, hath not God made *f.*
Gal. 3. 1, O *f.* Galatians.
3. 3, are ye so *f.*?
Eph. 5. 4, nor *f.* talking.
1 Tim. 6. 9, rich fall into *f.* lusts.
2 Tim. 2. 23; Tit. 3. 9, *f.* questions avoid.
Tit. 3. 3, we were sometimes *f.*
1 Pet. 2. 15, ignorance of *f.* men.
See Job 5. 3; Lam. 2. 14; Ezek. 13. 3.

Foolishness. 2 Sam. 15. 31, turn counsel into *f.*
Ps. 69. 5, thou knowest my *f.*
Prov. 22. 15, *f.* is bound in heart of child.
24. 9, thought of *f.* is sin. R. V. the foolish.
1 Cor. 1. 18, to them that perish *f.*
1. 21, by the *f.* of preaching.
1. 23, Christ crucified, to Greeks *f.*
1. 25, the *f.* of God is wiser than men.
2. 14, things of Spirit are *f.* to him.
3. 19, wisdom of world *f.* with God.

Fools, their character and conduct. Ps. 14. 1; 49. 13; 53. 1; 92. 6; Prov. 10. 8, 18, 23; 12. 15, 16; 13. 16; 14. 16; 15. 5; 17. 7, 10, 12, 16, 21, 28; 18. 2, 6, 7; 19. 1; 20. 3; 26. 4; 27. 3, 22; 28. 26; Eccl. 4. 5; 5. 1, 3; 7. 4, 9; 10. 2, 3, 14; Isa. 44. 25; Mat. 7. 26; 23. 17; 25. 2; Lu. 12. 20; Rom. 1. 22.

Foot. Gen. 41. 44, without thee no man lift *f.*
Deu. 2. 5, not so much as *f.* breadth.
11. 10, wateredst it with thy *f.*
Ps. 38. 16, when thy *f.* slippeth.
91. 12; Mat. 4. 6; Lu. 4. 11, dash *f.* against stone.
94. 18, my *f.* slippeth, thy mercy.
121. 3, not suffer *f.* to be moved.
Prov. 3. 23, thy *f.* shall not stumble.
25. 17, withdraw *f.* from neighbour's house.
Eccl. 5. 1, keep thy *f.* when thou goest.
Isa. 1. 6, from sole of *f.* to head no soundness.
Mat. 14. 13, people followed on *f.*
18. 8; Mk. 9. 45, if thy *f.* offend thee.
1 Cor. 12. 15, if the *f.* say, because I am not.
Heb. 10. 29, trodden under *f.* the Son of God.
See Jer. 12. 5; Mat. 5. 35; Jas. 2. 3.

Footstool of God: the temple called. 1 Chr. 28. 2; Ps. 99. 5; 132. 7.
the earth called. Isa. 66. 1; Mat. 5. 35; Acts 7. 49.
God's foes made. Ps. 110. 1; Mat. 22. 44; Heb. 10. 13.

Forbade. Mat. 3. 14; Mk. 9. 38; Lu. 9. 49.

Forbear. Ex. 23. 5, wouldest *f.* to help.
2 Chr. 35. 21, *f.* from meddling with God.
Neh. 9. 30, many years didst thou *f.* them.
Ezek. 2. 5; 3. 11, whether hear or *f.*
1 Cor. 9. 6, power to *f.* working.
Eph. 4. 2; Col. 3. 13, *f.* one another in love.
6. 9, *f.* threatening.
See Prov. 24. 11; Ezek. 3. 27; Zec. 11. 12.

Forbearance commended. Mat. 18. 33; Eph. 4. 2; 6. 9; Col. 3. 13; 2 Tim. 2. 24.
of God. Ps. 50. 21; Isa. 30. 18; Rom. 2. 4; 3. 25; 1 Pet. 3. 20; 2 Pet. 3. 9.

Forbid. Num. 11. 28, Joshua said, *f.* them.
Mk. 9. 39; Lu. 9. 50, *f.* him not.
10. 14; Lu. 18. 16, children, *f.* them not.
Lu. 6. 29, *f.* not to take coat.
23. 2, *f.* to give tribute.
Acts 10. 47, can any *f.* water?
1 Cor. 14. 39, *f.* not to speak with tongues.
1 Tim. 4. 3, *f.* to marry.
See Acts 16. 6; 28. 31; 1 Thes. 2. 16.

Force. Deu. 34. 7, nor natural *f.* abated.
Ez. 4. 23, made them cease by *f.*
Mat. 11. 12, violent take it by *f.*
John 6. 15, perceived they would take him by *f.*
Heb. 9. 17, a testament is of *f.* after.
See Deu. 20. 19; Prov. 30. 33; Am. 2. 14.

Forcible. Job 6. 25.

Ford. Gen. 32. 22; Jos. 2. 7; Isa. 16. 2.

Forecast. Dan. 11. 24, 25.

Forefathers. Jer. 11. 10; 2 Tim. 1. 3.

Forehead. Ex. 28. 38, it shall always be on his *f.*
1 Sam. 17. 49, smote Philistine in his *f.*
Ezek. 3. 8, made thy *f.* strong.
9. 4, set a mark on *f.* of them that sigh.

Rev. 7. 3; 9. 4, sealed in their *f.*
22. 4, his name shall be in their *f.*
See Rev. 13. 16; 14. 1; 17. 5; 20. 4.
Foreigner. Ex. 12. 45; Deu. 15. 3; Eph. 2. 19.
Foreknow. Rom. 8. 29; 11. 2; 1 Pet. 1. 2.
Foreknowledge. Acts 2. 23, delivered by *f.* of God.
Foremost. Gen. 32. 17; 33. 2; 2 Sam. 18. 27.
Foreordained. 1 Pet. 1. 20.
Forerunner. Heb. 6. 20.
Foresee. Prov. 22. 3; 27. 12; Gal. 3. 8.
Forest. Ps. 50. 10, every beast of *f.* is mine.
Isa. 29. 17; 32. 15, field esteemed as *f.*
Jer. 5. 6, lion out of *f.* shall slay them.
26. 18; Mic. 3. 12, high places of the *f.*
46. 23, they shall cut down her *f.*
Am. 3. 4, will lion roar in the *f.*?
See Ezek. 15. 6; 20. 46; Hos. 2. 12.
Foretell. Mk. 13. 23; Acts 3. 24; 2 Cor. 13. 2.
Forewarn. Lu. 12. 5; 1 Thes. 4. 6.
Forgat. Jud. 3. 7, they *f.* the Lord.
Ps. 78. 11, they *f.* his works.
106. 13, soon *f.* his works.
Lam. 3. 17, I *f.* prosperity.
See Gen. 40. 23; Hos. 2. 13.
Forgave. Mat. 18. 27, 32, and *f.* him the debt.
Lu. 7. 42, he frankly *f.* them both.
7. 43, he to whom he *f.* most.
2 Cor. 2. 10, if I *f.* any thing.
Col. 3. 13, even as Christ *f.* you.
See Ps. 32. 5; 78. 38; 99. 8.
Forge. Job 13. 4; Ps. 119. 69.
Forget. Deu. 4. 9, lest thou *f.* things thine eyes [have seen.
4. 23, lest ye *f.* the covenant.
6. 12; 8. 11, beware lest thou *f.* the Lord.
Job 8. 13, so are the paths of all that *f.* God.
Ps. 9. 17, all nations that *f.* God.
10. 12, *f.* not the humble.
45. 10, *f.* thine own people.
50. 22, consider, ye that *f.* God.
78. 7, that they might not *f.* works of God.
88. 12, in the land of *f.*
102. 4, I *f.* to eat my bread.
103. 2, *f.* not all his benefits.
119. 16, I will not *f.* thy word.
137. 5, if I *f.* thee, O Jerusalem.
Prov. 2. 17, *f.* the covenant of her God.
3. 1, *f.* not my law.
31. 5, lest they drink and *f.*
31. 7, let him drink, and *f.* his poverty.
Isa. 49. 15, can a woman *f.*?
51. 13, and *f.* the Lord thy Maker.
65. 11, *f.* my holy mountain.
Jer. 2. 32, maid *f.* her ornaments.
23. 27, cause my people to *f.* my name.
Am. 8. 7, I will never *f.* their works.
Phil. 3. 13, *f.* those things which are behind.
Heb. 6. 10, not unrighteous to *f.*
13. 2, not *f.* to entertain.
13. 16, to communicate *f.* not.
Jas. 1. 24, *f.* what manner of man.
See Gen. 41. 51; Lam. 5. 20.
Forgetfulness of God condemned. Deu. 4. 9; 6. 12; Ps. 78. 7; 103. 2; Prov. 3. 1; 4. 5; 31. 5; Hos. 4. 6; Heb. 13. 16.
punishment of. Job 8. 13; Ps. 9. 17; 50. 22; Isa. 17. 10; Jer. 2. 32; Hos. 8. 14.
Forgive. Ex. 32. 32, if thou wilt *f.* their sin.
34. 7; Num. 14. 18, *f.* iniquity, transgression.
1 Kn. 8. 30, 39; 2 Chr. 6. 21, 30, hearest, *f.*
2 Chr. 7. 14, then will I hear and *f.*
Ps. 32. 1; Rom. 4. 7, whose transgression is *f.*
86. 5, good, and ready to *f.*
103. 3, who *f.* all thine iniquities.
Mat. 6. 12; Lu. 11. 4, *f.* us, as we *f.*
6. 14, if ye *f.*
6. 15, if ye *f.* not.
9. 6; Mk. 2. 10; Lu. 5. 24, power to *f.* sin.
18. 21, how oft, and I *f.* him?
18. 35, if ye from your hearts *f.*
Mk. 2. 7, who can *f.* sins?
11. 25, *f.* that your Father may *f.*
11. 26, not *f.*, Father will not *f.*
Lu. 6. 37, *f.*, and ye shall be *f.* R. V. release, released.
7. 47, her sins which are many, are *f.*
7. 49, who is this *f.* sins also?
17. 3, 4, if brother repent, *f.* him.
23. 34, Father, *f.* them, they know not.
Acts 8. 22, thought of thine heart may be *f.*
2 Cor. 2. 7, ye ought rather to *f.*
2. 10, to whom ye *f.*, I *f.* also.
12. 13, *f.* me this wrong.
Eph. 4. 32, as God for Christ's sake hath *f.*
Col. 2. 13, quickened, having *f.*
1 John 1. 9, faithful and just to *f.*
Forgiveness. Ps. 130. 4, *f.* with thee, that thou mayest be feared.
Dan. 9. 9, to the Lord belong *f.*
Mk. 3. 29, hath never *f.*
Acts 5. 31, exalted to give *f.* R. V. remission.
Eph. 1. 7; Col. 1. 14, in whom we have *f.*
Forgiveness, mutual, commanded. Gen. 50. 17; Mat. 5. 23; 6. 14; 18. 21, 35; Mk. 11. 25; Lu. 11. 4; 17. 4; 2 Cor. 2. 7; Eph. 4. 32; Col. 3. 13; Jas. 2. 13.
of enemies. Mat. 5. 44; Lu. 6. 27; Rom. 12. 14, 19.
of sin, prayed for. Ex. 32. 32; 1 Kn. 8. 30; 2 Chr. 6. 21; Ps. 25. 18; 32.; 51.; 79. 9; 130.; Dan. 9. 19; Am. 7. 2; Mat. 6. 12.
promised. Lev. 4. 20; 2 Chr. 7. 14; Isa. 33. 24; 55. 7; Jer. 3. 12; 31. 20, 34; 33. 8; Ezek. 36. 25; Hos. 14. 4; Mic. 7. 18; Mat. 9. 2; 12. 31; Mk. 3. 28; Lu. 12. 10; 24. 47; Acts 5. 31; 13. 38; 26. 18; Eph. 1. 7; Col. 1. 14; Jas. 5. 15; 1 John 1. 9.
Forgotten. Deu. 24. 19, and hast *f.* a sheaf.
32. 18, *f.* God that formed thee.
Ps. 9. 18, needy not always *f.*
10. 11, said, God hath *f.*
31. 12, *f.* as a dead man.
42. 9, why hast thou *f.* me?
44. 20, if we have *f.* name of our God.
77. 9, hath God *f.* to be gracious?
Eccl. 2. 16, in days to come all *f.*
8. 10, wicked were *f.* in city.
9. 5, the memory of them is *f.*
Isa. 17. 10, *f.* the God of thy salvation.
44. 21, thou shalt not be *f.* of me.
49. 14, my Lord hath *f.* me.
65. 16, former troubles are *f.*
Jer. 2. 32; 13. 25; 18. 15, my people have *f.*
3. 21, *f.* the Lord their God.
44. 9, *f.* the wickedness of your fathers.
50. 6, *f.* their restingplace.
Ezek. 22. 12; 23. 35, thou hast *f.* me.
Mat. 16. 5; Mk. 8. 14, *f.* to take bread.
Lu. 12. 6, not one *f.* before God.
2 Pet. 1. 9, *f.* that he was purged.
See Lam. 2. 6; Hos. 4. 6; 13. 6.
Form (*n.*). Gen. 1. 2; Jer. 4. 23, without *f.*, and void. R. V. waste.
Job 4. 16, could not discern the *f.* R. V. appearance.
Isa. 52. 14, *f.* marred more than sons of men.
Ezek. 10. 8, the *f.* of a man's hand.
Dan. 3. 19, *f.* of visage changed.
3. 25, *f.* of fourth like Son of God. R. V. aspect.
Mk. 16. 12, appeared in another *f.*
Rom. 2. 20, hast *f.* of knowledge and truth.
Phil. 2. 6, being in the *f.* of God = possessing the essential attributes of Deity.
2. 7, the *f.* of a servant.
2 Tim. 1. 13, *f.* of sound words. R. V. pattern.
3. 5, having *f.* of godliness.
See 1 Sam. 28. 14; Ezek. 43. 11; Rom. 6. 17.
Form (*v.*). Deu. 32. 18, forgotten God that *f.* thee.
2 Kn. 19. 25; Isa. 37. 26, that I have *f.* it.
Job 26. 5, dead things are *f.* R. V. tremble.
26. 13, hath *f.* crooked serpent. R. V. pierced.
33. 6, I also am *f.* of clay.
Ps. 90. 2, or ever thou hadst *f.*
94. 9, he that *f.* the eye.
Prov. 26. 10, great God that *f.* all things. R. V. as an archer that woundeth all.
Isa. 43. 1, he that *f.* thee, O Israel.

Isa. 43. 7; 44. 21, I have *f.* him.
43. 10, before me was no God *f.*
43. 21, people have I *f.* for myself.
44. 10, who hath *f.* a god? R. V. fashioned.
54. 17, no weapon *f.* against thee.
Am. 7. 1, he *f.* grasshoppers.
Rom. 9. 20, shall thing *f.* say.
Gal. 4. 19, till Christ be *f.* in you.
See Gen. 2. 7, 19; Ps. 95. 5; Jer. 1. 5.

Former. Ru. 4. 7, manner in *f.* time.
Job 8. 8, enquire of the *f.* age.
Ps. 89. 49, where are thy *f.* lovingkindnesses?
Eccl. 1. 11, no remembrance of *f.* things.
7. 10, *f.* days better than these.
Isa. 43. 18, remember not the *f.* things.
46. 9, remember the *f.* things of old.
48. 3, declared *f.* things from beginning.
65. 7, measure their *f.* work. R. V. first measure their work.
65. 16, *f.* troubles are forgotten.
Jer. 5. 24; Hos. 6. 3; Joel 2. 23, *f.* and latter rain.
10. 16; 51. 19, the *f.* of all things.
Hag. 2. 9, glory of *f.* house.
Zec. 1. 4; 7. 7, 12, *f.* prophets have cried.
8. 11, I will not be as in *f.* days.
14. 8, half of them toward *f.* sea. R. V. eastern.
Mal. 3. 4, pleasant as in *f.* years. R. V. ancient.
Eph. 4. 22, concerning the *f.* conversation.
Rev. 21. 4, for the *f.* things are passed away. R. V. first.
See Gen. 40. 13; Dan. 11. 13; Acts 1. 1.

Fornication denounced. Ex. 22. 16; Lev. 19. 20; Num. 25.; Deu. 22. 21; 23. 17; Prov. 2. 16; 5. 3; 6. 25; 7.; 9. 13; 22. 14; 23. 27; 29. 3; 31. 3; Eccl. 7. 26; Hos. 4. 11; Mat. 15. 19; Mk. 7. 21; Acts 15. 20; Rom. 1. 29; 1 Cor. 5. 9; 6. 9; 2 Cor. 12. 21; Gal. 5. 19; Eph. 5. 5; Col. 3. 5; 1 Thes. 4. 3; 1 Tim. 1. 10; Heb. 13. 4; 1 Pet. 4. 3; Jude 7; Rev. 2. 14; 21. 8; 22. 15.
Spiritual. Ezek. 16. 29; Hos. 1.; 2.; 3.; Rev. 14. 8; 17. 2; 18. 3; 19. 2.

Forsake. Deu. 4. 31; 31. 6; 1 Chr. 28. 20, he will not *f.* R. V. fail.
12. 19, *f.* not the Levite.
32. 15, he *f.* God which made him.
Jos. 1. 5; Heb. 13. 5, I will not fail nor *f.*
Jud. 9. 11, *f.* my sweetness and fruit. R. V. leave.
1 Chr. 28. 9, if thou *f.* him, he will cast thee off.
2 Chr. 15. 2, if ye *f.* him, he will *f.* you.
Neh. 10. 39, we will not *f.* house of our God.
13. 11, why is house of God *f.*?
Job 6. 14, he *f.* the fear of the Almighty.
20. 19, oppressed and *f.* the poor. [*f.* me?
Ps. 22. 1; Mat. 27. 46; Mk. 15. 34, why hast thou
37. 25, yet have I not seen the righteous *f.*
37. 28, the Lord *f.* not his saints.
119. 8, *f.* me not utterly.
138. 8, *f.* not work of thine own hands.
Prov. 1. 8; 6. 20, *f.* not law of thy mother.
2. 17, *f.* the guide of her youth.
4. 6, *f.* her not, and she shall preserve thee.
27. 10, thy friend, and father's friend, *f.* not.
Isa. 6. 12, a great *f.* in the land.
17. 9, as a *f.* bough.
32. 14; Jer. 4. 29; Ezek. 36. 4, a *f.* city.
54. 6, as a woman *f.*
54. 7, for a small moment *f.*
62. 4, no more be termed *f.*
62. 12, a city not *f.*
Jer. 2. 13; 17. 13, *f.* fountain of living waters.
Mat. 19. 27; Lu. 5. 11, we have *f.* all. R. V. left.
19. 29, that hath *f.* houses. R. V. left.
26. 56; Mk. 14. 50, disciples *f.* him, and fled. R. V. left.
Mk. 1. 18, they *f.* their nets. R. V. left. [ceth.
Lu. 14. 33, whosoever *f.* not all. R. V. renoun-
2 Cor. 4. 9, persecuted, but not *f.*
2 Tim. 4. 10, Demas hath *f.* me.
4. 16, all men *f.* me.
Heb. 10. 25, not *f.* assembling of ourselves.
11. 27, by faith Moses *f.* Egypt.
See Ps. 71. 11; Isa. 49. 14; Ezek. 8. 12.

Forsaking God, danger of. Deu. 28. 20; Jud. 10. 13; 2 Chr. 15. 2; 24. 20; Ez. 8. 22; 9. 10; Isa. 1. 28; Jer. 1. 16; 5. 7, 19; 17. 13; 22. 9; Ezek. 6. 9.

Forswear. Mat. 5. 33.

Fortress. 2 Sam. 22. 2; Ps. 18. 2; Jer. 16. 19, Lord is my *f.*

Fortunatus, fôr-tū-nā'-tŭs, 'prosperous,' succours Paul. 1 Cor. 16. 17.

Forty days, as the flood. Gen. 7. 17.
giving of the law. Ex. 24. 18.
spying Canaan. Num. 13. 25.
Goliath's defiance. 1 Sam. 17. 16.
Elijah's journey to Horeb. 1 Kn. 19. 8.
Jonah's warning to Nineveh. Jon. 3. 4.
fasting of our Lord. Mat. 4. 2; Mk. 1. 13; Lu. 4. 2.
Christ's appearances during. Acts 1. 3.

Forty stripes. Deu. 25. 3, *f. s.* he may give him.
2 Cor. 11. 24, of the Jews five times received I *f. s.* save one.

Forty years. Ex. 16. 35, Israel did eat manna *f. y.*
Num. 14. 33, your children shall wander in the wilderness *f. y.*
Ps. 95. 10, *f. y.* long was I grieved.
See Jud. 3. 11; 5. 31; 8. 28.

Forward. Jer. 7. 24, backward, and not *f.*
Zec. 1. 15, helped *f.* the affliction.
See 2 Cor. 8. 8; 9. 2; 3 John 6.

Foul. Job 16. 16; Mat. 16. 3; Mk. 9. 25; Rev. 18. 2.

Found. Gen. 27. 20, *f.* it so quickly.
37. 32, this have we *f.*
44. 16, hath *f.* out iniquity.
1 Kn. 20. 36, a lion *f.* him.
21. 20, hast thou *f.* me?
2 Kn. 22. 8, I *f.* book of the law.
2 Chr. 19. 3, good things *f.* in thee.
Job 28. 12, 13, where shall wisdom be *f.*?
33. 24, I have *f.* a ransom.
Ps. 32. 6, when thou mayest be *f.*
36. 2, iniquity *f.* to be hateful.
84. 3, sparrow hath *f.* an house.
Prov. 25. 16, hast thou *f.* honey?
Eccl. 7. 28, one among a thousand have I *f.*
7. 29, this only have I *f.*
S. of S. 3. 4, but I *f.* him whom my soul loveth.
Isa. 65. 1; Rom. 10. 20, *f.* of them that sought me not.
Jer. 2. 26, thief ashamed when he is *f.*
2. 34, in thy skirts is *f.*
41. 8, ten men were *f.*
Ezek. 22. 30, I sought for a man, but *f.* none.
Dan. 5. 27, weighed and *f.* wanting.
Mal. 2. 6, iniquity not *f.* in his lips.
Mat. 7. 25; Lu. 6. 48, it was *f.* on a rock.
8. 10; Lu. 7. 9, have not *f.* so great faith.
13. 46, *f.* one pearl of great price.
20. 6, *f.* others standing idle.
21. 19; Mk. 14. 40; Lu. 22. 45, *f.* nothing thereon.
Mk. 7. 2, they *f.* fault.
7. 30, she *f.* the devil gone out.
Lu. 2. 46, they *f.* him in the temple.
8. 35, they *f.* the man clothed.
15. 5, 6, *f.* the sheep.
15. 9, *f.* the piece of money.
15. 24, 32, was lost, and is *f.*
23. 14, I have *f.* no fault.
24. 2, *f.* the stone rolled away.
24. 3, 23, *f.* not the body.
John 1. 41, 45, we have *f.* the Messias.
Acts 7. 11, our fathers *f.* no sustenance.
9. 2, if he *f.* any of this way.
17. 23, I *f.* an altar.
Rom. 7. 10, I *f.* to be unto death.
Gal. 2. 17, we ourselves also are *f.* sinners.
Phil. 2. 8, *f.* in fashion as a man.
Heb. 11. 5, Enoch was not *f.*
12. 17, he *f.* no place of repentance.
Rev. 3. 2, not *f.* thy works perfect.
12. 8, nor was their place *f.* any more.
16. 20, mountains were not *f.*
See Gen. 6. 8; 2 Chr. 15. 4; 2 Cor. 5. 3; Phil. 3. 9.

Foundation. Jos. 6. 26; 1 Kn. 16. 34, lay the *f.* in his firstborn.
Job 4. 19, them whose *f.* is in dust.
Ps. 11. 3, if *f.* be destroyed.
82. 5, all the *f.* of earth out of course.
102. 25, of old laid *f.* of earth.
137. 7, rase it even to the *f.*
Prov. 10. 25, righteous an everlasting *f.*
Isa. 28. 16, I lay in Zion a *f.*
58. 12, the *f.* of many generations.
Lu. 6. 48, laid the *f.* on a rock.
6. 49, without a *f.*
Rom. 15. 20, on another man's *f.*
1 Cor. 3. 10, I laid the *f.*
3. 11, other *f.* can no man lay.
3. 12, if any man build upon this *f.*
Eph. 2. 20, on the *f.* of the apostles and prophets.
1 Tim. 6. 19, laying up for themselves a good *f.*
2 Tim. 2. 19, the *f.* of God standeth sure.
Heb. 6. 1, not laying the *f.* of repentance.
11. 10, a city that hath *f.*
Rev. 21. 14, the wall had twelve *f.*
See Mat. 13. 35; John 17. 24; Acts 16. 26.

Fountain. Gen. 7. 11; 8. 2, *f.* of great deep.
Deu. 8. 7, a land of *f.*
2 Chr. 32. 3, took counsel to stop *f.* of water.
Ps. 36. 9, the *f.* of life.
Prov. 5. 16, let thy *f.* be dispersed.
8. 24, no *f.* abounding with water.
13. 14, law of the wise a *f.* of life.
14. 27, fear of the Lord a *f.* of life.
25. 26, a troubled *f.* and corrupt spring.
Eccl. 12. 6, pitcher broken at the *f.*
S. of S. 4. 12, a *f.* sealed.
4. 15, a *f.* of gardens.
Jer. 2. 13; 17. 13, forsaken *f.* of living waters.
9. 1, eyes a *f.* of tears.
Hos. 13. 15, his *f.* shall be dried up.
Zec. 13. 1, in that day shall be a *f.* opened.
Jas. 3. 11, 12, doth a *f.* send forth.
Rev. 7. 17, lead them to living *f.*
14. 7, worship him that made *f.* of waters.
21. 6, of the *f.* of life freely.
See Isa. 12. 3; 44. 3; 55. 1; Jer. 6. 7; Joel 3. 18; Mk. 5. 29; John 4. 10.

Four living creatures, vision of. Ezek. 1. 5; 10. 10; Rev. 4. 6; 5. 14; 6. 6.
kingdoms, Nebuchadnezzar's vision of. Dan. 2. 36.
Daniel's vision of. Dan. 7. 3, 16.

Fourfold compensation. Ex. 22. 1; 2 Sam. 12. 6; Lu. 19. 8.

Fowl, Fatted (1 Kn. 4. 23). Heb. *Barburîm, Abusîm*, 'fatted fowl.' Probably geese, which abound all over Palestine, as likewise domestic fowls.

Fowls. Gen. 1. 20, and *f.* that may fly above the earth.
7. 3, of *f.* also of the air by sevens.
Ps. 104. 12, the *f.* of heaven have their habitation.
148. 10, creeping things, and flying *f.*

Fox (Jud. 15. 4). Heb. *Shûâl*: Gk. ἀλώπηξ: R.V. marg. 'jackal.' The Hebrew word invariably translated 'fox' generally refers to the 'jackal' (*Canis aureus*), which is very abundant in Palestine; and the word seems a generic one, including both.
S. of S. 2. 15, take us the *f.*, the little *f.*
Lam. 5. 18, the *f.* walk upon it.
Mat. 8. 20, the *f.* have holes.
Lu. 13. 32, go ye, and tell that *f.*

Fragments. John 6. 12, 13, gather up *f.* that remain.
See Mat. 14. 20; Mk. 6. 43; 8. 19; Lu. 9. 17.

Frail. Ps. 39. 4.

Frame. (1) to contrive, manage. Jud. 12. 6, he could not *f.* to pronounce.
Ps. 94. 20, *f.* mischief by a law.
(2) Ps. 103. 14, he knoweth our *f.*
Isa. 29. 16, shall thing *f.* say of him that *f.* it?
Eph. 2. 21, building fitly *f.* together.
See Ezek. 40. 2; Hos. 5. 4; Heb. 11. 3.

Frankincense (Ex. 30. 34; Isa. 60. 6, R. V.). Heb. *Lĕbônah*: Gk. λίβανος: Bot. N. *Boswellia thurifera*, and other species of Boswellia. The frankincense tree, somewhat like a mountain ash, from which is distilled a fragrant gum, one of the ingredients of the sacred incense.
various uses for, Ex. 30. 34; Lev. 2. 1; S. of S. 3. 6; Mat. 2. 11.

Frankly. Lu. 7. 42.

Fraud, condemned. Lev. 19. 13; Ps. 10. 7; Mal. 3. 5; Mk. 10. 19; 1 Cor. 6. 8; 1 Thes. 4. 6; Jas. 5. 4.
See DECEIT.

Fray, to scare, frighten away. Deu. 28. 26; Jer. 7. 33; Zec. 1. 21.

Free. Gen. 2. 16, of every tree thou mayest *f.* eat.
Deu. 24. 5, shall be *f.* at home one year.
Jos. 9. 23, there shall none of you be *f.* R. V. never fail.
1 Sam. 14. 30, if people had eaten *f.*
2 Chr. 29. 31, of *f.* heart offered. R. V. willing.
Ez. 2. 68, chief fathers offered *f.* R. V. willingly.
7. 15, king and counsellors offered *f.* to God.
Ps. 51. 12, with thy *f.* spirit.
88. 5, *f.* among the dead. R. V. cast off.
Isa. 58. 6, let the oppressed go *f.*
Hos. 14. 4, I will love them *f.*
Mat. 10. 8, *f.* ye have received, *f.* give.
17. 26, then are the children *f.*
Mk. 7. 11, if a man say Corban, he shall be *f.*
John 8. 32, the truth shall make you *f.*
8. 33, how sayest thou, ye shall be *f.*?
8. 36, Son make you *f.*, ye shall be *f.* indeed.
Acts 22. 28, I was *f.* born. R. V. a Roman.
Rom. 3. 24, justified *f.* by his grace.
5. 15, the *f.* gift.
6. 18, 22, being made *f.* from sin.
6. 20, servants of sin, *f.* from righteousness.
8. 2, *f.* from the law of sin and death.
8. 32, with him *f.* give us all things.
1 Cor. 9. 1, am I not *f.*?
9. 19, though *f.* from all men.
12. 13; Eph. 6. 8, whether bond or *f.*
Gal. 3. 28; Col. 3. 11, there is neither bond nor *f.*
5. 1, wherewith Christ hath made us *f.*
2 Thes. 3. 1, word have *f.* course. R. V. run.
1 Pet. 2. 16, as *f.*, and not using liberty.
Rev. 21. 6, give of fountain of life *f.*
22. 17, let him take water of life *f.*
See Ex. 21. 2; Deu. 15. 13; Jer. 34. 9; Gal. 4. 22.

Freewill. Lev. 22. 18, and for all his *f.* offerings.
Num. 15. 3, or in a *f.* offering.
Deu. 16. 10, a tribute of a *f.* offering.
See Ez. 3. 5.

Freewoman. Gal. 4. 22.

Fresh. Num. 11. 8; Job 29. 20; 33. 25; Jas. 3. 12.

Fret. (1) to corrode, to eat away, as a moth (or an ulcer) does. Lev. 13. 51, 55.
(2) Ps. 37. 1, 7, 8; Prov. 24. 19, *f.* not thyself.
Prov. 19. 3, his heart *f.* against the Lord.
See 1 Sam. 1. 6; Isa. 8. 21; Ezek. 16. 43.

Friend. Ex. 33. 11, as a man to his *f.*
2 Sam. 19. 6, lovest thine enemies, and hatest *f.* R. V. them that love thee.
2 Chr. 20. 7, Abraham thy *f.* for ever.
Job 6. 27, ye dig a pit for your *f.*
42. 10, when he prayed for his *f.*
Ps. 35. 14, as though he had been my *f.*
41. 9, my familiar *f.* hath lifted.
88. 18, lover and *f.* hast thou put far from me.
Prov. 6. 1, if thou be surety for thy *f.* R. V. neighbour.
6. 3, make sure thy *f.* R. V. neighbour.
14. 20, the rich hath many *f.*
16. 28; 17. 9, whisperer separateth chief *f.*
17. 17, *f.* loveth at all times.
18. 24, a *f.* that sticketh closer than a brother.
19. 4, wealth maketh many *f.*
27. 6, faithful are wounds of a *f.*
27. 10, thine own *f.* and father's *f.* forsake not.
27. 17, man sharpeneth countenance of his *f.*
S. of S. 5. 16, this is my *f.*
Isa. 41. 8, seed of Abraham my *f.*
Jer. 20. 4, a terror to thy *f.*
Mic. 7. 5, trust not in a *f.*
Zec. 13. 6, wounded in house of my *f.*

Mat. 11. 19; Lu. 7. 34, a *f.* of publicans.
20. 13, *f.*, I do thee no wrong.
22. 12, *f.*, how camest thou hither?
26. 50, *f.*, wherefore art thou come?
Mk. 5. 19, go home to thy *f.*
Lu. 11. 5, which of you shall have a *f.*
11. 8, though he give not because he is his *f.*
14. 12, call not thy *f.*
15. 6, 9, calleth his *f.* and neighbours.
16. 9, *f.* of the mammon.
John 11. 11, our *f.* Lazarus sleepeth.
15. 13, lay down his life for his *f.*
15. 14, ye are my *f.*, if ye do whatsoever I command.
15. 15, not servants, but *f.*
19. 12, thou art not Cæsar's *f.*
Jas. 2. 23, Abraham was called the *f.* of God.
4. 4, a *f.* of the world.

Friends, value of. Prov. 18. 24; 27. 6, 9, 17; John 15. 13.
danger arising from evil. Deu. 13. 6; Prov. 22. 24; 25. 19; Mic. 7. 5; Zec. 13. 6.
Jesus calls His disciples. Lu. 12. 4; John 15. 14; 3 John 14.

Friendship of David and Jonathan. 1 Sam. 18. 1; 19.; 20.; 2 Sam. 1. 26.
with the world, unlawful. Rom. 12. 2; 2 Cor. 6. 17; Jas. 4. 4; 1 John 2. 15.

Fringes. Num. 15. 38, that they make them *f.*
Deu. 22. 12, thou shalt make thee *f.*

Frog (Ex. 8. 2; Ps. 78. 45; 105. 30; Rev. 16. 13). Heb. *Tzĕphardê'a:* Gk. *βάτραχος*: Zoöl. S. *Rana esculenta; Hyla arborea;* belongs to Zoological Class Amphibia.

Frontlets, something worn on the forehead. phylacteries bound on the forehead. Ex. 13. 16; Deu. 6. 8.

Froward, perverse, self-willed. Deu. 32. 20, a very *f.* generation.
Prov. 2. 12, man that speaketh *f.* things.
3. 32, the *f.* is abomination.
4. 24, put away *f.* mouth.
11. 20; 17. 20, of a *f.* heart.
16. 28, a *f.* man soweth strife.
21. 8, the way of man is *f.* R. V. laden with guilt.
22. 5, snares are in way of the *f.*
See Prov. 10. 32; Isa. 57. 17; 1 Pet. 2. 18.

Frowardness, results of. Deu. 32. 20; 2 Sam. 22. 27; Job 5. 13; Prov. 2. 12; 3. 32; 4. 24; 10. 31; 11. 20; 16. 28; 17. 20; 21. 8; 22. 5.

Fruit. Num. 13. 26, shewed them the *f.* of the land.
Deu. 26. 2, take the first of all *f.*
33. 14, precious *f.* brought forth.
Ps. 107. 37, yield *f.* of increase.
127. 3, the *f.* of the womb is his reward.
Prov. 8. 19, my *f.* is better than gold.
11. 30, *f.* of the righteous a tree of life.
12. 14; 18. 20, satisfied by the *f.* of his mouth.
S. of S. 2. 3, his *f.* was sweet to my taste.
4. 13, 16, orchard with pleasant *f.*
Isa. 3. 10; Mic. 7. 13, the *f.* of their doings.
27. 6, fill face of the world with *f.*
28. 4, the hasty *f.* before summer. R. V. first-ripe fig.
57. 19, I create the *f.* of the lips.
Jer. 17. 10; 21. 14; 32. 19, according to *f.* of doings.
Hos. 10. 13, eaten the *f.* of lies.
Am. 8. 1, basket of summer *f.*
Mic. 6. 7, *f.* of body for sin of soul.
Hab. 3. 17, neither shall *f.* be in vines.
Hag. 1. 10, earth is stayed from her *f.*
Mat. 3. 8; Lu. 3. 8, *f.* meet for repentance.
7. 16, 20, by their *f.* ye shall know them.
12. 33, make tree good, and his *f.* good.
13. 23, is he who beareth *f.*
21. 19, let no *f.* grow on thee.
21. 34, when time of *f.* drew near.
26. 29; Mk. 14. 25, drink of *f.* of vine.
Mk. 4. 28, earth bringeth forth *f.* of herself.
12. 2, receive the *f.* of the vineyard.
Lu. 13. 6, he sought *f.* thereon.
13. 7, I come seeking *f.* on this fig tree.
13. 9, if it bear *f.*, well.
John 4. 36, *f.* to life eternal.
John 15. 2, branch that beareth *f.*
15. 4, branch cannot bear *f.* of itself.
15. 8, that ye bear much *f.*
15. 16, ordained that ye should bring forth *f.*
Rom. 1. 13, have some *f.* among you.
6. 21, what *f.* had ye then.
7. 4, bring forth *f.* unto God.
2 Cor. 9. 10; Phil. 1. 11, the *f.* of righteousness.
Gal. 5. 22; Eph. 5. 9, the *f.* of the Spirit.
Phil. 1. 22, this is the *f.* of my labour.
4. 17, I desire *f.* that may abound.
Col. 1. 6, the gospel bringeth forth *f.* in you.
2 Tim. 2. 6, first partaker of the *f.*
Heb. 12. 11, peaceable *f.* of righteousness.
13. 15, the *f.* of our lips.
Jas. 3. 17, wisdom full of good *f.*
5. 7, waiteth for the precious *f.*
Jude 12, trees whose *f.* withereth, without *f.*
Rev. 22. 2, yielded her *f.* every month.
See Gen. 30. 2; Ps. 92. 14; Jer. 12. 2; Col. 1. 10.

Fruits, first three years to remain untouched. Lev. 19. 23.
of the obedient will be blessed. Deu. 7. 13; 28. 4.
of faith meet for repentance. Mat. 3. 8; 7. 16; John 4. 36; 15. 16; Rom. 7. 4; 2 Cor. 9. 10; Gal. 5. 22; Col. 1. 6; Heb. 12. 11; Jas. 3. 17.

Fruit trees saved in time of war. Deu. 20. 19.

Frustrate. Ez. 4. 5; Isa. 44. 25; Gal. 2. 21.

Fuel. Isa. 9. 5; Ezek. 15. 4; 21. 32.

Fugitive servant, law of. Deu. 23. 15.

Fulfil. Ps. 20. 4, the Lord *f.* all thy counsel.
20. 5, *f.* all thy petitions.
145. 19, he will *f.* the desire of them.
Mat. 3. 15, to *f.* all righteousness.
5. 17, not to destroy, but to *f.*
5. 18; 24. 34, till all be *f.* R. V. accomplished.
Mk. 13. 4, what the sign when these shall be *f.*? R. V. about to be accomplished.
Lu. 1. 20, my words shall be *f.* in season.
21. 24, times of the Gentiles be *f.*
22. 16, till it be *f.* in kingdom of God.
John 3. 29; 17. 13, this my joy is *f.*
Acts 13. 25, and as John *f.* his course.
13. 33, God hath *f.* the same unto us.
Rom. 13. 10, love is the *f.* of the law.
Gal. 5. 14, all the law is *f.* in one word.
6. 2, so *f.* the law of Christ.
Eph. 2. 3, *f.* the desires of the flesh. R. V. doing.
Phil. 2. 2, *f.* ye my joy.
Col. 4. 17, take heed thou *f.* the ministry.
2 Thes. 1. 11, *f.* good pleasure of his will.
Jas. 2. 8, if ye *f.* the royal law.
See Ex. 5. 13; 23. 26; Gal. 5. 16; Rev. 17. 17.

Full. Lev. 19. 29, land became *f.* of wickedness.
Deu. 6. 11, houses *f.* of good things.
34. 9, Joshua was *f.* of spirit of wisdom.
Ru. 1. 21, I went out *f.*
2 Kn. 6. 17, mountain was *f.* of horses.
1 Chr. 21. 22, 24, for the *f.* price.
Job 5. 26, come to grave in *f.* age.
11. 2, a man *f.* of talk.
14. 1, *f.* of trouble.
20. 11, *f.* of the sins of youth.
21. 23, dieth in his *f.* strength.
32. 18, I am *f.* of matter.
Ps. 10. 7; Rom. 3. 14, mouth *f.* of cursing.
65. 9, which is *f.* of water.
74. 20, *f.* of habitations of cruelty.
88. 3, soul *f.* of troubles.
119. 64, earth is *f.* of thy mercy.
127. 5, happy the man that hath his quiver *f.*
Prov. 27. 7, the *f.* soul loatheth an honeycomb.
27. 20, hell and destruction are never *f.* R. V. satisfied.
30. 9, lest I be *f.*, and deny thee.
Eccl. 1. 7, yet the sea is not *f.*
Hab. 3. 3, earth *f.* of his praise.
Zec. 8. 5, streets *f.* of boys and girls.
Mat. 6. 22; Lu. 11. 36, *f.* of light.
Lu. 6. 25, woe unto you that are *f.*!
11. 39, *f.* of ravening.
John 1. 14, *f.* of grace and truth.

John 15. 11; 16. 24, that your joy may be *f.*!
Acts 6. 3; 7. 55; 11. 24, men *f.* of the Holy Ghost.
9. 36, *f.* of good works.
Rom. 15. 14, ye also are *f.* of goodness.
1 Cor. 4. 8, now ye are *f.*
Phil. 4. 12, I am instructed to be *f.*
4. 18, I am *f.*
2 Tim. 4. 5, make *f.* proof of thy ministry.
Heb. 5. 14, meat to them of *f.* age. R. V. full-grown men.
1 Pet. 1. 8, with joy unspeakable and *f.* of glory.
Rev. 15. 7, *f.* of the wrath of God.
See Lev. 2. 14; 2 Kn. 4. 6; 10. 21; Am. 2. 13.

Fuller, a bleacher of cloth. Mal. 3. 2; Mk. 9. 3.

Fully. Num. 14. 24, Caleb hath followed me *f.*
Eccl. 8. 11, heart is *f.* set to do evil.
Rom. 14. 5, let every man be *f.* persuaded.
15. 19, I have *f.* preached the gospel.
Rev. 14. 18, her grapes are *f.* ripe.
See 1 Kn. 11. 6; Acts 2. 1; Rom. 4. 21.

Fulness. Ps. 16. 11, *f.* of joy.
John 1. 16, of his *f.* have we received.
Rom. 11. 25, the *f.* of the Gentiles.
Eph. 1. 23, the *f.* of him that filleth all in all.
3. 19, filled with the *f.* of God.
4. 13, the stature of the *f.* of Christ.
Col. 1. 19, in him should all *f.* dwell.
2. 9, the *f.* of the Godhead bodily.
See Num. 18. 27; Ps. 96. 11; Rom. 11. 12.

Furious. Prov. 22. 24, with a *f.* man thou shalt not go.
29. 22, a *f.* man aboundeth in transgression.
Nah. 1. 2, the Lord is *f.*
See 2 Kn. 9. 20; Ezek. 5. 15; 23. 25.

Furlong. Lu. 24. 13; John 11. 18 = a Roman stadium = 120 paces = ⅛ of a mile.
See Measures.

Furnace. Deu. 4. 20, Lord hath taken you out of *f.*
Ps. 12. 6, as silver tried in a *f.*
Isa. 48. 10, in the *f.* of affliction.
Mat. 13. 42, into a *f.* of fire.
See Gen. 15. 17; 19. 28; 1 Kn. 8. 51; Dan. 3. 6, 11, 15, &c.; Ezek. 22. 18.

Furnish. Ps. 78. 19; Mat. 22. 10; 2 Tim. 3. 17.

Furniture, equipment, harness. Gen. 31. 34.

Furrows. Ps. 65. 10; 129. 3; Hos. 10. 4; 12. 11.

Further. Ez. 8. 36, they *f.* the people.
Job 38. 11, hitherto shalt thou come, but no *f.*
Lu. 24. 28, as though he would have gone *f.*
Acts 4. 17, that it spread no *f.*
2 Tim. 3. 9, they shall proceed no *f.*
See Mk. 5. 35; Phil. 1. 12, 25.

Fury. Gen. 27. 44, till thy brother's *f.* turn.
Isa. 27. 4, *f.* is not in me.
63. 5, my *f.* upheld me.
Jer. 21. 5, I will fight against thee in *f.*
25. 15, the wine cup of this *f.*
Ezek. 21. 17, I will cause my *f.* to rest.
See Dan. 3. 13, 19; 8. 6; 9. 16; 11. 44.

Gaal, gā'-ăl, 'loathing.' Jud. 9. 26.

Gaash, gā'-ăsh, 'shaking.' Jos. 24. 30.

Gaba, gā'-bă, 'hill.' Jos. 18. 24.

Gabbai, găb-bā'-ī, 'a collector of tribute.' Neh. 11. 8.

Gabbatha, găb'-bă-thă, 'height' (pavement). John 19. 13.

Gabriel, gā'-brĭ-ĕl, 'man of God;' archangel, appears to Daniel. Dan. 8. 16; 9. 21.
to Zacharias. Lu. 1. 19.
to Mary. Lu. 1. 26.

Gad, găd, 'a troop' or 'good fortune.' (1) birth of. Gen. 30. 11.
his descendants. Gen. 46. 16.
blessed by Jacob. Gen. 49. 19.
(2) tribe of, blessed by Moses. Deu. 33. 20.
numbered. Num. 1. 24; 26. 15.
their possessions. Num. 32.; 34. 14.
divers commands to. Deu. 27. 13; Jos. 4. 12.
commended by Joshua. Jos. 22. 1.
charged with idolatry. Jos. 22. 11.
their defence. Jos. 22. 21.
(3) seer, his message to David. 2 Sam. 24. 11; 1 Chr. 21. 9; 2 Chr. 29. 25.

Gadara, the name of a city, and the surrounding district S. E. of the Sea of Galilee.

Gadarenes, găd'-ă-rēnes, inhabitants of Gadara; Christ's miracle in the country of. Mat. 8. 28; Mk. 5. 1; Lu. 8. 26.

Gaddi, găd'-dī, my fortune. Num. 13. 11.

Gaddiel, găd'-dĭ-ĕl, 'God is my fortune.' Num. 13. 10.

Gadfly. Probably the *Zebûb* of Eccl. 10. 1. *See* Fly.

Gadi, gā'dī. 2 Kn. 15. 14.

Gadites, găd'-ītes, persons belonging to the tribe of Gad. Deu. 3. 12.

Gaham, gā'-hăm, 'flame' (?). Gen. 22. 24.

Gahar, gā'-här, 'hiding-place.' Ez. 2. 47.

Gain. Job 22. 3, is it *g.* to him that thou makest thy ways perfect?
Prov. 1. 19; 15. 27; Ezek. 22. 12, greedy of *g.*
3. 14, the *g.* thereof better than gold.
28. 8, by usury and unjust *g.* R. V. usury and increase.
Ezek. 22. 13, 27, at thy dishonest *g.*
Dan. 11. 39, he shall divide the land for *g.* R. V. a price.
Mic. 4. 13, consecrate their *g.* to the Lord.
Mat. 16. 26; Mk. 8. 36; Lu. 9. 25, if he *g.* the world.
18. 15, thou hast *g.* thy brother.
25. 17, 22, had also *g.* other two.
Lu. 19. 15, 16, 18, had *g.* by trading.
Acts 16. 19, hope of their *g.* was gone.
19. 24, no small *g.* to the craftsmen. R. V. business.
1 Cor. 9. 19, that I might *g.* the more.
9. 20, that I might *g.* the Jews.
2 Cor. 12. 17, 18, did I make a *g.* of you? R. V. take advantage.
Phil. 1. 21, to die is *g.*
3. 7, *g.* to me, I counted loss.
1 Tim. 6. 5, supposing that *g.* is godliness. R. V. that godliness is a way of *g.*
6. 6, godliness with contentment is great *g.*
See Jud. 5. 19; Job 27. 8; Jas. 4. 13.

Gainsay, to speak against, i. e., contradict. Lu. 21. 15; Tit. 1. 9; Jude 11.

Gaius, gā'-ŭs. The Greek form of Caius. Acts 19. 29.
his piety. 3 John.

Galal, gā'-lăl, 'worthy' (?). 1 Chr. 9. 15.

Galatia, gă-lā'-tĭă, 'a place colonized by Gauls.' A Roman province in Asia Minor including both N. and S. Galatia, within the latter of which were probably the cities of Antioch, Iconium, Lystra, and Derbe.

Galatians, gă-lā'-tĭăns, inhabitants of Galatia. Gal. 3. 1.
Paul visits. Acts 16. 6.
reproved. Gal. 1. 6; 3.
exhorted. Gal. 5.; 6.
their love to Paul. Gal. 4. 13.

Galatians. An epistle of Paul to the churches of Galatia, probably to the cities of S. Galatia where he preached on his first missionary journey. Written about A. D. 57.

Galbanum (Ex. 30. 34). Heb. *Ḥelbĕnah:* Gk. *χαλβάνη*: Bot. N. *Opoidia galbanifera; Galbanum officinale.* A yellow resin, exuding from two umbelliferous plants; one of the ingredients of the sacred incense.

Galeed, gā'-lĕēd, 'witness-heap.' Gen. 31. 47.

Galilæans, găl-ĭ-læ'-ăns, i. e., natives of Galilee, were looked down upon by the southern Jews as an ignorant and rustic folk. Thus the name became a term of reproach. At the same time they were from a religious point of view the most liberal-minded people of Palestine; healthy, brave, industrious, and enterprising.
slaughter of. Lu. 13. 1.
disciples so called. Acts 1. 11; 2. 7.

Galilee, găl'-ĭ-lēe (circuit) (Jos. 20. 7). The northern of the three provinces of Palestine west of the Jordan, extending about 60 miles from north to south, and 30 miles from east to west. It was the scene of a considerable part of the ministry of Jesus.

Isaiah's prophecy concerning. Isa. 9. 1; Mat. 4. 15.
work of Christ there. Mat. 2. 22; 15. 29; 26. 32; 27. 55; 28. 7; Mk. 1. 9; Lu. 4. 14; 23. 5; 24. 6; Acts 10. 37; 13. 31.

Galilee, Sea of, called also Sea of Tiberias, Lake of Gennesaret, Sea of Chinnereth. About 13 miles long and 7 broad; 700 feet below the level of the Mediterranean. In the time of Christ the shore was a continuous garden, with several cities and villages, and was a favorite summer resort.

Gall. Heb. *Rôsh:* Gk. χολή, some poisonous bitter herb; it is twice translated 'poison,' and also 'hemlock.' Dr. Post of Syria thinks *Rôsh* is the poppy.
Ps. 69. 21; Jer. 9. 15; Lam. 3. 19; Am. 6. 12; Mat. 27. 34; Acts 8. 23.

Gallant, splendid. Isa. 33. 21.

Gallim, găl'-lĭm, 'heaps.' 1 Sam. 25. 44.

Gallio, găl'-lĭ-ō, dismisses Paul. Acts 18. 12.

Gallows. Esth. 7. 10, they hanged Haman on the *g.*

Gamaliel, gă-mā'-lĭ-ĕl, 'reward of God.' (1) Num. 1. 10.
(2) advises the council. Acts 5. 34.
Paul brought up at feet of. Acts 22. 3.

Games, public. 1 Cor. 9. 24; Phil. 3. 12; 1 Tim. 6. 12; 2 Tim. 2. 5; 4. 7; Heb. 12. 1.

Gammadims, găm'-mă-dĭms, 'warriors' (?). Ezek. 27. 11.

Gamul, găm'-ŭl, 'weaned.' 1 Chr. 24. 17.

Gap. Ezek. 13. 5; 22. 30.

Garden. Gen. 2. 8, God planted a *g.* eastward in Eden. 13. 10, as the *g.* of the Lord.
Deu. 11. 10; 1 Kn. 21. 2, as a *g.* of herbs.
S. of S. 4. 12, a *g.* enclosed.
4. 16, blow upon my *g.*
5. 1, I am come into my *g.*
6. 2, 11, gone down into his *g.*
Isa. 1. 8, as a lodge in a *g.*
1. 30, as a *g.* that hath no water.
51. 3, her desert like the *g.* of the Lord.
58. 11; Jer. 31. 12, like a watered *g.* [forth.
61. 11, as the *g.* causeth things sown to spring
Jer. 29. 5, plant *g.*, and eat the fruit.
Ezek. 28. 13, in Eden the *g.* of God.
31. 8. 9, cedars in *g.* of God.
36. 35, is become like the *g.* of Eden.
Joel 2. 3, land as the *g.* of Eden before them.
John 18. 1, where was a *g.*
18. 26, did not I see thee in the *g.* ?
19. 41, there was a *g.*, and in the *g.*
See Gen. 2. 15; Am. 4. 9; 9. 14; John 20. 15.

Garden house, a summer-house in a garden. 2 Kn. 9. 27.

Gareb, gā'-reb, 'scurfy' (?). 2 Sam. 23. 38; Jer. 31. 39.

Garlick (Num. 11. 5). Heb. *Shoom:* Gk. τὰ σκόρδα: Bot. N. *Allium sativum*, a kind of onion.

Garment. Gen. 39. 12, he left his *g.*, and fled.
49. 11, washed his *g.* in wine.
Jos. 7. 21, a goodly Babylonish *g.* R. V. mantle.
9. 5, Gibeonites took old *g.*
2 Kn. 5. 26, is it a time to receive *g.* ?
7. 15, all the way was full of *g.*
Job 37. 17, how thy *g.* are warm.
Ps. 22. 18, they part my *g.* among them. [*g.*
102. 26; Isa. 50. 9; 51. 6; Heb. 1. 11, wax old as a
104. 2, with light as with a *g.*
104. 6, coveredst it with the deep as with a *g.*
109. 18, clothed himself with cursing as with his *g.*
Prov. 20. 16, take his *g.* that is surety.
25. 20, a *g.* in cold weather.
30. 4, who hath bound the waters in a *g.* ?
Eccl. 9. 8, let thy *g.* be always white.
Isa. 52. 1, put on thy beautiful *g.*
61. 3, *g.* of praise for spirit of heaviness.
61. 10, the *g.* of salvation.
Joel 2. 13, rend your heart and not your *g.*
Zec. 13. 4, a rough *g.* to deceive. R. V. hairy mantle.
Mat. 9. 16; Mk. 2. 21; Lu. 5. 36, new cloth, old *g.*
Mat. 20. 14, 36; Mk. 5. 27; Lu. 8. 44, hem of *g.*
21. 8; Mk. 11. 8, spread *g.* in way.
22. 11, 12, wedding *g.*
23. 5, enlarge borders of *g.*
27. 35; Mk. 15. 24, parted *g.*, casting lots.
Mk. 11. 7; Lu. 19. 35, cast *g.* on colt. [cloke.
13. 16, not turn back again to take *g.* R. V.
Lu. 22. 36, let him sell his *g.* R. V. cloke.
24. 4, in shining *g.* R. V. dazzling apparel.
Acts 9. 39, shewing the coats and *g.*
Jas. 5. 2, your *g.* are motheaten.
Jude 23, the *g.* spotted by the flesh.
Rev. 3. 4, not defiled their *g.*
16. 15, that watcheth, and keepeth his *g.*

Garments (*of men*). The garments of Syrian men in the present day differ but little from those worn in the time of Moses. The chief are;—
(1) a coarse linen shirt;
(2) linen drawers;
(3) loose pantaloons with a girdle to sustain them;
(4) an inner vest buttoned to the throat;
(5) a long loose robe with a leathern girdle;
(6) an embroidered cloth or velvet jacket;
(7) a *keffiyeh* or silk handkerchief for the head;
(8) hose and
(9) sandals,
Besides these,
(10) a long loose robe with short sleeves was worn in full dress (instead of the jacket or girded robe), such as our Lord laid aside when He washed the disciples' feet (John 13. 4);
(11) the *aba*, a coarse cloak of goat's or camel's hair, very large, so as to form a covering by night as well as by day, with which Elijah smote the waters of Jordan (2 Kn. 2. 8).

Garments (*of women*). Women's dress varied according to their estate in life (e.g., maid, wife, or widow). It differed from the men's principally in the veil and cap, fitting close to the head, concealing the hair, and being profusely covered with gold and silver ornaments and with charms. The list of female clothing in Isa. 3. 18–23 is scarcely intelligible now.

Garments, priestly. Ex. 28. 39.
manner of purifying. Lev. 13. 47 (Eccl. 9. 8; Zec. 3. 3; Jude 23).
not of mixed materials. Lev. 19. 19; Deu. 22. 11.
of sexes, not to be exchanged. Deu. 22. 5.
of Christ, lots cast for (Ps. 22. 18); Mat. 27. 35; John 19. 23.

Garments, the hem of (Ex. 28. 33; Mat. 9. 20; 14. 36). The fringe which all Jews wore in obedience to the order given in Num. 15. 38. It is now represented by the *Tallith* or cloth worn by the Jews at prayers.

Garmite, gär'-mīte, 'bony.' 1 Chr. 4. 19.

Garner, a granary, barn. Ps. 144. 13; Joel 1. 17; Mat. 3. 12.

Garnish. Job 26. 13; Mat. 12. 44; 23. 29.

Gashmu, găsh'-mū, same as Geshem. Neh. 6. 6.

Gatam, gā'-tăm. Gen. 36. 11.

Gate (Jud. 5. 8; Ru. 4. 10). The gate of a city was frequently a considerable structure, near which was a public place of assembly, the exchange, court-house, and council-chamber of modern times. Hence the 'gate of a city' was so identified with the life of the community as to be synonymous with the city itself.
Gen. 28. 17, the *g.* of heaven.
Deu. 6. 9; 11. 20, write them on thy *g.*
Ps. 9. 13, the *g.* of death.
118. 19, the *g.* of righteousness.
Prov. 17. 19, exalteth *g.* seeketh destruction.
31. 23, her husband known in the *g.*
Isa. 26. 2, open the *g.*, that righteous may enter.
38. 10, the *g.* of the grave.
45. 1, open the two-leaved *g.*
60. 11, thy *g.* shall be open continually.
60. 18, walls Salvation, and *g.* Praise.

Mat. 7. 13; Lu. 13. 24, strait *g.*, wide *g.*
16. 18, *g.* of hell shall not prevail.
Heb. 13. 12, also suffered without the *g.*
Rev. 21. 25, *g.* not shut at all by day.
See Ps. 24. 7; Isa. 28. 6; Nah. 2. 6.

Gath, găth, 'wine-press.' Jos. 11. 22.
Goliath of. 1 Sam. 17. 4.
men of, smitten with emerods. 1 Sam. 5. 8.
David a refugee there. 1 Sam. 27. 4.
taken by David. 1 Chr. 18. 1.
by Hazael. 2 Kn. 12. 17.
Uzziah breaks down the wall of. 2 Chr. 26. 6.

Gather. Gen. 41. 35, let them *g.* all the food.
49. 10, to him shall *g.* of the people be. R. V. obedience.
Ex. 16. 17, *g.*, some more, some less.
Deu. 28. 38, carry much out, and *g.* little in.
30. 3; Ezek. 36. 24, will *g.* thee from all nations.
2 Sam. 14. 14, spilt, which cannot be *g.* up.
Job 11. 10, if he *g.* together, who can hinder? R. V. call to judgment.
Ps. 26. 9, *g.* not my soul with sinners.
39. 6, knoweth not who shall *g.* them.
Prov. 6. 8, the ant *g.* her food.
10. 5, he that *g.* in summer.
13. 11, he that *g.* by labour shall increase.
Isa. 27. 12, ye shall be *g.* one by one.
40. 11, he shall *g.* the lambs.
56. 8, yet will I *g.* others.
62. 10, *g.* out the stones.
Mat. 3. 12; Lu. 3. 17, *g.* wheat into garner.
6. 26, nor *g.* into barns.
7. 16; Lu. 6. 44, do men *g.* grapes of thorns?
12. 30; Lu. 11. 23, he that *g.* not scattereth.
13. 28, wilt thou that we *g.* them up?
13. 29, lest while ye *g.* up the tares.
13. 41, shall *g.* out of his kingdom.
25. 32, before him shall be *g.* all nations.
John 6. 12, *g.* up fragments.
15. 6, men *g.* them, and cast.
1 Cor. 16. 2, that there be no *g.* when I come. R. V. collections.
2 Thes. 2. 1, by our *g.* together unto him.
See Mat. 23. 37; John 4. 36; 11. 52.

Gath-hepher, găth-hē'-phĕr, 'the wine-press of digging.' 2 Kn. 14. 25.

Gath-rimmon, găth-rĭm'-mon, 'wine-press of the pomegranate.' Jos. 19. 45.

Gave. Gen. 3. 12, the woman *g.* me.
Jos. 21. 44; 2 Chr. 15. 15; 20. 30, Lord *g.* them rest.
1 Sam. 10. 9, *g.* to Saul another heart.
Neh. 8. 8, they read, and *g.* the sense.
Job 1. 21, the Lord *g.*
Ps. 21. 4, he asked life, and thou *g.* it.
68. 11, the Lord *g.* the word.
Eccl. 12. 7, to God who *g.* it.
Am. 2. 12, ye *g.* the Nazarites wine.
Mat. 21. 23; Mk. 11. 28; Lu. 20. 2, who *g.* thee this authority?
25. 35, 42, ye *g.* me meat.
Lu. 15. 16, no man *g.* unto him.
John 10. 29, my Father, who *g.* them.
Acts 2. 4, as the Spirit *g.* them utterance.
26. 10, I *g.* my voice against them.
Rom. 1. 28, God *g.* them over.
1 Cor. 3. 6, God *g.* the increase.
Eph. 4. 8, *g.* gifts unto men
4. 11, he *g.* some apostles.
See 2 Cor. 8. 5; Gal. 1. 4; Tit. 2. 14.

Gay. Jas. 2. 3.

Gaza, gā'-ză, same as AZZAH. Gen. 10. 19.
Samson carries away the gates of. Jud. 16.
destruction of, foretold. Jer. 47.; Am. 1. 6; Zep. 2. 4; Zec. 9. 5.

Gazathites, gā'-ză-thītes, 'inhabitants of Gaza.' Jos. 13. 3.

Gaze. Ex. 19. 21; Nah. 3. 6; Acts 1. 11; Heb. 10. 33.

Gazelle. Heb. *Tsĕbî*: Gk. δορκάς: A. V. 2 Sam. 2. 18; 1 Chr. 12. 8, 'roe;' in Deu. 12. 15, etc., 'roebuck.' The correct rendering in all cases is 'gazelle.'

Gazer, gā'-zĕr, 'portion.' 2 Sam. 5. 25.

Gazez, gā'-zĕz, 'shearer.' 1 Chr. 2. 46.

Gazites, gā'-zītes, 'inhabitants of Gaza.' Jud. 16. [2

Gazzam, găz'-zăm, 'locusts.' Ez. 2. 48.

Geba, gē'-bă, 'hill.' Jos. 21. 17.

Gebal, gē'-băl, 'boundary.' Ps. 83. 7.

Geber, gē'-bĕr, 'man.' 1 Kn. 4. 13. R. V. Ben-[geber.

Gebim, gē'-bĭm, 'trenches.' Isa. 10. 31.

Gecko (Lev. 11. 30). R. V. Heb. *Anâkah*: Gk. μυγάλη: A. V. 'ferret.' The gecko is one of the most repulsive-looking lizards in Palestine, black spotted with rows of rounded warts.

Gedaliah, gĕd-ă-lī'-ăh, 'Jehovah is great;' governor of the remnant of Judah. 2 Kn. 25. 22 (Jer. 40. 5).
treacherously killed by Ishmael. 2 Kn. 25. 25 (Jer. 41.).

Gedeon, gĕd'-ĕ-on, Greek form of Gideon. Heb. 11. 32.

Geder, gē'-dĕr, 'wall.' Jos. 12. 13.

Gederah, gĕ-dē'-răh, 'enclosure,' 'sheep-fold.' Jos. 15. 36. R. V. hedges.

Gederathite, gĕ-dē'-ră-thīte, an inhabitant of Gederah. 1 Chr. 12. 4.

Gederite, gĕ-dē'-rīte, native of Geder. 1 Chr. 27. 28.

Gederoth, gĕ-dē'-rōth, 'sheep-folds.' Jos. 15. 41.

Gederothaim, gĕ-dĕ-rō-thā'-ĭm, 'two sheep-folds.' Jos. 15. 36.

Gedor, gē'-dŏr, 'wall.' (1) Jos. 15. 58.
conquered by Simeonites. 1 Chr. 4. 41.
(2) 1 Chr. 4. 4; 8. 31.

Gehazi, gĕ-hā'-zī, 'valley of vision;' servant of Elisha. 2 Kn. 4. 12.
his covetousness. 2 Kn. 5. 20.

Geliloth, gĕ-lī'-lŏth, 'circles.' Jos. 18. 17.

Gemalli, gĕ-măl'-lī, 'possessor of camels.' Num. 13. 12.

Gemariah, gĕm-ă-rī'-ăh, 'Jehovah has completed.' Jer. 29. 3.

Gender, to produce, engender. 2 Tim. 2. 23.

Genealogies: generations of Adam. Gen. 3.; 1 Chr. 1.; Lu. 3.
of Noah. Gen. 10.; 1 Chr. 1. 4.
of Shem. Gen. 11. 10.
of Terah. Gen. 11. 27.
of Abraham. Gen. 25.; 1 Chr. 1. 28.
of Jacob. Gen. 29. 31; 30.; 46. 8; Ex. 1. 2; Num. 26.; 1 Chr. 2.
of Esau. Gen. 36.; 1 Chr. 1. 35.
of the tribes. 1 Chr. 2.; 4.; 5.; 6.; 7.
of David. 1 Chr. 3.
of CHRIST. Mat. 1.; Lu. 3. 23.
endless. 1 Tim. 1. 4. *See* FABLES.

Generation. (1) Deu. 1. 35, not one of this evil *g.*
32. 5, 20, a perverse and crooked *g.*
Ps. 14. 5, God is in the *g.* of the righteous.
22. 30, it shall be accounted for a *g.*
102. 18, written for the *g.* to come.
145. 4, one *g.* shall praise thy works.
Prov. 27. 24, crown endure to every *g.*
30. 11, there is a *g.* that curseth.
Eccl. 1. 4, one *g.* passeth away.
Isa. 34. 10, from *g.* to *g.* it shall lie waste.
Joel 1. 3, children tell another *g.*
Mat. 12. 41, in judgment with this *g.*
17. 17; Mk. 9. 19; Lu. 21. 32, perverse *g.*
23. 36, shall come on this *g.*
24. 34; Mk. 13. 30; Lu. 21. 32, this *g.* shall not [pass.
Lu. 16. 8, are in their *g.* wiser.
17. 25, rejected of this *g.*
1 Pet. 2. 9, a chosen *g.* R. V. elect race.
See Isa. 53. 8; Dan. 4. 3; Lu. 11. 30.
(2) offspring, brood. Mat. 3. 7; 12. 34; 23. 33; Lu. [3. 7.

Genesis, gĕn'-ĕ-sĭs, 'generation,' or beginning, name of first book of the Pentateuch.

Gennesaret, gĕn-nĕs'-ă-rĕt, 'garden of Princes.' Probably the fertile plain at the northwest corner of the Sea of Galilee. Mat. 14. 34.
A lake of Palestine; miracles wrought there. Mat. 17. 27; Lu. 5. 1; John 21. 6.

Gentiles, gĕn'-tīles, a name including all who are not Jews.
origin of. Gen. 10. 5.

Mat. 10. 5, go not in the way of the *G.*
John 7. 35, to the dispersed among *G.* R. V. Greeks.
Acts 9. 15, bear my name before the *G.*
13. 42, *G.* besought that these words. R. V. they.
13. 46, we turn to the *G.*
15. 3, declaring conversion of the *G.*
18. 6, from henceforth I will go to the *G.*
Rom. 3. 29, is he not also of the *G.*?
11. 11, salvation is come to the *G.*
11. 13, as the apostle of the *G.*
1 Cor. 5. 1, not so much as named among *G.*
Eph. 4. 17, walk not as other *G.* [omits *G.*
2 Tim. 1. 11, I am ordained a teacher of *G.* R. V.
3 John 7, taking nothing of the *G.*
See Rom. 2. 9; 1 Pet. 2. 12; Rev. 11. 2.

Gentiles, their state by nature. Rom. 1. 21; 1 Cor. 12. 2; Eph. 2.; 4. 17; 1 Thes. 4. 5.
God's judgments on. Joel 3. 9.
their conversion predicted. Isa. 11. 10; 42. 1; 49. 6 (Mat. 12. 18; Lu. 2. 32; Acts 13. 47); 62. 2; Jer. 16. 19; Hos. 2. 23; Mal. 1. 11; Mat. 8. 11.
prediction fulfilled. John 10. 16; Acts 8. 37; 10.; 14.; 15.; Eph. 2.; 1 Thes. 1. 1.
calling of. Rom. 9. 24. *See* Isa. 66. 19.
become fellow-citizens of the saints. Eph. 2. 11.
Christ made known to. Col. 1. 27.

Gentle. 1 Thes. 2. 7, we were *g.* among you.
2 Tim. 2. 24, servant of Lord be *g.*
Tit. 3. 2, *g.*, shewing all meekness.
Jas. 3. 17, wisdom is pure and *g.*
1 Pet. 2. 18, not only to be good and *g.*
See 2 Sam. 18. 5; 22. 36.

Gentleness: of Christ. 2 Cor. 10. 1; Mat. 11. 29 (Isa. 40. 11).
of Paul and Timotheus. 1 Thes. 2. 7.
the fruit of the Spirit. Gal. 5. 22.
exhortations to. 2 Tim. 2. 24; Tit. 3. 2.

Genubath, gĕ-nū'-băth. 1 Kn. 11. 20.

Geology of Palestine. Jerusalem is built on a platform of limestone. The maritime plain is formed of yellow sandstone and beds of calcareous sand. The central plateau is calcareous sandstone.

Gera, gē'-ră, 'a grain.' Gen. 46. 21.

Gerah, gē'-räh, 'a grain' = $\frac{1}{20}$ shekel = 11.2 grs. Ex. 30. 13. *See* Weights.

Gerar, gē'-rär, 'sojourning' (?). Gen. 10. 19.
herdmen of, strive with Isaac's. Gen. 26. 20.

Gerasa, a city of Gilead, with a large district probably including the smaller district of Gadara, in which was the city of Gergesa.

Gerasenes (Mk. 5. 1; Lu. 8. 26, 37). R. V. inhabitants of Gerasa. The Gadarenes were therefore also Gerasenes.

Gergesa, a city on the east shore of the Sea of Galilee, the modern Kersa.

Gergesenes, gĕr'-gĕ-sēnes, inhabitants of Gergesa, in the district of Gadara. Mat. 8. 28. R. V. Gadarenes.

Gerizim, gĕ-rī'-zĭm, persons living in a desert (?), the mountain opposite Ebal, mount of blessing. Deu. 11. 29; 27. 12; Jos. 8. 33.
site of Samaritan temple. John 4. 20.

Gershom, gĕr'-shŏm, 'expulsion' or 'a stranger there.'
(1) son of Moses. Ex. 2. 22; 18. 3. (2) Ez. 8. 2.

Gershon, gĕr'-shŏn, son of Levi. Gen. 46. 11; Num. 3. 17. Same as Gershom.

Gershonites, gĕr'-shŏn-ītes, descendants of Gershon. Num. 3. 21.
their duties in the service of the tabernacle. Num. 4.; 7.; 10. 17.

Gerzites, gĕr'-zītes. 1 Sam. 27. 8 (marg.).

Gesham, gē'-shăm. 1 Chr. 2. 47.

Geshem, gē'-shĕm, 'stout' (?). Neh. 2. 19.

Geshur, gē'-shūr, 'bridge' (?). 2 Sam. 3. 3.
Absalom takes refuge there after killing Amnon. 2 Sam. 13. 37; 14. 23 (Jos. 13. 13).

Geshuri, gĕ-shū'-rī, inhabitants of Geshur. Deu. 3. 14.

Geshurites, gĕ-shū'-rītes, same as preceding. Jos. 12. 5.

Gether, gē'-thĕr. Gen. 10. 23.

Gethsemane, gĕth-sĕm'-ă-nē, 'oil-press,' garden of, was across the brook Kidron (John 18. 1, R. V.), and probably at the foot of the Mount of Olives. The scene of our Lord's agony. Mat. 26. 36; Mk. 14. 32; Lu. 22. 39.

Getteth. Prov. 3. 13; 4. 7; 19. 8; Jer. 17. 1.

Geuel, gĕū'-ĕl, 'majesty of God.' Num. 13. 15.

Gezer, gē'-zĕr, 'precipice' (?), or 'portion' (?). Jos. 10. 33.

Gezrites, gĕz'-rītes, 'dwelling in a desert land' (?). 1 Sam. 27. 8.

Ghost, spirit; 'yield up the ghost' = to die. Mat. 27. 50.

Ghost, Holy. *See* Holy Spirit.

Giah, gī'-ăh, 'gushing forth.' 2 Sam. 2. 24.

Giants before the flood. Gen. 6. 4.
inhabit Canaan. Deu. 2. 10, 11, 19, 20; 9. 2.
spies discourage the people by stories of. Num. 13. 33; Deu. 1. 28.
several slain by David and his servants. 1 Sam. 17.; 2 Sam. 21. 16; 1 Chr. 20. 4.

Gibbar, gĭb'-bär, 'a hero.' Ez. 2. 20.

Gibbethon, gĭb'-bĕ-thŏn, 'a height.' Jos. 19. 44.

Gibea, gĭb'-ĕ-ă, 'hill.' 1 Chr. 2. 49.

Gibeah, gĭb'-ĕ-ăh, 'hill.' (1) a city of Judah. Jos. 15. 57.
(2) a city of Benjamin. Jud. 19. 14.
sin of its inhabitants. Jud. 19. 22.
their punishment. Jud. 20.
the city of Saul. 1 Sam. 10. 26; 11. 4; 14. 2; 15. 34; 2 Sam. 21. 6.

Gibeath, gĭb'-ĕ-ăth, 'hill.' Jos. 18. 28.

Gibeathite, gĭb'-ĕ-ă-thīte, inhabitant of Gibeah. 1 Chr. 12. 3.

Gibeon, gĭb'-ĕ-ŏn, situated on an isolated hill about five miles north of Jerusalem. Jos. 9. 3.
its inhabitants deceive Joshua. Jos. 9.
delivered by him from the five kings. Jos. 10.
Saul persecutes them. 2 Sam. 21. 1.
David makes atonement. 2 Sam. 21. 3-9.
Solomon's dream at. 1 Kn. 3. 5.
site of the tabernacle under David and Solomon. 1 Chr. 16. 39; 21. 29; 2 Chr. 1. 4-6.

Gibeonites, gĭb'-ĕ-ọn-ītes, inhabitants of Gibeon. 2 Sam. 21. 1.

Giblites, gĭb'-lītes, inhabitants of Gebal. Jos. 13. 5.

Giddalti, gĭd-dăl'-tī, 'I have magnified.' 1 Chr. 25. 4.

Giddel, gĭd'-dĕl, 'gigantic.' Ez. 2. 47.

Gideon, gĭd'-ĕ-ọn, 'one who cuts down.' God appoints him to deliver Israel from the Midianites. Jud. 6. 11, 14.
destroys the altar and grove of Baal. Jud. 6. 25, 27.
called Jerubbaal. Jud. 6. 32.
God gives him two signs. Jud. 6. 36-40.
his army reduced, and selected by a test of water. Jud. 7. 2-7.
his stratagem. Jud. 7. 16.
subdues the Midianites. Jud. 7. 19; 8.
makes an ephod of the spoil. Jud. 8. 24.
his death. Jud. 8. 32. *See* Heb. 11. 32.

Gideoni, gĭd-ĕ-ō'-nī, 'cutting down.' Num. 1. 11.

Gidom, gī'-dŏm. Jud. 20. 45.

Gift. Ex. 23. 8; Deu. 16. 19, a *g.* blindeth.
2 Sam. 19. 42, hath he given us any *g.*?
2 Chr. 19. 7, with the Lord no taking of *g.*
Ps. 68. 18; Eph. 4. 8, *g.* unto men.
72. 10, kings of Sheba and Seba offer *g.*
Prov. 6. 35, not content, though many *g.*
15. 27, he that hateth *g.* shall live.
17. 8, a *g.* is as a precious stone.
18. 16, man's *g.* maketh room for him.
21. 14, a *g.* in secret pacifieth anger.
Eccl. 3. 13; 5. 19, enjoy good, it is God's *g.*
7. 7, a *g.* destroyeth the heart.
Isa. 1. 23, every one loveth *g.*
Mat. 5. 23, bring thy *g.* to the altar.
5. 24, leave thy *g.* before the altar.
7. 11; Lu. 11. 13, know how to give good *g.*
Lu. 21. 1, casting *g.* into treasury.

John 4. 10, if thou knewest the *g.* of God.
Acts 8. 20, thought the *g.* of God may be purchased.
Rom. 1. 11, some spiritual *g.*
5. 15, free *g.*, *g.* by grace.
6. 23, the *g.* of God is eternal life.
11. 29, *g.* of God without repentance.
12. 6, *g.* differing according to grace.
1 Cor. 7. 7, his proper *g.* of God.
12. 4, diversities of *g.*
12. 31, covet best *g.*
14. 1, 12, desire spiritual *g.*
2 Cor. 9. 15, unspeakable *g.*
Eph. 2. 8, faith the *g.* of God.
Phil. 4. 17, not because I desire a *g.*
1 Tim. 4. 14, neglect not the *g.*
2 Tim. 1. 6, stir up the *g.*
Jas. 1. 17, good and perfect *g.*

Gifts, spiritual. Ps. 29. 11; 68. 18, 35; 84. 11; Prov. 2. 6; Ezek. 11. 19; John 3. 34; Acts 2. 38; 10. 45; 11. 17; Rom. 12. 6; 1 Cor. 1. 7; 12.; 13. 2; 14.; Eph. 2. 8; Jas. 1. 5, 17; 4. 6.
temporal. Gen. 1. 26; 9. 1; 27. 28; Lev. 26. 4; Ps. 34. 10; 65. 9; 104.; 136. 25; 145. 15; 147.; Isa. 30. 23; Acts 14. 17.
(Corban) Mat. 15. 5; Mk. 7. 11.

Gihon, gī′-hŏn, 'a bursting forth;' one of the rivers of Eden. Gen. 2. 13.

Gilalai, gĭl′ă-lāi. Neh. 12. 36.

Gilboa, gĭl-bō′-ă, a mountain in the south-eastern part of Galilee. 1 Sam. 28. 4.
the scene of Saul's death. 1 Sam. 31.; 2 Sam. 1. 21.

Gilead, gĭl′-ĕ-ăd, 'hill of witness,' according to Gen. 31. 21, or 'camel hump.' (1) Mountainous and richly wooded region east of Jordan, lying between Bashan on the north and Moab and Ammon on the south. In some passages the name is used for the whole country east of Jordan (Deu. 34. 1; Jos. 22. 9; Jud. 20. 1).
land of, granted to the Reubenites, &c. Num. 32.
invaded by the Ammonites. Jud. 10. 17.
Jephthah made captain of. Jud. 11.
(2) Mount Gilead (Jud. 7. 3) is evidently a mountain west of Jordan, probably Gilboa.
(3) persons. Num. 26. 29; Jud. 11. 1; 1 Chr. 5. 14.

Gileadite, gĭl′-ĕ-ăd-īte, an inhabitant of Gilead. Jud. 10. 3.

Gilgal, gĭl′-găl, 'a circle' with a play on a word meaning 'roll away.' (1) The first camping-place of the Israelites after crossing the Jordan (Jos. 4. 19; 9. 6), three miles east of Jericho.
(2) The residence of Elisha and site of a School of Prophets (2 Kn. 4. 38). Thirteen miles north-east of Joppa.
Saul made king there. 1 Sam. 10. 8; 11. 14.
Saul sacrifices at. 1 Sam. 13. 8; 15. 12.

Giloh, gī′-lōh. Jos. 15. 51.

Gilonite, gī′-lō-nīte, an inhabitant of Giloh. 2 Sam. 15. 12.

Gimzo, gĭm′-zō, 'sycamore.' 2 Chr. 28. 18.

Gin, a trap or snare. Am. 3. 5.

Ginath, gī′-năth, 'garden.' 1 Kn. 16. 21.

Ginnetho, gĭn′-nĕ-thō, 'gardener.' Neh. 12. 4.

Ginnethon, gĭn′-nĕ-thŏn, same as preceding. Neh. 10. 6.

Gird. 2 Sam. 22. 40; Ps. 18. 39, hast *g.* me with strength.
Isa. 45. 5, I *g.* thee, though thou hast not.
Joel 1. 13, *g.* yourselves, and lament.
Eph. 6. 14, having your loins *g.*
See Prov. 31. 17; John 13. 4; 21. 18; Rev. 15. 6.

Girdle. Ex. 28. 4, and a *g.*
Jer. 13. 1, go and get thee a linen *g.*
See Isa. 11. 5; Mat. 3. 4; Mk. 1. 6.

Girgashite, gĭr′-gă-shīte. 1 Chr. 1. 14.

Girgashites, gĭr′-gă-shītes, descendants of Canaan. Gen. 10. 15; 15. 21.
communion with, forbidden. Deu. 7. 1.
driven out. Jos. 3. 10; 24. 11.

Girgasite, gĭr′-gă-sīte, same as preceding. Gen. 10. 16.

Girl. Joel 3. 3; Zec. 8. 5.

Gispa, gĭs′-pă. Neh. 11. 21.

Gittah-hepher, gĭt′-tăh-hē′-phĕr, 'wine-press of digging.' Jos. 19. 13.

Gittaim, gĭt-tā′-ĭm, 'two wine-presses.' 2 Sam. 4. 3.

Gittites, gĭt′-tītes, inhabitants of Gath. Jos. 13. 3.

Gittith, gĭt′-tĭth = Gathite; 'after the manner of Gittites.' In the titles to Ps. 8., 81., 84., to the musician upon Gittith. Probably an instrument of music borrowed from Gath, possibly a mode or key in music.

Give. Gen. 28. 22, I will *g.* the tenth.
Ex. 30. 15, rich shall not *g.* more, poor not *g.* less.
Deu. 15. 10, thou shalt *g.* him thine heart.
16. 17; Ezek. 46. 5, *g.* as he is able.
1 Chr. 29. 14, of thine own have we *g.* thee.
Ez. 9. 9, to *g.* us a reviving.
Ps. 2. 8, I shall *g.* thee the heathen.
6. 5, in the grave who shall *g.* thanks?
29. 11, Lord will *g.* strength.
37. 4, *g.* thee the desires of thy heart.
37. 21, the righteous sheweth mercy and *g.*
84. 11, Lord will *g.* grace and glory.
109. 4, I *g.* myself unto prayer.
Prov. 23. 26, *g.* me thine heart.
Isa. 55. 10, *g.* seed to the sower.
Mat. 5. 42, *g.* to him that asketh.
6. 11; Lu. 11. 3, *g.* daily bread.
7. 9, will he *g.* him a stone?
10. 8, freely *g.*
13. 11; Mk. 4. 11; it is *g.* to you to know.
16. 26; Mk. 8. 37, *g.* in exchange.
19. 21; Mk. 10. 21, go sell, and *g.* to the poor.
20. 23; Mk. 10. 40, not mine to *g.*
26. 9; Mk. 14. 5, sold and *g.* to the poor.
Lu. 6. 38, *g.*, and it shall be *g.*
John 4. 7, 10, *g.* me to drink.
6. 37, all that the Father *g.* me.
6. 65, no man can come, except it were *g.* him.
10. 28, I *g.* to them eternal life.
13. 29, that he should *g.* something to poor.
14. 27, not as the world *g.*, *g.* I.
Acts 3. 6, such as I have *g.* I thee.
6. 4, we will *g.* ourselves to prayer.
20. 35, more blessed to *g.*
Rom. 12. 8, he that *g.*, let him do it.
12. 19, rather *g.* place unto wrath.
1 Cor. 3. 7, God *g.* the increase.
2 Cor. 9. 7, *g.* not grudgingly, a cheerful *g.*
Phil. 4. 15, concerning *g.* and receiving.
1 Tim. 4. 13, *g.* attendance to reading.
4. 15, *g.* thyself wholly to them.
6. 17, who *g.* us richly.
Jas. 1. 5, that *g.* to all men liberally.
4. 6, *g.* more grace, *g.* grace to humble.
2 Pet. 1. 5, *g.* all diligence. R. V. adding.
See Mk. 12. 15; Lu. 12. 48.

Give place, to give way, yield. Gal. 2. 5.

Gizonite, gī′-zŏn-īte. 1 Chr. 11. 34.

Glad. Ex. 4. 14, he will be *g.* in heart.
Job 3. 22, *g.* when they can find the grave.
Ps. 16. 9, therefore my heart is *g.*
34. 2; 69. 32, humble shall hear, and be *g.*
46. 4, make *g.* the city of God.
104. 15, maketh *g.* the heart of man.
122. 1, I was *g.* when they said.
126. 3, whereof we are *g.*
Prov. 10. 1; 15. 20, wise son maketh a *g.* father.
24. 17, let not thine heart be *g.*
Lam. 1. 21, they are *g.* that thou hast done it.
Lu. 15. 32, make merry and be *g.*
John 8. 56, saw my day and was *g.*
11. 15, I am *g.* for your sakes.
Acts 11. 23, when he had seen grace of God was *g.*
See Mk. 6. 20; 12. 37; Lu. 1. 19; 8. 1.

Gladness. Num. 10. 10, in day of your *g.*
Deu. 28. 47, servedst not with *g.* of heart.
Neh. 8. 17, there was very great *g.*
Ps. 4. 7, thou hast put *g.* in my heart.
45. 7; Heb. 1. 9, the oil of *g.*
97. 11, *g.* is sown for the upright.

Isa. 35. 10; 51. 11, they shall obtain joy and *g.*
Acts 2. 46, did eat with *g.* of heart.
12. 14, opened not for *g.* R. V. joy.
14. 17, filling our hearts with food and *g.*
See Ps. 100. 2; Prov. 10. 28; Isa. 51. 3.

Glass. 1 Cor. 13. 12, we see through a *g.* darkly. R. V. in a mirror.
2 Cor. 3. 18, beholding as in a *g.* the glory of the Lord. R. V. mirror.
Rev. 4. 6; 15. 2, a sea of *g.*, like unto crystal. [R. V. glassy sea.

Glean. Jer. 6. 9; 49. 9.

Gleaning, to be left for the poor and stranger. Lev. 19. 9, 10; 23. 22; Deu. 24. 19.
liberality of Boaz concerning. Ru. 2. 15.

Glede (Deu. 14. 13). Heb. *Râah:* Gk. γύψ. (Specimen, *Buteo ferox.*) Probably the buzzard, or kite. A. V. kite. R. V. vulture.

Glistering. 1 Chr. 29. 2, *g.* stones. R. V. stones for inlaid work. Lu. 9. 29. R. V. dazzling.

Glittering. Deu. 32. 41; Job 20. 25; 39. 23; Nah. 3. 3.

Gloominess. Joel 2. 2; Zep. 1. 15.

Glorify. Lev. 10. 3, before all people I will be *g.*
Ps. 50. 23, whoso offereth praise *g.* me.
86. 9, all nations shall *g.* thy name.
86. 12, I will *g.* thy name for evermore.
Isa. 24. 15, *g.* the Lord in the fires.
25. 3, a strong nation shall *g.* thee.
60. 7, I will *g.* house of my glory.
Ezek. 28. 22, I will be *g.* in midst of thee.
Dan. 5. 23, God hast thou not *g.*
Mat. 5. 16, *g.* your Father in heaven.
9. 8; 15. 31; Lu. 7. 16, they *g.* God.
Lu. 4. 15, being *g.* of all.
John 7. 39, because Jesus was not yet *g.*
11. 4, that the Son of God might be *g.*
12. 16, but when Jesus was *g.*, they remembered.
12. 28, Father, *g.* thy name . . . I have both *g.*
13. 32, God shall also *g.* him.
15. 8, herein is my Father *g.*
17. 1, *g.* thy Son.
17. 4, I have *g.* thee on earth.
21. 19, by what death he should *g.* God.
Rom. 1. 21, they *g.* him not as God.
8. 17, suffer with him, that we may be *g.*
8. 30, them he also *g.*
1 Cor. 6. 20, *g.* God in body and spirit.
Gal. 1. 24, they *g.* God in me.
2 Thes. 1. 10, to be *g.* in his saints.
Heb. 5. 5, so Christ *g.* not himself.

Glorifying God, exhortations to. 1 Chr. 16. 28; Ps. 22. 23; 50. 15; Rom. 15. 6; 1 Cor. 6. 20; 10. 31; 1 Pet. 2. 12; Rev. 15. 4.

Glorious. Ex. 15. 11, *g.* in holiness.
Deu. 28. 58; 1 Chr. 29. 13, this *g.* name.
Ps. 45. 13, all *g.* within.
66. 2, make his praise *g.*
72. 19, blessed be his *g.* name.
87. 3, *g.* things are spoken.
Isa. 11. 10, his rest shall be *g.*
28. 1, whose *g.* beauty is a fading flower.
60. 13, place of my feet *g.*
63. 1, *g.* in his apparel.
63. 14, to make thyself a *g.* name.
Jer. 17. 12, a *g.* high throne.
Dan. 11. 16, 41, stand in the *g.* land.
11. 45, in the *g.* holy mountain.
Lu. 13. 17, rejoiced for *g.* things done.
Rom. 8. 21, *g.* liberty of children of God.
2 Cor. 3. 7, 8, ministration *g.*
4. 4, light of *g.* gospel.
Eph. 5. 27, a *g.* church.
Phil. 3. 21, like to his *g.* body.
1 Tim. 1. 11, the *g.* gospel of the blessed God.
Tit. 2. 13, the *g.* appearing of the great God.
See Ex. 15. 1; 2 Sam. 6. 20; Isa. 24. 23.

Glory. Ex. 33. 18, shew me thy *g.*
Num. 14. 21; Ps. 72. 19; Isa. 6. 3, earth filled with *g.*
Ps. 8. 1, thy *g.* above the heavens.
16. 9, my *g.* rejoiceth.
24. 7, 10, the King of *g.*
73. 24, afterward receive me to *g.*
84. 11, will give grace and *g.*
108. 1, will give praise with my *g.*
145. 11, the *g.* of thy kingdom.
Prov. 3. 35, the wise shall inherit *g.*
17. 6, the *g.* of children are their fathers.
20. 29, the *g.* of young men is their strength.
25. 2, *g.* of God to conceal.
25. 27, for men to search their own *g.* is not *g.*
Isa. 10. 3, where will ye leave your *g.*?
24. 16, even *g.* to the righteous.
42. 8, my *g.* will I not give to another.
43. 7, have created him for my *g.*
60. 7, will glorify house of my *g.*
Jer. 2. 11, my people have changed their *g.*
Ezek. 20. 6, 15, the *g.* of all lands.
31. 18, to whom art thou thus like in *g.*?
Dan. 2. 37; 7. 14, God hath given power and *g.*
Hos. 4. 7, change *g.* into shame.
Hag. 2. 7, I will fill this house with *g.*
Mat. 6. 2, that ye may have *g.* of men.
6. 29; Lu. 12. 27, Solomon in all his *g.*
16. 27; Mk. 8. 38, in *g.* of his Father.
19. 28; Lu. 9. 26, Son of man sit in his *g.*
24. 30; Mk. 13. 26; Lu. 21. 27, power and great *g.*
Lu. 2. 14; 19. 38, *g.* to God in the highest.
9. 31, appeared in *g.*, and spake of his decease.
9. 32, they saw his *g.*
24. 26, to enter into his *g.*
John 1. 14, we beheld his *g.*
2. 11, thus did Jesus, and manifested his *g.*
8. 50, I seek not mine own *g.*
17. 5, the *g.* I had with thee.
17. 24, that they may behold my *g.*
Acts 12. 23, he gave not God the *g.*
Rom. 3. 23, come short of *g.* of God.
8. 18, not worthy to be compared with *g.*
11. 36; Gal. 1. 5; 2 Tim. 4. 18; Heb. 13. 21; 1 Pet. 5. 11, to whom be *g.*
1 Cor. 2. 8; Jas. 2. 1, the Lord of *g.*
10. 31, do all to *g.* of God.
11. 7, woman is the *g.* of the man.
11. 15, long hair, it is a *g.* to her.
15. 40, *g.* of celestial, *g.* of terrestrial.
15. 43, raised in *g.*
2 Cor. 3. 18, beholding as in a glass the *g.*
4. 17, eternal weight of *g.* R. V. glorying.
Eph. 1. 17, the Father of *g.*
3. 21, to him be *g.* in the church.
Phil. 3. 19, whose *g.* is in their shame.
4. 19, according to his riches in *g.*
Col. 1. 27, Christ in you, the hope of *g.*
3. 4, appear with him in *g.*
2 Thes. 1. 9, the *g.* of his power.
1 Tim. 3. 16, received up into *g.*
Heb. 1. 3, the brightness of his *g.*
2. 10, in bringing many sons to *g.*
3. 3, this man was counted worthy of more *g.*
1 Pet. 1. 8, joy unspeakable and full of *g.*
1. 11, the *g.* that should follow. R. V. glories.
1. 24, the *g.* of man as flower of grass.
4. 14, the spirit of *g.* and of God.
5. 10, called to eternal *g.*
2 Pet. 1. 17, voice from the excellent *g.*
Rev. 4. 11; 5. 12, worthy to receive *g.*
7. 12, blessing, and *g.*, and wisdom.
18. 1, earth lightened with his *g.*
21. 23, *g.* of God did lighten it.
See Lu. 17. 18; Jude 25.
See under God.

Glorying. 1 Cor. 5. 6; 9. 15; 2 Cor. 7. 4; 12. 11.

Gluttony condemned. Deu. 21. 20; Prov. 23. 1, 20; 25. 16; 1 Pet. 4. 3.

Gnash. Mat. 8. 12; 13. 42; 22. 13; 24. 51; 25. 30; Lu. 13. 28, *g.* of teeth.
Mk. 9. 18, he foameth, and *g.* with his teeth.
See Job 16. 9; Ps. 35. 16; Acts 7. 54.

Gnat (Mat. 23. 24). Gk. κώνωψ: Zool. S. *Culex.* Gnats and mosquitoes are among the most prevalent pests of Egypt and Palestine.

Gnaw. Zep. 3. 3; Rev. 16. 10.

Go. Gen. 32. 26, let me *g.*, for the day breaketh.
Ex. 14. 15; Job 23. 8, *g.* forward.
23. 23; 32. 34, angel shall *g.* before thee.

Ex. 33. 15, presence *g.* not with me.
Ru. 1. 16, whither thou *g.*, I will *g.*
Ps. 139. 7, whither shall I *g.*?
Prov. 22. 6, the way he should *g.*
30. 29, three things which *g.* well. R. V. are stately in their march.
Mat. 5. 41, to *g.* a mile, *g.* twain.
21. 30, I *g.*, sir, and went not.
Lu. 10. 37, *g.* and do likewise.
John 14. 12, I *g.* to the Father.
See Mat. 8. 9; Lu. 7. 8; 1 Cor. 9. 7; Rev. 14. 4.

Go about, to endeavour, try. John 7. 20; Rom. 10. 3.

Goad. Jud. 3. 31; 1 Sam. 13. 21; Eccl. 12. 11.

Goat. (1) (Isa. 14. 9). Heb. *'Attûd* (male); translated 'chief ones' (A. V. and R. V.), the metaphorical rendering of 'he-goats,' as in R. V. margin.
(2) (2 Chr. 29. 21). Heb. *Tsâphîr*, 'to leap' (male): Gk. τράγος, 'he-goats' (A. V. and R. V.).
(3) (Lev. 9. 3). Heb. *Sâîr* (rough, shaggy). The goat, especially the goat of the sin offering.
(4) (Gen. 30. 35). Heb. *Táyish:* Gk. τράγος, 'he-goat.'

Goat, wild (Deu. 14. 5; Job 39. 1; Ps. 104. 18). Heb. *Akko, yâ'êl:* Gk. ὄρυξ. This animal is the *Capra ibex.*

Goath, gō'-ăth, 'lowing.' Jer. 31. 39.

Gob, gŏb, 'pit,' 'cistern.' 2 Sam. 21. 18.

Go beyond, to overreach, cheat. 1 Thes. 4. 6.

God, Names of, in Old Testament.
To the Hebrews the *Name* of God meant the revelation of His Nature; hence the various names in O. T. are very important as showing the various conceptions of the Deity held by them in the successive stages of revelation.
El is the most primitive Semitic name: its root-meaning is probably 'strong:' in classical Hebrew it is mainly poetical. It is found in ancient compound proper names, such as Isra-el, Beth-el.
Elōhīm is a plural name, but the plural seems to be intensive, and often it implies 'fulness of might.' It occurs more than 2500 times, and is always rendered *God* in the Eng. versions.
Both El and Elohim are used of other gods than the God of Israel; hence we find such phrases as 'the El, Jehovah' (Isa. 42. 5, cf. Ps. 18. 30); 'Jehovah, he is the Elohim' (1 Kn. 18. 39); 'the Elohim of Elohim' (God of Gods) (Deu. 10. 17).
Elyon (the Most High) is found only in poetry (Num. 24. 16; Deu. 32. 8; Psalms). The Canaanite priest-king Melchizedek was priest of El-Elyon (Gen. 14. 18); the name was thus used by other nations than Israel.
El-Shaddai (God Almighty) expresses the omnipotence of God as contrasted with the impotence of heathen deities.
Jehovah, the name revealed to Moses at Horeb, is *the* Name of the God of Israel. Its real pronunciation is approximately *Yahweh*, but this Name might not, according to Rabbinical teaching, be pronounced: hence it was written with the vowel points of *Adonai* (Lord), which was substituted for it in reading. The Name itself was not pronounced Jehovah before the 16th century. The *meaning* of JHVH, as it was written, is probably not 'I am,' but 'I will become;' thus it appears to contain the promise of a gradual revelation. It is frequently found in composition with proper names, as e. g., Yehô-shua (Joshua), Yehonathan (Jonathan), Eliyahu (Elijah), Hizki-yahu (Hezekiah). It also occurs as a name of God in phrases such as Jehovah-Elohim (Eng. the Lord God), Jehovah-Sabaoth (the God of hosts: i. e., originally of the battle-hosts of God's people, then also of the 'hosts of heaven').
Adonai, Baal, Melekh, are names expressing the Divine dominion. **Adonai** is an intensive plural of *Adon* (= lord), and occurs not seldom in prophecy and poetry as a substitute for JHVH. It was applied by heathen nations to their gods (thus the Phœnician Tammuz has the title Adonis), and is found compounded with JHVH as a proper name (Adoni-yahu = Adonijah). **Baal** (= owner or master) was in late times remembered only as the title of the Canaanite local gods; but earlier it was used by worshippers of Jehovah. Thus one of Saul's sons was called Ishbaal: one of David's men of war was called Baaliah (Baal-Ya = Jehovah is Baal). In Hos. 2. 16, 17, we find a protest against this use of a title which had come to have degrading associations; and the older obnoxious proper names were changed, *bosheth* (shame) being substituted for *baal.* So we find Ishbosheth (2 Sam. 2. 8), Mephibosheth (2 Sam. 9. 6), Jerubbesheth (2 Sam. 11. 21). **Melekh** (= king) was, like Baal, employed as a religious term by non-Israelites: but the evidence of Hebrew proper names shows that it was freely used of Jehovah in early days; cf. the pairs of names, Abi-melech (the King is father) and Abi-jah, Eli-melech (God is King) and Eli-jah, Ahi-melech (the King is brother) and Ahi-jah.

God. Gen. 5. 22; 6. 9, walked with *G.*
16. 13, thou *G.* seest me.
32. 28, hath power with *G.*
48. 21, I die, but *G.* shall be with you.
Num. 23. 19, *G.* is not a man, that he should lie.
23. 23, what hath *G.* wrought?
Deu. 33. 27, the eternal *G.* is thy refuge.
1 Sam. 17. 46, may know there is a *G.* in Israel.
1 Kn. 18. 21, if the Lord be *G.*, follow him.
18. 39, he is the *G.*, he is the *G.*
Job 22. 13; Ps. 73. 11, how doth *G.* know?
Ps. 14. 1; 53. 1, hath said, there is no *G.*
22. 1; Mat. 27. 46, my *G.*, my *G.*, why hast.
56. 9, this I know, for *G.* is for me.
86. 10; Isa. 37. 16, thou art *G.* alone.
Eccl. 5. 2, *G.* is in heaven.
Isa. 44. 8, is there a *G.* beside me?
45. 22; 46. 9, I am *G.*, there is none else.
Hos. 11. 9, I am *G.*, and not man.
Am. 5. 27, whose name is the *G.* of hosts.
Jon. 1. 6, arise, call upon thy *G.*
Mic. 6. 8, walk humbly with thy *G.*
Mat. 1. 23, *G.* with us.
22. 32, *G.* is not *G.* of dead.
Mk. 12. 32, one *G.*, and none other. R. V. he is one.
John 3. 33, that *G.* is true.
4. 24, *G.* is a spirit.
13. 3, come from *G.*, and went to *G.*
20. 17, ascend to my *G.* and your *G.*
Rom. 3. 4, let *G.* be true.
8. 31, if *G.* be for us.
1 Cor. 1. 9; 10. 13, *G.* is faithful.
14. 25, that *G.* is in you.
14. 33, *G.* is not author of confusion.
Gal. 3. 20, but *G.* is one.
6. 7, *G.* is not mocked.
2 Thes. 2. 4, above all that is called *G.*
1 Tim. 3. 16, *G.* manifest in the flesh. R. V. he who was.
Heb. 8. 10, I will be to them a *G.*
11. 16, not ashamed to be called their *G.*
12. 23, but ye are come to *G.*
1 John 1. 5, *G.* is light.
4. 8, 16, *G.* is love.
4. 12, no man hath seen *G.*
5. 19, we know that we are of *G.*
Rev. 21. 3, *G.* himself shall be with them.
21. 4, *G.* shall wipe away all tears.
21. 7, I will be his *G.*

God:
THE LORD GOD ALMIGHTY. Gen. 17. 1; Ex. 6. 3; Num. 24. 4; Ru. 1. 20; Job 5. 17; Ps. 68. 14; 91. 1; Isa. 13. 6; Ezek. 1. 24; Joel 1. 15; 2 Cor. 6. 18; Rev. 1. 8.
THE CREATOR. Gen. 1.; 2.; Deu. 4. 19; Neh. 9. 6; Job 33. 4; 38.; Ps. 8.; 19. 1; 33. 6; 89. 11; 94. 9; 104.; 136.; 146. 6; 148.; Prov. 3. 19; 8. 22; Eccl. 12. 1; Isa. 37. 16; 40. 28; 43. 7, 13; 45. 8; Jer. 10. 12; 32. 17; Zec. 12. 1; John 1. 3; Acts

17. 24; Rom. 1. 25; Col. 1. 16; Heb. 1. 10; 3. 4; 11. 3; 1 Pet. 4. 19; Rev. 4. 11.

THE FATHER. Mat. 11. 25; 28. 19; Mk. 14. 36; Lu. 10. 21; 22. 42; 23. 34, 46; John 1. 14; Acts 1. 4; 2. 33; Rom. 6. 4; 8. 15; 15. 6; 1 Cor. 8. 6; 15. 24; 2 Cor. 1. 3; 6. 18; Gal. 1. 1, 3, 4; 4. 6; Eph. 1. 17; Phil. 2. 11; Col. 1. 19; 2. 2; 1 Thes. 1. 1; Heb. 12. 7, 9; Jas. 1. 27; 3. 9; 1 Pet. 1. 2, 17; 2 Pet. 1. 17; 1 John 1. 2; 2 John 3. 4, 9; Jude 1.

THE SON. Mat. 11. 27; Mk. 13. 32; Lu. 1. 32; John 1. 18; Acts 8. 37; 9. 20; Rom. 1. 4; 2 Cor. 1. 19; Gal. 2. 20; Eph. 4. 13; Heb. 4. 14; 1 John 2. 22; Rev. 2. 18. *See* CHRIST.

THE HOLY GHOST. Mat. 28. 19; John 15. 26; Acts 1. 2; 2 Cor. 3. 17; 1 Tim. 3. 16; Rev. 3. 1. *See* HOLY SPIRIT.

ATTRIBUTES OF:

Eternal. Gen. 21. 33; Ex. 3. 14; Deu. 32. 40; 33. 27; Job 10. 5; 36. 26; Ps. 9. 7; 90. 2; 92. 8; 93. 2; 102. 12; 104. 31; 135. 13; 145. 13; 146. 6, 10; Eccl. 3. 14; Isa. 9. 6; 40. 28; 41. 4; 43. 13; 48. 12; 57. 15; 63. 16; Jer. 10. 10; Lam. 5. 19; Dan. 4. 3, 34; 6. 26; Mic. 5. 2; Hab. 1. 12; Rom. 1. 20; 16. 26; Eph. 3. 9; 1 Tim. 1. 17; 6. 16; 2 Pet. 3. 8; Rev. 1. 8; 4. 9; 22. 13.

Faithfulness and truth. Num. 23. 19; Deu. 7. 8; Jos. 21. 45; 2 Sam. 7. 28; 1 Kn. 8. 56; Ps. 19. 9; 89. 34; 105. 8; 111. 7; 117.; 119. 89, 160; 146. 6; Isa. 25. 1; 31. 2; 46. 11; 65. 16; Jer. 4. 28; Lam. 2. 17; Ezek. 12. 25; Mat. 24. 35; John 7. 28; Rom. 3. 4; 1 Cor. 1. 9; 15. 58; 2 Cor. 1. 18; 1 Thes. 5. 24; 2 Thes. 3. 3; 2 Tim. 2. 13; Tit. 1. 2; Heb. 6. 18; 10. 23; 11. 11; 13. 5; 2 Pet. 3. 9; Rev. 1. 5; 3. 7; 15. 3; 16. 7.

Holiness. Gen. 35. 2; Ex. 3. 5; 14.; 15.; 19.; 20.; 28. 36; 34. 5; 39. 30; Lev. 11. 44; 21. 8; Jos. 5. 15; 1 Sam. 2. 2; 1 Chr. 16. 10; Ps. 22. 3; 30. 4; 60. 6. *See* PSALMS. Isa. 6. 3; 43. 15; 49. 7; 57. 15; Jer. 23. 9; Am. 4. 2; Lu. 1. 49; Acts 3. 14; Rom. 7. 12; 1 John 2. 20; Rev. 4. 8; 19. 1.

Immutable. Num. 23. 19; 1 Sam. 15. 29; Ps. 33. 11; 119. 89; Mal. 3. 6; Acts 4. 28; Eph. 1. 4; Heb. 1. 12; 6. 17; 13. 8; Jas. 1. 17.

Incomprehensible. Job 5. 9; 9. 10; 11. 7; 26. 14; 36. 26; 37. 5; Ps. 36. 6; 40. 5; 106. 2; 139. 6; Eccl. 3. 11; 8. 17; 11. 5; Isa. 40. 12; 45. 15; Mic. 4. 12; 1 Tim. 6. 16.

Invisible. Ex. 33. 20; Job 23. 8; John 1. 18; 4. 24; 5. 37; Col. 1. 15; 1 Tim. 1. 17; 6. 16; Heb. 11. 27; 1 John 4. 12.

Jealousy. Ex. 20. 5; 34. 14; Deu. 4. 24; 5. 9; 6. 15; 29. 20; 32. 16; Jos. 24. 19; Ps. 78. 58; 79. 5; Ezek. 16.; 23.; Hos. 1.; 2.; Joel 2. 18; Zep. 1. 18; Zec. 1. 14; 1 Cor. 10. 22.

Justice, &c. Gen. 2. 16; 3. 8; 4. 9; 6. 7; 9. 15; 18. 17, 19; Ex. 32. 33; Lev. 4.; 7. 20; 18. 4; 26. 21; Num. 11.; 14.; 16.; 17.; 20.; 25.; 26. 64; 27. 12; 35.; Deu. 1. 34–45; 4. 24; 5.; 6.; 9. 4; 10. 17; 25. 17; 28. 15; 31. 16; 32. 35, 41; Jos. 7. 1; Jud. 1. 7; 2. 14; 9. 56; 1 Sam. 2. 30; 3. 11; 6. 19; 15. 17; 2 Sam. 6. 7; 12. 1; 22.; 24. 11; 1 Kn. 8. 20; 2 Chr. 6. 17; 19. 7; Ez. 8. 22; Neh. 9. 33; Job 4. 17; 8.; 10. 3; 11. 11; 12. 6; 13. 15; 14. 15; 34. 10; 35. 13; 37. 23; 40. 8. *See* PSALMS. Prov. 11. 21; 15. 8; 28. 9; 30. 5; Eccl. 5. 8; 8. 12; 11. 9; Isa. 45. 21; Jer. 5. 3; 9. 24; 23. 20; 32. 19; 50. 7; 51. 9; Lam. 1. 18; Ezek. 7. 27; 16. 35; 18. 10; 33. 17; Dan. 4. 37; 9. 14; Hos. 4.; 5.; Nah. 1. 3; Hab. 1. 13; Zep. 3. 5; Mal. 2. 17; 4. 1; Mat. 10. 15; 20. 13; 23. 14; Lu. 12. 47; 13. 27; John 7. 18; Acts 10. 34; 17. 31; Rom. 2. 2; Gal. 6. 7; Eph. 6. 8; Col. 3. 25; Jas. 1. 13; 1 John 1. 9; Rev. 15. 3; 16. 7.

Knowledge, wisdom, and power. Gen. 1.; 3.; 6.–9.; 41. 16; Ex. 4. 1, 11; 7. 10; 12. 29; 14.; 15.; 33. 19; 34. 5; 35. 30; 36.; Num. 11. 23; 12.; 22. 9; 23. 4; 24. 16; Deu. 3.; 4. 32; 5. 24; 6. 22; 7.; 10.; 26.; 28. 58; 29. 29; 32. 4; Jos. 3.; 6.; 7. 10; 23. 9; 24.; Jud. 2.; 1 Sam. 2.; 4.; 5.; 12. 18; 14. 6; 16. 7; 17. 37, 46; 18. 10; 23.; 2 Sam. 7. 22; 1 Kn. 8. 27; 22. 22; 1 Chr. 16. 24; 17. 4; 22. 18; 28. 9; 29. 11; 2 Chr. 6. 18; 14. 11; 20. 6; Neh. 9. 5; Job 4. 9; 5. 9; 9.; 10. 4; 11. 12; 19. 6; 21. 17; 22. 23; 26. 6; 33.; 34. 22; 35.; 36. 5; 41. *See* PSALMS. Prov. 3. 19; 5. 21; 8. 22; 15. 3; 16. 9; 19. 21; 21. 30; Eccl. 3. 11; 7. 13; Isa. 2. 10; 6. 3; 12. 5; 14. 24; 28. 29; 29. 16; 30. 18; 33. 13; 40. 29; 41. 21; 42. 8; 43. 13; 44. 6, 23; 45. 20; 46. 5; 47. 4; 48. 3; 52. 10; 55. 11; 59. 1; 60. 1; 66. 1; Jer. 3. 14; 5. 22; 10. 6; 14. 22; 29. 23; 32. 17; Lam. 3. 37; Ezek. 8. 12; 11. 5; 22. 14; Dan. 2. 20; 3. 17, 29; 4. 34; 6. 26; Joel 2. 11; Am. 5. 12; 8. 7; Hab. 2. 14; Mal. 3. 16; Mat. 5. 48; 6. 13; 9. 38; 10. 29; 12. 25; 19. 26; 22. 29; Mk. 5. 30; 12. 15; Lu. 1. 48; 12. 5; 18. 27; John 1. 14; 2. 24; 5. 26; 6. 61; 11. 25; 16. 19; 18. 4; 19. 28; 20. 17; Acts 1. 24; 2. 17; 7. 55; 15. 18; Rom. 1. 20; 4. 17; 8. 29; 11. 34; 15. 19; 16. 27; 1 Cor. 2. 9, 16; 2 Cor. 4. 6; 12. 9; 13. 4; Gal. 2. 8; Eph. 1. 19; 3. 7; 6. 10; Phil. 1. 6; 3. 21; Col. 3. 4; 1 Tim. 1. 12, 17; Heb. 1. 3; 2. 10; 4. 12; Jas. 4. 6; 1 Pet. 2. 20; 1 John 1. 5; 3. 20; Jude 1, 24; Rev. 1. 8; 4. 11; 5. 13; 11. 17; 19. 6; 21. 3.

Mercy, goodness, and love. Gen. 1. 28; 3. 15; 4. 4; 8.; 9.; 15. 4; 16. 7; 17.; 18. 16; 19. 12; 21. 12; 22. 15; 24. 12; 26. 24; 28. 10; 29. 31; 32. 9, 24; 39. 2; 46.; Ex. 1. 20; 2. 23; 3. 7; 6.; 16.; 17.; 20. 6; 22. 27; 23. 20; 29. 45; 32. 14; 33. 12; 34. 6; Lev. 4. 35; 26. 3, 40; Num. 14. 18; 21. 7; Deu. 4. 29; 7. 7; 8.; 10. 15; 18. 15; 20. 4; 23. 5; 28. 1; 30.; 32. 7, 43; 33.; Jos. 20.; Jud. 2. 16; 6. 36; 10. 15; 13.; 15. 18; 1 Sam. 2. 9; 7.; 25. 32; 2 Sam. 7. 5; 12. 13; 1 Kn. 8. 56; 2 Chr. 16. 9; 30. 9; Ez. 8. 18; Neh. 2. 18; 9. 17; Job 5. 17; 7. 17; 11. 6; 33. 14; 36. 11; 37. 23; Ps. 34. 8; 36. 5; 69. 16; Prov. 8. 30; 11. 20; 18. 10; 28. 13; Eccl. 2. 26; 8. 11; Isa. 25. 4; 27. 3; 30. 18; 38. 17; 40. 29; 43. 1; 48. 9, 17; 49. 15; 54. 7; 55. 3; 63. 7; Jer. 3. 12; 9. 24; 16. 14; 17. 7; 31. 3, 12; 32. 39; 33. 11; 44. 28; Lam. 3. 22, 31; Ezek. 20. 17; 33. 11; Dan. 9. 9; Hos. 2. 19; 11. 4; 13. 14; 14. 3; Joel 2. 13; Mic. 7. 18; Nah. 1. 7; Hab. 3. 18; Zep. 3. 17; Mal. 3. 6, 16; 4.; Mat. 5. 45; 19. 17; 23. 37; Lu. 1. 50, 78; 5. 21; 6. 35; 13. 6; John 1. 4, 9; 3. 16; 4. 10; 14.; 15. 9; 16. 7; 17.; Acts 14. 17; Rom. 2. 4; 3. 25; 5. 5; 8. 32; 9. 22; 11.; 2 Cor. 1. 3; 12. 9; 13. 11; Gal. 1. 4; Eph. 2. 4, 17; 4. 6; 1 Tim. 2. 4; 6. 17; 2 Tim. 1. 9; Tit. 3. 4; Heb. 12. 6; Jas. 1. 5, 17; 5. 11; 1 Pet. 1. 3; 3. 20; 2 Pet. 3. 9, 15; 1 John 1.; Jude 21; Rev. 2. 3. *See* PSALMS.

Omnipresent. Job 23. 9; 26.; 28.; Ps. 139.; Prov. 15. 3; Acts 17. 27.

Omniscient. Job 26. 6; 34. 21; Ps. 139.; Prov. 15. 3; Isa. 44. 7; Ezek. 11. 5; Mat. 12. 25; John 2. 24; Rom. 1. 20.

Unsearchable. Job 11. 7; 26. 14; 37. 15; Ps. 145. 3; Eccl. 8. 17; Rom. 11. 33.

HIS CHARACTERS:

Disposer of events. Gen. 6.–9.; 11. 8; 12.; 14. 20; 18. 14; 22.; 25. 23; 26.; Ex. 9. 16; Deu. 7. 7; 1 Sam. 2. 6; 9. 15; 13. 14; 15. 17; 16.; 2 Sam. 7. 8; 22. 1; Ps. 10. 16; 22. 28; 24.; 33.; 74. 12; 75.; Isa. 40. 23; 43.–45.; 64. 8; Jer. 8. 19; 10. 10; 18.; 19.; Dan. 4.; 5.; Zec. 14. 9; Lu. 10. 21; Rom. 9.; Eph. 1.; 1 Tim. 1. 17; 6. 15; Jas. 4. 12.

Judge of all. Gen. 18. 25; Deu. 32. 36; Jud. 11. 27; Ps. 7. 11; 9. 7; 50.; 58. 11; 68. 5; 75. 7; 94. 2; Eccl. 3. 17; 11. 9; 12. 14; Isa. 2. 4; 3. 13; Jer. 11. 20; Acts 10. 42; Rom. 2. 16; 2 Tim. 4. 8; Heb. 12. 23; Jude 6; Rev. 11. 18; 18. 8; 19. 11.

Sanctuary and refuge. Deu. 33. 27; 2 Sam. 22. 3; Ps. 9. 9; 46. 1; 57. 1; 59. 16; 62.; 71. 7; 91.; 94. 22; 142. 5; Isa. 8. 14; Ezek. 11. 16; Heb. 6. 18.

Saviour. Ps. 106. 21; Isa. 43. 3, 11; 45. 15; 49. 26; 60. 16; 63. 8; Jer. 14. 8; Hos. 13. 4; Lu. 1. 47.

Searcher of hearts. 1 Chr. 28. 9; Ps. 7. 9; 44. 21; 139. 23; Prov. 17. 3; 24. 12; Jer. 17. 10; Acts 1. 24; Rom. 8. 27; Rev. 2. 23.

HIS DEALINGS WITH:

our first parents. Gen. 3. *See* ADAM, EVE.

Noah and the sinful world. Gen. 6.–9.

Abraham. Gen. 12.–24.

Lot. Gen. 19.

Isaac, Jacob, and Esau. Gen. 22.; 25.; 26.; 28.

Joseph. Gen. 39.

Moses and Aaron. Ex. 3.; 7.

Pharaoh and Egypt. Ex. 7.; 8.
causes the plagues of Egypt: blood, Ex. 7.; frogs, lice, and flies, Ex. 8.; murrain, boils, and hail, Ex. 9.; locusts and darkness, Ex. 10.; death of the firstborn, Ex. 12.
institutes the passover, Ex. 11.; 12.; 13.; and delivers the Israelites, Ex. 14.
the children of Israel during their forty years' wandering in the wilderness (Exodus, Leviticus, Numbers, Deuteronomy):
sends manna. Ex. 16. 15.
gives the ten commandments. Ex. 20.
reveals His glory to Moses, Aaron, and the elders. Ex. 24.
enters into covenant with Israel. Ex. 34.
directs the tabernacle to be made and erected. Ex. 35.; 40.

HIS DEALINGS WITH THE ISRAELITES:
propounds the law respecting sacrificial offerings. Lev. 1.; Num. 28.
sanctifies Aaron. Lev. 8.; 9.
institutes blessings and curses. Lev. 26.; Deu. 27.
punishes the revolt of Korah, Dathan, and Abiram. Num. 16.
causes Aaron's rod to blossom. Num. 17.
excludes Moses and Aaron from the Promised Land for unbelief. Num. 20. 12.
sends fiery serpents, and heals with brazen serpent. Num. 21.
Balaam and Balak. Num. 22.
Joshua at Jericho and Ai. Jos. 1.; 3.; 4.; 6.; 7.; 8.
kings of Canaan. Jos. 10.-12.
Gideon, Jud. 6.; Jephthah, Jud. 11.; Samson, Jud. 13.
Naomi and Ruth. Ru. 1.-4.
Hannah, Eli, and Samuel. 1 Sam. 1.-3.
Saul. 1 Sam. 9.-31.; 1 Chr. 10.
David. 1 Sam. 16.-31.; 2 Sam. 1.-24.; 1 Kn. 1.-2. 11; 1 Chr. 11.-23; 28.; 29.
Solomon. 1 Kn. 1.-11.; 2 Chr. 1.-9.
Rehoboam and Jeroboam. 1 Kn. 12.-15.; 2 Chr. 10.-12.
Ahab. 1 Kn. 16.-22.; 2 Chr. 18.
Elijah. 1 Kn. 17.-22.; 2 Kn. 1.; 2.
Elisha. 2 Kn. 2.-9.
Hezekiah. 2 Kn. 18.-20.; 2 Chr. 29.-32.; Isa. 36.-39.
Josiah. 2 Kn. 22.; 23.; 2 Chr. 34.; 35.
the captive Jews in Persia. Esth. 1.-10.
the liberated Jews. Ez. 1.-10.; Neh. 1.-13.
Job and his friends. Job 1.; 2.; 38.-42.
Isaiah. 2 Kn. 19.; 20.; 2 Chr. 26.; 32.
Jeremiah. 2 Chr. 35.; 36.; Jer. 26.; 34.-43.
Daniel at Babylon. Dan. 1.-10.
Shadrach, Meshach, and Abed-nego. Dan. 3.
Nebuchadnezzar. Dan. 4.
Jonah at Tarshish and Nineveh. Jon. 1.-4.

HIS GIFTS:
are free and abundant. Num. 14. 8; Rom. 8. 32.
are dispensed according to His will. Eccl. 2. 26; Dan. 2. 21; Rom. 12. 6; 1 Cor. 7. 7.
all blessings are. Jas. 1. 17; 2 Pet. 1. 3.

HIS SPIRITUAL GIFTS:—
acknowledge. Ps. 4. 7; 21. 2.
peace. Ps. 29. 11.
strength and power. Ps. 68. 35.
are through Christ. Ps. 68. 18, with Eph. 4. 7, 8; John 6. 27.
Christ the chief of. Isa. 42. 6; 55. 4; John 3. 16; 4. 10; 6. 32, 33.
a new heart. Ezek. 11. 19.
pray for. Mat. 7. 7, 11; John 16. 23, 24.
rest. Mat. 11. 28; 2 Thes. 1. 7.
the Holy Ghost. Lu. 11. 13; Acts 8. 20.
grace. Ps. 84. 11; Jas. 4. 6.
wisdom. Prov. 2. 6; Jas. 1. 5.
glory. Ps. 84. 11; John 17. 22.
repentance. Acts 11. 18.
righteousness. Rom. 5. 16, 17.
eternal life. Rom. 6. 23.
not repented of by Him. Rom. 11. 29.
faith. Eph. 2. 8; Phil. 1. 29.
to be used for mutual profit. 1 Pet. 4. 10.

HIS TEMPORAL GIFTS:
rain and fruitful seasons. Gen. 27. 28; Lev. 26. 4, 5; Isa. 30. 23; Acts 14. 17.
peace. Lev. 26. 6; 1 Chr. 22. 9.
should cause us to remember God. Deu. 8. 18.
wisdom. 2 Chr. 1. 10.
all good things. Ps. 34. 10; 1 Tim. 6. 17.
all creatures partake of. Ps. 136. 25; 145. 15, 16.
life. Isa. 42. 5.
to be used and enjoyed. Eccl. 3. 13; 5. 19, 20 Tim. 4. 4, 5.
pray for. Zec. 10. 1; Mat. 6. 11.
food and raiment. Mat. 6. 25-33.
illustrated. Mat. 25. 15-30.

HIS GLORY:
exhibited in Christ. John 1. 14; 2 Cor. 4. 6; Heb. 1. 3.
exhibited in His power. Ex. 15. 1, 6; Rom. 6. 4.
holiness, Ex. 15. 11. name, Deu. 28. 58; Neh. 9. 5. majesty, Job 37. 22; Ps. 93. 1; 104. 1; 145. 5, 12; Isa. 2. 10. works, Ps. 19. 1; 111. 3.
described as highly exalted, Ps. 8. 1; 113. 4. eternal, Ps. 104. 31. great, Ps. 138. 5. rich, Eph. 3. 16.
exhibited to Moses. Ex. 34. 5-7, with Ex. 33. 18-23.
His church, Deu. 5. 24; Ps. 102. 16. enlightens the church, Isa. 60. 1, 2; Rev. 21. 11, 23. Stephen, Acts 7. 55.
declare. 1 Chr. 16. 24; Ps. 145. 5, 11.
magnify. Ps. 57. 5.
saints desire to behold. Ps. 63. 2; 90. 16.
pleaded in prayer. Ps. 79. 9.
the earth is full of. Isa. 6. 3.
not to be given to others. Isa. 42. 8.
to be feared. Isa. 59. 19.
the knowledge of, shall fill the earth. Num. 14. 21; Hab. 2. 14.

HIS GOODNESS:
proclaimed. Ps. 25. 8; Nah. 1. 7; Mat. 19. 17.
is abundant, Ex. 34. 6; Ps. 33. 5. great, Neh. 9. 35; Zec. 9. 17. enduring, Ps. 23. 6; 52. 1. satisfying, Ps. 65. 4; Jer. 31. 12, 14. rich, Ps. 104. 24; Rom. 2. 4. universal, Ps. 145. 9; Mat. 5. 45.
Manifested:
in forgiving sins, 2 Chr. 30. 18; Ps. 86. 5. to His church, Ps. 31. 19; Lam. 3. 25, in providing for the poor, Ps. 68. 10. in doing good, Ps. 119. 68; 145. 9.
in supplying temporal wants. Acts 14. 17.
leads to repentance. Rom. 2. 4.

HIS JOY OVER HIS PEOPLE:
greatness of. Zep. 3. 17.
On account of their:
uprightness. 1 Chr. 29. 17; Prov. 11. 20.
fear of Him. Ps. 147. 11.
hope in His mercy. Ps. 147. 11.
meekness. Ps. 149. 4.
praying to Him. Prov. 15. 8.
repentance. Lu. 15. 7, 10.
faith. Heb. 11. 5, 6.
Leads Him to:
give them the inheritance. Num. 14. 8; 1 Pet. 1. 4.
do them good. Deu. 28. 63; Jer. 32. 41; Acts 14. 17.
prosper them. Deu. 30. 9.
deliver them. 2 Sam. 22. 20.
comfort them. Isa. 65. 19.
exemplified: Solomon. 1 Kn. 10. 9.
illustrated. Isa. 62. 5; Lu. 15. 23, 24.

HIS LAW:
is absolute and perpetual. Mat. 5. 18.
Given:
to Adam. Gen. 2. 16, 17, with Rom. 5. 12-14.
to Noah. Gen. 9. 6.
to the Israelites. Ex. 20. 2; Ps. 78. 5.
through Moses. Ex. 31. 18; John 7. 19.
through the ministration of angels. Acts 7. 53; Gal. 3. 19; Heb. 2. 2.
Described as:
perfect, Ps. 19. 7; Rom. 12. 2. pure, Ps. 19. 8. exceeding broad, Ps. 119. 96. truth, Ps. 119. 142. holy, just, and good, Rom. 7. 12. spiritual, Rom. 7. 14. not grievous, 1 John 5. 3.

requires perfect obedience. Deu. 27. 26; Gal. 3. 10; Jas. 2. 10.
requires obedience of the heart. Ps. 51. 6; Mat. 5. 28; 22. 37.
man cannot render perfect obedience to. 1 Kn. 8. 46; Eccl. 7. 20; Rom. 3. 10.
it is man's duty to keep. Eccl. 12. 13.
man cannot be justified by. Acts 13. 39; Rom. 3. 20, 28; Gal. 2. 16; 3. 11.
conscience testifies to. Rom. 2. 15.
all men have transgressed. Rom. 3. 9, 19.
gives the knowledge of sin. Rom. 3. 20; 7. 7.
worketh wrath. Rom. 4. 15.
man, by nature not in subjection to. Rom. 7. 5; 8. 7.
love is the fulfilling of. Rom. 13. 8, 10; Gal. 5. 14; Jas. 2. 8.
designed to lead to Christ. Gal. 3. 24.
sin is a transgression of. 1 John 3. 4.

Obedience to:
of prime importance. 1 Cor. 7. 19.
a test of love. 1 John 5. 3.
a characteristic of saints. Rev. 12. 17.
blessedness of keeping. Ps. 119. 1; Mat. 5. 19, 1 John 3. 22, 24; Rev. 22. 14.

CHRIST magnified. Isa. 42. 21.
came to fulfil. Mat. 5. 17.
explained. Mat. 7. 12; 22. 37–40.
the love of, produces peace. Ps. 119. 165.

Saints:
should make the subject of their conversation, Ex. 13. 9. prepare their hearts to seek, Ez. 7. 10. pledge themselves to walk in, Neh. 10. 29. pray to understand, Ps. 119. 18. pray for power to keep, Ps. 119. 34. keep, Ps. 119. 55. delight in, Ps. 119. 77; Rom. 7. 22. love, Ps. 119. 97, 113. lament over the violation of, by others, Ps. 119. 136. have, written on their hearts, Jer. 31. 33, with Heb. 8. 10. should remember, Mal. 4. 4. freed from the bondage of, Rom. 6. 14; 7. 4, 6; Gal. 3. 13. freed from the curse of, Gal. 3. 13.

The Wicked:
forsake, 2 Chr. 12. 1; Jer. 9. 13. refuse to walk in, Ps. 78. 10. cast away, Isa. 5. 24. refuse to hear, Isa. 30. 9; Jer. 6. 19. forget, Hos. 4. 6. despise, Am. 2. 4.
punishment for disobeying. Neh. 9. 26, 27; Isa. 65. 11–13; Jer. 9. 13–16.
is the rule of judgment. Rom. 2. 12.
is established by faith. Rom. 3. 31.
is the rule of life to saints. 1 Cor. 9. 21; Gal. 5. [13, 14.
to be used lawfully. 1 Tim. 1. 8.

HIS REVELATIONS TO:
Isaiah, warning Judah and Israel, Isa. 1.–12. surrounding nations, Isa. 13.–23. threatening impenitent Jews, Isa. 24.; 39.
Jeremiah, respecting Judah's overthrow on account of sin. Jer. 1.–25.; 27.–33.; 44.
Ezekiel, concerning Judah's captivity, Ezek. 3.–7. the defiled temple, Ezek. 8.–11. warnings to Judah, Ezek. 12.–19. impending judgments, Ezek. 20.–23. Jerusalem's overthrow, Ezek. 24. judgments upon other nations, Ezek. 25.–32. exhortations and promises, Ezek. 32.–39. the New Jerusalem, Ezek. 40.–48.

GOD AS A SPIRIT (John 4. 24; 2 Cor. 3. 17):
is declared to be: Omnipotent, Gen. 17. 1; Ex. 6. 3. Glorious, Ex. 15. 11; Ps. 145. 5. Gracious, Ex. 34. 6; Ps. 116. 5. Merciful, Ex. 34. 6, 7; Ps. 86. 5. Longsuffering, Num. 14. 18; Mic. 7. 18. Just, Deu. 32. 4; Isa. 45. 21. Eternal, Deu. 33. 27; Ps. 90. 2; Rev. 4. 8–10. Jealous, Jos. 24. 19; Nah. 1. 2. Compassionate, 2 Kn. 13. 23. Great, 2 Chr. 2. 5; Ps. 86. 10. Righteous, Ez. 9. 15; Ps. 145. 17. Unsearchable, Job 11. 7; 37. 23; Ps. 145. 3; Isa. 40. 28; Rom. 11. 33. Invisible, Job 23. 8, 9; John 1. 18; 5. 37; Col. 1. 15; 1 Tim. 1. 17. Good, Ps. 25. 8; 119. 68. Upright, Ps. 25. 8; 92. 15. Holy, Ps. 99. 9; Isa. 5. 16. Most High, Ps. 83. 18; Acts 7. 48. Immutable, Ps. 102. 26, 27; Jas. 1. 17. Omniscient, Ps. 139. 1–6; Prov. 5. 21. Omnipresent, Ps. 139. 7; Jer. 23. 23. Light, Isa. 60. 19; Jas. 1. 17; 1 John 1. 5. True, Jer. 10. 10; John 17. 3. Perfect, Mat. 5. 48. Incorruptible, Rom. 1. 23. Only-wise, Rom. 16. 27; 1 Tim. 1. 17. Faithful, 1 Cor. 10. 13; 1 Pet. 4. 19. Immortal, 1 Tim. 1. 17; 6. 16. a consuming fire, Heb. 12. 29. Love, 1 John 4. 8, 16.
none like to Him, Ex. 9. 14; Deu. 33. 26; 2 Sam. 7. 22; Isa. 46. 5, 9; Jer. 10. 6. beside Him, Deu. 4. 35; Isa. 44. 6. before Him, Isa. 43. 10. none good but God, Mat. 19. 17.
fills heaven and earth. 1 Kn. 8. 27; Jer. 23. 24.
should be worshipped in spirit and in truth. John 4. 24.

God (*an idol*). Gen. 31. 30, stolen my *g.*
Ex. 32. 1, make us *g.*, which shall go before us.
32. 4, these be thy *g.*
Jud. 5. 8, they chose new *g.*
6. 31, if he be a *g.*, let him plead.
10. 14, go and cry to the *g.* ye have chosen.
17. 5, Micah had a house of *g.*
18. 24, ye have taken away my *g.*
2 Kn. 17. 29, every nation made *g.*
17. 33, they feared the Lord, and served own *g.*
Isa. 44. 15, maketh a *g.* and worshippeth it.
45. 20, pray to a *g.* that cannot save.
Jon. 1. 5, cried every man to his *g.*
Acts 12. 22, the voice of a *g.*, not a man.
14. 11, the *g.* are come down.
1 Cor. 8. 5, there be *g.* many.
See Ex. 12. 12; Jer. 2. 11; Dan. 3. 28.

Goddess. 1 Kn. 11. 5; Acts 19. 27, 35, 37.

Godhead. Acts 17. 29; Rom. 1. 20; Col. 2. 9.

Godliness. 1 Tim. 3. 16, the mystery of *g.*
4. 7, exercise thyself to *g.*
4. 8, *g.* is profitable.
6. 3, doctrine according to *g.*
6. 5, supposing that gain is *g.*
2 Tim. 3. 5, a form of *g.*
Tit. 1. 1, the truth which is after *g.*
2 Pet. 1. 3, pertain to life and *g.*
1. 6, and to patience *g.*
3. 11, in all holy conversation and *g.*
See 1 Tim. 2. 2, 10; 6. 6, 11.

Godly. Ps. 12. 1, the *g.* man ceaseth.
Mal. 2. 15, seek a *g.* seed.
2 Cor. 1. 12, in *g.* sincerity.
7. 9, 10, *g.* sorrow worketh repentance.
2 Tim. 3. 12, all that will live *g.* in Christ.
Tit. 2. 12, live *g.* in this world.
Heb. 12. 28, reverence and *g.* fear. R. V. awe.
2 Pet. 2. 9, how to deliver the *g.*
3 John 6, bring forward after a *g.* sort. R. V. worthily of God.
See Ps. 4. 3; 32. 6; 2 Cor. 7. 9; 11. 2.

Godly conversation. *See* CONVERSATION.

Gods, judges described as. Ex. 22. 28; Ps. 82. 1; 138. 1; John 10. 34; 1 Cor. 8. 5.
false, worship of, forbidden. Ex. 20. 3, 23; 34. 17; Deu. 5. 7; 8. 19; 18. 20.

God save the king. 2 Sam. 16. 16, Hushai said unto Absalom, *G.*

Gog, gŏg. (1) 1 Chr. 5. 4.
(2) (and **Magog**). Ezek. 38.; 39.; Rev. 20. 8.

Going. Jos. 23. 14, *g.* the way of all the earth.
2 Sam. 5. 24; 1 Chr. 14. 15, sound of *g.* in trees. R. V. marching.
Job 33. 24, 28, from *g.* down to pit.
Ps. 17. 5, hold up my *g.* R. V. my steps have held.
40. 2, established my *g.*
Prov. 5. 21, pondereth all his *g.* R. V. maketh level all his paths.
20. 24, man's *g.* are of the Lord.
Dan. 6. 14, laboured till *g.* down of the sun.
Mic. 5. 2, whose *g.* forth have been from of old.
Mat. 26. 46, rise, let us be *g.*
1 Tim. 5. 24, *g.* before to judgment.
See Prov. 7. 27; 14. 15; Isa. 59. 8; Hos. 6. 3.

Golan, gō-lăn, 'circuit.' Deu. 4. 43.

Gold. Six different words are used for gold in the Old Testament;—

(1) (1 Kn. 9. 28). Heb. *Zâhâb:* Gk. χρυσίον. The commonest name, from its colour.

(2) (Job 28. 17). Heb. *Pâz*: Gk. χρυσίον: R. V. 'fine gold.' The native metal.
(3) (Job 22. 24). Heb. *Bétzer*: Gk. πέτρα Σωφίρ. Gold dust, fragments of ore.
(4) (Ps. 68. 13). Heb. *Ḥârûtz*: Gk. χρυσίον: R. V. 'yellow gold.' Referring to its lustre.
(5) (Job 28. 15). Heb. *Sâgûr*: Gk. περιουσιασμός. Treasure.
(6) (Job 28. 19). Heb. *Kéthem*: Gk. χρυσίον καθαρόν: R. V. 'pure gold.' *Kéthem* = concealed gold, denoting its high value.

Gold. Num. 31. 22, only *g.*, etc., that may abide fire.
Deu. 8. 13, when thy *g.* is multiplied.
17. 17, nor shall he greatly multiply *g.*
1 Kn. 20. 3, silver and *g.* is mine.
Job 28. 1, a vein for silver, a place for *g.*
31. 24, if I made *g.* my hope.
Ps. 19. 10, more to be desired than *g.*
21. 3, thou settest a crown of pure *g.* upon his [head.
Prov. 25. 11, like apples of *g.*
Isa. 46. 6, they lavish *g.* out of the bag.
60. 17, for brass I will bring *g.*
Hag. 2. 8, the silver is mine, and the *g.* is mine.
Zec. 4. 2, behold, a candlestick all of *g.*
13. 9, try them as *g.* is tried.
Mat. 10. 9, provide neither *g.* nor silver.
Acts 3. 6, silver and *g.* have I none.
17. 29, not think Godhead like to *g.*
20. 33, coveted no man's *g.*
2 Tim. 2. 20, in great house not only vessels of *g.*
Jas. 2. 2, man with a *g.* ring.
5. 3, your *g.* is cankered.
1 Pet. 1. 7, trial more precious than of *g.*
1. 18, not redeemed with *g.*
Rev. 3. 18, buy of me *g.* tried in the fire.
21. 18, city was pure *g.*
See Gen. 2. 11; Eccl. 12. 6; Isa. 13. 12.

Golden candlestick (Ex. 25. 31), the seven-branched candlestick of the Tabernacle and Temple.

Golgotha, gŏl'-gŏ-thă, 'a skull.' Called also Calvary, 'the place of a skull,' near the city, but outside the walls, with a garden adjoining. Probably the hill on the north of the city 250 yards west of the Damascus gate. Mat. 27. 33; Mk. 15. 22; Lu. 23. 33; John 19. 17.

Goliath, gō-lī'-ăth, 'conspicuous' (?); of Gath. 1 Sam. 17.; 21. 9; 22. 10.

Gomer, gō'-mĕr, 'complete.' Gen. 10. 2.

Gomorrah, gō-mŏr'-răh, 'submersion' (?); one of the five cities of the Plain, probably north of the Dead Sea. It was destroyed with Sodom. Gen. 10. 19; 18. 20; 19. 24, 28; Isa. 1. 9; Mat. 10. 15; Mk. 6. 11.

Gomorrha, gō-mŏr'-rhă, same as GOMORRAH. Mat. 10. 15.

Gone. Deu. 23. 23, that which is *g.* out of thy lips.
1 Kn. 20. 40, busy here and there, he was *g.*
Ps. 42. 4, I had *g.* with the multitude.
73. 2, my feet were almost *g.*
77. 8, mercy clean *g.* for ever.
103. 16, wind passeth, and it is *g.*
109. 23, I am *g.* like the shadow.
119. 176; Isa. 53. 6, *g.* astray like sheep.
Eccl. 8. 10, come and *g.* from place of the holy. R. V. went away from the holy place.
Jer. 15. 9, sun *g.* down while yet day.
Mat. 12. 43; Lu. 11. 24, spirit *g.* out.
25. 8, lamps are *g.* out.
Mk. 5. 30; Lu. 8. 46, virtue had *g.* out of him.
John 12. 19, the world is *g.* after him.
Acts 16. 19, hope of their gains *g.*
Rom. 3. 12, they are all *g.* out of the way. R. V. turned aside.
Jude 11, *g.* in the way of Cain.
See Ps. 89. 34; S. of S. 2. 11; Isa. 45. 23.

Good (*n.*). Gen. 50. 20, God meant it unto *g.*
Neh. 5. 19; 13. 31, think upon me for *g.*
Job 2. 10, shall we receive *g.*
22. 21, thereby *g.* shall come.
Ps. 4. 6, who will shew us any *g.*?
14. 1; 53. 1; Rom. 3. 12, none doeth *g.*
34. 12, loveth days that he may see *g.*
39. 2, held my peace even from *g.*
86. 17, a token for *g.*
Prov. 3. 27, withhold not *g.*
Eccl. 3. 12, I know there is no *g.* in them. R. V. nothing better for them.
9. 18, destroyeth much *g.*
Acts 10. 38, went about doing *g.*
Rom. 8. 28, work together for *g.*
13. 4, minister of God for *g.*
See Job 5. 27; 7. 7; Prov. 11. 17; 13. 21.

Good (*adj.*). Gen. 1. 4, 10, 12, 18, 21, 25, 31, God saw it was *g.*
Gen. 2. 18, not *g.* that man should be alone.
27. 46, what *g.* shall my life do me?
Deu. 2. 4; Jos. 23. 11, take *g.* heed.
1 Sam. 2. 24, no *g.* report I hear.
12. 23, I will teach you the *g.* way.
25. 15, men were very *g.* to us.
Ez. 7. 9; Neh. 2. 8, the *g.* hand of God on him.
Neh. 9. 20, thy *g.* spirit to instruct.
Ps. 34. 8, taste and see that the Lord is *g.*
45. 1, my heart is inditing a *g.* matter.
112. 5, a *g.* man sheweth favour. R. V. well is it with the man.
119. 68, thou art *g.*, and doest *g.*
145. 9, the Lord is *g.* to all.
Prov. 12. 25, a *g.* word maketh the heart glad.
15. 23, in season, how *g.* is it!
20. 18, with *g.* advice make war. R. V. wise guid-[ance.
22. 1, a *g.* name rather to be chosen.
25. 25, *g.* news from a far country.
Eccl. 6. 12, who knoweth what is *g.*?
Isa. 55. 2, eat ye that which is *g.*
Lam. 3. 26, it is *g.* that a man hope.
3. 27, *g.* that a man bear yoke.
Zec. 1. 13, answered with *g.* words.
Mat. 5. 13, it is *g.* for nothing.
7. 11; Lu. 11. 13, how to give *g.* gifts.
9. 22; Lu. 8. 48, be of *g.* comfort.
19. 16, what *g.* thing shall I do?
19. 17; Lu. 18. 19, none *g.*, save one.
20. 15, is thine eye evil because I am *g.*?
25. 21, *g.* and faithful servant.
26. 24, been *g.* for that man.
Mk. 9. 50; Lu. 14. 34, salt is *g.*, but.
Lu. 1. 53, filled the hungry with *g.* things.
6. 38, *g.* measure, pressed down.
10. 42, chosen that *g.* part.
12. 32, your Father's *g.* pleasure.
16. 25, thou in thy lifetime receivedst *g.* things.
23. 50, Joseph was a *g.* man and a just.
John 1. 46, can any *g.* thing come out of Nazareth?
2. 10, kept *g.* wine until now.
7. 12, some said, he is a *g.* man.
10. 11, I am the *g.* shepherd.
10. 33, for a *g.* work we stone thee not.
Rom. 7. 12, the commandment holy, just, and *g.*
7. 18, in my flesh dwelleth no *g.* thing.
12. 2, that *g.* and perfect will of God.
14. 21, it is *g.* neither to eat.
1 Cor. 7. 26, this is *g.* for the present.
15. 33, corrupt *g.* manners.
2 Cor. 9. 8, abound in every *g.* work.
Gal. 6. 6, communicate in all *g.* things.
Phil. 1. 6, hath begun a *g.* work.
Col. 1. 10, fruitful in every *g.* work.
1 Thes. 5. 15; 3 John 11, follow that which is *g.*
5. 21, hold fast that which is *g.*
1 Tim. 1. 8, the law is *g.*
3. 1, desireth a *g.* work.
4. 4, every creature of God is *g.*
2 Tim. 3. 3, despisers of *g.*
Tit. 2. 7, a pattern in *g.* works.
2. 14, zealous of *g.* works.
Heb. 6. 5, tasted the *g.* word of God.
13. 9, *g.* thing that the heart be established.
Jas. 1. 17, every *g.* gift.
See 2 Thes. 2. 17; Tit. 1. 16; 3. 8.

Goodliness. Isa. 40. 6.

Goodly. Gen. 49. 21, giveth *g.* words.

Ex. 2. 2, a *g*. child.
Deu. 8. 12, when thou hast built *g*. houses.
1 Sam. 9. 2, a choice young man, and a *g*.
16. 12, ruddy, and *g*. to look to.
Ps. 16. 6; Jer. 3. 19, a *g*. heritage.
Zec. 11. 13, a *g*. price I was prized at.
Mat. 13. 45, *g*. pearls.
Jas. 2. 2, a man in *g*. apparel. R. V. fine clothing.
See 1 Sam. 8. 16; 1 Kn. 20. 3; Lu. 21. 5.

Goodman, master, head of the family. Mat. 20. 11.

Goodness. Ex. 33. 19, make all my *g*. pass.
34. 6, abundant in *g*. and truth.
Ps. 16. 2, my *g*. extendeth not to thee.
23. 6, *g*. and mercy shall follow.
27. 13, believed to see the *g*. of the Lord.
31. 19; Zec. 9. 17, how great is thy *g*.
33. 5, earth full of thy *g*.
65. 11, crownest the year with thy *g*.
145. 7, the memory of thy *g*.
Prov. 20. 6, proclaim every one his own *g*. R. V. kindness.
Hos. 6. 4, your *g*. is as a morning cloud.
Rom. 2. 4, the riches of his *g*.
11. 22, the *g*. and severity of God.
See Neh. 9. 25; Isa. 63. 7; Gal. 5. 22; Eph. 5. 9.

Goods. Gen. 14. 21, take the *g*. to thyself.
24. 10, the *g*. of his master in his hand. R. V. goodly things.
Eccl. 5. 11, when *g*. increase.
Mat. 12. 29; Mk. 3. 27, spoil his *g*.
24. 47, ruler over all his *g*. R. V. all that he hath.
Lu. 6. 30, of him that taketh away thy *g*.
12. 19, much *g*. laid up.
15. 12, the portion of *g*. R. V. thy substance.
16. 1, accused that he had wasted his *g*.
19. 8, half of my *g*. I give.
1 Cor. 13. 3, bestow all my *g*. to feed.
Heb. 10. 34, joyfully the spoiling of your *g*. R. V. possessions.
1 John 3. 17, this world's *g*.
Rev. 3. 17, rich, and increased with *g*.

Gopher (Gen. 6. 14). Heb. *Gôpher:* Gk. ξύλα τετράγωνα. The wood used in building Noah's ark. Celsius thinks it was 'cypress;' Cheyne suggests 'cedar.'

Goshen, gō'-shĕn. (1) Fertile district in Egypt, immediately to the east of the ancient delta of the Nile. It was here that Jacob and his descendants settled until the Exodus (Gen. 45. 10; 46. 34; 47. 4; Ex. 8. 22; 9. 26).
(2) (Jos. 10. 41; 11. 16). District in southern Palestine, not identified.
(3) (Jos. 15. 51). Town in the highlands of Judah.

Gospel. The A. S. equivalent of the Greek εὐαγγέλιον, Lat. *evangelium*, 'good tidings;' the good tidings which Jesus brought from his Father. Hence the term was applied to a narrative of the facts concerning Jesus Christ (as in Mk. 1. 1).
Rom. 2. 16, according to my *g*.
2 Cor. 4. 3, if our *g*. be hid.
Gal. 1. 8, 9, any other *g*.
2. 7, the *g*. of uncircumcision, *g*. of circumcision.
Col. 1. 23, the hope of the *g*.
1 Tim. 1. 11, *g*. of the blessed God.
Rev. 14. 6, everlasting *g*.

Gospel of Christ, its teaching and accompaniments. Mat. 4. 23; 24. 14; Mk. 1. 14; Lu. 2. 10; 20. 21; Acts 13. 26; 14. 3; 20. 21; Rom. 1. 2, 9, 16; 2. 16; 10. 8; 16. 25; 1 Cor. 1. 18; 2. 13; 15. 1; 2 Cor. 4. 4; 5. 19; 6. 7; Eph. 1. 13; 3. 2; 6. 15; Phil. 2. 16; Col. 1. 5; 3. 16; 1 Thes. 1. 5; 2. 8; 3. 2; 1 Tim. 1. 11; 6. 3; Heb. 4. 2; 1 Pet. 1. 12, 25; 4. 17.
preached to Abraham. Gal. 3. 8.
to the poor and others. Mat. 11. 5; Mk. 1. 15; 13. 10; 16. 15; Lu. 4. 18; 24. 47; Acts 13. 46; 14.; 1 Cor. 1. 17; 9. 16; Gal. 2. 2; Rev. 14. 6.
its effects. Mk. 1. 15; 8. 35; Lu. 2. 10, 14; 19. 8; Acts 4. 32; Rom. 1. 16; 12.; 13.; 15. 29; 16. 26; 2 Cor. 8.; 9.; Gal. 1. 16; 2. 14; Eph. 4.-6.; Phil. 1. 5, 17, 27; Col. 1. 23; 3.; 4.; 1 Thes. 1.; 2.; Tit. 2.; 3.; Jas. 1.; 1 & 2 Pet.; 1 John 3.; Jude 3.
rejected by the Jews. Acts 13. 26; 28. 25; Rom. 9.-11.; 1 Thes. 2. 16.
from whom hid. 1 Cor. 1. 23; 2. 8; 2 Cor. 4. 3.

Go to, come now! Gen. 11. 3.

Gourd. (1) (Jon. 4. 6-9). Heb. *Kîkâyôn:* Gk. κολοκύνθη: Bot. N. *Cucurbita pepo:* R. V. marg. 'Palma Christi.' The rapidly growing 'bottle gourd' with large leaves.
(2) (The *wild*) (2 Kn. 4. 39). Heb. *Pakkuôh:* Gk. τολύπη ἀγρία: Bot. N. *Citrullus colocynthis*, the colocynth, a wild vine, with gourd-like melons, the pulp of which is a drastic cathartic, and, in quantities, an irritant poison. The 'vine of Sodom' (Deu. 32. 32) is probably the same plant.

Government. Isa. 9. 6; 1 Cor. 12. 28; 2 Pet. 2. 10.

Governor, steersman, pilot. Jas. 3. 4.

Gozan, gō'-zăn. 2 Kn. 17. 6.

Grace. Ps. 45. 2, *g*. is poured into thy lips.
Prov. 1. 9, an ornament of *g*.
3. 22, life to thy soul, and *g*. to thy neck.
3. 34; Jas. 4. 6, giveth *g*. to the lowly.
Zec. 4. 7, crying, *g*., *g*. unto it.
12. 10, spirit of *g*. and supplications.
John 1. 14, full of *g*. and truth.
1. 16, all received, and *g*. for *g*.
1. 17, *g*. and truth came by Jesus Christ.
Acts 4. 33, great *g*. was upon them all.
11. 23, when he had seen the *g*.
14. 3, the word of his *g*.
Rom. 1. 7; 1 Cor. 1. 3; 2 Cor. 1. 2; Gal. 1. 3; Eph. 1. 2; Phil. 1. 2; Col. 1. 2; 1 Thes. 1. 1; 2 Thes. 1. 2; Philem. 3; 1 Pet. 1. 2; 2 Pet. 1. 2; Rev. 1. 4. *g*. and peace.
3. 24, justified freely by his *g*.
4. 4, not reckoned of *g*., but of debt.
5. 2, access into this *g*.
5. 17, abundance of *g*.
5. 20, where sin abounded, *g*. did much more abound.
6. 14, 15, under *g*.
11. 5, the election of *g*.
2 Cor. 8. 9, know the *g*. of our Lord.
9. 8, able to make all *g*. abound.
12. 9, my *g*. is sufficient.
Gal. 1. 6, 15, who called you by his *g*.
5. 4, ye are fallen from *g*.
Eph. 2. 5, 8, by *g*. ye are saved.
3. 8, to me is this *g*. given.
4. 29, minister *g*. to hearers.
6. 24, *g*. be with all that love our Lord.
Col. 4. 6, let your speech be alway with *g*.
2 Thes. 2. 16, good hope through *g*.
1 Tim. 1. 2; 2 Tim. 1. 2; Tit. 1. 4; 2 John 3, *g*., mercy, and peace.
Heb. 4. 16, the throne of *g*.
10. 29, despite unto the Spirit of *g*.
12. 28, *g*. to serve God acceptably.
13. 9, heart established with *g*.
Jas. 1. 11, the *g*. of the fashion of it.
4. 6, he giveth more *g*.
1 Pet. 3. 7, heirs of *g*.
5. 5, giveth *g*. to the humble.
2 Pet. 3. 18, grow in *g*.
Jude 4, turning *g*. of God into lasciviousness.

Grace of God and Jesus Christ. Ps. 84. 11; Zec. 4. 7; Lu. 2. 40; John 1. 16; Acts 20. 24; Rom. 11. 5; 1 Cor. 15. 10; 2 Cor. 6. 1; 8. 9; Gal. 2. 21; 2 Tim. 1. 9; 1 Pet. 5. 5.
salvation through. Acts 15. 11; Rom. 3. 24; 4. 4; Eph. 2. 5; 2 Thes. 2. 16; Tit. 3. 7; 1 Pet. 1. 10.
effects of. 2 Cor. 1. 12; Tit. 2. 11; 1 Pet. 4. 10. *See* GOSPEL.
prayer for. Rom. 16. 20; 1 Tim. 1. 2; Heb. 4. 16.
danger of abusing, Rom. 6.; Jude 4. and departing from, Gal. 5. 4.
exhortations concerning. 2 Tim. 1. 9; Heb. 12. 15, 28; 2 Pet. 3. 18.

Gracious. Gen. 43. 29, God be *g*. to thee.
Ex. 22. 27, I will hear, for I am *g*.

Ex. 33. 19, I will be *g.* to whom I will be *g.*
Neh. 9. 17, 31, ready to pardon, *g.*, merciful.
Ps. 77. 9, hath God forgotten to be *g.*?
Prov. 11. 16, a *g.* woman retaineth honour.
Isa. 30. 18, wait, that he may be *g.*
Am. 5. 15, may be the Lord will be *g.*
Jon. 4. 2, I know thou art a *g.* God.
Lu. 4. 22, wondered at the *g.* words.
1 Pet. 2. 3, tasted that the Lord is *g.*
See Gen. 33. 5; Ex. 34. 6; 2 Chr. 30. 9; Hos. 14. 2.
Graffed, grafted. Rom. 11. 17, 19, 23, 24.
Grain. Mat. 13. 31; 17. 20; Mk. 4. 31; Lu. 13. 19; 17. 6, *g.* of mustard seed.
See Am. 9. 9; 1 Cor. 15. 37.
Grant. Ru. 1. 9, *g.* that you may find rest.
1 Chr. 4. 10, God *g.* him that which he requested.
Job 6. 8, *g.* the thing I long for.
Mat. 20. 21; Mk. 10. 37, *g.* that my two sons. R. V. command.
Rev. 3. 21, will I *g.* to sit with me.
See Ps. 20. 4; 85. 7; Acts 4. 29.
Grape. Gen. 49. 11, washed clothes in the blood of *g.*
Num. 6. 3, nor eat moist *g.*, or dried.
Deu. 23. 24, then thou mayest eat *g.* thy fill.
24. 21, when thou gatherest the *g.* of thy vineyard.
32. 14, drink the blood of the *g.*
S. of S. 2. 13, 15, vines with tender *g.*
Isa. 5. 2, looked it should bring forth *g.*
17. 6; 24. 13, yet gleaning *g.* R. V. gleanings.
Jer. 8. 13, there shall be no *g.*
31. 29, 30; Ezek. 18. 2, have eaten a sour *g.*
Am. 9. 13, treader of *g.* shall overtake.
See Lev. 19. 10; 25. 5; Lu. 6. 44; Rev. 14. 18.
Grass. (1) (Num. 22. 4). Heb. *Yérek:* Gk. τὰ χλωρά; general name for green herbage.
(2) (Gen. 1. 11). Heb. *Déshe:* Gk. βοτάνη; grass as distinguished from herbs.
(3) (Isa. 35. 7). Heb. *Ḥâtzîr:* Gk. χόρτος, πόα: R. V. marg. 'court,' fodder, grass, dried grass.
Grass. Deu. 32. 2, as showers upon the *g.*
2 Kn. 19. 26; Ps. 129. 6, as *g.* on housetops.
Ps. 72. 6, like rain upon mown *g.*
90. 5, like *g.* which groweth up.
102. 4, 11, withered like *g.*
103. 15, days are as *g.*
Isa. 40. 6; 1 Pet. 1. 24, all flesh is *g.*
Mat. 6. 30; Lu. 12. 28, if God so clothe the *g.*
See Prov. 27. 25; John 6. 10; Rev. 8. 7; 9. 4.
Grass brought forth. Gen. 1. 11.
man compared to. Ps. 37. 2; 90. 5; 103. 15; Isa. 40. 6; Jas. 1. 10; 1 Pet. 1. 24.
Grasshopper. (1) (Jud. 6. 5). Heb. *Arbeh:* Gk. ἀκρίς: R. V. 'locusts.' The generic name for locusts.
(2) (Lev. 11. 22; Isa. 40. 22). Heb. *Ḥâgâb:* Gk. ἀκρίς. Probably the smallest of the locust tribe.
(3) Am. 7. 1, and, behold, he formed *g.* R. V. locusts. Heb. *Gêb*, *see* Locust 8.
Grave (*n.*). Gen. 42. 38; 44. 31, with sorrow to the *g.*
Ex. 14. 11, no *g.* in Egypt.
Num. 19. 16, or a *g.*
Job 5. 26, come to *g.* in full age.
7. 9, he that goeth to the *g.* R. V. Sheol.
14. 13, hide me in the *g.* R. V. Sheol.
17. 1, the *g.* are ready for me.
17. 13, if I wait, the *g.* is mine house. R. V. look for Sheol as.
33. 22, his soul draweth near to the *g.* R. V. pit.
Ps. 6. 5, in the *g.* who shall give thee thanks? R. V. Sheol.
31. 17, let wicked be silent in the *g.* R. V. Sheol.
49. 14, like sheep laid in the *g.* R. V. Sheol.
49. 15; Hos. 13. 14, the power of the *g.* R. V. Sheol.
Eccl. 9. 10, no wisdom in the *g.*
Isa. 38. 18, the *g.* cannot praise thee.
53. 9, made his *g.* with the wicked.
Hos. 13. 14, O *g.*, I will be thy destruction.
John 5. 28, all in the *g.* shall hear. R. V. tombs.
11. 31, she goeth to the *g.* R. V. tomb.
1 Cor. 15. 55, O *g.*, where is thy victory? R. V. death.
See Mat. 27. 52; Lu. 11. 44; Rev. 11. 9; 20. 13.
Grave (*v.*). Isa. 49. 16, I have *g.* thee upon the palms.
Hab. 2. 18, that the maker hath *g.* it.
See Ex. 28. 9; 2 Chr. 2. 7; 3. 7.
Grave (*adj.*). 1 Tim. 3. 8; Tit. 2. 2.
Gravel. Prov. 20. 17; Isa. 48. 19; Lam. 3. 16.
Gravity. 1 Tim. 3. 4; Tit. 2. 7.
Gray. Ps. 71. 18; Prov. 20. 29; Hos. 7. 9.
Great. Gen. 12. 2; 18. 18; 46. 3, make a *g.* nation.
48. 19, he also shall be *g.*
Deu. 29. 24, the heat of his *g.* anger.
1 Sam. 12. 24, consider how *g.* things.
2 Kn. 5. 13, bid thee do some *g.* thing.
2 Chr. 2. 5, the house is *g.*, for *g.* is our God.
Neh. 6. 3, I am doing a *g.* work.
Job 32. 9, *g.* men not always wise.
36. 18, a *g.* ransom.
Ps. 14. 5; 53. 5, there were they in *g.* fear.
19. 11, there is *g.* reward.
31. 19, how *g.* is thy goodness!
92. 5, how *g.* are thy works!
139. 17, how *g.* is the sum of them!
Prov. 18. 16, gift bringeth before *g.* men.
25. 6, stand not in place of *g.* men.
Mat. 5. 12, *g.* is your reward.
5. 19, called *g.* in kingdom of heaven.
13. 46, pearl of *g.* price.
15. 28, *g.* is thy faith.
20. 26, whosoever will be *g.* among you.
22. 36, 38, the *g.* commandment.
Lu. 10. 2, the harvest is *g.* R. V. plenteous.
16. 26, a *g.* gulf fixed.
Acts 8. 9, giving out he was some *g.* one.
19. 28, 34, *g.* is Diana.
1 Tim. 3. 16, *g.* is the mystery.
Heb. 2. 3, so *g.* salvation.
12. 1, so *g.* a cloud of witnesses.
Jas. 3. 5, how *g.* a matter a little fire kindleth! R. V. how much wood.
See Deu. 9. 2; Eccl. 2. 9; Rev. 7. 9.
Greater. Gen. 4. 13, punishment *g.* than I can bear.
1 Chr. 11. 9; Esth. 9. 4, waxed *g.* and *g.*
Hag. 2. 9, glory of latter house *g.*
Mat. 11. 11; Lu. 7. 28, *g.* than he.
12. 6, one *g.* than the temple.
Mk. 12. 31, no commandment *g.* than these.
John 1. 50; 5. 20; 14. 12, shalt see *g.* things.
4. 12; 8. 53, art thou *g.* than our father?
10. 29; 14. 28, my father is *g.* than all.
13. 16; 15. 20, servant not *g.* than his lord.
15. 13, *g.* love hath no man.
1 Cor. 15. 6, the *g.* part remain.
Heb. 6. 13, he could swear by no *g.*
1 John 3. 20, God is *g.* than our hearts.
4. 4, *g.* is he in you than he in world.
3 John 4, no *g.* joy.
See Gen. 41. 40; 48. 19; Heb. 9. 11.
Greatest. Mat. 13. 32, is *g.* among herbs. R. V. greater than.
18. 1, 4, who is *g.* in kingdom?
Mk. 9. 34; Lu. 9. 46, disputed who should be *g.*
1 Cor. 13. 13, the *g.* of these is charity.
See Job 1. 3; Jer. 31. 34; Lu. 22. 24.
Greatly. 2 Sam. 24. 10; 1 Chr. 21. 8, I have sinned *g.*
1 Kn. 18. 3, Obadiah feared the Lord *g.*
Ps. 28. 7, my heart *g.* rejoiceth.
47. 9, God is *g.* exalted.
89. 7, *g.* to be feared. R. V. a God very terrible.
116. 10, I was *g.* afflicted.
Dan. 9. 23; 10. 11, thou art *g.* beloved.
Obad. 2, thou art *g.* despised.
Mk. 12. 27, ye do *g.* err.
See Ps. 62. 2; Mk. 9. 15; Acts 3. 11; 6. 7.
Greatness. 1 Chr. 29. 11, thine is the *g.*, power, and glory.
Ps. 145. 3, his *g.* is unsearchable.
Prov. 5. 23, in the *g.* of his folly.
Isa. 63. 1, travelling in *g.* of strength.

Eph. 1. 19, the exceeding *g.* of his power.
See 2 Chr. 9. 6; Ps. 66. 3; 79. 11; 150. 2.
Great Sea. The Mediterranean. Ezek. 47. 15, 19.
Greaves. Thin plates of metal to protect the front of the leg, below the knee. 1 Sam. 17. 6.
Grecia, grē'-çĭ-ā, same as GREECE. Dan. 8. 21.
Grecian, grē'-cĭăn, a Jew who speaks Greek. Acts 11. 20.
Greece, grēēçe, country of the Greeks. Called in Greek *Hellas.* Acts 20. 2.
prophecies of. Dan. 8. 21; 10. 20; 11. 2; Zec. 9. 13.
Paul preaches in. Acts 16.; 20.
Greedily. Prov. 21. 26; Ezek. 22. 12.
Greediness. Eph. 4. 19.
Greedy. Prov. 1. 19; 15. 27, *g.* of gain.
Isa. 56. 11, they are *g.* dogs.
See Ps. 17. 12; 1 Tim. 3. 3.
Greek, greēk, the language of Greece. Acts 21. 37.
Greeks, greēks, inhabitants of Greece. Acts 18. 17.
would see Jesus. John 12. 20.
believe in Him. Acts 11. 21; 17. 4.
Green. Lev. 23. 14; Jud. 16. 7; Lu. 23. 31.
Greyhound (Prov. 30. 31). Heb. *Zarzîr Mothnaim,* 'one girt in the loins:' Gk. ἀλέκτωρ: R. V. marg. 'war-horse.' (Uncertain.)
Grief. 2 Chr. 6. 29, every one shall know his own *g.*
Job 6. 2, oh that my *g.* were weighed! R. V. vexation.
Ps. 31. 10, life spent with *g.*
Eccl. 1. 18, in much wisdom is much *g.*
Isa. 53. 3, acquainted with *g.*
Jer. 10. 19, this is a *g.*, and I must bear it.
See Jon. 4. 6; Heb. 13. 17; 1 Pet. 2. 19.
Grieve. Gen. 6. 6, it *g.* him at his heart.
45. 5, be not *g.* that ye sold me.
1 Sam. 2. 33, the man shall be to *g.* thine heart.
Ps. 78. 40, they *g.* him in the desert.
95. 10, forty years was I *g.*
Lam. 3. 33, doth not willingly *g.*
Mk. 3. 5, being *g.* for the hardness.
10. 22, he went away *g.*
John 21. 17, Peter was *g.*
Rom. 14. 15, brother *g.* with meat.
Eph. 4. 30, *g.* not the holy Spirit of God.
See Neh. 2. 10; 13. 8; Ps. 119. 158; 139. 21.
Grievous. Gen. 21. 11, thing was *g.* in Abraham's sight.
50. 11, a *g.* mourning.
Ps. 10. 5, his ways are always *g.* R. V. firm at all times.
Prov. 15. 1, *g.* words stir up anger.
Isa. 15. 4, his life shall be *g.* R. V. his soul trembleth.
Jer. 30. 12; Nah. 3. 19, thy wound is *g.*
Mat. 23. 4; Lu. 11. 46, burdens *g.* to be borne.
Phil. 3. 1, to me is not *g.* R. V. irksome.
Heb. 12. 11, chastening *g.*
1 John 5. 3, commandments not *g.*
See Eccl. 2. 17; Jer. 16. 4; Acts 20. 29.
Grind. Isa. 3. 15, *g.* faces of the poor.
Lam. 5. 13, took young men to *g.*
Mat. 21. 44; Lu. 20. 18, it will *g.* him to powder. R. V. scatter him as dust.
See Eccl. 12. 3; Mat. 24. 41; Lu. 17. 35.
Grisled, of a gray colour, or mixed with gray. Gen. 31. 10.
Groan. Ex. 2. 24, God heard their *g.*
Job 24. 12, men *g.* from out the city.
Joel 1. 18, how do the beasts *g.*!
Rom. 8. 23, we ourselves *g.*
2 Cor. 5. 2, 4, in this we *g.*
See Job 23. 2; Ps. 6. 6; John 11. 33, 38.
Grope. Deu. 28. 29; Job 5. 14; 12. 25; Isa. 59. 10.
Gross. Isa. 60. 2; Jer. 13. 16; Mat. 13. 15; Acts 28. 27.
Ground. Ex. 3. 5; Acts 7. 33, holy *g.*
Job 5. 6, nor trouble spring out of the *g.*
Isa. 35. 7, parched *g.* become a pool. R. V. glowing sand.
Jer. 4. 3; Hos. 10. 12, break up fallow *g.*
Mat. 13. 8; Lu. 8. 8, good *g.*
Mk. 4. 16, stony *g.*
Lu. 13. 7, why cumbereth it the *g.*?
Lu. 14. 18, bought a piece of *g.* R. V. a field.
19. 44, lay thee even with the *g.*
John 8. 6, he wrote on the *g.*
See Zec. 8. 12; Mal. 3. 11; John 12. 24.
Grounded. Eph. 3. 17; Col. 1. 23.
Grove. (1) (Deu. 16. 21). Heb. *Ashêrah:* Gk. ἄλσος: R. V. 'Asherah.' A sacred tree or pole.
(2) (Gen. 21. 33). Heb. *Eshel:* Gk. ἄρουρα: Bot. N. *Tamarix Pallasii; Tamarix gallica:* R. V. 'tamarisk tree.'
Groves for worship. Gen. 21. 33.
idolatrous, forbidden. Deu. 16. 21; Jud. 6. 25; 1 Kn. 14. 15; 15. 13; 16. 33; 2 Kn. 17. 16; 21. 3; 23. 4.
Grow. Gen. 48. 16, let them *g.* into a multitude.
2 Sam. 23. 5, though he make it not to *g.*
Ps. 92. 12, *g.* like a cedar.
Isa. 53. 2, he shall *g.* up before him.
Hos. 14. 5, he shall *g.* as the lily. R. V. blossom.
Mal. 4. 2, *g.* up as calves of the stall. R. V. gambol.
Mat. 13. 30, let both *g.* together.
Mk. 4. 27, seed should *g.* up, he knoweth not.
Acts 5. 24, whereunto this would *g.*
Eph. 2. 21, *g.* unto an holy temple.
4. 15, may *g.* up into him.
2 Thes. 1. 3, your faith *g.* exceedingly.
1 Pet. 2. 2, that ye may *g.* thereby.
2 Pet. 3. 18, *g.* in grace.
See 2 Kn. 19. 26; Jer. 12. 2; Zec. 6. 12.
Grudge. (1) Lev. 19. 18; 2 Cor. 9. 7; 1 Pet. 4. 9.
(2) to grumble, murmur. Ps. 59. 15; Jas. 5. 9.
Guard. Gen. 40. 4; 2 Sam. 23. 23; 2 Kn. 11. 11; Neh. 4. 22; Ezek. 38. 7; Acts 28. 16.
Gudgodah, gŭd-gō'-dăh. Deu. 10. 7.
Guests. Zep. 1. 7; Mat. 22. 10; Lu. 19. 7.
Guide. Ps. 25. 9, meek will he *g.* in judgment.
32. 8, I will *g.* thee with mine eye. R. V. counsel.
48. 14, our *g.* even unto death.
73. 24, *g.* me with thy counsel.
Prov. 6. 7, having no *g.*, overseer, or ruler. R. V. chief.
Isa. 58. 11, the Lord shall *g.* thee.
Jer. 3. 4, the *g.* of my youth.
Mat. 23. 16, 24, ye blind *g.*
Lu. 1. 79, *g.* our feet into the way of peace.
John 16. 13, *g.* you into all truth.
See Gen. 48. 14; Prov. 11. 3; 23. 19.
Guile. Ps. 32. 2, in whose spirit is no *g.*
34. 13; 1 Pet. 3. 10, keep lips from speaking *g.*
John 1. 47, in whom is no *g.*
2 Cor. 12. 16, I caught you with *g.*
1 Pet. 2. 1, laying aside *g.*
2. 22, nor was *g.* found in his mouth.
3. 10, and his lips that they speak no *g.*
See Ex. 21. 14; 1 Thes. 2. 3; Rev. 14. 5.
Guiltless. Ex. 20. 7; Deu. 5. 11, will not hold him *g.*
Jos. 2. 19, we will be *g.*
2 Sam. 3. 28, are *g.* of blood.
Mat. 12. 7, ye would not have condemned the *g.*
See Num. 5. 31; 1 Sam. 26. 9; 1 Kn. 2. 9.
Guilty. Gen. 42. 21, verily *g.* concerning our brother.
Ex. 34. 7; Num. 14. 18, by no means clear the *g.*
Lev. 5. 3, when he knoweth of it, he shall be *g.*
Rom. 3. 19, all the world *g.* before God. R. V. brought under the judgement.
1 Cor. 11. 27, *g.* of the body and blood.
Jas. 2. 10, he is *g.* of all.
See Num. 35. 27; Prov. 30. 10; Mat. 26. 66.
Guilty of, worthy of, liable to. Mat. 26. 66.
Gulf. Lu. 16. 26.
Guni, gū'-nī, 'painted with colours.' (1) Gen. 46. 24. (2) 1 Chr. 5. 15.
Gunites, gū'-nītes, descendants of Guni. Num. 26. 48.
Gur, gŭr, 'a young lion.' 2 Kn. 9. 27.
Gur-baal, gŭr-bā'-ăl, 'Gur of Baal.' 2 Chr. 26. 7.
Gush. 1 Kn. 18. 28; Ps. 78. 20; 105. 41; Jer. 9. 18.

Haahashtari, hā-ă-hăsh'-tă-rī, 'the royal one' (?). 1 Chr. 4. 6.

Habaiah, hă-bai'-ăh, 'Jehovah hath hidden.' Ez. 2. 61.
Habakkuk, hă-băk'-kŭk, 'embrace,' a prophet of Judah; his burden, complaint to God, his answer, and faith. Hab. 1.; 2.; 3.
Habaziniah, hă-băz-ĭ-nī'-ăh. Jer. 35. 3. R. V. Habazziniah.
Habergeon, a coat of mail for the neck and breast. Job 41. 26.
Habitation. Ex. 15. 13, guided them to thy [holy *h*.
2 Chr. 6. 2, have built an house of *h*.
Ps. 26. 8, have loved the *h*.
33. 14, from the place of his *h*.
69. 25, let their *h*. be desolate.
74. 20, full of *h*. of cruelty.
89. 14, justice and judgment the *h*. of thy throne. R. V. foundation.
107. 7, 36, a city of *h*.
132. 13, the Lord desired it for his *h*.
Prov. 3. 33, he blesseth the *h*. of the just.
Isa. 32. 18, dwell in a peaceable *h*.
Jer. 21. 13, who shall enter into our *h*.? [folds.
25. 37, the peaceable *h*. are cut down. R. V.
Lu. 16. 9, into everlasting *h*. R. V. eternal tabernacles.
Eph. 2. 22, an *h*. of God through the Spirit.
Jude 6, angels which left their own *h*.
See Prov. 8. 31; Acts 1. 20; 17. 26; Rev. 18. 2.
Habor, hā'-bôr, 'joining together.' 2 Kn. 17. 6.
Hachaliah, hăch-ă-lī'-ăh, 'wait for Jehovah' (?). Neh. 1. 1.
Hachilah, hă-chī'-lăh, 'dark.' 1 Sam. 23. 19.
Hachmoni, hăch-mō'-nī, 'wise.' 1 Chr. 27. 32.
Hachmonite, hăch'-mō-nīte, a descendant of Hachmoni. 1 Chr. 11. 11.
Hadad, hā'-dăd, 'thunderer' (?). Gen. 36. 35. Edomite. 1 Kn. 11. 14.
Hadadezer, hăd-ă-dē'-zĕr, 'Hadad is help;' king of Zobah, David's wars with. 2 Sam. 8. *See* HADAREZER.
Hadadrimmon, hā'-dăd-rĭm'-mon, named from Hadad and Rimmon. Zec. 12. 11.
Hadar, hā'-dăr, 'enclosure.' Gen. 25. 15. R. V. Hadad.
Hadarezer, hăd-ă-rē'zĕr, same as HADADEZER. 2 Sam. 10. 16; 1 Chr. 18. 3.
Hadashah, hă-dăsh'-ăh, 'new.' Jos. 15. 37.
Hadassah, hă-dăs'-săh, 'myrtle.' Esth. 2. 7.
Hadattah, hă-dăt'-tăh, 'new.' Jos. 15. 25.
Hadid, hā'-dĭd, 'sharp.' Ez. 2. 33.
Hadlai, hăd-lā'-ī, 'rest.' 2 Chr. 28. 12.
Hadoram, hă-dôr'-ăm. Gen. 10. 27.
Hadrach, hā'-drăch. Zec. 9. 1.
Haft, handle of a knife, or dagger. Jud. 3. 22.
Hagab, hā'-găb, 'locust.' Ez. 2. 46.
Hagaba, hăg'-ă-bă, same as HAGAB. Neh. 7. 48.
Hagabah, hăg'-ă-băh, same as HAGAB. Ez. 2. 45.
Hagar, hā'-găr, 'flight,' mother of Ishmael. Gen. 16.
fleeing from Sarah is comforted by an angel. Gen. 16. 10, 11.
sent away with her son, Gen. 21. 14. allegory of, Gal. 4. 24.
Hagarenes, hăg'-ă-rēnes, inhabitants of Hagar. Ps. 83. 6.
Hagarites, hăg'-ă-rītes, same as HAGARENES. 1 Chr. 5. 10.
Hagerite, hă-gē'-rīte, same as HAGARENE. 1 Chr. 27. 31.
Haggai, hăg'-găi, 'festive,' prophet. Ez. 5.; 6. 14. *See* Hag. 1.; 2.
Haggeri, hăg-gē'-rī. 1 Chr. 11. 38.
Haggi, hăg'-gī, same as HAGGAI. Gen. 46. 16.
Haggiah, hăg-gī'-ăh, 'festival of Jehovah.' 1 Chr. 6. 30.
Haggites, hăg'-gītes, the posterity of Haggi. Num. 26. 15.
Haggith, hăg'-gĭth, 'festive.' 2 Sam. 3. 4.
Hai, hā'-ī, same as AI. Gen. 12. 8.
Hail. Job 38. 22, the treasures of the *h*.
Isa. 28. 17, *h*. sweep away refuge of lies.
Hail, plague of. Ex. 9. 23; Jos. 10. 11; Ps. 18. 12; 78. 47; Isa. 28. 2; Ezek. 13. 11; Hag. 2. 17; Rev. 8. 7; 11. 19; 16. 21.
Hair. Gen. 42. 38; 44. 29, bring down gray *h*. [with sorrow.
Jud. 20. 16, sling stones at *h*. breadth.
Job 4. 15, the *h*. of my flesh stood up.
Ps. 40. 12, more than the *h*. of my head.
Mat. 3. 4; Mk. 1. 6, raiment of camel's *h*.
5. 36, make one *h*. white or black.
10. 30, *h*. of head numbered.
1 Cor. 11. 14, 15, long *h*., it is a shame.
1 Tim. 2. 9, broided *h*.
1 Pet. 3. 3, plaiting the *h*. [14.
See 2 Sam. 14. 26; Hos. 7. 9; John 11. 2; Rev. 1.
Hairy. Gen. 27. 11, 23; Ps. 68. 21.
Hakkatan, hăk'-kă-tăn, 'the small.' Ez. 8. 12.
Hakkoz, hăk'-kŏz, 'the thorn.' 1 Chr. 24. 10.
Hakupha, hă-kū'-phă. Ez. 2. 51.
Halah, hā'-lăh. 2 Kn. 17. 6.
Halak, hā'-lăk, 'smooth.' Jos. 11. 17.
Hale, to drag forcibly, as an arrested person; to haul. Lu. 12. 58; Acts 8. 3.
Halhul, hăl'-hŭl. Jos. 15. 58.
Hali, hā'-lī, 'necklace.' Jos. 19. 25.
Hall. John 18. 28, then led they Jesus from Caiaphas unto the *h*. of judgment.
18. 33; 19. 9, then Pilate entered into the judgment *h*.
See Acts 25. 23.
Hallelujah. *See* Alleluia, praise ye Jehovah. Margin of Ps. 106.; 111.; 113.; 146.; 148.; 149.; 150.; Rev. 19. 1, 3, 4, 6.
Hallohesh, hăl-lō'-hĕsh, same as HALOHESH. Neh. 10. 24.
Hallow. Lev. 22. 32, I am the Lord which *h*. you.
25. 10, shall *h*. the fiftieth year.
Num. 5. 10, every man's *h*. things.
1 Kn. 9. 3, I have *h*. this house.
Jer. 17. 22; 24. 27, but *h*. ye the sabbath day.
Ezek. 20. 20; 44. 24, and *h*. my sabbaths.
Mat. 6. 9; Lu. 11. 2, *h*. be thy name.
Hallowed bread. *See* SHEWBREAD.
Halohesh, hă-lō'-hĕsh, 'the enchanter.' Neh. 3. [12.
Halt (*n*.), lame, crippled. Lu. 14. 21.
Halt (*v*.), to limp, go lamely (hence, hesitate).
1 Kn. 18. 21, how long *h*. ye?
Ps. 38. 17, I am ready to *h*.
Jer. 20. 10, my familiars watched for my *h*.
See Gen. 32. 31; Mic. 4. 6; Zep. 3. 19.
Ham, hăm, 'warm,' son of Noah. Gen. 9. 18.
cursed. Gen. 9. 22. [23.
his descendants. Gen. 10. 6; 1 Chr. 1. 8; Ps. 105.
smitten by the Simeonites. 1 Chr. 4. 40.
Haman, hā'-măn. Esth. 3. 1.
his advancement. Esth. 3.
anger against Mordecai. Esth. 3. 8.
his fall. Esth. 7.
Hamath, hā'-măth, 'fortress' (?). (Syria.) Num. 34. 8; Jos. 13. 5; 2 Kn. 14. 28; 17. 24.
conquered. 2 Kn. 18. 34; Isa. 37. 13; Jer. 49. 23.
Hamathite, hā'-măth-īte, a dweller at Hamath. Gen. 10. 18.
Hamath-zobah, hā'-măth-zō'-băh, 'fortress of Zobah.' 2 Chr. 8. 3.
Hammath, hăm'-măth, 'warm springs.' Jos. 19. 35.
Hammedatha, hăm-mĕ-dā'-thă, 'given by the moon' (?). Esth. 3. 1.
Hammelech, hăm'-mĕ-lĕch, 'the king.' Jer. 36. 26.
Hammer. Jud. 6. 21; 1 Kn. 6. 7; Jer. 23. 29.
Hammoleketh, hăm-mō'-lĕ-kĕth, 'the queen.' 1 Chr. 7. 18.
Hammon, hăm'-mŏn, 'warm.' Jos. 19. 28.
Hammoth-dor, hăm'-mŏth-dôr, 'warm springs of Dor.' Jos. 21. 32.
Hamonah, hă-mō'-năh, 'multitude.' Ezek. 39. 16.
Hamon-gog, hā'-mŏn-gŏg, 'multitude of Gog.' Ezek. 39. 11.
Hamor, hā'-môr, 'ass;' father of Shechem. Gen. 33. 19; Gen. 34.; Acts 7. 16.
Hamuel, hăm'-ū-ĕl. 1 Chr. 4. 26.
Hamul, hā'-mŭl, 'spared.' Gen. 46. 12.

Hamulites, hăm'-ū-lītes, the posterity of Hamul. Num. 26. 21.
Hamutal, hă-mū'-tăl, 'my husband's father is the dew' (?). 2 Kn. 23. 31.
Hanameel, hăn'-ă-meel, probably another form of HANANEEL. Jer. 32. 7.
Hanan, hā'-năn, 'gracious.' 1 Chr. 8. 23.
Hananeel, hăn'-ă-neel, 'God is gracious.' Neh. 3. 1.
Hanani, hă-nā'-nī, probably same as HANANIAH.
(1) 1 Kn. 16. 1.
(2) prophet. 2 Chr. 16. 7.
(3) brother of Nehemiah. Neh. 1. 2; 7. 2; 12. 36.
Hananiah, hăn-ă-nī'-ăh, 'Jehovah hath been gracious.' 1 Chr. 3. 19.
false prophet. Jer. 28.
his death. Jer. 28. 16.
Hand. Gen. 16. 12, *h.* against every man.
Gen. 24. 2; 47. 29, put thy *h.* under my thigh.
27. 22, the *h.* are the *h.* of Esau.
31. 29, in the power of my *h.* to do you hurt.
Ex. 21. 24; Deu. 19. 21, *h.* for *h.*, foot for foot.
33. 22, cover with my *h.* while I pass.
Num. 11. 23; Isa. 59. 1, Lord's *h.* waxed short.
22. 29, would there were sword in mine *h.*
Deu. 8. 17, my *h.* hath gotten this wealth.
33. 2, from right *h.* went fiery law.
Jud. 7. 2, saying, my own *h.* hath saved me.
1 Sam. 5. 11, *h.* of God was heavy.
6. 9, not his *h.* that smote us, but a chance.
12. 3, of whose *h.* have I received any bribe?
19. 5; 28. 21, put his life in his *h.*
23. 16, Jonathan strengthened his *h.* in God.
26. 18, what evil is in mine *h.*?
2 Sam. 14. 19, is not *h.* of Joab in this?
24. 14; 1 Chr. 21. 13, let us fall into *h.* of Lord.
1 Kn. 18. 44, cloud like a man's *h.*
2 Kn. 5. 11, strike his *h.* over the place.
1 Chr. 12. 2, could use right *h.* and left.
Ez. 7. 9; 8. 18; Neh. 2. 8, good *h.* of God.
10. 19, they gave their *h.* that they would.
Neh. 2. 18, strengthened their *h.* for work.
6. 5, with open letter in his *h.*
Job 12. 10, in whose *h.* is the soul.
19. 21, the *h.* of God hath touched me.
40. 14, that thine own *h.* can save.
Ps. 16. 11, at right *h.* pleasures for evermore.
24. 4, clean *h.* and pure heart.
68. 31, stretch out her *h.* unto God.
90. 17, establish thou the work of our *h.*
137. 5, let my right *h.* forget her cunning.
Prov. 3. 16, in left *h.* riches and honour.
6. 10; 24. 33, folding of *h.* to sleep.
10. 4, that dealeth with slack *h.*
11. 21; 16. 5, though *h.* join *h.*
12. 24, *h.* of diligent shall bear rule.
19. 24; 26. 15, slothful man hideth his *h.*
22. 26, be not of them that strike *h.*
Eccl. 2. 24, this I saw was from *h.* of God.
9. 10, whatsoever thy *h.* findeth.
11. 6, in evening withhold not thine *h.*
Isa. 1. 12, who hath required this at your *h.*?
5. 25; 9. 12; 10. 4; 14. 27, his *h.* stretched out still.
14. 26, this is the *h.* that is stretched out.
40. 12, measured waters in hollow of *h.*
44. 5, subscribe with his *h.* to the Lord.
53. 10, pleasure of Lord shall prosper in his *h.*
56. 2, keepeth his *h.* from evil.
Jer. 23. 14, strengthen *h.* of evil doers.
33. 13, shall pass under *h.* of him that telleth.
Lam. 2. 4, with his right *h.* as adversary.
4. 10, *h.* of pitiful women have sodden.
Ezek. 7. 17; 21. 7, all *h.* shall be feeble.
10. 2, fill *h.* with coals of fire.
17. 18, lo, he had given his *h.*
Dan. 4. 35, none can stay his *h.*
Hos. 7. 5, stretched out *h.* with scorners.
Mic. 7. 3, do evil with both *h.* earnestly.
Zep. 3. 16, let not thine *h.* be slack.
Zec. 13. 6, what are these wounds in thine *h.*?
Mat. 3. 2; 4. 17; 10. 7, kingdom of heaven at *h.*
3. 12; Lu. 3. 17, whose fan is in his *h.*
6. 3, let not left *h.* know.
Mat. 18. 8; Mk. 9. 43, if thy *h.* or foot offend.
26. 18, my time is at *h.*
26. 46; Mk. 14. 42, he is at *h.* that doth betray.
Mk. 14. 62, sitting on right *h.* of power.
16. 19, sat on right *h.* of God.
Lu. 9. 44, delivered into *h.* of men.
John 10. 28, nor pluck out of my *h.*
10. 29, my Father's *h.*
20. 27, reach hither thy *h.*
Acts 20. 34, these *h.* have ministered.
2 Cor. 5. 1, house not made with *h.*
Phil. 4. 5, moderation be known, the Lord is at *h.*
1 Thes. 4. 11, work with your own *h.*
2 Thes. 2. 2, the day of Christ is at *h.* R. V. now present.
1 Tim. 2. 8, lifting up holy *h.*
Heb. 10. 31, the *h.* of living God.
Jas. 4. 8, cleanse your *h.*
1 Pet. 4. 7, end of all things is at *h.*
1 John 1. 1, our *h.* have handled of the Word.
See Isa. 49. 16; Lu. 9. 62; John 18. 22; Col. 2. 14.
Hand of God, for blessing. 2 Chr. 30. 12; Ez. 7. 9; 8. 18; Neh. 2. 18.
for chastisement. Deu. 2. 15; Ru. 1. 13; Job 2. 10; 19. 21; 1 Pet. 5. 6.
Handbreadth. Ex. 37. 12; 2 Chr. 4. 5; Ps. 39. 5.
Handful. Gen. 41. 27; Ru. 2. 16; Ps. 72. 16.
Handle. Jud. 5. 14, that *h.* pen of the writer.
Ps. 115. 7, hands, but they *h.* not.
Prov. 16. 20, that *h.* a matter wisely. R. V. giveth heed unto the word.
Jer. 2. 8, they that *h.* the law.
Mk. 12. 4, sent away shamefully *h.*
Lu. 24. 39, *h.* me, and see.
2 Cor. 4. 2, not *h.* word deceitfully.
Col. 2. 21, taste not, *h.* not.
1 John 1. 1, have *h.* of Word of life.
See Gen. 4. 21; 1 Chr. 12. 8; Ezek. 27. 29.
Handmaid. Ps. 86. 16; 116. 16; Prov. 30. 23; Lu. 1. 38.
Hands, laying on of. Num. 8. 10; 27. 18; Acts 6. 6; 13. 3; 1 Tim. 4. 14; 2 Tim. 1. 6.
washing, declaratory of innocence. Deu. 21. 6; Ps. 26. 6; Mat. 27. 24.
lifting up, in prayer. Ex. 17. 11; Ps. 28. 2; 63. 4; 141. 2; 143. 6; 1 Tim. 2. 8.
Hanes, hā'-nĕs. Isa. 30. 4.
Hang. Deu. 21. 23; Gal. 3. 13, he that is *h.* is accursed.
Job 26. 7, *h.* the earth on nothing.
Ps. 137. 2, we *h.* our harps upon the willows.
Mat. 18. 6; Mk. 9. 42; Lu. 17. 2, millstone *h.* about neck.
22. 40, on these *h.* the law and the prophets.
27. 5, went and *h.* himself.
Heb. 12. 12, lift up the hands which *h.* down.
See Lu. 23. 39.
Hanging, a punishment. Gen. 40. 22; Num. 25. 4; Esth. 7. 10; 9. 14.
the hanged accursed. Deu. 21. 22; Gal. 3. 13.
Haniel, hăn'-ĭ-ĕl, 'favour of God.' 1 Chr. 7. 39.
Hannah, hăn'-năh, 'grace;' her song. 1 Sam. 2.
vow and prayer, 1 Sam. 1. 11. answered, 1 Sam. 1. 19.
Hannathon, hăn'-nă-thŏn, 'graceful' (?). Jos. 19. 14.
Hanniel, hăn'-nĭ-ĕl, same as HANIEL. Num. 34. 23.
Hanoch, hā'-nŏch, same as ENOCH. Gen. 25. 4.
Hanochites, hā'-nŏch-ītes, descendants of Hanoch. Num. 26. 5.
Hanun, hā'-nŭn, 'favoured;' king of the Ammonites. 2 Sam. 10. 1.
dishonours David's messengers. 2 Sam. 10. 4.
chastised. 2 Sam. 12. 30.
Haphraim, hăph'-rā-ĭm, 'two pits' (?). Jos. 19. 19.
Haply. 1 Sam. 14. 30; Mk. 11. 13; Acts 5. 39; 17. 27.
Happen. 1 Sam. 6. 9, it was a chance that *h.*
Prov. 12. 21, there shall no evil *h.* to the just.
Isa. 41. 22, let them shew us what shall *h.*
Jer. 44. 23, therefore this evil is *h.*
Mk. 10. 32, to tell what should *h.*
Lu. 24. 14, talked of things that had *h.*
Rom. 11. 25, blindness is *h.* to Israel. R. V. befallen.
1 Cor. 10. 11, things *h.* for ensamples.

Phil. 1. 12, things which *h.* to me.
1 Pet. 4. 12, as though some strange thing *h.*
2 Pet. 2. 22, it is *h.* according to proverb.
See Eccl. 2. 14; 8. 14; 9. 11; Acts 3. 10.

Happy. Gen. 30. 13, *h.* am I.
Deu. 33. 29, *h.* art thou.
Job 5. 17, *h.* is the man whom God correcteth.
Ps. 127. 5, *h.* is the man that hath quiver full
128. 2, *h.* shalt thou be.
144. 15, *h.* is that people.
Prov. 3. 13, 18, *h.* that findeth wisdom.
14. 21, he that hath mercy, *h.* is he.
28. 14, *h.* is the man that feareth alway.
Jer. 12. 1, why are they *h.* that deal treacherously? R. V. at ease.
Mal. 3. 15, now we call proud *h.* [blessed.
John 13. 17, if ye know, *h.* if ye do them. R. V.
Rom. 14. 22, *h.* is he that condemneth not.
1 Cor. 7. 40, *h.* if she so abide. [blessed.
Jas. 5. 11, we count them *h.* that endure. R. V.
1 Pet. 3. 14; 4. 14, *h.* are ye. R. V. blessed.

Happy, who so called. Deu. 33. 29; Job 5. 17; Ps. 127. 5; 144. 15; 146. 5; Prov. 3. 13; 14. 21; 28. 14; 29. 18; John 13. 17; Rom. 14. 22; Jas. 5. 11; 1 Pet. 3. 14; 4. 14.

Hara, hâr'-ă, 'mountainous.' 1 Chr. 5. 26.

Haradah, hă-rā'-dăh, 'fear.' Num. 33. 24.

Haran, hâr'-ăn, 'mountaineer.' (1) son of Terah. Gen. 11. 26, 27.
(2) (city of Nahor). Abraham comes to, Gen. 11. 31. departs from, Gen. 12. 4.
Jacob flees to Laban at. Gen. 27. 43; 28. 10; 29.

Hararite, hâr'-ă-rīte, 'a mountaineer.' 2 Sam. 23. 11.

Harbona, här-bō'-nă, 'ass-driver.' Esth. 1. 10.

Harbonah, här-bō'-năh, same as Harbona. Esth. 7. 9.

Hard. Gen. 18. 14, is any thing too *h.* for the Lord?
Deu. 1. 17; 17. 8, cause that is too *h.*
15. 18, it shall not seem *h.* to thee.
1 Kn. 10. 1; 2 Chr. 9. 1, prove with *h.* questions.
Job 41. 24, *h.* as piece of nether millstone. R. V. firm.
Prov. 13. 15, the way of transgressors is *h.* R. V. treacherous is rugged.
18. 19, brother offended *h.* to be won.
Jer. 32. 17, 27, there is nothing too *h.* for thee.
Ezek. 3. 5, 6, to a people of *h.* language.
Mat. 25. 24, thou art an *h.* man.
John 6. 60, this is an *h.* saying.
Acts 9. 5; 26. 14, *h.* to kick against the pricks.
Heb. 5. 11, many things *h.* to be uttered.
2 Pet. 3. 16, things *h.* to be understood.
See Deu. 15. 18; 2 Kn. 2. 10; Mk. 10. 24. [heart.

Harden. Ex. 4. 21; 7. 3; 14. 4, I will *h.* Pharaoh's
14. 17, *h.* hearts of Egyptians.
Job 6. 10, I would *h.* myself in sorrow. R. V. exult in pain that spareth not.
9. 4, who hath *h.* himself against him?
39. 16, she is *h.* against her young.
Prov. 21. 29, a wicked man *h.* his face.
28. 14, he that *h.* his heart.
29. 1, he that being often reproved *h.* his neck.
Isa. 63. 17, why hast thou *h.* our heart?
Mk. 6. 52; 8. 17, their heart was *h.*
John 12. 40, he hath *h.* their heart.
Acts 19. 9, when divers were *h.*
Rom. 9. 18, whom he will he *h.*
Heb. 3. 13, lest any of you be *h.*

Hardened heart deprecated. Deu. 15. 7; 1 Sam. 6. 6; 2 Kn. 17. 14; Ps. 95. 8; Heb. 3. 8. results of, Ex. 7. 13; 8. 15; Prov. 28. 14; Dan. 5. 20; John 12. 40.

Hardly. (1) Gen. 16. 6. [18. 24.
(2) with difficulty. Mat. 19. 34; Mk. 10. 23; Lu.

Hardness. (1) hardship. 2 Tim. 2. 3.
(2) Mk. 3. 5, grieved for *h.* of their hearts.
16. 14, upbraided them for *h.* of heart.
See Job 38. 38; Mat. 19. 8; Mk. 10. 5; Rom. 2. 5.

Hare (Lev. 11. 6). Heb. *Arnébeth:* Gk. χοιρογρύλλιος. Four kinds of hares are found in Palestine

Harel, här'-ĕl, 'mountain of God.' Ezek. 43. 15 (marg.).

Hareph, hâr'-ĕph, 'plucking' (?). 1 Chr. 2. 51.

Hareth, hâr'-ĕth. 1 Sam. 22. 5.

Harhaiah, här-hâi'-ăh. Neh. 3. 8.

Harhas, här'-hăs. 2 Kn. 22. 14.

Harhur, här'-hŭr, 'inflammation' (?), or 'free-born' (?). Ez. 2. 51.

Harim, hâr'-ĭm, 'consecrated.' 1 Chr. 24. 8.

Hariph, hâr'-ĭph, 'autumnal showers.' Neh. 7. 24.

Harlots. Gen. 34. 31; Lev. 19. 29; 21. 7; Deu. 23. 17; Isa. 57. 3; Jer. 3. 3; Mat. 21. 32; 1 Cor. 6. 15.
Rahab of Jericho. Jos. 2. 1.
priests forbidden to marry. Lev. 21. 14.
Solomon's judgment. 1 Kn. 3. 16.
figurative. Isa. 1. 21; Jer. 2. 20; Ezek. 16.; 23.; Hos. 2.; Rev. 17.; 18.

Harm. Lev. 5. 16, make amends for *h.* R. V. amiss.
Num. 35. 23, nor sought his *h.*
1 Sam. 26. 21, I will no more do thee *h.*
2 Kn. 4. 41, no *h.* in the pot.
1 Chr. 16. 22; Ps. 105. 15, do prophets no *h.*
Prov. 3. 30, if he have done thee no *h.*
Acts 16. 28, do thyself no *h.*
28. 5, he felt no *h.*
1 Pet. 3. 13, who will *h.* you?
See Gen. 31. 52; Jer. 39. 12; Acts 27. 21.

Harmless. Mat. 10. 16; Phil. 2. 15; Heb. 7. 26.

Harnepher, här'-nĕ-phĕr. 1 Chr. 7. 36.

Harness, body-armour of a soldier. 1 Kn. 22. 34.

Harnessed, armed, covered with armour. Ex. 13. 18.

Harod, hâr'-ŏd, 'trembling.' Jud. 7. 1. [23. 25.

Harodite, hâr'-ŏd-īte, inhabitant of Harod. 2 Sam.

Haroeh, hă-rō'-ĕh, 'the seer.' 1 Chr. 2. 52.

Harorite, hâr'-ō-rīte, probably another form of Harodite. 1 Chr. 11. 27.

Harosheth, hă-rō'-shĕth, 'carving.' Jud. 4. 2.

Harp, a stringed instrument, mainly used to accompany vocal music. (1) (Gen. 4. 21; 31. 27; 1 Sam. 16. 23; Job 21. 12; 30. 31; Ps. 137. 2; Isa. 5. 12). Heb. *Kinnôr:* Gk. κινύρα. The most ancient kind of harp, resembling the Greek kithara or lyre, played with the fingers or a plectrum. There were probably several varieties.
(2) (1 Sam. 10. 5; Neh. 12. 27; Ps. 33. 2; 57. 8; 71. 22; 81. 2; 92. 3; 150. 3; Isa. 5. 12). Heb. *Nébel:* Gk. ψαλτήριον, κιθάρα. A later improvement on the kinnôr, having ten strings, and thought to have supplied the bass. It is usually translated 'psaltery' (as in Ps. 57. 8; 81. 2, A. V. and R. V.); but is rendered 'lute' and 'viol' (Isa. 5. 12; Am. 5. 23; 6. 5).
(3) (Ps. 33. 2; 144. 9). Heb. *'Asôr:* Gk. δεκάχορδον. A smaller instrument of ten strings, thought to have supplied the treble.
(4) (Dan. 3. 5, 7). Heb. *Kaithrôs.* A later invention, of Greek origin (Eng. cithern or guitar). It was a lyre, with four strings.
1 Sam. 16. 16, cunning player on an *h.*
Ps. 49. 4, dark sayings on the *h.*
137. 2, hanged *h.* on the willows.
Isa. 5. 12, *h.* and viol are in their feasts.
24. 8, joy of the *h.* ceaseth.
1 Cor. 14. 7, what is piped or *h.*, except they give.
Rev. 14. 2, harping with their *h.*
See Ezek. 26. 13; Dan. 3. 5.

Harp (and organ). Gen. 4. 21. [6. 5.
played on by David. 1 Sam. 16. 16, 23; 2 Sam.
used in public worship. 1 Chr. 25. 3; Ps. 33. 2; 81. 2; 150. 3.
in heaven. Rev. 14. 2.

Harrow. 2 Sam. 12. 31; 1 Chr. 20. 3; Job 39. 10.

Harsha, här'-shă, 'enchanter,' 'magician' (?). Ez. 2. 52.

Hart, Hind (feminine) (Deu. 12. 15, 22). Heb. *Ayyâl:* Gk. ἔλαφος. The fallow deer. 'Hart' in Deu. 14. 5; 1 Kn. 4. 23, is *yahmûr,* 'roebuck.' *See* Ps. 42. 1; Isa. 35. 6.

Harum, hâr'-ŭm, 'high' (?). 1 Chr. 4. 8.
Harumaph, hă-rū'-măph, 'slit-nosed.' Neh. 3. 10.
Haruphite, hă-rū'-phīte. 1 Chr. 12. 5.
Haruz, hâr'-ŭz, 'active.' 2 Kn. 21. 19.
Harvest. Gen. 8. 22, *h.* shall not cease.
Ex. 23. 16; 34. 22, the feast of *h.*
Lev. 19. 9; 23. 10; Deu. 24. 19, when ye reap *h.*
1 Sam. 12. 17, is it not wheat *h.* to day?
Job 5. 5, whose *h.* the hungry eateth up.
Prov. 6. 8, the ant gathereth food in *h.*
10. 5, he that sleepeth in *h.*
25. 13, cold of snow in time of *h.*
26. 1, as rain in *h.*
Isa. 9. 3, according to joy in *h.*
16. 9, thy *h.* is fallen.
18. 4, dew in heat of *h.*
Jer. 5. 17, they shall eat up thine *h.*
5. 24, appointed weeks of *h.*
8. 20, the *h.* is past, the summer ended.
51. 33, the time of her *h.* shall come.
Joel 3. 13; Rev. 14. 15, the *h.* is ripe.
Mat. 9. 37, the *h.* is plenteous.
9. 38; Lu. 10. 2, the Lord of the *h.*
13. 30, in the time of *h.* I will say.
Mk. 4. 29, putteth in sickle, because *h.* is come.
Lu. 10. 2, the *h.* truly is great.
John 4. 35, the fields are white to *h.*
See Jos. 3. 15; Isa. 23. 3.
Harvest, promise concerning. Gen. 8. 22.
feast of. Ex. 23. 16; 34. 21; Lev. 19. 9; Isa. 9. 3; 16. 9.
of the world. Jer. 8. 20; Mat. 13. 30, 39; Rev. 14. 15.
Hasadiah, hăs-ă-dī'-ăh, 'Jehovah is kind.' 1 Chr. 3. 20.
Hasenuah, hăs-ĕ-nū'-ăh, 'she that is hated.' 1 Chr. 9. 7.
Hashabiah, hăsh-ă-bī'-ăh, 'Jehovah has taken account.' 1 Chr. 6. 45.
Hashabnah, hă-shăb'-năh, same as preceding (?). Neh. 10. 25.
Hashabniah, hăsh-ăb-nī'-ăh, same as Hashabiah. Neh. 3. 10.
Hashbadana, hăsh-bă-dā'-nă. Neh. 8. 4.
Hashem, hăsh'-ĕm. 1 Chr. 11. 34.
Hashmonah, hăsh-mō'-năh. Num. 33. 29.
Hashub, hăsh'-ŭb, 'thoughtful.' Neh. 3. 11.
Hashubah, hă-shū'-băh, 'consideration.' 1 Chr. 3. 20.
Hashum, hăsh'-ŭm, 'rich' (?). Ez. 2. 19.
Hashupha, hă-shū'-phă, another form of Hasupha. Neh. 7. 46.
Hasrah, hăs'-răh, probably same as Harhas. 2 Chr. 34. 22.
Hassenaah, hăs-sĕ-nā'-ăh, the same as Senaah. Neh. 3. 3.
Hasshub, hăs'-shŭb, same as Hashub. 1 Chr. 9. 14.
Haste. Ex. 12. 11, shall eat it in *h.*
1 Sam. 21. 8, king's business required *h.*
Ps. 31. 22; 116. 11, I said in my *h.*
Prov. 19. 2, he that *h.* with feet sinneth.
28. 22, he that *h.* to be rich.
Isa. 51. 14, captive exile *h.* to be loosed. R. V. shall speedily.
60. 22, will *h.* it in his time.
Jer. 1. 12, I will *h.* my word. R. V. watch over.
Zep. 1. 14, day of the Lord *h.* greatly.
See 2 Kn. 7. 15; Ps. 16. 4; 55. 8; Eccl. 1. 5.
Hastily. Prov. 20. 21; 25. 8.
Hasty. Prov. 14. 29; 21. 5; 29. 20; Eccl. 5. 2; 7. 9.
Hasupha, hă-sū'-phă, 'bare;' one of the Nethinim. Ez. 2. 43.
Hatach, hā'-tăch. Esth. 4. 5.
Hate. Gen. 37. 4, 5, 8, *h.* Joseph yet the more.
Lev. 19. 17, shall not *h.* thy brother.
1 Kn. 22. 8; 2 Chr. 18. 7, one man, but I *h.* him.
2 Chr. 19. 2, and love them that *h.* the Lord.
Ps. 34. 21, they that *h.* righteous shall be desolate.
97. 10, ye that love the Lord, *h.* evil.
139. 21, do not I *h.* them that *h.* thee?
Prov. 1. 22, how long will ye *h.* knowledge?
13. 24, he that spareth his rod *h.* his son.
Prov. 14. 20, the poor is *h.* of his neighbour.
15. 10, he that *h.* reproof shall die.
15. 27, he that *h.* gifts shall live.
Eccl. 2. 17, I *h.* life.
3. 8, a time to *h.*
Isa. 1. 14, your feasts my soul *h.*
61. 8, I *h.* robbery for burnt offering.
Am. 5. 15, *h.* the evil, and love the good.
Mic. 3. 2, who *h.* the good, and love the evil.
Zec. 8. 17, these are things that I *h.*
Mal. 1. 3; Rom. 9. 13, I loved Jacob, and *h.* Esau.
Mat. 5. 44; Lu. 6. 27, do good to them that *h.* you.
6. 24, either he will *h.* the one.
10. 22; Mk. 13. 13; Lu. 21. 17, ye shall be *h.*
24. 10, and shall *h.* one another.
Lu. 6. 22, blessed are ye when men shall *h.* you.
14. 26, and *h.* not his father.
John 3. 20, *h.* the light.
7. 7, the world cannot *h.* you.
12. 25, he that *h.* his life.
15. 18; 1 John 3. 13, marvel not if world *h.* you.
15. 24; they have both seen and *h.*
Eph. 5. 29, no man ever yet *h.* his own flesh.
1 John 2. 9, 11; 3. 15; 4. 20, *h.* his brother.
See Gen. 27. 41; Deu. 1. 27; Prov. 6. 16; Rev. 2. 6.
Hateful. Ps. 36. 2; Ezek. 23. 29; Tit. 3. 3.
Haters. Ps. 81. 15; Rom. 1. 30.
Hathath, hā'-thăth, 'terror.' 1 Chr. 4. 13.
Hatipha, hă-tī'-phă, 'seized' (?). Ez. 2. 54.
Hatita, hă-tī'-tă, 'dug.' Ez. 2. 42.
Hatred forbidden. Ex. 23. 5; Lev. 19. 17; Deu. 19. 11; Prov. 10. 12, 18; 15. 17; 26. 4; Mat. 5. 43; Gal. 5. 20; Tit. 3. 3; 1 John 2. 9; 3. 15; 4. 20.
Hattil, hăt'-tĭl, 'wavering' (?). Ez. 2. 57.
Hattush, hăt'-tŭsh. 1 Chr. 3. 22.
Haughtiness censured. 2 Sam. 22. 28; Prov. 6. 17; 16. 18; 21. 4, 24; Isa. 2. 11; 3. 16; 13. 11; 16. 6; Jer. 48. 29.
Haughty. 2 Sam. 22. 28, thine eyes are upon the *h.*
Ps. 131. 1, my heart is not *h.*
Prov. 16. 18, a *h.* spirit before a fall.
21. 24, proud and *h.* scorner.
Isa. 10. 33, the *h.* shall be humbled. R. V. lofty.
Zep. 3. 11, no more be *h.* because.
See Isa. 24. 4; Ezek. 16. 50.
Hauran, hau'-răn, 'hollow or black land.' Ezek. 47. 16.
Haven. Gen. 49. 13; Ps. 107. 30; Acts 27. 8.
Havilah, hăv'-ĭ-lăh. (1) men. Gen. 10. 7; 10. 29. (2) places. Gen. 2. 11; 25. 18; 1 Sam. 15. 7.
Havoth-Jair, hā'-vōth-jā'-ĭr, villages of Jair. Num. 32. 41.
Hawk (Job 39. 26). Heb. *Nêtz*: Gk. ἱέραξ. (Specimen, *Accipiter nisus*, found at Jericho.) A generic word for the whole hawk tribe.
Hawk, night (Lev. 11. 16). Heb. *Taḥmâs*: Gk. γλαῦξ. (Specimen, *Caprimulgus* (?).) An unclean bird, probably some kind of owl.
Hay (Prov. 27. 25). Heb. *Ḥâtzîr*: Gk. χόρτος. Fodder or grass = Grass No. 3.
Hazael, hă-zā'-ĕl, 'God hath seen;' king of Syria. 1 Kn. 19. 15.
Elisha's prediction. 2 Kn. 8. 7.
slays Ben-hadad. 2 Kn. 8. 15.
oppresses Israel. 2 Kn. 9. 14; 10. 32; 12. 17; 13. 22.
Hazaiah, hă-zai'-ăh, 'Jehovah hath seen.' Neh. 11. 5.
Hazar-addar, hā'-zăr-ăd'-dăr, 'Addar-village.' Num. 34. 4.
Hazar-enan, hā'-zăr-ē'-năn, 'fountain-village.' Num. 34. 9.
Hazar-gaddah, hā'-zăr-găd'-dăh, 'luck-village' (?). Jos. 15. 27.
Hazar-hatticon, hā'-zăr-hăt'-tĭ-cŏn, 'middle-village.' Ezek. 47. 16.
Hazarmaveth, hā'-zăr-mā'-vĕth, 'death-village.' Gen. 10. 26.
Hazar-shual, hā'-zăr-shū'-ăl, 'fox-village.' Jos. 15. 28.
Hazar-susah, hā'-zăr-sū'-săh, 'mare-village.' Jos. 19. 5.

Hazar-susim, hā'-zär-sū'-sĭm, 'horse-village.' 1 Chr. 4. 31.
Hazel (Gen. 30. 37). Heb. *Lûz*: Gk. *καρύα*: R. V. correctly, 'almond.'
Hazelelponi, hăz-ĕl-ĕl-pō'-nī. 1 Chr. 4. 3.
Hazerim, hă-zē'-rĭm, 'villages.' Deu. 2. 23.
Hazeroth, hă-zē'-rōth, same as HAZERIM. Num. 11. 35.
Hazezon-tamar, hăz'-ĕ-zŏn-tā'-mär, 'Hazezon (or pruning) of the palm.' Gen. 14. 7.
Haziel, hā'-zĭ-ĕl, 'vision of God.' 1 Chr. 23. 9.
Hazo, hā'-zō. Gen. 22. 22.
Hazor, hā'-zŏr, 'castle.' Jos. 11. 1.
Canaan, burnt. Jos. 11. 10; 15. 25.
Head. Gen. 3. 15, it shall bruise thy *h.*
Jos. 2. 19, blood be on his *h.*
Jud. 11. 9, shall I be your *h.*?
2 Kn. 2. 3, take thy master from thy *h.* to day.
4. 19, he said, my *h.*, my *h.*
Ps. 24. 7, 9, lift up your *h.*
66. 12, caused men to ride over our *h.*
110. 7, therefore shall he lift up the *h.*
141. 5, oil, which shall not break my *h.*
Prov. 10. 6, blessings on *h.* of the just.
11. 26, on *h.* of him that selleth corn.
25. 22; Rom. 12. 20, coals of fire on his *h.*
Eccl. 2. 14, a wise man's eyes are in his *h.*
Isa. 1. 5, the whole *h.* is sick.
35. 10; 51. 11, everlasting joy upon their *h.*
58. 5, to bow down *h.* as bulrush.
59. 17; Eph. 6. 17, helmet of salvation on *h.*
Jer. 9. 1, oh that my *h.* were waters.
14. 3, 4, ashamed, and covered their *h.*
Dan. 2. 38, thou art this *h.* of gold.
Am. 2. 7, that pant after dust on *h.*
9. 1, cut them in the *h.*
Zec. 1. 21, no man did lift up his *h.*
4. 7, the *h.*-stone with shoutings.
Mat. 5. 36, neither swear by *h.*
27. 39; Mk. 15. 29, reviled, wagging their *h.*
Lu. 7. 46, my *h.* thou didst not anoint.
21. 18, not hair of *h.* perish.
21. 28, then look up, and lift up your *h.*
John 13. 9, also my hands and my *h.*
1 Cor. 11. 3, the *h.* of every man is Christ.
11. 4, dishonoureth his *h.*
11. 10, woman to have power on her *h.*
Eph. 1. 22; 4. 15; Col. 1. 18, the *h.* of the church.
5. 23, husband is *h.* of the wife.
See Num. 6. 5; Jos. 7. 6; Acts 18. 6; Rev. 13. 1.
Head of the Church, Christ. Eph. 1. 22; 4. 15; 5. 23; Col. 1. 18; 2. 10.
not holding the. Col. 2. 19.
Heady, headstrong, wilful. 2 Tim. 3. 4.
Heal. Ex. 15. 26, I am the Lord that *h.* thee.
Deu. 32. 39, I wound, I *h.*
2 Kn. 2. 22, waters were *h.*
20. 5, 8, I will *h.* thee.
Ps. 6. 2, O Lord, *h.* me.
41. 4, *h.* my soul, for I have sinned.
103. 3, who *h.* all thy diseases.
107. 20, sent his word, and *h.* them.
Isa. 6. 10, lest they convert and be *h.*
53. 5, with his stripes we are *h.*
Jer. 6. 14; 8. 11, they have *h.* the hurt slightly.
15. 18, wound refuseth to be *h.*
17. 14, *h.* me, and I shall be *h.*
Lam. 2. 13, who can *h.* thee?
Hos. 5. 13, yet could he not *h.* thee.
6. 1, he hath torn, and he will *h.* us.
14. 4, I will *h.* their backslidings.
Mat. 8. 7, I will come and *h.* him.
8. 8, speak, and my servant shall be *h.*
10. 1, to *h.* all manner of sickness.
10. 8; Lu. 9. 2; 10. 9, *h.* the sick.
12. 10; Lu. 14. 3, is it lawful to *h.* on sabbath?
Mk. 3. 2; Lu. 6. 7, whether he would *h.* on the sabbath day.
Lu. 4. 18, to *h.* brokenhearted.
4. 23, physician, *h.* thyself.
5. 17, power of the Lord present to *h.*
John 4. 47, that he would come and *h.*
5. 13, he that was *h.* wist not.
Acts 4. 14, beholding the man which was *h.*
5. 16, they were *h.* every one.
14. 9, he had faith to be *h.*
Heb. 12. 13, let it rather be *h.*
Jas. 5. 16, pray that ye may be *h.*
1 Pet. 2. 24, by whose stripes ye were *h.*
Rev. 13. 3, his deadly wound was *h.*
See Eccl. 3. 3; Isa. 3. 7; Mat. 14. 14.
Healing. Jer. 14. 19, there is no *h.* for us.
Nah. 3. 19, no *h.* of thy bruise. R. V. assuaging of thy hurt.
Mal. 4. 2, with *h.* in his wings.
Mat. 4. 23, went about *h.* all.
Lu. 9. 11, that had need of *h.*
1 Cor. 12. 9, 28, 30, the gift of *h.*
Rev. 22. 2, for the *h.* of the nations.
See Jer. 30. 13; Lu. 9. 6; Acts 4. 22; 10. 38.
Health. 2 Sam. 20. 9, art thou in *h.*, my brother? R. V. is it well with thee?
Ps. 42. 11; 43. 5, the *h.* of my countenance.
Prov. 3. 8, *h.* to thy navel.
4. 22, they are *h.* to all their flesh.
16. 24, *h.* to the bones.
Isa. 58. 8, thy *h.* shall spring forth. R. V. healing.
Jer. 8. 15, looked for a time of *h.* R. V. healing.
8. 22, why is not *h.* recovered?
Acts 27. 34, it is for your *h.* R. V. safety.
3 John 2, mayest be in *h.*
Health, 'saving health' = salvation. Ps. 67. 2.
Health of body. Gen. 43. 28; 3 John 2.
spiritual, Ps. 42. 11; Prov. 3. 8; 12. 18; Isa. 58. 8; Jer. 8. 15; 30. 17; 33. 6.
Heap. Deu. 32. 23, *h.* mischiefs upon them.
Job 16. 4, I could *h.* up words. R. V. join together.
27. 16, though he *h.* up silver.
Ps. 39. 6, he *h.* up riches.
Prov. 25. 22; Rom. 12. 20, *h.* coals of fire.
Ezek. 24. 10, *h.* on wood.
Hab. 1. 10, they shall *h.* dust.
Mic. 3. 12, Jerusalem shall become *h.*
2 Tim. 4. 3, *h.* to themselves teachers.
Jas. 5. 3, ye have *h.* treasure for last days. R. V. laid up.
See Jud. 15. 16; Neh. 4. 2; Eccl. 2. 26.
Hear. Ex. 6. 12, how shall Pharaoh *h.* me?
1 Sam. 15. 14, lowing of oxen which I *h.*
1 Kn. 8. 42, they shall *h.* of thy great name.
18. 26, O Baal, *h.* us.
2 Kn. 18. 28; Isa. 36. 13, *h.* words of the great king.
1 Chr. 14. 15, when thou *h.* a sound of going.
Neh. 8. 2, all that could *h.* with understanding.
Job 31. 35, oh that one would *h.* me!
Ps. 4. 1; 39. 12; 54. 2; 84. 8; 102. 1; 143. 1; Dan. 9. 17, *h.* my prayer. R. V. answer.
4. 3; 17. 6; Zec. 10. 6, the Lord will *h.*
10. 17, cause thine ear to *h.*
49. 1, *h.* this, all ye people.
59. 7, who, say they, doth *h.*?
66. 18, if I regard iniquity, the Lord will not *h.* me.
85. 8, I will *h.* what God the Lord will speak.
102. 20, *h.* groaning of the prisoner.
Prov. 13. 8, the poor *h.* not rebuke.
18. 13, answereth a matter before he *h.*
22. 17, *h.* the words of the wise.
Eccl. 5. 1, more ready to *h.* than give.
7. 5, better to *h.* rebuke of wise.
12. 13, *h.* conclusion of the whole matter.
Isa. 1. 2, *h.*, O heavens, and give ear.
1. 15; Jer. 7. 16; 11. 14; 14. 12; Ezek. 8. 18, make many prayers, I will not *h.*
6. 9; Mk. 4. 12, *h.* but understand not.
29. 18, shall deaf *h.* words of the book.
33. 13, *h.*, ye that are afar off.
34. 1, let the earth *h.*
42. 20, opening ears, but he *h.* not.
55. 3; John 5. 25, *h.*, and your soul shall live.
Ezek. 3. 27, he that *h.*, let him *h.*
33. 31, they *h.* words, but will not do them.
Mat. 7. 24; Lu. 6. 47, whoso *h.* these sayings.
11. 4, shew things ye do *h.* and see.
11. 5; Mk. 7. 37; Lu. 7. 22, the deaf *h.*
13. 17; Lu. 10. 24, those things which ye *h.*
17. 5; Mk. 9. 7, my beloved Son, *h.* him.

Mat. 18. 16, if he will not *h.* thee.
Mk. 4. 24; Lu. 8. 18, take heed what ye *h.*
Lu. 9. 9, of whom I *h.* such things.
10. 16, he that *h.* you, *h.* me.
John 5. 25, dead shall *h.* voice of Son of God.
5. 30, as I *h.*, I judge.
6. 60, who can *h.* it?
8. 47, he that is of God *h.* God's words.
9. 31, God *h.* not sinners.
11. 42, I know thou *h.* me always.
12. 47, if any man *h.* my words.
14. 24, the word ye *h.* is not mine.
Acts 2. 8, how *h.* we every man?
13. 44, whole city came to *h.*
Rom. 10. 14, *h.* without a preacher.
1 Cor. 11. 18, I *h.* there be divisions.
1 Tim. 4. 16, save thyself, and them that *h.*
Jas. 1. 19, swift to *h.*
1 John 4. 5, the world *h.* them.
4. 6, he that knoweth God *h.* us.
5. 15, we know that he *h.* us.
Rev. 2. 7; 3. 6, 13, 22, let him *h.*
3. 20, if any man *h.* my voice.
See Deu. 30. 17; 2 Kn. 19. 16; 2 Chr. 6. 21.

Heard. Gen. 3. 8, they *h.* voice of the Lord.
21. 17, God *h.* voice of the lad.
45. 2, Joseph wept, and the Egyptians *h.*
Ex. 3. 7, I have *h.* their cry.
Num. 11. 1; 12. 2, the Lord *h.* it.
Deu. 4. 12, only ye *h.* a voice.
1 Kn. 6. 7, nor any tool of iron *h.*
10. 7; 2 Chr. 9. 6, exceedeth the fame I *h.*
2 Kn. 19. 25; Isa. 37. 26, hast thou not *h.* long ago?
Ez. 3. 13; Neh. 12. 43, the noise was *h.* afar off.
Job 15. 8, hast thou *h.* the secret of God?
16. 2, I have *h.* many such things.
19. 7, but I am not *h.*
26. 14, how little a portion is *h.*?
29. 11, when the ear *h.* me, it blessed me.
Ps. 6. 9, the Lord hath *h.* my supplication.
10. 17, hast *h.* the desire of the humble.
34. 4, I sought the Lord, and he *h.* R. V. answered.
38. 13, I, as a deaf man, *h.* not.
61. 5, thou hast *h.* my vows.
81. 5, I *h.* language I understood not.
116. 1, I love the Lord, because he hath *h.*
S. of S. 2. 12, voice of turtle is *h.*
Isa. 40. 21, 28, have ye not *h.*?
64. 4, not *h.* what he hath prepared.
65. 19, weeping no more be *h.*
66. 8, who hath *h.* such a thing?
Jer. 7. 13, rising early, but ye *h.* not.
8. 6, I *h.*, but they spake not aright.
51. 46; Obad. 1, a rumour that shall be *h.*
Dan. 12. 8, I *h.*, but understood not.
Zec. 8. 23, we have *h.* God is with you.
Mal. 3. 16, the Lord hearkened, and *h.* it.
Mat. 6. 7, *h.* for much speaking.
26. 65; Mk. 14. 64, ye have *h.* the blasphemy.
Lu. 12. 3, shall be *h.* in the light.
John 4. 42, we have *h.* him ourselves.
8. 6, as though he *h.* them not.
11. 41, I thank thee thou hast *h.* me.
Acts 4. 4, many which *h.* believed.
4. 20, cannot but speak things we have *h.*
16. 25, the prisoners *h.* them. R. V. were listening to.
22. 15, witness of what thou hast seen and *h.*
Rom. 10. 14, of whom they have not *h.*
10. 18, have they not *h.*?
1 Cor. 2. 9, eye hath not seen, nor ear *h.*
2 Cor. 12. 4, *h.* unspeakable words.
Eph. 4. 21, if so be ye have *h.* him.
Phil. 4. 9, things ye have *h.* and seen in me.
2 Tim. 2. 2, things thou hast *h.* of me.
Heb. 2. 3, confirmed by them that *h.*
4. 2, with faith in them that *h.*
5. 7, was *h.* in that he feared.
1 John 1. 1, 3, that which we have *h.* and seen.
Rev. 3. 3, remember how thou hast *h.*
10. 4; 14. 2; 18. 4, *h.* a voice from heaven.
See Jer. 31. 18; John 5. 37; Rev. 19. 6; 22. 8.

Hearer. Rom. 2. 13; Eph. 4. 29; Jas. 1. 23.

Hearing. Deu. 31. 11, read this law in their *h.*
2 Kn. 4. 31, neither voice nor *h.*
Job 42. 5, by the *h.* of the ear.
Prov. 20. 12, the *h.* ear.
Eccl. 1. 8, nor ear filled with *h.*
Am. 8. 11, a famine of *h.* the word.
Mat. 13. 13, *h.*, they hear not.
Acts 9. 7, *h.* a voice, but seeing no man.
Rom. 10. 17, faith cometh by *h.*
1 Cor. 12. 17, where were the *h.*?
Heb. 5. 11, ye are dull of *h.*
See Acts 28. 27; Gal. 3. 2; 2 Pet. 2. 8.

Hearken. Deu. 18. 15, unto him ye shall *h.*
Jos. 1. 17, so will we *h.* unto thee.
1 Sam. 15. 22, to *h.* than the fat of rams.
Prov. 29. 12, if a ruler *h.* to lies.
Isa. 55. 2, *h.* diligently unto me.
Dan. 9. 19, O Lord, *h.* and do.
Mk. 7. 14, *h.* to me, every one of you. R. V. hear me.
See Ps. 103. 20; Prov. 1. 33; 12. 15; Acts 4. 19.

Heart. Ex. 23. 9, ye know the *h.* of a stranger.
Deu. 11. 13; Jos. 22. 5; 1 Sam. 12. 20, 24, serve him with all your *h.*
13. 3; 30. 6; Mat. 22. 37; Mk. 12. 30, 33; Lu. 10. 27, love the Lord with all your *h.*
Jud. 5. 16, great searchings of *h.*
1 Sam. 10. 9, God gave him another *h.*
16. 7, the Lord looketh on the *h.*
1 Kn. 3. 9, 12, give an understanding *h.*
4. 29, gave Solomon largeness of *h.*
8. 17; 2 Chr. 6. 7, it was in the *h.* of David.
11. 4, not perfect, as was *h.* of David.
14. 8, followed me with all his *h.*
1 Chr. 12. 33, not of double *h.*
29. 17; Jer. 11. 20, I know thou triest the *h.*
2 Chr. 31. 21, he did it with all his *h.*
32. 25, his *h.* was lifted up.
Neh. 2. 2, nothing else but sorrow of *h.*
Job 23. 16, maketh my *h.* soft.
29. 13, caused the widow's *h.* to sing.
Ps. 10. 6; 11. 13; 14. 1; 53. 1, said in his *h.*
19. 8, rejoicing the *h.*
27. 3, my *h.* shall not fear.
28. 7, my *h.* trusted in him.
57. 7; 108. 1, my *h.* is fixed.
64. 6, the *h.* is deep.
73. 7, more than *h.* could wish.
78. 37, their *h.* was not right.
97. 11, gladness sown for upright in *h.*
119. 11, thy word have I hid in my *h.*
119. 80, let my *h.* be sound.
139. 23, search me and know my *h.*
Prov. 4. 23, keep thy *h.* with all diligence.
14. 10, the *h.* knoweth his own bitterness.
21. 1, king's *h.* is in the hand of the Lord.
23. 7, as he thinketh in his *h.*, so is he. R. V. reckoneth within himself.
25. 3, *h.* of kings is unsearchable.
25. 20, songs to a heavy *h.*
31. 11, *h.* of her husband doth trust.
Eccl. 8. 5, wise man's *h.* discerneth.
Isa. 35. 4, say to them of fearful *h.*
44. 20, a deceived *h.*
57. 1; Jer. 12. 11, no man layeth it to *h.*
57. 15, revive *h.* of contrite.
65. 14, sing for joy of *h.*
Jer. 11. 20; 20. 12, that triest the *h.*
17. 9, the *h.* is deceitful above all things.
20. 9, in mine *h.* as a burning fire.
24. 7, I will give them a *h.* to know me.
30. 21, that engaged his *h.* to approach. R. V. hath had boldness.
49. 16; Obad. 3, pride of *h.* deceived thee.
Ezek. 11. 19, take stony *h.*
18. 31, make you a new *h.*
36. 26, will give you a *h.* of flesh.
44. 7; Acts 7. 51, uncircumcised in *h.*
Dan. 1. 8, Daniel purposed in his *h.*
Joel 2. 13, rend your *h.*
Zec. 7. 12, made *h.* as adamant.
Mal. 2. 2, if ye will not lay it to *h.*

Mal. 4. 6, turn *h.* of fathers to children.
Mat. 5. 8, blessed are the pure in *h.*
6. 21; Lu. 12. 34, there will your *h.* be also.
11. 29, meek and lowly in *h.*
12. 34; Lu. 6. 45, out of abundance of the *h.*
15. 19, out of the *h.* proceed evil thoughts.
18. 35, if ye from your *h.* forgive not.
Mk. 2. 8, why reason ye in your *h.*?
8. 17, have ye your *h.* yet hardened?
10. 5; 16. 14, hardness of *h.*
Lu. 2. 19, 51, kept them in her *h.*
21. 14, settle it in your *h.*
24. 25, slow of *h.* to believe.
24. 32, did not our *h.* burn within us?
John 14. 1, 27, let not your *h.* be troubled.
Acts 5. 33; 7. 54, were cut to the *h.*
11. 23, with purpose of *h.*
Rom. 10. 10, with the *h.* man believeth.
1 Cor. 2. 9, neither have entered into *h.*
2 Cor. 3. 3, in fleshy tables of the *h.*
5. 12, glory in appearance, not in *h.*
Eph. 3. 17, that Christ dwell in your *h.* by faith.
5. 19, singing and making melody in your *h.*
6. 6, doing will of God from the *h.*
Phil. 4. 7, keep your *h.* and minds.
Col. 3. 15, let peace of God rule in your *h.*
3. 22, in singleness of *h.*
2 Thes. 3. 5, direct your *h.* into love of God.
Heb. 4. 12, discerner of intents of the *h.*
10. 22, draw near with true *h.*
13. 9, good that the *h.* be established.
Jas. 3. 14, if ye have strife in your *h.*
4. 8, purify your *h.*
1 Pet. 3. 4, the hidden man of the *h.*
3. 15, sanctify the Lord in your *h.*

Heart of man. Gen. 6. 5; 8. 21; Eccl. 8. 11; 9. 3; Jer. 17. 9; Mat. 12. 34; 15. 19; Lu. 6. 45; Rom. 2. 5.
searched and tried by God. 1 Chr. 28. 9; 29. 17; Ps. 44. 21; 139. 23; Prov. 21. 2; 24. 12; Jer. 12. 3; 17. 10; 20. 12; Rev. 2. 23.
enlightened, &c., by Him. 2 Cor. 4. 6; Ps. 27. 14; Prov. 16. 1; 1 Thes. 3. 13; 2 Pet. 1. 19.
a new, promised. Jer. 24. 7; 31. 32; 32. 39; Ezek. 11. 19; 36. 26.

Hearth. Gen. 18. 6; Ps. 102. 3; Isa. 30. 14; Jer. 36. 22.

Heartily. Col. 3. 23.

Heat. Deu. 29. 24, the *h.* of this great anger.
Ps. 19. 6, nothing hid from *h.* thereof.
Eccl. 4. 11, two together, then they have *h.* R. V. warmth.
Isa. 4. 6; 25. 4, a shadow from the *h.*
18. 4, *h.* upon herbs, dew in *h.* of harvest.
49. 10, neither shall *h.* smite them.
Hos. 7. 4, as oven *h.* by the baker.
Mat. 20. 12, burden and *h.* of the day. R. V. burden of the day and the scorching *h.*
Jas. 1. 11, sun no sooner risen with burning *h.* R. V. ariseth with the scorching wind.
2 Pet. 3. 10, melt with fervent *h.*
See Dan. 3. 19; Lu. 12. 55; Acts 28. 3.

Heath (Jer. 17. 6; 48. 6.) Heb. *'Ar'ar:* Gk. ἀγριομυρίκη: Bot. N. *Juniperus Sabina:* R. V. marg.. 'tamarisk,' a dwarf juniper growing in the desert. Not the true heath, which does not grow in Palestine south of the Lebanons.

Heathen. R. V. in O. T. nations; in N. T. Gentiles.
Ps. 2. 1; Acts 4. 25, why do the *h.* rage?
2. 8, give *h.* for inheritance.
102. 15, the *h.* shall fear name of the Lord.
Ezek. 36. 24, I will take you from among *h.*
Zec. 8. 13, ye were a curse among the *h.*
Mat. 6. 7, repetitions, as the *h.*
18. 17, let him be as *h.* man.
See Lev. 25. 44; Deu. 4. 27; Neh. 5. 8.

Heathen described. Eph. 2. 12; 4. 18; 5. 12; 1 Cor. 1. 21.
gospel preached to. Mat. 24. 14; 28. 19; Rom. 10. 14; 16. 26; Gal. 1. 16.
conversion of. Acts 10. 35; Rom. 15. 16.

Heaven. Gen. 28. 17, the gate of *h.*
Ex. 20. 22, have talked with you from *h.*
Deu. 10. 14; 1 Kn. 8. 27; Ps. 115. 16, the *h.* and *h.* of heavens.
Ps. 14. 2; 53. 2, had looked down from *h.*
73. 25, whom have I in *h.*? [R. V. skies.
89. 6, who in *h.* can be compared to the Lord?
119. 89, thy word is settled in *h.*
Eccl. 5. 2, for God is in *h.*
Jer. 7. 18, make cakes to queen of *h.*
23. 24, do not I fill *h.* and earth?
Mal. 3. 10, if I will not open windows of *h.*
Mat. 5. 18, till *h.* and earth pass.
11. 23, exalted to *h.*
24. 29; Mk. 13. 25, the powers of *h.*
Mk. 13. 32, no, not the angels in *h.*
Lu. 15. 18, I have sinned against *h.*
John 6. 31, 32, bread from *h.*
Rom. 1. 18, wrath of God revealed from *h.*
2 Cor. 5. 1, eternal in the *h.*
5. 2, our house that is from *h.*
Gal. 1. 8, though an angel from *h.* preach.
Eph. 1. 10, gather in one, things in *h.*
3. 15, whole family in *h.*
6. 9; Col. 4. 1, your master is in *h.*
Phil. 3. 20, our conversation is in *h.*
Heb. 12. 23, written in *h.*
1 John 5. 7, three that bear record in *h.*
Rev. 4. 1, door opened in *h.*
4. 2, throne set in *h.*
8. 1, silence in *h.*
12. 1, 3, a great wonder in *h.*
See 2 Cor. 12. 2; 1 Thes. 4. 16; 2 Thes. 1. 7.

Heaven, the firmament, created. Gen. 1. 1, 8; Ps. 8.; 19.; Isa. 40. 22; Rev. 10. 6.
dwelling-place of God. 1 Kn. 8. 30; Ps. 2. 4; 115. 3; 123. 1; Isa. 6. 1; 66. 1; Ezek. 1.; 10.; Mat. 6. 9; Acts 7. 49; Heb. 8. 1; Rev. 4.
happiness of. Ps. 16. 11; Isa. 49. 10; Dan. 12. 3; Mat. 5. 12; 13. 43; Lu. 12. 37; John 12. 26; 14. 1; 17. 24; 1 Cor. 2. 9; 13. 12; 1 Pet. 1. 4; Rev. 7. 16; 14. 13; 21. 4; 22. 3.
who enter. Mat. 5. 3; 25. 34; Rom. 8. 17; Heb. 12. 23; 1 Pet. 1. 4; Rev. 7. 9, 14.
who do not enter. Mat. 7. 21; 25. 41; Lu. 13. 27; 1 Cor. 6. 9; Gal. 5. 21; Rev. 21. 8; 22. 15.
the new. Rev. 21. 1.

Heavenly. Lu. 2. 13, multitude of the *h.* host.
John 3. 12, I tell you of *h.* things.
Acts 26. 19, the *h.* vision.
1 Cor. 15. 48, as is the *h.*, such are they.
Eph. 1. 3; 2. 6; 3. 10, in *h.* places.
Heb. 3. 1, partakers of the *h.* calling.
8. 5; 9. 23, shadow of *h.* things.
11. 16, an *h.* country.
See 2 Tim. 4. 18; Heb. 6. 4; 12. 22.

Heavenly Father. Mat. 6. 14, your *h. F.* also will forgive you.
Lu. 11. 13, how much more shall your *h. F.* give the Holy Spirit to them that ask him?

Heavens. Lev. 26. 19, make your *h.* as iron.
Deu. 33. 13, the precious things of *h.*
2 Kn. 7. 2, if the Lord make windows in *h.*
Job 15. 15, the *h.* are not clean in his sight.
22. 12, is not God in the height of *h.*?
Ps. 8. 3, when I consider thy *h.*
Prov. 8. 27, when he prepared the *h.* I was there.
25. 3, the *h.* for height.
Isa. 13. 13; Hag. 2. 6, will shake the *h.*
40. 12, meted out *h.* with the span.
65. 17; Rev. 21. 1, new *h.* and new earth.
Jer. 31. 37, if *h.* can be measured.
Ezek. 1. 1; Mat. 3. 16; Mk. 1. 10, the *h.* were [opened.
32. 7, I will cover the *h.*
Dan. 7. 13, with clouds of *h.*
Hag. 1. 10, *h.* over you is stayed from dew.
John 1. 51, ye shall see *h.* open.
Acts 4. 12, none other name under *h.*

Heave-offering. Ex. 29. 27; Num. 15. 19; 18. 8, [30.

Heaviness. Ps. 69. 20, I am full of *h.*
Prov. 12. 25, *h.* in the heart maketh it stoop.
14. 13, the end of that mirth is *h.*
Isa. 61. 3, garment of praise for spirit of *h.*

Jas. 4. 9, let your joy be turned to *h*.
See Ez. 9. 5; Prov. 10. 1; Rom. 9. 2.
Heavy. (1) Ex. 17. 12, Moses' hands were *h*.
Neh. 5. 18, the bondage was *h*.
Job 33. 7; Ps. 32. 4, hand *h*. [of the yoke.
Isa. 58. 6, to undo the *h*. burdens. R. V. bands
Mat. 11. 28, all ye that are *h*. laden.
23. 4, they bind *h*. burdens.
26. 43; Mk. 14. 33, their eyes were *h*.
See Prov. 27. 3; Isa. 59. 1; Lu. 9. 32.
(2) sad. 1 Kn. 14. 6, *h*. tidings.
Prov. 25. 20, songs to a *h*. heart. [ter in soul.
31. 6, wine to those of *h*. hearts. R. V. the bit-
Mat. 26. 37, he began to be very *h*. R. V. sore troubled.
Heber, hē'-bĕr. (1) 'fellowship.' Gen. 46. 17.
(2) the Kenite. Jud. 4. 11.
Heber, hē'-bĕr. Same as EBER. (1) 1 Chr. 5. 13.
(2) Lu. 3. 35 = Gen. 10. 21.
Heberites, hē'-bĕr-ītes, descendants of Heber. Num. 26. 45.
Hebrew, hē'-brew̄. (1) descendant of Heber (applied to Abraham). Gen. 14. 13.
(2) a Jew. Jer. 34. 9. [20.
(3) the language spoken by the Jews. John 19.
Hebrewess, hē'-brew̄-ĕss, a Jewess. Jer. 34. 9.
Hebrews, hē'-brew̄s. (1) descendants of Abraham. Gen. 40. 15; 43. 32; Ex. 2. 6; 2 Cor. 11. 22; Phil. 3. 5.
(2) Hebrew-speaking Jews. Acts 6. 1.
Hebron, hē'-brŏn, 'alliance.' (1) Man. Ex. 6. 18; 1 Chr. 2. 42.
(2) (Mamre). One of the most ancient cities of the world, its foundation being nearly contemporary with that of Damascus. As its other name, KIRJATH-ARBA, 'the city of four,' indicates, it consisted of four villages, situated on a cluster of heights about 19 miles S. W. of Jerusalem.
Abraham dwells there. Gen. 13. 18; 23. 2.
the spies come to. Num. 13. 22.
taken. Jos. 10. 36.
given to Caleb. Jos. 14. 13; 15. 13.
David reigns there. 2 Sam. 2. 1; 3. 2; 5. 1; 1 Chr. 11.; 12. 38; 29. 27.
Hebronites, hē'-brŏn-ītes, descendants of Hebron. Num. 3. 27.
Hedge. Job 3. 23, whom God hath *h*. in.
Prov. 15. 19, way of slothful an *h*. of thorns.
Eccl. 10. 8, whoso breaketh an *h*. R. V. fence.
Lam. 3. 7, he hath *h*. me about. R. V. fenced.
Hos. 2. 6, I will *h*. up thy way.
Mk. 12. 1, he set a *h*. about it.
Lu. 14. 23, the highways and *h*.
See Isa. 5. 5; Ezek. 13. 5; 22. 30; Nah. 3. 17.
Hedgehog (Lev. 11. 6). Heb. *Arnébeth:* Gk. χοιρογρύλλιος. This is the LXX. rendering in Lev. 11. 6 for *arnébeth* (hare).
Heed. 2 Sam. 20. 10, took no *h*. to the sword.
Ps. 119. 9, by taking *h*. thereto. [dered.
Eccl. 12. 9, preacher gave good *h*. R. V. pon-
Isa. 21. 7, hearkened diligently with much *h*.
Jer. 18. 18, let us not give *h*.
1 Tim. 1. 4; Tit. 1. 14, neither give *h*. to fables.
4. 1, giving *h*. to seducing spirits.
Heb. 2. 1, give more earnest *h*.
See Prov. 17. 4; Acts 3. 5; 8. 6.
Heel. Gen. 3. 15, thou shalt bruise his *h*.
Ps. 49. 5, when the iniquity of my *h*. shall compass me about.
Hegai, *or* **Hege**, hē'-gāī, hē'-gē. Esth. 2. 3, 8.
Heifer for sacrifice. Gen. 15. 9; Num. 19. 2; Deu. 21. 3; Heb. 9. 13.
Height. Ps. 102. 19, from *h*. of his sanctuary.
Prov. 25. 3, the heaven for *h*. [above.
Isa. 7. 11, ask it either in the depth, or in the *h*.
Eph. 3. 18, 19, the *h*. of the love of Christ.
See Job 22. 12; Ps. 148. 1; Am. 2. 9.
Heir. 2 Sam. 14. 7, we will destroy the *h*.
Prov. 30. 23, handmaid that is *h*. to her mistress.
Mat. 21. 38; Mk. 12. 7; Lu. 20. 14, this is the *h*.
Rom. 8. 17, *h*. of God, joint-*h*. with Christ.
Gal. 3. 29, *h*. according to the promise.
Gal. 4. 7, an *h*. of God through Christ.
Eph. 3. 6, Gentiles fellow-*h*.
Tit. 3. 7, *h*. according to hope of eternal life.
Heb. 1. 14, who shall be *h*. of salvation.
6. 17, the *h*. of promise.
11. 7, *h*. of the righteousness.
Jas. 2. 5, *h*. of the kingdom.
1 Pet. 3. 7, as *h*. together of the grace.
See Jer. 49. 1; Mic. 1. 15; Rom. 4. 13.
Helah, hē'-lăh, 'rust' (?). 1 Chr. 4. 5.
Helam, hē'-lăm, 'their army' (?). 2 Sam. 10. 16.
Helbah, hĕl'-băh, 'fatness.' Jud. 1. 31.
Helbon, hĕl'-bŏn, 'fertile.' Ezek. 27. 18.
Heldai, hĕl'-dāī, 'weasel' (?). 1 Chr. 27. 15.
Heleb, hē'-lĕb, 'fat' (?). 2 Sam. 23. 29.
Heled, hē'-lĕd, 'the world' (?). 1 Chr. 11. 30.
Helek, hē'-lĕk, 'portion.' Num. 26. 30.
Helekites, hē'-lĕk-ītes, descendants of Helek. Num. 26. 30.
Helem, hē'-lĕm, 'strength.' Zec. 6. 14.
Heleph, hē'-lĕph, 'exchange.' Jos. 19. 33.
Helez, hē'-lĕz, 'vigour.' 2 Sam. 23. 26.
Heli, hē'-lī, the Greek form of ELI. Lu. 3. 23.
Helkai, hĕl-kā'-ī, another form of HILKIAH. Neh. 12. 15.
Helkath, hĕl'-kăth, 'a portion.' Jos. 19. 25.
Helkath-hazzurim, hĕl'-kăth-hăz-zū'-rĭm, 'the field of swords' (?). 2 Sam. 2. 16.
Hell. In the O. T. this is the A. V. translation of the Heb. *Sheôl*, the dark, mysterious abode of the dead. The R. V. in general renders it 'grave' or 'pit,' with 'Sheol' in the margin. In the N. T. the word 'hell' is a translation of the Greek word *Hades*, the equivalent of the Hebrew *Sheôl*, or of *Gehenna*, the place of torment. The R. V. retains Hades and Gehenna in the text.
(1) *The grave*, *Sheol*. Deu. 32. 22, fire shall burn to lowest *h*.
2 Sam. 22. 6; Ps. 18. 5, sorrows of *h*. compassed me.
Job 11. 8, deeper than *h*.
26. 6, *h*. is naked before him.
Ps. 9. 17, wicked turned into *h*.
16. 10; Acts 2. 27, not leave soul in *h*.
55. 15, let them go down quick into *h*.
139. 8, if I make my bed in *h*.
Prov. 5. 5, her steps take hold on *h*.
7. 27, house is the way to *h*.
9. 18, her guests are in the depths of *h*.
15. 11, *h*. and destruction before the Lord.
15. 24, that he may depart from *h*. beneath.
23. 14, deliver his soul from *h*.
27. 20, *h*. and destruction are never full.
Isa. 14. 9, *h*. from beneath is moved.
28. 15, 18, with *h*. are we at agreement.
Ezek. 31. 16, when I cast him down to *h*.
32. 21, shall speak out of the midst of *h*.
Am. 9. 2, though they dig into *h*.
Jon. 2. 2, out of the belly of *h*.
Hab. 2. 5, enlargeth his desire as *h*.
(2) *Hades*, place of departed spirits.
Mat. 11. 23; Lu. 10. 15, brought down to *h*.
16. 18, gates of *h*. shall not prevail.
Lu. 16. 23, in *h*. he lift up.
Acts 2. 31, soul not left in *h*.
(3) *Gehenna*, place of torment.
Mat. 5. 22, in danger of *h*. fire.
5. 29, 30, whole body cast into *h*.
10. 28; Lu. 12. 5, destroy soul and body in *h*.
18. 9; Mk. 9. 47, having two eyes to be cast into *h*.
23. 15, more the child of *h*.
23. 33, how can ye escape the damnation of *h*.?
Jas. 3. 6, tongue set on fire of *h*.
2 Pet. 2. 4, cast angels down to *h*.
Hell (Hades), the grave. Acts 2. 31; 1 Cor. 15. 55; Rev. 20. 13.
place of torment. Mat. 11. 23; 13. 42; 25. 41, 46; Lu. 16. 23; 2 Pet. 2. 4; Rev. 14. 10; 20. 10, 15.
for whom reserved. Ps. 9. 17; Prov. 5. 5; 7. 27; 9. 18; Mat. 5. 22; 23. 15; 25. 41; Lu. 16. 23.
See Isa. 5. 14; 14. 9; 33. 14; Mat. 3. 12.

Hellenists (Acts 9. 29). A. V. Grecians: R. V. Grecian Jews. R. V. marg. Hellenists, i. e., Jews of the Dispersion who adopted Greek speech, habits, and culture. The word is carefully to be distinguished from 'Hellenes' = Gentiles. *See* John 7. 35, A. V. and R. V.

Helmet (1 Sam. 17. 5). Heb. *Kôbha.* Goliath's helmet was probably of leather. The Roman helmet (Eph. 6. 17; 1 Thes. 5. 8) was of leather or metal, and when closed showed little besides the eyes, nose, and mouth.

Helon, hē'lŏn, 'strong.' Num. 1. 9.

Help. Gen. 2. 18, 20, an *h.* meet for him.
Deu. 33. 29, the shield of thy *h.*
2 Chr. 26. 15, he was marvellously *h.*
Job 6. 13, is not my *h.* in me?
Ps. 22. 11, for there is none to *h.*
33. 20, he is our *h.* and our shield.
42. 5, the *h.* of his countenance. R. V. health.
46. 1, a very present *h.* in trouble.
60. 11; 108. 12, vain is the *h.* of man.
89. 19, laid *h.* on one that is mighty.
121. 1, the hills from whence cometh my *h.*
124. 8, our *h.* is in the name of the Lord.
Isa. 10. 3, to whom will ye flee for *h.*?
41. 6, they *h.* every one his neighbour.
Hos. 13. 9, in me is thine *h.*
Mat. 15. 25, Lord, *h.* me.
Mk. 9. 24, *h.* thou mine unbelief.
Acts 21. 28, men of Israel, *h.*
26. 22, having obtained *h.* of God.
Heb. 4. 16, grace to *h.* in time of need.
See Isa. 31. 3; Rom. 8. 26; 2 Cor. 1. 24.

Helper. Heb. 13. 6.

Helve, handle of an axe. Deu. 19. 5.

Hem. Mat. 9. 20, touched the *h.* of his garment. R. V. border.
14. 36, might only touch the *h.* of his garment. R. V. border.
See Num. 15. 38, 39; Mat. 23. 5. See GARMENT, Hem of.

Hemam, hē'-măm, same as HOMAM. Gen. 36. 22.

Heman, hē'-măn, 'faithful.' 1 Kn. 4. 31.

Hemath, hē'-măth. (1) 'hot spring.' 1 Chr. 2. 55. (2) same as HAMATH. Am. 6. 14.

Hemdan, hĕm'-dăn, 'pleasant.' Gen. 36. 26.

Hemlock. (1) (Deu. 29. 18, 'gall;' Hos. 10. 4, 'hemlock'). Heb. *Rôsh:* Gk. χολὴ ἄγρωστις. The same as *Gall* = a poisonous herb.
(2) (Am. 6. 12). Heb. *La'ănah:* Gk. πικρία: R. V. 'wormwood,' which *see.* Neither word refers to the poison hemlock or to the hemlock tree.

Hen. Mat. 23. 37; Lu. 13. 34. *See* FOWL.

Hen, hĕn, 'favour,' a man's name. Zec. 6. 14.

Hena, hē'-nă. 2 Kn. 18. 34.

Henadad, hĕn-ā'-dăd, 'favour of Hadad.' Ez. 3. 9.

Henceforth. 2 Cor. 5. 15; Gal. 6. 17; 2 Tim. 4. 8.

Henoch, hē'-nŏch, same as ENOCH. 1 Chr. 1. 3.

Hepher, hē'-phĕr, 'pit.' Jos. 12. 17.

Hepherites, hē'-phĕr-ītes, descendants of Hepher. Num. 26. 32.

Hephzi-bah, hĕph'-zĭ-băh, 'my delight is in her;' queen of Hezekiah, and mother of Manasseh. 2 Kn. 21. 1.
the restored Jerusalem. Isa. 62. 4.

Herb. (1) (Gen. 1. 11, 12). Heb. *Eseb:* Gk. χόρτος, herbage in general; χόρτος in the N. T. is 'grass.'
(2) (2 Kn. 4. 39). Heb. *Orôth:* Gk. ἀριώθ, 'herbs.'
(3) (Prov. 15. 17; 2 Kn. 19. 26). Heb. *Yârâk:* Gk. λάχανον, χλωρὰ βοτάνη, 'green things,' herbage in general.

Herbs, Bitter (Ex. 12. 8). Heb. *Mĕrôrîm:* Gk. πικρίδες. No specific plant, but such herbs as lettuce, endive, chicory, and nettles.

Heres, hē'-rĕs, 'destruction.' Jud. 1. 35.

Heresh, hē'-rĕsh, 'artificer' (?). 1 Chr. 9. 15.

Heresies deprecated. 1 Cor. 11. 19; Gal. 5. 20; 2 Pet. 2. 1. *See* Rom. 16. 17; 1 Cor. 1. 10; 3. 3; 14. 33; Phil. 2. 3; 4. 2; Tit. 3. 10; Jude 19.

Heritage. Job 20. 29, *h.* appointed by God.
Ps. 16. 6; Jer. 3. 19, a goodly *h.*
61. 5, the *h.* of those that fear.
127. 3, children are an *h.* of the Lord.
Isa. 54. 17, this is the *h.* of the servants.
Mic. 7. 14, feed flock of thine *h.*
1 Pet. 5. 3, lords over God's *h.* R. V. the charge allotted to you.
See Joel 2. 17; 3. 2; Mal. 1. 3.

Hermas and **Hermes,** hĕr'-măs and hĕr'-mēs, of Rome, saluted by Paul. Rom. 16. 14.

Hermogenes, hĕr-mŏg'-ĕ-nēs. 2 Tim. 1. 15.

Hermon, hĕr'-mon, 'sacred.' Mountain of the Lebanon range. Deu. 3. 8; 4. 48; Jos. 12. 5; 13. 5; Ps. 89. 12; 133. 3.

Hermonites, hĕr'-mō-nītes, 'the summits of Hermon.' Ps. 42. 6.

Herod, hĕr'-od. (1) (the Great) king of Judæa. [Mat. 2. 1.
troubled at Christ's birth. Mat. 2. 3.
slays the babes at Bethlehem. Mat. 2. 16.
(2) (Antipas) reproved by John the Baptist, imprisons him, Lu. 3. 19. beheads him, Mat. 14.; Mk. 6. 14.
desires to see Christ. Lu. 9. 9.
scourges Him, and is reconciled to Pilate. Lu. 23. 7; Acts 4. 27.
(3) (Agrippa) persecutes the church. Acts 12. 1.
his pride and miserable death. Acts 12. 23.
(4) (Agrippa II.) visits Festus. Acts 25.
Paul's defence before. Acts 26.

Herodians, hĕ-rō'-dĭ-ăns, partisans of Herod. They appear to have been a political party rather than a religious sect. It is thought that they looked with disfavour on the popular Messianic expectations and desired a restoration of Jewish independence under some member of the Herodian family. In Mat. 22. 16 we find them allied with the Pharisees, to whose general principles they were hostile, in a combined attack upon our Lord.
rebuked by Christ. Mat. 22. 16; Mk. 12. 13.
plot against him. Mk. 3. 6; 8. 15; 12. 13.

Herodias, hĕ-rō'-dĭ-ăs. Mat. 14. 3.
married to Herod Antipas. Mk. 6. 17.
plans the death of John the Baptist. Mat. 14.; Mk. 6. 24.

Herodion, hĕ-rō'-dĭ-on. Paul's kinsman. Rom. 16. 11.

Herods, Family of the. *See* p. 150.

Heron (Lev. 11. 19). Heb. *Anâphah:* Gk. χαραδριός. (Specimens, *Ardeola comata; Ardea cinerea.* T. Found in Jordan valley.) Especially frequent about the waters of Merom.

Hesed, hē'-sĕd, 'mercy.' 1 Kn. 4. 10.

Heshbon, hĕsh'-bŏn, 'counting.' city of Sihon, taken, Num. 21. 25, 26; Deu. 2. 24; Neh. 9. 22; Isa. 16. 8.

Heshmon, hĕsh'-mŏn, 'fatness.' Jos. 15. 27.

Heth, hĕth, sons of. Gen. 10. 15.
their kindness to Abraham. Gen. 23. 7; 25. 10.

Hethlon, hĕth'-lŏn. Ezek. 47. 15.

Hew. Ex. 34. 1; 1 Kn. 5. 6; 2 Kn. 12. 2; 2 Chr. 2. 2; Jer. 2. 13; Mat. 3. 10; Mk. 15. 46.

Hezeki, hĕz'-ĕ-kī, shortened from HIZKIAH. 1 Chr. 8. 17.

Hezekiah, hĕz-ĕ-kī'-ăh, 'Jehovah hath strengthened.' king of Judah. 2 Kn. 16. 19 (2 Chr. 28. 27).
abolishes idolatry. 2 Kn. 18.
attacked by the Assyrians, his prayer and deliverance. 2 Kn. 19.
his life lengthened, shadow of dial goes backward, displays his treasure, Isaiah's prediction, 2 Kn. 20. (Isa. 38.). his passover, 2 Chr. 30. 13.
his piety and good reign. 2 Chr. 29.
his death. 2 Kn. 20. 20.

Hezion, hē'-zĭ-ŏn, 'vision.' 1 Kn. 15. 18.

Hezir, hē'-zĭr, 'swine.' 1 Chr. 24. 15.

Hezrai, hĕz'-rā-ī, 'dwelling' (?). 2 Sam. 23. 35.

Hezro, hĕz'-rō, same as preceding. 1 Chr. 11. 37.

Hezron, hĕz'-rŏn. (1) same as HEZRAI. Gen. 46. 12.
(2) place. Jos. 15. 3.

Herods, Family of the.

(From Lewin's 'Life and Epistles of Saint Paul.')

- **Antipater**, of *Idumæa*. *m.* Cypros. *d.* B.C. 48.
  - **Phasaël.**
  - **HEROD the GREAT** ('Herod the king,' Mat. 2. 1). *d.* B.C. 4. *married*
    - **Doris.**
      - **Antipater.** *d.* B.C. 4.
    - **MARIAMNE,** dau. of Alexander *the Asmonæan.*
      - **Aristobulus.** *m.* Bernice. *d.* B.C. 6.
        - **AGRIPPA I.,** *K. of Judæa.* ('Herod the king,' Acts 12.). *m.* Cypros, dau. of Salampso. *d.* A.D. 44.
          - **Drusus.**
          - **AGRIPPA II.,** *K. of Trachonitis* ('King Agrippa,' Acts 25.). *d.* A.D. 99. *Last of the Herods.*
          - **Bernice** (Acts 25. 13). *m.* 1. Marcus. 2. Herod of Chalcis. 3. Polemo.
          - **Mariamne.** *m.* 1. Archelaus. 2. Demetrius.
          - **Drusilla** (Acts 24. 24), *m.* 1. Azizus. 2. Felix.
            - **Agrippa.**
        - **Herod,** *K. of Chalcis.* *d.* A.D. 48. *m.* 1. Mariamne. 2. Bernice.
          - **Aristobulus.**
          - **Bernice.**
          - **Hyrcanus.**
        - **Aristobulus.** *m.* Jotape.
        - **Herodias** (Mat. 14. 3). *m.* 1. Philip. 2. Antipas.
        - **Mariamne.** *m.* Antipater.
      - **Alexander.** *m.* Glaphyra. *d.* B.C. 6.
        - **Tigranes.**
        - **Alexander.**
          - **Tigranes,** *K. of Armenia.*
            - **Alexander,** *K. of Cilicia.*
      - **Herod.**
      - **Salampso.**
      - **Cypros.**
    - **Pallas.**
      - **Phasaël.**
    - **Phædra.**
      - **Roxana.**
    - **Mariamne,** dau. of Simon.
      - **Philip** (Mat. 14. 3). *m.* Herodias.
        - **Salome** (Mat. 14. 6). *m.* 1. Herod-Philip. 2. Aristobulus.
    - **Malthace.** *d.* B.C. 4.
      - **ARCHELAUS,** Ethnarch of Judæa (Mat. 2. 22). *deposed* A.D. 6.
      - **ANTIPAS,** Tetrarch of Galilee ('Herod the tetrarch,' Mat. 14. 3). *m.* 1. dau. of Aretas. 2. Herodias. *deposed* A.D. 40.
      - **Olympia.**
    - **Cleopatra.**
      - **HEROD-PHILIP,** Tetrarch of Trachonitis ('Philip,' Luke 3. 1). *m.* Salome. *d.* A.D. 33.
    - **Elpis.**
  - **Joseph.**
  - **Pheroras.**
  - **Salome.** *d.* A.D. 10.

Hezronites, hĕz'-rŏn-ītes, descendants of Hezron. Num. 26. 6.

Hid. 2 Kn. 4. 27, the Lord hath *h.* it from me.
Job 3. 21, more than for *h.* treasures.
Ps. 32. 5, mine iniquity have I not *h.*
69. 5, my sins are not *h.*
119. 11, thy word have I *h.* in mine heart.
Zep. 2. 3, it may be ye shall be *h.*
Mat. 10. 26; Mk. 4. 22, there is nothing *h.*
Lu. 19. 42, now they are *h.* from thine eyes.
1 Cor. 2. 7, even the *h.* wisdom.
2 Cor. 4. 3, if our gospel be *h.* R. V. veiled.
Col. 3. 3, your life is *h.* with Christ.
1 Pet. 3. 4, the *h.* man of the heart.
Rev. 2. 17, to eat of the *h.* manna.
See Gen. 3. 8; Mat. 5. 14; Mk. 7. 24.

Hiddai, hĭd-dā'-ī. 2 Sam. 23. 30.

Hiddekel, hĭd'-dĕ-kĕl (Gen. 2. 14; Dan. 10. 4), is the Hebrew form of *Hidiglat*, the Babylonian name for the Tigris.

Hide. Gen. 18. 17, shall I *h.* from Abraham?
Job 14. 13, *h.* me in the grave.
34. 29; Ps. 10. 11, he *h.* his face.
Ps. 17. 8, *h.* me under the shadow of thy wings.
27. 5, *h.* me in pavilion.
31. 20, *h.* them in secret of thy presence.

JERUSALEM AND THE
TEMPLE OF HEROD
FROM THE NORTH EAST

HEROD'S TEMPLE

A reconstruction of the Temple in the time of Christ based on the work of Professor W. Sanday and Paul Waterhouse, F.R.I.B.A. (*Clarendon Press*)

HEROD'S BUILDINGS AT SAMARIA

Herod the Great, who ruled by favour of the Romans, erected at Samaria (renamed Sebaste) impressive buildings in Greco-Roman style, of which these ruins remain. (*Donald McLeish*)

Ps. 89. 46, how long wilt thou *h.* thyself?
139. 12, darkness *h.* not from thee.
Isa. 1. 15, I will *h.* mine eyes from you.
3. 9, they *h.* not their sin.
26. 20, *h.* thyself for a little moment.
32. 2, a man shall be as an *h.* place.
45. 15, thou art a God that *h.* thyself.
Ezek. 28. 3, no secret they can *h.* from thee.
Jas. 5. 20, *h.* a multitude of sins. R. V. cover.
Rev. 6. 16, *h.* us from the face of him.
See Job 13. 24; Prov. 28. 28; Am. 9. 3.

Hid treasure, parable. Mat. 13. 44.

Hiel, hī'-ĕl, 'God liveth,' or 'brother of God.' 1 Kn. 16. 34.
See Jericho. [4. 13.

Hierapolis, hī-ĕr-ā'-pŏ-lĭs, 'a sacred city.' Col.

Higgaion, hĭg-gâi'-ŏn, 'meditation.' Ps. 9. 16.

High. Job 11. 8, it is as *h.* as heaven.
22. 12, behold stars, how *h.* they are!
41. 34, he beholdeth all *h.* things.
Ps. 62. 9, men of *h.* degree are a lie.
68. 18, thou hast ascended on *h.*
103. 11, as the heaven is *h.* above the earth.
131. 1, in things too *h.* for me.
138. 6, though the Lord be *h.*
139. 6, it is *h.*, I cannot attain unto it.
Eccl. 12. 5, afraid of that which is *h.*
Isa. 32. 15, spirit poured on us from on *h.*
33. 16, he shall dwell on *h.*
35. 8, an *h.*-way shall be there.
62. 10. cast up the *h.*-way.
Jer. 49. 16, though thou make thy nest *h.*
Mat. 22. 9; Lu. 14. 23, go into the *h.*-ways.
Lu. 1. 78, dayspring from on *h.*
24. 49, power from on *h.*
Rom. 12. 16, mind not *h.* things.
13. 11, it is *h.* time.
Phil. 3. 14, for prize of the *h.* calling.
See Isa. 57. 15; 2 Cor. 10. 5.

Higher. Isa. 55. 9, heavens *h.* than the earth.
Lu. 14. 10, friend, go up *h.*
Heb. 7. 26, made *h.* than the heavens.

High Places forbidden. Deu. 12. 2; 1 Kn. 3. 2; 12. 31; 13. 2; 14. 23; Jer. 3. 6.

High Priest. Ex. 28. 1.
his garments. Lev. 8. 7.

Highway. Jud. 5. 6; Prov. 16. 17; Isa. 35. 8.

Hilen, hī'-lĕn. 1 Chr. 6. 58. [Kn. 18. 18.

Hilkiah, hĭl-kī'-ăh, 'my portion is Jehovah.' 2
finds the book of the law. 2 Kn. 22. 8.

Hill. Gen. 49. 26, the everlasting *h.*
Deu. 11. 11, a land of *h.* and valleys.
Ps. 2. 6, set my king on holy *h.*
15. 1, who shall dwell in thy holy *h.*?
24. 3, who shall ascend the *h.* of the Lord?
43. 3, bring me to thy holy *h.*
50. 10, cattle on a thousand *h.*
95. 4, strength of the *h.* is his. [mountains.
121. 1, I will lift up mine eyes to the *h.* R. V.
Prov. 8. 25, before the *h.* was I brought forth.
Isa. 40. 12, weighed the *h.* in balance.
Jer. 3. 23, salvation hoped for from the *h.*
Hos. 10. 8; Lu. 23. 30, to the *h.*, fall on us.
Mat. 5. 14, city set on an *h.*
See Lu. 4. 29; 9. 37; Acts 17. 22.

Hillel, hĭl'-lĕl, 'he hath praised.' Jud. 12. 13.

Hin, hĭn, a liquid measure = nearly 6 quarts. Ex. 30. 24.
See Measures.

Hind. *See* Hart.

Hinder. Gen. 24. 56, *h.* me not.
Job 9. 12; 11. 10, who can *h.* him?
Lu. 11. 52, them that were entering ye *h.*
Acts 8. 36, what doth *h.* me to be baptized?
1 Cor. 9. 12, lest we *h.* the gospel.
Gal. 5. 7, who did *h.* you?
1 Thes. 2. 18, but Satan *h.* us.
1 Pet. 3. 7, that your prayers be not *h.*
See Num. 22. 16; Neh. 4. 8; Isa. 14. 6.

Hinges. 1 Kn. 7. 50; Prov. 26. 14.

Hinnom, hĭn'-nom, valley of (Neh. 11. 30; Jos. 15. 8). The Hebrew name is *Gê-hinnôm*, hence Gehenna (Mat. 5. 22, R. V., &c.). A valley S. of Jerusalem. The scene of Molech worship, the place into which the Jews cast all manner of refuse and the bodies of animals and criminals. To prevent infection great fires were kept always burning (the Gehenna of fire, R. V.), and the place became the type and symbol of the place of future punishment. 2 Kn. 23. 10; 2 Chr. 28. 3; 33. 6; Jer. 7. 31; 19. 11; 32. 35. *See* Tophet and Moloch.

Hirah, hī'-răh, 'nobility' (?). Gen. 38. 1.

Hiram, hī'-răm, 'brother of the exalted one.'
(1) (Huram) king of Tyre, sends aid to David and Solomon. 2 Sam. 5. 11; 1 Kn. 5.; 9. 11; 10. 11; 1 Chr. 14. 1; 2 Chr. 2. 11.
(2) principal brass-worker to Solomon. 1 Kn. 7. 13.

Hire. Deu. 24. 15, thou shalt give him his *h.*
Mic. 3. 11, priests teach for *h.*
Mat. 20. 7, no man hath *h.* us.
20. 8, give them their *h.*
Mk. 1. 20, in ship with *h.* servants.
Lu. 10. 7, labourer worthy of his *h.*
15. 17, how many *h.* servants.
Jas. 5. 4, *h.* of labourers which is kept back.
See Ex. 12. 45; Lev. 25. 40; Deu. 15. 18.

Hire for labour, not to be kept back. Lev. 19. 13; Deu. 24. 14, 15; Jas. 5. 4.

Hireling. Job 7. 1, like the days of an *h.*
7. 2, as *h.* looketh for reward.
14. 6, accomplish, as an *h.*, his day.
Mal. 3. 5. that oppress the *h.*
See Isa. 16. 14; 21. 16; John 10. 12.

His used for *neut.* 'its,' which occurs once only in A. V. (*see* Lev. 25. 5), where edit. of 1611 has 'it.' Acts 12. 10; 1 Cor. 15. 38, &c.

Hiss. 1 Kn. 9. 8; Job 27. 23; Jer. 18. 16. [me *h.*

Hitherto. Jos. 17. 14, the Lord hath blessed
1 Sam. 7. 12, *h.* hath the Lord helped us.
Job 38. 11, *h.* shalt thou come. [until now.
John 5. 17, my Father worketh *h.* R. V. even
16. 24, *h.* have ye asked nothing in my name.
1 Cor. 3. 2, *h.* ye were not able to bear it.
See Jud. 16. 13; 2 Sam. 15. 34; Isa. 18. 2.

Hittites, hĭt'-tītes, descendants of Heth. Gen. 15. 20; Jud. 1. 26; 3. 5.

Hivites, hī'-vītes, 'villagers' (?). Ex. 3. 8; Gen. 10. 17; Ex. 3. 17.
deceive Joshua. Jos. 9. [Zep. 1. 1.

Hizkiah, hĭz-kī'-ăh, 'Jehovah has strengthened.'

Hizkijah, hĭz-kī'-jăh, same as preceding. Neh. 10. 17.

Hoary. Job 41. 32. [Jethro.

Hobab, hō'-băb, 'beloved' (?). Num. 10. 29. *See*

Hobah, hō'-băh, 'a hiding-place.' Gen. 14. 15.

Hod, hŏd, 'splendour.' 1 Chr. 7. 37. [3. 24.

Hodaiah, hō-dâi'-ăh, 'praise of Jehovah.' 1 Chr.

Hodaviah, hō-dă-vī'-ăh, 'Jehovah is his praise.' 1 Chr. 5. 24.

Hodesh, hō'-dĕsh, 'new moon.' 1 Chr. 8. 9.

Hodevah, hō'-dĕ-văh, same as Hodaviah. Neh. 7. 43.

Hodiah, hō-dī'-ăh, same as Hodaiah. 1 Chr. 4. 19.

Hodijah, hō-dī'-jăh, same as preceding. Neh. 8. 7.

Hoglah, hŏg'-lăh, 'partridge.' Num. 26. 33.

Hoham, hō'-hăm. Jos. 10. 3.

Hoise, to hoist; 'hoised' = hoisted. Acts 27. 40.

Hold. (1) Gen. 21. 18, *h.* him in thine hand.
2 Kn. 7. 9, good tidings, and we *h.* our peace.
Esth. 4. 14, if thou altogether *h.* thy peace.
Job 36. 8, *h.* in cords of affliction. R. V. be taken.
Ps. 18. 35, thy right hand hath *h.* me up.
71. 6, by thee have I been *h.*
73. 23, thou hast *h.* me by my right hand.
119. 117, *h.* me up, and I shall be safe.
Prov. 11. 12, man of understanding *h.* his peace.
17. 28, a fool, when he *h.* his peace.
Isa. 41. 13, the Lord will *h.* thy hand.
62. 1, for Zion's sake will I not *h.* my peace.
Jer. 4. 19, I cannot *h.* my peace.
Am. 6. 10, *h.* thy tongue.

Mat. 6. 24; Lu. 16. 13, he will *h.* to the one.
Mk. 1. 25; Lu. 4. 35, *h.* thy peace, come out.
Rom. 1. 18, *h.* the truth in unrighteousness.
1 Cor. 14. 30, let the first *h.* his peace. R. V. keep.
Phil. 2. 16, *h.* forth the word of life.
2. 29, *h.* such in reputation.
Col. 2. 19, not *h.* the Head.
1 Thes. 5. 21, *h.* fast that which is good.
1 Tim. 1. 19, *h.* faith and good conscience.
3. 9, *h.* the mystery of faith.
2 Tim. 1. 13, *h.* fast form of sound words.
Tit. 1. 9, *h.* fast the faithful word.
Heb. 3. 14, *h.* beginning of confidence.
4. 14; 10. 23, *h.* fast our profession.
Rev. 2. 13, thou *h.* fast my name.
2. 25, *h.* fast till I come.
3. 3, *h.* fast, and repent. R. V. keep it.
3. 11, *h.* that fast which thou hast.
See Job 2. 3; Jer. 2. 13; 51. 30; Ezek. 19. 9.
(2) to consider, esteem, account. Ex. 20. 7; Deu. 5. 11, will not *h.* him guiltless.

Hole. Isa. 11. 8, child shall play on *h.* of the asp.
51. 1, *h.* of pit whence ye are digged.
Jer. 13. 4, hide in a *h.* of the rock.
Ezek. 8. 7, a *h.* in the wall.
Hag. 1. 6, a bag with *h.*
Mat. 8. 20; Lu. 9. 58, foxes have *h.*
See S. of S. 5. 4; Mic. 7. 17; Nah. 2. 12.

Holier. Isa. 65. 5.

Holiest. Heb. 9. 3; 10. 19.

Holily. 1 Thes. 2. 10.

Holiness. Ex. 15. 11, glorious in *h.*
28. 36; 39. 30; Zec. 14. 20, *h.* to the Lord.
1 Chr. 16. 29; 2 Chr. 20. 21; Ps. 29. 2; 96. 9; 110. 3, beauty of *h.*
Ps. 30. 4; 97. 12, at remembrance of his *h.*
47. 8, the throne of his *h.*
60. 6; 108. 7, God hath spoken in his *h.*
93. 5, *h.* becometh thine house.
Isa. 35. 8, the way of *h.*
63. 15, habitation of thy *h.*
Jer. 23. 9, the words of his *h.*
Obad. 17, upon mount Zion there shall be *h.*
Lu. 1. 75, might serve him in *h.*
Acts 3. 12, as though by our *h.* R. V. godliness.
Rom. 1. 4, according to the spirit of *h.*
6. 22, fruit unto *h.*
2 Cor. 7. 1, perfecting *h.* in fear of God.
Eph. 4. 24, created in righteousness and *h.*
1 Thes. 3. 13, unblameable in *h.*
4. 7, not called to uncleanness, but *h.* R. V. sanctification.
1 Tim. 2. 15, continue in faith and *h.* R. V. sanctification.
Tit. 2. 3, in behaviour as becometh *h.* R. V. reverent in demeanor.
Heb. 12. 10, partakers of his *h.* [fication.
12. 14, *h.*, without which no man. R. V. sancti-
See Ps. 89. 35; Isa. 23. 18; Jer. 2. 3.

Holiness enjoined. Ex. 19. 22; Lev. 11. 44; 20. 7; Num. 15. 40; Deu. 7. 6; 26. 19; 28. 9; Lu. 1. 75; Rom. 12. 1; 2 Cor. 7. 1; Eph. 1. 4; 4. 24; Col. 3. 12; 1 Thes. 2. 12; 1 Tim. 2. 15; Heb. 12. 14; 1 Pet. 1. 15, 16; 2 Pet. 3. 11; Rev. 22. 11.

Hollow. Gen. 32. 25; Jud. 15. 19; Isa. 40. 12.

Holon, hō´-lŏn, 'sandy.' Jos. 15. 51. [1. 54.

Holpen. Ps. 86. 17; Isa. 31. 3; Dan. 11. 34; Lu.

Holy. Ex. 3. 5; Jos. 5. 15, is *h.* ground.
19. 6; 1 Pet. 2. 9, an *h.* nation.
20. 8; 31. 14, sabbath day, to keep it *h.*
Lev. 10. 10, difference between *h.* and unholy.
20. 7, be ye *h.*
Num. 16. 5, Lord will shew who is *h.*
2 Kn. 4. 9, this is an *h.* man of God.
Ez. 9. 2; Isa. 6. 13, the *h.* seed.
Ps. 20. 6, hear from his *h.* heaven.
22. 3, thou art *h.* that inhabitest.
86. 2, preserve my soul, for I am *h.* R. V. godly.
98. 1, his *h.* arm hath gotten victory.
99. 9, worship at his *h.* hill. [gracious.
145. 17, the Lord is *h.* in all his works. R. V.
Prov. 20. 25, who devoureth that which is *h.*
Isa. 6. 3; Rev. 4. 8, *h.*, *h.*, *h.*, is the Lord.
52. 10, make bare his *h.* arm.
64. 10, thy *h.* cities are a wilderness.
64. 11, our *h.* and beautiful house. [profane.
Ezek. 22. 26, put no difference between *h.* and
Mat. 7. 6, give not that which is *h.*
Lu. 1. 35, that *h.* thing which shall be born of thee.
John 17. 11, *h.* Father, keep those.
Acts 4. 27, 30, against thy *h.* child Jesus.
Rom. 1. 2, promised in the *h.* scriptures.
7. 12, commandment is *h.*, just, and good.
11. 16, if firstfruit be *h.*, if root be *h.*
12. 1, a living sacrifice, *h.*, acceptable to God.
16. 16; 1 Cor. 16. 20; 2 Cor. 13. 12; 1 Thes. 5. 26; 1 Pet. 5. 14, with a *h.* kiss.
1 Cor. 3. 17, the temple of God is *h.*
7. 14, now are they *h.*
Eph. 1. 4; 5. 27, be *h.* and without blame.
2. 21, groweth to an *h.* temple in the Lord.
Col. 1. 22, present you *h.* and unblameable.
3. 12, elect of God, *h.* and beloved.
1 Thes. 5. 27, all the *h.* brethren.
1 Tim. 2. 8, lifting up *h.* hands.
2 Tim. 1. 9, called us with an *h.* calling.
Tit. 1. 8, bishop must be *h.*
Heb. 3. 1, *h.* brethren, partakers.
1 Pet. 1. 15; 2 Pet. 3. 11, *h.* in all conversation.
2. 5, an *h.* priesthood.
3. 5, the *h.* women, who trusted.
2 Pet. 1. 18, with him in the *h.* mount.
Rev. 3. 7, saith he that is *h.*
6. 10, O Lord, *h.* and true.
20. 6, *h.* is he that hath part.
21. 10, the *h.* Jerusalem.
22. 11, he that is *h.*, let him be *h.*
See 2 Tim. 3. 15; 2 Pet. 3. 2; Jude 20. [Ghost.

Holy Ghost. Mat. 1. 18, 20, with child of the *H.*
3. 11; Mk. 1. 8; Lu. 3. 16; John 1. 33; Acts 1. 5, baptize with *H.* Ghost.
Mat. 12. 31, blasphemy against *H.* Ghost. R. V. the Spirit.
Mk. 13. 11, not ye that speak, but *H.* Ghost.
Lu. 1. 15, shall be filled with the *H.* Ghost.
3. 22, *H.* Ghost descended in bodily shape.
4. 1, Jesus being full of the *H.* Ghost. R. V. *H.* Spirit.
12. 12, *H.* Ghost shall teach you. R. V. *H.* Spirit.
John 7. 39, the *H.* Ghost was not yet given. R. V. the Spirit.
14. 26, the Comforter, which is the *H.* Ghost. R. V. *H.* Spirit.
20. 22, receive ye the *H.* Ghost.
Acts 1. 8, after the *H.* Ghost is come.
2. 4, all filled with *H.* Ghost. R. V. *H.* Spirit.
5. 3, to lie to the *H.* Ghost.
6. 3, look out men full of the *H.* Ghost. R. V. the Spirit.
7. 51, ye do always resist the *H.* Ghost.
8. 15, prayed that they might receive *H.* Ghost.
9. 31, in comfort of the *H.* Ghost.
10. 44, *H.* Ghost fell on all which heard.
10. 47, received *H.* Ghost as well as we.
15. 8, giving them *H.* Ghost, as he did unto us.
15. 28, seemed good to the *H.* Ghost.
16. 6, forbidden of the *H.* Ghost.
19. 2, have ye received the *H.* Ghost?
20. 28, *H.* Ghost hath made you overseers.
Rom. 9. 1, bearing witness in *H.* Ghost.
14. 17, joy in the *H.* Ghost. [R. V. the Spirit.
1 Cor. 2. 13, words which the *H.* Ghost teacheth.
2 Cor. 13. 14, communion of the *H.* Ghost.
Tit. 3. 5, the renewing of the *H.* Ghost.
1 Pet. 1. 12, *H.* Ghost sent down from heaven.
2 Pet. 1. 21, *h.* men moved by *H.* Ghost.
See Holy Spirit.

Holy Gifts. Ex. 28. 38; Lev. 10. 12.

Holy Place, laws concerning. Ex. 28. 29; Lev. 6. 16; 16. 2; 2 Chr. 29. 5; Heb. 9. 12.
measure of the most. Ezek. 41. 4.

Holy Spirit, Eternal. Heb. 9. 14.
Omnipresent. Ps. 139. 7-13.

Omniscient. 1 Cor. 2. 10.
Omnipotent. Lu. 1. 35; Rom. 15. 19.
the Spirit of glory and of God. 1 Pet. 4. 14.
author of the new birth. John 3. 5, 6, with 1 John 5. 4.
inspiring scripture. 2 Tim. 3. 16, with 2 Pet. 1. 21.
the source of wisdom. Isa. 11. 2; John 14. 26; 16. 13; 1 Cor. 12. 8.
the source of miraculous power. Mat. 12. 28, with Lu. 11. 20; Acts 19. 11, with Rom. 15. 19.
appointing and sending ministers. Acts 13. 2, 4, with Mat. 9. 38; Acts 20. 28.
directing where the gospel should be preached. Acts 16. 6, 7, 10.
dwelling in saints. John 14. 17, with 1 Cor. 14. 25; 3. 16, with 1 Cor. 6. 19.
Comforter of the church. Acts 9. 31, with 2 Cor. 1. 3.
sanctifying the church. Ezek. 37. 28, with Rom. 15. 16.
the Witness. Heb. 10. 15, with 1 John 5. 9.
convincing of sin, of righteousness, and of judgment. John 16. 8-11.

COMFORTER:
proceeds from the Father. John 15. 26.
given:
by Christ. Isa. 61. 1; Lu. 4. 18.
by the Father. John 14. 16.
through Christ's intercession. John 14. 16.
sent in the name of Christ. John 14. 26.
sent by Christ from the Father. John 15. 26; 16. 7.
as such He:
abides for ever with saints. John 14. 16.
dwells with, and in saints. John 14. 17.
is known by saints. John 14. 17.
teaches saints. John 14. 26.
testifies of Christ. John 15. 26.
edifies the church. Acts 9. 31.
imparts the love of God. Rom. 5. 3-5.
communicates joy to saints. Rom. 14. 17; Gal. 5. 22; 1 Thes. 1. 6.
imparts hope. Rom. 15. 13; Gal. 5. 5.
the world cannot receive. John 14. 17.

EMBLEMS OF:
A Dove. Mat. 3. 16.
gentle. Mat. 10. 16, with Gal. 5. 22.
Fire. Mat. 3. 11.
illuminating. Ex. 13. 21; Ps. 78. 14; Zec. 4.; Rev. 4. 5.
purifying. Isa. 4. 4; Mal. 3. 2, 3.
searching. Zep. 1. 12, with 1 Cor. 2. 10.
Oil. Ps. 45. 7.
consecrating. Ex. 29. 7; 30. 30; Isa. 61. 1.
comforting. Isa. 61. 3; Heb. 1. 9.
illuminating. Mat. 25. 3, 4; 1 John 2. 20, 27.
healing. Lu. 10. 34; Rev. 3. 18.
Rain and Dew. Ps. 72. 6.
imperceptible. 2 Sam. 17. 12, with Mk. 4. 26-28.
refreshing. Ps. 68. 9; Isa. 18. 4.
abundant. Ps. 133. 3.
fertilizing. Ezek. 34. 26, 27; Hos. 6. 3; 10. 12; 14. 5.
A Seal. Rev. 7. 2.
authenticating. John 6. 27; 2 Cor. 1. 22.
securing. Eph. 1. 13, 14; 4. 30.
A Voice. Isa. 6. 8.
guiding. Isa. 30. 21, with John 16. 13.
speaking. Mat. 10. 20.
warning. Heb. 3. 7-11.
Water. John 3. 5; 7. 38, 39.
fertilizing. Ps. 1. 3; Isa. 27. 3, 6; 44. 3, 4; 58. 11.
refreshing. Ps. 46. 4; Isa. 41. 17, 18.
freely given. Isa. 55. 1; John 4. 14; Rev. 22. 17.
cleansing. Ezek. 16. 9; 36. 25; Eph. 5. 26; Heb. 10. 22.
abundant. John 7. 37, 38.
Wind.
powerful. 1 Kn. 19. 11, with Acts 2. 2.
reviving. Ezek. 37. 9, 10, 14.
independent. John 3. 8; 1 Cor. 12. 11.
sensible in its effects. John 3. 8.

GIFT OF:
by the Father. Neh. 9. 20; Lu. 11. 13.
to Christ without measure. John 3. 34.
by the Son. John 20. 22.
given:
for instruction. Neh. 9. 20.
upon the exaltation of Christ. Ps. 68. 18; John 7. 39.
in answer to prayer. Lu. 11. 13; Eph. 1. 16, 17.
through the intercession of Christ. John 14. 16.
for comfort of saints. John 14. 16.
to those who repent and believe. Acts 2. 38.
according to promise. Acts 2. 38, 39.
to those who obey God. Acts 5. 32.
to the Gentiles. Acts 10. 44, 45; 11. 17; 15. 8.
is abundant. Ps. 68. 9; John 7. 38, 39.
is fructifying. Isa. 32. 15.
is permanent. Isa. 59. 21; Hag. 2. 5; 1 Pet. 4. 14.
a pledge of the continued favour of God. Ezek. 39. 29.
an earnest of the inheritance of the saints. 2 Cor. 1. 22; 5. 5; Eph. 1. 14.
received through faith. Gal. 3. 14.
an evidence of union with Christ. 1 John 3. 24; 4. 13.

PERSONALITY OF:
He creates and gives life. Job 33. 4.
He appoints and commissions His servants. Isa. 48. 16; Acts 13. 2; 20. 28.
He directs where to preach. Acts 8. 29; 10. 19, 20.
He suffers Paul not to go to Bithynia. Acts 16. 6, 7.
He instructs Paul what to preach. 1 Cor. 2. 13.
He spoke in, and by, the prophets. Acts 1. 16; 1 Pet. 1. 11, 12; 2 Pet. 1. 21.
He strives with sinners, Gen. 6. 3. can be vexed, Isa. 63. 10. teaches, John 14. 26; 1 Cor. 12. 13. dwells with saints, John 14. 17. testifies of Christ, John 15. 26. reproves, John 16. 8. guides, John 16. 13. glorifies Christ, John 16. 14. can be tempted, Acts 5. 9. can be resisted, Acts 7. 51. comforts, Acts 9. 31. helps our infirmities, Rom. 8. 26. searches all things, Rom. 11. 33, 34, with 1 Cor. 2. 10, 11. has a power of His own, Rom. 15. 13. sanctifies, Rom. 15. 16; 1 Cor. 6. 11. works according to His own will, 1 Cor. 12. 11.

THE TEACHER:
promised. Prov. 1. 23.
as the Spirit of wisdom. Isa. 11. 2; 40. 13, 14.
given:
to saints. Neh. 9. 20; 1 Cor. 2. 12, 13.
in answer to prayer. Eph. 1. 16, 17.
necessity for. 1 Cor. 2. 9, 10.
as such He:
directs in the way of godliness. Isa. 30. 21; Ezek. 36. 27.
teaches saints to answer persecutors. Mk. 13. 11; Lu. 12. 12.
reveals the future. Lu. 2. 26; Acts 21. 11.
brings the words of Christ to remembrance. John 14. 26.
guides into all truth. John 14. 26; 16. 13.
reveals the things of Christ. John 16. 14.
directs the decisions of the church. Acts 15. 28.
reveals the things of God. 1 Cor. 2. 10, 13.
enables ministers to teach. 1 Cor. 12. 8.
the natural man will not receive the things of. 1 Cor. 2. 14.
all are invited to attend to the instruction of. Rev. 2. 7, 11, 29.

Holy Things, laws respecting. Ex. 28. 38; Lev. 5. 15; 22. 2; Num. 4. 19, 20; 1 Chr. 23. 28; Neh. 10. 33; Ezek. 20. 40; 22. 8.

Homam, hō'-măm, 'destruction' (?). 1 Chr. 1. 39.

Home. Ex. 9. 19, and shall not be brought *h*.
Lev. 18. 9, whether born at *h*. or abroad.
Deu. 24. 5, free at *h*. one year.
Ru. 1. 21, the Lord hath brought me *h*. empty.
2 Sam. 14. 13, fetch *h*. his banished.
1 Kn. 13. 7, come *h*. with me.
2 Kn. 14. 10; 2 Chr. 25. 19, tarry at *h*.
1 Chr. 13. 12, bring ark of God *h*.
Job 39. 12, he will bring *h*. thy seed.
Ps. 68. 12, she that tarried at *h*.
Eccl. 12. 5, man goeth to his long *h*.
Lam. 1. 20, at *h*. there is as death.

Hag. 1. 9, when ye brought it *h.* [house.
Mk. 5. 19, go *h.* to thy friends. R. V. to thy
John 19. 27, took her to his own *h.*
20. 10, went away to their own *h.*
1 Cor. 11. 34, let him eat at *h.*
14. 35, ask their husbands at *h.*
2 Cor. 5. 6, at *h.* in the body. [own family.
1 Tim. 5. 4, show piety at *h.* R. V. towards their
Tit. 2. 5, keepers at *h.*
See Jer. 2. 14; Lu. 9. 61; 15. 6.

Homer *or* **Cor.** Lev. 27. 16; Num. 11. 32. (1) A liquid measure = 10 baths = 388.8 litres = 86 gallons.
(2) A dry measure, of the same capacity = 388.8 litres = 10 bushels 3 pecks and 1 quart.
'Measure' in 1 Kn. 4. 22; 2 Chr. 2. 10 = homer.
See MEASURES.

Honest. (1) Lu. 8. 15, an *h.* and good heart.
Acts 6. 3, men of *h.* report.
Rom. 13. 13, let us walk *h.*, as in the day.
(2) honourable, comely. Rom. 12. 17; 2 Cor. 8. 21, provide things *h.*
Phil. 4. 8, whatsoever things are *h.*
1 Pet. 2. 12, conversation *h.* among Gentiles. R. V. behaviour seemly.

Honesty, honourable conduct. Rom. 12. 17; 13. 13; 2 Cor. 8. 21; 13. 7; Phil. 4. 8; 1 Thes. 4. 12; 1 Tim. 2. 2; Heb. 13. 18.

Honey. Gen. 43. 11; 1 Sam. 14. 25; Ps. 19. 10; Prov. 24. 13; 25. 16; 27. 7; Isa. 7. 15; S. of S. 4. 11; Rev. 10. 9.
not to be used in burnt sacrifices. Lev. 2. 11.

Honour (*n.*). Num. 22. 17, promote thee to *h.*
24. 11, hath kept thee back from *h.*
2 Sam. 6. 22, of them shall I be had in *h.*
1 Kn. 3. 13, also given thee riches and *h.*
1 Chr. 29. 28, died full of riches and *h.*
2 Chr. 1. 11, 12, thou hast not asked *h.*
26. 18, neither shall it be for thy *h.*
Esth. 1. 20, the wives shall give their husbands *h.*
Job 14. 21, his sons come to *h.*
Ps. 7. 5, lay mine *h.* in the dust. R. V. glory.
8. 5; Heb. 2. 7, crowned him with *h.* [glory.
26. 8, place where thine *h.* dwelleth. R. V.
49. 12, man being in *h.* abideth not.
96. 6, *h.* and majesty are before him.
149. 9, this *h.* have all his saints.
Prov. 3. 16, in left hand riches and *h.*
4. 8, she shall bring thee to *h.*
5. 9, lest thou give their *h.* to others. [glory.
14. 28, multitude of people is king's *h.* R. V.
20. 3, an *h.* to cease from strife.
25. 2, the *h.* of kings to search out. R. V. glory.
26. 1, 8, *h.* is not seemly for a fool.
31. 25, strength and *h.* are her clothing. R. V. dignity.
Eccl. 6. 2, to whom God hath given *h.*
Mal. 1. 6, where is mine *h.*?
Mat. 13. 57; Mk. 6. 4; John 4. 44, not without *h.*
John 5. 41, I receive not *h.* from men. R. V. glory.
5. 44, which receive *h.* one of another.
Rom. 2. 7, in well doing seek for *h.*
2. 10, *h.* to every man that worketh good.
12. 10, in *h.* preferring one another.
13. 7, *h.* to whom *h.*
2 Cor. 6. 8, by *h.* and dishonour. R. V. glory.
Col. 2. 23, not in any *h.* to satisfying. R. V. value against.
1 Thes. 4. 4, possess his vessel in *h.*
1 Tim. 5. 17, elders worthy of double *h.*
6. 1, count masters worthy of *h.*
6. 16, to whom be *h.* and power everlasting.
2 Tim. 2. 20, 21, some to *h.*, some to dishonour.
Heb. 3. 3, more *h.* than the house.
5. 4, no man taketh this *h.* unto himself.
1 Pet. 3. 7, giving *h.* to the wife.
Rev. 4. 11; 5. 12, thou art worthy to receive *h.*
21. 24, kings of the earth bring *h.* into it.

Honour (*v.*). Ex. 14. 4, I will be *h.* upon Pharaoh.
20. 12; Deu. 5. 16; Mat. 15. 4; 19. 19; Mk. 7. 10; 10. 19; Lu. 18. 20; Eph. 6. 2, *h.* thy father and mother.
Lev. 19. 32, thou shalt *h.* the face of the old man.
1 Sam. 2. 30, them that *h.* me I will *h.*
15. 30, *h.* me now before elders.
Esth. 6. 6, the king delighteth to *h.*
Ps. 15. 4, he *h.* them that fear the Lord.
Prov. 3. 9, *h.* the Lord with thy substance.
12. 9, better than he that *h.* himself.
Mal. 1. 6, a son *h.* his father. [lips.
Mat. 15. 8; Mk. 7. 6 (Isa. 29. 13), *h.* me with their
John 5. 23, *h.* the Son as they *h.* the Father.
Acts 28. 10, *h.* us with many *h.*
1 Tim. 5. 3, *h.* widows that are widows indeed.
1 Pet. 2. 17, *h.* all men, *h.* the king.

Honour due to God. Ps. 29. 2; 71. 8; 145. 5; Isa. 58. 13; Mal. 1. 6; 1 Tim. 1. 17; Rev. 4. 11; 5. 13; 7. 12; 19. 1.
granted by God. 1 Kn. 3. 13; Esth. 8. 16; Prov. 3. 16; 4. 8; 8. 18; 22. 4; 29. 23; Dan. 5. 18; John 12. 26.
due to parents. Ex. 20. 12; Deu. 5. 16; Mat. 15. 4; Eph. 6. 2.
to the aged. Lev. 19. 32; 1 Tim. 5. 1.
to the king. 1 Pet. 2. 17.

Honourable. Ps. 45. 9, among thy *h.* women.
Isa. 3. 3, take away the *h.* man.
9. 15, ancient and *h.*, he is the head.
42. 21, magnify the law, and make it *h.*
See Lu. 14. 8; 1 Cor. 4. 10; 12. 23; Heb. 13. 4.

Hoof. Ex. 10. 26; Deu. 14. 6; Mic. 4. 13.

Hook. Ex. 26. 32; 2 Kn. 19. 28; Mat. 17. 27.

Hoopoe. R. V. in Lev. 11. 19, for A. V. lapwing.

Hope (*n.*). Job 7. 6, my days are spent without *h.*
8. 13, the hypocrite's *h.* shall perish.
17. 15, where is now my *h.*?
19. 10, my *h.* hath he removed.
Ps. 16. 9; Acts 2. 26, my flesh also shall rest in *h.* R. V. dwell in safety.
39. 7, my *h.* is in thee.
119. 116, let me not be ashamed of my *h.*
Prov. 13. 12, *h.* deferred maketh the heart sick.
14. 32, hath *h.* in his death.
26. 12; 29. 20, more *h.* of a fool.
Eccl. 9. 4, to all the living there is *h.*
Jer. 17. 7, the man whose *h.* the Lord is.
31. 17, there is *h.* in thine end.
See Lam. 3. 18, my strength and *h.* is perished.
Hos. 2. 15, for a door of *h.*
Zec. 9. 12, ye prisoners of *h.*
Acts 28. 20, for the *h.* of Israel I am bound.
Rom. 4. 18, who against *h.* believed in *h.*
8. 24, we are saved by *h.*
12. 12, rejoicing in *h.*
1 Cor. 13. 13, faith, *h.*, charity.
15. 19, if in this life only we have *h.*
Eph. 1. 18, the *h.* of his calling.
2. 12, having no *h.*, and without God.
Col. 1. 27, Christ in you, the *h.* of glory.
1 Thes. 4. 13, even as others who have no *h.*
5. 8, for an helmet, the *h.* of salvation.
2 Thes. 2. 16, good *h.* through grace.
Tit. 3. 7, the *h.* of eternal life.
Heb. 6. 18, lay hold on *h.* set before us.
6. 19, *h.* as an anchor of the soul.
1 Pet. 1. 3, begotten to a lively *h.* [trust.

Hope (*v.*). Ps. 22. 9, thou didst make me *h.* R. V.
31. 24, all ye that *h.* in the Lord.
42. 5, 11; 43. 5, *h.* thou in God.
71. 14, I will *h.* continually.
Lam. 3. 26, good that a man both *h.* and wait.
Rom. 8. 25, if we *h.* for that we see not.
1 Pet. 1. 13, *h.* to the end.
See Acts 24. 26; Heb. 11. 1.

Hope (a good). Ps. 16. 9; 22. 9; 31. 24; Acts 24. 15; 28. 20; Rom. 15. 13.
of the wicked will perish. Job 8. 13; 11. 20; 27. 8.
comfort of. Job 11. 18; Ps. 146. 5; Prov. 10. 28; 14. 32; Jer. 17. 7; Lam. 3. 21; Acts 24. 15; Rom. 12. 12; 15. 4; 1 Cor. 13. 13; Eph. 1. 18; 4. 4; Col. 1. 5; Heb. 3. 6.
encouragement under. Ps. 31. 24; 42. 5; 130. 7; Lam. 3. 26; Rom. 8. 24; 15. 13; Col. 1. 23; Tit. 2. 13; Heb. 3. 6; 6. 11; 1 Pet. 1. 13.
prisoners of. Zec. 9. 12.

effect of. Rom. 5. 5; 8. 24; 15. 4; 1 Cor. 13. 7; 1 John 3. 3.
gift of God. Gal. 5. 5; 2 Thes. 2. 16; Tit. 1. 2; 1 Pet. 1. 3.
ready to give reason for. 1 Pet. 3. 15.

Hophni, hŏph'-nī, 'my fist;' and Phinehas, sons of Eli. 1 Sam. 1. 3.
their sin and death. 1 Sam. 2. 12, 22; 4. 11.

Hophra, hŏph'-ră, 'priest of the sun.' Jer. 44. 30.

Hor, hôr, a mountain on the border of the Edomite country S. of the Dead Sea.
(1) mount, Aaron dies on. Num. 20. 25.
(2) Num. 34. 7, boundary of land of Israel on the north, probably Mt. Hermon.

Horam, hôr'-ăm, 'elevated.' Jos. 10. 33.

Horeb, hôr'-ĕb, 'desert,' mount (Sinai). Ex. 3. 1; 17. 6; 33. 6; Deu. 1. 6; 4. 10.
law given. Ex. 19.; 20.; Deu. 4. 10; 5. 2; 18. 16; 1 Kn. 8. 9; Mal. 4. 4.
Moses twice there for forty days. Ex. 24. 18; 34. 28; Deu. 9. 9.
Elijah there for forty days. 1 Kn. 19. 8.

Horem, hôr'-ĕm, 'sacred.' Jos. 19. 38.

Hor-hagidgad, hôr-hă-gĭd'-găd, 'hollow of Gudgodah.' Num. 33. 32.

Hori, hôr'-ī, 'cave-dweller.' Gen. 36. 22.

Horims, hôr-'ĭms, 'cave-dwellers.' Deu. 2. 12.

Horites, hôr'-ītes, same as preceding. Gen. 14. 6.

Hormah, hôr'-măh, 'devoted,' 'a place laid waste.' Num. 14. 45.
destruction of. Num. 21. 3; Jud. 1. 17.

Hornet, Heb. *Tzir'ah*: Gk. σφηκία: Zool. S. *Vespa Crabro*. Hornets were abundant in Palestine. In Ex. 23. 28; Deu. 7. 20, and Jos. 24. 12, the hornet is mentioned as used by God to drive out the enemies of Israel. The author of the book of Wisdom took these places in a literal sense (Wisd. 12. 8-10), and some modern authorities, in view of the extreme savageness of the Palestinian hornet, have followed him: but it is more probable that the passages are metaphorical.

Horns. (1) figuratively mentioned. 1 Sam. 2. 1; 2 Sam. 22. 3; Ps. 75. 4.
vision of. Dan. 7. 7; 8. 3; Hab. 3. 4; Rev. 5. 6; 12. 3; 13. 1; 17. 3.
(2) of the altar. 1 Kn. 1. 50; 2. 28.
(3) of iron, Zedekiah makes. 1 Kn. 22.

Horonaim, hŏr-ō-nā'-ĭm, 'two caverns.' Isa. 15. 5.

Horonite, hôr'-ŏn-īte, native of Beth-horon. Neh. 2. 10.

Horrible. Ps. 11. 6; 40. 2; Jer. 2. 12; Ezek. 32. 10.

Horse (Nah. 3. 2, 3; Deu. 17. 16). Heb. *Sûs*: Gk. ἵππος. Horses were not used as beasts of burden, but only for chase and war (for riding, and in chariots).

Horse described. Job 39. 19; Prov. 21. 31; Jer. 8. 6.

Horseleech (Prov. 30. 15). Heb. *'Alûkah*: LXX.: Zool. S. *Hæmopis sanguisuga*. H.: *Hirudo medicinalis*. T.: R. V. marg. 'vampire.' Horseleech = large leech. Leeches are common in Palestine, in stagnant waters, where they cling to the feet and legs of those who wade in such waters.

Horses, kings forbidden to multiply. Deu. 17. 16; Ps. 33. 17; 147. 10.
vision of. Zec. 1. 8; 6.; Rev. 6.

Hosah, hō'-săh, 'refuge.' Jos. 19. 29.

Hosanna, hō-săn'-nă, 'save, we pray,' children sing to Christ. Mat. 21. 9, 15; Mk. 11. 9; John 12. 13 (Ps. 118. 25, 26).

Hosea, hō-sē'-ă, 'salvation;' prophet. declares God's judgment against idolatrous Israel, Hos. 1.; 2.; 4. and his reconciliation, Hos. 2. 14; 11.; 13.; 14.

Hosen, trousers and stockings in one piece. Dan. 3. 21.

Hoshaiah, hō-shā'-ăh, 'Jehovah has saved.' Neh. 12. 32.

Hoshama, hŏ'-shă-mă. 1 Chr. 3. 18.

Hoshea, hō-shē'-ă, same as Hosea. (1) Joshua, Deu. 32. 44.
(2) 1 Chr. 27. 20.
(3) last king of Israel, his wicked reign, defeat by the king of Assyria, and captivity. 2 Kn. 15. 30; 17.

Hospitality. Rom. 12. 13; 1 Tim. 3. 2; Tit. 1. 8; Heb. 13. 2; 1 Pet. 4. 9.
instances of: Abraham, Gen. 18. Lot, Gen. 19. Laban, Gen. 24. 31. Jethro, Ex. 2. 20. Manoah, Jud. 13. 15. Samuel, 1 Sam. 9. 22. David, 2 Sam. 6. 19. Barzillai, &c., 2 Sam. 17. 27; 19. 32. The Shunammite, 2 Kn. 4. 8. Nehemiah, Neh. 5. 18. Job, Job 31. 17. Matthew, Lu. 5. 29. Zacchæus, Lu. 19. 6. Lydia, Acts 16. 15. Publius, &c., Acts 28. 2. Gaius, 3 John 5.

Host, the heavenly. Lu. 2. 13. *See* 1 Chr. 12. 22; Ps. 103. 21; 148. 2.
of the Lord. Gen. 32. 2; Jos. 5. 14; 1 Chr. 9. 19.

Hot. Ps. 39. 3; Prov. 6. 28; 1 Tim. 4. 2; Rev. 3. 15.

Hotham, hō'-thăm, 'signet ring.' 1 Chr. 7. 32.

Hothan, hō'-thăn, same as preceding. 1 Chr. 11. 44.

Hothir, hō'-thĭr, 'abundance.' 1 Chr. 25. 4.

Hough, to cut the hamstrings or 'hocks' of animals. Jos. 11. 6, 9; 2 Sam. 8. 4.

Hour. Mat. 10. 19; Lu. 12. 12, shall be given you in that same *h.*
20. 12, have wrought but one *h.*
24. 36; Mk. 13. 32, that *h.* knoweth no man.
26. 40; Mk. 14. 37, could ye not watch one *h.*?
Lu. 12. 39, what *h.* the thief would come.
22. 53, but this is your *h.*
John 5. 25; 16. 32, the *h.* is coming, and now is.
11. 9, are there not twelve *h.* in the day?
12. 27, save me from this *h.*
Acts 3. 1, at the *h.* of prayer.
Gal. 2. 5, give place, no, not for an *h.*
Rev. 3. 10, the *h.* of temptation.

Hour, the third, of day. Mat. 20. 3; Mk. 15. 25; Acts 2. 15; 23. 23.
the sixth. Mat. 27. 45; Mk. 15. 33; Lu. 23. 44; John 4. 6; 19. 14; Acts 10. 9.
the ninth. Acts 3. 1; 10. 3, 30.
at hand, cometh. Mat. 26. 45; John 4. 21; 5. 25; 12. 23; 13. 1; 16. 21; 17. 1.
that very same. Mat. 8. 13; 9. 22; 10. 19; 15. 28; 17. 18; Lu. 12. 12; John 4. 53; Acts 16. 18, 33; 22. 13; 1 Cor. 4. 11; 8. 7.
knoweth no man. Mat. 24. 36, 42; 25. 13; Mk. 13. 32; Rev. 3. 3.
of temptation, Rev. 3. 10. judgment, Rev. 14. 7; 18. 10.
figurative. Rev. 8. 1; 9. 15.

House. Gen. 28. 17, none other but the *h.* of God.
Deu. 8. 12, when thou hast built goodly *h.*
2 Kn. 20. 1; Isa. 38. 1, set thine *h.* in order.
20. 15, what have they seen in thine *h.*?
Neh. 13. 11, why is the *h.* of God forsaken?
Job 30. 23, *h.* appointed for all living.
Ps. 26. 8, have loved the habitation of thy *h.*
65. 4, satisfied with goodness of thy *h.*
69. 9; John 2. 17, the zeal of thine *h.*
84. 3, the sparrow hath found an *h.*
92. 13, planted in the *h.* of the Lord.
118. 26, blessed you out of the *h.* of the Lord.
Prov. 2. 18, her *h.* inclineth to death.
9. 1, wisdom hath builded her *h.*
12. 7, *h.* of the righteous shall stand.
19. 14, *h.* and riches are inheritance.
Eccl. 7. 2, *h.* of mourning, *h.* of feasting.
12. 3, when keepers of the *h.* shall tremble.
Isa. 3. 14, spoil of poor in your *h.*
5. 8, woe unto them that join *h.* to *h.*
64. 11, our holy and beautiful *h.* is burned.
Hos. 9. 15, I will drive them out of mine *h.*
Hag. 1. 4, and this *h.* lie waste.
1. 9, because of mine *h.* that is waste.
Mal. 3. 10, that there may be meat in mine *h.*
Mat. 7. 25; Lu. 6. 48, beat upon that *h.*
10. 12, when ye come into an *h.*
12. 25; Mk. 3. 25, *h.* divided cannot stand.
23. 38, your *h.* is left desolate.
24. 17; Mk. 13. 15, to take anything out of *h.*
Lu. 10. 7, go not from *h.* to *h.*
14. 23, that my *h.* may be filled.

Lu. 18. 14, went down to his *h.* justified.
John 12. 3, *h.* filled with odour.
14. 2, in my Father's *h.* are many mansions.
Acts 2. 46, breaking bread from *h.* to *h.* R. V. at home.
5. 42, in every *h.* ceased not to preach. R. V. at home.
10. 2; 16. 34; 18. 8, with all his *h.*
20. 20, I taught you from *h.* to *h.*
1 Cor. 11. 22, have ye not *h.* to eat in?
2 Cor. 5. 1, *h.* not made with hands.
Col. 4. 15, church in his *h.*
1 Tim. 3. 4, 5, 12, ruleth well his own *h.*
5. 8, especially for those of his own *h.* R. V. household.
2 Tim. 3. 6, which creep into *h.*
Tit. 1. 11, subvert whole *h.*
See Mat. 9. 6; Lu. 7. 44; 19. 5; Acts 4. 34.

Household. Gen. 18. 19, command his *h.* after him.
1 Sam. 27. 3; 2 Sam. 2. 3, every man with his *h.*
2 Sam. 6. 20, returned to bless his *h.*
Prov. 31. 27, looketh well to her *h.*
Mat. 10. 36, a man's foes shall be of his own *h.*
Gal. 6. 10, the *h.* of faith.
Eph. 2. 19, of the *h.* of God.
See Gen. 31. 37; 47. 12; 2 Sam. 17. 23.

House of God. Gen. 28. 17; Jud. 20. 18; 2 Chr. 5. 14; Ez. 5. 8, 15; 7. 20, 23; Neh. 6. 10; Ps. 84. 10; Isa. 6. 11; 60. 7; 64. 7; Ezek. 41. 5, 13; 43. 5; Mic. 4. 2; Zec. 7. 2; Mat. 12. 4; 1 Tim. 3. 15; Heb. 10. 21; 1 Pet. 4. 17.
(heaven). Acts 7. 49.
(altars). *See* Altar.
(for worship). *See* Temple.

Housetop. Ps. 129. 6; Mat. 10. 27; Acts 10. 9.

Howbeit, nevertheless. Jud. 4. 17.

Howl. Deu. 32. 10; Am. 8. 3; Jas. 5. 1.

Hukkok, hŭk'-kŏk, 'decreed.' Jos. 19. 34.

Hukok, hū'-kŏk, same as preceding. 1 Chr. 6. 75.

Hul, hŭl, 'circle' (?). Gen. 10. 23.

Huldah, hŭl'-dăh, 'weasel.' 2 Kn. 22. 14.

Huleh, Lake of. *See* Merom.

Huleh Lily. *See* Lily.

Humble. Deu. 8. 2, to *h.* thee and prove thee.
2 Chr. 33. 12, *h.* himself greatly.
Ps. 9. 12; 10. 12, forgetteth not cry of the *h.* R. V. poor.
34. 2, the *h.* shall hear thereof. R. V. meek.
35. 13, I *h.* my soul with fasting. R. V. afflicted.
113. 6, *h.* himself to behold things in heaven.
Prov. 16. 19, better be of *h.* spirit. R. V. lowly.
Isa. 57. 15, of contrite and *h.* spirit.
Mat. 18. 4; 23. 12; Lu. 14. 11; 18. 14, *h.* himself.
Phil. 2. 8, he *h.* himself.
Jas. 4. 6; 1 Pet. 5. 5, God giveth grace to the *h.*
1 Pet. 5. 6, *h.* yourselves under mighty hand of God.
See Isa. 2. 11; 5. 15; Lam. 3. 20.

Humbly. 2 Sam. 16. 4; Mic. 6. 8.

Humility. Prov. 15. 33; 18. 12, before honour [is *h.*
22. 4, by *h.* are riches.

Humility. Prov. 15. 33; 18. 12; 22. 4; Col. 2. 18, 23.
enjoined. Mic. 6. 8; Mat. 18.; 20. 25; Mk. 9. 33; 10. 43; Lu. 9. 46; 14. 7; 22. 24; Eph. 4. 2; Col. 3. 12; Phil. 2. 3; Jas. 4. 10; 1 Pet. 5. 5.
benefits of. Ps. 34. 2; 69. 32; Prov. 3. 34; Isa. 57. 15; Mat. 18. 4; Lu. 14. 11; Jas. 4. 6.
profession of. Ps. 131.; Acts 20. 19.

Humtah, hŭm'-tăh, 'a lizard' (?). Jos. 15. 54.

Hunger. Deu. 8. 3, he suffered thee to *h.*
Job 18. 12, his strength shall be *h.*-bitten.
Ps. 34. 10, young lions do lack, and suffer *h.*
Prov. 19. 15, an idle soul shall suffer *h.*
Isa. 49. 10, shall not *h.* nor thirst.
Jer. 38. 9, he is like to die for *h.*
Mat. 5. 6; Lu. 6. 21, blessed are ye that *h.*
Lu. 6. 25, woe unto you that are full! for ye shall *h.*
John 6. 35, he that cometh to me shall never *h.*
Rom. 12. 20, if thine enemy *h.*
1 Cor. 4. 11, we both *h.* and thirst.
1 Cor. 11. 34, if any man *h.*, let him eat at home.
Rev. 7. 16, they shall *h.* no more.

Hunger. Ex. 16. 3; Ps. 34. 10; Jer. 38. 9; Lam. 4. 9; Lu. 15. 17; 2 Cor. 11 27; Rev. 6. 8.
(and thirst). Ps. 107. 5; Isa. 49. 10; 55.; Mat. 5. 6; John 6 35; Rev. 7. 16.

Hungred, an, very hungry. Mat. 4. 2; 12. 1; 25. 35 (Job 24. 10, R. V.).

Hungry. Job 22. 7, withholden bread from *h.*
24. 10, they take away the sheaf from the *h.*
Ps. 50. 12, if I were *h.*, I would not tell thee.
107. 5, *h.* and thirsty, their soul fainted in them.
107. 9, he filleth the *h.* soul with goodness.
146. 7, which giveth food to the *h.*
Prov. 25. 21, if thine enemy be *h.*, give him bread [to eat.
27. 7, to the *h.* every bitter thing is sweet.
Isa. 29. 8, when a *h.* man dreameth.
58. 7, is it not to deal thy bread to the *h.*?
65. 13, my servants eat but ye shall be *h.*
Ezek. 18. 7, given his bread to the *h.*
Lu. 1. 53, he hath filled the *h.* with good things.
Acts 10. 10, and he became very *h.*
1 Cor. 11. 21, one is *h.*, and another drunken.
Phil. 4. 12, instructed both to be full and to be *h.*
See Prov. 6. 30; Isa. 8. 21; 9. 20; Mk. 11. 12.

Hunt. 1 Sam. 26. 20, as when one doth *h.* a partridge.
Jer. 16. 16, *h.* them from every mountain.
Ezek. 13. 18, *h.* souls of my people.
Mic. 7. 2, they *h.* every man his brother.
See Gen. 10. 9; 27. 5; 1 Sam. 24. 11.

Hunting. Prov. 12. 27.

Hupham, hū'-phăm, 'inhabitant of the shore' (?). Num. 26. 39.

Huphamites, hū'-phăm-ītes, descendants of Hupham. Num. 26. 39.

Huppah, hŭp'-păh, 'covering.' 1 Chr. 24. 13.

Huppim, hŭp'-pĭm, 'coverings.' Gen. 46. 21.

Hur, hur, 'cavern.' Ex. 17. 10.

Hurai, hū-rā'-ī, another form of Hiddai. 1 Chr. 11. 32.

Huram, hū'-răm, another form of Hiram. 2 Chr. 2. 13.

Huri, hū'-rī, 'linen-weaver' (?). 1 Chr. 5. 14.

Hurl. Num. 35. 20; 1 Chr. 12. 2; Job 27. 21.

Hurt. Ps. 15. 4, that sweareth to his own *h.*
Eccl. 8. 9, ruleth over another to his own *h.*
Isa. 11. 9, shall not *h.* nor destroy.
Jer. 6. 14; 8. 11, have healed *h.* slightly.
8. 21, for the *h.* of my people.
25. 6, provoke not, I will do no *h.*
Dan. 3. 25, they have no *h.*
6. 23, no manner of *h.* found upon him.
Mk. 16. 18, deadly thing, it shall not *h.*
Lu. 10. 19, nothing shall by any means *h.* you.
Acts 18. 10, no man set on thee to *h.* thee. R. V. [harm.
Rev. 6. 6, *h.* not the oil and the wine.
See Rev. 7. 2; 9. 4; 11. 5.

Hurtful. Ez. 4. 15; Ps. 144. 10; 1 Tim. 6. 9.

Husband. Ex. 4. 25, a bloody *h.* art thou.
Prov. 12. 4, virtuous wife a crown to her *h.*
31. 11, 23, 28, her *h.* doth safely trust.
Isa. 54. 5, thy Maker is thy *h.*
John 4. 16, go, call thy *h.*
1 Cor. 7. 16, whether thou shalt save thy *h.*
14. 35, let them ask their *h.* at home.
Eph. 5. 22, submit yourselves to your *h.*
5. 25; Col. 3. 19, *h.*, love your wives.
1 Tim. 3. 12, the *h.* of one wife.
Tit. 2. 4, teach young women to love their *h.*
2. 5, obedient to their own *h.*
1 Pet. 3. 1, be in subjection to your *h.*
3. 7, ye *h.*, dwell with them.
See Gen. 3. 6; Ru. 1. 11; Esth. 1. 17, 20.

Husband, figuratively. Isa. 54. 5; Hos. 2. 7.

Husbandman. (1) a farmer. Gen. 9. 20.
(2) John 15. 1; 2 Tim. 2. 6; Jas. 5. 7.

Husbandmen, parable of. Mat. 21. 33; Mk. 12. 1; Lu. 20. 9.

Hushah, hū'-shăh, 'haste.' 1 Chr. 4. 4.

Hushai, hū'-shāi, 'hasting.' 2 Sam. 15. 32.
defeats Ahithophel's counsel. 2 Sam. 16. 16; 17. 5.

Husham, hū'-shăm, 'haste.' Gen. 36. 34.
Hushathite, hū'-shă-thīte, inhabitant of Hushah. 2 Sam. 23. 27.
Hushim, hū'-shĭm, 'those who make haste.' Gen. 46. 23.
Husks (Lu. 15. 16). Gk. κεράτια: Bot. N. *Ceratonia siliqua:* R. V. marg. correctly, 'the pods of the carob tree,' i. e., a locust tree. The pods are 6 to 12 inches long.
Huz, hŭz, same as Uz. Gen. 22. 21.
Huzzab, hŭz'-zăb, 'it is decreed.' Nah. 2. 7.
Hyæna (1 Sam. 13. 18; Isa. 13. 21; Jer. 12. 9). Heb. *Tsĕbûa* or *Tsĕbôa* (pl. *Tsĕbôïm*), [*Ôah*, pl. *Ôhim.*]
The word does not occur in the A. V.; but the hyæna is common in Palestine; and there are passages where some suppose it is meant; e. g., Isa. 13. 21, *ôchim*, 'doleful creatures'; and Jer. 12. 9, where *tsabûa* ('speckled bird,' A. V.) is rendered by many 'hyæna.'
Hymenæus, hȳ-mĕ-næ'-ŭs, 'belonging to Hymen.' 1 Tim. 1. 20; 2 Tim. 2. 17.
Hymn. The hymn sung by our Lord and His Apostles after the Last Supper (Mat. 26. 30; Mk. 14. 26) was very possibly part of the 'Great Paschal Hallel,' or 'Hymn of Praise,' consisting of Ps. 113.–118. But the singing of hymns as distinct from Psalms was from the first a feature in Christian worship, both public and private (Acts 16. 25, R. V.; Eph. 5. 19; Col. 3. 16). It is probable that Eph. 5. 14 contains a fragment of an early Christian hymn.
Hypocrisy. Mat. 23. 28, within ye are full of *h.*
Mk. 12. 15, he, knowing their *h.*
Lu. 12. 1, leaven of Pharisees, which is *h.*
Jas. 3. 17, wisdom is pure, and without *h.*
Hypocrisy. Isa. 29. 15; **Mat. 23. 28; Mk. 12. 15;** 1 Tim. 4. 2; Rev. 3. 1.
penalty of. Job 8. 13; 13. 16; 15. 34; 20. 5; 27. 8; 36. 13; Mat. 24. 51.
denounced. Mat. 6. 2; 7. 5; 1 Pet. 2. 1.
Hypocrite. Job 8. 13, the *h.* hope shall perish. R. V. of the godless man.
20. 5, the joy of the *h.* but for a moment.
36. 13, the *h.* in heart. R. V. godless.
Prov. 11. 9, the *h.* destroyeth his neighbour.
Isa. 9. 17, every one is an *h.* R. V. profane.
Mat. 6. 2, 5, 16, as the *h.* do.
7. 5; Lu. 6. 42; 13. 15, thou *h.*
15. 7; 16. 3; 22. 18; Mk. 7. 6; Lu. 12. 56, ye *h.*
23. 13; Lu. 11. 44, woe unto you, *h.*
24. 51, appoint his portion with the *h.*
Hypocritical. Ps. 35. 16; Isa. 10. 6.
Hyssop. Heb. *Ézôb:* Gk. ὕσσωπος: Bot. N. *Origanum maru.* Some labiate plant, like thyme, mint, sage, probably 'marjoram.' This is the hyssop of John 19. 29; tied to a reed, in Mat. 27. 48 and Mk. 15. 36.
See Ex. 12. 22; Lev. 14. 4; Num. 19. 6; 1 Kn. 4. 33; Ps. 51. 7; Heb. 9. 19.

I am. Ex. 3. 14; John 8. 58; Rev. 1. 18.
Ibhar, ĭb'-hăr, 'He (i. e., God) chooses.' 2 Sam. [5. 15.
Ibleam, ĭb'-lĕ-ăm, 'He destroys the people.' Jos. 17. 11.
Ibneiah, ĭb-nei'-ăh, 'Jehovah will build up.' 1 Chr. 9. 8.
Ibnijah, ĭb-nī'-jăh, same as preceding. 1 Chr. 9. 8.
Ibri, ĭb'-rī, 'Hebrew.' 1 Chr. 24. 27.
Ibzan, ĭb'-zăn, 'active' (?). Jud. 12. 8.
Ice. Job 6. 16; Ps. 147. 17. [14. 3.
I-chabod, ī'-chă-bŏd, 'inglorious.' 1 Sam. 4. 21;
Iconium, ī-cō'-nĭ-ŭm, a city on the table land of Lycaonia; gospel preached at. Acts 13. 51; 14. 1, 3; 16. 2.
Paul persecuted at. 2 Tim. 3. 11.
Idalah, ī'-dă-lăh, 'snares' (?). Jos. 19. 15.
Idbash, ĭd'-băsh, 'honeyed.' 1 Chr. 4. 3.
Iddo, ĭd'-dō. (1) 'loving' (?). 1 Chr. 27. 21. (2) Ez. 8. 17. (3) 'seasonable.' Zec. 1. 1.
Idle. Ex. 5. 8, 17, they be *i.*
Prov. 19. 15, an *i.* soul shall hunger.
31. 27, she eateth not bread of *i.*
Mat. 12. 36, every *i.* word men speak.
20. 3, 6, others standing *i.*
Idleness reproved. Prov. 6. 6; 18. 9; 24. 30; Rom. 12. 11; 1 Thes. 4. 11; 2 Thes. 3. 10; Heb. 6. 12.
evil of. Prov. 10. 4; 12. 24; 13. 4; 19. 15; 20. 4, 13; 21. 25; Eccl. 10. 18; Ezek. 16. 49; 1 Tim. 5. 13.
Idol. 1 Chr. 16. 26; Ps. 96. 5, all gods of the people are *i.*
Isa. 66. 3, as if he blessed an *i.*
Jer. 50. 38, they are mad upon their *i.*
Hos. 4. 17, Ephraim is joined to *i.*
Acts 15. 20, abstain from pollutions of *i.*
1 Cor. 8. 4, we know an *i.* is nothing.
8. 7, with conscience of the *i.*
1 Thes. 1. 9, ye turned to God from *i.*
1 John 5. 21, keep yourselves from *i.*
Idolaters not to be spared. Deu. 7. 16; 13. 8, 15.
Idolatry. The idolatry into which the Israelites fell, and against which the prophets protested, was of two forms. (1) The worship of heathen idols, with all the immoralities connected with it. (2) The worship of Jehovah by means of images.
The causes of the people's lapse into idolatry were twofold. (1) The seductive fascinations of the free immorality of much of the heathen worship; and (2) the great difficulty of realizing an unseen, spiritual God.
Idolatry. Ex. 20. 2; 22. 20; 23. 13; Lev. 26. 1; Deu. 4. 15; 5. 7; 11. 16; 17. 2; 18. 9; 27. 15; Ps. 97. 7; Jer. 2. 11; 1 Cor. 10. 7, 14; Gal. 5. 20; Col. 3. 5; 1 John 5. 21.
folly of. 1 Kn. 18. 26; Ps. 115. 4; 135. 15; Isa. 40. 19; 41.; 44. 9; 46. 1; Jer. 2. 26, 10.
monuments of, to be destroyed. Ex. 23. 24; 34. 13; Deu. 7. 5.
enticers to. Deu. 13. 1.
Israelites guilty of, Ex. 32.; Num. 25.; Jud. 2. 11; 3. 7; 8. 33; 18. 30; 2 Kn. 17. 12. also Micah, Jud. 17. Solomon, 1 Kn. 11. 5. Jeroboam, 1 Kn. 12. 28. Ahab, &c., 1 Kn. 16. 31; 18. 19. Manasseh, 2 Kn. 21. 4. Ahaz, 2 Chr. 28. 2. Nebuchadnezzar, &c., Dan. 3.; 5. inhabitants of Lystra, Acts 14. 11. Athens, Acts 17. 16. Ephesus, Acts 19. 28.
zeal of Asa against. 1 Kn. 15. 12.
of Jehoshaphat. 2 Chr. 17. 6.
of Hezekiah. 2 Chr. 30. 13.
of Josiah. 2 Chr. 34.
punishment of. Deu. 17. 2; Jer. 8. 1; 16. 1; 44. 21; Hos. 8. 5; 1 Cor. 6. 9; Eph. 5. 5; Rev. 14. 9; 21. 8; 22. 15.
Idols, meats offered to. Rom. 14.; 1 Cor. 8.
Idumæa, Idumea, ī-dū-mæ'-ă, ī-dū-mē'-ă, same as Edom. Isa. 34. 5.
Igal, ī'-găl, 'He redeems.' Num. 13. 7. [4.
Igdaliah, ĭg-dă-lī'-ăh, 'Jehovah is great.' Jer. 35.
Igeal, ī'-gĕ-ăl, same as Igal. 1 Chr. 3. 22.
Ignorance. Acts 3. 17, through *i.* ye did it.
17. 30, the times of *i.* God winked at.
Eph. 4. 18, alienated through *i.*
1 Pet. 2. 15, put to silence *i.* of foolish men.
Ignorance, sin offerings for. Lev. 4.; 5. 15, 16; Num. 15. 22, 24, 28.
effects of. Rom. 10. 3; 2 Pet. 3. 5.
Paul's deprecation of. 1 Cor. 10. 1; 12.; 2 Cor. 1. 8; 1 Thes. 4. 13.; 2 Pet. 3. 8.
Ignorant. Ps. 73. 22, so foolish was I, and *i.*
Isa. 63. 16, though Abraham be *i.* of us. R. V knoweth not.
Acts 4. 13, perceived they were *i.* men.
Rom. 10. 3, being *i.* of God's righteousness.
1 Cor. 14. 38, if any man be *i.*, let him be *i.*
2 Cor. 2. 11, not *i.* of his devices.
Heb. 5. 2, can have compassion on the *i.*
2 Pet. 3. 5, they willingly are *i.* R. V. forget.
See Acts 17. 23; 1 Tim. 1. 13.
Iim, ī'-ĭm. (1) 'ruins.' Num. 33. 45.
(2) i. e., 'wolves.' Isa. 13. 12 (marg.).
Ije-abarim, ī'-jĕ-ăb'-ă-rĭm, 'ruinous heaps of Abarim.' Num. 21. 11.

Ijon, ī'-jŏn, 'a ruin.' 1 Kn. 15. 20.
Ikkesh, ĭk'-kĕsh, 'perverse.' 2 Sam. 23. 26.
Ilai, ī'-lā-ī, 'most high' (?). 1 Chr. 11. 29.
Ill favoured, ill looking. Gen. 41. 3.
Illuminated, i. e., enlightened (R. V.). Heb. 10. 32.
Illyricum, ĭl-lўr'-ĭ-cŭm, gospel preached there. Rom. 15. 19.
Image. Gen. 1. 26; 5. 3; Ps. 73. 20; Mat. 22. 20; 1 Cor. 15. 49; Heb. 1. 3.
Images prohibited. Ex. 20. 4; Lev. 26. 1; Deu. 16. 22.
Imagination. Gen. 6. 5; 8. 21, *i.* of heart evil.
Deu. 29. 19; Jer. 23. 17, walk in *i.* of heart. R. V. stubbornness.
1 Chr. 28. 9, understandeth all the *i.* of thoughts.
Rom. 1. 21, vain in their *i.* R. V. reasonings.
2 Cor. 10. 5, casting down *i.*
See Deu. 31. 21; Prov. 6. 18; Lam. 3. 60.
Imagine. Ps. 62. 3, how long will ye *i.* mischief? R. V. set upon.
Nah. 1. 9, what do ye *i.* against the Lord?
1. 11, there is one that *i.* evil.
Zec. 7. 10; 8. 17, let none *i.* evil.
See Job 21. 27; Ps. 10. 2; 21. 11; Acts 4. 25.
Imla, ĭm'-lă, same as IMLAH. 2 Chr. 18. 7.
Imlah, ĭm-lăh, 'He will fill up.' 1 Kn. 22. 8.
Immanuel, ĭm-măn'-ū-ĕl (*see* EMMANUEL), 'God with us.' Isa. 7. 14; Mat. 1. 23.
Immer, ĭm'-mĕr, 'eloquent' (?). 1 Chr. 9. 12.
Immortal. 1 Tim. 1. 17. R. V. incorruptible.
Immortality. Rom. 2. 7; 1 Cor. 15. 53; 1 Tim. 6. 16; 2 Tim. 1. 10.
Immutability of GOD's counsel. Heb. 6. 17.
Imna, ĭm'-nă, 'He keeps back.' 1 Chr. 7. 35.
Imnah, ĭm'-năh, 'good fortune' (?). 1 Chr. 7. 30.
Impart. Job 39. 17; Lu. 3. 11; Rom. 1. 11; 1 Thes. 2. 8.
Impediment. Mk. 7. 32.
Impenitent. Rom. 2. 5.
Implacable. Rom. 1. 31.
Implead, to accuse, indict, plead against. Acts 19. 38.
Importable, insufferable, insupportable. Prayer of Manasses (Apoc.).
Impose. Ez. 7. 24; Heb. 9. 10.
Impossible. Mat. 19. 26; Mk. 10. 27; Lu. 18. 27, with men it is *i.*
Lu. 1. 37; 18. 27, with God nothing *i.* R. V. void of power.
See Mat. 17. 20; Lu. 17. 1; Heb. 6. 4, 18; 11. 6.
Impotent, powerless, without strength. John 5. 3; Acts 4. 9; 14. 8.
Impoverish. Jud. 6. 6; Isa. 40. 20; Jer. 5. 17.
Imprisonment. Ez. 7. 26; 2 Cor. 6. 5; Heb. 11. 36.
Impudent. Prov. 7. 13; Ezek. 2. 4; 3. 7.
Impute. Lev. 17. 4, blood shall be *i.* to that man.
Ps. 32. 2; Rom. 4. 8, to whom the Lord *i.* not iniquity.
Hab. 1. 11, *i.* his power to his god. R. V. even he whose might is.
Rom. 5. 13, sin is not *i.* when there is no law.
See 1 Sam. 22. 15; 2 Sam. 19. 19; 2 Cor. 5. 19.
Imrah, ĭm'-răh, 'stubbornness.' 1 Chr. 7. 36.
Imri, ĭm'-rī, 'eloquent.' 1 Chr. 9. 4.
Incense. Ex. 30. 22; 37. 29.
offered. Lev. 10. 1; 16. 13; Num. 16. 46.
figurative. Rev. 8. 3.
Incest condemned. Lev. 18.; 20. 17; Deu. 22. 30; 27. 20; Ezek. 22. 11; Am. 2. 7.
cases of. Gen. 19. 33; 35. 22; 38. 18; 2 Sam. 13.; 16. 21; Mk. 6. 17; 1 Cor. 5. 1.
Incline. Jos. 24. 23, *i.* your hearts to the Lord.
1 Kn. 8. 58, that he may *i.* hearts to keep law.
Ps. 40. 1; 116. 2, he *i.* unto me, and heard my cry.
119. 36, *i.* my heart to thy testimonies.
Jer. 7. 24; 11. 8; 17. 23; 34. 14, nor *i.* ear.
See Prov. 2. 18; Jer. 25. 4; 44. 5.
Inclosed. Ps. 17. 10; 22. 16; Lu. 5. 6.
Incontinency. 1 Cor. 7. 5.
Incontinent. 2 Tim. 3. 3. R. V. without self-control.
Incorruptible. 1 Cor. 9. 25, an *i.* crown.
1 Pet. 1. 4, inheritance *i.*
1. 23, born of *i.* seed.
See Rom. 1. 23; 1 Cor. 15. 42, 50, 52–54.

Increase (*n.*). Lev. 25. 36, take no usury or *i.*
26. 4, the land shall yield her *i.*
Deu. 14. 22, 28, tithe all *i.*
Ps. 67. 6; Ezek. 34. 27, earth shall yield her *i.*
Prov. 18. 20, with the *i.* of his lips.
Eccl. 5. 10, not satisfied with *i.*
Isa. 9. 7, *i.* of his government.
1 Cor. 3. 6, 7, God gave the *i.*
See Jer. 2. 3; Eph. 4. 16; Col. 2. 19.
Increase (*v.*). Job 8. 7, thy latter end shall greatly *i.*
Ps. 4. 7, that their corn and wine *i.*
62. 10, if riches *i.*, set not your heart upon them.
115. 14, Lord shall *i.* you more and more.
Prov. 1. 5; 9. 9, a wise man will *i.* learning.
11. 24, there is that scattereth, and yet *i.*
Eccl. 1. 18, he that *i.* knowledge *i.* sorrow.
Isa. 9. 3, multiplied the nation, and not *i.* the joy.
40. 29, he *i.* strength.
Ezek. 36. 37, *i.* them with men like a flock.
Dan. 12. 4, knowledge shall be *i.*
Hos. 12. 1, he daily *i.* lies. R. V. multiplieth.
Hab. 2. 6, that *i.* that which is not his.
Lu. 2. 52, Jesus *i.* in wisdom. R. V. advanced.
Acts 6. 7, word of God *i.*
16. 5, churches *i.* daily.
Rev. 3. 17, I am rich, and *i.* with goods. R. V. have gotten.
See Eccl. 2. 9; 5. 11; Mk. 4. 8; Col. 2. 19.
Incredible. Acts 26. 8.
Incurable. 2 Chr. 21. 18; Jer. 15. 18; Mic. 1. 9.
Indeed. 1 Kn. 8. 27; 2 Chr. 6. 18, will God *i.* dwell on the earth?
1 Chr. 4. 10, bless me *i.*
Mk. 11. 32, a prophet *i.*
Lu. 24. 34, the Lord is risen *i.*
John 1. 47, an Israelite *i.*
6. 55, my flesh is meat *i.*, and my blood is drink *i.*
8. 36, ye shall be free *i.*
1 Tim. 5. 3, that are widows *i.*
See Gen. 37. 8; Isa. 6. 9; Rom. 8. 7.
India, ĭn'-dĭ-ă. Esth. 1. 1.
Indifferent, fair, impartial. Ecclus. 42. 5.
Indignation. Ps. 78. 49, wrath, *i.*, and trouble.
Isa. 26. 20, till the *i.* be overpast.
Nah. 1. 6, who can stand before his *i.*?
Mat. 20. 24, moved with *i.*
26. 8, they had *i.*
2 Cor. 7. 11, yea, what *i.*
Heb. 10. 27, fearful looking for of fiery *i.* R. V. a fierceness of fire.
Rev. 14. 10, the cup of his *i.* R. V. anger.
See Zec. 1. 12; Acts 5. 17; Rom. 2. 8.
Inditing, dictating, composing. Ps. 45. 1.
Industry. Gen. 2. 15; 3. 23; Prov. 6. 6; 10. 4; 12. 24; 13. 4; 21. 5; 22. 29; 27. 23; Eph. 4. 28; 1 Thes. 4. 11; 2 Thes. 3. 12; Tit. 3. 14.
rewarded. 1 Kn. 11. 28; Prov. 13. 11; 31. 13.
Inexcusable. Rom. 2. 1.
Infant. Job 3. 16; Isa. 65. 20; Lu. 18. 15.
Infidel. 2 Cor. 6. 15; 1 Tim. 5. 8.
Infinite. Job 22. 5; Ps. 147. 5; Nah. 3. 9.
Infirmities, human, borne by Christ (Isa. 53. 4); Mat. 8. 17; Heb. 4. 15.
Infirmity. Ps. 77. 10, this is mine *i.*
Prov. 18. 14, spirit of man will sustain his *i.*
Mat. 8. 17, himself took our *i.*
Rom. 6. 19, the *i.* of your flesh.
8. 26, the Spirit helpeth our *i.*
15. 1, bear the *i.* of the weak.
2 Cor. 12. 5, 10, glory in mine *i.* R. V. weaknesses.
1 Tim. 5. 23, wine for thine often *i.*
Heb. 4. 15, touched with the feeling of our *i.*
See Lu. 5. 15; 7. 21; John 5. 5; Heb. 5. 2.
Inflame. Isa. 5. 11; 57. 5.
Inflicted. 2 Cor. 2. 6.
Influences. Job 38. 31.
Informed, instructed, taught. Dan. 9. 22.
Ingathering, feast of. Ex. 23. 16; 34. 22.
Ingrafted. Jas. 1. 21.
Ingratitude to God. Rom. 1. 21.
exemplified: Israel, Deu. 32. 18. Saul, 1 Sam. 15. 17. David, 2 Sam. 12. 7, 9. Nebuchadnezzar, Dan. 5. lepers, Lu. 17.

punished. Neh. 9. 27; Hos. 2. 8, 9. [3. 2.
characteristic of the wicked. Ps. 38. 20; 2 Tim.
its penalty. Prov. 17. 13; Jer. 18. 20.
Inhabit. Isa. 57. 15; 65. 21; Am. 9. 14.
Inhabitant. Num. 13. 32, land eateth up *i.*
Jud. 5. 23, curse bitterly the *i.*
Isa. 6. 11, cities wasted without *i.*
33. 24, *i.* shall not say, I am sick.
40. 22, the *i.* thereof are as grasshoppers.
Jer. 44. 22, land without an *i.*
See Jer. 2. 15; 4. 7; Zec. 8. 21.
Inherit. Ex. 32. 13, they shall *i.* it for ever.
Ps. 25. 13, shall *i.* the earth.
37. 11, the meek shall *i.* the earth.
Prov. 14. 18, the simple *i.* folly.
Mat. 19. 29, shall *i.* everlasting life.
25. 34, *i.* kingdom prepared.
Mk. 10. 17; Lu. 10. 25; 18. 18, *i.* eternal life.
1 Cor. 6. 9; 15. 50; Gal. 5. 21, not *i.* the kingdom.
Heb. 12. 17, when he would have *i.* the blessing.
Inheritance. Ps. 16. 5, Lord is portion of mine *i.*
47. 4, shall choose our *i.* for us.
Prov. 20. 21, an *i.* may be gotten hastily.
Eccl. 7. 11, wisdom good with an *i.*
Mk. 12. 7; Lu. 20. 14, the *i.* shall be ours.
Lu. 12. 13, that he divide the *i.* with me.
Acts 20. 32; 26. 18, an *i.* among the sanctified.
Eph. 1. 14, earnest of our *i.*
Heb. 9. 15, promise of eternal *i.* [6. 12.
Inheritance. Num. 27.; 36.; Deu. 21. 15; Heb.
in Christ. Eph. 1. 11, 14; 5. 5; Col. 1. 12; 3. 24;
1 Pet. 1. 4; 3. 9; Rev. 21. 7.
Iniquity. Ex. 20. 5; 34. 7; Num. 14. 18; Deu. 5.
9, visiting the *i.* of the fathers.
34. 7; Num. 14. 18, forgiving *i.* and transgression.
Job 4. 8, they that plow *i.* reap the same.
13. 26, to possess the *i.* of my youth.
34. 32, if I have done *i.*, I will do no more.
Ps. 25. 11, pardon mine *i.*, for it is great.
32. 5, mine *i.* have I not hid.
39. 11, when thou dost correct man for *i.*
51. 5, I was shapen in *i.*
66. 18, if I regard *i.* in my heart.
69. 27, add *i.* to their *i.*
79. 8, remember not former *i.*
90. 8, thou hast set our *i.*
103. 3, who forgiveth all thine *i.*
103. 10, not rewarded according to *i.*
107. 17, fools, because of *i.*, are afflicted.
119. 3, they also do no *i.* R. V. unrighteousness.
130. 3, if thou shouldest mark *i.*
Prov. 22. 8, he that soweth *i.* shall reap vanity.
Isa. 1. 4, a people laden with *i.*
6. 7, thine *i.* is taken away.
40. 2, her *i.* is pardoned.
53. 5, he was bruised for our *i.*
59. 2, your *i.* separated between you and God.
Jer. 5. 25, your *i.* turned away these things.
Ezek. 18. 30, repent, so *i.* shall not be your ruin.
Hab. 1. 13, canst not look on *i.* R. V. perverseness.
Mat. 24. 12, because *i.* shall abound.
Acts 1. 18, purchased with reward of *i.*
8. 23, in the bond of *i.*
Rom. 6. 19, servants to *i.* unto *i.*
2 Thes. 2. 7, the mystery of *i.* R. V. lawlessness.
2 Tim. 2. 19, depart from *i.* R. V. unrighteousness.
Jas. 3. 6, a world of *i.*
See Ps. 36. 2; Jer. 31. 30; Ezek. 3. 18; 18. 26.
Injurious, insolent, outrageous. 1 Tim. 1. 13.
Injustice. Ex. 22. 21; 23. 6; Lev. 19. 15; Deu. 16. 19; 24. 17; Job 31. 13; Ps. 82. 2; Prov. 22. 16; 29. 7; Jer. 22. 3; Lu. 16. 10.
results of. Prov. 11. 7; 28. 8; Mic. 6. 10; Am. 5. 11; 8. 5; 1 Thes. 4. 6; 2 Pet. 2. 9.
Ink. Jer. 36. 18; 2 Cor. 3. 3; 2 John 12; 3 John 13.
Inn was originally only a plot of ground, near a spring or well, and sometimes secured by a wall or fence, allotted as a camping-ground for the use of travellers. This was the 'inn' of the O. T. (Gen. 42. 27; 43. 21, &c., R. V. lodging place). In later times, some wealthy benefactor would raise the wall, build a few arches, unite them to the wall by a roof, close them with doors, and separate them by partitions, thus providing a separate room for each party; while the cattle were littered in the central open space, or in sheds abutting on the outside wall, or in natural caves around it. This is the modern khan or caravansary, and such, it is thought, was 'the inn' at Bethlehem (Lu. 2. 7); though the word translated 'inn' may simply mean 'guestchamber,' and is so rendered in Mk. 14. 14; Lu. 22. 11.
Innocent. Job 4. 7, who ever perished, being *i.*?
9. 23, laugh at trial of *i.*
27. 17, the *i.* shall divide the silver. [clear.
Ps. 19. 13, *i.* from the great transgression. R. V.
Prov. 28. 20, he that maketh haste to be rich shall not be *i.* R. V. unpunished.
Jer. 2. 34; 19. 4, blood of the *i.*
See Gen. 20. 5; Ex. 23. 7; Mat. 27. 24.
Innocents slain. Mat. 2. 16.
Innumerable. Job 21. 33; Ps. 40. 12; Heb. 12. 22.
Inordinate. Ezek. 23. 11; Col. 3. 5.
Inquisition, search, examination. Deu. 19. 18; Esth. 2. 23; Ps. 9. 12.
Inscription. Acts 17. 23.
Insects and the smaller animals of the Bible.

Ant	Horseleech
Bee	Lice
Beetle	Locust
Caterpillar	Manna
Cochineal	Mosquito
Flea	Moth
Fly	Scorpion
Gadfly	Snail
Gnat	Spider
Grasshopper	Worm
Hornet	

Inspiration. Job 32. 8. R. V. breath.
Inspiration of Scripture. Lu. 1. 70; 2 Tim. 3. 16; Heb. 1. 1; 2 Pet. 1. 21.
Instant. (1) Rom. 12. 12. R. V. stedfast. [4. 2.
(2) urgent, importunate. Lu. 23. 23, &c.; 2 Tim.
Instantly, with urgent importunity. Acts 26. 7.
Instruct. Neh. 9. 20, thy good spirit to *i.* them.
Ps. 16. 7, my reins *i.* me in night season.
32. 8, I will *i.* thee and teach thee.
Isa. 40. 14, who *i.* him?
Mat. 13. 52, every scribe *i.* unto the kingdom. R. V. made a disciple unto.
Phil. 4. 12, in all things I am *i.* R. V. have I learned the secret.
See Prov. 21. 11; Acts 18. 25; 2 Tim. 2. 25.
Instruction. Ps. 50. 17, thou hatest *i.*
Prov. 1. 7; 15. 5, fools despise *i.*
4. 13, take fast hold of *i.*
8. 33, hear *i.*, and be wise.
12. 1, whoso loveth *i.* loveth knowledge. R. V. correction.
16. 22, the *i.* of fools is folly.
24. 32, I looked upon it, and received *i.*
2 Tim. 3. 16, profitable for *i.*
See Jer. 35. 13; Zep. 3. 7.
Instruction promised. Job 33. 16; Ps. 32. 8; Prov. 10. 17; 12. 1; 13. 1; Mat. 13. 52; 2 Tim. 3. 16.
recommended. Prov. 1. 2, 8; 4. 13; 9. 9; 19. 20; 23. 12.
hated by wicked. Ps. 50. 17; Prov. 1. 22; 5. 12; Jer. 17. 23.
consequence of rejecting. Prov. 13. 18; 15. 32.
Instrument. Ps. 7. 13, hath prepared *i.* of death.
Isa. 41. 15, a new sharp threshing *i.*
Ezek. 33. 32, of one that can play on an *i.*
Rom. 6. 13, members *i.* of unrighteousness.
See Num. 35. 16; Ps. 68. 25; 150. 4.
Integrity. Job 2. 3, he holdeth fast his *i.*
31. 6, that God may know my *i.*
Ps. 25. 21, let *i.* preserve me.
26. 1, I walked in *i.*
Prov. 11. 3, the *i.* of the upright.
19. 1; 20. 7, that walketh in his *i.*
Integrity. Gen. 20. 5; 1 Sam. 12. 3; 2 Kn. 12.

15; 22. 7; Job 2. 3; Ps. 7. 8; 26. 1; 41. 12; 78. 72; Prov. 11. 3; 19. 1; 20. 7.

Intend, to meditate, plan, plot. Ps. 21. 11.

Intents. Jer. 30. 24; Heb. 4. 12.

Intercession. Isa. 53. 12, make *i.* for transgressors.
Rom. 8. 26, the Spirit itself maketh *i.*
Heb. 7. 25, ever liveth to make *i.*
See Jer. 7. 16; 27. 18.

Intercession of CHRIST. Lu. 23. 34; Rom. 8. 34; Heb. 7. 25; 1 John 2. 1.
predicted. Isa. 53. 12.
of the HOLY SPIRIT. Rom. 8. 26.
to be made for all men, 1 Tim. 2. 1; Eph. 6. 18.
for kings, 1 Tim. 2. 2.
asked for by Paul. Rom. 15. 30; 2 Cor. 1. 11; Col. 4. 3; 1 Thes. 5. 25; 2 Thes. 3. 1; Heb. 13. 18.

Intercessor. Isa. 59. 16.

Intermeddle. Prov. 14. 10; 18. 1.

Interpretation (of dreams) is of God. Gen. 40. 8; Prov. 1. 6; Dan. 2. 27.

Intreat. Ru. 1. 16, *i.* me not to leave thee.
1 Sam. 2. 25, if a man sin, who shall *i.* for him?
Ps. 119. 58, I *i.* thy favour.
Isa. 19. 22, he shall be *i.* of them.
1 Tim. 5. 1, but *i.* him as a father. R. V. exhort.
Jas. 3. 17, wisdom is easy to be *i.*
See Prov. 18. 23; Lu. 15. 28.

Intruding. Col. 2. 18.

Inventions. Ps. 106. 29; Prov. 8. 12; Eccl. 7. 29.

Invisible. Col. 1. 15; 1 Tim. 1. 17; Heb. 11. 27.

Inward. (1) Job 38. 36, wisdom in the *i.* parts.
Ps. 51. 6, truth in the *i.* parts.
64. 6, *i.* thought of every one is deep.
Jer. 31. 33, I will put my law in their *i.* parts.
Rom. 7. 22, delight in law of God after the *i.* man.
2 Cor. 4. 16, the *i.* man is renewed.
(2) intimate, close. Job 19. 19. R. V. marg. Heb. the men of my council.
See Ps. 62. 4; Mat. 7. 15; Rom. 2. 29.

Iphedeiah, Ĭph-ĕ-dēi'-ăh, 'Jehovah frees.' 1 Chr. 8. 25.

Ir, Ĭr, 'city.' 1 Chr. 7. 12.

Ira, Ī'-ră, 'watchful.' 2 Sam. 20. 26.

Irad, Ī'-răd, 'swift' (?). Gen. 4. 18.

Iram, Ī'-răm, 'belonging to a city' (?). Gen. 36. 43.

Iri, Ī'rī, same as IRAM. 1 Chr. 7. 7.

Irijah, Ī-rī'-jăh, 'Jehovah sees.' Jer. 37. 13.

Ir-nahash, Ĭr-nā'-hăsh, 'snake-town.' 1 Chr. 4. 12.

Iron, Ī'-rŏn, 'fear,' a city. Jos. 19. 38.

Iron and **Steel** (Gen. 4. 22: Deu. 8. 9). Heb. *Barzel*: Gk. σίδηρος. Iron seems to have come into use after copper, tin, and bronze, but in very early times. Steel is iron with a certain amount (0.6 to 2. per cent.) of carbon. 'Steel,' in A. V. of Jer. 15. 12, is an erroneous rendering for 'brass;' but steel is supposed to be meant by 'northern iron,' in the same verse; the most famous makers in old times being the Chalybes, near the Black Sea. In Nah. 2. 3, 'torches,' the translation of *pelâdoth* (rendered as 'steel' both in Arabic and Syriac, and also in R. V.) is conjectured to be an error for 'scythes' on the wheels of war-chariots.
2 Sam. 23. 7; Job 28. 2; Prov. 27. 17; Isa. 45. 2; Ezek. 27. 12; Dan. 2. 33, 40.
pen of. Job 19. 24.
rod of (figuratively used). Ps. 2. 9; Rev. 2. 27.

Irpeel, Ĭr'-pēel, 'God heals.' Jos. 18. 27.

Ir-shemesh, Ĭr-shē'-mĕsh, 'sun-town.' Jos. 19. 41.

Iru, Ī'-rū, same as IRAM. 1 Chr. 4. 15.

Isaac, Ī'-sāac, laughter; his birth promised, Gen. 15. 4; 17. 16, 19; 18. 10. born, Gen. 21. 2.
offered by Abraham. Gen. 22. 7.
marries Rebekah. Gen. 24. 67.
blesses his sons, Gen. 27. 28. dies, Gen. 35. 29.

Isaiah, Ī-sāi'-ăh, 'salvation of Jehovah' (Esaias).
(1) prophet. Isa. 1. 1; 2. 1.
sent to Ahaz, Isa. 7. and Hezekiah, Isa. 37. 6; 38. 4; 39. 3.
prophesies concerning various nations. Isa. 7.; 8.; 10.; 13.-23.; 45.-47.
referred to in Mat. 3. 3; 4. 14; 8. 17; 12. 17; 13. 14; 15. 7; Mk. 1. 3; Lu. 3. 4; 4. 17; John 1. 23; 12. 38; Acts 8. 32; 28. 25; Rom. 9. 27; 10. 16; 15. 12.
(2) others. 1 Chr. 25. 3; 26. 25; Ez. 8. 7; Neh. 11. 7.

Iscah, Ĭs'-căh. Gen. 11. 29.

Iscariot, Ĭs-căr'-ĭ-ŏt, 'man of Kerioth,' Judas. Mat. 10. 4; Mk. 3. 19.
his treachery. Mat. 26. 21; Mk. 14. 18; Lu. 22. 47; John 18. 3.
death. Mat. 27. 5; Acts 1. 18.

Ishbah, Ĭsh'-băh, 'praising.' 1 Chr. 4. 17.

Ishbak, Ĭsh'-băk. Gen. 25. 2.

Ishbi-benob, Ĭsh'-bī-bē'-nŏb, 'my dwelling is in Nob.' 2 Sam. 21. 16.

Ish-bosheth, Ĭsh-bŏsh'-eth, 'man of shame.' 2 Sam. 2. 8; 3. 7; 4. 5, 8.

Ishi, Ĭsh'-ī, 'my husband.' Hos. 2. 16.

Ishi, Ĭsh'-ī, 'my help.' 1 Chr. 2. 31.

Ishiah, Ĭsh-ī'-ăh, 'Jehovah lends.' 1 Chr. 7. 3.

Ishijah, Ĭsh-ī'-jăh, same as ISHIAH. Ez. 10. 31.

Ishma, Ĭsh'-mă, 'waste.' 1 Chr. 4. 3.

Ishmael, Ĭsh'-mā-ĕl, God hears. (1) son of Abram, Gen. 16. 15; 17. 20; 21. 17; 25. 17. his descendants, Gen. 25. 12; 1 Chr. 1. 29.
(2) son of Nethaniah, slays Gedaliah. 2 Kn. 25. 25; Jer. 40. 14; 41.
(3) others. 1 Chr. 8. 38; 2 Chr. 19. 11; Ez. 10. 22.

Ishmaelites, Ĭsh'-mā-ĕ-lītes, descendants of Ishmael. Jud. 8. 24.

Ishmaiah, Ĭsh-māi'-ăh, 'Jehovah hears.' 1 Chr. 27. 19.

Ishmeelites, Ĭsh'-mēe-lītes, same as ISHMAELITES. Gen. 37. 25.

Ishmerai, Ĭsh'-mĕ-rāi, 'Jehovah keeps.' 1 Chr. 8. 18.

Ishod, Ī'-shŏd, 'man of glory.' 1 Chr. 7. 18.

Ishpan, Ĭsh'-păn, 'cunning' (?). 1 Chr. 8. 22.

Ish-tob, Ĭsh'-tŏb, 'man of Tob.' 2 Sam. 10. 6.

Ishuah, Ĭsh'-ū-ăh, 'peaceful.' Gen. 46. 17.

Ishuai, Ĭsh'-ū-āi, same as ISUI. 1 Chr. 7. 30.

Ishui, Ĭsh'-ū-ī, same as ISHUAH. 1 Sam. 14. 49.

Ismachiah, Ĭs-mă-chī'-ăh, 'Jehovah upholds.' 2 Chr. 31. 13.

Ismaiah, Ĭs-māi'-ăh, same as ISHMAIAH. 1 Chr. 12. 4.

Ispah, Ĭs'-păh, 'bald' (?). 1 Chr. 8. 16.

Israel, Ĭs'-rā-ĕl, 'soldier of God' (?). (1) Jacob so called after wrestling with God. Gen. 32. 28; 35. 10; Hos. 12. 3.
(2) the name of the ten tribes as distinguished from Judah. 2 Sam. 2. 9.

Israelites, Ĭs'-rā-ĕl-ītes, descendants of Israel. Ex. 9. 7.
in Egypt. Ex. 1.-12.
the first passover instituted. Ex. 12.
flight from Egypt. Ex. 12. 31.
pass through the Red Sea. Ex. 14.
their journeys. Ex. 14. 1, 19; Num. 9. 15; Ps. 78. 14.
fed by manna and water in the wilderness. Ex. 16. 4; 17. 1; Num. 11.; 20.
God's covenant with, at Sinai. Ex. 19.; 20.; Deu. 29. 10.
their idolatry. Ex. 32. *See also* 2 Kn. 17.; Ez. 9.; Neh. 9.; Ezek. 20.; 22.; 23.; Acts 7. 39; 1 Cor. 10. 1.
their rebellious conduct rehearsed by Moses. Deu. 1.; 2.; 9.
conquer and divide Canaan under Joshua. Jos. 1.; 12.; 13.
governed by judges, Jud. 2. by kings, 1 Sam. 10.; 2 Sam.; 1 & 2 Kn.; 1 & 2 Chr.
their captivity in Assyria, 2 Kn. 17. in Babylon, 2 Kn. 25.; 2 Chr. 36.; Jer. 39.; 52. their return, Ez.; Neh.; Hag.; Zec.
God's wrath against, Ps. 78.; 106. deliverance of, Ps. 105.
their sufferings our examples. 1 Cor. 10. 6.

Israelitish, Ĭs-rā-ĕl-ī'-tĭsh, 'after the fashion of an Israelite.' Lev. 24. 10.

Issachar, Ĭs'-să-chăr, 'there is hire' (?). (1) son of Jacob. Gen. 30. 18; 35. 23.

(2) tribe, descendants of (1). Gen. 46. 13; Jud. 5. 15; 1 Chr. 7. 1.
(3) territory, occupied by tribe. Jos. 19. 7.
See Num. 1. 28; 26. 23; Gen. 49. 14; Deu. 33. 18; Jos. 19. 17; Ezek. 48. 33; Rev. 7. 7.

Isshiah, ĭs-shī'-ăh, same as ISHIAH. 1 Chr. 24. 21.
Issues. Ps. 68. 20; Prov. 4. 23.
Isuah, ĭs'-ū-ăh, same as ISHUAH. 1 Chr. 7. 30.
Isui, ĭs'-ū-ī, same as ISHUI. Gen. 46. 17. [1.
Italian, ī-tăl'-ĭăn, 'belonging to Italy.' Acts 10.
Italy, ĭt'-ă-lȳ. Acts 18. 2.
Itching. 2 Tim. 4. 3.
Ithai, ī-thā'-ī. 1 Chr. 11. 31.
Ithamar, ĭth'-ă-mär, 'island of palms.' Ex. 6. 23; Lev. 10. 6.
his charge. Num. 4.
Ithiel, ī'-thĭ-ĕl, 'God is with me.' Neh. 11. 7; Prov. 30. 1.
Ithmah, ĭth'-măh, 'bereavedness.' 1 Chr. 11. 46.
Ithnan, ĭth'-năn. Jos. 15. 23.
Ithra, ĭth'-ră, 'abundance' (?). 2 Sam. 17. 25.
Ithran, ĭth'-răn, 'profit.' Gen. 36. 26.
Ithream, ĭth'-rĕ-ăm, 'remainder of the people.' 2 Sam. 3. 5.
Ithrite, ĭth'-rīte, 'descendants of Jether' (?). 2 Sam. 23. 38.

Itinerary of the Israelites to the Land of Canaan.

The Itinerary of the Israelites, given in full in Num. 33., may be divided into four parts:—

A. From Goshen to the Red Sea.

1. At Rameses.	Ex. 12. 37. Num. 33. 3.
2. Succoth.	Ex. 12. 37–39.
3. Etham.	Ex. 13. 20.
4. Pi-hahiroth.	Ex. 14. 1–9. 1 Cor. 10. 1, 2.

Crossing the Red Sea.
Destruction of Pharaoh's host.

B. From the Red Sea to Sinai.

1. Marah (*'Ain Hawârah*).	Ex. 15. 23–25.
2. Elim (*Wady Gharandel*).	Ex. 15. 27.
3. The Wilderness of Sin.	Ex. 16. John 6. 31, 49. Rev. 2. 17.
4. Rephidim in the Horeb.	Ex. 17. 1–8. 1 Cor. 10. 4. Ex. 17. 13.
5. The Wilderness of Sinai. Mount of God (*Jebel Mûsa*).	Ex. 19. 1. Ex. 18. 5. Ex. 20. Ex. 32. 1 Cor. 10. 7. Ex. 40.

Giving of the Law from Mt. Sinai. } ONE YEAR.
Building of the Tabernacle. }

C. From Sinai to Kadesh-Barnea.

After a stay of nearly a year at Sinai, on the twentieth day of the second month of the second year, they move three days' journey to	Ex. 19. 1. Num. 10. 11, 12. Num. 10. 33.
1. Taberah (*burning*).	Num. 11. 1–3.
2. Kibroth-hattaavah (*the graves of lust*).	Num. 11. 1–34.
3. Hazeroth (*hudherah*).	Num. 11. 35.
4. Kadesh-Barnea (? *Ain-el-Weibeh*).	Num. 13. 26. Num. 14. 1–39. 1 Cor. 10. 10. Num. 16.

Thirty-eight years in the wilderness.

D. The New Start. From Kadesh-Barnea to the Border of the Jordan.

At the close of the wanderings they return to	Num. 33.
1. Kadesh-Barnea.	Num. 20. 14–21. Num. 27. 14.
2. Mount Hor, near Selah or Petra (Jos. *Ant.* iv. 4. 7).	Num. 20. 24–29.
3. The Arabah by way of Elath and Ezion-geber.	Deu. 2. 8 (R. V.). Num. 21. 5–9. John 3. 14. 1 Cor. 10. 9.
4. Zared (*the brook*), and Beer-Elim (*the well of heroes*).	Num. 21. 12, 16, 18.
5. Jahaz, they defeat Sihon, king of the Amorites, and at	Num. 21. 23, 24.
6. Edrei, Og, the king of Bashan. These two victories give to Israel possession of the whole country east of Jordan. They next go to	Num. 21. 33.
7. Abel-Shittim (*the meadow or oasis of the acacias*), the modern *Ghor es Seiseban*, over against Jericho.	Num. 33. 49. Num. 22. 4. Num. 23. 24. Num. 25. 1 Cor. 10. 9. Num. 31.
8. Plains of Moab opposite Jericho.	Deu. 32. Deu. 34. 6.

Moses' last charge and death.
Crossing the Jordan into the Promised Land.

Ittah-kazin, ĭt'-tăh-kā'-zĭn, 'time of a chief.' Jos. 19. 13.
Ittai, ĭt-tā'-ī, 'companionable.' 2 Sam. 15. 19; 18. 2.
Ituræa, ī-tū-ræ'-ă, a province so named from Jetur. Lu. 3. 1.
Ivah, ī'-văh. 2 Kn. 18. 34. [18. 12.
Ivory. 1 Kn. 10. 22; Ps. 45. 8; Ezek. 27. 15; Rev.
Solomon's throne of. 1 Kn. 10. 18; 2 Chr. 9. 17.
palaces. Ps. 45. 8; Am. 3. 15.
Izehar, ī'-zĕ-här, oil. Num. 3. 19.
Izeharites, ī'-zĕ-här-ītes, the descendants of Izehar. Num. 3. 27.
Izhar, ĭz'-här, same as IZEHAR. Ex. 6. 18.
Izharites, ĭz-här'-ītes, the same as IZEHARITES. 1 Chr. 26. 23.
Izrahiah, ĭz-ră-hī'-ăh, 'Jehovah will shine.' 1 Chr. 7. 3.
Izrahite, ĭz'-ră-hīte, probably same as ZARHITE. 1 Chr. 27. 8.
Izri, ĭz'-rī, 'a descendant of Jezer.' 1 Chr. 25. 11.

Jaakan, jā'-ă-kăn, 'one who turns' (?). Deu. 10. 6.
Jaakobah, jā-ă-kō'-băh, same as JACOB. 1 Chr. 4. 36.
Jaala, jā'-ă-lă, 'wild she-goat.' Neh. 7. 58.
Jaalah, jā'-ă-lăh, same as JAALA. Ez. 2. 56.
Jaalam, jā'-ă-lăm, 'He hides.' Gen. 36. 5.
Jaanai, jā'-ă-nāi, 'Jehovah answers.' 1 Chr. 5. 12.
Jaare-oregim, jā'-ă-rĕ-ŏr'-ĕ-gĭm, 'forests of the weavers.' 2 Sam. 21. 19.
Jaasau, jā'-ă-sāu, 'Jehovah works.' Ez. 10. 37.
Jaasiel, jā-ăs'-ĭ-ĕl, 'God works.' 1 Chr. 27. 21.
Jaazaniah, jā-ăz-ă-nī'-ăh, 'Jehovah hears.' 2 Kn. 25. 23.
Jaazer, jā-ā'-zĕr, 'He aids.' Num. 21. 32.
Jaaziah, jā-ă-zī'-ăh, 'Jehovah comforts.' 1 Chr. 24. 26.
Jaaziel, jā-ā'-zĭ-ĕl, 'God comforts.' 1 Chr. 15. 18.
Jabal, jā'-băl, 'leader.' Gen. 4. 20.
Jabbok, jăb'-bok, 'pouring out,' a river of Gilead,

flowing into the Jordan from the west. Boundary between Ammon and Moab; scene of Jacob's wrestling in prayer. Gen. 32. 22; Num. 21. 24; Deu. 3. 16; Jos. 12. 2.

Jabesh, jā'-bĕsh, 'dry.' 2 Kn. 15. 10.

Jabesh-gilead, jā'-bĕsh-gĭl'-ĕ-ăd, 'Jabesh of Gilead,' inhabitants smitten by Israel. Jud. 21. threatened by Ammonites, 1 Sam. 11. 1. delivered by Saul, 1 Sam. 11. 11.

Jabez, jā'-bĕz, 'causing pain' (?), prayer of. 1 Chr. 4. 9.

Jabin, jā'-bĭn, 'intelligent,' kings of Hazor. (1) conquered by Joshua. Jos. 11.
(2) destroyed by Barak. Jud. 4.

Jabneel, jăb'-nēēl, 'God causes to build.' Jos. 15. 11.

Jabneh, jăb'-nĕh, 'He causes to build.' 2 Chr. 26. 6.

Jachan, jā'-chăn, 'troubled.' 1 Chr. 5. 13.

Jachin, jā'-chĭn, 'He will establish,' one of the pillars of the porch of the temple. 1 Kn. 7. 21; 2 Chr. 3. 17.

Jachinites, jā'-chĭn-ītes, descendants of Jachin. Num. 26. 12.

Jacinth, or **Hyacinth** (Rev. 9. 17; 21. 20). Gk. ὑάκινθος: Italian *giacinto*: R. V. marg. 'sapphire,' the Oriental sapphire of modern jewelry. King, *Nat. Hist. of Gems*, says it was a yellow stone, sometimes tinged with blue or purple; such as the cairngorm and amethyst.

Jackal (Isa. 13. 22; S. of S. 2. 15; Lam. 5. 18). The jackal (*Canis aureus*) is very common in Palestine. Two words occur in the Hebrew: (1) *Shûal*, Gk. ἀλώπηξ, universally rendered 'fox,' though often meaning 'jackal.' (2) *Iyyîm*, Gk. ἐχῖνος (?=ἐχιναλώπηξ) (*pl.*), 'wild beasts of the islands,' which certainly seems to refer to jackals.

Jacob, jā'-cob, 'supplanter,' his birth. Gen. 25. 26.
birthright. Gen. 25. 33.
blessing. Gen. 27. 27.
sent to Padan-aram. Gen. 27. 43; 28. 1.
his vision of the ladder, and vow. Gen. 28. 10.
marriages. Gen. 29.
sons. Gen. 29. 31; 30.
dealings with Laban. Gen. 31.
his vision of God's host. Gen. 32. 1.
his prayer. Gen. 32. 9.
wrestles with an angel. Gen. 32. 24; Hos. 12. 4.
reconciled with Esau. Gen. 33.
builds an altar at Beth-el. Gen. 35. 1.
his grief for Joseph and Benjamin. Gen. 37.; 42. 38; 43.
goes down to Egypt. Gen. 46.
brought before Pharaoh. Gen. 47. 7.
blesses his sons. Gen. 48.; 49.
his death and burial. Gen. 49. 33; 50. *See* Ps. 105. 23; Mal. 1. 2; Rom. 9. 10; Heb. 11. 21.

Jacob's well. John 4. 5.

Jada, jā'-dă, 'wise.' 1 Chr. 2. 28.

Jadau, jā'-dau. Ez. 10. 43.

Jaddua, jăd'-dū-ă, 'known.' Neh. 10. 21.

Jadon, jā'-dŏn, 'a judge.' Neh. 3. 7.

Jael, jā'-ĕl, same as Jaala; kills Sisera. Jud. 4. 17; 5. 24.

Jagur, jā'-gûr, 'a lodging.' Jos. 15. 21.

Jah, jäh, poetic form of Jehovah. Ps. 68. 4.

Jahath, jā'-hăth, 'He will snatch up' (?). 1 Chr. 6. 20.

Jahaz, jā'-hăz, 'lowland.' Num. 21. 23.

Jahaza, jă-hā'-ză, same as Jahaz. Jos. 13. 18.

Jahazah, jă-hā'-zăh, same as Jahaza. Jos. 21. 36.

Jahaziah, jā-hă-zī'-ăh, 'Jehovah sees.' Ez. 10. 15.

Jahaziel, jă-hā'-zĭ'-ĕl, 'God sees.' 1 Chr. 16. 6.
comforts Jehoshaphat. 2 Chr. 19. 14.
prophesies against Moab and Ammon. 2 Chr. 20. 14.

Jahdai, jäh'-dā-ī, 'Jehovah leads' (?). 1 Chr. 2. 47.

Jahdiel, jäh'-dĭ-ĕl, 'God makes glad.' 1 Chr. 5. 24.

Jahdo, jäh'-dō, 'union.' 1 Chr. 5. 14.

Jahleel, jäh'-lēēl, 'wait for God.' Num. 26. 26.

Jahleelites, jäh'-lēēl-ītes, descendants of Jahleel. Num. 26. 26.

Jahmai, jäh'-mā-ī, 'may Jehovah protect.' 1 Chr. 7. 2.

Jahzah, jäh'-zăh, same as Jahaz. 1 Chr. 6. 78.

Jahzeel, jäh'-zēēl, 'God allots.' Gen. 46. 24.

Jahzeelites, jäh'-zēēl-ītes, descendants of Jahzeel. Num. 26. 48.

Jahzerah, jäh'-zĕ-răh, 'may he bring back.' 1 Chr. 9. 12.

Jahziel, jäh'-zĭ-ĕl, same as Jahzeel. 1 Chr. 7. 13.

Jair, jā'-ĭr, 'He (i. e., God) enlightens.' Num. 32. 41.
Gileadite, judge. Jud. 10. 3.

Jairite, jā'-ĭr-īte, a descendant of Jair. 2 Sam. 20. 26.

Jairus, jā-ī'-rŭs, Greek form of Jair; daughter of, raised. Mat. 9. 18; Mk. 5. 22; Lu. 8. 41.

Jakan, jā'-kăn, same as Jaakan. 1 Chr. 1. 42.

Jakeh, jā'-kĕh, 'pious' (?). Prov. 30. 1.

Jakim, jā'-kĭm, '(God) sets up.' 1 Chr. 8. 19.

Jalon, jā'-lŏn, 'passing the night.' 1 Chr. 4. 17.

Jambres, jăm'-brēs. 2 Tim. 3. 8. *See* Jannes.

James, jāmes, English form of Jacob in the N. T.
(1) (Apostle), son of Zebedee, called. Mat. 4. 21; Mk. 1. 19; Lu. 5. 10.
ordained one of the twelve. Mat. 10. 2; Mk. 3. 14; Lu. 6. 13.
witnessed Christ's transfiguration. Mat. 17. 1; Mk. 9. 2; Lu. 9. 28.
present at the passion. Mat. 26. 36; Mk. 14. 33.
slain by Herod. Acts 12. 2.
(2) (Apostle), son of Alphæus. Mat. 10. 3; Mk. 3. 18; 6. 3; Lu. 6. 15; Acts 1. 13; 12. 17.
his judgment respecting ceremonial. Acts 15. 13-29.
See 1 Cor. 15. 7; Gal. 1. 19; 2. 9.
his teaching. Jas. 1.-5.
mentioned. Acts 21. 18; 1 Cor. 15. 7; Gal. 1. 19; 2. 9.

Jamin, jā'-mĭn, 'right hand.' Gen. 46. 10.

Jaminites, jā'-mĭn-ītes, descendants of Jamin. Num. 26. 12.

Jamlech, jăm'-lĕch, 'He makes to reign.' 1 Chr. 4. 34.

Jangling, vain, babbling, vain talking. 1 Tim. 1. 6.

Janna, jăn'-nă, probably another form of John. Lu. 3. 24.

Jannes, jăn'-nēs, and **Jambres**, magicians of Egypt. 2 Tim. 3. 8 (Ex. 7. 11).

Janoah, jă-nō'-ăh, 'rest.' 2 Kn. 15. 29.

Janohah, jă-nō'-hăh, same as preceding. Jos. 16. 6.

Janum, jā'-nŭm, 'sleep.' Jos. 15. 53.

Japheth, jā'-phĕth, 'extension,' son of Noah. Gen. 5. 32.
blessed. Gen. 9. 27.
his descendants. Gen. 10. 1; 1 Chr. 1. 4.

Japhia, jă-phī'-ă, 'splendid.' Jos. 19. 12.

Japhlet, jăph'-lĕt, 'He delivers.' 1 Chr. 7. 32.

Japhleti, jăph'-lē-tī, the Japhletite, or descendant of Japhlet. Jos. 16. 3.

Japho, jā'-phō, 'beauty.' Jos. 19. 46.

Jarah, jâr'-ăh, 'forest.' 1 Chr. 9. 42.

Jareb, jâr'-ĕb, 'one who is contentious.' Hos. 5. 13.

Jared, jâr'-ĕd, 'descent.' Gen. 5. 15; Lu. 3. 37.

Jaresiah, jăr-ĕ-sī'-ăh, 'Jehovah nourishes.' 1 Chr. 8. 27.

Jarha, jăr'-hă. 1 Chr. 2. 34.

Jarib, jâr'-ĭb, 'adversary.' 1 Chr. 4. 24.

Jarmuth, jăr'-mŭth, 'height.' Jos. 10. 3.

Jaroah, jă-rō'-ăh, 'moon' (?). 1 Chr. 5. 14.

Jashen, jăsh'-ĕn, 'sleeping.' 2 Sam. 23. 32.

Jasher, jăsh'-ĕr, upright,' book of. Jos. 10. 13; 2 Sam. 1. 18.

Jashobeam, jă-shŏb'-ĕ-ăm, 'the people returns' (?), valour of. 1 Chr. 11. 11.

Jashub, jăsh'-ŭb, 'he returns.' Num. 26. 24.

Jashubi-lehem, jă-shū'-bī-lē'-hĕm, 'giving bread' (?). 1 Chr. 4. 22.

Jashubites, jăsh'-ū-bītes, 'descendants of Jashub.' Num. 26. 24.

Jasiel, jās'-ĭ-ĕl, 'God makes.' 1 Chr. 11. 47.

Jason, jā'-son, Græco-Judæan equivalent of Joshua; persecuted at Thessalonica. Acts 17. 5; Rom. 16. 21.

Jasper (Ex. 28. 20). Heb. *Yâshĕpheh:* Gk. ἴασπις. 'Among the ancients a bright-colored chalcedony, varying in color, green being the more common.' (*Cent. Dict.*)
Ezek. 28. 13, and a *j.*
Rev. 4. 3, he that sat was to look upon like a *j.*
21. 11, even like a *j.* stone.
21. 18, the building of the wall of it was of *j.*
21. 19, the first foundation was *j.*

Jathniel, jăth'-nĭ-ĕl, 'God gives.' 1 Chr. 26. 2.

Jattir, jăt'-tĭr, 'excelling' (?). Jos. 15. 48.

Javan, jā'-văn, 'wine' (?), son of Japheth, Ionians. Gen. 10. 2.

Javelin, a light spear, intended to be thrown by the hand. Wherever 'javelin' occurs in the A. V. the R. V. properly substitutes 'spear.'
Num. 25. 7, took a *j.* in his hand.
1 Sam. 18. 10, and there was a *j.* in Saul's hand.
19. 10, even to the wall with a *j.*

Jawbone of an ass, Samson uses, Jud. 15. 15. water flows from, Jud. 15. 19.

Jazer, jā'-zĕr, same as JAAZER. Num. 32. 1.

Jaziz, jā'-zĭz, 'shining' (?). 1 Chr. 27. 31.

Jealous. Ex. 20. 5; 34. 14; Deu. 4. 24; 5. 9; 6. 15; Jos. 24. 19, I am a *j.* God.
1 Kn. 19. 10, 14, I have been *j.* for the Lord.
Ezek. 39. 25, will be *j.* for my holy name.
2 Cor. 11. 2, I am *j.* over you.
See Num. 5. 14; Joel 2. 18; Zec. 1. 14; 8. 2.

Jealousy. Deu. 32. 16; 1 Kn. 14. 22, they provoked him to *j.*
Prov. 6. 34, *j.* is the rage of a man.
S. of S. 8. 6, *j.* is cruel as the grave.
Ezek. 36. 5, in fire of *j.* have I spoken.
1 Cor. 10. 22, do we provoke the Lord to *j.*

Jealousy (Ps. 79. 5; Prov. 6. 34; S. of S. 8. 6; Isa. 42. 13). trial and offering of, Num. 5. 11. provoking to. Ps. 78. 58; Ezek. 8. 3; 16. 38.

Jearim, jē'-ă-rĭm, 'forests.' Jos. 15. 10.

Jeaterai, jē-ăt'-ĕ-rāi, same as ETHNI. 1 Chr. 6. 21.

Jeberechiah, jĕ-bĕr-ĕ-chī'-ăh, 'Jehovah blesses.' Isa. 8. 2.

Jebus, jē'-bŭs, 'a place trodden down' (?), a name of Jerusalem. Jud. 19. 10.

Jebusi, jĕb'-ū-sī, 'a Jebusite.' Jos. 18. 16.

Jebusites, jĕb'-ū-sītes, the descendants of Jebus, the son of Canaan. Gen. 15. 21; Num. 13. 29; Jos. 15. 63; Jud. 1. 21; 19. 11; 2 Sam. 5. 6.

Jecamiah, jĕc-ă-mī'-ăh, 'may Jehovah set up.' 1 Chr. 3. 18.

Jecholiah, jĕch-ŏ-lī'-ăh, 'Jehovah is strong.' 2 Kn. 15. 2.

Jechonias, jĕch-ō-nī'-ăs, the Greek form of Jeconiah. Mat. 1. 11, 12; 1 Chr. 3. 17.

Jecoliah, jĕc-ŏ-lī'-ăh, same as JECHOLIAH. 2 Chr. 26. 3.

Jeconiah, jĕc-ō-nī'-ăh, 'Jehovah establishes.' 1 Chr. 3. 16.

Jedaiah, jĕ-dāi'-ăh. (1) 'He praiseth Jehovah.' 1 Chr. 4. 37. (2) 'Jehovah knoweth.' 1 Chr. 24. 7.

Jediael, jĕd-ĭ-ā'-ĕl, 'known of God.' 1 Chr. 7. 6.

Jedidah, jĕ-dī'-dăh, 'beloved.' 2 Kn. 22. 1.

Jedidiah, jĕd-ĭ-dī'-ăh, 'beloved of Jehovah,' a name of Solomon. 2 Sam. 12. 25.

Jeduthun, jĕ-dū'-thŭn, 'praise' (?), one of the famous singers of David. 1 Chr. 16. 38; 41.; 25. 6.

Jeduthun, To. 'Upon,' i. e., 'after the manner of Jeduthun.' [26. 30.

Jeezer, jē-ē'-zĕr, contracted from ABIEZER. Num. 26. 30.

Jeezerites, jē-ē'-zĕr-ītes, 'descendants of Jeezer.' Num. 26. 30.

Jegar-sahadutha, jē'-găr-să-hă-dū'-thă, 'mound of testimony.' Gen. 31. 47.

Jehaleleel, jĕ-hăl'-ĕ-lēĕl, 'he praises God.' 1 Chr. 4. 16.

Jehalelel, jĕ-hăl'-ĕ-lĕl, same as preceding. 2 Chr. 29. 12.

Jehdeiah, jĕh-dēi'-ăh, 'may Jehovah make glad.' 1 Chr. 24. 20.

Jehezekel, jĕ-hĕz'-ĕk-ĕl, same as EZEKIEL. 1 Chr. 24. 16.

Jehiah, jĕ-hī'-ăh, 'may Jehovah live.' 1 Chr. 15. 24.

Jehiel, jĕ-hī'-ĕl. (1) 'may God live.' 1 Chr. 15. 18. (2) 1 Chr. 9. 35.

Jehieli, jĕ-hī-ē'-lī, a Jehielite. 1 Chr. 26. 21.

Jehizkiah, jĕ-hĭz-kī'-ăh, same as HEZEKIAH. 2 Chr. 28. 12.

Jehoadah, jĕ-hō'-ă-dăh, 'Jehovah adorns' (?). 1 Chr. 8. 36.

Jehoaddan, jĕ-hō-ăd'-dăn, 'Jehovah is beauteous' (?). 2 Kn. 14. 2.

Jehoahaz, jĕ-hō'-ă-hăz, 'Jehovah holds fast.'
(1) son of Jehu, king of Israel. 2 Kn. 10. 35; 13. 4.
(2) (Shallum), king of Judah, his evil reign. 2 Kn. 23. 31; 2 Chr. 36. 1.

Jehoash, jĕ-hō'-ăsh, 'Jehovah is strong' (?). (1) 2 Kn. 11. 21. (2) 2 Kn. 13. 10.

Jehohanan, jē-hō-hā'-năn, 'Jehovah is gracious.' 1 Chr. 26. 3.

Jehoiachin, jĕ-hôi'-ă-chĭn, 'Jehovah has established;' king of Judah, his defeat and captivity. 2 Kn. 24. 6; 2 Chr. 36. 8.

Jehoiada, jĕ-hôi'-ă-dă, 'Jehovah knoweth.' 2 Sam. 8. 18.
high priest, deposes and slays Athaliah, and restores Jehoash. 2 Kn. 11. 4; 2 Chr. 23.
repairs the Temple. 2 Kn. 12. 7; 2 Chr. 24. 6.
abolishes idolatry. 2 Chr. 23. 16.

Jehoiakim, jĕ-hôi'-ă-kĭm, 'Jehovah has set up.' (Eliakim), made king of Judah by Pharaoh-nechoh: his evil reign and captivity. 2 Kn. 23. 34; 24. 1; 2 Chr. 36. 4; Dan. 1. 2. *See* Jer. 22. 18.

Jehoiarib, jĕ-hôi'-ă-rĭb, 'Jehovah will contend.' 1 Chr. 9. 10.

Jehonadab, jĕ-hŏn'-ă-dăb, 'Jehovah is bounteous' (?). 2 Kn. 10. 15.

Jehonathan, jĕ-hŏn'-ă-thăn, same as JONATHAN. 1 Chr. 27. 25.

Jehoram, jĕ-hôr'ăm, 'Jehovah is exalted.'
(1) (son of Jehoshaphat), king of Judah, 1 Kn. 22. 50; 2 Kn. 8. 16. his cruelty and death, 2 Chr. 21. 4, 18.
(2) (Joram), king of Israel, son of Ahab, 2 Kn. 1. 17; 3. 1. his evil reign, 2 Kn. 3. 2. slain by Jehu, 2 Kn. 9. 24.
(3) a priest. 2 Chr. 17. 8.

Jehoshabeath, jē-hō-shăb'-ĕ-ăth, 'Jehovah is an oath.' 2 Chr. 22. 11.

Jehoshaphat, jĕ-hŏsh'-ă-phăt, 'Jehovah judges.'
(1) king of Judah; his good reign, 1 Kn. 15. 24; 2 Chr. 17. his death, 1 Kn. 22. 50; 2 Chr. 21. 1.
(2) others. 2 Sam. 8. 16; 1 Kn. 4. 17; 2 Kn. 9. 2; 1 Chr. 11. 43; 15. 24.
(3) valley of. Joel 3. 2.

Jehosheba, jē-hŏsh'-ĕ-bă, same as JEHOSHABEATH. 2 Kn. 11. 2; 2 Chr. 22. 11.

Jehoshua, jĕ-hŏsh'-ū-ă, same as JOSHUA. Num. [13. 16.

Jehoshuah, jĕ-hŏsh'-ū-ăh, same as JOSHUA. 1 Chr. 7. 27.

Jehovah, jĕ-hō'-văh, 'the Eternal One' (ELOHIM, I AM THAT I AM). Ex. 6. 3; Ps. 83. 18; Isa. 12. 2; 26. 4.

Jehovah-jireh, jĕ-hō'-văh-jī'-rĕh, 'Jehovah will provide.' Gen. 22. 14.

Jehovah-nissi, jĕ-hō'-văh-nĭs'-sī, 'Jehovah is my banner.' Ex. 17. 15.

Jehovah-shalom, jĕ-hō'-văh-shā'-lŏm, 'Jehovah is peace.' Jud. 6. 24.

Jehovah-shammah, jĕ-hō'-văh-shăm'-măh, 'Jehovah is there.' Ezek. 48. 35.

Jehovah-tsidkenu, jĕ-hō'-vāh-tsĭd'-kĕ-nū, 'Jehovah is our righteousness.' Jer. 23. 6.
Jehozabad, jĕ-hō'-zā-băd, 'Jehovah gave.' 2 Kn. 12. 21.
Jehozadak, jĕ-hō'-zā-dăk, 'Jehovah is righteous.' 1 Chr. 6. 14.
Jehu, jē'-hū, 'Jehovah is He' (?). (1) son of Hanani, prophesies against Baasha. 1 Kn. 16. 1.
rebukes Jehoshaphat. 2 Chr. 19. 2; 20. 34.
(2) son of Nimshi, to be anointed king of Israel. 1 Kn. 19. 16; 2 Kn. 9. 1.
his reign. 2 Kn. 9. 10.
(3) others. 1 Chr. 2. 38; 4. 35; 12. 3. [34.
Jehubbah, jĕ-hŭb'-băh, 'beloved' (?). 1 Chr. 7.
Jehucal, jĕ-hū'-căl, 'Jehovah is able.' Jer. 37. 3.
Jehud, jē'-hŭd, 'praise' (?). Jos. 19. 45.
Jehudi, jĕ-hū'-dī, 'a Jew.' Jer. 36. 14.
Jehudijah, jĕ-hū-dī'-jăh, 'a Jewess.' 1 Chr. 4. 18.
Jehush, jē'-hŭsh, 'He hastens.' 1 Chr. 8. 39.
Jeiel, jē-ī'-ĕl. 1 Chr. 5. 7.
Jekabzeel, jĕ-kăb'-zēel, 'God gathers.' Neh. 11. 25.
Jekameam, jĕ-kăm'-ē-ăm, 'He raises up the people' (?). 1 Chr. 23. 19.
Jekamiah, jĕk-ă-mī'-ăh, same as Jecamiah. 1 Chr. 2. 41.
Jekuthiel, jĕ-kū'-thĭ-ĕl, 'preservation of God' (?). 1 Chr. 4. 18.
Jemima, jĕ-mī'-mă, 'dove.' Job 42. 14.
Jemuel, jĕ-mū'-ĕl, same as Nemuel. Gen. 46. 10.
Jeopard, hazard or risk, jeopardize. Jud. 5. 18.
Jephthæ, jĕph'-thǣ, Greek form of Jephthah. Heb. 11. 32.
Jephthah, jĕph'-thăh, 'He opens.' Jud. 11. 1.
judge, his dealings with the Gileadites. Jud. 11. 4.
defeats the Ammonites. Jud. 11. 14.
his rash vow. Jud. 11. 30, 34.
chastises the Ephraimites. Jud. 12.
Jephunneh, jĕ-phŭn'-nĕh. (1) Num. 13. 6.
(2) 1 Chr. 7. 38.
Jerah, jē'-răh, 'the moon' (?). Gen. 10. 26.
Jerahmeel, jĕ-răh'-mēel, 'God hath mercy.' 1 Chr. 2. 9.
Jerahmeelites, jĕ-răh'-mēel-ītes, descendants of Jerahmeel. 1 Sam. 27. 10.
Jered, jē'-rĕd, 'descent.' (1) 1 Chr. 1. 2.
(2) 1 Chr. 4. 18.
Jeremai, jĕr-ē-mā'-ī. Ez. 10. 33. [(?).
Jeremiah, jĕr-ē-mī'-ăh, 'Jehovah has appointed'
(1) prophet, his call and visions. Jer. 1.
his mission. Jer. 1. 17; 7.
his complaint. Jer. 20. 14.
his message to Zedekiah. Jer. 21. 3; 34. 1.
foretells the seventy years' captivity. Jer. 25. 8.
arraigned, condemned, but delivered. Jer. 26.
denounces the false prophet Hananiah. Jer. 28. 5.
writes to the captives in Babylon. Jer. 29.
his promises of comfort and redemption to Israel. Jer. 31.
writes a roll of a book, Jer. 36. 4. Baruch reads it, Jer. 36. 8.
imprisoned by Zedekiah. Jer. 32.; 37.; 38.
released. Jer. 38. 7.
predicts slaughter of innocents, Jer. 31. 15. fulfilled, Mat. 2. 17.
with all the remnant of Judah carried into Egypt. Jer. 43. 4.
various predictions. Jer. 46.–51.; 51. 59.
mentioned. Mat. 16. 14; 27. 9.
(2) others. 1 Chr. 5. 24; 12. 4; 12. 10; 2 Kn. 23. 31.
Jeremias, jĕr-ē-mī'-ăs, Greek form of Jeremiah. Mat. 16. 14.
Jeremoth, jĕr'-ē-mōth, 'high places' (?). 1 Chr. 8. 14.
Jeremy, jĕr'-ē-mȳ, shortened English form of Jeremiah. Mat. 2. 17.
Jeriah, jĕ-rī'-ăh, 'founded by Jehovah' (?). 1 Chr. 23. 19.
Jeribai, jĕr-ĭ-bā'-ī, 'Jehovah defends' (?). 1 Chr. 11. 46.
Jericho, jĕr'-ĭ-chō, 'a fragrant place' (?), 15 miles N. E. of Jerusalem, in the Jordan valley, 5 miles from the river. Num. 22. 1.
the spies at. Jos. 2. 1.
capture of. Jos. 6. 20 (Heb. 11. 30).
rebuilt by Hiel. 1 Kn. 16. 34. *See* Jos. 6. 26.
Jeriel, jĕr'-ĭ-ĕl, 'founded by God.' 1 Chr. 7. 2.
Jerijah, jĕ-rī'-jăh, same as Jeriah.' 1 Chr. 26. 31.
Jerimoth, jĕr'-ĭ-mōth, same as Jeremoth. 1 Chr. 7. 7.
Jerioth, jĕr'-ĭ-ōth, 'curtains' (?). 1 Chr. 2. 18.
Jeroboam I., jĕr'-ŏ-bō'-ăm, 'his people is many' (?). 1 Kn. 11. 26.
promoted by Solomon. 1 Kn. 11. 28.
Ahijah's prophecy to. 1 Kn. 11. 29.
made king. 1 Kn. 12. 20 (2 Chr. 10.).
his idolatry, withered hand, denunciation. 1 Kn. 12.; 13.; 14.
death. 1 Kn. 14. 20.
evil example. 1 Kn. 15. 34.
Jeroboam II. 2 Kn. 13. 13; 14. 23-29.
Jeroham, jĕ-rō'-hăm, 'beloved.' (1) Samuel's grandfather. 1 Sam. 1. 1.
(2) others. 1 Chr. 9. 8; 9. 12; 12. 7; 27. 22.
Jerubbaal, jĕr-ŭb-bā'-ăl, 'let Baal plead.' Jud. 6. 32.
Jerubbesheth, jĕ-rŭb'-bĕ-shĕth, 'let shame plead,' another name for Jerubbaal. 2 Sam. 11. 21.
Jeruel, jĕ-rū'-ĕl, same as Jeriel. 2 Chr. 20. 16.
Jerusalem, jĕ-rū'-să-lĕm, 'City of Salem,' or 'City of Peace.' (1) the religious capital of Palestine.
Adoni-zedec, king of, slain by Joshua. Jos. 10.
borders of. Jos. 15. 8.
David reigns there. 2 Sam. 5. 6.
the ark brought there. 2 Sam. 6.
saved from the pestilence. 2 Sam. 24. 16.
temple built at. 1 Kn. 5.–8.; 2 Chr. 1.–7.
sufferings from war. 1 Kn. 14. 25; 2 Kn. 14. 14 25.; 2 Chr. 12.; 25. 24; 36.; Jer. 39.; 52.
capture and destruction by Nebuchadrezzar. Jer. 52. 12–15.
captives return; and rebuilding of the temple begun by Cyrus, Ez. 1.–3. continued by Artaxerxes, Neh. 2.
wall rebuilt and dedicated by Nehemiah. Neh. 12. 38.
abominations there. Ezek. 16. 2.
presentation of Christ at. Lu. 2. 22.
the child Jesus tarries at. Lu. 2. 42.
Christ rides into. Mat. 21. 1; Mk. 11. 7; Lu. 19. 35; John 12. 14.
laments over it. Mat. 23. 37; Lu. 13. 34; 19. 41.
foretells its destruction. Mat. 24.; Mk. 13.; Lu. 13. 34; 17. 23; 19. 41; 21.
disciples filled with the Holy Ghost at. Acts 2. 4.
(2) which is above. Gal. 4. 26.
the new. Rev. 21. 2.
Jerusha, jĕ-rū'-shă, 'taken possession of.' 2 Kn. 15. 33.
Jerushah, jĕ-rū'-shăh, same as preceding. 2 Chr. 27. 1.
Jesaiah, jĕ-sāi'-ăh, same as Isaiah. 1 Chr. 3. 21.
Jeshaiah, jĕ-shāi'-ăh, same as preceding. 1 Chr. 25. 3.
Jeshanah, jĕ-shā'-năh, 'old.' 2 Chr. 13. 19.
Jesharelah, jĕsh-ă-rē'-lăh. 1 Chr. 25. 14.
Jeshebeab, jĕ-shĕb'-ē-ăb, 'the father brings back.' 1 Chr. 24. 13.
Jesher, jē'-shĕr, 'uprightness.' 1 Chr. 2. 18.
Jeshimon, jĕ-shī'-mon, 'the waste.' Num. 21. 20.
Jeshishai, jĕ-shĭsh'-āi, 'an old man.' 1 Chr. 5. 14.
Jeshohaiah, jĕsh-ō-hāi'-ăh, 'bowing before Jehovah' (?). 1 Chr. 4. 36.
Jeshua (Joshua), jĕsh'-ū-ă, 'Jehovah is salvation' (?). (1) Joshua (*q. v.*).
(2) others. 1 Chr. 24. 11; 2 Chr. 31. 15; Ez. 2. 2.
(3) village. Neh. 11. 26.
Jeshuah, jĕsh'-ū-ăh, same as Jeshua. 1 Chr. 24. 11.

Jeshurun, jĕ-shū'-rŭn, 'upright,' symbolical name of Israel. Deu. 32. 15; 33. 5, 26; Isa. 44. 2.
Jesiah, jĕ-sī'-ăh, 'Jehovah lends.' 1 Chr. 12. 6.
Jesimiel, jĕ-sĭm'-ĭ-ĕl. 1 Chr. 4. 36.
Jesse, jĕs'-sĕ. David's father. Ru. 4. 17, 22.
and his sons sanctified by Samuel. 1 Sam. 16. 5.
his son David anointed to be king. 1 Sam. 16. 13. *See* Isa. 11. 1.
his posterity. 1 Chr. 2. 13.
Jesting, evil, censured. Eph. 5. 4.
Jesui, jĕs'-ū-ī, same as ISHUI. Num. 26. 44.
Jesuites, jĕs'-ŭ-ītes, the posterity of Jesui. Num. 26. 44.
Jesurun, jĕs-ū'-rŭn, another form of Jeshurun. Isa. 44. 2.
Jesus, jē'-sŭs, 'Jehovah is salvation.' (1) Mat. 1. 21. *See* CHRIST.
(2) Joshua. Acts 7. 45; Heb. 4. 8.
(3) Justus. Col. 4. 11.
Jether, jē'-thĕr, same as ITHRA. Jud. 8. 20.
Jetheth, jē'-thĕth. Gen. 36. 40.
Jethlah, jĕth'-lăh. Jos. 19. 42.
Jethro, jĕth'-rō, same as ITHRA. Moses' father-in-law. Ex. 3. 1; 18. 12.
Jetur, jē'-tûr, 'an enclosure' (?). Gen. 25. 15.
Jeuel, jeū'-ĕl, same as JEIEL. 1 Chr. 9. 6.
Jeush, jē'-ŭsh, same as JEHUSH. Gen. 36. 5.
Jeuz, jē'-ŭz, 'counsellor.' 1 Chr. 8. 10.
Jew, jew̅, i. e., Judæan, an Israelite. Esth. 2. 5.
Jewels. Isa. 61. 10; Mal. 3. 17.
Jewess, jew̅'-ĕss, a female Jew. Acts 16. 1.
Jewish, jew̅'-ĭsh, of or belonging to Jews. Tit. 1. 14.

Jewish Sects and Parties.

The following is a list of the main distinctions in Biblical times:—

1. Pharisees 2. Sadducees 3. Essenes	Distinctions chiefly religious.
4. Herodians 5. Zealots 6. Galilæans 7. Assassins	Distinctions chiefly political.

Subordinate terms connected with the above.

8. Scribes.	12. Publicans.
9. Lawyers.	13. Samaritans.
10. Nazarites.	14. Sanhedrin.
11. Proselytes.	15. Synagogue.

See under each title.

Jewry, jew̅'-rȳ, 'Judæa properly so called; the part of Palestine occupied by the tribes of Judah and Benjamin after the Captivity.' Dan. 5. 13; John 7. 1, &c.
Jews, jew̅s. (1) inhabitants of Judæa (Israelites first so called). 2 Kn. 16. 6.
(2) Hebrew nation generally. Dan. 3. 8; Mat. 2. 2; Acts 13. 45.
Christ's mission to. Mat. 15. 24; 21. 37; Acts 3. 26.
Christ's compassion for. Mat. 23. 37; Lu. 19. 41.
Christ rejected by. Mat. 11. 20; 13. 15, 58; John 5. 16, 38, 43; Acts 3. 13; 13. 46; 1 Thes. 2. 15.
gospel first preached to. Mat. 10. 6; Lu. 24. 47; Acts 1. 8.
St. Paul's teaching rejected by. Acts 13. 46; 28. 24, 26, &c.
Jezaniah, jĕz-ă-nī'-ăh, 'Jehovah hears.' Jer. 40. 8.
Jezebel, jĕz'-ĕ-bĕl, 'unmarried,' wife of Ahab. 1 Kn. 16. 31.
kills the prophets. 1 Kn. 18. 4; 19. 2.
causes Naboth to be put to death. 1 Kn. 21.
her violent death. 2 Kn. 9. 30.
Jezer, jē'-zĕr, 'form.' Gen. 46. 24.
Jezerites, jē'-zĕr-ītes, descendants of Jezer. Num. 26. 49.

Jeziah, jĕ-zī'-ăh, 'Jehovah makes to spring up.' Ez. 10. 25.
Jeziel, jē'-zĭ-ĕl, 'the assembly of God.' 1 Chr. 12. 3.
Jezliah, jĕz-lī'-ăh. 1 Chr. 8. 18.
Jezoar, jĕ-zō'-ăr, 'splendid.' 1 Chr. 4. 7.
Jezrahiah, jĕz-ră-hī'-ăh, 'Jehovah shines forth.' Neh. 12. 42.
Jezreel, jĕz'-reēl, 'God sows.' (1) places, Jos. 15. 36; 19. 18.
(2) men. 1 Chr. 4. 3; Hos. 1. 4. *See* AHAB.
Jezreelite, jĕz'-reēl-īte, an inhabitant of Jezreel. 1 Kn. 21. 6.
Jezreelitess, jĕz-reēl-ī'-tĕss, feminine of preceding. 1 Sam. 27. 3.
Jibsam, jĭb'-săm, 'fragrant.' 1 Chr. 7. 2.
Jidlaph, jĭd'-lăph, 'he weepeth' (?). Gen. 22. 22.
Jimna, jĭm'-nă, same as IMNA. Num. 26. 44.
Jimnah, jĭm'-năh, same as IMNAH. Gen. 46. 17.
Jimnites, jĭm'-nītes, descendants of Jimnah. Num. 26. 44.
Jiphtah, jĭph'-tăh, same as JEPHTHAH. Jos. 15. 43.
Jiphthah-el, jĭph'-thăh-ĕl, 'God opens.' Jos. 19. 14.
Joab, jō'-ăb, 'Jehovah is father.' (1) 2 Sam. 2. 13.
nephew of David, and captain of the host. 2 Sam. 8. 16.
kills Abner. 2 Sam. 3. 23.
intercedes for Absalom, 2 Sam. 14. slays him in an oak, 2 Sam. 18. 14.
reproves David's grief. 2 Sam. 19. 5.
slays Amasa. 2 Sam. 20. 9.
unwillingly numbers the people. 2 Sam. 24. 3 (1 Chr. 21. 3).
joins Adonijah's usurpation. 1 Kn. 1. 7.
slain by Solomon's command. 1 Kn. 2. 5, 28.
(2) Othniel's grandson. 1 Chr. 4. 14.
(3) Ez. 2. 6; 8. 9; Neh. 7. 11.
Joah, jō'-ăh, 'Jehovah is brother.' 2 Kn. 18. 18; 2 Chr. 34. 8.
Joahaz, jō'-ă-hăz, 'Jehovah holds.' 2 Chr. 34. 8.
Joanna, jō-ăn'-nă, Greek way of writing Jehonan. Lu. 3. 27; 8. 2, 3; 24. 10.
Joash, jō'-ăsh, 'Jehovah is strong' (?). (1) father of Gideon. Jud. 6. 11.
(2) (Jehoash), king of Israel. 2 Kn. 13. 10.
visits Elisha sick. 2 Kn. 13. 14.
defeats the Syrians. 2 Kn. 13. 25.
chastises Amaziah. 2 Kn. 14. 8; 2 Chr. 25. 17.
(3) king of Judah. 2 Kn. 11. 4; 2 Chr. 23.
repairs the Temple. 2 Kn. 12.; 2 Chr. 24.
kills Zechariah. 2 Chr. 24. 17.
slain by his servants. 2 Kn. 12. 19; 2 Chr. 24. 23.
(4) a different Hebrew name. 1 Chr. 7. 8.
(5) others. 1 Chr. 4. 22; 12. 3; 27. 28; 1 Kn. 22. 26.
Joatham, jō'-ă-thăm, Greek form of Jotham. Mat. 1. 9.
Job, jōb. (1) Gen. 46. 13.
(2) one persecuted (?); his character. Job 1. 1, 8; 2. 3; (Ezek. 14. 14, 20).
his afflictions and patience. Job 1. 13, 20; 2. 7, 10 (Jas. 5. 11).
complains of his life. Job 3.
reproves his friends. Job 6.; 7.; 9.; 10.; 12.-14.; 16.; 17.; 19.; 21.; 23.; 24.; 26.-30.
solemnly protests his integrity. Job 31.
humbles himself. Job 40. 3; 42. 1.
God accepts and doubly blesses. Job 42. 10.
Jobab, jō'-băb, 'a desert' (?). Gen. 10. 29.
Jochebed, jŏch'-ĕ-bĕd, 'Jehovah is glorious;' mother of Moses. Ex. 6. 20; Num. 26. 59.
Joed, jō'-ĕd, 'Jehovah is witness.' Neh. 11. 7.
Joel, jō'-ĕl, 'Jehovah is God.' (1) son of Samuel. 1 Sam. 8. 2.
(2) prophet; delivers God's judgments. Joel 1.-3.
proclaims a fast, and declares God's mercy. Joel 1. 14; 2. 12; 3.
quoted. Acts 2. 16.
(3) others. 1 Chr. 6. 36; 7. 3; 11. 38; 15. 7; 27. 20.
Joelah, jō-ē'-lăh, 'may He help' (?). 1 Chr. 12. 7.

Joezer, jō-ē'-zĕr, 'Jehovah is help.' 1 Chr. 12. 6.
Jogbehah, jŏg'-bĕ-hăh, 'lofty.' Num. 32. 35.
Jogli, jŏg'-lī, 'led into exile' (?). Num. 34. 22.
Joha, jō'-hă. 1 Chr. 8. 16.
Johanan, jō-hā'-năn, 'Jehovah hath been gracious.' 2 Kn. 25. 23; Jer. 40. 8, 15; 41. 11; 42.; 43.
John, jŏhn, English form of Johanan. (1) the Apostle, called. Mat. 4. 21; Mk. 1. 19; Lu. 5. 10.
ordained. Mat. 10. 2; Mk. 3. 17.
enquires of Jesus. Mk. 13. 3.
reproved. Mat. 20. 20; Mk. 10. 35–40; Lu. 9. 50.
sent to prepare the passover. Lu. 22. 8.
declares the divinity and humanity of Jesus Christ. John 1.; 1 John 1.; 4.; 5.
Christ's love for. John 13. 23; 19. 26; 21. 7, 20, 24.
his care for Mary, the Lord's mother. John 19. 27.
meets for prayer. Acts 1. 13.
accompanies Peter before the council. Acts 3.; 4.
exhorts to obedience, and warns against false teachers. 1 John 1.–5.
sees Christ's glory in heaven. Rev. 1. 13.
writes the Revelation. Rev. 1. 19.
forbidden to worship the angel. Rev. 19. 10; 22. 8.
(2) (Mark). Acts 12. 12, 25. *See* Mark.
(3) the Baptist, his coming foretold. Isa. 40. 3; Mal. 4. 5; Lu. 1. 17.
his birth and circumcision. Lu. 1. 57.
office, preaching, and baptism. Mat. 3.; Mk. 1.; Lu. 3.; John 1. 6; 3. 26; Acts 1. 5; 13. 24.
baptizes Christ. Mat. 3.; Mk. 1.; Lu. 3.; John 1. 32; 3. 26.
imprisoned by Herod, Mat. 4. 12; Mk. 1. 14; Lu. 3. 20. and beheaded, Mat. 14.; Mk. 6. 14.
sends his disciples to Christ. Mat. 11. 1; Lu. 7. 18.
Christ's testimony to. Mat. 11. 11, 14; 17. 12; Mk. 9. 11; Lu. 7. 27.
his disciples receive the Holy Ghost. Acts 18. 24; 19. 1.
(4) Jewish dignitary. Acts 4. 6.
Joiada, joi'-ă-dă, 'Jehovah knows.' Neh. 12. 10.
Joiakim, joi'-ă-kĭm, shortened from Jehoiakim. Neh. 12. 10.
Joiarib, joi'-ă-rĭb, 'Jehovah pleads.' Ez. 8. 16.
Join. Prov. 11. 21; 16. 5, hand *j.* in hand.
Eccl. 9. 4, to him *j.* to living there is hope.
Isa. 5. 8, that *j.* house to house.
Jer. 50. 5, let us *j.* ourselves to the Lord.
Hos. 4. 17, Ephraim is *j.* to idols.
Mat. 19. 6; Mk. 10. 9, what God hath *j.*
Acts 5. 13, durst no man *j.* himself.
1 Cor. 1. 10, perfectly *j.* in same mind.
6. 17, *j.* to the Lord.
Eph. 4. 16, whole body *j.* together. R. V. framed.
See Acts 8. 29; 9. 26; 18. 7; Eph. 5. 31.
Joint. Gen. 32. 25; Ps. 22. 14; Prov. 25. 19, out of *j.* R. V. strained.
Eph. 4. 16, which every *j.* supplieth.
Heb. 4. 12, dividing asunder of *j.* and marrow.
See 1 Kn. 22. 34; Rom. 8. 17; Col. 2. 19.
Jokdeam, jŏk'-dĕ-ăm, 'burning of the people.' Jos. 15. 56.
Jokim, jō'-kĭm, shortened from Jehoiakim. 1 Chr. 4. 22.
Jokmeam, jŏk'-mĕ-ăm. 1 Chr. 6. 68.
Jokneam, jŏk'-nĕ-ăm. Jos. 12. 22.
Jokshan, jŏk'-shăn, 'fowler.' Gen. 25. 2.
Joktan, jŏk'-tăn. Gen. 10. 25.
Joktheel, jŏk'-thēel, 'subdued by God.' Jos. 15. 38.
Jona, jō'-nă, a Greek form of Johanan. John 1. 42. R. V. John.
Jonadab, jŏn'-ă-dăb, same as Jehonadab. (1) 2 Sam. 13. 3.
(2) (Jehonadab), son of Rechab. 2 Kn. 10. 15.
Jonah, jō'-năh, 'dove,' prophet. 2 Kn. 14. 25.
his disobedience, punishment, prayer, and repentance. Jon. 1.–4.
a type of Christ. Mat. 12. 39; Lu. 11. 29.
Jonan, jō'-năn, contracted from Johanan. Lu. 3. 30.
Jonas, jō'-năs. (1) same as Jona. John 21. 15.
(2) or Jonah. Mat. 12. 39.
Jonathan, jŏn'-ă-thăn, 'Jehovah gave.' (1) son of Saul, smites the Philistines. 1 Sam. 13. 2; 14.
his love for David. 1 Sam. 18. 1; 19.; 20.; 23. 16.
slain by the Philistines. 1 Sam. 31. 2.
David's lamentation for. 2 Sam. 1. 17.
(2) son of Abiathar. 2 Sam. 15. 27; 1 Kn. 1. 42.
(3) one of David's nephews; his deeds. 2 Sam. 21. 21; 1 Chr. 20. 7.
(4) a Levite, hired by Micah. Jud. 17. 7; 18.
Jonath-elem-rechokim, jō'-năth-ē'-lĕm-rĕ'-chō'-kĭm, 'after The Silent Dove in Far off Lands,' a popular melody of the time. Title of Ps. 56.
Joppa, jŏp'-pă, 'beauty' (?); the modern Jaffa (Yâfa), the seaport of Jerusalem, 30 miles to the west, and now connected with it by a railway. 2 Chr. 2. 16; Jon. 1. 3.
Tabitha raised at. Acts 9. 36.
Peter dwells at. Acts 10. 5; 11. 5.
Jorah, jôr'-ăh, 'watering' (?). Ez. 2. 18.
Jorai, jō'-rā-ī, 'Jehovah teaches.' 1 Chr. 5. 13.
Joram, jôr'-ăm, same as Jehoram (*q. v.*). 2 Sam. 8. 10; 1 Chr. 26. 25; 2 Chr. 17. 8.
Jordan, jôr'-dăn, 'descender,' the most important river in Palestine. It rises among the Lebanon Mountains, flows through Lake Merom to the Sea of Galilee, 13 miles long, then in a tortuous course of 200 miles through the Jordan valley, which is only 65 miles long in a straight line, to the Dead Sea. The direct course from the most northerly of its three sources is 125 miles, but the actual length of the stream is nearly 300 miles. Its width below the Sea of Galilee varies from 80 to 150 feet, its depth in summer 8 to 12 feet, in winter 17 to 21 feet. Gen. 13. 10.
river, waters of, divided for the Israelites, Jos. 3.; 4.; Ps. 114. 3. by Elijah and Elisha, 2 Kn. 2. 8, 13.
Naaman's leprosy cured at. 2 Kn. 5. 10.
John baptizes there. Mat. 3.; Mk. 1. 5; Lu. 3. 3. *See* Job 40. 23; Ps. 42. 6; Jer. 12. 5; 49. 19; Zec. 11. 3.
Jorim, jō'-rĭm, a form of Joram (?). Lu. 3. 29.
Jorkoam, jôr'-kō-ăm. 1 Chr. 2. 44.
Josabad, jŏs'-ă-băd, same as Jehozabad. 1 Chr. 12. 4.
Josaphat, jŏs'-ă-phăt, Greek form of Jehoshaphat. Mat. 1. 8.
Josedech, jŏs'-ĕ-dĕch, same as Jehozadak. Hag. 1. 1.
Joseph, jō'-sĕph, 'he shall add.' (1) son of Jacob. Gen. 30. 24. *See* Ps. 105. 17; Acts 7. 9; Heb. 11. 22.
his dreams, and the jealousy of his brethren. Gen. 37. 5.
sold to the Ishmeelites. Gen. 37. 28.
slave to Potiphar. Gen. 39.
resists Potiphar's wife. Gen. 39. 7.
interprets the dreams of Pharaoh's servants, Gen. 40. and of Pharaoh, predicting famine, Gen. 41. 25.
made ruler of Egypt. Gen. 41. 39.
prepares for the famine. Gen. 41. 48.
receives his brethren and father. Gen. 42.–46.
gives direction concerning his bones. Gen. 50. 25.
his death. Gen. 50. 26.
(2) son of Heli, husband of the Virgin. Mat. 1. 19; 2. 13, 19; Lu. 1. 27; 2. 4.
(3) of Arimathæa. Mat. 27. 57; Mk. 15. 42; Lu. 23. 50; John 19. 38.
(4) (Barsabas), Justus. Acts 1. 23.
(5) others. Num. 13. 7; Ez. 10. 42; Neh. 12. 14; Lu. 3. 24.
Joses, jō'-sĕs. (1) Mat. 13. 55. (2) Acts 4. 36. R. V. Joseph.
Joshah, jō'-shăh. 1 Chr. 4. 34.
Joshaphat, jŏsh'-ă-phăt, shortened from Jehoshaphat. 1 Chr. 11. 43.
Joshaviah, jŏsh-ă-vī'-ăh, same as Joshah (?). 1 Chr. 11. 46.
Joshbekashah, jŏsh-bĕ-kăsh'-ăh. 1 Chr. 25. 4.

Joshua, jŏsh'-ū-ă, 'Jehovah is salvation.'
(1) (Hoshea, Oshea, Jehoshua, Jeshua, and Jesus), son of Nun. Num. 14. 6; 1 Chr. 7. 27; Heb. 4. 8.
discomfits Amalek. Ex. 17. 9.
ministers to Moses. Ex. 24. 13; 32. 17; 33. 11.
spies out Canaan. Num. 13. 16.
ordained to succeed Moses. Num. 27. 18; 34. 17; Deu. 1. 38; 3. 28; 34. 9.
reassured by God. Jos. 1.
harangues his officers. Jos. 1. 10.
crosses river Jordan. Jos. 3.
erects memorial pillars. Jos. 4.
reenacts circumcision. Jos. 5.
assaults and destroys Jericho. Jos. 6.
condemns Achan. Jos. 7.
subdues Ai. Jos. 8.
his victories. Jos. 10.-12.
apportions the land. Jos. 14.-21.; Heb. 4. 8.
his charge to the Reubenites. Jos. 22.
exhortation to the people. Jos. 23.
reminds them of God's mercies. Jos. 24.
renews the covenant. Jos. 24. 14.
his death. Jos. 24. 29; Jud. 2. 8.
his curse, Jos. 6. 26. fulfilled, 1 Kn. 16. 34.
(2) others. 1 Sam. 6. 14; 2 Kn. 23. 8; Hag. 1. 1.

Josiah, jō-sī'-ăh, 'Jehovah supports.' (1) 2 Kn. 21. 24.
prophecy concerning, 1 Kn. 13. 2. fulfilled, 2 Kn. 23. 15.
reigns well. 2 Kn. 22.
repairs the temple. 2 Kn. 22. 3.
hears the words of the book of the law. 2 Kn. [22. 8.
Huldah's message from God to him. 2 Kn. 22. 15.
ordains the reading of the book. 2 Kn. 23.
keeps a signal passover to the Lord. 2 Chr. 35.
slain by Pharaoh-nechoh at Megiddo. 2 Kn. 23. 29.
(2) son of Zephaniah. Zec. 6. 10.

Josias, jō-sī'-ăs, Greek form of JOSIAH. Mat. 1. 10.

Josibiah, jŏs-ĭ-bī'-ăh, 'Jehovah causeth to dwell.' 1 Chr. 4. 35.

Josiphiah, jŏs-ĭ-phī'-ăh, 'Jehovah will add.' Ez. 8. 10.

Jot *or* **Yod**, the smallest letter of the Hebrew alphabet in its later form. Mat. 5. 18.

Jotbah, jŏt'-băh, 'pleasantness.' 2 Kn. 21. 19.

Jotbath, jŏt'-băth, same as JOTBAH. Deu. 10. 7.

Jotbathah, jŏt'-bă-thăh, same as JOTBAH. Num. 33. 33.

Jotham, jō'-thăm, 'Jehovah is perfect.' (1) son of Gideon; his apologue. Jud. 9. 5, 7.
(2) king of Judah. 2 Kn. 15. 32; 2 Chr. 27.
(3) son of Jahdai. 1 Chr. 2. 7.

Journey (*n.*). 1 Kn. 18. 27, or he is in a *j.*
Neh. 2. 6, for how long shall thy *j.* be?
Mat. 10. 10; Mk. 6. 8; Lu. 9. 3, nor scrip for your *j.*
John 4. 6, Jesus wearied with his *j.*

Journey (*v.*). Num. 10. 29, we are *j.* to the place.
See Gen. 12. 9; 13. 11.

Journeyings. Num. 10. 28, thus were the *j.*
2 Cor. 11. 26, in *j.* often.

Joy (*n.*). Ez. 3. 13, not discern noise of *j.*
Neh. 8. 10, *j.* of the Lord is your strength.
Job 20. 5, the *j.* of the hypocrite is but a moment.
29. 13, widow's heart sing for *j.*
33. 26, he will see his face with *j.* [danceth.
41. 22, sorrow is turned into *j.* R. V. terror
Ps. 16. 11, fulness of *j.*
30. 5, *j.* cometh in the morning.
48. 2, the *j.* of the whole earth.
51. 12, restore the *j.* of thy salvation.
126. 5, they that sow in tears shall reap in *j.*
137. 6, prefer Jerusalem above my chief *j.*
Prov. 14. 10, not intermeddle with his *j.*
21. 15, it is *j.* to the just to do judgment.
Eccl. 2. 10, I withheld not my heart from *j.*
9. 7, eat thy bread with *j.*
Isa. 9. 3, not increased the *j.*
Isa. 12. 3, with *j.* draw water.
24. 8, *j.* of the harp ceaseth.
29. 19, meek shall increase their *j.*
35. 10; 51. 11, and everlasting *j.*
56. 14, my servants sing for *j.* of heart.
Jer. 15. 16, thy word was the *j.* of my heart.
31. 13, will turn their mourning into *j.*
49. 25, the city of my *j.*
Lam. 2. 15, the *j.* of the whole earth.
Mat. 13. 20; Lu. 8. 13, with *j.* receiveth it.
13. 44, for *j.* goeth and selleth.
25. 21, 23, the *j.* of thy Lord.
Lu. 15. 7, *j.* in heaven over one sinner.
15. 10, there is *j.* in presence of angels.
24. 41, they believed not for *j.*
John 3. 29, this my *j.* is fulfilled.
15. 11; 16. 24, that your *j.* may be full.
Acts 8. 8, great *j.* in that city.
20. 24, finish my course with *j.*
2 Cor. 1. 24, helpers of your *j.*
Phil. 2. 2, fulfil ye my *j.*
Heb. 12. 2, for the *j.* that was set before him.
Jas. 1. 2, count it all *j.* when ye fall.
1 Pet. 1. 8, with *j.* unspeakable.
4. 13, glad also with exceeding *j.*
2 John 12, that our *j.* may be full.
Jude 24, faultless, with exceeding *j.*

Joy (*v.*), to rejoice. Ps. 21. 1.

Joy. 1 Chr. 12. 40; Ez. 6. 16; Neh. 8. 10; Ps. 16. 11; 89. 16; 149. 2; Isa. 35. 2; 60. 15; 61. 10; Hab. 3. 18; Lu. 10. 20; John 15. 11; Rom. 14. 17; Gal. 5. 22; Phil. 3. 3; Col. 1. 11; 1 Thes. 1. 6; Heb. 10. 34.
of the wicked, folly. Job 20. 5; Prov. 15. 21; Eccl. 2. 10; 7. 6; 11. 9; Isa. 16. 10; Jas. 4. 9.
follows grief. Ps. 30. 5; 126. 5; Prov. 14. 10; Isa. 35. 10; 61. 3; 66. 10; Jer. 31. 13; John 16. 20; 2 Cor. 6. 10; Jas. 1. 2.
in heaven over one repenting sinner. Lu. 15. 7, 10.
of Paul over the churches. 2 Cor. 1. 24; 2. 3; 7. 4, 13; Phil. 1. 4; 2. 2; 4. 1; 1 Thes. 2. 19; 3. 9; 2 Tim. 1. 4; Philem. 7.
of Paul and Titus. 2 Cor. 7. 13.
of John over his spiritual children. 3 John 4.
expressed by psalmody. Eph. 5. 19; Col. 3. 16; Jas. 5. 13.

Joyful. Ps. 35. 9, my soul shall be *j.* in the Lord.
63. 5, praise thee with *j.* lips.
66. 1; 81. 1; 95. 1; 98. 6, make a *j.* noise.
Eccl. 7. 14, in day of prosperity be *j.*
Isa. 56. 7, *j.* in my house of prayer. [12. 20.

Jozabad, jō'-ză-băd, same as JEHOZABAD. 1 Chr.

Jozachar, jō'-ză-chăr, 'Jehovah has remembered.' 2 Kn. 12. 21.

Jozadak, jō'-ză-dăk, same as JEHOZADAK. Ez. 3. 2.

Jubal, jū'-băl, inventor of harp and organ. Gen. 4. 21.

Jubilee, year of. At the end of seven times seven years, that is, forty-nine entire years, the fiftieth was observed as the year of *Jubilee*, a word of uncertain meaning. The directions for its observance are given in Lev. 25. 8-16, 23-55.

Jucal, jū'-căl, same as JEHUCAL. Jer. 38. 1.

Juda, jū'-dă. (1) Same as JUDAS. Lu. 3. 30.
(2) Same as JUDAH. Lu. 3. 33.

Judæa, jū-dæ'-ă, same as JUDEA. Mat. 19. 1.

Judah, jū'-dăh, 'praised.' (1) son of Jacob. Gen. 29. 35.
his descendants. Gen. 38.; 46. 12; Num. 1. 26; 26. 19; 1 Chr. 2.-4.
pledges himself for Benjamin. Gen. 43. 3.
his interview with Joseph. Gen. 44. 18-46. 28.
blessed by Jacob. Gen. 49. 8.
(2) tribe of, their blessing by Moses. Deu. 33. 7.
their inheritance. Jos. 15.
they make David king, 2 Sam. 2. 4. and adhere to his house, 1 Kn. 12.; 2 Chr. 10.; 11. *See* JEWS.
(3) others. Ez. 3. 9; 10. 23; Neh. 11. 9.

Judas, jū'-dăs, Greek form of Judah. (1) (JUDE, Lebbæus, Thaddæus), Apostle, brother of

James. Mat. 10. 3; Mk. 3. 18; Lu. 6. 16; Acts 1. 13.
his question to our Lord. John 14. 22.
enjoins perseverance. Jude 3, 20.
denounces false disciples. Jude 4.
(2) the Lord's brother. Mat. 13. 55; Mk. 6. 3.
(3) of Galilee. Acts 5. 37.
(4) (Barsabas). Acts 15. 22.
(5) others. Mat. 1. 2 (R. V. Judah); Acts 9. 11.

Judas Iscariot, jū'-dăs Ĭs-căr'-ĭ-ŏt. Mat. 10. 4; Mk. 3. 19; Lu. 6. 16; John 6. 70.
betrays Jesus. Mat. 26. 14, 47; Mk. 14. 10, 43; Lu. 22. 3, 47; John 13. 26; 18. 2.
hangs himself. Mat. 27. 5 (Acts 1. 18).

Jude, jūde, same as Judas. Jude 1.

Judea, jū-dē'-ă, 'land of Judah.' Ez. 5. 8. R. V. Judah.

Judge (*n.*). Gen. 18. 25; Ps. 94. 2, the *J.* of all the earth.
Ps. 50. 6, God is *j.* himself.
68. 5, a *j.* of the widows.
Mic. 7. 3, the *j.* asketh a reward.
Lu. 12. 14, who made me a *j.* over you?
18. 6, the unjust *j.*
Acts 10. 42, the *J.* of quick and dead.
2 Tim. 4. 8, the Lord, the righteous *j.*
Heb. 12. 23, to God the *J.* of all.
Jas. 5. 9, the *j.* standeth before the door.
See 2 Sam. 15. 4; Mat. 5. 25; Jas. 4. 11. [thee.

Judge (*v.*). Gen. 16. 5, Lord *j.* between me and
Deu. 32. 36; Ps. 7. 8, Lord *j.* the people.
Ps. 58. 11, he is a God that *j.* in the earth.
Isa. 1. 17, *j.* the fatherless.
Mat. 7. 1, *j.* not, that ye be not *j.*
Lu. 7. 43, thou hast rightly *j.*
John 7. 24, *j.* righteous judgment.
Rom. 14. 4, who art thou that *j.*?
See John 16. 11; Rom. 2. 16; 3. 6; 2 Tim. 4. 1.

Judges. The administration of justice amongst the Israelites, as in all early Eastern nations, rested with the heads of tribes, or of the chief families in a tribe (Job 29. 7–10; Ex. 18. 14–24). The judges of the period described in the book of Judges were 'a *succession of chiefs*, who arose in different parts of the land, *ruling with an authority* which was *personal and not hereditary*.' 'They were more like Peter the Hermit and Jeanne d'Arc than like Roman dictators.' 'The signification of the Hebrew word is much wider than that of the Greek κριτής, the Latin *judex*, or the English *judge*.' 'The judge was not only the *vindicator*, the *punisher*, but also the *defender*, the *deliverer*.' *Int. Crit. Com.*

Judges, appointment of. Deu. 16. 18; Ez. 7. 25.
their functions. Ex. 18. 21; Lev. 19. 15; Deu. 1. 16; 17. 8; 2 Chr. 19. 6; Ps. 82.; Prov. 18. 5; 24. 23.
unjust, 1 Sam. 8. 3; Isa. 1. 23; Lu. 18. 2. hateful to God, Prov. 17. 15; 24. 24; Isa. 10. 1.
Judges, Book of, is the record of the exploits of leaders, heroes, and deliverers of Israel, during the first two or three centuries of Israel as a nation up to the establishment of the kingdom. *See* Summaries.

Judgment. Deu. 1. 17, the *j.* is God's.
Ps. 1. 5, shall not stand in the *j.*
101. 1, I will sing of mercy and *j.*
Prov. 29. 26, *j.* cometh from the Lord.
Eccl. 11. 9; 12. 14, God will bring into *j.*
Isa. 28. 17, *j.* will I lay to the line.
53. 8, taken from prison and from *j.*
Jer. 5. 1, if there be any that executeth *j.* R. V. doeth justly.
10. 24, correct with *j.*, not in anger.
Hos. 12. 6, keep mercy and *j.*
Mat. 5. 21, in danger of the *j.*
John 5. 22, Father committed all *j.* to the Son.
9. 39, for *j.* I am come.
16. 8, reprove the world of *j.*
Acts 24. 25, reasoned of *j.* to come.
Rom. 14. 10, we shall all stand before the *j.* seat.
Heb. 9. 27, after this the *j.*
1 Pet. 4. 17, *j.* must begin at house of God.
See Mat. 12. 41; Heb. 10. 27; Jas. 2. 13.

Judgment, cautions respecting. Mat. 7. 1; Lu. 6. 37; 12. 57; John 7. 24; Rom. 2. 1; Jas. 4. 11.

Judgment, the Last, foretold. 1 Chr. 16. 33; Ps. 9. 7; 96. 13; 98. 9; Eccl. 3. 17; 11. 9; 12. 14; Acts 17. 31; Rom. 2. 16; 2 Cor. 5. 10; Heb. 9. 27; 2 Pet. 3. 7.
described. Ps. 50.; Dan. 7. 9; Mat. 25. 31; 2 Thes. 1. 8; Rev. 6. 12; 20. 11.
hope of Christians respecting. Rom. 8. 33; 1 Cor. 4. 5; 2 Tim. 4. 8; 1 John 2. 28; 4. 17.

Judith, jū'-dĭth, probably from same as Judea. Gen. 26. 34.

Julia, jū'-lĭ-ă, feminine form of Julius. Rom. 16. 15.

Julius, jū'-lĭ-ŭs, 'downy.' Acts 27. 1.

Junias *or* **Junia**, a kinsman, once a fellowprisoner of St. Paul, greeted by him as 'of note among the apostles.' Rom. 16. 7.

Juniper (1 Kn. 19. 4). Heb. *Rothem:* Gk. ῥαθμέν: Bot. N. *Retama rætam:* R. V. marg. 'broom.' A desert shrub (Arabic *retem*), growing about Sinai and the Jordan valley. Not a juniper, but a broom which grows to a height of ten feet.

Jupiter, jū'-pĭ-tĕr, Latin name corresponding to Zeus; Barnabas addressed as. Acts 14. 12; 19. 35.

Jushab-hesed, jū'-shăb-hĕs'-ĕd, 'love is returned.' 1 Chr. 3. 20.

Just. Job 9. 2, how should man be *j.* with God?
Prov. 3. 33, God blesseth the habitation of the *j.*
4. 18, path of *j.* as shining light. R. V. righteous.
10. 7, memory of *j.* is blessed.
Isa. 26. 7, way of the *j.* is uprightness.
Hab. 2. 4; Rom. 1. 17; Gal. 3. 11; Heb. 10. 38, the *j.* shall live by faith.
Mat. 5. 45, sendeth rain on *j.* and unjust.
Lu. 14. 14, recompensed at resurrection of *j.*
15. 7, ninety and nine *j.* persons. R. V. righteous.
Acts 24. 15, resurrection both of *j.* and unjust.
Rom. 3. 26, that he might be *j.*
Phil. 4. 8, whatsoever things are *j.*
Heb. 2. 2, a *j.* recompence of reward.
12. 23, spirits of *j.* men made perfect.
1 Pet. 3. 18, the *j.* for the unjust.
See Job 34. 17; Acts 3. 14.

Justice. 2 Sam. 15. 4, I would do *j.*
Ps. 89. 14, *j.* and judgment are the habitation. R. V. righteousness.
Prov. 8. 15, by me princes decree *j.*
Isa. 59. 4, none calleth for *j.* R. V. sueth in righteousness.
Jer. 23. 5, execute judgment and *j.* in the earth.
50. 7, the habitation of *j.*
See Job 36. 17; Isa. 9. 7.

Justice of God. Deu. 32. 4; Job 4. 17; 8. 3; 34. 12; Isa. 45. 21; Zep. 3. 5; 1 John 1. 9; Rev. 15. 3.
to do, enjoined. Lev. 19. 36; Deu. 16. 18; Ps. 82. 3; Prov. 3. 33; 11. 1; Isa. 56. 1; Jer. 22. 3; Ezek. 18. 5; 45. 9; Mic. 6. 8; Mat. 7. 12; Rom. 13. 7; 2 Cor. 8. 21; Phil. 4. 8; Col. 4. 1.

Justification by faith. Hab. 2. 4; Acts 13. 39; Rom. 1. 17; 3.–5.; Gal. 3. 11.
by works. Jas. 2. 14–26. [be *j.*?

Justify. (1) Job 11. 2, should a man full of talk
25. 4, how then can man be *j.* with God? R. V. just.
Ps. 51. 4, be *j.* when thou speakest.
143. 2, in thy sight shall no man living be *j.*
Isa. 5. 23, which *j.* the wicked for reward.
Mat. 11. 19; Lu. 7. 35, wisdom is *j.* of her children.
12. 37, by thy words thou shalt be *j.*
Lu. 10. 29, willing to *j.* himself.
18. 14, *j.* rather than the other.
Acts 13. 39, all that believe are *j.*
Rom. 3. 24; Tit. 3. 7, *j.* freely by his grace.
5. 1, being *j.* by faith.

Rom. 5. 9, being now *j.* by his blood.
Gal. 2. 16, man is not *j.* by works of the law.
1 Tim. 3. 16, *j.* in the Spirit.
(2) to acquit. Deu. 25. 1; Job 33. 32.
See Isa. 50. 8; Rom. 4. 5; 8. 33.

Justly. Mic. 6. 8; Lu. 23. 41; 1 Thes. 2. 10.

Justus, jŭs′-tŭs, 'upright.' Acts 1. 23.

Juttah, jŭt′-tăh, 'extended.' Jos. 15. 55.

Kabzeel, kăb′-zēēl, 'God has gathered.' Jos. 15. 21.

Kadesh, kā′-dĕsh, *or* **Kadesh-barnea,** kā′-dĕsh-bär′-nē-ă, was 'in the wilderness of Zin' (Num. 27. 14; Deu. 32. 51), which ran 'along by the *side of Edom*' (Num. 34. 3, 4; Jos. 15. 1-3). According to Num. 20. 16, and Josephus, *Ant.* iv. 4, 5, it was in the '*border*' of Edom, i. e., of Mount Seir. It is probably the modern *Ain Kadis*, 35 miles west of the Arabah, a stronghold at the base of the mountainous range which constitutes the southern border of Palestine.
Israelites murmur against Moses and Aaron, threaten to stone Caleb and Joshua, and provoke God's anger. Num. 13.; 14.; Deu. 1. 19; Jos. 14. 6.

Kadmiel, kăd′-mī-ĕl, 'eternity of God' (?). Ez. 2. 40.

Kadmonites, kăd′-mō-nītes, 'Orientals.' Gen. 15. 19.

Kallai, kăl-lā′-ī, 'swift.' Neh. 12. 20.

Kanah, kā′-năh, 'place of reeds' (Jos. 16. 8; 19. 28), a small river or wady on the boundary between Ephraim and Manasseh, flowing into a stream that enters the Mediterranean.

Kareah, kă-rē′-ăh, 'bald.' Jer. 40. 8.

Karkaa, kär′-kă-ă, 'floor.' Jos. 15. 3.

Karkor, kär′-kôr, 'plain' (?). Jud. 8. 10.

Karnaim, kär-nā′-ĭm, 'two horns.' Gen. 14. 5.

Kartah, kär′-tăh, 'city' (?). Jos. 21. 34.

Kartan, kär′-tăn, 'double city' (?). Jos. 21. 32.

Kattath, kăt′-tăth, 'small' (?). Jos. 19. 15.

Kedar, kē′-där, 'black-skinned.' (1) son of Ishmael. Gen. 25. 13; 1 Chr. 1. 29; Ps. 120. 5; S. of S. 1. 5; Jer. 2. 10; Ezek. 27. 21.
(2) tribe of, prophecies concerning. Isa. 21. 16; 42. 11; 60. 7; Jer. 49. 28.

Kedemah, kē′-dĕ-măh, 'eastward.' Gen. 25. 15.

Kedemoth, kē′-dĕ-mōth, 'eastern parts.' Jos. 13. 18.

Kedesh, kē′-dĕsh, 'sanctuary.' Jos. 12. 22.

Kedesh-naphtali, kē′-dĕsh-năph′-tă-lī. Jud. 4. 6.

Keep. Gen. 18. 19, they shall *k.* the way of the Lord.
Num. 6. 24, the Lord bless thee, and *k.* thee.
1 Sam. 2. 9, he will *k.* the feet of his saints.
25. 34, the Lord God hath *k.* me back from hurting thee.
Ps. 17. 8, *k.* me as the apple of the eye.
34. 13, *k.* thy tongue from evil.
91. 11, angels charge to *k.* thee in all thy ways.
121. 3, he that *k.* thee will not slumber.
127. 1, except the Lord *k.* the city.
141. 3, *k.* the door of my lips.
Prov. 4. 6, love wisdom, she shall *k.* thee.
4. 21, *k.* my sayings in midst of thine heart.
4. 23, *k.* thy heart with all diligence.
6. 20, my son, *k.* thy father's commandment.
Eccl. 3. 6, a time to *k.*
5. 1, *k.* thy foot when thou goest.
12. 13, fear God, and *k.* his commandments.
Isa. 26. 3, thou wilt *k.* him in perfect peace.
27. 3, I the Lord do *k.* it, I will *k.* it.
Jer. 3. 5, 12, will he *k.* his anger?
Hab. 2. 20, let the earth *k.* silence.
Mal. 3. 14, what profit that we have *k.*
Mat. 19. 17, if thou wilt enter life, *k.* the commandments.
Lu. 11. 28, blessed are they that *k.*
19. 43, enemies shall *k.* thee in on every side.
John 8. 51, 52, *k.* my sayings.
12. 25, he that hateth his life shall *k.* it.
14. 23, if a man love me, he will *k.* my words.
John 17. 11, holy Father, *k.* through thine own name.
17. 15, that thou shouldest *k.* them from the evil.
Acts 16. 4, delivered the decrees to *k.*
21. 25, *k.* from things offered to idols.
1 Cor. 5. 8, let us *k.* the feast.
9. 27, I *k.* under my body. R. V. buffet.
Eph. 4. 3, *k.* the unity of the Spirit.
Phil. 4. 7, the peace of God shall *k.* your hearts. R. V. guard.
1 Tim. 5. 22, *k.* thyself pure.
6. 20, *k.* that which is committed. R. V. guard.
Jas. 1. 27, *k.* himself unspotted.
1 John 5. 21, *k.* yourselves from idols. R. V. guard.
Jude 21, *k.* yourselves in the love of God. [guard.
24, him that is able to *k.* you from falling. R.V.
Rev. 3. 10, I will *k.* thee from hour of temptation.
22. 9, which *k.* the sayings of this book.
See 1 Pet. 1. 5; 4. 19; Jude 6; Rev. 3. 8.

Keeper. Ps. 121. 5, the Lord is thy *k.*
Eccl. 12. 3, when the *k.* of the house shall tremble.
S. of S. 1. 6, they made me *k.* of the vineyards.
Tit. 2. 5, chaste, *k.* at home. R. V. workers.
See Gen. 4. 2, 9; Mat. 28. 4; Acts 5. 23; 16. 27.

Kehelathah, kē-hĕ-lā′-thăh, 'assembly.' Num. 33. 22.

Keilah, kē-ī′-lăh, 'sling' (?). (1) a place. Jos. 15. 44.
David there. 1 Sam. 23. 1, 12.
(2) a man. 1 Chr. 4. 19.

Kelaiah, kĕ-lāī′-ăh, 'contempt' (?). Ez. 10. 23.

Kelita, kĕ-lī′-tă, 'dwarf' (?). Neh. 8. 7.

Kemuel, kĕ-mū′-ĕl, 'congregation of God' (?). (1) Gen. 22. 21. (2) Num. 34. 24. (3) 1 Chr. 27. 17.

Kenan, kē′-năn, 'smith' (?). 1 Chr. 1. 2.

Kenath, kē′-năth, 'possession.' Num. 32. 42.

Kenaz, kē′-năz, 'hunting.' Gen. 36. 11.

Kenezite, kē′-nĕz-īte, descendant of Kenaz. Num. 32. 12.

Kenites, kē′-nītes, descendants of an unknown man named Kain. Gen. 15. 19.
their fate foretold. Num. 24. 22. [Gen. 15. 19.

Kenizzites, kĕ-nĭz′-zītes, same as Kenezite.

Kerchief, a cloth worn over the head, a head-dress consisting of a simple square or oblong piece of linen, silk, etc.; woe respecting, Ezek. 13. 18.

Keren-happuch, kĕr′-ĕn-hăp′-pŭch, 'horn of antimony.'
one of Job's daughters. Job 42. 14.

Kerioth, kĕr′-ĭ-ŏth, 'cities;' a city of Judah. Jos. 15. 25; Jer. 48. 24, 41; Am. 2. 2.

Keros, kē′-rŏs, 'crook' (?). Ez. 2. 44.

Keturah, kĕ-tū′-răh, 'incense,' Abraham's wife, Gen. 25. her children, 1 Chr. 1. 32.

Key. Mat. 16. 19, the *k.* of kingdom of heaven.
Lu. 11. 52, ye have taken away *k.* of knowledge.
Rev. 1. 18, the *k.* of hell and of death.

Key of David. Isa. 22. 22; Rev. 3. 7.
keys of heaven. Mat. 16. 19.
of hell. Rev. 1. 18; 9. 1.

Kezia, kĕ-zī′-ă, 'cassia.' Job 42. 14.

Keziz, kē′-zĭz, 'cut off.' Jos. 18. 21.

Kibroth-hattaavah, kĭb′-rōth-hăt-tā′-ă-văh, 'graves of lust.' Num. 11. 34.

Kibzaim, kĭb′-zā-ĭm, 'two heaps.' Jos. 21. 22.

Kick. Deu. 32. 15; 1 Sam. 2. 29; Acts 9. 5.

Kid, laws about. Ex. 23. 19; Deu. 14. 21; Lev. 4. 23; 16. 5; 23. 19.

Kidneys, for sacrifices, burnt. Ex. 29. 13; Lev. 3. 4.
of wheat, fat of. Deu. 32. 14.

Kidron, kī′-drŏn *or* kĭd′-rŏn, the Brook. The torrent valley or wady of Kidron = Black; (Cedron, A. V. of John 18. 1). The deep valley east of Jerusalem, separating it from the Mt. of Olives; dry most of the year except after heavy rains (2 Sam. 15. 23); near garden of Gethsemane, frequented by our Lord, John 18. 1.
crossed by David. 2 Sam. 15. 23.
idols destroyed there. 1 Kn. 15. 13; 2 Kn. 23. 6; 2 Chr. 29. 16; Jer. 31. 40. *See* Cedron.

Kill. Num. 16. 13, to *k.* us in the wilderness.
2 Kn. 5. 7, am I a God to *k.*?
7. 4, if they *k.* us, we shall but die.
Eccl. 3. 3, a time to *k.*
Mat. 10. 28; Lu. 12. 4, fear not them that *k.* the [body.
Mk. 3. 4, is it lawful to save life, or to *k.*?
John 5. 18, the Jews sought the more to *k.* him.
7. 19, why go ye about to *k.* me?
8. 22, will he *k.* himself?
Rom. 8. 36, for thy sake we are *k.* all the day.
2 Cor. 3. 6, the letter *k.*
6. 9, chastened, and not *k.*
Jas. 4. 2, ye *k.*, and desire to have.
5. 6, ye condemned and *k.* the just.
See Mat. 23. 37; Mk. 12. 5; Lu. 22. 2.

Kinah, kī′-năh, 'song of mourning,' 'lamentation.' Jos. 15. 22.

Kind. (1) sort, species, class. Gen. 1. 11, 25.
Mat. 17. 21; Mk. 9. 29, this *k.* goeth not out.
(2) 2 Chr. 10. 7, if thou be *k.* to this people.
Lu. 6. 35, *k.* to unthankful and evil.
1 Cor. 13. 4, charity suffereth long, and is *k.*
See Mat. 13. 47; Eph. 4. 32; Jas. 3. 7.

Kindle. Ps. 2. 12, his wrath is *k.* but a little.
Prov. 26. 21, a contentious man to *k.* strife. R. V. inflame.
Isa. 50. 11, walk in sparks that ye have *k.*
Hos. 11. 8, my repentings are *k.* together.
Lu. 12. 49, what will I, if it be already *k.*?
Jas. 3. 5, how great a matter a little fire *k.*
See Job 19. 11; 32. 2; Ezek. 20. 48.

Kindly. Gen. 24. 49; 50. 21; Ru. 1. 8; Rom. 12. [10.

Kindness. Ru. 3. 10, thou hast shewed more *k.*
2 Sam. 2. 6, I will requite you this *k.*
9. 1, 7, show him *k.* for Jonathan's sake.
Ps. 17. 7; 92. 2, thy marvellous loving-*k.*
36. 7, how excellent is thy loving-*k.*!
63. 3, thy loving-*k.* is better than life.
117. 2; 119. 76, his merciful *k.*
141. 5, righteous smite me, it shall be a *k.*
Prov. 31. 26, in her tongue is the law of *k.*
Isa. 54. 8, with everlasting *k.*
Jer. 2. 2, I remember the *k.* of thy youth.
31. 3, with loving-*k.* have I drawn thee.
Col. 3. 12, put on *k.*, meekness.
2 Pet. 1. 7, to godliness, brotherly *k.* R. V. love of the brethren.

Kindness enjoined. Jos. 2. 12; Ru. 2.; 3.; Prov. 19. 22; 31. 26; Rom. 12. 10; 1 Cor. 13. 4; 2 Cor. 6. 6; Eph. 4. 32; Col. 3. 12; 2 Pet. 1. 7.
of God. Neh. 9. 17; Joel 2. 13; Jon. 4. 2.

Kindred. Acts 3. 25; Rev. 1. 7; 5. 9; 7. 9.

Kine, the old plural of 'cow;' 'milch kine' = milking-cows.
Pharaoh's dream of. Gen. 41. 2.
two take back the ark. 1 Sam. 6. 7.

King. Num. 23. 21, the shout of a *k.* is among [them.
Jud. 9. 8, the trees went forth to anoint a *k.*
17. 6, no *k.* in Israel.
1 Sam. 8. 5, now make us a *k.*
8. 19, we will have a *k.*
10. 24; 2 Sam. 16. 16, God save the *k.*
Job 18. 14, bring him to the *k.* of terrors.
34. 18, is it fit to say to a *k.*?
Ps. 5. 2; 84. 3, my *K.* and my God.
10. 16, the Lord is *K.* for ever.
20. 9, let the *k.* hear us when we call.
74. 12, God is my *K.* of old.
102. 15, the *k.* of the earth shall fear.
Prov. 8. 15, by me *k.* reign.
22. 29, the diligent shall stand before *k.*
31. 3, that which destroyeth *k.*
31. 4, it is not for *k.* to drink wine.
Eccl. 2. 12, what can the man do that cometh after the *k.*?
10. 16, woe to thee when thy *k.* is a child!
10. 20, curse not the *k.*
Isa. 32. 1, a *k.* shall reign in righteousness.
33. 17, thine eyes shall see the *k.* in his beauty.
49. 23, *k.* shall be thy nursing fathers.
Jer. 10. 10, the Lord is an everlasting *k.*
Mat. 22. 11, when the *k.* came in to see the guests.
Lu. 19. 38, blessed be the *K.* that cometh.
Lu. 23. 2, saying that he himself is Christ a *k.*
John 6. 15, by force, to make him a *k.*
19. 14, behold your *K.*!
19. 15, we have no *k.* but Cæsar.
1 Tim. 1. 17, now unto the *K.* eternal.
6. 15, the *K.* of *k.* and Lord of lords.
Rev. 1. 6; 5. 10, made us *k.* and priests unto God. R. V. to be a kingdom.
15. 3, thou *K.* of saints.

King, Israelites desire a. 1 Sam. 8. 5.
See ANOINTING.

Kingdom. Ex. 19. 6, a *k.* of priests.
1 Chr. 29. 11; Mat. 6. 13, thine is the *k.*
Ps. 22. 28, the *k.* is the Lord's.
103. 19, his *k.* ruleth over all.
145. 12, the glorious majesty of his *k.*
Isa. 14. 16, is this the man that did shake *k.*?
Dan. 4. 3, his *k.* is an everlasting *k.*
Mat. 4. 23; 9. 35; 24. 14, gospel of the *k.*
8. 12, children of the *k.* cast out.
12. 25; Mk. 3. 24; Lu. 11. 17, *k.* divided against [itself.
13. 38, good seed are children of the *k.*
25. 34, inherit the *k.*
Lu. 12. 32, Father's good pleasure to give you the [*k.*
22. 29, I appoint unto you a *k.*
John 18. 36, my *k.* is not of this world.
Acts 1. 6, wilt thou restore the *k.* to Israel?
1 Cor. 15. 24, when he shall have delivered up the [*k.*
Col. 1. 13, into the *k.* of his dear Son.
2 Tim. 4. 18, to his heavenly *k.*
Jas. 2. 5, heirs of the *k.* he hath promised.
2 Pet. 1. 11, entrance into everlasting *k.*
See Rev. 16. 10; 17. 17.

Kingdom of GOD. 1 Chr. 29. 11; Ps. 22. 28; 45. 6; 145. 11; Isa. 24. 23; Dan. 2. 44.
of CHRIST. Isa. 2.; 4.; 9.; 11.; 32.; 35.; 52.; 61.; 66.; Mat. 16. 28; 26. 29; John 18. 36; 2 Pet. 1. 11; Rev. 1. 9; 11. 15.
of heaven. Mat. 3. 2; 8. 11; 11. 11; 13. 11.
who shall enter. Mat. 5. 3; 7. 21; Lu. 9. 62; John 3. 3; Acts 14. 22; Rom. 14. 17; 1 Cor. 6. 9; 15. 50; 2 Thes. 1. 5.
parables concerning. Mat. 13. 24, &c.

King of kings. Ps. 2. 6; 10. 16; 24. 7; 110.; Zec. 9. 9; Lu. 23. 2; 1 Tim. 1. 17; 6. 15; Rev. 15. 3; 17. 14; 19. 16.

Kings chosen by God. Deu. 17. 14; 1 Sam. 9. 17; 1 Sam. 16. 1; 1 Kn. 11. 35; 1 Kn. 19. 15; 1 Chr. 28. 4; Dan. 2. 21.
admonished. Ps. 2. 10; Prov. 31. 4.
duty of. Prov. 25. 2; Isa. 49. 23.
honour due to. Prov. 24. 21; 25. 6; Eccl. 8. 2; 10. 20; Mat. 22. 21; Rom. 13.; 1 Pet. 2. 13, 17.
to be prayed for. 1 Tim. 2. 1, 2.
parable of the king and his servants, Mat. 18. 23.
of the king and his guests, Mat. 22. 2.

Kinsfolk. Job 19. 14; Lu. 2. 44; 21. 16.

Kinsman, right of. Ru. 3. 14; 4.

Kir, kĭr, 'town.' 2 Kn. 16. 9; Isa. 15. 1; 22. 6; Am. 1. 5; 9. 7.

Kir-haraseth, kĭr-hăr′-ă-sĕth, 'brick-town.' 2 Kn. 3. 25; Isa. 16. 7, 11.

Kir-hareseth, kĭr-hăr′-ĕ-sĕth, same as preceding. Isa. 16. 7.

Kir-haresh, kĭr-hăr′-ĕsh, same as preceding. Isa. 16. 11.

Kir-heres, kĭr-hē′-rĕs, same as preceding. Jer. 48. 31.

Kiriathaim, kĭr-ĭ-ă-thā′-ĭm, same as KIRJATHAIM. (1) Jos. 13. 19. (2) 1 Chr. 6. 76. (3) Ezek. 25. 9.

Kirioth, kĭr′-ĭ-ōth, 'cities.' Am. 2. 2.

Kirjath, kĭr′-jăth, 'city' (?). Jos. 18. 28.

Kirjathaim, kĭr-jă-thā′-ĭm, 'double city.' Num. 32. 37.

Kirjath-arba, kĭr′-jăth-ăr′-bă, 'city of Arba.' Gen. 23. 2.

Kirjath-arim, kĭr′-jăth-ăr′-ĭm, contracted from KIRJATH-JEARIM. Ez. 2. 25.

Kirjath-baal, kĭr′-jăth-bā′-ăl, 'city of Baal.' Jos. 15. 60.

Kirjath-huzoth, kĭr′-jăth-hū′-zŏth, 'city of streets.' Num. 22. 39.
Kirjath-jearim, kĭr′-jăth-jē′-ā-rĭm, 'city of woods.' Jos. 9. 17; 18. 14; 1 Chr. 13. 6.
the ark brought to. 1 Sam. 7. 1.
ark fetched from. 1 Chr. 13. 5; 2 Chr. 1. 4.
Kirjath-sannah, kĭr′-jăth-săn′-năh, 'city of thorns' (?). Jos. 15. 49.
Kirjath-sepher, kĭr′-jăth-sē′-phĕr, 'book-city' (?). Jos. 15. 15.
Kish, kĭsh, bow. (1) Saul's father. 1 Sam. 9. 1.
(2) others. 1 Chr. 8. 30; 24. 29; 2 Chr. 29. 12; Esth. 2. 5.
Kishi, kĭsh′-ī, 'bow of Jehovah' (?). 1 Chr. 6. 44.
Kishion, kĭsh′-jŏn, 'hardness.' Jos. 19. 20.
Kishon, kī′-shŏn, 'tortuous.' Jud. 4. 7; 5. 21; 1 Kn. 18. 40 = 'the waters of Megiddo.' A river which drains the plain of Esdraelon, flowing northwesterly along the base of Mt. Carmel to the Mediterranean.
Kison, kī′-sŏn, same as Kishon. Ps. 83. 9.
Kiss. Ps. 85. 10; Prov. 27. 6.
Kiss, holy, salute with. Rom. 16. 16; 1 Cor. 16. 20; 2 Cor. 13. 12; 1 Thes. 5. 26.
of charity. 1 Pet. 5. 14.
given as mark of affection. Gen. 27. 27; 29. 11; 45. 15; 48. 10; 1 Sam. 10. 1; 20. 41; Lu. 7. 38; 15. 20; Acts 20. 37.
given treacherously. 2 Sam. 20. 9; Mat. 26. 48; Lu. 22. 48.
idolatrous. 1 Kn. 19. 18; Job 31. 27; Hos. 13. 2.
Kite (Lev. 11. 14; Deu. 14. 13). Heb. *Ayyah:* Gk. ἰκτῖνος. (Specimen, *Milvus regalis.*) *Ayyah* is a generic term for 'keen-sighted' birds of the falcon tribe. There are three kinds of kite in Bible lands.
Kithlish, kĭth′-lĭsh. Jos. 15. 40.
Kitron, kĭt′-rŏn, 'burning.' Jud. 1. 30.
Kittim, kĭt′-tĭm, same as Chittim. Gen. 10. 4.
Knead. Gen. 18. 6; Ex. 8. 3; Hos. 7. 4.
Kneeling in prayer. 2 Chr. 6. 13; Ez. 9. 5; Ps. 95. 6; Dan. 6. 10; Acts 7. 60; 9. 40; 21. 5; Eph. 3. 14.
Knew. Gen. 28. 16, the Lord is in this place, and I *k*. it not.
Jer. 1. 5, before I formed thee I *k*. thee.
Mat. 7. 23, I never *k*. you, depart.
John 4. 10, if thou *k*. the gift of God.
2 Cor. 5. 21, who *k*. no sin.
See Gen. 3. 7; Deu. 34. 10; John 1. 10.
Knop, the bud of a flower, a carved imitation of one; now spelt 'knob.' Ex. 25. 33; 1 Kn. 6. 18.
Know. 1 Sam. 3. 7, Samuel did not yet *k*. the Lord.
1 Chr. 28. 9, *k*. thou the God of thy father.
Job 5. 27, *k*. thou it for thy good.
8. 9, we are but of yesterday, and *k*. nothing.
13. 23, make me to *k*. my transgression.
19. 25, I *k*. that my redeemer liveth.
22. 13; Ps. 73. 11, how doth God *k*.?
Ps. 39. 4, make me to *k*. mine end.
46. 10, be still, and *k*. that I am God.
56. 9, this I *k*., for God is for me.
103. 14, he *k*. our frame.
139. 23, *k*. my heart.
Eccl. 9. 5, the living *k*. they shall die.
11. 9, *k*. that for all these things.
Isa. 1. 3, the ox *k*. his owner.
Jer. 17. 9, the heart is deceitful, who can *k*. it?
31. 34; Heb. 8. 11, *k*. the Lord, for all shall *k*. me.
Ezek. 2. 5; 33. 33, *k*. there hath been a prophet.
Hos. 2. 20, thou shalt *k*. the Lord.
7. 9, yet he *k*. it not.
Mat. 6. 3, let not thy left hand *k*.
13. 11; Mk. 4. 11; Lu. 8. 10, given to you to *k*.
25. 12, I *k*. you not.
Mk. 1. 24; Lu. 4. 34, I *k*. thee, who thou art.
Lu. 19. 42, if thou hadst *k*.
22. 57, 60, I *k*. him not.
John 7. 17, he shall *k*. of the doctrine.
10. 14, I *k*. my sheep, and am *k*. of mine.
John 13. 7, *k*. not now, but shalt *k*. hereafter. R. V. understand.
13. 17, if ye *k*. these things.
13. 35, by this shall all men *k*. ye are my disciples.
Acts 1. 7, it is not for you to *k*.
Rom. 8. 28, we *k*. that all things work.
1 Cor. 2. 14, neither can he *k*. them.
13. 9, 12, we *k*. in part.
Eph. 3. 19, and to *k*. the love of Christ.
2 Tim. 1. 12, I *k*. whom I have believed.
3. 15, thou hast *k*. the scriptures.
1 John 2. 4, he that saith, I *k*. him.
3. 2, we *k*. that when he shall appear.
Rev. 2. 2, 9, 13, 19; 3. 1, 8, I *k*. thy works.
See Mat. 6. 8; 2 Tim. 2. 19; 2 Pet. 2. 9; Rev. 2. 17.
Knowledge. 1 Sam. 2. 3, the Lord is a God of *k*.
2 Chr. 1. 10–12, give me *k*.
Job 21. 14, we desire not *k*. of thy ways.
Ps. 94. 10, he that teacheth man *k*.
139. 6, such *k*. is too wonderful.
144. 3, that thou takest *k*. of him.
Prov. 10. 14, wise men lay up *k*.
14. 6, *k*. is easy to him that understandeth.
17. 27, he that hath *k*. spareth words.
24. 5, a man of *k*. increaseth strength.
30. 3, nor have the *k*. of the holy.
Eccl. 1. 18, increaseth *k*. increaseth sorrow.
9. 10, nor *k*. in the grave.
Isa. 11. 2, the spirit of *k*.
40. 14, who taught him *k*.?
53. 11, by his *k*. justify many.
Dan. 1. 17, God gave them *k*.
12. 4, *k*. shall be increased.
Hos. 4. 6, destroyed for lack of *k*.
Hab. 2. 14, earth shall be filled with the *k*.
Lu. 11. 52, taken away key of *k*.
Acts 4. 13, took *k*. of them.
24. 22, more perfect *k*. of that way.
Rom. 10. 2, zeal of God, but not according to *k*.
1 Cor. 8. 1, *k*. puffeth up.
13. 8, *k*. shall vanish away.
15. 34, some have not the *k*. of God.
Eph. 3. 19, love of Christ, which passeth *k*.
Phil. 3. 8, but loss for the *k*. of Christ.
Col. 2. 3, treasures of wisdom and *k*.
1 Tim. 2. 4; 2 Tim. 3. 7, the *k*. of the truth.
Heb. 10. 26, sin after we have received *k*.
2 Pet. 1. 5, 6, to virtue *k*. and to *k*. temperance.
3. 18, grow in grace and *k*.
Knowledge given by God. Ex. 8. 10; 18. 16; 31. 3; 2 Chr. 1. 12; Ps. 119. 66; Prov. 1. 4; 2. 6; Eccl. 2. 26; Isa. 28. 9; Jer. 24. 7; 31. 33; Dan. 2. 21; Mat. 11. 25; 13. 11; 1 Cor. 1. 5; 2. 12; 12. 8.
advantages of. Ps. 89. 15; Prov. 1. 4, 7; 3. 13; 4.; 9. 10; 10. 14; 12. 1; 13. 16; 18. 15; Eccl. 7. 12; Mal. 2. 7; Eph. 3. 18; 4. 13; Jas. 3. 13; 2 Pet. 2. 20.
want of. Prov. 1. 22; 19. 2; Jer. 4. 22; Hos. 4. 1, 6; Rom. 1. 28; 1 Cor. 15. 34.
prayed for. John 17. 3; Eph. 3. 18; Col. 1. 9; 2 Pet. 3. 18.
sought. 1 Cor. 14. 1; Heb. 6. 1; 2 Pet. 1. 5.
abuse of. 1 Cor. 8. 1.
its responsibility. Num. 15. 30; Deu. 17. 12; Lu. 12. 47; John 15. 22: Rom. 1. 21; 2. 21; Jas. 4. 17.
imperfection of human. Eccl. 1. 18; Isa. 44. 25; 1 Cor. 1. 19; 3. 19; 2 Cor. 1. 12.
knowledge of good and evil, tree of. Gen. 2. 9.
Koa, kō′-ā, 'prince' (?). Ezek. 23. 23.
Kohath, kō′-hăth, 'assembly;' son of Levi. Gen. 46. 11.
his descendants. Ex. 6. 18; 1 Chr. 6. 2. [34. 12.
their duties. Num. 4. 15; 10. 21; 2 Chr. 29. 12;
Kohathites, kō′-hăth-ītes, descendants of Kohath. Num. 3. 27.
Kolaiah, kō-lāī′-ăh, 'voice of Jehovah' (?). Neh. 11. 7.
Korah, kŏr′-ăh, 'bald.' (1) Gen. 36. 14.
(2) Dathan, &c., their sedition and punishment. Num. 16.; 26. 9; 27. 3.
(Core) Jude 11.

Korahites, kôr'-ă-hītes, descendants of Korah. 1 Chr. 9. 19.
Korathites, kôr'-ă-thītes, same as preceding. Num. 26. 58.
Kore, kôr'-ē, 'partridge.' 1 Chr. 9. 19. [20. 19.
Korhite, kôr'-hīte, same as KORATHITE. 2 Chr.
Koz, kŏz, 'thorn.' Ez. 2. 61.
Kushaiah, kū-shăĭ'-ăh, longer form of Kishi. 1 Chr. 15. 17.

Laadah, lā'-ă-dăh, 'order' (?). 1 Chr. 4. 21.
Laadan, lā'-ă-dăn, 'put in order' (?). 1 Chr. 7. 26.
Laban, lā'-băn, 'white.' (1) hospitality of. Gen. 24. 29.
gives Jacob his two daughters. Gen. 29.
envies and oppresses him. Gen. 30. 27; 31. 1.
his dream. Gen. 31. 24.
his covenant with Jacob. Gen. 31. 43.
(2) city. Deu. 1. 1.
Labour (*n.*). Ps. 90. 10, yet is their strength *l.* and sorrow.
104. 23, goeth to his *l.* till evening.
Prov. 13. 11, he that gathereth by *l.* shall increase.
14. 23, in all *l.* there is profit. [ness.
Eccl. 1. 8, all things are full of *l.* R. V. weari-
2. 22, what hath man of all his *l.*?
6. 7, all the *l.* of man is for his mouth.
John 4. 38, are entered into their *l.*
1 Cor. 15. 58, your *l.* is not in vain.
1 Thes. 1. 3; Heb. 6. 10, your *l.* of love.
Rev. 2. 2. I know thy *l.* and patience.
14. 13, rest from their *l.*
See Gen. 31. 42; Isa. 58. 3; 2 Cor. 6. 5; 11. 23.
Labour (*v.*). Ex. 20. 9; Deu. 5. 13, six days shalt thou *l.*
Neh. 4. 21, so we *l.* in the work. R. V. wrought.
Ps. 127. 1, they *l.* in vain.
144. 14, our oxen may be strong to *l.* R. V. well laden.
Prov. 16. 26, he that *l.* *l.* for himself.
23. 4, *l.* not to be rich. R. V. weary not thyself.
Eccl. 4. 8, for whom do I *l.*?
5. 12, the sleep of a *l.* man is sweet.
Mat. 11. 28, all ye that *l.*
John 6. 27, *l.* not for the meat which perisheth.
1 Cor. 3. 9, we are *l.* together with God. R. V. God's fellow-workers.
Eph. 4. 28, but rather *l.*, working with his hands.
1 Thes. 5. 12, which *l.* among you.
1 Tim. 5. 17, they who *l.* in word and doctrine.
See Mat. 9. 37; Lu. 10. 2.
Labour ordained for man. Gen. 3. 19; Ps. 104. 23; 1 Cor. 4. 12.
when blessed by God. Prov. 10. 16; 13. 11; Eccl. 2. 24; 4. 9; 5. 12, 19.
Labourer worthy of hire. Lu. 10. 7; 1 Tim. 5. 18.
Labourers, parable of. Mat. 20.
Lachish, lā'-chĭsh, 'impregnable' (?). Jos. 10. 3.
conquered. Jos. 10. 31; 12. 11.
Amaziah slain at. 2 Kn. 14. 19.
Lack, to be deficient in; as *sub.*, want. Mat. 19. 20; Mk. 10. 21; Lu. 22. 35; Acts 4. 34.
Lad. Gen. 21. 12; 22. 12; 44. 22; 48. 16; 1 Sam. 20. 21; 2 Kn. 4. 19; John 6. 9.
Ladanum (Gen. 37. 25; 43. 11). Heb. *Lôt:* Gk. *στακτή*: Bot. N. *Cistus villosus; Cistus salviæfolius:* R. V. marg. 'ladanum:' A.V. 'myrrh,' wrongly. It is the Arabic *ladan* (ladanum), the fragrant resinous gum of the *Cistus*, or rock rose.
Ladder, Jacob's. Gen. 28. 12.
Laden. Isa. 1. 4; Mat. 11. 28; 2 Tim. 3. 6.
Lael, lā'-ĕl, 'belonging to God.' Num. 3. 24.
Lahad, lā'-hăd, 'oppression.' 1 Chr. 4. 2.
Lahai-roi, lā'-hăi-rŏi, 'to the living One that seeth me.' Gen. 24. 62.
Lahmam, lăh'-măm. Jos. 15. 40.
Lahmi, lăh'-mī, 'warrior' (?). 1 Chr. 20. 5.
Laish, lā'-ĭsh, 'lion.' (1) man. 1 Sam. 25. 44.
(2) places. Jud. 18. 14; Isa. 10. 30.
Lake of fire. Rev. 19. 20; 20. 10; 21. 8.
Lakes and Seas of Scripture. *See* next column.

Lakes and Seas of Scripture.

Name.	Situation.	References.	Modern Name.
Galilee, Sea of ...	....	Mat. 15. 29.	Bahr.
Called also **Chinnereth.**	Jordan Valley.	Num. 34. 11.	Tubarîyeh.
Chinneroth	....	Jos. 11. 2.	
Gennesaret	....	Lu. 5. 1.	
Tiberias	....	John 6. 1.	
Great Sea	....	Eze. 47. 15, 19, 20.	Mediterranean.
Merom, Waters of	Upper Jordan.	Jos. 11. 5.	Huleh.
Salt Sea	Palestine, S. of the Jordan.	Gen. 14. 3.	Dead Sea, or Bahr-Lût.
Called also **Sea of the Arabah** *or* **Plain.**	....	Deu. 4. 49.	
East Sea	....	Joel 2. 20.	
The Sea	....	Ezek. 47. 8.	

Lakum, lā'-kŭm, 'fort' (?). Jos. 19. 33.
Lama, lä'-mä, 'why'? Mat. 27. 46.
Lamb. Isa. 5. 17, the *l.* feed after their manner.
11. 6, the wolf shall dwell with the *l.*
53. 7; Jer. 11. 19, as *l.* to the slaughter.
John 1. 29, 36, behold the *L.* of God.
1 Pet. 1. 19, as of a *l.* without blemish.
Rev. 5. 6; 13. 18, stood a *L.* slain.
12. 11, by the blood of the *L.*
22. 1, the throne of God and of the *L.*
See Isa. 40. 11; Lu. 10. 3; John 21. 15.
Lamb for sacrifices. Gen. 22. 7; Ex. 12. 3; Lev. 3. 7; Isa. 1. 11.
Lame. Job 29. 15; Prov. 26. 7; Isa. 35. 6; Heb. 12. 13.
Lame, the, excluded from the priest's office. Lev. 21. 18.
animals, not proper for sacrifices. Deu. 15. 21; Mal. 1. 8, 13.
healed by Christ, Mat. 11. 5; 21. 14; Lu. 7. 22.
by the apostles, Acts 3.; 8. 7.
Lamech, lā'-mĕch, 'destroyer,' descendant of Cain; father of Noah. Gen. 4. 18; 5. 25, 29.
Lament. Mat. 11. 17; John 16. 20; Acts 8. 2.
Lamentation for Jacob. Gen. 50. 10.
of David, for Saul and Jonathan, 2 Sam. 1. 17.
for Abner, 2 Sam. 3. 31.
for Josiah. 2 Chr. 35. 25.
for Tyrus. Ezek. 26. 17; 27. 30; 28. 12.
for Pharaoh. Ezek. 32.
for Christ. Lu. 23. 27.
for Stephen. Acts 8. 2.
for Babylon. Rev. 18. 10. [*See* SUMMARIES.
Lamentations, the title of a book by Jeremiah.
Lamp. Ps. 119. 105; Prov. 13. 9; Isa. 62. 1; Mat. 25. 1. *See* CANDLE.
Lamps in the tabernacle. Ex. 25. 37; 27. 20; 30. 7; Lev. 24. 2; Num. 8.
seen in visions. Gen. 15. 17; Zec. 4. 2; Rev. 4. 5.
parable referring to. Mat. 25. 1.
Land. Gen. 1. 9; 12. 1; Ex. 14. 21; Jos. 4. 22; Ps. 27. 13; 66. 1; Ezek. 34. 13; Mk. 15. 33.
Landmarks were usually a single block or small pile of stones laid upon the ground, and are still so in Palestine. They might easily be shifted by a dishonest landowner; hence the severe curse upon their removal.
See examples in the British Museum.
not to be removed. Deu. 19. 14; 27. 17; Job 24. 2; Prov. 22. 28; 23. 10.
Language. Neh. 13. 14; Ps. 19. 3; Isa. 19. 18.

TEMPLE VESSELS

Procession of Roman soldiers carrying the seven-branched candlestick (lamp-stand) and other objects from the Temple, taken at the capture of Jerusalem, A.D. 70. (*Arch of Titus: Donald McLeish*)

SCROLL OF THE LAW

A very ancient book (scroll) of the Law preserved in the Samaritan community at Shechem, displayed by a Samaritan high priest. (*Picture Post Library*)

Languages (Babel). Gen. 11.
gift of, by Holy Ghost. Acts 2. 7, 8; 10. 46; 19. 6; 1 Cor. 12. 10.
Lanterns are still commonly used in the East; any one going through the streets at night without a light is liable to be arrested as a dangerous character. A servant holds the lantern close to the ground, immediately in front of his master's feet — a practice rendered necessary by the entire absence of pavement, and by the numerous obstructions in the streets of Eastern cities; hence the force of the language, 'Thy word is a lamp unto my feet, and a light unto my path' (Ps. 119. 105).
Laodicea, lā-ŏd-ĭ-çē'-ă. An important city of Asia Minor on the river Lycus. Col. 2. 1. The seat of one of the 'Seven Churches of Asia' (Rev. 3. 14).
Laodiceans, lā-ŏd-ĭ-çē'-ăns, inhabitants of Laodicea. Rev. 1. 11; 3. 14.
Paul's epistle to. Col. 4. 16.
Lap. Jud. 7. 6; Prov. 16. 33.
Lapidoth, lăp'-ĭ-dōth, torches. Jud. 4. 4.
Lapwing (Lev. 11. 19). Heb. *Dûkîphath:* Gk. ἔποψ: R. V. 'hoopoe.' Doubtless the hoopoe, since the Arabic term is the same; in size similar to the thrush, but crested.
Lasciviousness, source of. Mk. 7. 21; Gal. 5. 19.
rebuked. 2 Cor. 12. 21; Eph. 4. 19; 1 Pet. 4. 3; Jude 4.
Lasea, lă-sē'-ă. Acts 27. 8.
Lasha, lā'-shă, 'fissure.' Gen. 10. 19.
Lasharon, lă-shâr'-on, 'of the plain.' Jos. 12. 18.
Last. Num. 23. 10, let my *l.* end be like his.
Prov. 23. 32, at the *l.* it biteth like a serpent.
Mat. 12. 45; Lu. 11. 26, *l.* state of that man.
19. 30; 20. 16; Mk. 10. 31; Lu. 13. 30, first shall be *l.*
John 6. 39; 11. 24; 12. 48, the *l.* day.
See Lam. 1. 9; 2 Tim. 3. 1; 1 Pet. 1. 5; 1 John 2. 18.
Latchet, a thong, lace. Mk. 1. 7.
Latin, lăt'-ĭn, the language spoken by Romans. John 19. 20.
Latter. Job 19. 25; Prov. 19. 20; Hag. 2. 9.
Laud, to praise. Rom. 15. 11.
Laugh. Prov. 1. 26; Eccl. 3. 4; Lu. 6. 21; Jas. 4. 9.
Laughter. Gen. 18. 13; Eccl. 2. 2; 3. 4; 7. 3; Ps. 126. 2.
Launch. Lu. 5. 4; 8. 22; Acts 21. 1; 27. 4.
Laver, a vessel for washing in. Ex. 38. 8.
Laver of brass, Ex. 30. 18; 38. 8; 40. 7. sanctified, Lev. 8. 11.
Lavers in the temple. 1 Kn. 7. 38.
Law. Jos. 8. 34, all the words of the *l.*
Ps. 37. 31, the *l.* of his God is in his heart.
40. 8, thy *l.* is within my heart.
119. 70, 77, 92, 174, I delight in thy *l.*
119. 97, 113, 163, 165, how I love thy *l.*
Prov. 13. 14, the *l.* of the wise is a fountain of life.
Isa. 8. 20, to the *l.* and to the testimony.
Mal. 2. 6, the *l.* of truth was in his mouth.
Mat. 5. 17, not come to destroy the *l.*
23. 23, the weightier matters of the *l.*
John 7. 51, doth our *l.* judge any man?
19. 7, we have a *l.*, and by our *l.*
Rom. 2. 14, are a *l.* unto themselves.
3. 20, by the deeds of the *l.*
7. 12, the *l.* is holy.
7. 14, the *l.* is spiritual.
7. 16; 1 Tim. 1. 8, the *l.* is good.
8. 3, what the *l.* could not do.
Gal. 3. 24, the *l.* was our schoolmaster.
5. 14, all the *l.* is fulfilled in one word.
5. 23, against such there is no *l.*
6. 2, so fulfil the *l.* of Christ.
1 Tim. 1. 9, the *l.* is not made for a righteous man.
Heb. 7. 16, the *l.* of a carnal commandment.
Jas. 1. 25; 2. 12, perfect *l.* of liberty.
2. 8, the royal *l.*
See Ps. 1. 2; Mat. 7. 12.
Law of God, given to Adam, Gen. 2. 16. to Noah, Gen. 9. 3. proclaimed through Moses. Ex. 19.; 20.; Deu. 1. 5; 5.; 6.
demands entire obedience. Deu. 27. 26; Gal. 3. 10; Jas. 2. 10.
described. Ps. 19. 7; 119.; Rom. 7. 12.
all guilty under. Rom. 3. 20.
(of Moses) ordained. Ex. 21.; Lev. 1.; Num. 3.; Deu. 12.
preserved on stone. Deu. 27. 1; Jos. 8. 32.
to be studied by the king. Deu. 17. 18.
read every seventh year. Deu. 31. 9.
preserved in the ark. Deu. 31. 24.
read by Joshua, Jos. 8. 34. by Ezra, Neh. 8.
book of, discovered by Hilkiah, 2 Kn. 22. 8. and read by Josiah, 2 Kn. 23. 2.
fulfilled by Christ. Mat. 5. 17; Rom. 5. 18; 10. 4.
abolished in Christ. Acts 15. 24; 28. 23; Gal. 2.-6.; Eph. 2. 15; Col. 2. 14; Heb. 7.
Christians redeemed from curse of. John 1. 17; Acts 13. 39; 15. 24, 28; Rom. 10. 4; Gal. 3. 13.
Lawful. Mat. 12. 2; John 5. 10; 1 Cor. 6. 12.
Lawgiver, God. Isa. 33. 22; Jas. 4. 12.
Lawless. 1 Tim. 1. 9.
Lawsuits censured. 1 Cor. 6. 1.
Lawyers (Gk. νομικός, from νόμος, 'law') are generally regarded as identical with the Scribes. The 'lawyer' of Mat. 22. 35 is called a 'scribe' in the parallel passage of Mk. 12. 28. *See* Scribes.
Lawyers, Christ reproves. Lu. 10. 25; 11. 46; 14. 3.
Lay at, to strike at. Job 41. 26.
Lazarus, lăz'-ă-rŭs, Greek form of Eleazar. (1) and the rich man. Lu. 16. 19.
(2) brother of Mary and Martha, raised from the dead. John 11.; 12. 1.
Lead (*n.*) (Ex. 15. 10). Heb. *Bedîl:* Gk. μόλιβος. Found in the Sinaitic rocks before the time of Moses.
Lead (*v.*). Deu. 4. 27; 28. 37, whither the Lord shall *l.* you.
Ps. 23. 2, he *l.* me beside still waters.
27. 11, *l.* me in a plain path.
31. 3, *l.* me, and guide me.
61. 2, *l.* me to the rock that is higher than I.
139. 10, there shall thy hand *l.* me.
139. 24, *l.* me in the way everlasting.
Prov. 6. 22, when thou goest, it shall *l.* thee.
Isa. 11. 6, a little child shall *l.* them.
42. 16, I will *l.* them in paths not known.
48. 17, I am the Lord which *l.* thee.
Mat. 6. 13; Lu. 11. 4, *l.* us not into temptation. R. V. bring.
15. 14; Lu. 6. 39, if the blind *l.* the blind.
Acts 13. 11, seeking some to *l.* him.
1 Tim. 2. 2, we may *l.* a quiet life.
See John 10. 3; 1 Cor. 9. 5; 2 Tim. 3. 6; Rev. 7. 17.
Leaf. Lev. 26. 36; Ps. 1. 3; Isa. 64. 6; Mat. 21. 19.
Leah, lē'-ăh, 'languid' (?), or 'wild-cow' (?). Gen. 29. 16, 31; 30. 17; 31. 4; 33. 2; 49. 31. *See* Ru. 4. 11.
Lean. Prov. 3. 5; Am. 5. 19; Mic. 3. 11; John 13. 23; 21. 20.
Leap. 2 Sam. 22. 30; Isa. 35. 6; Lu. 6. 23.
Learn. Deu. 31. 13, *l.* to fear the Lord.
Prov. 1. 5; 9. 9; 16. 21, will increase *l.*
22. 25, lest thou *l.* his ways.
Isa. 1. 17, *l.* to do well.
2. 4; Mic. 4. 3, neither shall they *l.* war.
29. 11, 12, deliver to one that is *l.*
John 6. 45, every one that hath *l.* of the Father.
7. 15, having never *l.*
Acts 7. 22, *l.* in all the wisdom of the Egyptians. R. V. instructed.
26. 24, much *l.* doth make thee mad.
Rom. 15. 4, written for our *l.*
Eph. 4. 20, ye have not so *l.* Christ.
2 Tim. 3. 14, in the things thou hast *l.*
Heb. 5. 8, though a Son, yet *l.* he obedience.
See Mat. 9. 13; 11. 29; Phil. 4. 11; Rev. 14. 3.
Learning, advantage of. Prov. 1. 5; 9. 9; 16. 21, 23; Rom. 15. 4.
Leasing, lying, falsehood. Ps. 4. 2; 5. 6.
Least. Mat. 5. 19, one of these *l.* commandments.
11. 11; Lu. 7. 28, he that is *l.* in kingdom of heaven. R. V. but little.

Mat. 25. 40, 45, done it to the *l.* of these.
Lu. 12. 26, not able to do that which is *l.*
16. 10, faithful in that which is *l.* R. V. a very little.
Eph. 3. 8, less than the *l.* of all saints.
See Gen. 32. 10; Jer. 31. 34; 1 Cor. 6. 4.

Leather. 2 Kn. 1. 8; Mat. 3. 4.

Leave. Gen. 2. 24; Mat. 19. 5; Mk. 10. 7; Eph. 5. 31, *l.* father and mother, and shall cleave.
Ps. 16. 10; Acts 2. 27, not *l.* my soul in hell.
27. 9; 119. 121, *l.* me not. R. V. cast off.
Mat. 23. 23, and not to *l.* the other undone.
John 14. 27, peace I *l.* with you.
Heb. 13. 5, I will never *l.* thee. R. V. fail.
See Ru. 1. 16; Mat. 5. 24; John 16. 28.

Leaven is any substance that promotes fermentation. In the N. T. a symbol of silent pervasive influence, usually of that which is corrupt; in a good sense, only in Mat. 13. 33; Lu. 13. 21.

Leaven, forbidden at the passover, Ex. 12. 15; 13. 7. and in meat offerings, Lev. 2. 11; 6. 17; 10. 12.
mentioned figuratively. Mat. 13. 33; 16. 6; Lu. 13. 21; 1 Cor. 5. 6.

Lebana, lĕ-bā'-nă, same as LEBANAH. Neh. 7. 48.

Lebanah, lĕ-bā'-năh, 'white.' Ez. 2. 45.

Lebanon, lĕb'-ă-non, 'white' from its snow-clad peaks. A double range of mountains north of Palestine. The two highest series of peaks vary in height from 9800 to 10,225 feet. Famous for its huge cedar trees. Deu. 1. 7.
forest and mountain. Deu. 3. 25; Jud. 3. 3; 1 Kn. 5. 14.
its cedars. 2 Kn. 14. 9; 2 Chr. 2. 8; Ps. 92. 12; S. of S. 3. 9; Isa. 40. 16; Hos. 14. 5.

Lebaoth, lĕ-bā'-ōth, 'lionesses.' Jos. 15. 32.

Lebbæus, lĕb-bǣ'-ŭs. Mat. 10. 3. *See* JUDE.

Lebonah, lĕ-bō'-năh, 'frankincense.' Jud. 21. 19.

Lecah, lē'-căh, journey (?). 1 Chr. 4. 21.

Leeks (Num. 11. 5). Heb. *Ḥâtzîr:* Gk. τὰ πράσα: Bot. N. *Allium porrum.* Usually translated 'grass' or 'hay,' but here 'leeks' in both A. V. and R. V. It is eaten raw as a salad.
Some modern writers prefer fenugreek (*Trigonella Fænum-græcum*), a strong-scented plant allied to clover, and a common article of food in Egypt.

Lees, dregs, sediment. Isa. 25. 6; Jer. 48. 11; Zep. 1. 12.

Left-handed slingers. Jud. 20. 16.

Legion (of devils). Mk. 5. 9; Lu. 8. 30.

Legions of angels. Mat. 26. 53.

Lehabim, lĕ-hā'-bĭm. Gen. 10. 13.

Lehi, lē'-hī, 'jaw-bone.' Jud. 15. 9.

Lemuel, lĕm'-ū-ĕl, '(devoted) to God' (?); king, his lesson. Prov. 31. 1.

Lend. Deu. 15. 6, thou shalt *l.* to many nations.
Ps. 37. 26; 112. 5, ever merciful, and *l.* [Lord.
Prov. 19. 17, he that hath pity on poor *l.* to the
22. 7, the borrower is servant to the *l.*
Lu. 6. 34, if ye *l.* to them of whom.
See 1 Sam. 1. 28; Isa. 24. 2; Lu. 11. 5.

Lending, regulations for. Ex. 22. 25; Lev. 25. 37; Deu. 15. 2; 23. 19; 24. 10. *See* Ps. 37. 26; Lu. 6. 34.

Lentils (Gen. 25. 34; 2 Sam. 23. 11). Heb. *'Adashim:* Gk. φακός: Bot. N. *Ervum lens.* Jacob's red pottage was of lentils, the small, dark-coloured, lens-like seeds of *Ervum lens*, a small, vetch-like plant still largely cultivated in the East.

Leopard (Jer. 5. 6; Hab. 1. 8). Heb. *Nâmêr:* Gk. πάρδαλις. The leopard is still common in parts of Palestine. In Scripture, illustrations are drawn from its 'spots,' its 'watching for prey,' its 'activity,' &c.

Leopard, vision of. Dan. 7. 6; Rev. 13. 2.
mentioned figuratively. Isa. 11. 6; Hos. 13. 7.

Lepers not to dwell in the camp. Lev. 13. 46; Num. 5. 2; 12. 14.
four, of Samaria. 2 Kn. 7. 3.

Leprosy in a house. Lev. 14. 33.
of Miriam. Num. 12. 10.
of Naaman and Gehazi. 2 Kn. 5.
of Uzziah. 2 Chr. 26. 19.
symptoms of. Lev. 13. [24. 8.
observances on healing. Lev. 14.; 22. 4; Deu.
cured by Christ. Mat. 8. 3; Mk. 1. 41; Lu. 5. 12; 17. 12.

Lepton. A. V. mite. Mk. 12. 42, the smallest Jewish bronze coin = ¼ farthing = ⅛ cent.

Leshem, lē'-shĕm, 'precious stone.' Jos. 19. 47.

Less. Ex. 30. 15; Job 11. 6; Isa. 40. 17.

Let, to hinder, prevent. 2 Thes. 2. 7. [6.

Letter and the spirit. Rom. 2. 27; 7. 6; 2 Cor. 3.

Letters: of David to Joab, 2 Sam. 11. 14. of Jezebel, 1 Kn. 21. 9. of king of Syria, 2 Kn. 5. 5. of Jehu, 2 Kn. 10. 1. of Elijah to Jehoram, 2 Chr. 21. 12. of Hezekiah, 2 Chr. 30. 1. of Bishlam and Rehum, Ez. 4. 7. of Artaxerxes, Ez. 4. 17. of Tatnai, Ez. 5. 6. of Sennacherib to Hezekiah, Isa. 37. 10, 14. of Jeremiah, Jer. 29. 1. of the Apostles, Acts 15. 23. of Claudius Lysias to Felix, Acts 23. 25.

Letushim, lĕ-tū'-shĭm, 'the hammered.' Gen. 25. 3.

Leummim, lĕ-ŭm'-mĭm, 'peoples.' Gen. 25. 3.

Levi, lē'-vī, 'joined' (?). (1) Son of Jacob. Gen. 29. 34.
avenges Dinah. Gen. 34. 25; 49. 5.
(2) same as MATTHEW, *q. v.* Mk. 2. 14.
(3) others. Lu. 3. 24, 29.

Levi and the Priesthood.

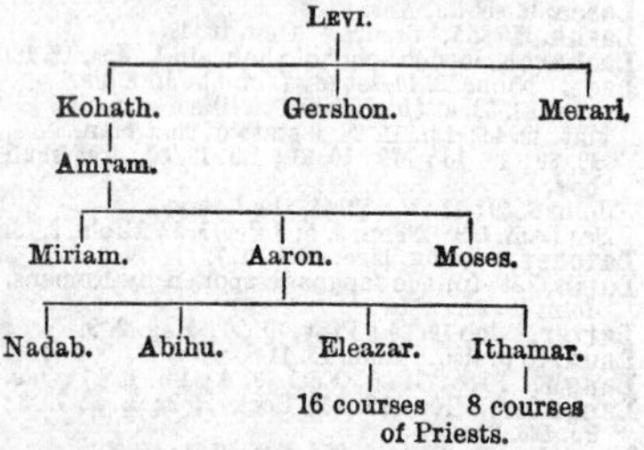

Leviathan, lē-vī'-ă-thăn (Ps. 74. 14; Job 41. 1). Heb. *Livyâthân:* Gk. δράκων: Zool. S. *Crocodilus vulgaris:* R. V. marg. 'crocodile.' The word occurs five times, and in every case but one (Ps. 104. 26) denotes the crocodile; there it denotes the whale. In Job 3. 8, 'their mourning' in A. V., but 'leviathan' in R. V. & A. V. marg., probably refers to the 'dragon.'

Levites, lē'-vītes, descendants of Levi. Ex. 6. 25; 32. 26.
their service. Ex. 38. 21.
appointed over the tabernacle. Num. 1. 47.
their divisions, Gershonites, Kohathites, Merarites. Num. 3.
duties of. Num. 3. 23; 4.; 8. 23; 18.
their consecration. Num. 8. 5.
inheritance of. Num. 35.; Deu. 18.; Jos. 21.
not to be forsaken. Deu. 12. 19; 14. 27.
their genealogies. 1 Chr. 6.; 9.
charged with the temple service. 1 Chr. 23.-27.
twenty-four courses, instituted by David, 1 Chr. 23. 6. redivided by Ezra, Ez. 6. 18.
their sin censured. Mal. 1. 2; Ezek. 22. 26.

Levitical, lē-vĭt'-ĭ-căl, belonging to Levi. Heb. 7. 11.

Leviticus, lē-vĭt'-ĭ-cŭs, the third book of the Pentateuch, which treats of the regulations of the Levitical law.

Lewd. (1) ignorant, vile, worthless. Acts 17. 5.
(2) wanton, lascivious. Ezek. 16. 27.

Lewdness, wickedness. Acts 18. 14.

Liars. Ps. 116. 11; John 8. 44; Rev. 2. 2.
their doom. Rev. 21. 8, 27; 22. 15.

instances: the devil, Gen. 3. 4. Cain, Gen. 4. 9. Sarah, Gen. 18. 15. Jacob, Gen. 27. 19. Joseph's brethren, Gen. 37. 31, 32. Gibeonites, Jos. 9. 9. Samson, Jud. 16. 10. Saul, 1 Sam. 15. 13. Michal, 1 Sam. 19. 14. David, 1 Sam. 21. 2. Prophet of Beth-el, 1 Kn. 13. 18. Gehazi, 2 Kn. 5. 22. Job's friends, Job 13. 4. Ninevites, Nah. 3. 1. Peter, Mat. 26. 72. Ananias, Acts 5. 4. Cretians, Tit. 1. 12.

Liberality enjoined. Deu. 15. 14; Prov. 11. 25; Isa. 32. 8; 2 Cor. 9. 13.
of the Israelites. Ex. 35. 21; Num. 7.
of the early Christians. Acts 2. 45; 4. 34.
of the Macedonians. 2 Cor. 8.; 9.; Phil. 4. 15.

Libertines, lĭb′-ĕr-tīnes, enfranchised slaves and their descendants. The synagogue of the *l.* at Jerusalem (Acts 6. 9) may have been founded by some of the 30,000 Jews whom Pompey took as slaves to Rome in B.C. 63; but perhaps the right reading there is *Libyatines*, in which case they would, like the Cyrenians in the same verse, be Jews of N. Africa.

Liberty. Lev. 25. 10, proclaim *l.* throughout the [land.
Ps. 119. 45, I will walk at *l.*
Isa. 61. 1; Jer. 34. 8; Lu. 4. 18, to proclaim *l.*
Rom. 8. 21, the glorious *l.* of the children of God.
1 Cor. 8. 9, take heed lest this *l.* of yours.
2 Cor. 3. 17, where the Spirit is, there is *l.*
Gal. 5. 1, stand fast in the *l.* R. V. freedom.
Jas. 1. 25; 2. 12, the law of *l.*

Liberty bestowed by the Gospel. Rom. 8. 21; 2 Cor. 3. 17; Gal. 5. 1; Jas. 1. 25; 2. 12 (Isa. 61. 1; Lu. 4. 18).
not to be misused. 1 Cor. 8. 9; Gal. 5. 13; 1 Pet. 2. 16; 2 Pet. 2. 19.

Libnah, lĭb′-năh, 'whiteness.' (1) Num. 33. 20. (2) subdued. Jos. 10. 29; 21. 13.
rebels. 2 Kn. 8. 22.
attacked by Assyrians. 2 Kn. 19. 8; Isa. 37. 8.

Libni, lĭb′-nī, 'white.' (1) Ex. 6. 17. (2) 1 Chr. 6. 29.

Libnites, lĭb′-nītes, descendants of Libni. Num. 3. 21.

Libya, lĭb′-y̆-ă. Ezek. 30. 5; Dan. 11. 43; Acts 2. 10.

Libyans, lĭb′-y̆-ăns, inhabitants of Libya. Jer. 46. 9.

Lice (Ex. 8. 16; Ps. 105. 31). Heb. *Kinnîm*: Gk. σκνῖφες: R. V. marg. 'sand-flies or fleas.' Parasitic insects abound in the East, and through the summer the Mohammedan men keep their heads shorn to avoid them.

Lien = lain (*p. p.* of 'lie'). Gen. 26. 10.

Life. Gen. 2. 7; 6. 17; 7. 22, the breath of *l.*
2. 9; 3. 24; Rev. 2. 7, the tree of *l.*
Deu. 30. 15; Jer. 21. 8, I have set before thee *l.*
Jos. 2. 14, our *l.* for yours.
1 Sam. 25. 29, bound in the bundle of *l.*
Ps. 16. 11, shew me the path of *l.*
17. 14; Eccl. 9. 9, their portion in this *l.*
26. 9, gather not my *l.* with bloody men.
27. 1, the strength of my *l.*
30. 5, in his favour is *l.*
34. 12, what man is he that desireth *l.*?
36. 9, the fountain of *l.*
91. 16, with long *l.* will I satisfy him.
133. 3, even *l.* for evermore.
Prov. 3. 22, so shall they be *l.* to thy soul.
8. 35, whoso findeth me findeth *l.*
15. 24, the way of *l.* is above to the wise.
Mat. 6. 25; Lu. 12. 22, take no thought for your *l.*
18. 8; 19. 17; Mk. 9. 43, to enter into *l.*
Lu. 12. 15, a man's *l.* consisteth not.
12. 23, the *l.* is more than meat.
John 1. 4, in him was *l.*
5. 24; 1 John 3. 14, passed from death to *l.*
5. 26, as the Father hath *l.* in himself.
5. 40; 10. 10, come that ye might have *l.*
6. 33, 47, 48, 54, the bread of *l.*
10. 15, 17; 13. 37, I lay down my *l.*
11. 25; 14. 6, the resurrection and the *l.*
Acts 5. 20, speak all the words of this *l.*
Rom. 6. 4, in newness of *l.*
Rom. 11. 15, *l.* from the dead.
2 Cor. 2. 16, the savour of *l.* unto *l.*
Gal. 2. 20, the *l.* that I now live.
Eph. 4. 18, alienated from the *l.* of God.
Col. 3. 3, your *l.* is hid.
1 Tim. 4. 8; 2 Tim. 1. 1, the promise of the *l.*
2 Tim. 1. 10, brought *l.* to light by gospel.
Jas. 4. 14, what is your *l.*?
1 John 1. 2, the *l.* was manifested.
2. 16, the pride of *l.*
5. 11, this *l.* is in his Son.
Rev. 22. 1, 17, river of water of *l.*

Life, the gift of God. Gen. 2. 7; Job 12. 10; Ps. 36. 6; 66. 9; Dan. 5. 23; Acts 17. 28.
long, to whom promised. Ex. 20. 12; Deu. 5. 33; 6. 2; Prov. 3. 2; 9. 11; 10. 27; Eph. 6. 3.
its vanity and uncertainty. Job 7. 1; 9. 25; 14. 1; Ps. 39. 5; 73. 19; 89. 47; 90. 5, 9; Eccl. 6. 12; Isa. 38. 12; Jas. 4. 14; 1 Pet. 1. 24.
mode of spending. Lu. 1. 75; Rom. 12. 18; 14. 8; Phil. 1. 21; 1 Pet. 1. 17.
of Hezekiah prolonged. 2 Kn. 20.; 2 Chr. 32. 24; Isa. 38.
SPIRITUAL. Rom. 6. 4; 8.; Gal. 2. 20; Eph. 2. 1; Col. 3. 3.
ETERNAL, the gift of God through Jesus Christ (Ps. 133. 3); Mat. 20. 28; John 6. 27, 54; 10. 28; 17. 3; Rom. 2. 7; 6. 23; 1 John 1. 2; 2. 25; Jude 21; Rev. 2. 7; 21. 6.
to whom promised. Mat. 10. 39; John 3. 16; 5. 24; 1 Tim. 1. 16.

Light. Ex. 10. 23, Israel had *l.* in their dwellings.
Job 18. 5, the *l.* of the wicked.
37. 21, men see not bright *l.* in clouds.
Ps. 4. 6; 90. 8, the *l.* of thy countenance.
27. 1, the Lord is my *l.*
36. 9, in thy *l.* shall we see *l.*
97. 11, *l.* is sown for the righteous.
119. 105, a *l.* to my path.
Eccl. 11. 7, the *l.* is sweet.
Isa. 5. 20, darkness for *l.*, and *l.* for darkness.
30. 26, the *l.* of the moon as *l.* of sun.
59. 9, we wait for *l.*
60. 1, arise, shine, for thy *l.* is come.
Zec. 14. 6, the *l.* shall not be clear.
Mat. 5. 14; John 8. 12; 9. 5, the *l.* of the world.
5. 16, let your *l.* so shine.
6. 22, the *l.* of the body is the eye.
Lu. 12. 35, your loins girded, and *l.* burning. R. V. lamps.
16. 8, wiser than children of *l.*
John 1. 9, that was the true *L.*
3. 19, *l.* is come into the world.
3. 20, hateth the *l.*
5. 35, burning and shining *l.*
12. 35, yet a little while is the *l.* with you.
12. 36, while ye have *l.*, believe in the *l.*
Acts 26. 18, turn from darkness to *l.*
1 Cor. 4. 5, bring to *l.* hidden things.
2 Cor. 4. 4, *l.* of the gospel.
4. 6, commanded *l.* to shine out of darkness.
11. 14, an angel of *l.*
Eph. 5. 8, now are ye *l.*, walk as children of *l.*
5. 14, Christ shall give thee *l.* R. V. shine upon thee.
1 Tim. 6. 16, in *l.* which no man can approach.
2 Pet. 1. 19, a *l.* shining in a dark place. R. V. lamp.
1 John 1. 5, God is *l.*
1. 7, walk in the *l.*, as he is in the *l.*
Rev. 22. 5, they need no candle, neither *l.* of the [sun.
See 2 Tim. 1. 10; Rev. 7. 16; 18. 23.

Light. Gen. 1. 3; Jer. 31. 35.
type of God's favour. Ex. 10. 23; Ps. 4. 6; 27. 1; 97. 11; Isa. 9. 2; 60. 19.
God's word produces. Ps. 19. 8; 119. 105, 130; Prov. 6. 23.
instances of miraculous. Mat. 17. 2; Acts 9. 3.
Christ the light of the world. Lu. 2. 32; John 1. 4; 3. 19; 8. 12; 12. 35; Rev. 21. 23.
children of, disciples. Eph. 5. 8; 1 Thes. 5. 5; 1 Pet. 2. 9.
God is. 1 Tim. 6. 16; 1 John 1. 5.

Lighten, to enlighten, illuminate. Lu. 2. 32.
Lightly, easily, carelessly. Mk. 9. 39.
Lightness, fickleness, levity. 2 Cor. 1. 17.
Lightning. Ex. 19. 16; 2 Sam. 22. 15; Job 28. 26; 38. 25; Ps. 18. 14; 144. 6; Mat. 24. 27; Lu. 10. 18. about God's throne. Ezek. 1. 13; Rev. 4. 5.
Ligure (Ex. 28. 19; 39. 12). Heb. *Léshem:* Gk. λιγύριον: R. V. 'jacinth,' marg. 'amber.' Probably the jacinth of modern jewelry.
Like. (1) to please. Deu. 23. 16.
(2) to approve of. 1 Chr. 28. 4.
Likeness. Ps. 17. 15, when I awake, with thy *l.*
Isa. 40. 18, what *l.* will ye compare?
Acts 14. 11, gods are come down in *l.* of men.
Rom. 6. 5, *l.* of his death, *l.* of his resurrection.
8. 3, in the *l.* of sinful flesh.
Phil. 2. 7, was made in the *l.* of men.
See Gen. 1. 26; 5. 1; Ex. 20. 4; Deu. 4. 16.
Likhi, lĭk'-hī, 'fond of learning' (?). 1 Chr. 7. 19.
Liking, attractive appearance, comeliness; 'worse liking,' less plump, in less favourable condition. Dan. 1. 10.
Lily (1 Kn. 7. 26; S. of S. 2. 16; 6. 2, 3). Heb. *Shûshan:* Gk. κρίνον. A general term for lily-like flowers, as the lily, iris, gladiolus, etc., and may include the poppy-anemone, which in spring paints with bright scarlet the plains of Palestine.
Lily of the valley. S. of S. 2. 1; Hos. 14. 5; Mat. 6. 28; Lu. 12. 27.
Limit. Ps. 78. 41; Ezek. 43. 12; Heb. 4. 7.
Line. Ps. 16. 6; Isa. 28. 10, 17; 34. 11; 2 Cor. 10. 16.
Linen, Fine. Gen. 41. 42; Lu. 16. 19, the Egyptian byssus, sometimes so fine and delicate that it was worth twice its weight in gold.
Linen for sacred vestments. Ex. 28. 42; Lev. 6. 10; 1 Sam. 2. 18; 22. 18. *See* Rev. 15. 6.
Linger. Gen. 19. 16; 43. 10; 2 Pet. 2. 3.
Linus, lī'-nŭs, 'flax.' 2 Tim. 4. 21.
Lion. (1) (Num. 24. 9; Jer. 49. 19). Heb. *Arî Aryeh:* Gk. λέων. The general term for 'lion.'
(2) (Am. 3. 4; Ps. 17. 12; Job 4. 10). Heb. *Kephîr:* Gk. σκύμνος δράκων, 'young lion.'
(3) (Job 4. 11). Heb. *Láyish:* Gk. μυρμηκολέων, 'old lion.'
(4) (Deu. 33. 20). Heb. *Lâbi:* Gk. λέων: R. V. 'lioness.'
(5) (Job 4. 10). Heb. *Shâhal:* Gk. λέαινα, 'fierce lion.' Besides mention of its depredations, the lion was the symbol of 'strength,' of the 'tribe of Judah,' and of 'Christ' (Rev. 5. 5).
Lions, Samson kills one, Jud. 14. 5. also David, 1 Sam. 17. 34.
Daniel in the den of. Dan. 6. 18.
Satan likened to a lion. 1 Pet. 5. 8 (Ps. 10. 9).
prophets slain by. 1 Kn. 13. 24; 20. 36.
parable of young. Ezek. 19.
mentioned figuratively. Gen. 49. 9 (Rev. 5. 5); Num. 24. 9; 2 Sam. 17. 10; Job 4. 10.
various visions of. Ezek. 1. 10; 10. 14; Dan. 7. 4; Rev. 4. 7.
Lip. 1 Sam. 1. 13, only her *l.* moved.
Job 27. 4, my *l.* shall not speak wickedness.
33. 3, my *l.* shall utter knowledge.
Ps. 12. 2, 3, flattering *l.*
12. 4, our *l.* are our own.
17. 1, goeth not out of feigned *l.*
31. 18; 120. 2; Prov. 10. 18; 12. 22; 17. 7, lying *l.*
Prov. 15. 7, the *l.* of the wise disperse knowledge.
Eccl. 10. 12, the *l.* of a fool will swallow himself.
S. of S. 7. 9, causing *l.* of those asleep to speak.
Isa. 6. 5, a man of unclean *l.*
Mat. 15. 8, honoureth me with their *l.*
See Ps. 51. 15; 141. 3; Dan. 10. 16; Hab. 3. 16.
List, please, choose, like. John 3. 8.
Little. Ez. 9. 8, for a *l.* space, a *l.* reviving.
Job 26. 14, how *l.* a portion is heard?
Ps. 8. 5; Heb. 2. 7, a *l.* lower than angels.
37. 16, a *l.* that a righteous man hath.
Prov. 6. 10; 24. 33, a *l.* sleep.
15. 16; 16. 8, better is a *l.* with fear of Lord.
Prov. 30. 24, four things *l.* on earth.
Isa. 28. 10, here a *l.* and there a *l.*
40. 15; Ezek. 16. 47, as a very *l.* thing.
Hag. 1. 6, bring in *l.*
Mat. 6. 30; 8. 26; 14. 31; 16. 8; Lu. 12. 28, *l.* faith.
10. 42; 18. 6; Mk. 9. 42; Lu. 17. 2, *l.* ones.
Lu. 7. 47, to whom *l.* is forgiven.
19. 3, *l.* of stature.
1 Cor. 5. 6; Gal. 5. 9, a *l.* leaven.
1 Tim. 4. 8, bodily exercise profiteth *l.*
5. 23, use a *l.* wine.
See John 7. 33; 14. 19; 16. 16; Rev. 3. 8; 6. 11.
Live. Gen. 17. 18, O that Ishmael might *l.* before thee!
45. 3, doth my father yet *l.*?
Lev. 18. 5; Neh. 9. 29; Ezek. 20. 11, if a man do, he shall *l.*
Deu. 8. 3; Mat. 4. 4; Lu. 4. 4, not *l.* by bread alone.
Job 7. 16, I would not *l.* alway.
14. 14, shall he *l.* again?
Ps. 118. 17, I shall not die, but *l.*
Isa. 38. 16, make me to *l.*
55. 3, hear, and your soul shall *l.*
Ezek. 3. 21; 18. 9; 33. 13, he shall surely *l.*
16. 6, when thou wast in thy blood, *l.*
Hos. 6. 2, we shall *l.* in his sight.
Hab. 2. 4, the just shall *l.* by faith.
Lu. 10. 28, this do, and thou shalt *l.*
John 11. 25, though he were dead, yet shall he *l.*
14. 19, because I *l.*, ye shall *l.* also.
Acts 17. 28, in him we *l.* and move.
Rom. 8. 12, *l.* after the flesh.
14. 8, whether we *l.*, we *l.* unto the Lord.
1 Cor. 9. 14, should *l.* of the gospel.
2 Cor. 6. 9, as dying, and behold we *l.*
Gal. 2. 19, that I might *l.* unto God.
5. 25, if we *l.* in the Spirit.
Phil. 1. 21, for me to *l.* is Christ.
2 Tim. 3. 12, all that will *l.* godly.
Jas. 4. 15, if the Lord will, we shall *l.*
Rev. 1. 18, I am he that *l.*, and was dead.
3. 1, a name that thou *l.*
See Rom. 6. 10; 1 Tim. 5. 6; Rev. 20. 4.
Lively, full of life, life-giving, living. Acts 7. 38; 1 Pet. 1. 3; 2. 5.
Living. Gen. 2. 7, a *l.* soul.
Job 28. 13; Ps. 27. 13; 52. 5; 116. 9, the land of [the *l.*]
33. 30; Ps. 56. 13, light of *l.*
Ps. 69. 28, the book of the *l.* R. V. life.
Eccl. 7. 2, the *l.* will lay it to heart.
9. 5, the *l.* know they shall die.
S. of S. 4. 15; Jer. 2. 13; 17. 13; Zec. 14. 8; John 4. 10, *l.* water.
Isa. 38. 19, the *l.* shall praise thee.
Lam. 3. 39, wherefore doth a *l.* man complain?
Mk. 12. 44, even all her *l.*
Lu. 8. 43, spent all her *l.*
John 6. 51, I am the *l.* bread.
Heb. 10. 20, a new and *l.* way.
See Mat. 22. 32; Mk. 12. 27; 1 Cor. 15. 43.
Living water, gift of Christ. John 4. 10; 7. 38; Rev. 7. 17.
Lizard (Lev. 11. 30). Heb. *Lĕtâah:* Gk. χαλαβώτης: Zool. S. generic term (?). Lizards abound everywhere, but they swarm in desert places.
Loadeth. Ps. 68. 19.
Lo-ammi, lō-ăm'-mī, 'not my people.' Hos. 1. 9.
Loan. 1 Sam. 2. 20.
Loathe. Num. 21. 5; Job 7. 16; Ezek. 6. 9; 20. 43; 36. 31.
Loaves, miraculous multiplication of. Mat. 14. 17; 15. 32; Mk. 6. 35; Lu. 9. 12; John 6. 5.
Locust. The 'locust' includes the insects called in our version by the different names 'beetle,' 'canker-worm,' 'caterpiller,' 'grasshopper,' 'locust,' 'bald locust,' 'palmerworm.' The Rabbis say there were 800 species; but only about forty have yet been identified in Palestine. In all stages of growth they are largely eaten by natives, and are a palatable food.
Nine Hebrew words are used to express the locust species. (1) (Ex. 10. 4-6; Lev. 11. 22).

Heb. *Arbeh* (multiplier): Gk. βροῦχος: Zool. S. *Œdipoda migratoria; Locusta peregrina.* This is the common migratory locust. It is always mentioned with reference either to its numbers or its destructiveness.
(2) locust (bald) (Lev. 11. 22). Heb. *Sal'am:* Gk. ἀττάκης: Zool. S. *Truxalis*, 'the devourer.'
(3) (Lev. 11. 22). Heb. *Ḥargôl:* Gk. ὀφιομάχη: R. V. 'cricket;' perhaps 'galloper.'
(4) (Lev. 11. 22). Heb. *Ḥâgâb:* Gk. ἀκρίς: perhaps 'concealer' of the sun. Generally translated 'grasshopper.'
(5) (Joel 1. 4). Heb. *Gâzâm*, 'shearer;' Gk. κάμπη: Zool. S. a lepidopterous larva. H.; *Œdipoda migratoria.* The 'palmerworm' of A. V., consuming what the locusts left. The larvæ of locusts and moths, before developing their wings; caterpillars.
(6) (Joel 1. 4; Nah. 3. 15; Ps. 105. 34; Jer. 51. 14, 27). Heb. *Yélek:* Gk. βροῦχος, the 'lopper' or 'licker.' The 'cankerworm' of A. V., in five passages; but rendered 'caterpiller' in three. The larvæ of the locust.
(7) (Deu. 28. 42). Heb. *Tzĕlâtzal:* Gk. ἐρυσίβη: the 'tinkler,' referring to the 'whirring' sound the locusts make.
(8) (Isa. 33. 4; Am. 7. 1). Heb. *Gêb:* Gk. ἀκρίς. Once translated 'locust,' and twice 'grasshoppers' (marg. 'green worms').
(9) (Ps. 78. 46). Heb. *Ḥâsîl;* 'finisher;' Gk. ἐρυσίβη. Translated 'caterpiller' in all passages; a destroying locust in some of its forms.

Locusts. Ex. 10. 4; Deu. 28. 38; Ps. 105. 34; Rev. 9. 3.
used as food. Lev. 11. 22; Mat. 3. 4.
described. Prov. 30. 27; Nah. 3. 17; Rev. 9. 7.

Lod, lŏd. 1 Chr. 8. 12. [Sam. 9. 4.

Lo-debar, lō'-dĕ-băr, 'without pasture' (?). 2

Lodge (*n.*), a hut. Isa. 1. 8.

Lodge (*v.*). Ru. 1. 16; Isa. 1. 21; 1 Tim. 5. 10.

Loft, an upper room. Acts 20. 9.

Lofty. Ps. 131. 1; Isa. 2. 11; 57. 15.

Log, a dry and also liquid measure = .54 litres, nearly a pint (.96). *See* MEASURES.

Loins. Prov. 31. 17; Eph. 6. 14; 1 Pet. 1. 13.

Lois, lō'-ĭs. 2 Tim. 1. 5.

Long. Job 3. 21, which *l.* for death.
6. 8, that God would grant the thing I *l.* for!
Ps. 63. 1, my flesh *l.* for thee in a dry land.
84. 2, my soul *l.* for courts of the Lord.
119. 174, I have *l.* for thy salvation.
See Deu. 12. 20; 28. 32; 2 Sam. 23. 15; Phil. 1. 8.

Look. (1) Gen. 19. 17, *l.* not behind thee.
Num. 21. 8, when he *l.* on the serpent. R. V. seeth.
Job 33. 27, he *l.* on men.
Ps. 5. 3, and will *l.* up. R. V. keep watch.
34. 5, they *l.* to him, and were lightened.
84. 9, *l.* upon the face of thine anointed.
Isa. 5. 7; 59. 11, he *l.* for judgment.
17. 7, at that day shall a man *l.* to his Maker.
45. 22, *l.* unto me, and be saved.
63. 5, I *l.*, and there was none to help.
66. 2, to this man will I *l.*
Jer. 8. 15; 14. 19, we *l.* for peace.
39. 12, *l.* well to him.
40. 4, come with me, and I will *l.* well to thee.
Hag. 1. 9, ye *l.* for much.
Mat. 11. 3; Lu. 7. 19, do we *l.* for another?
24. 50, in a day he *l.* not for.
Lu. 9. 62, no man *l.* back is fit for the kingdom.
10. 32, a Levite came and *l.* on him. R. V. saw.
22. 61, the Lord turned, and *l.* on Peter.
John 13. 22, disciples *l.* one on another.
Acts 3. 4, said *l.* on us.
6. 3, *l.* ye out seven men.
2 Cor. 4. 18, we *l.* not at things seen.
10. 7, *l.* upon things after outward appearance.
Phil. 2. 4, *l.* not every man on his own things.
Tit. 2. 13, *l.* for that blessed hope.
Heb. 11. 10, he *l.* for a city.
Heb. 12. 2, *l.* unto Jesus.
1 Pet. 1. 12, angels desire to *l.* into.
2 John 8, *l.* to yourselves.
(2) to expect. Isa. 5. 2.
See Prov. 14. 15; Mat. 5. 28; 2 Pet. 3. 12. [8, 11.

Look in the face, to meet in battle. 2 Kn. 14.

Loose. Job 38. 31, canst thou *l.* the bands of Orion?
Ps. 102. 20, *l.* those appointed to death.
116. 16, thou hast *l.* my bonds.
Eccl. 12. 6, or ever the silver cord be *l.*
Mat. 16. 19; 18. 18, *l.* on earth, be *l.* in heaven.
John 11. 44, *l.* him, and let him go.
Acts 2. 24, having *l.* the pains of death.
1 Cor. 7. 27, art thou *l.* from a wife?
See Deu. 25. 9; Isa. 45. 1; 51. 14; Lu. 13. 12.

Lord. Ex. 34. 6, the *L.*, the *L.* God, merciful.
Deu. 4. 35; 1 Kn. 18. 39, the *L.* is God.
6. 4, the *L.* our God is one *L.* [with you.
Ru. 2. 4; 2 Chr. 20. 17; 2 Thes. 3. 16, the *L.* be
1 Sam. 3. 18; John 21. 7, it is the *L.*
Neh. 9. 6; Isa. 37. 20, thou art *L.* alone.
Ps. 33. 12, whose God is the *L.*
100. 3, know that the *L.* he is God.
118. 23, this is the *L.* doing.
Zec. 14. 9, one *L.*, and his name one.
Mat. 7. 21, not every one that saith *L.*, *L.*
26. 22, *L.*, is it I?
Mk. 2. 28; Lu. 6. 5, the *L.* of the sabbath.
Lu. 6. 46, why call ye me *L.*, *L.*?
John 9. 36, who is he, *L.*?
20. 25, we have seen the *L.*
Acts 2. 36, both *L.* and Christ.
9. 5; 26. 15, who art thou, *L.*?
Eph. 4. 5, one *L.*
See Rom. 10. 12; 1 Cor. 2. 8; 15. 47; Rev. 11. 15.

Lord's Day. Rev. 1. 10.

Lordship. Mk. 10. 42; Lu. 22. 25.

Lord's Prayer. Mat. 6. 9.

Lord's Supper. *See* COMMUNION.

Lo-ruhamah, lō-rŭ-hä'-măh, 'not having obtained mercy.' Hos. 1. 6.

Lose. Mat. 10. 39; 16. 25; Mk. 8. 35; Lu. 9. 24, shall *l.* it.
16. 26; Mk. 8. 36; Lu. 9. 25, *l.* his own soul. R. V. forfeit.
John 6. 39, Father's will I should *l.* nothing.
See Jud. 18. 25; Eccl. 3. 6; Lu. 15. 4, 8.

Loss. 1 Cor. 3. 15; Phil. 3. 7, 8.

Lost. Ps. 119. 176; Jer. 50. 6, like *l.* sheep.
Ezek. 37. 11, our hope is *l.*
Mat. 10. 6; 15. 24, go to *l.* sheep of Israel.
18. 11; Lu. 19. 10, to save that which was *l.*
John 6. 12, that nothing be *l.*
17. 12, none of them is *l.*
18. 9, have I *l.* none.
See Lev. 6. 3; Deu. 22. 3; 2 Cor. 4. 3.

Lot. Ps. 16. 5, thou maintainest my *l.*
125. 3, not rest on the *l.* of the righteous.
Prov. 1. 14, cast in thy *l.* among us.
16. 33, *l.* is cast into the lap.
18. 18, *l.* causeth contentions to cease.
Dan. 12. 13, stand in thy *l.*
Acts 8. 21, neither part nor *l.* in this matter.

Lot, the, decided by God. Lev. 16. 8; Prov. 16. 33.
Canaan apportioned by. Num. 26. 55; Jos. 15.
Saul chosen king by. 1 Sam. 10. 17.
Jonathan taken by. 1 Sam. 14. 41, 42.
used to divide Christ's raiment. Mat. 27. 35; Mk. 15. 24 (Ps. 22. 18).
Matthias chosen apostle by. Acts 1. 26.

Lot, lŏt, 'veil' (?), Abram's nephew. Gen. 11. 27.
separates from Abram. Gen. 13. 10.
captured by four kings, and rescued by Abram. Gen. 14.
entertains angel visitors. Gen. 19. 1.
saved from Sodom. Gen. 19. 16; 2 Pet. 2. 7.
his wife turned into a pillar of salt. Gen. 19. 26; Lu. 17. 28, 32.

Lotan, lō'-tăn, 'veiling.' Gen. 36. 20.

Loud. Ez. 3. 13; Prov. 7. 11; 27. 14; Lu. 23. 23.

Love (*n.*). 2 Sam. 1. 26, wonderful, passing the *l.* of women.

Prov. 10. 12, *l.* covereth all sins.
15. 17, better a dinner of herbs where *l.* is.
S. of S. 2. 4, his banner over me was *l.*
8. 6, *l.* is strong as death.
Jer. 31. 3, loved thee with everlasting *l.*
Hos. 11. 4, the bands of *l.*
Mat. 24. 12, *l.* of many shall wax cold.
John 5. 42, ye have not the *l.* of God in you.
13. 35, if ye have *l.* one to another.
15. 13, greater *l.* hath no man than this.
Rom. 13. 10, *l.* worketh no ill.
2 Cor. 5. 14, the *l.* of Christ constraineth us.
13. 11, the God of *l.* shall be with you.
Eph. 3. 19, the *l.* of Christ, which passeth.
1 Tim. 6. 10, *l.* of money is the root of all evil.
Heb. 13. 1, let brotherly *l.* continue.
1 John 4. 7, *l.* is of God.
4. 8, 16, God is *l.*
4. 10, herein is *l.*, not that we loved God.
4. 18, no fear in *l.*
Rev. 2. 4, thou hast left thy first *l.*
See Gal. 5. 22; 1 Thes. 1. 3.

Love (*v.*). Lev. 19. 18; Mat. 19. 19; 22. 39; Mk. 12. 31, thou shalt *l.* thy neighbour.
Deu. 6. 5; 10. 12; 11. 1; 19. 9; 30. 6; Mat. 22. 37; Mk. 12. 30; Lu. 10. 27, *l.* the Lord thy God.
Ps. 18. 1, I will *l.* thee, O Lord, my strength.
26. 8, I have *l.* the habitation of thy house.
34. 12, what man is he that *l.* many days?
69. 36, they that *l.* his name.
97. 10, ye that *l.* the Lord.
109. 17, as he *l.* cursing.
122. 6, they shall prosper that *l.* thee.
Prov. 8. 17, I *l.* them that *l.* me.
17. 17, a friend *l.* at all times.
Eccl. 3. 8, a time to *l.*
Jer. 5. 31, my people *l.* to have it so.
31. 3, I have *l.* thee with an everlasting *l.*
Hos. 14. 4, I will *l.* them freely.
Am. 5. 15, hate the evil, and *l.* the good.
Mic. 6. 8, but to *l.* mercy, and walk humbly.
Mat. 5. 44; Lu. 6. 27, I say, *l.* your enemies.
5. 46, if ye *l.* them which *l.* you.
Lu. 7. 42, which will *l.* him most?
John 11. 3, he whom thou *l.* is sick.
15. 12, 17, that ye *l.* one another.
21. 15–17, *l.* thou me?
Rom. 13. 8, owe no man any thing, but to *l.*
Eph. 6. 24, grace be with all them that *l.* our Lord.
1 Pet. 1. 8, whom having not seen, ye *l.*
2. 17, *l.* the brotherhood.
1 John 4. 19, we *l.* him, because he first *l.* us.
Rev. 3. 19, as many as I *l.* I rebuke.
See Gen. 22. 2; John 14. 31.

Love to God commanded. Deu. 6. 5; 10. 12; 11. 1; Jos. 22. 5; Ps. 31. 23; Dan. 9. 4; Mat. 22. 37; 1 John 4.; 5.
blessings of. Neh. 1. 5; Ps. 145. 20; 1 Cor. 2. 9; 8. 3.
brotherly. Rom. 12. 9, 10. [25; Tit. 2. 4.
of husbands. Gen. 29. 20; 2 Sam. 1. 26; Eph. 5.
to Christ. Mat. 10. 37; Rev. 2. 4.
of the world, censured. 1 John 2. 15.

Lovely. 2 Sam. 1. 23; S. of S. 5. 16; Ezek. 33. 32; Phil. 4. 8.

Lover. 1 Kn. 5. 1; Ps. 88. 18; 2 Tim. 3. 4; Tit. 1. 8.

Lovingkindness. Ps. 17. 7; 36. 7, 10; 51. 1; 92. 2; 103. 4; 143. 8; Jer. 31. 3.

Low. Ps. 136. 23; Rom. 12. 16; Jas. 1. 9, 10.

Lower. Ps. 8. 5; 63. 9; Eph. 4. 9; Heb. 2. 7.

Lowest. Deu. 32. 22; Ps. 86. 13; Lu. 14. 9.

Lowliness. Eph. 4. 2; Phil. 2. 3.

Lowly. Prov. 11. 2, with the *l.* is wisdom.
Mat. 11. 29, I am meek and *l.*
See Ps. 138. 6; Prov. 3. 34; 16. 19; Zec. 9. 9.

Lubims, lū′-bĭms, same as Lehabim. 2 Chr. 12. 3.

Lucas, lū′-căs, same as Luke. Philem. 24.

Lucifer, lū′-çĭ-fĕr, 'light-bearer.' Isa. 14. 12.

Lucius, lū′-çĭ-ŭs, 'a noble' (?), of Cyrene, a teacher. Acts 13. 1; Rom. 16. 21.

Lucre, profit, 'filthy lucre' = base gain; greed of, forbidden. 1 Tim. 3. 3; Tit. 1. 7; 1 Pet. 5. 2.

Lud, lŭd, 'strife' (?). (1) Gen. 10. 22. (2) Isa. 66. 19.

Ludim, lū′-dĭm. Gen. 10. 13.

Luhith, lū′-hĭth. Isa. 15. 5.

Luke, lūke, 'of or belonging to Lucania' (?); the beloved physician, companion of Paul. Col. 4. 14; 2 Tim. 4. 11; Philem. 24 (Acts 16. 12; 20. 5).

Lukewarmness condemned. Rev. 3. 16.

Lust, desire, wish, pleasure. Deu. 12. 15, 20, 21; 14. 26, whatsoever thy soul *l.* after. R. V. desireth.
Ps. 81. 12, gave them up to their own hearts' *l.* R. V. stubbornness.
Rom. 7. 7, I had not known *l.* R. V. coveting.
Gal. 5. 24, Christ's have crucified flesh with *l.*
1 Tim. 6. 9, rich fall into hurtful *l.*
Tit. 2. 12, denying worldly *l.*
Jas. 1. 14, when he is drawn of his own *l.*
1 Pet. 2. 11, abstain from fleshly *l.*
1 John 2. 16, the *l.* of the flesh.
2. 17, the world passeth away, and the *l.* thereof.
Jude 16, 18, walking after *l.*
See Ex. 15. 9; Mat. 5. 28; 1 Cor. 10. 6; 2 Tim. 4. 3; Rev. 18. 14.

Lusty, vigorous, strong. Jud. 3. 29.

Lute, Heb. *Nébel*, a kind of harp, usually translated 'psaltery.'

Luz, lŭz, 'almond tree.' (1) Gen. 28. 19. (2) Jud. 1. 26.

Lycaonia, lȳ-cā-ō′-nĭ-ă. Acts 14. 6.

Lycia, lȳç′-ĭ-ă. Acts 27. 5.

Lydda, lȳd′-dă, Greek form of Lod (?), miracle at. Acts 9. 32.

Lydia, lȳd′-ĭ-ă, a Lydian, of Thyatira, piety of. Acts 16. 14, 40.

Lydians, lȳd′-ĭ-ăns, people of Lydia. Jer. 46. 9. R. V. Ludim.

Lying. 1 Kn. 22. 22; 2 Chr. 18. 21, a *l.* spirit in the mouth of the prophets.
Ps. 31. 18, let the *l.* lips be put to silence.
119. 163, I abhor *l.*, but thy law I love.
Prov. 6. 17, the Lord hateth a *l.* tongue.
12. 19, a *l.* tongue is but for a moment.
Jer. 7. 4, trust not in *l.* words.
Eph. 4. 25, putting away *l.*

Lying hateful to God. Prov. 6. 16, 19; 12. 22.
forbidden. Lev. 19. 11; Col. 3. 9.
devil father of. John 8. 44; Acts 5. 3. [3. 1.

Lysanias, lȳ-sā′-nĭ-ăs, 'ending sadness' (?). Lu.

Lysias, lȳs′-ĭ-ăs, a person of Lysia. Acts 23. 26.

Lystra, lȳs′-tră. Acts 14. 6.
miracle at. Acts 14. 8. [11.
Paul and Barnabas taken for gods at. Acts 14.
Paul stoned at, by Jews. Acts 14. 19.

Maacah, mā′-ă-căh, same as Maachah. 2 Sam. 3. 3.

Maachah, mā′-ă-chăh, 'royal' (?). (1) 1 Kn. 2. 39. (2) queen, her idolatry. 1 Kn. 15. 13; 2 Chr. 15. 16.

Maachathi, mā-ăch′-ă-thī, an inhabitant of Maachah. Deu. 3. 14.

Maachathites, mā-ăch′-ă-thītes, plural of preceding. Jos. 12. 5.

Maadai, mā-ă-dā′-ī, 'adorned.' Ez. 10. 34.

Maadiah, mā-ă-dī′-ăh, 'ornament of Jehovah.' Neh. 12. 5.

Maai, mā-ā′-ī, 'compassionate' (?). Neh. 12. 36.

Maaleh-acrabbim, mā′-ă-lĕh-ăc-răb′-bĭm, 'ascent of scorpions.' Jos. 15. 3.

Maarath, mā′-ă-răth. Jos. 15. 59.

Maaseiah, mā-ă-sēi′-ăh, 'work of Jehovah.' Ez. 10. 18.

Maasiai, mā-ăs-ĭ-ā′ī, same as Amashai (?). 1 Chr. 9. 12.

Maath, mā′-ăth, 'small' (?). Lu. 3. 26.

Maaz, mā′-ăz, 'wrath.' 1 Chr. 2. 27.

Maaziah, mā-ă-zī′-ăh. 1 Chr. 24. 18.

Macedonia, măç-ē-dō′-nĭ-ă, a Roman province lying to the north of Greece, the first country of Europe in which the gospel was preached by Paul. Acts 16. 9-12; 18. 5, 6.
liberality of. 2 Cor. 8.; 9.; 11. 9; Phil. 4. 15.
its churches. 1 & 2 Thes.

Macedonian, măç-ē-dō′-nĭ-ăn, an inhabitant of Macedonia. Acts 27. 2.
Machbanai, măch-bā′-nāi, 'cloak' (?). 1 Chr. 12. 13.
Machbenah, măch-bē′-năh, 'clad with a cloak' (?). 1 Chr. 2. 49.
Machi, mā′-chī. Num. 13. 15.
Machir, mā′-chĭr, 'sold.' (1) Gen. 50. 23; Jos. 17. 1. (2) 2 Sam. 9. 4.
Machirites, mā′-chĭr-ītes, the descendants of Machir. Num. 26. 29.
Machnadebai, măch-năd′-ĕ-bāi. Ez. 10. 40.
Machpelah, măch-pē′-lăh, 'a doubling' (?), field of. Gen. 23.
patriarchs buried there. Gen. 23. 19; 25. 9; 35. 29; 49. 30; 50. 12.
Mad. John 10. 20; Acts 26. 11, 24; 1 Cor. 14. 23.
Madai, mā′-dāi. Gen. 10. 2.
Made. Ex. 2. 14, who *m.* thee a prince over us?
Ps. 118. 24, this is the day the Lord hath *m.*
Prov. 16. 4, the Lord *m.* all things for himself.
Eccl. 3. 11, he hath *m.* every thing beautiful.
7. 29, God hath *m.* man upright.
Isa. 66. 2, all these things hath mine hand *m.*
John 1. 3, all things were *m.* by him.
5. 6, wilt thou be *m.* whole?
2 Cor. 5. 21, he hath *m.* him to be sin for us.
Eph. 2. 13, *m.* nigh by the blood of Christ.
3. 7; Col. 1. 23, I was *m.* a minister.
Col. 1. 20, having *m.* peace.
Heb. 2. 17, to be *m.* like his brethren.
See Ps. 95. 5; 149. 2; John 19. 7; Acts 17. 24.
Madian, mā′-dĭ-ăn, Greek form of MIDIAN. Acts 7. 29.
Madmannah, măd-măn′-năh, 'dunghill.' Jos. 15. 31.
Madmen, măd′-mĕn, 'dungheap.' Jer. 48. 2.
Madmenah, măd-mē′-năh, same as MADMEN. Isa. 10. 31.
Madness, David affects. 1 Sam. 21. 13.
threatened. Deu. 28. 28.
Madon, mā′-dŏn, contention. Jos. 11. 1.
Magbish, măg′-bĭsh, congregating. Ez. 2. 30.
Magdala, măg′-dă-lă, tower. Mat. 15. 39.
Magdalene, măg′-dă-lēne, inhabitant of Magdala. Mat. 27. 56.
Magdiel, măg′-dĭ-ĕl, 'praise of God' (?). Gen. 36. 43.
Magi, 'wise men.' In Jer. 13. 3, Rab-mag is probably 'chief of the Magi.' The Magi formed a religious caste in the East, of men deeply versed in science and philosophy. Such were led by the star to the infant Jesus. But in many cases the Magi became soothsayers, fortune-tellers, and sorcerers.
Magic, Magician. 'Magic is the profession and practice of the Magi.' 'It is the pretended art of controlling the actions of spiritual or superhuman beings.' The prophets habitually associate magic with idolatry. Mic. 5. 11, comp. 2 Kn. 9. 22; 2 Chr. 33. 6. Magic was forbidden. Isa. 8. 19–21. Magicians or 'engravers,' in Ex. 32. 4, were perhaps originally a literary caste. Comp. the case of the Magi.
of Egypt. Ex. 7. 11; 8. 19.
of Chaldæa preserved. Dan. 2.; 4. 7.
Magistrates. Ez. 7. 25.
to be obeyed. Ex. 22. 8; Rom. 13.; Tit. 3. 1; 1 Pet. 2. 14.
Magnifical, magnificent. 1 Chr. 22. 5.
Magnify. Jos. 3. 7, this day will I begin to *m.* thee.
Job 7. 17, what is man, that thou shouldest *m.* him?
Ps. 34. 3; 40. 16; Lu. 1. 46, *m.* the Lord.
Ps. 35. 26; 38. 16, that *m.* themselves.
138. 2, thou hast *m.* thy word above all.
Isa. 42. 21, *m.* the law.
Acts 19. 17, the name of Jesus was *m.*
Rom. 11. 13, I *m.* mine office.
See Dan. 8. 25; 11. 36; Acts 5. 13; Phil. 1. 20.
Magog, mā′-gŏg, 'land of Gog' (?). Gen. 10. 2.
Magor-missabib, mā′-gŏr-mĭs-să′-bĭb, 'fear round about.' Jer. 20. 3.

Magpiash, măg′-pĭ-ăsh. Neh. 10. 20.
Mahalah, mă-hā′-lăh, 'sickness.' 1 Chr. 7. 18.
Mahalaleel, mă-hăl′-ă-lēēl, 'praise of God.' Gen. 5. 12.
Mahalath, mā′-hă-lăth, 'a musical term.' (1) Gen. 28. 9; (2) 2 Chr. 11. 18.
(3) Ps. 53. title. 'After the manner of Mahalath,' in minor tones, mournfully. In Ps. 88. it is joined with Leannoth, 'to sing after the manner of Mahalath.'
Mahali, mā′-hă-lī, 'weak.' Ex. 6. 19.
Mahanaim, mā-hă-nā′-ĭm, 'two camps,' Jacob's vision at. Gen. 32.
Ish-bosheth made king at. 2 Sam. 2. 8.
David takes refuge from Absalom at. 2 Sam. 17. 24.
Mahaneh-dan, mā′-hă-nĕh-dăn, 'camp of Dan.' Jud. 18. 12.
Maharai, mā′-hă-rāi, 'impetuous.' 2 Sam. 23. 28.
Mahath, mā′-hăth, 'taking hold' (?). (1) 1 Chr. 6. 35. (2) 2 Chr. 31. 13.
Mahavite, mă-hā′-vīte. 1 Chr. 11. 46.
Mahazioth, mă-hā′-zĭ-ŏth, 'visions.' 1 Chr. 25. 4.
Maher-shalal-hash-baz, mā′-hĕr-shăl′-ăl-hăsh′-băz, 'the spoil hastens, the prey speeds.' Isa. 8. 1.
Mahlah, măh′-lăh, same as MAHALAH. Num. 26. 33.
Mahli, măh′-lī, same as MAHALI. (1) Num. 3. 20; 1 Chr. 6. 19. (2) 1 Chr. 23. 23.
Mahlites, măh′-lītes, the descendants of Mahli. Num. 3. 33.
Mahlon, măh′-lŏn, 'a sick person,' and Chilion die in Moab. Ru. 1. 2.
Mahol, mā′-hŏl, a dance. 1 Kn. 4. 31.
Maid. 2 Kn. 5. 2; Mat. 9. 24; 26. 71.
Maiden. Ex. 2. 5; Ps. 123. 2; 148. 12.
Maidservants. Ex. 20. 10, nor thy *m.*
21. 7, if a man sell his daughter to be a *m.*
Deu. 15. 17, unto thy *m.* thou shalt do likewise.
Mail. 1 Sam. 17. 5.
Maimed healed by Christ. Mat. 15. 30.
animal, unfit for sacrifice. Lev. 22. 22.
Maintain. 1 Kn. 8. 45; 49. 59; 2 Chr. 35. 39, *m.* their cause.
Ps. 16. 5, thou *m.* my lot.
Tit. 3. 8, 14, careful to *m.* good works.
See Job 13. 15; Ps. 9. 4; 140. 12.
Maintenance. Ez. 4. 14; Prov. 27. 27.
Majesty of God. 1 Chr. 29. 11; Job 37. 22; Ps. 93.; 96.; Isa. 24. 14; Nah. 1.; Hab. 3. *See* GOD.
of Christ. 2 Pet. 1. 16.
Makaz, mā′-kăz, 'end' (?). 1 Kn. 4. 9.
Maker. Job 4. 17, shall a man be more pure than his *m.*?
32. 22, my *m.* would soon take me away.
35. 10, none saith, where is God my *m.*?
36. 3, ascribe righteousness to my *m.*
Ps. 95. 6, kneel before the Lord our *m.*
Prov. 14. 31, 17. 5, reproacheth his *m.*
22. 2, the Lord is *m.* of them all.
Isa. 45. 9, that striveth with his *m.*
51. 13, forgettest the Lord thy *m.*
54. 5, thy *m.* is thine husband.
Heb. 11. 10, whose builder and *m.* is God.
See Isa. 1. 31; 17. 7; 22. 11; Hab. 2. 18.
Makest thou, doest thou. Jud. 18. 3.
Makheloth, măk-hē′-lŏth, 'assemblies.' Num. 33. 25.
Makkedah, măk-kē′-dăh, 'place of shepherds' (?). Jos. 10. 10.
cave of, five kings hide in. Jos. 10. 16.
Maktesh, măk′-tĕsh, 'a mortar.' Zep. 1. 11.
Malachi, măl′-ă-chī, 'the messenger of Jehovah;' deplores and reproves Israel's ingratitude. Mal. 1.; 2.
foretells the Messiah and His messenger. Mal. 3.; 4.
Malcham, măl′-chăm, 'their king.' (1) 1 Chr. 8. 9. (2) Zep. 1. 5.
Malchiah, măl-chī′-ăh, 'my king is Jehovah.' 1 Chr. 6. 40.
Malchiel, măl′-chĭ-ĕl, 'my king is God.' Gen. 46. 17.
Malchielites, măl′-chĭ-ē′-lītes, the descendants of Malchiel. Num. 26. 45.

Malchijah, măl-chī′-jăh, same as MALCHIAH. 1 Chr. 9. 12.
Malchiram, măl-chī′-răm, 'my king is exalted' (?). 1 Chr. 3. 18.
Malchi-shua, măl′-chī-shū′-ă, 'my king is prosperity.' 1 Chr. 8. 33.
Malchus, măl′-chŭs, Greek form of MALLUCH; wounded by Peter. John 18. 10; Mat. 26. 51; Mk. 14. 47.
healed by Jesus. Lu. 22. 51.
Male children saved from Pharaoh. Ex. 1. 15.
Malefactors, execution of. Deu. 21. 22.
crucified with Christ. Lu. 23. 32. [3. 37.
Maleleel, măl′-ĕ-lēel, same as MAHALALEEL. Lu.
Males to appear before the Lord thrice a year. Ex. 23. 17; Deu. 16. 16.
Malice condemned. Prov. 17. 5; 24. 17; 1 Cor. 5. 8; 14. 20; Eph. 4. 31; Col. 3. 8; Tit. 3. 3; Jas. 5. 9; 1 Pet. 2. 1.
Maliciousness. Rom. 1. 29; 1 Pet. 2. 16.
Mallothi, măl-lō′-thī. 1 Chr. 25. 4.
Mallow (Job 30. 4). Heb. *Mallûaḥ:* Gk. ἅλιμον: R. V. 'salt-wort;' *Atriplex Halimus*=sea purslane, a perennial shrub growing in salt marshes along the sea coast; the leaves were sometimes cooked as vegetables by the very poor.
Malluch, măl′-lŭch, 'counsellor.' 1 Chr. 6. 44.
Mammon, măm′-mŏn, 'riches' (*lit.* what is hidden); worship of. Mat. 6. 24; Lu. 16. 9.
Mamre, măm′-rē, 'fatness.' (1) a man. Gen. 14. 13.
(2) a place. [17; 35. 27.
Abram dwells there. Gen. 13. 18.; 14.; 18.; 23.
Man. Gen. 3. 22, the *m.* is become as one of us.
8. 21, for *m.* sake.
Num. 23. 19, God is not a *m.*
Neh. 6. 11, should such a *m.* as I flee?
Job 5. 7, *m.* is born to trouble.
10. 4, seest thou as *m.* seeth?
11. 12, vain *m.* would be wise.
14. 1, *m.* that is born of a woman.
15. 7, art thou the first *m.* that was born?
25. 6, *m.* that is a worm.
33. 12, God is greater than *m.*
Ps. 10. 18, the *m.* of earth.
49. 12, *m.* being in honour abideth not.
89. 48, what *m.* is he that liveth?
90. 3, thou turnest *m.* to destruction.
104. 23, *m.* goeth forth to his labour.
118. 6, I will not fear, what can *m.* do.
Prov. 12. 2, a good *m.* obtaineth favour.
Eccl. 6. 12, who knoweth what is good for *m.*
Isa. 2. 22, cease ye from *m.*
Jer. 10. 23, it is not in *m.* to direct his steps.
Lam. 3. 1, I am the *m.* that hath seen affliction.
Hos. 11. 9, I am God, and not *m.*
Mat. 6. 24; Lu. 16. 13, no *m.* can serve.
8. 4; Mk. 8. 26, 30; Lu. 5. 14; 9. 21, tell no *m.*
17. 8, they saw no *m.* R. V. one.
John 1. 18; 1 John 4. 12, no *m.* hath seen God.
7. 46, never *m.* spake like this *m.*
19. 5, behold the *m.*!
1 Cor. 2. 11, what *m.* knoweth things of a *m.*?
11. 8, *m.* is not of the woman.
2 Cor. 4. 16, though our outward *m.* perish.
Phil. 2. 8, in fashion as a *m.*
1 Tim. 2. 5, the *m.* Christ Jesus.
Man created. Gen. 1. 26; 2. 7.
his dignity. Gen. 1. 27; 2. 25; Eccl. 7. 29.
his fall. Gen. 3.
his iniquity. Gen. 6. 5, 12; 1 Kn. 8. 46; Job 14. 16; 15. 14; Ps. 14.; 51.; Eccl. 9. 3; Isa. 43. 27; 53. 6; Jer. 3. 25; 17. 9; John 3. 19; Rom. 3. 9; 5. 12; 7. 18; Gal. 3. 10; 5. 17; Jas. 1. 13; 1 John 1. 8.
his imperfection and weakness. 2 Chr. 20. 12; Mat. 6. 27; Rom. 9. 16; 1 Cor. 3. 7; 2 Cor. 3. 5.
liable to suffering. Job 5. 7; 14. 1; Ps. 39. 4; Eccl. 3. 2; Acts 14. 22; Rom. 8. 22; Rev. 7. 14.
ignorance of. Job 8. 9; 11. 12; 28. 12; Prov. 16. 25; 27. 1; Eccl. 8. 17; Isa. 59. 10; 1 Cor. 1. 20; 8. 2 (Isa. 47. 10); Jas. 4. 14.
mortality of. Job 14.; Ps. 39.; 49.; 62. 9; 78. 39; 89. 48; 103. 14; 144. 4; 146. 3; Eccl. 1. 4; 12. 7; Rom. 5. 12; Heb. 9. 27.
vanity of his life. Ps. 49.; Eccl. 1.; 2. [3. 23.
his whole duty. Eccl. 12. 13; Mic. 6. 8; 1 John
his redemption. Rom. 5.: 1 Cor. 15. 47, 49; Gal. 3.; 4.; Eph. 3.; 4. 24; 5. 25; Phil. 3. 21; Col. 1.; 1 Tim. 2. 4; Heb. 1.; 2.; Rev. 5.
Manaen, măn′-ā-ĕn, Greek form of MENAHEM. Acts 13. 1.
Manahath, măn′-ă-hăth, 'rest.' Gen. 36. 23.
Manahethites, măn-ă-hē′-thītes, inhabitants of Manahath (?). 1 Chr. 2. 52.
Manasseh, mă-năs′-sĕh, 'one who causes to forget.'
(1) firstborn son of Joseph. Gen. 41. 51.
his blessing. Gen. 48.
his descendants numbered, &c. Num. 1. 34; 26. 29; Jos. 22. 1; 1 Chr. 5. 23; 7. 14.
their inheritance. Num. 32. 33; 34. 14; Jos. 13. 29; 17.
incline to David's cause. 1 Chr. 9. 3; 12. 19; 2 Chr. 15. 9; 30. 11.
(2) king of Judah, his reign. 2 Kn. 21.; 2 Chr. 33.
(3) others. Jud. 18. 30; Ez. 10. 30, 33.
Manasses, mă-năs′-sēs, Greek form of MANASSEH. Mat. 1. 10.
Manassites, mă-năs′-sītes, members of the tribe of Manasseh. Deu. 4. 43.
Mandrake (Gen. 30. 14; S. of S. 7. 13). Heb. *Dûdâîm:* Gk. μανδραγόρας: Bot. N. *Mandragora officinarum:* R. V. marg. 'love-apples.' A stemless plant of the potato family, with a large tap root, dark green leaves spreading on the ground, blue flowers, and yellow pulpy fruit of the size of a large plum.
Maneh, mā′-nĕh, a weight. Ezek. 45. 12. The same as MINA, *q. v.*
Manger. Lu. 2. 7, laid him in a *m.* [be *m.*
Manifest. Mk. 4. 22, nothing hid that shall not
John 2. 11, and *m.* forth his glory.
14. 22, how is it thou wilt *m.* thyself?
17. 6, I have *m.* thy name. [the hearts.
1 Cor. 4. 5, who will make *m.* the counsels of
2 Cor. 2. 14, maketh *m.* savour of knowledge.
Gal. 5. 19, the works of the flesh are *m.*
2 Thes. 1. 5, a *m.* token of righteous judgment.
1 Tim. 3. 16, God was *m.* in the flesh.
5. 25, good works of some are *m.* beforehand. R. V. evident.
Heb. 4. 13, no creature that is not *m.*
1 John 1. 2, the life was *m.*
3. 5, he was *m.* to take away our sins.
4. 9, in this was *m.* the love of God.
Manifestation of Christ. Mat. 17.; John 1. 14; 2. 11; 1 John 3. 5.
of God's righteousness, Rom. 3. 21. of His love, 1 John 4. 9.
of the sons of God. Rom. 8. 19; 1 John 3. 10.
of the Spirit. 1 Cor. 12. 7.
Manifold. Ps. 104. 24, how *m.* are thy works!
Eph. 3. 10, the *m.* wisdom of God.
1 Pet. 1. 6, through *m.* temptations.
4. 10, stewards of the *m.* grace of God.
See Neh. 9. 19, 27; Am. 5. 12; Lu. 18. 30.
Manna, măn′-nă (Ex. 16. 15). Heb. *Man*, or *man hu:* Gk. μάννα. *Manna* (Heb. *Man hu*, 'What is it?') was the name by which the miraculous food given to Israel in the wilderness was known. It is described as a small round thing, like coriander seed, white, tasting like wafer and honey. A sweet semi-fluid substance called manna exudes from the tamarisk tree in the Sinaitic desert. The manna of commerce is a sickly smelling laxative exuding from the flowering ash.
Manna promised. Ex. 16. 4.
sent. Ex. 16. 14; Deu. 8. 3; Neh. 9. 20; Ps. 78. 24; John 6. 31.
an omer of it laid up in the ark. Ex. 16. 32; Heb. 9. 4.
Israelites murmur at it. Num. 11. 6.

it ceases on entering Canaan. Jos. 5. 12.
the hidden. Rev. 2. 17.
Manner. 2 Sam. 7. 19, is this the *m.* of man?
Ps. 144. 13, all *m.* of store.
Isa. 5. 17, lambs shall feed after their *m.* R. V. as in their pasture.
Mat. 8. 27; Mk. 4. 41; Lu. 8. 25, what *m.* of man is this!
12. 31, all *m.* of sin shall be forgiven. R. V. every.
Acts 26. 4, my *m.* of life from my youth.
1 Cor. 15. 33, evil communications corrupt good *m.* R. V. morals.
Heb. 10. 25, as the *m.* of some is. R. V. custom.
Jas. 1. 24, forgetteth what *m.* of man.
1 Pet. 1. 15, holy in all *m.* of conversation.
2 Pet. 3. 11, what *m.* of persons ought ye to be?
See Mat. 4. 23; 5. 11; Lu. 9. 55; Rev. 22. 2.
Manner, with the, 'taken with the manner' = caught in the very act. Num. 5. 13.
Manoah, mă-nō'-ăh, 'rest;' father of Samson. Jud. 13.; 16. 31.
Man of war, a soldier, a warrior. Lu. 23. 11.
Mansions, abiding places, dwelling places. John 14. 2.
Manslaughter. Gen. 9. 6; Ex. 21. 12; Num. 35. 6, 22; Deu. 19. 4; Jos. 20. 1; 1 Tim. 1. 9.
Manstealing. Ex. 21. 16; Deu. 24. 7.
Mantle. 2 Kn. 2. 8; Job 1. 20; Ps. 109. 29.
Maoch, mā'-ŏch, 'oppressed' (?). 1 Sam. 27. 2.
Maon, mā'-ŏn, 'habitation.' Jos. 15. 55.
Maonites, mā'-ŏn-ītes. Jud. 10. 12.
Mar. Lev. 19. 27, nor *m.* the corners of thy beard.
1 Sam. 6. 5, images of your mice that *m.* the land.
Job 30. 13, they *m.* my path.
Isa. 52. 14, visage *m.* more than any man.
Mk. 2. 22, wine spilled, and bottles *m.*
See Ru. 4. 6; 2 Kn. 3. 19; Jer. 13. 7; 18. 4.
Mara, mâr'-ă, 'sad' or 'bitter.' Ru. 1. 20.
Marah, mâr'-ăh, 'bitter;' bitter waters healed there. Ex. 15. 23.
Maralah, măr'-ă-lăh, 'trembling.' Jos. 19. 11.
Maranatha, măr-ăn-ä'-thă (*Mâran ethâ*). Two Chaldee words signifying, 'The Lord cometh' or 'The Lord is at hand.' It would seem probable that the phrase was used by the early Christians as a kind of watchword of mutual encouragement and hope. So the words in 1 Cor. 16. 22 are nearly equivalent to the similar expressions in Phil. 4. 5; Rev. 22. 20.
Marble. 1 Chr. 29. 2, and *m.* stones in abundance.
S. of S. 5. 15, his legs are as pillars of *m.*
Marcus, mär'-cŭs. Col. 4. 10. R. V. MARK.
Mareshah, mă-rē'-shăh, 'capital.' Jos. 15. 44.
Marish, marsh, swampy ground. Ezek. 47. 11.
Mark. Gen. 4. 15, the Lord set a *m.* on Cain. R. V. sign.
Job 22. 15, hast thou *m.* the old way? R. V. wilt thou keep?
Ps. 37. 37, *m.* the perfect man.
48. 13, *m.* well her bulwarks.
130. 3, if thou shouldest *m.* iniquities.
Jer. 2. 22, thine iniquity is *m.* before me.
23. 18, who hath *m.* his word?
Phil. 3. 14, I press toward the *m.* for the prize.
3. 17, *m.* them which walk so.
See Lu. 14. 7; Rom. 16. 17; Rev. 13. 16; 20. 4.
Mark, märk, English form of MARCUS; Evangelist. Acts 12. 12.
goes with Paul and Barnabas. Acts 12. 25; 13. 5.
leaves them at Perga. Acts 13. 13.
contention about him. Acts 15. 37.
approved by Paul. 2 Tim. 4. 11.
Maroth, mâr'-ōth, 'bitternesses.' Mic. 1. 12.
Marriage instituted. Gen. 2. 18.
honourable. Ps. 128.; Prov. 31. 10; Heb. 13. 4.
treated of by Christ. Mat. 19.; Mk. 10.
its obligations. Mat. 19. 4; Rom. 7. 2; 1 Cor. 6. 16; 7. 10; Eph. 5. 31.
parables concerning. Mat. 22.; 25. [12. 23.
belongs to this world only. Mat. 22. 30; Mk.
at Cana, miracle at. John 2.
Paul's opinion on. 1 Cor. 7.; 1 Tim. 5. 14.
of the Lamb, typical. Rev. 19. 7.
unlawful marriages. Lev. 18.; Deu. 7. 3; Jos. 23. 12; Ez. 9.; 10.; Neh. 13. 23.
Marrow. Job 21. 24; Ps. 63. 5; Prov. 3. 8; Heb. 4. 12.
Marry, forbidding to. 1 Tim. 4. 3. [17. 22.
Mars' (märs) **Hill,** English of AREOPAGUS. Acts
Marsena, mär-sē'-nă. Esth. 1. 14.
Martha, mär'-thă, 'lady,' instructed by Christ. John 11. 5, 21.
reproved by Him. Lu. 10. 38.
Martyr, Stephen the first. Acts 6.; 7.; 22. 20.
See Rev. 2. 13; 17. 6. R. V. (generally) witness.
Marvel. Mat. 8. 10; Mk. 6. 6; Lu. 7. 9, Jesus *m.*
Mk. 5. 20, all men did *m.*
John 3. 7; 5. 28; 1 John 3. 13, *m.* not.
See Eccl. 5. 8; John 7. 21; Gal. 1. 6. [ber.
Marvellous. Job 5. 9, *m.* things without num-
Ps. 17. 7, *m.* lovingkindness.
118. 23; Mat. 21. 42; Mk. 12. 11, *m.* in our eyes.
John 9. 30, herein is a *m.* thing.
1 Pet. 2. 9, into his *m.* light.
See Ps. 105. 5; 139. 14; Dan. 11. 36; Mic. 7. 15.
Mary, mâr'-ÿ, Greek form of MIRIAM. Mat. 1. 16.
(1) the Virgin, mother of Jesus, visited by the angel Gabriel. Lu. 1. 26.
believes, and magnifies the Lord. Lu. 1. 38, 46; John 2. 5.
Christ born of. Mat. 1. 18; Lu. 2.
witnesses the miracle at Cana. John 2. 1.
desires to speak with Christ. Mat. 12. 46; Mk. 3. 31; Lu. 8. 19.
commended to John by Christ at His crucifixion. Mat. 27. 56; John 19. 25.
(2) MAGDALENE, măg'-dă-lēne. Lu. 8. 2.
at the cross. Mat. 27. 56; Mk. 15. 40; John 19. 25.
Christ appears first to. Mat. 28. 1; Mk. 16. 1; Lu. 24. 10; John 20. 1.
(3) sister of Lazarus, commended. Lu. 10. 42.
Christ's love for. John 11. 5, 33.
anoints Christ's feet, John 12. 3. head, Mat. 26. 6; Mk. 14. 3.
(4) mother of Mark. Acts 12. 12.
(5) a Roman Christian. Rom. 16. 6.
Marys, the three, at the cross. John 19. 25.
Maschil, măs'-chĭl. Ps. 32.; 42.; 45., etc., titles. 'A finely constructed ode.'
Mash, măsh. Gen. 10. 23.
Mashal, mā'-shăl, 'proverb' (?). 1 Chr. 6. 74.
Masrekah, măs-rē'-kăh, 'vineyard.' Gen. 36. 36.
Massa, măs'-să, 'burden.' Gen. 25. 14.
Massah, măs'-săh, 'temptation;' the rebellion at. Ex. 17. 7; Deu. 9. 22; 33. 8.
Master. 2 Kn. 6. 32, sound of his *m.* feet behind him.
Mal. 1. 6, if I be a *m.*, where is my fear?
2. 12, the Lord will cut off the *m.* and the scholar.
Mat. 6. 24; Lu. 16. 13, no man can serve two *m.*
10. 24; Lu. 6. 40, disciple not above his *m.*
10. 25, enough for the disciple that he be as his *m.*
17. 24, doth not your *m.* pay tribute?
23. 8, 10, one is your *M.*, even Christ. R. V. teacher.
26. 25, *M.*, is it I? R. V. omits.
Mk. 5. 35; Lu. 8. 49, why troublest thou the *M.*?
9. 5; Lu. 9. 33, *M.*, it is good for us to be here. R. V. Rabbi.
10. 17; Lu. 10. 25, good *M.*, what shall I do?
Lu. 13. 25, when once the *m.* of the house is risen.
John 3. 10, art thou a *m.* of Israel? R. V. the teacher.
11. 28, the *M.* is come, and calleth.
13. 13, ye call me *M.*, and ye say well.
Rom. 14. 4, to his own *m.* he standeth or falleth. R. V. lord.
1 Cor. 3. 10, as a wise *m.*-builder.
Eph. 6. 5; Col. 3. 22; Tit. 2. 9; 1 Pet. 2. 18, be obedient to *m.*
6. 9; Col. 4. 1, *m.*, do the same things to them

1 Tim. 6. 1, count their *m.* worthy of honour.
6. 2, that have believing *m.*
Jas. 3. 1, be not many *m.* R. V. teachers.
See Gen. 24. 12; 39. 8; Prov. 25. 13; Eccl. 12. 11.

Masters, duty of. Ex. 20. 10; Lev. 19. 13; 25. 40; Deu. 24. 14; Job 31. 13; Jer. 22. 13; Eph. 6. 9; Col. 4. 1; Jas. 5. 4.

Mastery. Ex. 32. 18; 1 Cor. 9. 25; 2 Tim. 2. 5.

Mastick Tree (Hist. of Sus. 54). Gk. σχῖνος: Bot. N. *Pistacia lentiscus.* Its name occurs only in the Apocrypha; a small, evergreen, bushy tree.

Mathusala, mă-thū'-să-lă, Greek form of METHUSELAH. Lu. 3. 37.

Matred, mā'-trĕd, 'pushing forward' (?). Gen. 36. 39.

Matri, mā'-trī, 'rainy.' 1 Sam. 10. 21.

Mattan, măt'-tăn, 'a gift.' (1) slain. 2 Kn. 11. 18; 2 Chr. 23. 17. (2) Jer. 38. 1.

Mattanah, măt-tā'-năh, same as preceding. Num. 21. 18.

Mattaniah, măt-tă-nī'-ăh, 'gift of Jehovah.' 2 Kn. 24. 17.

Mattatha, măt'-tă-thă, same as following. Lu. 3. 31.

Mattathah, măt'-tă-thăh, 'gift.' Ez. 10. 33.

Mattathias, măt-tă-thī'-ăs, a Greek form of MATTITHIAH. Lu. 3. 26.

Mattenai, măt-tē'-nāī, 'liberal.' Ez. 10. 33.

Matter. Ez. 10. 4, arise, for this *m.* belongeth to thee.
Job 19. 28, the root of the *m.* is found in me.
32. 18, I am full of *m.* R. V. words.
Ps. 45. 1, my heart is inditing a good *m.*
Prov. 16. 20, handleth a *m.* wisely. R. V. giveth heed to the word.
18. 13, answereth a *m.* before he heareth it. R. V. giveth answer.
Eccl. 10. 20, that which hath wings shall tell the *m.*
12. 13, conclusion of the whole *m.*
Mat. 23. 23, the weightier *m.*
Acts 18. 14, if it were a *m.* of wrong.
1 Cor. 6. 2, to judge the smallest *m.*
2 Cor. 9. 5, as a *m.* of bounty.
Jas. 3. 5, how great a *m.* a little fire kindleth! R. V. how much wood.
See Gen. 30. 15; Dan. 3. 16; Acts 8. 21; 17. 32.

Matthan, măt'-thăn, 'gift.' Mat. 1. 15.

Matthat, măt'-thăt, another form of MATTHAN. (1) Lu. 3. 24. (2) Lu. 3. 29.

Matthew, măth'-ew, English form of MATTITHIAH. (Levi), Apostle and Evangelist, called. Mat. 9. 9; Mk. 2. 14; Lu. 5. 27.
sent out. Mat. 10. 3; Mk. 3. 18; Lu. 6. 15;—Acts 1. 13.

Matthias, măth-ī'-ăs, another Greek form of MATTITHIAH, apostle. Acts 1. 23; 26.

Mattithiah, măt-tĭ-thī'-ăh, another form of MATTITHIAS. 1 Chr. 9. 31.

Maul, heavy hammer (hence *mall-et*). Prov. 25. 18.

Mauzzim, mā-ŭz'-zĭm, 'fortresses.' Dan. 11. 38 (marg.).

Maw, the stomach of animals. Deu. 18. 3.

May. Mat. 9. 21; 26. 42; Acts 8. 37.

Mazzaroth, măz'-ză-rōth, 'the signs of the zodiac.' Job 38. 32.

Meah, mē'-ăh, 'a hundred.' Neh. 3. 1. R. V. Hammeah.

Mean. Ex. 12. 26; Jos. 4. 6, what *m.* ye by this service?
Deu. 6. 20, what *m.* the testimonies?
Prov. 22. 29, not stand before *m.* men.
Isa. 2. 9; 5. 15; 31. 8, the *m.* man.
Ezek. 17. 12, know ye not what these things *m.*?
Mk. 9. 10, what the rising from the dead should *m.*
Acts 21. 39, citizen of no *m.* city.
See Acts 10. 17; 17. 20; 21. 13.

Means. Ex. 34. 7; Num. 14. 18, by no *m.* clear guilty.
Ps. 49. 7, none can by any *m.* redeem.
Mal. 1. 9, this hath been by your *m.*
Mat. 5. 26, shalt by no *m.* come out.
Lu. 10. 19, nothing shall by any *m.* hurt you. R. V. in any wise.
John 9. 21, by what *m.* he now seeth.
1 Cor. 8. 9, lest by any *m.* this liberty.
9. 22, that I might by all *m.* save some.
Phil. 3. 11, by any *m.* attain.
2 Thes. 3. 16, give you peace always by all *m.* R. V. in all ways.
See Jer. 5. 31; 1 Cor. 9. 27; Gal. 2. 2.

Mearah, mē-âr'-ăh, cave. Jos. 13. 4.

Measure (*n.*). Deu. 25. 14; Prov. 20. 10, thou shalt not have divers *m.*
Job 11. 9, the *m.* is longer than the earth.
28. 25, he weigheth the waters by *m.*
Ps. 39. 4, the *m.* of my days.
Isa. 40. 12, the dust of the earth in a *m.*
Jer. 30. 11; 46. 28, I will correct thee in *m.* R. V. with judgement.
Ezek. 4. 11, thou shalt drink water by *m.*
Mat. 7. 2; Mk. 4. 24; Lu. 6. 38, with what *m.* ye mete.
13. 33; Lu. 13. 21, three *m.* of meal.
23. 32, fill up *m.* of your fathers.
Lu. 6. 38, good *m.*, pressed down.
John 3. 34, giveth not the Spirit by *m.*
Rom. 12. 3, to every man the *m.* of faith.
2 Cor. 12. 7, exalted above *m.* R. V. overmuch.
Eph. 4. 7, the *m.* of the gift of Christ.
4. 13, to the *m.* of the stature.
4. 16, in the *m.* of every part.
Rev. 6. 6, a *m.* of wheat for a penny.
21. 17, according to the *m.* of a man.
See Ps. 80. 5; Isa. 5. 14; Mic. 6. 10.

Measure (*v.*). Isa. 40. 12, who hath *m.* the waters?
65. 7, I will *m.* former work into bosom.
Jer. 31. 37, if heaven can be *m.*
33. 22; Hos. 1. 10, as the sand cannot be *m.*
2 Cor. 10. 12, *m.* themselves by themselves.
See Ezek. 40. 3; 42. 15; Zec. 2. 1.

Measures:—
of quantity:
log. Lev. 14. 10, 15, 21.
cab. 2 Kn. 6. 25.
omer. Ex. 16. 36; Lev. 5. 11; 14. 10.
hin. Ex. 29. 40.
bath or ephah. Isa. 5. 10; Ezek. 45. 11.
homer. Isa. 5. 10; Ezek. 45. 14.
firkin. John 2. 6.
of length:
handbreadth. Ex. 25. 25; Ps. 39. 5.
span. Ex. 28. 16; 1 Sam. 17. 4.
cubit. Gen. 6. 15, 16; Deu. 3. 11.
fathom. Acts 27. 28.
furlong. Lu. 24. 13; John 11. 18.
mile. Mat. 5. 41.

Measures.

I. Measures of Capacity (Liquid).

					Litres.	Gallons.	Quarts.	Pints.	Approximate gallons.	Approximate quarts.
Log.	Rom. Sextarius = Gk. *Xe'thēs*				.54	......	......	.96	......	½
4	Cab				2.16	......	......	3.84	......	2
12	3	Hin			6.48	1	1	1.5	......	6
72	18	6	Bath = Gk. *Mĕtrētēs'* = Ephah		38.88	8	2	1.	9	......
720	180	60	10	Homer or Cor..........	388.8	86	1	1.	86	......

'Measure' (Ps. 80. 5; Isa. 40. 12) = ⅓ Bath = 1 Seah of Dry Measure (nearly 3 gals.).
'Measure' (Lu. 16. 6) = Bath, 9 gals.
'Firkin' (John 2. 6) = Gk. *Mĕtrētēs'* = Bath = about 9 gallons (8 gals., 5.12 pints).
'Pot' (Mk. 7. 4) = Rom. *Sextarius* = about one pint (.96).

Note 1. These tables are in accord with the Greek and Roman Measures in Harper's *Classical Dictionary* (1897), and the *Temple Bible* (1901); and are as nearly as possible those used after the Exile and in New Testament times.

Note 2. The relations of these measures to one another are correct, but there is a double uncertainty as to the exact modern equivalents; for the capacity of the Hebrew measures cannot be accurately determined, and there is no uniformity as to the exact capacity of the English and American measures. There are, for instance, four different quarts in use named in the *Century Dictionary*.

Note 3. The Bath was the Unit of Liquid Measurement, as was its equivalent, the Ephah of Dry Measure = Gk. *Mĕtrētēs'*. 'According to Josephus it contained 72 Attic Sextarii = .96 pint × 72 = 8 gallons, 5.12 pints,' or one bushel and five pints Dry Measure. According to Colonel Conder, LL. D., in the Quarterly Statement of the Palestine Exploration Fund for April, 1902, the Bath occupied a cube of the small cubit, 13.33 inches; or the cube of 36 barleycorns = 12 inches.

Note 4. A Litre, the Unit of Capacity in the Metric System, is the volume of one kilogram of water = one cubic decimetre = 0.88 of an imperial quart, or 1.056 United States quarts.

II. Measures of Capacity (Dry).

						Litres.	Bushels.	Pecks.	Quarts.	Pints.	Gallons.	Pints.
Log.	Rom. Sextarius					.54	......	......	......	.96	......	.96
4	Cab..					2.16	......	......	1	1.84	......	3.84
7.2	1.8	Omer............................				3.89	......	......	3	1.	......	6.91
24	6	3⅓	Seah..........................			12.96	......	1	3	1.	2	7.
72	18	10	3	Ephah.............		38.88	1	......	2	1.	8	5.
720	180	100	60	10	Homer or Cor	388.8	10	3	1	0	86	3.

'Measure' (Rev. 6. 6) = Gk. *Choinix* = nearly one quart (.96).
'Measure' (1 Kin. 4. 22; 2 Chr. 2. 10) = homer.
'Bushel' (Mat. 5. 15) = Rom. *Modius* = nearly a peck (.96).
***See* Notes, p. 184.**

II. Measures of Capacity (Dry) — (*Continued*).

Note 1. The **Ephah** was the Unit of Dry Measure as the **Bath** was of Liquid.

Note 2. The equivalents here are in accord with Harper's *Classical Dictionary* (1897), and the *Temple Bible* (1901). The relations of the measures are correct, but there is considerable variation as to their modern equivalents, at different times, and according to different authorities.

Note 3. According to the careful calculations of Lieut.-Gen. Sir Charles Warren, an Ephah or Bath contained 2333.3 cubic inches. A Log contained 32.4 cubic inches, or a cube each of whose sides = 3.185 inches.

III. Measures of Length (the Smaller).

					Roman and Attic Standard. Metres.	Roman and Attic Standard. Feet.	Roman and Attic Standard. Inches.	Talmudic Standard. Metres.	Talmudic Standard. Feet.	Talmudic Standard. Inches.
1 Digit = finger-breadth					0.0185	..	0.728	0.023	..	0.91
4 " =	Palm = hand-breadth				0.074	..	2.912	0.092	..	3.64
12 " =	3 " =	Span			0.222	..	8.737	0.277	..	10.91
24 " =	6 " =	2 " =	**Cubit**		**0.444**	**1**	**5.48**	0.555	1	9.82
144 " =	36 " =	12 " =	6 " =	Reed	2.664	8	8.87	3.330	10	11.04
168 " =	42 " =	14 " =	6 " (of 7 palms)	Ezekiel's Reed	3.108	10	2.3	......	..	.....

Note 1. The Unit of measurement was the **Cubit**. The relations of the measures to one another are always as given, but the standards vary.

Note 2. The **Cubit** was originally the length of the human arm from the elbow to the tip of the middle finger (among the Greeks and Romans), and equalled **a foot and a half**.

Note 3. But as the length of the foot differed (the Greek foot being 308.3 millimetres, the Roman 295.7, the English 304.8), the Greek cubit was a little longer, and the Roman a little shorter, than a foot and a half English. See Harper's *Classical Dictionary*, "Cubitus," and table in the Appendix.

Note 4. The cubit in very early times was 25.19 inches; and after the Exile the legal cubit of the Talmudists was 21.85 inches. Col. Conder makes the cubit of 6 palms to be 16 inches, but gives five different lengths for the cubit according to the number of barleycorns, of which three = one inch.

According to Lieut.-Gen. Sir Charles Warren, K. C. B., F. R. S., the length of the cubit regulated everything connected with weights and measures, and even the weight of the gold, silver, and copper coinage. The building cubit of Egypt was 20.6 British inches, or 7 palms, while the common cubit was 6 palms, or 17.75 inches. " With this length Goliath at 6 cubits one span would have measured 9 feet 7.3 inches. The bedstead of Og (9 by 4 cubits) would have measured 13 feet 3.75 inches by 5 feet 11 inches."

IV. Measures of Length (Land and Distance).

					English Standard. Metres.	English Standard. Miles.	English Standard. Feet.	English Standard. Inches.
Foot = Rom. **Pes**					0.2968	......	......	11.65
1½ " =	**1 Cubit** = nearly 18 inches				0.444	......	1	5.934
5 " =	3⅓ " =	1 Pace, Passus			1.48	......	4	10.25
600 " =	400 " =	120 " =	Furlong, stadium		177.4	0.110	582	6
5000 " =	3333⅓ " =	1000 " =	8 " =	**Mile**, Mille Passuum.	1480	0.919	4854	......
5000 " =	3333⅓ " =	1000 " =	8 " =	A Sabbath day's journey.	1480	......	4854	......

IV. Measures of Length (Land and Distance) — (*Continued*).

Note 1. The relations of the measures to one another are correct, but the standards vary slightly, — the Roman stadium, or furlong, being 185 metres, the Attic 177, the Olympic 192.

Note 2. The Roman mile was a little more than nine tenths of an English mile.

Note 3. A metre, 39.37 English inches. The English foot is .3048 of a metre.

V. Measures of Surface (Roman). (Probably about the same as the Hebrew.)

			English Standard.			
			Sq. feet.	Acres.	Sq. rods.	Sq. feet.
Pes Quadratus, Roman square foot			0.9425	......	......	......
14,400 " =	**Actus Quadratus** 'furrow' 120 feet long, squared. Heb. Măănâh. 1 Sam. 14. 14.		13,571	5/16	49	231.7
28,800 " =	2 " =	Acre, **Jugerum** (Roman acre) Heb. Ṣĕmêd, 'yoke.' Isa. 5. 10.	27,143	5/8	99	190

Note 1. The **Actus** was the basis of the whole system of Roman land measurement. It was 120 Roman feet long, and 4 feet wide. The *Actus Quadratus*, or squared, was a square 120 feet each way.

Note 2. The **Jugerum**, 'yoke,' was the area which a yoke of oxen could plow in a day.

Note. The foregoing Tables will explain many texts in the Bible. Take, for instance, Isa. 5. 10: 'For ten acres of vineyard shall yield one bath (nearly 9 gallons, or 3½ quarts of wine to an acre), and a homer of seed (10 bushels 3 pecks) shall yield but an ephah' (one bushel 3 pints, or only one tenth as much as the seed sown).

Measuring of the holy city, and new Jerusalem. Ezek. 40.; Zec. 2. 1; Rev. 11. 1; 21. 15.

Meat, food of any kind. Gen. 1. 29, 30.
Gen. 27. 4, make me savoury *m.*
1 Kn. 19. 8, went in strength of that *m.*
Ps. 59. 15, wander up and down for *m.*
69. 21, they gave me also gall for my *m.*
78. 25, he sent them *m.* to the full.
145. 15, *m.* in due season.
Prov. 23. 3, dainties, for they are deceitful *m.*
30. 22, a fool when filled with *m.*
31. 15, she giveth *m.* to her household.
Isa. 65. 25, dust shall be the serpent's *m.*
Ezek. 4. 10, thy *m.* shall be by weight.
47. 12, fruit for *m.*
Dan. 1. 8, not defile himself with king's *m.*
Hab. 1. 16, because their *m.* is plenteous.
3. 17, fields yield no *m.*
Mal. 3. 10, bring tithes, that there may be *m.*
Mat. 6. 25; Lu. 12. 23, life more than *m.*? R. V. the food.
10. 10, workman worthy of his *m.* R. V. food.
15. 37; Mk. 8. 8, of broken *m.* R. V. broken pieces.
25. 35, ye gave me *m.*
Lu. 3. 11, he that hath *m.* let him do likewise. R. V. food.
24. 41; John 21. 5, have ye any *m.*? R. V. anything to eat.
John 4. 32, I have *m.* to eat.
4. 34, my *m.* is to do the will of him that sent me.
6. 27, labour not for the *m.* that perisheth.
Acts 2. 46, did eat *m.* with gladness. R. V. food.
15. 29, abstain from *m.* offered to idols. R. V. things.
Rom. 14. 15, destroy not him with thy *m.*
14. 17, kingdom of God is not *m.* and drink. R. V. eating.
14. 20, for *m.* destroy not the work of God.
1 Cor. 6. 13, *m.* for the belly.
8. 13, if *m.* make my brother to offend.
1 Cor. 10. 3, the same spiritual *m.*
1 Tim. 4. 3, to abstain from *m.*
Heb. 5. 12, 14, not of strong *m.* R. V. solid food.
12. 16, who for one morsel of *m.*
See Gen. 1. 29; 9. 3; Mat. 3. 4; Col. 2. 16.

Meat-offering. Lev. 2.; 3.; 6. 14; Num. 15.; Neh. 10. 33. R. V. meal-offering.

Meats, clean and unclean. Lev. 11.; Deu. 14.; Acts 15. 29; Rom. 14.; 1 Cor. 8. 4; Col. 2. 16; 1 Tim. 4. 3.

Mebunnai, mĕ-bŭn′-nāī, 'built' (?). 2 Sam. 23. 27.

Mecherathite, mĕ-chē′-ră-thīte, inhabitant of Mecherah (?). 1 Chr. 11. 36.

Medad, mē′-dăd. Prophesies. Num. 11. 26.

Medan, mē′-dăn, 'contention.' Gen. 25. 2.

Meddle. 2 Kn. 14. 10; 2 Chr. 25. 19, why *m.* to thy hurt?
Prov. 20. 3, every fool will be *m.* R. V. quarrelling.
20. 19, *m.* not with him that flattereth.
26. 17, that *m.* with strife. R. V. vexeth.

Meddling condemned. 2 Kn. 14. 10; Prov. 20. 3; 26. 17; 24. 21.

Medeba, mē′-dĕ-bă, 'flowing water' (?). Num. 21. 30.

Medes, mēdes, inhabitants of Media. 2 Kn. 17. 6. capture Babylon (Isa. 21. 2), Dan. 5. 28, 31.

Media, mē′-dĭ-ă, Greek form of Madai. Esth. 1. 3. Israel taken captive to. 2 Kn. 17. 6; 18. 11; Esth. 2. 6.
Daniel's prophecy of. Dan. 8. 20.

Median, mē′-dĭ-ăn, inhabitant of Media. Dan. 5. 31.

Mediator, one. Gal. 3. 19, 20; 1 Tim. 2. 5; Heb. 8. 6; 9. 15.
Jesus the. Heb. 12. 24.

Medicine, typical. Prov. 17. 22; Jer. 8. 22; 30. 13; 46. 11; Ezek. 47. 12.

Meditate. Gen. 24. 63, Isaac went out to *m.*
Jos. 1. 8, thou shalt *m.* therein.
Ps. 1. 2, in his law doth he *m.*
63. 6; 119. 148, *m.* in the night watches.

Ps. 77. 12; 143. 5, I will *m.* of thy works.
Isa. 33. 18, thine heart shall *m.* terror.
Lu. 21. 14, not to *m.* before.
1 Tim. 4. 15, *m.* upon these things. R. V. be diligent in.
Meditation encouraged. Ps. 1. 2; 19. 14; 77. 12; 107. 43; 119. 97, 99.
injunctions to. Jos. 1. 8; Ps. 4. 4; Prov. 4. 26; 1 Tim. 4. 15. *See* Gen. 24. 63.
Meek. Num. 12. 3, Moses was very *m.*
Ps. 22. 26, the *m.* shall eat and be satisfied.
25. 9, the *m.* will he guide.
37. 11; Mat. 5. 5, the *m.* shall inherit the earth.
149. 4, will beautify the *m.*
Isa. 29. 19, the *m.* shall increase their joy.
61. 1, good tidings to the *m.*
Mat. 11. 29, for I am *m*
1 Pet. 3. 4, a *m.* and quiet spirit.
Meekness. 2 Cor. 10. 1, by the *m.* of Christ.
Gal. 6. 1, restore in the spirit of *m.*
1 Tim. 6. 11, follow after *m.*
2 Tim. 2. 25, in *m.* instructing.
Tit. 3. 2, showing *m.* to all men.
1 Pet. 3. 15, give reason of hope in you with *m.*
Meekness, CHRIST an example of. Mat. 11. 29; 21. 5; Lu. 23. 34; 2 Cor. 10. 1 (Isa. 53. 2; John 18. 19).
exhortations to. Zep. 2. 3; Gal. 5. 23; 6. 1; Eph. 4. 2; Phil. 2. 2; Col. 3. 12; 1 Tim. 6. 11; 2 Tim. 2. 25; Tit. 3. 2; Jas. 1. 21; 3. 13; 1 Pet. 3. 4, 15.
blessed of God. Ps. 22. 26; 25. 9; 37. 11 (Mat. 5. 5); 69. 32; 76. 9; 147. 6; 149. 4; Isa. 11. 4; 29. 19; 61. 1.
examples of: Moses, Num. 12. 3. David, 2 Sam. 16. 9. Jeremiah, Jer. 26. 14.
Meet (*adj.*), suitable, fit. Prov. 11. 24, withholdeth more than is *m.*
Mat. 3. 8, fruits *m.* for repentance.
15. 26, not *m.* to take children's bread.
1 Cor. 15. 9, not *m.* to be called an apostle.
Meet (*v.*). Mat. 25. 1, 6, to *m.* the bridegroom.
1 Thes. 4. 17, to *m.* the Lord in the air.
See Prov. 22. 2; Am. 4. 12; Mat. 8. 34.
Megiddo, mĕ-gĭd'-dō, 'place of troops' (?). Jos. 12. 21; 17. 11; Jud. 1. 27; 5. 19.
Ahaziah and Josiah slain there. 2 Kn. 9. 27; 23. 29; Zec. 12. 11.
Megiddon, mĕ-gĭd'-dọn, same as preceding. Zec. 12. 11.
Mehetabeel, mĕ-hĕt'-ă-bēel, lengthened form of the following. Neh. 6. 10.
Mehetabel, mĕ-hĕt'-ă-bĕl, 'God benefits.' Gen. 36. 39.
Mehida, mĕ-hī'-dă. Ez. 2. 52.
Mehir, mē'-hĭr, 'price.' 1 Chr. 4. 11.
Meholathite, mĕ-hō'-lă-thīte, native of Meholah. 1 Sam. 18. 19.
Mehujael, mĕ-hū'-jā-ĕl, 'struck by God' (?). Gen. 4. 18.
Mehuman, mĕ-hū'-măn, 'faithful.' Esth. 1. 10.
Mehunim, mĕ-hū'-nĭm. Ez. 2. 50.
Mehunims, mĕ-hū'-nĭms, the people of Maon. 2 Chr. 26. 7.
Me-jarkon, mē-jär'-kŏn, 'waters of yellowness.' Jos. 19. 46.
Mekonah, mĕ-kō'-năh, 'a base.' Neh. 11. 28.
Melatiah, mĕl-ă-tī'-ăh, 'Jehovah has freed.' Neh. 3. 7.
Melchi, mĕl'-chī, Greek form of MELCHIAH. (1) Lu. 3. 24. (2) Lu. 3. 28.
Melchiah, mĕl-chī'-ăh, 'Jehovah is my king.' Jer. 21. 1.
Melchisedec, mĕl-chĭs'-ĕd-ĕc, Greek form of MELCHIZEDEK. Heb. 5. 6.
Melchi-shua, mĕl'-chī-shū'-ă, same as MALCHISHUA. 1 Sam. 14. 49.
Melchizedek, mĕl-chĭz'-ĕd-ĕk, 'king of righteousness;' king of Salem, blesses Abram. Gen. 14. 18.
his priesthood and Aaron's. Ps. 110. 4; Heb. 5. 6, 10; 6. 20; 7. 1.
Melea, mĕl'-ĕ-ă, 'fulness' (?). Lu. 3. 31.
Melech, mē'-lĕch, 'king.' 1 Chr. 8. 35.
Melicu, mĕl'-ĭ-cū, same as MALLUCH. Neh. 12. 14.
Melita, mĕl'-ĭ-tă, the island Malta; Paul shipwrecked near, and lands at. Acts 28. 1.
received kindly by the people. Acts 28. 2.
shakes off the viper at. Acts 28. 5.
heals Publius' father and others at. Acts 28.
Melody. Isa. 23. 16; 51. 3; Am. 5. 23; Eph. 5. 19.
Melons (Num. 11. 5). Heb. *Abattîchîm:* Gk. πέπονες: Bot. N. *Cucurbita citrullus; Cucumis melo.* The term includes watermelons, cantelopes, and muskmelons.
Melt. Ps. 46. 6, the earth *m.*
97. 5, the hills *m.*
107. 26, their soul *m.*
147. 18, he sendeth his word, and *m.* them.
Isa. 13. 7, every man's heart shall *m.*
64. 2, as when the *m.* fire burneth. R. V. fire kindleth the brushwood.
See Ex. 15. 15; Jos. 14. 8; Jer. 9. 7.
Melzar, mĕl'-zär, 'steward;' favours Daniel. Dan. 1. 11.
Member. Ps. 139. 16, all my *m.* were written.
Rom. 6. 13, 19, neither yield your *m.*
12. 4, as we have many *m.*
1 Cor. 6. 15, bodies *m.* of Christ.
Jas. 3. 5, the tongue is a little *m.*
4. 1, lusts which war in your *m.*
See Job 17. 7; Mat. 5. 29; Eph. 5. 30.
Members of the body, types of the Church. Rom. 12. 4; 1 Cor. 12. 12; Eph. 4. 25.
Memorials ordained. Ex. 17. 14; 28. 12; 30. 16; Num. 16. 40.
offerings of. Lev. 2. 2; Num. 5. 15.
Memory. Ps. 145. 7; Eccl. 9. 5.
Memory of the just, blessed. Prov. 10. 7.
of the wicked, cut off. Ps. 109. 15; Isa. 26. 14.
Memphis, mĕm'-phĭs, in Egypt. Hos. 9. 6.
Memucan, mĕ-mū'-căn. Esth. 1. 14.
Men. 1 Sam. 4. 9; 1 Cor. 16. 13, quit yourselves like *m.*
2 Chr. 6. 18, will God dwell with *m.*?
Ps. 9. 20, know themselves to be but *m.*
82. 7, but ye shall die like *m.*
Eccl. 12. 3, strong *m.* shall bow themselves.
Isa. 31. 3, the Egyptians are *m.*, and not God.
46. 8, show yourselves *m.*
Gal. 1. 10, do I now persuade *m.*?
1 Thes. 2. 4, not as pleasing *m.*, but God.
See Ps. 116. 11; 1 Pet. 2. 17.
Menahem, mĕn'-ă-hĕm, 'comforter;' king of Israel, his evil rule. 2 Kn. 15. 14, 18.
Menan, mē'-năn. Lu. 3. 31.
Mend. 2 Chr. 24. 12; 34. 10; Mat. 4. 21; Mk. 1. 19.
Mene, mē'-nē, 'numbered.' MENE, TEKEL, UPHARSIN. Dan. 5. 25–28.
Meni, mē'-nī, the God of luck. Isa. 65. 11 (marg.).
Mention. Gen. 40. 14, make *m.* of me to Pharaoh.
Ps. 71. 16, I will make *m.* of thy righteousness.
Isa. 12. 4, make *m.* that his name is exalted.
63. 7, I will *m.* the lovingkindnesses of the Lord.
Rom. 1. 9; Eph. 1. 16; 1 Thes. 1. 2, *m.* of you in my prayers.
See Isa. 62. 6; Ezek. 18. 22; 33. 16.
Meonenim, mē-ō'-nĕ-nĭm, 'enchanters.' Jud. 9. 37.
Meonothai, mē-ō'-nō-thāi, 'my habitations.' 1 Chr. 4. 14.
Mephaath, mĕph'-ā-ăth, 'beauty' (?). Jos. 13. 18.
Mephibosheth, mĕ-phĭb'-ō-shĕth, 'destroying shame.'
(1) Saul's son. 2 Sam. 21. 8.
(2) son of Jonathan, his lameness. 2 Sam. 4. 4.
cherished by David. 2 Sam. 9. 1.
slandered by Ziba. 2 Sam. 16. 1; 19. 24.
spared by David. 2 Sam. 21. 7.
Merab, mē'-răb, 'increase' (?); Saul's daughter. 1 Sam. 14. 49; 18. 17.
her five sons hanged by the Gibeonites. 2 Sam. 21. 8.
Meraiah, mĕ-rāi'-ăh, 'contumacy.' Neh. 12. 12.
Meraioth, mĕ-rāi'-ōth, 'rebellions.' (1) 1 Chr. 6. 6.
(2) Neh. 12. 15.

Merari, mĕ-râr´-ī, 'bitter.' Gen. 46. 11.
Merarites, mĕ-râr´-ītes, descendants of Levi. Ex. 6. 19; 1 Chr. 6. 1; 23. 21; 24. 26.
their duties and dwellings. Num. 4. 29; 7. 8; 10. 17; Jos. 21. 7; 1 Chr. 6. 63.
Merathaim, mĕr-ă-thā´-ĭm, 'double rebellion.' Jer. 50. 21.
Merchandise. Prov. 3. 14, *m.* of it better than *m.* of silver.
Isa. 23. 18, *m.* shall be holiness to the Lord.
Mat. 22. 5, one to his farm, another to his *m.*
John 2. 16, my father's house an house of *m.*
2 Pet. 2. 3, make *m.* of you.
See Deu. 21. 14; 24. 7; Ezek. 26. 12; Rev. 18. 11.
Merchant. Gen. 23. 16, current money with the *m.*
Isa. 23. 8, whose *m.* are princes.
47. 15, even thy *m.* shall wander.
Rev. 18. 3, 11, the *m.* of the earth.
18. 23, thy *m.* were great men of the earth.
See Prov. 31. 24; Isa. 23. 11.
Merchantman, merchant. Mat. 13. 45.
Merchants. Gen. 37. 25; 1 Kn. 10. 15; Neh. 13. 20; Isa. 23. 8; Ezek. 27.
parable of one seeking pearls. Mat. 13. 45.
Merciful. Ps. 37. 26, ever *m.*, and lendeth.
67. 1, God be *m.* to us, and bless us.
Prov. 11. 17, the *m.* doeth good to his own soul.
Isa. 57. 1, *m.* men are taken away.
Jer. 3. 12, return, for I am *m.*
Mat. 5. 7, blessed are the *m.*
Lu. 6. 36, be ye *m.*, as your Father is *m.*
18. 13, God be *m.* to me a sinner.
Heb. 2. 17, a *m.* High Priest.
See Ex. 34. 6; 2 Sam. 22. 26; 1 Kn. 20. 31.
Mercurius, mĕr-cū´-rĭ-ŭs, Latin name corresponding to Hermes; Paul so called. Acts 14. 12.
Mercy. Gen. 32. 10, not worthy the least of the *m.*
Ex. 33. 19, will shew *m.* on whom I will shew *m.*
34. 7; Dan. 9. 4, keeping *m.* for thousands.
Num. 14. 18; Ps. 103. 11; 145. 8, longsuffering and of great *m.*
1 Chr. 16. 34, 41; 2 Chr. 5. 13; 7. 3, 6; Ez. 3. 11; Ps. 106. 1; 107. 1; 118. 1; 136. 1; Jer. 33. 11, his *m.* endureth for ever.
Ps. 23. 6, surely goodness and *m.* shall follow.
25. 7, according to thy *m.* remember me. R. V. lovingkindness.
33. 22, let thy *m.* be upon us.
52. 8, I trust in the *m.* of God.
59. 10, the God of my *m.* R. V. with his lovingkindness.
66. 20, not turned his *m.* from me.
77. 8, is his *m.* clean gone for ever?
85. 10, *m.* and truth are met together.
89. 2, *m.* shall be built up for ever.
90. 14, satisfy us early with thy *m.*
101. 1, I will sing of *m.*
108. 4, thy *m.* is great above the heavens.
115. 1, for thy *m.*, and for thy truth's sake.
119. 64, the earth is full of thy *m.*
130. 7, with the Lord there is *m.*
Prov. 3. 3, let not *m.* and truth forsake thee.
14. 21, 31, he that hath *m.* on the poor. R. V. pity.
16. 6; 20. 28, *m.* and truth.
Isa. 54. 7, with great *m.* will I gather thee.
Jer. 6. 23, they are cruel, and have no *m.*
Lam. 3. 22, it is of the Lord's *m.*
Hos. 4. 1, because there is no *m.* in the land.
6. 6; Mat. 9. 13, I desired *m.*, and not sacrifice.
10. 12, sow in righteousness, reap in *m.*
14. 3, in thee the fatherless find *m.*
Mic. 6. 8, but to do justly, and love *m.*
7. 18, he delighteth in *m.*
Hab. 3. 2, in wrath remember *m.*
Mat. 5. 7, the merciful shall obtain *m.*
9. 27; 15. 22; 20. 30; Mk. 10. 47, 48; 18. 38, 39, thou son of David have *m.* on me.
Lu. 10. 37, he that shewed *m.*
Rom. 9. 15, 18, *m.* on whom I will have *m.*
9. 16, of God that sheweth *m.*
12. 1, beseech you by the *m.* of God.
12. 8, he that sheweth *m.*, with cheerfulness.
2 Cor. 1. 3, the Father of *m.*
Eph. 2. 4, God, who is rich in *m.*
1 Tim. 1. 13, 16, I obtained *m.*, because.
2 Tim. 1. 18, that he may find *m.* in that day.
Heb. 4. 16, obtain *m.*, and find grace.
Jas. 2. 13, without *m.*, that shewed no *m.*
1 Pet. 1. 3, according to his abundant *m.*
See Prov. 12. 10; 1 Tim. 1. 2.
Mercy, supplication for. Deu. 21. 8; 1 Kn. 8. 30; Neh. 9. 32; Ps. 51.; Dan. 9. 16; Hab. 3. 2; Mat. 6. 12.
injunctions to shew. Prov. 3. 3; Dan. 4. 27; Zec. 7. 9; Lu. 6. 36; Rom. 12. 19 (Prov. 25. 21); Phil. 2. 1; Col. 3. 12; Jas. 2. 13.
of God. Ps. 78. 38; 103. 9; Isa. 30. 18; 54. 7; Lam. 3. 32.
Mercy seat described. Ex. 25. 17; 26. 34; 37. 6; Lev. 16. 13; 1 Chr. 28. 11; Heb. 9. 5.
Mered, mē´-rĕd, 'rebellion.' 1 Chr. 4. 17.
Meremoth, mĕr´-ĕ-mōth, 'elevations.' Ez. 8. 33.
Meres, mē´-rĕs, 'worthy' (?). Esth. 1. 14.
Meribah, mĕr´-ĭ-băh, 'strife;' Israel rebels there. Ex. 17. 7; Num. 20. 13; 27. 14; Deu. 32. 51; 33. 8; Ps. 81. 7.
Merib-baal, mĕr´-ĭb-bā´-ăl, contender (?) against Baal. 1 Chr. 8. 34. Same as Mephibosheth (2).
Merodach, mĕr´-ō-dăch. Jer. 50. 2.
Merodach-baladan, mĕr´-ō-dăch-băl´-ă-dăn, 'Merodach gives a son;' (or Berodach) Baladan sends messengers to Hezekiah. 2 Kn. 20. 12; 2 Chr. 32. 31; Isa. 39.; —Jer. 50. 2.
Merom, mē´-rŏm, 'a high place,' waters of. Jos. 11. 5. A small reedy lake through which the Jordan runs, about twelve miles N. of the Sea of Galilee. The modern name is Huleh.
Meronothite, mĕ-rō´-nō-thīte, an inhabitant of Meronoth. (1) 1 Chr. 27. 30. (2) Neh. 3. 7.
Meroz, mē´-rŏz, 'refuge' (?); cursed. Jud. 5. 23.
Merry. Gen. 43. 34, were *m.* with him.
Jud. 16. 25, their hearts were *m.*
Prov. 15. 13, *m.* heart maketh cheerful countenance.
15. 15, *m.* heart hath a continual feast. R. V. cheerful.
Prov. 17. 22, *m.* heart doeth good like a medicine.
Eccl. 8. 15, nothing better than to eat and be *m.*
9. 7, drink thy wine with a *m.* heart.
10. 19, wine maketh *m.* R. V. glad the life.
Jas. 5. 13, is any *m.*? R. V. cheerful.
See Lu. 12. 19; 15. 23; Rev. 11. 10.
Mesech, mē´-sĕch, same as Meshech. Ps. 120. 5.
Mesha, mē´-shă. (1) 'retreat' (?). Gen. 10. 30. (2) 'deliverance.' 2 Kn. 3. 4. The king of Moab whose exploits are recorded on the Moabite stone, *q. v.*
Meshach, mē´-shăch. Dan. 1. 7. *See* Shadrach.
Meshech, mē´-shĕch, 'tall' (?); son of Japheth. Gen. 10. 2.
traders of. Ezek. 27. 13; 32. 26; 38. 2; 39. 1.
Meshelemiah, mĕ-shĕl-ĕ-mī´-ăh, 'Jehovah repays.' 1 Chr. 9. 21.
Meshezabeel, mĕ-shĕz´-ă-bēel, 'God delivers.' (1) Neh. 3. 4. (2) Neh. 10. 21. (3) Neh. 11. 24.
Meshillemith, mĕ-shĭl´-lĕ-mĭth, 'recompense.' 1 Chr. 9. 12.
Meshillemoth, mĕ-shĭl´-lĕ-mōth, 'retribution.' 2 Chr. 28. 12.
Meshobab, mĕ-shō´-băb, 'brought back.' 1 Chr. 4. 34.
Meshullam, mĕ-shŭl´-lăm, 'friend.' 2 Kn. 22. 3.
Meshullemeth, mĕ-shŭl´-lĕ-mĕth, feminine of preceding. 2 Kn. 21. 19.
Mesobaite, mĕ-sŏb´-ā-īte, inhabitant of Mesoba (?). 1 Chr. 11. 47.
Mesopotamia, mĕs-ō-pŏ-tā´-mĭ-ă, 'amidst the rivers.'
(Ur), country of the two rivers; Abram leaves. Gen. 11. 31; 12. 1; 24. 4, 10. *See* Acts 2. 9; 7. 2.
king of, slain by Othniel. Jud. 3. 8.
Mess, a quantity of food sufficient for a single occasion, a supply of anything to be eaten at one meal. Gen. 43. 34.
Messenger. Job 33. 23; Prov. 25. 13.

Messenger of the covenant. Mal. 3. 1; Isa. 42. 19.
Messiah, mĕs-sī′-ăh, 'anointed' (comp. CHRIST); Prince, prophecy about. Dan. 9. 25.
Messias, mĕs-sī′-ăs, Greek form of the above. John 1. 41; 4. 25. *See* Isa. 9. 6.
Metals of Scripture: Brass, bronze, Ex. 38. 8. Copper, Ez. 8. 27; 2 Tim. 4. 14. Gold, 1 Kn. 9. 28. Iron, Gen. 4. 22. Lead, Ex. 15. 10. Silver, Gen. 23. 15. Steel, 2 Sam. 22. 35. Tin, Num. 31. 22.
Mete, to measure. Isa. 40. 12; Mat. 7. 2; Mk. 4. 24; Lu. 6. 38.
Meteyard, a measuring rod. Lev. 19. 35.
Metheg-ammah, mĕth′-ĕg-ăm′-măh, 'bridle of Ammah.' 2 Sam. 8. 1.
Methusael, mĕ-thū′-sā-ĕl, 'man of God.' Gen. 4. 18.
Methuselah, mĕ-thū′-sĕ-lăh, 'man of a dart' (?). Gen. 5. 21.
his great age. Gen. 5. 27. [52.
Meunim, mĕ-ū′-nĭm, same as MEHUNIM. Neh. 7.
Mezahab, mĕ′-ză-hăb, 'water of gold.' Gen. 36. 39.
Mezuzeh, a case of metal or wood, containing the same summary of the Law as was enclosed in the Phylacteries (Ex. 13. 1-6; Deu. 6. 4-9; 11. 13-21), and affixed to the posts of the outer doors and gates.
Miamin, mī′-ă-mĭn, 'on the right hand.' Ez. 10. 25.
Mibhar, mĭb′-hăr, 'choice.' 1 Chr. 11. 38. [13.
Mibsam, mĭb′-săm, 'sweet odour.' (1) Gen. 25. (2) 1 Chr. 4. 25.
Mibzar, mĭb′-zăr, 'a fortress.' Gen. 36. 42.
Micah, mī′-căh, 'who (is) like unto Jehovah?'
(1) makes and worships idols. Jud. 17.; 18.
(2) prophet (Jer. 26. 18); denounces Israel's sin. Mic. 1.-3.; 6.; 7.
predicts the Messiah. Mic. 4.; 5.; 7.
(3) others. 1 Chr. 5. 5; 8. 34; 2 Chr. 34. 20.
Micaiah, mī-căi′-ăh, fuller form of MICAH; forewarns Ahab. 1 Kn. 22.; 2 Chr. 18.
Mice, golden. 1 Sam. 6. 11.
Micha, mī′-chă, a form of MICAH. (1) 2 Sam. 9. 12. (2) Neh. 11. 17.
Michael, mī′-chā-ĕl, 'who (is) like unto God?'
(1) Archangel. Dan. 10. 13, 21; 12. 1; Jude 9; Rev. 12. 7.
(2) others. Num. 13. 13; 1 Chr. 5. 13; 6. 40; 7. 3.; 8. 16; 12. 20; 27. 18.
Michah, mī′-chăh, same as MICAH. 1 Chr. 24. 24.
Michaiah, mī-chăi′-ăh, same as MICAIAH. Neh. 12. 35.
Michal, mī′-chăl, 'brook.' 1 Sam. 14. 49.
David's wife. 1 Sam. 18. 20.
given to another. 1 Sam. 25. 44.
restored to David. 2 Sam. 3. 13.
mocks his religious dancing, and is rebuked. 2 Sam. 6. 16, 20; 1 Chr. 15. 29.
Michmas, mĭch′-măs, later form of MICHMASH. Ez. 2. 27.
Michmash, mĭch′-măsh, 'treasured.' 1 Sam. 13. 2.
Michmethah, mĭch-mē′-thăh. Jos. 16. 6.
Michri, mĭch′-rī, 'precious' (?). 1 Chr. 9. 8.
Michtam, mĭch′-tăm. Ps. 16.; 56.-69., titles. 'A Golden Poem' or 'A song of deep import.'
Midian, mĭd′-ĭ-ăn, 'strife.' (1) Gen. 25. 2.
sons of. Gen. 25. 4.
(2) land of. Ex. 2. 15. *See* 1 Kn. 11. 18; Isa. 60. 6; Hab. 3. 7.
Midianites, mĭd′-ĭ-ă-nītes, people of Midian. Gen. 37. 28.
their cities destroyed by Moses. Num. 31. 1.
subdued by Gideon. Jud. 6.-8. *See* Ps. 83. 9; Isa. 9. 4; 10. 26.
Midianitish, mĭd-ĭ-ă-nī′-tĭsh, belonging to Midian. Num. 25. 6, 14.
Midnight, Egyptians smitten at. Ex. 12. 29.
prayer at. Ps. 119. 62; Acts 16. 25; 20. 7.
bridegroom cometh at. Mat. 25. 6.
master of house cometh at. Mk. 13. 35.

Midst. Ps. 102. 24, in the *m.* of my days.
Prov. 23. 34, lieth down in *m.* of the sea.
Dan. 9. 27, in the *m.* of the week. R. V. for the half.
Mat. 18. 2; Mk. 9. 36, a little child in the *m.*
18. 20, there am I in the *m.*
Lu. 24. 36; John 20. 19, Jesus himself in the *m.*
Phil. 2. 15, in the *m.* of a crooked nation.
Rev. 2. 7, in the *m.* of the Paradise of God.
4. 6; 5. 6; 7. 17, in the *m.* of the throne.
See Gen. 2. 9; Isa. 12. 6; Hos. 11. 9.
Midwives of Egypt. Ex. 1. 16, 20. [38.
Migdal-el, mĭg′-dăl-ĕl, 'tower of God.' Jos. 19.
Migdal-gad, mĭg′-dăl-găd, 'tower of Gad.' Jos. 15. 37.
Migdol, mĭg′-dŏl. Ex. 14. 2; Jer. 44. 1.
Might. Deu. 6. 5, love God with all thy *m.*
8. 17, the *m.* of mine hand hath gotten.
2 Sam. 6. 14, David danced with all his *m.*
Eccl. 9. 10, do it with thy *m.*
Isa. 40. 29, to them that have no *m.*
Jer. 9. 23, mighty man glory in his *m.*
51. 30, their *m.* hath failed.
Zec. 4. 6, not by *m.*, nor by power.
Eph. 3. 16; Col. 1. 11, strengthened with *m.*
See Eph. 6. 10; 2 Pet. 2. 11; Rev. 7. 12. [1. 29.
Mightily. Jon. 3. 8; Acts 18. 28; 19. 20; Col.
Mighty. Gen. 10. 9, he was a *m.* hunter.
Jud. 5. 23, to the help of the Lord against the *m.*
2 Sam. 1. 19, 25, how are the *m.* fallen!
23. 8, these be the names of the *m.* men whom David had.
1 Chr. 11. 10, the chief of the *m.* men.
Job 9. 4, wise in heart and *m.* in strength.
Ps. 24. 8, strong and *m.*, *m.* in battle.
89. 13, thou hast a *m.* arm.
89. 19, help upon one that is *m.*
93. 4, the *m.* waves of the sea.
Isa. 1. 24; 30. 29; 49. 26; 60. 16, the *m.* One of Israel.
5. 22, *m.* to drink wine.
63. 1, *m.* to save.
Jer. 32. 19, *m.* in work.
Am. 2. 14, neither shall *m.* deliver himself.
Mat. 11. 20; 13. 54; 14. 2; Mk. 6. 2, *m.* works.
Lu. 9. 43, the *m.* power of God. R. V. majesty.
24. 19, prophet *m.* in deed and word.
Acts 18. 24, *m.* in the scriptures.
1 Cor. 1. 26, not many *m.*
2 Cor. 10. 4, weapons *m.* through God.
Eph. 1. 19, the working of his *m.* power.
See Num. 14. 12; Eccl. 6. 10; Mat. 3. 11.
Migron, mĭg′-rŏn, 'a precipice' (?). Isa. 10. 28.
Mijamin, mĭ′-jă-mĭn, same as MIAMIN. 1 Chr. 24. 9.
Mikloth, mĭk′-lōth, 'staves,' 'lots.' (1) 1 Chr. 8. 32. (2) 1 Chr. 27. 4.
Mikneiah, mĭk-nĕi′-ăh, 'possession of Jehovah.' 1 Chr. 15. 18.
Milalai, mĭl′-ă-lăi, 'eloquent' (?). Neh. 12. 36.
Milcah, mĭl′-căh, 'counsel' (?). (1) Gen. 11. 29; 22. 20. (2) Num. 26. 33.
Milch, giving milk (as cows). Gen. 32. 15.
Milcom, mĭl′-cŏm, same as MOLOCH; false God. 1 Kn. 11. 5, 33; 2 Kn. 23. 13.
Mile (Mat. 5. 41). Gk. μίλιον = 'a thousand' (Roman paces) = 5000 feet, a little less than an English mile. *See* MEASURES.
Miletum, mī-lē′-tŭm, improper form of MILETUS. 2 Tim. 4. 20.
Miletus, mī-lē′-tŭs, the ancient capital of Ionia in Asia Minor.
Paul takes leave of elders at. Acts 20. 15.
Trophimus left at. 2 Tim. 4. 20.
Milk. Palestine is better adapted to the pasturage of goats than of cows, and the milk with which the land 'flowed' (Ex. 3. 8; Lev. 20. 24) must have been chiefly the product of goats.
Gen. 49. 12, teeth white with *m.*
Prov. 30. 33, churning of *m.*
Isa. 55. 1, buy wine and *m.*
Lam. 4. 7, Nazarites were whiter than *m.*

Ezek. 25. 4, shall eat thy fruit and drink thy *m*.
Heb. 5. 12, 13, such as have need of *m*.
1 Pet. 2. 2, the sincere *m*. of the word.
See Jud. 4, 19; 5. 25; Job 21. 24; Joel 3. 18.
Milk (and honey). Jos. 5. 6; Isa. 55. 1.
mentioned. S. of S. 4. 11; Isa. 7. 22; 1 Cor. 3. 2; Heb. 5. 12; 1 Pet. 2. 2.
Mill was not a building, but a pair of millstones of granite or basalt, placed one upon the other, the upper loose, with a hole through its centre into which the corn was put. The grinding was done by women, usually two at a time. Mat. 24. 41.
Millet (Ezek. 4. 9). Heb. *Dôḥan:* Gk. κέγχρος: Bot. N. *Panicum miliaceum; Sorghum vulgare.* A cereal grass still largely grown in the East. It has very small seeds, is used for cakes, and is also eaten, uncooked, by the poor.
Millo, mĭl'-lō, 'a mound;' house of. Jud. 9. 6; 2 Sam. 5. 9.
Millstones. Ex. 11. 5; Mat. 24. 41; Rev. 18. 21.
Mina *or* **Maneh**, pound = 50 shekels in weight = 11,225 grs. = nearly two lbs. Troy of silver = £6 16s. 8d. = $32.30, heavy standard of the Old Test. The lighter standard of the New Test. is just one half of this. The pound of Lu. 19. 13 being therefore 5612½ grs. = £3 8s. 4d. = $16.15. The gold mina weighs 12,630 grs. *See* MONEY and WEIGHTS.
Mincing, walking with very short steps, affectedly elegant. Isa. 3. 16.
Mind (*n.*). Neh. 4. 6, the people had a *m*. to work.
Job 23. 13, he is in one *m*., who can turn him?
34. 33, should it be according to thy *m*.? R. V. as thou wilt.
Ps. 31. 12, as a dead man out of *m*.
Prov. 29. 11, a fool uttereth all his *m*. R. V. anger.
Isa. 26. 3, whose *m*. is stayed on thee.
Mk. 5. 15; Lu. 8. 35, sitting, in his right *m*.
Lu. 12. 29, neither be of doubtful *m*.
Rom. 8. 7, the carnal *m*. is enmity against God.
12. 16, be of the same *m*.
14. 5, fully persuaded in his own *m*.
2 Cor. 8. 12, if there be first a willing *m*. R. V. the readiness is there.
13. 11; Phil. 1. 27; 2. 2, be of one *m*.
Phil. 2. 3, in lowliness of *m*.
2. 5, let this *m*. be in you.
4. 7, peace of God keep your *m*. R. V. thoughts.
1 Tim. 6. 5; 2 Tim. 3. 8, men of corrupt *m*.
2 Tim. 1. 7, spirit of sound *m*. R. V. discipline.
Tit. 3. 1, put them in *m*. to be subject.
1 Pet. 1. 13, the loins of your *m*.
2 Pet. 3. 1, stir up your pure *m*.
See Rom. 11. 20; 1 Thes. 5. 14; Jas. 1. 8.
Mind (*v.*). (1) to care for, attend to. Rom. 8. 5; 12. 16; Phil. 3. 16, 19.
(2) to intend. Acts 20. 13.
Mind devoted to God. Mat. 22. 37; Mk. 12. 30; Rom. 7. 25.
a willing. 1 Chr. 28. 9; Neh. 4. 6; 2 Cor. 8. 12.
united. 1 Cor. 1. 10; 2 Cor. 13. 11; Phil. 2. 2; 1 Pet. 3. 8. *See* Heb. 8. 10.
Minded, disposed, determined. Ru. 1. 18; Rom. 8. 6.
Mindful. Ps. 8. 4; 111. 5; Isa. 17. 10; 2 Pet. 3. 2.
Mineral substances of Scripture.
Bitumen. Gen. 11. 3.
Clay. (1) Isa. 29. 16. (2) 41. 25.
Earth. (1) Gen. 1. 22. (2) Gen. 9. 20. (3) Isa. 47. 1.
Nitre. Jer. 2. 22.
Salt. 1 Chr. 18. 12.
Sand. Prov. 27. 3.
Sulphur. Gen. 19. 24.
Mingle. Lev. 19. 19; Isa. 5. 22; Mat. 27. 34; Lu. 13. 1.
Miniamin, mĭn-ī'-ă-mĭn, full form of MIAMIN. 2 Chr. 31. 15.
Minish, diminish, lessen. Ex. 5. 19.
Minister (*n.*). servant, attendant. Ps. 103. 21, ye *m*. of his.
104. 4; Heb. 1. 7, his *m*. a flame of fire.
Isa. 61. 6, men shall call you the *m*. of God.
Joel 1. 9, the Lord's *m*. mourn.
Mat. 20. 26; Mk. 10. 43, let him be your *m*.
Lu. 4. 20, gave it to the *m*. R. V. attendant.
Rom. 13. 4, he is the *m*. of God to thee.
2 Cor. 3. 6, able *m*. of new testament.
Gal. 2. 17, is Christ the *m*. of sin?
Eph. 3. 7; Col. 1. 23, whereof I was made a *m*.
6. 21; Col. 1. 7; 4. 7, a faithful *m*.
1 Tim. 4. 6, a good *m*.
Minister (*v.*). (1) 1 Sam. 2. 11, the child did *m*. unto the Lord.
1 Chr. 15. 2, chosen to *m*. for ever.
Dan. 7. 10, thousand thousands *m*. to him.
Mat. 4. 11; Mk. 1. 13, angels *m*. to him.
20. 28; Mk. 10. 45, not to be *m*. unto but to *m*.
Lu. 8. 3, which *m*. of their substance.
Acts 20. 34, these hands have *m*.
(2) 2 Cor. 9. 10; 2 Pet. 1. 11. R. V. supply.
Ministering spirits. Heb. 1. 14. *See* Rom. 15. 25, 27.
Ministers, GOD'S. Ps. 103. 21; 104. 4; Heb. 1. 7.
(priests). Ex. 28.; 1 Thes. 3. 2; Heb. 10. 11.
worthy of honour and obedience. 1 Thes. 5. 12, 13; 1 Tim. 5. 17; Heb. 13. 17.
CHRIST'S. 1 Cor. 3. 5; 4. 1; 2 Cor. 3. 6; 6.; 11. 23; Eph. 3. 7; 6. 21.
how qualified. 1 Tim. 3.; Tit. 1.; 1 Pet. 5.
Ministration. Lu. 1. 23; Acts 6. 1; 2 Cor. 3. 7; 9. 13.
Ministry. Acts 6. 4, give ourselves to the *m*.
2 Cor. 4. 1, seeing we have this *m*.
5. 18, the *m*. of reconciliation.
6. 3, that the *m*. be not blamed. R. V. our ministration.
Eph. 4. 12, for the work of the *m*.
Col. 4. 17, take heed to the *m*.
2 Tim. 4. 5, make full proof of thy *m*.
Heb. 8. 6, obtained a more excellent *m*.
Ministry of the Gospel. Acts 1. 17; 6. 4; 12. 25; 20. 24; Rom. 12. 7; 1 Cor. 16. 15; 2 Cor. 4. 1; 5. 18; Eph. 6. 21; Col. 1. 7; 4. 17; 1 Tim. 1. 12.
Minni, mĭn'-nī, a part of Armenia. Jer. 51. 27.
Minnith, mĭn'-nĭth, 'allotment' (?). Jud. 11. 33.
Minstrel. 2 Kn. 3. 15; Mat. 9. 23.
Mint (Lu. 11. 42). Gk. ἡδύοσμον: Bot. N. *Mentha sativa.* Several species grow in Palestine.
Miphkad, mĭph'-kăd, 'number' (?). Neh. 3. 31.
Miracle. Jud. 6. 13, where be all his *m*.? R. V. wondrous works.
Mk. 9. 39, no man which shall do a *m*. in my name. R. V. mighty work.
Lu. 23. 8, hoped to have seen some *m*.
John 2. 11, beginning of *m*. R. V. his signs.
4. 54, this is the second *m*. R. V. sign.
10. 41, said, John did no *m*. R. V. sign.
Acts 2. 22, approved of God by *m*. and signs. R. V. mighty works.
1 Cor. 12. 10, to another, the working of *m*.
See Gal. 3. 5; Heb. 2. 4.

Miracles in the Old Testament.

MIRACLES.	REFERENCES.
In Egypt.	
Aaron's rod turned into a serpent	Ex. 7. 10-12.
The ten plagues: —	
1. Water made blood	7. 20-25.
2. Frogs	8. 5-14.
3. Lice	8. 16-18.
4. Flies	8. 20-24.
5. Murrain	9. 3-6.
6. Boils and blains	9. 8-11.
7. Thunder and hail	9. 22-26.
8. Locusts	10. 12-19.
9. Darkness	10. 21-23.
10. Firstborn slain	12. 29, 30.
Parting of the Red Sea	14. 21-31.
In the Wilderness.	
The curing of the waters of Marah	15. 23-25.
Feeding with manna	16. 14-35.
Water from the rock, at Rephidim	17. 5-7.
Death of Nadab and Abihu	Lev. 10. 1, 2.
Burning of the congregation at Taberah	Num. 11. 1-3.
Death of Korah, Dathan, and Abiram, &c.	16. 31-35.
Budding of Aaron's rod, at Kadesh	17. 8.
Water from the rock, at Meribah	20. 7-11.
The brazen serpent	21. 8, 9.
Stoppage of the Jordan stream	Jos. 3. 14-17.
In Canaan. — Under Joshua.	
Fall of Jericho	6. 6-25.
Staying of sun and moon	10. 12-14.
Under the Kings.	
Death of Uzzah	2 Sam. 6. 7.
Withering of Jeroboam's hand, and destruction of the altar at Beth-el	1 Kn. 13. 4-6.
By Elijah.	
The staying of the cruse of oil and meal at Zarephath	17. 14-16.
The raising of the widow's son at Zarephath	17. 17-24.
The burning of the sacrifice on Mount Carmel	18. 30-38.
Burning of the captains and their companies	2 Kn. 1. 10-12.
Dividing of Jordan	2. 7, 8.
By Elisha.	
Dividing of Jordan	2. 14.
Cure of waters of Jericho	2. 21, 22.
Destruction of mocking children at Beth-el	2. 24.
Supply of water to the allied armies in Moab	3. 16-20.
Increase of the widow's oil	4. 2-7.
Raising the Shunammite's son	4. 32-37.
Healing the deadly pottage	4. 38-41.
Feeding one hundred men with twenty loaves	4. 42-44.
Cure of Naaman's leprosy, and its transfer to Gehazi	5. 10-14, 27.
Making an iron axe swim	6. 5-7.
Smiting the Syrian army	6. 18-20.
Resurrection of dead man by touching Elisha's bones	13. 21.
Recorded by Isaiah.	
Destruction of Sennacherib's army	19. 35.
Return of sun by the dial of Ahaz	20. 9-11.
During Captivity.	
Deliverance of the Three Children from the fiery furnace	Dan. 3. 19-27.
Deliverance of Daniel from the lions	6. 16-23.
Miscellaneous.	
Smiting of Philistines, and fall of Dagon	1 Sam. 5. 3-12.
Smiting of Uzziah with leprosy	2 Chr. 26. 16-21.
Deliverance of Jonah from the great fish	Jon. 2. 1-10.

Miracles of our Lord.

MIRACLES.	MAT.	MARK.	LUKE.	JOHN.
I. *Narrated in one Gospel only.*				
Two blind men healed	9. 27			
A dumb demoniac healed	9. 32			
Stater in the mouth of the fish	17. 24			
The deaf and dumb man healed	....	7. 31		
A blind man healed	....	8. 22		
When Christ passed unseen through the multitude	....	....	4. 30	
Draught of fishes	....	....	5. 1	
Raising the widow's son	....	....	7. 11	
Healing the crooked woman	....	....	13. 11	
Healing the man with the dropsy	....	....	14. 1	
Healing the ten lepers	....	....	17. 11	
Healing the ear of Malchus, servant of the high priest	....	....	22. 50	
Turning water into wine	....	....	....	2. 1
Healing the nobleman's son (of fever)	....	....	....	4. 46
Healing the impotent man at Bethesda	....	....	....	5. 1
Healing the man born blind	....	....	....	9. 1
Raising of Lazarus	....	....	....	11. 43
Draught of fishes	....	....	....	21. 1
II. *Narrated in two Gospels.*				
Demoniac in synagogue cured	....	1. 23	4. 33	
Healing centurion's servant (of palsy)	8. 5	....	7. 1	
The blind and dumb demoniac	12. 22	....	11. 14	
Healing the daughter of the Syrophenician	15. 21	7. 24		
Feeding the four thousand	15. 32	8. 1		
Cursing the fig tree	21. 18	11. 12		
III. *Narrated in three Gospels.*				
Healing the leper	8. 2	1. 40	5. 12	
Healing Peter's mother-in-law	8. 14	1. 30	4. 38	
Stilling the storm	8. 26	4. 37	8. 22	
The legion of devils entering swine	8. 28	5. 1	8. 27	
Healing the man sick of the palsy	9. 2	2. 3	5. 18	
Healing woman with issue of blood	9. 20	5. 25	8. 43	
Raising of Jairus' daughter	9. 23	5. 38	8. 49	
Healing the man with a withered hand	12. 10	3. 1	6. 6	
Walking on the sea	14. 25	6. 48	....	6. 19
Curing demoniac child	17. 14	9. 17	9. 38	
Curing blind Bartimæus (two blind men, Mat. 20.)	20. 30	10. 46	18. 35	
IV. *Narrated in four Gospels.*				
Feeding the five thousand	14. 19	6. 35	9. 12	6. 5

Miracles performed: by Moses and Aaron at God's command, Ex. 4. 3; 7. 10; 7.–12.; 14. 21; 15. 25; 17. 6; Num. 16. 28; 20. 11; 21. 8. by Joshua, Jos. 3.; 4.; 6.; 10. 12. by Samson, Jud. 14.–16. by Samuel, 1 Sam. 12. 18. by a prophet, 1 Kn. 13. 4. by Elijah, 1 Kn. 17.; 18.; 2 Kn. 1. 10–12. by Elisha, 2 Kn. 2.–6.; 13. 21. by Isaiah, 2 Kn. 20. 9. by the disciples, Lu. 10. 17. by Peter, Acts 3.; 5.; 9. 32. by Stephen, Acts 6. 8. by Philip, Acts 8. 6. by Paul, Acts 13.; 14.; 16.; 19.; 20.; 28. by sorcerers and evil spirits, Ex. 7. 11; 8. 7; Mat. 24. 24; 2 Thes. 2. 9; Rev. 13. 14; 16. 14; 19. 20.

Miriam, mĭr'-ĭ-ăm, 'their rebellion' (?).
(1) sister of Moses and Aaron. Ex. 15. 20; Num. 26. 59.
song of. Ex. 15. 20, 21.
murmurs against Moses. Num. 12. 1, 2.
is smitten with leprosy, and shut out of the camp. Num. 12. 10, 15.
her death. Num. 20. 1.
(2) 1 Chr. 4. 17.

Mirma, mĭr'-mă, 'fraud.' 1 Chr. 8. 10.

Mirth. Ps. 137. 3; Prov. 14. 13; Eccl. 8. 15.

Mirth, vanity of. Eccl. 2.; 7. 4. *See* Jer. 7. 34; 16. 9; Hos. 2. 11.

Miry. Ps. 40. 2; Ezek. 47. 11; Dan. 2. 41.

Mischief. Job 15. 35; Ps. 7. 14; Isa. 59. 4, they conceive *m.*
Ps. 28. 3, *m.* is in their hearts.
94. 20, frameth *m.* by a law. [V. wickedness.
Prov. 10. 23, it is as sport to a fool to do *m.* R.
11. 27, he that seeketh *m.*
24. 2, lips talk of *m.*
Ezek. 7. 26, *m.* shall come upon *m.* [V. villany.
Acts 13. 10, O full of all subtilty and all *m.* R.
See Prov. 24. 8; Eccl. 10. 13; Mic. 7. 3.

Mischief, punishment of. Ps. 7. 14; 9. 15; 140. 2; Prov. 26. 27; Isa. 33. 1; Acts 13. 10.

Miserable. Job 16. 2; Mat. 21. 41; 1 Cor. 15. 19; Rev. 3. 17.

Misery. Prov. 31. 7, drink, and remember his *m.* no more.
Eccl. 8. 6, the *m.* of man is great upon him.
Lam. 1. 7, remembered in days of her *m.*
Jas. 5. 1, howl for your *m.* that shall come.
See Jud. 10. 16; Job 3. 20; 11. 16; Rom. 3. 16.

Misgab, mĭs'-găb, 'height.' Jer. 48. 1.

Mishael, mī'-shā-ĕl, 'who is what God is?' Ex. 6. 22.
Mishal, mī'-shăl, 'prayer.' Jos. 21. 30.
Misham, mī'-shăm, 'cleansing.' 1 Chr. 8. 12.
Misheal, mī'-shĕ-ăl, same as MISHAL. Jos. 19. 26.
Mishma, mĭsh'-mă, 'report.' (1) Gen. 25. 14. (2) 1 Chr. 4. 25.
Mishmannah, mĭsh-măn'-năh, 'fatness.' 1 Chr. 12. 10.
Mishraites, mĭsh'-rā-ītes. 1 Chr. 2. 53.
Mispereth, mĭs'-pĕ-rĕth, 'number.' Neh. 7. 7.
Misrephoth - maim, mĭs'-rĕ-phōth-mā'-ĭm, 'burning of waters' (?). Jos. 11. 8.
Missionary journeys of Paul. *See* under PAUL and *Summary of* ACTS.
Mite (Gr. *lepton*) (Mk. 12. 42; Lu. 12. 59; 21. 2). From the same root as *minute*, anything very small. The coin=½ English farthing=⅛ of a cent. Not current in the market, but, as now, used for alms to beggars, and known as 'beggars' money.' *See* MONEY.
Mithcah, mĭth'-căh, 'sweetness.' Num. 33. 28.
Mithnite, mĭth'-nīte. 1 Chr. 11. 43.
Mithredath, mĭth'-rĕ-dăth, 'given by Mithra.' Ez. 1. 8.
Mitre, a head-dress or turban of the high priest. Ex. 28. 4; 29. 6; 39. 28.
Mitylene, mĭt-ў-lē'-nē (Acts 20. 14), the chief town of Lesbos, an island on the coast of Asia Minor.
Mixed. Prov. 23. 30, they seek *m.* wine.
Isa. 1. 22, thy wine *m.* with water.
Heb. 4. 2, not being *m.* with faith. R. V. united by.
See Ex. 12. 38; Num. 11. 4; Neh. 13. 3.
Mizar, mī'-zär, 'smallness.' Ps. 42. 6.
Mizpah, mĭz'-păh, 'a look out,' places in Gilead and Moab.
(1) Jacob and Laban meet at. Gen. 31. 49.
(2) Jephthah at. Jud. 10. 17; 11. 11; 20. 1.
(3) Jos. 11. 3.
(4) Samuel at. 1 Sam. 7. 5.
(5) (in Moab). 1 Sam. 22. 3.
Mizpar, mĭz'-pär, 'number.' Ez. 2. 2.
Mizpeh, mĭz'-pĕh, 'watch-tower.' Jos. 11. 3.
Mizraim, mĭz'-rā-ĭm. Gen. 10. 6; 1 Chr. 1. 8.
Mizzah, mĭz'-zăh. Gen. 36. 13.
Mnason, mnā'-son, name of an early disciple. Acts 21. 16.
Moab, mō'-ăb, 'progeny of a father' (?) Gen. 19. 37.
his descendants, and territory. Deu. 2. 9, 18; 34. 5.
Moabites, mō'-ăb-ītes, people of Moab. Deu. 2. 9.
excluded from the congregation. Deu. 23. 3.
conquered by Ehud, Jud. 3. 12. by David, 2 Sam. 8. 2. by Jehoshaphat and Jehoram, 2 Kn. 1. 1; 3.
their overthrow. 2 Chr. 20. 23.
prophecies concerning. Ex. 15. 15; Num. 21. 29; 42. 17; Ps. 60. 8; 83. 6; Isa. 11. 14; 15.; 16.; 25. 10; Jer. 9. 26; 25. 21; 48.; Ezek. 25. 8; Am. 2. 1; Zep. 2. 8.
Moabitess, mō-ăb-ī'-tĕss, a woman of Moab. Ru. 4. 5.
Moabite Stone. This wonderful monument, the oldest in the Phœnician character, was discovered by the Rev. F. Klein at Dibhân in the land of Moab, Aug. 19, 1868. It measures 3 ft. 10 in. by 2 ft. by 14½ in., and is inscribed with thirty-four lines. It contains a record of Mesha, King of Moab, concerning his wars with Israel and Judah. *See* 2 Kn. 3. 25. A cast of the inscription is in the British Museum.
Moabitish, mō-ăb-ī'-tĭsh, belonging to Moab. Ru. 2. 6.
Moadiah, mō-ă-dī'-ăh, 'festival of Jehovah.' Neh. 12. 17.
Mock. Gen. 19. 14, he seemed as one that *m.*
Num. 22. 29; Jud. 16. 10, 13, 15, thou hast *m.* me.
1 Kn. 18. 27, at noon Elijah *m.* them.
2 Chr. 36. 16, they *m.* the messengers of God.
Prov. 1. 26, I will *m.* when your fear cometh.
17. 5, whoso *m.* the poor.
30. 17, the eye that *m.* at his father.
Mat. 2. 16, Herod *m.* by the wise men.
Gal. 6. 7, God is not *m.*
Mocker. Ps. 35. 16; Prov. 20. 1; Isa. 28. 22; Jude 18.
Mocking condemned. Prov. 17. 5; 30. 17; Jer. 15. 17; Jude 18.
punished. Gen. 21. 9; 2 Kn. 2. 23. *See* 2 Chr. 30. 10; 36. 16.
(of Christ). Mat. 27. 29; Mk. 15. 16; Lu. 23. 11.
Moderation. Phil. 4. 5.
Modest apparel. 1 Tim. 2. 9; 1 Pet. 3. 3.
Moisture. Ps. 32. 4; Lu. 8. 6.
Moladah, mō-lā'-dăh, 'birth.' Jos. 15. 26.
Mole. (1) (Lev. 11. 30). Heb. *Tinshĕmeth:* Gk. ἀσπάλαξ: R. V. chameleon. Probably the mole-rat, about the size and shape of a common rat, but in habit and appearance like a mole.
(2) (Isa. 2. 20). Heb. *Ḥâphôr-pêrôth:* Gk. ματαίοι. Probably a generic term for small animals which burrow in waste places, as rats, mice, sand-rats, mole-rats, dormice.
Molech, mō'-lĕch (Lev. 18. 21; 20. 2). A deity worshipped by the Ammonites, one feature of his worship being the burning of children.
worship of. 1 Kn. 11. 7; 2 Kn. 23. 10; Jer. 32. 35; Am. 5. 26; Acts 7. 43.
Molid, mō'-lĭd, 'begetter.' 1 Chr. 2. 29.
Mollified. Isa. 1. 16.
Moloch, mō'-lŏch, 'king.' Am. 5. 26; another form of MOLOCH.
Molten. Ex. 32. 4; Mic. 1. 4; Hab. 2. 18.
Moment. Num. 16. 21, 45, consume them in a *m.*
Job 7. 18, try him every *m.*
21. 13, and in a *m.* they go down.
Ps. 30. 5, his anger endureth but a *m.*
Isa. 26. 20, hide thyself as it were a *m.*
27. 3, I will water it every *m.*
54. 7, for a small *m.* have I forsaken thee.
1 Cor. 15. 51, 52, we shall all be changed, in a *m.*
2 Cor. 4. 17, affliction, which is but for a *m.*
See Ex. 33. 5; Ezek. 26. 16; 32. 10; Lu. 4. 5.
Money. *See* pages 193-195.
Money. 2 Kn. 5. 26, is it a time to receive *m.*?
Eccl. 7. 12, *m.* is a defence.
10. 19, *m.* answereth all things.
Isa. 52. 3, redeemed without *m.*
55. 1, he that hath no *m.*
55. 2, wherefore do ye spend *m.*?
Mat. 17. 24; 22. 19, the tribute *m.* R. V. the half-shekel.
25. 18, hid his lord's *m.*
Acts 8. 20, thy *m.* perish with thee. R. V. silver.
1 Tim. 6. 10, the love of *m.*
Money. Gen. 17. 27; 23. 9; 42. 25; Jer. 32. 9; Mat. 22. 19; Mk. 6. 8; 12. 41; 14. 11; Lu. 9. 3; Acts 4. 37.
love of, censured. 1 Tim. 6. 10.

THE MOABITE STONE

Inscribed stone set up by Mesha, king of Moab, to record his victories over the Israelites *c.* 850 B.C.

(1)

(2)

(3)

(4)

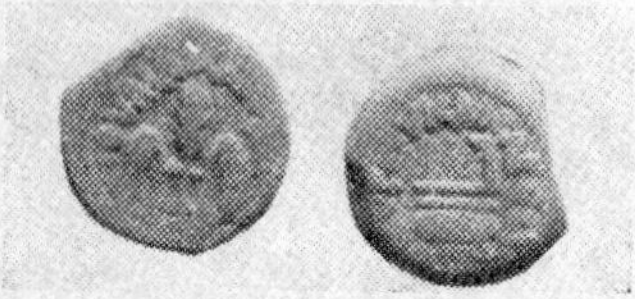

MONEY

Coins in use in Palestine in the time of Christ: (1) silver stater of Augustus ('piece of money' Matt. xvii. 27); (2) silver denarius of Tiberius ('penny' Matt. xviii. 28, &c.); (3) bronze assarion ('farthing' Matt. x. 29); (4) bronze lepton ('mite' Mark xii. 42).

Money.

Money of the Old Testament.

Gold and Silver Values.	Heavy or Common Standard. Weight in Grains.	£	s.	d.	$	Cents.	Light Standard. Weight in Grains.	£	s.	d.	$	Cents.
Shekel (silver) = 4 drachmas or denarii	$224\frac{1}{2}$		2	9 nearly		64.6	$112\frac{1}{4}$		1	$4\frac{1}{2}$ nearly		$32\frac{1}{3}$
15 " = **Shekel** (gold)	$252\frac{2}{3}$	2	1	0	9	69	$126\frac{1}{3}$	1	0	6	4	85
50 " = **Mina** (silver)	11,225	6	16	8	32	30	$5,612\frac{1}{2}$	3	8	4	16	15
50 " = **Mina** (gold)	12,630	102	10	0	484	75	6,315	51	5	0	242	38
3000 " = 60 " = **Talent** (silver)	673,500 $=96\frac{1}{2}$ lbs. avdps.	410	0	0	1,940 nearly	00	336,750	205	0	0	970 nearly	00
3000 " = 60 " = **Talent** (gold)	758,000 =108 lbs. avdps.	6,150	0	0	29,085	00	379,000	3,075	0	0	14,542	50
Dram, A. V., Daric, R. V. (Ez. 8. 27; Neh. 7. 22), a gold Persian coin	130	1	1	1	5	60						

Note 1. **The Shekel** was the unit of value in common use.

Note 2. **The value of the Shekel** = 4 Greek drachmas = 4 Roman denarii. The best specimens extant of silver shekels weigh 218 to 220 grains, showing the correctness of the theoretical standard of $224\frac{1}{2}$ grs. So Hastings' *Bib. Dict.* But Harper's *Classical Dictionary* gives the weight of the denarius in Augustus' time, up to Nero, as 60 grs. A shekel therefore (4 denarii) = 240 grs.

Note 3. The reason for the different weights of the gold and silver shekels and their multiples lies in the fact that the ratio of silver to gold being 13.3 to 1, which was very inconvenient for commercial transactions, the ratio of the coins was made 15 to 1 by increasing the number of grains in a gold shekel to $252\frac{2}{3}$, so that 15 silver shekels = 1 gold shekel in value.

Note 4. There are no coins mentioned in the Bible before the Exile, and only one, the gold Daric, in the O. T. But there were ingots or bars of gold and silver of definite weights for convenience of trade.

Note 5. These tables have been computed by a careful comparison of the article by Prof. A. R. S. Kennedy, D. D., in Hastings' *Bib. Dict.*, who conferred with Mr. G. F. Hill of the Department of Coins and Medals in the British Museum, with the tables in Harper's *Classical Dictionary.* The equivalents in English money are given on English authorities. Those in dollars and cents are in accordance with the denarius of 60 grains, as in the *Classical Dictionary.*

Note 6. One pound avoirdupois contains 7000 grains. One pound troy contains 5760 grains.

Money of the New Testament (from Augustus to Nero).

		£	s.	d.	$	Cents.	Weight in Grains. *Classical Dict.*	Weight in Grains. Hastings.
	I. Copper or Brass Coins.							
	Mite (Gk. *Lepton*). Mat. 12. 2; Lu. 21. 2; 12. 59			¼ farthing		⅛ cent		
2 "	**Farthing** (Gk. *Kodrantes*), the Roman Quadrans. Mat. 5. 26; Mk. 12. 42.			½ farthing		¼ cent		
8 " / 4 "	**Farthing,** Assarion = As. Mat. 10. 29; Lu. 12. 6			2 farthings ½ d.		1 cent	4	
32 " / 16 " / 4 "	**Sestertius** (Roman)			2		4		
128 " / 64 " / 16 " / 4 "	**Denarius** (Roman), the silver penny; **Drachma** (Gk.). Mat. 22. 19; Lu. 20. 24.			8½		16	60	56
	II. Silver Coins and Values.							
	Denarius *or* **Drachma**. Lu. 15. 8; Acts 19. 19			8½		16	60	56
2 "	**Didrachma,** 'Tribute Money.' Mat. 22. 19. Half shekel = shekel of the sanctuary		1	4½		32⅓	120	112¼
4 " / 2 "	**Shekel** (Jewish); Stater (Roman). Mat. 17. 27; Tetradrachm (Greek); Argurion, 'piece of silver.' Mat. 26. 15.		2	9		64.6	240	224½
100 " / 50 " / 25 "	**Mina** (= Maneh). Lu. 19. 13–25. Pound	3	8	4	16	15	6,000 nearly a lb. avdps.	5,612
6000 " / 3000 " / 1500 " / 60 "	**Talent.** Mat. 25	205	0	0	970	00	360,000	336,750
26 "	= **Aureus,** the gold coin current in Palestine in the time of Augustus = nearly ¼ Mina. Mat. 10. 9	1	0	0	4 to 5			

Money — (*Continued*).

NOTE 1. The **Denarius** was the standard coin of Rome, as the **Shekel** was of Jewish currency. The coin shekel was about the size of an English half crown, and a little larger than a half dollar.

NOTE 2. Since in all our coins the pure silver and gold are alloyed with harder metals to render them more enduring, the calculations of the equivalents in English money are based upon the price at which the Royal Mint buys pure gold, viz., £3 17 s. 10½ d. per oz. of 480 grains.

The equivalents in dollars and cents are based upon the amount of pure silver in the standard dollar of 416 grs., of which 371½ grs. are pure silver. Silver is 16 to 1 of gold in the United States coinage. The denarius is calculated as 60 grs. in weight, for the American equivalents, and as 56 grs. for English money.

NOTE 3. **The variations** in values are very perplexing. In some cases the proportions of one coin to another varied in different ages. Before B. C. 210 a denarius (which means 'ten asses') consisted of ten asses, but in the time of Augustus it consisted of 16. There were differences often between current and tariff values. The mina of silver was of a different weight from the mina of gold. The mina of the Old Testament consisted of 50 shekels, but in New Testament times of 25 shekels, or of 50 shekels of the sanctuary, each of which was the half of a common shekel.

The tables therefore are approximate only, for any particular age, but the proportions of the different coins are correct.

Money changers were a necessity, for coins of many countries were in circulation. They were especially necessary in connection with the temple offerings, which must be made in Hebrew money, while those who made the offerings came from all parts of the world. *See* Mat. 21. 12, John 2. 14.

NOTE 4. (From Lieut.-Gen. Sir Charles Warren, K. C. B., F. R. S., in *Palestine Exploration Fund.*) The standard weight of a talent was the weight of $\frac{2}{3}$ of an ancient cubit cubed (or a cubic foot) in rain water. This was the standard at a very early period. But it did not become a standard of linear measure till the length of the cubit was reduced in Greece and Rome, when the side of this cube became the Roman foot. The $\frac{2}{3}$ cubic cubit or cubic foot was divided into 80 parts, or logs, or Roman pounds. The $\frac{2}{3}$ cubit cubed or cubic foot of Greece, Rome, and of Europe generally is about two thirds the capacity of that of Babylon, and the question arises whether this is due to the gradual depreciation of the cubit of 20.6109 inches to about 18 inches, or to a deliberate change of unit for purposes of convenience. No doubt the old system of working in palms had many inconveniences, and the new unit of 70,000 to a double cubit cubed could not be fairly brought into use generally so long as the standard of length remained a broken number of inches, viz., 20.6109. The change that was made was a very simple one, by which the new pound (80 to a cubic foot) became half the monetary mina, of which there were 60 to an ancient cubic foot or talent, and by which the standard cubit of 20.6109 inches became 18 inches, and the double cubit became a yard or 36 inches. This change consisted simply of reducing the content of the double cubit cubed by one third, and using the side cube of this remaining bulk as the new standard of length. It was discovered that 70,000 is nearly exactly $\frac{3}{2}(36)^3$. It has been shown that the inch is almost exactly equivalent to $\frac{1}{70000}$ double cubit cubed of the ancients, and that the foot and yard cubed are almost exactly two thirds respectively of the $\frac{2}{3}$ cubit and double cubit cubed. The Hebrew kor (= 10 baths) is exactly half an English cubic yard. If the contents of a cubic yard are shaped in the form of a sphere, and a cylinder enclose it, and a cone be erected on the base of the cylinder with the same height, the cone will represent exactly a kor, the sphere will represent a cubic yard, and the cylinder will represent an Egyptian chest, and their proportions respectively will be 1, 2, and 3. The English pounds Troy and avoirdupois appear to have been derived from different sources. The pound Troy would appear to have the same relation to the cubic foot as the Roman pound has to the Roman cubic foot and thus to have been derived from the Babylonian measures.

Comparative Table of Values.

(Silver to gold, 16 to 1.)

From Col. C. R. Conder, LL. D., in *Palestine Exploration Fund*, April, 1902, showing the variations in values.

	Hebrew.			Babylonian.			Phœnician.			Persian.			Attic.			Roman.		
	£	s.	d.	£	s.	d.	£	s.	d.	£	s.	d.	£	s.	d.	£	s.	d.
Quarter shekel.....	0	0	10	0	0	8½	0	0	7½	0	0	8	0	0	8½	0	0	6½
Half shekel........	0	1	8	0	1	5½	0	1	3	0	1	4	0	1	5½		—	
Three-quarter shekel	0	2	6	0	2	1½	0	1	10½	0	2	0	0	2	1½		—	
Shekel............	0	3	4	0	2	10	0	2	6	0	2	8	0	2	10		—	
Maneh, silver	4	3	4	4	3	4	5	0	0	4	0	0	3	8	6	3	2	6
Maneh, silver	8	6	8	8	6	8		—		8	0	0		—			—	
Talent............	250	0	0	250	0	0		—		247	10	0		—			—	
Talent............	500	0	0	500	0	0	500	0	0	495	0	0	436	12	8		—	
Maneh, gold	66	13	4	66	13	4	80	0	0	64	0	0	55	1	0	41	13	4
Maneh, gold	133	6	8	133	6	8	100	0	0	128	0	0		—			—	
Talent, gold........	4000	0	0	4000	0	0		—		3840	0	0	3334	0	0		—	
Talent, gold........	8000	0	0	8000	0	0	8000	0	0	7680	0	0		—			—	
Gold unit..........	1	0	10	1	0	10		—		1	1	0	0	18	0	1	1	0

Months: Jewish Calendar.

Year. Sacred.	Year. Civil.	Month.	Festivals.	English Month (nearly)	Corresponding Dates for 1902, 3.	1910, 11.	1915, 16.	Seasons and Productions.
I.	7.	ABIB, or NISAN. (Green ears.) Days 30. Ex. 12. 2.	1. New Moon. 14. The Passover (Ex. 12.1–51; 13. 3–10). 16. Firstfruits of Barley harvest (Lev. 23. 10–12).	**April.**	Ap. 8. " 22. " 24.	Ap. 10. " 24. " 26.	Mch. 16. " 30.	Fall of the latter or spring rains (Deu. 11. 14). Floods (Jos. 3. 15). Barley ripe at Jericho.
II.	8.	ZIF. (Blossom.) Days 29. Later IYAR. 1 Kn. 6. 1.	1. New Moon. 14. Second Passover, for those who could not keep the first (Num. 9. 10, 11).	**May.**	May 7, 8. " 21.	May 9. " 22.	Ap. 14, 15 " 28.	HARVEST. Wheat partly in the ear. Barley harvest general (Ru 1. 22). Wheat ripens.
III.	9.	SIVAN. Days 30. Esth. 8. 9.	1. New Moon. 6. Pentecost, or Feast of Weeks. Firstfruits of Wheat harvest (Lev. 23. 17, 20), and Firstfruits of all the ground (Ex. 23. 19; Deu. 26. 2, 10).	**June.**	June 6. " 11.	June 8. " 13.	May 14. " 19.	Wheat harvest. Summer begins. No rain from April to Sept. (1 Sam. 12. 17).
IV.	10.	THAMMUZ. Days 29. Zec. 8. 19.	1. New Moon. 17. Taking of Jerusalem Fast.	**July.**	July 5, 6. " 22.	July 7, 8. " 24.	Ju. 12, 13 " 29.	HOT SEASON. Heat increases.
V.	11.	AB. Days 30. Ez. 7. 9.	1. New Moon. 9. Destruction of Temple Fast.	**Aug.**	Aug. 4. " 12.	Aug. 6. " 14.	July 12. " 20.	Streams dry up. Heat intense. Vintage (Lev. 26. 5).
VI.	12.	ELUL. Days 29. Neh. 6. 15.	1. New Moon.	**Sept.**	Sept. 2, 3.	Sept. 4, 5.	Aug. 10, 11.	Heat still intense (2 Kn. 4. 18–20). Grape harvest general (Num. 13. 23).
VII.	1.	TISRI, or ETHANIM. Days 30. 1 Kn. 8. 2. 2 Chr. 5. 3.	1. Feast of Trumpets (Num. 29. 1). New Year. 10. Day of Atonement (Lev. 16.). 15. Feast of Tabernacles (Lev. 23. 34), 1st day. Firstfruits of Wine and Oil (Deu. 16. 13).	**Oct.**	Oct. 2. " 11. " 16.	Oct. 4. " 13. " 18.	Sept. 9. " 18. " 23.	SEED TIME. Former or early rains begin (Joel 2. 23). Plowing and sowing begin.
VIII.	2.	BUL, or MARCHESVAN (Rain.) Days 29. 1 Kn. 6. 38.	1. New Moon.	**Nov.**	Oct. 31, Nov. 1.	Nov. 2, 3.	Oct. 8, 9.	Rain continues. Wheat and barley sown. Vintage in N. Palestine.

Months: Jewish Calendar — (*Continued*).

Year. Sacred.	Year. Civil.	Month.	Festivals.	English Month (nearly).	Corresponding Dates for 1902, 3.	1910, 11.	1915, 16.	Seasons and Productions.
IX.	3.	CHISLEU. Days 30. Neh. 1. 1.	1. New Moon. 25. Feast of Dedication (1 Macc. 4. 52–59; John 10. 22, 23).	**Dec.**	Nov. 30, Dec. 1. Dec. 25.	Dec. 2. " 26.	Nov.7, 8. Dec. 3.	WINTER. Winter begins. Snow on the mountains.
X.	4.	TEBETH. Days 29. Esth. 2. 16.	1. New Moon.	**Jan.**	Dec. 30, Jan. 1, 1903.	Dec. 31.	Dec.7, 8.	Coldest month. Hail, snow (Jos. 10. 11).
XI.	5.	SHEBAT. Days 30. Zec. 1. 7.	1. New Moon.	**Feb.**	Jan. 29, 1903.	Jan. 30, 1911.	Jan. 6, 1916.	Weather gradually becomes warmer.
XII.	6.	ADAR. Days 29. Esth. 3. 7. Esth. 9. 27.	1. New Moon. 14, 15. Feast of Purim (Esth. 3. 7; 9. 21–24).	**March.**	Feb. 27, 28. Mch. 13, 14, 1903.	Feb. 28, Mch. 1. Mch. 14, 15, 1911.	Feb. 4, 5, 1916.	COLD SEASON. Thunder and hail frequent. Almond tree blossoms.
XIII. VEADAR (Intercalary). Latter part of March and beginning of April.			1. New Moon. 11. Fast of Esther. 14, 15. Purim.	— — —	— — —	— — —	Mch. 5, 6. " 18, 19. " 20, 1916.	

NOTE 1. This calendar has been adapted to the three years, 1902, 1910, 1915, by Dr. Solomon Schindler, late Rabbi of Temple Adath-Israel, Boston, U. S. A., in order to shew the variations of the months from the corresponding ones given in the column of modern months. They vary nearly as our Eastertide. Out of eight years, the calculations for which are before me, in four Nisan (April) begins in March and in four in April.

NOTE 2. The Jewish year is strictly lunar, and contains 354 days, or 12 lunations of the moon; but in a cycle of 19 years an intercalary month (Veadar) is seven times introduced, to render the average length of the year nearly correct. 'This thirteenth month was added to the year whenever on the 16th of Nisan the barley was not yet ripe, but this was forbidden in the sabbatical years, as two intercalary years in succession were not allowed.' H. von Soden, in *Encyc. Bib.*

Months of the Hebrews. Ex. 12. 2; 13. 4; Deu. 16. 1; 1 Kn. 6. 1; 8. 2.
of the Chaldæans. Neh. 1. 1; 2. 1.

Moon (the lesser light). Gen. 1. 16.
referred to. Deu. 33. 14; Jos. 10. 12; Ps. 8. 3; 89. 37; 104. 19; 121. 6.
idolatrously worshipped. Deu. 17. 3; Job 31. 26; Jer. 44. 17.
feasts of the new. 1 Sam. 20. 5; 1 Chr. 23. 31; Ps. 81. 3; Isa. 1. 13; Hos. 2. 11.

Morasthite, mō-răs'-thīte, 'native of Moresheth.' Jer. 26. 18.

Mordecai, mŏr-dĕ-cā'-ī, 'worshipper of Merodach' (?). Esth. 2. 5.
reveals conspiracy against king Ahasuerus. Esth. 2. 21.
is hated by Haman. Esth. 3. 5.
honoured by the king. Esth. 6.
advanced. Esth. 8.–10. (Ez. 2. 2; Neh. 7. 7).

Moreh, mō'-rĕh, 'teacher.' Gen. 12. 6; Jud. 7. 1.

More part, greater part, majority. Acts 27. 12.

Moresheth-gath, mō'-rĕsh-ĕth-găth, 'the possession of Gath.' Mic. 1. 14.

Moriah, mō-rī'-ăh, provided by Jehovah,' the hill of Jerusalem on which the temple was builded, and on which Abraham offered Isaac. Abraham's sacrifice. Gen. 22.
David's sacrifice there. 2 Sam. 24. 18; 1 Chr. 21. 18; 22. 1.
temple built on. 2 Chr. 3. 1.

Morning. Gen. 1. 5; Ps. 30. 5; 90. 5; 130. 6; Eccl. 11. 6; Hos. 6. 4; Mk. 16. 2; Acts 5. 21.

Morrow. Prov. 27. 1, boast not thyself of to *m.*
Isa. 22. 13; 1 Cor. 15. 32, for to *m.* we die.
56. 12, to *m.* shall be as this day.
Mat. 6. 34, take no thought for the *m.*
Jas. 4. 14, ye know not what shall be on the *m.*
See Jos. 5. 12; 2 Kn. 7. 1; Prov. 3. 28.

Morsel. Job 31. 17; Ps. 147. 17; Prov. 17. 1; Heb. 12. 16.

Mortal. Deu. 19. 11, smite his neighbour *m.*
Job 4. 17, shall *m.* man be more just?
Rom. 6. 12; 8. 11, in your *m.* body.
1 Cor. 15. 53, 54, this *m.* must put on immortality.

Mortality of man. Job 19. 26; Rom. 8. 11; 1 Cor. 15. 53; 2 Cor. 4. 11; 5. 4.

Mortar. Prov. 27. 22; Ezek. 13. 11, 22, 28.

Mortgages. Neh. 5. 3.

Mortify, to kill (metaphorically), subdue, bring into subjection. Rom. 8. 13; Col. 3. 5.

Mosera, mō'-sĕ-rā, 'bond.' Deu. 10. 6.

Moseroth, mō'-sĕ-rōth, 'bonds.' Num. 33. 30.

Moses, mō'-sĕs, connected in Ex. 2. 10, by a play on the words, with a Hebrew verb meaning 'to draw out.'
born, and hidden. Ex. 2. (Acts 7. 20; Heb. 11. 23).
escapes to Midian. Ex. 2. 15.
revelation from God. Ex. 3.; confirmed by signs. Ex. 4.
returns to Egypt. Ex. 4. 20.
intercedes with Pharaoh for Israel. Ex. 5.–12.

leads Israel forth. Ex. 14.
meets God in mount Sinai. Ex. 19. 3 (24. 18).
brings the law to the people. Ex. 19. 25; 20.-23.; 34. 10; 35. 1; Lev. 1.; Num. 5.; 6.; 15.; 27.-30.; 36.; Deu. 12.-26.
instructed to build the tabernacle. Ex. 25.-31.; 35.; 40.; Num. 4.; 8.-10.; 18.; 19.
his grief at Israel's idolatry. Ex. 32. 19.
his intercession. Ex. 32. 11 (33. 12).
again meets God in the mount. Ex. 34. 2.
skin of his face shines. Ex. 34. 29 (2 Cor. 3. 7, 13).
sets apart Aaron. Lev. 8.; 9.
numbers the people. Num. 1.; 26.
sends out the spies to Canaan. Num. 13. [13.
intercedes for the murmuring people. Num. 14.
Korah's sedition against. Num. 16.
for his unbelief suffered not to enter Canaan. Num. 20. 12; 27. 12; Deu. 1. 35; 3. 23.
his government of Israel in the wilderness. Num. 20.; 21.
makes the brazen serpent. Num. 21. 9 (John 3. 14).
recounts Israel's history, and exhorts to obedience. Deu. 1.; 3.-12.; 27.-31.
his charge to Joshua. Deu. 3. 28; 31. 7, 23.
his death, Deu. 34. 5. his body, Jude 9.
seen at Christ's transfiguration. Mat. 17. 3; Mk. 9. 4; Lu. 9. 30.
his meekness. Num. 12. 3.
dignity. Deu. 34. 10.
faithfulness. Num. 12. 7; Heb. 3. 2.

Mote, a minute particle, as of dust. Mat. 7. 3.

Moth (Lu. 6. 41). Heb. *Âsh:* Gk. σής: Zool. S. *Tinea.*
Job 13. 28, a garment that is *m.* eaten.
27. 18, he buildeth his house as a *m.*
Ps. 39. 11, consume away like a *m.*
Isa. 50. 9, the *m.* shall eat them up.
Hos. 5. 12, unto Ephraim as a *m.*
Mat. 6. 19, where *m.* and rust doth corrupt.
In eight of the nine passages where 'moth' occurs in the Bible the reference is to the destructiveness of the common clothes-moth, or *Tinea:* but in Job 27. 18 the reference is to the larvæ of the *Tortrix*, which twist up leaves and bind them with the thread which they spin, to make a hiding-place in which they may change to the pupa state.

Mother. Jud. 5. 7; 2 Sam. 20. 19, a *m.* in Israel.
1 Kn. 22. 52, Ahaziah walked in the way of his *m.*
2 Chr. 22. 3, his *m.* was his counsellor.
Job 17. 14, to the worm, thou art my *m.*
Ps. 113. 9, a joyful *m.* of children.
Isa. 66. 13, as one whom his *m.* comforteth.
Ezek. 16. 44, as is the *m.*, so is her daughter.
Mat. 12. 48; Mk. 3. 33, who is my *m.*?
John 2. 1; Acts 1. 14, the *m.* of Jesus.
See Gen. 17. 16; Gal. 4. 26; 1 Tim. 1. 9; 5. 2.

Mother of all living, Eve. Gen. 3. 20.

Mothers, love of, Isa. 49. 15; 66. 13. instances, Gen. 21. 10; Ex. 2.; 1 Sam. 1. 22; 2 Sam. 21. 10; 1 Kn. 3. 26; 2 John.
love to, enforced. Ex. 20. 12; Prov. 1. 8; 19. 26; 23. 22; Eph. 6. 1.

Motions, emotions, passions, workings. Rom. 7. 5.

Mouldy. Jos. 9. 5, 12.

Mount. Ex. 18. 5, the *m.* of God.
Ps. 107. 26, they *m.* up to heaven.
Isa. 40. 31, *m.* with wings, as eagles.
See Job 20. 6; 39. 27; Isa. 27. 13.

Mount to be cast against Jerusalem. Jer. 6. 6.

Mountains of Scripture:

Name.	References.	Associations.
Abarim	Num. 33. 47, 48	Balaam's blessing.
Ararat	Gen. 8. 4	The region where Noah's ark rested.
Bashan	Deu. 3. 13	Part of Og's territory; famous for its oaks and wild cattle.
Carmel	1 Kn. 18. 19	Elijah's sacrifice (distinct from the southern town called Carmel).
Ebal	Deu. 27. 4; Jos. 8. 32, 33	Cursing of law-breakers; site of the stones inscribed with the Law.
Gerizim	John 4. 20	Blessing of the keepers of the Law; site of Samaritan temple.
Gilboa	1 Sam. 31. 8	Scene of Saul's death.
Gilead	Gen. 31. 48	Scene of the covenant between Laban and Jacob.
Hermon	Deu. 4. 48	The conjectured site of the Transfiguration.
Hor	Num. 20. 27, 28	Scene of Aaron's death. Now Jebel Haroûn (*Aaron's mount*).
Hor	Num. 34. 7	The boundary of the Land of Israel towards the north; in all probability Hermon.
Horeb *	Ex. 3. 1; Deu. 5. 2; 1 Kn. 19. 8	Scene of burning bush; giving of the Law; Elijah's vision.
Lebanon	2 Chr. 2. 8–10	Source of timber for Solomon's Temple.
Moriah	2 Chr. 3. 1	Place of Abraham's intended sacrifice (Gen. 22. 2); site of Solomon's Temple.
Nebo	Deu. 34. 1	The range from whose summit (Pisgah) Moses saw the Promised Land.
Olivet	2 Sam. 15. 30; Mat. 24. 3; Acts 1. 9–12	Scene of David's flight from Absalom; of Christ's weeping over Jerusalem; and of His Ascension.
Seir	Gen. 32. 3; 36. 8; Deu. 2. 22	A mountain range practically coextensive with Edom; taken by Esau from the Horites.
Sinai *	Ex. 19. 1–11	In Arabia; scene of Israelite encampment for nearly a year, and of giving of the Law.
Tabor	Jud. 4. 14; Mk. 9. 2	Scene of Barak's camp, and, possibly, of Christ's transfiguration.
Zion (spelt **Sion** in N.T.)	2 Sam. 5. 7	Stronghold of Jebusites, stormed by Joab; site of David's palace.

* Probably Horeb is the name of the district, Sinai of the mountain.

Mourn. Gen. 37. 35, down to the grave *m.*
Prov. 5. 11, and thou *m.* at the last.
Isa. 61. 2, to comfort all that *m.*
Jer. 31. 13, I will turn their *m.* into joy.
Mat. 5. 4, blessed are they that *m.*
24. 30, then shall all the tribes of the earth *m.*
Lu. 6. 25, woe to you that laugh, for ye shall *m.*
See Neh. 8. 9; Zec. 7. 5; Jas. 4. 9.
Mourner. 2 Sam. 14. 2; Eccl. 12. 5; Hos. 9. 4.
Mourners, comfort for. Job 29. 25; Rom. 12. 15; 2 Cor. 1. 4; 1 Thes. 4. 18.
Mournfully. Mal. 3. 14.
Mourning, when blessed. Eccl. 7. 2; Mat. 5. 4; Lu. 6. 21.
for the dead. Gen. 50. 3; Num. 20. 29; Deu. 14. 1; 2 Sam. 1. 17; 3. 31; 12. 16; 18. 33; 19. 1; Eccl. 12. 5; Jer. 6. 26; 9. 17; 22. 18.
of the priests. Lev. 21. 1; Ezek. 44. 25.
Mouse (Lev. 11. 29; 1 Sam. 6. 4, 5). Heb. *'Akhbar:* Gk. μῦς. The mice of 1 Sam. 6. 4, 5, were probably the short-tailed field mice. Tristram found 25 species of rats and mice in Palestine and Syria.
Mouth. Job 9. 20, mine own *m.* shall condemn me.
40. 4, I will lay my hand on my *m.*
Ps. 8. 2; Mat. 21. 16, out of the *m.* of babes.
39. 1, I will keep my *m.* with a bridle.
49. 3, my *m.* shall speak of wisdom.
55. 21, words of his *m.* smoother than butter.
81. 10, open thy *m.* wide.
Prov. 10. 14; 14. 3; 15. 2, the *m.* of the foolish.
13. 2, good by the fruit of his *m.*
13. 3; 21. 23, he that keepeth his *m.*
Eccl. 6. 7, all the labour of a man is for his *m.*
Isa. 29. 13; Mat. 15. 8, this people draw near with *m.*
Ezek. 33. 31, with their *m.* they shew much love.
Mal. 2. 6, the law of truth was in his *m.*
Mat. 12. 34; Lu. 6. 45, the *m.* speaketh.
13. 35, I will open my *m.* in parables.
Lu. 21. 15, I will give you a *m.* and wisdom.
Rom. 10. 10, with the *m.* confession is made.
Tit. 1. 11, whose *m.* must be stopped.
Jas. 3. 10, out of the same *m.* proceedeth.
See Lam. 3. 29; John 19. 29; 1 Pet. 2. 22.
Mouth of God. Deu. 8. 3; Mat. 4. 4.
of babes. Ps. 8. 2; Mat. 21. 16.
of the wicked. Ps. 32. 9; 63. 11; 107. 42; 109. 2; 144. 8; Prov. 4. 24; 5. 3; 6. 12; 19. 28; Rom. 3. 15; Rev. 13. 5.
of the righteous, &c. Ps. 37. 30; Prov. 10. 31; Eccl. 10. 12.
of fools. Prov. 14. 3; 15. 2; 18. 7; 26. 7.
Move. Ps. 10. 6; 16. 8; 30. 6; 62. 2, I shall not be *m.*
Mat. 21. 10; Acts 21. 30, all the city was *m.* R. V. stirred.
John 5. 3, waiting for the *m.* of the water. R. V. omits.
Acts 17. 28, in him we live, and *m.*
20. 24, none of these things *m.* me.
See Prov. 23. 31; Isa. 7. 2; 2 Pet. 1. 21.
Moza, mō'-ză, 'fountain.' (1) 1 Chr. 2. 46. (2) 1 Chr. 8. 36.
Mozah, mō'-zăh, same as Moza (?). Jos. 18. 26.
Much. Ex. 16. 18; 2 Cor. 8. 15, he that gathered *m.*
Num. 16. 3, ye take too *m.* upon you.
Lu. 7. 47, for she loved *m.*
12. 48, to whom *m.* is given.
16. 10, faithful in *m.*
See Prov. 25. 16; Eccl. 5. 12; Jer. 2. 22.
Muffler, a covering for the lower part of the face. Isa. 3. 19.
Mulberry (2 Sam. 5. 23; Lu. 17. 6). Heb. *Bĕcâîm:* Gk. ἄπισι, συκάμινος: Bot. N. *Populus Euphratica.* The tree meant is the poplar. The Greek συκάμινος, 'sycamine,' is the black mulberry. Lu. 17. 6.
Mule (2 Sam. 13. 29). Heb. *Péred:* Gk. ἡμίονος. Three Hebrew words (*péred, rekesh, yêmîm*) are translated 'mule' in our A. V.; of which the first only is correct; the second ought to be 'the horse or ass,' and the third (*yêmîm*) (Gen. 36. 24) is doubtful; possibly it means 'warm springs' of water.
Multiply. Isa. 9. 3, thou hast *m.* the nation, and not increased the joy.
Jer. 3. 16, when ye be *m.* they shall say.
Dan. 4. 1; 6. 25; 1 Pet. 1. 2; 2 Pet. 1. 2; Jude 2, peace be *m.*
Nah. 3. 16, thou hast *m.* thy merchants.
See Acts 6. 1; 7. 17; 9. 31; 12. 24.
Multitude. Ex. 23. 2, a *m.* to do evil.
Job 32. 7, *m.* of years should teach wisdom.
Ps. 5. 7; 51. 1; 69. 13; 106. 7, in the *m.* of thy mercy.
33. 16, no king saved by the *m.* of an host.
94. 19, in the *m.* of my thoughts.
Prov. 10. 19, in *m.* of words there wanteth not sin.
11. 14; 15. 22; 24. 6, in the *m.* of counsellors.
Eccl. 5. 3, through the *m.* of business.
Jas. 5. 20; 1 Pet. 4. 8, hide a *m.* of sins.
See Deu. 1. 10; Jos. 11. 4; Lu. 2. 13.
Munition, fortress, fortifications. Nah. 2. 1.
Muppim, mŭp'-pĭm, probably written for Shupham. Gen. 46. 21.
Murder. Gen. 9. 6; Ex. 20. 13; Lev. 24. 17; Deu. 5. 17; 21. 9; Mat. 5. 21; 1 John 3. 15.
examples; Gen. 4.; Jud. 9.; 2 Sam. 3. 27; 4.; 12. 9; 20. 8; 1 Kn. 16. 9; 21.; 2 Kn. 15. 10; 21. 23; 2 Chr. 24. 21.
its penalty. Gen. 4. 12; 9. 6; Num. 35. 30; Jer. 19. 4; Ezek. 16. 38; Gal. 5. 21; Rev. 22. 15.
source of. Mat. 15. 19; Gal. 5. 21.
Murmuring rebuked. Num. 14. 27; Lam. 3. 39; 1 Cor. 10. 10; Phil. 2. 14; Jude 16.
of Israel, instances of. Ex. 15. 23; 16.; 17.; Num. 11.; 16.; 20.; 21.
Murrain, cattle plague. Ex. 9. 3; Ps. 78. 50.
Muse, meditate. Ps. 39. 3; 143. 5; Lu. 3. 15.
Mushi, mū'-shī, 'withdrawn.' Ex. 6. 19.
Mushites, mū'-shītes, descendants of **Mushi.** Num. 3. 33.
Music, invention of. Gen. 4. 21.
its effects on Saul. 1 Sam. 16. 14.
used for worship. 2 Sam. 6. 5; 1 Chr. 15. 28; 16. 42; 2 Chr. 7. 6; 29. 25; Ps. 33.; 81.; 92.; 108.; 150.; Dan. 3. 5.
at festivities. Isa. 5. 12; 14. 11; Am. 6. 5; Lu. 15. 25; 1 Cor. 14. 7.
in heaven. Rev. 5. 8; 14. 2.

Musical Instruments.

(1) Stringed instruments.

Harp.	Sackbut.
Lute.	Viol.
Psaltery.	

(2) Wind instruments.

Cornet.	Pipe.
Dulcimer.	Trumpet.
Flute.	Shawm.
Organ.	

(3) Instruments of percussion.

Bells.	Tabret.
Cymbals.	

(*See* under each name.)

Mustard (Mat. 13. 31). Gk. σίναπι: Bot. N. *Sinapis nigra.* The annual herb 'mustard' grows 10 or 12 feet high in Palestine.
Mustard seed, parable of. Mat. 13. 31; Mk. 4. 30; Lu. 13. 18.
Muth-labben, Upon (mŭth-lăb'-bĕn). Ps. 9., title. Meaning sung to an air beginning with the words, 'Death of the Son;' or 'Death makes wise.'
Mutter. Isa. 8. 19; 59. 3.
Mutual. Rom. 1. 12.
Muzzling the ox that treadeth out the corn forbidden. Deu. 25. 4; 1 Cor. 9. 9; 1 Tim. 5. 18.
Myra, mȳ'-ră. Acts 27. 5.
Myrrh. (1) (Ex. 30. 23; Prov. 7. 17). Heb. *Môr:* Gk. σμύρνα: Bot. N. *Balsamodendron myrrha,*

a domestic perfume, a gum resin from a small thorny tree.
(2) (Gen. 37. 25). Heb. *Lôt:* Gk. στακτή : R. V. marg. 'ladanum,' which see.
See Esth. 2. 12; Ps. 45. 8; S. of S. 1. 13; Mat. 2. 11; Mk. 15. 23; John 19. 39.
Myrtle (Isa. 55. 13). Heb. *Hădas:* Gk. μυρσίνη: Bot. N. *Myrtus communis.* A small tree growing 20 feet high, the dried flowers and berries of which are used as a perfume. Esther's Heb. name Hadassah = Myrtle.
Myrtles (Isa. 41. 19; 55. 13), vision of. Zec. 1. 8.
Mysia, mȳs'-ĭ-ă, a vaguely defined district in the northwest of Asia Minor, part of the Roman province of Asia, and bordering on the province of Bithynia. Acts 16. 7.
Mystery of the kingdom of God made known by Christ. Mat. 13. 11; Mk. 4. 11; Eph. 1. 9; 3. 3; 1 Tim. 3. 16.
by the disciples to the world. 1 Cor. 2. 7; 4. 1; 13. 2; 15. 51; Eph. 5. 22; 6. 19; Col. 2. 2.
of the raising of the dead. 1 Cor. 15. 51.
of iniquity. 2 Thes. 2. 7; Rev. 17. 5.

Naam, nā'-ăm, 'pleasantness.' 1 Chr. 4. 15.
Naamah, nā'-ă-măh, 'pleasant.' (1) women. Gen. 4. 22; 1 Kn. 14. 21.
(2) town. Jos. 15. 41.
Naaman, nā'-ă-măn, 'pleasantness.' (1) Gen. 46. 21; Num. 26. 40.
(2) The Syrian. 2 Kn. 5.
his leprosy healed. 2 Kn. 5. 14.
his request. 2 Kn. 5. 17. *See* Lu. 4. 27.
Naamathite, nā-ăm'-ă-thīte. Job 2. 11.
Naamites, nā-ă'-mītes, descendants of Naaman. Num. 26. 40.
Naarah, nā'-ă-răh, 'a girl.' 1 Chr. 4. 5.
Naarai, nā'-ă-răi, 'youthful.' 1 Chr. 11. 37.
Naaran, nā'-ă-răn, same as Naarah. 1 Chr. 7. 28.
Naarath, nā'-ă-răth, 'to Naarah.' Jos. 16. 7.
Naashon, nā-ăsh'-ŏn, 'enchanter.' Ex. 6. 23.
Naasson, nā-ăs'-sŏn, Greek form of Naashon. Mat. 1. 4.
Nabal, nā'-băl, 'foolish.' 1 Sam. 25. 3.
conduct to David. 1 Sam. 25. 10.
Abigail, intercedes for. 1 Sam. 25. 18.
his death. 1 Sam. 25. 38.
Naboth, nā'-bŏth, 'fruits' (?); slain by Jezebel. [1 Kn. 21.
his murder avenged. 2 Kn. 9. 21.
Nachon, nā'chŏn, 'prepared.' 2 Sam. 6. 6.
Nachor, nā'-chôr, 'snorting.' Jos. 24. 2.
Nadab, nā'-dăb, 'liberal.' (1) son of Aaron. Ex. 6. [23.
offers strange fire. Lev. 10. 1, 2.
(2) 1 Chr. 2. 28.
(3) king of Israel, slain by Baasha. 1 Kn. 14. 20; [15. 25, 28.
Nagge, năg'-gē, Greek form of Nogah. Lu. 3. 25.
Nahalal, nā'-hă-lăl, 'a pasture.' Jos. 21. 35.
Nahaliel, nă-hăl'-ĭ-ĕl, 'valley of God.' Num. 21. 19.
Nahallal, nă-hăl'-lăl, same as Nahalal. Jos. 19. 15.
Nahalol, nā'-hă-lŏl, same as preceding. Jud. 1. 30.
Naham, nā'-hăm, 'consolation.' 1 Chr. 4. 19.
Nahamani, nā-hă-mā'-nī, 'comforter.' Neh. 7. 7.
Naharai, nā'-hă-răi, 'one who snores.' 1 Chr. 11. 39.
Nahari, nā'-hă-rī, same as preceding. 2 Sam. 23. 37.
Nahash, nā'-hăsh, 'serpent.' (1) Amasa's father. 2 Sam. 17. 25.
(2) the Ammonite, invades Jabesh-Gilead. 1 Sam. 11.
(3) another Ammonite king. 2 Sam. 10. 2.
Nahath, nā'-hăth, 'descent.' Gen. 36. 13.
Nahbi, năh'-bī, 'hidden.' Num. 13. 14.
Nahor, nā'-hôr, same as Nachor. (1) Gen. 11. 22.
(2) Abram's brother. Gen. 11. 26; 22. 20; 24. 10.
Nahshon, năh'-shŏn, same as Naashon. Num. 1. 7.
Nahum, nā'-hŭm, 'comforter,' vision of. Nah. 1. 1-3.
Nail. Ez. 9. 8, give us a *n.* in his holy place.
Isa. 22. 23, fasten as a *n.* in sure place.
John 20. 25, put finger into print of *n.*
Col. 2. 14, *n.* it to his cross.
See Jud. 4. 21; Eccl. 12. 11; Dan. 4. 33.
Nain, nā'-ĭn, 'pasture,' miracle at. Lu. 7. 11.
Naioth, nāi'-ŏth, 'habitations.' 1 Sam. 19. 18.
school of prophets. 1 Sam. 19. 23; 20. 1.
Naked. Ex. 32. 25, made *n.* to their shame. R. V. broken loose.
Job 1. 21, *n.* came I out, and *n.* shall I return.
Mat. 25. 36, *n.*, and ye clothed me.
1 Cor. 4. 11, to this present hour we are *n.*
2 Cor. 5. 3, we shall not be found *n.*
Heb. 4. 13, all things are *n.* to eyes of him.
See John 21. 7; Jas. 2. 15; Rev. 3. 17; 16. 15.
Nakedness. Rom. 8. 35; 2 Cor. 11. 27; Rev. 3. 18.
Name (*n.*). Gen. 32. 29; Jud. 13. 18, wherefore dost thou ask after my *n.*?
Ex. 3. 15, this is my *n.* for ever.
23. 21, my *n.* is in him.
Jos. 7. 9, what wilt thou do to thy great *n.*?
2 Chr. 14. 11, in thy *n.* we go.
Neh. 9. 10, so didst thou get thee a *n.*
Job 18. 17, he shall have no *n.* in the street.
Ps. 20. 1, the *n.* of God defend thee.
20. 5, in the *n.* of God set up banners.
22. 22; Heb. 2. 12, I will declare thy *n.*
48. 10, according to thy *n.* so is thy praise.
69. 36, they that love his *n.*
111. 9, holy and reverend is his *n.*
115. 1, unto thy *n.* give glory.
138. 2, thy word above all thy *n.*
Prov. 10. 7, the *n.* of the wicked shall rot.
18. 10, the *n.* of the Lord a strong tower.
22. 1; Eccl. 7. 1, good *n.* rather to be chosen.
S. of S. 1. 3, thy *n.* is as ointment poured forth.
Isa. 42. 8, I am the Lord, that is my *n.*
55. 13, it shall be to the Lord for a *n.*
56. 5; 63. 12, an everlasting *n.*
57. 15, whose *n.* is Holy.
62. 2, called by a new *n.*
64. 7, there is none that calleth on thy *n.*
Jer. 10. 6, thou art great, and thy *n.* is great.
14. 14; 23. 25; 27. 15, prophesy lies in my *n.*
44. 26, sworn by my great *n.*
Zec. 10. 12, walk up and down in his *n.*
14. 9, one Lord, and his *n.* one.
Mal. 1. 6, wherein have we despised thy *n.*?
4. 2, to you that fear my *n.*
Mat. 6. 9; Lu. 11. 2, hallowed be thy *n.*
10. 22; 19. 29; Mk. 13. 13; Lu. 21. 12; John 15. 21; Acts 9. 16, for my *n.* sake.
12. 21, in his *n.* shall the Gentiles trust.
18. 5; Mk. 9. 37; Lu. 9. 48, receive in my *n.*
18. 20, gathered together in my *n.*
24. 5; Mk. 13. 6; Lu. 21. 8, many shall come in [my *n.*
Mk. 5. 9; Lu. 8. 30, what is thy *n.*?
9. 39, do a miracle in my *n.*
Lu. 10. 20, *n.* written in heaven.
John 5. 43, if another shall come in his own *n.*
14. 13; 15. 16; 16. 23, 24, 26, whatsoever ye ask in my *n.*
Acts 3. 16, his *n.* through faith in his *n.*
4. 12, none other *n.* under heaven.
5. 28, that ye should not teach in this *n.*
5. 41, worthy to suffer for his *n.* R. V. the Name.
Eph. 1. 21, far above every *n.*
Phil. 2. 9, 10, a *n.* above every *n.*
4. 3, whose *n.* are in the book of life.
Col. 3. 17, do all in the *n.* of the Lord Jesus.
Heb. 1. 4, obtained a more excellent *n.*
Jas. 2. 7, that worthy *n.*
Rev. 2. 13, holdest fast my *n.*
2. 17, a *n.* written, which no man knoweth.
3. 1, thou hast a *n.* that thou livest.
3. 4, a few *n.* in Sardis.
13. 1, the *n.* of blasphemy.
14. 1; 22. 4, Father's *n.* in their foreheads.
See Gen. 2. 20; Ex. 28. 9; Isa. 45. 3; John 10. 3.
Name (*v.*). Eccl. 6. 10, that which hath been is *n.* already.
Isa. 61. 6, ye shall be *n.* Priests of the Lord.

Rom. 15. 20, not where Christ was *n*. [Christ.
2 Tim. 2. 19, every one that *n*. the name of
See 1 Sam. 16. 3; Isa. 62. 2; Lu. 2. 21; 6. 13.

Name of God. Ex. 34. 5, 14. *See* Ex. 6. 3; 15. 3; Ps. 83. 18.
honour due to. Ex. 20. 7; Deu. 5. 11; 28. 58; Ps. 34. 3; 72. 17; 111. 9; Mic. 4. 5; 1 Tim. 6. 1.
of Christ, prayer in, John 14. 13; 16. 23; Rom. 1. 8; Eph. 5. 20; Col. 3. 17; Heb. 13. 15. miracles performed in, Acts 3. 6; 4. 10; 19. 13.
responsibilities of bearing. 2 Tim. 2. 19.

Name given to children at circumcision. Lu. 1. 59; 2. 21.

Name, value of a good. Prov. 22. 1; Eccl. 7. 1.

Names changed by God. Gen. 17. 5, 15; 32. 27; 2 Sam. 12. 25. by man, Dan. 1. 7. by Christ, Mk. 3. 16, 17.

Names of Christ. *See* under Christ.

Naomi, nā′-ō-mī, 'pleasant.' Ru. 1. 2. [15.

Naphish, nā′-phĭsh, 'refreshment' (?). Gen. 25.

Naphtali, năph′-tă-lī, 'my wrestling.' (1) son of Jacob. Gen. 30. 8; 35. 25; 46. 24; 49. 21; Deu. 33. 23.
(2) tribe of, numbered. Num. 1. 42; 10. 27; 13. 14; 26. 48; Jud. 1. 33.
subdue the Canaanites. Jud. 4. 10; 5. 18; 6. 35; 7. 23.
carried captive. 2 Kn. 15. 29. *See* Isa. 9. 1; Mat. 4. 13.

Naphtuhim, năph-tū′-hĭm. Gen. 10. 13.

Napkin. Lu. 19. 20; John 11. 44; 20. 7.

Narcissus, när-çĭs′-sŭs, 'benumbing' (?); household of. Rom. 16. 11.

Nard. *See* Spikenard.

Narrow. Isa. 28. 20; 49. 19; Mat. 7. 14. [7.

Nathan, nā′-thăn, 'gift.' (1) the prophet. 2 Sam. shews David his sin. 2 Sam. 12. 1.
anoints Solomon king. 1 Kn. 1. 34; 1 Chr. 29. 29; 2 Chr. 9. 29.
(2) son of David. 2 Sam. 5. 14; Zec. 12. 12; Lu. 3. 31.
(3) others. 2 Sam. 23. 36; 1 Kn. 4. 5; Ez. 8. 16; 10. 39.

Nathanael, nă-thăn′-ă-ĕl, 'God gave;' 'Israelite indeed.' John 1. 45; 21. 2.

Nathan-melech, nā′-thăn-mē′-lĕch, 'the king's gift.' 2 Kn. 23. 11.

Nation. Gen. 10. 32, by these were the *n*. divided.
20. 4, wilt thou slay a righteous *n*.?
Num. 14. 12; Deu. 9. 14, I will make thee a greater *n*.
2 Sam. 7. 23; 1 Chr. 17. 21, what *n*. like thy people?
Ps. 33. 12, blessed is the *n*. whose God is the Lord.
147. 20, he hath not dealt so with any *n*.
Prov. 14. 34, righteousness exalteth a *n*. [*n*.
Isa. 2. 4; Mic. 4. 3, *n*. shall not lift sword against
18. 2, a *n*. scattered and peeled.
26. 2, that the righteous *n*. may enter in.
34. 1, come near, ye *n*., to hear.
52. 15, so shall he sprinkle many *n*.
Jer. 10. 7, O King of *n*.
Zec. 2. 11, many *n*. shall be joined to the Lord.
8. 22, strong *n*. shall seek the Lord.
Mat. 24. 7; Mk. 13. 8; Lu. 21. 10, *n*. against *n*.
Lu. 7. 5, he loveth our *n*.
21. 25, distress of *n*.
John 11. 50, that the whole *n*. perish not.
Acts 2. 5, devout men of every *n*.
10. 35, in every *n*. he that feareth.
Phil. 2. 15, crooked and perverse *n*. R. V. generation.
Rev. 5. 9, redeemed out of every *n*.
See Deu. 4. 27; 15. 6; Jer. 2. 11; 4. 2; 31. 10.

Nations, origin of. Gen. 10. [23. 15.

Nativity. Gen. 11. 28; Jer. 46. 16; Ezek. 21. 30;

Natural. Deu. 34. 7, nor his *n*. force abated.
Rom. 1. 31; 2 Tim. 3. 3, without *n*. affection.
1 Cor. 2. 14, the *n*. man receiveth not.
See 1 Cor. 15. 44; Phil. 2. 20; Jas. 1. 23.

Nature. 1 Cor. 11. 14, doth not even *n*. itself teach?
Eph. 2. 3, by *n*. children of wrath.
Heb. 2. 16, the *n*. of angels.
2 Pet. 1. 4, partakers of the divine *n*.
See Rom. 1. 26; 2. 14, 27; Gal. 2. 15; 4. 8.

Naught. Prov. 20. 14, it is *n*., saith the buyer.
Isa. 49. 4, spent strength for *n*.
52. 3, ye have sold yourselves for *n*.
Mal. 1. 10, shut the doors for *n*. R. V. omits.
Acts 5. 38, if of men, it will come to *n*. R. V. be overthrown.
See Deu. 15. 9; Job 1. 9; Rom. 14. 10; 1 Cor. 1. 28.

Naughtiness. 1 Sam. 17. 28; Prov. 11. 6; Jas. 1. 21.

Naughty, bad, worthless, good for nothing. Prov. 6. 12; 17. 4; Jer. 24. 2.

Naum, nā′-ŭm, same as Nahum. Lu. 3. 25.

Navy of Solomon. 1 Kn. 9. 26; 2 Chr. 8. 17.
of Jehoshaphat. 1 Kn. 22. 48.

Nay. Mat. 5. 37; 2 Cor. 1. 17-19; Jas. 5. 12.

Nazarene, năz-ă-rēne′, an inhabitant of Nazareth; applied to Jesus to distinguish him from others of the same name, Mat. 2. 23, and to his followers, Acts 24. 5.

Nazareth, năz′-ă-rĕth, 'branch,' in Galilee; the home of our Lord for eight and twenty years (Lu. 2. 4, 39, 51). Hence His familiar title of 'the Nazarene' (Mat. 1. 23). Mat. 2. 23; 21. 11; Lu. 1. 26; 2. 39, 51; 4. 16; John 1. 45; 18. 5; Acts 2. 22; 3. 6.

Nazarites, năz′-ă-rītes, R. V. Nazirites (Heb. *nāzar*, 'to separate or consecrate,' whence *nāzīr*, 'a separated one'), were not a brotherhood, but individuals under a personal vow, some for life, as Samson, Samuel, John the Baptist; others for 30 to 60 days or even longer, referred to in Am. 2. 11, 12; Acts 21. 23-26. The vow was the outward symbol of consecration to God, expressed by abstinence from wine and strong drink, and by the hair being allowed to grow long. *See* Num. 6.

Neah, nē′-ăh, 'of a slope.' Jos. 19. 13.

Neapolis, nē-ăp′-ŏ-lĭs, 'new city.' Acts 16. 11; the seaport of Philippi, and the first place in Europe at which Paul touched; now Kavala.

Near. Jud. 20. 34, knew not evil was *n*. R. V. close upon.
Ps. 22. 11, trouble is *n*.
148. 14, a people *n*. to him.
Prov. 27. 10, better a neighbour that is *n*.
Isa. 50. 8, he is *n*. that justifieth.
55. 6, call upon the Lord while he is *n*.
Obad. 15; Zep. 1. 14, the day of the Lord is *n*.
Mat. 24. 33, it is *n*., even at the doors.
Mk. 13. 28, ye know that summer is *n*.
See Ezek. 11. 3; 22. 5; Rom. 13. 11.

Neariah, nē-ă-rī′-ăh, 'servant of Jehovah.' 1 Chr. 3. 22.

Nebai, nē-bā′-ī, 'fruitful.' Neh. 10. 19.

Nebaioth, nĕ-bāi′-ōth, 'high places.' 1 Chr. 1. 29.

Nebajoth, nĕ-bā′-jōth, same as Nebaioth. Gen. 25. 13.

Neballat, nĕ-băl′-lăt. Neh. 11. 34.

Nebat, nē′-băt, 'aspect.' 1 Kn. 11. 26.

Nebo, nē′-bō, 'the prophet.' (1) (Deu. 32. 49; 34. 1). One of the peaks of the Abarim mountains east of the Jordan opposite Jericho, either the same as Pisgah, or one peak of Mt. Pisgah. From its top Moses saw the Promised Land.
(2) (Isa. 46. 1). Babylonian city.
(3) (Num. 32. 3). a town in Moab.

Nebuchadnezzar, nĕb-ū-chăd-nĕz′-zär, same as the following. 2 Kn. 24. 1.
king of Babylon. Jer. 20.; 21.; 25.; 27.; 28.; 32.; 34.; Ezek. 26. 7; 29. 19.
captures Jerusalem. 2 Kn. 24.; 25.; 2 Chr. 36.; Jer. 37.-39.; 52.; Dan. 1. 1.
his dreams. Dan. 2.; 4.
sets up the golden image. Dan. 3.
his madness. Dan. 4. 33.
his restoration and confession. Dan. 4. 34.

Nebuchadrezzar, nĕb-ū-chăd-rĕz′-zär, 'Nebo protect the landmark.' Jer. 21. 2.

Nebushasban, nĕb-ū-shăs′-băn, 'Nebo will save me.' Jer. 39. 13.

Nebuzar-adan, nĕb-ū'-zär-ăd'-ăn, 'Nebo gives posterity.' 2 Kn. 25. 8.
his care of Jeremiah. Jer. 39. 11; 40. 1. [3. 14.
Necessary. Job 23. 12; Acts 15. 28; 28. 10; Tit.
Necessities. 2 Cor. 6. 4, as the ministers of God, in *n*.
Necessity. Rom. 12. 13, distributing to the *n*. of saints.
1 Cor. 9. 16, *n*. is laid upon me. [of *n*.
2 Cor. 9. 7; Philem. 14, give, not grudgingly, or
See Acts 20. 34; 2 Cor. 12. 10; Phil. 4. 16.
Necho, nē'-chō, 'conqueror' (?). Jer. 46. 2.
Nechoh, nē'-chōh, same as NECHO. 2 Kn. 23. 29.
Neck. Prov. 3. 3; 6. 21, bind them about thy *n*.
Mat. 18. 6; Mk. 9. 42; Lu. 17. 2, millstone about his *n*.
Lu. 15. 20; Acts 20. 37, fell on his *n*.
Acts 15. 10, yoke on the *n*. of disciples.
See Neh. 9. 29; Isa. 3. 16; Lam. 5. 5; Rom. 16. 4.
Necromancer, one who pretends to call up the dead for purposes of divination (Deu. 18. 11), as the witch of Endor (1 Sam. 28. 7). *See* DIVINATION.
Nedabiah, nĕd-ă-bī'-ăh, 'Jehovah is bountiful' (?). 1 Chr. 3. 18.
Need. 2 Chr. 20. 17, ye shall not *n*. to fight.
Prov. 31. 11, he shall have no *n*. of spoil. R. V. lack of gain.
Mat. 6. 8; Lu. 12. 30, what things ye have *n*. of.
9. 12; Mk. 2. 17; Lu. 5. 31, *n*. not a physician.
14. 16, they *n*. not depart. [them.
21. 3; Mk. 11. 3; Lu. 19. 31, 34, the Lord hath *n*. of
Lu. 11. 8, as many as he *n*.
Acts 2. 45; 4. 35, as every man had *n*.
1 Cor. 12. 21, cannot say, I have no *n*. of thee.
Phil. 4. 12, to abound and to suffer *n*.
4. 19, God shall supply all your *n*.
2 Tim. 2. 15, that *n*. not to be ashamed.
Heb. 4. 16, grace to help in time of *n*.
5. 12, ye have *n*. that one teach you.
1 John 3. 17, seeth his brother have *n*.
Rev. 3. 17, rich, and have *n*. of nothing.
21. 23; 22. 5, city had no *n*. of the sun.
See Deu. 15. 8; Lu. 9. 11; John 2. 25; Acts 17. 25.
Needful. Lu. 10. 42; Phil. 1. 24; Jas. 2. 16.
Needle. Mat. 19. 24; Mk. 10. 25; Lu. 18. 25.
Needlework. Ex. 26. 36; Jud. 5. 30; Ps. 45. 14.
Needs of necessity. Gen. 17. 13.
Needy. Deu. 15. 11, thou shalt open thine hand to thy *n*.
Job 24. 4, they turn the *n*. out of the way.
Ps. 9. 18, the *n*. shall not alway be forgotten.
40. 17; 70. 5; 86. 1; 109. 22, I am poor and *n*.
74. 21, let the poor and *n*. praise thy name.
Prov. 31. 9, plead the cause of the poor and *n*.
Isa. 41. 17, when the *n*. seek water.
See Ezek. 16. 49; 18. 12; 22. 29; Am. 8. 4, 6.
Neesing, an old form of sneezing. Job. 41. 18.
Neginah, nĕ-gī'-năh, 'a stringed instrument,' singular of NEGINOTH. Ps. 61., title.
Neginoth, On, nĕ-gī'-nōth, 'upon stringed instruments.' Ps. 4.; 54.; 55.; 76.; 77., title.
Neglect. Mat. 18. 17; Acts 6. 1; 1 Tim. 4. 14; Heb. 2. 3.
Negligent. 2 Chr. 29. 11; 2 Pet. 1. 12.
Nehelamite, nĕ-hĕl'-ă-mīte. Jer. 29. 24.
Nehemiah, nē-hĕm-ī'-ăh, 'Jehovah comforts.' (1) Ez. 2. 2. (2) Neh. 3. 16.
(3) son of Hachaliah.
his grief for Jerusalem. Neh. 1.
his prayer for. Neh. 1. 5.
his visit to. Neh. 2. 5, 9, 17.
his conduct at. Neh. 4.-6.; 8.-10.; 13.
Nehiloth, Upon, nē'-hĭ-lōth, Heb. *Nĕ-hī'-lōth*. Ps. 5., title. 'To the flutes,' or 'with flute accompaniment;' or 'to wind instruments.'
Nehum, nē'-hŭm, 'consolation.' Neh. 7. 7.
Nehushta, nĕ-hŭsh'-tă, 'bronze.' 2 Kn. 24. 8.
Nehushtan, nĕ-hŭsh'-tăn, 'brazen;' the brazen serpent of Moses, idolatrously used by Israelites, so called by Hezekiah, and destroyed by him. 2 Kn. 18. 4.

Neiel, neî'-ĕl, 'moved by God.' Jos. 19. 27.
Neighbour. Prov. 3. 28, say not to thy *n*., go and come again.
14. 20, the poor is hated even of his *n*.
21. 10, his *n*. findeth no favour.
Eccl. 4. 4, envied of his *n*.
Jer. 22. 13, that useth his *n*. service without wages.
Hab. 2. 15, that giveth his *n*. drink.
Zec. 8. 16; Eph. 4. 25, speak every man truth to his *n*.
Lu. 10. 29, who is my *n*.?
14. 12, call not thy rich *n*.
Neighbour, how to treat our. Ex. 20. 16; 22. 26; Lev. 19. 13, 18; Deu. 15. 2; 27. 17; Prov. 3. 28; 24. 28; 25. 8, 17; Mk. 12. 31; Rom. 13. 9, 10; Gal. 5. 14; Jas. 2. 8.
Nekeb, nē'-kĕb, 'cavern.' Jos. 19. 33.
Nekoda, nĕ-kō'-dă, 'a herdman.' Ez. 2. 48.
Nemuel, nĕm'-ū-ĕl, same as JEMUEL (?). (1) Num. 26. 9. (2) 1 Chr. 4. 24.
Nemuelites, nĕm-ū-ĕ'-lītes, descendants of Nemuel. Num. 26. 12.
Nepheg, nĕph'-ĕg, 'sprout.' (1) Ex. 6. 21. (2) 2 Sam. 5. 15.
Nephew, Lat. *Nepos*. A grandson. Jud. 12. 14; 1 Tim. 5. 4. This is the original meaning.
Nephish, nĕph'-ĭsh, same as NAPHISH. 1 Chr. 5. 19.
Nephishesim, nĕ-phĭsh'-ĕ-sĭm, 'expansions.' Neh. 7. 52.
Nephthalim, nĕph'-thă-lĭm, Greek form of NAPHTALI. Mat. 4. 13.
Nephtoah, nĕph-tō'-ăh, 'opened.' Jos. 15. 9.
Nephusim, nĕ-phū'-sĭm, a better form for NEPHISHESIM. Ez. 2. 50.
Nepthalim, nĕp'-thă-lĭm, same as NEPHTHALIM. Rev. 7. 6.
Ner, nĕr, 'lamp.' 1 Sam. 14. 50.
Nereus, nē'-reūs, 'liquid' (?). Rom. 16. 15.
Nergal, nĕr'-găl, the god of Kutha (2 Kn. 17. 30), has been identified in the Assyrian inscriptions as a lion-god.
Nergal-sharezer, nĕr'-găl-shă-rē'-zĕr, 'Nergal protect the king.' Jer. 39. 3.
Neri, nē'-rī, Greek form of NERIAH. Lu. 3. 27.
Neriah, nē-rī'-ăh, 'Jehovah is my lamp.' Jer. 32. 12.
Nest. Num. 24. 21, thou puttest thy *n*. in a rock.
Deu. 32. 11, as an eagle stirreth up her *n*.
Job 29. 18, I shall die in my *n*.
Ps. 84. 3, the swallow hath found a *n*.
Mat. 8. 20; Lu. 9. 58, birds of the air have *n*.
See Prov. 27. 8; Isa. 16. 2; Jer. 49. 16; Obad. 4.; Hab. 2. 9.
Net. Ps. 141. 10, let the wicked fall into their own *n*.
Prov. 1. 17, in vain the *n*. is spread.
Eccl. 9. 12, as fishes taken in an evil *n*.
Hab. 1. 16, they sacrifice unto their *n*.
Mat. 13. 47, kingdom of heaven like a *n*.
Mk. 1. 18, they forsook their *n*.
Lu. 5. 5, at thy word I will let down the *n*.
See Mat. 4. 21; Mk. 1. 16; John 21. 6.
Net, parable of. Mat. 13. 47. [Num. 1. 8.
Nethaneel, nĕth'-ă-nēel, same as NATHANAEL.
Nethaniah, nĕth-ă-nī'-ăh, 'Jehovah gave.' 2 Kn. 25. 23.
Nether, lower (comp. *be-neath*). Ex. 19. 17; Deu. 24. 6; Job 41. 24.
Nethermost, lowest of all. 1 Kn. 6. 6.
Nethinims, nĕth'-ĭ-nĭms. R. V. correctly Nethinim, 'the appointed' (1 Chr. 9. 2; Ez. 2. 58), were the descendants of those Gibeonites whom Joshua reduced to slavery, making them hewers of wood and drawers of water for the sanctuary (Jos. 9. 27). They were employed as servants in the drudgery of the temple. Ez. 2. 43; 7. 7, 24; 8. 17; Neh. 10. 28.
Netophah, nĕ-tō'-phăh, 'dropping.' Ez. 2. 22.
Netophathi, nĕ-tŏph'-ă-thī, an inhabitant of Netophah. Neh. 12. 28.
Netophathite, nĕ-tŏph'-ă-thīte, same as the preceding. 2 Sam. 23. 28.

Nettles. (1) (Isa. 34. 13). Heb. *Kimmôsh:* Gk. ἄκανθα, ὄλεθρος: Bot. N. *Urtica pilulifera.* The stinging nettles, twice translated 'thorns.'
(2) (Prov. 24. 31). Heb. *Ḥârûl:* Gk. φρύγανα ἄγρια: R. V. marg. 'wild vetches.' Probably a general term for weeds.
Never. Lev. 6. 13, the fire shall *n.* go out. R. V. not.
Job 3. 16, as infants which *n.* saw light.
Ps. 10. 11, he will *n.* see it.
15. 5; 30. 6, shall *n.* be moved.
Prov. 27. 20; 30. 15, *n.* satisfied.
Isa. 56. 11, which can *n.* have enough.
Mat. 7. 23, I *n.* knew you.
9. 33, it was *n.* so seen in Israel.
26. 33, yet will I *n.* be offended.
Mk. 2. 12, we *n.* saw it on this fashion.
3. 29, hath *n.* forgiveness.
14. 21, if he had *n.* been born. R. V. not.
John 4. 14; 6. 35, shall *n.* thirst.
7. 46, *n.* man spake like this man.
8. 51; 10. 28; 11. 26, shall *n.* see death.
1 Cor. 13. 8, charity *n.* faileth.
Heb. 13. 5, I will *n.* leave thee. R. V. in no wise.
2 Pet. 1. 10, ye shall *n.* fall.
See Jud. 2. 1; Ps. 58. 5; Jer. 33. 17; Dan. 2. 44.
New. Num. 16. 30, if the Lord make a *n.* thing.
Ps. 33. 3; 40. 3; 96. 1; 98. 1; 144. 9; 149. 1; Isa. 42. 10; Rev. 5. 9; 14. 3, a *n.* song.
Eccl. 1. 9; no *n.* thing under the sun.
Isa. 65. 17; 66. 22; Rev. 21. 1, *n.* heavens and *n.* earth.
Lam. 3. 23, *n.* every morning.
Mat. 9. 16; Mk. 2. 21; Lu. 5. 36, *n.* cloth to old garment. R. V. undressed.
13. 52, things *n.* and old.
Mk. 1. 27; Acts 17. 19, what *n.* doctrine is this?
John 13. 34; 1 John 2. 7, 8, a *n.* commandment.
Acts 17. 21, to tell or hear some *n.* thing.
2 Cor. 5. 17; Gal. 6. 15, a *n.* creature.
Eph. 2. 15; 4. 24; Col. 3. 10, *n.* man.
Heb. 10. 20, *n.* and living way.
Rev. 2. 17; 3. 12, a *n.* name.
21. 5, I make all things *n.*
See Isa. 24. 7; 43. 19; 65. 8; Acts 2. 13.
New birth (born again), John 3. 3, 6; 1 Pet. 1. 23.
Newly. Deu. 32. 17; Jud. 7. 19.
Newness. Rom. 6. 4; 7. 6.
News. Prov. 25. 25.
Neziah, nĕ-zī'-ăh, 'illustrious.' Ez. 2. 54.
Nezib, nĕz'-ĭb, 'garrison.' Jos. 15. 43.
Nibhaz, nĭb'-hăz. 2 Kn. 17. 31.
Nibshan, nĭb'-shăn, 'level' (?). Jos. 15. 62.
Nicanor, nī-cā'-nŏr, one of the seven deacons. Acts 6. 5.
Nicodemus, nĭc-ŏ-dē'-mŭs, Pharisee and ruler; goes to Jesus by night. John 3. 1.
takes His part. John 7. 50.
assists at Christ's burial. John 19. 39.
Nicolaitanes, nĭc-ō-lā-ī'-tānes, named after Nicolas. Rev. 2. 6.
Nicolas, nĭc'-ŏ-lăs. Acts 6. 5.
Nicopolis, nī-cŏp'-ŏ-lĭs, 'city of victory.' Tit. 3. 12.
Niger, nī'-gĕr, 'black.' Acts 13. 1.
Nigh. Num. 24. 17, but not *n.*
Deu. 30. 14; Rom. 10. 8, the word is *n.* unto thee.
Ps. 34. 18, *n.* to them of broken heart.
145. 18, *n.* to all that call upon him.
Eph. 2. 13, made *n.* by the blood of Christ.
See Joel 2. 1; Lu. 21. 20; Heb. 6. 8.
Night. Ex. 12. 42, a *n.* to be much observed.
Job 7. 4, when shall I arise, and the *n.* be gone?
35. 10; Ps. 77. 6, songs in the *n.*
Ps. 30. 5, weeping may endure for a *n.*
91. 5, the terror by *n.*
136. 9; Jer. 31. 35, moon and stars to rule by *n.*
139. 11, the *n.* shall be light about me.
Isa. 21. 4, the *n.* of my pleasure. R. V. twilight.
21. 11, watchman, what of the *n.*?
Lu. 6. 12, he continued all *n.* in prayer.
John 9. 4, the *n.* cometh, when no man can work.
11. 10, walk in the *n.*, he stumbleth.
Rom. 13. 12, the *n.* is far spent.
1 Thes. 5. 2; 2 Pet. 3. 10, cometh as a thief in the *n.*
Rev. 21. 25; 22. 5, no *n.* there.
Night. Gen. 1. 5; Job 7. 3; Ps. 121. 6; 19. 2; Mat. 27. 64; John 3. 2. figurative, John 9. 4; Rom. 13. 12; 1 Thes. 5. 5. none in heaven, Rev. 21. 25 (Isa. 60. 20).
Night, divisions of. *See* DAY.
Nimrah, nĭm'-răh, 'panther.' Num. 32. 3.
Nimrim, nĭm'-rĭm. Isa. 15. 6.
Nimrod, nĭm'-rŏd, 'an inhabitant of Marad' (?); mighty hunter. Gen. 10. 8, 9.
Nimshi, nĭm'-shī, 'discloser' (?). 1 Kn. 19. 16.
Nineve, nĭn'-ĕ-vē, same as NINEVEH. Lu. 11. 32.
Nineveh, nĭn'-ĕ-vĕh, 'dwelling' (?). The capital of Assyria. Built on the river Tigris by Nimrod (Gen. 10. 11; Jon. 4. 11). A very great city at one time, it was destroyed in 606 B. C. so thoroughly that when Xenophon passed the spot, all recollection of the place had disappeared. Within a century the ruins have been discovered, and from the remains of the old royal libraries there found, a great deal of information has been gained concerning the past.
Jonah's mission to. Jon. 1. 1; 3. 2.
denounced by Jonah. Jon. 3. 4.
repenting, is spared by God. Jon. 3. 5-10 (Mat. 12. 41; Lu. 11. 32).
the burden of. Nah. 1. 1; 2.; 3. [Lu. 11. 30.
Ninevites, nĭn'-ĕ-vītes, inhabitants of Nineveh.
Nisan, nī'-săn. Neh. 2. 1; Esth. 3. 7, the same as Abib, the first month of the Jewish sacred year = April. *See* MONTHS.
Nisroch, nĭs'-rŏch, 'eagle' (?). 2 Kn. 19. 37; Isa. 37. 38.
Nitre (Prov. 25. 20; Jer. 2. 22). Heb. *Nĕther:* Gk. νίτρον: R. V. 'lye.' Natron = carbonate of soda; not the modern nitre, which = saltpetre.
No, nō, 'abode' (?), Nah. 3. 8. multitude of, threatened, Jer. 46. 25; Ezek. 30. 14.
Noadiah, nō-ă-dī'-ăh, 'Jehovah meets.' (1) Ez. 8. 33. (2) Neh. 6. 14.
Noah, nō'-ăh. (1) 'rest;' son of Lamech. Gen. 5. 29.
finds grace with God. Gen. 6. 8.
ordered to build the ark. Gen. 6. 14.
with his family and living creatures enters into the ark. Gen. 7.
flood assuaging, goes forth. Gen. 8. 18.
God blesses and makes a covenant with. Gen. 9. 1, 8.
is drunken, and mocked of Ham. Gen. 9. 22.
his death. Gen. 9. 29.
(2) 'wandering.' Num. 26. 33.
No Amon, nō ā'-mŏn, 'abode of Amon' (i. e., 'the hidden one'). Jer. 46. 25 (marg.).
Nob, nŏb, 'high place,' city of; David comes to, and eats hallowed bread at. 1 Sam. 21. 1.
smitten by Saul. 1 Sam. 22. 19.
Nobah, nō'-băh, 'a barking.' (1) Num. 32. 42. (2) Jud. 8. 11.
Noble. Neh. 3. 5, the *n.* put not their neck.
Job 29. 10, the *n.* held their peace.
Jer. 2. 21, planted thee a *n.* vine.
14. 3, their *n.* sent their little ones to the waters.
Acts 17. 11, Bereans were more *n.*
1 Cor. 1. 26, not many *n.*
See Num. 21. 18; Ps. 149. 8; Eccl. 10. 17.
Nod, nŏd, 'flight,' 'wandering.' Gen. 4. 16.
Nodab, nō'-dăb, 'nobility.' 1 Chr. 5. 19.
Noe, nō'-ē, Greek form of NOAH. Mat. 24. 37.
Nogah, nō'-gäh, 'brightness.' 1 Chr. 3. 7.
Nohah, nō'-häh, 'rest.' 1 Chr. 8. 2.
Noise. Ez. 3. 13, not discern *n.* of joy.
Ps. 66. 1; 81. 1; 95. 1; 98. 4; 100. 1, joyful *n.*
Ezek. 1. 24; 43. 2, *n.* of great waters.
2 Pet. 3. 10, pass away with great *n.*
See Jos. 6. 27; Mat. 9. 23; Mk. 2. 1.
Noise abroad, to spread a report everywhere. Lu. 1. 65; Acts 2. 6.
Noisome, noxious, hurtful. Ps. 91. 3; Ezek. 14. 21; Rev. 16. 2.
Non, nŏn, same as NUN. 1 Chr. 7. 27.
Noonday. Deu. 28. 29; Job 11. 17; Ps. 37. 6.

Noph, nŏph, same as MEMPHIS; city, warned, Isa. 19. 13; Jer. 2. 16; 46. 14; Ezek. 30. 13.
Nophah, nō'-phăh, 'windy.' Num. 21. 30.
North and south, conflicts of. Dan. 11.
Nose. Ps. 115. 6; Prov. 30. 33; Isa. 3. 21.
Nostrils. Gen. 2. 7; Job 4. 9; Isa. 2. 22.
Note. Isa. 30. 8; 2 Thes. 3. 14; Rom. 16. 7. [n.
Nothing. Deu. 2. 7; Neh. 9. 21, thou hast lacked
2 Sam. 24. 24, neither offer of that which doth cost *n*.
2 Chr. 14, 11, it is *n*. with thee to help. R. V. there is none beside thee. [pared.
Neh. 8. 10, portions to them for whom *n*. is pre-
Job 8. 9, but of yesterday, and know *n*.
Ps. 49. 17, he shall carry *n*. away.
119. 165, *n*. shall offend them.
Prov. 13. 4, the sluggard desireth, and hath *n*.
13. 7, there is that maketh himself rich, yet hath *n*.
Lam. 1. 12, is it *n*. to you?
Mat. 17. 20; Lu. 1. 37, *n*. shall be impossible.
21. 19; Mk. 11. 13, *n*. but leaves. [spairing.
Lu. 6. 35, hoping for *n*. again. R. V. never de-
7. 42, they had *n*. to pay.
John 15. 5, without me ye can do *n*.
1 Cor. 4. 4, I know *n*. by myself.
2 Cor. 6. 10, as having *n*.
13. 8, we can do *n*. against the truth.
1 Tim. 4. 4, *n*. to be refused.
6. 7, brought *n*. into this world, can carry *n*. out.
See Phil. 4. 6; Jas. 1. 4; 3 John 7.
Nothing, in no degree, not at all. Jas. 1. 6.
Nourish. Isa. 1. 2, I have *n*. and brought up children.
1 Tim. 4. 6, *n*. in words of faith.
Jas. 5. 5, have *n*. your hearts.
See Gen. 45. 11; 50. 21; Acts 12. 20; Col. 2. 19.
Novice, 'newly arrived,' one newly admitted into the Christian body. 1 Tim. 3. 6.
Now. Job 4. 5, *n*. it is come upon thee.
Ps. 119. 67, but *n*. have I kept thy word.
Hos. 2. 7, then was it better than *n*.
Lu. 14. 17, all things are *n*. ready.
John 13. 7, thou knowest not *n*.
16. 12, ye cannot bear them *n*.
1 Cor. 13. 12, *n*. I know in part.
Gal. 2. 20, the life I *n*. live.
1 Tim. 4. 8, the life that *n*. is.
1 Pet. 1. 8, though *n*. ye see him not.
1 John 3. 2, *n*. are we sons of God.
See Rom. 6. 22; Gal. 3. 3; Heb. 2. 8. [without *n*.
Number (*n*.). Job 5. 9; 9. 10, marvellous things
25. 3, is there any *n*. of his armies?
Ps. 139. 18, more in *n*. than the sand.
147. 4, he telleth the *n*. of the stars.
Acts 11. 21, a great *n*. believed.
16. 5, the churches increased in *n*. daily.
Rev. 13. 17, 18, the *n*. of his name.
See Deu. 7. 7; Hos. 1. 10; Rom. 9. 27. [left *n*.
Number (*v*.). Gen. 41. 49, gathered corn till he
2 Sam. 24. 2; 1 Chr. 21. 2, *n*. the people.
Ps. 90. 12, so teach us to *n*. our days.
Eccl. 1. 15, that which is wanting cannot be *n*.
Isa. 53. 12; Mk. 15. 28, he was *n*. with transgressors.
Mat. 10. 30; Lu. 12. 7, hairs are all *n*.
Rev. 7. 9, multitude which no man could *n*.
See Ex. 30. 12; Job 14. 16; Ps. 40. 5; Acts 1. 17.
Numbering of the people: by Moses, Num. 1. 18; 26. 4. by David, 2 Sam. 24.; 1 Chr. 21.
of the Levites. Num. 3. 15; 4. 34; 26. 57.
Nun, nŭn, 'fish.' Ex. 33. 11.
Nurse. Gen. 35. 8, Deborah Rebekah's *n*. died.
2 Sam. 4. 4, and his *n*. took him up and fled.
1 Thes. 2. 7, even as a *n*. cherisheth her children.
See Ex. 2. 7, 9; Isa. 60. 4.
Nursing. Isa. 49. 23, kings shall be thy *n*. fathers, and their queens thy *n*. mothers.
Nurture, education, training, discipline. Eph. 6. 4. R. V. chastening.
Nuts. (1) (S. of S. 6. 11). Heb. *Egôz:* Gk. *καρύα*: Bot. N. *Juglans regia*, probably the walnut.
(2) (Gen. 43. 11). Heb. *Botnîm:* Gk. *τερέβινθος*: Bot. N. *Pistacia vera:* R. V. marg. correctly, 'pistachio nuts.'
Nymphas, nўm'-phăs, shortened form of Nymphodorus. Col. 4. 15.

Oak. (1) (Gen. 35. 8; Jos. 24. 26). Heb. *Allâh, allôn:* Gk. *δρῦς, βάλανος, τερέβινθος*: Bot. N. *Quercus pseudococcifera* and *Quercus ægilops*. The common oak.
(2) (Isa. 1. 29; Gen. 35. 4; Deu. 11. 30, R. V.). Heb. *El, êlah, êlôn, ûlan*. The terebinth, a tree of the general appearance of the oak.
Oar. Isa. 33. 21; Ezek. 27. 6, 29.
Oath, God ratifies his purpose by. Ps. 132. 11; Lu. 1. 73; Acts 2. 30; Heb. 6. 17.
of the forty Jews. Acts 23. 12, 21.
Oaths, directions about. Lev. 5. 4; 6. 3; 19. 12; Num. 30. 2; Ps. 15. 4; Mat. 5. 33; Jas. 5. 12.
examples of. Gen. 14. 22; 21. 31; 24. 2; Jos. 14. 9; 1 Sam. 20. 42; 28. 10; Ps. 132. 2.
demanded. Ex. 22. 11; Num. 5. 21; 1 Kn. 8. 31; Ez. 10. 5.
rash: of Esau. Gen. 25. 33.
Israel to the Gibeonites. Jos. 9. 19.
Jephthah. Jud. 11. 30.
Saul at Beth-aven. 1 Sam. 14. 24.
Herod to Herodias' daughter. Mat. 14. 7.
Obadiah, ō-bă-dī'-ăh, 'worshipper of Jehovah.'
(1) prophet, his prediction. Obad. 1–21.
(2) Levite, porter in the temple. Neh. 12. 25.
(3) sent by Ahab to find water. 1 Kn. 18. 3.
meets Elijah. 1 Kn. 18. 7.
how he hid a hundred prophets. 1 Kn. 18. 4, 13.
(4) others. 1 Chr. 7. 3; 8. 38; 9. 16; 12. 9; 27. 19; 2 Chr. 17. 7; 34. 12; Ez. 8. 9.
Obal, ō'-băl, 'hill' (?). Gen. 10. 28.
Obed, ō'-bĕd, 'worshipping' (God). (1) Ru. 4. 17.
(2) others. 1 Chr. 2. 37; 11. 47; 26. 7; 2 Chr. 23. 1.
Obed-edom, ō'-bĕd-ē'-dom, 'serving Edom.' (1) prospered while taking charge of the ark. 2 Sam. 6. 10; 1 Chr. 13. 14; 15. 18, 24; 16. 5.
his sons. 1 Chr. 26. 4, 5
(2) others. 1 Chr. 15. 18; 16. 5, 38; 2 Chr. 25. 34.
Obedience. Rom. 5. 19, by the *o*. of one.
16. 26, the *o*. of faith.
Heb. 5. 8, yet learned he *o*. [Heb. 5. 8.
Obedience of CHRIST. Rom. 5. 19; Phil. 2. 8;
Obedience to God enjoined. Ex. 19. 5; 23. 21; Lev. 26. 3; Deu. 4.-8.; 11.; 29.; Isa. 1. 19; Jer. 7. 23; 26. 13; 38. 20; Acts 5. 29; Jas. 1. 25.
its blessings. Ex. 23. 22; Deu. 28.; 30.; Prov. 25. 12; Isa. 1. 19; Heb. 11. 8; 1 Pet. 1. 22; Rev. 22. 14.
preferred before sacrifice. 1 Sam. 15. 22; Ps. 50. 8; Mic. 6. 6.
to the faith. Rom. 1. 5; 16. 19, 26; 2 Cor. 7. 15; 10. 5; 1 Pet. 1. 2.
of children to parents. Eph. 6. 1; Col. 3. 20.
to masters. Eph. 6. 5; Col. 3. 22; Tit. 2. 9.
of wives to husbands. Tit. 2. 5. [13. 17.
of people to rulers. Num. 27. 20; Tit. 3. 1; Heb.
Obedient. Ex. 24. 7, all will we do, and be *o*.
Prov. 25. 12, wise reprover upon an *o*. ear.
Isa. 1. 19, if *o*. ye shall eat.
2 Cor. 2. 9, *o*. in all things.
Eph. 6. 5; Tit. 2. 9, be *o*. to your masters.
Phil. 2. 8, *o*. unto death.
1 Pet. 1. 14, as *o*. children.
Obeisance (Gen. 37. 7; 43. 28; 2 Sam. 15. 5) was the salutation of an inferior to a superior. It consisted of bowing the head and body forward, with the hands extended, and their palms turned downwards.
Obey. Deu. 11. 27, a blessing if ye *o*. R. V. hearken to.
Jos. 24. 24, his voice will we *o*. R. V. hearken.
1 Sam. 15. 22, to *o*. is better than sacrifice.
Jer. 7. 23, *o*. my voice, and I will be your God.
Acts 5. 29, we ought to *o*. God rather than men.
Rom. 6. 16, his servants ye are to whom ye *o*.
Eph. 6. 1; Col. 3. 20, *o*. your parents in the Lord.
2 Thes. 1. 8; 1 Pet. 4. 17, that *o*. not the gospel.

Heb. 13. 17, *o.* them that have rule over you.
1 Pet. 1. 22, purified your souls in *o.* the truth.
See Ex. 5. 2; 23. 21; Dan. 9. 10; Mat. 8. 27.
Obil, ō'-bĭl, 'camel-driver.' 1 Chr. 27. 30.
Object. Acts 24. 19. R. V. make accusation.
Oblations, offerings (in sacrifice). Lev. 2.; 3.; 7. 38.
of the spoil. Num. 31. 28.
Oboth, ō'-bōth, 'water-skins.' Num. 21. 10.
Obscure. Prov. 20. 20.
Obscurity. Isa. 29. 18; 58. 10; 59. 9.
Observation. Lu. 17. 20.
Observe. Gen. 37. 11, his father *o.* the saying. R. V. kept in mind.
Ps. 107. 43, whoso is wise, and will *o.* these things. R. V. give heed to.
Prov. 23. 26, let thine eyes *o.* my ways. R. V. delight in.
Eccl. 11. 4, he that *o.* the wind.
Jon. 2. 8, that *o.* lying vanities. R. V. regard.
Mat. 28. 20, teaching them to *o.* all things.
Mk. 6. 20, Herod feared John, and *o.* him. R. V. kept him safe.
10. 20, all these have I *o.*
See Ex. 12. 42; 31. 16; Ezek. 20. 18; Gal. 4. 10.
Observer. Deu. 18. 10.
Obstinate. Deu. 2. 30; Isa. 48. 4.
Obtain. Prov. 8. 35, shall *o.* favour of the Lord.
Isa. 35. 10; 51. 11, shall *o.* joy and gladness.
Lu. 20. 35, worthy to *o.* that world. R. V. attain to.
Acts 26. 22, having *o.* help of God.
1 Cor. 9. 24, so run that ye may *o.* R. V. attain.
1 Thes. 5. 9; 2 Tim. 2. 10, to *o.* salvation.
1 Tim. 1. 13, I *o.* mercy. [V. receive.
Heb. 4. 16; *o.* mercy, and find grace to help. R.
9. 12, having *o.* eternal redemption. [have *o.*
1 Pet. 2. 10, which had not *o.* mercy, but now
2 Pet. 1. 1, *o.* like precious faith.
See Dan. 11. 21; Hos. 2. 23; Acts 1. 17; 22. 28.
Occasion. 2 Sam. 12. 14, great *o.* to enemies to blaspheme.
Dan. 6. 4, sought to find *o.*
Rom. 7. 8, sin, taking *o.* by the commandment.
14. 13, an *o.* to fall in his brother's way.
1 Tim. 5. 14, give none *o.* to the adversary.
See Gen. 43. 18; Ez. 7. 20; Ezek. 18. 3. [19. 25.
Occupation. Gen. 46. 33; Jon. 1. 8; Acts 18. 3;
Occupier, a trader. Ezek. 27. 27.
Occupy, to take possession, to make use of. Ezek. 27. 9; Lu. 19. 13.
Occurrent, a person or thing that comes against another; occurrence. 1 Kn. 5. 4.
Ochim, ō'-chĭm, 'jackals.' Isa. 13. 21 (marg.).
Ocran, ŏc'-răn, 'troublesome.' Num. 1. 13.
Oded, ō'-dĕd, 'setting up' (?). (1) prophet. 2 Chr. 28. 9.
(2) father of prophet Azariah. 2 Chr. 15. 1.
Odour. John 12. 3; Phil. 4. 18; Rev. 5. 8.
Of, used in various senses. (1) instead of 'by.' Mk. 1. 9.
(2) for 'concerning.' Acts 13. 29.
(3) 'out of' or 'from.' 1 Cor. 15. 47.
Offence. (1) that against which one stumbles. Isa. 8. 14; Rom. 9. 33; 1 Pet. 2. 8, a rock of *o.*
Mat. 16. 23, thou art an *o.* to me. R. V. stumblingblock.
18. 7; Lu. 17. 1, woe to the world because of *o.*! R. V. occasions of stumbling.
1 Cor. 10. 32; 2 Cor. 6. 3, give none *o.* R. V. occasion of stumbling.
(2) Eccl. 10. 4, yielding pacifieth great *o.*
Acts 24. 16, conscience void of *o.*
Rom. 14. 20, that man who eateth with *o.*
Phil. 1. 10, without *o.* till the day of Christ.
See 1 Sam. 25. 31; Rom. 5. 15; Gal. 5. 11.
Offence, giving of, deprecated. 1 Cor. 10. 32; 2 Cor. 6. 3; Phil. 1. 10.
Offences, woe because of. Mat. 18. 7.
how to remedy. Eccl. 10. 4; Mat. 5. 29; 18. 8; Mk. 9. 43; Rom. 16. 17.
Christ was delivered for our. Rom. 4. 25.

Offend. (1) to cause to stumble, make to sin. Ps. 119. 165, nothing shall *o.* them. R. V. none occasion of stumbling.
Mat. 5. 29; 18. 9; Mk. 9. 47, if thine eye *o.* thee. R. V. cause thee to stumble.
13. 41, gather all things that *o.* R. V. cause stumbling.
13. 57; Mk. 6. 3, they were *o.* in him.
26. 33, though all shall be *o.*, yet will I never be.
Rom. 14. 21, whereby thy brother is *o.* R. V. omits.
(2) Job 34. 31, I will not *o.* any more.
Prov. 18. 19, brother *o.* is harder to be won.
Jas. 2. 10, yet *o.* in one point. R. V. stumbleth.
See Gen. 20. 9; Jer. 37. 18. R. V. sinned against.
Offender. 1 Kn. 1. 21; Isa. 29. 21; Acts 25. 11.
Offer. Jud. 5. 2, people willingly *o.* themselves.
Ps. 50. 23, whoso *o.* praise.
Mat. 5. 24, then come and *o.* thy gift.
Lu. 6. 29, one cheek, *o.* also the other.
1 Cor. 8. 1, 4, 7; 10. 19, things *o.* to idols.
Phil. 2. 17, *o.* in the service of your faith.
2 Tim. 4. 6, now ready to be *o.*
Heb. 9. 28, Christ once *o.* to bear the sins of many.
See 2 Chr. 17. 16; Ez. 1. 6; 2. 68; Mal. 1. 8.
Offering (of Christ). Heb. 9. 14, 28; 10. 10, 12, 14.
Offerings for the Altar.
(1) Burnt offerings, expressing consecration to God, a means of worship.
(2) Peace offerings.
i. Thanksgiving.
ii. In payment of vows.
iii. Freewill, expressing love to God.
(3) Incense offerings, expressing and aiding worship.
Each of these was accompanied by:
i. a meal offering.
ii. a drink offering.
(4) Sin offerings.
i. Sin offerings for wrongs the effect of which terminates primarily on the sinner.
ii. Trespass offerings for wrongs to others.
These were aids to, and expressions of, repentance, showing the evil of sin against God, and the need of atonement, and the assurance of forgiveness.
Offerings, laws for. Lev. 1.; 22. 21; Deu. 15. 21; Mal. 1. 13.
Office. 1 Sam. 2. 36, put me into one of the priests' *o.*
Rom. 11. 13, I magnify mine *o.* R. V. ministry.
1 Tim. 3. 1, the *o.* of a bishop.
Heb. 7. 5, the *o.* of the priesthood.
See Gen. 41. 13; Ps. 109. 8; Rom. 12. 4.
Offscouring. Lam. 3. 45; 1 Cor. 4. 13.
Offspring. Job 27. 14; Acts 17. 28; Rev. 22. 16.
Often. Prov. 29. 1, being *o.* reproved.
Mal. 3. 16, spake *o.* one to another. R. V. omits.
Mat. 23. 37; Lu. 13. 34, how *o.* would I have gathered.
1 Cor. 11. 26, as *o.* as ye eat.
1 Tim. 5. 23, thine *o.* infirmities.
See 2 Cor. 11. 26; Heb. 9. 25; 10. 11.
Og, ŏg, 'circle' (?); king of Bashan. Num. 21. 33; Deu. 3. 1; Ps. 135. 11; 136. 20.
Ohad, ō'-hăd, 'might' (?). Gen. 46. 10.
Ohel, ō'-hĕl, 'tent.' 1 Chr. 3. 20.
Oil. Ps. 45. 7; Heb. 1. 9, with *o.* of gladness.
92. 10, be anointed with fresh *o.*
104. 15, *o.* to make his face to shine.
Isa. 61. 3, *o.* of joy for mourning.
Mat. 25. 3, took no *o.* with them.
Lu. 10. 34, pouring in *o.* and wine.
Oil for lamps. Ex. 27. 20; Lev. 24. 1.
for anointing. Ex. 30. 31; 37. 29; Lu. 7. 46.
used in meat offerings. Lev. 2. 1; Mic. 6. 7.
miracles of. 1 Kn. 17. 12; 2 Kn. 4. 1.
figurative. Ps. 23. 5; 141. 5; Isa. 61. 3; Zec. 4. 12; Mat. 25. 1.
Oil tree (Isa. 41. 19). Heb. *'Etz Shémen:* Gk. *ξύλα κυπαρίσσινα*: Bot. N. *Eleagnus angustifolia.* R. V. marg. 'oleaster.' The Heb. means

'oily trees,' or 'trees of oil.' It occurs three times, each with a different translation. 1 Kn. 6. 33, 'olive tree.' Neh. 8. 15, A. V. 'pine,' R. V. 'wild olive.' Isa. 41. 19, 'oil tree.' The only translation that meets all the conditions referred to in the Bible is 'fat wood trees,' or 'oil trees,' i. e., resinous trees, referring to the pine.

Ointment, Christ anointed with. Mat. 26. 7; Mk. 14. 3; Lu. 7. 37; John 11. 2; 12. 3.

Old. Deu. 8. 4; 29. 5; Neh. 9. 21, waxed not *o.*
Jos. 5. 11, did eat of the *o.* corn.
Ps. 37. 25, I have been young, and now am *o.*
71. 18, when I am *o.* forsake me not.
Prov. 22. 6, when he is *o.* he will not.
Isa. 58. 12, build the *o.* waste places.
Jer. 6. 16, ask for the *o.* paths.
Lu. 5. 39, he saith, the *o.* is better.
2 Cor. 5. 17, *o.* things are passed away.
2 Pet. 2. 5, God spared not the *o.* world. R. V. ancient.
1 John 2. 7, the *o.* commandment is the word.
Rev. 12. 9; 20. 2, that *o.* serpent.
See Job 22. 15; Ps. 77. 5; Mat. 5. 21; Rom. 7. 6.

Old age. Job 30. 2; Ps. 90. 10; Eccl. 12.; Tit. 2. 2. reverence due to. Lev. 19. 32; Prov. 23. 22; 1 Tim. 5. 1.

Old man, to put off. Rom. 6. 6; Eph. 4. 22; Col. 3. 9.

Old prophet, the. 1 Kn. 13. 11.

Old Testament Quotations in N. T.

Matthew.

Behold, a virgin shall be with child	1. 23. — Isa. 7. 14.
Thou Bethlehem, in the land of Juda	2. 6. — Mic. 5. 2.
Out of Egypt have I called my son	2. 15. — Hos. 11. 1.
In Rama was there a voice heard	2. 18. — Jer. 31. 15.
The voice of one crying in the wilderness	3. 3. — Isa. 40. 3.
Man shall not live by bread alone	4. 4. — Deu. 8. 3.
He shall give his angels charge	4. 6. — Ps. 91. 11, 12.
Thou shall not tempt the Lord	4. 7. — Deu. 6. 16.
Thou shalt worship the Lord thy God	4. 10. — Deu. 6. 13.
The land of Zabulon, and the land of Nephthalim	4. 15, 16. — Isa. 9. 1, 2; 42. 7.
Thou shalt not kill	5. 21. — Ex. 20. 13.
Thou shalt not commit adultery	5. 27. — Ex. 20. 14.
Whosoever shall put away his wife	5. 31. — Deu. 24. 1.
Thou shalt not forswear thyself	5. 33. — Lev. 19. 12.
An eye for an eye, and a tooth for a tooth	5. 38. — Ex. 21. 24.
Thou shalt love thy neighbour	5. 43. — Lev. 19. 18.
Be ye therefore perfect	5. 48. — Gen. 17. 1.
Depart . . . ye that work iniquity	7. 23. — Ps. 6. 8.
Himself took our infirmities	8. 17. — Isa. 53. 4.
I will have mercy, and not sacrifice	9. 13; 12. 7. — Hos. 6. 6.
Behold, I send my messenger	11. 10. — Mal. 3. 1.
Behold my servant, whom I have chosen	12. 18–21. — Isa. 42. 1–4.
By hearing ye shall hear, and shall not understand	13. 14, 15. — Isa. 6. 9, 10.
I will open my mouth in parables	13. 35. — Ps. 78. 2.
Honour thy father and mother	15. 4. — Ex. 20. 12.
He that curseth father or mother	15. 4. — Ex. 21. 17.
This people draweth nigh unto me	15. 8, 9. — Isa. 29. 13.
He . . . made them male and female	19. 4. — Gen. 1. 27.
For this cause shall a man leave father and mother	19. 5. — Gen. 2. 24.
Thou shalt do no murder	19. 18. — Ex. 20. 13.
Honour thy father and thy mother	19. 19. — Ex. 20. 12.
Thou shalt love thy neighbour as thyself	19. 19. — Lev. 19. 18.
Tell ye the daughter of Sion, Behold, thy King cometh	21. 5. — Isa. 62. 11; Zec. 9. 9.
Blessed is he that cometh in the name of the Lord	21. 9. — Ps. 118. 26.
My house shall be called the house of prayer	21. 13. — Isa. 56. 7.
Ye have made it a den of thieves	21. 13. — Jer. 7. 11.
Out of the mouth of babes	21. 16. — Ps. 8. 2.
The stone which the builders rejected	21. 42. — Ps. 118. 22, 23.
If a man die, having no children	22. 24. — Deu. 25. 5.
I am the God of Abraham	22. 32. — Ex. 3. 6.
Thou shalt love the Lord thy God	22. 37. — Deu. 6. 5.
Thou shalt love thy neighbour as thyself	22. 39. — Lev. 19. 18.
The Lord said . . . Sit thou on my right hand	22. 44. — Ps. 110. 1.
Blessed is he that cometh in the name of the Lord	23. 39. — Ps. 118. 26.
I will smite the shepherd	26. 31. — Zec. 13. 7.
And they took the thirty pieces of silver	27. 9, 10. — Zec. 11. 12, 13.
They parted my garments	27. 35. — Ps. 22. 18.
My God, my God, why hast thou forsaken me?	27. 46. — Ps. 22. 1.

Mark.

Behold, I send my messenger	1. 2. — Mal. 3. 1.
Prepare ye the way of the Lord	1. 3. — Isa. 40. 3.
Seeing they may see, and not perceive	4. 12. — Isa. 6. 9, 10.
This people honoureth me with their lips	7. 6, 7. — Isa. 29. 13.
Honour thy father and thy mother	7. 10. — Ex. 20. 12.

Whoso curseth father or mother	7. 10. — Ex. 21. 17.
Where their worm dieth not	9. 44. — Isa. 66. 24.
God made them male and female	10. 6. — Gen. 1. 27.
They twain shall be one flesh	10. 7, 8. — Gen. 2. 24.
Do not commit adultery, Do not kill	10. 19. — Ex. 20. 13, 14.
Hosanna; Blessed is he that cometh	11. 9. — Ps. 118. 26.
My house shall be called the house of prayer	11. 17. — Isa. 56. 7.
Ye have made it a den of thieves	11. 17. — Jer. 7. 11.
The stone which the builders rejected	12. 10, 11. — Ps. 118. 22, 23.
If a man's brother die, and leave no children	12. 19. — Deu. 25. 5.
I am the God of Abraham	12. 26. — Ex. 3. 6.
The Lord our God is one Lord	12. 29. — Deu. 6. 4.
Thou shalt love the Lord thy God	12. 30. — Deu. 6. 5.
Thou shalt love thy neighbour	12. 31. — Lev. 19. 18.
The Lord said to my Lord, Sit thou on my right hand	12. 36. — Ps. 110. 1.
I will smite the shepherd	14. 27. — Zec. 13. 7.
He was numbered with the transgressors	15. 28. — Isa. 53. 12.
My God, my God, why hast thou forsaken me?	15. 34. — Ps. 22. 1.

Luke.

To turn the hearts of the fathers	1. 17. — Mal. 4. 6.
Every male that openeth the womb	2. 23. — Ex. 13. 2, 12.
A pair of turtle doves, &c	2. 24. — Lev. 12. 8.
The voice of one crying in the wilderness	3. 4–6. — Isa. 40. 3–5.
Man shall not live by bread alone	4. 4. — Deu. 8. 3.
Thou shalt worship the Lord thy God	4. 8. — Deu. 6. 13.
He shall give his angels charge over thee	4. 10, 11. — Ps. 91. 11, 12.
Thou shalt not tempt the Lord thy God	4. 12. — Deu. 6. 16.
The Spirit of the Lord is upon me	4. 18, 19. — Isa. 61. 1, 2; 58. 6.
Behold, I send my messenger	7. 27. — Mal. 3. 1.
That seeing they might not see	8. 10. — Isa. 6. 9.
Thou shalt love the Lord thy God	10. 27. — Deu. 6. 5; Lev. 19. 18.
And thy neighbour as thyself	10. 27. — Lev. 19. 18.
Blessed is he that cometh in the name of the Lord	13. 35. — Ps. 118. 26.
Do not commit adultery, Do not kill	18. 20. — Ex. 20. 12–16.
My house is the house of prayer	19. 46. — Isa. 56. 7.
Ye have made it a den of thieves	19. 46. — Jer. 7. 11.
The stone which the builders rejected	20. 17. — Ps. 118. 22, 23.
If a man's brother die, having a wife	20. 28. — Deu. 25. 5.
The Lord said unto my Lord, Sit thou on my right hand	20. 42, 43. — Ps. 110. 1.
He was reckoned among the transgressors	22. 37. — Isa. 53. 12.
Say to the mountains, Fall on us	23. 30. — Hos. 10. 8.
Into thy hands I commend my spirit	23. 46. — Ps. 31. 5.

John.

The voice of one crying in the wilderness	1. 23. — Isa. 40. 3.
The zeal of thine house hath eaten me up	2. 17. — Ps. 69. 9.
He gave them bread from heaven	6. 31. — Ps. 78. 24.
They shall be all taught of God	6. 45. — Isa. 54. 13.
I said, Ye are gods	10. 34. — Ps. 82. 6.
Hosanna: Blessed is the King of Israel	12. 13. — Ps. 118. 26.
Fear not, daughter of Zion: Behold, thy King	12. 15. — Zec. 9. 9.
Lord, who hath believed our report?	12. 38. — Isa. 53. 1.
He hath blinded their eyes	12. 40. — Isa. 6. 9, 10.
He that eateth bread with me	13. 18. — Ps. 41. 9.
They hated me without a cause	15. 25. — Ps. 35. 19; 69. 4.
They parted my raiment among them	19. 24. — Ps. 22. 18.
A bone of him shall not be broken	19. 36. — Ex. 12. 46; Ps. 34. 20.
They shall look on him whom they pierced	19. 37. — Zec. 12. 10.

Acts.

Let his habitation be desolate	1. 20. — Ps. 69. 25.
His bishoprick let another take	1. 20. — Ps. 109. 8.
I will pour out my Spirit upon all flesh	2. 17–21. — Joel 2. 28–32.
I foresaw the Lord always before my face	2. 25–28. — Ps. 16. 8–11.
The Lord said . . . Sit thou on my right hand	2. 34, 35. — Ps. 110. 1.
A prophet shall the Lord . . . raise up . . . like unto me	3. 22, 23. — Deu. 18. 18, 19.
In thy seed shall all the kindreds of the earth	3. 25. — Gen. 12. 3; 22. 18.
This is the stone which was set at nought	4. 11. — Ps. 118. 22.
Why did the heathen rage	4. 25, 26. — Ps. 2. 1, 2.
[1] Get thee out of thy country	7. 3. — Gen. 12. 1.

[1] St. Stephen, in this chapter (Acts 7. 2–50), refers to God's dealings with His people, in support of

Old Testament Quotations in N. T. — (*Continued*).

Who made thee a ruler and a judge over us?	7. 27, 28. — Ex. 2. 14.
I am the God of thy fathers	7. 32. — Ex. 3. 6.
Put off thy shoes from thy feet	7. 33, 34. — Ex. 3. 5, 7, 8, 10.
A prophet shall the Lord your God raise up	7. 37. — Deu. 18. 15.
Make us gods to go before us	7. 40. — Ex. 32. 1.
O ye house of Israel, have ye offered to me slain beasts	7. 42, 43. — Am. 5. 25-27.
Heaven is my throne, and earth is my footstool	7. 49, 50. — Isa. 66. 1, 2.
He was led as a sheep to the slaughter	8. 32, 33. — Isa. 53. 7, 8.
I have found David the son of Jesse	13. 22. — Ps. 89. 20.
Thou art my Son, this day have I begotten thee	13. 33. — Ps. 2. 7.
I will give you the sure mercies of David	13. 34. — Isa. 55. 3.
Thou shalt not suffer thy Holy One to see corruption	13. 35. — Ps. 16. 10.
Behold, ye despisers, and wonder, and perish	13. 41. — Hab. 1. 5.
I have set thee to be a light of the Gentiles	13. 47. — Isa. 49. 6.
After this I will return, and will build . . . the tabernacle	15. 16, 17. — Am. 9. 11, 12.
Thou shalt not speak evil of the ruler of thy people	23. 5. — Ex. 22. 28.
Go unto this people, and say, Hearing ye shall hear	28. 26, 27. — Isa. 6. 9, 10.

Romans.

The just shall live by faith	1. 17. — Hab. 2. 4.
The name of God is blasphemed	2. 24. — Isa. 52. 5.
Thou mightest be justified in thy sayings	3. 4. — Ps. 51. 4.
There is none righteous, no, not one	3. 10. — Ps. 14. 1, 3.
There is none that understandeth	3. 11. — Ps. 14. 2.
They are all gone out of the way	3. 12. — Ps. 14. 3.
Their throat is an open sepulchre	3. 13. — Ps. 5. 9; 140. 3.
Whose mouth is full of cursing	3. 14. — Ps. 10. 7.
Their feet are swift to shed blood	3. 15. — Isa. 59. 7.
Destruction and misery are in their ways	3. 16, 17. — Isa. 59. 7, 8.
There is no fear of God before their eyes	3. 18. — Ps. 36. 1.
Abraham believed God, and it was counted unto him for righteousness	4. 3. — Gen. 15. 6.
Blessed are they whose iniquities are forgiven	4. 7, 8. — Ps. 32. 1, 2.
I have made thee a father of many nations	4. 17. — Gen. 17. 5.
So shall thy seed be	4. 18. — Gen. 15. 5.
Thou shalt not covet	7. 7. — Ex. 20. 17.
For thy sake we are killed all the day	8. 36. — Ps. 44. 22.
In Isaac shall thy seed be called	9. 7. — Gen. 21. 12.
At this time . . . Sarah shall have a son	9. 9. — Gen. 18. 10.
The elder shall serve the younger	9. 12. — Gen. 25. 23.
Jacob have I loved, but Esau have I hated	9. 13. — Mal. 1. 2, 3.
I will have mercy on whom I will have mercy	9. 15. — Ex. 33. 19.
Even for this same purpose have I raised	9. 17. — Ex. 9. 16.
I will call them my people, which were not my people	9. 25. — Hos. 2. 23.
Ye are not my people	9. 26. — Hos. 1. 10.
Though the number of the children of Israel	9. 27, 28. — Isa. 10. 22, 23.
Except the Lord of Sabaoth had left us a seed	9. 29. — Isa. 1. 9.
Behold, I lay in Sion a stumbling-stone	9. 33. — Isa. 28. 16.
The man which doeth those things shall live	10. 5. — Lev. 18. 5.
Who shall ascend into heaven	10. 6, 7. — Deu. 30. 12, 13.
The word is nigh thee, even in thy mouth	10. 8. — Deu. 30. 14.
Whosoever believeth on him shall not be ashamed	10. 11. — Isa. 28. 16.
Whosoever shall call on the name of the Lord	10. 13. — Joel 2. 32.
How beautiful are the feet of them that preach	10. 15. — Isa. 52. 7.
Lord, who hath believed our report?	10. 16. — Isa. 53. 1.
Their sound went into all the earth	10. 18. — Ps. 19. 4.
I will provoke you to jealousy	10. 19. — Deu. 32. 21.
I was found of them that sought me not	10. 20. — Isa. 65. 1.
All day long I have stretched forth my hands	10. 21. — Isa. 65. 2.
Lord, they have killed thy prophets	11. 3. — 1 Kn. 19. 10, 14.
I have reserved to myself seven thousand	11. 4. — 1 Kn. 19. 18.
God hath given them the spirit of slumber	11. 8. — Isa. 29. 10.
Let their table be made a snare	11. 9, 10. — Ps. 69. 22.
There shall come out of Sion the Deliverer	11. 26, 27. — Isa. 59. 20, 21.
Who hath known the mind of the Lord?	11. 34. — Isa. 40. 13.
Who hath first given to him	11. 35. — Job 41. 11.
Vengeance is mine; I will repay	12. 19. — Deu. 32. 35.
If thine enemy hunger, feed him	12. 20. — Prov. 25. 21, 22.

his argument that God's favour has never been limited to one particular place. He glances cursorily at the sacred records, and does not quote literally (see next Table, 'Acts').

Thou shalt not commit adultery........13. 9.—Ex. 20. 13-17; Lev. 19. 18.
Every knee shall bow to me........14. 11.—Isa. 45. 23.
The reproaches of them that reproached thee........15. 3.—Ps. 69. 9.
For this cause I will confess to thee among the Gentiles........15. 9.—Ps. 18. 49.
Rejoice, ye Gentiles, with his people........15. 10.—Deu. 32. 43.
Praise the Lord, all ye Gentiles........15. 11.—Ps. 117. 1.
There shall be a root of Jesse........15. 12.—Isa. 11. 1, 10.
To whom he was not spoken of, they shall see........15. 21.—Isa. 52. 15.

1 Corinthians.

I will destroy the wisdom of the wise........1. 19.—Isa. 29. 14.
He that glorieth, let him glory in the Lord........1. 31.—Jer. 9. 24.
Who hath known the mind of the Lord?........2. 16.—Isa. 40. 13.
He taketh the wise in their own craftiness........3. 19.—Job 5. 13.
The Lord knoweth the thoughts of the wise........3. 20.—Ps. 94. 11.
Two shall be one flesh........6. 16.—Gen. 2. 24.
Thou shalt not muzzle the mouth of the ox........9. 9.—Deu. 25. 4.
The people sat down to eat and drink........10. 7.—Ex. 32. 6.
The earth is the Lord's, and the fulness thereof........10. 26.—Ps. 24. 1.
With men of other tongues and other lips........14. 21.—Isa. 28. 11, 12.
He must reign, till he hath put all enemies under his feet........15. 25.—Ps. 110. 1.
All things are put under him........15. 27.—Ps. 8. 6.
Let us eat and drink, for to morrow we die........15. 32.—Isa. 22. 13.
The first man Adam was made a living soul........15. 45.—Gen. 2. 7.
Death is swallowed up in victory........15. 54.—Isa. 25. 8.
O death, where is thy sting?........15. 55.—Hos. 13. 14.

2 Corinthians.

Moses . . . put a veil over his face........3. 13.—Ex. 34. 33.
I believed, and therefore have I spoken........4. 13.—Ps. 116. 10.
I have heard thee in a time accepted........6. 2.—Isa. 49. 8.
I will dwell in them, and walk in them........6. 16.—Lev. 26. 11, 12.
Wherefore come out from among them........6. 17.—Isa. 52. 11.
He that had gathered much had nothing over........8. 15.—Ex. 16. 18.
He hath dispersed abroad........9. 9.—Ps. 112. 9.
He that glorieth, let him glory in the Lord........10. 17.—Jer. 9. 24.
In the mouth of two or three witnesses,........13. 1.—Deu. 19. 15.

Galatians.

Abraham believed God, and it was accounted........3. 6.—Gen. 15. 6.
In thee shall all nations be blessed........3. 8.—Gen. 12. 3.
Cursed is every one that continueth not........3. 10.—Deu. 27. 26.
The just shall live by faith........3. 11.—Hab. 2. 4.
The man that doeth them shall live in them........3. 12.—Lev. 18. 5.
Cursed is every one that hangeth on a tree........3. 13.—Deu. 21. 23.
Rejoice, thou barren that bearest not........4. 27.—Isa. 54. 1.
Cast out the bondwoman and her son........4. 30.—Gen. 21. 10.
Thou shalt love thy neighbour as thyself........5. 14.—Lev. 19. 18.

Ephesians.

When he ascended up on high, he led captivity captive........4. 8.—Ps. 68. 18.
Speak every man truth with his neighbour........4. 25.—Zec. 8. 16.
Be ye angry, and sin not........4. 26.—Ps. 4. 4.
For this cause shall a man leave........5. 31.—Gen. 2. 24.
Honour thy father and thy mother........6. 2, 3.—Ex. 20. 12; Deu. 5. 16.

1 Timothy.

Thou shalt not muzzle the ox........5. 18.—Deu. 25. 4.

2 Timothy.

The Lord knoweth them that are his........2. 19.—Num. 16. 5.

Hebrews.

Thou art my Son, this day have I begotten thee........1. 5.—Ps. 2. 7.
I will be to him a Father........1. 5.—2 Sam. 7. 14.
Let all the angels of God worship him........1. 6.—Ps. 97. 7.
Who maketh his angels spirits........1. 7.—Ps. 104. 4.
Thy throne, O God, is for ever and ever........1. 8, 9.—Ps. 45. 6, 7.
Thou, Lord, in the beginning hast laid . . . the earth........1. 10-12.—Ps. 102. 25-27.

Old Testament Quotations in N. T. — (*Continued*).

Sit on my right hand, until I make . . . thy footstool.............. 1. 13. — Ps. 110. 1.
What is man, that thou art mindful of him .... 2. 6–8. — Ps. 8. 4–6.
I will declare thy name unto my brethren.............................. 2. 12. — Ps. 22. 22.
I will put my trust in him.. 2. 13. — Isa. 8. 18.
Behold I and the children which God hath given me.................. 2. 13. — Isa. 8. 18.
To day if ye will hear his voice.. 3. 7–11. — Ps. 95. 7–11.
As I have sworn in my wrath.. 4. 3. — Ps. 95. 11.
And God did rest the seventh day.. 4. 4. — Gen. 2. 2.
Thou art my Son, to day have I begotten thee............................ 5. 5. — Ps. 2. 7.
Thou art a priest after the order of Melchisedec........................ 5. 6. — Ps. 110. 4.
Blessing I will bless thee.. 6. 14. — Gen. 22. 17.
See . . . that thou make all things according to the pattern............ 8. 5. — Ex. 25. 40.
Behold, the days come, saith the Lord... 8. 8–12. — Jer. 31. 31–34.
This is the blood of the testament.. 9. 20 — Ex. 24. 8.
Sacrifice and offering thou wouldest not ....10. 5–7. — Ps. 40. 6–8.
For ever sat down on the right hand of God..................................10. 12, 13. — Ps. 110. 1.
I will put my laws into their hearts..10. 16, 17. — Jer. 31. 33, 34.
Vengeance belongeth unto me ....10. 30. — Deu. 32. 35, 36.
He that shall come will come, and will not tarry...........................10. 37, 38. — Hab. 2. 3, 4.
In Isaac shall thy seed be called..11. 18. — Gen. 21. 12.
My son, despise not thou the chastening of the Lord.....................12. 5, 6. — Prov. 3. 11, 12.
Lift up the hands that hang down...12. 12.— Isa. 35. 3.
Yet once more I shake not the earth only ....12. 26. — Hag. 2. 6.
I will never leave thee, nor forsake thee.......................................13. 5. — Jos. 1. 5.
The Lord is my helper, I will not fear...13. 6. — Ps. 118. 6.

James.

Thou shalt love thy neighbour.. 2. 8. — Lev. 19. 18.
Do not commit adultery... 2. 11. — Ex. 20. 13, 14.
Abraham believed God, and it was imputed unto him for righteousness 2. 23. — Gen. 15. 6.
God resisteth the proud, but giveth grace unto the humble............ 4. 6. — Prov. 3. 34.

1 Peter.

Be ye holy; for I am holy... 1. 16. — Lev. 11. 44.
All flesh is as grass, and . . . glory of man as . . . grass................ 1. 24, 25. — Isa. 40. 6–8.
Behold, I lay in Sion a chief corner stone..................................... 2. 6. — Ps. 118. 22; Isa. 28. 16.
The stone which the builders disallowed.. 2. 7. — Ps. 118. 22.
Who did no sin, neither was guile found in his mouth..................... 2. 22. — Isa. 53. 9.
Who his own self bare our sins . . . on the tree .... 2. 24. — Isa. 53. 4.
He that will love life, and see good days.. 3. 10–12. — Ps. 34. 12–16.
God resisteth the proud, and giveth grace to the humble.................. 5. 5. — Prov. 3. 34.

2 Peter.

The dog is turned to his own vomit.. 2. 22. — Prov. 26. 11.

Revelation.

The whole of this book is a reflex of the prophetic visions of the Old Testament. It contains pictures of that heavenly form of worship divinely manifested to Moses (of which the Tabernacle ritual was only a pattern), reproduced, and further developed, by its fulfilment in the Atonement of Christ; while it also repeats the mysterious predictions, uttered by Isaiah, Ezekiel, and Daniel, portraying the philosophy of history, the recurrence of its cycles, and the supremacy over all other powers of the kingdom of Christ. It is, therefore, full of references and allusions to the writings of Moses and the prophets, too numerous to be tabulated, and often allusive rather than literal; but the marginal references will better aid the reader in working out the connection between this Revelation, which closes Holy Scripture, and the inspirations vouchsafed to the earlier dispensation, which prepared the way for the fulness of the glory of Christ.

References to the Old Testament in N. T., not being exact quotations.

Matthew.

[1] He shall be called a Nazar ne... 2. 23. — Isa. 11. 1; Zec. 3. 8; 6. 12; Ps. 22. 6; Isa. 53. 3.
The meek shall inherit the earth.. 5. 5. — Ps. 37. 11.

[1] This exact term is not found in any prophecy. Chrysostom and others suppose it to be quoted from some lost book. Jerome refers it to the Hebrew word *Nezer*, 'a sprout,' and identifies it with 'the Branch,' by which the Messiah is designated by Isaiah and Ezekiel. This view is adopted by most modern expositors. Others consider it to be equivalent to 'a reproach,' or 'scorn of men' (Isa. 53.; Ps. 22.), and recognize the fulfilment of those prophecies in the low estimation in which the people of Nazareth were held by the other Jews (John 1. 46).

Shew thyself to the priest	8. 4. — Lev. 14. 3.
The blind receive their sight	11. 5. — Isa. 29. 18.
Elias, which was for to come	11. 14; 17. 10. — Mal. 4. 5.
David . . . did eat the shewbread	12. 3, 4. — 1 Sam. 21. 6.
Priests profane the sabbath, and are blameless	12. 5. — Num. 28. 9.
Teaching for doctrines the commandments of men	15. 9. — Isa. 29. 13.
If thy brother trespass . . . tell him . . . alone	18. 15. — Lev. 19. 17.
In the mouth of two or three witnesses	18. 16. — Deu. 19. 15.
Moses' command to give a writing of divorcement	19. 7. — Deu. 24. 1.
With God all things are possible	19. 26. — Jer. 32. 17.
The parable of a vineyard	21. 33. — Isa. 5. 1.
Your house is left unto you desolate	23. 38. — Jer. 22. 5.
The abomination of desolation	24. 15. — Dan. 12. 11.
Wheresoever the carcase is, there will the eagles	24. 28. — Job 39. 30.
Immediately after . . . shall the sun be darkened	24. 29. — Isa. 13. 10; Ezek. 32. 7; Joel 2. 10; 3. 15.
Heaven and earth shall pass away	24. 35. — Isa. 51. 6.
Depart from me, ye cursed	25. 41. — Ps. 6. 8.
The Son of man goeth, as it is written	26. 24. — Ps. 22.
At last came two false witnesses	26. 60. — Ps. 35. 11.
They did spit in his face	26. 67. — Isa. 50. 6.
He trusted in God	27. 43. — Ps. 22. 8.
All power is given unto me	28. 18. — Dan. 7. 14.

MARK.

Shew thyself to the priest	1. 44. — Lev. 14. 3.
David did eat the shewbread	2. 26. — 1 Sam. 21. 6.
Elias must first come	9. 11. — Mal. 4. 5.
Moses suffered . . . bill of divorcement	10. 4. — Deu. 24. 1.
A certain man planted a vineyard	12. 1. — Isa. 5. 1.
More than all whole burnt offerings	12. 33. — 1 Sam. 15. 22.
Take heed lest any man deceive you	13. 5. — Jer. 29. 8.
The brother shall betray brother	13. 12. — Mic. 7. 6.
Abomination of desolation	13. 14. — Dan. 12. 2.
The sun shall be darkened	13. 24. — Isa. 13. 10.
My words shall not pass away	13. 31. — Isa. 40. 8.

LUKE.

Shall give unto him the throne of . . . David	1. 32. — Ps. 132. 11.
Of his kingdom there shall be no end	1. 33. — Dan. 4. 3.
As he spake to . . . Abraham, and to his seed for ever	1. 55. — Gen. 17. 19.
Oath he sware to . . . Abraham	1. 73. — Gen. 12. 3.
The dayspring from on high	1. 78. — Num. 24. 17; Mal. 4. 2.
Give light to them that sit in darkness	1. 79. — Isa. 9. 2.
Eight days were accomplished for the circumcising	2. 21. — Lev. 12. 3.
The days of her purification	2. 22. — Lev. 12. 2–4.
For the fall and rising again	2. 34. — Isa. 8. 14.
Shew thyself unto the priest	5. 14. — Lev. 14. 3.
David . . . did take and eat the shewbread	6. 4. — 1 Sam. 21. 6.
This do, and thou shalt live	10. 28. — Lev. 18. 5.
Depart, ye workers of iniquity	13. 27. — Ps. 6. 8.
Your house is left unto you desolate	13. 35. — Jer. 22. 25.
If thy brother trespass against thee	17. 3. — Lev. 19. 17.
Parable of the vineyard	20. 9. — Isa. 5. 1.
Blessed are the barren	23. 29. — Isa. 54. 1.
It behoved Christ to suffer	24. 46. — Isa. 53. 5.

JOHN.

One soweth and another reapeth	4. 37. — Mic. 6. 15.
If any . . . thirst . . . come unto me	7. 37. — Isa. 55. 1.
Wells of living water (illustration of the Spirit)	7. 38. — Prov. 18. 4; Isa. 12. 3.
Of the Spirit . . . they should receive	7. 39. — Isa. 44. 3.
Christ's birth at Bethlehem, and of David's house	7. 42. — Mic. 5. 2.
The testimony of two men is true	7. 17. — Deu. 19. 15.
Christ abideth for ever	12. 34. — Ps. 89. 36, 37; Isa. 9. 7.
God's command to the Christ, what he shall say	12. 49. — Deu. 18. 18.
None shall be lost, but the son of perdition	17. 12. — Ps. 109. 8.
They filled a sponge with vinegar, &c.	19. 29. — Ps. 69. 21.
He must rise again from the dead	20. 9. — Ps. 16. 10.

References to the Old Testament in N. T. — (*Continued*).

Acts.

God promised to give Canaan for a possession to Abraham, and to his seed after him....... 7. 5. — Gen. 12. 7; 13. 15.
That his seed should sojourn in a strange land; and that they should bring them into bondage, and entreat them evil four hundred years. 7. 6. — Gen. 15. 13.
After that shall they come forth, and serve me in this place....... 7. 7. — Gen. 15. 16.
Abraham begat Isaac....... 7. 8. — Gen. 21. 3.
And circumcised him the eighth day....... 7. 8. — Gen. 21. 4.
Isaac begat Jacob....... 7. 8. — Gen. 25. 26.
Jacob begat the twelve patriarchs....... 7. 8. — Gen. 42. 13.
The patriarchs . . . sold Joseph into Egypt....... 7. 9. — Gen. 37. 4, 11, 28.
But God was with him....... 7. 9. — Gen. 39. 2, 21.
I have seen the affliction of my people....... 7. 34. — Ex. 3. 7.
Have ye offered to me slain beasts....... 7. 42. — Am. 5. 25, 26.
I will carry you away beyond Babylon....... 7. 43. — Am. 5. 27; Jer. 20. 4.
God is no respecter of persons....... 10. 34. — Job 34. 19.

Romans.

Who will render to every man according to his deeds....... 2. 6. — Ps. 62. 12.
There is no respect of persons with God....... 2. 11. — Deu. 10. 17.
Shall the thing formed say to him that formed it....... 9. 20. — Isa. 45. 9.
The potter has power over the clay....... 9. 21. — Jer. 18. 6.
Eyes that they should not see....... 11. 8. — Isa. 29. 10.

1 Corinthians.

Eye hath not seen....... 2. 9. — Isa. 64. 4.

Ephesians.

Helmet of salvation....... 6. 17. — Isa. 59. 17.

Philippians.

Every knee should bow....... 2. 10. — Isa. 45. 23.

2 Thessalonians.

Exalteth himself above all that is called God....... 2. 4. — Dan. 11. 36.

1 Timothy.

We brought nothing into the world....... 6. 7. — Job 1. 21.

Hebrews.

Abraham's seed . . . as the stars of the sky in multitude, and as the sand by the seashore....... 11. 12. — Gen. 22. 17.
The patriarchs . . . confessed themselves strangers and pilgrims on the earth....... 11. 13. — Gen. 23. 4; 47. 9.
Moses' parents . . . saw he was 'a proper child'....... 11. 23. — Ex. 2. 2.

James.

As the flower of the grass he shall pass away....... 1. 10. — Job 14. 2.

1 Peter.

Tasted that the Lord is gracious....... 2. 3. — Ps. 34. 8.
A chosen generation....... 2. 9. — Deu. 10. 15.
Which in time past were not a people....... 2. 10. — Hos. 1. 10.
Fear God. Honour the king....... 2. 17. — Prov. 24. 21.
Charity shall cover the multitude of sins....... 4. 8. — Prov. 10. 12.

2 Peter.

A thousand years as ono day....... 3. 8. — Ps. 90. 4.
The heavens shall pass away....... 3. 10. — Ps. 102. 25, 26.
A new heaven and a new earth....... 3. 13. — Isa. 65. 17; 66. 22.

1 John.

If we say we have no sin....... 1. 8. — Prov. 20. 9.

Old Testament, Incidents in the, referred to in N. T.

David's visit to Ahimelech, at Nob....... Mat. 12. 3, 4. — 1 Sam. 21. 1.
Jonah's entombment for three days and nights in the belly of the fish { Mat. 12. 40. Mat. 16. 4. } — Jon. 1. 17.

The Queen of Sheba's visit to Solomon	Mat. 12. 42. — 1 Kn. 10. 1.
The death of Abel	Mat. 23. 35. — Gen. 4. 8.
[1] Death of Zacharias	Mat. 23. 35. — 2 Chr. 24. 20.
Elijah's visit to the widow of Zarephath	Lu. 4. 26. — 1 Kn. 17. 9.
The healing of Naaman's leprosy	Lu. 4. 27. — 2 Kn. 5. 14.
Jonah's mission to Nineveh	Lu. 11. 30. — Jon. 3.; 4.
The Queen of Sheba's visit to Solomon	Lu. 11. 31. — 1 Kn. 10. 1.
The murder of Abel and Zacharias	Lu. 11. 51. — Gen. 4. 8; 2 Chr. 24. 20, 21.
The deluge in the days of Noah	Lu. 17. 26. — Gen. 7.
The destruction of Sodom	Lu. 17. 29. — Gen. 19. 16.
The fate of Lot's wife	Lu. 17. 32. — Gen. 19. 21.
Moses' vision of the burning bush	Lu. 20. 37. — Ex. 3.
Moses lifting up the brazen serpent	John 3. 14. — Num. 21. 9.
Manna in the wilderness	John 6. 31. — Ex. 16. 15.
Mosaic enactment of circumcision	John 7. 22. — Lev. 12. 3.
Mosaic enactment of stoning, as punishment for adultery	John 8. 5. — Lev. 20. 10.
God appeared unto Abraham, when he was in Mesopotamia, before he dwelt in Charran	Acts 7. 2. — Gen. 15. 7; Neh. 9. 7.
Abraham's residence in Charran	Acts 7. 4. — Gen. 11. 31.
Abraham's migration from Charran to Canaan	Acts 7. 4. — Gen. 12. 4, 5.
God's promise to give Canaan to Abraham and his seed	Acts 7. 5. — Gen. 10. 1-7; 13. 15.
Israel's bondage in Egypt	Acts 7. 6. — Gen. 15. 13.
The birth of Isaac from Abraham	Acts 7. 8. — Gen. 21. 3.
His circumcision the eighth day	Acts 7. 8. — Gen. 21. 4.
Jacob's birth from Isaac	Acts 7. 8. — Gen. 25. 26.
The birth of the twelve patriarchs from Jacob	Acts 7. 8. — Gen. 42. 13.
Joseph sold into Egypt by his brethren	Acts 7. 9. — Gen. 37. 4, 11, 28.
God's favour to Joseph in Egypt	Acts 7. 9. — Gen. 39. 2, 21.
Joseph's deliverances from affliction by God's favour, and his divine gift of wisdom	Acts 7. 10. — Gen. 41. 37-39.
Pharaoh's promotion of Joseph to be ruler over Egypt and over his house	Acts 7. 10. — Gen. 41. 40.
The famine over Egypt and Canaan	Acts 7. 11. — Gen. 41. 54.
Jacob sending his sons to Egypt to buy corn	Acts 7. 12. — Gen. 42. 2.
Joseph makes himself known to his brethren in Egypt	Acts 7. 13. — Gen. 45. 1.
The descent of Jacob and his family into Egypt	Acts 7. 14, 15. — Gen. 45. 9; 46. 5, 6.
Jacob's death in Egypt	Acts 7. 15. — Gen. 49. 33.
The burial of the patriarchs at Shechem	Acts 7. 16. — Gen. 33. 19; Jos. 24. 32.
The great increase of the Israelites	Acts 7. 17. — Ex. 1. 7.
The accession of a king of Egypt hostile to the Israelites	Acts 7. 18. — Ex. 1. 8.
Pharaoh dealt subtilly with them	Acts 7. 19. — Ex. 1. 10.
The casting of their sons into the river	Acts 7. 19. — Ex. 1. 22.
The concealment of Moses' birth for three months	Acts 7. 20. — Ex. 2. 2.
His being cast out, and his adoption by Pharaoh's daughter	Acts 7. 21. — Ex. 2. 3-10.
His murder of an Egyptian, and flight into Midian	Acts 7. 24-29. — Ex. 2. 12-15.
The birth of his two sons in Midian	Acts 7. 29. — Ex. 18. 3.
The appearance of an angel to him in a burning bush, in the wilderness of Sinai	Acts 7. 30. — Ex. 3. 2.
God's mission to Moses	Acts 7. 35. — Ex. 3. 15-18; 4.
The miracles in Egypt by Moses' mission	Acts 7. 36. — Ex. 7.-12.
The miracle by Moses in the Red Sea	Acts 7. 36. — Ex. 14. 21, &c.
The Exodus	Acts 7. 36. — Ex. 12. 41.
Miracles in the wilderness	Acts 7. 36. — Ex. 15. 23; 16. &c
The forty years' wandering in the wilderness	Acts 7. 36. — Num. 14. 33; Ps. 95. 10, 11.
The giving of the Law to Moses on Mount Sinai	Acts 7. 38. — Ex. 20.-24. 18.
The worship of the golden calf	Acts 7. 41. — Ex. 32. 19.
The making of the tabernacle in the wilderness	Acts 7. 44. — Ex. 25. 40; 26. 30.
The erection of the tabernacle in Canaan	Acts 7. 45. — Jos. 18. 1.
David's desire to build a tabernacle	Acts 7. 46. — 2 Sam. 7.
The building of Solomon's Temple	Acts 7. 47. — 1 Kn. 8.
The exodus	Acts 13. 17. — Ex. 12. 41.
The forty years' wandering in the wilderness	Acts 13. 18. — Num. 14. 33; Ps. 95. 10.
God's expulsion of seven nations from Canaan	Acts 13. 19. — Deu. 7. 1.
The division of Canaan among the Israelites by lot	Acts 13. 19. — Jos. 14. 2.
The rule of the judges	Acts 13. 20. — Jud. 2. 16.

[1] This Zacharias has likewise been identified with Zechariah the prophet, with Zacharias the father of John the Baptist, and also with Zechariah the son of Jeberechiah (Isa. 8. 2).

Old Testament, Incidents in the, referred to in N. T.—(*Continued*).

The judgeship of Samuel the prophet	Acts 13. 20.—1 Sam. 3. 20.
The desire of Israel for a kingdom	Acts 13. 21.—1 Sam. 8. 5.
The forty years' reign of Saul, son of Kish, the Benjamite	Acts 13. 21.—1 Sam. 10. 21.
God's removal of Saul from the kingdom, and selection of David to succeed him	Acts 13. 22.—1 Chr. 10. 14.
The pillar of a cloud, guiding Israel	1 Cor. 10. 1.—Ex. 13. 21.
The passage through the Red Sea	1 Cor. 10. 1.—Ex. 14. 22.
The Israelites fed by manna	1 Cor. 10. 3.—Ex. 16. 3-35.
Moses bringing water out of the rock	1 Cor. 10. 4.—Ex. 17. 6.
Birth of Ishmael from Abraham and Hagar	Gal. 4. 23, 25.—Gen. 16. 15.
The creation of Adam and Eve	1 Tim. 2. 13.—Gen. 2. 7, 21, 22.
The priority of Eve's fall	1 Tim. 2. 14.—Gen. 3. 12.
The opposition of the Egyptian magicians to Moses	2 Tim. 3. 8.—Ex. 7. 11.
The tabernacle and its furniture	Heb. 9. 2, 3.—Ex. 25. and 26.
The pot of manna, Aaron's rod, and the two tables, in the Ark of the Covenant	Heb. 9. 4.—Ex. 16. 33, 34; 25. 16; Num. 17. 10.
The high priest's offering on the Day of Atonement	Heb. 9. 7.—Ex. 30. 10.
Moses sprinkling the people with the blood of the testament	Heb. 9. 19, 20.—Ex. 24. 8.
The daily sacrifice	Heb. 10. 11.—Ex. 29. 38.
The creation of the world	Heb. 11. 3.—Gen. 1.
God's acceptance of Abel's sacrifice	Heb. 11. 4.—Gen. 4. 4.
Enoch's translation	Heb. 11. 5.—Gen. 5. 24.
Noah's preparation of the ark, and preservation of himself and family	Heb. 11. 7.—Gen. 6. 15-18.
The call of Abraham	Heb. 11. 8.—Gen. 12. 1.
His sojourn in Canaan	Heb. 11. 9.—Gen. 12. 5, &c.
Isaac and Jacob in Canaan	Heb. 11. 9.—Gen. 27.
The birth of Isaac from Sarah in her old age	Heb. 11. 11.—Gen. 18. 11, 12, 14.
Abraham offering up Isaac	Heb. 11. 17.—Gen. 22.
Isaac blessing Jacob and Esau	Heb. 11. 20.—Gen. 27.
Jacob blessing Joseph's sons before his death	Heb. 11. 21.—Gen. 48. 15.
Joseph's dying command concerning his bones, &c.	Heb. 11. 22.—Gen. 50. 25.
Moses' return to his own people from Pharaoh's daughter	Heb. 11. 25.—Ex. 2. 11.
His flight from Egypt	Heb. 11. 27.—Ex. 2. 15.
The Passover in Egypt, and slaughter of the first-born	Heb. 11. 28.—Ex. 12. 21-29.
The passage of the Red Sea, and destruction of the Egyptian army	Heb. 11. 29.—Ex. 14.
The compassing of Jericho for seven days, and the fall of its walls	Heb. 11. 30.—Jos. 6. 12-20.
The sparing of Rahab and her household	Heb. 11. 31.—Jos. 6. 23.
The exploits of the judges, Gideon, Barak, Samson, Jephthah, Samuel	Heb. 11. 32.—Jud. and 1 Sam.
The exploits of David	Heb. 11. 32.—2 Sam.
Deliverance of Daniel in the lions' den	Heb. 11. 33.—Dan. 6. 22.
Deliverance of the Three Children from the fiery furnace	Heb. 11. 34.—Dan. 3. 27.
Restoration of children to life by Elijah and Elisha	Heb. 11. 35.—1 Kn. 17. 23; 2 Kn. 4. 34.
The visit of angels to Abraham and Lot	Heb. 13. 2.—Gen. 18. 2; 19. 1.
Rahab's reception and deliverance of the spies	Jas. 2. 25.—Jos. 2. 1.
The patience of Job	Jas. 5. 11.—Job 1. 21.
Elijah's prayer for a dearth on Israel	Jas. 5. 17.—1 Kn. 17. 1.
The deluge, the disobedience of the world, and preservation of Noah and his family	1 Pet. 3. 20.—Gen. 6. 3. 2 Pet. 2. 5.—Gen. 7. 1.
Sarah's deference to Abraham, calling him lord	1 Pet. 3. 6.—Gen. 18. 12.
The destruction of Sodom and the cities of the plain	2 Pet. 2. 6.—Gen. 19.
Balaam rebuked by his ass	2 Pet. 2. 15.—Num. 22.
Cain's murder of Abel	1 John 3. 12.—Gen. 4. 8.
The exodus of Israel from Egypt	Jude 5.—Ex. 12. 41.
The death of unbelievers in the wilderness	Jude 5.—Num. 14. 32.
The destruction of Sodom, Gomorrha, &c.	Jude 7.—Gen. 19.
The body of Moses	Jude 9.—Deu. 34. 5, 6.
'The way of Cain'	Jude 11.—Gen. 4. 8.
The error of Balaam for reward	Jude 11.—Num. 22.
The gainsaying of Core (Korah)	Jude 11.—Num. 16.
Enoch, the seventh from Adam	Jude 14.—Gen. 5. 18.

Olive (Gen. 8. 11; Deu. 8. 8). **Heb.** *Zayith*: **Gk.** *ἐλαία*: **Bot. N.** *Olea europæa*. **Very abundant in Palestine, and valued for the oil from its fruit, and for its beautiful wood.**

Olive (wild) (Rom. 11. 17). Gk. *ἀγριέλαιος*. The wild olive produces a small and inferior fruit; good fruit is obtained by grafting.

Olivet, ŏl'-ĭ-vĕt, from the Latin *Olivetum*, 'olive-yard.' The mountain east of Jerusalem beyond the Kidron ravine. So named from the olive trees which grew upon it. It has associations with many events both of Old and New Test. history. 2 Sam. 15. 30; 1 Kn. 11. 7; Zec. 14. 4; Mat. 21. 1; 24. 3; Mk. 11. 1; 13. 3; Lu. 21. 37; John 8. 1; Acts 1. 12.

NAZARETH

Modern photograph showing the site among the Galilean hills. (*Picture Post Library*)

THE MOUNT OF OLIVES

The Garden of Gethsemane in the foreground. (*Paul Popper*)

Olive trees, vision of. Zec. 4. 3; Rev. 11. 4. *See* Jud. 9. 9; Ps. 52. 8; Rom. 11. 17.
Olympas, ō-lym'-pās. Rom. 16. 15.
Omar, ō'-mär, 'eloquent' (?). Gen. 36. 11.
Omega, ō-mĕg'-ă, 'great O,' the last letter of the Greek alphabet. Rev. 1. 8, 11; 21. 6; 22. 13.
Omer, ō'-mĕr (Ex. 16. 33). A dry measure = $\frac{1}{10}$ of an ephah = about 3 quarts.
See MEASURES.
Omitted. Mat. 23. 23.
Omri, ŏm'-rī, 'like a sheaf' (?). (1) king of Israel. 1 Kn. 16. 16, &c.; Mic. 6. 16.
(2) others. 1 Chr. 7. 8; 9. 4; 27. 18.
On, ŏn. (1) 'the sun-god.' Gen. 41. 45.
(2) 'vigour.' Num. 16. 1.
Onam, ō'-năm, 'strong.' (1) Gen. 36. 23.
(2) 1 Chr. 2. 26.
Onan, ō'-năn, 'strong.' Gen. 38. 4.
Once. Gen. 18. 32, yet but this *o.*
Num. 13. 30, let us go up at *o.*
Job 33. 14; Ps. 62. 11, speaketh *o.*, yea twice.
Isa. 66. 8, shall a nation be born at *o.*?
Heb. 6. 4, *o.* enlightened.
9. 27. *o.* to die.
See Rom. 6. 10; Heb. 10. 10; 1 Pet. 3. 18.
One. Job 9. 3, *o.* of a thousand.
Eccl. 7. 27; Isa. 27. 12, *o.* by *o.*
Mk. 10. 21; Lu. 18. 22, *o.* thing thou lackest.
Lu. 10. 42, *o.* thing is needful.
John 9. 25, *o.* thing I know.
17. 11, 21, 22, that they may be *o.*
Gal. 3. 28, all *o.* in Christ.
Eph. 4. 5, *o.* Lord, *o.* faith, *o.* baptism.
See Deu. 6. 4; Mk. 12. 32; 1 Tim. 2. 5.
Onesimus, ō-nĕs'-ĭ-mŭs, 'profitable.' Col. 4. 9; Philem. 10.
Onesiphorus, ō-nĕs-ĭph'-ŏ-rŭs, 'bringing profit.' 2 Tim. 1. 16.
Onions (Num. 11. 5). Heb. *Bĕtzâlîm*: Gk. κρόμμυα: Bot. N. *Allium cepa*. Named among the vegetables of Egypt, where it is still extensively grown, and is as large as a Portugal onion.
Ono, ō'-nō, 'strong.' 1 Chr. 8. 12.
Onyx. (1) (Ex. 28. 20). Heb. *Tarshîsh*: Gk. ὀνύχιον: A. V. and R. V. 'beryl:' R. V. marg. 'chalcedony,' probably the banded agate, a variety of quartz. (2) (Ex. 35. 9; Ezek. 28. 13). Heb. *Shōham*: R. V. marg. sometimes 'beryl' (Ex. 28. 9). Onyx is probably correct, but scholars are divided between beryl, carbuncle, chalcedony, onyx, and turquoise.
Open. (1) Num. 16. 30, if the earth *o.* her mouth.
Ps. 51. 15, *o.* thou my lips.
81. 10, *o.* thy mouth wide.
104. 28; 145. 16, thou *o.* thine hand.
119. 18, *o.* thou mine eyes.
Prov. 31. 8, *o.* thy mouth for the dumb.
Isa. 22. 22, he shall *o.*, and none shall shut.
42. 7, to *o.* the blind eyes.
60. 11, thy gates shall be *o.* continually.
Ezek. 16. 63, never *o.* thy mouth.
Mal. 3. 10, *o.* windows of heaven.
Mat. 25. 11; Lu. 13. 25, Lord *o.* to us.
27. 52, graves were *o.*
Mk. 7. 34, that is, be *o.*
Lu. 24. 45, then *o.* he their understanding.
Acts 26. 18, to *o.* their eyes, and turn them.
1 Cor. 16. 9, great door and effectual is *o.*
Col. 4. 3, *o.* to us a door of utterance.
(2) to explain clearly.
Ps. 49. 4, I will *o.* my dark saying.
Lu. 24. 32, while he *o.* to us the scriptures.
See Acts 16. 14; 2 Cor. 2. 12; Heb. 4. 13; Rev. 5. 2.
Operation. Ps. 28. 5; Isa. 5. 12; 1 Cor. 12. 6; Col. 2. 12.
Ophel, ō'-phĕl, 'a hill.' 2 Chr. 27. 3.
Ophir, ō'-phĭr. (1) son of Joktan. Gen. 10. 29.
gold of. 1 Kn. 9. 28; 10. 11; 22. 48; 1 Chr. 29. 4; 2 Chr. 8. 18; Job 22. 24; Ps. 45. 9; Isa. 13. 12.
Ophni, ŏph'-nī, 'man of the hill.' Jos. 18. 24.
Ophrah, ŏph'-răh, 'fawn.' (1) man. 1 Chr. 4. 14.
(2) towns. Jos. 18. 23; Jud. 6. 11.
Opinion. 1 Kn. 18. 21; Job 32. 6.
Opportunity. Gal. 6. 10; Phil. 4. 10; Heb. 11. 15.
Oppose. Job 30. 21; 2 Thes. 2. 4; 2 Tim. 2. 25.
Oppositions. 1 Tim. 6. 20.
Oppress. Ex. 22. 21; 23. 9, *o.* a stranger.
Lev. 25. 14, 17, ye shall not *o.* one another. R. V. wrong.
1 Sam. 12. 3, whom have I *o.*?
Ps. 10. 18, that the man of earth may no more *o.* R. V. be terrible.
Prov. 14. 31; 22. 16, he that *o.* the poor.
28. 3, a poor man that *o.* the poor.
Jer. 7. 6, if ye *o.* not the stranger.
Hos. 12. 7, he loveth to *o.*
Zec. 7. 10, *o.* not the widow.
See Acts 7. 24; 10. 38; Jas. 2. 6.
Oppression. Deu. 26. 7, the Lord looked on our *o.*
Ps. 62. 10, trust not in *o.*
119. 134, deliver me from the *o.* of man.
Eccl. 4. 1, I considered the *o.*
7. 7, *o.* maketh a wise man mad. R. V. extortion.
Isa. 30. 12, ye trust in *o.*
See Isa. 33. 15; Zec. 9. 8; 10. 4.
Oppression forbidden by God. Ex. 22. 21; Lev. 25. 14; Deu. 23. 16; 24. 14; Ps. 12. 5; 62. 10; Prov. 14. 31; 22. 16; Eccl. 4. 1; 5. 8; Isa. 1. 17; 10.; 58. 6; Jer. 22. 17; Ezek. 22. 7; Am. 4. 1; 8. 4; Mic. 2. 2; Mal. 3. 5; Jas. 5. 4.
Oracle of the temple. 1 Kn. 6. 16; 8. 6; 2 Chr. 4. 20; Ps. 28. 2.
Oracles. (1) Divine utterances for man's guidance. 2 Sam. 16. 23.
(2) The places where such utterances were usually given. 1 Kn. 6. 16; 2 Chr. 3. 16.
(3) (the Holy Scriptures). Acts 7. 38; Rom. 3. 2; Heb. 5. 12; 1 Pet. 4. 11.
See also URIM.
Orator. Isa. 3. 3; Acts 24. 1.
Ordain, appoint, order, arrange, establish. 1 Chr. 17. 9, I will *o.* a place for my people. R. V. appoint.
Ps. 8. 2, hast thou *o.* strength. R. V. established.
81. 5, this he *o.* in Joseph. R. V. appointed.
132. 17, I have *o.* a lamp for mine anointed.
Isa. 26. 12, thou wilt *o.* peace for us.
30. 33, Tophet is *o.* of old. R. V. prepared.
Jer. 1. 5, I *o.* thee a prophet. R. V. appointed.
Mk. 3. 14, Jesus *o.* twelve. R. V. appointed.
John 15. 16, have *o.* you, that ye should bring forth.
Acts 1. 22, one be *o.* to be a witness. R. V. become.
10. 42, *o.* of God to be the Judge.
13. 48, *o.* to eternal life.
14. 23; Tit. 1. 5, *o.* elders. R. V. appointed.
16. 4, decrees that were *o.*
17. 31, by that man whom he hath *o.*
Rom. 13. 1, the powers that be are *o.* of God.
Gal. 3. 19, the law was *o.* by angels.
Eph. 2. 10, good works which God hath before *o.* R. V. prepared.
Jude 4, of old *o.* to this condemnation. R. V. set forth.
See 1 Cor. 2. 7; 9. 14; Heb. 5. 1.
Order. Jud. 13. 12, how shall we *o.* the child?
2 Kn. 20. 1; Isa. 38. 1, set thine house in *o.*
Job 10. 22, land without any *o.*
23. 4, I would *o.* my cause.
37. 19, we cannot *o.* our speech.
Ps. 40. 5, they cannot be reckoned in *o.*
50. 21, I will set them in *o.*
50. 23, to him that *o.* his conversation aright.
110. 4; Heb. 5. 6; 6. 20; 7. 11, the *o.* of Melchisedec.
1 Cor. 14. 40, decently and in *o.*
Tit. 1. 5, that thou shouldest set in *o.*
See Ps. 37. 23; Acts 21. 24; 1 Cor. 15. 23.
Ordinance. Isa. 58. 2; Rom. 13. 2, the *o.* of their God.
Mal. 3. 14, what profit that we have kept *o.*? R. V. charge.
Eph. 2. 15, commandments contained in *o.*

Col. 2. 14, handwriting of *o*.
Heb. 9. 10, in carnal *o*.
See Jer. 31. 36; Lu. 1. 6; 1 Pet. 2. 13.
Ordination, mode and use of. Acts 6. 6; 14. 23; 1 Tim. 2. 7; 3.; 4. 14; 5. 22; 2 Tim. 2. 2; Tit. 1. 5.
Oreb, ŏr'-ĕb, 'raven.' Jud. 7. 20, 25.
Oren, ō'-rĕn, 'fir tree.' 1 Chr. 2. 25.
Or ever, before ever, before at all. Dan. 6. 24; Acts 23. 15.
Organ (Gen. 4. 21; Job 21. 12; 30. 31; Ps. 150. 4). Heb. *Ugâb*: R. V. 'pipe.' The Gk. is various, — κιθάρα (Gen. 4. 21), ψαλμός (Job 21. 12; 30. 31), ὄργανον (Ps. 150. 4). It is probably a general term for wind instruments. Thus Jubal (Gen. 4. 21) is the inventor of stringed and wind instruments, and the orchestra in Ps. 150. has the same two divisions.
Orion, ō-rī'-on. Job 9. 9.
Ornaments, of apparel, &c. Gen. 24. 22; Prov. 1. 9; 4. 9; 25. 12; Isa. 3. 18; Jer. 2. 32; 1 Pet. 3. 3.
Ornan, ŏr'-năn, same as ARAUNAH. 2 Sam. 26. 14; 1 Chr. 21. 15.
Orpah, ŏr'păh, 'hind' (?). Ru. 1. 4.
Orphans. Lam. 5. 3.
Osee, ō'-sēē, same as HOSEA. Rom. 9. 25.
Oshea, ō-shē'-ă, 'salvation,' same as JOSHUA. Num. 13. 8.
Osprey (Lev. 11. 13). Heb. *Oznîyyâh*: Gk. ἁλιαίετος. (Specimen, *Pandion haliaëtos*.) A fish-eating eagle.
Ossifrage, 'bone-breaker' (Lev. 11. 13). Heb. *Péres*, 'breaker:' Gk. γύψ: R. V. 'gier eagle.' (Specimen, *Gypaëtus barbatus*.) The 'Lämmergeier,' most magnificent of the vulture species.
Ostentation condemned. Prov. 25. 14; 27. 2; Mat. 6. 1.
Ostrich. (1) (Lam. 4. 3). Heb. *Ya'ănâh*: 'the voracious:' Gk. στρουθίον. (Specimen, *Struthio camelus*.)
(2) (Job 39. 13). Heb. *Rĕnânîm*: R. V. 'ostrich:' A. V. 'peacock.' The ostrich, from the twanging cry of the female.
Othni, ŏth'-nī, 'lion' (?). 1 Chr. 26. 7.
Othniel, ŏth'-nĭ-ĕl, 'lion of God.' Jos. 15. 17; Jud. 1. 13; 3. 9.
Ouches, settings of gold or silver for precious stones (*lit.* sockets). Ex. 28. 11.
Ought. 1 Chr. 12. 32, to know what Israel *o*. to do.
Mat. 23. 23; Lu. 11. 42, these *o*. ye to have done.
Lu. 24. 26, *o*. not Christ to have suffered?
John 4. 20, the place where men *o*. to worship.
Acts 5. 29, we *o*. to obey God. R. V. must.
Rom. 8. 26, what we should pray for as we *o*.
Heb. 5. 12, when ye *o*. to be teachers.
Jas. 3. 10, these things *o*. not so to be.
2 Pet. 3. 11, what manner of persons *o*. ye to be?
See Rom. 12. 3; 15. 1; 1 Tim. 3. 15.
Ours. Mk. 12. 7; Lu. 20. 14; 1 Cor. 1. 2; 2 Cor. 1. 14.
Out. Num. 32. 23, be sure your sin will find you *o*.
Ps. 82. 5, are *o*. of course. R. V. moved.
Prov. 4. 23, *o*. of it are the issues of life.
Mat. 12. 34; 15. 19, *o*. of abundance of heart the mouth speaketh.
2 Tim. 3. 11, *o*. of them all the Lord delivered me.
4. 2, instant in season, *o*. of season.
See Gen. 2. 9, 23; 3. 19; John 15. 19; Acts 2. 5.
Outcasts of Israel, promised restoration. Ps. 147. 2; Isa. 11. 12; 16. 3; 27. 13; Jer. 30. 17; Rom. 11.
Outgoings, utmost limits or boundaries. Jos. 17. 18; Ps. 65. 8.
Outlandish, foreign. Neh. 13. 26.
Outrageous. Prov. 27. 4.
Outrun. John 20. 4.
Outside. Jud. 7. 11; Mat. 23. 25; Lu. 11. 39.
Outstretched. Deu. 26. 8; Jer. 21. 5; 27. 5.
Outward. 1 Sam. 16. 7, looketh on *o*. appearance.
Mat. 23. 27, appear beautiful *o*.
Rom. 2. 28, not a Jew, which is one *o*.
2 Cor. 4. 16, though our *o*. man perish.
See Mat. 23. 28; Rom. 2. 28; 1 Pet. 3. 3.

Overcharge, overburden. Lu. 21. 34; 2 Cor. 2. 5.
Overcome. Gen. 49. 19, he shall *o*. at last. R. V. press upon their heel.
Jer. 23. 9, like a man whom wine hath *o*.
John 16. 33, I have *o*. the world.
Rom. 12. 21, be not *o*. of evil, but *o*. evil.
1 John 5. 4, 5, victory that *o*. the world.
Rev. 2. 7, 17, 26; 3. 12, 21, to him that *o*.
See S. of S. 6. 5; 2 Pet. 2. 19; Rev. 12. 11.
Overcoming, glory and reward of. 1 John 2. 13; Rev. 2. 7, 11, 17, 26; 3. 5, 12, 21; 21. 7.
Overflow. Deu. 11. 4; Ps. 78. 20; Isa. 43. 2.
Overmuch. Eccl. 7. 16; 2 Cor. 2. 7.
Overpass, pass over, take no notice of. Jer. 5. 28.
Overpast. Ps. 57. 1; Isa. 26. 20.
Overplus. Lev. 25. 27.
Overseer. Gen. 41. 34; Prov. 6. 7; Acts 20. 28.
Overseers in building the temple. 1 Chr. 9. 29; 2 Chr. 2. 18.
Overshadow. Mat. 17. 5; Mk. 9. 7; Lu. 1. 35; Acts 5. 15.
Oversight. Gen. 43. 12; Neh. 11. 16; 1 Pet. 5. 2.
Overspread. Gen. 9. 19; Dan. 9. 27.
Overtake. Am. 9. 13, plowman shall *o*. the reaper.
Gal. 6. 1, if a man be *o*. in a fault.
1 Thes. 5. 4, day should *o*. you as a thief.
See Deu. 19. 6; Isa. 59. 9; Jer. 42. 16.
Overthrow. Ex. 23. 24, utterly *o*. them.
Job 19. 6, God hath *o*. me.
Ps. 140. 4, purposed to *o*. my goings.
Prov. 13. 6, wickedness *o*. the sinner.
Jon. 3. 4, yet forty days, and Nineveh shall be *o*.
Acts 5. 39, if it be of God, ye cannot *o*. it.
See Gen. 19. 21; Prov. 29. 4; 2 Tim. 2: 18.
Overturn. Job 9. 5; 12. 15; 28. 9; Ezek. 21. 27.
Overwhelm. Job 6. 27, ye *o*. the fatherless. R. V. cast lots upon.
Ps. 61. 2, when my heart is *o*.
77. 3; 142. 3; 143. 4, my spirit was *o*.
See Ps. 55. 5; 78. 53; 124. 4.
Overwise. Eccl. 7. 16.
Owe. Lu. 16. 5, 7, how much *o*. thou?
Rom. 13. 8, *o*. no man any thing.
See Mat. 18. 24, 28; Lu. 7. 41; Philem. 18.
Owl. (1) (Isa. 34. 13). Heb. *Bath-haya'ănâh*, 'daughter of the *ya'ănâh*,' ostrich. Gk. στρουθός. The A. V. renders 'owl' in Lev. 11. 16; Deu. 14. 15; Jer. 30. 59; Mic. 1. 8; Isa. 34. 13; 43. 20; Job 30. 29. In all cases the R. V. renders correctly 'ostrich.'
(2) **Great** (Lev. 11. 17). Heb. *Yanshooph*: Gk. ἶβεις, probably the 'ibis.' (Specimen, *Bubo Ascalaphus*, found at Jericho.)
(3) (Isa. 34. 15). Heb. *Kippôz*: Gk. ἐχῖνος: R. V. arrowsnake. Probably some species of owl.
(4) **Little** (Lev. 11. 17). Heb. *Kôs*: Gk. νυκτικόραξ. (Specimen, *Athene meridionalis*, found at Bethlehem.) A general name for 'owl.'
(5) **of Desert** (Ps. 102. 6). Heb. *Kôs*: Gk. νυκτικόροξ, 'owl.'
(6) **Screech** (Isa. 34. 14). Heb. *Lîlîth*: Gk. ὀνοκένταυρος: A. V. marg. and R. V. 'night monster.' (Specimen, *Otus vulgaris*, found at Jericho.) Cheyne translates, 'night-fairy.' It refers probably 'to a female demon of popular superstition, especially hostile to children.'
Own. Num. 32. 42, called it after his *o*. name.
1 Chr. 29. 14, of thine *o*. have we given thee.
Ps. 12. 4, our lips are our *o*.
67. 6, even our *o*. God shall bless us.
Mat. 20. 15, do what I will with mine *o*.
John 1. 11, to his *o*., and his *o*. received him not.
13. 1, having loved his *o*.
1 Cor. 6. 19, ye are not your *o*.
See Acts 5. 4; Phil. 3. 9; 1 Tim. 5. 8; Rev. 1. 5.
Owner. Ex. 21. 28; 22. 11; Eccl. 5. 13; Isa. 1. 3.
Ox. (1) (Gen. 12. 16). Heb. *Bâkâr*: Gk. μόσχος. The general name of the bovine species without reference to age or sex.

(2) (Deu. 22. 10). Heb. *Shôr :* Gk. μόσχος. The unit, the individual of the bovine species.
(3) (Deu. 21. 3). Heb. *Ēgel*, or *Eglâh* (fem.). The young of the bovine species irrespective of sex ; calf, heifer.
(4) (Ps. 22. 12). Heb. *Abîrîm :* Gk. ταῦροι, πίονες, 'the strong ones' = bulls.
(5) (Ps. 69. 31). Heb. *Par* (fem. *Pârâh*), usually employed to designate bulls or heifers for sacrifice.

Ox, treatment of. Ex. 21. 28 ; 22. 1 ; 23. 4 ; Lev. 17. 3 ; Deu. 5. 14 ; 22. 1 ; Lu. 13. 15.
that treadeth out the corn, unlawful to muzzle. Deu. 25. 4 ; 1 Cor. 9. 9 ; 1 Tim. 5. 18.

Ozem, ō'-zĕm. (1) 1 Chr. 2. 15. (2) 1 Chr. 2. 25.

Ozias, ō-zī'-ăs, Greek form of Uzziah. Mat. 1. 8.

Ozni, ŏz'-nī, 'my hearing.' Num. 26. 16.

Oznites, ŏz'-nītes, descendants of Ozni. Num. 26. 16.

Paarai, pā'-ă-rāi, 'devoted to Peor' (?). 2 Sam. 23. 35.

Pacify. Prov. 16. 14 ; 21. 14 ; Eccl. 10. 4 ; Ezek. 16. 63.

Padan, pā'-dăn, short for the following. Gen. 48. 7.

Padan-aram, pā'-dăn-âr'-ăm, 'the plain of Syria.' Gen. 25. 20 ; 28. 2.

Padon, pā'-dŏn, 'redemption.' Ez. 2. 44.

Pagiel, pā'-ġĭ-ĕl, 'intervention of God.' Num. 1. 13.

Pahath-moab, pā'-hăth-mō'-ăb, 'governor of Moab.' Ez. 2. 6.

Pai, pā'-ī, 'bleating.' 1 Chr. 1. 50.

Pain. Ps. 55. 4, my heart is sore *p.*
116. 3, the *p.* of hell gat hold upon me.
Acts 2. 24, having loosed the *p.* of death.
Rom. 8. 22, creation travaileth in *p.*
Rev. 21. 4, neither shall there be any more *p.*
See Ps. 73. 16 ; Jer. 4. 19 ; 2 Cor. 11. 27.

Painful, that which gives or is characterized by pain ; laborious, difficult. Ps. 73. 16.

Painfulness, unsparing toil. 2 Cor. 11. 27.

Painted. 2 Kn. 9. 30 ; Jer. 4. 30 ; 22. 14 ; Ezek. 23. 40.

Palace. Ps. 48. 13, consider her *p.*
122. 7, prosperity within thy *p.*
144. 12, the similitude of a *p.*
Jer. 9. 21, death is entered into our *p.*
Lu. 11. 21, a strong man keepeth his *p.* R. V. own court.
Phil. 1. 13, manifest in all the *p.* R. V. whole prætorian guard.
See 1 Chr. 29. 1 ; Neh. 1. 1 ; 2. 8 ; Isa. 25. 2.

Palace, the temple so called. 1 Chr. 29. 1 ; Ps. 48. 3 ; 71. 69 ; 122. 7.

Palal, pā'-lăl, 'judge.' Neh. 3. 25.

Pale. Isa. 29. 22 ; Jer. 30. 6 ; Rev. 6. 8.

Palestina, păl-ĕs-tī'-nă. Ex. 15. 14 ; Isa. 14. 29, 31. R. V. Philistia, same as following.

Palestine, păl'-ĕs-tīne (Joel 3. 4). R. V. Philistia. The land of the Philistines, the name in the early Christian period being extended to the whole of the Holy Land.

Pallu, păl'-lū, 'distinguished.' Ex. 6. 14.

Palluites, păl'-lū-ītes, descendants of Pallu. Num. 26. 5.

Palm. (1) a measure = the width of the hand = ⅛ of a cubit = 3½ inches.
(2) Isa. 49. 16 ; Mat. 26. 67 ; Mk. 14. 65.
See Measures.

Palm tree (Ex. 15. 27). Heb. *Tâmâr :* Gk. φοῖνιξ : Bot. N. *Phœnix dactylifera.* The date palm. Its tall stem (from 30 to 80 feet high), surmounted by feathery foliage, was the symbol of elegance and grace ; hence it became a favourite woman's name, 'Tamar' (Gen. 38. 6 ; 2 Sam. 13. 1 ; 14. 27). The evergreen foliage and abundance of delicious fruit make it a type of the righteous man (Ps. 92. 12). Bethany (the 'house of Dates') received its name from their abundance there. Lev. 23. 40 ; Deu. 34. 3 ; Jud. 1. 16 ; 3. 13 ; 2 Chr. 28. 15 ; John 12. 13 ; Rev. 7. 9.

Palmerworm. *See* Caterpillar.

Palsy cured by Christ. Mat. 4. 24 ; 8. 6 ; 9. 2 ; Mk. 2. 3 ; Lu. 5. 18.
by His disciples. Acts 8. 7 ; 9. 33.

Palti, păl'-tī, 'my deliverance.' Num. 13. 9.

Paltiel, păl'-tĭ-ĕl, 'God is my deliverance.' Num. 34. 26.

Paltite, păl'-tīte, a descendant of Palti. 2 Sam. 23. 26.

Pamphylia, păm-phy̆l'-ĭ-ă. Paul preaches there. Acts 13. 13 ; 14. 24 ; 27. 5.

Pannag (Ezek. 27. 17). Heb. *Pannag :* Gk. κασία : R. V. marg. 'perhaps a kind of confection.' Perhaps the Turkish *pĕk-mĕs*, a considerable article of commerce. Composed of 'syrup, carob-honey, dibs (grape-honey) or date honey, boiled with a decoction of soapwort roots and sesame oil.' Dr. G. E. Post, in *Hastings' Bib. Dict.*

Pant. Ps. 38. 10 ; 42. 1 ; 119. 131 ; Am. 2. 7.

Paper reeds of Egypt. Isa. 19. 7. R. V. meadows.

Paphos, pā'-phŏs, Paul at. Acts 13. 6.
Elymas the sorcerer at. Acts 13. 8.

Parable taken up. Hab. 2. 6.

Parables as discourses. Num. 23. 7 ; 24. 5, 16 ; Ps. 78. 2 ; Job 27. ; Prov. 26. 9.

Parables, list of. *See* p. 218.

Parabolic symbols of the prophets. Isa. 5. 1 ; Jer. 13. 1 ; 18. ; 24. ; 27. ; Ezek. 16. ; 17. ; 19. ; 23. ; 24. ; 31. ; 33. ; 37.

Paradise. Probably a Persian word signifying a park, and used by the LXX. as a translation of the Heb. *Eden.* It is used as a symbol of the region of heavenly blessedness. 2 Cor. 12. 3, 4 ; Rev. 2. 7.
promised by Christ to the penitent thief. Lu. 23. 43.
Paul caught up into. 2 Cor. 12. 4.

Parah, pâr'-ăh, 'heifer.' Jos. 18. 23.

Paran, pâr'-ăn, 'cavernous ;' mount. Gen. 21. 21 ; Num. 10. 12 ; 12. 16 ; 13. 26 ; Deu. 33. 2 ; Hab. 3. 3.

Parbar, păr'-băr, 'outside place.' 1 Chr. 26. 18.

Parcel, a piece, portion. Gen. 33. 19.

Parched. Ru. 2. 14 ; Isa. 35. 7 ; Jer. 17. 6.

Parchments. 2 Tim. 4. 13, but especially the *p.*

Pardon. Ex. 23. 21, he will not *p.*
2 Kn. 5. 18, the Lord *p.* thy servant.
2 Chr. 30. 18, the good Lord *p.* every one.
Neh. 9. 17, a God ready to *p.*
Isa. 55. 7, he will abundantly *p.*

Pardon of sin. 2 Chr. 30. 18 ; Neh. 9. 17 ; Job 7. 21 ; Ps. 25. 11 ; Isa. 55. 7 ; Jer. 33. 8 ; 50. 20 ; Lam. 3. 42 ; Mic. 7. 18.

Parents. Mat. 10. 21 ; Mk. 13. 12, children rise up against *p.*
Lu. 18. 29, no man that hath left *p.*
21. 16, ye shall be betrayed by *p.*
John 9. 2, who did sin, this man, or his *p.* ?
Rom. 1. 30 ; 2 Tim. 3. 2, disobedient to *p.*
2 Cor. 12. 14, not to lay up for *p.*, but *p.* for children.
Eph. 6. 1 ; Col. 3. 20, children, obey your *p.*
See Lu. 2. 27 ; 8. 56 ; Heb. 11. 23.

Parents, duty of. Prov. 13. 24 ; 19. 18 ; 22. 6, 15 ; 23. 13 ; 29. 15, 17 ; Lu. 11. 13 ; Eph. 6. 4 ; Col. 3. 21 ; 1 Tim. 5. 8 ; Tit. 2. 4.
duty to. 1 Tim. 5. 4. *See* Obedience.

Parmashta, păr-măsh'-tă, 'superior' (?) Esth. 9. 9.

Parmenas, păr'-mĕ-năs, 'standing firm.' Acts 6. 5.

Parnach, păr'-năch. Num. 34. 25.

Parosh, pâr'-ŏsh, 'flea.' Ez. 2. 3.

Parshandatha, păr-shăn-dā'-thă, 'given by prayer' (?). Esth. 9. 7.

Part (*n.*). Jos. 22. 25, 27, ye have no *p.* in the Lord.
Ps. 5. 9, their inward *p.* is very wickedness.
51. 6, in hidden *p.* make me to know.
118. 7, the Lord taketh my *p.*
139. 9, dwell in the uttermost *p.*
Mk. 9. 40, he that is not against us is on our *p.*
Lu. 10. 42, that good *p.*
John 13. 8, thou hast no *p.* with me.

Acts 8. 21, neither *p.* nor lot.
2 Cor. 6. 15, what *p.* hath he that believeth ?
See Tit. 2. 8; Rev. 20. 6; 21. 8; 22. 19. [and me.

Part (*v.*). Ru. 1. 17, if ought but death *p.* thee
2 Sam. 14. 6, there was none to *p.* them.
Ps. 22. 18, they *p.* my garments.
Lu. 24. 51, while he blessed them he was *p.*
Acts 2. 45, *p.* them to all men.
See Mat. 27. 35; Mk. 15. 24; Lu. 23. 34; John 19. 24.

Partaker. Ps. 50. 18, hast been *p.* with adulterers.
Rom. 15. 27, *p.* of their spiritual things.
1 Cor. 9. 10, *p.* of his hope.
9. 13; 10. 18, *p.* with the altar.
10. 17, *p.* of that one bread.
10. 21, *p.* of the Lord's table.
1 Tim. 5. 22, neither be *p.* of other men's sins.
Heb. 3. 1, *p.* of the heavenly calling.
1 Pet. 4. 13, *p.* of Christ's sufferings.
5. 1, a *p.* of the glory.
2 Pet. 1. 4, *p.* of the divine nature.
See Eph. 3. 6; Phil. 1. 7; Col. 1. 12; Rev. 18. 4.

Parthians, pär'-thĭ-ăns. Acts 2. 9.

Partiality condemned. Lev. 19. 15; Deu. 1. 17; 16. 19; Prov. 18. 5; 24. 23; Mal. 2. 9; 1 Tim. 5. 21; Jas. 2. 4; 3. 17; Jude 16.

Particular. 1 Cor. 12. 27; Eph. 5. 33.

Particularly, in detail, one by one. Acts 21. 10.

Partition. 1 Kn. 6. 21; Eph. 2. 14.

Partner. Prov. 29. 24; Lu. 5. 7; 2 Cor. 8. 23.

Partridge (Jer. 17. 11; 1 Sam. 26. 20). Heb. *Kôrè*: Gk. πέρδιξ. (Specimens, *Caccabis Græcus; Ammoperdix Heyii,* found at Jericho.) The sand partridge suits David's comparison in 1 Sam. 26. 20.

Parables.

Parables in the Old Testament.

Parables.	By whom spoken.	References.
The ewe lamb	Nathan to David	2 Sam. 12. 1-4.
The two brethren, and avengers of blood.	Widow of Tekoah	2 Sam. 14. 1-11.
Escaped captive	Man of the sons of the prophets to Ahab	1 Kn. 20. 35-40.
Vineyard and grapes	Isaiah to Judah and Jerusalem	Isa. 5. 1-7.
Eagles and vine	Ezekiel to Israel	Ezek. 17. 3-10.
Lions' whelps	Ezekiel to Israel	Ezek. 19. 2-9.
The boiling pot	Ezekiel to Israel	Ezek. 24. 3-5.
Parabolic Fables.		
Trees choosing a king	Jotham to Shechemites	Jud. 9. 7-15.
Micaiah's vision		1 Kn. 22. 19-23.
Thistle and cedar	Jehoash to Amaziah	2 Kn. 14. 9; 2 Chr. 25. 18.

Parables of our Lord.

Parables.	Mat.	Mark.	Luke.	Leading Lessons.
I. *Recorded in one Gospel only.*				
The tares	13. 24			Good and evil in life and judgment.
The hid treasure	13. 44			Value of the gospel.
The goodly pearl	13. 45			The seeker finding salvation.
The draw-net	13. 47			Visible Church a mixed body.
The unmerciful servant	18. 23			Duty of forgiveness.
The labourers in the vineyard	20. 1			Precedence in service gives no claim for priority in reward.
The two sons	21. 28			Insincerity and repentance.
The marriage of the king's son	22. 2			Necessity of the robe of righteousness.
The ten virgins	25. 1			Watchful preparation and careless security.
The talents	25. 14			Use of advantages.
The sheep and goats	25. 31			Love the test of life.
The seed growing secretly		4. 26		The law of growth in religion.
The householder		13. 34		Watchfulness.
The two debtors			7. 41	Gratitude for pardon.
The good Samaritan			10. 30	Active benevolence.
The importunate friend			11. 5	Perseverance in prayer.
The rich fool			12. 16	Worldly-mindedness.
Servants watching			12. 35	Expectancy of the Second Coming.
The wise steward			12. 42	Conscientiousness in trust.
The barren fig tree			13. 6	Unprofitableness under grace.
The great supper			14. 16	Universality of the Divine call.

Parables of our Lord — (*Continued*).

Parables.	Mat.	Mark.	Luke.	Leading Lessons.
Tower; king going to war........	....	....	14. 28	Prudence and self-denial.
The piece of money	....	....	15. 8	Joy over penitence.
The prodigal son........	....	....	15. 11	Fatherly love to returning sinner.
The unjust steward........	....	....	16. 1	Faithfulness to trust.
The rich man and Lazarus........	....	....	16. 19	Hopeless future of the unfaithful.
Unprofitable servants........	....	....	17. 7	God's claim on all our service.
The unjust judge........	....	....	18. 2	Advantage of persevering prayer.
The Pharisee and publican........	....	....	18. 10	Self-righteousness and humility.
The pounds........	....	....	19. 12	Diligence rewarded, sloth punished.
II. *Recorded in two Gospels.*				
House on rock, and on the sand...	7. 24	....	6. 47	Consistent and false profession.
The leaven........	13. 33	....	13. 20	Pervading influence of religion.
The lost sheep........	18. 12	....	15. 4	Joy over penitent.
III. *Recorded in three Gospels.*			[11. 33	
Candle under a bushel........	5. 15	4. 21	8. 16;	Dissemination of truth.
New cloth on old garment........	9. 16	2. 21	5. 36	New doctrine on old prejudices.
New wine in old bottles........	9. 17	2. 22	5. 37	New spirit in unregenerate heart.
The sower........	13. 3	4. 3	8. 5	Hearers divided into classes.
The mustard-seed........	13. 31	4. 30	13. 18	Spread of the gospel.
The wicked husbandmen........	21. 33	12. 1	20. 9	Rejection of Christ by the Jews.
The fig tree and all the trees......	24. 32	13. 28	21. 29	Indications of Second Advent.

N. B. These 40 parables are grouped according to their record by the Evangelists. For their approximate chronological position, *see* Harmony of the Gospels.

Paruah, pă-rū'-ăh, 'flourishing.' 1 Kn. 4. 17.
Parvaim, pär-vā'-ĭm, 'oriental regions' (?). 2 Chr. 3. 6.
Pasach. pā'-săch, 'divider.' 1 Chr. 7. 33.
Pas-dammim, păs-dăm'-mĭm, shortened from Ephes-dammim. 1 Chr. 11. 13.
Paseah, pă-sē'-ăh, 'lame.' (1) 1 Chr. 4. 12. (2) Neh. 3. 6.
Pashur, păsh'-ŭr, his cruelty to Jeremiah. (1) Jer. 20. (2) Jer. 21.
Pass. (1) Ex. 12. 13, when I see the blood I will *p.* over.
Isa. 43. 2, when thou *p.* through waters.
Mat. 26. 39; Mk. 14. 36, let this cup *p.*
Lu. 16. 26, neither can they *p.* to us.
1 Cor. 7. 31; 1 John 2. 17, fashion of this world *p.*
(2) to surpass, exceed. Ezek. 32. 19, *p.* in beauty.
Eph. 3. 19, love of Christ, which *p.* knowledge.
Phil. 4. 7, which *p.* all understanding.
See Jer. 2. 6; Lu. 13. 37; Rom. 5. 12; Rev. 21. 1.
Passage. (1) a ford. Jud. 12. 6.
(2) a pass. 1 Sam. 14. 4.
Passion. Acts 1. 3; 14. 15; Jas. 5. 17.
Passover. The Passover was a great Historical Festival. Year after year it recalled, as in 'a living drama,' the great facts of the national deliverance from Egyptian bondage. The directions for its yearly celebration are given in Ex. 23. 15; Lev. 23. 5–8; Num. 28. 16–25. It lasted from the 14th to the 21st of Nisan or Abib. *See* Feasts.
Passover ordained. Ex. 12. 3, 11. [Deu. 16.
laws relating to. Lev. 23. 4; Num. 9.; 28. 16;
kept under Moses in Egypt, Ex. 12. 12. at Sinai, Num. 9. 5. under Joshua in Canaan, Jos. 5. 10. by Hezekiah after the captivity of Israel, 2 Chr. 30. 13. by Josiah before the captivity of Judah, 2 Kn. 23. 21; 2 Chr. 35. by Ezra on return from the captivity, Ez. 6. 19.
kept by Christ. Mat. 26. 19; Mk. 14. 12; Lu. 22. 7; John 13.
a type of Christ's death. 1 Cor. 5. 7.
Past. Job 29. 2, as in months *p.* R. V. of old.
Eccl. 3. 15, God requireth that which is *p.*
S. of S. 2. 11, the winter is *p.*
Jer. 8. 20, the harvest is *p.*
Rom. 3. 25, of sins that are *p.*
11. 33, ways *p.* finding out.
2 Cor. 5. 17, old things *p.* away.
Eph. 4. 19, being *p.* feeling.
See Eph. 2. 2; 2 Tim. 2. 18; 1 Pet. 2. 10.
Pastor, a shepherd. Jer. 3. 15; 17. 16; Eph. 4. 11.
Pastors transgressing. Jer. 2. 8; 10. 21; 23.
Pasture, spiritual. Ps. 23. 2; 74. 1; 79. 13; 95. 7; 100.; Ezek. 34. 14; John 10. 9.
Patara, păt'-ă-ră. Acts 21. 1.
Pate. Ps. 7. 16. [knoweth.
Path. Job 28. 7, there is a *p.* which no fowl
Ps. 16. 11, shew me the *p.* of life.
27. 11, lead me in a plain *p.*
65. 11, thy *p.* drop fatness.
77. 19, thy *p.* is in the great waters.
119. 105, a light to my *p.*
Prov. 4. 18, the *p.* of the just.
Isa. 2. 3; Mic. 4. 2, we will walk in his *p.*
42. 16, in *p.* they have not known.
58. 12, restorer of *p.* to dwell in.
Jer. 6. 16, ask for the old *p.*
Mat. 3. 3; Mk. 1. 3; Lu. 3. 4, make his *p.* straight.
See Ps. 139. 3; Prov. 3. 17; Lam. 3. 9; Heb. 12. 13.
Pathros, păth'-rŏs, in Egypt. Isa. 11. 11; Jer. 44. 1, 15; Ezek. 29. 14; 30. 14.
Pathrusim, păth-rū'-sĭm, people of Pathros. Gen. 10. 14.
Patience. Mat. 18. 26, 29, have *p.* with me.
Lu. 8. 15, bring forth fruit with *p.*
21. 19, in your *p.* possess ye your souls.
Rom. 5. 3, tribulation worketh *p.*
8. 25, with *p.* wait for it.
15. 4, through *p.* and comfort.
15. 5, the God of *p.*
2 Cor. 6. 4, as ministers of God in much *p.*
Col. 1. 11 strengthened with all might to all *p.*
1 Thes. 1. 3, your *p.* of hope.
2 Thes. 1. 4, glory in you for your *p.*
1 Tim. 6. 11, follow after *p.*

Tit. 2. 2, sound in faith, charity, *p.*
Heb. 10. 36, ye have need of *p.*
12. 1, run with *p.*
Jas. 1. 3, trying of your faith worketh *p.*
1. 4, let *p.* have her perfect work.
5. 7, the husbandman hath long *p.*
5. 10, for an example of *p.*
5. 11, ye have heard of the *p.* of Job.
2 Pet. 1. 6, add to temperance *p.*
Rev. 2. 2, 19, I know thy *p.*
3. 10, thou hast kept word of *p.*
13. 10; 14. 12, here is the *p.* of saints.

Patience commended. Ps. 37. 7; Eccl. 7. 8; Isa. 30. 15; 40. 31; Lu. 21. 19; Rom. 12. 12; 1 Thes. 5. 14; 2 Thes. 3. 5; 1 Tim. 3. 3; 6. 11; Heb. 12. 1; Jas. 1. 3; 5. 7; 1 Pet. 2. 20; 2 Pet. 1. 6.
blessed results of. Rom. 5. 3; 15. 4; Heb. 6. 12; Rev. 2. 2; 3. 10.
Patiently. Ps. 37. 7; 40. 1; Heb. 6. 15; 1 Pet. 2. 20.
Patmos, păt′-mŏs, place of St. John's exile. Rev. 1. 9.
Patriarchs, their genealogy. Gen. 5.

Patriarchs, The, and their Descendants.

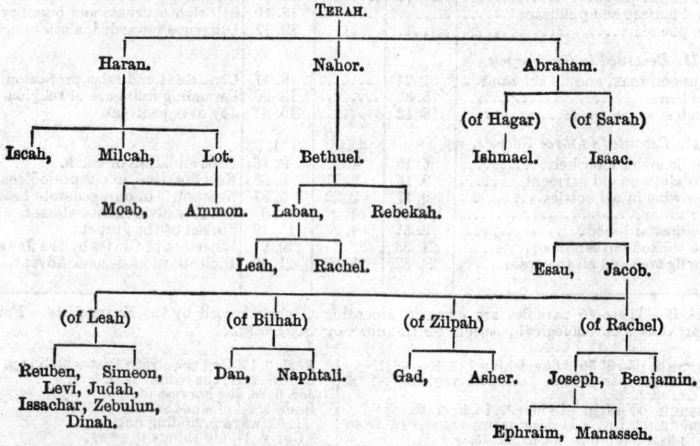

Patrobas, păt′-rō-băs. Rom. 16. 14.
Pattern. 1 Tim. 1. 16; Tit. 2. 7.
Pattern of the tabernacle, &c. Ex. 25. 9, 40 (Ezek. 43. 10); Heb. 8. 5; 9. 23.
Pau, pā′-ū, older form of PAI. Gen. 36. 39.
Paul, paûl, *or* **Paulus**, paû′-lŭs, 'little.' Acts 13. 9.
as a persecutor. Acts 7. 58; 8. 1; 9. 1; 22. 4; 26. 9; 1 Cor. 15. 9; Gal. 1. 13; Phil. 3. 6; 1 Tim. 1. 13.
as a convert to the gospel. Acts 9. 3; 22. 6; 26. 12.
as a preacher. Acts 9. 19, 29; 13. 1, 4, 14; 17. 18 (2 Cor. 11. 32; Gal. 1. 17).
stoned at Lystra. Acts 14. 8, 19.
contends with Barnabas. Acts 15. 36.
is persecuted at Philippi. Acts 16.
the Holy Ghost given by his hands to John's disciples at Ephesus. Acts 19. 6.
restores Eutychus. Acts 20. 10.
his charge to the elders of Ephesus, at Miletus. [Acts 20. 17.
his return to Jerusalem, and persecution there. Acts 21.
his defence before the people and the council. Acts 22.; 23.
before Felix, Acts 24. Festus, Acts 25. and Agrippa, Acts 26.
appeals to Cæsar at Rome. Acts 25.
his voyage and shipwreck. Acts 27.
miracles by, at Melita. Acts 28. 3, 8.
at Rome, reasons with the Jews. Acts 28. 17.
his love to the churches. Rom. 1. 8; 15.; 1 Cor. 1. 4; 4. 14; 2 Cor. 1.; 2.; 6.; 7.; Phil. 1.; Col. 1.; 1 & 2 Thes.
his sufferings. 1 Cor. 4. 9; 2 Cor. 11. 23; 12. 7; Phil. 1. 12; 2 Tim. 2. 11.
divine revelations to. 2 Cor. 12. 1.
defends his apostleship. 1 Cor. 9.; 2 Cor. 11.; 12.; 2 Tim. 3. 10.
commends Timothy, &c. 1 Cor. 16. 10; Phil. 2. 19; 1 Thes. 3. 2.
commends Titus. 2 Cor. 7. 13; 8. 23.
blames Peter. Gal. 2. 14.
pleads for Onesimus. Philem.
his epistles mentioned by St. Peter. 2 Pet. 3. 15.

Paul's Missionary Journeys. *See* ACTS, CHRONOLOGY OF.

I. First Journey with Barnabas and John Mark. Acts 13., 14. Two or more years, from A. D. 47 to A. D. 49. Sent forth A. D. 47, from
SYRIA { Antioch, the capital. Seleucia, the seaport.
CYPRUS { Salamis. Paphos.
ASIA MINOR { PAMPHYLIA — Perga. PISIDIA — Antioch. LYCAONIA { Iconium. Lystra. Derbe, the farthest point.
RETURNS via
Lystra.
Iconium.
Antioch.
Perga.
Attalia.
to
ANTIOCH IN SYRIA, A. D. 49.

II. St. Paul's Second Missionary Journey with Silas. Acts 15. 36–18. 22. Three or more years, from close of A. D. 50 to A. D. 52.
SYRIA { Antioch, the starting-point; and the towns to the North.
CILICIA — by land from Syria.

Lycaonia { Derbe. Lystra. Iconium.
Phrygia.
Galatia. South Galatia, including the cities above named.
Mysia — Troas.
Macedonia { Neapolis. Philippi. Thessalonica. Berea.
Greece { Athens. Corinth. Cenchræa.
Returns via
Ephesus.
Cæsarea.
Jerusalem.
to
Antioch in Syria. A. D. 52.

III. St. Paul's Third Missionary Journey with Timothy and others. Acts 18. 23–21. 17. Three or four years, from A. D. 53 to 56.
Syria — Antioch, the starting-point.
Galatia, and its churches.
Phrygia.
Asia — Ephesus, and vicinity; nearly three years.
Mysia — Troas.
Macedonia — Philippi.
Greece — Corinth.
Returns through:
Philippi.
Troas.
Assos.
Mitylene.
Trogyllium.
Miletus.
Patara.
Tyre.
Ptolemais.
Cæsarea.
to
Jerusalem.

Paul's voyage to Rome, with St. Luke, Aristarchus, and certain prisoners under charge of Julius, a Centurion of the Augustan Cohort. Acts 27. 28. A. D. 59 and 60.
Sailed from Cæsarea to
Mediterranean Sea. { Sidon. Cyprus. Myra. Cnidus. Salmone. Fair Havens. Phœnix. Cauda. Malta. Syracuse.
Italy. { Rhegium. Puteoli. Appii Forum. The Three Taverns. Rome.

Pavement. 2 Kn. 16. 17; Ezek. 40. 17, 18; John [19. 13.
Pavilion. 2 Sam. 22. 12, and he made darkness *p.*
See Ps. 18. 11; 27. 5; 31. 20; Jer. 43. 10.
Pay. Ex. 22. 7, let him *p.* double. [the price.
Num. 20. 19, water, I will *p.* for it. R. V. give
2 Kn. 4. 7, sell the oil, and *p.* thy debt.
Ps. 22. 25; 66. 13; 116. 14, will *p.* my vows.
Prov. 22. 27, if thou hast nothing to *p.*
Eccl. 5. 4, defer not to *p.* it.
Mat. 18. 26, I will *p.* thee all.
18. 28, *p.* that thou owest.
23. 23, ye *p.* tithe of mint.
See Ex. 21. 19; Mat. 17. 24; Rom. 13. 6; Heb. 7. 9.
Peace. Gen. 41. 16, an answer of *p.*
Num. 6. 26, the Lord give thee *p.*
25. 12, my covenant of *p.*
Deu. 20. 10, proclaim *p.* to it.
23. 6, thou shalt not seek their *p.*
1 Sam. 25. 6; Lu. 10. 5, *p.* be to this house.
2 Kn. 9. 19, what hast thou to do with *p.*?
9. 31, had Zimri *p.*, who slew his master?
Job 5. 23, beasts shall be at *p.* with thee.
22. 21, acquaint thyself with him, and be at *p.*
Ps. 4. 8, I will lay me down in *p.*
29. 11, the Lord will bless his people with *p.*
34. 14; 1 Pet. 3. 11, seek *p.*, and pursue it.
37. 37, the end of that man is *p.*
85. 8, will speak *p.* to his people.
122. 6, pray for *p.* of Jerusalem.
Eccl. 3. 8, a time of *p.*
Isa. 26. 3, keep him in perfect *p.*
32. 17, work of righteousness shall be *p.*
45. 7, I make *p.*, and create evil.
48. 18, thy *p.* as a river.
48. 22; 57. 21, no *p.* to the wicked.
52. 7; Nah. 1. 15, that publisheth *p.*
59. 8; Rom. 3. 17, the way of *p.* they know not.
Jer. 6. 14; 8. 11, saying *p.*, *p.*, when there is no *p.*
8. 15; 14. 19, we looked for *p.*
34. 5, thou shalt die in *p.*
Ezek. 7. 25, they shall seek *p.* [be multiplied.
Dan. 4. 1; 6. 25; 1 Pet. 1. 2; 2 Pet. 1. 2; Jude 2, *p.*
Hag. 2. 9, in this place will I give *p.*
Mat. 10. 13, let your *p.* come upon it.
10. 34; Lu. 12. 51, to send *p.* on earth.
Mk. 9. 50, have *p.* one with another.
Lu. 1. 79, to guide our feet into way of *p.*
2. 14, on earth *p.*
19. 42, things which belong to thy *p.*
24. 36; John 20. 19, *p.* be unto you.
John 14. 27, *p.* I leave, my *p.* I give you.
16. 33, that in me ye might have *p.*
Rom. 1. 7; 1 Cor. 1. 3; 2 Cor. 1. 2; Gal. 1. 3; Eph. 1. 2; Phil. 1. 2, *p.* from God our Father.
5. 1, we have *p.* with God.
10. 15; Eph. 6. 15, the gospel of *p.*
14. 19, follow after the things which make for *p.*
15. 33; 16. 20; 2 Cor. 13. 11; Phil. 4. 9; 1 Thes. 5. 23; Heb. 13. 20, the God of *p.*
1 Cor. 14. 33, author of *p.*
2 Cor. 13. 11, live in *p.*
Eph. 2. 14, he is our *p.*
2. 17, *p.* to you which were afar off.
4. 3, in the bond of *p.* [standing.
Phil. 4. 7, *p.* of God which passeth all under-
Col. 1. 2; 1 Thes. 1. 1; 2 Thes. 1. 2; 1 Tim. 1. 2; 2 Tim. 1. 2; Tit. 1. 4; Philem. 3; 2 John 3, grace and *p.* from God.
3. 15, let the *p.* of God rule in your hearts.
1 Thes. 5. 13, be at *p.* among yourselves.
2 Thes. 3. 16, Lord of *p.* give you *p.* always.
2 Tim. 2. 22; Heb. 12. 14, follow *p.* with all men.
Heb. 7. 2, king of *p.*
Jas. 2. 16, depart in *p.*
3. 18, fruit of righteousness is sown in *p.*
2 Pet. 3. 14, found of him in *p.* [1 Tim. 2. 2.
Peace to be sought of God. Ez. 6. 10; Jer. 29. 7;
bestowed by God. Lev. 26. 6; 1 Kn. 2. 33; 4. 24; 2 Kn. 20. 19; Prov. 16. 7; Isa. 45. 7; Jer. 14. 13.
exhortations to maintain. Ps. 34. 14; Mat. 5. 9; Rom. 12. 18; 14. 19; 1 Cor. 7. 15; Eph. 4. 3; 1 Thes. 5. 13; 2 Tim. 2. 22; Jas. 3. 18; 1 Pet. 3. 11.
spiritual, gift of God (John 14. 27). Acts 10. 36; Rom. 1. 7; 5. 1; 8. 6; 14. 17; Phil. 4. 7; Col. 3. 15; 1 Thes. 5. 23; 2 Thes. 3. 16; Rev. 1. 4.
proclaimed to the Gentiles. Zec. 9. 10; Eph. 2. 14, 17; 3.
produced by the Spirit. Gal. 5. 22.
denied to the wicked. 2 Kn. 9. 31; Isa. 48. 22; 59. 8 (Rom. 3. 17); Jer. 12. 12; Ezek. 7. 25.
to whom promised. Ps. 29. 11; 85. 8; 122. 6; 125. 5; 128. 6; 147. 14; John 14. 27; Gal. 6. 16; Eph. 6. 23.
on earth. Lu. 2. 14.
in heaven. Lu. 19. 38.
Peace (Salem), king of (Melchisedec). Heb. 7. 2.
Peace, the prince of (Christ). Isa. 9. 6.
Peaceable. Isa. 32. 18; 1 Tim. 2. 2; Heb. 12. 11; Jas. 3. 17.
Peaceably. Gen. 37. 4; 1 Sam. 16. 4; Jer. 9. 8; Rom. 12. 18.

Peace offerings, laws pertaining to. Ex. 20. 24; 24. 5; Lev. 3.; 6.; 7. 11; 19. 5.
Peacock (1 Kn. 10. 22). Heb. *Tucciyyim* (plural); Gk. ταώς. (Specimen, *Pavo cristatus.*) 2 Chr. 9. 21, the ships of Tarshish bringing *p.*
Job 39. 13, gavest thou the goodly wings unto the *p.* R. V. ostrich.
Pearl, parable of. Mat. 7. 6; 13. 45. *See* 1 Tim. 2. 9; Rev. 17. 4.
Peculiar people of God. Deu. 14. 2; Ps. 135. 4. *See* Tit. 2. 14; 1 Pet. 2. 9.
Pedahel, pĕ-däh'-ĕl, 'God redeemed.' Num. 34. 28.
Pedahzur, pĕ-däh'-zûr, 'the Rock redeemed.' Num. 1. 10.
Pedaiah, pĕ-dāī'-ăh, 'Jehovah redeemed.' 1 Chr. 27. 20.
Pedigree. Num. 1. 18.
Peeled, stripped of the skin. Isa. 18. 2; Ezek. 29. [18.
Peep, to chirp, to utter low sounds. Isa. 8. 19; 10. 14.
Pekah, pē'-käh, 'open-eyed' (?); king of Israel. 2 Kn. 15. 25.
his victory over Judah. 2 Chr. 28. 6.
denounced in prophecy. Isa. 7. 1.
Pekahiah, pĕk-ă-hī'-ăh, 'Jehovah opened;' king of Israel. 2 Kn. 15. 22.
Pekod, pē'-kŏd, 'visitation.' Jer. 50. 21.
Pelaiah, pĕ-lāī'-ăh, 'Jehovah distinguished.' 1 Chr. 3. 24.
Pelaliah, pĕl-ă-lī'-ăh, 'Jehovah judged.' Neh. 11. 12.
Pelatiah, pĕl-ă-tī'-ăh, 'Jehovah delivered.' Ezek. 11. 1.
Peleg, pē'-lĕg, 'division.' Gen. 10. 25.
Pelet, pē'-lĕt, 'liberation.' (1) 1 Chr. 2. 47. (2) 1 Chr. 12. 3.
Peleth, pē'-lĕth, 'swiftness.' (1) Num. 16. 1. (2) 1 Chr. 2. 33.
Pelethites, pĕl'-ĕ-thītes, 'runners.' 2 Sam. 8. 18.
Pelican. Heb. *Kâath*: Gk. πελεκᾶς, an unclean bird of uninhabited places. Spends the winter in Palestine; migrates in the summer to Russia.
Lev. 11. 18, and the swan, and the *p.*
Deu. 14. 17, the *p.*, and the gier eagle.
Ps. 102. 6, I am like a *p.* of the wilderness.
Pelonite, pē'-lō-nīte. 1 Chr. 11. 27.
Pen. Jud. 5. 14, they that handle the *p.* R. V. marshal's staff.
Job 19. 24, graven with an iron *p.*
Ps. 45. 1, my tongue is the *p.* of a ready writer.
Isa. 8. 1, write in it with a man's *p.*
Jer. 8. 8, the *p.* of the scribes is in vain.
17. 1, is written with a *p.* of iron.
3 John 13, I will not with ink and *p.* write.
Pence. Mat. 18. 28; Mk. 14. 5; Lu. 7. 41; 10. 35.
Peniel, pĕn'-ĭ-ĕl, 'the face of God;' scene of Jacob's wrestling with an angel. Gen. 32. 30.
Gideon's vengeance upon. Jud. 8. 17.
Peninnah, pĕ-nĭn'-năh, 'coral.' 1 Sam. 1. 2.
Penny. Mat. 20. 13, didst not thou agree with me for a *p.*?
22. 19, they brought him a *p.*
Mk. 12. 15, bring me a *p.*
Rev. 6. 6, a measure of wheat for a *p.*
Pentecost, pĕn'-tē-cŏst (Acts 2. 1), so named from the Greek word for *fiftieth* day after the Passover, counting seven complete weeks from the 16th of Nisan. It is called the 'Feast of Weeks' (Ex. 34. 22), and the 'Feast of Harvest' (Ex. 23. 16). It was a kind of Thanksgiving Day, and lasted but one day. The passages bearing on it will be found in Ex. 23. 16; Lev. 23. 15-21; Num. 28. 26-31; Deu. 16. 9-13. *See* Feasts.
Holy Spirit given at. Acts 2. [32. 31.
Penuel, pĕn-ū'ĕl. (1) old form of Peniel. Gen. (2) persons. 1 Chr. 4. 4; 8. 25.
Penury. Prov. 14. 23; Lu. 21. 4.
People. Ex. 6. 7; Deu. 4. 20; 2 Sam. 7. 24; Jer. 13. 11, I will take you to me for a *p.*
Lev. 20. 24, 26, separated from other *p.*
Deu. 4. 33, did ever *p.* hear voice of God and live?
33. 29, O *p.* saved by the Lord.
2 Sam. 22. 44; Ps. 18. 43, a *p.* I knew not.
Ps. 81. 11, my *p.* would not hearken.
144. 15, happy is that *p.*
Prov. 30. 25, the ants are a *p.* not strong.
Isa. 1. 4, a *p.* laden with iniquity.
27. 11, a *p.* of no understanding.
43. 4, I will give *p.* for thy life.
43. 8, blind *p.* that have eyes.
Jer. 6. 22; 50. 41, a *p.* cometh from the north.
Jon. 1. 8, of what *p.* art thou?
Lu. 1. 17, a *p.* prepared for the Lord.
Tit. 2. 14, purify unto himself a peculiar *p.*
People of God, their blessings and privileges. Deu. 7. 6; 32. 9; 33.; 1 Sam. 12. 22; 2 Sam. 7. 23; Ps. 3. 8; 29. 11; 33. 12; 77. 15; 85.; 89. 15; 94. 14; 95. 7; 100.; 110.; 111. 6; 121.; 125.; 144. 15; 148. 14; 149. 4; Isa. 11. 11; 14. 32; 30. 19; 33. 24; 49. 13; 51. 22; 65. 18; Dan. 7. 27; Joel 2. 18; 3. 16; Zep. 3. 9, 20; Mat. 1. 21; Lu. 1. 17; Acts 15. 14; Rom. 11.; 2 Cor. 6. 16; Tit. 2. 14; Heb. 4. 9; 8. 10; 1 Pet. 2. 9; Rev. 5. 9; 21. 3.
Peor, pē'-ŏr, 'point' (Baal). Num. 23. 28; 25. 3, 18; Jos. 22. 17.
Peradventure, perhaps. Gen. 31. 31.
Perazim, pĕ-rā'-zĭm, 'breaches.' Isa. 28. 21.
Perceive. Deu. 29. 4, a heart to *p.* R. V. know.
Jos. 22. 31, we *p.* the Lord is among us. R. V. know.
Job 9. 11, I *p.* him not.
23. 8, I cannot *p.* him.
Isa. 6. 9, see indeed, but *p.* not.
33. 19, deeper speech than thou canst *p.*
64. 4, nor *p.* by the ear what God hath.
Mat. 22. 18, Jesus *p.* their wickedness.
Mk. 8. 17, *p.* ye not yet?
Lu. 8. 46, I *p.* that virtue is gone out.
John 4. 19, I *p.* thou art a prophet.
Acts 10. 34, I *p.* God is no respecter of persons.
1 John 3. 16, hereby *p.* we the love of God. R. V. know.
See 1 Sam. 3. 8; Neh. 6. 12; Job 33. 14; Mk. 12. 28.
Perdition, what results in. Phil. 1. 28; 1 Tim. 6. 9; Heb. 10. 39; 2 Pet. 3. 7; Rev. 17. 8.
the son of. John 17. 12; 2 Thes. 2. 3.
Peres, pē'-rĕs, 'divided.' Dan. 5. 28.
Peresh, pē'-rĕsh, 'distinction.' 1 Chr. 7. 16.
Perez, pē'-rĕz, 'breach.' 1 Chr. 27. 3.
Perez-uzza, pē'-rĕz-ŭz'-ză, same as following. 1 Chr. 13. 11.
Perez-uzzah, pē'-rĕz-ŭz'-zăh, 'breach of Uzzah.' 2 Sam. 6. 8.
Perfect. Gen. 6. 9, Noah was *p.*
Gen. 17. 1, walk before me, and be thou *p.*
Deu. 18. 13, thou shalt be *p.* with the Lord.
32. 4, his work is *p.*
2 Sam. 22. 31; Ps. 18. 30, his way is *p.*
Ps. 19. 7, law of the Lord is *p.*
37. 37, mark the *p.* man.
Prov. 4. 18, more and more to *p.* day.
Ezek. 28. 15, thou wast *p.* in thy ways.
Mat. 5. 48; 2 Cor. 13. 11, be ye *p.*
19. 21, if thou wilt be *p.*
John 17. 23, be made *p.* in one.
Rom. 12. 2, that *p.* will of God.
1 Cor. 2. 6, wisdom among them that are *p.*
2 Cor. 12. 9, strength made *p.* in weakness.
Eph. 4. 13, unto a *p.* man. R. V. fullgrown.
Phil. 3. 12, not as though I were already *p.*
3. 15, let us, as many as be *p.*
Col. 1. 28, present every man *p.*
4. 12, may stand *p.* and complete.
2 Tim. 3. 17, that the man of God may be *p.* R. V. complete.
Heb. 2. 10, make *p.* through suffering.
11. 40, without us should not be made *p.*
12. 23, spirits of just men made *p.*
13. 21, make you *p.* in every good work.
Jas. 1. 4, patience have her *p.* work.
1. 17, every good and *p.* gift.
1. 25, *p.* law of liberty.
3. 2, the same is a *p.* man.
1 John 4. 18, *p.* love casteth out fear.
See 2 Chr. 8. 16; 2 Cor. 7. 1.

Perfection. Job 11. 7; 2 Cor. 13. 9.
Perfection of God. Deu. 32. 4; 2 Sam. 22. 31; Job 36. 4; Mat. 5. 48.
of Christ. Heb. 2. 10; 5. 9; 7. 28.
of God's law. Ps. 19. 7; 119.; Jas. 1. 25.
of saints. 1 Cor. 2. 6; Eph. 4. 12; Col. 1. 28; 3. 14; 2 Tim. 3. 17. *See* Mat. 5. 48; Lu. 6. 40; 2 Cor. 12. 9; Heb. 6. 1; 11. 40.
Perfectly. Jer. 23. 20; Acts 18. 26; 1 Cor. 1. 10.
Perfectness. Col. 3. 14.
Perform. Ex. 18. 18, not able to *p.* it thyself alone.
Esth. 5. 6; 7. 2, to half of kingdom it shall be *p.*
Job 5. 12, cannot *p.* their enterprise.
Ps. 65. 1, unto thee shall the vow be *p.*
119. 106, I have sworn, and I will *p.* it. R. V. have confirmed.
Isa. 9. 7, zeal of the Lord will *p.* this.
44. 28, shall *p.* all my pleasure.
Jer. 29. 10; 33. 14, I will *p.* my good word.
Rom. 4. 21, able also to *p.*
7. 18, how to *p.* that which is good I find not.
Phil. 1. 6, *p.* it until day of Christ.
See Job 23. 14; Ps. 57. 2; Jer. 35. 14; Mat. 5. 33.
Performance. Lu. 1. 45; 2 Cor. 8. 11.
Perfume, the most holy. Ex. 30. 34. [25.
Perga, pĕr′-gă, visited by Paul. Acts 13. 13; 14.
Pergamos, pĕr′-gă-mŏs, 'citadel' (?), epistle to. Rev. 1. 11; 2. 12.
Perida, pĕ-ri′-dă, 'a recluse.' Neh. 7. 57.
Peril. Lam. 5. 9; Rom. 8. 35; 2 Cor. 11. 26.
Perilous. 2 Tim. 3. 1.
Perish. Num. 17. 12, we die, we *p.*, we all *p.* R. V. are undone.
Deu. 26. 5. a Syrian ready to *p.*
Job 4. 7, who ever *p.*, being innocent?
29. 13, blessing of him that was ready to *p.*
34. 15, all flesh shall *p.* together.
Ps. 1. 6, way of ungodly shall *p.*
37. 20, the wicked shall *p.*
49. 12, like the beasts that *p.*
80. 16, they *p.* at rebuke of thy countenance.
102. 26, they shall *p.*, but thou shalt endure.
Prov. 11. 10; 28. 28, when the wicked *p.*
29. 18, no vision, the people *p.* R. V. cast off restraint.
31. 6, strong drink to him that is ready to *p.*
Isa. 27. 13, they shall come that were ready to *p.*
Jer. 7. 28, truth is *p.*
Jon. 1. 6; 3. 9, God will think on us, that we *p.* not.
1. 14, let us not *p.* for this man's life.
Mat. 8. 25; Lu. 8. 24, save us, we *p.*
18. 14, that one of these little ones should *p.*
26. 52, shall *p.* with the sword.
Mk. 4. 38, carest thou not that we *p.*?
Lu. 13. 3, 5, ye shall all likewise *p.*
15. 17, I *p.* with hunger.
21. 18, there shall not an hair of your head *p.*
John 6. 27, labour not for the meat which *p.*
Acts 8. 20, thy money *p.* with thee.
Col. 2. 22, which are to *p.* with the using.
2 Pet. 3. 9, not willing that any should *p.*
See Ps. 2. 12; Jer. 6. 21; John 10. 28; Rom. 2. 12.
Perizzites, pĕ-rĭz′-zītes, 'belonging to a village.' Gen. 13. 7; 15. 20; 34. 30; Jud. 1. 4; 2 Chr. 8. 7.
Perjury condemned. Ex. 20. 16; Lev. 6. 3; 19. 12; Deu. 5. 20; Ezek. 17. 16; Zec. 5. 4; 8. 17; 1 Tim. 1. 10.
Permission. 1 Cor. 7. 6.
Permit. 1 Cor. 14. 34; 16. 7; Heb. 6. 3.
Pernicious. 2 Pet. 2. 2.
Perpetual. Ex. 31. 16, sabbath for a *p.* covenant.
Lev. 25. 34, their *p.* possession.
Ps. 9. 6, destructions are come to a *p.* end. R. V. desolate forever.
74. 3; Jer. 25. 9; Ezek. 35. 9, the *p.* desolations.
Jer. 8. 5, a *p.* backsliding.
15. 18, why is my pain *p.*?
Hab. 3. 6, the *p.* hills. R. V. everlasting.
See Gen. 9. 12; Jer. 5. 22; 50. 5; 51. 39; Ezek. 46. 14.
Perpetually. 1 Kn. 9. 3; 2 Chr. 7. 16; Am. 1. 11.

Perplexed. Lu. 9. 7; 24. 4; 2 Cor. 4. 8.
Perplexity. Isa. 22. 5; Mic. 7. 4; Lu. 21. 25.
Persecute. (1) Job 19. 22, why do ye *p.* me?
Ps. 143. 3, the enemy hath *p.* my soul.
Mat. 5. 11, 12, blessed are ye when men *p.* you.
5. 44, pray for them that *p.* you.
John 15. 20, if they have *p.* me.
Acts 9. 4; 22. 7; 26. 14, why *p.* thou me?
22. 4, I *p.* this way unto death.
26. 11, I *p.* them even to strange cities.
1 Cor. 4. 12, being *p.*, we suffer it.
15. 9; Gal. 1. 13, I *p.* the church of God.
Phil. 3. 6, concerning zeal, *p.* the church.
(2) to pursue. Ps. 7. 1, save me from them that *p.* me. R. V. pursue.
10. 2, the wicked doth *p.* the poor. R. V. poor is pursued.
71. 11, *p.* and take him. R. V. pursue.
2 Cor. 4. 9, *p.* but not forsaken. R. V. pursued.
See John 5. 16; Acts 7. 52; Gal. 1. 23; 4. 29.
Persecution. Mat. 13. 21; Mk. 4. 17, when *p.* ariseth.
2 Cor. 12. 10, take pleasure in *p.*
2 Tim. 3. 12, all that will live godly shall suffer *p.*
See Lam. 5. 5; Acts 8. 1; Gal. 6. 12; 1 Tim. 1. 13.
Persecution, coming of. Mat. 13. 21; 23. 34; Mk. 10. 30; Lu. 11. 49; John 15. 20; 2 Cor. 4. 9; 2 Tim. 3. 12.
conduct under. Mat. 5. 44; 10. 22; Acts 5. 41; Rom. 12. 14; Phil. 1. 28; Heb. 10. 34; 1 Pet. 4. 13–19.
results of. Mat. 5. 10; Lu. 6. 22; 9. 24; Jas. 1. 2; 1 Pet. 4. 14; Rev. 6. 9; 7. 13.
Perseverance enjoined. Mat. 24. 13; Mk. 13. 13; Lu. 9. 62; Acts 13. 43; 1 Cor. 15. 58; 16. 13; Eph. 6. 18; Col. 1. 23; 2 Thes. 3. 13; 1 Tim. 6. 14; Heb. 3. 6, 13; 10. 23, 38; 2 Pet. 3. 17; Rev. 2. 10, 25.
Persia, pĕr′sĭă, kingdom of. 2 Chr. 36. 20; Esth. 1. 3; Ezek. 27. 10; 38. 5; Dan. 6.
prophecies concerning. Isa. 21. 2; Dan. 5. 28; 8. 20; 10. 13; 11. 2.
Persian, pĕr′-sĭăn, belonging to Persia. Dan. 6. 28.
Persis, pĕr′-sĭs, a Persian woman; the beloved. Rom. 16. 12.
Person. Deu. 10. 17; 2 Sam. 14. 14, God, which regardeth not *p.*
2 Sam. 17. 11, go to battle in thine own *p.*
Ps. 15. 4; Isa. 32. 5, 6, vile *p.* R. V. a reprobate.
26. 4; Prov. 12. 11; 28. 19, with vain *p.*
105. 37, not one feeble *p.*
Mat. 22. 16; Mk. 12. 14, regardest not *p.* of men.
2 Cor. 2. 10, forgave I it in the *p.* of Christ.
Heb. 1. 3, the express image of his *p.* R. V. substance.
2 Pet. 3. 11, what manner of *p.* ought ye to be?
See Mal. 1. 8; Lu. 15. 7; Heb. 12. 16; Jude 16.
Persons, God no respecter of. Deu. 10. 17; 2 Chr. 19. 7; Job 34. 19; Acts 10. 34; Rom. 2. 11; Gal. 2. 6; Eph. 6. 9; Col. 3. 25; 1 Pet. 1. 17.
Persuade. 1 Kn. 22. 20, who shall *p.* Ahab? R. V. entice.
Prov. 25. 15, by long forbearing is a prince *p.*
Mat. 28. 14, we will *p.* him, and secure you.
Acts 26. 28, almost thou *p.* me. [sured.
Rom. 14. 5, let every man be fully *p.* R. V. as-
2 Cor. 5. 11, we *p.* men.
Gal. 1. 10, do I now *p.* men or God?
Heb. 6. 9, we are *p.* better things of you.
See 2 Kn. 18. 32; 2 Chr. 18. 2; 2 Tim. 1. 12.
Pertain. Rom. 15. 17; 1 Cor. 6. 3; 2 Pet. 1. 3.
Peruda, pĕ-rū′-dă, same as Perida. Ez. 2. 55.
Perverse. Deu. 32. 5, a *p.* and crooked generation.
Job 6. 30, cannot my taste discern *p.* things? R. V. mischievous.
Prov. 4. 24, *p.* lips put far from thee.
12. 8, *p.* heart shall be despised.
17. 20, *p.* tongue falleth into mischief.
23. 33, thine heart shall utter *p.* things.
Phil. 2. 15, in the midst of a *p.* nation.
See Num. 23. 21; Isa. 30. 12; 1 Tim. 6. 5.

Pervert. Deu. 16. 19, a gift doth *p.* words.
Job 8. 3, doth God *p.* judgment?
Prov. 10. 9, he that *p.* his ways shall be known.
19. 3, the foolishness of man *p.* his way.
Jer. 3. 21, they have *p.* their way.
23. 36, ye have *p.* the words of God.
Acts 13. 10, wilt thou not cease to *p.* right ways?
Gal. 1. 7, would *p.* the gospel.
See Eccl. 5. 8; Mic. 3. 9; Lu. 23. 2.

Pestilence, the penalty of disobedience. Ex. 5. 3; 9. 15; Lev. 26. 25; Num. 14. 12; Deu. 28. 21; Jer. 14. 12; 27. 13; Jer. 42. 17; 44. 13; Ezek. 5. 12; 6. 11; 7. 15; Mat. 24. 7; Lu. 21. 11.
Israel visited with. Num. 14. 37; 16. 46; 25. 9; 2 Sam. 24. 15.
removed. Num. 16. 47; 2 Sam. 24. 16.

Pestilent. Acts 24. 5.

Peter, pē′-tĕr, 'a stone;' Apostle, called. Mat. 4. 18; Mk. 1. 16; Lu. 5.; John 1. 35.
sent forth. Mat. 10. 2; Mk. 3. 16; Lu. 6. 14.
tries to walk to Jesus on the sea. Mat. 14. 29.
confesses Jesus to be the Christ. Mat. 16. 16; Mk. 8. 29; Lu. 9. 20.
witnesses the transfiguration. Mat. 17.; Mk. 9.; Lu. 9. 28; 2 Pet. 1. 16.
his self-confidence reproved. Lu. 22. 31; John 13. 36.
thrice denies Christ. Mat. 26. 69; Mk. 14. 66; Lu. 22. 57; John 18. 17.
his repentance. Mat. 26. 75; Mk. 14. 72; Lu. 22. 62.
the assembled disciples addressed by. Acts 1. 15.
the Jews preached to by. Acts. 2. 14; 3. 12.
brought before the council. Acts 4.
condemns Ananias and Sapphira. Acts 5.
denounces Simon the sorcerer. Acts 8. 18.
restores Æneas and Tabitha. Acts 9. 32, 40.
sent for by Cornelius. Acts 10.
instructed by a vision not to despise the Gentiles. Acts 10. 9.
imprisoned, and liberated by an angel. Acts 12.
his decision about circumcision. Acts 15. 7.
rebuked by Paul. Gal. 2. 14.
bears witness to Paul's teaching. 2 Pet. 3. 15.
comforts the church, and exhorts to holy living by his epistles. 1 & 2 Pet.
his martyrdom foretold by Christ. John 21. 18; 2 Pet. 1. 14.

Pethahiah, pĕth-ă-hī′-ăh, 'Jehovah opens.' 1 Chr. 24. 16.

Pethor, pē′-thŏr. Num. 22. 5.

Pethuel, pĕ-thū′-ĕl, 'God's opening' (?). Joel 1. 1.

Petition. 1 Sam. 1. 17, God of Israel grant thee thy *p.*
1 Kn. 2. 20, one small *p.*
Esth. 5. 6; 7. 2; 9. 12, what is thy *p.*?
Dan. 6. 7, whosoever shall ask a *p.*
6. 13, maketh his *p.* three times a day.
See Esth. 7. 3; Ps. 20. 5; 1 John 5. 15.

Peulthai, pē-ŭl′-thāī, 'deed of Jehovah.' 1 Chr. 26. 5.

Phalec, phā′-lĕc, Greek form of PELEG. Lu. 3. 35.

Phallu, phăl′-lū, an English form of PALLU. Gen. 46. 9.

Phalti, phăl′-tī, 'deliverance of Jehovah.' 1 Sam. 25. 44.

Phaltiel, phăl′-tĭ-ĕl, 'God is my deliverance.' 2 Sam. 3. 15.

Phanuel, phă-nū′-ĕl, Greek form of PENUEL. Lu. 2. 36.

Pharaoh, phâr′-āōh, is a title of the Kings of Egypt, as Cæsar was of the Emperors of Rome, and represents the Egyptian words *Per-āa*, or *Āa-perti*,— It means 'great house [in which all men live].'

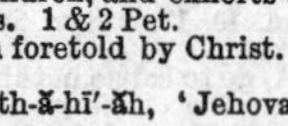

, or

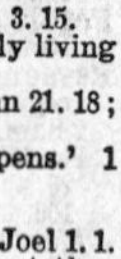

(1) Abram's wife taken into house of. Gen. 12. 15.
Pharaoh plagued because of her. Gen. 12. 17.
(2) (patron of Joseph), his dreams, &c. Gen. 40.
his hospitality to Joseph's father and brethren. Gen. 47.
(3) (oppressor of the Israelites). Ex. 1. 8.
daughter preserves Moses. Ex. 2. 5, 10; Acts 7. 21.
miracles performed before, and plagues sent. Ex. 7.-10.
grants Moses' request. Ex. 12. 31.
repenting, pursues Israel, and perishes in the Red Sea. Ex. 14. (Neh. 9. 10; Ps. 135. 9; 136. 15; Rom. 9. 17).
(4) (father-in-law of Solomon). 1 Kn. 3. 1.
shelters Hadad, Solomon's adversary. 1 Kn. 11. 19.

Pharaoh-hophra, phâr′-āōh-hŏph′-ră, 'Pharaoh the priest of the sun;' his fate predicted. Jer. 44. 30. *See* Ezek. 30.-32.
compared to a dragon. Ezek. 29. 3.

Pharaoh-necho, and **-nechoh**, phâr′-āōh-nē′-chō and -nē′-chōh, 'Pharaoh the lame;' slays Josiah. 2 Kn. 23. 29; 2 Chr. 35. 20.
his wars with Israel. 2 Kn. 23. 33; 2 Chr. 36. 3.

Phares, phâr′-ĕs, Greek form of PHAREZ. Lu. 3. 33.

Pharez, phâr′-ĕz, 'breach.' Gen. 38. 29; Ru. 4. 18.

Pharisees, phăr′-ĭ-sēēs. Heb. *Perushim*, 'separated ones,' a name apparently bestowed upon them by their opponents in substitution for the self-chosen title Ḥăsīdīm ('pious ones'). They 'separated' themselves from the heathen by a scrupulous adherence to the letter of the law, but often without its true spirit. See Mat. 23. 25; Lu. 11. 39, 42; Phil. 3. 5. They formed an association numbering 6000 members (Josephus), but it was religious rather than political.
celebrated ones: Nicodemus, John 3. 1. Simon, Lu. 7. Gamaliel, Acts 5. 34. Saul of Tarsus, Acts 23. 6; 26. 5; Phil. 3. 5.
Christ entertained by. Lu. 7. 36; 11. 37; 14. 1.
Christ utters woes against. Mat. 23. 13; Lu. 11. 42.
Christ questioned by, about: divorce, Mat. 19. 3. eating, Mat. 9. 11; 15. 1; Mk. 2. 16; Lu. 5. 30. forgiveness of sin, Lu. 5. 21. sabbath, Mat. 12. 2, 10. fasting, Mk. 2. 18. tribute, Mat. 22. 17.
deride Christ. Lu. 16. 14.
murmur against Christ. Mat. 9. 34; Lu. 15. 2.
denounced by Christ. Mat. 5. 20; 16. 6; 21. 43; 23. 2; Lu. 11. 39.
people cautioned against. Mk. 8. 15; Lu. 12. 1.
seek a sign from Christ. Mat. 12. 38; 16. 1.
take counsel against Christ. Mat. 12. 14; Mk. 3. 6.
Nicodemus remonstrates with. John 7. 51.
cast out the man cured of blindness. John 9. 13.
dissensions about. John 9. 16.
send officers to take Christ. John 7. 32.
contend about circumcision. Acts 15. 5.
their belief in the resurrection, &c. Acts 23. 8.
and publican. Lu. 18.

Pharosh, phâr′-ŏsh, same as PAROSH. Ez. 8. 3.

Pharpar, phär′-pär, 'swift,' one of the rivers of Damascus. 2 Kn. 5. 12.

Pharzites, phär′-zītes, 'descendants of Pharez.' Num. 26. 20.

Phaseah, phă-sē′-ăh, same as PASEAH. Neh. 7. 51.

Phebe, phē′-bē, 'moon' (?). Rom. 16. 1.

Phenice. (1) phē-nī′-çē, 'land of the date palm,' or 'of purple dyeing' or 'of dark-skinned people.' Same as PHENICIA. Acts 11. 19; 15. 3.
(2) phē′-nīçe. Acts 27. 12. R. V. Phœnix, a harbour of Crete.

Phenicia, phē-nĭç′-ĭă, 'land of palms' (Acts 21. 2), *see* PHENICE. A narrow country bordering on the Mediterranean, N. W. of Palestine.

Phichol, phī′-chŏl. Gen. 21. 22.

Philadelphia, Phĭl-ă-dĕl′-phĭ-ă, 'brotherly love;' church of, commended. Rev. 1. 11; 3. 7.

Philemon, phī-lē′-mon, 'friendly;' Paul's letter to, concerning Onesimus. Philem.

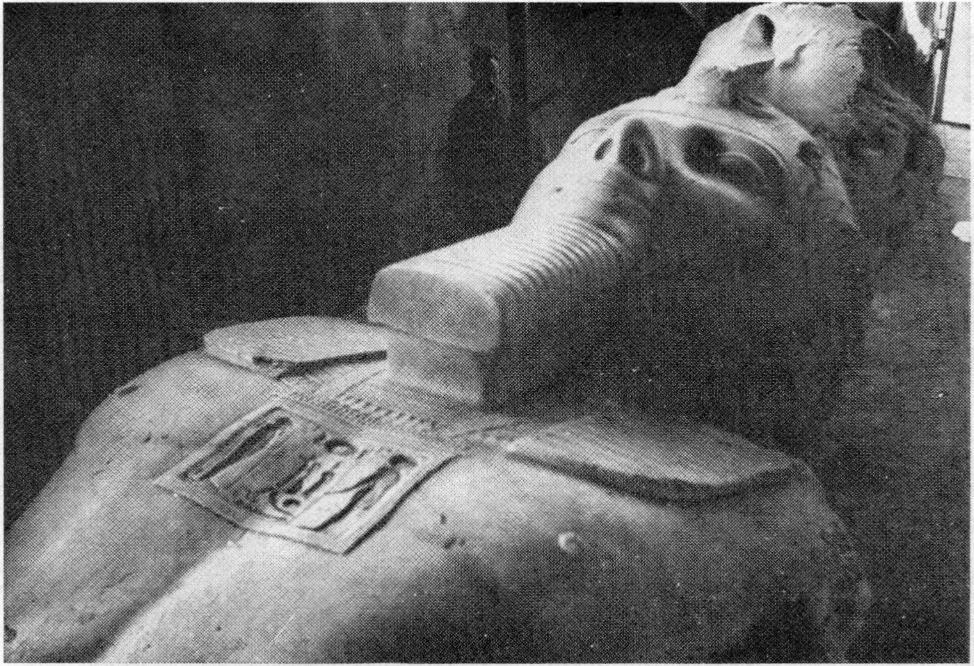

THE PHARAOH RAMESES II

A colossal statue of Rameses, probably the Pharaoh of the oppression. (*L. A. Fereday*)

THE ROSETTA STONE

Inscription in honour of a Greek king of Egypt, set up 195 B.C. in both Egyptian (hieroglyphic and demotic scripts) and Greek: it provided the first key to the reading of ancient Egyptian inscriptions. (*Picture Post Library*)

Philetus, phĭ-lē'-tŭs, 'worthy of love.' 2 Tim. 2. 17.
Philip, phĭl'-ĭp, 'lover of horses.' (1) Apostle, called. John 1. 43.
sent forth. Mat. 10. 3; Mk. 3. 18; Lu. 6. 14; John 12. 22; Acts 1. 13.
remonstrated with by Christ. John 14. 8.
(2) deacon, elected. Acts 6. 5.
preaches in Samaria. Acts 8. 5.
baptizes the eunuch. Acts 8. 27.
his four virgin daughters prophesy. Acts 21. 8.
(3) Herod-Philip, half-brother of Herod Antipas, and tetrarch of Trachonitis. Lu. 3. 1. married his niece Salome.
(4) half-brother of (3) and of Herod Antipas; first husband of Herodias, and father of Salome. Mat. 14. 3; Mk. 6. 17; Lu. 1. 19.
Philippi, phĭ-lĭp'-pī. A city of Macedonia, where St. Paul first preached the gospel in Europe; where Lydia and the jailer were converted (Acts 16. 12–40); and which became the seat of a Christian Church addressed by the Apostle in one of his Epistles; called after Philip of Macedonia.
Paul persecuted at. Acts 16. 12.
church at, commended and exhorted. Phil. 1.–4.
Philippians, phĭ-lĭp'-pĭăns, the people of Philippi. Phil. 4. 15.
Philistia, phĭl-ĭs'-tĭ-ă, the land of the Philistines. Gen. 21. 34; Ex. 13. 17; Jos. 13. 2 2 Kn. 8. 2; Ps. 60. 8.
Philistim, phĭl'-ĭs-tĭm, 'wanderers.' Gen. 10. 14.
Philistines, phĭl-ĭs'-tĭnes, same as PHILISTIM. A warlike race dwelling on the plains and low hills bordering on the Mediterranean W. and S. W. of Judæa. Gen. 21. 34.
origin of. Gen. 10. 14; 1 Chr. 1. 12.
fill up Isaac's wells. Gen. 26. 15.
contend with Joshua, Jos. 13. Shamgar, Jud. 3. 31. Samson, Jud. 14.–16. Samuel, 1 Sam. 4.; 7. Jonathan, 1 Sam. 14. Saul, 1 Sam. 17. David, 1 Sam. 18.
their wars with Israel. 1 Sam. 4. 1; 28.; 29.; 31.; 2 Chr. 21. 16.
mentioned. Ps. 60. 8; 83. 7; 87. 4; 108. 9; Isa. 2. 6; 9. 12; 11. 14; Jer. 25. 20.
their destruction predicted. Jer. 47.; Ezek. 25. 15; Am. 1. 8; Obad. 19; Zep. 2. 5; Zec. 9. 6.
Philologus, phĭ-lŏl'-ŏ-gŭs, 'fond of words.' Rom. 16. 15, Salute *P*. . . . and all the saints.
Philosophers. Acts 17. 18, then certain *p*. of the Epicureans.
Philosophy. Col. 2. 8.
Phinehas, phĭn'-ĕ-hăs, 'serpent's mouth' (?). (1) slays Zimri and Cozbi. Num. 25. 7, 11; Ps. 106. 30. sent against the Midianites, Reubenites, and Benjamites. Num. 31. 6; Jos. 22. 13; Jud. 20. 28. [Ex. 6. 25.
(2) son of Eli, his sin and death. 1 Sam. 1. 3; 2. 22; 4. 11.
Phlegon, phlĕg'-ŏn, 'burning.' Rom. 16. 14.
Phrygia, phrȳg'-ĭ-ă. Acts 2. 10; 16. 6; 18. 23.
Phurah, phū'-răh, 'branch' (?). Jud. 7. 10.
Phut, phŭt. Gen. 10. 6.
Phuvah, phū'-văh, 'mouth.' Gen. 46. 13.
Phygellus, phȳ-gĕl'-lŭs, 'little fugitive;' and Hermogenes turned away from Paul. 2 Tim. 1. 15.
Phylacteries (Gk. 'safeguards'). The Hebrews were commanded to bind the enactments of the Law on their hands, and as frontlets between their eyes, and to write them on the door posts of their houses (Deu. 6. 8, 9). Adopting a strictly literal interpretation of these words, they wrote a summary of the Moral Law (Ex. 13. 1–16; Deu. 6. 4–9; 11. 13–21) on strips of parchment, and placed them in small cubical cases which were called Phylacteries. They were bound one on the forehead, and one on the back of the right hand, by the Israelites, and worn as they still are at their prayers. The Pharisees made them as conspicuous as possible (Mat. 23. 5), and wore them always.
Physician. Jer. 8. 22, is there no *p*. there?
Mat. 9. 12; Mk. 2. 17; Lu. 5. 31, they that be whole need not a *p*.
Lu. 4. 23, *p*., heal thyself.
Pi-beseth, pī-bē'-sĕth, 'the city of Bast.' Ezek. 30. 17.
Pick. Prov. 30. 17.
Pictures. Num. 33. 52; Prov. 25. 11; Isa. 2. 16.
Piece. 1 Sam. 2. 36; Prov. 6. 26; 28. 21, a *p*. of bread. R. V. morsel.
15. 33, Samuel hewed Agag in *p*.
Ps. 7. 2, rending in *p*. while none to deliver.
50. 22, consider, lest I tear you in *p*.
Jer. 23. 29, hammer that breaketh rock in *p*.
Am. 4. 7, one *p*. was rained upon.
Zec. 11. 12, weighed for my price thirty *p*.
11. 13; Mat. 27. 6, 9, took thirty *p*. of silver.
See Lu. 14. 18; Acts 19. 19; 23. 10; 27. 44.
Pierce. 2 Kn. 18. 21; Isa. 36. 6, into his hand and *p*. it.
Zec. 12. 10; John 19. 37, they shall look on me whom they have *p*.
1 Tim. 6. 10, *p*. themselves with many sorrows.
See Isa. 27. 1; Lu. 2. 35; Heb. 4. 12; Rev. 1. 7.
Piety. 1 Tim. 5. 4, let them learn first to shew *p*. at home.
Pigeon. (1) (Ps. 68. 13; Mat. 3. 16). Heb. *Yônah:* Gk. περιστερά. Called 'dove' in A. V. and R. V. There are four species of pigeon, and three of the turtle-dove, in Palestine.
(2) (Gen. 15. 9). Heb. *Gôzâl:* Gk. περιστερά, a young pigeon; properly any young bird.
Pigeons as offerings. Lev. 1. 14; 12. 6; Num. 6. 10; Lu. 2. 24.
Pi-hahiroth, pī-hă-hī'-rōth, 'where sedge grows.' Ex. 14. 2.
Pilate, pī'-lăte, 'armed with a javelin' (?). Pontius, governor of Judæa during our Lord's ministry, sufferings, and death. Lu. 3. 1.
Christ delivered to, admonished by his wife, examines Jesus, washes his hands, but delivers Him to be crucified. Mat. 27.; Mk. 15.; Lu. 23.; John 18.; 19.
grants request of Joseph of Arimathæa. Mat. 27. 57; Mk. 15. 42; Lu. 23. 50; John 19. 38. *See* Acts 3. 13; 4. 27; 13. 28; 1 Tim. 6. 13.
Pildash, pĭl'-dăsh, 'steel' (?). Gen. 22. 22.
Pile. Isa. 30. 33; Ezek. 24. 9.
Pileha, pī'-lĕ-hă, 'plowman' (?). Neh. 10. 24.
Pilgrimage, typical. Gen. 47. 9; Ex. 6. 4; Ps. 119. 54; Heb. 11. 13; 1 Pet. 2. 11.
Pill, to strip off the bark, to peel. Gen. 30. 37, 38.
Pillar. Gen. 19. 26, a *p*. of salt.
Job 9. 6; 26. 11, the *p*. thereof tremble.
Prov. 9. 1, she hath hewn out her seven *p*.
Gal. 2. 9, Cephas and John, who seemed to be *p*.
1 Tim. 3. 15, the *p*. and ground of the truth.
Rev. 3. 12, him that overcometh will I make a *p*.
See Isa. 19. 19; Jer. 1. 18; Joel 2. 30; Lu. 17. 32; Rev. 10. 1.
Pillars: erected by Jacob, Gen. 28. 18; 35. 20. and Absalom, 2 Sam. 18. 18.
in porch of the temple. 1 Kn. 7. 21; 2 Chr. 3. 17; Rev. 3. 12.
of cloud and fire in wilderness. Ex. 13. 21; 33. 9; Neh. 9. 12; Ps. 99. 7.
Pillow. Gen. 28. 11; 1 Sam. 19. 13; Ezek. 13. 18; Mk. 4. 38.
Pilots. Ezek. 27. 8.
Piltai, pĭl-tā'-ī, 'Jehovah delivers.' Neh. 12. 17.
Pin. Jud. 16. 14; Ezek. 15. 3.
Pine. Lev. 26. 39; Lam. 4. 9; Isa. 38. 12; Ezek. 24. 23.
Pine tree. (1) (Isa. 41. 19; 60. 13). Heb. *Tidhâr:* Gk. βραθυδαάρ, πεύκη: R. V. marg. 'or, plane.' It is very uncertain what tree is referred to.
(2) (Neh. 8. 15). Heb. *Etz-shĕmĕn.* R. V. wild olive, but probably a term including all resinous trees; oil trees.
Pinon, pī'-nŏn, darkness. Gen. 36. 41.
Pipe. (1) (1 Kn. 1. 40; Isa. 5. 12; 30. 29). Heb. *Ḥâlîl:* Gk. αὐλός. Some kind of flute-like instrument. These were of different kinds: (*a*) those played by blowing in a hole at the side;

(*b*) those played by blowing at the end without reeds; (*c*) the same with reeds. To which kind the Ḥâlîl refers is uncertain.
(2) (Ex. 15. 20; Ps. 30. 11; 150. 4; Jer. 31. 4, 13); Heb. *Mâḥol:* Gk. χοροί, χαρά, 'dancing' or 'dances,' usually. This is thought to have been a small flute to accompany the dance.
Isa. 5. 12, the harp and *p.* are in their feasts.
Mat. 11. 17; Lu. 7. 32, we have *p.* unto you.
1 Cor. 14. 7, how shall it be known what is *p.*?
Rev. 18. 22, voice of *p.* shall be heard no more.

Piram, pī'-răm, 'like a wild ass.' Jos. 10. 3.

Pirathon, pī-rā'-thon, 'leader.' Jud. 12. 15.

Pirathonite, pī-rā'thŏn-īte, 'an inhabitant of Pirathon.' Jud. 12. 13.

Pisgah, pĭs'-găh, 'a part, boundary;' mount. Num. 21. 20; 23. 14; Deu. 3. 27; 34. 1.

Pisidia, pī-sĭd'-ĭ-ă. Acts 13. 14; 14. 24.

Pison, pī'-sŏn. Heb. *Pîshôn*, one of the rivers of Eden. Gen. 2. 11.

Pispah, pĭs'-păh, 'expansion.' 1 Chr. 7. 38.

Pit. Gen. 37. 20, cast him into some *p.*
Ex. 21. 33, 34, if a man dig a *p.*
Num. 16. 30, 33, go down quick into the *p.*
Job 33. 24, deliver him from going down to the *p.*
Ps. 28. 1; 143. 7, like them that go down into the *p.*
40. 2, out of an horrible *p.*
Prov. 22. 14; 23. 27, a deep *p.*
28. 10, shall fall into his own *p.*
Isa. 38. 17, the *p.* of corruption.
Mat. 12. 11; Lu. 14. 5, fall into a *p.* on sabbath.

Pit, the grave, death. Job 17. 16; 33. 18; Ps. 28. 1; 30. 9; 88. 4; 143. 7; Isa. 14. 15; 38. 17; Ezek. 26. 20; 32. 18.
as a prison. Isa. 24. 22; Zec. 9. 11. [Isa. 34. 9.

Pitch, used for the ark, &c. Gen. 6. 14; Ex. 2. 3;

Pitcher. Gen. 24. 14, let down thy *p.*
Jud. 7. 16, lamps within the *p.*
Eccl. 12. 6, or the *p.* be broken.
Lam. 4. 2, esteemed as earthen *p.* [water.
Mk. 14. 13; Lu. 22. 10, a man, bearing a *p.* of

Pithom, pī'-thŏm (and Raamses), cities built by Israelites in Egypt. Ex. 1. 11.

Pithon, pī'-thŏn, 'simple' (?). 1 Chr. 8. 35.

Pitiful. Lam. 4. 10; Jas. 5. 11; 1 Pet. 3. 8.

Pity. Deu. 7. 16; 13. 8; 19. 13, thine eye shall have no *p.*
2 Sam. 12. 6, because he had no *p.*
Job 19. 21, have *p.* on me, my friends.
Ps. 69. 20, I looked for some to take *p.*
Prov. 19. 17, that hath *p.* on the poor lendeth.
28. 8, gather for him that will *p.* the poor.
Isa. 13. 18, they shall have no *p.* on fruit.
63. 9, in his *p.* he redeemed them.
Jer. 13. 14, I will not *p.* nor spare.
Ezek. 16. 5, none eye *p.* thee.
24. 21, I will profane what your soul *p.*
Joel 2. 18, the Lord will *p.* his people.
Zec. 11. 5, their own shepherds *p.* them not.
Mat. 18. 33, as I had *p.* on thee. R. V. mercy.
See Ps. 103. 13; Jer. 15. 5; Lam. 2. 2; Jon. 4. 10.

Place. Ex. 3. 5; Jos. 5. 15, *p.* whereon thou standest is holy.
Jud. 18. 10, a *p.* where there is no want.
2 Kn. 5. 11, strike his hand over the *p.*
6. 1; Isa. 49. 20, the *p.* is too strait for us.
Ps. 26. 8, the *p.* where thine honour dwelleth.
32. 7; 119. 114, thou art my hiding *p.*
37. 10, thou shalt diligently consider his *p.*
74. 20, the dark *p.* of the earth.
90. 1, our dwelling *p.*
Prov. 14. 26, his children have a *p.* of refuge.
15. 3, the eyes of the Lord in every *p.*
Eccl. 3. 20, all go to one *p.*
Isa. 5. 8, lay field to field, till there be no *p.*
60. 13, the *p.* of my feet.
66. 1, where is the *p.* of my rest?
Jer. 6. 3, they shall feed every one in his *p.*
Mic. 1. 3, the Lord cometh out of his *p.*
Zec. 10. 19, *p.* shall not be found for them.
Mal. 1. 11, in every *p.* incense shall be offered.
Mat. 28. 6; Mk. 16. 6, see the *p.* where the Lord lay.
Lu. 10. 1, two and two into every *p.*
14. 9, give this man *p.*
John 8. 37, my word hath no *p.* in you. R. V. not free course.
18. 2, Judas knew the *p.*
Acts 2. 1, with one accord in one *p.*
4. 31, the *p.* was shaken.
Rom. 12. 19, rather give *p.* to wrath.
Eph. 4. 27, neither give *p.* to the devil.
Heb. 12. 17, found no *p.* of repentance.
Rev. 20. 11, there was found no *p.* for them.
See Ps. 16. 6; Isa. 40. 4; Eph. 1. 3; 2. 6; 3. 10.

Places, idolatrous, 1 Kn. 11. 7; 12. 31; 13.; Ps. 78. 58; Ezek. 16. 24. destruction of, Lev. 26. 30; 2 Kn. 18. 4; 23.; 2 Chr. 14. 3; 17. 6; 34. 3; Ezek. 6. 3.

Plague. Lev. 26. 21, I will bring seven times more *p.*
Deu. 28. 59, will make thy *p.* wonderful.
29. 22, when they see the *p.* of that land.
1 Kn. 8. 38, every man the *p.* of his own heart.
Ps. 73. 5, nor are they *p.* like other men.
91. 10, nor any *p.* come nigh thy dwelling.
Hos. 13. 14, O death, I will be thy *p.*
Rev. 18. 4, that ye receive not of her *p.*
22. 18, shall add to him the *p.* written.
See Lev. 14. 35; Num. 8. 19; 16. 46; Mk. 3. 10.

Plagues. (1) of Egypt. *See* Miracles in the O. T. (2) of Israel. *See* Pestilence.

Plain. Gen. 25. 27, Jacob was a *p.* man.
Ps. 27. 11, lead me in a *p.* path. [eth.
Prov. 8. 9, they are *p.* to him that understand-
15. 19, the way of the righteous is made *p.*
Isa. 40. 4, rough places *p.*
Hab. 2. 2, write the vision, make it *p.*
See Gen. 13. 10; 19. 17; Isa. 28. 25; Mk. 7. 35.

Plainly. Deu. 27. 8, write the words very *p.*
Isa. 32. 4, stammerers shall speak *p.*
John 10. 24, tell us *p.*
16. 25, I shall shew you *p.* of the Father.
16. 29, now speakest thou *p.*
See Ex. 21. 5; Ez. 4. 18; John 11. 14; 2 Cor. 3. 12.

Plaiting. 1 Pet. 3. 3.

Planes. Isa. 44. 13.

Plant (*n.*). Job 14. 9, bring forth boughs like a *p.*
Ps. 128. 3, children like olive *p.*
144. 12, sons as *p.* grown up.
Isa. 5. 7; 17. 10, his pleasant *p.*
16. 8, broken down principal *p.*
53. 2, as a tender *p.*
Ezek. 34. 29, a *p.* of renown.
Mat. 15. 13, every *p.* my Father hath not planted.
See Gen. 2. 5; 1 Chr. 4. 23. R. V. Netaim.

Plant (*v.*). Num. 24. 6, as trees which the Lord hath *p.*
2 Sam. 7. 10; 1 Chr. 17. 9, I will *p.* them.
Ps. 1. 3; Jer. 17. 8, like a tree *p.*
80. 15, the vineyard thy right hand hath *p.*
92. 13, *p.* in the house of the Lord.
94. 9, he that *p.* the ear.
Jer. 2. 21, I had *p.* thee a noble vine.
Ezek. 17. 10, being *p.* shall it prosper?
Lu. 17. 6, be thou *p.* in the sea.
Rom. 6. 5, if we have been *p.* together. R. V. become united with him.
1 Cor. 3. 6, I have *p.*
See Mat. 21. 33; Mk. 12. 1; Lu. 20. 9.

Plant, used figuratively. Ps. 128. 3; 144. 12; S. of S. 4. 13; Isa. 5. 7; 53. 2; Jer. 2. 21; 48. 32; Ezek. 34. 29; Mat. 15. 13.

Plat, a small patch of ground, plot. 2 Kn. 9. 26.

Plate. Ex. 28. 36; 39. 30; Jer. 10. 9.

Platted. Mat. 27. 29; Mk. 15. 17; John 19. 2.

Platter, a dish. Mat. 23. 25; Lu. 11. 39. [*p.*

Play. (1) Ex. 32. 6; 1 Cor. 10. 7, people rose up to
1 Sam. 16. 17, a man that can *p.* well.
2 Sam. 6. 21, I will *p.* before the Lord.
10. 12, let us *p.* the men.
Job 41. 5, wilt thou *p.* with him?
Ps. 33. 3, *p.* skilfully with a loud noise.
Isa. 11. 8, the sucking child shall *p.*

Ezek. 33. 32, can *p.* well on an instrument.
(2) to fence, fight with swords. 2 Sam. 2. 14; 14. 26.
See 1 Chr. 15. 29; Ps. 68. 25; Zec. 8. 5.

Plea. Deu. 17. 8.

Plead. Jud. 6. 31, 32, will ye *p.* for Baal?
Job 9. 19, who shall set me a time to *p.*?
13. 19, who will *p.* with me?
16. 21, that one might *p.* for a man.
23. 6, will he *p.* against me with his great power?
Isa. 1. 17, *p.* for the widow.
3. 13, the Lord standeth up to *p.*
43. 26, let us *p.* together.
59. 4, none *p.* for truth.
Jer. 2. 9, I will yet *p.* with you.
Lam. 3. 58, thou hast *p.* the causes of my soul.
Joel 3. 2, I will *p.* with them for my people.
See 1 Sam. 25. 39; Job 13. 6; Isa. 66. 16.

Pleading of God with Israel. Isa. 1.; 3. 13; 43. 26; Jer. 2.-6.; 13.; Ezek. 17. 20; 20. 36; 22.; Hos. 2. &c.; Joel 3. 2; Mic. 2.
of Job with God. Job 9. 19; 16. 21.

Pleasant. Gen. 3. 6, *p.* to the eyes. R. V. a delight.
2 Sam. 1. 23, were *p.* in their lives.
1. 26, very *p.* hast thou been to me.
Ps. 16. 6, lines fallen in *p.* places.
106. 24, they despised the *p.* land.
133. 1, how *p.* for brethren to dwell together.
Prov. 2. 10, knowledge is *p.* to thy soul.
15. 26, the words of the pure are *p.* words.
16. 24, *p.* words are as honeycomb.
Eccl. 11. 7, it is *p.* to behold the sun.
S. of S. 4. 13, 16; 7. 13, with *p.* fruits.
Isa. 64. 11, our *p.* things are laid waste.
Jer. 31. 20, is Ephraim a *p.* child?
Ezek. 33. 32, of one that hath a *p.* voice.
Dan. 10. 3, I ate no *p.* bread.
See Am. 5. 11; Mic. 2. 9; Nah. 2. 9; Zec. 7. 14.

Pleasantness. Prov. 3. 17.

Please. 1 Kn. 3. 10, the speech *p.* the Lord.
Ps. 51. 19. then shalt thou be *p.* with sacrifices.
115. 3; 135. 6; Jon. 1. 14, he hath done whatsoever he *p.*
Prov. 16. 7, when a man's ways *p.* the Lord.
Isa. 2. 6, they *p.* themselves in children of strangers.
53. 10, it *p.* the Lord to bruise him.
55. 11, accomplish that which I *p.*
Mic. 6. 7, will the Lord be *p.* with rams
Mal. 1. 8, offer it, will he be *p.* with thee?
John 8. 29, I do always those things that *p.* him.
Rom. 8. 8, in the flesh cannot *p.* God.
15. 1, to bear, and not to *p.* ourselves.
15. 3, even Christ *p.* not himself.
1 Cor. 1. 21, it *p.* God by the foolishness of preaching.
10. 33, as I *p.* men in all things.
Gal. 1. 10, do I seek to *p.* men?
Eph. 6. 6; Col. 3. 22, as men-*p.*
Heb. 11. 6, without faith it is impossible to *p.* God.
See 1 Cor. 7. 32; Col. 1. 19; 1 Thes. 2. 4; 1 John 3. 22.

Pleasure. 1 Chr. 29. 17, hast *p.* in uprightness.
Esth. 1. 8, do according to every man's *p.*
Job 21. 21, what *p.* hath he in his house?
21. 25, another never eateth with *p.* R. V. tasteth of good.
22. 3, is it any *p.* to the Almighty?
Ps. 16. 11, *p.* for evermore.
35. 27, hath *p.* in the prosperity of his servants.
51. 18, do good in thy good *p.*
102. 14, thy servants take *p.* in her stones.
103. 21, ye ministers of his that do his *p.*
111. 2, of all them that have *p.* therein.
147. 11, taketh *p.* in them that fear him.
149. 4, the Lord taketh *p.* in his people.
Prov. 21. 17, he that loveth *p.* shall be poor.
Eccl. 5. 4, he hath no *p.* in fools.
12. 1, I have no *p.* in them.
Isa. 44. 28, Cyrus shall perform all my *p.*
53. 10, the *p.* of the Lord shall prosper.
58. 3, in the day of your fast ye find *p.*
58. 13, doing thy *p.* on my holy day.
Jer. 22. 28; 48. 38; Hos. 8. 8, a vessel wherein is no *p.*
Ezek. 18. 23; 33. 11, have I any *p.*?
Mal. 1. 10, I have no *p.* in you, saith the Lord.
Lu. 8. 14, choked with *p.* of this life.
12. 32, Father's good *p.*
Eph. 1. 5, the good *p.* of his will.
Phil. 2. 13, to will and to do of his good *p.*
1 Tim. 5. 6, she that liveth in *p.*
2 Tim. 3. 4, lovers of *p.*
Heb. 10. 38, my soul shall have no *p.* in him.
11. 25, the *p.* of sin for a season.
12. 10, chastened us after their own *p.*
Jas. 5. 5, ye have lived in *p.* on earth. R. V. delicately.
Rev. 4. 11, for thy *p.* they were created. R. V. because of thy will.
See Gen. 18. 12; Ps. 5. 4.

Pleasures, vanity of worldly. Eccl. 2.
effects of. Lu. 8. 14; Jas. 5.; 2 Pet. 2. 13.
exhortations against. 2 Tim. 3. 4; Tit. 3. 3; Heb. 11. 25; 1 Pet. 4.

Pledges, limitations of. Ex. 22. 26; Deu. 24. 6.
See Job 22. 6; 24. 3; Ezek. 18. 7; Am. 2. 8.

Pleiades, plē′-ă-dēs. Employed in LXX. and Eng. versions as a rendering of the Heb. *Kîma*, though LXX. in Job 9. 9 renders it 'Arcturus.' The stars referred to may be the Pleiads, or Arcturus, or Sirius: in the last case the 'refreshing influences' of Kima are taken as referring to the rise of the Nile, which corresponds with the heliacal rising of Sirius.

Plenteous. Ps. 86. 5; 103. 8, *p.* in mercy.
130. 7, *p.* redemption.
Hab. 1. 16, portion fat and meat *p.*
Mat. 9. 37, the harvest truly is *p.*
See Gen. 41. 34; Prov. 21. 5.

Plentiful. Ps. 31. 23; Jer. 2. 7; 48. 33, Lu. 12. 16.

Plenty. Gen. 27. 28, *p.* of corn and wine.
Job 22. 25, *p.* of silver. R. V. precious silver.
37. 23, *p.* of justice.
Prov. 3. 10, barns filled with *p.*
See 2 Chr. 31. 10; Prov. 28. 19; Jer. 44. 17.

Plenty, the gift of God. Gen. 27. 28; Deu. 16. 10; 28. 11; 30. 9; Ps. 65. 8; 68. 9; 104. 10; 144. 13; Isa. 30. 23; Joel 2. 26; Acts 14. 17.

Plow. Job 4. 8, that *p.* iniquity shall reap.
Prov. 20. 4, not *p.* by reason of cold.
21. 4, the *p.* of the wicked is sin. R. V. lamp.
Isa. 2. 4; Mic. 4. 3, beat swords into *p.*-shares.
28. 24, doth plowman *p.* all day to sow?
Joel 3. 10, beat your *p.*-shares into swords.
Am. 9. 13, the *p.*-man overtake the reaper.

Plowing. Deu. 22. 10; Job 1. 14; 1 Cor. 9. 10.
figuratively mentioned. Job 4. 8; Hos. 10. 13; 1 Cor. 9. 10.

Plowshares beaten into swords. Joel 3. 10.
swords to be beaten into plowshares. Isa. 2. 4; Mic. 4. 3.

Pluck. Deu. 23. 25, mayest *p.* the ears with thy hand.
2 Chr. 7. 20, then will I *p.* them up.
Job 24. 9, they *p.* the fatherless from the breast.
Ps. 25. 15, he shall *p.* my feet out of the net.
74. 11, *p.* it out of thy bosom.
Prov. 14. 1, foolish *p.* it down with her hands.
Eccl. 3. 2, a time to *p.* up.
Isa. 50. 6, my cheeks to them that *p.*
Jer. 22. 24, yet I would *p.* thee thence.
Am. 4. 11; Zec. 3. 2, a firebrand *p.* out.
Mat. 5. 29; 18. 9; Mk. 9. 47, offend thee, *p.* it out.
12. 1; Mk. 2. 23; Lu. 6. 1, began to *p.* ears.
John 10. 28, nor shall any *p.* out of my hand.
See Gen. 8. 11; Lu. 17. 6; Gal. 4. 15; Jude 12.

Plumbline and plummet. 2 Kn. 21. 13; Isa. 28. 17; Am. 7. 8; Zec. 4. 10.

Pochereth of Zebaim, pō-chĕ-rĕth of zĕ-bā′-ĭm, 'offspring of gazelles' (?). Ez. 2. 57.

Poets, heathen, quoted. Acts 17. 28; Tit. 1. 12.

Point. Jer. 17. 1, written with the *p.* of a diamond.
Heb. 4. 15, in all *p.* tempted.
Jas. 2. 10, yet offend in one *p.*
See Gen. 25. 32; Eccl. 5. 16; Mk. 5. 23; John 4. 47.

Poison of serpents. Ps. 58. 4; 140. 3; Rom. 3. 13; Jas. 3. 8.
Pole. Num. 21. 8.
Policy. Dan. 8. 25.
Polished. Ps. 144. 12; Isa. 49. 2; Lam. 4. 7; Dan. 10. 6.
Politarchs (Acts 17. 6). This word, rendered literally 'rulers of the city,' has been found, from an inscription on one of the arches of Thessalonica, to have been the official title of its chief magistrates. The stones of the arch are now in the British Museum.
Poll, to cut the hair of the head. 2 Sam. 14. 26; Ezek. 44. 20; Mic. 1. 16.
Pollutions under the Law. Lev. 5.; 11.; 13.; 15.; 21.; 22.; Num. 5.; 9. 6; Ezek. 22.
of the heathen. Lev. 18. 24; 19. 31; 20. 3; Acts 15. 20.
of the sabbath. Neh. 13. 15; Isa. 56. 2; Ezek. 20. 13.
of God's altar, &c. Ex. 20. 25; 2 Chr. 33. 7.; 36. 14; Ezek. 8. 6; 44. 7; Dan. 8. 11; Zep. 3. 4; Mal. 1. 7.
Pollux, pŏl'-lŭx. Acts 28. 11.
Pomegranate (Num. 20. 5; Deu. 8. 8). Heb. *Rimmôn:* Gk. ῥοά, ῥοιά, κώδων: Bot. N. *Punica granatum.* One of the pleasant fruits of Egypt, and of the promised blessings of Palestine. A refreshing drink was made from the juicy pulp of its fruit. S. of S. 8. 2.
Pomegranates on the priest's robe. Ex. 28. 33; 39. 24.
on the pillars of the temple. 1 Kn. 7. 18; 2 Kn. 25. 17; 2 Chr. 3. 16.
Pomp. Isa. 5. 14; 14. 11; Ezek. 7. 24; 30. 18; Acts 25. 23.
Ponder. Prov. 4. 26, *p.* the path of thy feet. R. V. make level.
5. 6, lest thou shouldest *p.* R. V. she findeth.
5. 21, the Lord *p.* all his goings. R. V. maketh level.
See Prov. 21. 2; 24. 12 (R. V. weigheth); Lu. 2. 19.
Pontius, pŏn'-tiŭs, 'belonging to the sea.' Mat. 27. 2.
See PILATE.
Pontus, pŏn'-tŭs, 'sea.' Acts 2. 9.
Pools. Jerusalem, being on the top of a mountain, had an insufficient water supply. Hence a number of reservoirs were built to supply the city with water. One never-failing spring, issuing from near Mount Moriah, is collected in the pool of Siloam. The two pools of Gihon and the pool of Hezekiah on the west of Jerusalem were probably supplied by an aqueduct seven miles long from reservoirs at Etam near Bethlehem. The pool of Bethesda was probably north-east of Jerusalem near the sheep gate. Here in 1888 was discovered the remains of a building with five porches (John 5. 2, etc.). Ps. 84. 6; Isa. 35. 7; 41. 18; John 5. 2; 9. 7. For Pool of Siloam, *see* SILOAM.
Poor. Ex. 30. 15, the *p.* shall not give less.
Deu. 15. 11, the *p.* shall never cease. R. V. needy.
2 Kn. 24. 14, none remained, save *p.* sort.
Job 24. 4, the *p.* of the earth hide.
29. 16, I was a father to the *p.* R. V. needy.
Ps. 10. 14, the *p.* committeth himself to thee. R. V. helpless.
34. 6, this *p.* man cried.
40. 17; 69. 29; 70. 5; 86. 1; 109. 22, I am *p.*
49. 2, rich and *p.* together.
Prov. 10. 4, becometh *p.* that dealeth with slack hand.
13. 23, food in the tillage of the *p.*
18. 23, the *p.* useth entreaties.
22. 2, rich and *p.* meet together.
30. 9, lest I be *p.* and steal.
Isa. 41. 17, when *p.* and needy seek water.
Am. 2. 6, they sold the *p.*
Zec. 11. 7, 11, I will feed even you, O *p.* of the flock.
Mat. 5. 3, blessed are the *p.* in spirit.
2 Cor. 6. 10, as *p.*, yet making many rich.
8. 9, for your sakes he became *p.*
See Lev. 27. 8; Rev. 3. 17; 13. 16.
Poor, always to be found. Deu. 15. 11; 1 Sam. 2. 7; Mat. 26. 11; Mk. 14. 7; John 12. 8.
their condition described. Job 24. 4; Prov. 13. 8; 14. 20; 18. 23; 19. 4; 30. 9; Eccl. 9. 15; Jas. 2.
comfort for. Job 31. 19; Prov. 31. 6; 1 John 3. 17.
causes of poverty. Prov. 6. 11; 10. 4; 13. 4; 19. 15; 20. 13; 23. 21; 28. 19.
oppression of, described and condemned. Ex. 22. 25; Deu. 15. 7; 24. 12; Job 24. 9; Ps. 12. 5; 14. 6; 82. 3; Prov. 14. 31; 17. 5; 22. 16, 22; 28. 3; Eccl. 5. 8; Isa. 3. 14; Jer. 22. 3; Am. 2. 6; 4.; 5. 11; 8. 4; Zec. 7. 10; Jas. 2. 2.
kindly treatment of. Ex. 23. 11; Lev. 19. 10; 23. 22; 25. 25; Deu. 15. 7; Ps. 41. 1; Prov. 14. 21; Isa. 58. 7; 2 Cor. 8.; 9.; Gal. 2. 10.
their right to justice. Lev. 19. 15; Deu. 1. 17; 16. 19; Prov. 24. 23; 28. 21; Jas. 2.
God's consideration for. Job 5. 15; Ps. 9. 18; 68. 10; 69. 33; 72. 2; 102. 17; 113. 7; 132. 15; Zec. 11. 7.
when blessed by God. Prov. 15. 16; 16. 8; 19. 1; 28. 6, 11.
to be cared for by the church. Acts 6. 1; 1 Cor. 16. 2; 2 Cor. 8.; 9.; Gal. 2. 10.
not to be encouraged in litigation. Ex. 23. 3.
in spirit, blessed by Christ. Mat. 5. 3; Lu. 6. 20 (Isa. 66. 2).
Poplar (Gen. 30. 37; Hos. 4. 13). Heb. *Libneh:* 'white:' Gk. στύραξ λεύκη: Bot. N. *Populus alba; Populus Euphratica.* R. V. marg. 'storax tree,' a resinous shrub 10 to 20 feet high. The LXX. understands the white poplar in Hos. 4. 13.
Populous. Deu. 26. 5; Nah. 3. 8.
Poratha, pôr-ā'-thă, 'having many chariots' (?). Esth. 9. 8.
Porch. 1 Chr. 28. 11; John 5. 2; 10. 23.
Porcius Festus, pôr'-cĭ-ŭs fĕs'-tŭs. Acts 24. 27.
Port, a gate. Neh. 2. 13.
Porters were 'the doorkeepers' and police of the Temple (2 Chr. 31. 14). They lived on the adjoining Mount Ophel. They were divided into companies, under the command of the 'Captain of the Temple,' and one division was always on duty, keeping guard day and night. Josephus says that it took twenty of them to shut the great brazen gates (Acts 21. 30).
Portion. Gen. 31. 14, is there yet any *p.* for us?
48. 22, one *p.* above thy brethren.
Deu. 32. 9, the Lord's *p.* is his people.
2 Kn. 2. 9, a double *p.* of thy spirit.
Neh. 8. 10; Esth. 9. 19, send *p.* to them.
Job 20. 29, this is the *p.* of a wicked man.
24. 18, their *p.* is cursed.
26. 14; 27. 13, how little a *p.* is heard of him? R. V. whisper.
31. 2, what *p.* of God is there from above?
Ps. 11. 6, this shall be the *p.* of their cup.
16. 5, Lord is the *p.* of mine inheritance.
17. 14, have their *p.* in this life.
73. 26, God is my *p.*
119. 57; 142. 5, thou art my *p.*, O Lord.
Prov. 31. 15, giveth a *p.* to her maidens. R. V. task.
Eccl. 2. 10, this was my *p.* of all my labour.
3. 22; 5. 18; 9. 9, rejoice, for that is his *p.*
5. 19, God hath given power to take *p.*
9. 6, nor have they any more *p.* for ever.
11. 2, give a *p.* to seven.
Isa. 53. 12, divide a *p.* with the great.
61. 7, they shall rejoice in their *p.*
Jer. 10. 16; 51. 19, *p.* of Jacob not like them.
12. 10, my pleasant *p.* a wilderness.
52. 34, every day a *p.*
Dan. 1. 8, with *p.* of king's meat.
Mic. 2. 4, he hath changed the *p.* of my people.
Mat. 24. 51, appoint him *p.* with hypocrites.
Lu. 12. 42, their *p.* in due season.
12. 46, his *p.* with unbelievers.
15. 12, the *p.* of goods that falleth.
See Gen. 47. 22; Jos. 17. 14; Dan. 4. 15; 11. 26.
Possess. Gen. 22. 17; 24. 60, thy seed shall *p.* the gate.

Job 7. 3, made to *p.* months of vanity.
13. 26, *p.* iniquities of my youth. R. V. inherit.
Prov. 8. 22, the Lord *p.* me in beginning.
Lu. 18. 12, I give tithes of all I *p.* R. V. get.
21. 19, in patience *p.* your souls. R. V. ye shall win.
See Lu. 12. 15; Acts 4. 32; 1 Cor. 7. 30; 2 Cor. 6. 10.

Possession. Gen. 17. 8; 48. 4, an everlasting *p.*
Prov. 28. 10, good things in *p.* R. V. inherit good.
Eccl. 2. 7; Mat. 19. 22; Mk. 10. 22, great *p.*
Acts 2. 45, and sold their *p.*
Eph. 1. 14, redemption of purchased *p.*
See Lev. 25. 10; 27. 16; 1 Kn. 21. 15.

Possible. Mat. 19. 26; Mk. 10. 27, with God all things are *p.*
24. 24; Mk. 13. 22, if *p.* deceive elect.
26. 39; Mk. 14. 35, 36, if *p.* let this cup.
Mk. 9. 23, all things are *p.* to him that believeth.
14. 36; Lu. 18. 27, all things are *p.* to thee.
Rom. 12. 18, if *p.* live peaceably.
See Acts 2. 24; 20. 16; Gal. 4. 15; Heb. 10. 4.

Post. (1) a messenger, letter carrier. 2 Chr. 30. 6; Job 9. 25; Jer. 51. 31.
(2) Deu. 6. 9; Am. 9. 1.

Posterity. Gen. 45. 7; Ps. 49. 13; 109. 13; Dan. 11. 4.

Pot. 2 Kn. 4. 2, not any thing save a *p.* of oil.
4. 40, there is death in the *p.*
Job 41. 31, maketh the deep boil like a *p.*
Zec. 14. 21, every *p.* shall be holiness.
Mk. 7. 4, the washing of cups and *p.*
John 2. 6, six water-*p.*
See Ex. 16. 33; Jer. 1. 13; John 4. 28; Heb. 9. 4.

Potentate. 1 Tim. 6. 15.

Potiphar, pŏt'-ĭ-phăr, 'belonging to the sun,' or 'gift of the risen one;' Joseph's master. Gen. 37. 36; 39.

Poti-pherah, pŏt-ĭ-phē'-răh, 'the gift of the sun-god;' the priest of On, father-in-law of Joseph. Gen. 41. 45.

Pots. Mk. 7. 4 = the Roman sextarius = one pint (.96).

Potsherd, a fragment of broken pottery. Ps. 22. 15.

Pottage, porridge, or thick soup, made of red lentils boiled in water, is a savoury and highly nutritious dish, of which the Arabs at the present day are especially fond.
Esau's mess of. Gen. 25. 29.
injurious, healed by Elisha. 2 Kn. 4. 38.

Potter, as a type of God's power. Isa. 64. 8; Jer. 18. 2; Rom. 9. 21.

Potters, turning the tables with their feet, and moulding with their hands the clay as it spins round upon the table, are constantly to be seen in the East. 1 Chr. 4. 23; Jer. 18. 2; 19. 1.

Pound. (1) In Lu. 19. 13, the pound is a mina = 2 lbs. Troy = £3 8s. 4d. = $16.15.
(2) In John 12. 3; 19. 39, the pound is 11½ oz. avoirdupois.
See Money and Weights.

Pour. Job 10. 10, hast thou not *p.* me out as milk.
29. 6, rock *p.* out rivers of oil.
30. 16, my soul is *p.* out upon me.
Ps. 45. 2, grace is *p.* into thy lips.
62. 8, *p.* out your heart before him.
Prov. 1. 23; Isa. 44. 3; Joel 2. 28, 29; Acts 2. 17, 18, I will *p.* out my Spirit.
S. of S. 1. 3, as ointment *p.* forth.
Isa. 26. 16, *p.* out prayer when chastening.
32. 15, till the spirit be *p.* on us.
44. 3, I will *p.* water on thirsty.
53. 12, *p.* out his soul unto death.
Jer. 7. 20; 42. 18, my fury shall be *p.* out.
Lam. 2. 19, *p.* out thine heart like water.
Nah. 1. 6, fury is *p.* out like fire.
Mal. 3. 10, if I will not *p.* out a blessing.
Mat. 26. 7; Mk. 14. 3, *p.* ointment on his head.
John 2. 15, he *p.* out the changers' money.
See 2 Sam. 23. 16; 2 Kn. 3. 11.

Pouring out of God's wrath. Ps. 69. 24; 79. 6; Jer. 10. 25; Ezek. 7. 8; Hos. 5. 10; Rev. 14. 10.
of the Holy Spirit. Isa. 32. 15; 44. 3; Ezek. 39. 29; Joel 2. 28; Zec. 12. 10; Acts 2.; 10. 45.
of the vials. Rev. 16.

Pourtray. Ezek. 4. 1; 8. 10; 23. 14.

Poverty. Gen. 45. 11; Prov. 20. 13, lest thou come to *p.*
Prov. 6. 11; 24. 34, thy *p.* come as one that travelleth.
10. 15, destruction of poor is *p.*
11. 24, it tendeth to *p.*
13. 18, *p.* to him that refuseth instruction.
28. 19, shall have *p.* enough.
30. 8, give me neither *p.* nor riches.
31. 7, drink and forget his *p.*
See Prov. 23. 21; 2 Cor. 8. 2; Rev. 2. 9.

Powder. Ex. 32. 20; 2 Kn. 23. 6; Mat. 21. 44.

Power. (1) Gen. 32. 28; Hos. 12. 3, hast thou *p.* with God. R. V. striven (in Gen.).
Ex. 15. 6, glorious in *p.*
Lev. 26. 19, the pride of your *p.*
Deu. 8. 18, he giveth thee *p.* to get wealth.
2 Sam. 22. 33, God is my strength and *p.* R. V. fortress.
1 Chr. 29. 11; Mat. 6. 13, thine is the *p.* and glory.
2 Chr. 25. 8, God hath *p.* to help.
Job 26. 2, him that is without *p.*
Ps. 49. 15, from the *p.* of the grave.
65. 6, being girded with *p.* R. V. might.
90. 11, who knoweth *p.* of thine anger.
Prov. 3. 27, when it is in *p.* to do it.
18. 21, in the *p.* of the tongue.
Eccl. 5. 19; 6. 2, *p.* to eat thereof.
8. 4, where word of king is, there is *p.*
Isa. 40. 29, he giveth *p.* to the faint.
Mic. 3. 8, full of *p.* by the spirit.
Hab. 3. 4, the hiding of his *p.*
Zec. 4. 6, not by might, nor by *p.*
Mat. 9. 6; Mk. 2. 10; Lu. 5. 24, *p.* on earth to forgive.
9. 8, who had given such *p.* to men.
24. 30; Lu. 21. 27, coming in clouds with *p.*
28. 18, all *p.* is given to me.
Lu. 1. 35, the *p.* of the Highest.
4. 6, all this *p.* will I give thee.
4. 14, Jesus returned in the *p.* of the Spirit.
4. 32, his word was with *p.* R. V. authority.
5. 17, the *p.* of the Lord was present.
9. 43, amazed at the mighty *p.* of God. R. V. majesty.
12. 5, that hath *p.* to cast into hell.
12. 11, bring you unto magistrates and *p.* R. V. authorities.
22. 53, your hour and the *p.* of darkness.
24. 49, with *p.* from on high.
John 1. 12, *p.* to become sons of God.
10. 18, I have *p.* to lay it down.
17. 2, *p.* over all flesh. R. V. authority.
19. 10, I have *p.* to crucify thee.
Acts 1. 8, *p.* after the Holy Ghost is come.
3. 12, as though by our own *p.*
5. 4, was it not in thine own *p.*
8. 10, this man is the great *p.* of God.
8. 19, give me also this *p.*
26. 18, from the *p.* of Satan unto God.
Rom. 1. 20, his eternal *p.* and Godhead.
9. 17, that I might shew my *p.* in thee.
13. 2, whosoever resisteth the *p.*
1 Cor. 15. 43, it is raised in *p.*
Eph. 2. 2, prince of the *p.* of the air.
3. 7, the effectual working of his *p.*
Phil. 3. 10, the *p.* of his resurrection.
2 Thes. 1. 9, from the glory of his *p.* R. V. might.
2 Tim. 1. 7, spirit of *p.* and love.
3. 5, form of godliness, but denying the *p.*
Heb. 2. 14, him that had *p.* of death.
6. 5, the *p.* of the world to come.
7. 16, the *p.* of an endless life.
Rev. 2. 26, to him will I give *p.* R. V. authority.
4. 11, worthy to receive *p.*
(2) an army, host. 2 Chr. 32. 9.
See Mat. 22. 29; Lu. 22. 69; Rom. 1. 16.

Power bestowed by God. Isa. 40. 29; Acts 6. 8; Rom. 15. 18; 1 Cor. 5. 4; 2 Cor. 12. 9; Eph. 1. 19.

Powerful. Ps. 29. 4; 2 Cor. 10. 10; Heb. 4. 12.

Powers, heavenly. Mat. 24. 29; Eph. 3. 10.
earthly to be obeyed. Rom. 13.; Tit. 3.; 1 Pet. 2. 13.
Praetorium, prǣ-tôr′-ĭ-ŭm, the headquarters of the governor. Mk. 15. 16.
Praise (*n.*). Ex. 15. 11, fearful in *p.*
Deu. 10. 21, he is thy *p.* and thy God.
Jud. 5. 3; Ps. 7. 17; 9. 2; 57. 7; 61. 8; 104. 33, I will sing *p.*
Neh. 9. 5, above all blessing and *p.*
Ps. 22. 3, that inhabitest the *p.* of Israel.
22. 25, my *p.* shall be of thee.
33. 1; 147. 1, *p.* is comely for the upright.
34. 1, his *p.* continually be in my mouth.
50. 23, whoso offereth *p.* glorifieth me.
65. 1, *p.* waiteth for thee.
66. 2, make his *p.* glorious.
109. 1, O God of my *p.*
148. 14, the *p.* of all his saints.
Prov. 27. 21, so is a man to his *p.*
Isa. 60. 18, call thy gates *P.*
61. 3, garment of *p.*
62. 7, a *p.* in the earth.
Jer. 13. 11, that they might be to me for a *p.*
49. 25, how is the city of *p.*
Hab. 3. 3, earth was full of his *p.*
Zep. 3. 30, a *p.* among all people.
John 9. 24, give God the *p.*
12. 43, the *p.* of men.
Rom. 2. 29, whose *p.* is not of men.
13. 3, thou shalt have *p.*
1 Cor. 4. 5, every man have *p.* of God.
2 Cor. 8. 18, whose *p.* is in the gospel.
Eph. 1. 6, 12, *p.* of glory of his grace.
Phil. 4. 8, if there be any *p.*
Heb. 13. 15, offer sacrifice of *p.*
1 Pet. 2. 14, *p.* of them that do well.
4. 11, to whom be *p.* and dominion.
See 2 Chr. 29. 30; Acts 16. 25; 1 Pet. 2. 9.
Praise (*v.*). Gen. 49. 8, whom thy brethren shall [*p.*
2 Sam. 14. 25, none to be so much *p.*
Ps. 30. 9, shall the dust *p.* thee?
42. 5, 11; 43. 5, I shall yet *p.* him.
45. 17, therefore shall the people *p.* thee.
49. 18, men will *p.* thee when thou doest well.
63. 3, my lips shall *p.* thee.
67. 3. 5, let the people *p.* thee.
71. 14, I will yet *p.* thee more and more.
72. 15, daily shall he be *p.*
76. 10, the wrath of man shall *p.* thee.
88. 10, shall the dead arise and *p.* thee?
107. 32, *p.* him in the assembly.
115. 17, the dead *p.* not.
119. 164, seven times a day do I *p.* thee.
145. 4, one generation shall *p.* thy works.
145. 10, all thy works shall *p.* thee.
Prov. 27. 2, let another *p.* thee.
31. 31, her own works *p.* her in the gates.
Isa. 38. 19, the living shall *p.* thee.
See Lu. 2. 13; 24. 53; Acts 2. 47; 3. 8.
Praise, God worthy of. Deu. 10. 21; Jud. 5. 2; Isa. 12.; 25.; 38. 19; 42. 10; Jer. 31. 7; Dan. 2. 23; Joel 2. 26; Hab. 3. 3; Lu. 1. 46, 68; Eph. 1. 6; Rev. 19. 5.
of man, vanity of. Prov. 27. 2; Mat. 6. 1.
Prancing. Jud. 5. 22; Nah. 3. 2.
Prating. Prov. 10. 8; 3 John 10.
Pray. Gen. 20. 7, a prophet and shall *p.* for thee.
1 Sam. 7. 5, I will *p.* for you to the Lord.
12. 23, sin in ceasing to *p.* for you.
2 Chr. 7. 14, if my people shall *p.*
Ez. 6. 10, *p.* for the life of the king.
Job 21. 15, what profit if we *p.* to him.
Ps. 5. 2, to thee will I *p.*
55. 17, evening, morning, and at noon will I *p.*
122. 6, *p.* for the peace of Jerusalem.
Isa. 45. 20, *p.* to a god that cannot save.
Jer. 7. 16; 11. 14; 14. 11, *p.* not for this people.
37. 3; 42. 2, 20, *p.* now to the Lord for us.
Zec. 7. 2, they sent men to *p.* R. V. intreat the favour.
Mat. 5. 44, and *p.* for them which despitefully use you.
Mat. 6. 5, they love to *p.* standing.
14. 23; Mk. 6. 46; Lu. 6. 12; 9. 28, apart to *p.*
26. 36; Mk. 14. 32, while I *p.* yonder.
Mk. 11. 25, and when ye stand *p.*, forgive.
Lu. 11. 1, Lord, teach us to *p.*
18. 1, men ought always to *p.*
John 14. 16; 16. 26, I will *p.* the Father.
17. 9, I *p.* for them, I *p.* not for the world.
17. 20, neither *p.* I for these alone.
Acts 9. 11, behold he *p.*
Rom. 8. 26, know not what we should *p.* for.
1 Cor. 14. 15, I will *p.* with the spirit, and *p.* with understanding also.
Eph. 6. 18, *p.* always with all prayer.
1 Thes. 5. 17, *p.* without ceasing.
1 Tim. 2. 8, that men *p.* everywhere.
Jas. 5. 13, is any afflicted? let him *p.*
5. 16, *p.* one for another.
1 John 5. 16, I do not say he shall *p.* for it.
See Lu. 9. 29; 1 Cor. 11. 4; 14. 14; 1 Thes. 5. 25.
Prayer. 2 Chr. 7. 15, ears shall be attent to the *p.*
Job 15. 4, thou restrainest *p.* R. V. devotion.
16. 17; Ps. 4. 1; 5. 3; 6. 9; 17. 1; 35. 13; 39. 12; 66. 19; Lam. 3. 8, my *p.*
Ps. 65. 2, thou that hearest *p.*
72. 15, *p.* shall be made continually.
109. 4, I give myself to *p.*
Prov. 15. 8, the *p.* of the upright.
Isa. 1. 15, when ye make many *p.*
56. 7; Mat. 21. 13; Mk. 11. 17; Lu. 19. 46, house [of *p.*
Mat. 21. 22, whatever ye ask in *p.*, believing.
23. 14; Mk. 12. 40; Lu. 20. 47, long *p.*
Lu. 6. 12, all night in *p.* to God.
Acts 3. 1, the hour of *p.*
6. 4, give ourselves continually to *p.*
12. 5, *p.* was made without ceasing.
16. 13, where *p.* was wont to be made.
Phil. 4. 6, in every thing by *p.*
Jas. 5. 15, *p.* of faith shall save the sick.
5. 16, effectual fervent *p.* of a righteous man.
1 Pet. 4. 7, watch unto *p.*
Rev. 5. 8; 8. 3, the *p.* of the saints.
See Ps. 72. 20; Dan. 9. 21.
Prayer, occasions, objects, examples of. 1 Chr. 16. 35; Job 33. 26; Ps. 122. 6; Mat. 5. 44; 9. 38; 26. 41; Lu. 18. 3, 38; Rom. 15. 30; 1 Cor. 7. 5; Jas. 5. 13; 1 Pet. 3. 7; 4. 7.
commanded. Isa. 55. 6; Mat. 7. 7; 26. 41; Lu. 18. 1; 21. 36; Rom. 12. 12; Eph. 6. 18; Phil. 4. 6; Col. 4. 2; 1 Thes. 5. 17, 25; 1 Tim. 2. 1, 8.
encouragements to. Job 33. 26; Ps. 6. 9; 32. 6; 66. 19; Isa. 65. 24; Zec. 13. 9; Mat. 18. 19; 21. 22; Mk. 11. 24; Lu. 11. 9; Rom. 10. 13; Jas. 1. 5.
God hears and answers. Ps. 10. 17; 65. 2; 99. 6; Isa. 58. 9; John 11. 42.
how to be offered. Ps. 145. 18; Prov. 15. 29; Eccl. 5. 2; Mat. 6. 5, 7; 21. 22; Mk. 11. 24; Lu. 11. 5; 18. 1; John 9. 31; 15. 7; Rom. 12. 12; Eph. 6. 18; Col. 4. 2; 1 Tim. 2. 8; 5. 5; Heb. 11. 6; Jas. 1. 6; 4. 8.
through Christ. Eph. 2. 18; Heb. 10. 19.
in the name of Christ. John 16. 26.
promises for. Isa. 65. 24; Am. 5. 4; Zec. 13. 9; Mat. 6. 6; Lu. 11. 9; John 14. 13.
posture for. Num. 16. 22; Jos. 5. 14; 1 Kn. 8. 22; 1 Chr. 21. 16; 2 Chr. 6. 13; Ps. 28. 2; 95. 6; Isa. 1. 15; Lam. 2. 19; Mat. 26. 39; Mk. 11. 25; Lu. 22. 41; Acts 20. 36; 1 Tim. 2. 8.
(public). Ex. 20. 24; 2 Chr. 7. 14, 16; Isa. 56. 7; Mat. 12. 9; 18. 19, 20; Lu. 4. 16; 11. 2.
instances of: Joshua, Jos. 7. 6-9. David, 1 Chr. 29. 10, 12; 2 Sam. 6. 18. Solomon, 2 Chr. 6. 12. Jews, Lu. 1. 10. early church, Acts 2. 46; 4. 24; 12. 5, 12. Peter and John, Acts 3. 1. church at Antioch, Acts 13. 3. Paul and Silas, Acts 16. 16. Paul with the elders, Acts 20. 36; 21. 5.
(private). Ps. 55. 17; 88. 1; Dan. 6. 10; 1 Thes. 5. 17.
instances of: Abraham, Gen. 18. 23-32. Lot, Gen. 19. 19. Eliezer, Gen. 24. 12. Jacob, Gen. 32. 9. Gideon, Jud. 6. 13, 22, 36, 39. Hannah, 1 Sam. 1. David, 2 Sam. 7. 18; 1 Chr. 29. 10.

Elijah, 1 Kn. 18. 36. Hezekiah, 2 Kn. 20. 2. Isaiah, 2 Kn. 20. 11. Jabez, 1 Chr. 4. 10. Manasseh, 2 Chr. 33. 19. Ezra, Ez. 9. 5, 6. Nehemiah, Neh. 2. 4. Jeremiah, Jer. 32. 16. Daniel, Dan. 9. 3. Jonah, Jon. 2. 1. Anna, Lu. 2. 37. Paul, Acts 9. 11; 1 Thes. 5. 23. Cornelius, Acts 10. 2, 30. Peter, Acts 9. 40; 10. 9.

of the hypocrite condemned. Ps. 109. 7; Prov. 1. 28; 28. 9; Mat. 6. 5.
the Lord's. Mat. 6. 9; Lu. 11. 2.
of malefactor on the cross. Lu. 23. 42.

Prayers (of Christ). Mat. 14. 23; 26. 36; 27. 46; Mk. 6. 46; 14. 32; 15. 34; Lu. 6. 12; 9. 28; 23. 34, 46; John 17. 9.

Prayers (Special) in the Old Testament.

(See also under headings PRAYER, PSALMS, &c.)

OF WHOM RECORDED.	REFERENCES.	SUBJECTS.
Aaron and priests	Num. 6. 22–26	The Aaronic blessing of Israel.
Abraham	Gen. 15. 2	For a son.
Abraham	Gen. 17. 17, 18	For Ishmael's acceptance.
Abraham	Gen. 18. 23	For mercy on Sodom.
Abraham's servant	Gen. 24. 12	Success in his mission, when sent to find a wife for Isaac.
Agur	Prov. 30. 1	For moderation in his desires.
Asa	2 Chr. 14. 11	When going to battle with Zerah the Ethiopian.
Daniel	Dan. 9. 4	For restoration of Jerusalem.
David	2 Sam. 7. 18	Prayer for blessing on his house.
David	Ps. 51	After his sin with Bath-sheba.
David	2 Sam. 24. 17	After numbering the people.
David	1 Chr. 29. 10–19	Thanksgiving at close of life.
Elijah	1 Kn. 17. 20	For the restoration of the widow's son.
Elijah	1 Kn. 18. 36	For Divine attestation of his mission.
Elijah	1 Kn. 19. 4	For death.
Elisha	2 Kn. 6. 17	For his servant's eyes to be opened.
Elisha	2 Kn. 6. 18	That the army sent to take him may be blinded.
Ezekiel	Ezek. 9. 8	Intercession for his people.
Ezra	Ez. 9. 6	Confession of sin in the people's alliances with the heathen.
Habakkuk	Hab. 3. 1–16	For revival of God's work.
Hannah	1 Sam. 1. 11	For the gift of a son.
Hezekiah	2 Kn. 19. 15; Isa. 37. 16.	For protection against Sennacherib.
Hezekiah	2 Kn. 20. 3; Isa. 38. 3	When dangerously ill.
Hezekiah	2 Chr. 30. 18	For the unprepared who had eaten of the Passover.
Israel	Deu. 21. 6–8	Expiation of undiscovered murder.
Israel	Deu. 26. 5–10	Confession on presenting firstfruits.
Israel	Deu. 26. 13–15	The prayer of the tithing year.
Jabez	1 Chr. 4. 10	For the Divine blessing.
Jacob	Gen. 32. 9	For deliverance from Esau.
Jehoshaphat	2 Chr. 20. 6	For protection against armies of Moabites and Ammonites.
Jeremiah	Jer. 14. 7	In a great famine.
Jeremiah	Jer. 15. 15–18	For comfort.
Jonah	Jon. 2. 2	For deliverance from the great fish.
Joshua	Jos. 7. 7–9	After Achan's sin.
Levites	Neh. 9. 5	Confession of God's goodness, and their nation's sins.
Manoah	Jud. 13. 8, 9	For Divine guidance in training his child.
Moses	Ex. 32. 11; Deu. 9. 26	Forgiveness for the people's idolatry.
Moses	Ex. 33. 12	For the Divine presence.
Moses	Num. 10. 35, 36	At the setting forth and stopping of the ark.
Moses	Num. 11. 11–15	For Divine help to govern the Israelites.
Moses	Num. 12. 13	For Miriam, for cure from leprosy.
Moses	Num. 14. 13–19	For the people disappointed at the spies' report.
Moses	Num. 27. 15	For a successor.
Moses	Deu. 3. 24	To enter Canaan.
Nehemiah	Neh. 1. 5	For the remnant in captivity.
Nehemiah	Neh. 4. 4	For protection against Sanballat and Tobiah.
Samson	Jud. 16. 28	To be avenged on his enemies.
Solomon	1 Kn. 3. 5–9	For wisdom to govern Israel.
Solomon	1 Kn. 8. 23; 2 Chr. 6. 14.	Dedication of the Temple.

Prayers and Thanksgivings (Special) in the New Testament.

(See also the Special Songs of Thanksgiving in Lu. 1., 2.; Rev. 4., 5., 7., 11., 12., 15., 18., 19.)

Of whom recorded.	References.	Subjects.
Apostles	Lu. 17. 5.	For more faith.
Apostles	Acts 1. 24, 25.	On choosing an Apostle.
Blind Bartimæus	Mk. 10. 47	For sight.
Early Church	Acts 4. 24–30.	For support under persecution.
Father of the lunatic boy	Mat. 17. 15	For his only son.
Jairus	Mat. 9. 18.	For his little daughter.
Jesus	Mat. 11. 25, 26; Lu. 10. 21.	Thanksgiving.
Jesus	Mat. 26. 39; Lu. 22. 42.	Under suffering in Gethsemane.
Jesus	Mat. 27. 46	Under suspension of Divine consolation.
Jesus	Lu. 23. 34.	For His murderers.
Jesus	Lu. 23. 46.	Commending His spirit to God.
Jesus	John 11. 41, 42	Thanksgiving for the Father's acceptance of His prayer.
Jesus	John 12. 27, 28	Imploring His Father's aid.
Jesus	John 17.	For His Apostles, and all believers. For unity.
Lord's prayer	Mat. 6. 9; Lu. 11. 2.	The model of supplication for relief of human needs.
Penitent thief	Lu. 23. 42.	To be remembered by Jesus.
Pharisee's prayer	Lu. 18. 11.	Thanksgiving for his own righteousness.
Prodigal son	Lu. 15. 18, 19.	For forgiveness.
Publican's prayer	Lu. 18. 13.	For Divine mercy.
St. Paul	Acts 9. 6, 11.	For instruction and grace.
St. Paul	2 Cor. 12. 8.	For relief from personal trial.
St. Paul	Eph. 1. 17–20; 3. 14–21; Phil. 1. 9–11; Col. 1. 9–11; 1 Thes. 3. 10–13; 2 Thes. 1. 11, 12; 2. 16, 17; 3. 5; Heb. 13. 20, 21.	Intercession for the Churches.
Samaritan woman	John 4. 15.	For the Living Water.
Stephen	Acts 7. 59, 60.	Commendation of his soul; forgiveness of his murderers.
Syrophenician woman	Mat. 15. 22	For her daughter.
Ten lepers	Lu. 17. 13.	For cleansing.
The centurion	Mat. 8. 6	For his servant.
The disciples	Mat. 8. 25	To be saved from the storm.
The leper	Mat. 8. 2	For cleansing.
The nobleman	John 4. 49	For his child.
The waiting Church	Rev. 22. 20	For the coming of Christ.
Two blind men	Mat. 9. 27.	For sight.

Preach. Neh. 6. 7, appointed prophets to *p.* of thee.
Isa. 61. 1, to *p.* good tidings.
Jon. 3. 2, *p.* the preaching I bid thee.
Mat. 4. 17; 10. 7, Jesus began to *p.*
11. 1, to *p.* in their cities.
11. 5, the poor have the gospel *p.*
Mk. 2. 2, he *p.* the word to them. R. V. spake.
16. 20, and *p.* every where.
Lu. 9. 60, go thou and *p.* kingdom of God.
Acts 8. 5, and *p.* Christ unto them.
10. 36, *p.* peace by Jesus Christ.
13. 38, through this man is *p.* forgiveness.
17. 18, he *p.* Jesus and the resurrection.
Rom. 2. 21, thou that *p.* a man should not steal.
10. 15, how shall they *p.* except.
1 Cor. 1. 18, the *p.* of the cross is foolishness.
1. 21, by the foolishness of *p.*
1. 23, but we *p.* Christ crucified.
9. 27, lest when I have *p.* to others.
15. 11, so we *p.* and so ye believed.
15. 14, then is our *p.* vain.
2 Cor. 4. 5, we *p.* not ourselves.
Phil. 1. 15, some *p.* Christ of envy and strife.
2 Tim. 4. 2, *p.* the word; be instant.
Heb. 4. 2, word *p.* did not profit. R. V. of hearing.
1 Pet. 3. 19, *p.* to spirits in prison.
See Ps. 40. 9; 2 Cor. 11. 4.

Preacher. Rom. 10. 14, how shall they hear without a *p.*?
1 Tim. 2. 7, whereunto I am ordained a *p.*
2 Pet. 2. 5, Noah, a *p.* of righteousness.
See 2 Tim. 1. 11. [Ecclesiastes.

Preacher, The, Ecclesiastes, title of the book

Preaching, the gospel of Christ. Mat. 4. 17; 5.; 28. 19; Mk. 1. 14; 16. 15; Lu. 4. 18 (Isa. 61. 1); 9. 60; 24. 47; Acts 2. 14; 3. 12; 4. 8; 10. 42; 13. 16. *See* Rom. 10. 8; 1 Cor. 1. 17; 2.; 15. 1; Gal. 1.; Eph. 1. 3.
gospel manifested through. Tit. 1. 3.
repentance, by John the Baptist. Mat. 3.; Mk. 1.; Lu. 3.
of Noah. 2 Pet. 2. 5, &c.
of Jonah. Jon. 3.; Mat. 12. 41; Lu. 11. 32.

Precept. Neh. 9. 14, commandedst them *p.*
Isa. 28. 10, 13, *p.* must be upon *p.*
29. 13, taught by *p.* of men.
Jer. 35. 18, ye have kept Jonadab's *p.* [9. 19.
See Ps. 119. 4, etc.; Dan. 9. 5; Mk. 10. 5; Heb.

Precious. Deu. 33. 13-16, *p.* things.
1 Sam. 3. 1, the word was *p.* in those days.
26. 21, my soul was *p.* in thine eyes.
2 Kn. 1. 13, let my life be *p.*
Ez. 8. 27, fine copper, *p.* as gold. [V. costly.
Ps. 49. 8, the redemption of their soul is *p.* R.
72. 14, *p.* shall their blood be in his sight.
116. 15, *p.* in sight of the Lord is death of saints.
126. 6, bearing *p.* seed. R. V. forth the seed.
133. 2, like *p.* ointment upon the head.
139. 17, how *p.* are thy thoughts.
Prov. 3. 15, wisdom more *p.* than rubies.
Eccl. 7. 1, good name better than *p.* ointment.
Isa. 13. 12, I will make a man more *p.*
28. 16; 1 Pet. 2. 6, a *p.* corner stone.
43. 4, since thou wast *p.* in my sight.
Jer. 15. 19, take the *p.* from the vile.
Lam. 4. 2, the *p.* sons of Zion.
1 Pet. 1. 7, trial of faith more *p.* than gold.
1. 19, the *p.* blood of Christ.
2. 7, to you which believe he is *p.*
2 Pet. 1. 1, like *p.* faith.
1. 4, great and *p.* promises.
See Mat. 26. 7; Mk. 14. 3; Jas. 5. 7; Rev. 21. 11.

Precious Stones of the Bible.

Adamant.	Emerald.
Agate.	Jacinth.
Amber.	Jasper.
Amethyst.	Ligure.
Beryl.	Onyx.
Carbuncle.	Sapphire.
Chalcedony.	Sardius.
Chrysolite.	Sardonyx.
Chrysoprase.	Topaz.
Diamond.	

Predestination. Rom. 8. 29; 9.-11.; Eph. 1. 5.
Preeminence. Eccl. 3. 19; Col. 1. 18; 3 John 9.
Prefer. Ps. 137. 6; John 1. 15; Rom. 12. 10; 1 Tim. 5. 21.
Premeditate. Mk. 13. 11.
Preparation. Prov. 16. 1, *p.* of the heart.
Eph. 6. 15, feet shod with *p.* of gospel. [14.
See Mat. 27. 62; Mk. 15. 42; Lu. 23. 54; John 19.
Prepare. 1 Sam. 7. 3, *p.* your hearts to the Lord.
2 Chr. 20. 33, as yet the people had not *p.* R. V. set.
Ps. 68. 10, thou hast *p.* of thy goodness.
107. 36, that they may *p.* a city.
Prov. 8. 27, when he *p.* the heavens I was there. R. V. established.
Isa. 40. 3; Mal. 3. 1; Mat. 3. 3; Mk. 1. 2; Lu. 1. 76, *p.* way of the Lord.
62. 10, *p.* the way of the people.
Am. 4. 12, *p.* to meet thy God.
Jon. 1. 17, Lord had *p.* a great fish.
Mat. 20. 23; Mk. 10. 40, to them for whom *p.*
John 14. 2, I go to *p.* a place for you.
Rom. 9. 23, afore *p.* to glory.
1 Cor. 2. 9, things God hath *p.*
Heb. 10. 5, a body hast thou *p.* me.
See 1 Chr. 22. 5; Ps. 23. 5; Rev. 21. 2.
Presbytery. 1 Tim. 4. 14.
Prescribe. Ez. 7. 22; Isa. 10. 1.
Presence. Gen. 4. 16, Cain went out from the *p.* of the Lord.
47. 15, why should we die in thy *p.*
Ex. 33. 15, if thy *p.* go not with me.
Job 23. 15, I am troubled at his *p.*
Ps. 16. 11, in thy *p.* is fulness of joy.
17. 2, my sentence come forth from thy *p.*
31. 20, in the secret of thy *p.*
51. 11, cast me not away from thy *p.*
139. 7, whither shall I flee from thy *p.*?
Prov. 14. 7, go from *p.* of a foolish man.
Isa. 63. 9, angel of his *p.* saved them.
Jer. 23. 39; 52. 3, I will cast you out of my *p.*
Jon. 1. 3, to flee from *p.* of the Lord.
Zep. 1. 7, hold thy peace at *p.* of the Lord.
Lu. 13. 26, we have eaten and drunk in thy *p.*
Acts 3. 19, times of refreshing from the *p.*
2 Cor. 10. 1, 10, who in *p.* am base.
2 Thes. 1. 9, destruction from the *p.* of the Lord.
See Gen. 16. 12; Ps. 23. 5; Prov. 25. 6; Lu. 15. 10.
Presence of God. 1 Chr. 16. 27; Ps. 16. 11; 18. 7; 68. 8; Isa. 64. 1; Jer. 5. 22; Ezek. 1.; Dan. 7. 9; Nah. 1.; Hab. 3.; Rev. 1.
Christ has entered. Heb. 9. 24. [8, 11.
angels and elders stand in. Lu. 1. 19; Rev. 5.
Present. 1 Sam. 10. 27, they brought him no *p.*
Ps. 46. 1, a very *p.* help in trouble.
John 14. 25, being yet *p.* with you. R. V. abiding.
Acts 10. 33, all here *p.* before God.
Rom. 7. 18, to will is *p.* with me.
7. 21, evil is *p.* with me.
8. 18, sufferings of this *p.* time.
12. 1, *p.* your bodies a living sacrifice.
1 Cor. 7. 26, good for the *p.* distress. [home.
2 Cor. 5. 8, to be *p.* with the Lord. R. V. at
5. 9, whether *p.* or absent. R. V. at home.
Gal. 1. 4, deliver us from this *p.* world.
Col. 1. 28, *p.* every man perfect.
2 Tim. 4. 10, having loved this *p.* world.
Tit. 2. 12, live godly in this *p.* world.
Heb. 12. 11, no chastening for *p.* seemeth joyous.
2 Pet. 1. 12, established in the *p.* truth.
Jude 24, able to *p.* you faultless. R. V. set.
See Ps. 72. 10; Lu. 2. 22.
Presently, immediately, in a short time. Prov. 12. 16; Mat. 21. 19; 26. 53.
Presents made. Gen. 32. 13; 33. 10; 43. 11; Jud. 3. 15; 1 Sam. 9. 7; 2 Kn. 8. 8; 20. 12; Mat. 2. 11.
Preserve. Gen. 32. 30, I have seen God, and my life is *p.*
45. 5, did send me before you to *p.* life.
Job 29. 2, as in days when God *p.* me.
Ps. 36. 6, thou *p.* man and beast.
121. 7, the Lord *p.* thee from evil.
121. 8, *p.* thy going out and coming in.
Prov. 2. 8, he *p.* the way of his saints.
2. 11, discretion shall *p.* thee.
20. 28, mercy and truth *p.* the king.
Jer. 49. 11, I will *p.* them alive.
Lu. 17. 33, lose his life shall *p.* it.
See Neh. 9. 6; Isa. 49. 6; Hos. 12. 13; Jude 1.
Preserver (God) of the faithful. Ps. 31. 23; 37. 28; 97. 10; 145. 20; Prov. 2. 8.
of men. Jos. 24. 17; 2 Sam. 8. 6; Job 7. 20; Ps. 36. 6; 116. 6; 146. 9.
Press. Prov. 3. 10, *p.* burst with new wine.
Am. 2. 13, I am *p.* under you as a cart is *p.*
Mk. 3. 10, they *p.* on him to touch him.
Lu. 6. 38, good measure, *p.* down. [violently.
16. 16, every man *p.* into it. R. V. entereth
Phil. 3. 14, I *p.* toward the mark.
See Mk. 2. 4; 5. 27; Lu. 8. 19; 19. 3.
Pressfat, the vat of a winepress. Hag. 2. 16.
Presumption: of Israelites, Num. 14. 44; Deu. 1. 43, prophets, Deu. 18. 20. builders of Babel, Gen. 11. Korah, &c., Num. 16. Beth-shemites, 1 Sam. 6. 19. Hiel, the Beth-elite, 1 Kn. 16. 34. Uzzah, 2 Sam. 6. 6. Uzziah, 2 Chr. 26. 16. Jewish exorcists, Acts 19. 13. Diotrephes, 3 John 9.
Presumptuous sins. Ex. 21. 14; Num. 15. 30; Deu. 17. 12; Ps. 19. 13; 2 Pet. 2. 10.
Pretence. Mat. 23. 14; Mk. 12. 40; Phil. 1. 18.
Prevail. Gen. 32. 28; Hos. 12. 4, power with God, and hast *p.*
Ex. 17. 11, Moses held up hand, Israel *p.*
1 Sam. 2. 9, by strength shall no man *p.*
Ps. 9. 19, let not man *p.*
65. 3, iniquities *p.* against me.
Eccl. 4. 12, if one *p.* against him.
Mat. 16. 18, gates of hell shall not *p.*
Acts 19. 20, grew word of God and *p.*
See Job 14. 20; Jer. 20. 7; Lam. 1. 16; John 12. 19.
Prevent, to go before, anticipate, precede. 2 Sam. 22. 6; Ps. 18. 5, snares of death *p.* me.
Ps. 88. 13, in the morning shall my prayer *p.* thee.
119. 147, I *p.* the dawning of the morning.
See Ps. 21. 3; 79. 8; Isa. 21. 14; 1 Thes. 4. 15.
Prey. Isa. 49. 24, shall the *p.* be taken from the mighty?
Jer. 21. 9; 38. 2; 39. 18; 45. 5, his life shall be for a *p.*

Ezek. 34. 22, my flock shall no more be a *p*.
See Gen. 49. 9; Num. 14. 3; Neh. 4. 4; Am. 3. 4.
Price. Lev. 25. 52, the *p*. of his redemption.
Deu. 23. 18, *p*. of a dog. R. V. wages.
2 Sam. 24. 24; 1 Chr. 21. 22, I will buy it at a *p*.
Acts 5. 2, kept back part of the *p*.
1 Cor. 6. 20; 7. 23, bought with a *p*.
1 Pet. 3. 4, meek spirit of great *p*.
Price of Him that was valued. *See* Mat. 26. 15; cf. Zec. 11. 12.
of virtue, Prov. 31. 10. of wisdom, Job 28. 13.
of redemption. 1 Cor. 6. 20; 7. 23.
pearl of great, Mat. 13. 46. ornament of, 1 Pet. 3. 4.
Pricks, goads (for driving cattle). Num. 33. 55; Acts 9. 5; 26. 14.
Pride. Ps. 31. 20, hide them from *p*. of man. R. V. plottings.
Prov. 8. 13, *p*. do I hate.
14. 3, in mouth of foolish is rod of *p*.
Isa. 28. 1, woe to the crown of *p*.
Jer. 49. 16, *p*. of thine heart hath deceived thee.
Pride. 1 Sam. 2. 3; Prov. 6. 16; 8. 13; 16. 5; 21. 4; Dan. 5. 20; Mk. 7. 20; Rom. 12. 3, 16.
origin of. 2 Kn. 20. 13; Zep. 3, 11; Lu. 18. 11; 1 Cor. 8. 1; 1 Tim. 3. 6; 1 John 2. 16.
evil results of. Ps. 10. 2; Prov. 13. 10; 21. 24; 28. 25; Jer. 43. 2; 49. 16; Obad. 3.
followed by shame and destruction. Prov. 11. 2; 16. 18; 18. 12; 29. 23; Isa. 28. 3.
exhortations against. Isa. 28. 1; Jer. 13. 15.
Priest (Heb. *Côhên*: Gk. ἱερεύς). Heb. 5. 10; 2 Pet. 2. 9. 'Priest' is a contraction of the Greek *presbyteros*, Lat. *presbyter*, 'an elder,' or 'elderly.' The word has a noteworthy history. 'Presbyter' was first a name for the officials of the Jewish religious community: it then became a title of office in the Christian Church and ultimately came to = the Lat. *sacerdos* and Gk. ἱερεύς, losing its original connotation of 'elder,' and acquiring that of 'sacrificing minister.' The essential idea of the Jewish *Cohen* was that of a mediator between God and man, (1) by ministering at the sanctuary, (2) by teaching the law of God, (3) by inquiring for the people the Divine will.
Gen. 14. 18; Heb. 7. 1, *p*. of most high God.
Ex. 19. 6, a kingdom of *p*.
1 Sam. 2. 35, I will raise up a faithful *p*.
2 Chr. 6. 41; Ps. 132. 16, *p*. clothed with salvation.
13. 9, *p*. of them that are no gods.
15. 3, without a teaching *p*.
Isa. 24. 2, as with the people, so with the *p*.
28. 7, *p*. and prophet have erred.
61. 6, shall be named the *p*. of the Lord.
Jer. 13. 13, will fill *p*. with drunkenness.
Mic. 3. 11, the *p*. teach for hire.
Mal. 2. 7, the *p*. lips should keep knowledge.
Lu. 17. 14, shew yourselves to the *p*.
Acts 6. 7, *p*. were obedient to the faith.
Rev. 1. 6; 5. 10; 20. 6, kings and *p*. to God.
Priest, high. Ex. 28.; 39.; Lev. 8.; 16.
Priesthood. Ex. 40. 15; Num. 25. 13, an everlasting *p*.
Num. 16. 10, seek ye the *p*. also.
Heb. 7. 24, an unchangeable *p*.
1 Pet. 2. 5, an holy *p*.
2. 9, ye are a royal *p*.
See Num. 18. 1; Jos. 18. 7; Neh. 13. 29.
Priesthood of Christ, Aaron, and Melchizedec. Rom. 8. 34; Heb. 2. 17; 3.; 4. 15; 5.; 7.; 1 John 2. 1.
Priests, Levitical, Ex. 28. 1; Lev. 8. their duties, offerings, rites, Lev. 1.; 9.; 21.; 22.; Num. 3.; Deu. 31. 9; Jos. 3.; 4.; 1 Kn. 8. 3.
fourscore and five slain by command of Saul. 1 Sam. 22. 17.
divided by lot by David. 1 Chr. 24.
denounced for unfaithfulness. Jer. 1. 18; 5. 31; Hos. 5.; 6.; Mic. 3. 11; Zep. 3. 4; Mal. 2.
of Baal, slain. 1 Kn. 18. 40; 2 Kn. 10. 19; 11. 18.
Christians called. 1 Pet. 2. 5; Rev. 1. 6; 5. 10; 20. 6.

Prince. Gen. 32. 28, as a *p*. hast thou power. R. V. omits.
Ex. 2. 14; Num. 16. 13, who made thee a *p*. over us?
1 Sam. 2. 8; Ps. 113. 8, to set them among *p*.
2 Sam. 3. 38, a *p*. fallen in Israel.
Job 12. 21; Ps. 107. 40, poureth contempt on *p*.
21. 28, where is the house of the *p*.?
31. 37, as a *p*. would I go near him.
Ps. 45. 16, make *p*. in all the earth.
118. 9, than to put confidence in *p*.
146. 3. put not your trust in *p*.
Prov. 8. 15, by me *p*. decree justice.
31. 4, nor for *p*. strong drink.
Eccl. 10. 7, *p*. walking as servants.
10. 16, when thy *p*. eat in the morning.
10. 17, blessed when *p*. eat in due season.
Isa. 34. 12; 40. 23, all her *p*. shall be nothing.
Hos. 3. 4, abide many days without a *p*.
Mat. 9. 34; 12. 24; Mk. 3. 22, by *p*. of devils.
John 12. 31; 14. 30; 16. 11, the *p*. of this world.
Acts 3. 15, and killed the *P*. of life.
5. 31, exalted to be a *P*. and Saviour.
1 Cor. 2. 6, wisdom of the *p*. of this world. R. V. rulers.
2. 8, which none of *p*. of this world knew. R. V. rulers.
Eph. 2. 2, the *p*. of the power of the air.
See Isa. 3. 4; Hos. 7. 5; Mat. 20. 25.
Prince: of peace, Isa. 9. 6. of life, Acts 3. 15.
of this world, John 12. 31; 14. 30; 16. 11. of the power of the air, Eph. 2. 2.
of devils, Christ's miracles ascribed to. Mat. 9. 34; 12. 24; Mk. 3. 22; Lu. 11. 15.
Princes of the tribes. Num. 1. 5.
their offerings. Num. 7.
Principal. Prov. 4. 7; Isa. 28. 25; Acts 25. 23.
Principalities. Eph. 6. 12, we wrestle against *p*. and powers.
Tit. 3. 1, to be subject to *p*. R. V. rulers.
Principalities and powers. Rom. 8. 38; Eph. 3. 10; 6. 12; Col. 2. 15.
Christ the head of all. Eph. 1. 21; Col. 1. 16; 2. 10.
Principles. Heb. 5. 12; 6. 1.
Print. Lev. 19. 28; Job 13. 27; 19. 23; John 20. 25.
Prisca, prĭs′-că, 'ancient.' 2 Tim. 4. 19.
Priscilla, prĭs-çĭl′-lă, diminutive of PRISCA (and AQUILA). Acts 18.; Rom. 16. 3; 1 Cor. 16. 19.
Prison. Ps. 142. 7, bring my soul out of *p*.
Eccl. 4. 14, out of *p*. he cometh to reign.
Isa. 53. 8, taken from *p*. and from judgment. R. V. by oppression.
61. 1, opening of the *p*.
Mat. 5. 25; Lu. 12. 58, thou be cast into *p*.
11. 2, John heard in the *p*.
25. 36, 39, in *p*. and ye came unto me.
Lu. 22. 33, to go with thee to *p*. and to death.
2 Cor. 11. 23, in *p*. more frequent.
1 Pet. 3. 19, spirits in *p*.
See Jer. 32. 2; 39. 14; Lu. 3. 20; Acts 5. 18.
Prisoner. Ps. 79. 11; Zec. 9. 12; Mat. 27. 16; Eph. 3. 1.
Private. 2 Pet. 1. 20.
Privately. Mat. 24. 3; Mk. 9. 28; Lu. 10. 23; Gal. 2. 2.
Privily. Mat. 1. 19; 2. 7; Acts 16. 37; Gal. 2. 4; 2 Pet. 2. 1.
Prize. 1 Cor. 9. 24; Phil. 3. 14.
Proceed. Gen. 24. 50, the thing *p*. from the Lord.
Deu. 8. 3; Mat. 4. 4, that *p*. out of mouth of God.
Job 40. 5, I will *p*. no further.
Isa. 29. 14, I will *p*. to do a marvellous work.
51. 4, a law shall *p*. from me.
Jer. 9. 3, they *p*. from evil to evil.
Mat. 15. 18; Mk. 7. 21, *p*. out of the mouth.
John 8. 42, I *p*. forth from God. R. V. came.
Jas. 3. 10, *p*. blessing and cursing.
See Lu. 4. 22; John 15. 26; Eph. 4. 29; Rev. 22. 1.
Prochorus, prŏch′-ō-rŭs, one of the seven 'deacons.' Acts 6. 5.
Proclaim. Ex. 33. 19; 34. 5, I will *p*. the name of the Lord.

Isa. 61. 1, to *p.* liberty to captives.
61. 2, to *p.* acceptable year.
62. 11, Lord hath *p.*, thy salvation cometh.
Jer. 34. 15, in *p.* liberty every man to his neighbour.
Lu. 12. 3, *p.* upon the housetops.
See Deu. 20. 10; Prov. 20. 6; Jer. 3. 12; Joel 3. 9.

Procure. Prov. 11. 27; Jer. 2. 17; 4. 18; 26. 19; 33. 9.

Prodigal son, parable of. Lu. 15. 11.

Produce. Isa. 41. 21.

Profane. Lev. 18. 21; 19. 12; 20. 3; 21. 6; 22. 2, *p.* name of God.
Jer. 23. 11, prophet and priest are *p.*
Ezek. 22. 26, no difference between holy and *p.* R. V. common.
Mat. 12. 5, priests in temple *p.* sabbath.
Acts 24. 6, hath gone about to *p.* temple.
1 Tim. 1. 9, law for unholy and *p.*
4. 7, refuse *p.* and old wives' fables.
6. 20; 2 Tim. 2. 16, avoiding *p.* babblings.
Heb. 12. 16, any *p.* person.
See Ps. 89. 39; Jer. 23. 15; Mal. 2. 10.

Profanity. Lev. 18. 21; 19. 12; Neh. 13. 18; Ezek. 22. 8; Mal. 1. 12.

Profess, to declare openly. Mat. 7. 23; Rom. 1. 22; 2 Cor. 9. 13; 1 Tim. 2. 10; 6. 12.

Profession of Christ, to hold fast. 1 Tim. 6. 12; Heb. 3. 1; 4. 14; 10. 23.

Profit (*n.*). Gen. 25. 32, what *p.* shall birthright do me?
37. 26, what *p.* if we slay?
Job 21. 15, what *p.* if we pray?
Prov. 14. 23, in all labour there is *p.*
Eccl. 1. 3; 3. 9; 5. 16, what *p.* of labour?
2. 11, there was no *p.* under the sun.
5. 9, *p.* of the earth for all.
7. 11, by wisdom there is *p.*
Jer. 16. 19, things wherein is no *p.*
Mal. 3. 14, what *p.* that we have kept.
1 Cor. 10. 33, not seeking own *p.* but *p.* of many.
2 Tim. 2. 14, about words to no *p.*
Heb. 12. 10, he chasteneth us for our *p.*
See Esth. 3. 8; Ps. 30. 9; Isa. 30. 5; 1 Tim. 4. 15.

Profit (*v.*). 1 Sam. 12. 21, vain things which cannot *p.*
Job 33. 27, I have sinned, and it *p.* not.
34. 9, *p.* nothing to delight in God.
Prov. 10. 2, treasures of wickedness *p.* nothing.
11. 4, riches *p.* not in the day of wrath.
Isa. 30. 5, 6, people that could not *p.*
48. 17, the Lord which teacheth thee to *p.*
Jer. 2. 11, changed for that which doth not *p.*
23. 32, they shall not *p.* this people.
Mat. 16. 26; Mk. 8. 36, what is a man *p.*?
1 Cor. 12. 7, to every man to *p.* withal.
Gal. 5. 2, Christ shall *p.* you nothing.
1 Tim. 4. 8, bodily exercise *p.* little.
Heb. 4. 2, the word preached did not *p.* [14.
See Mat. 15. 5; Rom. 2. 25; 1 Cor. 13. 3; Jas. 2.

Profitable. Job 22. 2, can a man be *p.* to God?
Eccl. 10. 10, wisdom is *p.* to direct.
Acts 20. 20, I kept back nothing *p.*
1 Tim. 4. 8, godliness is *p.* to all things.
2 Tim. 3. 16, scripture is *p.* for doctrine.
See Mat. 5. 29; 2 Tim. 4. 11; Tit. 3. 8; Philem. 11.

Prolong. Deu. 4. 26; 30. 18, ye shall not *p.* your days.
Job 6. 11, what is mine end that I should *p.* my life? R. V. be patient.
Prov. 10. 27, fear of the Lord *p.* days.
Eccl. 8. 12, though a sinner's days be *p.*
See Ps. 61. 6; Prov. 28. 2; Isa. 13. 22; 53. 10.

Promise (*n.*). Num. 14. 34, ye shall know my breach of *p.*
1 Kn. 8. 56, hath not failed one word of *p.*
Ps. 77. 8, doth his *p.* fail?
Lu. 24. 49; Acts 1. 4, *p.* of Father.
Acts 2. 39, the *p.* is to you and your children.
26. 6, for hope of the *p.*
Rom. 4. 14, the *p.* made of none effect.
4. 20, staggered not at the *p.*
9. 4, to whom pertain the *p.*
Rom. 9. 8; Gal. 4. 28, the children of the *p.*
2 Cor. 1. 20, *p.* are yea and Amen.
Gal. 3. 21, is the law against the *p.* of God?
1 Tim. 4. 8; 2 Tim. 1. 1, *p.* of the life that now is.
Heb. 6. 12, through faith and patience inherit the *p.*
9. 15; 10. 36, the *p.* of eternal inheritance.
11. 13, died, not having received *p.*
2 Pet. 1. 4, great and precious *p.*
3. 4, where is the *p.* of his coming?
3. 9, not slack concerning his *p.* [*p.*

Promise (*v.*). Ex. 12. 25, will give you as he hath
Num. 14. 40, will go to place the Lord *p.*
Deu. 1. 11; 15. 6, the Lord bless you as he hath *p.*
9. 28, not able to bring into land *p.*
19. 8; 27. 3, give the land he *p.* to give.
Jos. 23. 15, all good things which the Lord *p.*
2 Kn. 8. 19; 2 Chr. 21. 7, he *p.* to give him light.
Mk. 14. 11, they *p.* to give him money.
Rom. 4. 21, what he *p.* he was able to perform.
Heb. 10. 23; 11. 11, he is faithful that *p.*
1 John 2. 25, he hath *p.* eternal life.

Promises of God. 1 Kn. 8. 24; Neh. 9. 15; Ps. 89. 3; Rom. 1. 2; Eph. 1. 13; 2. 12; 3. 6; 6. 2; 2 Tim. 1. 1; Heb. 4. 1; 6. 17; 8. 6; 11. 9.
inviolable and precious. Num. 23. 19; Deu. 7. 9; Jos. 23. 14; 1 Kn. 8. 56; Ps. 77. 8; 89. 3; 105. 42; 2 Cor. 1. 20; Gal. 3. 21; Heb. 6. 17; 2 Pet. 1. 4.
God faithful to His. Ps. 105. 42; Lu. 1. 54; Tit. 1. 2; Heb. 10. 23.
pleaded in prayer. Gen. 32. 9, 12; 1 Chr. 17. 23; Isa. 43. 26.
to the repentant and returning. Ex. 34. 7; Ps. 65. 3; 103. 9, 13; 130. 4; Isa. 1. 18; 27. 5; 43. 25; 44. 22; 45. 25; 46. 13; 53.; 55.; Jer. 31. 34; 33. 8; Ezek. 33. 16; 36. 25; Mic. 7. 18; Rom. 4.; 5.; 2 Cor. 6. 18; 7. 1; Eph. 2. 13.
to uphold and perfect. Ps. 23.; 37. 17; 42. 8; 73. 26; 84. 11; 94. 14; 103. 13; Isa. 25. 8; 30. 18; 40. 29; 41. 10; 43. 4; 46. 3; 49. 14; 63. 9; Jer. 31. 3; Hos. 13. 10; 14. 4; Zep. 3. 17; Zec. 2. 8; 10.; Rom. 16. 20; 1 Cor. 10. 13; 15. 57; 2 Cor. 6. 18; 12. 9; Eph. 1. 3; 1 Pet. 1. 3; 5. 7.
to Adam, Gen. 3. 15. to Noah, Gen. 8. 21; 9. 9. to Abraham, Gen. 12. 7; 13. 14; 15.; 17.; 18. 10; 22. 15. to Hagar, Gen. 16. 10; 21. 17. to Isaac, Gen. 26. 2. to Jacob, Gen. 28. 13; 31. 3; 32. 12; 35. 11; 46. 3. to David, 2 Sam. 7. 11; 1 Chr. 17. 10. to Solomon, 1 Kn. 9.; 2 Chr. 1. 7; 7. 12.
of Christ to His disciples. Mat. 6. 4, 33; 7. 7; 10.; 11. 28; 12. 50; 16. 18, 24; 17. 20; 19. 28; 28. 20; Lu. 9.-12.; 12. 32; 22. 29; John 14.-16.; 20. 21.
Gentiles partakers of. Eph. 3.
fulfilled in Christ. 2 Sam. 7. 12 (with Acts 13. 23); Lu. 1. 69-73.
to the poor, fatherless, &c. Deu. 10. 18; Ps. 9. 8; 10. 14; 12. 5; 68. 5; 69. 33; 72. 12; 102. 17; 107. 41; 109. 31; 113. 7; 146. 9; Prov. 15. 25; 23. 10; Jer. 49. 11; Hos. 14. 3.
of temporal blessings. Ex. 23. 25; Lev. 26. 6; Ps. 34. 9; 37. 3; 91.; 102. 28; 112.; 121. 3; 128.; Prov. 3. 10; Isa. 32. 18; 33. 16; Mat. 6. 25; Phil. 4. 19; 1 Tim. 4. 8.
exhortation concerning. Heb. 4. 1.

Promote. Num. 22. 17; 24. 11; Prov. 4. 8.

Promotion. Ps. 75. 6; Prov. 3. 35.

Pronounce. Jud. 12. 6; Jer. 34. 5.

Proof. 2 Cor. 2. 9; 8. 24; 13. 3; Phil. 2. 22; 2 Tim. 4. 5.

Proper, comely, fair. 1 Chr. 29. 3; 1 Cor. 7. 7; Heb. 11. 23.

Prophecies and their Fulfilment, respecting Christ: Prophecy, Ps. 2. 7; fulfilled, Lu. 1. 32, 35. Gen. 3. 15—(Gal. 4. 4). Gen. 17. 7; 22. 18—(Gal. 3. 16). Gen. 21. 12—(Heb. 11. 17-19). Ps. 132. 11; Jer. 23. 5—(Acts 13. 23; Rom. 1. 3). Gen. 49. 10; Dan. 9. 24, 25—(Lu. 2. 1). Isa. 7. 14—(Mat. 1. 18; Lu. 2. 7). Isa. 7. 14—(Mat. 1. 22, 23). Mic. 5. 2—(Mat. 2. 1; Lu. 2. 4-6). Ps. 72. 10—(Mat. 2. 1-11). Jer. 31. 15—(Mat. 2. 16-18). Hos. 11. 1—(Mat. 2. 15). Isa. 40. 3; Mal. 3. 1—(Mat. 3. 1, 3; Lu. 1. 17). Ps. 45. 7; Isa. 11. 2; 61. 1—(Mat. 3. 16; John 3. 34; Acts 10. 38). Deu.

18. 15-18 — (Acts 3. 20-22). Ps. 110. 4 — (Heb. 5. 5, 6). Isa. 61. 1, 2 — (Lu. 4. 16-21, 43). Isa. 9. 1, 2 — (Mat. 4. 12-16, 23). Zec. 9. 9 — (Mat. 21. 1-5). Hag. 2. 7, 9; Mal. 3. 1 — (Mat. 21. 12; Lu. 2. 27-32; John 2. 13-16). Isa. 53. 2 — Mk. 6. 3; Lu. 9. 58). Isa. 42. 2 — (Mat. 12. 15, 16, 19). Isa. 40. 11; 42. 3 — (Mat. 12. 15, 20; Heb. 4. 15). Isa. 53. 9 — (1 Pet. 2. 22). Ps. 69. 9 — (John 2. 17). Ps. 78. 2 — (Mat. 13. 34, 35). Isa. 35. 5, 6 — (Mat. 11. 4-6; John 11. 47). Ps. 22. 6; 69. 7, 9, 20 — (Rom. 15. 3). Ps. 69. 8; Isa. 63. 3 — (John 1. 11; 7. 3). Isa. 8. 14 — (Rom. 9. 32; 1 Pet. 2. 8). Ps. 69. 4; Isa. 49. 7 — (John 15. 24, 25). Ps. 118. 22 — (Mat. 21. 42; John 7. 48). Ps. 2. 1, 2 — (Lu. 23. 12; Acts 4. 27). Ps. 41. 9; 55. 12-14 — (John 13. 18, 21). Zec. 13. 7 — (Mat. 26. 31, 56). Zec. 11. 12 — (Mat. 26. 15). Zec. 11. 13 — (Mat 27. 7). Ps. 22. 14, 15 — (Lu. 22. 42, 44). Isa. 53. 4-6, 12; Dan. 9. 26 — (Mat. 20. 28). Isa. 53. 7 — (Mat. 26. 63; 27. 12-14). Mic. 5. 1 — (Mat. 27. 30). Isa. 52. 14; 53. 3 — (John 19. 5). Isa. 50. 6 — (Mk. 14. 65; John 19. 1). Ps. 22. 16 — (John 19. 18; 20. 25). Ps. 22. 1 — (Mat. 27. 46). Ps. 22. 7, 8 — (Mat. 27. 39-44). Ps. 69. 21 — (Mat. 27. 34). Ps. 22. 18 — (Mat. 27. 35). Isa. 53. 12 — (Mk. 15. 28). Isa. 53. 12 — (Lu. 23. 34). Isa. 53. 12 — (Mat. 27. 50). Ex. 12. 46; Ps. 34. 20 — (John 19. 33, 36). Zec. 12. 10 — (John 19. 34, 37). Isa. 53. 9 — (Mat. 27. 57-60). Ps. 16. 10 — (Acts 2. 31). Ps. 16. 10; Isa. 26. 19 — (Lu. 24. 6, 31, 34). Ps. 68. 18 — (Lu. 24. 51; Acts 1. 9). Ps. 110. 1 — (Heb. 1. 3). Zec. 6. 13 — (Rom. 8. 34). Isa. 28. 16 — (1 Pet. 2. 6, 7). Ps. 2. 6 — (Lu. 1. 32; John 18. 33-37). Isa. 11. 10; 42. 1 — (Mat. 1. 17, 21; John 10. 16; Acts 10. 45, 47). Ps. 45. 6, 7 — (John 5. 30; Rev. 19. 11). Ps. 72. 8; Dan. 7. 14 — (Phil. 2. 9, 11). Isa. 9. 7; Dan. 7. 14 — (Lu. 1. 32, 33). *See* Christ, Prophecies relating to.

Prophecy, prŏph′-ĕ-cȳ. 1 Cor. 13. 8, whether *p.*, shall fail.
2 Pet. 1. 19, sure word of *p.*
1. 21, *p.* came not in old time.
Rev. 1. 3; 22. 7, the words of this *p.*
See Neh. 6. 12; Prov. 31. 1; 1 Tim. 4. 14.

Prophecy, God author of. Isa. 44. 7; 45. 21; Lu. 1. 70; 2 Pet. 1. 19, 21; Rev. 1. 1.
gift of Christ. Eph. 4. 11; Rev. 11. 3.
of Holy Ghost. 1 Cor. 12. 10.
Christ the great subject of. Lu. 24. 44; Acts 3. 22-24; 10. 43; 1 Pet. 1. 10, 11.
to be received with faith and reverence. 2 Chr. 20. 20; Lu. 24. 25; 1 Thes. 5. 20; 2 Pet. 1. 19.
pretended, guilt of. Jer. 14. 14; 23. 13; Ezek. 13. 3.
how tested. Deu. 13. 1; 18. 20; Jer. 14. 15; 23. 16.

Prophesy, prŏph′-ĕ-sȳ. (1) to speak by divine inspiration; (2) to foretell; (3) to explain religious subjects, to preach, to exhort.
Num. 11. 25, they *p.* and did not cease.
2 Chr. 18. 7, he never *p.* good to me.
Isa. 30. 10, *p.* not to us right things.
Jer. 5. 31, prophets *p.* falsely.
14. 14; 23. 25, prophets *p.* lies.
28. 9, the prophet which *p.* of peace.
Ezek. 37. 9, *p.* to the wind.
Joel 2. 28; Acts 2. 17, your sons shall *p.*
Am. 3. 8, who can but *p.*
7. 13, *p.* not again any more.
Mic. 2. 11, I will *p.* of wine.
Mat. 26. 68; Mk. 14. 65; Lu. 22. 64, *p.*, thou Christ.
Rom. 12. 6, let us *p.* according to the proportion.
1 Cor. 13. 9, we *p.* in part.
14. 39, covet to *p.*
1 Thes. 5. 20, despise not *p.*
See Am. 2. 12; 1 Cor. 11. 5; Rev. 10. 11.

Prophet. The literal meaning of the Greek word (προφήτης, from πρόφημι, 'to speak forth') is a *forth-teller*, i. e., one who speaks forth the message which has been communicated to him through Divine inspiration, whether of practical duties or future events. The emphasis of the prophet's work lay on the former. The Heb. words are: (1) *nâbî'*, from a verb meaning 'to boil forth' as a fountain, hence one who speaks out freely from a full heart impelled by an inspiration from God. (2) *rō'eh*, from a verb meaning to see, hence a seer (1 Sam. 9. 10), one who saw Divine visions, Divine truths, and spoke what he had seen from God.
Ex. 7. 1, Aaron shall be thy *p.*
Num. 11. 29, would all Lord's people were *p.*
12. 6, if there be a *p.* among you.
Deu. 13. 1, if there arise a *p.* or dreamer.
18. 15; Acts 3. 22; 7. 37, the Lord will raise up a [*P.*
34. 10, there arose not a *p.* like Moses.
1 Sam. 10. 12; 19. 24, is Saul among *p.*?
1 Kn. 13. 11, there dwelt an old *p.* in Beth-el.
18. 22, I only remain a *p.*
22. 7; 2 Kn. 3. 11, is there not a *p.* besides?
2 Kn. 5. 8, he shall know there is a *p.*
1 Chr. 16. 22; Ps. 105. 15, do my *p.* no harm.
2 Chr. 20. 20, believe his *p.*, so shall ye prosper.
Ps. 74. 9, there is no more any *p.*
Isa. 3. 2, the Lord taketh away the *p.*
Jer. 29. 26, mad, and maketh himself a *p.*
37. 19, where are now your *p.*?
Ezek. 2. 5; 33. 33, there hath been a *p.* among [them.
Hos. 9. 7, the *p.* is a fool.
Am. 7. 14, I was no *p.*, nor *p.* son.
Zec. 1. 5, the *p.*, do they live for ever?
Mat. 7. 15, beware of false *p.*
10. 41, that receiveth a *p.* in name of a *p.*
13. 57; Mk. 6. 4; Lu. 4. 24; John 4. 44, a *p.* not without honour.
23. 29; Lu. 11. 47, ye build the tombs of the *p.*
Lu. 1. 76, be called the *p.* of the Highest.
7. 16, a great *p.* is risen.
7. 28, not a greater *p.* than John.
7. 39, if he were a *p.* would have known.
13. 33, it cannot be that a *p.* perish out of.
24. 19, Jesus, who was a *p.* mighty.
John 4. 19, I perceive thou art a *p.*
7. 40, of a truth this is the *P.*
7. 52, out of Galilee ariseth no *p.*
Acts 26. 27, believest thou the *p.*?
1 Cor. 12. 29, are all *p.*?
14. 37, if any man think himself a *p.*
Eph. 2. 20, built on foundation of *p.*
4. 11, he gave some *p.*
1 Pet. 1. 10, of which salvation the *p.* enquired.
Rev. 22. 9, I am of thy brethren the *p.*
See 1 Kn. 20. 35; Neh. 6. 14; 1 Cor. 14. 32.

Prophets sent by God. Isa. 58. 1; Jer. 1. 4; 23. 28; 25. 4; Ezek. 2. 3.
Christ predicted as a Prophet, Deu. 18. 15. called one, Mat. 21. 11; Lu. 7. 16. mocked at as, Lu. 22. 64.
persons so called: Aaron, Ex. 7. 1. Abraham, Gen. 20. 7. Agabus, Acts 21. 10. Ahijah, 1 Kn. 11. 29. Amos, Am. 7. 14. Balaam, Num. 24. 2. Daniel, Dan. 10.; Mat. 24. 15. David, Mat. 13. 35; Acts 2. 30. Eldad, Num. 11. 26. Elijah, 1 Kn. 18. 36. Elisha, 2 Kn. 6. 12. Ezekiel, Ezek. 1. 3. Gad, 1 Sam. 22. 5. Habakkuk, Hab. 1. 1. Haggai. Ez. 5. 1; 6. 14, Hag. 1. 1. Hananiah, Jer. 28. 17. Hosea, Hos. 1. 1; Rom. 9. 25. Iddo, 2 Chr. 13. 22. Isaiah, 2 Kn. 20. 11; Isa. 1. 1; Mat. 3. 3. Jehu, 1 Kn. 16. 7. Jeremiah, 2 Chr. 36. 12; Jer. 1. 5. Joel, Joel 1. 1; Acts 2. 16. John the Baptist, Lu. 7. 28. Joshua, 1 Kn. 16. 34. Jonah, 2 Kn. 14. 25; Jon. 1. 1; Mat. 12. 39. Malachi, Mal. 1. 1. Medad, Num. 11. 26. Micah, Jer. 26. 18; Mic. 1. 1. Moses, Deu. 34. 10. Nahum, Nah. 1. 1. Nathan, 1 Kn. 1. 32. Obadiah, Obad. 1. Oded, 2 Chr. 15. 8. Paul, Acts 13. 9; 27. 10. Samuel, 1 Sam. 3. 20. Shemaiah, 2 Chr. 12. 5. Zacharias, Lu. 1. 67. Zechariah, Zec. 1. 1. Zephaniah, Zep. 1. 1.
false. Zedekiah, 1 Kn. 22. 11; Jer. 29. 21. Bar-jesus, Acts 13. 6. denounced, Deu. 13.; 18. 20; Isa. 9. 15; Jer. 6. 13; 14. 13; 23. 9, 34; 28. 15; 29. 20, 31; Ezek. 13. 3; 14. 9; Mat. 7. 15; 24. 11; 2 Pet. 2. 1; 1 John 4. 1.

Prophetesses: Anna, Lu. 2. 36. Deborah, Jud. 4. 4.

Huldah, 2 Kn. 22. 14. Miriam, Ex. 15. 20. Noadiah, Neh. 6. 14.

Propitiation for sin. Rom. 3. 25; 1 John 2. 2; 4. 10.

Proportion. 1 Kn. 7. 36; Job 41. 12; Rom. 12. 6.

Proselytes (Gk. προσήλυτος, 'an approacher, newcomer') were Gentiles converted to Judaism. Mat. 23. 15; Acts 2. 10; 13. 43. They are said to have been of two kinds: (1) 'Proselytes of Righteousness,' who were admitted to the full religious privileges, and charged with the entire obligations of the Mosaic covenant, but were not esteemed to be heirs of the promises made to Abraham and his seed.

(2) 'Proselytes of the Gate,' who were allowed to join in the worship of God, standing in the outer 'court of the Gentiles,' but were not bound by the ceremonial laws of Moses, but only by the moral ones.

Prosper. Gen. 24. 56, the Lord hath *p.* my way.
39. 3, the Lord made all Joseph did to *p.*
Num. 14. 41, transgress, but it shall not *p.*
Deu. 28. 29, thou shalt not *p.* in thy ways.
1 Chr. 22. 11, *p.* thou, and build.
2 Chr. 20. 20, believe, so shall ye *p.*
26. 5, God made him to *p.*
Ez. 5. 8, this work *p.* in their hands.
Neh. 2. 20, the God of heaven will *p.* us.
Job 9. 4, who hardened himself and *p.*
Ps. 1. 3, whatsoever he doeth shall *p.*
37. 7, fret not because of him who *p.*
73. 12, the ungodly who *p.* in the world. R. V. being always at ease.
122. 6, they shall *p.* that love thee.
Prov. 28. 13, he that covereth sins shall not *p.*
Eccl. 11. 6, knowest not whether shall *p.*
Isa. 53. 10, pleasure of the Lord shall *p.*
54. 17, no weapon against thee shall *p.*
55. 11, it shall *p.* in the thing.
Jer. 2. 37, thou shalt not *p.* in them.
12. 1, wherefore doth way of wicked *p.*?
22. 30, no man of his seed shall *p.*
Ezek. 17. 9, 10, shall it *p.*?
17. 15, shall he *p.*, shall he escape?
1 Cor. 16. 2, lay by as God hath *p.* him.
3 John 2, in health, even as thy soul *p.*
See Prov. 17. 8; Dan. 6. 28; 8. 12.

Prosperity. Deu. 23. 6, thou shalt not seek their [*p.*
1 Sam. 25. 6, say to him that liveth in *p.*
Job 15. 21, in *p.* the destroyer shall come.
Ps. 30. 6, in my *p.* I said, I shall never.
73. 3, when I saw the *p.* of the wicked.
Prov. 1. 32, *p.* of fools shall destroy them.
Eccl. 7. 14, in day of *p.* be joyful.
Jer. 22. 21, I spake to thee in thy *p.*
See 1 Kn. 10. 7; Ps. 35. 27; 122. 7.

Prosperity of the righteous. Job 36. 11; Ps. 36. 8; 37. 11, 18; 75. 10; 84. 11; 92. 12; Prov. 3. 2; Eccl. 8. 12.
of the wicked. Job 12. 6; 20. 5; 21. 7; Ps. 17. 10; 37.; 73. 3; 92. 7; Eccl. 8. 14; 9. 2; Jer. 12.
dangers of. Deu. 6. 10; Prov. 1. 32; 30. 8; Lu. 6. 24; 12. 16; 16. 19; Jas. 5. 1.

Prosperous. Gen. 39. 2, he was a *p.* man.
Jos. 1. 8, then thou shalt make thy way *p.*
Job 8. 6, make habitation of thy righteousness *p.*
Zec. 8. 12, the seed shall be *p.* R. V. the seed of peace.
See Gen. 24. 21; Jud. 18. 5; 2 Chr. 7. 11; Rom. 1. 10.

Protection. Deu. 32. 38.

Protest. Gen. 43. 3; Jer. 11. 7; Zec. 3. 6; 1 Cor. [15. 31.

Proud. Job 38. 11, here shall thy *p.* waves be stayed.
40. 11, every one that is *p.*, and abase him.
Ps. 31. 23, rewardeth the *p.* doer.
40. 4, man that respecteth not the *p.*
94. 2, render a reward to the *p.*
101. 5, him that hath a *p.* heart will not I suffer.
123. 4, soul filled with contempt of the *p.*
138. 6, the *p.* he knoweth afar off. R. V. haughty.
Prov. 6. 17, the Lord hateth a *p.* look. R. V. haughty eyes.
Prov. 15. 25, the Lord will destroy house of the *p.*
16. 5, *p.* in heart is abomination.
21. 4, a *p.* heart is sin.
Eccl. 7. 8, patient better than *p.* in spirit.
Hab. 2. 5, he is a *p.* man. R. V. haughty.
Mal. 3. 15, we call the *p.* happy.
Lu. 1. 51, scattered the *p.*
1 Tim. 6. 4, he is *p.*, knowing nothing. R. V. puffed up.
Jas. 4. 6; 1 Pet. 5. 5, God resisteth the *p.*
See Job 9. 13; 26. 12; Rom. 1. 30; 2 Tim. 3. 2.

Proudly. Ex. 18. 11; 1 Sam. 2. 3; Neh. 9. 10; Isa. 3. 5; Obad. 12.

Prove, to test, try, put to the proof. Ex. 15. 25, there he *p.* them.
Jud. 6. 39, let me *p.* thee but this once.
1 Sam. 17. 39, I have not *p.* them.
1 Kn. 10. 1; 2 Chr. 9. 1, she came to *p.* Solomon.
Ps. 17. 3, thou hast *p.* mine heart.
81. 7, I *p.* thee at the waters.
95. 9; Heb. 3. 9, when your fathers *p.* me.
Mal. 3. 10, *p.* me now herewith.
Lu. 14. 19, I go to *p.* them.
2 Cor. 8. 22, whom we have often *p.* diligent.
13. 5, *p.* your own selves.
1 Thes. 5. 21, *p.* all things.
See Eccl. 2. 1; 7. 23; Dan. 1. 14; John 6. 6.

Proverb. Deu. 28. 37, a *p.* and a byword.
Ps. 69. 11, I became a *p.* to them.
Eccl. 12. 9, set in order many *p.*
Ezek. 16. 44, every one that useth *p.*
Lu. 4. 23, will surely say this *p.* R. V. parable.
John 16. 29, speakest plainly, and no *p.*
See Num. 21. 27; Prov. 1. 6.

Proverbs of Solomon, Book of Proverbs; collected under Hezekiah. Prov. 25.-29.
various. 1 Sam. 10. 12; 24. 13; Lu. 4. 23; 2 Pet. 2. 22.

Provide. Gen. 22. 8, God will *p.* himself a lamb.
30. 30, when shall I *p.* for mine own house?
Ps. 78. 20, can he *p.* flesh?
Mat. 10. 9, *p.* neither gold nor silver. R. V. get you no.
Lu. 12. 20, whose shall those things be thou hast *p.*? R. V. prepared.
12. 33, *p.* yourselves bags that wax not old. R. V. make for.
Rom. 12. 17; 2 Cor. 8. 21, *p.* things honest. R. V. take thought for.
1 Tim. 5. 8, if any *p.* not for his own.
Heb. 11. 40, having *p.* some better thing for us.
See Job 38. 41; Prov. 6. 8; Acts 23. 24.

Providence. Acts 24. 2.

Providence of God. Gen. 8. 22; Jos. 7. 14; 1 Sam. 6. 7; Ps. 36. 6; 104.; 136.; 145.; 147.; Prov. 16.; 19.; 20.; 33.; Mat. 6. 26; 10. 29, 30; Lu. 21. 18; Acts 1. 26; 17. 26.

Provision. Gen. 42. 25; 45. 21, *p.* for the way.
Ps. 132. 15, I will abundantly bless her *p.*
Rom. 13. 14, make not *p.* for the flesh.
See Jos. 9. 5; 1 Kn. 4. 7; 2 Kn. 6. 23.

Provocation. Job 17. 2; Ps. 95. 8; Ezek. 20. 28.

Provoke. (1) Ex. 23. 21, obey his voice and *p.* him not.
Num. 14. 11, how long will this people *p.* me? R. V. despise.
Deu. 31. 20, *p.* me and break my covenant. R. V. despise.
Job 12. 6, they that *p.* God are secure.
Ps. 106. 7, they *p.* him at the sea.
106. 29, they *p.* him with their inventions.
1 Cor. 13. 5, is not easily *p.*
Gal. 5. 26, *p.* one another.
(2) to stimulate, incite.
Lu. 11. 53, began to urge and *p.* him to speak.
Rom. 10. 19; 11. 11, I will *p.* to jealousy.
Gal. 5. 26, *p.* one another.
Eph. 6. 4, *p.* not your children to wrath.
Heb. 10. 24, to *p.* to love and good works.
See Prov. 20. 2; Isa. 65. 3; Jer. 7. 19; 44. 8.

Prudence. 2 Chr. 2. 12; Prov. 8. 12; 12. 16, 23; 13. 16; 14. 8, 15, 18; 15. 5; 16. 21; 18. 15; 19. 14; 22. 3; Hos. 14. 9; Am. 5. 13; Eph. 1. 8.

Prudent. Prov. 12. 16, a *p.* man covereth shame.
12. 23, a *p.* man concealeth knowledge.
14. 15, the *p.* looketh well to his going.
16. 21, wise in heart called *p.*
19. 14, *p.* wife is from the Lord.
22. 3; 27. 12, *p.* man foreseeth evil. [sight.
Isa. 5. 21, woe unto them that are *p.* in their own
Jer. 49. 7, counsel perished from *p.*
Hos. 14. 9, who is *p.*?
Mat. 11. 25; Lu. 10. 21, hast hid things from *p.* R. V. understanding.
See Isa. 52. 13; Am. 5. 13; Acts 13. 7.

Prune. Lev. 25. 3; Isa. 2. 4; Joel 3. 10; Mic. 4. 3.

Psalmody, singing, service of song, Jewish. Ex. 15. 1; 1 Chr. 6. 31; 13. 8; 2 Chr. 5. 13; 20. 22; 29. 30; Neh. 12. 27.
Christian. Mat. 26. 30; Mk. 14. 26; Jas. 5. 13.
spiritual songs. Eph. 5. 19; Col. 3. 16.

The Psalms.

May be divided into Five Books, each ending with a doxology, as follows:—

I. 1.-41. II. 42.-72. III. 73.-89. IV. 90.-106. V. 107.-150.

Or may be classified according to their subjects, thus:—

(I.) Psalms of Supplication.

1. on account of sin. Ps. 6.; 25.; 32.; 38.; 51.; 102.; 130.
2. suffering. Ps. 7.; 10.; 13.; 17.; 22.; 31.; 35.; 41.-43.; 54.-57.; 59.; 64.; 69.-71.; 77.; 86.; 88.; 94.; 109.; 120.; 140.-143.
3. persecution. Ps. 44.; 60.; 74.; 79.; 80.; 83.; 89.; 94.; 102., 123.; 137.
4. public worship. Ps. 26.; 27.; 42.; 43.; 63.; 65.; 84.; 92.; 95.-100.; 118.; 122.; 132.; 144.; 145.-150.
5. trust in God. Ps. 3.-5.; 11.; 12.; 16.; 20.; 23.; 27.; 28.; 31.; 42.; 43.; 52.; 54.; 56.; 57.; 59.; 61.-64.; 71.; 77.; 86.; 108.; 115.; 118.; 121.; 125.; 131.; 138.; 141.
6. the Psalmist's piety. Ps. 7.; 17.; 26.; 35.; 101; 119.

(II.) Gratitude.

1. the Psalmist personally. Ps. 9.; 18.; 30.; 32.; 34.; 40.; 61.-63.; 75.; 103.; 108.; 116.; 118.; 138.; 144.
2. relative to the Church. Ps. 33.; 46.; 47.; 65.; 66.; 68.; 75.; 76.; 81.; 85.; 87.; 95.; 98.; 105.-107.; 124.; 126; 129.; 134.-136.; 149.

(III.) Adoration.

1. of God's goodness and mercy. Ps. 3.; 4.; 9.; 16.; 18.; 30.-34.; 36.; 40.; 46.; 65.-68.; 84.; 85.; 91.; 99.; 100., 103.; 107.; 111.; 113.; 116.; 117.; 121.; 126.; 145.; 146.
2. of God's power, majesty, and glory. Ps. 2.; 3.; 8.; 18.; 19.; 24.; 29.; 33.; 45.-48; 50.; 65.-68.; 76.; 77.; 89.; 91.-100.; 104.-108.; 110.; 111.; 113.-118.; 135.; 136.; 139.; 145.-150.

(IV.) Didactic.

1. shewing the blessings of God's people and the misery of His enemies. Ps. 1.; 3.; 4.; 5.; 7.; 9.-15.; 17., 24.; 25.; 32.; 34.; 36.; 37.; 41.; 50.; 52.; 53.; 58.; 62.; 73.; 75.; 82.; 84.; 91.; 92.; 94.; 101.; 112.; 119.; 121.; 125.; 127.-129.; 133.; 149.
2. the excellence of God's law. Ps. 19.; 119.
3. the vanity of human life, &c. Ps. 14.; 39.; 49.; 53.; 73.; 90.

(V.). Prophetical, Typical, and Historical.
Ps. 2.; 16.; 22.; 24.; 31.; 35.; 40., 41.; 45.; 50.; 55.; 68.; 69.; 72.; 78.; 87.; 88.; 102.; 105.; 106.; 109.; 110.; 118.; 132.; 135.; 136.
See Summaries.

Psaltery. (1) (1 Chr. 13. 8; 15. 16; 25. 1; 2 Chr. 5. 12; 29. 25; 2 Sam. 6. 5). Heb. *Nébel:* Gk. *νάβλα*, a kind of harp, of which the Greek name is also *Psalterion.*
(2) (Dan. 3. 5, 7). Chald. *Psantêrîn:* Gk. *ψαλτήριον*. Probably a harp 'played with both hands,' one that could be 'played in octaves.'

Ptolemais (Acts 21. 7), same as Accho, a town on the Mediterranean just north of Mt. Carmel.

Pua, pū'-ă, same as Phuvah; R. V. Puvah. Num. 26. 23.

Puah, pū'-ăh, 'splendour.' Ex. 1. 15.

Public. Mat. 1. 19; Acts 18. 28; 20. 20.

Publican, parable of Pharisee and. Lu. 18. 10.

Publicans, the, were the tax-collectors of the civil power. The taxes were farmed by rich Roman citizens of the Equestrian Order, or sometimes by a joint-stock company at Rome, who had agents in the provinces (*portitores*) to arrange the actual collection from the people. These agents were the Publicans of the Gospels. They were universally despised. They had large opportunities for unscrupulous gains. Mat. 5. 46; 9. 11; 11. 19; 18. 17; Lu. 3. 12.
become believers in Jesus. Mat. 21. 32; Lu. 5. 27; 7. 29; 15. 1; 19. 2.

Publish. Deu. 32. 3, I will *p.* the name of the Lord. R. V. proclaim.
2 Sam. 1. 20, *p.* it not in Askelon.
Ps. 68. 11, great was the company that *p.* it.
Isa. 52. 7; Nah. 1. 15, that *p.* peace.
Mk. 1. 45; 5. 20, he began to *p.* it much.
Lu. 8. 39, *p.* throughout the whole city.
See Esth. 1. 20; 3. 14; Jon. 3. 7; Mk. 13. 10.

Publius, pŭb'-lĭ-ŭs, a prominent inhabitant of Malta; entertains Paul. Acts 28. 7.

Pudens, pū'-dĕns, 'shamefaced.' 2 Tim. 4. 21.

Puffed. 1 Cor. 4. 6; 5. 2; 13. 4; Col. 2. 18.

Puffeth. Ps. 10. 5; 12. 5; 1 Cor. 8. 1.

Puhites, pū'-hītes. 1 Chr. 2. 53.

Pul, pŭl. (1) a short name for Tiglath-Pileser, King of Assyria. 2 Kn. 15. 19; 1 Chr. 5. 26.
(2) an African country (Isa. 66. 19). Probably Put (Phut, Gen. 10. 6).

Pull. Lam. 3. 11, *p.* me in pieces.
Am. 9. 15, shall no more be *p.* up. R. V. plucked.
Zec. 7. 11, they *p.* away the shoulder.
Mat. 7. 4; Lu. 6. 42, *p.* mote out of thine eye. R. V. cast.
Lu. 12. 18, will *p.* down barns.
14. 5, will not *p.* him out on sabbath. R. V. draw up.
2 Cor. 10. 4, to the *p.* down of strong holds. R. V. casting.
Jude 23, *p.* them out of the fire. R. V. snatching.
See Gen. 8. 9; Ez. 6. 11; Ps. 31. 4; Isa. 22. 19.

Pulpit. Neh. 8. 4.

Pulse (2 Sam. 17. 28; Dan. 1. 12). Heb. *Kâlî, Zêrôîm:* Gk. *ὄσπρια*. Translated 'parched *pulse*' (2 Sam. 17. 28), but the latter word is inserted in the A. V. and R. V.: the Hebrew has only 'parched.' In Daniel, *zêrôîm* signifies seed of any kind; it may be that of grain generally, or perhaps specially of leguminous plants, as peas and beans. In both cases it implies simple plain food.

Punish. Ez. 9. 13, *p.* less than iniquities deserve.
Prov. 17. 26, to *p.* the just is not good.
Isa. 13. 11, I will *p.* the world for their evil.
26. 21, Lord cometh to *p.* inhabitants.
Jer. 13. 21, what wilt thou say when he *p.* R. V. set thy friends over thee.
Acts 26. 11, I *p.* them in every synagogue.
2 Thes. 1. 9, *p.* with everlasting destruction.
2 Pet. 2. 9, to day of judgment to be *p.*
See Lev. 26. 18; Prov. 21. 11; 22. 3; 27. 12.

Punishment. Gen. 4. 13, my *p.* is greater than I can bear.
Lev. 26. 41, accept the *p.* of their iniquity.
1 Sam. 28. 10, no *p.* shall happen to thee.
Lam. 3. 39, a man for the *p.* of his sins.
4. 6, *p.* greater than *p.* of Sodom.
4. 22, the *p.* is accomplished.

Ezek. 14. 10, shall bear *p.* of their iniquity. R. V. omits.
Mat. 25. 46, everlasting *p.*
Heb. 10. 29, of how much sorer *p.*
1 Pet. 2. 14, the *p.* of evildoers. R. V. vengeance [on.
See Prov. 19. 19; Am. 1. 3; 2. 1; 2 Cor. 2. 6.

Punishments:
burning. Gen. 38. 24; Lev. 20. 14; 21. 9.
hanging. Gen. 40. 22; Deu. 21. 23; Ez. 6. 11; Esth. 2. 23; 7. 10.
scourging. Lev. 19. 20; Deu. 25. 1; Mat. 27. 26; Acts 22. 25.
stoning. Lev. 20. 2; 24. 14; 1 Kn. 21. 10; John 8. 59; Acts 7. 58; 14. 19.
beheading. 2 Kn. 6. 31; 10. 7; Mat. 14. 10. *See* Heb. 11. 36.
crucifying. Mat. 20. 19; 27. 31, &c.

Punites, pū′-nītes, descendants of Pua. Num. [26. 23.
Punon, pū′-nŏn, same as Pinon. Num. 33. 42.
Pur, pūr, 'a lot.' Esth. 3. 7.
Purchase. Ru. 4. 10, have I *p.* to be my wife.
Ps. 74. 2, congregation thou hast *p.*
Acts 1. 18, *p.* a field with reward of iniquity. R. V. obtained.
8. 20, gift of God *p.* by money. R. V. obtain.
20. 28, he hath *p.* with his own blood.
Eph. 1. 14, redemption of *p.* possession. R. V. God's own.
1 Tim. 3. 13, *p.* to themselves a good degree. R. V. gain.
See Gen. 49. 32; Ex. 15. 16; Lev. 25. 33.
Purchases. Gen. 23.; Ru. 4.; Jer. 32. 6.
Pure. Deu. 32. 14, the *p.* blood of the grape.
2 Sam. 22. 27; Ps. 18. 26, with *p.* shew thyself *p.*
Job 4. 17, shall man be more *p.*?
8. 6, if thou wert *p.* and upright.
11. 4, my doctrine is *p.*
16. 17, my prayer is *p.*
25. 5, stars are not *p.* in his sight.
Ps. 12. 6, the words of the Lord are *p.*
19. 8, commandment of the Lord is *p.*
119. 140, thy word is very *p.*
Prov. 15. 26, words of the *p.* are pleasant. R. V. pleasant words are *p.*
20. 9, who can say, I am *p.*?
Mic. 6. 11, shall I count them *p.*?
Zep. 3. 9, turn to the people a *p.* language.
Acts 20. 26, *p.* from blood of all men.
Rom. 14. 20, all things indeed are *p.* R. V. clean.
Phil. 4. 8, whatsoever things are *p.*
1 Tim. 3. 9; 2 Tim. 1. 3, in a *p.* conscience.
5. 22, keep thyself *p.*
Tit. 1. 15, unto the *p.* all things are *p.*
Jas. 1. 27, *p.* religion.
3. 17, first *p.*, then peaceable.
2 Pet. 3. 1, stir up your *p.* minds. R. V. sincere.
1 John 3. 3, even as he is *p.*
Rev. 22. 1, a *p.* river of water of life. R. V. omits.
See Ex. 27. 20; Ez. 6. 20; Mal. 1. 11.
Purely. Isa. 1. 25.
Pureness. Job 22. 30; Prov. 22. 11; 2 Cor. 6. 6.
Purer. Lam. 4. 7; Hab. 1. 13.
Purge, to purify, remove by cleansing. 2 Chr. 34. 8, when he had *p.* the land.
Ps. 51. 7, *p.* me with hyssop.
65. 3, transgressions, thou shalt *p.* them.
Isa. 1. 25, and purely *p.* away thy dross.
6. 7, thy sin is *p.*
22. 14, this iniquity shall not be *p.*
Ezek. 24. 13, I have *p.* thee and thou wast not *p.*
Mal. 3. 3, *p.* them as gold.
Mat. 3. 12; Lu. 3. 17, *p.* his floor. R. V. cleanse.
John 15. 2, he *p.* it, that it may bring forth. R. V. cleanseth.
1 Cor. 5. 7, *p.* out the old leaven.
2 Tim. 2. 21, if a man *p.* himself from these.
Heb. 9. 14, *p.* your conscience. R. V. cleanse.
9. 22, all things are *p.* with blood. R. V. cleansed.
See Prov. 16. 6; Heb. 1. 3; 10. 2; 2 Pet. 1. 9.
Purification, laws concerning. Lev. 13.-16; Num. 9. 4; 19.; 31. 19 (Mal. 3. 3; Acts 21. 24; Heb. 9. 13).
of women. Lev. 12.; Esth. 2. 12; Lu. 2. 22.
of the heart by faith. Acts 15. 9; 1 Pet. 1. 22; 1 John 3. 3. *See* Dan. 12. 10.
Purify. Tit. 2. 14; Jas. 4. 8.
Purim, pū′-rĭm. The Feast of Purim, or *Lots* (from the lots cast by Haman, Esth. 4. 16), was instituted to commemorate the preservation of the Jews in Persia from the massacre with which they were threatened by the machinations of Haman (Esth. 9. 24-26). It began on the 14th day of the twelfth month, Adar, and lasted two days. *See* Feasts.
Purity, moral, enjoined. Gal. 5. 16; Eph. 5. 3; Phil. 2. 15; 4. 8; Col. 3. 5; 1 Tim. 4. 12; 5. 2, 22; Tit. 1. 15; 1 Pet. 2. 11; 2 Pet. 3. 1; 1 John 3. 3.
of God's word and law. Ps. 12. 6; 19. 8; 119. 140; Prov. 30. 5.
Purloining. Tit. 2. 10.
Purpose. Job 17. 11, my *p.* are broken off.
Prov. 20. 18, every *p.* established by counsel.
Isa. 14. 27, the Lord hath *p.*, who shall disannul?
46. 11, I have *p.*, I will also do it.
Mat. 26. 8, to what *p.* is this waste?
Acts 11. 23, with *p.* of heart.
Rom. 8. 28, called according to his *p.*
9. 11, that the *p.* of God might stand.
Eph. 1. 11, according to the *p.*
3. 11, eternal *p.* in Christ.
See 2 Cor. 1. 17; 2 Tim. 1. 9; 1 John 3. 8.
Purse. Prov. 1. 14; Mat. 10. 9; Mk. 6. 8; Lu. 10. 4.
Pursue. Lev. 26. 17; Prov. 28. 1, shall flee when none *p.*
Deu. 19. 6; Jos. 20. 5, lest avenger *p.*
Job 13. 25, wilt thou *p.* the stubble?
30. 15, terrors *p.* my soul. R. V. chase.
Ps. 34. 14, seek peace and *p.* it.
Prov. 11. 19, he that *p.* evil *p.* it to death.
13. 21, evil *p.* sinners.
Jer. 48. 2, the sword shall *p.* thee.
See Ex. 15. 9; 2 Sam. 24. 13; 1 Kn. 18. 27.
Push. Ex. 21. 29; 1 Kn. 22. 11; Job 30. 12.
Put. Ex. 23. 1, *p.* not thine hand with the wicked.
Lev. 26. 8; Deu. 32. 30, *p.* ten thousand to flight. R. V. chase.
Jud. 12. 3; 1 Sam. 28. 21, I *p.* my life in my hands.
1 Sam. 2. 36, *p.* me into one of priests' offices.
1 Kn. 9. 3; 14. 21, to *p.* my name there.
Eccl. 10. 10, must he *p.* to more strength.
Isa. 43. 26, *p.* me in remembrance.
Mat. 19. 6; Mk. 10. 9, let not man *p.* asunder.
Mk. 10. 16, *p.* his hands on them and blessed. R. V. laying.
Philem. 18, *p.* that on mine account.
2 Pet. 1. 14, I must *p.* off this tabernacle.
See Lu. 9. 62; John 13. 2; 1 Thes. 5. 8.
Put, pŭt, same as Phut (of Gen. 10. 6). 1 Chr. 1. 8.
Puteoli, pū-tē′-ŏ-lĭ, 'wells' (Pozzuoli), seaport of Italy. Acts 28. 13.
Putiel, pū-tĭ-ĕl. Ex. 6. 25.
Putrifying. Isa. 1. 6.
Pygarg (Deu. 14. 5). Gk. πύγαργος. Probably a kind of gazelle. *See* Antelope.

Quail (Ex. 16. 13). Heb. *Shĕlâv*: Gk. ὀρτυγομήτρα. (Specimen, *Coturnix vulgaris.*)
Quails: Israel fed with, Ex. 16. 12. sent in wrath, Num. 11. 31; Ps. 78. 27; 105. 40.
Quake. Joel 2. 10; Nah. 1. 5; Mat. 27. 51; Heb. 12. 21.
Quantity. Isa. 22. 24.
Quarrel. Lev. 26. 25; 2 Kn. 5. 7; Mk. 6. 19; Col. 3. 13.
Quarrelling. *See* Strife.
Quarter. Ex. 13. 7; Mk. 1. 45; Rev. 20. 8.
Quartus, quar′-tŭs, 'fourth.' Rom. 16. 23.
Quarternion. A Roman guard of four soldiers, detailed to act as sentries over a prisoner (Acts 12. 4). In the strictest custody (as in the case of Peter), each hand of the prisoner was handcuffed to a separate soldier, inside the cell,

while the other two kept sentry outside the door.

Queen. Jer. 44. 17, 25, burn incense unto the *q*.

Quench. Num. 11. 2, the fire was *q*.
2 Sam. 21. 17, *q*. not light of Israel.
S. of S. 8. 7, many waters cannot *q*. love.
Isa. 34. 10, shall not be *q*. night nor day.
42. 3; Mat. 12. 20, smoking flax not *q*.
66. 24, neither shall their fire be *q*.
Mk. 9. 43, 48, fire that never shall be *q*.
Eph. 6. 16, able to *q*. fiery darts.
1 Thes. 5. 19, *q*. not the Spirit.
Heb. 11. 34, *q*. violence of fire.
See Ps. 104. 11; 118. 12; Ezek. 20. 47; Am. 5. 6.

Question. 1 Kn. 10. 1; 2 Chr. 9. 1, to prove him with *q*.
Mat. 22. 46, neither durst ask him *q*.
Mk. 9. 16, what *q*. ye with them?
11. 29, I will ask you one *q*.
1 Cor. 10. 25. asking no *q*. for conscience.
1 Tim. 1. 4, which minister *q*. rather.
6. 4, doting about *q*.
2 Tim. 2. 23; Tit. 3. 9, unlearned *q*. avoid.
See Mk. 1. 27; 9. 10; Acts 18. 15; 19. 40.

Quick. Num. 16. 30; Ps. 55. 15, go down *q*. R. V. alive.
Isa. 11. 3, of *q*. understanding. R. V. and his delight shall be.
Acts 10. 42; 2 Tim. 4. 1; 1 Pet. 4. 5, Judge of *q*. and dead.
Heb. 4. 12, the word is *q*. and powerful. R. V. living.
See Lev. 13. 10, 24; Ps. 124. 3.

Quicken, to revive, make alive. Ps. 71. 20, thou shalt *q*. me again.
80. 18, *q*. us and we will call.
119. 25, *q*. me according to thy word.
119. 37, *q*. me in thy way.
119. 50, thy word hath *q*. me.
Rom. 8. 11, shall also *q*. your bodies.
1 Cor. 15. 36, that thou sowest is not *q*.
Eph. 2. 1, you hath he *q*.
2. 5; Col. 2. 13, *q*. us together with Christ.
1 Pet. 3. 18, to death in flesh, *q*. by Spirit.

Quickening, spiritual. Ps. 71. 20; 80. 18; John 5. 21; 6. 63; Rom. 4. 17; 8. 11; 1 Cor. 15. 45; 2 Cor. 3. 6; Eph. 2. 1; 1 Tim. 6. 13; 1 Pet. 3. 18.

Quickly. Ex. 32. 8; Deu. 9. 12, have turned aside *q*.
Num. 16. 46, go *q*. to congregation.
Jos. 10. 6, come *q*. and save us.
Eccl. 4. 12, threefold cord not *q*. broken.
Mat. 5. 25, agree with adversary *q*.
Lu. 14. 21, go *q*. into streets and lanes.
John 13. 27, that thou doest, do *q*.
Rev. 2. 5, 16, repent, else I will come *q*.
3. 11; 22. 7, 12, I come *q*.
22. 20, surely I come *q*.
See Gen. 18. 6; 27. 20; Lu. 16. 6; Acts 22. 18.

Quicksands, sands which move, i. e., unstable (quick = living). The greater and lesser Syrtis, near Tunis, on the N. E. coast of Africa (Acts 27. 17). These were the terror of Mediterranean sailors.

Quiet. Ps. 107. 30, then are they glad because *q*.
131. 2, I have *q*. myself as a child.
Eccl. 9. 17, words of wise are heard in *q*.
Isa. 7. 4, be *q*., fear not.
14. 7, earth is at rest and *q*.
32. 18, in *q*. resting places.
33. 20, a *q*. habitation.
Jer. 49. 23, sorrow on the sea, it cannot be *q*.
Ezek. 16. 42, I will be *q*.
Acts 19. 36, ye ought to be *q*.
1 Thes. 4. 11, study to be *q*.
1 Tim. 2. 2, a *q*. and peaceable life. R. V. tranquil.
1 Pet. 3. 4, ornament of a meek and *q*. spirit.
See 2 Kn. 11. 20; 2 Chr. 14. 1; Job 3. 13; 21. 23.

Quiet, the faithful shall dwell in. Prov. 1. 33; Isa. 30. 15; 32. 17, 18.
to be, enjoined. 1 Thes. 4. 11; 2 Thes. 3. 12; 1 Tim. 2. 2; 1 Pet. 3. 4.

Quietly. 2 Sam. 3. 27; Lam. 3. 26.

Quietness. Job 34. 29, when he giveth *q*.
Prov. 17. 1, better a dry morsel and *q*.
Eccl. 4. 6, better handful with *q*. than both.
Isa. 30. 15, in *q*. and confidence strength.
32. 17, effect of righteousness *q*.
See Jud. 8. 28; 1 Chr. 22. 9; 2 Thes. 3. 12.

Quit, to acquit one's self, behave. Ex. 21. 19; Jos. 2. 20; 1 Sam. 4. 9; 1 Cor. 16. 13.

Quite. Gen. 31. 15; Job 6. 13; Hab. 3. 9.

Quiver. Ps. 127. 5; Jer. 5. 16; Lam. 3. 13.

Quotations from the Old Testament in the New Testament. *See* OLD TESTAMENT.

Raamah, rā′-ă-mäh, 'trembling.' Gen. 10. 7.

Raamiah, rā-ă-mī′-ăh, 'trembling of Jehovah.' Neh. 7. 7.

Raamses, rā-ăm′-sēs, 'son of the sun.' Same as RAMESES. Ex. 1. 11.

Rabbah, răb′-băh, 'capital city.' Jos. 13. 25; 2 Sam. 11.; 12. 26; Jer. 49. 2; Ezek. 21. 20; 25. 5; Am. 1. 14.

Rabbath, răb′-băth, same as RABBAH. Deu. 3. 11.

Rabbi, răb′-bī, 'master.' Mat. 23. 7, 8; John 1. 38; 3. 2.

Rabbith, răb′-bĭth, 'populous.' Jos. 19. 20.

Rabboni, răb-bō′-nī, 'my master,' title addressed to Christ by Mary. John 20. 16.

Rab-mag, răb′-măg, 'most exalted' (?). Jer. 39. 3.

Rabsaris, răb′-să-rĭs, 'chief eunuch.' 2 Kn. 18. 17.

Rab-shakeh, răb-shā′-kĕh, 'chief of the cupbearers.' The title of an Assyrian military leader or general. 2 Kn. 18. 17.
reviles Hezekiah. 2 Kn. 18. 19; 19. 1; Isa. 36. 4.

Raca, rā′-că, 'vain fellow,' a term of reproach. 2 Sam. 6. 20; Mat. 5. 22.

Race. Ps. 19. 5; Eccl. 9. 11; 1 Cor. 9. 24; Heb. 12. 1.

Rachab, rā′-chăb, Greek form of RAHAB. Mat. 1. 5.

Rachal, rā′-chăl, 'traffic.' 1 Sam. 30. 29.

Rachel, rā′-chĕl, 'ewe' (and Jacob). Gen. 29. 6, 10, 28; 30.; 31. 4, 19, 34; 35. 16.

Raddai, răd′-dā-ī, 'subduing.' 1 Chr. 2. 14.

Ragau, rā′-gâu, Greek form of REU. Lu. 3. 35.

Rage. 2 Kn. 5. 12, went away in a *r*.
Ps. 2. 1; Acts 4. 25, why do the heathen *r*.
Prov. 14. 16, the fool *r*. and is confident. R. V. beareth himself insolently.
See Prov. 6. 34; 29. 9; Dan. 3. 13; Hos. 7. 16.

Ragged. Isa. 2. 21.

Raging. Ps. 89. 9; Prov. 20. 1; Lu. 8. 24; Jude 13.

Rags. Prov. 23. 21; Isa. 64. 6; Jer. 38. 11.

Raguel, ră-gū′-ĕl, 'friend of God.' Num. 10. 29.

Rahab, rā′-hăb. (1) 'broad;' the harlot. Jos. 2.; 6. 22.
See Mat. 1. 5; Heb. 11. 31; Jas. 2. 25.
(2) 'violence' (EGYPT). Ps. 87. 4; 89. 10; Isa. 51. 9.

Raham, rā′-hăm. 1 Chr. 2. 44.

Rahel, rā′-hĕl, same as RACHEL. Jer. 31. 15.

Railing. 1 Sam. 25. 14; 2 Sam. 16. 7; Mk. 15. 29; 1 Cor. 5. 11; 1 Tim. 6. 4; 1 Pet. 3. 9; 2 Pet. 2. 11; Jude 9.

Raiment. Gen. 28. 20, if the Lord will give me *r*.
Deu. 8. 4, thy *r*. waxed not old.
24. 13, that he may sleep in his *r*. R. V. garment.
24. 17, nor take a widow's *r*. to pledge.
Job 27. 16, though he prepare *r*. as the clay.
Isa. 63. 3, I will stain all my *r*.
Zec. 3. 4, I will clothe thee with *r*. R. V. rich apparel.
Mat. 6. 25; Lu. 12. 23, the body more than *r*.
6. 28, why take thought for *r*.
11. 8; Lu. 7. 25, man clothed in soft *r*.
17. 2; Mk. 9. 3; Lu. 9. 29, his *r*. was white as light. R. V. garments.
1 Tim. 6. 8, having food and *r*., be content. R. V. covering.
Jas. 2. 2, poor man in vile *r*. R. V. clothing.

Rev. 3. 18, buy white *r.* R. V. garments.
See Mat. 3. 4; Lu. 10. 30; 23. 34; Acts 22. 20.
Rain (*n.*). Lev. 26. 4; Deu. 11. 14; 28. 12, *r.* in due season.
Deu. 11. 11, drinketh water of the *r.* of heaven.
32. 2, my doctrine shall drop as the *r.*
2 Sam. 23. 4, clear shining after *r.*
1 Kn. 18. 41, sound of abundance of *r.*
Ez. 10. 13, a time of much *r.*
Job 5. 10, who giveth *r.* on earth.
37. 6, to small *r.* and to great *r.*
38. 28, hath the *r.* a father?
Ps. 72. 6, like *r.* on mown grass.
Prov. 25. 14, like clouds and wind without *r.*
25. 23, north wind driveth away *r.*
26. 1, as *r.* in harvest.
28. 3, that oppresseth poor is like sweeping *r.*
Eccl. 11. 3, if clouds be full of *r.*
12. 2, nor clouds return after *r.*
S. of S. 2. 11, the *r.* is over and gone.
Isa. 4. 6, covert from storm and *r.*
55. 10, as the *r.* cometh down.
Ezek. 38. 22, I will *r.* an overflowing *r.*
Hos. 6. 3, he shall come unto us as the *r.*
Mat. 5. 45, *r.* on just and unjust.
7. 25, the *r.* descended and floods came.
See Acts 28. 2; Heb. 6. 7.
Rain (*v.*). Ex. 16. 4, I will *r.* bread from heaven.
Job 20. 23, God shall *r.* his fury on him.
Ps. 11. 6, on wicked he shall *r.* snares.
78. 24, 27, and *r.* down manna.
Ezek. 22. 24, thou art the land not *r.* upon.
Hos. 10. 12, till he come and *r.* righteousness.
See Gen. 2. 5; Rev. 11. 6.
Rain. the deluge. Gen. 7.; Ex. 9. 34; 1 Sam. 12. 17; Ps. 105. 32.
the gift of God. Jer. 5. 24; Mat. 5. 45; Acts 14. 17.
withheld. 1 Kn. 17.; Jer. 14.; Am. 4. 7; Zec. 14. 17; Jas. 5. 17.
emblematic. Lev. 26. 4; Deu. 32. 2; 2 Sam. 23. 4; Ps. 68. 9; Hos. 10. 12.
Rainbow, God's covenant with Noah. Gen. 9. 12; Ezek. 1. 28.
in heaven. Rev. 4. 3; 10. 1.
Rainy. Prov. 27. 15.
Raise. Deu. 18. 15; Acts 3. 22, will *r.* up a Prophet.
Jud. 2. 16, 18, the Lord *r.* up judges.
1 Sam. 2. 8; Ps. 113. 7, he *r.* poor out of dust.
Job 41. 25, when he *r.* himself, mighty are.
Ps. 145. 14; 146. 8, he *r.* those that be bowed down.
Isa. 45. 13, I have *r.* him in righteousness.
Hos. 6. 2, in third day he will *r.* us up.
Mat. 10. 8; 11. 5; Lu. 7. 22, *r.* the dead.
16. 21; 17. 23; Lu. 9. 22, be *r.* the third day.
John 2. 19, in three days I will *r.* it up.
6. 39, 40, 44, 54, I will *r.* him up at last day.
Acts 2. 24, 32; 3. 15; 4. 10; 5. 30; 10. 40; 13. 30, 33, 34; 17. 31; Rom. 10. 9; 1 Cor. 6. 14; 2 Cor. 4. 14; Gal. 1. 1; Eph. 1. 20, whom God hath *r.* up.
26. 8, why incredible that God should *r.* the dead.
Rom. 4. 25, *r.* again for our justification.
6. 4, like as Christ was *r.* from the dead.
8. 11, Spirit of him that *r.* up Jesus.
1 Cor. 6. 14, and will also *r.* up us by his power.
15. 15, *r.* up Christ, whom he *r.* not up.
15. 16, then is not Christ *r.*
15. 17, if Christ be not *r.*
15. 35, how are the dead *r.* up?
15. 43, it is *r.* in glory, it is *r.* in power.
2 Cor. 1. 9, trust in God which *r.* the dead.
4. 14, he shall *r.* up us also.
Eph. 2. 6, and hath *r.* us up together.
Heb. 11. 19, accounting God was able to *r.* him.
11. 35, women received dead *r.* to life.
Jas. 5. 15, and the Lord shall *r.* him up.
See Lu. 20. 37; John 5. 21; 2 Tim. 2. 8.
Raisins. 1 Sam. 25. 18; 30. 12; 2 Sam. 16. 1.
Rakem, rā'-kĕm, 'variegated.' 1 Chr. 7. 16.
Rakkath, răk'-kăth, 'shore.' Jos. 19. 35.
Rakkon, răk'-kŏn, same as RAKKATH. Jos. 19. 46.
Ram, răm, 'high.' Ru. 4. 19.
Ram (Gen. 15. 9). Heb. *Ayil:* Gk. κριός. in sacrifices. Gen. 15. 9; 22. 13; Ex. 29. 15; Lev. 9.; Num. 5. 8.
typical. Dan. 8. 20.
Ram, battering. Ezek. 4. 2; 21. 22.
Rama, rā'-mă, Greek form of RAMAH. Mat. 2. 18.
Ramah, rā'-măh, 'high place.' Jos. 18. 25; Jud. 4. 5; 1 Sam. 1. 19; 7. 17; 8. 4; 19. 18; 25. 1; Jer. 31. 15.
Ramath, rā'-măth, same as preceding. Jos. 19. 8.
Ramathaim-zophim, rā-mă-thā'-ĭm-zō'-phĭm, 'double high place.' 1 Sam. 1. 1.
Ramathite, rā'-măth-īte, a native of Ramah. 1 Chr. 27. 27.
Ramath-lehi, rā'-măth-lē'-hī, 'height of Lehi.' Jud. 15. 17.
Ramath-mizpeh, rā'-măth-mĭz'-pēh, 'height of Mizpeh. Jos. 13. 26.
Rameses, răm'-ĕ-sēś, or **Ramses**, răm'-sēś, 'son of the sun.' (1) the name of several Pharaohs of Egypt.
(2) the name of a store city in the land of Goshen in Egypt, built by the forced labour of the Hebrews for Pharaoh (Ramses II.) (Ex. 1. 11): the rendezvous of the Israelites at the beginning of the Exodus (Ex. 12. 37; Num. 33. 3.)
Ramiah, ră-mī'-ăh, 'Jehovah is high.' Ez. 10. 25.
Ramoth, rā'-mŏth, plural of RAMAH. 1 Chr. 6. 73.
Ramoth-gilead, rā'-mŏth-gĭl'-ĕ-ăd, 'heights of Gilead.' Deu. 4. 43; 1 Kn. 4. 13, 22; 2 Kn. 8. 28; 9. 1; 2 Chr. 18., 22. 5.
Rams' horns, trumpets of. Jos. 6. 4.
Ran. Ex. 9. 23; Num. 16. 47; Jer. 23. 21.
Rang. 1 Sam. 4. 5; 1 Kn. 1. 45.
Range, to roam in search of prey. Prov. 28. 15.
Ranges. (1) furnaces of masonry arranged to receive cooking utensils on top. Lev. 11. 35.
(2) ranks of soldiers. 2 Kn. 11. 8.
Ranks. 1 Kn. 7. 4; Joel 2. 7; Mk. 6. 40.
Ransom. Ex. 21. 30, give for the *r.* of his life. R. V. redemption.
30. 12, every man a *r.* for his soul.
Job 33. 24, I have found a *r.*
36. 18, a great *r.* cannot deliver.
Ps. 49. 7, nor give a *r.* for him.
Prov. 13. 8, the *r.* of a man's life are his riches.
Isa. 35. 10, the *r.* of the Lord shall return.
43. 3, I gave Egypt for thy *r.*
Hos. 13. 14, I will *r.* them from the grave.
Mat. 20. 28; Mk. 10. 45, to give his life a *r.*
1 Tim. 2. 6, gave himself a *r.* for all.
See Prov. 6. 35; Isa. 51. 10; Jer. 31. 11.
Rapha, rā'-phă, 'giant' (?). 1 Chr. 8. 37.
Raphu, rā'-phū, 'healed.' Num. 13. 9.
Rare. Dan. 2. 11.
Rase, raze, to lay level with the ground. Ps. 137. 7.
Rash. Eccl. 5. 2; Acts 19. 36.
Rate. Ex. 16. 4; 2 Kn. 25. 30; 2 Chr. 8. 13.
Rather. Job 7. 15; Jer. 8. 3, death *r.* than life.
Ps. 84. 10, *r.* be a doorkeeper.
Mat. 10. 6, go *r.* to lost sheep.
10. 28, *r.* fear him that is able.
25. 9, go *r.* to them that sell.
Mk. 5. 26, but *r.* grew worse.
Lu. 18. 14, justified *r.* than the other.
John 3. 19, loved darkness *r.* than light.
Acts 5. 29, obey God *r.* than men.
Rom. 8. 34, that died, yea *r.*, that is risen.
12. 19, *r.* give place to wrath. R. V. omits.
1 Cor. 6. 7, why do ye not *r.* take wrong?
Heb. 11. 25, choosing *r.* to suffer.
12. 13, let it *r.* be healed.
See Jos. 22. 24; 2 Kn. 5. 13; Phil. 1. 12.
Raven. Heb. *'Oreb:* Gk. κόραξ. The term includes the whole tribe of the crow family. Gen. 8. 7; Lev. 11. 15; Deu. 14. 14; 1 Kn. 17. 4; Job 38. 41; Ps. 147. 9; Prov. 30. 17; Lu. 12. 24.
Ravening (*n.*), greediness, rapacity. Lu. 11. 39.
Ravening (*p.*). Ps. 22. 13; Ezek. 22. 25; Mat. 7. 15.
Ravenous. Isa. 35. 9; 46. 11; Ezek. 39. 4.
Ravin (*n.*), plunder. Nah. 2. 12.

Ravin (*v.*), to seize upon prey. Gen. 49. 27.
Razor. Num. 6. 5; Ps. 52. 2; Ezek. 5. 1.
Reach. Gen. 11. 4; John 20. 27; 2 Cor. 10. 13.
Read. Deu. 17. 19, king shall *r.* all his life.
Isa. 34. 16, seek out of book of Lord and *r.*
Mat. 12. 3; 19. 4; 21. 16; 22. 31; Mk. 2. 25; 12. 10; Lu. 6. 3, have ye not *r.*
Lu. 4. 16, Jesus stood up to *r.*
2 Cor. 3. 2, epistle known and *r.* of all men.
1 Tim. 4. 13, give attendance to *r.*
See Hab. 2. 2; 2 Cor. 3. 14; Rev. 1. 3; 5. 4.
Readiness. Acts 17. 11; 2 Cor. 8. 11; 10. 6.
Reading of the Law. Ex. 24. 7; Jos. 8. 34; 2 Kn. 23.; Neh. 8.; 9.
of the Prophets. Lu. 4. 16.
of the Epistles. Col. 4. 16; 1 Thes. 5. 27.
See Acts 13. 15.
Ready. Num. 32. 17, we will go *r.* armed.
Deu. 26. 5, a Syrian *r.* to perish.
2 Sam. 18. 22, wherefore run, no tidings *r.* R. V. no reward for the tidings.
Neh. 9. 17, thou art a God *r.* to pardon.
Job 12. 5, *r.* to slip with his feet.
17. 1, the graves are *r.* for me.
29. 13, blessing of him *r.* to perish.
Ps. 38. 17, I am *r.* to halt.
45. 1, pen of a *r.* writer.
86. 5, good and *r.* to forgive.
88. 15, *r.* to die from my youth.
Prov. 24. 11, deliver those *r.* to be slain.
31. 6, give strong drink to *r.* to perish.
Eccl. 5. 1, be more *r.* to hear. R. V. for to draw nigh to hear is better.
Isa. 27. 13, shall come that were *r.* to perish.
32. 4, stammerers *r.* to speak plainly.
38. 20, the Lord was *r.* to save me.
Dan. 3. 15, if ye be *r.* to fall down.
Mat. 22. 4; Lu. 14. 17, all things are *r.*
22. 8, the wedding is *r.*
24. 44; Lu. 12. 40, be ye also *r.*
25. 10, they that were *r.* went in.
Mk. 14. 38, the Spirit is *r.* R. V. willing.
Lu. 22. 33, I am *r.* to go with thee.
John 7. 6, your time is alway *r.*
Acts 21. 13, *r.* not to be bound only, but.
Rom. 1. 15, I am *r.* to preach at Rome.
2 Cor. 8. 19, declaration of your *r.* mind.
9. 2, Achaia was *r.* a year ago.
1 Tim. 6. 18, *r.* to distribute.
2 Tim. 4. 6, *r.* to be offered.
Tit. 3. 1, *r.* to every good work.
1 Pet. 1. 5, *r.* to be revealed.
3. 15, *r.* always to give an answer.
5. 2, but of a *r.* mind.
Rev. 3. 2, things that are *r.* to die.
See Ex. 17. 4; 19. 11; Ez. 7. 6; Job 15. 23.
Reaia, rē-ā̤ī'-ă, 'Jehovah has seen.' 1 Chr. 5. 5.
Reaiah, rē-ā̤ī'-ăh, correct form of Reaia. 1 Chr. 4. 2.
Reap. Lev. 25. 11, in jubilee neither sow nor *r.*
Eccl. 11. 4, regardeth clouds shall not *r.*
Jer. 12. 13, sown wheat, but shall *r.* thorns.
Hos. 8. 7, shall *r.* the whirlwind.
10. 12, sow in righteousness, *r.* in mercy.
Mic. 6. 15, shalt sow, but not *r.*
Mat. 6. 26; Lu. 12. 24, sow not, neither *r.*
25. 26; Lu. 19. 21, *r.* where I sowed not.
John 4. 38, *r.* whereon ye bestowed no labour.
1 Cor. 9. 11, if we shall *r.* your carnal things.
2 Cor. 9. 6, shall *r.* sparingly.
Gal. 6. 7, that shall he also *r.*
Jas. 5. 4, cries of them which *r.* R. V. moved.
Reaping. Lev. 19. 9; 23. 10, 22; 25. 5.
figurative. Job 4. 8; Ps. 126. 5; Prov. 22. 8; Isa. 17. 5; Mat. 13. 30; John 4. 36; 1 Cor. 9. 11; 2 Cor. 9. 6; Gal. 6. 7; Rev. 14. 15.
Reason (*n.*). Job 32. 11, I gave ear to your *r.*
Prov. 26. 16, seven men that can render a *r.*
Eccl. 7. 25, to search out the *r.* of things.
Isa. 41. 21, bring forth your strong *r.*
1 Pet. 3. 15, a *r.* of the hope in you.
See 1 Kn. 9. 15; Dan. 4. 36; Acts 6. 2.
Reason (*v.*). Job 9. 14, choose words to *r.* with him.
Job 13. 3, I desire to *r.* with God.
15. 3, should he *r.* with unprofitable talk.
Isa. 1. 18, let us *r.* together.
Mat. 16. 7; 21. 25; Mk. 8. 16; 11. 31; Lu. 20. 5, they *r.* among themselves.
Lu. 5. 22, what *r.* ye in your hearts?
24. 15, while they *r.* Jesus drew near. R. V. questioned.
Acts 24. 25, as he *r.* of righteousness.
See 1 Sam. 12. 7; Mk. 2. 6; 12. 28; Acts 28. 29.
Reasonable. Rom. 12. 1.
Reba, rē'-bă, 'a fourth part.' (1) Num. 31. 8, a king of Midian.
(2) *Rebah*, 'a fourth part' of a shekel = 56 gr. *See* Weights.
Rebecca, rĕ-bĕc'-că, Greek form of Rebekah. Rom. 9. 10.
Rebekah, rĕ-bĕk'-ăh, 'a noose;' history of. Gen. 22. 23; 24. 15, 67; 27. 6, 42; 49. 31; Rom. 9. 10.
Rebel. Num. 14. 9, only *r.* not against the Lord.
Jos. 1. 18, whosoever doth *r.* he shall die.
Neh. 2. 19, will ye *r.* against the king?
Job 24. 13, that *r.* against the light.
Ps. 105. 28, they *r.* not against his word.
Isa. 1. 2, have nourished children and they *r.*
63. 10, they *r.* and vexed his holy Spirit.
Lam. 3. 42, we have *r.*, thou hast not pardoned.
Dan. 9. 9, though we have *r.* against him.
See 1 Sam. 12. 14; Ezek. 2. 3; Hos. 7. 14; 13. 16.
Rebellion. 1 Sam. 15. 23, *r.* is as the sin of witchcraft.
Job 34. 37, he addeth *r.* to his sin.
Prov. 17. 11, an evil man seeketh *r.*
Jer. 28. 16, thou hast taught *r.*
See Deu. 31. 27; Ez. 4. 19; Neh. 9. 17.
Rebellious. Deu. 21. 18, 20, a stubborn and *r.* son.
1 Sam. 20. 30, son of perverse *r.* woman.
Ps. 66. 7, let not the *r.* exalt themselves.
68. 6, the *r.* dwell in a dry land.
Isa. 1. 23, *r.*, companions of thieves.
Jer. 5. 23, this people hath a *r.* heart.
See Ezek. 2. 3; 3. 9; 12. 2; 17. 12; 24. 3.
Rebels. Num. 17. 10; 20. 10; Ezek. 20. 38.
Rebuke (*n.*). 2 Kn. 19. 3; Isa. 37. 3, this is a day of *r.*
Ps. 39. 11, when thou with *r.* dost correct.
80. 16, perish at *r.* of thy countenance.
104. 7, at thy *r.* they fled.
Prov. 13. 8, the poor heareth not *r.* R. V. no threatening.
27. 5, open *r.* is better than secret love.
Eccl. 7. 5, better to hear *r.* of wise.
Isa. 30. 17, thousand flee at *r.* of one.
Jer. 15. 15, for thy sake I suffered *r.* R. V. reproach.
Phil. 2. 15, without *r.* R. V. blemish.
See Deu. 28. 20; Isa. 25. 8; 50. 2.
Rebuke (*v.*). Ps. 6. 1; 38. 1, *r.* me not in anger.
Prov. 9. 7, he that *r.* a wicked man getteth a blot.
9. 8, *r.* a wise man, and he will love thee.
28. 23, he that *r.* a man shall find favour.
Isa. 2. 4; Mic. 4. 3, he shall *r.* many nations.
Zec. 3. 2; Jude 9, the Lord *r.* thee.
Mal. 3. 11, I will *r.* the devourer for your sakes.
Mat. 8. 26; Mk. 4. 39; Lu. 8. 24, he *r.* wind.
16. 22; Mk. 8. 32, Peter began to *r.* him.
Lu. 4. 39, he *r.* the fever.
17. 3, if thy brother trespass, *r.* him.
19. 39, Master, *r.* thy disciples.
1 Tim. 5. 1, *r.* not an elder.
5. 20, them that sin, *r.* before all. R. V. reprove.
2 Tim. 4. 2, *r.*, exhort, with longsuffering.
Tit. 1. 13; 2. 15, *r.* them sharply. R. V. reprove.
Heb. 12. 5, nor faint when thou art *r.* R. V. reproved.
See Ru. 2. 16; Neh. 5. 7; Am. 5. 10.
Recall. Lam. 3. 21.
Receipt of custom, 'place of toll' as in R. V. Mat. 9. 9; Mk. 2. 14; Lu. 5. 27.
Receive. 2 Kn. 5. 26, is it a time to *r.* money.
Job 4. 12, mine ear *r.* a little.
22. 22, *r.* law from his mouth.
Ps. 6. 9, the Lord will *r.* my prayer.

Ps. 49. 15, he shall *r*. me.
68. 18, hast *r*. gifts for men.
73. 24, afterwards *r*. me to glory.
Prov. 2. 1, if thou wilt *r*. my words.
Isa. 40. 2, she hath *r*. double.
Jer. 2. 30, your children *r*. no correction.
Hos. 10. 6, Ephraim shall *r*. shame.
14. 2, *r*. us graciously. R. V. accept.
Mat. 11. 5, the blind *r*. their sight.
11. 14, if ye will *r*. it, this is Elias.
18. 5, whoso shall *r*. one such little child.
19. 12, he that is able, let him *r*. it.
21. 22, ask, believing ye shall *r*.
Mk. 15. 23, but he *r*. it not.
16. 19; Acts 1. 9, he was *r*. up into heaven.
Lu. 16. 9, *r*. you into everlasting habitations.
18. 42; Acts 22. 13, *r*. thy sight.
John 1. 11, his own *r*. him not.
1. 12, to as many as *r*. him.
3. 27, can *r*. nothing, except.
5. 43, in his own name, him ye will *r*.
5. 44, which *r*. honour one of another.
16. 24, ask, and ye shall *r*.
20. 22, *r*. ye the Holy Ghost.
Acts 7. 59, *r*. my spirit.
8. 17, they *r*. the Holy Ghost.
10. 43, shall *r*. remission of sins.
19. 2, have ye *r*. the Holy Ghost.
20. 24, which I have *r*. of the Lord.
Rom. 5. 11, by whom we *r*. atonement.
14. 3, for God hath *r*. him.
15. 7, *r*. ye one another.
1 Cor. 3. 8, every man shall *r*. his own reward.
11. 23, I *r*. of the Lord that which also I delivered.
2 Cor. 4. 1, as we have *r*. mercy we faint not.
5. 10, every one may *r*. things done.
7. 2, *r*. us; we have wronged no man. R. V. open your hearts to.
Phil. 2. 29, *r*. him in the Lord.
4. 15, as concerning giving and *r*.
Col. 2. 6, as ye have *r*. Christ.
1 Tim. 3. 16, *r*. up into glory.
4. 4, if it be *r*. with thanksgiving.
1 John 3. 22, whatsoever we ask we *r*.
See Ezek. 3. 10; Acts 20. 35; Jas. 4. 3.

Rechab, rē´-c͟hăb, 'horseman.' 2 Kn. 10. 15.

Rechabites, rē´-c͟hăb-ītes, descendants of Rechab. Jer. 35. 2.

Rechah, rē´-c͟hăh, 'side' (?). 1 Chr. 4. 12.

Reckon. Lev. 25. 50, he shall *r*. with him that bought him.
Ps. 40. 5, thy thoughts cannot be *r*. up. R. V. set.
Mat. 18. 24, when he had begun to *r*.
25. 19, lord of servants *r*. with them.
Rom. 4. 4, reward is not *r*. of grace.
6. 11, *r*. yourselves dead to sin.
8. 18, I *r*. the sufferings of this present time.
See 2 Kn. 22. 7; Isa. 38. 13; Lu. 22. 37.

Recommended. Acts 14. 26; 15. 40.

Recompence (recompense in R. V. in N. T.).
Deu. 32. 35, to me belongeth *r*.
Job 15. 31, vanity shall be his *r*.
Isa. 35. 4, God will come with a *r*.
Hos. 9. 7, days of *r*. are come.
Joel 3. 4, will ye render me a *r*.?
Lu. 14. 12, and a *r*. be made thee.
2 Cor. 6. 13, for a *r*., be ye also enlarged.
Heb. 2. 2; 10. 35; 11. 26, just *r*. of reward.
See Prov. 12. 14; Isa. 34. 8; Jer. 51. 56.

Recompense. Num. 5. 7, he shall *r*. his trespass. R. V. make restitution for his guilt in full.
Ru. 2. 12, the Lord *r*. thy work.
2 Sam. 19. 36, why should the king *r*. me?
Job 34. 33, he will *r*. it, whether.
Prov. 20. 22, say not, I will *r*. evil.
Isa. 65. 6, but will *r*., even *r*. into their bosom.
Jer. 25. 14; Hos. 12. 2, will *r*. according to deeds.
Lu. 14. 14, for they cannot *r*. thee.
Rom. 11. 35, it shall be *r*. to him again.
12. 17, *r*. to no man evil for evil. R. V. render.
See 2 Chr. 6. 23; Jer. 32. 18; Heb. 10. 30.

Reconcile. 1 Sam. 29. 4, wherewith should he *r*. himself.
Ezek. 45. 20, so shall ye *r*. the house. R. V. make atonement for.
Mat. 5. 24, first be *r*. to thy brother.
Rom. 5. 10, if when enemies we were *r*.
Eph. 2. 16, that he might *r*. both.

Reconciliation with God. Isa. 53. 5; Dan. 9. 24; Rom. 5.; 11. 15; 2 Cor. 5. 19; Eph. 2. 16; Col. 1. 20; Heb. 2. 17.

Record. Ex. 20. 24, in places where I *r*. my name.
Deu. 30. 19; 31. 28, I call heaven to *r*. R. V. witness.
Job 16. 19, my *r*. is on high. R. V. he that voucheth for me.
John 8. 13, thou bearest *r*. of thyself. R. V. witness.
Rom. 10. 2, I bare them *r*. R. V. witness.
Phil. 1. 8, God is my *r*. how greatly I long. R. V. witness.
1 John 5. 7, three that bare *r*. R. V. omits.
5. 10, he believeth not the *r*. R. V. witness.
5. 11, this is the *r*., that God hath given. R. V. witness.
3 John 12, we bare *r*., and our *r*. is true. R. V. witness.
See Acts 20. 26; John 1. 19; Rev. 1. 2.

Recount. Nah. 2. 5, *r*. his worthies. R. V. remembereth.

Recover. 2 Kn. 5. 3, the prophet would *r*. him.
Ps. 39. 13, that I may *r*. strength.
Isa. 11. 11, to *r*. remnant of his people.
Hos. 2. 9, and I will *r*. my wool and flax. R. V. pluck away.
Mk. 16. 18, lay hands on sick, and they shall *r*.
Lu. 4. 18, preach *r*. of sight to blind.
See Isa. 38. 16; Jer. 8. 22; 41. 16; 2 Tim. 2. 16.

Red. Gen. 25. 30, *r*. pottage.
49. 12, eyes *r*. with wine.
2 Kn. 3. 22, water *r*. as blood.
Ps. 75. 8, wine is *r*., full of mixture. R. V. foameth.
Prov. 23. 31, look not on wine when *r*.
Isa. 1. 18, though your sins be *r*. like crimson.
27. 2, a vineyard of *r*. wine. R. V. omits.
63. 2, *r*. in thine apparel.
Mat. 16. 2, fair weather, for the sky is *r*.
See Lev. 13. 19; Num. 19. 2; Nah. 2. 3; Rev. 6. 4.

Red Dragon. Rev. 12. 3.

Redeem. Gen. 48. 16, angel which *r*. me.
Ex. 6. 6, I will *r*. you.
15. 13, people whom thou hast *r*.
Lev. 27. 28, no devoted thing, shall be *r*.
2 Sam. 4. 9, the Lord hath *r*. my soul.
Neh. 5. 5, nor is it in our power to *r*. them. R. V. help it.
5. 8, after our ability have *r*. Jews.
Job 5. 20, in famine he shall *r*. thee.
6. 23, to *r*. me from hand of mighty.
Ps. 25. 22, *r*. Israel out of all his troubles.
34. 22, the Lord *r*. the soul of his servants.
44. 26, *r*. us for thy mercies' sake.
49. 7, none can *r*. his brother.
49. 15, God will *r*. my soul from the grave.
72. 14, he shall *r*. their soul from deceit.
107. 2, let the *r*. of the Lord say so.
130. 8, he shall *r*. Israel.
Isa. 1. 27, Zion shall be *r*. with judgment.
35. 9, the *r*. shall walk there.
44. 22, return, for I have *r*. thee.
50. 2, is my hand shortened that it cannot *r*.?
51. 11, the *r*. of the Lord shall return.
52. 3, *r*. without money.
63. 4, the year of my *r*. is come.
Hos. 7. 13, though I *r*. them, they have spoken lies.
13. 14, I will *r*. them from death.
Lu. 1. 68, hath visited, and *r*. his people.
24. 21, he who should have *r*. Israel.
Gal. 3. 13, *r*. us from curse of the law.
4. 5, *r*. them that were under the law.
Tit. 2. 14, that he might *r*. us from iniquity.
1 Pet. 1. 18, not *r*. with corruptible things.

Rev. 5. 9, thou hast *r.* us by thy blood. R. V. didst purchase.
See Num. 18. 15; 2 Sam. 7. 23; Eph. 5. 16; Col. 4. 5.

Redeemer. Job 19. 25, I know that my *r.* liveth.
Ps. 19. 14, O Lord, my strength and my *r.*
78. 35, God was their *r.*
Prov. 23. 11, their *r.* is mighty.
Isa. 47. 4, as for our *r.*, the Lord of hosts is his name.
49. 26; 60. 16, know that I am thy *R.*
59. 20, the *R.* shall come to Zion.
63. 16, thou art our *r.*

Redeemer, the Lord. Job 19. 25; Ps. 19. 14; 78. 35; Prov. 23. 11; Isa. 41. 14; 44. 6; 47. 4; 48. 17; 54. 5; 59. 20; 63. 16; Jer. 50. 34; Hos. 13. 14.

Redemption. Lev. 25. 24, grant a *r.* for the land.
Ps. 49. 8, the *r.* of their soul is precious.
111. 9, he sent *r.* to his people.
130. 7, plenteous *r.*
Jer. 32. 7, the right of *r.* is thine.
Lu. 2. 38, that looked for *r.* in Jerusalem.
21. 28, your *r.* draweth nigh.
Rom. 8. 23, the *r.* of our body.
Eph. 4. 30, sealed unto the day of *r.*

Redemption by Christ. Rom. 3. 24; 5.; 1 Cor. 1. 30; Gal. 1. 4; 3.; 4.; Eph. 1.; 2.; Col. 1.; Heb. 9.; 10.; Tit. 2. 14; 1 Pet. 1. 18; Rev. 5. 9.

Redemption of land, &c. Lev. 25.; Neh. 5. 8.
of the firstborn. Ex. 13. 11; Num. 3. 12, 46.

Red horse, vision of. Zec. 1. 8; 6. 2; Rev. 6. 4.

Redound. 2 Cor. 4. 15, grace might *r.*

Red Sea. Ex. 14.; 15.; 1 Kn. 9. 26.

Reed. (1) (*See* BULRUSH). bruised, 2 Kn. 18. 21; Isa. 42.; Mat. 12. 20.
(2) A measure = 6 cubits = 8 ft. 9. in. Rev. 11. 1; 21. 15.
(3) Ezekiel's reed = 6 cubits of 7 palms = 10 ft. 2.3 in. Ezek. 40. 3.

Reelaiah, rē-ĕl-āī′-ăh, 'trembling of Jehovah.' Ez. 2. 2.

References in the New Testament to incidents and passages, not exact quotations, in the Old Testament. *See* OLD TESTAMENT.

Refiner, the. Isa. 48. 10; Zec. 13. 9; Mal. 3. 2.

Reformation. Heb. 9. 10, time of *r.*

Reformed. Lev. 26. 23, if ye will not be *r.*

Refrain. Gen. 45. 1, Joseph could not *r.* himself.
Job 7. 11, I will not *r.* my mouth.
29. 9, princes *r.* talking.
Ps. 40. 9, I have not *r.* my lips.
119. 101, *r.* my feet from every evil way.
Prov. 1. 15, *r.* thy foot from their path.
10. 19, he that *r.* his lips is wise.
Acts 5. 38, *r.* from these men. [10.
See Gen. 43. 31; Isa. 64. 12; Jer. 31. 16; 1 Pet. 3.

Refresh. Ex. 31. 17, he rested and was *r.*
Job 32. 20, I will speak that I may be *r.*
Prov. 25. 13, he *r.* the soul of his masters.
Acts 3. 19, times of *r.* shall come.
1 Cor. 16. 18, they *r.* my spirit. [7. 13.
See 1 Kn. 13. 7; Isa. 28. 12; Rom. 15. 32; 2 Cor.

Refuge, the divine. Deu. 33. 27; 2 Sam. 22. 3; Ps. 9. 9; 46. 1; 48. 3; Heb. 6. 18.

Refuge, Cities of, six Levitical cities designed to shelter those who had accidentally slain any person, from the Avenger of blood. Num. 35. 9–14; Ex. 21. 13. The cities appointed for this purpose were HEBRON (in *Judah*), SHECHEM (in *Ephraim*), KEDESH (in *Naphtali*), BEZER (in *Reuben*), GOLAN (in *Manasseh*), RAMOTH (in *Gad*). Jos. 20. 7–9.

Refuse (*n.*). 1 Sam. 15. 9; Lam. 3. 45; Am. 8. 6.

Refuse (*v.*). Gen. 37. 35, Jacob *r.* to be comforted.
Num. 22. 13, the Lord *r.* to give me leave.
1 Sam. 16. 7, look not on him, for I have *r.* him. R. V. rejected.
Job 6. 7, things my soul *r.* to touch.
Ps. 77. 2, my soul *r.* to be comforted.
78. 10, they *r.* to walk in his law.
118. 22, stone the builders *r.* R. V. rejected.
Prov. 1. 24, I have called and ye *r.*
8. 33, be wise and *r.* it not.
10. 17, he that *r.* reproof. R. V. forsaketh.
13. 18, shame to him that *r.* instruction.
15. 32, he that *r.* instruction despiseth his soul.
21. 25, his hands *r.* to labour.
Isa. 7. 15, 16, may know to *r.* the evil.
Jer. 8. 5, they *r.* to return.
9. 6, they *r.* to know me.
15. 18, my wound *r.* to be healed.
25. 28, if they *r.* to take the cup.
38. 21, if thou *r.* to go forth.
Zec. 7. 11, they *r.* to hearken.
Acts 7. 35, this Moses whom they *r.*
1 Tim. 4. 4, nothing to be *r.* R. V. rejected.
4. 7, *r.* profane and old wives' fables.
5. 11, the younger widows *r.*
Heb. 11. 24, Moses *r.* to be called.
12. 25, *r.* not him that speaketh.
See Ex. 4. 23; 10. 3; 1 Kn. 20. 35; 2 Kn. 5. 16.

Regard. Gen. 45. 20, *r.* not your stuff.
Ex. 5. 9, let them not *r.* vain words.
Deu. 10. 17, that *r.* not persons.
1 Kn. 18. 29, neither voice, nor any that *r.*
Job 4. 20, they perish without any *r.* it.
34. 19, nor *r.* rich more than poor.
39. 7, neither *r.* crying of the driver. R. V. heareth.
Ps. 28. 5; Isa. 5. 12, they *r.* not works of the Lord,
66. 18, if I *r.* iniquity in my heart.
102. 17, he will *r.* prayer of the destitute.
106. 44, he *r.* their affliction.
Prov. 1. 24, and no man *r.* [serve.
5. 2, that thou mayest *r.* discretion. R. V. pre-
6. 35, he will not *r.* any ransom.
12. 10, *r.* the life of his beast.
13. 18; 15. 5, he that *r.* reproof.
Eccl. 11. 4, he that *r.* the clouds.
Lam. 4. 16, the Lord will no more *r.* them.
Dan. 11. 37, *r.* God of his fathers, nor *r.* any god.
Mal. 1. 9, will he *r.* your persons. R. V. accept of.
Mat. 22. 16; Mk. 12. 14, *r.* not the person of men.
Lu. 18. 2, neither *r.* man.
Rom. 14. 6, he that *r.* the day, *r.* it to the Lord.
See Deu. 28. 50; 2 Kn. 3. 14; Am. 5. 22; Phil. 2. 30.

Regem, rē′gĕm, 'friend.' 1 Chr. 2. 47.

Regem-melech, rē′-gĕm-mĕl′-ĕch, 'friend of the king.' Zec. 7. 2.

Regeneration. Mat. 19. 28, in the *r.*
Tit. 3. 5, by the washing of *r.*
See John 1. 13; 3. 3.

Region. Deu. 3. 4; Mat. 3. 5; 4. 16; Acts 8. 1; 16. 6; 2 Cor. 10. 16.

Register. Ez. 2. 62; Neh. 7. 5, 64.

Rehabiah, rē-hă-bī′-ăh, 'Jehovah enlarges.' 1 Chr. 23. 17.

Rehearse. Jud. 5. 11, *r.* the righteous acts.
Acts 14. 27, they *r.* all God had done.
See Ex. 17. 14; 1 Sam. 8. 21; 17. 31; Acts 11. 4.

Rehob, rē′-hŏb, 'street.' (1) men. 2 Sam. 8. 3; Neh. 10. 11.
(2) places. Num. 13. 21; Jos. 19. 28, 30.

Rehoboam, rē-hŏ-bō′-ăm, 'who enlarges the people.' 1 Kn. 11. 43.
king of Judah. 1 Kn. 11.; 12.; 14.; 2 Chr. 9.–12.

Rehoboth, rē′-hŏ-bōth, 'roominess.' Gen. 10. 11; 26. 22.

Rehum, rē′hŭm, 'merciful.' Ez. 4. 8.

Rei, rē′-ī, 'friendly.' 1 Kn. 1. 8.

Reign. Gen. 37. 8, shalt thou *r.* over us.
Ex. 15. 18; Ps. 146. 10, Lord shall *r.* for ever.
Lev. 26. 17, that hate you shall *r.* over you.
Deu. 15. 6, thou shalt *r.* over many nations.
Jud. 9. 8, the trees said, *r.* thou over us.
1 Sam. 11. 12, shall Saul *r.* over us.
12. 12, nay, but a king shall *r.* over us.
2 Sam. 16. 8, in whose stead thou hast *r.*
Job 34. 30, that the hypocrite *r.* not.
Ps. 47. 8, God *r.* over the heathen.
93. 1; 96. 10; 97. 1; 99. 1, the Lord *r.*
Prov. 8. 15, by me kings *r.*
30. 22, for a servant when he *r.* R. V. is king.

Eccl. 4. 14, out of prison he cometh to *r*. R. V. to be king.
Isa. 32. 1, a king shall *r*. in righteousness.
52. 7, that saith unto Zion, thy God *r*.
Jer. 22. 15, shalt thou *r*. because thou closest?
23. 5, a king shall *r*. and prosper.
Mic. 4. 7, the Lord shall *r*. over them.
Lu. 19. 14, not have this man to *r*. over us.
19. 27, that would not I should *r*.
Rom. 5. 14, death *r*. from Adam to Moses.
5. 17, death *r*. by one.
5. 21, as sin hath *r*., so might grace *r*.
6. 12, let not sin *r*. in your bodies.
1 Cor. 4. 8, ye have *r*. as kings without us.
15. 25, for he must *r*.
2 Tim. 2. 12, if we suffer we shall also *r*. with him.
Rev. 5. 10, we also shall *r*. on the earth.
11. 15, he shall *r*. for ever and ever.
19. 6, the Lord God omnipotent *r*.
See Isa. 24. 23; Lu. 1. 33; Rev. 20. 4; 22. 5.

Reins, the kidneys (spoken of as if the seat of joy, pain, &c.). Job 16. 13, he cleaveth my *r*. asunder.
19. 27, though my *r*. be consumed.
Ps. 7. 9, God trieth the *r*.
16. 7, my *r*. instruct me.
26. 2, examine me, try my *r*.
73. 21, thus I was pricked in my *r*.
139. 13, thou hast possessed my *r*.
Prov. 23. 16, my *r*. shall rejoice.
Isa. 11. 5, faithfulness the girdle of his *r*.
Rev. 2. 23, I am he who searcheth the *r*.
See Jer. 11. 20; 12. 2; 17. 10; 20. 12; Lam. 3. 13.

Reject. 1 Sam. 8. 7, they have not *r*. thee, but they have *r*. me.
10. 19, ye have *r*. God who saved you.
15. 23, because thou hast *r*. the word of the Lord.
16. 1, I have *r*. him from being king.
Isa. 53. 3, despised and *r*. of men.
Jer. 2. 37, the Lord hath *r*. thy confidence.
7. 29, the Lord hath *r*. the generation.
8. 9, they have *r*. the word of the Lord.
14. 19, thou hast utterly *r*. Judah.
Lam. 5. 22, thou hast utterly *r*. us.
Hos. 4. 6, because thou hast *r*. knowledge, I will *r*. thee.
Mat. 21. 42; Mk. 12. 10; Lu. 20. 17, the stone which builders *r*.
Mk. 7. 9, full well ye *r*. the commandment.
Lu. 7. 30, lawyers *r*. the counsel of God.
17. 25, must first be *r*. of this generation.
Tit. 3. 10, after admonition *r*. R. V. refuse.
Heb. 12. 17, when he would have inherited was *r*.
See Jer. 6. 19; Mk. 6. 26; 8. 31; Lu. 9. 22; John 12. 48.

Rejoice. Deu. 12. 7, shall *r*. in all ye put your hand to.
16. 14, thou shalt *r*. in thy feast.
26. 11, thou shalt *r*. in every good thing.
28. 63; 30. 9, the Lord will *r*. over you.
30. 9, *r*. for good as he *r*. over thy fathers.
1 Sam. 2. 1, because I *r*. in thy salvation.
1 Chr. 16. 10, let the heart of them *r*. that seek the Lord.
2 Chr. 6. 41, let thy saints *r*. in goodness.
Job 21. 12, they *r*. at sound of the organ.
31. 25, if I *r*. because my wealth was great.
31. 29, if I *r*. at destruction of him that.
39. 21, the horse *r*. in his strength.
Ps. 2. 11, *r*. with trembling.
5. 11, let all that trust in thee *r*.
9 14, I will *r*. in thy salvation.
19. 5, *r*. as a strong man to run a race.
33. 21, our heart shall *r*. in him.
35. 15, in mine adversity they *r*.
35. 26, let them be ashamed that *r*. at my hurt.
38. 16, hear me, lest they should *r*. over me.
51. 8, bones thou hast broken may *r*.
58. 10, righteous shall *r*. when he seeth.
63. 7, in shadow of thy wings will I *r*. [exult.
68. 3, let righteous *r*., yea, exceedingly *r*. R. V.
Ps. 85. 6, that thy people may *r*. in thee.
89. 16, in thy name shall they *r*. all the day.
96. 11, let the heavens *r*. R. V. be glad,
97. 1, the Lord reigneth, let the earth *r*.
104. 31, the Lord shall *r*. in his works.
107. 42, the righteous shall see it and *r*. R. V. be glad.
109. 28, let thy servant *r*.
149. 2, let Israel *r*. in him that made him.
Prov. 2. 14, who *r*. to do evil.
5. 18, *r*. with the wife of thy youth. [be glad.
23. 15, if thine heart be wise, mine shall *r*. R. V.
23. 24, father of the righteous shall greatly *r*.
23. 25, she that bare thee shall *r*.
24. 17, *r*. not when thine enemy falleth.
29. 2, when righteous are in authority people *r*.
31. 25, she shall *r*. in time to come. R. V. laugheth at the.
Eccl. 2. 10, my heart *r*. in all my labour.
3. 12, for a man to *r*. and do good.
3. 22; 5. 19, that a man should *r*. in his works.
11. 9, *r*. O young man in thy youth.
Isa. 9. 3, as men *r*. when they divide the spoil.
24. 8, noise of them that *r*. endeth.
29. 19, poor among men shall *r*.
35. 1, the desert shall *r*.
62. 5, as the bridegroom *r*. over the bride.
64. 5, him that *r*. and worketh righteousness.
65. 13, my servants shall *r*., but ye.
66. 14, when ye see this, your heart shall *r*.
Jer. 11. 15, when thou doest evil, then thou *r*.
32. 41, I will *r*. over them to do them good.
51. 39, that they may *r*. and sleep.
Ezek. 7. 12, let not buyer *r*.
Am. 6. 13, which *r*. in a thing of nought.
Mic. 7. 8, *r*. not against me.
Hab. 3. 18, yet I will *r*. in the Lord.
Mat. 18. 13, he *r*. more of that sheep.
Lu. 1. 14, many shall *r*. at his birth.
6. 23, *r*. ye in that day, and leap for joy.
10. 20, in this *r*. not, but rather *r*. because.
10. 21, in that hour Jesus *r*. in spirit.
15. 6, 9, *r*. with me.
John 5. 35, willing for a season to *r*. in his light.
8. 56, Abraham *r*. to see my day.
14. 28, if ye loved me, ye would *r*.
16. 20, ye shall weep, but the world shall *r*.
16. 22, I will see you again, and your heart shall *r*.
Rom. 5. 2, and *r*. in hope.
12. 15, *r*. with them that do *r*.
1 Cor. 7. 30, they that *r* as though they *r*. not.
13. 6, *r*. not in iniquity, but *r*. in the truth.
Phil. 1. 18, I therein do *r*. and will *r*
2. 16, that I may *r*. in the day of Christ. R. V. have whereof to glory.
3. 1, finally, *r*. in the Lord.
4. 4, *r*. in the Lord alway, and again I say *r*.
1 Thes. 5. 16, *r*. evermore. [glory.
Jas. 1. 9, let the brother of low degree *r*. R. V.
2. 13, mercy *r*. against judgment. R. V. glorieth.
1 Pet. 1. 8, *r*. with joy unspeakable.
See 1 Kn. 1. 40; 5. 7; 2 Kn. 11. 14; 1 Chr. 29. 9.

Rejoicing. Job 8. 21, till he fill thy lips with *r*. R. V. shouting.
Ps. 107. 22, declare his works with *r*. R. V. singing.
118. 15, voice of *r*. is in tabernacles of the righteous.
119. 111, they are the *r*. of my heart. [joy.
126. 6, shall doubtless come again with *r*. R. V.
Prov. 8. 31, *r*. in the habitable part of his earth.
Isa. 65. 18, I create Jerusalem a *r*.
Jer. 15. 16, thy word was to me the *r*. of my heart.
Zep. 2. 15, this is the *r*. city. R. V. joyous.
Acts 5. 41, *r*. that they were counted worthy.
Rom. 12. 12, *r*. in hope.
2 Cor. 6. 10, as sorrowful, yet alway *r*.
1 Thes. 2. 19, what is our crown of *r*. R. V. glorying.
See Hab. 3. 14; Acts 8. 39; Gal. 6. 4; Jas. 4. 16.

Rejoicing of the faithful. Lev. 23. 40; Deu. 12.

10; 16. 11; 1 Chr. 16. 10; 2 Chr. 6. 41; Ps. 5. 11; 33.; 48. 11; 68. 4; 89. 16; 97. 12; 103.; Isa. 41. 16; Joel 2. 23; Hab. 3. 18; Zec. 10. 7; Rom. 12. 15; Phil. 3. 1; 4. 4; 1 Thes. 5. 16; Jas. 1. 9; Rev. 12. 12; 18. 20.

Rekem, rē'-kĕm, same as Rakem. Num. 31. 8.

Release. Esth. 2. 18; Mat. 27. 17; Mk. 15. 11; John 19. 10.

Release, year of. Ex. 21. 2; Deu. 15. 1; 31. 10; Jer. 34. 14.

Relief sent to the brethren. Acts 11. 29; 24. 17.

Relieve. Lev. 25. 35, then thou shalt *r.* him. R. V. uphold.
Ps. 146. 9, he *r.* the fatherless and widow. R. V. upholdeth.
Isa. 1. 17, *r.* the oppressed.
Lam. 1. 16, comforter that should *r.* my soul is far from me. R. V. refresh.
See Acts 11. 29: 1 Tim. 5. 10, 16.

Religion. Acts 26. 5; Gal. 1. 13; Jas. 1. 26, 27.

Religious. Acts 13. 43; Jas. 1. 26.

Rely. 2 Chr. 13. 18; 16. 7, 8.

Remain. Gen. 8. 22, while earth *r.*
14. 10, they that *r.* fled to the mountain.
Ex. 12. 10, let nothing of it *r.* until morning.
Jos. 13. 1, there *r.* yet much land to be possessed.
1 Kn. 18. 22, I only *r.* a prophet. R. V. am left.
Job 21. 32, yet shall he *r.* in the tomb. R. V. keep watch over.
Prov. 2. 21, the perfect shall *r.* in the land.
Eccl. 2. 9, my wisdom *r.* with me.
Jer. 17. 25, this city shall *r.* for ever.
37. 10, there *r.* but wounded men.
Lam. 2. 22, in day of anger none *r.*
Mat. 11. 23, would have *r.* until this day.
John 6. 12, gather up the fragments that *r.*
9. 41, ye say, we see, therefore your sin *r.*
Acts 5. 4, whiles it *r.*, was it not thine own?
1 Cor. 15. 6, the greater part *r.* to this present.
1 Thes. 4. 15, we which are alive and *r.* unto coming of the Lord. R. V. are left.
Heb. 4. 9, there *r.* a rest to the people of God.
10. 26, there *r.* no more sacrifice for sins.
Rev. 3. 2, things which *r.* ready to die.
See Ps. 76. 10; Lam. 5. 19; John 1. 33; 1 John 3. 9.

Remaliah, rĕm-ă-lī'-ăh, 'Jehovah adorned.' 2 Kn. 15. 25.

Remedy. 2 Chr. 36. 16; Prov. 6. 15; 29. 1.

Remember. Gen. 40. 23, yet did not the butler *r.*
41. 9, I do *r.* my faults this day.
Ex. 13. 3, *r.* this day ye came out of Egypt.
20. 8, *r.* the sabbath day.
Num. 15. 39, *r.* all the commandments.
Deu. 5. 15; 15. 15; 16. 12; 24. 18, 22, *r.* thou wast a servant.
8. 2, *r.* all the way the Lord led thee.
32. 7, *r.* the days of old.
1 Chr. 16. 12, *r.* his marvellous works.
Neh. 13. 14, *r.* me, O God, concerning this.
Job 7. 7, O *r.* my life is wind.
11. 16, *r.* it as waters that pass away.
14. 13, appoint me a set time and *r.* me.
24. 20, the sinner shall be no more *r.*
Ps. 9. 12, when he maketh inquisition he *r.*
20. 7, we will *r.* the name of the Lord. R. V. make mention of.
25. 6, *r.* thy mercies, they have been ever of old.
25. 7, *r.* not sins of my youth, by mercy *r.* me.
63. 6, when I *r.* thee upon my bed.
77. 3, I *r.* God and was troubled.
78. 39, he *r.* that they were but flesh.
79. 8, *r.* not against us former iniquities.
89. 47, *r.* how short my time is.
105. 8, he hath *r.* his covenant for ever.
119. 55, I have *r.* thy name in the night.
136. 23, who *r.* us in our low estate.
137. 1, we wept when we *r.* Zion.
Prov. 31. 7, drink and *r.* his misery no more.
Eccl. 5. 20, not much *r.* the days of his life.
11. 8, let him *r.* the days of darkness.
12. 1, *r.* now thy Creator.
S. of S. 1. 4, we will *r.* thy love. R. V. make mention of.
Isa. 23. 16, sing songs that thou mayest be *r.*
43. 18; 46. 9, *r.* ye not the former things.
57. 11, thou hast not *r.* me.
65. 17, the former heavens shall not be *r.*
Jer. 31. 20, I do earnestly *r.* him still.
51. 50, ye that have escaped *r.* the Lord.
Lam. 1. 9, she *r.* not her last end.
Ezek. 16. 61; 20. 43; 36. 31, then shalt thou *r.* thy ways.
Am. 1. 9, and *r.* not the brotherly covenant.
Hab. 3. 2, in wrath *r.* mercy.
Zec. 10. 9, they shall *r.* me in far countries.
Mat. 26. 75, Peter *r.* the word of Jesus.
Lu. 16. 25, son, *r.* that thou in thy lifetime.
17. 32, *r.* Lot's wife.
23. 42, Lord, *r.* me when thou comest.
24. 8, and they *r.* his words.
John 2. 22, when he was risen, they *r.*
15. 20, *r.* the word I said unto you.
Acts 11. 16, then *r.* I the word of the Lord.
20. 35, *r.* the words of the Lord Jesus.
Gal. 2. 10, that we should *r.* the poor.
Col. 4. 18, *r.* my bonds.
1 Thes. 1. 3, *r.* your work of faith.
Heb. 13. 3, *r.* them that are in bonds.
13. 7, *r.* them that have the rule over you.
Rev. 2. 5, *r.* from whence thou art fallen.
3. 3, *r.* how thou hast received.
See Ps. 88. 5; 103. 14; Mat. 5. 23; John 16. 21.

Remembrance. Num. 5. 15, bringing iniquity to *r.*
2 Sam. 18. 18, no son to keep my name in *r.*
1 Kn. 17. 18, art thou come to call my sin to *r.*
Job 18. 17, his *r.* shall perish.
Ps. 6. 5, in death there is no *r.* of thee.
30. 4; 97. 12, give thanks at *r.* of his holiness. R. V. to his holy name.
77. 6, I call to *r.* my song in the night.
112. 6, righteous shall be in everlasting *r.*
Eccl. 1. 11, there is no *r.* of former things.
2. 16, no *r.* of wise more than the fool.
Isa. 43. 26, put me in *r.*
57. 8, behind doors hast thou set up thy *r.* R. V. memorial.
Lam. 3. 20, my soul hath them still in *r.*
Ezek. 23. 19, calling to *r.* days of youth. R. V. remembering.
Mal. 3. 16, a book of *r.*
Lu. 22. 19; 1 Cor. 11. 24, this do in *r.* of me.
John 14. 26, bring all things to your *r.*
Acts 10. 31, thine alms are had in *r.*
2 Tim. 1. 3, I have *r.* of thee in my prayers.
2. 14, of these things put them in *r.*
See Heb. 10. 3; 2 Pet. 1. 12; 3. 1; Jude 5; Rev. 16. 19.

Remeth, rĕm'-ĕth, 'a high place.' Jos. 19. 21.

Remission of sins. Mat. 26. 28; Mk. 1. 4; Lu. 24. 47; Acts 2. 38; 10. 43; Heb. 9. 22; 10. 18.

Remit. John 20. 23, whose soever sins ye *r.*, are *r.*

Remmon, rĕm'-mŏn, more correctly spelt Rimmon. Jos. 19. 7.

Remmon-methoar, rĕm'-mŏn-mĕ-thō'-ăr, '*R.* reaching (to Neah).' Jos. 19. 13.

Remnant. Lev. 5. 13, the *r.* shall be the priest's.
2 Kn. 19. 4; Isa. 37. 4, lift up prayer for the *r.*
Ez. 9. 8, grace shewed to leave us a *r.*
Isa. 1. 9, unless the Lord had left a *r.*
11. 11, to recover the *r.* of his people.
16. 14, the *r.* shall be very small and feeble.
Jer. 44. 28, *r.* shall know whose words shall stand.
Ezek. 6. 8, yet will I leave a *r.*
Joel 2. 32, the *r.* whom the Lord shall call.
See Mic. 2. 12; Hag. 1. 12; Rom. 11. 5; Rev. 11. 13.

Remove. Deu. 19. 14, shall not *r.* landmark.
Job 9. 5, *r.* the mountains and they know not.
14. 18, the rock is *r.* out of his place.
Ps. 36. 11, let not hand of wicked *r.* me. R. V. drive me away.
39. 10, *r.* thy stroke away from me.
46. 2, not fear though the earth be *r.* R. V. do change.
81. 6, I *r.* his shoulder from burden.
103. 12, so far hath he *r.* our transgressions.
119. 22, *r.* from me reproach. R. V. take away.

Ps. 125. 1, as mount Zion, which cannot be *r*. R. V. moved.
Prov. 4. 27, *r*. thy foot from evil.
10. 30, the righteous shall never be *r*.
Eccl. 11. 10, *r*. sorrow from thy heart.
Isa. 13. 13, earth shall *r*. out of her place. R. V. be shaken.
24. 20, earth shall be *r*. like a cottage. R. V. moved to and fro.
29. 13, have *r*. their heart far from me.
54. 10, the hills shall be *r*.
Jer. 4. 1, return unto me, then shalt thou not *r*.
Lam. 3. 17, thou hast *r*. my soul from peace.
Mat. 17. 20, ye shall say, *r*. hence, and it shall *r*.
Lu. 22. 42, *r*. this cup from me.
Gal. 1. 6, I marvel ye are so soon *r*.
Rev. 2. 5, or else I will *r*. thy candlestick. R. V. move. [27.
See Job 19. 10; Eccl. 10. 9; Ezek. 12. 3; Heb. 12.
Remphan, rĕm′-phăn. R. V. Rephan. Acts 7. 43.
Rend. 1 Kn. 11. 11, I will *r*. the kingdom.
Isa. 64. 1, that thou wouldest *r*. the heavens.
Hos. 13. 8, I will *r*. the caul of their heart.
Joel 2. 13, *r*. your heart.
Mat. 7. 6, lest they turn again and *r*. you.
See Ps. 7. 2; Eccl. 3. 7; John 19. 24.
Render. Deu. 32. 41, *r*. vengeance.
1 Sam. 26. 23, *r*. to every man his faithfulness.
Job 33. 26, he will *r*. to man his righteousness. R. V. restoreth.
34. 11, the work of a man shall be *r*. to him.
Ps. 28. 4, *r*. to them their desert.
38. 20, they that *r*. evil for good.
79. 12, and *r*. to our neighbour sevenfold.
94. 2, *r*. a reward to the proud.
116. 12, what shall I *r*. to the Lord. [ing.
Prov. 24. 12; Rom. 2. 6, *r*. to every man accord-
26. 16, wiser than seven men who can *r*. a reason.
Hos. 14. 2, so will we *r*. the calves of our lips.
Joel 3. 4, will ye *r*. me a recompence?
Zec. 9. 12, I will *r*. double.
Mat. 21. 41, *r*. fruits in their seasons.
22. 21; Mk. 12. 17; Lu. 20. 25, *r*. unto Cæsar.
Rom. 13. 7, *r*. to all their dues.
1 Thes. 3. 9, what thanks can we *r*.
5. 15, see that none *r*. evil for evil.
1 Pet. 3. 9, not *r*. evil for evil, or railing.
See Num. 18. 9; Jud. 9. 56; Ps. 62. 12; Isa. 66. 6.
Rending the clothes, Gen. 37. 34; 2 Sam. 13. 19; 2 Chr. 34. 27; Ez. 9. 5; Job 1. 20; 2. 12; Joel 2. 13.
by the high priest, Mat. 26. 65; Mk. 14. 63.
Renew. Job 10. 17, thou *r*. thy witnesses.
29. 20, my bow was *r*. in my hand.
Ps. 51. 10, and *r*. a right spirit within me.
103. 5, thy youth is *r*. like the eagle's.
104. 30, thou *r*. the face of the earth.
Isa. 40. 31, wait on Lord shall *r*. strength.
41. 1, let the people *r*. their strength.
Lam. 5. 21, *r*. our days as of old.
2 Cor. 4. 16, the inward man is *r*. day by day.
Eph. 4. 23, be *r*. in spirit of your mind.
Col. 3. 10, new man which is *r*. in knowledge.
Heb. 6. 6, if they fall away, to *r*. them again.
See 2 Chr. 15. 8; Rom. 12. 2; Tit. 3. 5.
Renounced. 2 Cor. 4. 2, have *r*. hidden things.
Renown. Gen. 6. 4; Num. 16. 2, men of *r*.
Num. 1. 16, the *r*. of the congregation. R. V. they that were called.
Isa. 14. 20, evildoers shall never be *r*. R. V. not be named for ever.
Ezek. 16. 14, thy *r*. went forth among the heathen.
34. 29, a plant of *r*.
See Ezek. 23. 23; 26. 17; 39. 13; Dan. 9. 15.
Rent. Gen. 37. 33, Joseph is *r*. in pieces.
Jos. 9. 4, bottles old and *r*.
Jud. 14. 5, 6, *r*. lion as he would have *r*. a kid.
1 Kn. 13. 3, the altar shall be *r*.
Job 26. 8, the cloud is not *r*. under them.
Mat. 9. 16; Mk. 2. 21, the *r*. is made worse.
27. 51; Mk. 15. 38; Lu. 23. 45, vail was *r*. in twain.
See 1 Sam. 15. 27; Job 1. 20; 2. 12; Jer. 36. 24.

Repaid. Prov. 13. 21, to righteous good shall be *r*. R. V. recompensed with good.
Repair. 2 Chr. 24. 5, gather money to *r*. the house.
Isa. 61. 4, they shall *r*. the waste cities.
See 2 Kn. 12. 5; Ez. 9. 9; Neh. 3. 4; Isa. 58. 12.
Repay. Deu. 7. 10, he will *r*. to his face.
Lu. 10. 35, when I come I will *r*. thee.
Rom. 12. 19, vengeance is mine, I will *r*.
Philem. 19, I have written it, I will *r*. it.
See Job 21. 31; 41. 11; Isa. 59. 18. [harpeth on.
Repeateth. Prov. 17. 9, he that *r*. a matter. R. V.
Repent. Gen. 6. 6, it *r*. the Lord.
Ex. 13. 17, lest the people *r*.
32. 14; 2 Sam. 24. 16; 1 Chr. 21. 15; Jer. 26. 19, Lord *r*. of evil he thought to do.
Num. 23. 19, neither son of man that he should *r*.
Deu. 32. 36, Lord shall *r*. for his servants.
1 Sam. 15. 29, will not *r*., for he is not a man that he should *r*.
Job 42. 6, I *r*. in dust and ashes.
Ps. 90. 13, let it *r*. thee concerning thy servants.
106. 45, Lord *r*. according to his mercies.
110. 4; Heb. 7. 21, Lord hath sworn and will not *r*.
Jer. 8. 6, no man *r*. of his wickedness.
18. 8; 26. 13, if that nation turn I will *r*.
31. 19, after that I was turned I *r*.
Joel 2. 13, he is slow to anger and *r*. him.
Mat. 12. 41; Lu. 11. 32, they *r*. at the preaching.
21. 29, afterward he *r*. and went.
27. 3, Judas *r*. himself.
Lu. 13. 3, except ye *r*.
15. 7, joy over one sinner that *r*.
17. 3, if thy brother *r*., forgive him.
Acts 8. 22, *r*. of this thy wickedness.
Rev. 2. 21, space to *r*., and she *r*. not.
Repentance. Hos. 13. 14, *r*. shall be hid.
Mat. 3. 8; Lu. 3. 8; Acts 26. 20, fruits meet for *r*.
Rom. 2. 4, goodness of God leadeth thee to *r*.
11. 29, gifts of God are without *r*.
2 Cor. 7. 10, *r*. not to be repented of.
Heb. 6. 1, not laying again the foundation of *r*.
6. 6, to renew them again to *r*.
12. 17, no place of *r*., though he sought it.
See Acts 20. 21; 2 Tim. 2. 25; 2 Pet. 3. 9.
Repentance preached by John the Baptist. Mat. 3.; Mk. 1. 4; Lu. 3. 3.
by JESUS CHRIST. Mat. 4. 17; Mk. 1. 15; 6. 12; Lu. 13. 3; 15.; 24. 47; Acts 2. 38; 3. 19; 17. 30.
exhortations to. Job 11. 13; Isa. 1.; Jer. 3.–5.; 26.; 31. 18; Ezek. 14. 6; 18.; Hos. 6.; 12.; 14.; Joel 1. 8; 2.; Zep. 2.; Zec. 1.; Mal. 1.–4.; Rev. 2. 5, 16, 21; 3. 3, 19.
Repetitions, vain, forbidden. Mat. 6. 7. *See* 1 Kn. 18. 26.
Rephael, rĕph′-ā-ĕl, 'God has healed.' 1 Chr. 26. 7.
Rephah, rē′-phăh, 'riches.' 1 Chr. 7. 25.
Rephaiah, rĕ-phāī′-ăh, 'Jehovah has healed.' 1 Chr. 3. 21.
Rephaim, rĕph′-ā-ĭm, 'giants.' 2 Sam. 5. 18.
Rephaims, rĕph′-ā-ĭms, same as REPHAIM. Gen. 14. 5.
Rephidim, rĕph′-ĭ-dĭm, 'expanses,' 'stretches.' The camping ground of Israel between the wilderness of Sin and Sinai (Ex. 17. 1). Here the rock brought forth water (Ex. 17. 5, 6), and the battle with the Amalekites was fought (Ex. 17. 8–16).
Replenish. Gen. 1. 28; 9. 1; Jer. 31. 25; Ezek. 26. 2.
Repliest. Rom. 9. 20, that *r*. against God.
Report (*n*.). Gen. 37. 2, their evil *r*.?
Ex. 23. 1, thou shalt not *r*. a false *r*.
Num. 13. 32, an evil *r*. of the land.
1 Sam. 2. 24, it is no good *r*. I hear.
1 Kn. 10. 6; 2 Chr. 9. 5, it was a true *r*. I heard.
Prov. 15. 30, good *r*. maketh the bones fat. R. V. tidings.
Isa. 28. 19, a vexation only to understand *r*. R. V. message.

Isa. 53. 1, who hath believed our *r.*?
Acts 6. 3, men of honest *r.*
10. 22, of good *r.* among the Jews.
2 Cor. 6. 8, by evil *r.* and good *r.*
Phil. 4. 8, whatsoever things are of good *r.*
1 Tim. 3. 7, a bishop must have a good *r.* R. V. testimony.
See Deu. 2. 25; Heb. 11. 2, 39; 3 John 12.

Report (*v.*). Neh. 6. 6, it is *r.* among heathen.
Jer. 20. 10, *r.*, say they, and we will *r.* it. R. V. denounce.
Mat. 28. 15, saying is commonly *r.* R. V. was spread abroad.
Acts 16. 2, well *r.* of by the brethren.
1 Cor. 14. 25, he will *r.* that God is in you. R. V. declaring.
See Ezek. 9. 11; Rom. 3. 8; 1 Tim. 5. 10; 1 Pet. 1. 12.

Reproach (*n.*). Gen. 30. 23, hath taken away my *r.*
34. 14, that were a *r.* to us.
1 Sam. 11. 2, lay it for a *r.* upon all Israel.
Neh. 2. 17, build that we be no more a *r.*
Ps. 15. 3, that taketh not up a *r.*
22. 6, a *r.* of men.
31. 11, I was a *r.* among mine enemies.
44. 13; 79. 4; 89. 41, a *r.* to our neighbours.
69. 9; Rom. 15. 3, the *r.* of them that reproached thee.
78. 66, put them to a perpetual *r.*
Prov. 6. 33, his *r.* shall not be wiped away.
14. 34, sin is a *r.* to any people.
18. 3, with ignominy cometh *r.*
Isa. 43. 28, I have given Israel to *r.* R. V. revilings.
51. 7, fear not the *r.* of men.
Jer. 23. 40, I will bring an everlasting *r.*
31. 19, I did bear the *r.* of my youth.
Lam. 3. 30, he is filled full with *r.*
Ezek. 5. 14, I will make thee a *r.* among nations.
5. 15, Jerusalem shall be a *r.* and a taunt.
Mic. 6. 16, ye shall bear the *r.* of my people.
2 Cor. 11. 21, I speak as concerning *r.* R. V. by way of disparagement.
12. 10, pleasure in *r.* for Christ's sake. R. V. injuries.
1 Tim. 3. 7, good report lest he fall into *r.*
4. 10, we labour and suffer *r.* R. V. strive.
Heb. 11. 26, the *r.* of Christ greater riches.
13. 13, without the camp bearing his *r.*
See Ps. 69. 10; 119. 39; Jer. 6. 10; 20. 8; 24. 9.

Reproach (*v.*). Num. 15. 30, *r.* the Lord. R. V. blasphemeth.
Ru. 2. 15, *r.* her not.
2 Kn. 19. 22; Isa. 37. 23, whom hast thou *r.*
Job 19. 3, these ten times have ye *r.* me.
27. 6, my heart shall not *r.* me.
Ps. 42. 10, as with a sword mine enemies *r.* me.
44. 16, the voice of him that *r.*
74. 22, how the foolish man *r.* thee.
119. 42; Prov. 27. 11, to answer him that *r.* me.
Prov. 14. 31; 17. 5, oppresseth poor *r.* his Maker.
Lu. 6. 22, men shall *r.* you for my sake.
1 Pet. 4. 14, if ye be *r.* for Christ's sake.
See Ps. 55. 12; 74. 18; 79. 12; 89. 51; Zep. 2. 8.

Reproachfully. Job 16. 10; 1 Tim. 5. 14.

Reprobate. Jer. 6. 30; Rom. 1. 28; 2 Tim. 3. 8; Tit. 1. 16. *See* 2 Cor. 13. 5.

Reproof. Prov. 6. 23; 13. 18; 15. 5, 31; 17. 10; 19. 25; 25. 12; 27. 5; 29. 15; Eccl. 7. 5; Eph. 5. 13; 2 Tim. 3. 16.
necessary. Lev. 19. 17; Isa. 58. 1; Ezek. 2. 3; 33.; 2 Thes. 3. 15; 1 Tim. 5. 20; 2 Tim. 4. 2; Tit. 1. 13; 2. 15.
beneficial. Ps. 141. 5; Prov. 9. 8; 10. 17; 15. 5; 24. 25.
not to be despised. Prov. 1. 25; 5. 12; 10. 17; 12. 1; 15. 10; 29. 1.

Reprove. (1) 1 Chr. 16. 21, *r.* kings for their sakes.
Job 13. 10, he will *r.* you if ye accept.
22. 4, will he *r.* thee for fear.
40. 2, he that *r.* God let him answer it. R. V. argueth with.
Ps. 50. 8, I will not *r.* thee for burnt offerings.
Ps. 141. 5, let him *r.* me, it shall be excellent oil.
Prov. 9. 8, *r.* not a scorner lest he hate thee.
15. 12, a scorner loveth not one that *r.*
19. 25, *r.* one that hath understanding.
29. 1, he that being often *r.*
30. 6, lest he *r.* thee and thou be found.
Isa. 11. 4, *r.* with equity for the meek.
Jer. 2. 19, thy backslidings shall *r.* thee.
John 3. 20, lest his deeds should be *r.*
16. 8, he will *r.* the world of sin. R. V. convict.
(2) to refute, to disprove, prove to be wrong, Job 6. 25.

Reprover. Prov. 25. 12; Ezek. 3. 26.

Reptiles and Amphibia of the Bible.

Adder.	Gecko.
Asp.	Leviathan.
Chameleon.	Lizard.
Cockatrice.	Serpent.
Crocodile.	Toad.
Dabba.	Tortoise.
Dragon.	Viper.
Frog.	

Reputation. Eccl. 10. 1, folly him that is in *r.* for wisdom. R. V. folly outweigh wisdom.
Acts 5. 34, had in *r.* among the people. R. V. honour of.
Phil. 2. 7, made himself of no *r.* R. V. emptied himself.
2. 29, hold such in *r.* R. V. honour.
See Job 18. 3; Dan. 4. 35; Gal. 2. 2.

Request. Jud. 8. 24, I would desire a *r.* of thee.
Ez. 7. 6, the king granted all his *r.*
Job 6. 8, Oh that I might have my *r.*
Ps. 21. 2, hast not withholden *r.* of his lips.
106. 15, he gave them their *r.*
Phil. 1. 4, in every prayer making *r.* with joy. R. V. my supplication.
4. 6, let your *r.* be made known.
See 2 Sam. 14. 15; Neh. 2. 4; Esth. 4. 8; 5. 3.

Requested. 1 Kn. 19. 4, Elijah *r.* that he might die.

Require. Gen. 9. 5, blood of your lives will I *r.*
31. 39, of my hand didst thou *r.* it.
Deu. 10. 12; Mic. 6. 8, what doth the Lord *r.*
Jos. 22. 23; 1 Sam. 20. 16, let the Lord himself *r.* it.
Ru. 3. 11, I will do all thou *r.* R. V. sayest.
1 Sam. 21. 8, the king's business *r.* haste.
2 Sam. 3. 13, one thing I *r.* of thee.
19. 38, whatsoever thou shalt *r.* I will do.
2 Chr. 24. 22, the Lord look on it and *r.* it.
Neh. 5. 12, we will restore and *r.* nothing of them.
Ps. 10. 13, he hath said thou wilt not *r.* it.
40. 6, sin offering hast thou not *r.*
137. 3, they that wasted us *r.* of us mirth.
Prov. 30. 7, two things have I *r.* of thee.
Eccl. 3. 15, God *r.* that which is past. R. V. seeketh again.
Isa. 1. 12, who hath *r.* this at your hand?
Ezek. 3. 18; 33. 6, his blood will I *r.* at thine hand.
34. 10, I will *r.* my flock at their hand.
Lu. 11. 50, may be *r.* of this generation.
12. 20, this night thy soul shall be *r.*
12. 48, of him shall much be *r.*
19. 23, I might have *r.* mine own with usury.
1 Cor. 1. 22, the Jews *r.* a sign. R. V. ask for.
4. 2, it is *r.* in stewards.
See 2 Chr. 8. 14; Ez. 3. 4; Neh. 5. 18; Esth. 2. 15.

Requite. Gen. 50. 15, Joseph will certainly *r.* us.
Deu. 32. 6, do ye thus *r.* the Lord.
Jud. 1. 7, as I have done so God hath *r.* me.
2 Sam. 2. 6, I also will *r.* you this kindness.
16. 12, it may be the Lord will *r.* good for this.
1 Tim. 5. 4, learn to *r.* their parents.
See Ps. 10. 14; 41. 10; Jer. 51. 56.

Rereward, rear-guard (*lit.* rear-ward). Jos. 6. 9; Isa. 52. 12; 58. 8.

Rescue. Ps. 35. 17, *r.* my soul.
Hos. 5. 14, none shall *r.* him. R. V. deliver.
See Deu. 28. 31; 1 Sam. 14. 45; Dan. 6. 27; Acts 23. 27.

Resemblance. Zec. 5. 6, this is their *r.*
Resemble. Jud. 8. 18; Lu. 13. 18.
Resen, rē′-sĕn, 'bridle.' Gen. 10. 12.
Reserve. Gen. 27. 36, hast thou not *r.* a blessing.
Ru. 2. 18, gave her mother in law that she had *r.* R. V. left.
Job 21. 30, the wicked is *r.* to day of destruction.
38. 23, which I have *r.* against time of trouble.
Jer. 3. 5, will he *r.* anger for ever? R. V. retain.
5. 24, he *r.* the weeks of harvest.
50. 20, I will pardon them whom I *r.* R. V. leave as a remnant.
Nah. 1. 2, the Lord *r.* wrath for his enemies.
1 Pet. 1. 4, an inheritance *r.* in heaven.
2 Pet. 2. 4, to be *r.* to judgment.
3. 7, the heavens and earth are *r.* unto fire.
See Num. 18. 9; Rom. 11. 4; 2 Pet. 2. 9; Jude 6, 13.
Resheph, rē′-shĕph, 'flame.' 1 Chr. 7. 25.
Residue, the rest, the remainder. Ex. 10. 5, locusts shall eat the *r.*
Isa. 38. 10, I am deprived of the *r.* of my years.
Jer. 15. 9, *r.* of them will I deliver to the sword.
Ezek. 9. 8, wilt thou destroy all the *r.*
Zec. 8. 11, I will not be to the *r.* as in former days. R. V. remnant.
Mal. 2. 15, yet had he the *r.* of the Spirit.
Acts 15. 17, that the *r.* might seek the Lord.
See Neh. 11. 20; Jer. 8. 3; 29. 1; 39. 3.
Resist. Zec. 3. 1, at his right hand to *r.*
Mat. 5. 39, *r.* not evil.
Lu. 21. 15, adversaries shall not be able to *r.* R. V. withstand.
Rom. 9. 19, who hath *r.* his will. R. V. withstandeth.
13. 2, whoso *r.* power, *r.* ordinance of God. R. V. withstand.
Jas. 4. 6; 1 Pet. 5. 5, God *r.* the proud.
4. 7, *r.* the devil, and he will flee.
1 Pet. 5. 9, whom *r.* stedfast in the faith. R. V. withstand.
See Acts 6. 10; 7. 51; 2 Tim. 3. 8; Heb. 12. 4.
Resort. Neh. 4. 20, *r.* hither to us.
Ps. 71. 3, whereunto I may continually *r.*
John 18. 2, Jesus ofttimes *r.* thither.
See Mk. 2. 13; 10. 1; John 18. 20; Acts 16. 13.
Respect (*n.*). Gen. 4. 4, Lord had *r.* to Abel.
Ex. 2. 25, God had *r.* unto them. R. V. took knowledge of.
1 Kn. 8. 28; 2 Chr. 6. 19, have *r.* unto their prayer.
2 Chr. 19. 7; Rom. 2. 11; Eph. 6. 9; Col. 3. 25, there is no *r.* of persons with God.
Ps. 74. 20, have *r.* unto thy covenant.
119. 15, I will have *r.* unto thy ways.
138. 6, yet hath he *r.* to the lowly.
Prov. 24. 23; 28. 31, not good to have *r.* of persons.
Isa. 17. 7, his eyes shall have *r.* to Holy One.
22. 11, nor had *r.* to him that fashioned it.
Phil. 4. 11, not that I speak in *r.* of want.
See Heb. 11. 26; Jas. 2. 1, 3, 9; 1 Pet. 1. 17.
Respect (*v.*). Lev. 19. 15, shalt not *r.* person of poor.
Deu. 1. 17, ye shall not *r.* persons in judgment.
Job 37. 24, he *r.* not any that are wise of heart. R. V. regardeth.
See Num. 16. 15; 2 Sam. 14. 14; Ps. 40. 4; Lam. 4. 16.
Respite. Ex. 8. 15; 1 Sam. 11. 3.
Rest (*n.*). Gen. 49. 15, Issachar saw that *r.* was good. R. V. a resting place.
Ex. 31. 15; 35. 2; Lev. 16. 31; 23. 3, 32; 25. 4, the sabbath of *r.*
33. 14, my presence shall go with thee, and I will give thee *r.*
Lev. 25. 5, a year of *r.* to the land.
Deu. 12. 10, when he giveth you *r.* from your enemies.
Jud. 3. 30, the land had *r.* fourscore years.
Ru. 3. 1, shall not I seek *r.* for thee.
1 Chr. 22. 9, a man of *r.*, and I will give him *r.*
22. 18, hath he not given you *r.* on every side?
1 Chr. 28. 2, to build a house of *r.*
Neh. 9. 28, after they had *r.* they did evil.
Esth. 9. 16, the Jews had *r.* from their enemies.
Job 3. 17, there the weary be at *r.*
11. 18, thou shalt take thy *r.* in safety.
17. 16, when our *r.* together is in the dust.
Ps. 55. 6, then would I fly away and be at *r.*
95. 11; Heb. 3. 11, not enter into my *r.*
116. 7, return to thy *r.*, O my soul.
132. 8, arise into thy *r.* R. V. resting place.
132. 14, this is my *r.* for ever. R. V. resting place.
Eccl. 2. 23, his heart taketh not *r.* in the night.
Isa. 11. 10, his *r.* shall be glorious.
14. 7; Zec. 1. 11, earth is at *r.* and quiet.
18. 4, I will take my *r.* R. V. be still.
30. 15, in returning and *r.* shall ye be saved.
66. 1, where is the place of my *r.*?
Jer. 6. 16, ye shall find *r.* for your souls.
Ezek. 38. 11, I will go to them that are at *r.* R. V. quiet.
Mic. 2. 10, depart, this is not your *r.*
Mat. 11. 28, I will give you *r.*
11. 29, ye shall find *r.* to your souls.
12. 43; Lu. 11. 24, seeking *r.* and finding none.
26. 45; Mk. 14. 41, sleep on and take your *r.*
John 11. 13, of taking *r.* in sleep.
Acts 9. 31. then had the churches *r.*
See Prov. 29. 17; Eccl. 6. 5; Dan. 4. 4; 2 Thes. 1. 7.
Rest (*v.*). Gen. 2. 2, he *r.* on seventh day.
Num. 11. 25, when the Spirit *r.* upon them.
2 Chr. 32. 8, people *r.* on the words.
Job 3. 18, there the prisoners *r.* together. R. V. are at ease.
Ps. 16. 9; Acts 2. 26, my flesh shall *r.* in hope. R. V. dwell.
37. 7, *r.* in the Lord.
Eccl. 7. 9, anger *r.* in bosom of fools.
Isa. 11. 2, the spirit of the Lord shall *r.* upon him.
28. 12, ye may cause the weary to *r.*
57. 20, like the sea when it cannot *r.*
62. 1, for Jerusalem's sake I will not *r.*
63. 14, Spirit of the Lord caused him to *r.*
Jer. 47. 6, *r.* and be still.
Dan. 12. 13, thou shalt *r.* and stand in thy lot.
Mk. 6. 31, come and *r.* awhile.
2 Cor. 12. 9, power of Christ may *r.* on me.
Rev. 4. 8, they *r.* not day and night.
6. 11, *r.* yet for a little season.
14. 13, that they may *r.* from their labours.
See Prov. 14. 33; S. of S. 1. 7; Isa. 32. 18; Lu. 10. 6.
Rest, future, promised. Heb. 3. 11; 4. *See* Isa. 11. 10; 14. 3; 30. 15; Jer. 6. 16; Mat. 11. 28.
Restitution, Ex. 22. 1; Lev. 5. 16; 6. 4; 24. 21; Num. 5. 5 (Lu. 19. 8). times of, Acts 3. 21.
Restore. Ex. 22. 4, he shall *r.* double.
Lev. 6. 4, he shall *r.* that he took away.
Deu. 22. 2, things strayed thou shalt *r.* again.
Ps. 23. 3, he *r.* my soul.
51. 12, *r.* to me the joy of thy salvation.
69. 4, I *r.* that which I took not away.
Isa. 1. 26, I will *r.* thy judges as at the first.
Jer. 27. 22, I will *r.* them to this place.
30. 17, I will *r.* health to thee.
Ezek. 33. 15, if wicked *r.* pledge.
Mat. 17. 11; Mk. 9. 12, Elias shall *r.* all things.
Lu. 19. 8, I *r.* him fourfold.
Acts 1. 6, wilt thou at this time *r.* the kingdom.
Gal. 6. 1. *r.* such an one in meekness.
See Ru. 4. 15; Isa. 58. 12; Joel 2. 25; Mk. 8. 25.
Restrain. Gen. 11. 6, nothing will be *r.* R. V. withholden.
Ex. 36. 6, people were *r.* from bringing.
1 Sam. 3. 13, his sons made themselves vile, and he *r.* them not.
Job 15. 4, thou *r.* prayer before God.
15. 8, dost thou *r.* wisdom to thyself?
Ps. 76. 10, remainder of wrath shalt thou *r.* R. V. gird upon thee.
See Gen. 8. 2; Isa. 63. 15; Ezek. 31. 15; Acts 14. 18.
Resurrection of the body foretold. Job 19. 26;

Ps. 17. 15; Isa. 26. 19; Dan. 12. 2. typical, Ezek. 37.
proclaimed by Christ. Mat. 22. 31; Lu. 14. 14; John 5. 28; 11. 23.
preached by the apostles. Acts 4. 2; 17. 18; 24. 15; 26. 8; Rom. 6. 5; 8. 11; 1 Cor. 15.; 2 Cor. 4. 14; Phil. 3. 20; Col. 3. 3; 1 Thes. 4. 15; 5. 23; Heb. 6. 2; 2 Pet. 1. 11; 1 John 3. 2.

Retain. Job 2. 9, dost thou still *r.* integrity? R. V. hold fast.
Prov. 3. 18, happy is every one that *r.* her.
4. 4, let thine heart *r.* my words.
11. 16, a gracious woman *r.* honour.
Eccl. 8. 8, no man hath power to *r.* the spirit.
John 20. 23, whose soever sins ye *r.* they are *r.*
See Mic. 7. 18; Rom. 1. 28; Philem. 13.

Retire. Jud. 20. 39; 2 Sam. 11. 15; Jer. 4. 6.

Return. Gen. 3. 19, to dust shalt thou *r.*
Ex. 14. 27, the sea *r.* to his strength.
Jud. 7. 3, whosoever is fearful, let him *r.*
Ru. 1. 16, entreat me not to leave thee or
2 Sam. 12. 23, he shall not *r.* to me.
2 Kn. 20. 10, let the shadow *r.* backward.
Job 1. 21, naked shall I *r.* thither.
7. 10, he shall *r.* no more.
10. 21; 16. 22, I go whence I shall not *r.*
15. 22, he believeth not he shall *r.* out of darkness.
33. 25, he shall *r.* to the days of his youth.
Ps. 35. 13, my prayer *r.* into mine own bosom.
73. 10, his people *r.* hither.
90. 3, thou sayest, *r.*, ye children of men.
104. 29, they die and *r.* to their dust.
116. 7, *r.* to thy rest, O my soul.
Prov. 2. 19, none that go to her *r.* again.
26. 11, as a dog *r.* to his vomit.
26. 27, he that rolleth a stone, it will *r.*
Eccl. 1. 7, whence rivers come, thither they *r.* again. R. V. go.
5. 15, naked shall he *r.* to go as he came. R. V. go again.
12. 2, nor the clouds *r.* after the rain.
12. 7, dust *r.* to earth and spirit *r.* to God.
Isa. 21. 12, *r.*, come. R. V. turn ye.
35. 10; 51. 11, the ransomed of the Lord shall *r.*
44. 22, *r.* unto me, for I have redeemed thee.
45. 23, word is gone out and shall not *r.*
55. 11, it shall not *r.* to me void.
Jer. 4. 1, if thou wilt *r.*, saith the Lord, *r.* unto me.
15. 19, let them *r.* unto thee, but *r.* not thou.
24. 7, they shall *r.* with whole heart.
31. 8, a great company shall *r.* thither.
36. 3, *r.* every man from his evil way.
Ezek. 46. 9, he shall not *r.* by the way he came.
Hos. 2. 7, I will *r.* to my first husband.
5. 15, I will *r.* to my place.
7. 16, they *r.*, but not to the most High.
14. 7, they that dwell under his shadow shall *r.*
Am. 4. 6, yet have ye not *r.* to me.
Joel 2. 14, who knoweth if he will *r.* and repent. R. V. not turn.
Zec. 1. 16, I am *r.* to Jerusalem with mercies.
8. 3, I am *r.* to Zion and will dwell.
Mal. 3. 7, *r.* to me and I will *r.* to you.
3. 18, then shall ye *r.* and discern.
Mat. 12. 44; Lu. 11. 24, I will *r.* into my house.
24. 18, neither let him in the field *r.* back.
Lu. 9. 10, apostles *r.* and told him all.
10. 17, the seventy *r.* with joy.
12. 36, when he will *r.* from wedding.
17. 18, not found that *r.* to give glory.
Acts 13. 34, now no more to *r.* to corruption.
Heb. 11. 15, might have had opportunity to *r.*
1 Pet. 2. 25, now *r.* to the Shepherd of your souls.
See Gen. 31. 3; Ex. 4. 18; Lev. 25. 10; Isa. 55. 7.

Return from captivity. Ez. 1.; Neh. 2.; Jer. 16. 14; 23.; 24.; 30.; 31.; 32.; 50. 4, 17, 33; Am. 9. 14; Hag. 1.; Zec. 1.

Reu, rē'-ū, same as Raguel. Gen. 11. 18.

Reuben, reû'-bĕn, 'behold a son'(?); son of Jacob. Gen. 29.; 30.; 35.; 37.; 42.; 49.; 1 Chr. 5. 1.

Reubenites, reû'-bĕn-ītes, descendants of Reuben; their number and possessions. Num. 1.; 2.; 26.; 32.; Deu. 3. 12; Jos. 13. 15; 1 Chr. 5. 18.
dealings of Moses and Joshua with. Num. 32.; Deu. 33.; Jos. 1.; 22.
go into captivity. 1 Chr. 5. 26 (Rev. 7. 5).

Reuel, reû'-ĕl, 'friend of God.' (1) Gen. 36. 4. (2) Ex. 2. 18. (3) 1 Chr. 9. 8.

Reumah, reû'-măh, 'exalted.' Gen. 22. 24.

Reveal. Deu. 29. 29, things *r.* belong unto us and to our children.
1 Sam. 3. 7, nor was word of Lord *r.* to him.
Job 20. 27, the heaven shall *r.* his iniquity.
Prov. 11. 13; 20. 19, a talebearer *r.* secrets.
Isa. 22. 14, it was *r.* in mine ears.
40. 5, glory of the Lord shall be *r.*
53. 1; John 12. 38, to whom is arm of Lord *r.*
56. 1, my righteousness is near to be *r.*
Jer. 11. 20, unto thee have I *r.* my cause.
33. 6, I will *r.* abundance of peace.
Dan. 2. 22, he *r.* deep and secret things.
2. 28, there is a God that *r.* secrets.
Am. 3. 7, he *r.* his secrets to the prophets.
Mat. 10. 26; Lu. 12. 2, nothing covered that shall not be *r.*
11. 25, hast *r.* them unto babes.
16. 17, flesh and blood hath not *r.* it.
Lu. 2. 35, that thoughts of many hearts may be *r.*
17. 30, in day when Son of man is *r.*
Rom. 1. 17, righteousness of God *r.*
1. 18, wrath of God is *r.* from heaven.
8. 18, glory which shall be *r.* in us.
1 Cor. 2. 10, God hath *r.* them by his Spirit.
3. 13, it shall be *r.* by fire.
14. 30, if any thing be *r.* to another.
Gal. 1. 16, to *r.* his Son in me.
2 Thes. 1. 7, when Lord Jesus shall be *r.*
2. 3, man of sin be *r.*
2. 8, that wicked one be *r.*
1 Pet. 1. 5, ready to be *r.* in last time.
4. 13, when his glory shall be *r.*
5. 1, partaker of glory that shall be *r.*

Revelation. Rom. 2. 5, *r.* of righteous judgment.
16. 25, *r.* of the mystery.
1 Cor. 14. 26, every one hath a *r.* R. V. tongue.
2 Cor. 12. 1, to visions and *r.*
See Gal. 2. 2; Eph. 1. 17; 1 Pet. 1. 13.

Revelation of Jesus Christ to John. *See* book of Revelation throughout.

Revelations, merciful, from God. Deu. 29. 29; Job 33. 16; Isa. 40. 5; 53. 1; Jer. 33. 6; Dan. 2. 22; Am. 3. 7; Mat. 11. 25; 16. 17; 1 Cor. 2. 10; 2 Cor. 12.; Gal. 1. 12; Eph. 3. 9; Phil. 3. 15; 1 Pet. 1. 5; 4. 13.
wrathful. Rom. 1. 18; 2. 5; 2 Thes. 1. 7.

Revellings. Gal. 5. 21; 1 Pet. 4. 3.

Revenge. Jer. 15. 15, O Lord, *r.* me. R. V. avenge.
20. 10, we shall take our *r.* on him.
Nah. 1. 2, the Lord *r.* and is furious. R. V. avengeth.
2 Cor. 7. 11, what *r.* it wrought in you. R. V. avenging.
10. 6, in readiness to *r.* R. V. avenge.
See Ps. 79. 10; Ezek. 25. 12; Rom. 13. 4.

Revenge deprecated. Lev. 19. 18; Prov. 20. 22; 24. 29; Mat. 5. 39; Rom. 12. 19; 1 Thes. 5. 15; 1 Pet. 3. 9.

Revenue. Prov. 8. 19, my *r.* better than silver.
16. 8, better than great *r.* without right.
Jer. 12. 13, ashamed of your *r.* R. V. fruits.
See Ez. 4. 13; Prov. 15. 6; Isa. 23. 3; Jer. 12. 13.

Reverence. Mat. 21. 37; Mk. 12. 6; Heb. 12. 9.

Reverence to God. Ex. 3. 5; Ps. 89. 7; 111. 9; Heb. 12. 28.
to God's sanctuary. Lev. 19. 30.
from wives to husbands. Eph. 5. 33.

Reverend. Ps. 111. 9, holy and *r.* is his name.

Reverse. Num. 23. 20; Esth. 8. 5, 8.

Revile. Isa. 51. 7, neither be afraid of *r.*
Mat. 27. 39, they that passed by *r.* him. R. V. railed on.

Mk. 15. 32, they that were crucified *r.* him. R. V. reproached.
1 Cor. 4. 12, being *r.* we bless.
1 Pet. 2. 23, when he was *r.*, *r.* not again.
Reviling condemned. Ex. 21. 17; 22. 28; Mat. 5. 22; 1 Cor. 6. 10.
examples of enduring. Isa. 51. 7; Mat. 5. 11; 27. 39; John 9. 28; 1 Cor. 4. 12; 1 Pet. 2. 23.
Revive. Neh. 4. 2, will they *r.* the stones.
Ps. 85. 6, wilt thou not *r.* us. R. V. quicken.
138. 7, thou wilt *r.* me.
Isa. 57. 15, to *r.* spirit of the humble.
Hos. 6. 2, after two days will he *r.* us.
14. 7, they shall *r.* as corn.
Hab. 3. 2, *r.* thy work in midst of years.
Rom. 7. 9, when commandment came sin *r.*
14. 9, Christ both died, rose, and *r.*
See Gen. 45. 27; 2 Kn. 13. 21; Ez. 9. 8. R. V. lived again.
Revolt. Isa. 1. 5; 31. 6; 59. 13; Jer. 5. 23.
Revolt, instances of: cities of the plain, Gen. 14. 1. Korah, Dathan, Abiram, Num. 16. 1. Israel from Mesopotamia, Jud. 3. 9 (under Othniel). southern tribes from the Philistines, Jud. 3. 31. eastern tribes from Eglon, Jud. 3. 12. Deborah and Barak, Jud. 4. 4. southern tribes from Midian, Jud. 6.; 7.; 8. southern tribes from Ammon, Jud. 11. Samson, Jud. 15. Ishbosheth, 2 Sam. 2. 8. Abner, 2 Sam. 3. Absalom, 2 Sam. 15. 10. Adonijah, 1 Kn. 1. 5; 2. 13. Hadad and Rezon, 1 Kn. 11. 14, 23. ten tribes, 1 Kn. 12. 19; 2 Chr. 10. 19. Moab, 2 Kn. 1.; 3. 5, 7. Edom, 2 Kn. 8. 20; 2 Chr. 21. 8. Libnah, 2 Kn. 8. 22; 2 Chr. 21. 10. Jehu, 2 Kn. 9. 11. Hoshea, 2 Kn. 17. 4. Hezekiah, 2 Kn. 18. 4. Jehoiakim, 2 Kn. 24. 1. Zedekiah, 2 Kn. 24. 20; 2 Chr. 36. 13; Jer. 52. 3. Theudas, Acts 5. 36. Judas of Galilee, Acts 5. 37.
Reward (*n.*). Gen. 15. 1, thy exceeding great *r.*
Num. 22. 7, *r.* of divination in their hand.
Deu. 10. 17, God who taketh not *r.*
Ru. 2. 12, full *r.* be given thee of the Lord.
2 Sam. 4. 10, thought I would have given *r.*
Job 6. 22, did I say, give a *r.* R. V. offer a present.
7. 2, as an hireling looketh for *r.* R. V. his wages.
Ps. 19. 11, in keeping them there is great *r.*
58. 11, there is a *r.* for the righteous.
91. 8, thou shalt see the *r.* of the wicked.
127. 3, fruit of womb is his *r.*
Prov. 11. 18, soweth righteousness a sure *r.*
21. 14, a *r.* in the bosom. R. V. present.
24. 20, no *r.* to the evil man.
Eccl. 4. 9, they have a good *r.* for labour.
9. 5, neither have they any more a *r.*
Isa. 1. 23, every one followeth after *r.*
5. 23, justify wicked for *r.*
40. 10; 62. 11, his *r.* is with him.
Ezek. 16. 34, thou givest *r.*, and no *r.* is given thee. R. V. hire.
Dan. 5. 17, give thy *r.* to another.
Hos. 9. 1, thou hast loved a *r.* R. V. hire.
Mic. 3. 11, the heads thereof judge for *r.*
7. 3, judge asketh for a *r.*
Mat. 5. 12; Lu. 6. 23, great is your *r.* in heaven.
5. 46, what *r.* have ye.
6. 1, ye have no *r.* of your father.
6. 2, 5, 16, they have their *r.*
10. 41, a prophet's *r.*, a righteous man's *r.*
10. 42; Mk. 9. 41, in no wise lose *r.*
Lu. 6. 35, do good and your *r.* shall be great.
23. 41, we receive due *r.* of our deeds.
Acts 1. 18, purchased with *r.* of iniquity.
Rom. 4. 4, the *r.* is not reckoned.
1 Cor. 3. 8, every man shall receive his own *r.*
9. 18, what is my *r.* then.
Col. 2. 18, let no man beguile you of your *r.* R. V. prize.
3. 24, the *r.* of the inheritance. R. V. recompense.
1 Tim. 5. 18, labourer worthy of his *r.*
Heb. 2. 2; 10. 35; 11. 26, recompence of *r.*
2 Pet. 2. 13, the *r.* of unrighteousness. R. V. hire.
See 2 John 8.; Jude 11; Rev. 11. 18.
Reward (*v.*). Gen. 44. 4, wherefore have ye *r.*
Deu. 32. 41, I will *r.* them that hate me. R. V. recompense.
1 Sam. 24. 17, thou hast *r.* me good. R. V. rendered to.
2 Chr. 15. 7, be strong, and your work shall be *r.*
20. 11, behold how they *r.* us.
Job 21. 19, he *r.* him and he shall know it. R. V. recompensed.
Ps. 31. 23, plentifully *r.* the proud doer.
35. 12; 109. 5, they *r.* me evil for good.
103. 10, nor *r.* us according to our iniquities.
137. 8, happy is he that *r.* thee.
Prov. 17. 13, whoso *r.* evil, evil shall not depart.
25. 22, heap coals, and the Lord shall *r.* thee.
26. 10, both *r.* the fool and *r.* transgressors. R. V. hireth.
Jer. 31. 16, thy work shall be *r.*
See 2 Sam. 22. 21; 16. 27; 2 Tim. 4. 14.
Reward to the righteous. Gen. 15. 1; Ps. 19. 11; 58. 11; Prov. 11. 18; 25. 22; Mat. 5. 12; 6. 1; 10. 41; Lu. 6. 35; 1 Cor. 3. 8; Col. 2. 18; 3. 24; Heb. 10. 35; 11. 6; Rev. 22. 12.
threatened to the wicked. Deu. 32. 41; 2 Sam. 3. 39; Ps. 54. 5; 91. 8; 109.; Obad. 15; 2 Pet. 2. 13; Rev. 19. 17; 20. 15; 22. 15.
exceeding great. Gen. 15. 1.
Rezeph, rē´-zĕph, 'a stone.' 2 Kn. 19. 12.
Rezia, rē´-zī-ă, 'delight.' 1 Chr. 7. 39.
Rezin, rē´-zĭn, 'firm,' king of Syria. 2 Kn. 15. 37; 16. 5, 9; Isa. 7. 1.
Rezon, rē´-zŏn, 'lean,' of Damascus. 1 Kn. 11. 23.
Rhegium, rhē´-gĭ-ŭm, on the extreme S. W. coast of Italy, the first port in Italy which Paul reached on his way to Rome. Acts 28. 13.
Rhesa, rhē´-să, 'chieftain' (?). Lu. 3. 27.
Rhoda, rhō´-dă, 'a rose.' Acts 12. 13.
Rhodes, rhōdes, island of. Acts 21. 1.
Ribai, rī-bā´-ī, 'contentious.' 2 Sam. 23. 29.
Riblah, rĭb´-lăh, 'fertility,' in Syria. 2 Kn. 23. 33; 25. 6; Jer. 39. 5; 52. 9.
Rich. Gen. 13. 2, Abram was very *r.*
14. 23, lest thou shouldest say, I have made Abram *r.*
Ex. 30. 15, the *r.* shall not give more.
Ru. 3. 10, followedst not poor or *r.*
1 Sam. 2. 7, the Lord maketh poor and *r.*
Job 15. 29, he shall not be *r.*
27. 19, *r.* man shall lie down, but shall not be gathered.
Ps. 45. 12, the *r.* shall entreat thy favour.
49. 16, be not afraid when one is made *r.*
Prov. 10. 4, hand of diligent maketh *r.*
10. 22, blessing of the Lord maketh *r.*
18. 23, the *r.* answereth roughly.
21. 17, he that loveth wine shall not be *r.*
28. 11, *r.* man is wise in his own conceit.
Eccl. 10. 20, curse not *r.* in thy bedchamber.
Isa. 53. 9, with the *r.* in his death.
Jer. 9. 23, let not *r.* man glory in his *r.*
Hos. 12. 8, Ephraim said, I am become *r.*
Zec. 11. 5, blessed be the Lord, for I am *r.*
Mk. 12. 41, *r.* cast in much.
Lu. 1. 53, *r.* he hath sent empty away.
6. 24, woe to you *r.* for ye have received.
12. 21, not *r.* toward God.
14. 12, call not thy *r.* neighbours.
18. 23, sorrowful, for he was very *r.*
Rom. 10. 12, the Lord is *r.* to all that call.
1 Cor. 4. 8, now ye are full, now ye are *r.*
2 Cor. 6. 10, poor, yet making many *r.*
8. 9, *r.*, yet for your sakes.
Eph. 2. 4, God, who is *r.* in mercy.
1 Tim. 6. 9, they that will be *r.* fall into temptation.
6. 18, do good and be *r.* in good works.
Jas. 1. 10, let *r.* rejoice that he is made low.
2. 5, hath not God chosen the poor, *r.* in faith.
Rev. 2. 9, but thou art *r.*
3. 17, because thou sayest, I am *r.*

Rev. 3. 18, buy of me gold that thou mayest be r.
See Lev. 25. 47; Rev. 6. 15.
Riches. Gen. 13. 2.
Jos. 22. 8, return with much r. to your tents. R. V. wealth.
1 Kn. 3. 11; 2 Chr. 1. 11, neither hast asked r.
3. 13, I have given thee both r. and honour.
10. 23; 2 Chr. 9. 22, Solomon exceeded all for r.
1 Chr. 29. 12, both r. and honour come of thee.
Job 20. 15, he swallowed down r.
36. 19, will he esteem thy r. [abundance.
Ps. 37. 16, better than r. of many wicked. R. V.
39. 6, he heapeth up r.
52. 7, trusted in abundance of r.
62. 10, if r. increase, set not your heart.
73. 12, the ungodly increase in r.
104. 24, the earth is full of thy r.
112. 3, wealth and r. shall be in his house.
Prov. 3. 16, in left hand r. and honour.
8. 18, r. and honour are with me.
11. 4, r. profit not in day of wrath.
13. 7, poor yet hath great r. R. V. wealth.
23. 5, r. make themselves wings.
30. 8, give me neither poverty nor r.
Eccl. 5. 13, r. kept for owners to their hurt.
Isa. 45. 3, I will give thee hidden r.
Jer. 9. 23, let not r. man glory in his r.
17. 11, getteth r. and not by right.
Ezek. 28. 5, heart lifted up because of r.
Mat. 13. 22; Mk. 4. 19; Lu. 8. 14, deceitfulness of r.
Mk. 10. 23, hardly shall they that have r.
Rom. 2. 4, the r. of his goodness.
9. 23, make known the r. of his glory.
11. 12, fall of them the r. of the world.
11. 33, the depth of the r. of the wisdom.
Eph. 1. 7, redemption according to the r. of grace.
2. 7, that he might shew the exceeding r. of grace.
3. 8, unsearchable r. of Christ.
Phil. 4. 19, according to his r. in glory by Christ.
Col. 1. 27, r. of the glory of this mystery.
2. 2, the r. of the full assurance.
1 Tim. 6. 17, nor trust in uncertain r.
Heb. 11. 26, reproach of Christ greater r.
Jas. 5. 2, your r. are corrupted.
Rev. 5. 12, worthy is the Lamb to receive r.
Riches, God gives. 1 Sam. 2. 7; Prov. 10. 22; Eccl. 5. 19.
the true. Prov. 3. 14; Mat. 13. 44; Lu. 16. 11; Eph. 3. 8; Col. 2. 3.
earthly. Deu. 8. 17; 1 Chr. 29. 12; Ps. 49. 6; Prov. 11. 4; 15. 16; 23. 5; 27. 24; Eccl. 4. 8; 5. 10; 6.; Jer. 9. 23; 48. 36; Ezek. 7. 19; Zep. 1. 18; Mat. 6. 19; 13. 22; 1 Tim. 6. 17; Jas. 1. 11; 5. 2; 1 Pet. 1. 18.
uncertain. Prov. 23. 5.
dangers of. Deu. 8. 13; 32. 15; Neh. 9. 25; Prov. 15. 16; 18. 23; 28. 11; 30. 8; Eccl. 5. 12; Hos. 12. 8; Mic. 6. 12; Mat. 13. 22; 19. 23; Mk. 10. 22; Lu. 12. 15; 1 Tim. 6. 10; Jas. 2. 6; 5. 1.
proper use of. 1 Chr. 29. 3; Job 31. 16, 24; Ps. 62. 10; Jer. 9. 23; Mat. 6. 19; 19. 21; Lu. 16. 9; 1 Tim. 6. 17; Jas. 1. 9; 1 John 3. 17.
evil use of. Job 20. 15; 31. 24; Ps. 39. 6; 49. 6; 73. 12; Prov. 11. 28; 13. 7, 11; 15. 6; Eccl. 2. 26; 5. 10; Jas. 5. 3.
end of the wicked rich. Job 20. 16; 21. 13; 27. 16; Ps. 52. 7; Prov. 11. 4; 22. 16; Eccl. 5. 14; Jer. 17. 11; Mic. 2. 3; Hab. 2. 6; Lu. 6. 24; 12. 16; 16. 19; Jas. 5. 1.
Richly. Col. 3. 16; 1 Tim. 6. 17.
Riddance. Lev. 23. 22; Zep. 1. 18.
Riddle. Jud. 14. 12; Ezek. 17. 2.
Ride. Deu. 32. 13, r. on high places of the earth.
33. 26, who r. upon the heaven.
Jud. 5. 10, ye that r. on white asses.
2 Kn. 4. 24, slack not thy r. for me.
Job 30. 22, causest me to r. upon the wind.
Ps. 45. 4, in thy majesty r. prosperously.
66. 12, hast caused men to r. over our heads.
68. 4, 33, extol him that r. on the heavens.
Isa. 19. 1, the Lord r. on a swift cloud.
See Hos. 14. 3; Am. 2. 15; Hab. 3. 8; Hag. 2. 22.

Rider. Gen. 49. 17; Ex. 15. 1; Job 39. 18; Zec. 10. 5.
Ridges. Ps. 65. 10, waterest the r. thereof.
Right (*n*). Deu. 21. 17, the r. of the firstborn is his.
2 Sam. 19. 28, what r. have I to cry to the king.
Neh. 2. 20, ye have no r. in Jerusalem.
Job 34. 6, should I lie against my r.
Job 36. 6, he giveth r. to the poor.
Ps. 9. 4, thou maintainest my r.
17. 1, hear the r., O Lord.
140. 12, Lord will maintain r. of the poor.
Prov. 16. 8, great revenues without r. R. V. with injustice.
Jer. 17. 11, that getteth riches and not by r.
Ezek. 21. 27, till he come whose r. it is.
See Am. 5. 12; Mal. 3. 5; Heb. 13. 10. [do r.
Right (*adj.*). Gen. 18. 25, shall not Judge of all
24. 48, the Lord led me in r. way.
Deu. 6. 18; 12. 25; 21. 9, shalt do that is r.
32. 4, God of truth, just and r. is he.
1 Sam. 12. 23, I will teach you the good and r. way.
2 Sam. 15. 3, thy matters are good and r.
Neh. 9. 13, thou gavest them r. judgments.
Job 6. 25, how forcible are r. words. R. V. words of uprightness.
34. 23, he will not lay on man more than r. (*see* R. V.).
Ps. 19. 8, the statutes of the Lord are r.
45. 6, sceptre is a r. sceptre. R. V. sceptre of equity.
51. 10, renew a r. spirit within me.
107. 7, he led them by the r. way. R. V. straight.
119. 75, thy judgments are r. R. V. righteous.
Prov. 4. 11, I have led thee in r. paths. R. V. paths of uprightness.
8. 6, opening of my lips shall be r. things.
12. 5, thoughts of the righteous are r. R. V. just.
12. 15, way of a fool is r. in his own eyes.
14. 12; 16. 25, there is a way that seemeth r.
21. 2, every way of man is r. in his own eyes.
24. 26, kiss his lips that giveth a r. answer.
Isa. 30. 10, prophesy not r. things.
Jer. 2. 21, planted wholly a r. seed.
Ezek. 18. 5, if a man do that which is r.
18. 19; 21. 27; 33. 14, that which is lawful and r.
Hos. 14. 9, the ways of the Lord are r.
Am. 3. 10, they know not how to do r.
Mat. 20. 4, whatsoever is r. I will give you.
Mk. 5. 15; Lu. 8. 35, in his r. mind.
Lu. 10. 28, thou hast answered r.
Eph. 6. 1, obey your parents, this is r.
See Jud. 17. 6; Lu. 12. 57; Acts 8. 21; 2 Pet. 2. 15.
Righteous. Gen. 7. 1, thee have I seen r. before me.
Gen. 18. 23, wilt thou destroy r. with wicked.
20. 4, wilt thou slay also a r. nation?
38. 26, she hath been more r. than I.
Ex. 23. 8, gift perverteth words of the r.
Num. 23. 10, let me die the death of the r.
Deu. 25. 1; 2 Chr. 6. 23, they shall justify the r.
1 Sam. 24. 17, thou art more r. than I.
1 Kn. 2. 32, two men more r. than he.
Job 4. 7, where were the r. cut off. R. V. upright.
9. 15, though I were r. yet would I not answer.
15. 14, what is man that he should be r.
17. 9, r. shall hold on his way.
22. 3, is it any pleasure that thou art r.
23. 7, there the r. might dispute with him. R. V. upright.
34. 5, Job hath said, I am r.
Ps. 1. 5, the congregation of the r.
1. 6, the Lord knoweth the way of the r.
7. 9, the r. God trieth the hearts.
11. 3, what can the r. do.
34. 17, the r. cry, and the Lord heareth them.
34. 19, many are the afflictions of the r.
37. 16, a little that a r. man hath.
37. 21, the r. sheweth mercy and giveth.
37. 25, have not seen the r. forsaken.
37. 29, the r. shall inherit the land.

Ps. 37. 30, mouth of *r.* speaketh wisdom.
37. 39, salvation of *r.* is of the Lord.
55. 22, never suffer the *r.* to be moved.
58. 11, there is a reward for the *r.*
69. 28, let them not be written with the *r.*
92. 12, the *r.* shall flourish like palm tree.
97. 11, light is sown for the *r.*
112. 6, *r.* shall be in everlasting remembrance.
125. 3, rod shall not rest on lot of *r.*
140. 13, the *r.* shall give thanks.
141. 5, let the *r.* smite me.
146. 8, the Lord loveth the *r.*
Prov. 2. 7, he layeth up wisdom for the *r.* R. V. upright.
3. 32, his secret is with the *r.* R. V. upright.
10. 3, the Lord will not suffer *r.* to famish.
10. 11, the mouth of *r.* is a well of life.
10. 16, labour of *r.* tendeth to life.
10. 21, lips of *r.* feed many.
10. 24, desire of the *r.* shall be granted.
10. 25, the *r.* is an everlasting foundation.
10. 28, hope of the *r.* shall be gladness.
10. 30, the *r.* shall never be removed.
11. 8, the *r.* is delivered out of trouble.
11. 10, when it goeth well with the *r.*
11. 21, seed of the *r.* shall be delivered.
12. 3, the root of the *r.* shall not be moved.
12. 5, thoughts of the *r.* are right.
12. 7, house of the *r.* shall stand.
12. 10, *r.* man regardeth the life of his beast.
12. 26, the *r.* is more excellent than his neighbour.
13. 9, the light of the *r.* rejoiceth.
13. 21, to the *r.* good shall be repaid.
13. 25, *r.* eateth to the satisfying of his soul.
14. 9, among the *r.* there is favour. R. V. upright.
14. 32, the *r.* hath hope in his death.
15. 6, in the house of the *r.* is much treasure.
15. 19, the way of the *r.* is made plain. R. V. upright.
15. 28, the heart of the *r.* studieth to answer.
15. 29, he heareth the prayer of the *r.*
16. 13, *r.* lips are delight of kings.
18. 10, *r.* runneth into it and is safe.
28. 1, the *r.* are bold as a lion.
29. 2, when the *r.* are in authority, people rejoice.
Eccl. 7. 16, be not *r.* overmuch.
9. 1, the *r.* and the wise are in the hand of God.
9. 2, one event to *r.* and wicked.
Isa. 3. 10, say to *r.*, it shall be well.
24. 16, songs, even glory to the *r.*
26. 2, that the *r.* nation may enter.
41. 2, raised up a *r.* man. R. V. whom he calleth in righteousness.
53. 11, shall my *r.* servant justify.
57. 1, *r.* perisheth, and no man layeth it.
60. 21, thy people shall be all *r.*
Jer. 23. 5, raise to David a *r.* branch.
Ezek. 13. 22, with lies ye have made *r.* sad.
16. 52, thy sisters are more *r.* than thou.
33. 12, the righteousness of the *r.* shall not.
Am. 2. 6, they sold the *r.* for silver.
Mal. 3. 18, discern between the *r.* and wicked.
Mat. 9. 13; Mk. 2. 17; Lu. 5. 32, not come to call *r.*
13. 17, many *r.* men have desired.
13. 43, then shall the *r.* shine forth.
23. 28, outwardly appear *r.* to men.
23. 29, garnish sepulchres of the *r.*
25. 46, the *r.* unto life eternal.
Lu. 1. 6, they were both *r.* before God.
18. 9, trusted they were *r.* and despised others.
23. 47, certainly this was a *r.* man.
John 7. 24, judge *r.* judgment.
Rom. 3. 10, there is none *r.*, no not one.
5. 7, scarcely for a *r.* man will one die.
5. 19, many be made *r.*
2 Thes. 1. 6, it is a *r.* thing with God.
2 Tim. 4. 8, the Lord, the *r.* Judge.
Heb. 11. 4, obtained witness that he was *r.*
1 Pet. 3. 12, eyes of the Lord are over the *r.*
1 Pet. 4. 18, if the *r.* scarcely be saved.
2 Pet. 2. 8, Lot vexed his *r.* soul.
1 John 2. 1, Jesus Christ the *r.*
3. 7, *r.* as he is *r.*
Rev. 22. 11, he that is *r.* let him be *r.* still.
See Ezek. 3. 20; Mat. 10. 41; 1 Tim. 1. 9.

Righteous, blessings and privileges of the. Job 36. 7; Ps. 1.; 5. 12; 14. 5; 15.; 16. 3, 11; 32. 11; 34. 15; 37.; 52. 6; 55. 22; 58. 10; 64. 10; 89.; 92. 12; 97. 11; 112.; 125. 3; 146. 8; Prov. 2. 7; 3. 32; 10.-13.; 12. 26; 28. 1; Isa. 3. 10; 26. 2; 60. 21; Ezek. 18.; Mat. 13. 43; Acts 10. 35; Rom. 2. 10; Jas. 5. 16; 1 Pet. 3. 12; 1 John 3. 7; Rev. 22. 11.

Righteously. Deu. 1. 16; Prov. 31. 9, judge *r.*
Ps. 67. 4; 96. 10, thou shalt judge the people *r.* R. V. with equity.
Isa. 33. 15, he that walketh *r.* shall dwell on high.
See Jer. 11. 20; Tit. 2. 12; 1 Pet. 2. 23.

Righteousness. Gen. 30. 33, so shall my *r.* answer for me.
Deu. 33. 19, offer sacrifices of *r.*
1 Sam. 26. 23; Job 33. 26, render to every man his *r.*
Job 6. 29, return again, my *r.* is in it.
27. 6, my *r.* I hold fast.
29. 14, I put on *r.* and it clothed me.
35. 2, thou saidst, my *r.* is more than God's?
36. 3, I will ascribe *r.* to my Maker.
Ps. 4. 1, hear me, O God of my *r.*
4. 5, offer the sacrifices of *r.*
9. 8, he shall judge the world in *r.*
15. 2, he that worketh *r.* shall never be moved.
17. 15, as for me, I will behold thy face in *r.*
23. 3, leadeth me in paths of *r.*
24. 5, and *r.* from the God of his salvation.
40. 9, I have preached *r.*
45. 7; Heb. 1. 9, thou lovest *r.*
50. 6; 97. 6, heavens shall declare his *r.*
72. 2, he shall judge thy people with *r.*
85. 10, *r.* and peace have kissed each other.
94. 15, judgment shall return unto *r.*
97. 2, *r.* is the habitation of his throne.
111. 3; 112. 3, 9, his *r.* endureth for ever.
118. 19, open to me the gates of *r.*
132. 9, let thy priests be clothed with *r.*
Prov. 8. 18, durable riches and *r.* are with me.
10. 2; 11. 4, but *r.* delivereth from death.
11. 5, *r.* of the perfect shall direct his way.
11. 6, *r.* of the upright shall deliver.
11. 19, *r.* tendeth to life.
12. 28, in the way of *r.* is life.
14. 34, *r.* exalteth a nation.
16. 8, better is a little with *r.*
16. 12, the throne is established by *r.*
16. 31, crown of glory if found in way of *r.*
Eccl. 7. 15, a just man that perisheth in his *r.*
Isa. 11. 5, *r.* the girdle of his loins.
26. 10, yet will he not learn *r.*
32. 1, a king shall reign in *r.*
32. 17, the work of *r.* peace, and the effect of *r.*
41. 10, uphold thee with right hand of my *r.*
46. 12, ye that are far from *r.*
58. 8, thy *r.* shall go before thee.
59. 16, his *r.* sustained him.
62. 2, the Gentiles shall see thy *r.*
64. 6, our *r.* are as filthy rags.
Jer. 23. 6; 33. 16, this is his name, The Lord our *r.*
33. 15, cause the branch of *r.* to grow.
51. 10, the Lord hath brought forth our *r.*
Ezek. 3. 20; 18. 24, righteous man turn from *r.*
14. 14, deliver but their own souls by *r.*
18. 20, the *r.* of the righteous shall be upon him.
33. 13, if he trust to his own *r.*
Dan. 4. 27, break off thy sins by *r.*
9. 7, *r.* belongeth to thee.
9. 24, to bring in everlasting *r.*
12. 3, they that turn many to *r.*
Hos. 10. 12, till he rain *r.* upon you.
Am. 5. 24, let *r* run down as a stream.
6. 12, turned fruit of *r.* into hemlock.
Zep. 2. 3, ye meek of the earth, seek *r.*

Mal. 4. 2, shall the Sun of *r.* arise.
Mat. 3. 15, to fulfil all *r.*
5. 6, hunger and thirst after *r.*
5. 10, persecuted for *r.* sake.
5. 20, except your *r.* exceed the *r.*
21. 32, John came to you in the way of *r.*
Lu. 1. 75, in *r.* before him.
John 16. 8, reprove the world of *r.*
Acts 10. 35, he that worketh *r.*
13. 10, thou enemy of all *r.*
24. 25, as he reasoned of *r.*
Rom. 1. 17; 3. 5; 10. 3, the *r.* of God.
4. 6, to whom God imputeth *r.*
4. 11, seal of the *r.* of faith.
5. 17, which receive the gift of *r.*
5. 18, by the *r.* of one.
5. 21, so might grace reign through *r.*
6. 13, yield your members as instruments of *r.*
6. 20, ye were free from *r.*
8. 10, the Spirit is life, because of *r.*
9. 30, the *r.* which is of faith.
10. 3, going about to establish their own *r.*
10. 4, Christ is the end of the law for *r.*
10. 10, with the heart man believeth unto *r.*
14. 17, kingdom of God not meat and drink, but *r.*
1 Cor. 1. 30, Christ is made unto us *r.*
15. 34, awake to *r.*
2 Cor. 5. 21, that we might be made the *r.*
6. 7, the armour of *r.*
6. 14, what fellowship hath *r.*
Gal. 2. 21, if *r.* come by the law.
5. 5, we wait for the hope of *r.*
Eph. 6. 14, the breastplate of *r.*
Phil. 1. 11, filled with the fruits of *r.*
3. 6, touching the *r.* in the law, blameless.
3. 9, not having mine own *r.*, but the *r.* of God.
1 Tim. 6. 11, follow after *r.*
2 Tim. 3. 16, for instruction in *r.*
4. 8, laid up for me a crown of *r.*
Tit. 3. 5, not by works of *r.*
Heb. 1. 8, a sceptre of *r.* R. V. uprightness.
5. 13, unskilful in the word of *r.*
7. 2, by interpretation, King of *r.*
11. 7, heir of the *r.* which is by faith.
11. 33, through faith wrought *r.*
12. 11, the peaceable fruit of *r.*
Jas. 1. 20, wrath of man worketh not *r.* of God.
3. 18, the fruit of *r.* is sown in peace.
1 Pet. 2. 24, dead to sins should live unto *r.*
2 Pet. 2. 5, a preacher of *r.*
2. 21, better not to have known way of *r.*
3. 13, new earth, wherein dwelleth *r.*
1 John 2. 29, every one that doeth *r.*
See Isa. 54. 14; 63. 1; Zec. 8. 8; Rev. 19. 8.

Righteousness by faith. Gen. 15. 6; Ps. 106. 31; Rom. 4. 3; Gal. 3. 6; Jas. 2. 23.
of Christ, imputed to the Church. Isa. 54. 17; Jer. 23. 6; 33. 16; Hos. 2. 19; Mal. 4. 2; Rom. 1. 17; 3. 22; 10. 3; 1 Cor. 1. 30; 2 Cor. 5. 21; Phil. 3. 9; Tit. 2. 14; 2 Pet. 1. 1.
of the law and faith. Rom. 10.
of man. Deu. 9. 4; Isa. 64. 6; Dan. 9. 18; Phil. 3. 9.

Rightly. Gen. 27. 36; Lu. 7. 43; 20. 21; 2 Tim. 2. 15.

Rigour. Ex. 1. 13, 14; Lev. 25. 43, 46, 53.

Rimmon, rĭm'-mon. (1) 'pomegranate.' 2 Sam. 4. 2.
(2) an idol. 2 Kn. 5. 18.

Rimmon-parez, rĭm'-mŏn-păr'-ĕz, 'pomegranate of the breach.' Num. 33. 19.

Ringleader. Acts 24. 5, a *r.* of the sect of the Nazarenes.

Rings. Gen. 41. 42; Ex. 25. 12; 26. 29; Esth. 3. 10; Ezek. 1. 18; Lu. 15. 22.

Ringstraked, streaked with rings. Gen. 30. 35.

Rinnah, rĭn'-năh, 'shout.' 1 Chr. 4. 20.

Rioting *and* **Revelling.** Prov. 23. 20; 28. 7; Lu. 15. 13; Rom. 13. 13; 1 Pet. 4. 4; 2 Pet. 2. 13.

Riotous, dissolute, wanton. Prov. 23. 20 (R. V. gluttonous). Lu. 15. 13.

Ripe. Gen. 40. 10, brought forth *r.* grapes.
Ex. 22. 29, offer the first of thy *r.* fruits.
Num. 18. 13, whatsoever is first *r.* be thine.
Joel 3. 13, put in sickle, for the harvest is *r.*
Mic. 7. 1, my soul desired the first-*r.* fruit.
Rev. 14. 5, time to reap, for harvest of earth is *r.*
See Num. 13. 20; Jer. 24. 2; Hos. 9. 10; Nah. 3. 12.

Riphath, rī'-phăth. Gen. 10. 3.

Rise. Gen. 19. 2, ye shall *r.* up early.
19. 23, the sun was *r.* when Lot entered Zoar.
Num. 24. 17, a sceptre shall *r.* out of Israel.
32. 14, ye are *r.* up in your fathers' stead.
Job 9. 7, commandeth the sun and it *r.* not.
14. 12, man lieth down and *r.* not.
24. 22, he *r.* up, and no man is sure of life.
31. 14, what shall I do when God *r.* up?
Ps. 27. 3, though war should *r.* against me.
119. 62, at midnight I will *r.* to give thanks.
127. 2, it is vain to *r.* up early.
Prov. 31. 15, she *r.* up while it is yet night.
31. 28, her children *r.* up and call her blessed.
Eccl. 12. 4, he shall *r.* at the voice of the bird.
Isa. 33. 10, now will I *r.*, saith the Lord.
58. 10, then shall thy light *r.* in obscurity.
60. 1, the glory of the Lord is *r.* upon thee.
Jer. 7. 13; 25. 3; 35. 14, I spake unto you, *r.* up early.
7. 25; 25. 4; 26. 5; 29. 19; 35. 15; 44. 4, I sent my servants, *r.* early.
11. 7, *r.* early and protesting.
25. 27, fall and *r.* no more.
Lam. 3. 63, sitting down and *r.* up, I am their music.
Mat. 5. 45, maketh sun to *r.* on evil and good.
17. 9; Mk. 9. 9, until Son of man be *r.*
20. 19; Mk. 9. 31; 10. 34; Lu. 18. 33; 24. 7, the third day he shall *r.* again.
26. 32; Mk. 14. 28, after I am *r.* I will go before you.
26. 46, *r.*, let us be going.
Mk. 4. 27, should sleep, and *r.* night and day.
9. 10, what the *r.* from dead should mean.
10. 49, *r.*, he calleth thee.
Lu. 2. 34, this child is set for the fall and *r.*
11. 7, I cannot *r.* and give thee.
22. 46, why sleep ye? *r.* and pray.
24. 34, the Lord is *r.* indeed.
John 11. 23, thy brother shall *r.* again.
Acts 10. 13, *r.*, Peter, kill and eat.
26. 16, *r.*, and stand upon thy feet.
26. 23, the first that should *r.* from the dead.
Rom. 8. 34, that died, yea rather, that is *r.*
1 Cor. 15. 15, if so be the dead *r.* not.
15. 20, but now is Christ *r.*
Col. 3. 1, if ye then be *r.* with Christ.
1 Thes. 4. 16, the dead in Christ shall *r.* first.
See Prov. 30. 31; Isa. 60. 3; Mk. 16. 2; Col. 2. 12.

Rissah, rĭs'-săh, 'a ruin,' or 'rain.' Num. 33. 21.

Rites. Num. 9. 3, according to all the *r.* of it.

Rithmah, rĭth'-măh, 'broom.' Num. 33. 18.

River. Ex. 7. 19; 8. 5, stretch out hand on *r.*
2 Sam. 17. 13, that city, and we will draw it into the *r.*
2 Kn. 5. 12, are the *r.* of Damascus better.
Job 20. 17, ye shall not see the *r.* of honey.
28. 10, he cutteth out *r.* among the rocks. R. V. channels.
29. 6, the rock poured out *r.* of oil.
40. 23, he drinketh up a *r.*, and hasteth not.
Ps. 1. 3, tree planted by the *r.* R. V. streams.
36. 8, the *r.* of thy pleasures.
46. 4, *r.*, the streams whereof make glad.
65. 9, enrichest it with *r.* of God.
107. 33, turneth *r.* into a wilderness.
119. 136, *r.* of waters run down mine eyes.
137. 1, by the *r.* of Babylon we sat.
Eccl. 1. 7, all the *r.* run into the sea.
Isa. 32. 2, shall be as *r.* of water in a dry place.
43. 2, through the *r.*, they shall not overflow.
43. 19, I will make *r.* in the desert.
48. 18, then had thy peace been as a *r.*

Isa. 66. 12, I will extend peace like a *r.*
Lam. 2. 18, let tears run down like *r.*
Mic. 6. 7, be pleased with *r.* of oil.
John 7. 38, shall flow *r.* of living water.
Rev. 22. 1, a pure *r.* of water of life.

River of life. Rev. 22. *See* Ps. 36. 8 ; 46. 4 ; 65. 9 ; Ezek. 47.
of Egypt (Nile), Gen. 41. 1 ; Ex. 1. 22 ; Ezek. 29. 3, 10. Moses hidden in, Ex. 2. 5. waters of, turned into blood, Ex. 7. 15.

Rivers and Brooks of Scripture.

R. = *river* ; B. = *brook.*

Name.	Situation.	References.	Modern Name.
Abana, R. (R. V. **Abanah** or **Amanah.**)	Damascus, *Syria*	2 Kn. 5. 12	Abanias.
Arnon, R.	E. of Salt Sea	Num. 21. 13–15	El-Mojib.
Chebar, R.	Chaldæa	Ezek. 1. 1, 3	Nahr Malcha ?
Cherith, B.	'Before Jordan' (uncertain)	1 Kn. 17. 5	
Egypt, River of. (R. V. **Brook.**)		Num. 34. 5 ; 1 Kn. 8. 65	El-Arish.
Egypt, Stream of		Isa. 27. 12	El-Arish.
Euphrates, R.	Mesopotamia	Gen. 2. 14	Euphrates.
Gihon, R.	Eden	Gen. 2. 13	
Hiddekel, R.	Eden	Gen. 2. 14	Tigris, or Dijlah.
Jabbok, R.	Gilead	Gen. 32. 22	Zerka.
Jordan, R.	The great river of Palestine	2 Kn. 5. 10	Esh-Sheriah.
Kanah, R. (R. V. **Brook.**)	Palestine	Jos. 16. 8	
Kidron, B.	Judæa	2 Sam. 15. 23 ; John 18. 1	Wady en-Nâr.
Kishon, R.	Palestine	Jud. 4. 7 ; 5. 21 ; 1 Kn. 18. 40	Nahr Mukutta.
Pharpar, R.	Damascus, *Syria*	2 Kn. 5. 12	Taura, or Nahr el-Awaj ?
Pison, R.	Eden	Gen. 2. 11	
Zared, B.		Num. 21. 12	El-Hesi.

Rizpah, rĭz'-păh, 'hot stone.' 2 Sam. 3. 7.
Road. 1 Sam. 27. 10, whither have ye made a *r.* R. V. raid.
Roar. 1 Chr. 16. 32 ; Ps. 96. 11 ; 98. 7, let the sea *r.*
Job 3. 24, my *r.* are poured out.
Ps. 46. 3, will not fear, though waters *r.*
104. 21, young lions *r.* after their prey.
Prov. 19. 12 ; 20. 2, king's wrath as the *r.* of a lion.
Isa. 59. 11, we *r.* like bears.
Jer. 6. 23, their voice *r.* like the sea.
25. 30, the Lord shall *r.* from on high.
Hos. 11. 10, he shall *r.* like a lion.
Joel 3. 16 ; Am. 1. 2, the Lord shall *r.* out of Zion.
Am. 3. 4, will a lion *r.* when he hath no prey ?
See Ps. 22. 1 ; 32. 3 ; Zec. 11. 3 ; Rev. 10. 3.
Roaring. Prov. 28. 15, as a *r.* lion, is a wicked ruler.
Lu. 21. 25, distress, the sea and waves *r.*
1 Pet. 5. 8, the devil as a *r.* lion.
See Ps. 22. 13 ; Isa. 31. 4 ; Ezek. 22. 25 ; Zep. 3. 3.
Roast. Ex. 12. 9, not raw, but *r.* with fire.
Prov. 12. 27, slothful man *r.* not that he took.
Isa. 44. 16, he *r. r.*, and is satisfied.
See Deu. 16. 7 ; 1 Sam. 2. 15 ; 2 Chr. 35. 13.
Rob. Prov. 22. 22, *r.* not the poor.
Isa. 10. 2, that they may *r.* the fatherless. R. V. make . . . their prey.
10. 13, I have *r.* their treasures.
42. 22, this is a people *r.* and spoiled.
Ezek. 33. 15, if he give again that he had *r.*
Mal. 3. 8, ye have *r.* me.
2 Cor. 11. 8, I *r.* other churches.
See Jud. 9. 25 ; 2 Sam. 17. 8 ; Ps. 119. 61 ; Prov. 17. [12.
Robber. Job 12. 6, tabernacles of *r.* prosper.
Isa. 42. 24, who gave Israel to the *r.*
Jer. 7. 11, is this house become a den of *r.*
John 10. 1, the same is a thief and a *r.*
10. 8, all that came before me are *r.*
Acts 19. 37, these men are not *r.* of churches.
2 Cor. 11. 26, in perils of *r.*
See Ezek. 7. 22 ; 18. 10 ; Dan. 11. 14 ; Hos. 6. 9.
Robbery. Phil. 2. 6, thought it not *r.* to be equal. R. V. a prize.
Robbery. Lev. 19. 13 ; Ps. 62. 10 ; Prov. 21. 7 ; 22. 22 ; 28. 24 ; Isa. 10. 2 ; 61. 8 ; Ezek. 22. 29 ; Am. 3. 10 ; 1 Cor. 6. 8 ; 1 Thes. 4. 6.
Robe. 1 Sam. 24. 4, cut off skirt of Saul's *r.*
Job 29. 14, my judgment was as a *r.*
Isa. 61. 10, covered me with *r.* of righteousness.
Lu. 15. 22, bring forth the best *r.*
20. 46, desire to walk in long *r.*
See Ex. 28. 4 ; Mic. 2. 8 ; Rev. 6. 11.
Robe, scarlet, gorgeous, purple. Mat. 27. 28 ; Lu. 23. 11 ; John 19. 2.
Roboam, rō-bō'-ăm, Greek form of Rehoboam. Mat. 1. 7.
Rock. Ex. 33. 22, I will put thee in a clift of *r.*
Num. 20. 8, speak to the *r.* before their eyes.
20. 10, must we fetch you water out of this *r.* ?
23. 9, from the top of the *r.* I see him.
24. 21, thou puttest thy nest in a *r.*
Deu. 8. 15, who brought thee water out of the *r.*
32. 4, he is the *R.*
32. 15, lightly esteemed the *R.* of his salvation.
32. 18, of the *R.* that begat thee.
32. 30, except their *R.* had sold them.
32. 31, their *r.* is not as our *R.*
32. 37, where is their *r.* in whom they trusted ?
1 Sam. 2. 2, neither is there any *r.* like our God.
2 Sam. 22. 2 ; Ps. 18. 2 ; 92. 15, the Lord is my *r.*
22. 3, the God of my *r.*
22. 32 ; Ps. 18. 31, who is a *r.*, save our God ?
23. 3, the *R.* of Israel spake.

1 Kn. 19. 11, strong wind brake in pieces the *r*.
Job 14. 18, the *r*. is removed out of his place.
19. 24, graven in the *r*. for ever.
24. 8, embrace the *r*. for want of shelter.
Ps. 27. 5; 40. 2, shall set me up upon a *r*.
31. 3; 71. 3, thou art my *r*. and my fortress.
61. 2, lead me to the *r*. that is higher than I.
81. 16, with honey out of the *r*.
Prov. 30. 26, yet make their houses in the *r*.
S. of S. 2. 14, that art in the clefts of the *r*.
Isa. 8. 14, for a *r*. of offence.
17. 10, not mindful of the *r*. of thy strength.
32. 2, as the shadow of a great *r*.
33. 16, defence shall be munitions of *r*.
Jer. 5. 3, they made their faces harder than *r*.
23. 29, hammer that breaketh the *r*. in pieces.
Nah. 1. 6, the *r*. are thrown down by him.
Mat. 7. 25; Lu. 6. 48, it was founded upon a *r*.
16. 18, upon this *r*. I will build my church.
27. 51, and the *r*. rent.
Lu. 8. 6, some fell upon a *r*.
Rom. 9. 33; 1 Pet. 2. 8, I lay a *r*. of offence.
1 Cor. 10. 4, spiritual *R*., and that *R*. was Christ.
Rev. 6. 16, said to the *r*., Fall on us.
See Jud. 6. 20; 13. 19; 1 Sam. 14. 4; Prov. 30. 19.

Rock, water brought out of, by Moses. Ex. 17. 6; Num. 20. 10. *See* 1 Cor. 10. 4.
figuratively used. Deu. 32. 4, 15; 2 Sam. 22. 2; 23. 3; Ps. 18. 2; 28. 1; 31. 2; 61. 2; Isa. 17. 10; 26. 4; 32. 2. *See* Mat. 7. 24.

Rod. Job 9. 34, let him take his *r*. from me.
21. 9, neither is the *r*. of God upon them.
Ps. 2. 9, break them with a *r*. of iron.
23. 4, thy *r*. and thy staff comfort me.
Prov. 10. 13; 26. 3, *r*. for the back of fools.
13. 24, he that spareth his *r*.
22. 8, the *r*. of his anger shall fail.
23. 14, thou shalt beat him with the *r*.
29. 15, the *r*. and reproof give wisdom.
Isa. 10. 15, as if the *r*. should shake itself.
11. 1, shall come forth a *r*. R. V. shoot.
Jer. 48. 17, how is the beautiful *r*. broken.
Ezek. 20. 37, cause you to pass under the *r*. [it.
Mic. 6. 9, hear ye the *r*., and who hath appointed
2 Cor. 11. 25, thrice was I beaten with *r*.
See Gen. 30. 37; 1 Sam. 14. 27; Rev. 2. 27; 11. 1.

Rod of Moses, Ex. 4. of Aaron, Num. 17.; Heb. 9. 4.

Rode. 2 Sam. 18. 9; 2 Kn. 9. 25; Neh. 2. 12; Ps. 18. 10.

Roe, roebuck (Deu. 12. 15). Heb. *Tsĕbî*: Gk. δορκάς. The gazelle (*Gazella dorcas*). Still abundant in Syria.

Rogelim, rō′-gĕ-lĭm, 'fullers.' 2 Sam. 17. 27.

Rohgah, rōh′-găh, 'outcry.' 1 Chr. 7. 34.

Roll. Jos. 5. 9, I have *r*. away reproach.
Job 30. 14, they *r*. themselves on me.
Isa. 9. 5, with garments *r*. in blood.
34. 4; Rev. 6. 14, the heavens shall be *r*. together.
Mk. 16. 3, who shall *r*. us away the stone?
Lu. 24. 2, they found the stone *r*. away. [60.
See Gen. 29. 8; Prov. 26. 27; Isa. 17. 13; Mat. 27.

Roll of prophecy. Isa. 8. 1; Jer. 36. 2; Ezek. 2. 9; 3. 1; Zec. 5. 1. Roll was the ancient form of a book. *See* Book.

Romamti-ezer, rō-măm′-tī-ē′-zĕr, 'I have exalted help.' 1 Chr. 25. 4.

Romans, rō′-măns, men of Rome. John 11. 48.
St. Paul's teaching to. *See* Epistle to Romans.

Rome, rōme, 'strength' (?). The capital of Italy and the Roman Empire, situated on the Tiber, fifteen miles from its mouth. It was the residence of many Jews (Acts 2. 10; 18. 2), and of many Christians, whom St. Paul was anxious to visit (Acts 19. 21), and to whom he wrote an Epistle. It was the scene of his first and second imprisonment, and of his martyrdom.
strangers of, at Pentecost. Acts 2. 10.
Jews ordered to depart from. Acts 18. 2.
Paul preaches there. Acts 28.

Rome, Paul's voyage to. *See* under Paul.

Roof. Gen. 19. 8, under the shadow of my *r*.
Deu. 22. 8, make a battlement for thy *r*.
Job 29. 10; Ps. 137. 6; Lam. 4. 4; Ezek. 3. 26, tongue cleaveth to *r*. of mouth.
Mat. 8. 8; Lu. 7. 6, I am not worthy that thou shouldest come under my *r*.
Mk. 2. 4, they uncovered the *r*.
See Jos. 2. 6; Jud. 16. 27; 2 Sam. 11. 2; Jer. 19. 13.

Room. Gen. 24. 23, is there *r*. for us.
26. 22, the Lord hath made *r*. for us.
Ps. 31. 8, set my feet in a large *r*. R. V. place.
80. 9, thou preparedst *r*. before it.
Prov. 18. 16, a man's gift maketh *r*. for him.
Mal. 3. 10, there shall not be *r*. enough.
Mat. 23. 6; Mk. 12. 39; Lu. 20. 46, love uppermost *r*. R. V. chief place.
Mk. 2. 2, there was no *r*. to receive them.
Lu. 2. 7, no *r*. for them in the inn.
12. 17, no *r*. to bestow my goods. [seats.
14. 7, how they chose out the chief *r*. R. V.
14. 9, begin with shame to take the lowest *r*. R. V. place.
14. 22, it is done, and yet there is *r*.
See Gen. 6. 14; 1 Kn. 8. 20; 19. 16; Mk. 14. 15.

Root (*n*.). Deu. 29. 18, a *r*. that beareth gall.
2 Kn. 19. 30, shall again take *r*. downward.
Job 5. 3, I have seen the foolish taking *r*.
8. 17, his *r*. are wrapped about the heap.
14. 8, the *r*. thereof wax old in the earth.
18. 16, his *r*. shall be dried up.
19. 28, the *r*. of the matter.
29. 19, my *r*. was spread out by the waters.
Prov. 12. 3, *r*. of righteous shall not be moved.
12. 12, *r*. of righteous yieldeth fruit.
Isa. 5. 24, their *r*. shall be rottenness.
11. 1, a Branch shall grow out of his *r*.
11. 10; Rom. 15. 12, there shall be a *r*. of Jesse.
27. 6; 37. 31, them that come of Jacob to take *r*.
53. 2, as a *r*. out of a dry ground.
Ezek. 31. 7, his *r*. was by great waters.
Hos. 14. 5, cast forth his *r*. as Lebanon.
Mal. 4. 1, leave them neither *r*. nor branch.
Mat. 3. 10; Lu. 3. 9, axe laid to *r*. of trees.
13. 6; Mk. 4. 6; Lu. 8. 13, because they had no *r*.
Mk. 11. 20, fig tree dried up from the *r*.
Rom. 11. 16, if the *r*. be holy.
1 Tim. 6. 10, love of money the *r*. of all evil.
Heb. 12. 15, lest any *r*. of bitterness.
Jude 12, twice dead, plucked up by the *r*.
Rev. 22. 16, *r*. and offspring of David.
See 2 Chr. 7. 20; Dan. 4. 15; 7. 8; 11. 7.

Root (*v*.). Deu. 29. 28, Lord *r*. them out.
1 Kn. 14. 15, he shall *r*. up Israel.
Job 18. 14, confidence shall be *r*. out.
31. 8, let my offspring be *r*. out.
31. 12, *r*. out all mine increase.
Ps. 52. 5, *r*. thee out of land of the living.
Mat. 13. 29, lest ye *r*. up also the wheat.
15. 13, hath not planted shall be *r*. up.
Eph. 3. 17, being *r*. and grounded in love.
Col. 2. 7, *r*. and built up in him.
See Prov. 2. 22; Jer. 1. 10; Zep. 2. 4.

Rose (Isa. 35. 1; S. of S. 2. 1). Heb. *Ḥăbatzĕleth*: Gk. κρίνον, ἄνθος: Bot. N. *Narcissus tazetta*: R. V. marg. 'autumn crocus.' Only mentioned twice. As the word is derived from a root meaning 'a bulb,' it is no doubt a bulbous plant, of which there are many kinds in Palestine, as the lily, the crocus, the narcissus, any of which may be the plant referred to. No true roses are found, except on the Lebanons.

Rose (*v*.). Gen. 32. 31, the sun *r*. upon him.
Jos. 3. 16, waters *r*. up on an heap.
Lu. 16. 31, though one *r*. from the dead.
Rom. 14. 9, to this end Christ both died and *r*.
1 Cor. 15. 4, buried, and *r*. the third day.
2 Cor. 5. 15, live to him who died and *r*.
See Lu. 24. 33; Acts 10. 41; 1 Thes. 4. 14; Rev. 19. 3.

Rosh, rōsh, 'head.' Gen. 46. 21.

Rot. Num. 5. 21; Prov. 10. 7; Isa. 40. 20.

Rotten. Job 41. 27; Jer. 38. 11; Joel 1. 17.

Rottenness. Prov. 12. 4; 14. 30; Isa. 5. 24.

ROME: THE APPIAN WAY

The road leading out from Rome along which the brethren came to meet St. Paul at Appii Forum (Acts xxviii. 15). (*Donald McLeish*)

ROME: THE FORUM

Centre of the City's life in the time when Christianity was first brought there; in the background the Arch of Titus, conqueror of Jerusalem, A.D. 70. (*Donald McLeish*)

Rough. Isa. 27. 8, stayeth his *r.* wind.
40. 4; Lu. 3. 5, *r.* places made plain.
Zec. 13. 4, wear a *r.* garment to deceive. R. V. hairy.
See Deu. 21. 4; Jer. 51. 27; Dan. 8. 21.
Roughly. Gen. 42. 7, Joseph spake *r.*
Prov. 18. 23, the rich answereth *r.*
See 1 Sam. 20. 10; 1 Kn. 12. 13; 2 Chr. 10. 13.
Round. Ex. 16. 14; Isa. 3. 18; Lu. 19. 43.
Rowed. Jon. 1. 13; Mk. 6. 48; John 6. 19.
Royal. Gen. 49. 20, yield *r.* dainties.
Esth. 1. 7, *r.* wine in abundance.
5. 1; 6. 8; 8. 15; Acts 12. 21, *r.* apparel.
Jas. 2. 8, fulfil the *r.* law.
1 Pet. 2. 9, a *r.* priesthood.
See 1 Chr. 29. 25; Isa. 62. 3; Jer. 43. 10.
Rubies. Job 28. 18; Prov. 8. 11; 31. 10.
Rudders. Ancient vessels were steered by two oars or paddles, passed through the vessel on each side of the stern (Acts 27. 40).
Ruddy. 1 Sam. 16. 12; S. of S. 5. 10; Lam. 4. 7.
Rude. 2 Cor. 11. 6, *r.* in speech.
Rudiments. Col. 2. 8, 20, *r.* of the world.
Rue (Lu. 11. 42). Gk. πήγανον: Bot. N. *Ruta bracteosa; Ruta graveolens.* A half shrubby plant two or three feet high, of powerful odour, cultivated, but of small value.
Rufus, rū'-fŭs, 'red.' Mk. 15. 21; Rom. 16. 13.
Ruhamah, rū-hä'-măh, 'compassionated.' Hos. 2. 1.
Ruin. 2 Chr. 28. 23, they were the *r.* of him.
Ps. 89. 40, hast brought his strong holds to *r.*
Prov. 24. 22, who knoweth the *r.* of both. R. V. destruction.
26. 28, a flattering mouth worketh *r.*
Ezek. 18. 30, so iniquity shall not be your *r.*
21. 15, that their *r.* may be multiplied. R. V. stumbling.
Lu. 6. 49, the *r.* of that house was great.
See Isa. 3. 8; Ezek. 36. 35; Am. 9. 11; Acts 15. 16.
Rule (*n.*). Esth. 9. 1, Jews had *r.* over them.
Prov. 17. 2, a wise servant shall have *r.*
19. 10, servant to have *r.* over princes.
25. 28, no *r.* over his own spirit. R. V. without restraint.
Isa. 63. 19, thou never barest *r.* over them.
1 Cor. 15. 24, when he shall put down all *r.*
Gal. 6. 16, as many as walk according to this *r.*
Heb. 13. 7, 17, them that have the *r.* over you.
See Eccl. 2. 19; Isa. 44. 13; 2 Cor. 10. 13.
Rule (*v.*). Gen. 1. 16, to *r.* the day.
3. 16, thy husband shall *r.* over thee.
Jud. 8. 23, I will not *r.* over you.
2 Sam. 23. 3, that *r.* over men must be just.
Ps. 66. 7, he *r.* by his power for ever.
89. 9, thou *r.* the raging of the sea.
103. 19, his kingdom *r.* over all.
Prov. 16. 32, that *r.* his spirit.
22. 7, rich *r.* over the poor.
Eccl. 9. 17, him that *r.* among fools.
Isa. 3. 4, babes *r.* over them.
32. 1, princes shall *r.* in judgment.
40. 10, his arm shall *r.* for him.
Ezek. 29. 15, shall no more *r.* over nations.
Rom. 12. 8, he that *r.* with diligence.
Col. 3. 15, peace of God *r.* in your hearts.
1 Tim. 3. 4, one that *r.* well his own house.
5. 17, elders that *r.* well.
See Dan. 5. 21; Zec. 6. 13; Rev. 2. 27; 12. 5.
Ruler. Num. 13. 2, every one a *r.* among them. R. V. prince.
Prov. 6. 7, ant having no guide, overseer, or *r.*
23. 1, when thou sittest to eat with a *r.*
28. 15, a wicked *r.* over the poor.
Isa. 3. 6, be thou our *r.*
Mic. 5. 2, out of thee shall come *r.*
Mat. 25. 21, I will make thee *r.* R. V. set thee.
John 7. 26, do the *r.* know that this is Christ?
7. 48, have any of the *r.* believed.
Rom. 13. 3, *r.* not a terror to good works.
See Gen. 41. 43; Neh. 5. 7; Ps. 2. 2; Isa. 1. 10.
Rulers of the Jews (as Nicodemus). John 3. 1; 7. 48; 12. 42, &c.
of the synagogue: Jairus, Lu. 8. 41. Crispus, Acts 18. 8. Sosthenes, Acts 18. 17. *See* Synagogue.
chosen by Moses. Ex. 18. 25.
Rumah, rū'-măh, 'height.' 2 Kn. 23. 36.
Rumour. Jer. 49. 14, I have heard a *r.* R. V. tidings.
Ezek. 7. 26, *r.* shall be upon *r.*
Mat. 24. 6; Mk. 13. 7, wars and *r.* of wars.
See 2 Kn. 19. 7; Obad. 1; Lu. 7. 17.
Run. 2 Sam. 18. 27, the *r.* of the foremost is like.
2 Chr. 16. 9, eyes of Lord *r.* to and fro.
Ps. 19. 5, as a strong man to *r.* a race.
23. 5, my cup *r.* over.
147. 15, his word *r.* very swiftly.
S. of S. 1. 4, draw me, we will *r.* after thee.
Isa. 40. 31, they shall *r.* and not be weary.
55. 5, nations shall *r.* to thee.
Jer. 12. 5, if thou hast *r.* with the footmen.
51. 31, one post shall *r.* to meet another.
Dan. 12. 4, many shall *r.* to and fro.
Hab. 2. 2, that he may *r.* that readeth.
Zec. 2. 4, *r.*, speak to this young man.
Lu. 6. 38, good measure *r.* over.
Rom. 9. 16, nor of him that *r.*
1 Cor. 9. 24, they which *r.* in a race *r.* all.
9. 26, I therefore so *r.*
Gal. 2. 2, lest I should *r.* or had *r.* in vain.
5. 7, ye did *r.* well.
Heb. 12. 1, let us *r.* with patience.
1 Pet. 4. 4, that ye *r.* not to same excess.
See Prov. 4. 12; Jer. 5. 1; Lam. 2. 18; Am. 8. 12.
Rush (*n.*). Heb. *Gômé:* Gk. πάπυρος. Egyptian Papyrus. *See* Bulrush. (1) *Gômé.* Job 8. 11; Isa. 9. 14; 19. 15; 35. 7.
Rush (*v.*). Isa. 17. 13; Jer. 8. 6; Ezek. 3. 12; Acts 2. 2.
Rust. Mat. 6. 19, 20; Jas. 5. 3.
Ruth, rūth, 'a friend'(?); story of. Ru. 1.-4.
Christ descended from. Mat. 1. 5.
Rye (Ex. 9. 32; Isa. 28. 25). Heb. *Cussémeth:* Gk. ζέα, ὀλύρα: Bot. N. *Triticum spelta:* R. V. spelt. An inferior kind of wheat. Rye is a northern, not a Syrian, plant.

Sabachthani, să-băch'-thă-nī, 'thou hast forsaken me.' Mk. 15. 34.
Sabaoth, să-bā'-ōth, 'Hosts,' the Lord of. Rom. 9. 29; Jas. 5. 4.
Sabbath, 'cessation,' 'rest,' a divinely instituted day of rest, for all men, for which the seventh day was set apart. Ex. 16. 23.
See Feasts.
Lev. 25. 8, number seven *s.* of years.
2 Kn. 4. 23, it is neither new moon nor *s.*
2 Chr. 36. 21, as long as desolate she kept *s.*
Ezek. 46. 1, on the *s.* it shall be opened.
Am. 8. 5, when will the *s.* be gone.
Mk. 2. 27, the *s.* was made for man.
2. 28; Lu. 6. 5, the Son of man is Lord of the *s.*
Lu. 13. 15, doth not each on *s.* loose.
See Isa. 1. 13; Lam. 1. 7; 2. 6; John 5. 18.
Sabbath, day of rest. Gen. 2. 2 (Heb. 4. 4).
to be kept holy. Ex. 16. 23; 20. 8; 23. 12; 31. 13; 34. 21; 35. 2; Lev. 25. 3; Num. 15. 32; Deu. 5. 12; Neh. 10. 31; 13. 15; Isa. 56.; 58. 13; Jer. 17. 21; Ezek. 20. 12.
offerings. Num. 28. 9.
the seventh year kept as. Ex. 23. 10; Lev. 25. 1.
Christ the Lord of. Mk. 2. 27; Lu. 6. 5.
Sabeans, să-bē'-ăns, 'people of Sheba.' Job 1. 15; Isa. 45. 14.
Sabta, săb'-tă, same as following. 1 Chr. 1. 9.
Sabtah, săb'-tăh, 'rest' (?). Gen. 10. 7.
Sabtecha, săb-tē'-chă. 1 Chr. 1. 9.
Sabtechah, săb-tē'-chăh. Gen. 10. 7.
Sacar, sā'-căr, 'hire,' 'reward.' 1 Chr. 11. 35.
Sack. Gen. 42. 25; 43. 21; 44. 1, 11, 12; Jos. 9. 4.
Sackbut (Dan. 3. 5, 7, &c.). Chald. *Sabběca:* Gk. σαμβύκη. The Heb. and Gk. refer to a kind of a harp, or lyre, but with only four strings. The translation 'sackbut' is wrong,

for a sackbut is a wind instrument with a movable slide, as in the trombone.

Sackcloth. 2 Sam. 3. 31, gird you with *s.*
1 Kn. 20. 32, they girded *s.* on their loins.
Neh. 9. 1, assembled with fasting and *s.*
Esth. 4. 1, put on *s.* with ashes.
Ps. 30. 11, thou hast put off my *s.*
35. 13, my clothing was *s.*
Jon. 3. 5, and put on *s.*

Sacrifice (*n.*). Gen. 31. 54, Jacob offered *s.*
Ex. 5. 17, let us go and do *s.* to the Lord.
Num. 25. 2, called people to the *s.* of their gods.
1 Sam. 2. 29, wherefore kick ye at my *s.*
9. 13, he doth bless the *s.*
15. 22, to obey is better than *s.*
Ps. 4. 5, offer the *s.* of righteousness.
27. 6, will I offer *s.* of joy.
40. 6; 51. 16, *s.* thou didst not desire.
51. 17, the *s.* of God are a broken spirit.
118. 27, bind the *s.* with cords.
Prov. 15. 8, *s.* of wicked an abomination.
17. 1, than a house full of *s.* with strife. R. V. feasting.
21. 3, to do justice is more acceptable than *s.*
Eccl. 5. 1, the *s.* of fools.
Isa. 1. 11, to what purpose is multitude of *s.*
Jer. 6. 20, nor are your *s.* sweet unto me.
33. 18, nor want a man to do *s.*
Dan. 8. 11; 9. 27; 11. 31, daily *s.* taken away. R. V. burnt offering.
Hos. 3. 4, many days without a *s.*
6. 6; Mat. 9. 13; 12. 7, I desired mercy and not *s.*
Am. 4. 4, bring your *s.* every morning.
Zep. 1. 7, the Lord hath prepared a *s.*
Mal. 1. 8, ye offer the blind for *s.*
Mk. 9. 49, every *s.* shall be salted.
12. 33, to love the Lord is more than *s.*
Lu. 13. 1, blood Pilate mingled with *s.*
Acts 7. 42, have ye offered *s.* forty years.
14. 13, and would have done *s.*
Rom. 12. 1, present your bodies a living *s.*
1 Cor. 8. 4; 10. 19, 28, offered in *s.* to idols.
Eph. 5. 2, a *s.* to God for sweet-smelling savour.
Phil. 2. 17, upon the *s.* of your faith.
4. 18, a *s.* acceptable, well pleasing.
Heb. 9. 26, put away sin by *s.* of himself.
10. 12, offered one *s.* for sins.
10. 26, there remaineth no more *s.* for sin.
11. 4, a more excellent *s.*
13. 15, let us offer the *s.* of praise.
13. 16, with such *s.* God is well pleased.
1 Pet. 2. 5, to offer up spiritual *s.*

Sacrifice (*v.*). Ex. 22. 20, he that *s.* to any god.
Neh. 4. 2, will they *s.*
Ps. 54. 6, I will freely *s.* to thee.
106. 37, they *s.* their sons to devils.
107. 22, let them *s.* sacrifices of thanksgiving. R. V. offer.
Eccl. 9. 2, to him that *s.* and that *s.* not.
Isa. 65. 3, people that *s.* in gardens.
Hos. 8. 13, they *s.*, but the Lord accepteth not.
Hab. 1. 16, they *s.* unto their net.
1 Cor. 5. 7, Christ our passover is *s.* for us.
10. 20, things Gentiles *s.*, they *s.* to devils.

Sacrifices, types of Christ. Heb. 9.; 10.

Sacrilege. Rom. 2. 22, dost thou commit *s.* R. V. rob temples.

Sad. 1 Kn. 21. 5, why is thy spirit so *s.*
Eccl. 7. 3, by *s.* of countenance the heart is made better.
Mat. 6. 16, be not of a *s.* countenance.
Mk. 10. 22, he was *s.* at that saying. R. V. his countenance fell.
Lu. 24. 17, as ye walk and are *s.*
See Gen. 40. 6; 1 Sam. 1. 18; Neh. 2. 1; Ezek. 13. 22.

Saddle. 2 Sam. 19. 26; 1 Kn. 13. 13.

Sadducees, săd′-dū-çēēs. A religious party of the Jews, in opposition to the Pharisees. The name is derived either from *Zadok* (Gk. often *Sad-douk*), a Rabbi who lived about 300 B. C., or from *Sadoc*, 'just,' 'righteous,' as a retort against the arrogant title of 'pious' adopted by the Pharisees. They were very conservative in theology, and refused to admit any doctrine which could not be traced to Moses. (Hence their address to our Lord — 'Master, Moses said . . .') Thus they retained the vague ideas of a future life held by the earlier Hebrews, denying the doctrine of resurrection; and in consequence their creed was rationalistic in tone; they held that there was 'neither angel nor spirit.' In our Lord's time the high-priestly aristocracy was largely Sadducæan (Acts 5. 17).
their controversies with Christ, Mat. 16. 1; 22. 23; Mk. 12. 18; Lu. 20. 27. with the apostles, Acts 4. 1; with Paul, Acts 23. 6.
their doctrines. Mat. 22. 23; Mk. 12. 18; Acts 23. 8.

Sadoc, sā′-dŏc. Greek form of ZADOK. Mat. 1. 14.

Safe. 2 Sam. 18. 29, is the young man *s.*? R. V. is it well with.
Job 21. 9, their houses are *s.* from fear.
Ps. 119. 117, hold me up and I shall be *s.*
Prov. 18. 10, righteous run and are *s.*
29. 25, whoso trusteth in the Lord shall be *s.*
Ezek. 34. 27, they shall be *s.* in their land. R. V. secure.
Acts 27. 44, so they escaped all *s.*
See 1 Sam. 12. 11; Isa. 5. 29; Lu. 15. 27; Phil. 3. 1.

Safeguard. 1 Sam. 22. 23, with me thou shalt be in *s.*

Safely. Ps. 78. 53, he led them on *s.*
Prov. 1. 33, shall dwell *s.* R. V. securely.
3. 23, shalt thou walk *s.* R. V. securely.
31. 11, doth *s.* trust in her. R. V. omits.
Hos. 2. 18, I will make them to lie down *s.*
See Isa. 41. 3; Zec. 14. 11; Mk. 14. 44; Acts 16. 23.

Safety. Job 3. 26, I was not in *s.* R. V. ease.
5. 4, his children are far from *s.*
11. 18, thou shalt take thy rest in *s.*
Prov. 11. 14; 24. 6, in the multitude of counsellors is *s.* 21. 31, *s.* is of the Lord. R. V. victory.
1 Thes. 5. 3, when they say peace and *s.*
See Job 24. 23; Ps. 12. 5; 33. 17; Isa. 14. 30.

Saffron (S. of S. 4. 14). Heb. *Karkôm*: Gk. *κρόκος*: Bot. N. *Crocus sativus*. The saffron crocus, esteemed for its fragrance, and used in the East for colouring and seasoning.

Sail. Isa. 33. 23; Ezek. 27. 7; Lu. 8. 23; Acts 27. 9.

Saints. 1 Sam. 2. 9, he will keep feet of *s.* R. V. holy ones.
Job 5. 1, to which of the *s.* wilt thou turn? R. V. holy ones.
15. 15, he putteth no trust in his *s.* R. V. holy ones.
Ps. 16. 3, but to the *s.* that are in the earth.
30. 4, sing to the Lord, O ye *s.* of his.
37. 28, the Lord forsaketh not his *s.*
50. 5, gather my *s.* together.
89. 5, the congregation of the *s.* R. V. holy ones.
89. 7, to be feared in assembly of *s.* R. V. holy ones.
97. 10, preserveth the souls of his *s.*
116. 15, precious is the death of his *s.*
132. 9, let thy *s.* shout for joy.
149. 9, this honour have all his *s.*
Dan. 7. 18, but the *s.* shall take the kingdom.
8. 13, then I heard one *s.* speaking. R. V. a holy one.
Mat. 27. 52, many bodies of *s.* arose.
Acts 9. 13, evil he hath done to thy *s.*
Rom. 1. 7; 1 Cor. 1. 2, called to be *s.*
8. 27, he maketh intercession for the *s.*
12. 13, distributing to the necessity of *s.*
16. 2, receive her as becometh *s.*
1 Cor. 6. 1, dare any go to law, and not before *s.*
6. 2, the *s.* shall judge the world.
16. 1, concerning collection for *s.*
16. 15, the ministry of *s.*
Eph. 1. 18, his inheritance in the *s.*
2. 19, fellowcitizens with the *s.*
3. 8, less than least of all *s.*
4. 12, perfecting of the *s.*
5. 3, not named among you, as becometh *s.*

Col. 1. 12, the *s.* in light.
1 Thes. 3. 13, at coming of our Lord with *s.*
2 Thes. 1. 10, to be glorified in his *s.*
1 Tim. 5. 10, if she have washed the *s.* feet.
Jude 3, faith once delivered to *s.*
Rev. 5. 8; 8. 3, 4, the prayers of *s.*
See Phil. 4. 21; Rev. 11. 18; 13. 7; 14. 12; 15. 3.

Saints of God. Deu. 33. 2; 1 Sam. 2. 9; Ps. 145. 10; 148. 14; 149.; Prov. 2. 8; Dan. 7. 18; Zec. 14. 5.
believers. Rom. 8. 27; Eph. 2. 19; Col. 1. 12; Jude 3; Rev. 5. 8.
obligations of. 2 Chr. 6. 41; Ps. 30. 4; 31. 23; 34. 9; 132. 9; Rom. 16. 2, 15; 1 Cor. 6.; 2 Cor. 8.; 9.; Eph. 4.; 6. 18; Philem.; Heb. 6. 10; 13. 24.

Sake. Gen. 3. 17, cursed for thy *s.*
8. 21, not curse ground for man's *s.*
12. 13, be well with me for thy *s.*
18. 26, I will spare for their *s.*
30. 27, the Lord hath blessed me for thy *s.*
Num. 11. 29, enviest thou for my *s.*?
Deu. 1. 37; 3. 26; 4. 21, angry with me for your *s.*
2 Sam. 9. 1, shew kindness for Jonathan's *s.*
18. 5, deal gently for my *s.* [fold mercies.
Neh. 9. 31, for thy great mercies' *s.* R. V. mani-
Ps. 6. 4; 31. 16, save me for thy mercies' *s.*
23. 3, he leadeth me for his name's *s.*
44. 22, for thy *s.* are we killed.
106. 8, he saved them for his name's *s.*
Mat. 5. 10, persecuted for righteousness' *s.*
10. 18; Mk. 13. 9; Lu. 21. 12, for my *s.*
24. 22; Mk. 13. 20, for the elect's *s.*
John 11. 15, I am glad for your *s.* [R. V. me.
13. 38, wilt thou lay down thy life for my *s.*?
Rom. 13. 5; 1 Cor. 10. 25, for conscience *s.*
Col. 1. 24, for his body's *s.* which is the church.
1 Thes. 5. 13, for their work's *s.*
1 Tim. 5. 23, for thy stomach's *s.*
Tit. 1. 11, for lucre's *s.*
2 John 2, for the truth's *s.*
See Rom. 11. 28; 2 Cor. 8. 9; 1 Thes. 3. 9.

Sala, sā'-lă, Greek form of SALAH. Lu. 3. 35.

Salah, sā'-lăh, 'sprout' (?). Gen. 10. 24.

Salamis, săl'-ă-mĭs, a port at the eastern end of Cyprus. Acts 13. 5.

Salathiel, să-lā'-thĭ-ĕl, Greek form of SHEALTIEL. 1 Chr. 3. 17.

Salcah *or* **Salchah,** săl'-căh *or* săl'-chăh, 'road.' Deu. 3. 10.

Salem, sā'-lĕm, 'perfect.' Gen. 14. 18; Heb. 7. 1.

Salim, sā'-lĭm, Greek form of SALEM (?). John 3. 23.

Sallai, săl-lā'-ī, 'exaltation.' Neh. 11. 8.

Sallu, săl'-lū, same as SALLAI. 1 Chr. 9. 7.

Salma, săl'-mă, 'garment.' 1 Chr. 2. 11.

Salmon, săl'-mŏn. (1) 'shady.' Ps. 68. 14. R. V. Zalmon.
(2) 'garment.' Ru. 4. 20; Mat. 1. 4.

Salmone, săl-mō'-nĕ. The eastern promontory of Crete. Acts 27. 7.

Salome, să-lō'-mē, 'perfect.' Mk. 15. 40; 16. 1.

Salt (1 Chr. 18. 12). Heb. *Melaḥ:* Gk. ἅλς. Salt pits are referred to in Zep. 2. 9; a city of salt in Jos. 15. 62; and the valley of salt in 2 Sam. 8. 13.

Salt. Lev. 2. 13; Mk. 9. 49.
Lot's wife becomes a pillar of. Gen. 19. 26.
salt of the earth. Mat. 5. 13 (Lu. 14. 34; Col. 4. 6).

Salt sea (SIDDIM), the same as the Dead Sea. Gen. 14. 3; Num. 34. 3, 12; Deu. 3. 17; Jos. 3. 16; 12. 3; 15. 1, 2.

Salu, sā'-lū, same as SALLU (?). Num. 25. 14.

Salutations, between one wayfarer and another, and to labourers in the field (such as 'Peace be to you!' 'The Lord prosper you!' 'We wish you good luck,' &c.), are in daily use in Syria (comp. Ru. 2. 4; Ps. 129. 8). But often the forms of salutation were very elaborate and prolonged. Hence the injunction in Lu. 10. 4, to 'salute no man by the way.' Mk. 12. 38; Lu. 1. 29; Col. 4. 18; 2 Thes. 3. 17.

Salute. 1 Sam. 10. 4; 2 Kn. 4. 29; Mk. 15. 18.

Salvation. Gen. 49. 18, I have waited for thy *s.*
Ex. 14. 13; 2 Chr. 20. 17, see the *s.* of the Lord.
15. 2, he is become my *s.*
Deu. 32. 15, lightly esteemed the rock of his *s.*
1 Sam. 11. 13; 19. 5, the Lord wrought *s.* in Israel.
14. 45, Jonathan, who hath wrought this *s.*
2 Sam. 22. 51, he is the tower of *s.* for his king. R. V. great deliverance giveth he.
1 Chr. 16. 23, shew forth from day to day his *s.*
2 Chr. 6. 41, let thy priests be clothed with *s.*
Ps. 3. 8, *s.* belongeth to the Lord.
9. 14, I will rejoice in thy *s.*
14. 7, O that the *s.* of Israel were come.
25. 5, thou art the God of my *s.*
27. 1; 62. 6; Isa. 12. 2, my light and my *s.*
35. 3, say unto my soul, I am thy *s.*
37. 39, the *s.* of the righteous is of the Lord.
40. 10, I have declared thy faithfulness and *s.*
50. 23, to him will I shew the *s.* of God.
51. 12; 70. 4, restore the joy of thy *s.*
68. 20, he that is our God, is the God of *s.* R. V. deliverances.
69. 13, hear me in the truth of thy *s.*
69. 29, let thy *s.* set me up on high.
71. 15, my mouth shall shew forth thy *s.*
74. 12, working *s.* in the midst of the earth.
78. 22, they trusted not in his *s.*
85. 9, his *s.* is nigh them that fear him.
91. 16, will satisfy him and shew him my *s.*
96. 2, shew forth his *s.* from day to day.
98. 3, ends of the earth have seen the *s.*
116. 13, the cup of *s.*
118. 14; Isa. 12. 2, the Lord is become my *s.*
119. 41, let thy *s.* come.
119. 81, my soul fainteth for thy *s.*
119. 123, mine eyes fail for thy *s.*
119. 155, *s.* is far from the wicked.
119. 174, I have longed for thy *s.*
132. 16, I will clothe her priests with *s.*
144. 10, that giveth *s.* unto kings.
149. 4, beautify the meek with *s.*
Isa. 12. 3, the wells of *s.*
26. 1, *s.* will God appoint for walls.
33. 2, be thou our *s.* in time of trouble.
45. 8, earth open and let them bring forth *s.*
45. 17, saved with an everlasting *s.*
49. 8, in a day of *s.* have I helped thee.
51. 5, my *s.* is gone forth.
52. 7, feet of him that publisheth *s.*
52. 10, ends of the earth shall see *s.*
56. 1, my *s.* is near to come.
59. 11, we look for *s.*, but it is far off.
59. 16, his arm brought *s.*
59. 17, an helmet of *s.* on his head.
60. 18, call thy walls *S.*
61. 10, the garments of *s.*
62. 1, the *s.* thereof as a lamp.
63. 5, mine own arm brought *s.*
Jer. 3. 23, in vain is *s.* hoped for. R. V. help.
Lam. 3. 26, wait for the *s.* of the Lord.
Jon. 2. 9, *s.* is of the Lord.
Hab. 3. 8, ride on thy chariots of *s.*
3. 18, I will joy in the God of my *s.*
Zec. 9. 9, thy King, just, and having *s.*
Lu. 1. 69, an horn of *s.* for us.
1. 77, give knowledge of *s.* to his people.
2. 30, mine eyes have seen thy *s.*
3. 6, all flesh shall see the *s.* of God.
19. 9, this day is *s.* come to this house.
John 4. 22, *s.* is of the Jews.
Acts 4. 12, neither is there *s.* in any other.
13. 26, to you is the word of *s.* sent.
16. 17, these men shew to us the way of *s.*
Rom. 1. 16, the power of God to *s.*
10. 10, confession is made to *s.*
13. 11, now is our *s.* nearer.
2 Cor. 1. 6, comforted, it is for your *s.*
6. 2, the day of *s.*
7. 10, sorrow worketh repentance to *s.*
Eph. 1. 13, the Gospel of your *s.*
6. 17; 1 Thes. 5. 8, the helmet of *s.* and sword.
Phil. 1. 19, this shall turn to my *s.*
1. 28, an evident token of *s.*
2. 12, work out your own *s.*

1 Thes. 5. 9, hath appointed us to obtain *s.*
2 Thes. 2. 13, God hath chosen you to *s.*
2 Tim. 3. 15, wise unto *s.*
Tit. 2. 11, grace of God that bringeth *s.*
Heb. 1. 14, for them who shall be heirs of *s.*
2. 3, if we neglect so great *s.*
2. 10, the captain of their *s.*
5. 9, author of eternal *s.*
6. 9, things that accompany *s.*
9. 28, without sin unto *s.*
1 Pet. 1. 5, kept through faith unto *s.*
1. 9, end of faith, *s.* of your souls.
1. 10, of which *s.* the prophets enquired.
2 Pet. 3. 15, longsuffering of the Lord is *s.*
Jude 3, of the common *s.*
Rev. 7. 10, saying, *s.* to our God.
See Job 13. 16; 1 Sam. 2. 1; 2 Sam. 22. 36.

Salvation. Ex. 14. 13; 15.; 1 Sam. 11. 13; Ps. 3. 8; 37. 39; 62. 1; 68. 19; Isa. 33. 2; 46. 13; 59. 1; 63. 5; Lam. 3. 26; Mic. 7. 7; Hab. 3. 18; Lu. 1. 69; Phil. 1. 19, 28; Rev. 7. 10; 12. 10; 19. 1.
to be wrought out with fear and trembling. Phil. 2. 12.

Samaria, să-mâ′-rĭ-ă. (1) The province between Judæa and Galilee. Lu. 17. 11; John 4.
(2) The city built by Omri, king of Israel. 1 Kn. 16. 24; 20. 1; 2 Kn. 6. 24. It was destroyed by the Assyrians, B. C. 721-2, and rebuilt by Herod. Gospel preached there. Acts 8.

Samaritan, să-măr′-ĭ-tăn, belonging to Samaria.
parable of the good. Lu. 10. 33.
miracle performed on. Lu. 17. 16.

Samaritans, să-măr′-ĭ-tăns, inhabitants of Samaria. They were by origin a mixed heathen people, derived from the colonists whom the king of Assyria sent to inhabit the land of Samaria after he had carried the Israelites captive (2 Kn. 17. 24-41). Having been refused an alliance with the Jews after the Return from Exile, they built a temple on Mt. Gerizim. They accepted the Pentateuch and the books of Joshua and Judges. The Samaritans now number about 150. For the hostility between Jews and Samaritans, comp. John 4. 9. St. Luke lays special stress on our Lord's tolerance to these people (*parable of the good Samaritan: incident of the grateful Samaritan leper*).

Same. Job 4. 8, sow wickedness, reap the *s.*
Ps. 102. 27; Heb. 1. 12, thou art the *s.*
Mat. 5. 46, do not the publicans the *s.*?
Acts 1. 11, this *s.* Jesus shall come. R. V. omits.
Rom. 10. 12, the *s.* Lord over all.
12. 16; 1 Cor. 1. 10; Phil. 4. 2, be of *s.* mind.
Heb. 13. 8, *s.* yesterday, to day, and for ever.
See 1 Cor. 10. 3; 12. 4; 15. 39; Eph. 4. 10.

Samgar-nebo, săm′-găr-nē′-bō, 'Be gracious, Nebo' (?). Jer. 39. 3.

Samlah, săm′-lăh, 'garment.' Gen. 36. 36.

Samos, sā′-mŏs, 'a height' (?). Acts 20. 15.

Samothracia, săm-ō-thrā′-çĭ-ă. Acts 16. 11.

Samson, săm′-sǫn, 'like the sun.' Jud. 13.-16.
delivered up to Philistines. Jud. 16. 21.
his death. Jud. 16. 30.

Samuel, săm′-ū-ĕl, 'name of God,' or 'heard of God.' 1 Sam. 1. 20.
born, and presented to the Lord. 1 Sam. 1. 19, 26.
ministers to the Lord. 1 Sam. 3.
the Lord speaks to. 1 Sam. 3. 11.
judges Israel. 1 Sam. 7.; 8. 1; Acts 13. 20.
anoints Saul king. 1 Sam. 10. 1.
rebukes Saul for sin. 1 Sam. 13. 13; 15. 16.
anoints David. 1 Sam. 16.; 19. 18.
his death. 1 Sam. 25. 1; 28. 3.
his spirit consulted by Saul. 1 Sam. 28. 12.
as a prophet. Ps. 99. 6; Acts 3. 24; Heb. 11. 32.

Sanballat, săn-băl′-lăt, 'Sin (the moon) giveth life' (?). Neh. 2. 10; 4.; 6. 2; 13. 28.

Sanctification by Christ. John 17. 19; 1 Cor. 1. 2, 30; 6. 11; Eph. 5. 26; Heb. 2. 11; 10. 10; Jude 1.
by the Spirit. Rom. 15. 16; 2 Thes. 2. 13; 1 Pet. 1. 2.

Sanctified: the seventh day, Gen. 2. 3. the firstborn to be, Ex. 13. 2. the people, Ex. 19. 10; Num. 11. 18; Jos. 3. 5. the tabernacle, Ex. 29.; 30.; Lev. 8. 10. the priests, Lev. 8. 30; 9.; 2 Chr. 5. 11.

Sanctify. Lev. 11. 44; 20. 7; Num. 11. 18; Jos. 3. 5; 7. 13; 1 Sam. 16. 5, *s.* yourselves.
Isa. 5. 16, God shall be *s.* in righteousness.
13. 3, I have commanded my *s.* ones. R. V. consecrated.
29. 23, they shall *s.* the Holy One.
66. 17, *s.* themselves in gardens.
Jer. 1. 5, I *s.* and ordained thee a prophet.
Ezek. 20. 41; 36. 23, I will be *s.* in you.
28. 25; 39. 27, *s.* in them in sight of heathen.
Joel 1. 14; 2. 15, *s.* ye a fast.
John 10. 36, him whom the Father *s.*
17. 17, *s.* them through thy truth.
17. 19, for their sakes I *s.* myself.
Acts 20. 32; 26. 18, inheritance among them that are *s.*
Rom. 15. 16, being *s.* by the Holy Ghost.
1 Cor. 1. 2, to them that are *s.*
6. 11, but now ye are *s.*
7. 14, husband is *s.* by the wife, and the wife is *s.*
Eph. 5. 26, *s.* and cleanse the church.
1 Thes. 5. 23, the very God of peace *s.* you.
1 Tim. 4. 5, it is *s.* by the word of God.
2 Tim. 2. 21, a vessel *s.* for the Master's use.
Heb. 2. 11, he that *s.* and they who are *s.*
10. 10, by the which will we are *s.*
10. 14, perfected for ever them that are *s.*
13. 12, that he might *s.* the people.
1 Pet. 3. 15, *s.* the Lord God in your hearts.
Jude 1, to them that are *s.* by God the Father. R. V. beloved in.
See Job 1. 5; Mat. 23. 17.

Sanctuary. Ex. 15. 17, plant them in the *s.*
25. 8, let them make me a *s.*
36. 1; 3. 4, work for the *s.*
Num. 7. 9, service of *s.* belongeth to them.
Neh. 10. 39, where are the vessels of the *s.*
Ps. 74. 7, they have cast fire into thy *s.*
Isa. 60. 13, beautify the place of my *s.*
Lam. 2. 7, the Lord hath abhorred his *s.*
See Dan. 8. 11; 9. 17.

Sanctuary, God, of His people. Isa. 8. 14; Ezek. 11. 16. *See* Ps. 20. 2; 63. 2; 68. 24; 73. 17; 77. 13; 78. 54; 96. 6; 134.; 150.; Heb. 8.; 9. *See* TEMPLE.

Sand (Prov. 27. 3; Jer. 5. 22). Heb. *Ḥôl*: Gk. ἄμμος. Sand abounds along the seaboard of Palestine, and is used to symbolize abundance, insecurity, extensiveness, and weight.
Gen. 22. 17, as the *s.* which is upon the sea shore.
Hos. 1. 10; Rev. 20. 8, as the *s.* of the sea.
Heb. 11. 12, the *s.* which is by the sea.
See Job 6. 3; Prov. 27. 3; Mat. 7. 26.

Sandals. Mk. 6. 9, be shod with *s.*
Acts 12. 8, bind on thy *s.*

Sang. Ex. 15. 1; Neh. 12. 42; Job 38. 7.

Sanhedrin, The (Gk. συνέδριον, lit., 'a sitting together;' in A. V. and R. V. 'council'), was the great 'Council' of the Jewish Church and people, which, after Alexander's conquest, if not before, held chief authority 'in all causes and over all persons, ecclesiastical and civil.' It was suggested by the old institution of seventy-two elders (six from each tribe), appointed by Moses (Ex. 18. 14; Num. 11. 16). It consisted of an equal number (twenty-four) of priests, scribes, and elders, all of whom were required to be married, above thirty years of age, well instructed in the Law, and of good report among the people. This constituted the Supreme Court of Judicature and Administrative Council, taking cognizance of false doctrine and teaching, as well as of breaches of the Mosaic Law, and regulating both civil and ecclesiastical observances peculiar to the Jewish nation.

Sank. Ex. 15. 5, they *s.* into the bottom.

Sansannah, săn-săn′-năh, 'palm branch.' Jos. 15. 31.
Sap. Ps. 104. 16, trees full of *s.*
Saph, săph, 'threshold.' 2 Sam. 21. 18.
Saphir, sā′-phĭr, 'beautiful.' Mic. 1. 11.
Sapphira, săpph-ī′-ră, Greek form of SAPHIR (feminine). Acts 5. 1.
Sapphire. Heb. *Sappîr:* Gk. *σάπφειρος*. The Hebrew denotes that on which something is engraved or inscribed. According to the Targum, the Tables of the Law were made of it. Esp., one of the gems in the breastplate of the high priest. It is one of the three varieties of corundum, of bluish colour, obtained by the ancients from Ethiopia and India. Job 28. 16; Lam. 4. 7; Ezek. 28. 13; Rev. 21. 19.
Ex. 24. 10, a paved work of a *s.* stone.
Ezek. 1. 26, as the appearance of a *s.* stone.
10. 1, as it were a *s.* stone.
Sara, sâr′-ă, Greek form of SARAH. Heb. 11. 11.
Sarah, sâr′-ăh. (1) 'princess.' Gen. 17. 15. (Sarai). Gen. 11.; 12.; 20. 2. *See* ABRAHAM.
her death and burial. Gen. 23. (Heb. 11. 11; 1 Pet. 3. 6.
(2) for SERAH. Num. 26. 46.
Sarai, sâr′-ā-ī, 'contentious' (?). Gen. 11. 29.
Saraph, sâr′-ăph, 'burning.' 1 Chr. 4. 22.
Sardine. Rev. 4. 3, like a jasper and *s.* stone. R. V. sardius.
Sardis, sär′-dĭs, church of. Rev. 1. 11; 3. 1.
Sardites, sär′-dītes, descendants of Sered. Num. 26. 26.
Sardius, Sardine (Ezek. 28. 13; Rev. 4. 3). Heb. *Odêm*, 'reddish gem:' Gk. *σάρδιος*, 'from Sardis.' R. V. marg. ruby. A variety of chalcedony, of many colours, each variety receiving a different name. The Hebrew *Odêm* refers probably to the red or brownish red carnelian.
Ex. 28. 17, the first row shall be a *s.*
Sardonyx (Rev. 21. 20). Gk. *σαρδόνυξ*, 'finger-nail onyx.' Sardonyx is a chalcedony with at least three stripes of different colours.
Sarepta, să-rĕp′-tă, Greek form of ZAREPHATH. Lu. 4. 26.
Sargon, sär′-gŏn, '[God] appoints the king' (?). Isa. 20. 1.
Sarid, sâr′-ĭd, 'survivor.' Jos. 19. 10.
Saron, sâr′-ŏn, Greek form of SHARON. Acts 9. 35.
Sarsechim, sär′-sĕ-chĭm. Jer. 39. 3.
Saruch, sâr′-ŭch, Greek form of SERUG. Lu. 3. 35.
Sat. Jud. 20. 26, they *s.* before the Lord.
Job 29. 25, I *s.* chief.
Ps. 26. 4, have not *s.* with vain persons.
Jer. 15. 17, I *s.* alone because of thy hand.
Ezek. 3. 15, I *s.* where they *s.* R. V. to where they sat.
Mat. 4. 16, the people who *s.* in darkness.
Mk. 16. 19, he *s.* on the right hand of God.
Lu. 7. 15, he that was dead *s.* up.
10. 39, Mary *s.* at Jesus' feet.
John 4. 6, *s.* thus on the well.
Acts 2. 3, cloven tongues *s.* upon each.
See Ez. 10. 16; Neh. 1. 4; Ps. 137. 1; Rev. 4. 3.
Satan, sā′-tăn, 'adversary.' 1 Chr. 21. 1, *S.* provoked David.
Ps. 109. 6, let *S.* stand at his right hand.
Mat. 12. 26; Mk. 3. 23; Lu. 11. 18, if *S.* cast out *S.*
16. 23; Mk. 8. 33; Lu. 4. 8, get behind me, *S.*
Lu. 10. 18, I beheld *S.* as lightning fall.
Acts 5. 3, why hath *S.* filled thine heart.
26. 18, turned them from power of *S.*
2 Cor. 12. 7, messenger of *S.* to buffet me.
2 Thes. 2. 9, after the working of *S.*
1 Tim. 1. 20, whom I have delivered unto *S.*
5. 15, already turned aside after *S.*
See Rom. 16. 20; 1 Cor. 5. 5; 2 Cor. 2. 11; 11. 14.
See also DEVIL.
Satiate. Jer. 31. 14, 25; 46. 10.
Satisfy. Job 38. 27, to *s.* the desolate.
Ps. 17. 15, I shall be *s.* when I awake.
22. 26, the meek shall eat and be *s.*
Ps. 36. 8, they shall be *s.* with fatness.
37. 19, in days of famine be *s.*
59. 15, and grudge if they be not *s.*
63. 5, my soul shall be *s.*
81. 16, with honey should I have *s.* thee.
90. 14, *s.* us early with thy mercy.
91. 16, with long life will I *s.* him.
103. 5, who *s.* thy mouth with good.
104. 13, the earth is *s.*
105. 40, he *s.* them with bread from heaven.
107. 9, he *s.* the longing soul.
132. 15, I will *s.* her poor with bread.
Prov. 6. 30, if he steal to *s.* his soul.
12. 11, he that tilleth his land shall be *s.* R. V. have plenty.
14. 14, a good man shall be *s.* from himself.
19. 23, he that hath it shall abide *s.*
20. 13, open thine eyes and thou shalt be *s.*
30. 15, three things never *s.*
Eccl. 1. 8, the eye is not *s.* with seeing.
4. 8, neither is his eye *s.* with riches.
5. 10, shall not be *s.* with silver.
Isa. 9. 20; Mic. 6. 14, shall eat and not be *s.*
53. 11, travail of his soul and be *s.*
58. 10, if thou *s.* the afflicted soul.
58. 11, the Lord shall *s.* thy soul in drought.
Jer. 31. 14, shall be *s.* with my goodness.
Ezek. 16. 28, yet thou couldest not be *s.*
Am. 4. 8, wandered to drink, but were not *s.*
Hab. 2. 5, as death and cannot be *s.*
See Ex. 15. 9; Deu. 14. 29; Job 19. 22; 27. 14.
Saul, saul, 'asked for.' (1) king of Israel, his parentage, anointing by Samuel, prophesying, and acknowledgment as king. 1 Sam. 9.; 10.
his disobedience, and rejection by God. 1 Sam. 14. 31; 15.
possessed by an evil spirit, quieted by David. 1 Sam. 16. 14, 15, 23.
favours David, 1 Sam. 18. 5. seeks to kill him, 1 Sam. 18. 10. pursues him, 1 Sam. 20.; 23.; 24.; 26.
slays priests for succouring David. 1 Sam. 22. 9.
enquires of the witch of En-dor. 1 Sam. 28. 7.
his ruin and suicide. 1 Sam. 28. 15; 31.; 1 Chr. 10.
his posterity. 1 Chr. 8. 33.
(2) of Tarsus. *See* PAUL.
Save (*v.*). Gen. 45. 7, to *s.* your lives.
47. 25, thou hast *s.* our lives.
Deu. 28. 29, spoiled and no man shall *s.* thee.
33. 29, O people, *s.* by the Lord.
Jos. 10. 6, come up quickly and *s.* us.
Jud. 6. 15, wherewith shall I *s.* Israel?
1 Sam. 4. 3, the ark may *s.* us.
10. 27, how shall this man *s.* us?
11. 3, if there be no man to *s.* us, we will come.
14. 6, no restraint to *s.* by many or by few.
2 Sam. 19. 9, the king *s.* us, and now he is fled. R. V. delivered.
2 Kn. 6. 10, *s.* himself there, not once nor twice.
Job 2. 6, in thine hand, but *s.* his life. R. V. spare.
22. 29, he shall *s.* the humble.
Job 26. 2, how *s.* thou.
Ps. 7. 10, God who *s.* the upright.
20. 6, the Lord *s.* his anointed.
34. 18, he *s.* such as be of a contrite spirit.
44. 3, neither did their own arm *s.* them.
60. 5, *s.* with thy right hand.
72. 4, he shall *s.* the children of the needy.
80. 3; Prov. 28. 18; Jer. 17. 14; Mat. 10. 22; 24. 13; Mk. 13. 13; 16. 16; John 10. 9; Acts 2. 21; 16. 31; Rom. 5. 9; 9. 27; 10. 9; 11. 26, shall be *s.*
86. 2, *s.* thy servant that trusteth.
109. 31, *s.* him from those that condemn.
118. 25, *s.*, I beseech thee, send prosperity.
119. 94, *s.* me, for I have sought.
119. 146, *s.* me, and I shall keep thy testimonies.
138. 7, thy right hand shall *s.*
Prov. 20. 22, wait on Lord and he shall *s.* thee.
Isa. 35. 4, your God will come and *s.* you.
43. 12, I have declared and have *s.*
45. 20, pray to a god that cannot *s.*
45. 22, look unto me and be ye *s.*

THE ROAD THROUGH SAMARIA

The road from Galilee to Jerusalem winds through the hilly country of central Palestine.
(*L. A. Fereday*)

DEAD SEA SCROLL

Ancient Hebrew manuscript discovered in 1947 in a cave near the Dead Sea. This is a chapter from a collection of Psalms known as the Thanksgiving Scroll. (*Friends of the Hebrew University of Jerusalem*)

Job 18. 15, brimstone shall be *s.* on his habitation.
37. 11, he *s.* his bright cloud. R. V. spreadeth abroad.
38. 24, which *s.* the east wind.
Ps. 68. 30, *s.* thou the people that delight in war.
92. 9, the workers of iniquity shall be *s.*
147. 16, he *s.* the hoar frost.
Prov. 11. 24, there is that *s.* and yet increaseth.
20. 8, a king *s.* evil with his eyes.
20. 26, a wise king *s.* the wicked.
Jer. 10. 21, all their flocks shall be *s.*
23. 1, woe to pastors that *s.* the sheep.
50. 17, Israel is a *s.* sheep. [be *s.*
Zec. 13. 7; Mat. 26. 31; Mk. 14. 27, sheep shall
Mat. 9. 36, *s.* as sheep having no shepherd.
12. 30; Lu. 11. 23, he that gathereth not with me *s.*
See John 11. 52; 16. 32; Acts 8. 1; Jas. 1. 1.

Scent. Job 14. 9; Jer. 48. 11; Hos. 14. 7.

Sceptre. Gen. 49. 10; Num. 24. 17; Esth. 5. 2; Ps. 45. 6; Heb. 1. 8.

Sceva, scē´-vă, 'left-handed.' Acts 19. 14.

Schism condemned. 1 Cor. 1.; 3.; 11. 18; 12. 25; 2 Cor. 13. 11.

Scholar. 1 Chr. 25. 8; Mal. 2. 12.

School. Acts 19. 9, *s.* of one Tyrannus (i. e., a lecture-hall).

Schoolmaster. Gal. 3. 24, the law was our *s.* R. V. tutor.

Science. Dan. 1. 4; 1 Tim. 6. 20.

Scoff. Hab. 1. 10, shall *s.* at kings.

Scoffers, their sin. Ps. 1.; 2.; 123. 4; Prov. 1. 22; 3. 34; 9. 7, 12; 13. 1; 14. 6; 15. 12; 19. 25, 29; 21. 24; 24. 9; Isa. 28. 14; 29. 20; 2 Pet. 3. 3.

Scorch. Mat. 13. 6; Mk. 4. 6; Rev. 16. 8.

Scorn. Esth. 3. 6; Job 16. 20; Ps. 44. 13; 79. 4.

Scorner. Prov. 9. 8, reprove not a *s.*
13. 1, a *s.* heareth not rebuke.
19. 25, smite a *s.* [mocketh at.
19. 28, an ungodly witness *s.* judgment. R. V.
19. 29, judgments are prepared for *s.*
21. 11, when *s.* is punished simple is made wise.
24. 9, the *s.* is an abomination.
Isa. 29. 20, the *s.* is consumed.
Hos. 7. 5, stretched out hands with *s.*
See Ps. 1. 1; Prov. 1. 22; 3. 34; 9. 12.

Scorpion. Heb. *Akrâb:* Gk. σκορπίος: Zool. S. numerous. Ten distinct species are found in Palestine, where they swarm in many parts.
Deu. 8. 15, fiery serpents and *s.*
Lu. 10. 19, power to tread on *s.*
Rev. 9. 3, as the *s.* of the earth.

Scourge. Job 5. 21, the *s.* of the tongue.
9. 23, if the *s.* slay suddenly.
Isa. 28. 15, the overflowing *s.*
Mat. 10. 17; 23. 34, they will *s.* you.
John 2. 15, a *s.* of small cords.
Acts 22. 25, is it lawful to *s.* a Roman?
Heb. 12. 6, the Lord *s.* every son.
See Jos. 23. 13; Isa. 10. 26; John 19. 1.

Scourging. Lev. 19. 20; Deu. 25. 3; 2 Cor. 11. 24. of Christ. Mat. 27. 26; Lu. 23. 16.

Scrabble, to scratch, paw with the hands, make marks. 1 Sam. 21. 13.

Scrape. Lev. 14. 41; Job 2. 8; Ezek. 26. 4.

Scribes. Gk. γραμματεύς, a term which means more than 'writer,' and implies learning, the Latin *litteratus;* the Hebrew equivalent is *Sōpherim.* Their functions were to guard, transcribe, and interpret the Scriptures.
1 Chr. 27. 32, a wise man and a *s.* [counted.
Isa. 33. 18, where is the *s.*? R. V. he that
Jer. 8. 8, the pen of the *s.* is in vain.
Mat. 5. 20, exceed righteousness of the *s.*
7. 29, authority, and not as the *s.*
13. 52, every *s.* instructed unto kingdom.
Mk. 12. 38; Lu. 20. 46, beware of the *s.*

Scribes. 2 Sam. 8. 17; 20. 25; 1 Kn. 4. 3; 2 Kn. 19. 2; 22. 8; 1 Chr. 27. 32; Ez. 4. 8; 7. 6; Neh. 8. 4; Jer. 36. 26; Mat. 8. 19; 17. 10; Mk. 12. 35.
and Pharisees, censured by Christ. Mat. 15. 3; 23. 2; Mk. 2. 16; 3. 22; Lu. 11. 15, 53; 20. 1.
conspire against Christ. Mk. 11. 18; Lu. 20. 19; 22. 2; 23. 10.
persecute Stephen. Acts 6. 12.

Scrip, a small bag or wallet, made of a 'scrap' of stuff (Skeat). 1 Sam. 17. 40; Mat. 10. 10; Lu. 10. 4; 22. 35.

Scriptures, the Holy, given by inspiration of God through the Holy Ghost. Acts 1. 16; 2 Tim. 3. 16; Heb. 3. 7; 2 Pet. 1. 21.
Christ confirms and teaches out of. Mat. 4. 4; Mk. 12. 10; Lu. 24. 27; John 7. 42.
testify of Christ. John 5. 39; Acts 10. 43; 18. 28; 1 Cor. 15. 3.
profitable for doctrine, instruction, and rule of life. Ps. 19. 7; 119. 9; John 17. 17; Acts 20. 32; Rom. 15. 4; 16. 26; 2 Tim. 3. 16, 17.
make wise unto salvation. John 20. 31; Rom. 1. 2; 2 Tim. 3. 15; Jas. 1. 21; 2 Pet. 1. 19.
to be taught diligently. Deu. 6. 9; 17. 19; 1 Pet. 2. 2.
to be kept unaltered. Deu. 4. 2; Prov. 30. 6; 2 Tim. 1. 13 (Jude 3); Rev. 22. 18.
to be searched, John 5. 39. example, Acts 17. 11.
formerly given by God through the prophets, Lu. 16. 31; Rom. 3. 2; 9. 4; Heb. 1. 1. in the last days through Jesus Christ, Heb. 1. 2. fulfilled by Him, Mat. 5. 17; Lu. 24. 27; John 19. 24; Acts 13. 29.
appealed to by the apostles. Acts 2.; 3.; 8. 32; 17. 2; 18. 24; 28. 23.
rejecters will be judged by. John 12. 48; Heb. 2. 3; 10. 28; 12. 25.

Scroll, the heavens compared to. Isa. 34. 4; Rev. 6. 14.

Scythian, scўth´-ĭ-ăn. Col. 3. 11.

Sea, God's power over. Ex. 14. 6; 15.; Neh. 9. 11; Job 38. 11; Ps. 65. 7; 66. 6; 89. 9; 93. 4; 107. 23; 114.; Prov. 8. 29; Isa. 51. 10; 50. 2; Nah. 1. 4.
the molten, 1 Kn. 7. 23; 2 Chr. 4. 2. of glass, Rev. 4. 6; 15. 2.
no more. Rev. 21. 1.

Seah, a dry measure = ⅓ of an ephah = 12.96 litres = 1 peck 3½ quarts.

Seal of righteousness. Rom. 4. 11.

Sealed believers, 2 Cor. 1. 22; Eph. 1. 13; 4. 30.
in heaven, number of, Rev. 7.
book opened. Rev. 5. 6.
utterances of the seven thunders. Rev. 10. 4.

Seals. Gen. 38. 18; Ex. 28. 11; 1 Kn. 21. 8; Job 38. 14; S. of S. 8. 6; Jer. 32. 10; Dan. 12. 4; Mat. 27. 66.

Seam. John 19. 23, coat was without *s.*

Sear, to scorch (as with a hot iron). 1 Tim. 4. 2.

Search (*n.*). Job 11. 7; Ps. 64. 6; 77. 6; Jer. 2. 34.

Search (*v.*). Num. 13. 2, that they may *s.* the land. R. V. spy out.
1 Chr. 28. 9, the Lord *s.* all hearts.
Job 13. 9, is it good that he should *s.* you out?
28. 27, he prepared it and *s.* it out.
29. 16, the cause I knew not I *s.* out.
32. 11, I waited whilst ye *s.* out what to say.
36 26, can number of his years be *s.* out.
Ps. 44. 21, shall not God *s.* this out?
139. 1, thou hast *s.* me and known me.
139. 23, *s.* me and know my heart.
Prov. 25. 2, honour of kings to *s.* out a matter.
25. 27, for men to *s.* out their own glory.
Eccl. 1. 13; 7. 25, I gave my heart to *s.* wisdom.
Isa. 40. 28, no *s.* of his understanding.
Jer. 17. 10, I the Lord *s.* the heart.
29. 13, when ye shall *s.* for me with all.
31. 37, foundations of the earth *s.* out.
Lam. 3. 40, let us *s.* our ways, and turn.
Ezek. 34. 6, none did *s.* or seek after them.
34. 8, neither did my shepherds *s.* for my flock.
34. 11, I will *s.* my sheep.
Am. 9. 3, I will *s.* and take them out thence.
Zep. 1. 12, I will *s.* Jerusalem with candles.
John 5. 39; Acts 17. 11, *s.* the scriptures.
Rom. 8. 27, that *s.* hearts knoweth mind.
1 Cor. 2. 10, the Spirit *s.* all things. [gently.
1 Pet. 1. 10, which salvation prophets *s.* dili-
See Job 10. 6; 28. 3; Prov. 2. 4; 1 Pet. 1. 11.

Searcher of hearts, God. 1 Chr. 28. 9; 29. 17; Ps. 7. 9; Jer. 17. 10.
Season. (1) Gen. 1. 14, for signs, and *s.*, and days.
Deu. 28. 12, give rain in his *s.*
Job 5. 26, as a shock of corn in his *s.*
Ps. 1. 3, that bringeth forth fruit in his *s.*
104. 19, appointed the moon for *s.*
Eccl. 3. 1, to every thing there is a *s.* and a time.
Jer. 5. 24, former and latter rain in his *s.*
33. 20, day and night in their *s.*
Ezek. 34. 26, cause shower to come down in *s.*
Dan. 2. 21, changeth the times and *s.*
Hos. 2. 9, take away my wine in *s.*
Mat. 21. 41, render the fruits in their *s.*
Lu. 20. 10, at the *s.* he sent servant.
Acts 1. 7, not for you to know times and *s.*
(2) a period of time, awhile. Gen. 40. 4, continued a *s.* in ward.
2 Chr. 15. 3, for long *s.* without true God.
Ps. 22. 2, I cry in the night *s.*
Prov. 15. 23, word spoken in due *s.*
Isa. 50. 4, know how to speak a word in *s.* R. V. sustain with words.
Dan. 7. 12, lives prolonged for a *s.*
Lu. 1. 20, my words shall be fulfilled in *s.*
23. 8, desirous to see him of a long *s.* R. V. time.
John 5. 4, angel went down at certain *s.* R. V. omits.
5. 35, willing for a *s.* to rejoice.
Acts 13. 11, not seeing the sun for a *s.*
24. 25, a convenient *s.*
2 Tim. 4. 2, be instant in *s.*
Heb. 11. 25, pleasures of sin for a *s.*
See 1 Thes. 5. 1; 1 Pet. 1. 6; Rev. 6. 11; 20. 3.
Seasons, continuance of. Gen. 8. 22.
Seat. 1 Sam. 20. 18, thy *s.* will be empty.
Job 23. 3, that I might come even to his *s.*
29. 7, when I prepared my *s.* in the street.
Ps. 1. 1, the *s.* of the scornful.
Am. 6. 3, cause *s.* of violence to come near.
Mat. 21. 12, *s.* of them that sold doves.
23. 2, scribes sit in Moses' *s.*
23. 6; Mk. 12. 39, chief *s.* in synagogues.
See Ezek. 8. 3; 28. 2; Lu. 1. 52; Rev. 2. 13; 4. 4.
Seaweed, 'weeds' in Jon. 2. 5. *See* BULRUSH (4) *Sûph.*
Seba, sē'-bă, 'man'(?). (1) Gen. 10. 7. (2) Isa. 43. 3; 45. 14.
Sebat, sē'-băt, 'rest'(?). Zec. 1. 7. R. V. Shebat, *q. v.*
Secacah, sĕ-cā'-căh, 'enclosure.' Jos. 15. 61.
Sechu, sē'-chû, 'watch-tower.' 1 Sam. 19. 22.
Second coming, Christ's. Acts 1. 11.
Second death. Rev. 20. 14.
Secret (*n.*). Gen. 49. 6, come not into their *s.* R. V. council.
Job 11. 6, the *s.* of wisdom.
15. 8, hast thou heard the *s.* of God?
29. 4, the *s.* of God was upon my tabernacle.
Ps. 25. 14, *s.* of Lord is with them that fear.
27. 5, in *s.* of his tabernacle will he hide. R. V. covert.
139. 15, when I was made in *s.*
Prov. 3. 32, his *s.* is with the righteous.
9. 17, bread eaten in *s.*
21. 14, a gift in *s.* pacifieth anger.
Isa. 45. 19; 48. 16, I have not spoken in *s.*
Mat. 6. 4, thy Father who seeth in *s.*
6. 6, pray to thy Father which is in *s.*
24. 26, he is in the *s.* chambers. R. V. inner.
John 18. 20, in *s.* have I said nothing.
See Prov. 11. 13; 20. 19; Dan. 2. 18; 4. 9.
Secret (*adj.*). Deu. 29. 29, *s.* things belong to God.
Jud. 3. 19, I have a *s.* errand.
13. 18, my name, seeing it is *s.* R. V. wonder-[ful.
Ps. 19. 12, cleanse thou me from *s.* faults. R. V. hidden.
Ps. 90. 8, our *s.* sins. [V. hidden.
Prov. 27. 5, open rebuke better than *s.* love. R.
See S. of S. 2. 14; Isa. 45. 3; Jer. 13. 17.
Secretly. Gen. 31. 27, flee away *s.*
Deu. 13. 6, entice thee *s.*, saying.
1 Sam. 18. 22, commune with David *s.*
23. 9, Saul *s.* practised mischief. R. V. devised.
2 Sam. 12. 12, for thou didst it *s.*
Job 4. 12, a thing was *s.* brought to me.
13. 10, if you *s.* accept persons.
31. 27, my heart hath been *s.* enticed.
Ps. 10. 9, he lieth in wait *s.* R. V. in the covert.
31. 20, keep them *s.* from the strife.
John 11. 28, she called her sister *s.*
19. 38, *s.* for fear of the Jews.
See Deu. 27. 24; Lev. 28. 57; 2 Kn. 17. 9. [18. 15.
Secrets, not to be revealed. Prov. 25. 9; Mat.
Secret things belong to God. Deu. 29. 29; Job 15. 8.
revealed by Him. Ps. 25. 14; Prov. 3. 32; Am. 3. 7; Mat. 11. 25; 13. 35; Rom. 16. 25; 2 Cor. 3. 13.
all known to Him. Ps. 44. 21; 90. 8; Eccl. 12. 14; Mat. 6. 4; Mk. 4. 22; Rom. 2. 16.
Sect. Acts 5. 17; 15. 5; 24. 5; 26. 5; 28. 22.
Secundus, sĕ-cŭn'-dŭs, 'second.' Acts 20. 4.
Secure, without care, free from apprehension or danger. Jud. 8. 11; Job 11. 18; 12. 6; Mat. 28. 14.
Securely. Prov. 3. 29; Mic. 2. 8.
Sedition. Ez. 4. 15; Lu. 23. 19; Acts 24. 5.
Seduce. Mk. 13. 22, shew signs to *s.* R. V. that they may lead astray.
1 John 2. 26, concerning them that *s.* you. R. V. would lead you astray.
Rev. 2. 20, to *s.* my servants.
See Prov. 12. 26; 1 Tim. 4. 1; 2 Tim. 3. 13.
See. Gen. 11. 5, came down to *s.* the city.
44. 23, you shall *s.* my face no more.
45. 28, I will go and *s.* him before I die.
Ex. 12. 13, when I *s.* the blood.
14. 13, *s.* the salvation of the Lord.
33. 20, there shall no man *s.* me and live.
Deu. 3. 25, let me *s.* the good land.
34. 4, I have caused thee to *s.* it.
2 Kn. 6. 17, open his eyes, that he may *s.*
10. 16, *s.* my zeal for the Lord.
Job 7. 7, mine eye shall no more *s.* good.
19. 26, yet in my flesh shall I *s.* God.
Ps. 27. 13, believed to *s.* the goodness.
66. 5, come and *s.* the works of God.
94. 9, shall he not *s.*?
Isa. 6. 10, lest they *s.* with their eyes.
32. 3, eyes of them that *s.* shall not be dim.
33. 17, shall *s.* the king in his beauty.
40. 5, all flesh shall *s.* it together.
52. 8, they shall *s.* eye to eye.
Jer. 5. 21; Ezek. 12. 12, eyes and *s.* not.
Mat. 5. 8, they shall *s.* God.
12. 38, we would *s.* a sign.
13. 14; Mk. 4. 12; Acts 28. 26, *s.* ye shall *s.*
27. 4, *s.* thou to that.
28. 6, *s.* the place where the Lord lay.
Mk. 8. 18, having eyes *s.* ye not.
Lu. 17. 23, *s.* here or *s.* there. R. V. lo.
John 1. 39; 11. 34; Rev. 6. 1, come and *s.*
1. 50, thou shalt *s.* greater things.
9. 25, I was blind, now I *s.*
9. 39, that they who *s.* not might *s.*
Heb. 2. 9, but we *s.* Jesus. R. V. behold him.
1 Pet. 1. 8, though now we *s.* him not.
1 John 3. 2, we shall *s.* him as he is.
See Mat. 27. 24; John 1. 51.
Seed. Gen. 3. 15, enmity between thy *s.*
47. 19, give us *s.*
Ex. 16. 31, manna like coriander *s.*
Lev. 19. 19, thou shalt not sow mingled *s.*
26. 16, ye shall sow your *s.* in vain.
Num. 20. 5, it is no place of *s.*
Deu. 1. 8, to give it to their *s.* after them.
11. 10, not as Egypt where thou sowedst *s.*
14. 22, tithe all the increase of your *s.*
28. 38, thou shalt carry much *s.* into field.
Ps. 126. 6, bearing precious *s.*
Eccl. 11. 6, in the morning sow thy *s.*
Isa. 5. 10, the *s.* of an homer shall yield.
17. 11, in morning make thy *s.* to flourish.

Isa. 55. 10, give *s.* to the sower.
61. 9, the *s.* which the Lord hath blessed.
Jer. 2. 21, I had planted thee wholly a right *s.*
Joel 1. 17, the *s.* is rotten.
Am. 9. 13, overtake him that soweth *s.*
Hag. 2. 19, is the *s.* yet in the barn?
Zec. 8. 12, the *s.* shall be prosperous..
Mal. 2. 15, that he might seek a godly *s.*
See 1 Cor. 15. 38; 1 Pet. 1. 23.

Seed: of the woman, Gen. 3. 15; Rev. 12. of the serpent, Gen. 3. 15.
parables about. Mat. 13.; Lu. 8. 5.

Seek. Gen. 37. 15, what *s.* thou?
Num. 15. 39, that ye *s.* not after your own heart. R. V. go not about.
16. 10, *s.* ye the priesthood also.
Deu. 4. 29, if thou *s.* him with all thy heart.
12. 5, even to his habitation shall ye *s.* and come.
23. 6; Ez. 9. 12, thou shalt not *s.* their peace.
Ru. 3. 1, shall I not *s.* rest for thee.
1 Chr. 28. 9; 2 Chr. 15. 2, if thou *s.* him, he will be found.
2 Chr. 19. 3, hast prepared thine heart to *s.* God.
34. 3, Josiah began to *s.* after God.
Ez. 4. 2, we *s.* your God as ye do.
Neh. 2. 10, to *s.* the welfare of Israel.
Job 5. 8, I would *s.* unto God.
8. 5, *s.* unto God betimes.
20. 10, children shall *s.* to please the poor.
39. 29, from thence she *s.* the prey. R. V. spieth out.
Ps. 9. 10, hast not forsaken them that *s.* thee.
10. 4, the wicked will not *s.* after God. R. V. saith, He will not require it.
10. 15, *s.* out his wickedness till thou find none.
14. 2; 53. 2, if there were any that did *s.* God.
24. 6, generation of them that *s.* him.
27. 4, desired, that will I *s.* after.
27. 8, *s.* ye my face, thy face will I *s.*
34. 14; 1 Pet. 3. 11, *s.* peace and pursue it.
63. 1, early will I *s.* thee.
69. 32, your heart shall live that *s.* God.
83. 16, that they may *s.* thy name.
122. 9, I will *s.* thy good.
Prov. 1. 28, they shall *s.* me, but not find.
8. 17, those that *s.* me early shall find me.
11. 27, that diligently *s.* good.
21. 6, of them that *s.* death.
23. 30, they that go to *s.* mixed wine.
23. 35, I will *s.* it yet again.
Eccl. 1. 13; 7. 25, gave my heart to *s.* wisdom.
S. of S. 3. 2, I will *s.* him whom my soul loveth.
Isa. 1. 17, learn to do well, *s.* judgment.
8. 19, should not a people *s.* unto their God?
19. 3, they shall *s.* to charmers.
34. 16, *s.* ye out of the book of the Lord.
41. 17, when the needy *s.* water.
45. 19, I said not, *s.* ye my face in vain.
Jer. 5. 1, any that *s.* the truth.
29. 13, ye shall *s.* me and find when ye search.
30. 17, Zion whom no man *s.* after.
38. 4, this man *s.* not welfare of people. [him.
Lam. 3. 25, the Lord is good to the soul that *s.*
Ezek. 7. 25, they shall *s.* peace.
34. 16, I will *s.* that which was lost.
Dan. 9. 3, I set my face to *s.* by prayer.
Am. 5. 4, *s.* me and ye shall live.
Zep. 2. 3, *s.* ye the Lord, all ye meek.
Mal. 2. 7, they should *s.* the law at his mouth.
Mat. 6. 32, after these things do Gentiles *s.*
6. 33; Lu. 12. 31, *s.* first the kingdom of God.
7. 7; Lu. 11. 9, *s.* and ye shall find.
12. 39; 16. 4, adulterous generation *s.* a sign.
28. 5; Mk. 16. 6, I know that ye *s.* Jesus.
Mk. 1. 37, all men *s.* for thee.
8. 11, *s.* of him a sign from heaven.
Lu. 13. 7, I come *s.* fruit.
13. 24, many will *s.* to enter in.
15. 8, doth she not *s.* diligently.
19. 10, is come to *s.* and to save.
24. 5, why *s.* ye the living among the dead?
John 1. 38, what *s.* ye?
4. 23, the Father *s.* such to worship him.
John 7. 25, is not this he whom they *s.* to kill?
7. 34, ye shall *s.* me and shall not find me.
18. 8, if ye *s.* me, let these go their way.
20. 15, woman, whom *s.* thou?
Rom. 3. 11, there is none that *s.* after God.
1 Cor. 1. 22, the Greeks *s.* after wisdom.
10. 24, let no man *s.* his own.
13. 5, charity *s.* not her own.
2 Cor. 12. 14, I *s.* not yours, but you.
Phil. 2. 21, all *s.* their own things.
Col. 3. 1, *s.* those things which are above.
Heb. 11. 6, a rewarder of them that *s.* him.
11. 14, declare plainly that they *s.* a country.
13. 14, but we *s.* one to come.
1 Pet. 5. 8, *s.* whom he may devour.
Rev. 9. 6, in those days shall men *s.* death.
See Jer. 45. 5; Mat. 13. 45; John 6. 24; 1 Cor. 10. 33.

Seem. Gen. 19. 14, he *s.* as one that mocked.
29. 20, they *s.* to him but a few days.
Num. 16. 9, *s.* it but a small thing.
Prov. 14. 12, there is a way that *s.* right.
Lu. 8. 18, taken away that he *s.* to have. R. V. thinketh he hath.
24. 11, words *s.* as idle tales. R. V. appeared.
1 Cor. 3. 18, if any *s.* to be wise. R. V. thinketh that he is.
11. 16, if any man *s.* to be contentious.
Heb. 4. 1, lest any *s.* to come short.
12. 11, now no chastening *s.* to be joyous.
See Gen. 27. 12; Eccl. 9. 13; Acts 17. 18; Gal. 2. 6.

Seemly. Prov. 19. 10; 26. 1.

Seen. Gen. 32. 30, I have *s.* God face to face.
Ex. 14. 13, Egyptians whom ye have *s.* to day.
Jud. 6. 22, because I have *s.* an angel.
2 Kn. 20. 15, what have they *s.*
Job 13. 1, mine eye hath *s.* all this.
28. 7, a path the vulture's eye hath not *s.*
Ps. 37. 25, have I not *s.* righteous forsaken.
90. 15, years wherein we have *s.* evil.
Eccl. 6. 5, he hath not *s.* the sun.
Isa. 9. 2, have *s.* a great light.
64. 4; 1 Cor. 2. 9, neither hath eye *s.*
66. 8, who hath *s.* such things.
Mat. 6. 1; 23. 5, to be *s.* of men.
9. 33, never so *s.* in Israel.
Mk. 9. 1, till they have *s.* the kingdom of God.
Lu. 5. 26, we have *s.* strange things to day.
John 1. 18, no man hath *s.* God.
8. 57, hast thou *s.* Abraham?
John 14. 9, he that hath *s.* me hath *s.* the Father.
Acts 11. 23, when he had *s.* the grace of God.
1 Cor. 9. 1, have I not *s.* Jesus Christ.
1 Tim. 6. 16, whom no man hath *s.*, nor can see.
Heb. 11. 1, evidence of things not *s.*
1 Pet. 1. 8, whom having not *s.*, ye love.
See John 5. 37; 9. 37; 15. 24; 20. 29; Rom. 1. 20.

Seer. 1 Sam. 9. 9, a prophet was beforetime called a *s.*
2 Sam. 24. 11, the prophet Gad, David's *s.*

Seethe, to boil; *perf.* sod, *p. p.* sodden. Ex. 23. 19; 2 Kn. 4. 38; Ezek. 24. 5.

Segub, sē′-gŭb, 'elevated.' 1 Kn. 16. 34.

Seir, sē′-ĭr, 'rough.' (1) a man. Gen. 36. 20.
(2) mount, Edom, land of Esau. Gen. 14. 6; 32. 3; 36. 8; Deu. 33. 2; Jos. 24. 4; Isa. 21. 11; Ezek. 25. 8.
predictions about. Num. 24. 18; Ezek. 35. 2.

Seirath, sē-ī′-răth, 'well wooded.' Jud. 3. 26.

Seize. Job 3. 6; Ps. 55. 15; Jer. 49. 24; Mat. 21. 38.

Sela, sē′-lă, 'rock,' *or* **Selah.** Petra (2 Kn. 14. 7; Isa. 16. 1). The ancient capital of Arabia, founded by descendants of Esau.

Sela-hammahlekoth, sĕ-lă-hăm-măh′-lē-kōth, 'rock of escapes.' 1 Sam. 23. 28.

Selah, sē′-lăh, a musical direction, meaning probably an 'interlude.' Ps. 3. 2; 4. 2; 24. 6; 39. 5, 11; 46. 3; 48. 8; 50. 6; Hab. 3. 3, 9, 12, &c.

Seled, sē′-lĕd, 'exultation, or burning.' 1 Chr. 2. 30.

Seleucia, sĕ-leū′-çĭ-ă, the port of Antioch; named after Seleucus, a king of Syria. apostles at, Acts 13. 4.

Self. Tit. 1. 7; 2 Pet. 2. 10.
Self-denial. Prov. 23. 2; Jer. 35.; Lu. 3. 11; 14. 33; Acts 2. 45; 20. 24; Rom. 6. 12; 8. 13; 14. 20; 15. 1; Gal. 5. 24; Phil. 2. 4; Tit. 2. 12; Heb. 11. 24; 1 Pet. 2. 11.
Christ an example of. Mat. 4. 8; 8. 20; Rom. 15. 3; Phil. 2. 6.
incumbent on His followers. Mat. 10. 38; 16. 24; Mk. 8. 34; Lu. 9. 23.
Self-examination enjoined. Lam. 3. 40; Ps. 4. 4; 1 Cor. 11. 28; 2 Cor. 13. 5.
Selfishness. Isa. 56. 11; Rom. 15. 1; 1 Cor. 10. 24; 2 Cor. 5. 15; Phil. 2. 4, 21; 2 Tim. 3. 2; Jas. 2. 8.
Selfwill. Num. 14. 44; Deu. 1. 43; Ps. 75. 5; Tit. 1. 7; 2 Pet. 2. 10.
Sell. Gen. 25. 31, *s.* me thy birthright?
37. 27, come, let us *s.* him.
1 Kn. 21. 25, Ahab did *s.* himself to work.
Neh. 5. 8, will ye even *s.* your brethren?
Prov. 23. 23, buy the truth, and *s.* it not.
Joel 3. 8, I will *s.* your sons and daughters.
Am. 8. 5, that we may *s.* corn.
8. 6, and *s.* the refuse of the wheat.
Mat. 19. 21; Mk. 10. 21; Lu. 12. 33; 18. 22, *s.* that thou hast.
Lu. 22. 36, let him *s.* his garment.
Jas. 4. 13, we will buy and *s.*, and get gain. R. V. trade.
See Ps. 44. 12; Prov. 11. 26; 31. 24; Mat. 13. 44.
Seller. Isa. 24. 2; Ezek. 7. 12, 13; Acts 16. 14.
Sem, sĕm, Greek form of SHEM. Lu. 3. 36.
Semachiah, sĕm-ă-chī′-ăh, 'Jehovah sustains.' 1 Chr. 26. 7.
Semei, sĕm′-ĕ-ī, Greek form of SHIMEI. Lu. 3. 26.
Senaah, sĕn′-ă-ăh, perhaps 'thorny.' Ez. 2. 35.
Senators. Ps. 105. 22.
Send. Gen. 24. 7, God shall *s.* his angel.
24. 12, *s.* me good speed this day.
45. 5, God did *s.* me.
Ex. 4. 13, *s.* by hand of him whom thou wilt *s.*
2 Chr. 7. 13; Ezek. 14. 9, if I *s.* pestilence.
Ps. 20. 2, *s.* thee help from the sanctuary.
43. 3, *s.* out thy light and truth.
118. 25, *s.* now prosperity.
Isa. 6. 8, whom shall I *s.*? *s.* me.
Mat. 9. 38; Lu. 10. 2, *s.* labourers.
12. 20, till he *s.* forth judgment.
15. 23, *s.* her away, for she crieth after us.
Mk. 3. 14, that he might *s.* them to preach.
John 14. 26, whom the Father will *s.* in my name.
17. 8, believed that thou didst *s.* me.
Rom. 8. 3, God *s.* his Son in likeness.
See Lu. 10. 3; 24. 49; John 20. 21; 2 Thes. 2. 11.
Seneh, sĕn′-ĕh, 'crag-thorn.' 1 Sam. 14. 4.
Senir, sē′-nĭr, 'coat of mail.' 1 Chr. 5. 23.
Sennacherib, sĕn-năch′-ĕr-ĭb, 'Sin (the moon) multiplies brethren.' A great Assyrian king, son of Sargon, reigned B. C. 705–681. A cylinder has been found recording his expedition against Hezekiah. It is now in the British Museum. 2 Kn. 18. 13; 2 Chr. 32.; Isa. 36.; 37.
Sensual. Jas. 3. 15; Jude 19.
Sent. Jud. 6. 14, have not I *s.* thee?
Ps. 77. 17, the skies *s.* out a sound.
106. 15, he *s.* leanness into their soul.
107. 20, he *s.* his word and healed them.
Jer. 23. 21, I have not *s.* these prophets.
Mat. 15. 24, I am not *s.* but to lost sheep.
John 4. 34, the will of him that *s.* me.
9. 4, work the works of him that *s.* me.
17. 3, life eternal to know him whom thou hast [*s.*
Acts 10. 29, as soon as I was *s.* for.
Rom. 10. 15, preach, except they be *s.*
See Isa. 61. 1; John 1. 6; 3. 28; 1 Pet. 1. 12.
Sentence. Ps. 17. 2, let my *s.* come forth.
Prov. 16. 10, a divine *s.* in the lips of the king.
Eccl. 8. 11, because *s.* is not executed speedily.
2 Cor. 1. 9, *s.* of death in ourselves. R. V. answer.
See Deu. 17. 9; Jer. 4. 12; Dan. 5. 12; 8. 23; Acts 15. 19.
Senuah, sĕn′-ū-ăh, 'bristling' (?). Neh. 11. 9.

Seorim, sē-ōr′-ĭm, 'barley.' 1 Chr. 24. 8.
Separate. Gen. 13. 9, *s.* thyself from me.
Deu. 19. 2, thou shalt *s.* three cities.
Prov. 16. 28; 17. 9, whisperer *s.* chief friends.
19. 4, the poor is *s.* from his neighbour.
Mat. 25. 32, he shall *s.* them.
Rom. 8. 35, who shall *s.* us from love of God?
2 Cor. 6. 17, be ye *s.*
Heb. 7. 26, *s.* from sinners.
See Num. 6. 2; Ez. 10. 11; Isa. 56. 3; 59. 2.
Separation. Num. 6. 8; 19. 9; 31. 23; Ezek. 42. 20.
Separation of women. Lev. 12.
Sephar, sē′-phär, 'a numbering.' Gen. 10. 30.
Sepharad, sĕ-phâr′-ăd. Obad. 20.
Sepharvaim, sē-phär-vā′-ĭm. 2 Kn. 17. 24; 18. 34; 19. 13.
Sepharvites, sē-phär′-vītes, people of Sepharvaim. 2 Kn. 17. 31.
Sepulchre. Gen. 23. 6; 2 Kn. 23. 17; Ps. 5. 9; Jer. 5. 16; Mat. 23. 27; 27. 60; Lu. 11. 47.
Serah, sē′-räh, 'abundance.' Gen. 46. 17.
Seraiah, sĕ-râī′-ăh, 'soldier of Jehovah' (?). (1) Joab's father. 1 Chr. 4. 13, 14.
(2) son of Neraiah. Jer. 51. 59.
(3) others. 2 Sam. 8. 17; 2 Kn. 25. 18, 23; 1 Chr. 4. 35; Ez. 2. 2; Neh. 11. 11; Jer. 36. 26.
Seraphims, sĕr′-ă-phĭms, 'burning ones.' Isa. 6. 2.
Sered, sē′-rĕd, 'fear.' Gen. 46. 14.
Sergius, sĕr′-gĭ-ŭs. Acts 13. 7.
Sermon on the mount. Mat. 5.-7.; Lu. 6. 20.
Serpent. (1) (Ps. 58. 4; Prov. 30. 19). Heb. *Nâhâsh*: Gk. ὄφις: Zool. S. generic term denoting serpents in general.
(2) (Ex. 7. 9, 10). Heb. *Tannîn:* Gk. δράκων, any sea or land monster.
(3) (Ps. 58. 4). Heb. *Péthen:* Gk. ἀσπίς: Zool. S. *Cobra Ægyptiaca.* The asp of the Romans, of the same species as the cobra of India.
(4) (Gen. 49. 17). Heb. *Shĕphîphôn:* Gk. ὄφις: Zool. S. *Cerastes Hasselquistii.* Poisonous adder of sandy deserts, the horned sand-snake, 3 to 6 ft. long.
(5) (Job 20. 16). Viper. Heb. *Eph'eh:* Gk. ἀσπίς: Zool. S. *Echis arenicola.* A venomous serpent of uncertain species.
(6) (Ps. 140. 3). Heb. *Akshûb:* Gk. βασιλίσκος: Zool. S. *Vipera Euphratica,* or *Vipera ammodytes.* The common adder.
(7) (Prov. 23. 32; Isa. 11. 8). Heb. *Tzeph'a:* Gk. ἀσπίς: Zool. S. *Daboia xanthina* (?). T.: R. V. 'adder' or 'basilisk:' A. V. 'adder' or 'cockatrice.' It may be the large yellow-streaked serpent, not uncommon in Palestine.
(8) **Fiery** (Num. 21. 6-8). Heb. *Sârâph:* Gk. ὄφις θανατῶν: Zool. S. *Daboia xanthina* (?). So called from the fiery, burning fever caused by their bites.
(9) **Fiery Flying** (Isa. 14. 29). Gk. ἀσπίς, ὄφις πετάμενος: Zool. S. *Daboia xanthina* (?). 'Flying' is poetic imagery, perhaps from the swiftness of its stroke.
Gen. 3. 1, the *s.* was more subtil.
49. 17, Dan shall be a *s.* by the way.
Job 26. 13, his hand formed the crooked *s.*
Ps. 58. 4, like the poison of a *s.*
140. 3, sharpened their tongues like a *s.*
Prov. 23. 32, at last it biteth like a *s.*
Eccl. 10. 8, breaketh a hedge, a *s.* shall bite him.
10. 11, *s.* will bite without enchantment.
Isa. 27. 1, the Lord shall punish the *s.*
65. 25, dust shall be the *s.* meat.
Jer. 8. 17, I will send *s.* among you.
Am. 9. 3, I will command the *s.*
Mic. 7. 17, they shall lick dust like a *s.*
Mat. 7. 10; Lu. 11. 11, will he give him a *s.*?
10. 16, be ye wise as *s.*
23. 33, ye *s.*, how can ye escape.
Mk. 16. 18, they shall take up *s.*
John 3. 14, as Moses lifted up the *s.*

Rev. 12. 9; 20. 2, that old *s.* called the Devil.
See Ex. 4. 3; Jas. 3. 7.
Serpent cursed by God. Gen. 3. 14 (2 Cor. 11. 3; Rev. 12. 9).
Serpents, fiery, sent by God, and brazen one made by Moses, Num. 21. 8 (John 3. 14). the latter destroyed, 2 Kn. 18. 4.
Serug, sē'-rŭg, 'shoot.' Gen. 11. 20.
Servant. Gen. 9. 25, a *s.* of *s.* shall he be.
Job 3. 19, the *s.* is free.
7. 2, as a *s.* desireth the shadow.
Ps. 116. 16; 119. 125; 143. 12, I am thy *s.*
Prov. 22. 7, the borrower is *s.* to the lender.
29. 19, a *s.* will not be corrected with words.
Isa. 24. 2, as with *s.* so with master.
Mat. 10. 25, enough for *s.* to be as his lord.
25. 21, good and faithful *s.*
Lu. 12. 47, that *s.* which knew his lord's will.
17. 10, unprofitable *s.*
John 8. 35, *s.* abideth not in house for ever.
15. 15, *s.* knoweth not what his lord doeth.
1 Cor. 7. 21, art thou called, being a *s.*
7. 23, be not ye the *s.* of men.
Eph. 6. 5; Col. 3. 22; Tit. 2. 9; 1 Pet. 2. 18, *s.* be obedient.
See Rom. 6. 16; Rev. 22. 3.
Servants. Ex. 20. 10; 21.; Deu. 5. 14; Col. 4. 1.
advice to. Mal. 1. 6; Eph. 6. 5; Col. 3. 22; 1 Tim. 6. 1; Tit. 2. 9; 1 Pet. 2. 18.
Serve. Gen. 25. 23, elder shall *s.* the younger.
Deu. 6. 13; 10. 12, 20; 11. 13; 13. 4; Jos. 22. 5; 24. 14; 1 Sam. 7. 3; 12. 14, thou shalt fear the Lord and *s.* him.
Jos. 24. 15, choose ye whom ye will *s.*
1 Chr. 28. 9, *s.* him with a perfect heart.
Job 21. 15, what is the Almighty, that we should *s.* him?
Ps. 22. 30, a seed shall *s.* him.
72. 11, all nations shall *s.* him.
Isa. 43. 23, I have not caused thee to *s.*
43. 24, thou hast made me to *s.* with thy sins.
Jer. 5. 19, so shall ye *s.* strangers.
Dan. 6. 16, thy God whom thou *s.* will deliver.
Zep. 3. 9, to *s.* him with one consent.
Mal. 3. 17, spareth his son that *s.* him.
3. 18, between him that *s.* God and him that.
Mat. 6. 24; Lu. 16. 13, no man can *s.* two masters.
Lu. 10. 40, hath left me to *s.* alone.
15. 29, these many years do I *s.* thee.
John 12. 26, if any man *s.* me, let him.
Acts 6. 2, leave word of God and *s.* tables.
Rom. 6. 6, henceforth we should not *s.* sin. R. V. be in bondage to.
Gal. 5. 13, by love *s.* one another.
Col. 3. 24, for ye *s.* the Lord Christ.
1 Thes. 1. 9, from idols to *s.* living God.
Rev. 7. 15, they *s.* him day and night.
See Lu. 22. 27; Acts 13. 36; Heb. 9. 14; 12. 28.
Service. Ex. 12. 26, what mean ye by this *s.*?
1 Chr. 29. 5, who is willing to consecrate his *s.* R. V. himself.
John 16. 2, will think he doeth God *s.*
Rom. 12. 1, your reasonable *s.*
Eph. 6. 7, doing *s.* as to the Lord.
Phil. 2. 30, to supply your lack of *s.*
See Ez. 6. 18; Ps. 104. 14; Jer. 22. 13.
Servile work forbidden on holy days. Lev. 23. 7; Num. 28. 18; 29. 1.
Servitor, a servant or attendant. 2 Kn. 4. 43.
Set. Gen. 4. 15, the Lord *s.* a mark on Cain. R. V. appointed.
9. 13, I do *s.* my bow in the cloud.
Deu. 1. 8, I have *s.* the land before thee.
Job 33. 5, *s.* thy words in order.
Ps. 16. 8, I have *s.* the Lord before me.
20. 5, we will *s.* up our banners.
91. 14, he hath *s.* his love upon me.
Eccl. 7. 14, hath *s.* the one against the other. R. V. made . . . side by side with.
S. of S. 8. 6, *s.* me as a seal upon thine heart.
Mat. 5. 14, a city *s.* on a hill.
Heb. 6. 18, the hope *s.* before us.
See Ps. 75. 7; 107. 41; Mat. 5. 1; Eph. 1. 20; Col. 3. 2.

Set by, valued, esteemed. 1 Sam. 18. 30.
Seth, sĕth, 'appointed;' son of Adam. Gen. 4. 25; 5. 3.
Sethur, sē'-thûr, 'hidden.' Num. 13. 13.
Set on, to attack. Acts 18. 10.
Settle. (1) 'a bench or seat.' Ezek. 43. 14.
(2) Zep. 1. 12; Lu. 21. 14; Col. 1. 23.
Set to his seal, attached his seal to, attested. John 3. 33.
Seventy elders, the. Ex. 18. 25; 24.; Num. 11. 16.
years' captivity foretold. Jer. 25. 11.
weeks, Daniel's prophecy concerning. Dan. 9. 24.
disciples, Christ's charge to. Lu. 10.
Sever. Lev. 20. 26; Ezek. 39. 14; Mat. 13. 49.
Severally, separately, individually. 1 Cor. 12. 11.
Sew. Gen. 3. 7; Job 14. 17; Eccl. 3. 7; Mk. 2. 21.
Shaalabbin, shā-ă-lăb'-bĭn, 'earths of foxes' (?). Jos. 19. 42.
Shaalbim, shā-ăl'-bĭm, same as preceding. Jud. 1. 35.
Shaalbonite, shā-ăl-bō'-nīte, 'inhabitant of Shaalbim' (?). 2 Sam. 23. 32.
Shaaph, shā'-ăph, 'anger' (?). 1 Chr. 2. 47.
Shaaraim, shā-ă-rā'-ĭm, 'two gates.' 1 Sam. 17. 52.
Shaashgaz, shā-ăsh'-găz, 'beauty's servant' (?). Esth. 2. 14.
Shabbethai, shăb'-bĕ-thāī, 'born on the sabbath.' Ez. 10. 15.
Shachia, shă-chī'-ă, 'lustful' (?). 1 Chr. 8. 10.
Shade. Ps. 121. 5, the Lord is thy *s.*
Shadow. Gen. 19. 8, the *s.* of my roof.
Job 7. 2, as servant earnestly desireth the *s.*
14. 2, he fleeth as a *s.* and continueth not.
17. 7, all my members are as a *s.*
Ps. 91. 1, under the *s.* of the Almighty.
102. 11, my days are like a *s.*
144. 4; Eccl. 8. 13, his days are as a *s.*
Eccl. 6. 12, life which he spendeth as a *s.*
S. of S. 2. 3, under his *s.* with great delight.
2. 17; 4. 6, till the *s.* flee away.
Isa. 4. 6, for a *s.* in the daytime.
25. 4, a *s.* from the heat.
32. 2, as the *s.* of a great rock.
49. 2; 51. 16, in the *s.* of his hand.
Jer. 6. 4, the *s.* of evening are stretched out.
Lam. 4. 20, under his *s.* we shall live.
Hos. 14. 7, they that dwell under his *s.* shall return.
Acts 5. 15, the *s.* of Peter might overshadow.
Jas. 1. 17, with whom is no *s.* of turning.
Shadow. Jud. 9. 15, 36; 1 Chr. 29. 15; Job 8. 9; Ps. 17. 8; 36. 7; 63. 7; Isa. 38. 8; Jon. 4. 5.
of heavenly things. Heb. 8. 5; 10. 1.
Shadrach, shā'-drăch, Meshach, and Abed-nego, their faith and suffering and deliverance. Dan. 1.; 3.
Shaft. Ex. 25. 31; 37. 17; Isa. 49. 2.
Shage, shā'-gē, 'wanderer.' 1 Chr. 11. 34.
Shaharaim, shā-hă-rā'-ĭm, 'two dawns.' 1 Chr. 8. 8.
Shahazimah, shā-hă-zī'-măh, 'lofty places' (?). Jos. 19. 22.
Shake. Jud. 16. 20, I will *s.* myself.
Ps. 29. 8, voice of Lord *s.* wilderness.
72. 16, fruit thereof shall *s.* like Lebanon.
Isa. 2. 19, when he ariseth to *s.* the earth.
13. 13; Joel 3. 16; Hag. 2. 6, 21, I will *s.* the heavens.
52. 2, *s.* thyself from the dust.
Hag. 2. 7, I will *s.* all nations.
Mat. 11. 7; Lu. 7. 24, a reed *s.* with the wind.
Lu. 6. 38, good measure, *s.* together.
2 Thes. 2. 2, be not soon *s.* in mind.
Heb. 12. 26, I *s.* not earth only.
12. 27, things which cannot be *s.*
See Job 9. 6; Ezek. 37. 7; Mat. 24. 29.
Shalem, shā'-lĕm, 'safe,' 'perfect.' Gen. 33. 18.
Shalim, shā'-lĭm, 'foxes.' 1 Sam. 9. 4.
Shalisha, shăl'-ĭ-shă, 'a third part.' 1 Sam. 9. 4.
Shallecheth, shăl'-lĕ-chĕth, 'felling' (?). 1 Chr. 26. 16.

Shallum, shăl'-lŭm, 'retribution.' (1) King of Judah, same as Jehoahaz, 1 Chr. 3. 15.
(2) others, 2 Kn. 15. 10; 22. 14; 2 Chr. 34. 22; Jer. 22. 11.
Shallun, shăl'-lŭn, 'spoliation.' Neh. 3. 15.
Shalmai, shăl'-măi, 'peaceful' (?). Ez. 2. 46.
Shalman, shăl'-măn, shortened form of following. Hos. 10. 14.
Shalmaneser, shăl-măn-ē'-sĕr, 'Shalman, be propitious.' 2 Kn. 17. 3.
carries ten tribes captive. 2 Kn. 17.; 18. 9.
Shama, shā'-mă, 'obedient.' 1 Chr. 11. 44.
Shamariah, shăm-ă-rī'-ăh, 'Jehovah guards.' 2 Chr. 11. 19.
Shame. Ps. 4. 2, turn my glory into *s.* R. V. dishonour.
40. 14; 83. 17, let them be put to *s.* R. V. dishonour.
Prov. 10. 5; 17. 2, a son that causeth *s.*
Isa. 61. 7, for your *s.* ye shall have double.
Jer. 51. 51, *s.* hath covered our faces. R. V. confusion.
Ezek. 16. 52, bear thine own *s.*
Dan. 12. 2, awake, some to *s.*
Zep. 3. 5, the unjust knoweth no *s.*
Lu. 14. 9, with *s.* to take lowest room.
Acts 5. 41, worthy to suffer *s.*
1 Cor. 6. 5; 15. 34, I speak this to your *s.*
Eph. 5. 12, a *s.* to speak of those things.
Phil. 3. 19, whose glory is in their *s.*
Heb. 6. 6, put him to an open *s.*
12. 2, despising the *s.*
See 1 Cor. 11. 6; 14. 35; 1 Thes. 2. 2.
Shame. Gen. 2. 25; 3. 10; Ex. 32. 25. *See* Prov. 3. 35; 11. 2; 13. 5; Ezek. 16. 63; Rom. 6. 21. of God's enemies, Ps. 40. 14; 109. 29; Ezek. 7. 18; Dan. 12. 2.
subdued by hope, Rom. 5. 5.
Shamed, shā'-mĕd, 'destroyer' (?). 1 Chr. 8. 12.
Shamefacedness (better 'shamefastness,' as in R. V.); modesty. 1 Tim. 2. 9.
Shamefully. Hos. 2. 5; Mk. 12. 4; 1 Thes. 2. 2.
Shamer, shā'-mĕr, 'keeper.' 1 Chr. 6. 46.
Shamgar, shăm'-găr, 'destroyer' (?); judges Israel. Jud. 3. 31; 5. 6.
Shamhuth, shăm'-hŭth, 'notoriety' (?). 1 Chr. 27. 8.
Shamir, shā'-mĭr, 'a thorn.' 1 Chr. 24. 24.
Shamma, shăm'-mă, 'desert.' 1 Chr. 7. 37.
Shammah, shăm'-măh, same as SHAMMA. (1) Gen. 36. 13. (2) 2 Sam. 23. 11.
Shammai, shăm'-mā-ī, 'wasted.' 1 Chr. 2. 28.
Shammoth, shăm'-mŏth, 'deserts.' 1 Chr. 11. 27.
Shammua, shăm'-mū-ă, 'famous.' (1) Num. 13. 4. (2) Neh. 11. 17.
Shammuah, shăm'-mū-ăh, same as preceding. 2 Sam. 5. 14.
Shamsherai, shăm'-shĕ-răi. 1 Chr. 8. 26.
Shape. Lu. 3. 22; John 5. 37; Rev. 9. 7.
Shapham, shā'-phăm, 'bald.' 1 Chr. 5. 12.
Shaphan, shā'-phăn, 'coney;' repairs the temple. 2 Kn. 22. 3; 2 Chr. 34. 8.
Shaphat, shā'-phăt, 'judge.' (1) the spy. Num. 13. 5.
(2) father of Elisha. 1 Kn. 19. 16-19.
(3) others. 1 Chr. 3. 22; 5. 12; 27. 29.
Shapher, shā'-phĕr, 'pleasantness.' Num. 33. 23.
Sharai, shâr-ā'-ī, 'free.' Ez. 10. 40.
Sharaim, shă-rā'-ĭm, same as SHAARAIM. Jos. 15. 36.
Sharar, shâr'-ăr, 'firm' (?). 2 Sam. 23. 33.
Sharezer, shă-rē'-zĕr, '[God] protect the king.' 2 Kn. 19. 37.
Sharon, shâr'-on, 'plain.' 1 Chr. 27. 29.
rose of. S. of S. 2. 1.
Sharonite, shâr'-on-īte, one who lives in Sharon. 1 Chr. 27. 29.
Sharp. 1 Sam. 13. 20, to *s.* every man his share.
13. 21, a file to *s.* the goads. R. V. set.
Ps. 52. 2, tongue like a *s.* razor.
140. 3, they *s.* their tongues like a serpent.
Prov. 25. 18, false witness is *s.* arrow.
Prov. 27. 17, iron *s.* iron, so a man *s.* his friend.
Isa. 41. 15, a *s.* threshing instrument.
Acts 15. 39, the contention was so *s.*
Heb. 4. 12, *s.* than any two-edged sword.
See Mic. 7. 4; 2 Cor. 13. 10; Rev. 1. 16; 14. 14.
Sharuhen, shă-rū-hĕn. Jos. 19. 6.
Shashai, shā'-shăi, 'pale.' Ez. 10. 40.
Shashak, shā'-shăk, 'activity' (?). 1 Chr. 8. 14.
Shaul, shā'-ŭl, same as SAUL. Gen. 46. 10.
Shaulites, shā-ŭ'-lītes, the family of Shaul. Num. 26. 13.
Shaveh, shā'-vĕh, 'plain' (?). Gen. 14. 17.
Shaveh Kiriathaim, shā'-vĕh kĭr-ī-ă-thā'-ĭm, 'plain (?) of Kiriathaim.' Gen. 14. 5.
Shaving the head. Lev. 13. 33; 14. 8; Num. 6. 9; 8. 7.
See Job 1. 20; Ezek. 44. 20; Acts 21. 24; 1 Cor. 11. 5 (Lev. 21. 5).
Shavsha, shăv'-shă, another name of SERAIAH. 1 Chr. 18. 16.
Shawm (Ps. 98. 7, Prayer-book Version). The A. V. (Ps. 98. 6) has 'cornet.' *See* TRUMPET, *Shôphâr*, a trumpet, for rallying people.
Sheal, shē'-ăl, 'prayer.' Ez. 10. 29.
Shealtiel, shē-ăl'-tī-ĕl, 'I asked God.' Ez. 3. 2.
Shearers. Gen. 38. 12; 1 Sam. 25. 7; Isa. 53. 7.
Sheariah, shē-ă-rī'-ăh, 'whom Jehovah hath esteemed.' 1 Chr. 8. 38.
Shearing sheep, rejoicing at. 1 Sam. 25. 4; 2 Sam. 13. 23.
Shear-jashub, shē'-ăr-jăsh'-ŭb, 'the remnant shall return.' Isa. 7. 3.
Sheath. 1 Sam. 17. 51; 1 Chr. 21. 27; Ezek. 21. 3.
Sheaves of corn, Joseph's dream. Gen. 37. 7.
of the firstfruits of harvest. Lev. 23. 10-12.
forgotten, to be left in the field. Deu. 24. 19; Job 24. 10.
typical. Ps. 126. 6; Mic. 4. 12; Mat. 13. 30.
Sheba, shē'-bă, 'an oath,' or 'seven.' (1) men. Gen. 25. 3; 2 Sam. 20. 1.
(2) places. Job 6. 19; Ps. 72. 10; Jer. 6. 20; Ezek. 27. 22; 38. 13.
queen of, visits Solomon. 1 Kn. 10.; 2 Chr. 9.; Mat. 12. 42.
Shebah, shē'-băh, 'an oath.' Gen. 26. 33. R. V. Shibah.
Shebam, shē'-băm, 'fragrance.' Num. 32. 3. R. V. Sebam.
Shebaniah, shĕb-ă-nī'-ăh, 'Jehovah hides.' 1 Chr. 15. 24.
Shebarim, shĕb'-ă-rĭm, 'breaches.' Jos. 7. 5.
Shebat, shē'-băt, the eleventh month of the Jewish sacred year = February. Zec. 1. 7. *See* MONTHS.
Sheber, shē'-bĕr, 'breaking.' 1 Chr. 2. 48.
Shebna, shĕb'-nă, 'youth' (?); the scribe. 2 Kn. 18. 18; 19. 2; Isa. 22. 15; 36. 3; 37. 2.
Shebuel, shĕ-bū'-ĕl, 'captive of God.' 1 Chr. 23. 16.
Shecaniah, shĕc-ă-nī'-ăh, same as following. 1 Chr. 24, 11.
Shechaniah, shĕch-ă-nī'-ăh, 'Jehovah dwells.' 1 Chr. 3. 21.
Shechem, shē'-chĕm, 'back,' 'shoulder.' (1) a city (*Nablous*) on the side of Gerizim, the first spot on which Abraham built an altar (Gen. 12. 6, 7); hence it is the most ancient sacred place in Hebrew history. It was rebuilt by Jeroboam as his capital (1 Kn. 12. 25), but was superseded in the time of Baasha by Tirzah (1 Kn. 15. 33). *See* Gen. 34. 25; 48. 22; Jos. 17. 7; 24. 26; Ps. 60. 6; John 4.; Acts 7. 16.
charge of Joshua at. Jos. 24.
its treachery and penalty. Jud. 9. 1, 41.
(2) the Hivite. Gen. 34. [Num. 26. 31.
Shechemites, shē'-chĕm-ītes, people of Shechem.
Shechinah, shē-chī'-năh. The term does not occur in Scripture, but the word is used by the later Jews to express the visible symbol of God's glory, which anciently dwelt in the tabernacle and in Solomon's temple (Num. 14. 10; 1 Kn. 8. 10-13).

Shed. Gen. 9. 6, shall his blood be *s.*
Mat. 26. 28, *s.* for many for remission of sins.
Rom. 5. 5, love of God *s.* in our hearts.
Tit. 3. 6, which he *s.* on us abundantly. R. V. poured out upon.
Heb. 9. 22, without *s.* of blood is no remission.
See Ezek. 18. 10; 22. 3; Acts 2. 33.

Shedeur, shĕd'-ē-ûr, 'giving forth of light.' Num. 1. 5.

Sheep. Heb. *Tsôn:* Gk. πρόβατα. Shepherding is used as a symbol of God's pastoral care for man, both in the Old and the New Testament (Ps. 23.).
Gen. 4. 2, Abel was a keeper of *s.*
Num. 27. 17; 1 Kn. 22. 17; 2 Chr. 18. 16; Mat. 9. 36; Mk. 6. 34, as *s.* which have no shepherd.
1 Sam. 15. 14, what meaneth this bleating of *s.*
Ps. 49. 14, like *s.* are laid in the grave. R. V. they are appointed as a flock.
95. 7; 100. 3, we are the *s.* of his hand.
Isa. 53. 6, all we like *s.* have gone astray.
Jer. 12. 3, pull them out like *s.* for slaughter.
Ezek. 34. 6, my *s.* wandered.
Mat. 7. 15, false prophets in *s.* clothing.
10. 6, go rather to lost *s.*
12. 12, how much is a man better than a *s.*?
John 10. 2, that entereth by door is shepherd of *s.*
10. 11, good shepherd giveth his life for the *s.*
21. 16, feed my *s.*
See Mat. 10. 16; 12. 11; 18. 12.

Sheep for sacrifice. Lev. 1. 10; 1 Kn. 8. 63; 2 Chr. 30. 24.
the people spoken of as. 2 Sam. 24. 17; Ps. 74. 1.
the church compared to. Ps. 74. 1; 79. 13; 95. 7; 100. 3; Ezek. 34.; 36. 38; Mic. 2. 12; Mat. 15. 24; 25. 32; John 10. 2; Heb. 13. 20; 1 Pet. 2. 25.
emblem of Christ. Isa. 53. 7; Acts 8. 32.
of His people. Ps. 95. 7; John 21. 16.

Sheepfold. Jud. 5. 16; Ps. 78. 70; John 10. 1.

Sheet. Jud. 14. 12; Acts 10. 11; 11. 5.

Shehariah, shē-hă-rī'-ăh, 'Jehovah seeks.' 1 Chr. 8. 26.

Shekel, shē'-kĕl. (1) a weight = 224½ grs. *See* WEIGHTS.
(2) a silver coin = stater = 4 denarii = 65 cts. *See* MONEY.
See Gen. 23. 15; Ex. 30. 13; Jos. 7. 21; 2 Sam. 14. 26; 1 Kn. 10. 16; Neh. 5. 15; Jer. 32. 9; Ezek. 4. 10.

Shelah, shē'-lăh. (1) 'petition;' a son of Judah. Gen. 38. 5.
(2) 'a shoot,' or 'sprout,' a different name from (1). 1 Chr. 1. 18.

Shelanites, shē-lā'-nītes, descendants of Shelah. Num. 26. 20.

Shelemiah, shĕl-ē-mī'-ăh, 'Jehovah repays.' 1 Chr. 26. 14.

Sheleph, shē'-lĕph, 'drawing out.' Gen. 10. 26.

Shelesh, shē'-lĕsh, 'triad.' 1 Chr. 7. 35.

Shelomi, shĕ-lō'-mī, 'peaceful.' Num. 34. 27.

Shelomith, shĕ-lō'-mīth, 'peacefulness.' Lev. 24. 11.

Shelomoth, shĕ-lō'-mōth, same as SHELOMITH. 1 Chr. 24. 22.

Shelter. Job 24. 8; Ps. 61. 3.

Shelumiel, shĕ-lū'-mĭ-ĕl, 'friend of God.' Num. 1. 6.

Shem, shĕm, 'name.' Gen. 5. 32; 9. 26; 10. 21; 11. 10; 1 Chr. 1. 17.

Shema, shē'-mă. (1) 'echo' (?). Jos. 15. 26.
(2) 'fame.' 1 Chr. 2. 43.

Shemaah, shĕm'-ā-ăh, 'fame.' 1 Chr. 12. 3.

Shemaiah, shĕm-āī'-ăh, 'Jehovah has heard;' prophet. 1 Kn. 12. 22; 2 Chr. 11. 2; 12. 5 (Jer. 29. 24).

Shemariah, shĕm-ă-rī'-ăh, 'Jehovah guards.' 1 Chr. 12. 5.

Shemeber, shĕm-ē'-bĕr, 'soaring on high' (?). Gen. 14. 2.

Shemer, shē'-mĕr, 'guardian.' 1 Kn. 16. 24.

Shemida, shĕ-mī'-dă, 'fame of wisdom' (?). Num. 26. 32.

Shemidah, shĕm-ī'-dăh, same as preceding. 1 Chr. 7. 19.

Shemidaites, shĕ-mī'-dā-ītes, descendants of Shemida. Num. 26. 32.

Sheminith, Upon, shĕm'-ĭ-nĭth, Heb. Shĕm-ī'-nĭth. Ps. 6., 12, title, 'Upon the octave below,' that is, 'for bass singers.' 1 Chr. 15. 21.

Shemiramoth, shĕ-mī'-ră-mōth, 'most high name' (?). 1 Chr. 15. 18.

Shemuel, shĕ-mū'-ĕl, same as SAMUEL. Num. 34. 20.

Shen, shĕn, 'tooth.' 1 Sam. 7. 12.

Shenazar, shĕn-ā'-zär. 1 Chr. 3. 18.

Shenir, shē'-nĭr, same as SENIR. Deu. 3. 9.

Shepham, shē'-phăm, 'nakedness.' Num. 34. 10.

Shephathiah, shĕph-ă-thī'-ăh, an incorrect way of spelling the next word. 1 Chr. 9. 8.

Shephatiah, shĕph-ă-tī'-ăh, 'Jehovah has judged.'
(1) one of David's sons. 2 Sam. 3. 4.
(2) a prince hostile to Jeremiah. Jer. 38. 1–4.
(3) others. 1 Chr. 12. 5; 27. 16; 2 Chr. 21. 2; Ez. 2. 4, 57.

Shepherd. Gen. 46. 34, *s.* abomination to Egyptians.
Ps. 23. 1, the Lord is my *s.*
Isa. 13. 20, nor shall *s.* make their fold there.
40. 11, he shall feed his flock like a *s.*
56. 11, they are *s.* that cannot understand.
Jer. 23. 4, I will set *s.* over them who shall feed.
50. 6, their *s.* have caused them to go astray.
Am. 3. 12, as the *s.* taketh out of the mouth.
Zec. 11. 17, woe to the idol *s.*
John 10. 14, I am the good *s.*

Shepherd, the Good (Christ). John 10. 14; Heb. 13. 20; 1 Pet. 2. 25; 5. 4 (Isa. 40. 11; Zec. 11. 16; 13. 7).
(of Israel). Ps. 23. 1; 80. 1; Ezek. 34. 11.
shepherd of his flock. Isa. 63. 11.
idol shepherd. Zec. 11. 17. R. V. worthless.
hireling. John 10. 12.

Shepherds. Gen. 46. 32, 34; 47. 3; Jer. 33. 12; Ezek. 34. 2; Zec. 11. 3; Lu. 2. 8.

Shephi, shē'-phī, 'baldness.' 1 Chr. 1. 40.

Shepho, shē'-phō, same as SHEPHI. Gen. 36. 23.

Shephuphan, shĕ-phū'-phăn, 'serpent' (?). 1 Chr. 8. 5.

Sherah, shē'-răh, 'consanguinity.' 1 Chr. 7. 24.

Sherd, a fragment, shred, broken piece. Isa. 30. 14.

Sherebiah, shĕr-ē-bī'-ăh, 'heat of Jehovah.' Ez. 8. 18.

Sheresh, shē'-rĕsh, 'root.' 1 Chr. 7. 16.

Sherezer, shĕr-ē'-zĕr, same as SHAREZER. Zec. 7. 2.

Sheshach, shē'-shăch, a name for Babel. Jer. 25. 26; 51. 41.

Sheshai, shē'-shāī, 'clothed in white' (?). Num. 13. 22.

Sheshan, shē'-shăn, 'lily' (?). 1 Chr. 2. 31.

Sheshbazzar, shĕsh-băz'-zär. Ez. 1. 8; 5. 14.

Sheth, shĕth. (1) same as SETH. 1 Chr. 1. 1.
(2) tumult. Num. 24. 17.

Shethar, shē'-thär, 'star.' Esth. 1. 14.

Shethar-boznai, shē'-thär-bŏz'-nāī, 'bright star.' Ez. 5. 3.
and Tatnai oppose rebuilding of temple. Ez. 5. 6.

Sheva, shē'-vă, 'vanity.' (1) 1 Chr. 2. 49. (2) 2 Sam. 20. 25.

Shewbread. Ex. 25. 30; Lev. 24. 5; Heb. 9. 2.
David takes. 1 Sam. 21. 6 (Mat. 12. 4; Mk. 2. 26; Lu. 6. 4).

Shibboleth, shĭb'-bō-lĕth, 'an ear of corn,' or 'a flood.' Jud. 12. 6.

Shibmah, shĭb'-măh, 'fragrant.' Num. 32. 38.

Shicron, shĭc'-rŏn, 'drunkenness.' Jos. 15. 11.

Shield. Shields were (1) large, translated 'buckler,' 'target,' worn by heavy armed soldiers; (2) light, translated 'shield,' 'buckler,' used by archers. They were made of leather or metal.
Jud. 5. 8, was there a *s.* seen.
Ps. 5. 12, compass him as with a *s.*
33. 20; 59. 11; 84. 9, the Lord is our *s.*
84. 11, a sun and *s.*
91. 4, truth shall be thy *s.*

Isa. 21. 5, anoint the *s.*
Eph. 6. 16, taking the *s.* of faith.
Shield, God, of His people. Gen. 15. 1; Deu. 33. 29; Ps. 33. 20; 84. 11; 115. 9; Prov. 30. 5.
of faith. Eph. 6. 16.
Goliath's. 1 Sam. 17. 41.
Shields (Jer. 51. 11; Ezek. 39. 9). Solomon's. 1 Kn. 10. 17.
Shiggaion, shĭg-gā'-ŏn. Ps. 7., title, 'an irregular or Dithyrambic Ode,' or, as Ewald, 'To dithyrambic measure.'
Shigionoth, shĭg-ĭ-ō'-nōth. Hab. 3. 1.
Shihon, shī'-hŏn, 'ruin.' Jos. 19. 19.
Shihor, shī'-hôr, 'black.' 1 Chr. 13. 5.
Shihor-libnath, shī'-hôr-lĭb'-năth. Jos. 19. 26.
Shilhi, shĭl'-hī, 'darter.' 1 Kn. 22. 42.
Shilhim, shĭl'-hĭm, 'aqueducts.' Jos. 15. 32.
Shillem, shĭl'-lĕm, 'requital.' Gen. 46. 24.
Shillemites, shĭl'-lĕm-ītes, descendants of Shillem. Num. 26. 49.
Shiloah, shī-lō'-ăh, 'outlet of water.' Isa. 8. 6.
Shiloh, shī'-lōh, 'tranquillity,' 'rest.' (1) a sacred place 10 miles north of Bethel, the modern Seilûn. Jos. 18. 1; Jud. 21. 19; 1 Sam. 1. 3; 2. 14; 3. 21; Ps. 78. 60; Jer. 7. 12; 26. 6.
(2) in Gen. 49. 10, either (*a*) a proper name for the Messiah, referring to the peacefulness of his kingdom; or (*b*) the town of Shiloh, a type of the rest and peace of the Messiah's reign.
Shiloni, shī-lō'-nī, native of Shiloh. Neh. 11. 5.
Shilonite, shī'-lō-nīte, same as preceding. 1 Kn. 11. 29.
Shilshah, shĭl'-shăh, 'triad.' 1 Chr. 7. 37.
Shimea, shĭm'-ĕ-ă, 'famous.' (1) son of David. 1 Chr. 3. 5.
(2) Levites. 1 Chr. 6. 30, 39.
Shimeah, shĭm'-ĕ-ăh, same as preceding. (1) 2 Sam. 21. 21. (2) 1 Chr. 8. 32.
Shimeam, shĭm'-ĕ-ăm, same as preceding. 1 Chr. 9. 38.
Shimeath, shĭm'-ĕ-ăth, 'fame.' 2 Kn. 12. 21.
Shimeathites, shĭm'-ĕ-ă-thītes. 1 Chr. 2. 55.
Shimei, shĭm'-ĕ-ī, 'my fame.' (1) Num. 3. 18.
(2) a Benjamite.
curses David. 2 Sam. 16. 5.
slain by Solomon. 1 Kn. 2. 36.
(3) others. 1 Kn. 2. 46; 1 Chr. 3. 19; 4. 26; 5. 4; 6. 42; 27. 27; 2 Chr. 29. 14; 31. 12; Ez. 10. 23; Zec. 12. 13.
Shimeon, shĭm'-ĕ-on, 'a hearkening.' Ez. 10. 31.
Shimhi, shĭm'-hī, same as Shimei. 1 Chr. 8. 21.
Shimi, shĭm'-ī, same as preceding. Ex. 6. 17.
Shimites, shĭm'-ītes, descendants of Shimei. Num. 3. 21.
Shimma, shĭm'-mă, 'rumour.' 1 Chr. 2. 13.
Shimon, shī'-mŏn. 1 Chr. 4. 20.
Shimrath, shĭm'-răth, 'watchfulness.' 1 Chr. 8. 21.
Shimri, shĭm'-rī, 'watchful.' 1 Chr. 4. 37.
Shimrith, shĭm'-rĭth, 'vigilant.' 2 Chr. 24. 26.
Shimrom, shĭm'-rŏm, 'watch-post.' 1 Chr. 7. 1.
Shimron, shĭm'-rŏn, 'watchful.' Jos. 11. 1.
Shimronites, shĭm'-rŏn-ītes, descendants of Shimron. Num. 26. 24.
Shimron-meron, shĭm'-rŏn-mē'-rŏn. Jos. 12. 20.
Shimshai, shĭm'-shāi, 'sunny.' Ez. 4. 8.
Shinab, shī'-năb, 'hostile' (?). Gen. 14. 2.
Shinar, shī'-när. Gen. 10. 10.
Shine. Job 22. 28, the light shall *s.* upon thy ways.
29. 3, when his candle *s.* upon my head.
Ps. 104. 15, oil to make his face *s.*
139. 12, the night *s.* as the day.
Prov. 4. 18, light that *s.* more and more.
Isa. 9. 2, upon them hath the light *s.*
60. 1, arise, *s.*, for thy light is come.
Dan. 12. 3, wise shall *s.* as the brightness.
Mat. 5. 16, let your light so *s.*
13. 43, the righteous *s.* as the sun.
2 Cor. 4. 6, God who commanded the light to *s.*
See John 1. 5; 2 Pet. 1. 19; 1 John 2. 8.
Shining of God's face. Num. 6. 25; Ps. 31. 16; 50. 2; 67. 1; 80. 1; Dan. 9. 17.
skin of Moses' face. Ex. 34. 29; 2 Cor. 3.
of Christ's face. Mat. 17. 2; Lu. 9. 29; Acts 9. 3; Rev. 1. 16.
of believers, as lights of the world, Mat. 5. 16; Phil. 2. 15; John 5. 35. and in the kingdom of heaven, Dan. 12. 3; Mat. 13. 43.
of the gospel. 2 Cor. 4. 4; Isa. 9. 2.
Shiphi, shī'-phī, 'abundant.' 1 Chr. 4. 37.
Shiphmite, shĭph'-mīte, a native of Shepham. 1 Chr. 27. 27.
Shiphrah, shĭph'-răh, 'beauty' (?). Ex. 1. 15.
Shiphtan, shĭph'-tăn, 'judicial.' Num. 34. 24.
Shipmaster, captain of a ship. Jon. 1. 6.
Shipmen, sailors. Acts 27. 27.
Ships, Gen. 49. 13; Num. 24. 24. Solomon's, 1 Kn. 9. 26. Jehoshaphat's, 1 Kn. 22. 48.
Ships of Tarshish were probably Phœnician trading vessels, plying between Tyre and Tartessus in Spain.
See Ps. 48. 7; Isa. 2. 16; 23. 1; 60. 9; Ezek. 27. 25; Jon. 1. 3.
Shisha, shī'-shă, 'brightness.' 1 Kn. 4. 3.
Shishak, shī'-shăk, 'illustrious.' 1 Kn. 11. 40.
invades and spoils Jerusalem. 1 Kn. 14. 25; 2 Chr. 12.
Shitrai, shĭt-rā'-ī, 'official.' 1 Chr. 27. 29.
Shittah, shĭt'-tăh (Isa. 41. 19). Heb. *Shittah*: Gk. ξύλον ἄσηπτον: Bot. N. *Acacia seyal*: R. V. acacia.
Shittim, shĭt'-tĭm, 'acacias.' Num. 25. 1.
Shittim wood for the tabernacle (Ex. 25. 5; 26. 15; 27. 1). Heb. *Shittîm*: Gk. ξύλον ἄσηπτον: R. V. acacia wood, a very hard wood, used for the tabernacle and its fittings. It is one of the trees from which gum arabic is obtained.
Shiza, shī'-ză, 'cheerful' (?). 1 Chr. 11. 42.
Shoa, shō'-ă, 'opulent.' Ezek. 23. 23.
Shobab, shō'-băb, 'apostate.' 2 Sam. 5. 14.
Shobach, shō'-băch, 'pouring.' 2 Sam. 10. 16.
Shobai, shō-bā'-ī, 'bright' (?). Ez. 2. 42.
Shobal, shō'-băl, 'stream.' Gen. 36. 20.
Shobek, shō'-bĕk, 'forsaker.' Neh. 10. 24.
Shobi, shō'-bī, 'taking captive.' 2 Sam. 17. 27.
Shocho, shō'-chō, same as the next word. 2 Chr. 28. 18.
Shochoh, shō'-chōh, 'a hedge.' 1 Sam. 17. 1.
Shock. Jud. 15. 5; Job 5. 26.
Shoco, shō'-cō, same as Shochoh. 2 Chr. 11. 7.
Shod. Mk. 6. 9; Eph. 6. 15.
Shoe. Hebrew shoes were, as a rule, simply sandals affixed to the foot by straps. They were not worn in the sitting-room, or at the table. Lu. 7. 38; Mk. 1. 7.
Shoe latchet, lace of a shoe, strap, fastening. Gen. 14. 23.
Shoes taken off. Ex. 3. 5; Deu. 25. 9; Jos. 5. 15; Ru. 4. 7; 2 Sam. 15. 30.
Shoham, shō'-hăm, 'onyx.' 1 Chr. 24. 27.
Shomer, shō'-mĕr, 'watchman.' 2 Kn. 12. 21.
Shoot. Ps. 22. 7, they *s.* out the lip.
64. 3, to *s.* their arrows, even bitter words.
144. 6, *s.* out thine arrows and destroy them.
See 1 Chr. 12. 2; Mk. 4. 32; Lu. 21. 30.
Shophach, shō'-phăch, same as Shobak. 1 Chr. 19. 16.
Shophan, shō'-phăn, 'baldness.' Num. 32. 35.
Short. Job 17. 12, the light is *s.* R. V. near unto.
20. 5, triumphing of wicked is *s.*
Ps. 89. 47, remember how *s.* my time is.
Rom. 3. 23, come *s.* of the glory of God.
1 Cor. 7. 29, the time is *s.*
See Num. 11. 23; Isa. 50. 2; 59. 1; Mat. 24. 22.
Shorter. Isa. 28. 20, the bed is *s.*
Shortly. Gen. 41. 32; Ezek. 7. 8; Rom. 16. 20.
Shoshannim, Upon, shō-shăn'-nĭm. Ps. 45., 69., title, 'After the popular song, The Lilies.'
Soshannim-Eduth, Upon, shō-shăn'-nĭm-ē'-dûth. Ps. 80., title, 'After the song, The Lilies of the Testimony.'
Shoulder, sacrificial. Ex. 29. 22, 27; Lev. 7. 34; 10. 14; Num. 6. 19.
Shout. Ps. 47. 5, God is gone up with a *s.*

Lam. 3. 8, when I *s.* he shutteth out my prayer. R. V. call for help.
1 Thes. 4. 16, shall descend with a *s.*
See Num. 23. 21; Isa. 12. 6.
Shouting, in war. Jos. 6. 5; 1 Sam. 4. 5; 2 Chr. 13. 15.
in worship. 2 Sam. 6. 15; Ez. 3. 11; Ps. 47. 1; Zep. 3. 14.
Shower. Ps. 65. 10, makest it soft with *s.*
72. 6, like *s.* that water the earth.
Ezek. 34. 26, will cause *s.* to come in season.
See Deu. 32. 2; Job 24. 8; Jer. 3. 3; 14. 22.
Shroud, foliage (of a tree). A. S. *scrúd.* Ezek. 31. 3.
Shrubs. Gen. 21. 15.
Shua, shū'-ă, 'wealth.' 1 Chr. 2. 3.
Shuah, shū'-ăh, 'depression.' Three different names in Hebrew: (1) Gen. 25. 2. (2) Shuhah in R. V. 1 Chr. 4. 11. (3) Shua in R. V., 'wealth.' Gen. 38. 2.
Shual, shū'-ăl, 'jackal.' 1 Chr. 7. 36.
Shubael, shū'-bā-ĕl, same as SHEBUEL (?). 1 Chr. 24. 20.
Shuham, shū'-hăm, 'pitman' (?). Num. 26. 42.
Shuhamites, shū'-hăm-ītes, the descendants of Shuham. Num. 26. 42.
Shuhite, shū'-hīte, a descendant of Shua. Job 8. 1.
Shulamite, shū'-lă-mīte, same as SHELOMITH. S. of S. 6. 13.
Shumathites, shū'-mă-thītes, people of Shumah. 1 Chr. 2. 53.
Shun. Acts 20. 27; 2 Tim. 2. 16.
Shunammite, shū-năm'-mīte, an inhabitant of Shunem. 1 Kn. 1. 3.
Shunem, shū'-nĕm, 'two resting places.' Jos. 19. 18; 1 Sam. 28. 4; 2 Kn. 4. 8.
Shuni, shū'-nī, 'quiet.' Gen. 46. 16.
Shunites, shū'-nītes, descendants of Shuni. Num. 26. 15.
Shupham, shū'-phăm, 'serpent.' Num. 26. 39.
Shuphamites, shū'-phăm-ītes, the descendants of Shupham. Num. 26. 39.
Shuppim, shŭp'-pĭm. 1 Chr. 7. 12.
Shur, shûr, 'a fort' (?). Gen. 16. 7.
Shushan, shū'-shăn, 'a lily;' city. Artaxerxes at. Neh. 1. 1; Esth. 2. 8; 3. 15.
Shushan-Eduth, Upon, shū'-shăn-ē'-dūth. Ps. 60., title, 'After The Lily of the Testimony.' Probably a popular song.
Shut. Gen. 7. 16, the Lord *s.* him in.
Isa. 22. 22, he shall open and none shall *s.*
60. 11, gates shall not be *s.* day nor night.
Jer. 36. 5, I am *s.* up, I cannot go to the house of the Lord.
Lam. 3. 8, he *s.* out my prayer.
See Gal. 3. 23; 1 John 3. 17; Rev. 3. 7; 20. 3.
Shut: the door was, Mat. 25. 10. eyes, Isa. 6. 10; 44. 18. heaven, Rev. 11. 6; 21. 25.
Shuthalhites, shū-thăl'-hītes, the descendants of Shuthelah. Num. 26. 35.
Shuthelah, shū-thē'-lăh, 'plantation' (?). Num. 26. 35.
Sia, sī'-ă, 'assembly.' Neh. 7. 47.
Siaha, sī'-ă-hă, 'council.' Ez. 2. 44.
Sibbecai, sĭb'-bĕ-căi, 'entangling.' 1 Chr. 11. 29.
Sibbechai, sĭb'-bĕ-chăi, same as preceding. 2 Sam. 21. 18.
Sibboleth, sĭb'-bŏ-lĕth, same as SHIBBOLETH. Jud. 12. 6.
Sibmah, sĭb'-măh, same as SHIBMAH. Jos. 13. 19.
Sibraim, sĭb'-rā-ĭm, 'two hills' (?). Ezek. 47. 16.
Sichem, sī'-chĕm, 'the shoulder-blade.' Gen. 12. 6.
Sick. Prov. 13. 12, maketh the heart *s.*
23. 35, stricken me and I was not *s.* R. V. hurt.
S. of S. 2. 5, I am *s.* of love.
Isa. 1. 5, the whole head is *s.*
Hos. 7. 5, made him *s.* with bottles of wine.
Mat. 8. 14, wife's mother *s.*
Jas. 5. 14, is any *s.* ? call elders of the church.
5. 15, prayer of faith shall save the *s.*
Sick: Hezekiah, 2 Kn. 20. 1; 2 Chr. 32. 24. Lazarus, John 11. 1. Dorcas, Acts 9. 37. Peter's wife's mother, Mat. 8. 14; Mk. 1. 30; Lu. 4. 38.
healing the. Mat. 8. 16; 10. 8; Mk. 16. 18; Lu. 7. 10.
when saw we thee. Mat. 25. 39.
unto death. Phil. 2. 27.
Sickle. Deu. 16. 9; 23. 25.
typical. Joel 3. 13; Mk. 4. 29; Rev. 14. 14.
Sickness. Lev. 26. 16; Deu. 28. 27; 2 Sam. 12. 15; 2 Chr. 21. 15; Ps. 41. 3; Eccl. 5. 17; Mat. 8. 17.
conduct under. Ps. 35. 13; Isa. 38. 12; Mat. 25. 36; Jas. 5. 14. *See* AFFLICTION.
Siddim, sĭd'-dĭm, 'the plains' (?). Gen. 14. 3.
Sidon, sī'-dŏn, 'fishing.' R. V. Zidon.
(1) son of Canaan. Gen. 10. 15.
(2) city, a seaport on the Mediterranean, 22 miles N. of Tyre. Jos. 19. 28; 1 Kn. 5. 6; Acts 27. 3.
Sidonians, sī-dō'-nĭ-ăns, persons living in Sidon. Deu. 3. 9.
Siege. Deu. 20. 19; 2 Chr. 32. 9; Isa. 29. 3; Ezek. 4. 7; Zec. 12. 2.
Sieve. Isa. 30. 28; Am. 9. 9.
Sift. Isa. 30. 28; Am. 9. 9; Lu. 22. 31.
Sight. Ex. 3. 3, this great *s.*
Deu. 28. 34, for *s.* of thine eyes.
Eccl. 6. 9, better is *s.* of eyes.
Mat. 11. 5; 20. 34; Lu. 7. 21, blind receive *s.*
11. 26; Lu. 10. 21, it seemed good in thy *s.*
Lu. 18. 42; Acts 22. 13, receive thy *s.*
21. 11, fearful *s.* and signs from heaven. R. V. terrors.
Rom. 12. 17, things honest in *s.* of all men.
2 Cor. 5. 7, walk by faith, not by *s.*
See Eccl. 11. 9; Isa. 43. 4; Dan. 4. 11; Heb. 4. 13.
Sight of God, in. Acts 4. 19; 8. 21; 10. 31; 2 Cor. 2. 17; 4. 2; 7. 12; Gal. 3. 11; 1 Thes. 1. 3; 1 Tim. 2. 3; 6. 13; 1 Pet. 3. 4.
Sign. Isa. 7. 11, ask thee a *s.* of the Lord.
55. 13, for an everlasting *s.*
Ezek. 12. 6, I have set thee for a *s.*
Dan. 4. 3, how great are his *s.*
Mat. 16. 3, *s.* of the times.
Mk. 16. 20, with *s.* following.
Lu. 2. 34, for a *s.* which shall be spoken against.
John 4. 48, except ye see *s.*
Acts 2. 22, man approved of God by *s.*
4. 30, that *s.* may be done by the name.
See Rom. 4. 11; 15. 19; 1 Cor. 1. 22; Rev. 15. 1.
Sign, Pharisees ask a. Mat. 12. 38; Mk. 8. 11.
Signet, a seal. Gen. 38. 18.
Signify. John 12. 33; Heb. 9. 8; 1 Pet. 1. 11.
Signs: sun and moon, Gen. 1. 14. rainbow, Gen. 9. 13. circumcision, Gen. 17. 10. Moses, Ex. 3. 12; 4. 8. Sabbath, Ex. 31. 13. Jonas, Mat. 12. 39. apostles, Acts 2. 43. *See also* 1 Kn. 13. 3; Isa. 7. 11; 8. 18; 20. 3; Ezek. 24. 24.
false. Deu. 13. 1; Mat. 24. 24; 2 Thes. 2. 9.
of the times. Mat. 16. 3.
Sihon, sī'-hŏn, 'brush;' king of the Amorites. Num. 21. 21; Deu. 1. 4; 2. 26; Ps. 135. 11; 136. 19.
Sihor, sī'-hôr, same as SHIHOR. Jos. 13. 3.
Silas, sī'-lăs, shortened form of SILVANUS. Acts 15. 22; 16. 19; 17. 4. *See* 2 Cor. 1. 19; 1 Thes. 1. 1; 1 Pet. 5. 12.
Silence. Job 2. 13; Ps. 39. 2; Prov. 10. 19; 11. 12; 17. 28; Mat. 22. 34; 1 Tim. 2. 11; 1 Pet. 2. 15.
women to keep. 1 Tim. 2. 11.
in heaven for half an hour. Rev. 8. 1.
Silent. 1 Sam. 2. 9, *s.* in darkness.
Ps. 28. 1, be not *s.* to me. R. V. deaf unto.
31. 17, let the wicked be *s.* in the grave.
Zec. 2. 13, be *s.*, all flesh, before the Lord.
See Ps. 22. 2; 30. 12; Isa. 47. 5; Jer. 8. 14.
Silk. Prov. 31. 22, her clothing is *s.* and purple. R. V. fine linen.
Ezek. 16. 10, I covered thee with *s.*
Silla, sĭl'-lă, 'way,' 'highway' (?). 2 Kn. 12. 20.
Silly, simple, innocent. Job 5. 2; Hos. 7. 11; 2 Tim. 3. 6.
Siloah, sī-lō'-ăh, same as SHILOAH. Neh. 3. 15.
Siloam, sī-lō'-ăm, 'sent,' especially of water sent

through an aqueduct. (1) Pool of. A reservoir 58 ft. long by 18 broad and 19 deep, under the S. E. wall of Jerusalem (John 9. 7); probably identical with Shiloah, the waters of which go softly (Isa. 8. 6), and the pool of Shelah by the king's garden (Neh. 3. 15).
(2) the tower. Lu. 13. 4.

Siloam Inscription, discovered in 1880 by Mr. C. Schick, consists of six lines, dating from the time of Ahaz or Hezekiah. It is a description of the making of the tunnel, recording how the workmen began at both ends and met in the middle.

Silvanus, sĭl-vā'-nŭs, 'of the forest.' 2 Cor. 1. 19.

Silver (Gen. 23. 15). Heb. *Késeph:* Gk. ἀργύριον. Largely imported into Egypt, and afterwards into Palestine, from Spain and Arabia.
1 Kn. 10. 27, king made *s.* as stones.
Job 22. 25, thou shalt have plenty of *s.*
Ps. 12. 6; 66. 10, as *s.* is tried.
Prov. 8. 10, receive instruction and not *s.*
Eccl. 5. 10, he that loveth *s.* shall not be satisfied.
Isa. 1. 22, thy *s.* is become dross.
Jer. 6. 30, reprobate *s.* shall men call them.
Mal. 3. 3, sit as a refiner and purifier of *s.*

Silver. Gen. 44. 2; Ex. 26. 19; Num. 7. 13; Eccl. 12. 6; Mat. 27. 6; Acts 19. 24.
as money. Gen. 23. 15; 44. 2; Deu. 22. 19; 2 Kn. 5. 22.

Silverling, a small silver coin. Isa. 7. 23.

Silversmith. Acts 19. 24, Demetrius, a *s.*

Simeon, sĭm'-ĕ-ọn, same as SHIMEON.
(1) son of Jacob. Gen. 29. 33; 34. 7, 25; 42. 24.
his descendants. Gen. 46. 10; Ex. 6. 15; Num. 1. 22; 26. 12; 1 Chr. 4. 24; 12. 25.
prophecy concerning. Gen. 49. 5.
(2) blesses Christ. Lu. 2. 25.
(3) (Niger). Acts 13. 1.

Simeonites, sĭm'-ĕ-ọn-ītes, members of the family of Simeon. Num. 26. 14.

Similitude. (1) Num. 12. 8, the *s.* of the Lord. R. V. form.
Deu. 4. 12, saw no *s.* R. V. form.
Ps. 144. 12, after the *s.* of a palace. R. V. fashion.
Rom. 5. 14, after the *s.* of Adam's transgression. R. V. likeness.
Jas. 3. 9, made after the *s.* of God. R. V. likeness.
(2) parable. Hos. 12. 10; Dan. 10. 16; Heb. 7. 15.

Simon, sī'-mon, same as SIMEON.
(1) brother of Christ. Mat. 13. 55; Mk. 6. 3.
(2) (Zelotes), APOSTLE. Mat. 10. 4; Mk. 3. 18; Lu. 6. 15.
(3) (Pharisee), reproved. Lu. 7. 36.
(4) (leper). Mat. 26. 6; Mk. 14. 3.
(5) (of Cyrene), bears the cross of Jesus. Mat. 27. 32; Mk. 15. 21; Lu. 23. 26.
(6) (a tanner), Peter's vision in his house. Acts 9. 43; 10. 6.
(7) (a sorcerer), baptized, Acts 8. 9. rebuked by Peter, Acts 8. 18.
(8) PETER. *See* PETER.

Simple, innocent, guileless, or foolish. Ps. 19. 7, making wise the *s.*
116. 6, the Lord preserveth the *s.*
119. 130, it giveth understanding to the *s.*
Prov. 1. 22, how long, ye *s.* ones?
1. 32, the turning away of the *s.*
7. 7, and beheld among the *s.*
8. 5, O ye *s.*, understand wisdom.
9. 4, whoso is *s.*
14. 15, the *s.* believeth every word.
19. 25, and the *s.* will beware.
22. 3; 27. 12, the *s.* pass on, and are punished.
Rom. 16. 18, deceive the hearts of the *s.* R. V. innocent.

Simplicity. 2 Cor. 1. 12, that in *s.* and godly sincerity. R. V. holiness.
11. 3, from the *s.* that is in Christ.

Simri, sĭm'-rī, same as SHIMRI. 1 Chr. 26. 10.

Sin, sĭn, 'clay' (Ex. 16. 1). (Zin), wilderness of. Ex. 16.; Num. 13. 21; 20.; 27. 14.

Sin (*n.*). Gen. 4. 7, *s.* lieth at the door.
Num. 27. 3, died in his own *s.*
Deu. 24. 16; 2 Kn. 14. 6; 2 Chr. 25. 4, put to death for his own *s.*
Job 10. 6, thou searchest after my *s.*
Ps. 19. 13, from presumptuous *s.*
25. 7, remember not *s.* of my youth.
32. 1, blessed is he whose *s.* is covered.
38. 18, I will be sorry for my *s.*
51. 3, my *s.* is ever before me.
90. 8, our secret *s.*
103. 10, hath not dealt with us according to our *s.*
Prov. 5. 22, holden with cords of *s.*
10. 19, in multitude of words wanteth not *s.* R. V. transgression.
14. 9, fools make a mock at *s.* R. V. guilt.
14. 34, *s.* is a reproach to any people.
Isa. 30. 1, to add *s.* to *s.*
43. 25; 44. 22, not remember *s.*
53. 10, offering for *s.*
53. 12, bare the *s.* of many.
Jer. 51. 5, land filled with *s.* R. V. guilt.
Ezek. 33. 16, none of his *s.* shall be mentioned.
Hos. 4. 8, they eat up *s.* of my people.
Mic. 6. 7, fruit of my body for *s.* of my soul.
Mat. 12. 31, all manner of *s.* shall be forgiven.
John 1. 29, the *s.* of the world.
8. 7, he that is without *s.*
16. 8, will reprove the world of *s.*
19. 11, hath the greater *s.*
Acts 7. 60, lay not this *s.* to their charge.
22. 16, wash away thy *s.*
Rom. 5. 20, where *s.* abounded.
6. 1, shall we continue in *s.*
7. 7, I had not known *s.*
14. 23, whatsoever is not of faith is *s.*
2 Cor. 5. 21, made him to be *s.* for us.
2 Thes. 2. 3, that man of *s.*
1 Pet. 2. 24, his own self bare our *s.*
See 1 John 4. 10; Rev. 1. 5.

Sin (*v.*). Gen. 42. 22, do not *s.* against the child.
Ex. 9. 27; 10. 16; Num. 22. 34; Jos. 7. 20; 1 Sam. 15. 24; 26. 21; 2 Sam. 12. 13; Job 7. 20; Ps. 41. 4; Mat. 27. 4; Lu. 15. 18, I have *s.*
Job 10. 14, if I *s.*, thou markest me.
Ps. 4. 4, stand in awe and *s.* not.
39. 1, that I *s.* not with my tongue.
Prov. 8. 36, he that *s.* against me.
Isa. 43. 27, thy first father hath *s.*
Ezek. 18. 4, the soul that *s.* it shall die.
Hos. 13. 2, now they *s.* more and more.
Mat. 18. 21, how oft shall my brother *s.*
John 5. 14; 8. 11, *s.* no more.
Rom. 6. 15, shall we *s.* because.
1 Cor. 15. 34, awake to righteousness and *s.* not.
Eph. 4. 26, be ye angry, and *s.* not.
1 John 3. 9, he cannot *s.* because born of God.
See Num. 15. 28; Job 1. 5, 22; Rom. 3. 23.

Sin, what it is. Deu. 9. 7; Jos. 1. 18; Prov. 24. 9; Rom. 14. 23; Jas. 4. 17; 1 John 3. 4; 5. 17.
origin of. Gen. 3. 6, 7; Mat. 15. 19; John 8. 44; Rom. 5. 12; 1 John 3. 8.
characteristics of. Prov. 14. 34; 15. 9; 30. 12; Isa. 1. 18; 59. 3; Jer. 44. 4; Eph. 5. 11; Heb. 3. 13, 15; 6. 1; 9. 14; Jas. 1. 15.
sting of death. 1 Cor. 15. 56.
all born in, and under. Gen. 5. 3; Job 15. 14; 25. 4; Ps. 51. 5; Rom. 3. 9; Gal. 3. 22.
Christ alone without. 2 Cor. 5. 21; Heb. 4. 15; 7. 26; 1 John 3. 5. His blood alone redeems from, John 1. 29; Eph. 1. 7; 1 John 1. 7; 3. 5.
fountain for. Zec. 13. 1.
repented of, and confessed. Job 33. 27; Ps. 38. 18; 97. 10; Prov. 28. 13; Jer. 3. 21; Rom. 12. 9; 1 John 1. 9.
prayed, striven against, and mortified. Ps. 4. 4; 19. 13; 39. 1; 51. 2; 139. 23, 24; Mat. 6. 13; Rom. 8. 13; Col. 3. 5; Heb. 12. 4.
excludes from heaven. 1 Cor. 6. 9; Gal. 5. 19; Eph. 5. 5; Rev. 21. 27.
wages of, death. Rom. 6. 23.
punishment of. Gen. 2. 17; Ezek. 18. 4; Rom. 5. 13; Heb. 10. 26; Jas. 1. 15.

Sina, sī'-nă, Greek form of SINAI. Acts 7. 30.

Sinai, sī'-nāl *or* sī'-nā, 'pointed' (?). The mountain, also called Horeb, in the peninsula between the arms of the Red Sea, from which the Law was given. Ex. 19. 1; Deu. 33. 2; Jud. 5. 5; Ps. 68. 8, 17; Gal. 4. 24.
Sincere, pure, lit. without wax, as honey. Phil. 1. 10; 1 Pet. 2. 2.
Sincerity. Jos. 24. 14; 1 Cor. 5. 8; Eph. 6. 24.
Sinful. Lu. 5. 8; 24. 7; Rom. 7. 13; 8. 3.
Sing. Ex. 15. 21; 1 Chr. 16. 23; Ps. 66. 2; 95. 1; Eph. 5. 19; Rev. 15. 3.
Singers. 1 Chr. 15. 19; Ps. 68. 25; 87. 7; Eccl. 2. 8; Ezek. 40. 44; Hab. 3. 19.
Singing. Ps. 100. 2; 126. 2; S. of S. 2. 12; Eph. 5. 19. *See* PSALMODY.
Single. Mat. 6. 22; Lu. 11. 34.
Singleness. Acts 2. 46; Eph. 6. 5; Col. 3. 22.
Sinim, sī'-nĭm, 'Chinese' (?). Isa. 49. 12.
Sinite, sī'-nīte. Gen. 10. 17
Sink. Ps. 69. 2; Mat. 14. 30; Lu. 9. 44.
Sinner. Gen. 13. 13, men of Sodom *s.* exceedingly.
Ps. 1. 1, standeth not in way of *s.*
25. 8, teach *s.* in the way.
26. 9, gather not my soul with *s.*
51. 13, *s.* shall be converted.
Prov. 1. 10, if *s.* entice thee.
13. 21, evil pursueth *s.*
Eccl. 9. 18, one *s.* destroyeth much good.
Isa. 33. 14, the *s.* in Zion are afraid.
Mat. 9. 11; Mk. 2. 16; Lu. 5. 30; 15. 2, eat with *s.*
9. 13; Mk. 2. 17; Lu. 5. 32, call *s.* to repentance.
11. 19; Lu. 7. 34, a friend of *s.*
Lu. 7. 37, woman who was a *s.*
13. 2, suppose ye these were *s.* above all?
15. 7, 10, joy over one *s.*
18. 13, be merciful to me a *s.*
John 9. 16, how can a man that is a *s.* do such [miracles?
9. 25, whether he be a *s.* I know not.
Rom. 5. 8, while we were yet *s.*
5. 19, many were made *s.*
Heb. 7. 26, separate from *s.*
See Jas. 4. 8; 5. 20; 1 Pet. 4. 18; Jude 15.
Sins, National, bring judgments, Mat. 23. 35, 36; 27. 25.
denounced, Isa. 1. 24; 30. 1; Jer. 5. 9; 6. 27.
Sion, sī'-on. (1) 'lifted up.' Deu. 4. 48.
(2) Greek name for Mount Zion. Mat. 21. 5.
Siphmoth, sĭph'-mōth, 'bare places' (?). 1 Sam. 30. 28.
Sippai, sĭp'-pā-ī, 'belonging to the doorstep' (?). 1 Chr. 20. 4.
Sirah, sī'-rāh, withdrawing.' 2 Sam. 3. 26.
Sirion, sĭ'-rĭ-on, 'a coat of mail;' mount. Deu. 3. 9; Ps. 29. 6.
Sisamai, sĭs'-ă-māī, 'fragrant' (?). 1 Chr. 2. 40.
Sisera, sĭs'-ĕ-rā. (1) Jud. 4. 2, 21; 5. 24; 1 Sam. 12. 9; Ps. 83. 9. (2) Ez. 2. 53; Neh. 7. 55.
Sister. Job 17. 14; Prov. 7. 4; Mat. 12. 50; 1 Tim. 5. 2.
Sit. 2 Kn. 7. 3, why *s.* we here until we die?
Ps. 69. 12, they that *s.* in the gate.
107. 10, such as *s.* in darkness. R. V. sat.
Isa. 30. 7, their strength is to *s.* still.
Jer. 8. 14, why do we *s.* still?
Ezek. 33. 31, they *s.* before thee as thy people.
Mic. 4. 4, they *s.* every man under his vine.
Mal. 3. 3, he shall *s.* as a refiner.
Mat. 20. 23; Mk. 10. 37, to *s.* on my right hand.
See Prov. 23. 1; Lam. 3. 63; Acts 2. 2.
Sith, since, forasmuch as. Ezek. 35. 6.
Sitnah, sĭt'-nāh, 'contention.' Gen. 26. 21.
Situation. 2 Kn. 2. 19; Ps. 48. 2.
Sivan, sī'-văn, 'bright.' The third month of the Jewish sacred year = June. Pentecost is on the 6th of Sivan. Lev. 23. 15, 16; Esth. 8. 9. *See* MONTHS.
Skilful. 1 Chr. 28. 21; Ps. 33. 3; Ezek. 21. 31; Dan. 1. 4.
Skill (*n.*). Eccl. 9. 11; Dan. 1. 17; 9. 22.
Skill (*v.*), to have skill in, understand. 1 Kn. 5. 6; 2 Chr. 2. 7.

Skin. Ex. 34. 29, wist not that *s.* of his face shone.
Job 2. 4, *s.* for *s.*
10. 11, thou hast clothed me with *s.* and flesh.
19. 26, though after my *s.* worms destroy.
Jer. 13. 23, can the Ethiopian change his *s.*
Ezek. 37. 6, I will cover you with *s.*
Heb. 11. 37, wandered in sheep-*s.*
See Gen. 3. 21; 27. 16; Ps. 102. 5; Mic. 3. 2; MK. [1. 6.
Skip. Ps. 29. 6; 114. 4; Jer. 48. 27.
Skirt. Ps. 133. 2; Jer. 2. 34; Zec. 8. 23.
Skull. Mat. 27. 33; Mk. 15. 22.
Sky. Job 37. 18; Isa. 48. 8; Mat. 16. 2; Lu. 12. 56; Heb. 11. 12.
Slack. Deu. 7. 10; Prov. 10. 4; Zep. 3. 16; 2 Pet. 3. 9.
Slain. Gen. 4. 23, I have *s.* a man.
Prov. 7. 26, strong men have been *s.* by her.
22. 13, the slothful man saith, I shall be *s.*
24. 11, deliver those ready to be *s.*
Isa. 22. 2, thy *s.* men are not *s.* with the sword.
26. 21, earth shall no more cover her *s.*
66. 16, the *s.* of the Lord shall be many.
Jer. 9. 1, weep for the *s.* of my people.
Lam. 4. 9, *s.* with sword better than *s.* with hun- [ger.
Ezek. 37. 9, breathe upon these *s.*
Eph. 2. 16, having *s.* the enmity.
Rev. 5. 6, a Lamb as it had been *s.*
See 1 Sam. 18. 7; 22. 21; Lu. 9. 22; Heb. 11. 37.
Slander. Ex. 23. 1; Ps. 15. 3; 31. 13; 34. 13 (1 Pet. 3. 10); 50. 20; 64. 3; 101. 5; Prov. 10. 18; Jer. 6. 28; 9. 4; Eph. 4. 31; 1 Tim. 3. 11; Tit. 3. 2.
effects of, and conduct under. Prov. 16. 28; 17. 9; 18. 8; 26. 20, 22; Jer. 38. 4; Ezek. 22. 9; Mat. 5. 11; 26. 59; Acts 6. 11; 17. 7; 24. 5; 1 Cor. 4. 12.
Slanderously. Rom. 3. 8, as we be *s.* reported.
Slaughter. Ps. 44. 22, as sheep for the *s.*
Isa. 53. 7; Jer. 11. 19, brought as a lamb to the *s.*
Jer. 7. 32; 19. 6, valley of *s.*
Ezek. 9. 2, every man a *s.* weapon.
See Hos. 5. 2; Zec. 11. 4; Acts 9. 1; Jas. 5. 5.
Slave. Jer. 2. 14; Rev. 18. 13.
Slavery. The Mosaic Law made various humane provisions as to the status and treatment of slaves. The N. T. nowhere forbids slavery. But it inculcates principles which must prove fatal to an institution based on a supposed inferiority in individual and social rights. And the modern disappearance of slavery in Christianized societies testifies to the sure working of the N. T. principles. *See esp.*, 1 Cor. 7. 21-24; Eph. 6. 5-9; Col. 3. 22-4. 1, and the Epistle to Philemon.
Slay. Gen. 18. 25, far from thee to *s.* the righteous.
Job 9. 23, if scourge *s.* suddenly.
13. 15, though he *s.* me.
See Gen. 4. 15; Ex. 21. 14; Neh. 4. 11; Lu. 11. 49; [19. 27.
Slaying unpremeditatedly. Num. 35. 11; Deu. 4. 42; 19. 3; Jos. 20. 3.
Sleep (*n.*). 1 Sam. 26. 12, deep *s.* from God.
Job 4. 13; 33. 15, when deep *s.* falleth.
Ps. 13. 3, lest I sleep the *s.* of death.
127. 2, giveth his beloved *s.*
Prov. 3. 24, thy *s.* shall be sweet.
6. 10; 24. 33, yet a little *s.*
20. 13, love not *s.*, lest.
Eccl. 5. 12, the *s.* of a labouring man.
Jer. 51. 39, sleep a perpetual *s.*
Lu. 9. 32, heavy with *s.*
John 11. 13, of taking rest in *s.*
Rom. 13. 11, high time to awake out of *s.*
See Dan. 2. 1; 6. 18; 8. 18; Acts 16. 27; 20. 9.
Sleep (*v.*). Ex. 22. 27, raiment, wherein shall he *s.*
Job 7. 21, now shall I *s.* in the dust.
Ps. 4. 8, I will lay me down and *s.*
121. 4, shall neither slumber nor *s.*
Prov. 4. 16, they *s.* not, except they have done.
6. 22, when thou *s.* it shall keep thee.
10. 5, he that *s.* in harvest is a son that causeth shame.
S. of S. 5. 2, I *s.*, but my heart waketh.
Dan. 12. 2, many that *s.* in the dust.

Mat. 9. 24; Mk. 5. 39; Lu. 8. 52, not dead but *s.*
13. 25, while men *s.* the enemy sowed.
26. 45; Mk. 14. 41, *s.* on now.
Mk. 13. 36, coming suddenly he find you *s.*
Lu. 22. 46, why *s.* ye? rise and pray.
John 11. 11, our friend Lazarus *s.*
1 Cor. 11. 30, for this cause many *s.*
15. 51, we shall not all *s.*
Eph. 5. 14, awake thou that *s.*
1 Thes. 4. 14, them which *s.* in Jesus.
5. 6, let us not *s.* as do others.
5. 7, they that *s. s.* in the night.
5. 10, that whether we wake or *s.*

Sleep. Gen. 2. 21; 15. 12; 28. 11; 1 Sam. 26. 12; 1 Kn. 18. 27; Job 4. 13; Prov. 6. 4-11; 19. 15; 20. 13; Acts 12. 6.
figurative. Ps. 13. 3; Dan. 12. 2; Mk. 13. 36; Rom. 13. 11; 1 Cor. 11. 30; 15. 20, 51; 1 Thes. 4. 13-15.

Sleight, artifice, trick, deceitfulness. Eph. 4. 14, the *s.* of men.

Slew. Jud. 9. 54, a woman *s.* him. [V. smote.
1 Sam. 17. 36, *s.* both the lion and the bear. R.
29. 5, Saul *s.* his thousands.
2 Kn. 10. 9, who *s.* all these? R. V. smote.
Ps. 78. 34, when he *s.* them, then they sought him.
Isa. 66. 3, killeth an ox is as if he *s.* a man.
Dan. 5. 19, whom he would he *s.*
Mat. 23. 35, whom ye *s.* between temple and altar.
Acts 5. 30; 10. 39, whom ye *s.* and hanged on a tree.
22. 20, kept raiment of them that *s.* him.
Rom. 7. 11, sin by the commandment *s.* me.
See Gen. 4. 8; Ex. 2. 12; 13. 15; Neh. 9. 26; Lam. 2. 4.

Slide. Deu. 32. 35; Ps. 26. 1; 37. 31; Hos. 4. 16.

Slightly. Jer. 6. 14; 8. 11, healed hurt *s.*

Slime, any soft viscous substance; here, bitumen. Gen. 11. 3; 14. 10; Ex. 2. 3.

Sling, a simple weapon consisting of a piece of leather with two strings attached, for hurling stones, Jud. 20. 16. Goliath slain by, 1 Sam. 17. 49. *See* 2 Kn. 3. 25; 2 Chr. 26. 14.
figurative. 1 Sam. 25. 29; Prov. 26. 8.

Slip. 2 Sam. 22. 37; Ps. 18. 36, feet did not *s.*
Job 12. 5, he that is ready to *s.*
Ps. 17. 5, that my footsteps *s.* not.
38. 16, when my foot *s.* they magnify.
73. 2, my steps had well nigh *s.*
Heb. 2. 1, lest we should let them *s.* R. V. should drift away from them.
See Deu. 19. 5; 1 Sam. 19. 10; Ps. 94. 18.

Slippery. Ps. 35. 6; 73. 18; Jer. 23. 12.

Slothful. Jud. 18. 9, be not *s.* to possess.
Mat. 25. 26, thou *s.* servant.
Rom. 12. 11, not *s.* in business.
Heb. 6. 12, that ye be not *s.* R. V. sluggish.

Slothfulness. Prov. 12. 24, 27; 15. 19; 18. 9; 19. 15, 24; 21. 25; 22. 13; 24. 30; 26. 13-16; Eccl. 10. 18; Mat. 25. 26; Rom. 11. 8.
condemned. Prov. 6. 4; Rom. 12. 11; 13. 11; 1 Thes. 5. 6; Heb. 6. 12.

Slow. Ex. 4. 10, I am *s.* of speech.
Neh. 9. 17, a God *s.* to anger.
Prov. 14. 29, *s.* to wrath is of great understanding.
Lu. 24. 25, *s.* of heart.
See Acts 27. 7; Tit. 1. 12; Jas. 1. 19.

Sluggard. Prov. 6. 6, go to the ant, thou *s.*
10. 26, so is the *s.* to them that send him.
13. 4, the soul of the *s.* desireth.
20. 4, the *s.* will not plow. R. V. slothful.
26. 16, the *s.* is wiser in his own conceit.

Slumber. Ps. 121. 3, that keepeth thee will not *s.*
Prov. 6. 4, give not *s.* to thine eyelids.
6. 10; 24. 33, a little more *s.*
Isa. 5. 27, none shall *s.* among them.
56. 10, loving to *s.*
Nah. 3. 18, thy shepherds *s.*
Rom. 11. 8, hath given them the spirit of *s.* R. V. stupor.
See Job 33. 15; Mat. 25. 5; 2 Pet. 2. 3.

Small. Ex. 16. 14, *s.* round thing, *s.* as hoar frost.
18. 22, every *s.* matter they shall judge.
Num. 16. 9, a *s.* thing that God hath separated.
16. 13, a *s.* thing that thou hast brought us.
Deu. 9. 21, I ground the calf *s.*, even as *s.* as dust. R. V. fine.
32. 2, doctrine distil as *s.* rain. [sight.
2 Sam. 7. 19; 1 Chr. 17. 17, yet a *s.* thing in thy
1 Kn. 2. 20, one *s.* petition of thee.
2 Kn. 19. 26, inhabitants of *s.* power.
Job 8. 7, thy beginning was *s.*
15. 11, are consolations of God *s.*?
36. 27, he maketh *s.* the drops of water. R. V. draweth up.
Ps. 119. 141, I am *s.*
Prov. 24. 10, thy strength is *s.*
Isa. 7. 13, is it a *s.* thing to weary men?
16. 14, remnant very *s.* and feeble.
40. 15, nations as the *s.* dust.
54. 7, for a *s.* moment.
60. 22, a *s.* one shall become a strong nation.
Jer. 49. 15, I will make thee *s.* among heathen.
Dan. 11. 23, strong with a *s.* people.
Am. 7. 2, by whom shall Jacob arise? for he is *s.*
Zec. 4. 10, the day of *s.* things.
Mk. 8. 7; John 6. 9, a few *s.* fishes.
Acts 12. 18; 19. 23, no *s.* stir.
15. 2, had no *s.* dissension.
Jas. 3. 4, turned with very *s.* helm.
See Jer. 44. 28; Ezek. 34. 18; 1 Cor. 6. 2.

Smart. Prov. 11. 15, shall *s.* for it.

Smell. Gen. 27. 27, as *s.* of field which the Lord hath blessed.
Deu. 4. 28, gods that neither see nor *s.*
Job 39. 25, he *s.* the battle.
Ps. 45. 8, thy garments *s.* of myrrh.
115. 6, noses have they, but they *s.* not.
Isa. 3. 24, instead of sweet *s.* R. V. spices.
Dan. 3. 27, nor the *s.* of fire.
1 Cor. 12. 17, hearing, where were the *s.*?
Eph. 5. 2, sacrifice for sweet-*s.* savour.
Phil. 4. 18, an odour of a sweet *s.*
See S. of S. 1. 12; 2. 13; 4. 10; 7. 8; Am. 5. 21.

Smite. Ex. 2. 13, wherefore *s.* thou.
21. 12, he that *s.* a man.
1 Sam. 26. 8, I will not *s.* him the second time.
2 Kn. 6. 18, *s.* this people with blindness.
6. 21, shall I *s.* them?
Ps. 121. 6, the sun shall not *s.* thee by day.
141. 5, let the righteous *s.* me.
Prov. 19. 25, *s.* a scorner.
Isa. 10. 24, he shall *s.* thee with a rod.
49. 10, neither shall heat *s.* thee.
50. 6, gave my back to the *s.*
58. 4, to *s.* with the fist of wickedness.
Jer. 18. 18, let us *s.* him with the tongue.
Lam. 3. 30, giveth his cheek to him that *s.*
Ezek. 7. 9, know that I am the Lord that *s.*
21. 14, prophesy, and *s.* thine hands together.
Nah. 2. 10, the knees *s.* together.
Zec. 13. 7, awake, O sword, and *s.* the shepherd.
Mal. 4. 6, lest I *s.* the earth with a curse.
Mat. 5. 39, *s.* thee on the right cheek.
24. 49, shall begin to *s.* his fellowservants.
Lu. 22. 49, shall we *s.* with sword?
John 18. 23, why *s.* thou me?
See Lu. 6. 29; Acts 23. 2; 2 Cor. 11. 20; Rev. 11. 6.

Smith. 1 Sam. 13. 19; Isa. 44. 12; Jer. 24. 1.

Smitten. Num. 22. 28, that thou hast *s.*
Deu. 28. 25, cause thee to be *s.*
1 Sam. 4. 3, wherefore hath the Lord *s.* us?
2 Kn. 13. 19, thou shouldest have *s.* five or six times.
Ps. 3. 7, thou hast *s.* all mine enemies.
102. 4, my heart is *s.*
Isa. 24. 12, the gate is *s.* with destruction.
53. 4, *s.* of God.
Jer. 2. 30, in vain have I *s.* your children.
Hos. 6. 1, he hath *s.* and he will bind.
Am. 4. 9, I have *s.* you.
See Job 16. 10; Ezek. 22. 13; Acts 23. 3.

Smoke. Gen. 19. 28, as the *s.* of a furnace.
Deu. 29. 20, the anger of the Lord shall *s.*

Ps. 37. 20, wicked consume into *s.*
68. 2, as *s.* is driven away.
74. 1, why doth thy anger *s.*?
102. 3, my days are consumed like *s.*
104. 32; 144. 5, he toucheth the hills, and they *s.*
119. 83, like a bottle in the *s.*
Prov. 10. 26, as *s.* to the eyes.
Isa. 6. 4, the house was filled with *s.*
34. 10, the *s.* thereof shall go up for ever.
51. 6, the heavens shall vanish like *s.*
65. 5, these are a *s.* in my nose.
Hos. 13. 3, as the *s.* out of a chimney.
See Rev. 9. 2; 14. 11; 15. 8; 18. 9; 19. 3.

Smoking. Gen. 15. 17; Ex. 20. 18; Isa. 42. 3; Mat. 12. 20.

Smooth. Gen. 27. 11, I am a *s.* man.
1 Sam. 17. 40; Isa. 57. 6, five *s.* stones.
Isa. 30. 10, speak unto us *s.* things.
Lu. 3. 5, rough ways shall be made *s.*
See Ps. 55. 21; Prov. 5. 3; Isa. 41. 7.

Smote. Num. 20. 11, Moses *s.* the rock twice.
Jud. 15. 8, Samson *s.* them hip and thigh.
1 Sam. 24. 5, David's heart *s.* him.
Isa. 60. 10, in my wrath I *s.* thee.
Jer. 31. 19, I *s.* upon my thigh.
Hag. 2. 17, I *s.* you with blasting and mildew.
Mat. 26. 68; Lu. 22. 64, who is he that *s.* thee? R. V. struck.
Lu. 18. 13, *s.* upon his breast.
Acts 12. 23, immediately angel *s.* him.
See 2 Sam. 14. 7; Dan. 2. 34; Mat. 27. 30.

Smyrna, smy̆r'-nă, 'myrrh.' Rev. 1. 11.

Snail. (1) (Lev. 11. 30). Heb. *Ḥômet*, 'one prostrate on the ground:' Gk. *σαύρα*: Zool. S. generic. Probably same as R. V. 'sand lizard.' (2) (Ps. 58. 8). Heb. *Shablûl*, 'moist,' 'slimy one:' Gk. *κηρός*: Zool. S. generic. The genuine snail.

Snake. *See* SERPENT.

Snare. Ex. 10. 7, this man be a *s.* unto us.
Deu. 7. 25, nor take silver of idols, lest thou be *s.*
12. 30, take heed that thou be not *s.* by them.
Jos. 23. 13, they shall be *s.* unto you.
Jud. 8. 27, which thing became a *s.* to Gideon.
1 Sam. 18. 21, that she may be a *s.*
28. 9, wherefore layest thou a *s.* for my life?
2 Sam. 22. 6; Ps. 18. 5, *s.* of death prevented me.
Job 18. 8, he walketh on a *s.* R. V. the toils.
22. 10, *s.* are round about thee.
Ps. 11. 6, upon the wicked he shall rain *s.*
38. 12, they lay *s.* for me.
64. 5, commune of laying *s.* privily.
69. 22, let their table become a *s.*
91. 3, deliver thee from *s.* of fowler.
124. 7, the *s.* is broken.
Prov. 6. 2; 12. 13, *s.* with words of thy mouth.
7. 23, as a bird hasteth to the *s.*
13. 14; 14. 27, the *s.* of death.
18. 7, a fool's lips are the *s.* of his soul.
22. 25, learn his ways, and get a *s.* to thy soul.
29. 8, bring city into *s.* R. V. in a flame.
29. 25, fear of man bringeth a *s.*
Eccl. 9. 12, *s.* in an evil time.
Isa. 24. 17; Jer. 48. 43, the *s.* are upon thee.
Lam. 3. 47, fear and a *s.* is come upon us. R. V. the pit.
Ezek. 12. 13, he shall be taken in my *s.*
Hos. 9. 8, the prophet is a *s.*
Am. 3. 5, can a bird fall in a *s.*?
Lu. 21. 35, as a *s.* shall it come. R. V. so.
1 Tim. 3. 7, lest he fall into the *s.*
6. 9, they that will be rich fall into a *s.*
2 Tim. 2. 26, recover out of the *s.* of the devil.
See Ex. 23. 33; Deu. 7. 16; Jud. 2. 3; Eccl. 7. 26.

Snatch. Isa. 9. 20, shall *s.* and be hungry.

Sneezed. 2 Kn. 4. 35, child *s.* seven times.

Snout. Prov. 11. 22, jewel in swine's *s.* [as *s.*

Snow. Ex. 4. 6; Num. 12. 10; 2 Kn. 5. 27, leprous
2 Sam. 23. 20, slew lion in time of *s.*
Job 6. 16, wherein the *s.* is hid.
9. 30, wash myself in *s.* water.
24. 19, drought and heat consume *s.* waters.
Job 37. 6, saith to *s.*, be thou on the earth.
38. 22, the treasures of the *s.*
Ps. 51. 7, I shall be whiter than *s.*
147. 16, he giveth *s.* like wool.
Prov. 25. 13, cold of *s.* in harvest.
26. 1, as *s.* in summer.
31. 21, she is not afraid of the *s.*
Isa. 1. 18, your sins shall be white as *s.*
Isa. 55. 10, as the *s.* from heaven returneth not.
Jer. 18. 14, will a man leave the *s.* of Lebanon?
Lam. 4. 7, Nazarites purer than *s.*
Dan. 7. 9; Mat. 28. 3; Mk. 9. 3, garment white [as *s.*
See Ps. 68. 14; 148. 8; Rev. 1. 14.

Snuffed. Jer. 14. 6; Mal. 1. 13.

Snuffers, gold. Ex. 25. 38; 37. 23.

So, sō, Hebrew form of Egyptian word *Sevech.* 2 [Kn. 17. 4.

Soaked. Isa. 34. 7, land *s.* with blood. R. V. drunken.

Soap (Jer. 2. 22; Mal. 3. 2). Heb. *Bôrîth*: Gk. *πόα*, 'grass,' translated 'soap' in the A. V. It was some cleansing preparation of a vegetable alkali (the *Kali* of the desert). The alkali was used for washing the person. (Job 9. 30. R. V. marg. lye.) It was not the composition in modern domestic use.

Sober. Acts 26. 25, words of truth and *s.*
2 Cor. 5. 13, *s.* for your cause.
1 Thes. 5. 6, let us watch and be *s.*
1 Tim. 3. 2; Tit. 1. 8, a bishop must be *s.*
Tit. 2. 2, aged men be *s.* R. V. temperate.
2. 4, teach young women to be *s.* R. V. omits.
1 Pet. 4. 7, be ye therefore *s.*, and watch.

Sobriety. Rom. 12. 3; 1 Thes. 5. 6; 1 Tim. 2. 9; 3. 2; Tit. 1. 8; 2. 12; 1 Pet. 1. 13; 4. 7; 5. 8.

Socho, sō'-c̲h̲ō, same as SHOCHO. 1 Chr. 4. 18.

Sochoh, sō'-c̲h̲ōh, same as SHOCHOH. 1 Kn. 4. 10.

Socoh, sō'-cōh, same as SHOCO. Jos. 15. 35.

Sod, sodden, boiled, from 'seethe.' Gen. 25. 29; Ex. 12. 9; 1 Sam. 2. 15; Lam. 4. 10.

Sodi, sō'-dī, 'an acquaintance.' Num. 13. 10.

Sodom, sŏd'-om, 'burning' (?). Gen. 10. 19.
its iniquity and destruction. Gen. 13. 13; 18. 20; 19. 4-24; Deu. 23. 17; 1 Kn. 14. 24.
Lot's deliverance from. Gen. 19.
a warning. Deu. 29. 23; 32. 32; Isa. 1. 9; 13. 19; Lam. 4. 6; Mat. 10. 15; Lu. 17. 29; Jude 7; Rev. 11. 8.

Sodoma, sŏd'-ŏ-mă, Greek form of the preceding. Rom. 9. 29. R. V. Sodom.

Sodomites, sŏd'-om-ītes, persons who imitated the sin of the men of Sodom. 1 Kn. 15. 12.

Sodom, vine of (Deu. 32. 32). Heb. *Géphen, Sĕdom*: Gk. *ἄμπελος Σοδόμων*: Bot. N. *Citrullus colocynthis.* The *Colocynth* grows near the Dead Sea; it has long straggling tendrils like a vine, and a fruit of tempting appearance, like a beautiful orange, and its bitter nauseous taste—bitter as gall—agrees with the description of the grapes of the vine of Sodom.

Soft. Job 23. 16, God maketh my heart *s.* R. V. faint.
41. 3, will he speak *s.* words?
Ps. 65. 10, thou makest it *s.* with showers.
Prov. 15. 1, a *s.* answer turneth away wrath.
25. 15, a *s.* tongue breaketh the bone.
See Ps. 55. 21; Mat. 11. 8; Lu. 7. 25.

Softly. Gen. 33. 14; Jud. 4. 21; 1 Kn. 21. 27; Isa. 38. 15.

Soil. Ezek. 17. 8, planted in a good *s.*

Sojourn, to dwell for a time. Gen. 19. 9, this fellow came in to *s.*
26. 3, *s.* in this land, and I will be with thee.
47. 4, to *s.* in the land are we come.
Deu. 26. 5, *s.* with a few, and became a nation.
Jud. 17. 9, I go to *s.* where I may find place.
2 Kn. 8. 1, *s.* wheresoever thou canst *s.*
Ps. 120. 5, woe is me, that I *s.*
Isa. 23. 7, feet carry her afar off to *s.*
Jer. 42. 22, die in place whither ye desire to *s.*
Lam. 4. 15, they shall no more *s.* there.
Heb. 11. 9, by faith he *s.* in land of promise.
1 Pet. 1. 17 pass time of your *s.* here in fear.

up from Babylon on their return to Jerusalem, or sung by those who went up to Jerusalem to attend the annual feasts.

Songs: of Moses, Red Sea, Ex. 15. for water, Num. 21. 17. God's mercy, Deu. 32. and of the Lamb, Rev. 15. 3.
of Deborah, Jud. 5. of Hannah, 1 Sam. 2. of David, 2 Sam. 22. (*see* PSALMS). of Mary, Lu. 1. 46. of Zacharias, Lu. 1. 68. of the angels, Lu. 2. 13. of Simeon, Lu. 2. 29. of the redeemed, Rev. 5. 9; 19.

Sons of God. Job 1. 6; 38. 7; John 1. 12; Rom. 8. 14; 2 Cor. 6. 18; Heb. 2. 10; 12. 5; Jas. 1. 18; 1 John 3. 1.
obligations of. Eph. 5. 1; Phil. 2. 15; 1 Pet. 1. 14; 2. 9.

Soon. Ex. 2. 18, how is it ye are come so *s.*?
Job 32. 22, my Maker would *s.* take me away.
Ps. 37. 2, shall *s.* be cut down.
58. 3, go astray as *s.* as born.
68. 31, Ethiopia shall *s.* stretch out her hands. R. V. haste to.
90. 10, it is *s.* cut off.
Ps. 106. 13, they *s.* forgat his works.
Prov. 14. 17, he that is *s.* angry.
See Mat. 21. 20; Gal. 1. 6; 2 Thes. 2. 2; Tit. 1. 7.

Soothsayer, a diviner, foreteller of future events. Dan. 2. 27.

Soothsaying, divination, pretence of predicting. Acts 16. 16. *See* DIVINATION.

Sop. John 13. 26, 27, 30.

Sopater, sŏ′-pă-tĕr. Acts 20. 4.

Sophereth, sŏ′-phĕ-rĕth, 'scribe.' Ez. 2. 55.

Sorcerer, a fortune-teller (originally by casting lots); hence, one who uses magic arts, a wizard, a conjurer. Ex. 7. 11.

Sorcery. Isa. 47. 9; 57. 3; Acts 8. 9; 13. 6; Rev. 21. 8; 22. 15. *See* DIVINATION.

Sore (*adv.*), greatly, severely; as *adj.* severe. Gen. 19. 9; 2 Chr. 6. 29; Isa. 1. 6; Lu. 16. 20.

Sorek, sôr′-ĕk, 'choice vine.' Jud. 16. 4.

Sorrow. Gen. 3. 16, multiply thy *s.*
42. 38, with *s.* to the grave.
Job 6. 10, I would harden myself in *s.* R. V. pain.
21. 17, God distributeth *s.* in his anger.
41. 22, *s.* is turned into joy. R. V. terror.
Ps. 13. 2, having *s.* in my heart daily.
90. 10, yet is their strength labour and *s.*
116. 3, I found trouble and *s.*
127. 2, to eat the bread of *s.* R. V. toil.
Prov. 10. 22, maketh rich, addeth no *s.*
23. 29, who hath *s.*?
Eccl. 2. 23, all his days are *s.*
7. 3, *s.* is better than laughter.
11. 10, remove *s.* from thy heart.
Isa. 17. 11, day of desperate *s.*
35. 10; 51. 11, *s.* and sighing shall flee away.
53. 3, a man of *s.*
Jer. 30. 15, thy *s.* is incurable.
49. 23, there is *s.* on the sea.
Lam. 1. 12, any *s.* like unto my *s.*
Mat. 24. 8; Mk. 13. 8, beginning of *s.* R. V. travail.
Lu. 22. 45, sleeping for *s.*
John 16. 6, *s.* hath filled your heart.
2 Cor. 2. 7, with overmuch *s.*
7. 10, godly *s.* worketh repentance.
1 Thes. 4. 13, *s.* not as others.
1 Tim. 6. 10, pierced with many *s.*
See Prov. 15. 13; Hos. 8. 10; Rev. 21. 4.

Sorrow: godly, 2 Cor. 7. 10. earthly, Gen. 42. 38; Job 17. 7; Ps. 13. 2; 90. 10; Prov. 10. 22; Isa. 35. 10; Lu. 22. 45; Rom. 9. 2; 1 Thes. 4. 13. consequence of sin, Gen. 3. 16, 17; Ps. 51.

Sorrowful. 1 Sam. 1. 15, woman of a *s.* spirit.
Ps. 69. 29, I am poor and *s.*
Prov. 14. 13, even in laughter the heart is *s.*
Jer. 31. 25, replenished every *s.* soul.
Zep. 3. 18, I will gather them that are *s.*
Mat. 19. 22; Lu. 18. 23, went away *s.*
26. 37, he began to be *s.*
26. 38; Mk. 14. 34, my soul is exceeding *s.*
John 16. 20, ye shall be *s.*
See Job 6. 7; 2 Cor. 6. 10; Phil. 2. 28.

Sorry. Ps. 38. 18, I will be *s.* for my sin.
Isa. 51. 19, who shall be *s.* for thee?
See 1 Sam. 22. 8; Neh. 8. 10; Mat. 14. 9.

Sort. Gen. 6. 19, two of every *s.*
1 Chr. 29. 14, to offer after this *s.*
Dan. 3. 29, deliver after this *s.*
Acts 17. 5, fellows of the baser *s.* R. V. rabble.
2 Cor. 7. 11; 3 John 6, after a godly *s.*
2 Tim. 3. 6, of this *s.* are they. R. V. these.
See Deu. 22. 11; Eccl. 2. 8; Ezek. 27. 24; 38. 4.

Sosipater, sō-sĭp′-ă-tĕr. Rom. 16. 21.

Sosthenes, sŏs′-thĕ-nēs. Acts 18. 17.

Sotai, sō-tā′-ī, 'deviator.' Ez. 2. 55.

Sottish. Jer. 4. 22, they are *s.* children.

Sought. Gen. 43. 30, he *s.* where to weep.
Ex. 4. 24, the Lord *s.* to kill him.
1 Sam. 13. 14, the Lord hath *s.* him a man.
1 Chr. 15. 13, we *s.* him not after due order.
2 Chr. 15. 4, when they *s.* him he was found.
15. 15, they *s.* him with their whole desire.
16. 12, in his disease he *s.* not the Lord.
26. 5, as long as he *s.* the Lord.
Ps. 34. 4; 77. 2, I *s.* the Lord, and he heard me.
111. 2, *s.* out of all that have pleasure.
Eccl. 7. 29, *s.* out many inventions.
12. 10, the preacher *s.* to find acceptable words.
Isa. 62. 12, shalt be called, *S.* out.
65. 1, *s.* of them that asked not. R. V. inquired of by.
Jer. 10. 21, pastors have not *s.* the Lord. R. V. inquired of.
Lam. 1. 19, they *s.* meat to relieve their souls.
Ezek. 22. 30, I *s.* for a man among them.
34. 4, neither have ye *s.* that which was lost.
Lu. 11. 16, *s.* of him a sign.
13. 6, he *s.* fruit thereon.
19. 3, *s.* to see Jesus.
Rom. 9. 32, *s.* it not by faith.
Heb. 12. 17, though he *s.* it carefully with tears.
See S. of S. 3. 1; Lu. 2. 44; 1 Thes. 2. 6.

Soul. Gen. 2. 7, a living *s.*
Ex. 30. 12, a ransom for his *s.*
Deu. 11. 13, serve him with all your *s.*
13. 6, thy friend, which is as thine own *s.*
30. 2; Mat. 22. 37, obey with all thy *s.*
Jud. 10. 16, his *s.* was grieved.
1 Sam. 18. 1; 20. 17, loved him as his own *s.*
1 Kn. 8. 48, return with all their *s.*
1 Chr. 22. 19, set your *s.* to seek the Lord.
Job 3. 20, life unto the bitter in *s.*
12. 10, in whose hand is the *s.*
16. 4, if your *s.* were in my *s.* stead.
23. 13, what his *s.* desireth, even that he doeth.
31. 30, wishing a curse to his *s.* R. V. asking his life with a curse.
33. 22, his *s.* draweth near to the grave.
Ps. 33. 19, to deliver their *s.* from death.
34. 22, redeemeth the *s.* of his servants.
49. 8, the redemption of their *s.* is precious.
62. 1, my *s.* waiteth upon God.
63. 1, my *s.* thirsteth for thee.
74. 19, the *s.* of thy turtledove.
103. 1; 104. 1, bless the Lord, O my *s.*
116. 7, return to thy rest, O my *s.*
116. 8, thou hast delivered my *s.* from death.
119. 175, let my *s.* live.
142. 4, no man cared for my *s.*
Prov. 11. 25, the liberal *s.* shall be made fat.
19. 2, *s.* without knowledge.
25. 25, cold waters to thirsty *s.*
Isa. 55. 3, hear, and your *s.* shall live.
58. 10, if thou wilt satisfy the afflicted *s.*
Jer. 20. 13, hath delivered the *s.* of the poor.
31. 12, their *s.* shall be as a watered garden.
Ezek. 18. 4, all *s.* are mine.
22. 25, they have devoured *s.*
Hab. 2. 10, thou hast sinned against thy *s.*
Mat. 10. 28, to destroy both *s.* and body.
16. 26; Mk. 8. 36, lose his own *s.* R. V. life.
26. 38; Mk. 14. 34, my *s.* is exceeding sorrowful.
Lu. 21. 19, in your patience possess ye your *s.*
Acts 4. 32, of one heart and *s.*
Rom. 13. 1, let every *s.* be subject.

1 Thes. 5. 23, that your s. and body be preserved.
Heb. 6. 19, an anchor of the s.
13. 17, they watch for your s.
Jas. 5. 20, shall save a s. from death.
1 Pet. 2. 11, which war against the s.
4. 19, commit keeping of s. to him.
2 Pet. 2. 14, beguiling unstable s.
3 John 2, even as thy s. prospereth.
See Prov. 3. 22; Ezek. 3. 19; Acts 15. 24.
Soul, man endowed with. Gen. 2. 7.
atonement for. Lev. 17. 11.
redemption of. Ps. 34. 22; 49. 8, 15.
worth of. Mat. 16. 26; Mk. 8. 37.
Sound (*n.*). Lev. 26. 36, the s. of a shaken leaf.
1 Kn. 18. 41, s. of abundance of rain.
Job 15. 21, a dreadful s. is in his ears.
Ps. 89. 15, that know the joyful s.
92. 3, harp with a solemn s.
Eccl. 12. 4, s. of grinding is low.
Jer. 50. 22, s. of battle in the land.
51. 54, s. of a cry cometh.
Ezek. 33. 5, he heard s., and took not warning.
John 3. 8, thou hearest the s. R. V. voice.
Acts 2. 2, suddenly a s. from heaven.
Rom. 10. 18, s. went into all the earth.
1 Cor. 14. 8, an uncertain s. R. V. voice.
See 2 Kn. 6. 32; Rev. 1. 15; 9. 9; 18. 22.
Sound (*adj.*). Prov. 2. 7; 3. 21; 8. 14, s. wisdom.
Prov. 14. 30, a s. heart is life of the flesh.
1 Tim. 1. 10; 2 Tim. 4. 3; Tit. 1. 9; 2. 1, s. doctrine.
2 Tim. 1. 7, spirit of a s. mind. R. V. discipline.
1. 13, form of s. words.
See Ps. 119. 80; Lu. 15. 27; Tit. 2. 2, 8. [omits.
Sound (*v.*). Ex. 19. 19, the trumpet s. long. R. V.
Joel 2. 1, s. an alarm in holy mountain.
Mat. 6. 2, do not s. a trumpet before thee.
1 Thes. 1. 8, from you s. out word of the Lord.
See Neh. 4. 18; 1 Cor. 13. 1; 15. 52; Rev. 8. 7.
Sour. Isa. 18. 5; Jer. 31. 29; Ezek. 18. 2; Hos. 4. 18.
South, the king of. Dan. 11.
queen of. Mat. 12. 42.
Sow. Job 4. 8, they that s. wickedness.
Ps. 97. 11, light is s. for the righteous.
126. 5, s. in tears.
Prov. 6. 19, he that s. discord. [not s.
Eccl. 11. 4, he that observeth the wind shall
11. 6, in morning s. thy seed.
Isa. 32. 20, that s. beside all waters.
Jer. 4. 3, s. not among thorns.
12. 13, they have s. wheat, but shall reap thorns.
Hos. 10. 12, s. in righteousness, reap in mercy.
Nah. 1. 14, that no more of thy name be s.
Hag. 1. 6, ye have s. much, and bring in little.
Mat. 6. 26, they s. not.
13. 37, he that s. good seed.
John 4. 36, both he that s. and he that reapeth.
1 Cor. 15. 36, that which thou s. is not quickened.
2 Cor. 9. 6, he which s. sparingly.
Gal. 6. 7, whatsoever a man s., that shall he reap.
See Lev. 26. 5; Deu. 11. 10; Jer. 2. 2; Jas. 3. 18.
Sower. Isa. 55. 10; Jer. 50. 16; Mat. 13. 3; Mk. 4. 3; Lu. 8. 5; 2 Cor. 9. 10.
Spain, spain. Rom. 15. 24.
Spake. Ps. 39. 3, then s. I with my tongue.
106. 33, he s. unadvisedly with his lips.
Mal. 3. 16, s. often one to another.
John 7. 46, never man s. like this man.
1 Cor. 13. 11, I s. as a child.
Heb. 12. 25, refused him that s. on earth.
2 Pet. 1. 21, holy men s. as they were moved.
See Gen. 35. 15; John 9. 29; Heb. 1. 1.
Span. A measure of length, originally the extent between the tips of the thumb and the little finger when stretched out = 3 palms = ½ a cubit = 9 or 10 inches. The English span = 9 inches. *See* Measures.
Ex. 28. 16; Isa. 40. 12; 48. 13; Lam. 2. 20 (*see* R. V.).
Spare. Gen. 18. 26, I will s. for their sakes.
Neh. 13. 22, s. me according to thy mercy.
Ps. 39. 13, s. me, that I may recover strength.
Prov. 13. 24, he that s. the rod.
19. 18, let not thy soul s. for his crying. R. V. set not thy heart on.
Joel 2. 17, s. thy people.
Mal. 3. 17, I will s. them as a man s.
Lu. 15. 17, bread enough and to s.
Rom. 8. 32, s. not his own Son.
11. 21, if God s. not the natural branches.
2 Pet. 2. 4, if God s. not the angels.
See Prov. 17. 27; 21. 26; Isa. 54. 2; 58. 1.
Spark. Job 5. 7; 18. 5; Isa. 1. 31; 50. 11.
Sparrow (Ps. 84. 3; 102. 7). Heb. *Tzippôr*, 'chirper:' Gk. στρουθίον. (Specimens, *Passer salicarius*, found at Ain Fasail; *Fringilla patronia*, found at Jericho.) The word occurs forty times in the Bible; and is always, with two exceptions, translated 'bird' or 'fowl.' The Greek, στρουθίον, denotes any small bird.
Speak. Gen. 18. 27, to s. unto the Lord.
Ex. 4. 14, I know he can s. well.
33. 11, spake to Moses as a man s. to his friend.
Num. 20. 8, s. to the rock.
1 Sam. 25. 17, a man cannot s. to him.
Job 11. 5, oh that God would s. against thee.
13. 7, will ye s. wickedly for God?
32. 7, days should s.
33. 14, God s. once, yea, twice.
37. 20, if a man s. he shall be swallowed up.
Ps. 85. 8, I will hear what the Lord will s.
Prov. 23. 9, s. not in the ears of a fool.
S. of S. 7. 9, causing lips of those asleep to s. R. V. gliding through the lips.
Isa. 19. 18, shall s. language of Canaan.
63. 1, I that s. in righteousness.
65. 24, while they are yet s., I will hear.
Jer. 20. 9, I will not s. any more in his name.
Hab. 2. 3, at the end it shall s. R. V. it hasteth toward the end.
Zec. 8. 16; Eph. 4. 25, s. every man the truth.
Mat. 8. 8, s. the word only, and my servant.
10. 19; Mk. 13. 11, how or what ye shall s.
12. 34; Lu. 6. 45, of abundance of heart mouth s.
12. 36, every idle word that men shall s.
Mk. 9. 39, can lightly s. evil of me.
Lu. 6. 26, when all men s. well of you.
John 3. 11, we s. that we do know.
Acts 4. 17, that they s. to no man in this name.
4. 20, we cannot but s.
26. 25, I s. words of truth and soberness.
1 Cor. 1. 10, that ye all s. the same thing.
14. 28, let him s. to himself and to God.
2 Cor. 4. 13, we believe and therefore s.
Eph. 4. 15, s. the truth in love.
Heb. 11. 4, he being dead yet s.
12. 24, that s. better things than that of Abel.
Jas. 1. 19, slow to s.
See 1 Cor. 14. 2; 1 Pet. 2. 1; 2 Pet. 2. 12.
Spear. An offensive weapon consisting of a shaft with a metal head, used for thrusting; but it could be hurled, especially the smaller kind called javelin. Jos. 8. 18, stretch out the s. R. V. javelin.
Jud. 5. 8, was there a shield or s. seen?
1 Sam. 13. 22, nor s. with any but Saul.
17. 7, the staff of his s.
17. 45, thou comest to me with a s.
Ps. 46. 9, he cutteth the s. in sunder.
Isa. 2. 4; Mic. 4. 3, beat s. into pruninghooks.
See Job 41. 29; Jer. 6. 23; Hab. 3. 11; John 19. 34.
Special. Deu. 7. 6; Acts 19. 11.
Spectacle. 1 Cor. 4. 9, made a s. to the world.
Sped, succeeded. Jud. 5. 30, have they not s. R. V. found.
Speech. Gen. 11. 1, earth was of one s.
Ex. 4. 10, I am slow of s.
Num. 12. 8, not in dark s.
Deu. 32. 2, my s. shall distil as dew.
1 Kn. 3. 10, Solomon's s. pleased the Lord.
Job 6. 26, the s. of one that is desperate.
15. 3, or with s. wherewith he can do no good.
Ps. 19. 2, day unto day uttereth s. [heard.
19. 3, there is no s. where their voice is not

Prov. 17. 7, excellent *s.* becometh not a fool.
S. of S. 4. 3, thy *s.* is comely.
Isa. 33. 19, of deeper *s.* than thou canst perceive.
Mat. 26. 73, thy *s.* bewrayeth thee.
1 Cor. 2. 1, not with excellency of *s.*
4. 19, not the *s.*, but the power. R. V. word.
2 Cor. 3. 12, we use great plainness of *s.*
10. 10, his *s.* is contemptible.
Col. 4. 6, let your *s.* be alway with grace.
Tit. 2. 8, sound *s.*, that cannot be condemned.
See Ezek. 3. 5; Rom. 16. 18; 2 Cor. 11. 6.

Speechless. Mat. 22. 12; Lu. 1. 22; Acts 9. 7.

Speed, success, good fortune. Gen. 24. 12, send me good *s.*
2 John 10, receive him not, neither bid him God *s.* R. V. give him no greeting.
See Ez. 6. 12; Isa. 5. 26; Acts 17. 15.

Speedily. Ps. 31. 2, deliver me *s.*
69. 17; 143. 7, hear me *s.*
79. 8, let thy mercies *s.* prevent us.
102. 2, when I call, answer me *s.*
Eccl. 8. 11, because sentence is not executed *s.*
Isa. 58. 8, thy health shall spring forth *s.*
Zec. 8. 21, let us go *s.* to pray.
Lu. 18. 8, he will avenge them *s.*
See 1 Sam. 27. 1; Ez. 6. 13; 7. 17; Joel 3. 4.

Spelt. Isa. 28. 25; Ezek. 4. 9, marg. An inferior kind of wheat.

Spend. Job 21. 13, they *s.* their days in wealth.
36. 11, they *s.* their days in prosperity.
Ps. 90. 9, we *s.* our years as a tale that is told. R. V. bring our years to an end as.
Isa. 55. 2, why *s.* money for that which is not bread?
2 Cor. 12. 15, very gladly *s.* and be spent for you.
See Prov. 21. 20; Eccl. 6. 12; Lu. 10. 35.

Spent. Gen. 21. 15, water was *s.* in the bottle.
Job 7. 6, days *s.* without hope.
Ps. 31. 10, my life is *s.* with grief.
Isa. 49. 4, I have *s.* my strength for nought.
Lu. 15. 14, when he had *s.* all.
Acts 17. 21, *s.* their time to tell some new thing.

Spent: night is far, Rom. 13. 12. day, Jud. 19. 11; Mk. 6. 35; Lu. 24. 29.

Spice. (1) Heb. *Bosem*, used generically for spices and fragrant stuff. Ex. 25. 6 with 30. 23, 24; 1 Kn. 10. 10.
(2) Heb. *Nĕcôth*. *See* SPICERY.
(3) Heb. *Sammim*, fragrant odours used for making incense. Ex. 30. 7.
(4) Gk. ἄρωμα, 'aroma.' Mk. 16. 1; John 19. 40. a generic term for spices.

Spicery (*spice tree*) (Gen. 37. 25; 43. 11). Heb. *Nĕcôth:* Gk. θυμίαμα: Bot. N. *Astragalus tragacantha:* R. V. marg. 'gum tragacanth, or storax.' *See* STACTE. The Heb. here is probably a specific term for tragacanth, but a form of this word may be used in 2 Kn. 20. 13; Isa. 39. 2, for spices in general.

Spices for religious rites. Ex. 25. 6; 30. 23, 34; 37. 29; Esth. 2. 12; Ps. 45. 8.
for funeral. 2 Chr. 16. 14; Mk. 16. 1; Lu. 23. 56; John 19. 40.

Spider. (1) (Isa. 59. 5). Heb. *Accâbîsh:* Gk. αράχνη. There are more than 700 species of spiders in Palestine.
(2) (Prov. 30. 28). Heb. *Semamith*, 'poisonous thing;' R. V. lizard. The statement 'taking hold with her hands' is true both of the spider and the gecko lizard.

Spies sent into Canaan, by Moses. Num. 13. 3, 17, 26; 14. 36; Deu. 1. 22; Heb. 3. 17.
sent to Jericho, by Joshua. Jos. 2. 1, 4, 17, 23; 6. 17, 23.

Spikenard (S. of S. 1. 12). Heb. *Nerd:* Gk. νάρδος: Bot. N. *Nardostachys jatamansi:* R. V. marg. Mk. 14. 3, pistic nard (πιστικός νάρδος); i. e., genuine or liquid nard. A plant with very fragrant roots growing on the Himalaya Mts. 11,000 to 17,000 feet above the sea. The nard made from this root was worth from 25 to 400 denarii ($4 to $65) a pound.
Mary anoints Christ with. Mk. 14. 3; Lu. 7. 37; John 12. 3.

Spilt. 2 Sam. 14. 14, as water *s.*

Spin. Ex. 35. 25; Mat. 6. 28; Lu. 12. 27.

Spirit. Gen. 6. 3, my *s.* shall not always strive.
Ex. 35. 21, every one whom his *s.* made willing.
Num. 11. 17, take of the *s.* that is on thee.
14. 24, he had another *s.* with him.
16. 22; 27. 16, the God of the *s.* of all flesh.
27. 18, a man in whom is the *s.*
Jos. 5. 1, nor was there any more *s.* in them.
1 Kn. 22. 21; 2 Chr. 18. 20, there came forth a *s.*
2 Kn. 2. 9, let a double portion of thy *s.*
Neh. 9. 20, thou gavest thy good *s.* to instruct.
Job 4. 15, a *s.* passed before my face.
15. 13, thou turnest thy *s.* against God.
26. 4, whose *s.* came from thee?
32. 8, there is a *s.* in man.
Ps. 31. 5; Lu. 23. 46, into thine hand I commit [my *s.*
32. 2, in whose *s.* there is no guile.
51. 10, renew a right *s.* within me.
78. 8, whose *s.* was not stedfast.
104. 4; Heb. 1. 7, who maketh his angels *s.*
106. 33, they provoked his *s.*
139. 7, whither shall I go from thy *s.*?
Prov. 16. 2, the Lord weigheth the *s.*
16. 18, an haughty *s.* goeth before a fall.
16. 19; 29. 23; Isa. 57. 15, an humble *s.*
16. 32, he that ruleth his *s.* better than he.
Eccl. 3. 21, who knoweth *s.* of man, and *s.* of beast?
7. 8, the patient in *s.* better than the proud.
8. 8, no man hath power over *s.* to retain *s.*
11. 5, the way of the *s.*
12. 7, the *s.* shall return to God.
Isa. 4. 4; 28. 6, *s.* of judgment.
11. 2; Eph. 1. 17, the *s.* of wisdom.
34. 16, his *s.* it hath gathered them.
42. 1, I have put my *s.* upon him.
57. 16, the *s.* should fail before me.
61. 1; Lu. 4. 18, the *S.* of the Lord is upon me.
Ezek. 3. 14; 8. 3; 11. 1, I went in the heat of my *s.*
11. 19; 18. 31; 36. 26, a new *s.*
Mic. 2. 11, a man walking in the *s.* and falsehood.
Mat. 14. 26; Mk. 6. 49, it is a *s.* R. V. an apparition.
26. 41; Mk. 14. 38, the *s.* is willing.
Mk. 1. 10; John 1. 32, the *S.* descending on him.
8. 12, sighed deeply in his *s.*
Lu. 1. 17, go before him in *s.* and power of Elias.
2. 27, came by the *S.* into the temple.
8. 55, her *s.* came again.
9. 55, ye know not what manner of *s.* R. V. omits.
10. 21, Jesus rejoiced in *s.* R. V. the Holy Spirit.
24. 39, a *s.* hath not flesh and bones.
John 3. 34, God giveth not the *S.* by measure.
4. 24, God is a *S.*, worship him in *s.* and in truth.
6. 63, it is the *s.* that quickeneth.
14. 17; 15. 26; 16. 13; 1 John 4. 6, *S.* of truth.
Acts 2. 4, began to speak as the *S.* gave utterance.
6. 10, not able to resist the wisdom and *s.*
17. 16, his *s.* was stirred within him.
23. 8, say that there is neither angel nor *s.*
Rom. 8. 1, walk not after the flesh, but after the [*S.*
8. 2, the law of the *S.* of life.
8. 11, the *S.* of him that raised up Jesus.
8. 16, the *S.* itself beareth witness.
8. 26, the *S.* maketh intercession.
12. 11, fervent in *s.*
1 Cor. 2. 4, in demonstration of the *S.*
2. 10, the *S.* searcheth all things.
4. 21; Gal. 6. 1, in the *s.* of meekness.
6. 17, he that is joined to the Lord is one *s.*
6. 20, glorify God in body and *s.* R. V. omits.
12. 4, diversities of gifts, but the same *S.*
12. 10, to another discerning of *s.*
14. 2, in the *s.* he speaketh mysteries.
15. 45, the last Adam made a quickening *s.*
2 Cor. 3. 6, the letter killeth, but the *s.* giveth life.
3. 17, where the *S.* of the Lord is, there is liberty.

Gal. 3. 3, having begun in the *S.*
5. 16, walk in the *S.*
5. 22; Eph. 5. 9, the fruit of the *S.*
5. 25, if we live in the *S.*, let us walk in the *S.*
6. 8, he that soweth to the *S.* shall of the *S.* reap.
Eph. 2. 2, the *s.* that worketh in children of disobedience.
2. 18, access by one *S.*
2. 22, habitation of God through the *S.*
3. 16, strengthened by his *S.* in inner man.
4. 3, the unity of the *S.*
4. 4, one body and one *S.*
4. 23, renewed in *s.* of your mind.
4. 30, grieve not the holy *S.* of God.
5. 18, be filled with the *S.*
6. 17, take sword of the *S.*
Phil. 1. 27, stand fast in one *s.*
2. 1, if any fellowship of the *S.*
Col. 1. 8, your love in the *s.*
2. 5, absent in flesh, yet with you in the *s.*
1 Thes. 5. 19, quench not the *S.* [the *S.*
2 Thes. 2. 13, chosen through sanctification of
1 Tim. 3. 16, justified in the *S.*
4. 1, giving heed to seducing *s.*
4. 12, be thou an example in *s.*
2 Tim. 4. 22, the Lord Jesus be with thy *s.*
Heb. 1. 14, ministering *s.*
4. 12, dividing asunder of soul and *s.*
9. 14, who through the eternal *S.*
12. 9, in subjection to the Father of *s.*
12. 23, to *s.* of just men made perfect.
Jas. 2. 26, the body without the *s.* is dead.
4. 5, the *s.* lusteth to envy.
1 Pet. 1. 2, through sanctification of the *S.*
3. 4, ornament of a meek and quiet *s.*
3. 18, but quickened by the *S.*
3. 19, preached to *s.* in prison.
4. 6, live according to God in the *s.*
1 John 3. 24, by the *S.* he hath given us.
4. 1, believe not every *s.*, but try the *s.*
4. 2, hereby know ye the *S.* of God.
4. 3, every *s.* that confesseth not.
5. 6, it is the *S.* that beareth witness.
5. 8, the *s.*, the water, and the blood.
Jude 19, sensual, having not the *S.*
Rev. 1. 10, I was in the *S.* on the Lord's day.
2. 7, 11, 17, 29; 3. 6, 13, 22, hear what the *S.* saith.
4. 2, I was in the *s.*, and, behold.
11. 11, the *S.* of life from God entered. R. V. breath.
14. 13, blessed are the dead: Yea, saith the *S.*
22. 17, the *S.* and the bride say, Come.
See Mat. 8. 16; Acts 7. 59; Rom. 7. 6.

Spirit of CHRIST. Rom. 8. 9; 1 Pet. 1. 11.
of Antichrist. 1 John 4. 3. [2. 11.
of man. Eccl. 3. 21; 12. 7; Zec. 12. 1; 1 Cor.
broken. Ps. 51. 17; Prov. 15. 13; 17. 22.
born of. John 3. 5; Gal. 4. 29.
fruit of. Gal. 5. 22; Eph. 5. 9.
of truth. John 14. 17; 15. 26; 16. 13.
bondage. Rom. 8. 15.
divination. Acts 16. 16.
dumbness, &c. Mk. 9. 17.
fear. 2 Tim. 1. 7.
jealousy. Num. 5. 14.
slumber. Rom. 11. 8.

Spirit of God. *See* HOLY SPIRIT.

Spiritual. Hos. 9. 7, the *s.* man is mad. R. V. man that hath the spirit.
Rom. 1. 11, impart some *s.* gift.
7. 14, the law is *s.*
15. 27, partakers of their *s.* things.
1 Cor. 2. 13, comparing *s.* things with *s.*
2. 15, he that is *s.* judgeth all things.
3. 1, not speak unto you as unto *s.*
10. 3, all eat the same *s.* meat.
12. 1; 14. 1, concerning *s.* gifts.
15. 44, it is raised a *s.* body.
15. 46, that was not first which is *s.*
Gal. 6. 1, ye which are *s.*, restore such an one.
Eph. 5. 19, in psalms and hymns and *s.* songs.
6. 12, *s.* wickedness in high places.
1 Pet. 2. 5, a *s.* house, to offer up *s.* sacrifices.
See 1 Cor. 9. 11; Col. 1. 9; 3. 16.

Spiritual body, gifts, &c. Rom. 1. 11; 1 Cor. 12.; 14.; 15. 44; Phil. 3. 21; 1 John 3. 2 (1 Cor. 2. 13; 1 Pet. 2. 5).

Spiritually. Rom. 8. 6; 1 Cor. 2. 14; Rev. 11. 8.

Spite. Ps. 10. 14, thou beholdest mischief and *s.*

Spitefully. Mat. 22. 6; Lu. 8. 32.

Spitting. Num. 12. 14; Deu. 25. 9; Job 30. 10. suffered by Christ (Isa. 50. 6). Mat. 26. 67; 27. 30; Mk. 10. 34; 14. 65; 15. 19.

Spoil (*n.*). Jud. 5. 30, necks of them that take *s.*
1 Sam. 14. 32, people flew upon the *s.*
2 Chr. 15. 11, offered to the Lord of the *s.*
20. 25, three days gathering the *s.*
28. 15, with the *s.* they clothed the naked.
Esth. 3. 13; 8. 11, take the *s.* of them for a prey.
9. 10, on the *s.* laid they not their hand.
Job 29. 17, I plucked the *s.* out of his teeth. R. V. prey.
Ps. 119. 162, rejoice as one that findeth great *s.*
Prov. 16. 19, than to divide *s.* with the proud.
31. 11, he shall have no need of *s.*
Isa. 3. 14, the *s.* of the poor is in your houses.
42. 24, who gave Jacob for a *s.*?
53. 12, divide the *s.* with the strong. [14. 1.
See Isa. 9. 3; Ezek. 7. 21; 38. 13; Nah. 2. 9; Zec.

Spoil (*v.*). Ex. 3. 22, ye shall *s.* the Egyptians.
Ps. 76. 5, the stouthearted are *s.*
S. of S. 2. 15, the little foxes that *s.* the vines.
Isa. 33. 1, woe to thee that *s.*, and thou wast not *s.*!
42. 22, this is a people robbed and *s.*
Jer. 4. 30, when *s.*, what wilt thou do?
Hab. 2. 8, thou hast *s.* many nations.
Zec. 11. 2, howl because the mighty are *s.*
Col. 2. 15, having *s.* principalities.
See Ps. 35. 10; Isa. 22. 4; Col. 2. 8; Heb. 10. 34.

Spoil, its division. Num. 31. 27; 1 Sam. 30. 22.

Spoken. Num. 23. 19, hath he *s.*, and shall he not make it good?
1 Sam. 1. 16, out of my grief have I *s.*
1 Kn. 18. 24, the people said, It is well *s.*
2 Kn. 4. 13, wouldest thou be *s.* for to the king?
Ps. 62. 11, God hath *s.* once.
66. 14, my mouth hath *s.* when in trouble.
87. 3, glorious things are *s.* of thee.
Prov. 15. 23, a word *s.* in due season.
25. 11, a word fitly *s.* is like.
Eccl. 7. 21, take no heed to all words *s.*
Isa. 48. 15, I, even I, have *s.*
Mal. 3. 13, what have we *s.* so much against?
Mk. 14. 9, shall be *s.* of for a memorial.
Lu. 2. 34, for a sign which shall be *s.* against.
Acts 19. 36, these things cannot be *s.* against. R. V. gainsaid.
Rom. 1. 8, your faith is *s.* of. R. V. proclaimed.
14. 16, let not your good be evil *s.* of.
Heb. 2. 2, the word *s.* by angels.
See Heb. 13. 7; 1 Pet. 4. 14; 2 Pet. 3. 2.

Spoken for, asked (for) in marriage. S. of S. 8. 8.

Spokesman. Ex. 4. 16, he shall be thy *s.*

Spoons. Ex. 25. 29; 1 Kn. 7. 50; 2 Kn. 25. 14.

Sport, to disport or amuse one's self. Gen. 26. 8; Isa. 57. 4; 2 Pet. 2. 13.

Spot. Num. 28. 3; 9. 11; 29. 17, lambs without *s.* R. V. blemish.
Deu. 32. 5, their *s.* is not the *s.* of his children. R. V. they are not his . . . it is their blemish.
Job 11. 15, lift up thy face without *s.*
Jer. 13. 23, or the leopard his *s.*
Eph. 5. 27, glorious church, not having *s.*
1 Tim. 6. 14, commandment without *s.*
Heb. 9. 14, offered himself without *s.* R. V. blemish.
1 Pet. 1. 19, lamb without blemish or *s.*
2 Pet. 3. 14, that ye may be found without *s.*
Jude 12, these are *s.* in your feasts. R. V. hidden rocks.
See S. of S. 4. 7; 2 Pet. 2. 13; Jude 23.

Spouse. S. of S. 4. 8; 5. 1; Hos. 4. 13.

Sprang. Mk. 4. 8; Acts 16. 29; Heb. 7. 14; 11. 12.

Spread. Deu. 32. 11, eagle *s.* abroad her wings.

2 Kn. 19. 14; Isa. 37. 14, *s.* letter before the Lord.
Job 9. 8, God who alone *s.* out the heavens.
26. 9, he *s.* his cloud upon it.
29. 19, my root was *s.* out by waters.
36. 30, he *s.* his light upon it.
37. 18, hast thou with him *s.* out the sky?
Ps. 105. 39, he *s.* a cloud for a covering.
140. 5, they have *s.* a net by the wayside.
Isa. 1. 15, when ye *s.* forth your hands I will hide.
33. 23, they could not *s.* the sail.
65. 2, *s.* out hands to a rebellious people.
Jer. 8. 2, they shall *s.* them before the sun.
Ezek. 26. 14, a place to *s.* nets upon.
Mat. 21. 8; Mk. 11. 8; Lu. 19. 36, *s.* garments.
Acts 4. 17, but that it *s.* no further.
See Jud. 8. 25; 1 Kn. 8. 54; Ez. 9. 5.

Sprigs. Isa. 18. 5; Ezek. 17. 6. [1 Sam. 9. 26.

Spring. (1) to dawn, as *sub.* dawn. Jud. 19. 25;
(2) Num. 21. 17, *s.* up, O well.
Job 5. 6, neither doth trouble *s.* out of the ground.
38. 16, hast thou entered into the *s.* of the sea?
Ps. 87. 7, all my *s.* are in thee. R. V. fountains.
104. 10, he sendeth the *s.* into valleys.
107. 33, he turneth water-*s.* into dry ground.
107. 35, turneth dry ground into water-*s.*
Prov. 25. 26, a troubled fountain, and a corrupt *s.*
Isa. 42. 9, before they *s.* forth I tell you.
43. 19, a new thing, now it shall *s.* forth.
45. 8, let righteousness *s.* up together.
58. 8, thine health shall *s.* forth.
58. 11, shall be like a *s.* of water.
Mk. 4. 27, seed should *s.* he knoweth not how.
See Joel 2. 22; John 4. 14; Heb. 12. 15.

Sprinkle. Job 2. 12; Isa. 52. 15; Ezek. 36. 25.

Sprinkling of blood, the passover. Ex. 12. 22; Heb. 11. 28.
the covenant of. Ex. 24. 8; Heb. 9. 13.
cleansing the leper by. Lev. 14. 7.
of oil. Lev. 14. 16. [1. 2.
of the blood of Christ. Heb. 10. 22; 12. 24; 1 Pet.

Sprout. Job 14. 7, a tree will *s.* again.

Spunge. Mat. 27. 48; Mk. 15. 36; John 19. 29.

Spy. Num. 13. 16; Jos. 2. 1; Gal. 2. 4.

Stability. Isa. 33. 6, the *s.* of thy times.

Stable. 1 Chr. 16. 30; Ezek. 25. 5.

Stablish, to establish, confirm. 2 Sam. 7. 13.

Stachys, stăch'-ўs, 'an ear of corn.' Rom. 16. 9.

Stacte (Ex. 30. 34). Heb. *Nâtâph:* Gk. στακτή: Bot. N. *Styrax officinale:* R. V. marg. 'opobalsamum.' Lit. 'a drop' of some exuding gum; one ingredient in the holy incense; translated Job 36. 27, 'drop *of water*.' Probably the gum of the storax tree (styrax); or opobalsam, a resinous juice from the balm or balsam of Gilead.

Staff. Gen. 32. 10, with my *s.* I passed over.
Ex. 12. 11, eat it with *s.* in hand.
Num. 13. 23, bare grapes between two on a *s.*
Jud. 6. 21, the angel put forth end of his *s.*
2 Sam. 3. 29, not fail one that leaneth on a *s.*
2 Kn. 4. 29, lay my *s.* on face of the child.
18. 21; Isa. 36. 6, thou trustest on *s.*
Ps. 23. 4, thy rod and *s.* comfort me.
Isa. 3. 1, the stay and *s.*, the whole stay of bread.
9. 4, thou hast broken the *s.* of his shoulder.
10. 5, the *s.* in their hand is mine indignation.
10. 15, as if the *s.* should lift up itself.
14. 5, the Lord hath broken the *s.* of the wicked.
Jer. 48. 17, how is the strong *s.* broken?
Zec. 11. 10, took my *s.*, even Beauty.
Mk. 6. 8, take nothing, save *s.* only.
Heb. 11. 21, leaning on the top of his *s.*
See Ex. 21. 19; Num. 22. 27; Isa. 28. 27.

Stagger. (1) Job 12. 25; Ps. 107. 27, *s.* like a drunken man.
Isa. 19. 14, as a drunken man *s.*
29. 9, they *s.*, but not with strong drink.
(2) to stumble, to hesitate. Rom. 4. 20. R. V. wavered.

Stain. Job 3. 5; Isa. 23. 9; 63. 3.

Stairs. 1 Kn. 6. 8; Neh. 9. 4; S. of S. 2. 14.

Stakes. Isa. 33. 20; 54. 2.

Stalk. Gen. 41. 5; Jos. 2. 6; Hos. 8. 7.

Stall. Prov. 15. 17; Hab. 3. 17; Mal. 4. 2.

Stammering. Isa. 28. 11; 32. 4; 33. 19.

Stamp. Deu. 9. 21; 2 Sam. 22. 43; Jer. 47. 3.

Stand. (1) Ex. 14. 13; 2 Chr. 20. 17, *s.* still, and see.
Deu. 29. 10, ye *s.* this day all of you before the Lord.
1 Sam. 9. 27, *s.* thou still a while. [minister.
1 Kn. 8. 11; 2 Chr. 5. 14, priests could not *s.* to
17. 1; 18. 15; 2 Kn. 3. 14; 5. 16, the Lord before whom I *s.*
2 Kn. 10. 4, two kings stood not, how shall we *s.*?
Esth. 8. 11, to *s.* for their life.
Job 8. 15, shall lean on his house, but it shall not *s.*
19. 25, he shall *s.* at the latter day.
Ps. 1. 1, nor *s.* in the way of sinners.
1. 5, the ungodly shall not *s.* in judgment.
4. 4, *s.* in awe, and sin not.
10. 1, why *s.* thou afar off?
24. 3, who shall *s.* in his holy place?
33. 11, the counsel of the Lord *s.* for ever.
35. 2, *s.* up for my help.
76. 7, who may *s.* in thy sight?
94. 16, who will *s.* up for me?
109. 31, shall *s.* at right hand of the poor.
122. 2, our feet shall *s.* within thy gates. [*s.*?
130. 3, if thou, Lord, mark iniquities, who shall
147. 17, who can *s.* before his cold?
Prov. 22. 29, shall *s.* before kings.
27. 4, who is able to *s.* before envy?
Eccl. 8. 3, *s.* not in an evil thing. R. V. persist.
Isa. 7. 7; 8. 10, thus saith the Lord, it shall not *s.*
21. 8, I *s.* continually on watchtower.
28. 18, your agreement with hell shall not *s.*
40. 8, the word of God shall *s.* for ever.
65. 5, *s.* by thyself, I am holier than thou.
Jer. 6. 16, *s.* ye in the ways, ask for the old paths.
35. 19, shall not want a man to *s.* before me.
Dan. 11. 16, he shall *s.* in the glorious land.
12. 13, and shall *s.* in thy lot.
Mic. 5. 4, he shall *s.* and feed in strength.
Nah. 2. 8, *s.*, *s.*, shall they cry.
Zec. 3. 1, Satan *s.* at his right hand.
Mal. 3. 2, who shall *s.* when he appeareth?
Mat. 12. 25; Mk. 3. 24, 25; Lu. 11. 18, house divided shall not *s.*
16. 28; Lu. 9. 27, there be some *s.* here.
20. 3, others *s.* idle in the marketplace.
Rom. 5. 2, this grace wherein we *s.*
14. 4, God is able to make him *s.*
1 Cor. 2. 5, faith should not *s.* in wisdom.
16. 13, *s.* fast in the faith. [plexed.
Gal. 4. 20, I *s.* in doubt of you. R. V. am per-
5. 1, *s.* fast in the liberty.
Phil. 1. 27, *s.* fast in one spirit.
4. 1; 1 Thes. 3. 8, *s.* fast in the Lord.
Jas. 5. 9, the judge *s.* before the door.
Rev. 3. 20, I *s.* at the door, and knock.
6. 17, is come, and who shall be able to *s.*?
20. 12, the dead, small and great, *s.* before God.
(2) to stand firm. Eph. 6. 13; 2 Tim. 2. 19.
(3) to consist. 1 Cor. 2. 5.
See Rom. 14. 4; 1 Cor. 10. 12; Rev. 15. 2.

Standard. Isa. 10. 18, as when *s.*-bearer fainteth.
49. 22, I will set up my *s.* to the people. R. V. ensign.
59. 19, Spirit of the Lord shall lift up *s.* against. R. V. breath of the Lord driveth.
62. 10, go through, lift up a *s.* R. V. ensign.
Jer. 4. 6; 50. 2; 51. 12, set up a *s.*
See Num. 1. 52; 2. 3; 10. 14. [34. 32.

Stand to, to agree to, abide by. Deu. 25. 8; 2 Chr.

Star at Christ's birth. Mat. 2. 2.
morning star, Christ, Rev. 22. 16. predicted, Num. 24. 17.
great star falls from heaven. Rev. 8. 10; 9. 1.

Stars created. Gen. 1. 16.
mentioned. Gen. 15. 5; 37. 9; Jud. 5. 20; 1 Cor. 15. 41; Heb. 11. 12; Jude 13; Rev. 8. 12; 12. 1.
not to be worshipped. Deu. 4. 19.
morning. Job 38. 7.

State. Ps. 39. 5; Mat. 12. 45; Lu. 11. 26.

Stater, stā'-tĕr, a silver coin. A. V. 'piece of money' (Mat. 17. 27) = shekel = 4 denarii or drachmas = 34 d. = 65 cts. *See* Money.
Stature. Num. 13. 32, men of great *s.*
1 Sam. 16. 7, look not on height of his *s.*
Isa. 10. 33, high ones of *s.* hewn down.
45. 14, men of *s.* shall come.
Mat. 6. 27; Lu. 12. 25, not add to *s.*
Lu. 2. 52, Jesus increased in *s.*
19. 3, little of *s.*
Eph. 4. 13, *s.* of the fulness of Christ.
See 2 Sam. 21. 20; S. of S. 7. 7; Ezek. 17. 6; 31. 3.
Statute. Ex. 18. 16, the *s.* of God.
Lev. 3. 17; 16. 34; 24. 9, a perpetual *s.*
2 Kn. 17. 8, *s.* of the heathen.
Neh. 9. 14, *s.* and laws.
Ps. 19. 8, the *s.* of the Lord are right. R. V. [precepts.
50. 16, to declare my *s.*
Ezek. 5. 6, hath changed my *s.*
20. 25, *s.* that were not good.
33. 15, walk in the *s.* of life.
Zec. 1. 6, my *s.*, did they not take hold?
See Ps. 18. 22; 105. 45; Ezek. 18. 19.
Statutes of the Lord. 1 Chr. 29. 19; Ps. 19. 8; 119. 12, 16.
Staves. Num. 21. 18, nobles digged with *s.*
1 Sam. 17. 43, am I a dog, that thou comest with *s.*?
Hab. 3. 14, strike through with his *s.*
Zec. 11. 7, took unto me two *s.*
Mat. 10. 10; Lu. 9. 3, neither two coats, nor *s.*
See Mat. 26. 47; Mk. 14. 43; Lu. 22. 52.
Staves for the tabernacle. Ex. 25. 13; 37. 15; 40. 20; Num. 4. 6.
Stay (*n.*), a support. 2 Sam. 22. 19; Ps. 18. 18, the Lord was my *s.*
Isa. 3. 1, take away the *s.* and staff.
See Lev. 13. 5; 1 Kn. 10. 19; Isa. 19. 13.
Stay (*v.*). (1) (*tr.*) to support.
S. of S. 2. 5, *s.* me with flagons.
Isa. 26. 3, whose mind is *s.* on thee.
(2) (*intr.*) to rely or depend on.
Isa. 30. 12, ye trust in oppression, and *s.* thereon.
50. 10, trust in name of the Lord, and *s.* on his God.
(3) (*tr.*) to stop, hold back.
Num. 16. 48; 25. 8; 2 Sam. 24. 25; 1 Chr. 21. 22; Ps. 106. 30, the plague was *s.*
2 Sam. 24. 16; 1 Chr. 21. 15, *s.* now thine hand.
Job 37. 4, he will not *s.* them.
38. 11, here shall thy proud waves be *s.*
38. 37, who can *s.* the bottles of heaven? R. V. pour out.
Prov. 28. 17, let no man *s.* him.
Isa. 27. 8, he *s.* his rough wind. R. V. hath removed her with.
29. 9, *s.* yourselves, and wonder. R. V. tarry.
Dan. 4. 35, none can *s.* his hand.
Hag. 1. 10, heaven is *s.*, earth is *s.*
(4) (*intr.*) to remain. Gen. 19. 17, neither *s.* in plain.
Ex. 9. 28, ye shall *s.* no longer.
See Jos. 10. 13; 1 Sam. 24. 7; Jer. 4. 6; 20. 9.
Stead, place. Num. 32. 14, risen in your fathers' *s.*
1 Chr. 5. 22, dwelt in their *s.*
Job 16. 4, if your soul were in my soul's *s.*
34. 24, he shall set others in their *s.*
Prov. 11. 8, the wicked cometh in his *s.*
2 Cor. 5. 20, we pray you in Christ's *s.* R. V. on behalf of Christ.
See Gen. 30. 2; 2 Kn. 17. 24; 1 Chr. 5. 22.
Steadfastness of the disciples. Acts 2. 42; Col. 2. 5, urged. Deu. 10. 20; Job 11. 15; 1 Cor. 15. 58; 1 Thes. 5. 21; Heb. 3. 14; 4. 14; 10. 23; 1 Pet. 5. 9; 2 Pet. 3. 17.
Steady. Ex. 17. 12, Moses' hands were *s.*
Steal. Gen. 31. 27, wherefore didst thou *s.* away?
44. 8, how then should we *s.* silver or gold?
Prov. 6. 30, if he *s.* to satisfy his soul.
30. 9, lest I be poor, and *s.*
Jer. 23. 30, prophets that *s.* my words.
Mat. 6. 19, thieves break through and *s.*
John 10. 10, thief cometh not, but to *s.*

Stealing. Ex. 20. 15; 21. 16; Lev. 19. 11; Deu. 5. 19; 24. 7; Ps. 50. 18; Hos. 4. 2; Zec. 5. 4; Mat. 19. 18; 27. 64; Rom. 2. 21; 13. 9; Eph. 4. 28; 1 Pet. 4. 15.
restoration inculcated. Ex. 22. 1; Lev. 6. 4; Prov. 6. 30, 31.
Stealth. 2 Sam. 19. 3, by *s.* into city.
Stedfast. Ps. 78. 8, not *s.* with God.
Dan. 6. 26, living God, and *s.* for ever.
Heb. 2. 2, word spoken by angels was *s.*
3. 14, hold our confidence *s.* to end. R. V. firm.
6. 19, hope as anchor, sure and *s.*
1 Pet. 5. 9, resist *s.* in the faith.
See Acts 2. 42; Col. 2. 5; 2 Pet. 3. 17.
Steel. 2 Sam. 22. 35; Job 20. 24; Jer. 15. 12.
Steep. Ezek. 38. 20; Mic. 1. 4; Mat. 8. 32.
Step. 1 Sam. 20. 3, but a *s.* between me and death.
Job 14. 16, thou numberest my *s.*
23. 11, my foot hath held his *s.*
29. 6, I washed my *s.* with butter.
31. 4, doth not he count my *s.*?
31. 7, if my *s.* hath turned out of the way.
Ps. 37. 23, the *s.* of a good man are ordered.
37. 31, none of his *s.* shall slide.
44. 18, nor have our *s.* declined.
56. 6, they mark my *s.*
73. 2, my *s.* had well nigh slipped.
85. 13, set us in the way of his *s.*
119. 133, order my *s.* in thy word.
Prov. 4. 12, thy *s.* shall not be straitened.
5. 5, her *s.* take hold on hell.
16. 9, the Lord directeth his *s.*
Isa. 26. 6, the *s.* of the needy shall tread it down.
Jer. 10. 23, not in man to direct his *s.*
Rom. 4. 12, walk in *s.* of that faith.
2 Cor. 12. 18, walked we not in same *s.*?
1 Pet. 2. 21, that ye should follow his *s.*
See Ex. 20. 26; 2 Sam. 22. 37; Lam. 4. 18; Ezek. 40. 22.
Stephanas, stĕph'-ă-năs, 'crowned.' 1 Cor. 1. 16.
Stephen, stē'-phĕn, 'a crown,' deacon and protomartyr. Acts 6. 5, 8; 7. 58.
Steward. 1 Kn. 16. 9, drunk in house of his *s.*
Lu. 12. 42, that faithful and wise *s.*
See Gen. 15. 2; Lu. 8. 3; 1 Cor. 4. 1; 1 Pet. 4. 10.
Steward, parable of. Lu. 16. 1.
of God, a bishop is. Tit. 1. 7 (1 Cor. 4. 1; 1 Pet. 4. 10).
Stick. Num. 15. 32, gathered *s.* on sabbath.
1 Kn. 17. 12, I am gathering two *s.*
Job 33. 21, his bones *s.* out.
Ps. 38. 2, thine arrows *s.* fast in me.
Prov. 18. 24, a friend that *s.* closer than a brother.
Ezek. 37. 16, take *s.*, and write on it.
See 2 Kn. 6. 6; Lam. 4. 8; Ezek. 29. 4.
Stiff. Ex. 32. 9; 33. 3; 34. 9; Deu. 9. 6, 13; 10. 16, *s.*-necked people.
Ps. 75. 5, speak not with *s.* neck.
Jer. 17. 23, obeyed not, but made their neck *s.*
Ezek. 2. 4, impudent and *s.*-hearted.
Acts 7. 51, ye *s.*-necked, ye do always resist.
See Deu. 31. 27; 2 Chr. 30. 8; 36. 13.
Still. Ex. 15. 16, as *s.* as a stone.
Num. 14. 38, Joshua and Caleb lived *s.*
Jos. 24. 10, Balaam blessed you *s.*
Jud. 18. 9, the land is good, and are ye *s.*?
2 Sam. 14. 32, good to have been there *s.*
2 Kn. 7. 4, if we sit *s.* here, we die also.
2 Chr. 22. 9, no power to keep *s.* the kingdom. R. V. hold.
Job 2. 9, dost thou *s.* retain thine integrity?
Ps. 4. 4, commune with thine heart, and be *s.*
8. 2, *s.* the enemy and avenger.
23. 2, beside the *s.* waters.
46. 10, be *s.*, and know that I am God.
76. 8, earth feared, and was *s.*
83. 1, hold not thy peace, and be not *s.*, O God.
84. 4, they will be *s.* praising thee.
107. 29, so that the waves thereof are *s.*
139. 18, when I awake, I am *s.* with thee.
Eccl. 12. 9, he *s.* taught knowledge.

Isa. 5. 25; 9. 12; 10. 4, his hand is stretched out *s.*
30. 7, their strength is to sit *s.*
42. 14, I have been *s.*, and refrained.
Jer. 8. 14, why do we sit *s.*?
31. 20, I do earnestly remember him *s.*
Zec. 11. 16, nor feed that that standeth *s.* R. V. which is sound.
Mk. 4. 39, arose, and said, Peace, be *s.*
Rev. 22. 11, unjust *s.*, filthy *s.*, holy *s.*
See Num. 13. 30; Ps. 65. 7; 89. 9; 92. 14.

Sting. Prov. 23. 32; 1 Cor. 15. 55; Rev. 9. 10.

Stir. Num. 24. 9, who shall *s.* him up? R. V. rouse.
Deu. 32. 11, as an eagle *s.* up her nest.
1 Sam. 22. 8, my son hath *s.* up my servant.
26. 19, if the Lord have *s.* thee up.
1 Kn. 11. 14, the Lord *s.* up an adversary. R. V. raised.
1 Chr. 5. 26; 2 Chr. 36. 22; Hag. 1. 14, God *s.* up the spirit.
Job 17. 8, the innocent shall *s.* up himself.
41. 10, none dare *s.* him up.
Ps. 35. 23, *s.* up thyself.
39. 2, my sorrow was *s.*
Prov. 10. 12, hatred *s.* up strifes.
15. 18; 29. 22, a wrathful man *s.* up strife.
Isa. 10. 26, the Lord shall *s.* up a scourge.
14. 9, hell from beneath *s.* up the dead.
64. 7, none *s.* up himself to take hold.
Lu. 23. 5, he *s.* up the people.
Acts 17. 16, his spirit was *s.* in him. R. V. provoked.
19. 23, no small *s.* about that way.
2 Tim. 1. 6, *s.* up gift of God in thee.
2 Pet. 1. 13, I think it meet to *s.* you up.
See S. of S. 2. 7; 3. 5; 8. 4; Isa. 22. 2; Acts 12. 18.

Stock. Job 14. 8, though the *s.* thereof die.
Isa. 40. 24, their *s.* shall not take root.
44. 19, shall I fall down to the *s.* of a tree?
Hos. 4. 12, my people ask counsel at their *s.*
Nah. 3. 6; Heb. 10. 33, a gazing-*s.*
Acts 13. 26, children of the *s.* of Abraham.
See Jer. 2. 27; 10. 8; Phil. 3. 5.

Stocks. Job 13. 27; 33. 11; Prov. 7. 22.
Jeremiah in. Jer. 20. 2.
Paul and Silas in. Acts 16. 24.

Stoicks. Same as STOICS.

Stoics, stō'-ics, philosophers whose founder taught in a famous porch or Stoa at Athens. They taught that the universe is permeated by a principle of reason: that this reason was man's highest possession and made him (*a*) essentially independent of pleasure and pain, (*b*) a cosmopolitan being, i. e., member of a world-wide commonwealth. It was from a Stoic poet (Aratus or Cleanthes) that St. Paul quoted the words 'For we also are his offspring.' Acts 17. 28.

Stole. 2 Sam. 15. 6, Absalom *s.* the hearts.
Eph. 4. 28, let him that *s.* steal no more.
See Gen. 31. 20; 2 Kn. 11. 2; 2 Chr. 22. 11; Mat. 28. 13.

Stolen. Jos. 7. 11, they have *s.*, and dissembled.
2 Sam. 21. 12, men had *s.* the bones of Saul.
Prov. 9. 17, *s.* waters are sweet.
Obad. 5, *s.* till they had enough.
See Gen. 30. 33; 31. 19; Ex. 22. 7; 2 Sam. 19. 41.

Stomach. (1) 1 Tim. 5. 23, for thy *s.* sake.
(2) courage. 2 Mac. 7. 21.

Stomacher, part of a woman's dress, generally forming the lower part of the bodice. Isa. 3. 24.

Stone. Gen. 11. 3, they had brick for *s.*
28. 18, 22; 31. 45; 35. 14, set up a *s.* for a pillar.
Deu. 8. 9, a land whose *s.* are iron.
Jos. 24. 27, this *s.* shall be a witness.
2 Sam. 17. 13, till there be not one small *s.* found there.
2 Kn. 3. 25, cast every man his *s.*
Job 5. 23, in league with *s.* of the field.
6. 12, is my strength the strength of *s.*?
14. 19, the waters wear the *s.*
28. 3, he searcheth out the *s.* of darkness.
41. 24, his heart is as firm as a *s.*
Ps. 91. 12; Mat. 4. 6; Lu. 4. 11, lest thou dash thy foot against a *s.*
118. 22; Mat. 21. 42; Mk. 12. 10, the *s.* which the builders refused is become the head *s.*
Prov. 27. 3, a *s.* is heavy, a fool's wrath heavier.
Isa. 54. 11, I will lay thy *s.* with fair colours.
60. 17, bring for *s.* iron.
62. 10, gather out the *s.*
Jer. 2. 27, and to a *s.*, thou hast brought me forth.
Dan. 2. 34, a *s.* was cut out of the mountain.
Hab. 2. 11, the *s.* shall cry out of the wall.
2. 19, that saith to the dumb *s.*, Arise.
Hag. 2. 15, before *s.* was laid upon *s.*
Zec. 3. 9, upon one *s.* shall be seven eyes.
4. 7, bring forth the head-*s.* thereof.
7. 12, they made their hearts as *s.*
Mat. 7. 9; Lu. 11. 11, will he give him a *s.*?
21. 44; Lu. 20. 18, whosoever shall fall on this *s.*
24. 2; Mk. 13. 2; Lu. 19. 44; 21. 6, not one *s.* upon another.
Mk. 13. 1, see what manner of *s.* are here!
16. 4; Lu. 24. 2, found *s.* rolled away.
Lu. 4. 3, command this *s.* that it be made bread.
John 1. 42, Cephas, by interpretation a *s.* R. V. Peter.
8. 7, first cast a *s.*
11. 39, take ye away the *s.*
Acts 17. 29, that the Godhead is like to *s.*
1 Pet. 2. 5, as lively *s.*, are built up.
See 1 Sam. 30. 6; 1 Cor. 3. 12; 2 Cor. 3. 3; Rev. 2. 17.

Stone, corner, Christ is (Ps. 118. 22; Isa. 28. 16). Mat. 21. 42; Mk. 12. 10; 1 Pet. 2. 6.

Stone bow, a cross-bow for shooting stones. Wisd. 5. 22.

Stones, precious: in the high priest's breastplate, Ex. 28. 17. in the temple, 1 Chr. 29. 2; 2 Chr. 3. 6. in the new Jerusalem, Rev. 21. 19.

Stoning: Lev. 20. 2; 24. 14; Deu. 13. 10; 17. 5; 22. 21.
of Achan, Jos. 7. 25. Naboth, 1 Kn. 21. Stephen, Acts 7. 58. Paul, Acts 14. 19; 2 Cor. 11. 25.

Stony. Ps. 141. 6; Ezek. 11. 19; 36. 26; Mat. 13. 5.

Stood. Gen. 18. 22, *s.* yet before the Lord.
Ex. 14. 19, *s.* behind them.
Jos. 3. 16, waters *s.* upon an heap.
2 Kn. 23. 3, all the people *s.* to the covenant.
Esth. 9. 16, Jews *s.* for their lives.
Ps. 33. 9, he commanded, and it *s.* fast.
Lu. 24. 36, Jesus himself *s.* in the midst.
2 Tim. 4. 16, no man *s.* with me. R. V. took my part.
See Gen. 23. 3; Job 29. 8; Ezek. 37. 10; Rev. 7. 11.

Stoop. Gen. 49. 9, Judah *s.* down.
Prov. 12. 25, heaviness maketh the heart *s.*
John 8. 6, *s.* down, and wrote on the ground.
See 2 Chr. 36. 17; Job 9. 13; Mk. 1. 7; John 20. 11.

Stop. Gen. 8. 2, windows of heaven were *s.*
1 Kn. 18. 44, that the rain *s.* thee not.
Ps. 107. 42, iniquity shall *s.* her mouth.
Zec. 7. 11, refused, and *s.* their ears.
Acts 7. 57, *s.* their ears, and ran upon him.
Rom. 3. 19, that every mouth may be *s.*
Tit. 1. 11, whose mouths must be *s.*
Heb. 11. 33, through faith *s.* mouths of lions.
See Gen. 26. 15; Job 5. 16; Ps. 58. 4; Prov. 21. 13.

Store. Lev. 25. 22; 26. 10, eat of the old *s.*
Deu. 28. 5, blessed be thy basket and *s.* R. V. kneading-trough.
2 Kn. 20. 17, thy fathers have laid up in *s.*
Ps. 144. 13, affording all manner of *s.*
Nah. 2. 9, none end of the *s.* and glory.
Mal. 3. 10, bring tithes into *s.*-house.
Lu. 12. 24, neither have *s.*-house nor barn.
1 Cor. 16. 2, every one lay by him in *s.*
1 Tim. 6. 19, laying up in *s.* a good foundation.
2 Pet. 3. 7, by same word are kept in *s.*
See 1 Kn. 10. 10; 1 Chr. 29. 16; Ps. 33. 7.

Stork. Heb. *Hăsîdâh:* Gk. ἀσίδα. (Specimen, *Ciconia alba.*) Both the black and the white stork occur.

Ps. 104. 17, as for the *s.*, the fir trees are her house.
Jer. 8. 7, yea, the *s.* in the heaven.
Zec. 5. 9, like the wings of a *s.*
Storm. Ps. 55. 8, escape from windy *s.*
83. 15, make them afraid with thy *s.*
107. 29, he maketh the *s.* a calm.
Isa. 4. 6; 25. 4, a covert from *s.*
28. 2, as a destroying *s.*
Ezek. 38. 9, shalt ascend and come like a *s.*
Nah. 1. 3, the Lord hath his way in the *s.*
See Job 21. 18; 27. 21; Mk. 4. 37; Lu. 8. 23.
Stormy. Ps. 107. 25; 148. 8; Ezek. 13. 11.
Story. 2 Chr. 13. 22; 24. 27. R. V. commentary.
Stout. Dan. 7. 20, whose look was more *s.*
Mal. 3. 13, words have been *s.* against me.
See Ps. 76. 5; Isa. 9. 9; 10. 12; 46. 12.
Straight. Ps. 5. 8, make thy way *s.* R. V. plain.
Prov. 4. 25, let eyelids look *s.* before thee.
Eccl. 1. 15; 7. 13, crooked cannot be made *s.*
Isa. 40. 3, make *s.* a highway.
40. 4; 42. 16; 45. 2; Lu. 3. 5, crooked shall be made *s.*
Jer. 31. 9, cause them to walk in a *s.* way.
Mat. 3. 3; Mk. 1. 3; Lu. 3. 4; John 1. 23, make his paths *s.*
Lu. 13. 13, she was made *s.*
Acts 9. 11, street which is called *S.*
Heb. 12. 13, make *s.* paths for your feet.
See Jos. 6. 5; 1 Sam. 6. 12; Ezek. 1. 7; 10. 22.
Straightway, immediately, at once. Prov. 7. 22, he goeth after her *s.*
Mat. 4. 20; Mk. 1. 18, they *s.* left their nets.
Jas. 1. 24, *s.* forgetteth what manner of man.
See Lu. 14. 5; John 13. 32; Acts 9. 20; 16. 33.
Strain. Mat. 23. 24, *s.* at a gnat. More correctly, as in R. V., '*s.* out;' i. e., to get rid of by using a strainer.
Strait (*n.*). 2 Sam. 24. 14, I am in a great *s.*
Job 20. 22, he shall be in *s.*
Phil. 1. 23, I am in a *s.* betwixt two.
See Jer. 19. 9.
Strait. (1) narrow. Isa. 49. 20, the place is too *s.* for me, give place.
Mic. 2. 7, is spirit of the Lord *s.*?
Mat. 7. 13; Lu. 13. 24, enter in at the *s.* gate.
Lu. 12. 50, how am I *s.* till it be accomplished!
2 Cor. 6. 12, ye are not *s.* in us.
(2) strict. Acts 26. 5.
See 2 Kn. 6. 1; Job 18. 7; 37. 10.
Straitly, strictly, closely. Gen. 43. 7; Jos. 6. 1; Acts 4. 17.
Straitness, distress from narrow circumstances; hence, want, famine, scarcity of food. Deu. 28. 53; Job 36. 16.
Strake (*n.*), a streak. Gen. 30. 37.
Strake (*v.*), did strike. Acts 27. 27. R. V. lowered the gear.
Strange. Gen. 42. 7, Joseph made himself *s.*
Ex. 2. 22; 18. 3; Ps. 137. 4, in a *s.* land.
Lev. 10. 1; Num. 3. 4; 26. 61, offered *s.* fire.
1 Kn. 11. 1, Solomon loved many *s.* women.
Job 19. 17, my breath is *s.* to my wife.
31. 3, a *s.* punishment to workers. R. V. disaster.
Prov. 2. 16, to deliver thee from the *s.* woman.
5. 3, 20, for the lips of a *s.* woman.
21. 8, the way of man is froward and *s.* R. V. exceeding crooked.
23. 27, a *s.* woman is a narrow pit.
Isa. 28. 21, his *s.* work, his *s.* act.
Ezek. 3. 5, not sent to people of a *s.* speech.
Zep. 1. 8, clothed with *s.* apparel. R. V. foreign.
Lu. 5. 26, we have seen *s.* things to day.
Acts 17. 20, thou bringest *s.* things to our ears.
26. 11, persecuted them even to *s.* cities. R. V. foreign.
Heb. 13. 9, carried about with *s.* doctrines.
1 Pet. 4. 4, they think it *s.* ye run not.
4. 12, not *s.* concerning the fiery trial. [you.
Stranger. Gen. 23. 4; Ps. 39. 12, I am a *s.* with
Ex. 23. 9, ye know the heart of a *s.*
1 Chr. 29. 15, we are *s.*, as were all our fathers.
Job 15. 19, no *s.* passed among them.
31. 32, the *s.* did not lodge in the street.
Ps. 54. 3, for *s.* are risen up against me.
109. 11, let the *s.* spoil his labour.
146. 9, the Lord preserveth the *s.*
Prov. 2. 16, to deliver thee even from the *s.*
5. 10, lest *s.* be filled with thy wealth. R. V. an alien.
5. 17, let them be thine own, not *s.* with thee.
6. 1, stricken thy hand with a *s.*
7. 5, from the *s.* which flattereth.
11. 15, he that is surety for a *s.* shall smart.
14. 10, a *s.* doth not intermeddle.
20. 16; 27. 13, garment that is surety for a *s.*
27. 2, let a *s.* praise thee.
Isa. 1. 7, your land, *s.* devour it.
2. 6, please themselves in children of *s.*
14. 1, the *s.* shall be joined with them.
56. 3, neither let the son of the *s.* speak.
Jer. 14. 8, why be as a *s.* in the land? R. V. sojourner.
Ezek. 28. 10, thou shalt die by the hand of *s.*
Hos. 7. 9, *s.* have devoured his strength.
Mat. 25. 35, I was a *s.*, and ye took me in.
Lu. 17. 18, that returned, save this *s.*
Eph. 2. 12, *s.* from the covenant.
2. 19, no more *s.*, but fellowcitizens.
Heb. 11. 13, confessed they were *s.*
13. 2, be not forgetful to entertain *s.*
See Mat. 17. 25; John 10. 5.
Strangers (among the Israelites), how to be treated, Ex. 22. 21; 23. 9; Lev. 19. 33; Deu. 1. 16; 10. 18; 23. 7; 24. 14; Mal. 3. 5.
regulations as to the passover, the priest's office, marriage, and the laws concerning them. Ex. 12. 43; 34. 16; Lev. 17. 10; 22. 10; 24. 16; Num. 1. 51; 18. 7; 19. 10; 35. 15; Deu. 7. 3; 17. 15; 25. 5; 31. 12; Jos. 8. 33; Ez. 10. 2; Neh. 13. 27; Ezek. 44. 9. *See* HOSPITALITY.
and pilgrims. 1 Pet. 2. 11.
Strangled. Nah. 2. 12; Acts 15. 20; 21. 25.
Straw, to strew, scatter. Mat. 21. 8.
Stream. Ps. 124. 4; Isa. 35. 6; 66. 12; Am. 5. 24.
Street. Prov. 1. 20; Lu. 14. 21; Rev. 21. 21; 22. 2.
Strength. Ex. 15. 2; 2 Sam. 22. 33; Ps. 18. 2; 28. 7; 118. 14; Isa. 12. 2, the Lord is my *s.*
Jud. 5. 21, thou hast trodden down *s.*
1 Sam. 2. 9, by *s.* shall no man prevail.
15. 29, the *S.* of Israel will not lie.
Job 9. 19, if I speak of *s.*, lo, he is strong.
12. 13, with him is wisdom and *s.* R. V. might.
Ps. 18. 32, girded me with *s.*
27. 1, the Lord is the *s.* of my life.
29. 11, the Lord will give *s.* to his people.
33. 16, mighty not delivered by much *s.*
39. 13, spare me, that I may recover *s.*
46. 1; 81. 1, God is our refuge and *s.*
68. 34, ascribe *s.* to God, his *s.* is in the clouds.
68. 35, God giveth *s.* and power.
73. 26, God is the *s.* of my heart.
84. 5, the man whose *s.* is in thee.
84. 7, they go from *s.* to *s.*
96. 6, *s.* and beauty are in his sanctuary.
138. 3, strengthenedst me with *s.* in my soul.
Prov. 10. 29, the way of the Lord is *s.* R. V. a stronghold.
Eccl. 9. 16, wisdom is better than *s.*
10. 17, princes eat for *s.*
Isa. 25. 4, a *s.* to the poor, a *s.* to the needy. R. V. stronghold.
40. 29, he increaseth *s.*
51. 9, awake, put on *s.*
Hag. 2. 22, I will destroy the *s.* of the kingdoms.
Lu. 1. 51, he hath shewed *s.* with his arm.
Rom. 5. 6, when ye were without *s.* R. V. weak.
1 Cor. 15. 56, the *s.* of sin is the law. R. V. power.
Rev. 3. 8, thou hast a little *s.* R. V. power.
See Job 21. 23; Prov. 20. 29.
Strength of Israel, the Lord. Ex. 15. 2; 1 Sam. 15. 29; Ps. 27. 1; 28. 8; 29. 11; 46. 1; 81. 1; Isa. 26. 4; Joel 3. 16; Zec. 12. 5.

of sin. Rom. 7.; 1 Cor. 15. 56.
made perfect in weakness. 2 Cor. 12. 9; Heb. 11. 34; Ps. 8. 2.

Strengthen. Job 15. 25, he *s.* himself against. R. V. behaveth proudly.
Ps. 20. 2, *s.* thee out of Zion.
104. 15, bread which *s.* man's heart.
Eccl. 7. 19, wisdom *s.* the wise.
Isa. 35. 3, *s.* ye the weak hands.
Lu. 22. 32, when converted, *s.* thy brethren. R.V. stablish.
Eph. 3. 16; Col. 1. 11, to be *s.* with might.
Phil. 4. 13, all things through Christ which *s.* me.
See Lu. 22. 43; 1 Pet. 5. 10; Rev. 3. 2.

Stretch. Ps. 68. 31, *s.* out her hands to God.
Isa. 28. 20, shorter than a man can *s.* himself.
Jer. 10. 12; 51. 15, he *s.* out the heavens.
Ezek. 16. 27, I have *s.* out my hand over thee.
Mat. 12. 13, *s.* forth thine hand.
See Ps. 104. 2; Prov. 1. 24; Rom. 10. 21; 2 Cor. 10. 14.

Stricken, advanced (in years). Lu. 1. 7.

Strife. Prov. 3. 30; 17. 14; 25. 8; 26. 17; Rom. 13. 13; 1 Cor. 3. 3; Gal. 5. 20; Phil. 2. 3, 14; 2 Tim. 2. 23; Tit. 3. 9; Jas. 3. 14.
its origin. Prov. 10. 12; 13. 10; 15. 18; 16. 28; 22. 10; 23. 29; 26. 20; 28. 25; 30. 33; 1 Tim. 6. 4; 2 Tim. 2. 23; Jas. 4. 1.
its results. Lev. 24. 10; Gal. 5. 15; Jas. 3. 16.
deprecated. 1 Cor. 1. 11; 3. 3; 6.; 11. 17.

Strike. (1) Job 17. 3; Prov. 22. 26, *s.* hands.
Ps. 110. 5, shall *s.* through kings.
Prov. 7. 23, till a dart *s.* through his liver.
(2) to pass the hand over lightly, to stroke. 2 Kn. 5. 11. R. V. wave.
See Prov. 23. 35; Isa. 1. 5; 1 Tim. 3. 3; Tit. 1. 7.

Stripes. Deu. 25. 3, forty *s.* he may give.
2 Cor. 11. 24, five times received I forty *s.*

Stripling. 1 Sam. 17. 56, whose son the *s.* is.

Strive. Gen. 6. 3, shall not always *s.*
Prov. 3. 30, *s.* not without cause.
Lu. 13. 24, *s.* to enter in at strait gate.
2 Tim. 2. 5, if a man *s.* for mastery. R. V. contend.
2. 24, the servant of the Lord must not *s.*
See Isa. 45. 9; Jer. 50. 24; Mat. 12. 19; Heb. 12. 4.

Strong. 1 Sam. 4. 9; 1 Kn. 2. 2; 2 Chr. 15. 7; Isa. 35. 4; Dan. 10. 19, be *s.*
Job 9. 19, if I speak of strength, lo, he is *s.* R. V. omits.
Ps. 19. 5, as a *s.* man to run a race.
24. 8, the Lord is *s.*
31. 2, be thou my *s.* rock.
71. 7, thou art my *s.* refuge.
Prov. 10. 15, the rich man's wealth is his *s.* city.
18. 10, the name of the Lord is a *s.* tower.
Eccl. 9. 11, the battle is not to the *s.*
Isa. 40. 26, for that he is *s.* in power.
Mat. 12. 29, first bind the *s.* man.
Rom. 4. 20, *s.* in faith.
1 Cor. 4. 10, we are weak, ye are *s.* [error.
2 Thes. 2. 11, *s.* delusion. R. V. a working of
Heb. 5. 12, of milk, and not of *s.* meat. R. V. solid.
6. 18, we have a *s.* consolation.
See Prov. 14. 26; Joel 3. 10; Rom. 15. 1; Rev. 5. 2.

Stubble. Ps. 83. 13, make them as *s.*
Isa. 33. 11, conceive chaff, bring forth *s.*
41. 2, as driven *s.*
Jer. 13. 24, I will scatter them as *s.*
See Joel 2. 5; Nah. 1. 10; Mal. 4. 1; 1 Cor. 3. 12.

Stubbornness, penalty of. Deu. 21. 18; Prov. 1. 24; 29. 1.
forbidden. 2 Chr. 30. 8; Ps. 32. 9; 75. 4.
of the Jews. 2 Kn. 17. 14; Jer. 5. 3; 7. 28; 32. 33.

Study. Eccl. 12. 12, much *s.* is a weariness of the flesh.
See 1 Thes. 4. 11; 2 Tim. 2. 15.

Stuff, the furniture or baggage (of an army, &c.). 1 Sam. 30. 24.

Stumble. Prov. 4. 19, know not at what they *s.*
Isa. 28. 7, they *s.* in judgment.
Isa. 59. 10, we *s.* at noonday.
Jer. 46. 6; Dan. 11. 19, *s.* and fall.
Mal. 2. 8, have caused many to *s.*
1 Pet. 2. 8, that *s.* at the word.
See John 11. 9; Rom. 11. 11. [27. 18.

Stumblingblock, the blind. Lev. 19. 14; Deu.
figurative of offence. Isa. 8. 14; Rom. 9. 32; 14. 21; 1 Cor. 1. 23; 8. 9; 1 Pet. 2. 8.

Stump. Isa. 5. 4; Dan. 4. 15.

Suah, sū′-ăh, 'sweepings.' 1 Chr. 7. 36.

Subdue. Ps. 47. 3, he shall *s.* the people.
Mic. 7. 19, he will *s.* our iniquities. R. V. tread under foot.
Phil. 3. 21, able to *s.* all things. R. V. subject.
Heb. 11. 33, through faith *s.* kingdoms.
See Dan. 2. 40; Zec. 9. 15; 1 Cor. 15. 28.

Subject. Lu. 10. 17, devils are *s.* unto us.
Rom. 8. 7, not *s.* to law of God.
8. 20, creature *s.* to vanity.
13. 1, *s.* to the higher powers.
1 Cor. 14. 32, spirits of prophets *s.* to prophets.
15. 28, then shall the Son also be *s.* to him.
Eph. 5. 24, as the church is *s.* to Christ.
Heb. 2. 15, all their lifetime *s.* to bondage.
Jas. 5. 17, a man *s.* to like passions.
1 Pet. 2. 18, servants, be *s.* to your masters.
3. 22, angels and powers *s.* to him.
5. 5, all of you be *s.* one to another. R. V. serve one another.
See Lu. 2. 51; Col. 2. 20; Tit. 3. 1.

Submission to God. Rom. 10. 3; Jas. 4. 7.
to rulers. Eph. 5. 21; Heb. 13. 17; 1 Pet. 2. 13; 5. 5.

Submit. 2 Sam. 22. 45, *s.* themselves.
Ps. 68. 30, till every one *s.* himself. R. V. trampling under foot.
Eph. 5. 22, wives *s.* yourselves.
Jas. 4. 7, *s.* yourselves to God. [man.
1 Pet. 2. 13, *s.* yourselves to every ordinance of

Suborned. Acts 6. 11, *s.* men which said.

Subscribe. Isa. 44. 5; Jer. 32. 44.

Substance. Gen. 13. 6, their *s.* was great.
Deu. 33. 11, bless his *s.*
Job 30. 22, thou dissolvest my *s.* R. V. me in the storm.
Ps. 17. 14, they leave their *s.* to babes. [frame.
139. 15, my *s.* was not hid from thee. R. V.
Prov. 3. 9, honour the Lord with thy *s.*
28. 8, he that by usury increaseth his *s.*
S. of S. 8. 7, give all his *s.* for love.
Jer. 15. 13; 17. 3, thy *s.* will I give to spoil.
Hos. 12. 8, I have found me out *s.* R. V. wealth.
Mic. 4. 13, I will consecrate their *s.*
Lu. 8. 3, ministered to him of their *s.*
15. 13, wasted his *s.*
Heb. 10. 34, a better *s.* R. V. possession.
11. 1, the *s.* of things hoped for. R. V. assurance.
See Prov. 1. 13; 6. 31; 8. 21; 12. 27; 29. 3.

Subtil. Gen. 3. 1; 2 Sam. 13. 3; Prov. 7. 10.

Subtilty. Gen. 27. 35; Mat. 26. 4; Acts 13. 10.

Subvert. Lam. 3. 36; 2 Tim. 2. 14; Tit. 1. 11; 3. 11.

Success. Jos. 1. 8, have good *s.*

Succoth, sŭc′-cōth, 'booths.' (1) (Canaan). Gen. 33. 17; Jos. 13. 27; 1 Kn. 7. 46; Ps. 60. 6.
punished by Gideon. Jud. 8. 5, 16.
(2) (in Egypt). Ex. 12. 37; 13. 20. [30.

Succoth-benoth, sŭc′-cōth-bē′-nōth. 2 Kn. 17.

Succour. 2 Cor. 6. 2; Heb. 2. 18.

Suchathites, sū′-chă-thītes. 1 Chr. 2. 55.

Suck. Deu. 32. 13, *s.* honey out of rock.
33. 19, *s.* abundance of the seas.
Job 20. 16, *s.* poison of asps.
Isa. 60. 16, *s.* the milk of the Gentiles.
See Mat. 24. 19; Mk. 13. 17; Lu. 21. 23; 23. 29.

Suckling. Deu. 32. 25; Ps. 8. 2; Mat. 21. 16.

Sudden. Job 22. 10; Prov. 3. 25; 1 Thes. 5. 3.

Suddenly. Prov. 29. 1, be *s.* destroyed.
Eccl. 9. 12, when it falleth *s.*
Mal. 3. 1, shall *s.* come to his temple.
Mk. 13. 36, lest coming *s.* he find you sleeping.

1 Tim. 5. 22, lay hands *s.* on no man. R. V. hastily.
Suffer. Job 21. 3, *s.* me that I may speak.
Ps. 55. 22, never *s.* righteous to be moved.
89. 33, nor *s.* my faithfulness to fail.
Prov. 19. 15, the idle soul shall *s.* hunger.
Eccl. 5. 12, not *s.* him to sleep.
Mat. 3. 15, *s.* it to be so now.
8. 21; Lu. 9. 59, *s.* me first to bury my father.
16. 21; 17. 12; Mk. 8. 31; Lu. 9. 22, *s.* many things.
19. 14; Mk. 10. 14; Lu. 18. 16, *s.* little children.
23. 13, neither *s.* ye them that are entering to go in.
Lu. 24. 46; Acts 3. 18, behoved Christ to *s.*
Rom. 8. 17, if we *s.* with him.
1 Cor. 3. 15, he shall *s.* loss.
10. 13, will not *s.* you to be tempted.
12. 26, whether one member *s.*, all *s.* with it.
Gal. 6. 12, lest they should *s.* persecution.
2 Tim. 2. 12, if we *s.*, we shall also reign. R. V. endure.
3. 12, shall *s.* persecution.
Heb. 13. 3, remember them who *s.*
1 Pet. 2. 21, *s.* for us, leaving an example.
4. 1, he that hath *s.* in the flesh.
See Gal. 3. 4; Phil. 3. 8; Heb. 2. 18; 5. 8.
Suffering for Christ. Phil. 1. 29.
Sufferings. *See* CHRIST.
of His followers. Acts 5. 40; 12.; 13. 50; 14. 19; 16. 23; 20. 23; 21.; 22.; 1 Cor. 4. 11; 2 Cor. 1. 4; 4. 8; 6. 4; 11. 23; Phil. 1.; 1 Tim. 4. 10; 2 Tim. 3. 10; 1 Pet. 2. 19; 3. 14; 4. 12.
Sufficiency. Job 20. 22; 2 Cor. 3. 5; 9. 8.
Sufficient. Isa. 40. 16, not *s.* to burn.
Mat. 6. 34, *s.* for the day is the evil.
2 Cor. 2. 16, who is *s.* for these things?
See Deu. 15. 8; John 6. 7; 2 Cor. 3. 5; 12. 9.
Sukkiims, sŭk'-kĭ-ĭms, 'nomads.' 2 Chr. 12. 3.
Sulphur (Gen. 19. 24; Ps. 11. 6). Heb. *Gophrith:* Gk. *θεῖον*. Sulphur, or brimstone, is found in some of the valleys entering the Vale of Siddim, and in the plain of the Ghôr.
Sum. Ps. 139. 17; Acts 22. 28; Heb. 8. 1.
Summer. Gen. 8. 22; Ps. 74. 17, *s.* and winter.
Prov. 6. 8; 30. 25, provideth meat in *s.*
10. 5, he that gathereth in *s.* is a wise son.
26. 1, as snow in *s.*
Jer. 8. 20, the *s.* is ended.
Mat. 24. 32; Mk. 13. 28, ye know *s.* is nigh.
See Dan. 2. 35; Zec. 14. 8; Lu. 21. 30.
Sumptuously. Lu. 16. 19, fared *s.* every day.
Sun. Jos. 10. 12, *s.*, stand thou still.
Jud. 5. 31. as the *s.* in his might.
Job 8. 16, hypocrite is green before the *s.*
Ps. 58. 8, that they may not see the *s.*
84. 11, a *s.* and shield.
121. 6, the *s.* shall not smite thee.
Eccl. 1. 9, no new thing under the *s.*
11. 7, a pleasant thing it is to behold the *s.*
12. 2, while the *s.* or stars be not darkened.
S. of S. 1. 6, because the *s.* hath looked upon me.
6. 10, clear as the *s.*
Jer. 15. 9, her *s.* is gone down while yet day.
Joel 2. 10; 3. 15, the *s.* be darkened.
Mat. 5. 45, maketh his *s.* to rise on evil.
13. 43, then shall righteous shine as *s.*
Eph. 4. 26, let not *s.* go down on your wrath.
See 1 Cor. 15. 41; Jas. 1. 11; Rev. 7. 16; 21. 23.
Sun created. Gen. 1. 14; Ps. 19. 4; 74. 16; 1 Cor. 15. 41.
not to be worshipped. Deu. 4. 19; Job 31. 26; Ezek. 8. 16.
stayed by Joshua, Jos. 10. 12. brought backward for Hezekiah, 2 Kn. 20. 9. darkened at crucifixion, Lu. 23. 44.
Sun of righteousness. Mal. 4. 2.
Sunder, to separate, part asunder. Job 41. 17.
Sundry, several, various, separate. Heb. 1. 1.
Sung. Isa. 26. 1; Mat. 26. 30; Rev. 5. 9.
Sunk. 1 Sam. 17. 49; Ps. 9. 15; Jer. 38. 22.
Sunrising. Num. 21. 11; Deu. 4. 41; Jud. 20. 43.

Sup. Lu. 17. 8; 1 Cor. 11. 25; Rev. 3. 20.
Superfluity. Jas. 1. 21, *s.* of naughtiness. R. V. overflowing.
Superscription. Mat. 22. 20; Lu. 20. 24; 23. 38.
Superstition. Acts 17. 22; 25. 19.
Supper, parable of. Lu. 14. 16.
marriage supper of the Lamb. Rev. 19. 9.
Lord's Supper. *See* COMMUNION.
Supple, to make or render pliant. Ezek. 16. 4. R. V. correctly 'cleanse.'
Supplication. 1 Kn. 9. 3, I have heard thy *s.*
Job 9. 15, I would make *s.* to my judge.
Ps. 6. 9, the Lord hath heard my *s.*
Dan. 9. 3, to seek by prayer and *s.*
Zec. 12. 10, spirit of grace and *s.*
Eph. 6. 18, with all prayer and *s.*
1 Tim. 2. 1, that *s.* be made for all men.
See Ps. 28. 6; 31. 22; Phil. 4. 6; Heb. 5. 7.
Supply. Phil. 1. 19; 2. 30; 4. 19.
Support. Acts 20. 35; 1 Thes. 5. 14.
Supreme. 1 Pet. 2. 13, to the king as *s.*
Sur, sur. 2 Kn. 11. 6.
Sure. Num. 32. 23, be *s.* your sin will find you out.
Job 24. 22, no man is *s.* of life.
Prov. 6. 3, make *s.* thy friend. R. V. importune.
Isa. 55. 3; Acts 13. 34, the *s.* mercies of David.
2 Tim. 2. 19, the foundation of God standeth *s.* R. V. omits.
See Isa. 33. 16; Heb. 6. 19; 2 Pet. 1. 10, 19.
Surely, securely. Prov. 10. 9.
Suretiship, evils of. Prov. 6. 1; 11. 15; 17. 18; 20. 16; 22. 26; 27. 13.
Surfeiting, excess in eating or drinking. Lu. 21. 34, overcharged with *s.*
Surprised. Isa. 33. 14; Jer. 48. 41; 51. 41.
Susanchites, sū-săn'-chītes, inhabitants of Susa or Susinak. Ez. 4. 9.
Susanna, sū-săn'-nă, 'lily.' Lu. 8. 3.
Susi, sū'-sī, 'horseman.' Num. 13. 11.
Sustain. Ps. 3. 5; 55. 22; Prov. 18. 14; Isa. 59. 16.
Sustenance. Jud. 6. 4; Acts 7. 11.
Swaddle, to swathe, bandage (as infants). Ezek. 16. 4.
Swallow. (1) (Prov. 26. 2; Ps. 84. 3). Heb. *Dĕrôr:* 'shooting straight out,' or 'freedom:' Gk. *στρουθός*. (Specimen, *Hirundo rustica*, found in the Jordan valley.) The barn-swallow of Great Britain is abundant in Palestine.
(2) (Isa. 38. 14). Heb. *Agûr:* Gk. *χελιδών*: R. V. 'crane.' 'Swallow' (A. V.) is thought to be a mistranslation for 'crane.'
(3) (Isa. 38. 14). Heb. *sûs*, a bird with a chattering note, is translated 'swallow' in R. V. Tristram believes that the swift is intended.
Swan (Lev. 11. 18; Deu. 14. 16). Heb. *Tinshémeth*, 'breathing,' 'inflation:' Gk. *κύκνος*: R. V. 'horned owl,' marg. 'stork.' Tristram thinks the bird is the purple gallinule, or the glossy ibis.
Swarm. Ex. 8. 24; Jud. 14. 8.
Swear. (1) to cause to swear. Ex. 13. 19.
(2) Ps. 15. 4, that *s.* to his hurt.
Eccl. 9. 2, he that *s.*, as he that feareth an oath.
Isa. 45. 23, to me every tongue shall *s.*
65. 16, shall *s.* by the God of truth.
Jer. 4. 2, *s.*, the Lord liveth, in truth.
23. 10, because of *s.* the land mourneth.
Hos. 4. 2, by *s.*, and lying, they break out.
10. 4, *s.* falsely in making a covenant.
Zec. 5. 3, every one that *s.* shall be cut off.
Mal. 3. 5, a witness against false *s.*
See Zep. 1. 5; Mat. 26. 74; Heb. 6. 13.
Swear (and curse). Lev. 5. 1, 4.
falsely. Lev. 6. 3, 5; Ex. 22. 28.
Swearing. Mat. 5. 34; Jas. 5. 12.
Sweat. Gen. 3. 19; Ezek. 44. 18; Lu. 22. 44.
Sweet. Job 20. 12, though wickedness be *s.*
Ps. 55. 14, we took *s.* counsel together.
104. 34, my meditation shall be *s.*
Prov. 3. 24, thy sleep shall be *s.*
9. 17, stolen waters are *s.*
13. 19, desire accomplished is *s.*

Prov. 16. 24, pleasant words are *s.*
27. 7, to the hungry every bitter thing is *s.*
Eccl. 5. 12, sleep of labouring man is *s.*
11. 7, truly the light is *s.*
S. of S. 2. 3, his fruit was *s.* to my taste.
Isa. 5. 20, put bitter for *s.*, and *s.* for bitter.
23. 16, make *s.* melody.
Jas. 3. 11, at same place *s.* water and bitter.
See Jud. 14. 18; Mic. 6. 15; Mk. 16. 1.

Swelling. Jer. 12. 5; 2 Pet. 2. 18; Jude 16.

Swift (Isa. 38. 14). Heb. *Sîs, Sûs:* Gk. περιστερά: R. V. 'swallow.' (Specimens, *Cypselus apus; C. affinis; C. melba*, found in the Jordan valley.) *See* SWALLOW.

Swift. Eccl. 9. 11, the race is not to the *s.*
Am. 2. 15, the *s.* of foot shall not deliver.
Rom. 3. 15, feet *s.* to shed blood.
See Job 7. 6; 9. 25; Jer. 46. 6; Mal. 3. 5.

Swim. 2 Kn. 6. 6, iron did *s.*
Ezek. 47. 5, waters to *s.* in.
See Ps. 6. 6; Isa. 25. 11; Ezek. 32. 6; Acts 27. 42.

Swine (Lev. 11. 7; Deu. 14. 8; Isa. 65. 4; Mat. 7. 6). Heb. *Ḥêzîr;* Gk. ὗς. The Hebrews and Phœnicians abhorred swine, and the Mosaic Law classed them with unclean animals, their flesh when badly cooked being productive of trichinosis.

Swine, devils sent into herd of. Mat. 8. 32; Mk. 5. 13; Lu. 8. 33.
typical of unbelievers and apostates. Mat. 7. 6; 2 Pet. 2. 22.

Swollen. Acts 28. 6, when he should have *s.*

Swoon. Lam. 2. 11, children *s.* in the streets.

Sword. Ps. 57. 4, their tongue a sharp *s.*
Isa. 2. 4, nation shall not lift up *s.*
Ezek. 7. 15, the *s.* is without, pestilence within.
Mat. 10. 34, not to send peace, but a *s.*
Lu. 2. 35, a *s.* shall pierce thy own soul.
Rom. 13. 4, he beareth not the *s.* in vain.
Eph. 6. 17, the *s.* of the Spirit.
Heb. 4. 12, sharper than twoedged *s.*
Rev. 1. 16; 19. 15, out of his mouth a sharp *s.*
13. 10, that killeth with *s.* must be killed with *s.*
See Isa. 2. 4; Joel 3. 10; Mic. 4. 3; Lu. 22. 38.

Sword of the LORD. Gen. 3. 24; Deu. 32. 41; Jud. 7. 18; 1 Chr. 21. 12; Ps. 45. 3; Isa. 34. 5; 66. 16; Jer. 12. 12; 47. 6; Ezek. 21. 4; 30. 24; 32. 10; Zep. 2. 12.

Sycamine (Lu. 17. 6). Gk. συκάμινος: Bot. N. *Morus nigra.* The black mulberry, still called *sycominos* in Greece, useful for its fruit, and for its leaves on which the silkworm feeds.

Sychar, sȳ'-chär, 'drunken' (?). John 4. 5.

Sychem, sȳ'-chĕm, Greek form of SHECHEM. Acts 7. 16.

Sycomore (Ps. 78. 47; 1 Chr. 27. 28; Lu. 19. 4). Heb. *Shikmîm, Shikmôth:* Gk. συκομορέα: Bot. N. *Ficus sycomorus.* A species of fig, and consequently quite different from the British sycamore, which is a maple. It is an evergreen timber tree, of large growth.

Syene, sȳ-ē'-nē, 'opening.' Ezek. 29. 10.

Synagogue, The (Gk. συναγωγή, 'a gathering together;' Heb. *Keneseth*), was a term applied both to the congregation in a provincial town, and to the room in which it met during the week for mutual instruction, disputation, and administration of justice, and on the sabbath for prayer and praise, not sacrifice. The institution of the synagogue dates probably from the Captivity in Babylon. There are said to have been 480 synagogues in Jerusalem, but this is probably an exaggeration.

The principal officers of the Synagogue were:—

(1) **The Batlanim** (*men of leisure*). These were the 'Rulers of the Synagogue,' also called the 'shepherds' and the 'elders:' they had special seats of honour assigned them during divine worship (Acts 13. 15; Mat. 23. 6). They also formed the local Sanhedrin or tribunal.

(2) **The Sheliach** (*Delegate*). He was one of the elders, delegated by the Chief Shepherd (*Parnas*) to recite the most sacred portions of the liturgy, and be the mouthpiece of the congregation.

(3) **The Chazzan** (literally *Inspector*), the permanent minister or attendant (Lu. 4. 20), whose duties were partly ecclesiastical, partly civil. He frequently acted as schoolmaster.

(4) **The Methurgeman** (*Interpreter*). As the synagogue came principally into use in later times, when Hebrew was not well known and Greek and Aramaic were more generally used in common life, the Law was expounded to the congregation by an interpreter. This word *Methurgeman*, or *Turgeman*, has been corrupted into the modern *Dragoman.*

Synagogues: Christ teaches in, Mat. 12. 9; Lu. 4. 16; John 6. 59; 18. 20. Paul preaches in, Acts 13. 5; 14. 1; 18. 4.

Syntyche, sȳn'-tȳ-chē, 'fortunate.' Phil. 4. 2.

Syracuse, sȳr'-ă-cūse, the chief city of Sicily. Acts 28. 12.

Syria, sȳr'-ĭ-ă, was a country along the eastern coast of the Mediterranean, and extending inland to Mesopotamia. In early times its capital was Damascus. After the Roman conquest the capital was Antioch. Jud. 10. 6.

Syriack, sȳr'-ĭ-ăck, belonging to Syria. Dan. 2. 4.

Syria-damascus, sȳr'-ĭ-ă-dă-măs'-cŭs. 1 Chr. 18. 6.

Syria-maachah, sȳr'-ĭ-ă-mā'-ă-chăh. 1 Chr. 19. 6.

Syrians, sȳr'-ĭ-ăns, *or* **Aramæans.** Heb. *Arâm:* Gk. σύροι: Lat. *Syri.* Aram is in O. T. the name for a large region extending from Mesopotamia, of which it included a part, to Syria and Arabia Petræa. The Syrians are one branch of the Semites, and their language, Aramaic, a dialect of the Semitic language, which became the language of western Assyria, and the common language of Palestine. For the relations of Israel and Judah with Syria *see* BABYLONIA AND ASSYRIA. Gen. 25. 20; Deu. 26. 5.
subdued by David. 2 Sam. 8.; 10.
contend with Israel. 1 Kn. 10. 29; 11. 25; 20.; 22.; 2 Kn. 6. 24; 7.; 8. 13; 13. 7; 16. 6; 2 Chr. 18.
employed to punish Joash. 2 Chr. 24. 23. *See* 2 Chr. 28. 23; Isa. 7. 2; Ezek. 27. 16; Hos. 12. 12; Am. 1. 5.
gospel preached to. Mat. 4. 24; Acts 15. 23; 18. 18; Gal. 1. 21.

Syrophenician, sȳ-rō-phē-nĭç'-ĭ-ăn, Phœnician living in Syria. Mk. 7. 26.

Taanach, tā'-ă-năch, 'castle' (?). Jos. 12. 21.

Taanath-shiloh, tā'-ă-năth-shī'-lōh, 'fig tree of Shiloh' (?). Jos. 16. 6.

Tabbaoth, tăb-bā'-ōth, 'rings.' Ez. 2. 43.

Tabbath, tăb'-băth, 'pleasantness.' Jud. 7. 22.

Tabeal, tā'-bĕ-ăl, 'good for nothing' (?). Isa. 7. 6.

Tabeel, tăb'-ēel, 'God is good.' Ez. 4. 7.

Taberah, tăb'-ĕ-răh, 'burning.' Num. 11. 3.

Tabering, beating (as on a tabor or drum). Nah. 2. 7.

Tabernacle. Ps. 15. 1, abide in thy *t.*
27. 5, in secret of his *t.* shall he hide me.
84. 1, how amiable are thy *t.*!
Isa. 33. 20, a *t.* that shall not be taken down.
See Job 5. 24; Prov. 14. 11.

Tabernacle (Ex. 25. 8, 9). An oblong tent, with a wooden framework covered with cloth and skins, made by divine command as a movable place of worship in the wilderness, called also the Tent of Meeting, R. V., and Tent, or Tabernacle of the Congregation, A. V.

Tabernacle of GOD, its construction. Ex. 25.-27.; 36.-39.; 40.; Num. 9. 15.
consecrated by Moses. Lev. 8. 10.
directions concerning its custody and removal. Num. 1. 50, 53; 3.; 4.; 9. 18; 1 Chr. 6. 48.
set up at Shiloh, Jos. 18. 1. at Gibeon, 1 Chr. 21. 29; 2 Chr. 1. 3.
David's love for. Ps. 27.; 42.; 43.; 84.; 132.

of witness. Num. 17. 7; 18. 2; 2 Chr. 24. 6; Acts 7. 44.
of testimony, Ex. 38. 21, &c. in heaven, Rev. 15. 5.
parallels from its history. Heb. 8. 2; 9. 2.
Tabernacle, the human body compared to. 2 Cor. 5. 1; 2 Pet. 1. 13.
Tabernacles, Feast of. *See* FEASTS. Deu. 16. 13-15; 2 Chr. 8. 13; Ez. 3. 4; Zec. 14. 16; John 7. 2.
Tabitha, tăb'-ĭ-thă, 'gazelle.' Acts 9. 36.
Table (John 12. 2; 13. 28). The Hebrews in the time of our Lord had adopted the Roman custom of reclining at table on cushioned divans, resting themselves on the left arm. The tables were in three portions, forming three sides of a square, the seats being placed along the outer sides, and the servants waiting in the inside.
Ps. 23. 5, thou preparest a *t.*
69. 22, let their *t.* become a snare.
78. 19, can God furnish a *t.* in the wilderness?
128. 3, like olive plants about thy *t.*
Prov. 9. 2, wisdom hath furnished her *t.*
Mat. 15. 27; Mk. 7. 28, from their masters' *t.*
Acts 6. 2, leave word of God, and serve *t.*
2 Cor. 3. 3, fleshy *t.* of the heart.
See Prov. 3. 3; Jer. 17. 1; Mal. 1. 7; 1 Cor. 10. 21.
Table of the Lord (Jewish). Ex. 25. 23; 31. 8; 37. 10; 40. 4; Ezek. 41. 22.
its holiness. Mal. 1. 7, 12; 1 Cor. 10. 21.
of shewbread. Ex. 25. 30; Lev. 24. 6; Num. 4. 7.
the Lord's. *See* COMMUNION.
Table (writing). (Ex. 32. 15; 34. 1.) The Law was engraved upon two stone slabs. Subsequently 'writing tables' (or tablets) were in common use, made of wood, whitened, and written upon with a black fluid, like the modern Arab slate, or covered with wax, and written upon with a metal pencil or style.
Tables of stone, the law. Ex. 24. 12; 31. 18.
broken. Ex. 32. 19; Deu. 9. 15.
renewed. Ex. 34.; Deu. 10.
of stone and the heart. 2 Cor. 3. 3.
Tablets, mentioned by Isaiah (3. 20) among a woman's ornaments, are still in use. They are little cylinders (like bodkin-cases) of wood or metal, attached to chains and used as charms, in which women place little rolls of parchment on which their secret wishes are written. The R. V., however, renders the Hebrew word 'perfume boxes.'
Tabor, tā'-bôr. (1) A mountain of Galilee, 1843 feet above the sea. Here Barak assembled his forces for battle against Sisera. Jud. 4. 6, 12, 14.
(2) An oak (1 Sam. 10. 3). Probably somewhere in the tribe of Benjamin.
See Jos. 19. 22; Jud. 8. 18; 1 Sam. 10. 3; Ps. 89. 12; Jer. 46. 18; Hos. 5. 1.
Tabret (Gen. 31. 27; 1 Sam. 10. 5; 18. 6; Isa. 5. 12; 24. 8; 30. 32; Jer. 31. 4; Ezek. 28. 13). Heb. *Tôph*: Gk. τύμπανον (ψαλτήριον, Job 21. 12). The simple tambourine, used with cymbals as an accompaniment to dancing and singing.
Tabrimon, tăb-rĭm'-on, 'Rimmon is good.' 1 Kn. 15. 18.
Taches, attachments, fastenings. Ex. 26. 6. R. V. clasps.
Tachmonite, tăch'-mō-nīte, same as HACHMONITE (?). 2 Sam. 23. 8.
Tackling. Isa. 33. 23; Acts 27. 19.
Tadmor, tăd'-môr, 'city of palms' (?). (Palmyra), built by Solomon. 1 Kn. 9. 18.
Tahan, tā'-hăn, 'camp.' Num. 26. 35.
Tahanites, tā'-hăn-ītes, descendants of Tahan. Num. 26. 35.
Tahapanes, tă-hăp'-ă-nēs. Jer. 2. 16. [33. 26.
Tahath, tā'-hăth, 'substitute.' (1) a place. Num. (2) men. 1 Chr. 6. 24; 7. 20.
Tahpanhes, täh'-păn-hēs, same as TAHAPANES. Jer. 43. 7.
Tahpenes, täh'-pĕn-ēs. 1 Kn. 11. 19.
Tahrea, täh'-rē-ă, 'cunning' (?). 1 Chr. 9. 41.
Tahtim-hodshi, täh'-tĭm-hŏd'-shī, 'nether land newly inhabited' (?). 2 Sam. 24. 6.
Take. Ex. 6. 7, I will *t.* you to me for a people.
34. 9, *t.* us for thine inheritance.
Jud. 19. 30, *t.* advice, and speak your minds.
2 Kn. 19. 30; Isa. 37. 31, shall yet *t.* root.
Job 23. 10, he knoweth the way that I *t.*
Ps. 51. 11, *t.* not thy holy spirit from me.
116. 13, I will *t.* the cup of salvation.
S. of S. 2. 15, *t.* us the foxes, the little foxes.
Isa. 33. 23, the lame *t.* the prey.
Hos. 14. 2, *t.* with you words.
Am. 9. 2, thence shall mine hand *t.* them.
Mat. 6. 25, 28, 31, 34; 10. 19; Mk. 13. 11; Lu. 12. 11, 22, 26, *t.* no thought.
11. 29, *t.* my yoke.
16. 5; Mk. 8. 14, forgotten to *t.* bread.
18. 16, then *t.* with thee one or two more.
20. 14, *t.* that thine is, and go thy way.
26. 26; Mk. 14. 22; 1 Cor. 11. 24, *t.*, eat; this is my body.
Lu. 6. 29, forbid him not to *t.* thy coat also.
12. 19, soul, *t.* thine ease.
John 16. 15, he shall *t.* of mine.
1 Cor. 6. 7, why do ye not rather *t.* wrong?
1 Tim. 3. 5, how shall he *t.* care of the church?
1 Pet. 2. 20, if ye *t.* it patiently.
Rev. 3. 11, that no man *t.* thy crown.
See John 1. 29; 10. 18; 1 Cor. 10. 13; Rev. 22. 19.
Tale. (1) Ps. 90. 9; Lu. 24. 11.
(2) a (fixed) number, a total. Ex. 5. 8, 18.
Talebearers. Lev. 19. 16; Prov. 11. 13; 18. 8; 26. 20; Ezek. 22. 9; 1 Tim. 5. 13; 1 Pet. 4. 15.
Talent, a weight of about 108 lbs. avoirdupois, for gold, or 96½ lbs. silver. The light weight talent is one half of these numbers. *See* WEIGHTS. gold, Ex. 25. 39 = £6150 = $29,940. silver, 1 Kn. 20. 39 = £410 = $1940. common O. T. standard = in N. T. £205 or $970. lead, Zec. 5. 7. *See* MONEY.
Talents, parables of. Mat. 18. 24; 25. 14.
Talitha, tăl'-ĭ-thă, 'girl.' Mk. 5. 41. [speak.
Talk. Deu. 5. 24, God doth *t.* with man. R. V. 6. 7, *t.* of them when thou sittest.
Job 11. 2, a man full of *t.*
13. 7, will ye *t.* deceitfully for him?
15. 3, reason with unprofitable *t.*
Ps. 71. 24, *t.* of thy righteousness.
145. 11, *t.* of thy power.
Prov. 6. 22, it shall *t.* with thee.
Jer. 12. 1, let me *t.* with thee of thy judgments. R. V. would I reason the cause.
Ezek. 3. 22, arise, and I will *t.* with thee there.
Mat. 22. 15, they might entangle him in his *t.*
Lu. 24. 32, while he *t.* with us by the way.
John 9. 37, it is he that *t.* with thee.
See Prov. 14. 23; John 14. 30.
Talking, vain, censured. 1 Sam. 2. 3; Job 11. 2; Prov. 13. 3; 24. 2; Eccl. 10. 14; Ezek. 33. 30; 36. 3; Eph. 5. 4; Tit. 1. 10. *See* SLANDER, TALEBEARERS, &c.
Tall. Deu. 1. 28; 2. 10; 2 Kn. 19. 23.
Talmai, tăl'-māi, 'abounding in furrows.' (1) Num. 13. 22; Jos. 15. 14. (2) 2 Sam. 3. 3.
Talmon, tăl'-mōn, 'oppressed.' 1 Chr. 9. 17.
Tamah, tā'-măh, 'joy.' Neh. 7. 55.
Tamar, tā'-mär, 'a palm tree.' (1) a place. Ezek. 47. 19.
(2) daughter-in-law of Judah. Gen. 38. 6.
(3) daughter of David. 2 Sam. 13.
(4) daughter of Absalom. 2 Sam. 14. 27.
Tame. Mk. 5. 4; Jas. 3. 7, 8.
Tammuz, tăm'-mŭz, is the Hebrew name of the Babylonian god *Duzu* (also called *Adonis*), the son of *Ea*, whose death was mourned by women (Ezek. 8. 14).
Tanach, tā'-năch, same as TAANACH. Jos. 21. 25.
Tanhumeth, tăn-hū'-mĕth, 'consolation.' 2 Kn. 25. 23.
Tanner. Acts 9. 43; 10. 6.
Tapestry. Prov. 7. 16; 31. 22.
Taphath, tā'-phăth. 1 Kn. 4. 11.

TADMOR (PALMYRA)

These ruins of the 2nd–3rd cent. A.D. show the riches of Palmyra (Tadmor), due to its strategic position on an important desert trade-route. (*L. A. Fereday*)

TIBERIAS ON THE LAKE OF GALILEE

Ruins and modern houses at Tiberias, which in the time of Christ was the most important city on the Lake, hence called the 'Sea of Tiberias'. (*Picture Post Library*)

Tappuah, tăp′-pū-ăh, 'apple.' (1) Hebron's son. 1 Chr. 2. 43.
(2) places. Jos. 15. 34; 16. 8; 17. 8.
Taran, târ′-ăh, 'station.' Num. 33. 27.
Taralah, tăr′-ă-lăh, 'reeling' (?). Jos. 18. 27.
Tare. 2 Sam. 13. 31; 2 Kn. 2. 24; Mk. 9. 20.
Tarea, târ′-ĕ-ă, same as TAHREA. 1 Chr. 8. 35.
Tares (Mat. 13. 25-27). Gk. ζιζάνια: Bot. N. *Lolium temulentum;* R. V. marg. 'darnel.' The Arabic *zawân*, the bearded darnel, which is found as a weed among corn crops in Britain. It is a grass almost undistinguishable from wheat while the two are in blade, but bears poisonous grains.
Target, a light shield, buckler. 1 Sam. 17. 6.
Tarpelites, tär′-pē-lītes, people of Tarpel. Ez. 4. 9.
Tarry. Gen. 27. 44, and *t.* a few days.
Ex. 12. 39, were thrust out, and could not *t.*
2Kn. 7. 9, if we *t.* till morning light.
9. 3, flee, and *t.* not.
Ps. 68. 12, she that *t.* at home divided the spoil.
101. 7, he that telleth lies shall not *t.* in my sight. R. V. be established.
Prov. 23. 30, they that *t.* long at the wine.
Isa. 46. 13, my salvation shall not *t.*
Jer. 14. 8, that turneth aside to *t.* for a night.
Hab. 2. 3, though it *t.*, wait for it.
Mat. 25. 5, while the bridegroom *t.*
26. 38; Mk. 14. 34, *t.* here and watch. R. V. abide.
Lu. 24. 29, he went in to *t.* with them. R. V. abide.
24. 49, *t.* ye in city of Jerusalem until endued.
John 21. 22, if I will that he *t.*
Acts 22. 16, why *t.* thou? arise, and be baptized.
1 Cor. 11. 33, *t.* one for another.
Heb. 10. 37, will come, and will not *t.*
See 1 Sam. 30. 24; Mic. 5. 7; John 3. 22.
Tarshish, tär′-shĭsh. Gen. 10. 4; 1 Kn. 10. 22; 2 Chr. 9. 21; 20. 36; Jer. 10. 9; Ezek. 27. 12; 38. 13.
Jonah going there. Jon. 1. 3.
prophecies concerning. Ps. 48. 7; 72. 10; Isa. 2. 16; 23.; 60. 9; 66. 19.
Tarsus, tär′-sŭs, city of the apostle Paul. Acts 9. 11; 11. 25; 21. 39.
Tartak, tär′-tăk. 2 Kn. 17. 31.
Tartan, tär′-tăn (2 Kn. 18. 17; Isa. 20. 1), is the Hebrew form of the Accadian *tur-dan*, a title of the chief officer in the army.
Task. Ex. 5. 13, 14, 19.
Taskmasters. Ex. 1. 11, they did set over them.
5. 6, the *t.* of the people.
Taste. Num. 11. 8, the *t.* of it as *t.* of fresh oil.
Job 6. 6, is any *t.* in white of egg?
12. 11, doth not the mouth *t.* his meat?
34. 3, trieth words as mouth *t.* meat.
Ps. 34. 8, *t.* and see that the Lord is good.
119. 103, how sweet are thy words to my *t.*!
Jer. 48. 11, his *t.* remained in him.
Mat. 16. 28; Mk. 9. 1; Lu. 9. 27, some, which shall not *t.* death.
Lu. 14. 24, none bidden shall *t.* of my supper.
John 8. 52, keep my saying, shall never *t.* of death.
Col. 2. 21, touch not, *t.* not.
Heb. 2. 9, *t.* death for every man.
6. 4, and have *t.* of the heavenly gift.
1 Pet. 2. 3, have *t.* that the Lord is gracious.
See 1 Sam. 14. 43; 2 Sam. 19. 35; Mat. 27. 34.
Tatnai, tăt′-naī, 'gift' (?), and Shethar-boznai hinder the rebuilding of the temple. Ez. 5. 3; 6. 13.
Tattlers. 1 Tim. 5. 13, *t.* and busybodies.
Taught. Jud. 8. 16, he *t.* the men of Succoth.
2 Chr. 6. 27, thou hast *t.* them the good way.
23. 13, such as *t.* to sing praise. R. V. led the singing.
Ps. 71. 17; 119. 102, thou hast *t.* me.
Prov. 4. 4, he *t.* me also, and said.
4. 11, I have *t.* thee in way of wisdom.
Eccl. 12. 9, he still *t.* the people knowledge.
Isa. 29. 13, their fear is *t.* by precept of men.
54. 13, all thy children shall be *t.* of God.
Jer. 12. 16, as they *t.* my people to swear by Baal.
32. 33, *t.* them, rising up early.
Zec. 13. 5, *t.* me to keep cattle. R. V. I have been made a bondman.
Mat. 7. 29; Mk. 1. 22, *t.* as one having authority.
28. 15, and did as they were *t.*
Lu. 13. 26, thou hast *t.* in our streets.
John 6. 45, they shall be all *t.* of God.
8. 28, as my Father hath *t.* me.
Gal. 1. 12, nor was I *t.* it, except by revelation.
6. 6, let him that is *t.* in the word.
Eph. 4. 21, if so be ye have been *t.* by him.
2 Thes. 2. 15, the traditions ye have been *t.*
See Col. 2. 7; 1 Thes. 4. 9; Tit. 1. 9; 1 John 2. 27.
Taunt. Jer. 24. 9; Ezek. 5. 15; Hab. 2. 6.
Taverns, shops, inns, from a word meaning 'a table.' The Three Taverns was a town on the Appian Way 30 miles south of Rome, where a company of Christians from Rome met and welcomed Paul on his way to that city. Acts 28. 15.
Taxation of all the world, under Cæsar Augustus (Lu. 2. 1). The R. V. 'enrolment' more nearly gives the sense of the Greek: this 'enrolment' was a census of the whole Roman empire.
Teach. Ex. 4. 15, I will *t.* you.
Deu. 4. 10, that they may *t.* their children.
6. 7; 11. 19, *t.* them diligently.
Jud. 13. 8, *t.* us what we shall do to the child.
1 Sam. 12. 23, I will *t.* you the good way.
2 Sam. 1. 18, bade them *t.* the use of the bow.
2 Chr. 15. 3, without a *t.* priest.
Job 6. 24, *t.* me, and I will hold my tongue.
8. 10, thy fathers, shall not they *t.* thee?
12. 7, ask the beasts, and they shall *t.* thee.
34. 32, that which I see not *t.* thou me.
36. 22, God exalteth, who *t.* like him?
Ps. 25. 4, *t.* me thy paths.
25. 8, he will *t.* sinners in the way.
27. 11; 86. 11, *t.* me thy way, and lead me.
34. 11, I will *t.* you the fear of the Lord.
51. 13, then will I *t.* transgressors.
90. 12, so *t.* us to number our days.
94. 12, blessed is the man whom thou *t.*
Prov. 6. 13, the wicked man *t.* with his fingers. R. V. maketh signs.
Isa. 2. 3; Mic. 4. 2, he will *t.* us of his ways.
28. 9, whom shall he *t.* knowledge?
28. 26, God doth *t.* him discretion.
48. 17, I am thy God which *t.* thee to profit.
Jer. 9. 20, and *t.* your daughters wailing.
Ezek. 44. 23, *t.* my people the difference.
Mic. 3. 11, priests *t.* for hire.
Mat. 28. 19, *t.* all nations. R. V. make disciples of.
Lu. 11. 1, *t.* us to pray.
12. 12, the Holy Ghost shall *t.* you.
John 9. 34, dost thou *t.* us?
14. 26, shall *t.* you all things.
Acts 5. 42, they ceased not to *t.* and preach.
Rom. 12. 7, he that *t.*, on *t.*
1 Cor. 4. 17, as I *t.* every where.
11. 14, doth not even nature *t.* you?
14. 19, that by my voice I might *t.* others.
Col. 1. 28, *t.* every man in all wisdom.
3. 16, *t.* and admonishing one another.
1 Tim. 1. 3, charge some that they *t.* no other.
2. 12, I suffer not a woman to *t.*
3. 2; 2 Tim. 2. 24, apt to *t.*
4. 11, these things command and *t.*
6. 2, these things *t.* and exhort.
2 Tim. 2. 2, faithful men, able to *t.*
Tit. 1. 11, *t.* things they ought not.
2. 4, *t.* young women to be sober.
2. 12, *t.* us, that denying ungodliness.
Heb. 5. 12, ye have need that one *t.* you again.
See Mat. 22. 16; Mk. 6. 34; 12. 14; Rev. 2. 20.
Teacher. 1 Chr. 25. 8, as well *t.* as scholar.
Ps. 119. 99, more understanding than all my *t.*
Prov. 5. 13, have not obeyed the voice of my *t.*
Isa. 30. 20, thine eyes shall see thy *t.*

l

Hab. 2. 18, a *t.* of lies.
John 3. 2, a *t.* come from God.
Rom. 2. 20, thou art a *t.* of babes.
1 Cor. 12. 29, are all *t.*?
Eph. 4. 11, evangelists, pastors, and *t.*
1 Tim. 1. 7, desiring to be *t.* of the law.
Tit. 2. 3, aged women, *t.* of good things.
See 1 Tim. 2. 7; 2 Tim. 1. 11; Heb. 5. 12.

Teachers appointed in Judah. 2 Chr. 17. 7; Ez. 7. 10.
Christian (Bishops, Deacons, Elders). Acts 13. 1; Rom. 12. 7; 1 Cor. 12. 28; Eph. 4. 11; Col. 1. 28; 3. 16; 1 Tim. 3.; Tit. 1. 5.
worthy of honour and benevolence. 1 Cor. 9. 9; Gal. 6. 6; 1 Tim. 5. 17.
False, foretold and described, Jer. 5. 13; 6. 13; Ezek. 14. 9; 22. 25; Hos. 9. 7; Mic. 2. 11; 3. 11; Zep. 3. 4; Mat. 24. 4; Acts 13. 6; 20. 29; 2 Cor. 11. 13; 1 Tim. 1. 6; 4. 1; 6. 3; 2 Tim. 3. 8; Tit. 1. 11; 2 Pet. 2.; Jude 4; Rev. 2. 14, 20. not to be hearkened to, Deu. 13. 1; Mat. 24. 5; Col. 2. 8; 1 Tim. 1. 4; 4. 1; Heb. 13. 9; 2 Pet. 2.; 1 John 4. 1; 2 John 10; Jude; Rev. 2. 14. how to be tested and avoided, Isa. 8. 20; Rom. 16. 17; Tit. 3. 10; 1 John 4. 2, 3; 2 John 10. their condemnation, Deu. 13. 1; 18. 20; Isa. 8. 20; 9. 15; Jer. 28. 15; Ezek. 13. 8; 14. 10; Mic. 3. 6; Gal. 1. 8; 2 Tim. 3. 9; 2 Pet. 2. 1; Jude 4, 10, 16.

Teaching from God. Ps. 71. 17; Isa. 54. 13; Jer. 31. 34; John 6. 45; Gal. 1. 12; Eph. 4. 21; 1 Thes. 4. 9; 1 John 2. 27.
of Christ. Mat. 5.; 7. 29.

Tear. Job 16. 9, he *t.* me in his wrath.
Job 18. 4, he *t.* himself in his anger.
Ps. 7. 2, lest he *t.* my soul.
35. 15, they did *t.* me, and ceased not.
50. 22, lest I *t.* you in pieces.
Hos. 5. 14, I will *t.* and go away.
See Mic. 5. 8; Zec. 11. 16; Mk. 9. 18; Lu. 9. 39.

Tears. 2 Kn. 20. 5; Isa. 38. 5, I have seen thy *t.*
Job 16. 20, mine eye poureth out *t.*
Ps. 6. 6, I water my couch with *t.*
39. 12, hold not thy peace at my *t.*
42. 3, *t.* have been my meat.
56. 8, put thou my *t.* into thy bottle.
80. 5, the bread of *t.*, and *t.* to drink.
116. 8, thou hast delivered mine eyes from *t.*
126. 5, they that sow in *t.*
Isa. 16. 9, I will water thee with my *t.*
25. 8, will wipe away *t.*
Jer. 9. 1, oh that mine eyes were a fountain of *t.*!
13. 17; 14. 17, mine eyes run down with *t.*
31. 16, refrain thine eyes from *t.*
Lam. 1. 2, her *t.* are on her cheeks.
2. 11, mine eyes do fail with *t.*
Ezek. 24. 16, neither shall thy *t.* run down.
Mal. 2. 13, covering the altar with *t.*
Lu. 7. 38, to wash his feet with her *t.*
Acts 20. 19, serving the Lord with many *t.*
20. 31, ceased not to warn with *t.*
2 Tim. 1. 4, being mindful of thy *t.*
See 2 Cor. 2. 4; Heb. 5. 7; 12. 17; Rev. 7. 17.

Tebah, tē′-bäh, 'slaughter.' Gen. 22. 24.

Tebaliah, tĕb-ă-lī′-ăh, 'Jehovah has immersed.' 1 Chr. 26. 11.

Tebeth, tē′-bĕth, the tenth month of the Jewish sacred year = January. Esth. 2. 16. See Months.

Tedious. Acts 24. 4, that I be not further *t.*

Teeth. Gen. 49. 12, *t.* white with milk.
Num. 11. 33, flesh yet between their *t.*
Job 19. 20, escaped with the skin of my *t.*
Prov. 10. 26, as vinegar to the *t.*
Isa. 41. 15, an instrument having *t.*
Jer. 31. 29; Ezek. 18. 2, *t.* set on edge.
Am. 4. 6, cleanness of *t.*
See Mic. 3. 5; Zec. 9. 7; Mat. 27. 44; Rev. 9. 8.

Tehaphnehes, tĕ-hăph′-nĕ-hēs, same as Tahapanes. Ezek. 30. 18.

Tehinnah, tĕ-hĭn′-năh, 'cry for mercy.' 1 Chr. 4. 12.

Teil tree (Isa. 6. 13). Heb. *Elâh*: Gk. τερέβινθος: Bot. N. *Pistacia terebinthus.* The Hebrew *Elâh* is translated 'teil tree' here in A. V., but elsewhere 'oak,' except in Hos. 4. 13, 'elm.' R. V. correctly, 'terebinth,' which see. The teil tree is the linden or lime, and is not found in Palestine.

Tekel, tē′-kĕl, 'weighed.' Dan. 5. 25.

Tekoa, tĕ-kō′-ă, 'sound of trumpet.' 1 Chr. 2. 24; 4. 5.
widow of. 2 Sam. 14 (Jer. 6. 1).

Tekoah, tĕ-kō′-ăh, same as Tekoa. 2 Sam. 14. 2.

Tekoite, tĕ-kō′-īte, inhabitant of Tekoah. 2 Sam. 23. 26.

Tel-abib, tĕl-ā′-bĭb, 'hill of ears of corn.' Ezek. 3. 15.

Telah, tē′-läh. 1 Chr. 7. 25.

Telaim, tĕ-lā′-ĭm, 'lambs.' 1 Sam. 15. 4.

Telassar, tĕ-lăs′-sär, 'hill of Asshur.' Isa. 37. 12.

Telem, tē′-lĕm, 'oppression.' Ez. 10. 24.

Tel-haresha, tĕl-hă-rē′-shă, 'forest-hill.' Neh. 7. 61.

Tel-harsa, tĕl-här′-să, same as preceding. Ez. 2. 59.

Tell. (1) Gen. 32. 29, *t.* me thy name.
2 Sam. 1. 20, *t.* it not in Gath.
Ps. 50. 12, if I were hungry, I would not *t.* thee.
Eccl. 6. 12; 10. 14, who can *t.* what shall be after?
10. 20, that which hath wings shall *t.*
Jon. 3. 9, who can *t.* if God will turn? R. V. knoweth.
Mat. 18. 15, *t.* him his fault. R. V. shew.
18. 17, *t.* it unto the church.
21. 27; Mk. 11. 33; Lu. 20. 8, neither *t.* I you.
Mk. 5. 19, *t.* how great things.
11. 33; Lu. 20. 7, we cannot *t.* R. V. know not.
Lu. 13. 32, *t.* that fox. R. V. say to.
John 3. 8, canst not *t.* whence. R. V. knowest not.
3. 12, if I *t.* you of heavenly things.
4. 25, he will *t.* us all things.
18. 34, did others *t.* it thee of me?
Acts 17. 21, either to *t.* or hear some new thing.
(2) to number. Gen. 15. 5, *t.* the stars.
Ps. 48. 12, *t.* the towers thereof.
See Ps. 56. 8; Isa. 19. 12; Mat. 28. 7; 2 Cor. 12. 2.

Tel-melah, tĕl-mē′-lăh, 'salt-hill.' Ez. 2. 59.

Tema, tē′-mă, 'a desert.' (1) Gen. 25. 15. (2) Job 6. 19. (3) Isa. 21. 14; Jer. 25. 23.

Teman, tē′-măn, 'on the right hand.' Gen. 36. 11; Jer. 49. 7, 20; Ezek. 25. 13; Am. 1. 12; Obad. 9; Hab. 3. 3.

Temani, tē′-măn-ī, descendants of Teman. Gen. 36. 34.

Temanite, tē′-măn-īte, same as preceding. Job 2. 11.

Temeni, tē′-mĕ-nī, same as Temani. 1 Chr. 4. 6.

Temper, to modify by mixing, to mix, to compound. Ex. 29. 2; 30. 35; Ezek. 46. 14; 1 Cor. 12. 24.

Temperance commended. Prov. 23. 1; 1 Cor. 9. 25; Gal. 5. 23; Eph. 5. 18; Tit. 1. 8; 2. 2; 2 Pet. 1. 6.

Tempest. Job 9. 17, breaketh me with a *t.*
Ps. 11. 6, on wicked he shall rain a *t.* R. V. burning wind.
55. 8, hasten from windy storm and *t.*
Isa. 32. 2, a covert from the *t.*
Heb. 12. 18, not come to darkness and *t.*
2 Pet. 2. 17, clouds carried with a *t.*

Tempestuous. Ps. 50. 3; Jon. 1. 11; Acts 27. 14.

Temple, house of the Lord, or place for worship.
2 Sam. 22. 7, hear my voice out of his *t.*
Neh. 6. 10, meet together in the *t.*
Ps. 27. 4, to enquire in his *t.*
29. 9, in his *t.* doth every one speak of his glory.
Isa. 6. 1, his train filled the *t.*
Am. 8. 3, songs of the *t.* shall be howlings.
Mal. 3. 1, the Lord shall suddenly come to his *t.*
Mat. 12. 6, one greater than the *t.*
John 2. 19, destroy this *t.*
1 Cor. 3. 16; 6. 19; 2 Cor. 6. 16, ye are the *t.* of God.
See Hos. 8. 14; Rev. 11. 19.
See also Altar and Tabernacle.

Temple of God and Holy Ghost, Christians are.

1 Cor. 3. 16, 17; 6. 19; 2 Cor. 6. 16. *See also* Rev. 3. 12; 7. 15; 15. 8; 21. 22.
Temple (house of GOD). Ps. 65. 4; Eccl. 5. 1; 1 Tim. 3. 15; Heb. 10. 21; 1 Pet. 4. 17.
blessedness of frequenting. Ps. 65. 4; 84. 1, 10; 100. 4; 122 (Isa. 2. 3).
Temple of Jerusalem. Temple was the name given to the whole sacred precincts on Mount Moriah, including the sanctuary and the various 'courts.'
in David's heart to build. 2 Sam. 7. 3; 1 Chr. 17. 2; 28. 2.
David forbidden to build. 2 Sam. 7. 5; 1 Chr. 17. 4; 28. 3.
Solomon to build. 2 Sam. 7. 12; 1 Chr. 17. 11; 28. 5.
David's preparations for. 1 Chr. 28. 11.
Solomon builds. 1 Kn. 6.; 2 Chr. 3.; 4.
no hammer or axe heard in building. 1 Kn. 6. 7.
dimensions and ornaments of. 2 Chr. 3. 4.
its solemn dedication. 1 Kn. 8.; 2 Chr. 6.; 7.
glory of the Lord fills. 2 Chr. 5. 14.
plundered by Shishak, king of Egypt. 1 Kn. 14. 25; 2 Chr. 12. 9.
restored by Joash. 2 Kn. 12. 5, 12.
cleansed by Hezekiah. 2 Chr. 29. 5.
polluted by Manasseh. 2 Chr. 33. 7.
repaired by Josiah. 2 Chr. 34.
spoiled by the Chaldæans. 2 Kn. 25. 9; 2 Chr. 36.
decrees of Cyrus and Darius for rebuilding. Ez. 6. 3, 12.
commenced. Ez. 3. 8.
suspended by order of Artaxerxes. Ez. 4. 24.
resumed under Darius. Ez. 6. 7.
finished and dedicated. Ez. 6. 15, 16.
purified by Nehemiah. Neh. 13. 30.
made a den of thieves. Mat. 21. 12; Mk. 11. 15; Lu. 19. 46.
Christ drives out buyers and sellers. Mat. 21. 12; Mk. 11. 15; Lu. 19. 45; John 2. 14.
Christ foretells its destruction. Mat. 24. 2; Mk. 13. 2; Lu. 21. 6.
Christ teaches in. Lu. 21. 37.
disciples continue there daily. Acts 2. 46.
Peter and John pray and teach in. Acts 3. 1, 12.
Paul enters, and is assaulted in. Acts 21. 26.
Temple, symbolical. Ezek. 40.-44.
symbolical of the body of Christ. John 2. 21.
Temporal. 2 Cor. 4. 18, things seen are *t.*
Tempt. (1) to incite, entice to evil. 1 Cor. 10. 13, will not suffer you to be *t.*
Gal. 6. 1, considering thyself, lest thou be *t.*
Heb. 2. 18, hath suffered, being *t.*
4. 15, in all points *t.* like as we are.
Jas. 1. 13, cannot be *t.*, neither *t.* he any man.
(2) to try, to put to the test. Gen. 22. 1, God did *t.* Abraham. R. V. prove.
Ex. 17. 2, wherefore do ye *t.* the Lord?
Num. 14. 22, have *t.* me these ten times.
Deu. 6. 16; Mat. 4. 7; Lu. 4. 12, ye shall not *t.* the Lord your God.
Ps. 78. 18, they *t.* God in their heart.
Isa. 7. 12, I will not ask, neither *t.* the Lord.
Mal. 3. 15, they that *t.* God are delivered.
Mat. 22. 18; Mk. 12. 15; Lu. 20. 23, why *t.* ye me?
Lu. 10. 25, a lawyer, *t.* him.
Acts 5. 9, agreed together to *t.* the Spirit.
15. 10, why *t.* ye God to put a yoke?
See Mat. 4. 1; Mk. 1. 13; Lu. 4. 2; John 8. 6.
Temptation. Mat. 6. 13, lead us not into *t.*
26. 41; Mk. 14. 38; Lu. 22. 46, lest ye enter into *t.*
Lu. 8. 13, in time of *t.* fall away.
1 Cor. 10. 13, there hath no *t.* taken you.
Gal. 4. 14, my *t.* in flesh ye despised not.
1 Tim. 6. 9, they that will be rich fall into *t.*
Jas. 1. 2, when ye fall into divers *t.*
2 Pet. 2. 9, how to deliver out of *t.*
See Lu. 11. 4; Acts 20. 19; Rev. 3. 10.
Temptation, trial of faith and life. Gen. 22.; Dan. 12. 10; Zec. 13. 9; Lu. 22. 31, 40; Heb. 11. 17; Jas. 1. 12; 1 Pet. 1. 7; 4. 12.
none excessive. 1 Cor. 10. 13.
of Christ, by the devil. Mat. 4.; Mk. 1. 13; Lu. 4.

Tempter. Mat. 4. 3, and when the *t.* came to him.
1 Thes. 3. 5, the *t.* have tempted you.
Tend. Prov. 11. 19; 14. 23; 19. 23; 21. 5.
Tender. Deu. 28. 54, man that is *t.*
32. 2, distil as small rain on *t.* herb.
2 Kn. 22. 19; 2 Chr. 34. 27, thy heart was *t.*
Job 14. 7, the *t.* branch will not cease.
Prov. 4. 3, *t.* in sight of my mother.
S. of S. 2. 13, 15; 7. 12, vines with *t.* grapes. R. V. are in blossom.
Isa. 47. 1, no more be called *t.*
53. 2, grow up before him as a *t.* plant.
Dan. 1. 9, God brought Daniel into *t.* love. R. V. compassion.
Lu. 1. 78, through the *t.* mercy of our God.
Eph. 4. 32, be kind and *t.*-hearted.
Jas. 5. 11, the Lord is pitiful, and of *t.* mercy.
See 1 Chr. 22. 5; Ezek. 17. 22; Mk. 13. 28.
Tender (*v.*), to be careful for, to regard. 2 Mac. 4. 2.
Tenor. Gen. 43. 7; Ex. 34. 27.
Tent. Gen. 9. 21, was uncovered within his *t.*
9. 27, he shall dwell in the *t.* of Shem.
12. 8, and pitched his *t.*
25. 27, a plain man, dwelling in *t.*
Num. 24. 5, how goodly are thy *t.*!
1 Sam. 4. 10; 2 Sam. 18. 17, fled every man to his *t.*
1 Kn. 12. 16, to your *t.*, O Israel.
Ps. 84. 10, than to dwell in *t.* of wickedness.
Isa. 38. 12, removed as a shepherd's *t.*
54. 2, enlarge the place of thy *t.*
Jer. 10. 20, there is none to stretch forth my *t.*
Acts 18. 3, by occupation they were *t.*-makers.
See Isa. 40. 22; Jer. 4. 20; 35. 7; Zec. 12. 7; Heb. 11. 9.
Tent of Meeting. (1) the same as TABERNACLE. (2) the provisional tent used while the permanent tabernacle was erected. Ex. 33. 7-11.
Tenth. Gen. 28. 22; Lev. 27. 32; Isa. 6. 13.
Terah, tē'-răh, 'a station' (?). Gen. 11. 24.
Teraphim, tĕr'-ă-phĭm, 'nourishers' (?); of Laban, Gen. 31. 34.
of Micah. Jud. 17. 5; 18. 14.
of Michal. 1 Sam. 19. 13.
Terebinth (Isa. 6. 13; Hos. 4. 13, R. V.). Heb. *Elâh:* Gk. τερέβινθος: Bot. N. *Pistacia terebinthus:* elsewhere rendered 'oak' in R. V. text and 'terebinth' in margin. The Hebrew *Elâh* is probably the terebinth, a turpentine tree, resembling the oak, but smaller.
Teresh, tē'-rĕsh, 'severe' (?). Esth. 2. 21.
Terrible. Ex. 34. 10, a *t.* thing I will do.
Deu. 1. 19; 8. 15, that *t.* wilderness.
7. 21; 10. 17; Neh. 1. 5; 4. 14; 9. 32, a mighty God and *t.*
10. 21, hath done for thee *t.* things.
Jud. 13. 6, like an angel of God, very *t.*
Job 37. 22, with God is *t.* majesty.
39. 20, the glory of his nostrils is *t.*
Ps. 45. 4, thy right hand shall teach thee *t.* things.
65. 5, by *t.* things in righteousness.
66. 3, say unto God, how *t.* art thou!
66. 5, *t.* in his doing.
68. 35, *t.* out of thy holy places.
76. 12, he is *t.* to the kings of the earth.
99. 3, thy great and *t.* name.
145. 6, the might of thy *t.* acts.
S. of S. 6. 4, *t.* as an army with banners.
Isa. 25. 4, blast of the *t.* ones.
64. 3, when thou didst *t.* things.
Jer. 15. 21, redeem thee out of hand of the *t.*
Joel 2. 11, the day of the Lord is very *t.*
Heb. 12. 21, so *t.* was the sight. R. V. fearful.
See Lam. 5. 10; Ezek. 1. 22; 28. 7; Dan. 7. 7.
Terribleness. Deu. 26. 8; 1 Chr. 17. 21; Jer. 49. 16.
Terribly. Isa. 2. 19, 21; Nah. 2. 3.
Terrify. Job 9. 34, let not his fear *t.*
Lu. 21. 9, when ye hear of wars, be not *t.*
24. 37, they were *t.* and affrighted.
Phil. 1. 28, in nothing *t.* by adversaries.
See Job 7. 14; 2 Cor. 10. 9.
Terror. Gen. 35. 5; Job 6. 4, the *t.* of God.

Deu. 32. 25, the sword without and *t.* within.
Jos. 2. 9, your *t.* is fallen upon us.
Job 18. 11, *t.* shall make him afraid.
24. 17, in the *t.* of the shadow of death.
31. 23, destruction was a *t.* to me.
33. 7, my *t.* shall not make thee afraid.
Ps. 55. 4, the *t.* of death are fallen upon me.
73. 19, utterly consumed with *t.*
91. 5, afraid for the *t.* by night.
Jer. 17. 17, be not a *t.* to me.
20. 4, a *t.* to thyself.
Ezek. 26. 21; 27. 36; 28. 19, I will make thee a *t.*
Rom. 13. 3, rulers are not *t.* to good works.
2 Cor. 5. 11, knowing the *t.* of the Lord. [3. 14.
See Jer. 15. 8; Lam. 2. 22; Ezek. 21. 12; 1 Pet.

Tertius, tĕr′-tiŭs, 'the third.' Rom. 16. 22.

Tertullus, tĕr-tŭl′-lŭs (*dim.* of TERTIUS). Acts 24. 1.

Testament, a will; also a covenant, as in the N. T.

Testament, the New, of Christ's blood. Mat. 26. 28; Mk. 14. 24; Lu. 22. 20; 1 Cor. 11. 25; 2 Cor. 3. 6; Heb. 7. 22.
better than the first covenant. Heb. 8. 6, 7; 9.; 10.; 12. 24.
For quotations from and references to O. T. in, *see* NEW TEST., etc.

Testify. Num. 35. 30, one witness shall not *t.*
Deu. 31. 21, this song shall *t.* against them.
Ru. 1. 21, seeing the Lord hath *t.* against me.
2 Sam. 1. 16, thy mouth hath *t.* against thee.
Neh. 9. 30, *t.* against them by thy spirit.
Job 15. 6, thine own lips *t.* against thee.
Isa. 59. 12, our sins *t.* against us.
Hos. 5. 5; 7. 10, the pride of Israel doth *t.*
Mic. 6. 3, what have I done? *t.* against me.
Lu. 16. 28, send Lazarus, that he may *t.*
John 2. 25, needed not that any should *t.* R. V. bear witness concerning.
3. 32, seen and heard, that he *t.* R. V. beareth witness.
5. 39, they *t.* of me. R. V. bear witness.
7. 7, because I *t.* of it.
15. 26, he shall *t.* of me. R. V. bear witness.
21. 24, the disciple which *t.* of these things. R. V. beareth witness.
Acts 23. 11, as thou hast *t.* in Jerusalem.
1 Tim. 2. 6, gave himself to be *t.* in due time.
1 Pet. 1. 11, it *t.* beforehand the sufferings.
1 John 4. 14, we have seen and do *t.* R. V. bear witness.
See 1 Cor. 15. 15; 1 Thes. 4. 6; Rev. 22. 16.

Testimony. 2 Kn. 17. 15, rejected his *t.*
Ps. 93. 5, thy *t.* are sure.
119. 22, I have kept thy *t.*
119. 24, thy *t.* are my delight.
119. 46, I will speak of thy *t.*
119. 59, I turned my feet to thy *t.*
119. 119, I love thy *t.*
119. 129, thy *t.* are wonderful.
Isa. 8. 16, bind up the *t.*
8. 20, to the law and to the *t.*
Mat. 10. 18; Mk. 13. 9, for a *t.* against them.
Lu. 21. 13, it shall turn to you for a *t.*
John 3. 32, no man receiveth his *t.*
21. 24, we know that his *t.* is true. R. V. witness.
Acts 14. 3, *t.* to the word of his grace. R. V. witness.
1 Cor. 2. 1, declaring the *t.* of God. R. V. mystery.
2 Cor. 1. 12, the *t.* of our conscience.
2 Tim. 1. 8, be not ashamed of the *t.*
Heb. 11. 5, Enoch had this *t.* R. V. witness.

Testimony. Ex. 25. 16, 21; Rev. 1. 2; 6. 9; 11. 7; 12. 11; 19. 10.
of the apostles. Acts 22. 18; 2 Thes. 1. 10; 2 Tim. 1. 8; Rev. 1. 2; 11. 7; 12. 17.

Tetrarch, tē′-trärch, ruler of a fourth part of a country. Mat. 14. 1.

Thaddæus, thăd-dæ′-ŭs, Greek form of THEUDAS. Mat. 10. 3.

Thahash, thā′-hăsh, 'seal' (?). Gen. 22. 24.

Thamah, thā′-măh, 'laughter.' Ez. 2. 53.

Thamar, thā′-mär, Greek equivalent of TAMAR. Mat. 1. 3.

Thammuz, thăm′-mŭz (Zec. 8. 19). The fourth month of the Jewish sacred year = July. *See* MONTHS.

Thank. Mat. 11. 25; Lu. 10. 21; 18. 11; John 11. 41, I *t.* thee.
Acts 28. 15, *t.* God, and took courage.
1 Cor. 1. 4, I *t.* God on your behalf.
2 Thes. 1. 3, we are bound to *t.* God.
1 Tim. 1. 12, I *t.* Jesus Christ.
See 1 Chr. 23. 30; Dan. 2. 23; Rom. 6. 17.

Thanks. Neh. 12. 31, companies that gave *t.*
Mat. 26. 27; Lu. 22. 17, took the cup, and gave *t.*
Lu. 2. 38, Anna gave *t.* to the Lord.
Rom. 14. 6, eateth to the Lord, for he giveth *t.*
1 Cor. 15. 57, *t.* be to God, who giveth us the victory.
Eph. 5. 20, giving *t.* always for all things.
1 Thes. 3. 9, what *t.* can we render? R. V. thanksgiving.
Rev. 4. 9, give *t.* to him that sat on the throne.
See 2 Cor. 1. 11; 2. 14; 8. 16; 9. 15; Heb. 13. 15.

Thanks, giving of, at the Lord's Supper, Mat. 26. 27; Mk. 14. 23; Lu. 22. 17; 1 Cor. 11. 24. at meals, Mk. 8. 6; John 6. 11; Acts 27. 35; Rom. 14. 6; Eph. 5. 20; 1 Tim. 4. 3.

Thanksgiving. Ps. 26. 7, the voice of *t.*
95. 2, come before his face with *t.*
Isa. 51. 3, *t.* and melody shall be found therein.
Am. 4. 5, offer a sacrifice of *t.*
Phil. 4. 6, with *t.* let your requests be made.
Col. 4. 2, watch in the same with *t.*
1 Tim. 4. 3, to be received with *t.*
See Neh. 11. 17; 12. 8; 2 Cor. 4. 15.

Thanksgiving, exhortations to. Ps. 34. 3; 50. 14; 95. 2; 100. 4; 107. 22; 136.; 2 Cor. 9. 12; Phil. 4. 6; Col. 2. 7; 4. 2; Rev. 7. 12. *See* PSALMS, PRAISE.

Thara, thâr′-ă, Greek form of TERAH. Lu. 3. 34.

Tharshish, thär′-shĭsh, same as TARSHISH. 1 Kn. 10. 22.

That. Gen. 18. 25, *t.* be far from thee.
Num. 24. 13; 1 Kn. 22. 14, *t.* will I speak.
Job 23. 13, even *t.* he doeth.
Ps. 27. 4, *t.* will I seek after.
Zec. 11. 9, *t. t.* dieth, let it die.
Mat. 10. 15; Mk. 6. 11, than for *t.* city.
13. 12; 25. 29; Mk. 4. 25, *t.* he hath.
John 1. 8, he was not *t.* light.
5. 12, what man is *t.* which said?
13. 27, *t.* thou doest, do quickly.
21. 22, what is *t.* to thee?
Rom. 7. 19, the evil which I would not, *t.* I do.
Jas. 4. 15, we shall live, and do this or *t.* [18.
See Mk. 13. 11; 1 Cor. 11. 23; 2 Cor. 8. 12; Philem.

Theatre at Ephesus, Paul's danger there. Acts 19. 29.

Thebez, thē′-bĕz, 'brightness.' Abimelech wounded at. Jud. 9. 50.

Theft, whence proceeding. Mat. 15. 19; Mk. 7. 22. *See* STEALING.

Thelasar, thĕl′-ă-sär, same as TELASSAR. 2 Kn. 19. 12.

Then. Gen. 4. 26, *t.* began men to call.
Jos. 14. 12, if the Lord be with me, *t.* I shall be able.
Ps. 27. 10, *t.* the Lord will take me up. R. V. but.
55. 12, *t.* I could have borne it.
Isa. 58. 8, *t.* shall thy light break forth.
Ezek. 39. 28, *t.* shall they know.
Mat. 5. 24, *t.* come and offer thy gift.
19. 25; Mk. 10. 26, who *t.* can be saved?
24. 14, *t.* shall the end come.
2 Cor. 12. 10, *t.* am I strong.
See 1 Cor. 4. 5; 13. 12; 1 Thes. 5. 3; 2 Thes. 2. 8.

Theophilus, thē-ŏph′-ĭ-lŭs, 'loved of God.' Lu. 1. 3.

These. Ex. 32. 4, *t.* be thy gods, O Israel.
Eccl. 7. 10, former days better than *t.*
Isa. 60. 8, who are *t.* that fly?

Mat. 5. 37, whatsoever is more than *t.*
23. 23, *t.* ought ye to have done.
25. 40, one of the least of *t.*
John 17. 20, neither pray I for *t.* alone.
21. 15, lovest thou me more than *t.*?
See Job 26. 14; Ps. 73. 12; Jer. 7. 4.

Thessalonians, thĕss-ă-lō´-nĭ-ănṡ, people of Thessalonica, to whom Paul wrote two epistles. *See* SUMMARIES. 1 & 2 Thes.

Thessalonica, thĕss-ă-lō-nī´-că, the metropolis of Macedonia. Now Saloniki in Turkey; Paul at. Acts 17.

The Three Taverns. Acts 28. 15. *See* TAVERNS.

Theudas, theū´-dăs, 'praise'(?). Acts 5. 36.

Thick. Deu. 32. 15, thou art grown *t.*
2 Sam. 18. 9, the mule went under the *t.* boughs.
Ps. 74. 5, lifted up axes on the *t.* trees.
Ezek. 31. 3, top was among *t.* boughs.
Hab. 2. 6, ladeth himself with *t.* clay. R. V. pledges.
See 1 Kn. 12. 10; 2 Chr. 10. 10; Neh. 8. 15; Job 15. 26.

Thicket. Gen. 22. 13; Isa. 9. 18; Jer. 4. 7, 29.

Thick trees (Lev. 23. 40). Heb. *'Etz 'âbôth:* Gk. *κλάδοι δασεῖς.* 'Thick trees are mentioned among those from whose branches the booths were to be made at the Feast of Tabernacles.' Doubtless the myrtle.

Thief. Ps. 50. 18, when thou sawest a *t.*
Jer. 2. 26, as the *t.* is ashamed.
Joel 2. 9, enter at windows like a *t.*
Lu. 12. 33, where no *t.* approacheth.
John 10. 1, the same is a *t.* and a robber.
1 Pet. 4. 15, let none suffer as a *t.*
See Prov. 6. 30; 29. 24.

Thief, punishment of. Ex. 22. 2; Deu. 24. 7; Zec. 5. 4; 1 Cor. 6. 10; 1 Pet. 4. 15.
conduct of, described. Job 24. 14; Jer. 2. 26; 49. 9; Lu. 10. 30; John 10. 1.
in the night, Christ's second coming typified by. Mat. 24. 43; Lu. 12. 39; 1 Thes. 5. 2; 2 Pet. 3. 10; Rev. 3. 3; 16. 15.

Thieves. Isa. 1. 23; Lu. 10. 30; John 10. 8; 1 Cor. 6. 10.

Thieves at crucifixion. Mat. 27. 38; Mk. 15. 27; Lu. 23. 40.

Thigh. Gen. 24. 2; 47. 29, put hand under *t.*
32. 25, touched hollow of Jacob's *t.*
Jud. 15. 8, smote them hip and *t.*
S. of S. 3. 8, every man hath sword on his *t.*
See Ps. 45. 3; Jer. 31. 19; Ezek. 21. 12; Rev. 19. 16.

Thimnathah, thĭm´-nă-thăh, 'portion.' Jos. 19. 43.

Thine. Gen. 31. 32, discern what is *t.*
1 Sam. 15. 28, to a neighbour of *t.*
1 Kn. 20. 4, I am *t.*, and all I have.
1 Chr. 29. 11, *t.* is the greatness.
Ps. 74. 16, the day is *t.*, the night also is *t.*
119. 94, I am *t.*, save me.
Isa. 63. 19, we are *t.* R. V. become as they.
Mat. 20. 14, take that is *t.*
Lu. 4. 7, worship me, all shall be *t.*
22. 42, not my will, but *t.* be done.
John 17. 6, *t.* they were, and thou gavest them me.
17. 10, all mine are *t.*, and *t.* are mine.
See Gen. 14. 23; Jos. 17. 18; 1 Chr. 12. 18; Lu. 15. 31.

Thing. Gen. 21. 11, the *t.* was very grievous.
Ex. 18. 17, the *t.* thou doest is not good.
2 Sam. 13. 33, let not my lord take the *t.* to heart.
2 Kn. 2. 10, thou hast asked a hard *t.*
Eccl. 1. 9, the *t.* that hath been.
Isa. 7. 13, is it a small *t.* to weary?
41. 12, as a *t.* of nought.
43. 19; Jer. 31. 22, a new *t.*
Mk. 1. 27, what *t.* is this?
John 5. 14, lest a worse *t.* come unto thee.
Phil. 3. 16, let us mind the same *t.* R. V. omits.
See Heb. 10. 29; 1 Pet. 4. 12; 1 John 2. 8.

Things devoted, Lev. 27.; Num. 18. 14; Ezek. 44. 29. not to be redeemed, Lev. 27. 33. abuse of (Corban), Mat. 15. 5; Mk. 7. 11.

Think. Gen. 40. 14, but *t.* on me when it shall be well.
Neh. 5. 19, *t.* on me, O my God, for good. R. V. remember.
Ps. 40. 17, I am poor, yet the Lord *t.* on me.
Prov. 23. 7, as he *t.* in his heart, so is he.
Isa. 10. 7, nor doth his heart *t.* so.
Jon. 1. 6, if God will *t.* upon us.
Mat. 3. 9, *t.* not to say within yourselves.
6. 7, *t.* they shall be heard.
9. 4, why *t.* ye evil in your hearts?
17. 25; 22. 17, what *t.* thou?
22. 42; 26. 66; Mk. 14. 64, what *t.* ye of Christ?
Rom. 12. 3, more highly than he ought to *t.*
1 Cor. 10. 12, that *t.* he standeth.
2 Cor. 3. 5, to *t.* any thing as of ourselves. R. V. account.
Gal. 6. 3, if a man *t.* himself to be something.
Eph. 3. 20, able to do above all we ask or *t.*
Phil. 4. 8, *t.* on these things.
Jas. 1. 7, let not that man *t.* he shall receive.
1 Pet. 4. 12, *t.* it not strange.
See Job 35. 2; Jer. 29. 11; Ezek. 38. 10; Lu. 10. 36.

Thirst (*n.*). Ex. 17. 3, to kill us with *t.*
Deu. 29. 19, to add drunkenness to *t.* R. V. destroy the moist with the dry.
Jud. 15. 18, now I shall die for *t.*
2 Chr. 32. 11, doth persuade you to die by *t.*
Ps. 69. 21, in my *t.* they gave me vinegar.
Isa. 41. 17, when their tongue faileth for *t.*
Am. 8. 11, not a *t.* for water, but of hearing.
2 Cor. 11. 27, in hunger and *t.* often.
See Deu. 28. 48; Job 24. 11; Ps. 104. 11.

Thirst (*v.*). Ps. 42. 2; 63. 1; 143. 6, my soul *t.* for God.
Isa. 49. 10; Rev. 7. 16, shall not hunger nor *t.*
55. 1, every one that *t.*
Mat. 5. 6, *t.* after righteousness.
John 4. 14; 6. 35, shall never *t.*
7. 37, if any man *t.*, let him come unto me.
19. 28, I *t.*
See Ex. 17. 3; Isa. 48. 21; Rom. 12. 20; 1 Cor. 4. 11.

Thirsty. Ps. 63. 1; 143. 6, in a *t.* land.
107. 5, hungry and *t.*, their soul fainted.
Prov. 25. 25, as cold waters to a *t.* soul.
Isa. 21. 14, brought water to him that was *t.*
29. 8, as when a *t.* man dreameth.
44. 3, pour water on him that is *t.*
65. 13, but ye shall be *t.*
See Jud. 4. 19; Isa. 32. 6; Ezek. 19. 13; Mat. 25. 35.

Thistle. Heb. *Dardar:* Gk. *τρίβολος*, probably the *Tribulus terrestris*, one of the plants called caltrop, common by the roadside. Not our *thistle*, which is one of the Compositæ. *See* BRAMBLE.
Gen. 3. 18, thorns and *t.* shall it bring forth.
Job 31. 40, let *t.* grow instead of wheat.
Mat. 7. 16, do men gather figs of *t.*?
See 2 Kn. 14. 9; 2 Chr. 25. 18; Hos. 10. 8.

Thomas, thŏm´-ăs, 'a twin,' Apostle. Mat. 10. 3; Mk. 3. 18; Lu. 6. 15; Acts 1. 13.
his zeal. John 11. 16.
his doubt and confession. John 20. 24.

Thorn. Num. 33. 55; Jud. 2. 3, *t.* in your sides.
Jud. 8. 7, 16, *t.* of the wilderness.
Ps. 118. 12, quenched as the fire of *t.*
Prov. 15. 19, way of slothful man is as an hedge of *t.*
24. 31, it was all grown over with *t.*
26. 9, as a *t.* goeth into hand of drunkard.
Eccl. 7. 6, crackling of *t.* under a pot.
S. of S. 2. 2, as the lily among *t.*
Isa. 33. 12, as *t.* cut up shall they be burned.
34. 13, and *t.* shall come up in her palaces.
55. 13, instead of the *t.* shall come up the fir tree.
Jer. 4. 3, sow not among *t.*
12. 13, but shall reap *t.*
Hos. 2. 6, I will hedge up thy way with *t.*
9. 6, *t.* shall be in their tabernacles.
10. 8, the *t.* shall come up on their altars.
Mic. 7. 4, most upright is sharper than *t.* hedge.
Mat. 13. 7, among *t.* and the *t.* sprung up.

2 Cor. 12. 7, a *t.* in the flesh.
See also BRAMBLE.

Thorns, crown of (Mat. 27. 29; Mk. 15. 17; John 19. 2), is generally believed to have been made of *Zizyphus spina Christi*, a species of jujube or lotus tree, with pliant branches, sharp thorns, and leaves resembling the ivy with which emperors and victors were crowned.

Thought (*n.*). 1 Chr. 28. 9, the Lord understandeth the *t.*
Job 4. 13, in *t.* from the visions of the night.
12. 5, despised in *t.* of him that is at ease.
42. 2, no *t.* can be withholden from thee.
Ps. 10. 4, God is not in all his *t.*
40. 5, thy *t.* cannot be reckoned.
92. 5, thy *t.* are very deep.
94. 11, the Lord knoweth the *t.* of man.
94. 19, in the multitude of my *t.*
139. 2, thou understandest my *t.* afar off.
139. 17, how precious are thy *t.* to me!
139. 23, try me, and know my *t.*
Prov. 12. 5, the *t.* of the righteous are right.
16. 3, thy *t.* shall be established.
24. 9, the *t.* of foolishness is sin.
Isa. 55. 7, and the unrighteous man his *t.*
55. 8, my *t.* are not your *t.*
55. 9, so are my *t.* higher than your *t.*
Mic. 4. 12, they know not the *t.* of the Lord.
Mat. 9. 4; 12. 25; Lu. 5. 22; 6. 8; 9. 47; 11. 17, Jesus knowing their *t.*
15. 19; Mk. 7. 21, out of the heart proceed evil *t.*
Lu. 2. 35, the *t.* of many hearts may be revealed.
24. 38, why do *t.* arise in your hearts?
Acts 8. 22, if the *t.* of thine heart may be forgiven.
1 Cor. 3. 20, the Lord knoweth the *t.* of the wise.
2 Cor. 10. 5, bringing into captivity every *t.*
Heb. 4. 12, the word of God is a discerner of the *t.*
Jas. 2. 4, ye are become judges of evil *t.*
See Gen. 6. 5; Jer. 4. 14; 23. 20; Am. 4. 13.

Thought (*v.*). Gen. 48. 11, I had not *t.* to see thy face.
Num. 24. 11, I *t.* to promote thee.
Deu. 19. 19, do to him as he *t.* to have done.
2 Kn. 5. 11, I *t.*, he will surely come out.
Neh. 6. 2, they *t.* to do me mischief.
Ps. 48. 9, we have *t.* of thy lovingkindness.
50. 21, thou *t.* I was such an one as thyself.
73. 16, when I *t.* to know this.
119. 59, I *t.* on my ways.
Prov. 30. 32, if thou hast *t.* evil.
Isa. 14. 24, as I have *t.*, so shall it come.
Jer. 18. 8, I will repent of the evil I *t.* to do.
Zec. 8. 14, as I *t.* to punish you.
8. 15, I *t.* to do well.
Mal. 3. 16, for them that *t.* on his name.
Mat. 1. 20, but while he *t.* on these things.
Mk. 14. 72, when he *t.* thereon, he wept.
Lu. 12. 17, he *t.* within himself, what shall I do? R. V. reasoned.
19. 11, *t.* the kingdom of God should appear. R. V. supposed.
John 11. 13, they *t.* he had spoken of taking of rest.
Acts 10. 19, while Peter *t.* on the vision.
26. 8, why should it be *t.* a thing incredible? R. V. judged.
1 Cor. 13. 11, I *t.* as a child.
Phil. 2. 6, *t.* it not robbery to be equal with God. R. V. counted.
See Gen. 20. 11; 50. 20; 1 Sam. 1. 13; Heb. 10. 29.

Thought, great anxiety, excessive care. Mat. 6. 25, 31, 34; 10. 19; Mk. 13. 11; Lu. 12. 11, 22.

Thread. Gen. 14. 23; Jos. 2. 18; Jud. 16. 9.

Threaten. Acts 4. 17; 9. 1; Eph. 6. 9; 1 Pet. 2. 23.

Threefold. Eccl. 4. 12, a *t.* cord.

Thresh. Isa. 41. 15, thou shalt *t.* the mountains.
Jer. 51. 33, it is time to *t.* her. R. V. at the . . . when it is trodden.
Mic. 4. 13, arise and *t.*
Hab. 3. 12, thou didst *t.* the heathen.
1 Cor. 9. 10, *t.* in hope.
See Lev. 26. 5; 1 Chr. 21. 20; Isa. 21. 10; 28. 28.

Threshold. 1 Sam. 5. 5; Ezek. 47. 1; Zep. 2. 14.

Threw. 2 Kn. 9. 33; Mk. 12. 42; Lu. 9. 42; Acts 22. 23.

Throat. Ps. 5. 9; 115. 7; Prov. 23. 2; Mat. 18. 28.

Throne. Ps. 11. 4, the Lord's *t.* is in heaven.
94. 20, shall *t.* of iniquity have fellowship with thee?
122. 5, there are set *t.* of judgment.
Prov. 20. 28, his *t.* is upholden by mercy.
Isa. 66. 1; Acts 7. 49, heaven is my *t.*
Jer. 17. 12, a glorious high *t.* from the beginning.
Dan. 7. 9, his *t.* was like the fiery flame.
Mat. 19. 28; 25. 31, the Son of man shall sit in the *t.*
Col. 1. 16, whether they be *t.*
Heb. 4. 16, the *t.* of grace.
Rev. 3. 21, to him will I grant to sit on my *t.*
4. 2, a *t.* was set in heaven.
See Rev. 6. 16; 7. 9; 14. 3; 19. 4; 20. 11; 22. 1.

Throng. Mk. 3. 9; 5. 31; Lu. 8. 42, 45.

Throughly. Ps. 51. 2; Jer. 7. 5; Mat. 3. 12.

Throw. Mic. 5. 11; Mal. 1. 4; Mat. 24. 2.

Thrust. Job 32. 13, God *t.* him down, not man. R. V. may vanquish.
Joel 2. 8, neither shall one *t.* another.
Lu. 10. 15, shall be *t.* down to hell. R. V. brought.
13. 28, and you yourselves *t.* out. R. V. cast forth without.
John 20. 25, and *t.* my hand into his side. R. V. put.
Rev. 14. 15, *t.* in thy sickle. R. V. send forth.
See Ex. 11. 1; 1 Sam. 31. 4; Ezek. 34. 21.

Thumb. Ex. 29. 20; Lev. 8. 23, 24; Jud. 1. 6.

Thummim, thŭm'-mĭm, 'perfection,' on high priest's breastplate. Ex. 28. 30; Lev. 8. 8; Deu. 33. 8; Ez. 2. 63; Neh. 7. 65. *See* URIM.

Thunder. Ex. 9. 23; 1 Sam. 7. 10; 12. 18; Ps. 78. 48.
See Ex. 19. 16; Rev. 4. 5; 16. 18.

Thunders, seven. Rev. 10.

Thyatira, thȳ-ā-tī'-rā. Acts 16. 14.
angel of. Rev. 1. 11; 2. 18.

Thyine wood (Rev. 18. 12). Gk. **ξύλον θύϊνον**: Bot. N. *Callitris quadrivalvis:* A. V. marg. 'sweet wood.' 'Thyine wood' is one of the priceless commodities of the Babylon of the book of Revelation. It is a large tree of the Cypress family, reddish brown, hard and fragrant.

Tiberias, tī-bē'-rĭ-ăs (*Tubariya*). A town on the west shore of the Sea of Galilee. It gave its name to the sea. John 6. 1; 21. 1.

Tiberius, tī-bē'-rĭ-ŭs. Lu. 3. 1.

Tibhath, tĭb'-hăth, 'butchery.' 1 Chr. 18. 8.

Tibni, tĭb'-nī, 'made of straw' (?). 1 Kn. 16. 21.

Tidal, tī'-dăl, 'dread.' Gen. 14. 1.

Tidings. Ps. 112. 7, afraid of evil *t.*
Jer. 20. 15, cursed be the man who brought *t.*
Dan. 11. 44, *t.* out of the east.
Lu. 1. 19; 2. 10; 8. 1; Acts 13. 32; Rom. 10. 15, glad *t.*
See Ex. 33. 4; 1 Kn. 14. 6; Jer. 49. 23.

Tiglath-pileser, tĭg'-lăth-pī-lē'-sĕr, 'the son of the temple of Sarra is a ground of confidence' (?). 2 Kn. 15. 29; 16. 7.

Tikvah, tĭk'-văh, 'expectation.' 2 Kn. 22. 14.

Tikvath, tĭk'-văth, same as TIKVAH. 2 Chr. 34. 22.

Tile. Ezek. 4. 1; Lu. 5. 19.

Tilgath-pilneser, tĭl'-găth-pĭl-nē'-sĕr, same as TIGLATH-PILESER. 1 Chr. 5. 6, 26; 2 Chr. 28. 20.

Till. Gen. 2. 5; Prov. 12. 11; 28. 19; Ezek. 36. 9.

Tillage. 1 Chr. 27. 26; Neh. 10. 37; Prov. 13. 23.

Tilon, tī'-lŏn, 'gift' (?). 1 Chr. 4. 20.

Timæus, tī-mæ'-ŭs, 'polluted' (?). Mk. 10. 46.

Timbrel (Ex. 15. 20; Jud. 11. 34; 2 Sam. 6. 5; Job 21. 12; Ps. 81. 2; 149. 3; 150. 4). The same Hebrew word (*sing.* and *pl.*) represents 'tabret' and 'timbrel;' therefore only one instrument is meant, viz., a simple tambourine.

Time. Gen. 47. 29, the *t.* drew nigh.
Job 22. 16, cut down out of *t.*
38. 23, reserved against the *t.* of trouble.
Ps. 32. 6, in a *t.* when thou mayest be found.
37. 19, not ashamed in the evil *t.* [day.
41. 1, deliver him in *t.* of trouble. R. V. the
56. 3, what *t.* I am afraid.
69. 13; Isa. 49. 8; 2 Cor. 6. 2, acceptable *t.*
89. 47, remember how short my *t.* is.
Eccl. 3. 1, there is a *t.* to every purpose.
9. 11, *t.* and chance happeneth to all.
Isa. 60. 22, I will hasten it in his *t.*
Jer. 46. 21, the *t.* of their visitation.
Ezek. 16. 8, thy *t.* was the *t.* of love.
Dan. 7. 25, a *t.* and *t.* and the dividing of *t.*
Hos. 10. 12, it is *t.* to seek the Lord. [the *t.*
Mal. 3. 11, neither shall vine cast fruit before
Mat. 16. 3, the signs of the *t.*
Lu. 19. 44, the *t.* of thy visitation.
Acts 3. 19, the *t.* of refreshing. R. V. seasons.
3. 21, the *t.* of restitution.
Rom. 13. 11, it is high *t.* to awake.
1 Cor. 7. 29, the *t.* is short.
Eph. 5. 16; Col. 4. 5, redeeming the *t.*
Heb. 4. 16, help in *t.* of need.
1 Pet. 1. 11, what manner of *t.*
Rev. 1. 3, the *t.* is at hand.
10. 6, *t.* no longer.
See Prov. 17. 17; Eph. 1. 10.

Time, redemption of. Ps. 39. 4; 90. 12; Eccl. 12. 1; Isa. 55. 6; Mat. 5. 25; Lu. 19. 42; John 9. 4; 12. 35; Rom. 13. 11; 2 Cor. 6. 2; Gal. 6. 9; Eph. 5. 16; Col. 4. 5.
the end of. Rev. 10. 6.
for all things. Eccl. 3.
See DAY and MONTHS.

Times, signs of. Mat. 16. 3; Acts 3. 21; 1 Thes. 5. 1; 2 Thes. 2.; 1 Tim. 4. 1; 2 Tim. 3. 1.

Timna, tĭm'-nă, 'unapproachable' (?). Gen. 36. 12.

Timnah, tĭm'-năh, 'a portion.' (1) a 'duke' of Edom. Gen. 36. 40; 1 Chr. 1. 51.
(2) places. Jos. 15. 10 and 57.

Timnath, tĭm'-năth, same as TIMNAH. (1) Gen. 38. 12. (2) Jud. 14. 1.

Timnath-heres, tĭm'-năth-hē'-rĕs, 'portion of the sun.' Jud. 2. 9.

Timnath-serah, tĭm'-năth-sē'-răh, 'portion of the remainder.' Jos. 19. 50.
Joshua buried there. Jos. 24. 30.

Timnite, tĭm'-nīte, a man of Timna. Jud. 15. 6.

Timon, tī'-mŏn. Acts 6. 5.

Timotheus, tĭ-mŏth'-ē-ŭs, 'honouring God.' Acts 16. 1.

Timothy, tĭm'-ō-thȳ, English form of the above; accompanies Paul. Acts 16. 3; 17. 14, 15; Rom. 16. 21; 2 Cor. 1. 1, 19.
commended. 1 Cor. 16. 10; Phil. 2. 19.
instructed in letters by Paul. 1 & 2 Tim.

Tin (Num. 31. 22). Heb. *'Ophéreth:* Gk. κασσίτερος. Tin was early known to the Hebrews, being one of the imports of Egypt from Spain. Later it was obtained from Britain. So Herodotus and Strabo. It was used for the preparation of bronze, its alloy with copper.

Tingle. 1 Sam. 3. 11; 2 Kn. 21. 12; Jer. 19. 3.

Tinkling. Isa. 3. 16, 18; 1 Cor. 13. 1.

Tip. Ex. 29. 20; Lu. 16. 24.

Tiphsah, tĭph'-săh, 'passage.' 1 Kn. 4. 24.

Tiras, tī'-răs. Gen. 10. 2.

Tirathites, tī'-ră-thītes. 1 Chr. 2. 55.

Tire (*n.*), a head-dress. Isa. 3. 18.

Tire (*v.*), to adorn with a head-dress. 2 Kn. 9. 30.

Tirhakah, tĭr-hā'-kăh. Sennacherib's war with. 2 Kn. 19. 9.

Tirhanah, tĭr-hā'-năh, 'murmuring' (?). 1 Chr. 2. 48.

Tiria, tī'-rĭ-ă, 'fear.' 1 Chr. 4. 16.

Tirshatha, tĭr'-shă-thă, 'the stern' (?). Ez. 2. 63; Neh. 7. 70.

Tirzah, tĭr'-zăh, 'pleasantness.' (1) a woman. Num. 26. 33.
(2) the second capital of Israel, eleven miles N. E. of Shechem. 1 Kn. 14. 17; 15. 21; 16. 8, 15; 2 Kn. 15. 16; S. of S. 6. 4 (Jos. 12. 24).

Tishbite, tĭsh'-bīte, inhabitant of Tishbe. 1 Kn. 17. 1.

Tishri, tĭsh'-rī, called *Ethanim* in 1 Kn. 8. 2. The seventh month of the Jewish sacred year, October, in which were the Feast of Trumpets, the Day of Atonement, and the Feast of Tabernacles. *See* MONTHS.

Tisri, tĭs'-rī, same as TISHRI.

Tithes paid by Abraham to Melchizedek. Gen. 14. 20; Heb. 7. 6.
due to God. Gen. 28. 22; Lev. 27. 30; Prov. 3. 9; Mal. 3. 8.
to the Levites. Num. 18. 21; 2 Chr. 31. 5; Neh. 10. 37; Heb. 7. 5.
for the feasts, and poor. Deu. 14. 23, 28.

Title *or* **superscription.** Over every crucified malefactor were inscribed, on a white tablet smeared with gypsum, his name, residence, and offence. This was the official warrant for his execution, and was copied from the register in which his sentence was recorded. What Pilate 'had written' on the cross of Jesus (John 19. 19-22) he 'had written' also in the official record, which it was illegal for him to alter.

Titles of Christ. *See* CHRIST.

Tittle (Gk. κεραία, a little horn) was the minute projecting line which serves to distinguish certain of the Hebrew letters from others (Mat. 5. 18).

Titus, tī'-tŭs, 'protected' (?). Gal. 2. 3.
Paul's love for. 2 Cor. 2. 13; 7. 6, 13.
instructed by Paul. Tit. 1.-3.

Tizite, tī'-zīte. 1 Chr. 11. 45.

To, used in sense of 'for.' Mat. 3. 9.

Toah, tō'-ăh, 'low.' 1 Chr. 6. 34.

Tob, tŏb, 'good.' Jud. 11. 3.

Tob-adonijah, tŏb-ăd-ō-nī'-jăh, 'good is my lord Jehovah.' 2 Chr. 17. 8.

Tobiah, tō-bī'-ăh, 'Jehovah is good.' Ez. 2. 60.
the Ammonite, vexes the Jews. Neh. 4. 3; 6. 1, 12, 14; 13. 4.

Tobijah, tō-bī'-jăh, same as TOBIAH. 2 Chr. 17. 8.

To brake, should be one word 'tobrake' or 'to-brake,' i. e., broke in pieces. Jud. 9. 53, 'and entirely broke his skull.' *See* ALL TO BRAKE.

Tochen, tō'-chĕn, 'a measure.' 1 Chr. 4. 32.

Toes. 2 Sam. 21. 20; Dan. 2. 41, 42.

Togarmah, tō-găr'-măh, 'rugged.' (1) Gen. 10. 3. (2) Ezek. 27. 14.

Together. Prov. 22. 2, meet *t.*
Am. 3. 3, can two walk *t.*?
Mat. 18. 20, where two or three are gathered *t.*
Rom. 8. 28, work *t.* for good.
1 Thes. 4. 17, caught up *t.*
See Mat. 19. 6; Eph. 2. 21; 2 Thes. 2. 1.

Tohu, tō'-hū, same as TOAH (?). 1 Sam. 1. 1.

Toi, tō'-ī, 'wanderer.' 2 Sam. 8. 9.

Toil. Gen. 5. 29; 41. 51; Mat. 6. 28; Lu. 12. 27.

Token. Ex. 3. 12; Ps. 65. 8; 86. 17; Mk. 14. 44; Phil. 1. 28; 2 Thes. 1. 5.

Tola, tō'-lă, 'worm.' (1) Gen. 46. 13. (2) Jud. 10. 1.

Tolad, tō'-lăd, 'birth.' 1 Chr. 4. 29.

Tolaites, tō'-lă-ītes, 'descendants of Tola.' Num. 26. 23.

Tolerable. Mat. 10. 15; 11. 24; Mk. 6. 11; Lu. 10. 12.

Toll. Ez. 4. 13, 20; 7. 24.

Tomb. Job 21. 32; Mat. 8. 28; 23. 29; 27. 60; Mk. 5. 3; 6. 29; Lu. 8. 27.

Tongs. Ex. 25. 38; Num. 4. 9; Isa. 6. 6.

Tongue. Job 5. 21, hid from scourge of the *t.*
20. 12, hide wickedness under his *t.*
Ps. 34. 13; 1 Pet. 3. 10, keep thy *t.* from evil.
Prov. 10. 20, *t.* of the just as choice silver.
12. 18; 31. 26, *t.* of the wise is health.
12. 19, the lying *t.* is but for a moment.
15. 4, a wholesome *t.* is a tree of life.
18. 21, death and life are in the power of the *t.*
21. 23, whoso keepeth his *t.* keepeth his soul.

Prov. 25. 15, a soft *t.* breaketh the bone.
Isa. 30. 27, his *t.* as a devouring fire.
50. 4, hath given me the *t.* of the learned.
Jer. 9. 5, taught their *t.* to speak lies.
18. 18, let us smite him with the *t.*
Mk. 7. 35, his *t.* was loosed.
Jas. 1. 26, and bridleth not his *t.*
3. 5, the *t.* is a little member.
3. 6, the *t.* is a fire.
3. 8, the *t.* can no man tame.
1 John 3. 18, not love in word, neither in *t.*
See Ps. 45. 1; Lu. 16. 24; Rom. 14. 11; Phil. 2. 11.

Tongue, unruly. Jas. 3.
must be bridled. Ps. 39. 1; Prov. 4. 24; 10. 10, 19; 14. 23; 15. 4; 17. 20; 18. 6; Eccl. 3. 7; 10. 12; Mat. 5. 22; 12. 36; Eph. 4. 29; 5. 4; Col. 3. 8; 4. 6; 1 Thes. 5. 11; Tit. 1. 10; 2. 8; 3. 2; Jas. 1. 26; 3.; 1 Pet. 3. 10; Jude 16.

Tongues, confusion of. Gen. 11.
(gift of). (1) The symbolical expression of the presence and power of the Holy Spirit on the day of Pentecost. Acts 2. 4–11.
(2) certain ecstatic utterances under the influence of the Holy Spirit. 1 Cor. 12. and 14.
See Acts 10. 46; 19. 6.

Tool. Ex. 20. 25; 32. 4; Deu. 27. 5; 1 Kn. 6. 7.

Tooth. Ex. 21. 24; Prov. 25. 19; Mat. 5. 38.

Top. Gen. 11. 4; Ex. 19. 20; Jud. 15. 8; 2 Sam. 5. 24; Ezek. 17. 4; Mat. 27. 51.

Topaz (Ex. 28. 17; Rev. 21. 20). Heb. *Pitdâh:* Gk. *τοπάζιον*. The topaz of the ancients was a yellow variety of corundum. Found in Egypt and an island of the Red Sea.

Tophel, tō′-phĕl, 'lime.' Deu. 1. 1.

Tophet, tō′-phĕt, was the furnace in the Valley of the Sons of Hinnom, south of Jerusalem, in which human sacrifices were offered (2 Kn. 23. 10; Isa. 30. 33; Jer. 7. 31). It derived its name from the tabrets (*Topheth*) with which they drowned the cries of the victims; or perhaps from its shape. The Valley (*Ge*) of Hinnom was subsequently called in Greek *Gehenna*, and this word was used to indicate the doom of the ungodly (Mat. 5. 22; 10. 28; Mk. 9. 47; Lu. 12. 5), because of those horrible sins committed there, and because it was the place where continual fires were burning up the refuse and offal of the city.

Topheth, tō′-phĕth, same as Tophet. 2 Kn. 23. 10. *See* Moloch.

Torches. Nah. 2. 3; Zec. 12. 6; John 18. 3.

Tormah, tôr′-măh, 'privily.' Jud. 9. 31 (marg.).

Torment. Mat. 8. 29, to *t.* before the time.
Lu. 16. 23, being in *t.*
Heb. 11. 37, destitute, afflicted, *t.* R. V. evil entreated.
1 John 4. 18, fear hath *t.* R. V. punishment.
Rev. 9. 5, *t.* as *t.* of a scorpion.
14. 11, the smoke of their *t.*
See Mat. 4. 24; Mk. 5. 7; Lu. 8. 28.

Tormentor, a torturer, executioner. Mat. 18. 34.

Torn. Gen. 44. 28, surely he is *t.* in pieces.
Ezek. 4. 14, have not eaten of that which is *t.*
Hos. 6. 1, he hath *t.*, and he will heal us.
See Isa. 5. 25; Mal. 1. 13; Mk. 1. 26.

Torn beasts not to be eaten. Ex. 22. 31; Lev. 22. 8; Ezek. 4. 14; 44. 31.

Tortoise (Lev. 11. 29). R. V. Great lizard. *See* (3). Heb. *Tzâb:* Gk. *κροκόδειλος χερσαῖος*: Zool. S. (1) *Testudo ibera*, the land tortoise, found everywhere. (2) *Testudo Kleinmanni.* A larger kind of tortoise found on Mt. Carmel. (3) *Emys Caspica:* the 'great lizard' of the R. V. The animal referred to in Lev. 11. 29; green in colour, spotted with brown, with rows of strong spines around its tail; attains the length of two to two and a half feet.

Tortured. Heb. 11. 35.

Toss. Ps. 109. 23, I am *t.* up and down.
Isa. 22. 18, he will *t.* thee like a ball.
54. 11, afflicted, *t.* with tempest.
Eph. 4. 14, no more children, *t.* to and fro.
See Mat. 14. 24; Acts 27. 18; Jas. 1. 6.

Tou, tō′-ū, older form of Toi. 1 Chr. 18. 9.

Touch. Gen. 3. 3, nor *t.* it lest ye die.
1 Sam. 10. 26, a band whose hearts God had *t.*
1 Chr. 16. 22; Ps. 105. 15, *t.* not mine anointed.
Job 5. 19, there shall no evil *t.* thee.
6. 7, things my soul refused to *t.*
Isa. 6. 7, lo, this hath *t.* thy lips.
Jer. 1. 9, the Lord *t.* my mouth.
Zec. 2. 8, he that *t.* you, *t.* the apple of his eye.
Mat. 9. 21; Mk. 5. 28, if I may but *t.* his garment.
Mk. 10. 13; Lu. 18. 15, children, that he should *t.* them.
John 20. 17, *t.* me not.
2 Cor. 6. 17, *t.* not the unclean thing.
Col. 2. 21, *t.* not, taste not.
See Job 19. 21; Lu. 7. 14; 11. 46; 1 Cor. 7. 1.

Touching, concerning as touching = with regard to. Mat. 18. 19.

Touching Christ's garment. Mk. 5. 28; 6. 56; Lu. 6. 19.

Tow. Jud. 16. 9; Isa. 1. 31; 43. 17.

Towel. John 13. 4, 5, took a *t.* and girded himself.

Tower. 2 Sam. 22. 3; Ps. 18. 2; 144. 2, my high *t.*
Ps. 61. 3, a strong *t.* from the enemy.
Prov. 18. 10, the name of the Lord is a strong *t.*
Isa. 33. 18, where is he that counted the *t.*?
See Isa. 2. 15; 5. 2; Mic. 4. 8; Mat. 21. 33.

Tower: of Babel, Gen. 11. Penuel, Jud. 8. 17. Shechem, Jud. 9. 46. Siloam, Lu. 13. 4.

Town. Gen. 25. 16; 1 Sam. 16. 4; Mat. 10. 11; Mk. 8. 26; Lu. 5. 17; 9. 6; John 7. 42; 11. 1.

Townclerk. Acts 19. 35, *t.* had appeased the people.

Trachonitis, trăch-ō-nī′-tĭs, 'rugged district.' Lu. 3. 1.

Trade. Gen. 34. 10; 46. 32; Lu. 19. 15.

Traders in Tyre. Ezek. 27.

Tradition. Mat. 15. 2; Mk. 7. 3, thy disciples transgress the *t.*
Gal. 1. 14, zealous of the *t.* of my fathers.
Col. 2. 8, after the *t.* of men.
1 Pet. 1. 18, received by *t.* from your fathers.

Traffick. Gen. 42. 34; 1 Kn. 10. 15; Ezek. 17. 4.

Train. 1 Kn. 10. 2; Prov. 22. 6; Isa. 6. 1.

Traitor. Lu. 6. 16; 2 Tim. 3. 4.

Trample. Ps. 91. 13; Isa. 63. 3; Mat. 7. 6.

Trance: of Balaam, Num. 24. 4. Peter, Acts 10. 10; 11. 5. Paul, Acts 22. 17.

Tranquillity. Dan. 4. 27, lengthening of thy *t.*

Transferred. 1 Cor. 4. 6, in a figure *t.* to myself.

Transfiguration of Christ. Mat. 17.; Mk. 9. 2; Lu. 9. 29; John 1. 14; 2 Pet. 1. 16.

Transform. Rom. 12. 2, *t.* by the renewing.

Transformation of Satan and his ministers. 2 Cor. 11. 13, 15.

Transgress. Num. 14. 41, wherefore do ye *t.*?
1 Sam. 2. 24, make the Lord's people to *t.*
Neh. 1. 8, if ye *t.*, I will scatter you abroad. R. V. trespass.
Ps. 17. 3, my mouth shall not *t.*
Prov. 28. 21, for a piece of bread that man will *t.*
Jer. 2. 8, the pastors *t.*
3. 13, only acknowledge that thou hast *t.*
Hab. 2. 5, he *t.* by wine. R. V. wine is a treacherous dealer.
See Mat. 15. 2; Rom. 2. 27; 1 John 3. 4; 2 John 9.

Transgression. Ex. 34. 7; Num. 14. 18, forgiving *t.*
1 Chr. 10. 13, Saul died for his *t.* R. V. trespass.
Ez. 10. 6, he mourned because of their *t.* R. V. trespass.
Job 7. 21, why dost thou not pardon my *t.*?
13. 23, make me to know my *t.*
14. 17, my *t.* is sealed up.
31. 33, if I covered my *t.*
Ps. 19. 13, innocent from the great *t.*
25. 7, remember not my *t.*
32. 1, blessed is he whose *t.* is forgiven.
51. 1, blot out all my *t.*
65. 3, as for our *t.*, thou shalt purge them.
107. 17, fools because of their *t.* are afflicted.
Prov. 17. 9, he that covereth a *t.*
Isa. 43. 25; 44. 22, blotteth out thy *t.*
53. 5, he was wounded for our *t.*

Isa. 53. 8, for the *t.* of my people was he smitten.
58. 1, shew my people their *t.*
Ezek. 18. 22, his *t.* shall not be mentioned.
Mic. 1. 5, what is the *t.* of Jacob?
See Rom. 4. 15; 5. 14; 1 Tim. 2. 14; Heb. 2. 2.
Also under SIN.

Transgressor. Ps. 51. 13, teach *t.* thy ways.
59. 5, be not merciful to any wicked *t.*
Prov. 13. 15, the way of *t.* is hard. R. V. treacherous.
21. 18, the *t.* shall be ransom for the upright. R. V. treacherous.
Isa. 48. 8, thou wast called a *t.* from the womb.
53. 12; Mk. 15. 28; Lu. 22. 37, numbered with the *t.*
See Dan. 8. 23; Hos. 14. 9; Gal. 2. 18.

Translate, to transfer. 2 Sam. 3. 10; Col. 1. 13; Heb. 11. 5.

Translation: the removal of a person to heaven without death. of Enoch, Gen. 5. 24; Heb. 11. 5. of Elijah, 2 Kn. 2.

Transparent. Rev. 21. 21, streets as *t.* glass.

Trap. Job 18. 10; Ps. 69. 22; Jer. 5. 26; Rom. 11. 9.

Travail, labour, pain, also trouble. (*v.*). to be in pain, to be troubled. Ps. 7. 14, he *t.* with iniquity.
Isa. 23. 4, I *t.* not.
53. 11, the *t.* of his soul.
Rom. 8. 22, the whole creation *t.* in pain.
Gal. 4. 19, my children, of whom I *t.*
See Job 15. 20; Isa. 13. 8; Mic. 5. 3; Rev. 12. 2.

Travel. Eccl. 1. 13; 2. 23; 1 Thes. 2. 9; 2 Thes. 3. 8.

Traveller. Jud. 5. 6; 2 Sam. 12. 4; Job 31. 32.

Treacherous. Isa. 21. 2; Jer. 9. 2; Zep. 3. 4.

Treacherously. Isa. 33. 1, thou dealest *t.*
Jer. 12. 1, why are they happy that deal *t.*?
Lam. 1. 2, her friends have dealt *t.* with her.
See Hos. 5. 7; 6. 7; Mal. 2. 10, 15.

Treachery, instances of. Gen. 34. 13; Jud. 9.; 1 Sam. 21. 7; 22. 9 (Ps. 52.); 2 Sam. 3. 27; 11. 14; 16.; 20. 9; 1 Kn. 21. 5; 2 Kn. 10. 18; Esth. 3.; Mat. 26. 47; Mk. 14. 43; Lu. 22. 47; John 18. 3.

Tread. Deu. 11. 24, whereon soles of feet *t.*
25. 4; 1 Cor. 9. 9; 1 Tim. 5. 18, not muzzle the ox when he *t.*
Ps. 7. 5, let him *t.* down my life.
44. 5, through thy name will we *t.* them under.
60. 12; 108. 13, shall *t.* down our enemies.
91. 13, thou shalt *t.* upon lion and adder.
Isa. 10. 6, to *t.* them down like mire.
16. 10, shall *t.* out no wine.
63. 3, I will *t.* them in mine anger.
Jer. 48. 33, none shall *t.* with shouting.
Ezek. 34. 18, but ye must *t.* the residue.
Hos. 10. 11, loveth to *t.* out corn.
Mal. 4. 3, ye shall *t.* down the wicked.
See Job 9. 8; Isa. 41. 25; 63. 2; Rev. 19. 15.

Treason, instances of. 2 Sam. 15.–18.; 20.; 1 Kn. 1.; 16. 10; 2 Kn. 11.; 15. 10; 2 Chr. 22. 10; Esth. 2. 21.

Treasure. Gen. 43. 23, God hath given you *t.*
Ex. 19. 5; Ps. 135. 4, a peculiar *t.* to me.
Deu. 28. 12, open to thee his good *t.*
Job 3. 21; Ps. 17. 14; Prov. 2. 4, for hid *t.*
38. 22, the *t.* of the snow. R. V. treasuries.
Prov. 8. 21, I will fill *t.* of those that love me. R. V. treasuries.
10. 2, *t.* of wickedness profiteth nothing.
15. 16, than great *t.* and trouble therewith.
21. 20, there is a *t.* to be desired.
Eccl. 2. 8, I gathered the peculiar *t.* of kings.
Isa. 2. 7, neither is there any end of their *t.*
45. 3, I will give thee the *t.* of darkness.
Jer. 41. 8, slay us not, for we have *t.* R. V. stores hidden.
51. 13, waters abundant in *t.*
Dan. 11. 43, power over the *t.* of gold.
Mic. 6. 10, the *t.* of wickedness.
Mat. 6. 21; Lu. 12. 34, where your *t.* is.
12. 35, out of the good *t.* of the heart.
13. 44, like unto *t.* hid in a field.
Mat. 13. 52, out of his *t.* things new and old.
19. 21; Mk. 10. 21; Lu. 18. 22, thou shalt have *t.* in heaven.
Lu. 12. 21, that layeth up *t.* for himself.
2 Cor. 4. 7, we have this *t.* in earthen vessels.
Col. 2. 3, in whom are hid *t.* of wisdom.
Heb. 11. 26, greater riches than the *t.* in Egypt.
Jas. 5. 3, ye have heaped *t.*
See Deu. 32. 34; 33. 19; Isa. 33. 6; Mat. 2. 11.

Treasurer. Neh. 13. 13; Isa. 22. 15; Dan. 3. 2.

Treasury, the (Mk. 12. 41), in the temple consisted of alms-boxes with trumpet-shaped openings, in the Court of the Women.
Mk. 12. 41, the people cast money into the *t.*
Lu. 21. 1, rich men casting their gifts into the *t.*
See Jos. 6. 19; Jer. 38. 11; Mat. 27. 6.

Treatise. Acts 1. 1, the former *t.*

Tree. Deu. 20. 19, the *t.* is man's life.
Job 14. 7, there is hope of a *t.*
24. 20, wickedness shall be broken as a *t.*
Ps. 1. 3; Jer. 17. 8, like a *t.* planted.
104. 16, the *t.* of the Lord are full of sap.
Eccl. 11. 3, where the *t.* falleth.
Isa. 56. 3, I am a dry *t.*
61. 3, called *t.* of righteousness.
Ezek. 15. 2, what is the vine *t.* more than any *t.*?
31. 9, all the *t.* of Eden envied him.
See Mk. 8. 24; Rev. 7. 3.

Tree of life. Gen. 2. 9; 3. 22; Prov. 3. 18; 11. 30; Ezek. 47. 7, 12; Rev. 2. 7; 22. 2, 14.
of knowledge of good and evil. Gen. 2. 17; 3.

Trees, laws concerning. Lev. 19. 23; 27. 30; Deu. 20. 19.
Jotham's parable of the. Jud. 9. 8.
Nebuchadnezzar's vision. Dan. 4. 10.
figuratively mentioned. Num. 24. 6; 1 Chr. 16. 33; Ps. 1. (Jer. 17. 8); 92. 12; Eccl. 11. 3; S. of S. 2. 3; Isa. 41. 19; Ezek. 17. 24; 31. 5; Mat. 3. 10; 7. 17; 12. 33; Lu. 3. 9; 6. 43; 21. 29; Jude 12.

Tremble. Deu. 2. 25, the nations shall *t.*
Jud. 5. 4; 2 Sam. 22. 8; Ps. 18. 7; 77. 18; 97. 4, the earth *t.*
Ez. 9. 4, then assembled to me every one that *t.*
Job 9. 6, the pillars thereof *t.*
26. 11, the pillars of heaven *t.*
Ps. 2. 11, rejoice with *t.*
60. 2, thou hast made earth to *t.*
99. 1, the Lord reigneth, let the people *t.*
104. 32, he looketh on the earth, and it *t.*
Eccl. 12. 3, the keepers of the house shall *t.*
Isa. 14. 16, is this the man that made earth *t.*?
64. 2, that the nations may *t.* at thy presence.
66. 5, ye that *t.* at his word.
Jer. 5. 22, will ye not *t.* at my presence?
33. 9, they shall *t.* for all the goodness.
Am. 8. 8, shall not the land *t.* for this?
Acts 24. 25, Felix *t.* R. V. was terrified.
Jas. 2. 19, devils also believe, and *t.* R. V. shudder.
See Acts 9. 6; 16. 29; 1 Cor. 2. 3; Eph. 6. 5; Phil. 2. 12.

Trench. 1 Sam. 17. 20; 26. 5; 1 Kn. 18. 32; Lu. 19. 43.

Trespass, transgression, sin. Gen. 31. 36, what is my *t.*?
50. 17, we pray thee forgive the *t.* R. V. transgression.
Ez. 9. 2, rulers have been chief in this *t.*
Ps. 68. 21, goeth on still in his *t.* R. V. guiltiness.
Mat 6. 14, if ye forgive men their *t.*
18. 15, if thy brother *t.*, tell him his fault. R. V. sin.
Lu. 17. 3, if thy brother *t.* against thee. R. V. sin.
2 Cor. 5. 19, not imputing their *t.*
Eph. 2. 1, dead in *t.* and sins.
Col. 2. 13, having forgiven you all *t.*
See Num. 5. 6; 1 Kn. 8. 31; Ezek. 17. 20; 18. 24.

Trespass offerings, laws concerning. Lev. 5.; 6.; Num. 5.

Trial. Job 9. 23, the *t.* of the innocent.
2 Cor. 8. 2, a great *t.* of affliction. R. V. much [proof.
See Ezek. 21. 13; Heb. 11. 36; 1 Pet. 1. 7.

Trial of the heart, by God alone. Ps. 26. 2; 66. 10; Prov. 17. 3; Jer. 11. 20; 1 Thes. 2. 4.
of faith. Job 23. 10; Zec. 13. 9; Heb. 11. 17; Jas. 1. 3; 1 Pet. 4. 12; Rev. 3. 10. *See* TEMPTATION.
Tribes. Ps. 105. 37, not one feeble person among their *t.*
122. 4, whither the *t.* go up.
Isa. 19. 13, they that are the stay of the *t.*
49. 6, my servant to raise up the *t.*
Hab. 3. 9, according to oaths of the *t.*
Mat. 24. 30, then shall all *t.* of the earth mourn.
See Deu. 1. 13; 12. 5; 18. 5.
Tribes of Israel, blessed. Gen. 49.; Num. 23. 20; 24.; Deu. 33.
their order and numbering. Num. 1.; 2.; 10. 14; 26.; 2 Sam. 24.; 1 Chr. 21.
number of those sealed. Rev. 7. 4.
Tribulation. Deu. 4. 30, when thou art in *t.*
Jud. 10. 14, let them deliver you in *t.* R. V. distress.
Mat. 13. 21, when *t.* ariseth.
24. 21, then shall be great *t.*
John 16. 33, in the world ye shall have *t.*
Acts 14. 22, through much *t.*
Rom. 5. 3, we glory in *t.* also.
12. 12, patient in *t.*
See 2 Cor. 1. 4; 7. 4; Eph. 3. 13; 1 Thes. 3. 4; Rev. 7. 14.
Tributary. Deu. 20. 11; Jud. 1. 30; Lam. 1. 1.
Tribute was of two kinds: (1) The half-shekel, which every Jew, wherever resident, was expected to contribute for the maintenance of the temple (Mat. 17. 24). (2) The tax, custom, dues, &c., exacted from them by their Roman subjugators for the maintenance of the civil authorities (Mat. 22. 17). The former was, if possible (but not necessarily), paid in Jewish, the latter in Roman coin.
Gen. 49. 15, a servant to *t.* R. V. task-work.
Num. 31. 37, the Lord's *t.*
Deu. 16. 10, *t.* of freewill offering.
Ez. 7. 24, not lawful to impose *t.*
Neh. 5. 4, borrowed money for king's *t.*
Prov. 12. 24, the slothful shall be under *t.* R. V. task-work.
See Mat. 22. 21; Lu. 20. 25; Rom. 13. 6; 1 Pet. 2. 13.
Tribute paid by Christ. Mat. 17. 24.
Trim. 2 Sam. 19. 24; Jer. 2. 33; Mat. 25. 7.
Triumph. Ex. 15. 1, he hath *t.* gloriously.
Ps. 25. 2, let not mine enemies *t.*
92. 4, I will *t.* in the works of thy hands.
2 Cor. 2. 14, which always causeth us to *t.*
Col. 2. 15, a shew of them openly, *t.* over them.
See 2 Sam. 1. 20; Ps. 47. 1.
Triumph of wicked, short. Job 20. 5; Ps. 37. 10.
Troas, trō'-ăs, the district of Troy and a seaport in the district; visited by Paul. Acts 16. 8; 20. 5; 2 Cor. 2. 12; 2 Tim. 4. 13.
Trodden. Job 22. 15, the old way which wicked men have *t.*
Ps. 119. 118, thou hast *t.* down all that err. R. V. set at nought.
Isa. 5. 5, the vineyard shall be *t.* down.
63. 3, I have *t.* the winepress alone.
Mic. 7. 10, now shall she be *t.* as mire.
Mat. 5. 13, salt to be *t.* under foot.
Lu. 21. 24, Jerusalem shall be *t.* down.
Heb. 10. 29, hath *t.* under foot the Son of God.
See Deu. 1. 36; Jud. 5. 21; Isa. 18. 2.
Trode. 2 Kn. 14. 9; 2 Chr. 25. 18; Lu. 12. 1.
Trogyllium, trō-gȳl'-lĭ-ŭm. Acts 20. 15.
Troop. 2 Sam. 22. 30; Ps. 18. 29; Hos. 7. 1.
Trophimus, trŏph'-ĭ-mŭs, companion of Paul. Acts 20. 4; 21. 29; 2 Tim. 4. 20.
Trouble (*n.*). Deu. 31. 17, many *t.* shall befall.
1 Chr. 22. 14, in my *t.* I prepared for the house. R. V. affliction.
Neh. 9. 32, let not the *t.* seem little. R. V. travail.
Job 3. 26, yet *t.* came.
5. 6, neither doth *t.* spring out of the ground.
5. 7, man is born to *t.*
Job 5. 19, shall deliver thee in six *t.*
14. 1, of few days, and full of *t.*
30. 25, weep for him that was in *t.*
34. 29, he giveth quietness, who can make *t.*? R. V. condemn.
38. 23, I have reserved against the time of *t.*
Ps. 9. 9, a refuge in time of *t.*
22. 11, for *t.* is near.
25. 17, the *t.* of mine heart are enlarged.
25. 22, redeem Israel out of all his *t.*
27. 5, in time of *t.* he shall hide me.
46. 1, a very present help in *t.*
73. 5, they are not in *t.* as other men.
88. 3, my soul is full of *t.*
119. 143, *t.* and anguish have taken hold on me.
138. 7, though I walk in the midst of *t.*
Isa. 17. 14, at eveningtide *t.* R. V. behold terror.
30. 6, into the land of *t.* they will carry riches.
65. 16, because former *t.* are forgotten.
65. 23, they shall not bring forth for *t.* R. V. calamity.
Jer. 2. 27, in time of *t.* they will say, save us.
8. 15, we looked for health, and behold *t.* R. V. dismay.
1 Cor. 7. 28, such shall have *t.* in the flesh. R. V. tribulation.
2 Cor. 1. 4, able to comfort them in *t.* R. V. affliction.
See Prov. 15. 6; 25. 19; Jer. 11. 12; 30. 7; Lam. 1. 21.
Trouble (*v.*). Jos. 7. 25, why hast thou *t.* us?
1 Kn. 18. 17, art thou he that *t.* Israel?
18. 18, I have not *t.* Israel, but thou.
Job 4. 5, now it toucheth thee, and thou art *t.*
Ps. 3. 1, how are they increased that *t.* me! R. V. mine adversaries.
77. 4, I am so *t.* that I cannot speak.
Prov. 25. 26, is as a *t.* fountain.
Isa. 57. 20, the wicked are like the *t.* sea.
Dan. 5. 10, let not thy thoughts *t.* thee.
11. 44, tidings out of the north shall *t.* him.
Mat. 24. 6, see that ye be not *t.*
26. 10; Mk. 14. 6, why *t.* ye the woman?
John 5. 4, an angel *t.* the water. R. V. omits.
11. 33; 12. 27; 13. 21, Jesus groaned, and was *t.*
2 Cor. 4. 8; 7. 5, we are *t.* on every side. R. V. pressed.
Gal. 1. 7, there be some that *t.* you.
6. 17, let no man *t.* me.
See 2 Thes. 1. 7; 2. 2; Heb. 12. 15; 1 Pet. 3. 14.
Troubling. Job 3. 17; John 5. 4.
Trough. Gen. 24. 20; 30. 38; Ex. 2. 16.
Trow, think, imagine, suppose. Lu. 17. 9.
Truce. 2 Tim. 3. 3, men shall be *t.*-breakers. R. V. implacable.
True. Gen. 42. 11, we are *t.* men.
1 Kn. 22. 16, tell me nothing but that which is *t.*
2 Chr. 15. 3, Israel hath been without the *t.* God.
Neh. 9. 13, thou gavest them *t.* laws.
Ps. 119. 160, thy word is *t.* from the beginning.
Prov. 14. 25, a *t.* witness delivereth souls.
Jer. 10. 10, the Lord is the *t.* God.
Mat. 22. 16; Mk. 12. 14, we know that thou art *t.*
Lu. 16. 11, the *t.* riches.
John 1. 9, that was the *t.* light.
4. 23, when the *t.* worshippers.
5. 31, if I bear witness of myself, my witness is not *t.*
6. 32, the *t.* bread.
10. 41, all things that John spake were *t.*
15. 1, I am the *t.* vine.
17. 3; 1 John 5. 20, to know thee the only *t.* God.
2 Cor. 6. 8, as deceivers, and yet *t.*
Eph. 4. 24, created in *t.* holiness.
Phil. 4. 8, whatsoever things are *t.*
Heb. 10. 22, draw near with a *t.* heart.
See Rev. 3. 7; 6. 10; 15. 3; 16. 7; 19. 9, 11; 21. 5.
Trump = trumpet. 1 Cor. 15. 52; 1 Thes. 4. 16.
Trumpet. (1) (Lev. 23. 24; Jos. 6. 4). Heb. *Kéren*: Gk. κέρας, σάλπιγξ. The primitive trumpet, formed of a ram's horn.
(2) (Ex. 19. 16; Jos. 6. 4; Jud. 3. 27; 7. 16; 1 Sam. 13. 3; Ps. 47. 5; 81. 3; 98. 6; Joel 2. 1). Heb.

Shôphâr: Gk. κερατίνη, σάλπιγξ. A very long horn, *turned up* at the extremity. The national trumpet for rallying the people, and rousing political or religious enthusiasm. In 1 Chr. 15. 28, &c., it is rendered 'cornet,' as also in Ps. 98. 6, where in the version of the Book of Common Prayer it is rendered 'shawm.'

(3) (Num. 10. 2; 2 Kn. 11. 14; 1 Chr. 15. 28; 2 Chr. 5. 12; Ps. 98. 6; Hos. 5. 8). Heb. *Chătzôtzĕrah:* Gk. σάλπιγξ. A *straight* trumpet of silver, terminating in a bell-mouth. This was a sacred rather than a martial trumpet.

Trumpet, giving uncertain sound. 1 Cor. 14. 8.
the last. 1 Cor. 15. 52; 1 Thes. 4. 16.

Trumpets, their use. Num. 10.; Jos. 6. 4; Jud. 7. 16; Ps. 81. 3; Ezek. 7. 14; 33. 3; Joel 2. 1.
used in the temple. 1 Chr. 13. 8; 15. 24; 2 Chr. 5. 12; 29. 27; Ps. 98. 6.
feast of. Lev. 23. 24; Num. 29.
the seven. Rev. 8.; 9.; 11.

Trust. Job 13. 15, though he slay me, yet will I *t.* R. V. wait for.
39. 11, wilt thou *t.* him, because his strength is great?
Ps. 25. 2; 31. 6; 55. 23; 56. 3; 143. 8, I *t.* in thee.
37. 3; 40. 3; 62. 8; 115. 9; Prov. 3. 5; Isa. 26. 4, *t.* in the Lord.
118. 8, better to *t.* in the Lord.
144. 2, he in whom I *t.*
Prov. 28. 26, he that *t.* in his own heart is a fool.
Isa. 50. 10, let him *t.* in the name of the Lord.
Jer. 49. 11, let thy widows *t.* in me.
Mic. 7. 5, *t.* ye not in a friend.
Nah. 1. 7, the Lord knoweth them that *t.* in him.
Mat. 27. 43, he *t.* in God, let him deliver him.
Lu. 18. 9, certain which *t.* in themselves.

Trust in God. Ps. 4. 5; 34.; 37. 3; 40. 3, 4; 62. 8; 64. 10; 84. 12; 115. 9; 118. 8; Prov. 3. 5; 16. 20; Isa. 26. 4; 50. 10; 51. 5; Jer. 17. 7; 1 Tim. 4. 10.
exemplified. 1 Sam. 17. 45; 30. 6; 2 Kn. 18. 5; 2 Chr. 20. 12; Dan. 3. 28; 2 Tim. 1. 12; 4. 18.
blessings resulting from. Ps. 5. 11; 26. 1; 32. 10; 33. 21; 34. 8, 22; 37. 5, 40; 56. 11; 112. 7; 125.; Prov. 16. 20; 28. 25; 29. 25; Isa. 12. 2; 26. 3; 57. 13; Heb. 13. 6.

Trust in man, riches, vain. Job 31. 24; Ps. 20. 7; 33. 16; 44. 6; 49. 6; 52. 7; 62. 10; 118. 8; 146. 3; Prov. 11. 28; 28. 26; Isa. 30.; 31.; Jer. 7. 4; 9. 4; 17. 5; 46. 25; 49. 4; Ezek. 33. 13; Mk. 10. 24; 2 Cor. 1. 9; 1 Tim. 6. 17.

Truth. Deu. 32. 4, a God of *t.* R. V. faithfulness.
Ps. 15. 2, speaketh the *t.* in his heart.
51. 6, desirest *t.* in inward parts.
91. 4, his *t.* shall be thy shield.
117. 2, his *t.* endureth for ever.
119. 30, I have chosen the way of *t.* R. V. faithfulness.
Prov. 23. 23, buy the *t.*
Isa. 59. 14, *t.* is fallen in the streets.
Jer. 9. 3, they are not valiant for the *t.*
Zec. 8. 16, speak every man *t.* to his neighbour.
Mal. 2. 6, the law of *t.* was in his mouth.
John 1. 14, full of grace and *t.*
8. 32, know the *t.*, and the *t.* shall make you free.
14. 6, I am the way, the *t.*, and the life.
16. 13, Spirit of *t.* will guide you into all *t.*
18. 38, what is *t.*?
Rom. 1. 18, who hold the *t.* in unrighteousness.
1 Cor. 5. 8, unleavened bread of sincerity and *t.*
2 Cor. 13. 8, can do nothing against *t.*, but for the *t.*
Eph. 4. 15, speaking the *t.* in love.
1 Tim. 3. 15, the pillar and ground of *t.*
2 Tim. 2. 15, rightly dividing the word of *t.*
Jas. 5. 19, if any err from the *t.*
See 2 Tim. 3. 7; 1 John 3. 19; 5. 6.

Truth of God. Ex. 34. 6; Num. 23. 19; Deu. 32. 4; Ps. 19. 9; 25. 10; 33. 4; 57. 3, 10; 85. 10; 86. 15; 89. 14; 91. 4; 96. 13; 100. 5; 119. 160; 146. 6; Isa. 25. 1; 65. 16; Dan. 4. 37; Mic. 7. 20; John 17. 17; 2 Cor. 1. 20; Rev. 15. 3; 16. 7.
the, the Gospel. John 1. 17; 4. 24; 5. 33; 17. 17; 18. 37; Rom. 2. 8; 1 Cor. 13. 6; 2 Cor. 4. 2; Gal. 3. 1; Eph. 6. 14; 2 Thes. 2. 10; 1 Tim. 2. 7; 3. 15; 4. 3; 6. 5; 2 Tim. 3. 8; 4. 4; Tit. 1. 1; 1 Pet. 1. 22.
word of. Ps. 119. 43; 2 Cor. 6. 7; Eph. 1. 13; Col. 1. 5; 2 Tim. 2. 15; Jas. 1. 18. *See* SCRIPTURES, GOSPEL.

Truthfulness. Prov. 12. 17; Zec. 8. 16; Eph. 4. 25; 1 John 1. 8.

Try. 2 Chr. 32. 31, God left him, to *t.* him.
Job 23. 10, when he hath *t.* me.
Ps. 26. 2, *t.* my reins and my heart.
Jer. 9. 7; Zec. 13. 9, I will melt them and *t.* them.
1 Cor. 3. 13, shall *t.* every man's work. R. V. prove.
Jas. 1. 12, when *t.* he shall receive the crown. R. V. hath been approved.
1 John 4. 1, *t.* the spirits. R. V. prove.
See Prov. 17. 3; Isa. 28. 16; 1 Pet. 4. 12; Rev. 3. 18.

Tryphena, trȳ-phē'-nă, 'delicate.' Rom. 16. 12.

Tryphosa, trȳ-phō'-să, 'delicate.' Rom. 16. 12.

Tubal, tū'-băl, 'production' (?). (1) Gen. 10. 2.
(2) Isa. 66. 19; Ezek. 27. 13; 32. 26; 38.; 39.

Tubal-cain, tū'-băl-cain, 'producer of weapons' (?). Gen. 4. 22.

Tumults: under David, 2 Sam. 20. 1. Rehoboam, 1 Kn. 12. 16. against Christ, Mat. 27. 24. Paul, Acts 14. 5; 17. 5; 18. 12; 19. 24; 21. 27.

Turn. Job 23. 13, who can *t.* him?
Ps. 7. 12, if he *t.* not, he will whet his sword.
Prov. 1. 23, *t.* at my reproof.
Jer. 31. 18; Lam. 5. 21, *t.* thou me, and I shall be *t.*
Ezek. 14. 6; 18. 30; 33. 9; Hos. 12. 6; Joel 2. 12, repent, and *t.*
Zec. 9. 12, *t.* you to the strong hold, ye prisoners.
Mat. 5. 39, *t.* the other also.
Acts 26. 18, to *t.* them from darkness to light.
2 Tim. 3. 5, from such *t.* away.
See Prov. 21. 1; 26. 14; Hos. 7. 8; Lu. 22. 61; Jas. 1. 17.

Turtle, turtledove (Gen. 15. 9; Lev. 1. 14). Heb. *Tôr, Yônah:* Gk. τρυγών. (Specimens, *Turtur auritus*, found at Yebua; *Turtur risorius*, found at Jericho.) A species of pigeon. It abounds in Palestine, and was readily obtained by the poor.

Turtledove, used for offerings. Gen. 15. 9; Lev. 1. 14; 12. 6; Num. 6. 10; Lu. 2. 24.

Tutor, Gk. παιδαγωγός: the slave whose duty it was to conduct his master's children to school. Gal. 4. 2.

Twain, two. Isa. 6. 2; Mat. 5. 41; 19. 5; Eph. 2. 15.

Twelve, the, ordained. Mk. 3. 14.

Twice. Job 33. 14; Mk. 14. 30; Lu. 18. 12; Jude 12.

Twilight. 2 Kn. 7. 7; Job 3. 9; Prov. 7. 9.

Twinkling. 1 Cor. 15. 52, in the *t.* of an eye.

Two-edged. Ps. 149. 6; Prov. 5. 4; Heb. 4. 12; Rev. 1. 16.

Tychicus, tȳch'-ĭ-cŭs, 'fortuitous;' companion of Paul. Acts 20. 4; 2 Tim. 4. 12; Tit. 3. 12. commended. Eph. 6. 21; Col. 4. 7.

Types of Christ. *See* CHRIST.

Tyrannus, tȳ-răn'-nŭs, 'tyrant;' a philosopher at Ephesus whose lecture-room was used by St. Paul. Acts 19. 9.

Tyranny, instances of. Ex. 1.; 5.; 1 Sam. 22. 9; 1 Kn. 12. 4; 21.; Jer. 26. 20; Mat. 2.; Acts 12.

Tyre, tȳre (*Tsor*, 'the rock'). An ancient Phœnician city, on the Mediterranean. Its marvellous wealth and commerce are described by Ezekiel (27.), and its destruction by Nebuchadnezzar foretold (Ezek. 26. 7), which happened after thirteen years' siege. Our Lord once visited this neighbourhood (Mat. 15. 21), and St. Paul landed at its port (Acts 21. 3).

Tyrus, tȳ'-rŭs, Latin name of TYRE. Jer. 25. 22.

Ucal, ū'-căl. Prov. 30. 1.

Uel, ū'-ĕl, 'will of God.' Ez. 10. 34.

Uknaz, ŭk'-năz, and KENAZ. 1 Chr. 4. 15 (marg.).

Ulai, ū'-lāi. Dan. 8. 2.

Ulam, ū'-lăm, 'foremost' (?). 1 Chr. 7. 16.

Ulla, ŭl'-lă, 'yoke.' 1 Chr. 7. 39.

Ummah, ŭm'-măh, 'community.' Jos. 19. 30.

Unadvisedly. Ps. 106. 33, he spake *u.*
Unawares. Lu. 21. 34; Gal. 2. 4; Heb. 13. 2; Jude 4.
Unbelief. Mk. 9. 24, help thou mine *u.*
Rom. 3. 3, shall *u.* make faith without effect? R. V. want of faith.
11. 32, concluded all in *u.* R. V. unto disobedience.
Heb. 3. 12, evil heart of *u.*
See Mk. 6. 6; 1 Tim. 1. 13.
Unbelief, sin. John 16. 9; Rom. 11. 32; Tit. 1. 15; 1 John 5. 10.
its source. Mk. 16. 14; Lu. 8. 12; 24. 25; John 5. 38; 8. 45; 10. 26; 12. 39; Acts 19. 9; 2 Cor. 4. 4; Eph. 2. 2; 2 Thes. 2. 12; Heb. 3. 12.
the world condemned for. John 3. 18; 5. 24.
its effects. 1 Kn. 17. 18; 2 Kn. 7. 2; Ps. 78. 19; 106. 24; Isa. 53. 1; Mat. 24. 11; John 12. 37; 16. 9; Acts 14. 2; 19. 9; Heb. 3. 12.
deprecated. Mat. 17. 17; John 20. 27, 29; Heb. 3. 12; 4. 11.
instances of. Gen. 3. 4; Num. 13.; 14.; 20. 12; Deu. 9. 23; 2 Kn. 7. 2, 17; Ps. 78.; 106.; Mat. 13. 58; Lu. 1. 20; 22. 67; John 5. 38; 7. 5; 12. 37; 20. 25; Acts 14. 2; 17. 5; Rom. 3. 3; 11. 20; Heb. 3. 19.
Unbelievers. Rom. 16. 17; 2 Cor. 6. 14; Phil. 3. 2; 1 Tim. 6. 5.
fate of. Mk. 16. 16; John 3. 18; 8. 24; Rom. 11. 20; Eph. 5. 6; 2 Thes. 2. 12; Heb. 3. 19; 4. 11; 11. 6; Jas. 5.; 2 Pet. 2.; 3.; Jude 5; Rev. 21. 8.
Unblameable. Col. 1. 22; 1 Thes. 3. 13.
Uncertain. 1 Cor. 9. 26; 14. 8; 1 Tim. 6. 17.
Unchangeable. Heb. 7. 24, an *u.* priesthood.
Uncircumcised. Gen. 17. 14; Ex. 6. 12; 12. 48; 1 Sam. 31. 4; 2 Sam. 1. 20; Ezek. 44. 7; Acts 7. 51.
Uncle. Lev. 25. 49; Esth. 2. 7; Am. 6. 10.
Unclean. Acts 10. 28; Rom. 14. 14; 2 Cor. 6. 17.
Uncleanness. Lev. 5.; 7.; 11.; 12.; 15.; 22.; Num. 5.; 19.; Deu. 23. 10; 24. 1.
typical of sin. Zec. 13. 1; Mat. 23. 27.
Unclean spirits. Mat. 10. 1; 12. 43, 45; Acts 5. 16; Rev. 16. 13.
animals. Lev. 11.; 20. 25; Deu. 14. 3.
Unclothed. 2 Cor. 5. 4, not that we would be *u.*
Uncomely. 1 Cor. 7. 36; 12. 23.
Uncondemned. Acts 16. 37; 22. 25.
Uncorruptible. Rom. 1. 23, glory of the *u.*
Uncorruptness. Tit. 2. 7, in doctrine shewing *u.*
Unction. 1 John 2. 20, an *u.* from the Holy One. R. V. anointing.
Undefiled. Ps. 119. 1, blessed are the *u.* R. V. they that are perfect.
Jas. 1. 27, pure religion and *u.*
1 Pet. 1. 4, an inheritance *u.*
See S. of S. 5. 2; 6. 9; Heb. 7. 26; 13. 4.
Under. Rom. 3. 9; 1 Cor. 9. 27; Gal. 3. 10.
Undergird (Acts 27. 17). The device of passing ropes or chains around a vessel, when the ship was strained by a storm pressing against the great sails.
Undersetters, pedestals, support. 1 Kn. 7. 30, 34.
Understand. Ps. 19. 12, who can *u.* his errors? R. V. discern.
73. 17, then *u.* I their end. R. V. considered.
119. 100, I *u.* more than the ancients.
139. 2, thou *u.* my thought afar off.
Prov. 8. 9, all plain to him that *u.*
20. 24, how can a man *u.* his own way?
29. 19, though he *u.* he will not answer.
Isa. 6. 9, hear ye indeed, but *u.* not.
28. 19, a vexation only to *u.* the report.
Jer. 9. 24, let him glory in this, that he *u.* me.
Dan. 10. 12, thou didst set thine heart to *u.*
12. 10, wicked shall not *u.*, the wise shall *u.*
Hos. 14. 9, who is wise, and he shall *u.* these things?
Mat. 13. 51, have ye *u.* all these things?
24. 15, whoso readeth, let him *u.*
Lu. 24. 45, that they might *u.* the scriptures.
John 8. 43, why do ye not *u.* my speech?
Rom. 3. 11, there is none that *u.*
15. 21, they that have not heard shall *u.*
1 Cor. 13. 2, though I *u.* all mysteries. R. V. know.
13. 11, I *u.* as a child. R. V. felt.
See 1 Cor. 14. 2; Heb. 11. 3; 2 Pet. 2. 12; 3. 16.
Understanding. Ex. 31. 3; Deu. 4. 6, wisdom and *u.*
1 Kn. 3. 11, hast asked for thyself *u.*
4. 29, gave Solomon wisdom and *u.*
7. 14, filled with wisdom and *u.*
1 Chr. 12. 32, men that had *u.* of the times.
2 Chr. 26. 5, had *u.* in visions.
Job 12. 13, he hath counsel and *u.*
12. 20, he taketh away the *u.* of the aged.
17. 4, thou hast hid their heart from *u.*
28. 12, where is the place of *u.*?
32. 8, the Almighty giveth them *u.*
38. 36, who hath given *u.* to the heart?
39. 17, neither imparted to her *u.*
Ps. 47. 7, sing ye praises with *u.*
49. 3, the meditation of my heart shall be of *u.*
119. 34, 73, 125, 144, 169, give me *u.*
119. 99, I have more *u.* than my teachers.
119. 104, through thy precepts I get *u.*
147. 5, his *u.* is infinite.
Prov. 2. 2, apply thine heart to *u.*
2. 11, *u.* shall keep thee.
3. 5, lean not to thine own *u.*
3. 19, by *u.* hath he established the heavens.
4. 5, 7, get wisdom, get *u.*
8. 1, doth not *u.* put forth her voice?
9. 6, go in the way of *u.*
9. 10, the knowledge of the holy is *u.*
14. 29, he that is slow to wrath is of great *u.*
16. 22, *u.* is a wellspring of life.
17. 24, wisdom is before him that hath *u.*
19. 8, he that keepeth *u.* shall find good.
21. 30, there is no *u.* against the Lord.
24. 3, by *u.* an house is established.
30. 2, have not the *u.* of a man.
Eccl. 9. 11, nor yet riches to men of *u.*
Isa. 11. 2, the spirit of *u.* shall rest on him.
27. 11, it is a people of no *u.*
29. 14, the *u.* of prudent men shall be hid.
40. 14, who shewed him the way of *u.*?
40. 28, there is no searching of his *u.*
Jer. 3. 15, pastors shall feed you with *u.*
Ezek. 28. 4, with thy *u.* thou hast gotten riches.
Dan. 4. 34, mine *u.* returned.
Mat. 15. 16; Mk. 7. 18, are ye also without *u.*?
Mk. 12. 33, to love him with all the *u.*
Lu. 2. 47, astonished at his *u.*
24. 45, then opened he their *u.*
1 Cor. 1. 19, bring to nothing *u.* of prudent.
14. 15, I will pray with the *u.* also.
14. 20, be not children in *u.* R. V. mind.
Eph. 4. 18, having the *u.* darkened.
Phil. 4. 7, peace of God, which passeth all *u.*
See Col. 1. 9; 2. 2; 2 Tim. 2. 7; 1 John 5. 20.
Undertake. Isa. 38. 14, *u.* for me. R. V. be thou my surety.
Undone. Jos. 11. 15; Isa. 6. 5; Mat. 23. 23; Lu. 11. 42.
Unequal. (1) unjust. Ezek. 18. 25, 29. (2) 2 Cor. 6. 14.
Unfaithful. Ps. 78. 57; Prov. 25. 19.
Unfeigned. 2 Cor. 6. 6; 1 Tim. 1. 5; 2 Tim. 1. 5; 1 Pet. 1. 22.
Unfruitful. Mat. 13. 22; Eph. 5. 11; Tit. 3. 14; 2 Pet. 1. 8.
Ungirded. Gen. 24. 32, he *u.* his camels.
Ungodliness. Rom. 1. 18; 11. 26; 2 Tim. 2. 16; Tit. 2. 12.
Ungodly. 2 Chr. 19. 2, shouldest thou help the *u.*? R. V. wicked.
Job 16. 11, God hath delivered me to the *u.*
Ps. 1. 1, counsel of *u.* R. V. wicked.
1. 6, the way of the *u.* shall perish. R. V. [wicked.
43. 1, plead my cause against an *u.* nation.
Prov. 16. 27, an *u.* man diggeth up evil. R. V. worthless.

Rom. 5. 6, Christ died for the *u*.
1 Pet. 4. 18, where shall the *u*. appear?
2 Pet. 3. 7, perdition of *u*. men.
See Rom. 4. 5; 1 Tim. 1. 9; 2 Pet. 2. 5; Jude 15.

Unholy. Lev. 10. 10; 1 Tim. 1. 9; 2 Tim. 3. 2; Heb. 10. 29.

Unicorn. (1) any one-horned animal, as the rhinoceros. Isa. 34. 7, marg.
(2) (Job 39. 9–12). Heb. *Rĕēm:* Gk. μονοκέρως: R. V. 'wild-ox;' marg. 'ox-antelope.' The Greek in Num. 23. 22 is ἁδροί. The translation 'unicorn' is erroneous, as the mention of *two* horns on one *rĕēm* (Deu. 33. 17) proves. It was a very strong wild-ox, untameable, having two tall horns, with which it gored. It is distinct from oxen and bulls, and is used figuratively for 'prince' or 'chieftain' (Isa. 34. 7).
Num. 23. 22, he hath as it were the strength of an *u*.
Deu. 33. 17, his horns are like the horns of an *u*.
Job 39. 9, will the *u*. be willing to serve thee?
Isa. 34. 7, the *u*. shall come down with them.

Union in worship and prayer. Ps. 34. 3; 55. 14; 122.; Rom. 15. 30; 2 Cor. 1. 11; Eph. 6. 18; Col. 1. 3; 3. 16; Heb. 10. 25.

Unite. Gen. 49. 6; Ps. 86. 11.

Unity of the Church. John 10. 16; Rom. 12. 5; 1 Cor. 10. 17; 12. 13; Gal. 3. 28; Eph. 1. 10; 2. 19; 4. 4; 5. 23, 30.
of brethren. Ps. 133.; John 17. 21; Acts 2. 42.
enforced. Ps. 133.; Rom. 12. 16; 15. 5; 1 Cor. 1. 10; 2 Cor. 13. 11; Eph. 4. 3; Phil. 1. 27; 2. 2; 1 Pet. 3. 8.

Unjust. Ps. 43. 1; Prov. 11. 7; 29. 27, *u*. man.
Prov. 28. 8, he that by *u*. gain. R. V. increase.
Zep. 3. 5, the *u*. knoweth no shame.
Mat. 5. 45, he sendeth rain on the just and *u*.
Lu. 18. 6, hear what the *u*. judge saith. R. V. unrighteous.
18. 11, not as other men, *u*.
Acts 24. 15, a resurrection both of the just and *u*.
1 Cor. 6. 1, go to law before the *u*. R. V. unrighteous.
1 Pet. 3. 18, suffered, the just for the *u*. R. V. unrighteous.
Rev. 22. 11, he that is *u*., let him be *u*. still. R. V. unrighteous, . . . do unrighteousness.
See Ps. 82. 2; Isa. 26. 10; Lu. 16. 8; 2 Pet. 2. 9.

Unknown. Acts 17. 23; 1 Cor. 14. 2; 2 Cor. 6. 9; Gal. 1. 22.

Unlade. Acts 21. 3, the ship was to *u*.

Unlawful. Acts 10. 28; 2 Pet. 2. 8.

Unlearned. Acts 4. 13; 1 Cor. 14. 16; 2 Tim. 2. 23; 2 Pet. 3. 16.

Unleavened bread. Ex. 12. 39; 13. 7; 23. 18; Lev. 2. 4; 7. 12; 8. 26; Num. 6. 19 (1 Cor. 5. 7).

Unloose. Mk. 1. 7; Lu. 3. 16.

Unmarried (virgins), Paul's exhortation to. 1 Cor. 7. 8, 11, 25, 32.

Unmindful. Deu. 32. 18, thou art *u*.

Unmoveable. Acts 27. 41; 1 Cor. 15. 58.

Unni, ŭn′-nī, 'depressed.' 1 Chr. 15. 18.

Unoccupied. Jud. 5. 6, the highways were *u*.

Unperfect. Ps. 139. 16, yet being *u*. R. V. unformed.

Unprepared. 2 Cor. 9. 4, find you *u*.

Unprofitable. Job 15. 3, *u*. talk.
Mat. 25. 30; Lu. 17. 10, *u*. servant. [18; 13. 17.
See Rom. 3. 12; Tit. 3. 9; Philem. 11; Heb. 7.

Unpunished. Prov. 11. 21; 16. 5; 17. 5; 19. 5; Jer. 25. 29; 49. 12, shall not be *u*.
See Jer. 30. 11; 46. 28.

Unquenchable. Mat. 3. 12; Lu. 3. 17.

Unreasonable. Acts 25. 27; 2 Thes. 3. 2.

Unreproveable. Col. 1. 22, *u*. in his sight.

Unrighteous. Ex. 23. 1, an *u*. witness.
Isa. 10. 1, decree *u*. decrees.
55. 7, let the *u*. man forsake his thoughts.
Rom. 3. 5, is God *u*.?
Heb. 6. 10, God is not *u*. to forget your work.
See Deu. 25. 16; Ps. 71. 4; Lu. 16. 11; 1 Cor. 6. 9.

Unrighteousness. Lu. 16. 9, mammon of *u*.
Rom. 1. 18, hold the truth in *u*.
2. 8, to them that obey *u*.
3. 5, if our *u*. commend righteousness.
6. 13, instruments of *u*.
9. 14, is there *u*. with God? [iniquity.
2 Cor. 6. 14, what fellowship with *u*.? R. V.
2 Thes. 2. 12, had pleasure in *u*.
2 Pet. 2. 13, receive the reward of *u*. R. V. wrong-doing.
1 John 1. 9, cleanse us from all *u*.
5. 17, all *u*. is sin.
See Lev. 19. 15; Ps. 92. 15; Jer. 22. 13; John 7. 18.

Unripe. Job 15. 33, *u*. grape.

Unruly. 1 Thes. 5. 14; Tit. 1. 6; Jas. 3. 8.

Unsavoury. (1) Job 6. 6, can that which is *u*. be eaten?
(2) without savour; foolish. 2 Sam. 22. 27. R. V. froward.

Unsearchable. Job 5. 9; Ps. 145. 3; Rom. 11. 33; Eph. 3. 8.

Unseemly. Rom. 1. 27; 1 Cor. 13. 5.

Unskilful. Heb. 5. 13, is *u*. in the word. R. V. without experience of.

Unspeakable. 2 Cor. 9. 15; 12. 4; 1 Pet. 1. 8.

Unspotted. Jas. 1. 27, *u*. from the world.

Unstable. Gen. 49. 4; Jas. 1. 8; 2 Pet. 2. 14.

Unstopped. Isa. 35. 5, ears of the deaf *u*.

Untempered. Ezek. 13. 10, 11, 14.

Unthankful. Lu. 6. 35; 2 Tim. 3. 2.

Untimely. Ps. 58. 8; Rev. 6. 13. [crooked.

Untoward, obstinate, perverse. Acts 2. 40. R. V.

Unwalled. Deu. 3. 5; Esth. 9. 19; Ezek. 38. 11.

Unwashen. Mat. 15. 20; Mk. 7. 2, 5. [Eph. 5. 17.

Unwise. Deu. 32. 6; Hos. 13. 13; Rom. 1. 14;

Unwittingly, unconsciously, unintentionally. Lev. 22. 14; Josh. 20. 3, 5.

Unworthy. Acts 13. 46; 1 Cor. 6. 2; 11. 27.

Upbraid. Mat. 11. 20; Mk. 16. 14; Jas. 1. 5.

Upharsin, ū-phär′-sĭn, 'and dividers.' Dan. 5. 25.

Uphaz, ū′-phăz. Jer. 10. 9; Dan. 10. 5.

Uphold. Ps. 51. 12, *u*. me with thy free spirit.
54. 4, with them that *u*. my soul.
119. 116, *u*. me according to thy word.
145. 14, the Lord *u*. all that fall.
Isa. 41. 10, I will *u*. thee with right hand.
42. 1, my servant, whom I *u*.
63. 5, wondered there was none to *u*.
Heb. 1. 3, *u*. all things by the word of his power.
See Ps. 37. 17; 41. 12; 63. 8; Prov. 20. 28.

Uppermost. Matt. 23. 6; Mk. 12. 39; Lu. 11. 43.

Upright. Job 12. 4, the *u*. man is laughed to scorn. R. V. perfect.
17. 8, *u*. men shall be astonied.
Ps. 19. 13, then shall I be *u*. R. V. perfect.
25. 8; 92. 15, good and *u*. is the Lord.
37. 14, such as be of *u*. conversation.
49. 14, the *u*. shall have dominion.
111. 1, the assembly of the *u*.
112. 4, to the *u*. ariseth light.
125. 4, that are *u*. in their hearts.
Prov. 2. 21, the *u*. shall dwell in the land.
11. 3, the integrity of the *u*. [fect.
11. 20, such as are *u*. in their way. R. V. per-
14. 11, the tabernacle of the *u*.
15. 8, the prayer of the *u*. is his delight.
28. 10, the *u*. shall have good things.
Eccl. 7. 29, God hath made man *u*. [they.
S. of S. 1. 4, the *u*. love thee. R. V. rightly do
See Isa. 26. 7; Jer. 10. 5; Mic. 7. 2; Hab. 2. 4.

Uprightly. Ps. 58. 1; 75. 2, do ye judge *u*.?
84. 11, withhold no good from them that walk *u*.
Prov. 10. 9; 15. 21; 28. 18, he that walketh *u*.
Isa. 33. 15, he that speaketh *u*.
See Ps. 15. 2; Am. 5. 10; Mic. 2. 7; Gal. 2. 14.

Uprightness. 1 Kn. 3. 6, in *u*. of heart.
1 Chr. 29. 17, thou hast pleasure in *u*.
Job 4. 6, the *u*. of thy ways. R. V. integrity.
33. 23, to shew unto man his *u*. R. V. what is right for him.
Ps. 25. 21, let *u*. preserve me.
143. 10, lead me into the land of *u*.

Prov. 2. 13, who leave the paths of *u*.
See Ps. 111. 8; Prov. 14. 2; 28. 6; Isa. 26. 7, 10.
Uprising. Ps. 139. 2, thou knowest mine *u*.
Uproar. Mat. 26. 5; Mk. 14. 2; Acts 17. 5; 21. 31.
Upside. 2 Kn. 21. 13; Ps. 146. 9; Acts 17. 6.
Upward. Job 5. 7; Eccl. 3. 21; Isa. 38. 14.
Ur, ûr, 'flame;' land of. Gen. 11. 28; 15. 7.
Urbane, ûr'-bāne, 'pleasant.' Rom. 16. 9.
Urge. Gen. 33. 11; 2 Kn. 2. 17; Lu. 11. 53.
Urgent. Ex. 12. 33; Dan. 3. 22.
Uri, ū'-rī, 'fiery.' Ex. 31. 2.
Uriah, ū-rī'-ăh, 'Jehovah is my light.' (1) the Hittite. 2 Sam. 11.; 1 Kn. 15. 5. (2) Ez. 8. 33. (3) Isa. 8. 2.
Urias, ū-rī'-ăs, Greek form of URIAH. Mat. 1. 6. R. V. Uriah.
Uriel, ū'-rĭ-ĕl, 'God is my light.' 1 Chr. 6. 24.
Urijah, ū-rī'-jăh, same as URIAH. (1) priest. 2 Kn. 16. 10, 16.
(2) prophet. Jer. 26. 20.
(3) priest. Neh. 8. 4. R. V. Uriah.
Urim, ū'-rĭm, **and Thummim,** 'Lights and Perfections.' Ex. 28. 30; Lev. 8. 8. Sacred symbols worn upon the breastplate of the high priest, 'upon his heart,' by which God gave oracular responses for the guidance of His people in temporal matters. What they were is unknown.
Use. Mat. 6. 7, *u*. not vain repetitions.
1 Cor. 7. 31, they that *u*. this world.
Gal. 5. 13, *u*. not liberty for an occasion.
1 Tim. 1. 8, if a man *u*. it lawfully.
See Ps. 119. 132; 1 Cor. 9. 12; 1 Tim. 5. 23.
Usurp. 1 Tim. 2. 12, I suffer not a woman to *u*. R. V. have dominion.
Usury. Ex. 22. 25, neither shalt thou lay upon him *u*.
Lev. 25. 36, take thou no *u*. of him.
Deu. 23. 20, thou mayest lend upon *u*.
Neh. 5. 7, ye exact *u*.
Ezek. 18. 8, not given forth upon *u*.
18. 13, hath given forth upon *u*.
18. 17, that hath not received *u*.
22. 12, thou hast taken *u*.
Uthai, ū'-thăī, 'helpful.' 1 Chr. 9. 4.
Utter. Ps. 78. 2, I will *u*. dark sayings.
106. 2, who can *u*. the mighty acts?
119. 171, my lips shall *u*. praise.
Prov. 1. 20, wisdom *u*. her voice.
23. 33, thine heart shall *u*. perverse things.
29. 11, a fool *u*. all his mind.
Eccl. 5. 2, let not thine heart be hasty to *u*.
Rom. 8. 26, which cannot be *u*.
2 Cor. 12. 4, not lawful for a man to *u*.
Heb. 5. 11, many things hard to be *u*. R. V. of interpretation.
See Job 33. 3; Isa. 48. 20; Joel 2. 11; Mat. 13. 35.
Utterance. Acts 2. 4, as the Spirit gave *u*.
See 1 Cor. 1. 5; 2 Cor. 8. 7; Eph. 6. 19; Col. 4. 3.
Utterly. Ps. 119. 8, forsake me not *u*.
Jer. 23. 39, I will *u*. forget you.
Zep. 1. 2, I will *u*. consume all things.
2 Pet. 2. 12, these shall *u*. perish. R. V. surely.
See Deu. 7. 2; Neh. 9. 31; Isa. 40. 30; Rev. 18. 8.
Uttermost, last. Mat. 5. 26; 1 Thes. 2. 16; Heb. 7. 25.
Uz, ŭz, 'fertile.' (1) Gen. 10. 23. (2) Gen. 36. 28. (3) Job 1. 1; Jer. 25. 20; Lam. 4. 21.
Uzai, ū'-zăī. Neh. 3. 25.
Uzal, ū'-zăl, 'wanderer.' Gen. 10. 27.
Uzza, ŭz'-ză, 'strength.' 2 Kn. 21. 18.
Uzzah, ŭz'-zăh, another form of UZZA; his trespass. 2 Sam. 6. 3.
his death. 1 Chr. 13. 7.
Uzzen-sherah, ŭz'-zĕn-shē'-răh, 'portion of Sherah.' 1 Chr. 7. 24.
Uzzi, ŭz'-zī, shortened form of UZZIAH. 1 Chr. 6. 5.
Uzzia, ŭz-zī'-ă, another form of UZZIAH. 1 Chr. 11. 44.
Uzziah, ŭz-zī'-ăh, 'Jehovah is my strength.' (1) 2 Kn. 15. 13. *See* AZARIAH.
(2) 1 Chr. 27. 25.
Uzziel, ŭz'-zī-ĕl, 'power of God.' Ex. 6. 18.
Uzzielites, ŭz-zī-ē'-lītes, descendants of Uzziel. Num. 3. 27.

Vagabond. Gen. 4. 12, a *v*. shalt thou be in the earth. R. V. wanderer.
See Ps. 109. 10; Acts 19. 13.
Vail. Mat. 27. 51; 2 Cor. 3. 14; Heb. 6. 19.
Vain. Ex. 5. 9, not regard *v*. words. R. V. lying.
20. 7; Deu. 5. 11, shalt not take name of the Lord in *v*.
Deu. 32. 47, it is not a *v*. thing for you.
2 Sam. 6. 20, as one of the *v*. fellows.
2 Kn. 18. 20; Isa. 36. 5, they are but *v*. words.
Job 11. 12, *v*. man would be wise.
16. 3, shall *v*. words have an end?
21. 34, how then comfort ye me in *v*.?
Ps. 2. 1; Acts 4. 25, the people imagine a *v*. thing.
26. 4, I have not sat with *v*. persons.
33. 17, an horse is a *v*. thing for safety.
39. 6, every man walketh in a *v*. shew.
60. 11; 108. 12, *v*. is the help of man.
89. 47, wherefore hast thou made men in *v*.? R. V. for what vanity.
127. 1, labour in *v*., the watchman waketh in *v*.
Prov. 12. 11; 28. 19, followeth *v*. persons.
31. 30, beauty is *v*.
Eccl. 6. 12, all the days of his *v*. life.
Isa. 1. 13, bring no more *v*. oblations.
45. 18, he created it not in *v*. R. V. a waste.
45. 19, I said not, seek ye me in *v*.
49. 4; 65. 23, laboured in *v*. R. V. vanity.
Jer. 3. 23, in *v*. is salvation hoped for.
10. 3. the customs of the people are *v*. R. V. [vanity.
46. 11, in *v*. shalt thou use medicines.
Mal. 3. 14, ye have said, it is *v*. to serve God.
Mat. 6. 7, use not *v*. repetitions.
15. 9; Mk. 7. 7, in *v*. do they worship me.
Rom. 13. 4, he beareth not the sword in *v*.
1 Cor. 15. 2, unless ye have believed in *v*.
2 Cor. 6. 1, receive not the grace of God in *v*.
Gal. 2. 2, lest I should run in *v*.
Tit. 1. 10, unruly and *v*. talkers.
Jas. 1. 26, this man's religion is *v*.
1 Pet. 1. 18, redeemed from *v*. conversation.
See Prov. 1. 17; Rom. 1. 21; Gal. 5. 26; Phil. 2. 3.
Vainglory. Gal. 5. 26; Phil. 2. 3.
Vajezatha, vă-jĕz'-ă-thă, 'strong as the wind' (?). Esth. 9. 9.
Vale. Deu. 1. 7; 1 Kn. 10. 23; Jer. 33. 13.
Valiant. 1 Sam. 18. 17, be *v*. for me.
1 Kn. 1. 42, for thou art a *v*. man. R. V. worthy.
Isa. 10. 13, put down inhabitants like a *v*. man.
Jer. 9. 3, not *v*. for truth. R. V. grown strong.
Heb. 11. 34, waxed *v*. in fight. R. V. mighty in war.
See Ps. 60. 12; 118. 15; Isa. 33. 7; Nah. 2. 3.
Valley. Jos. 8. 13; 12. 8; 18. 31; 1 Sam. 17. 3; 17. 19; Ps. 23. 4; 65. 13; 84. 6; Isa. 22. 1; 28. 1; 40. 4; Jer. 21. 13; Ezek. 37. 1; Joel 3. 14; Lu. 3. 5.
Valour. Jos. 1. 14; 10. 7; Jud. 6. 12.
Value. Job 13. 4, physicians of no *v*.
Mat. 10. 31; Lu. 12. 7, of more *v*.
See Lev. 27. 16; Job 28. 16; Mat. 27. 9.
Vaniah, vă-nī'-ăh, 'distress' (?). Ez. 10. 36.
Vanish. Isa. 51. 6; 1 Cor. 13. 8; Heb. 8. 13.
Vanity. Job 7. 3, to possess months of *v*.
15. 31, *v*. shall be his recompence.
35. 13, God will not hear *v*.
Ps. 12. 2, speak *v*. every one with his neighbour.
39. 5, every man at his best state is *v*.
62. 9, are *v*. lighter than *v*.
144. 4, man is like to *v*.
Prov. 13. 11, wealth gotten by *v*.
30. 8, remove from me *v*.
Eccl. 6. 11, many things increase *v*.
11. 10, childhood and youth are *v*.
Isa. 30. 28, with the sieve of *v*.
Jer. 18. 15, they have burned incense to *v*.
Hab. 2. 13, people shall weary themselves for *v*.
Rom. 8. 20, the creature was made subject to *v*.
Eph. 4. 17, walk in *v*. of mind.
2 Pet. 2. 18, great swelling words of *v*.

Vanity of worldly things. Ps. 39. 5, 11; 49.; 90.; Eccl. 1.; Isa. 40. 17, 23.
of idolatry. Deu. 32. 21; 2 Kn. 17. 15; Jer. 10. 8; 14. 22; 18. 15; Acts 14. 15.
Vapours. Job 36. 27, according to the *v.* thereof.
Ps. 135. 7; Jer. 10. 13, he causeth the *v.* to ascend.
148. 8, snow and *v.*
Variableness. Jas. 1. 17, with whom is no *v.* R. V. variation.
Variance. Mat. 10. 35; Gal. 5. 20.
Vashni, văsh′-nī, 'strong' (?); but perhaps not a proper name. 1 Chr. 6. 28. R. V. Joel.
Vashti, văsh′-tī, 'beautiful.' Esth. 1. 9.
Vaunt. Jud. 7. 2; 1 Cor. 13. 4.
Veadar, vē′-ă-dăr, an intercalary month introduced seven times in a cycle of 19 years to render the average length of the year nearly correct. *See* MONTHS.
Vehement. S. of S. 8. 6; Mk. 14. 31; 2 Cor. 7. 11.
Veil (of women). Gen. 24. 65; Ru. 3. 15; 1 Cor. 11. 10.
of Moses. Ex. 34. 33; 2 Cor. 3. 13.
of the tabernacle and temple. Ex. 26. 31; 36. 35; 2 Cor. 3. 14. *See* Heb. 6. 19; 9. 3; 10. 20.
of temple, rent at crucifixion. Mat. 27. 51; Mk. 15. 38; Lu. 23. 45.
Vengeance. Deu. 32. 35, to me belongeth *v.*
Prov. 6. 34; Isa. 34. 8; 61. 2; Jer. 51. 6, the day of *v.*
Isa. 59. 17, garments of *v.* for clothing.
Acts 28. 4, whom *v.* suffereth not to live. R. V. Justice.
Jude 7, the *v.* of eternal fire. R. V. punishment.
See Mic. 5. 15; Lu. 21. 22; Rom. 12. 19.
Vengeance belongs to God. Deu. 32. 35; Ps. 94. 1; 99. 8; Isa. 34. 8; 35. 4; Jer. 50. 15; Ezek. 24.; 25.; Nah. 1. 2; 2 Thes. 1. 8; Heb. 10. 30; Jude 7.
Venison. Gen. 25. 28, he did eat of his *v.*
27. 3, take me some *v.*
Venom. Deu. 32. 33, cruel *v.* of asps.
Venture. 1 Kn. 22. 34, drew a bow at a *v.*
Verified. Gen. 42. 20; 1 Kn. 8. 26; 2 Chr. 6. 17.
Verily. Gen. 42. 21; Ps. 58. 11; 73. 13; Mk. 9. 12.
Verity. Ps. 111. 7; 1 Tim. 2. 7.
Vermilion. Jer. 22. 14; Ezek. 23. 14. Vermilion (Heb. *Shâshar*, Gk. *μίλτος*) is a red pigment obtained from cinnabar. The Greek *μίλτος* denotes any red mineral coloring matter.
Very, true, real, actual. John 7. 26.
Vessel. 2 Kn. 4. 6, there is not a *v.* more.
Ps. 2. 9, them in pieces like a potter's *v.*
31. 12, I am like a broken *v.*
Jer. 22. 28, a *v.* wherein is no pleasure.
25. 34, fall like a pleasant *v.*
Mat. 13. 48, gathered the good into *v.*
25. 4, the wise took oil in their *v.*
Acts 9. 15, he is a chosen *v.* unto me.
Rom. 9. 22, the *v.* of wrath.
9. 23, the *v.* of mercy.
1 Thes. 4. 4, to possess his *v.* in sanctification.
2 Tim. 2. 21, he shall be a *v.* to honour.
1 Pet. 3. 7, giving honour to the wife as to weaker *v.*
See Isa. 52. 11; 65. 4; Jer. 14. 3; Mk. 11. 16.
Vessels: of temple, 1 Kn. 7. 40. carried to Babylon, 2 Kn. 25. 14. profaned, Dan. 5. restored, Ez. 1. 7.
Vestment. It was and still is customary for every Jew, on entering the synagogue for religious worship, to put on the *Tallith* or scarf of white lamb's wool with blue stripes and fringes at each end. It marked the worshipper as being a true Israelite. It was perhaps some similar vestment which Jehu ordered 'him that was over the vestry' to supply to each worshipper of Baal (2 Kn. 10. 22), the acceptance of which was the profession of being a true Baalite.
Vestry. 2 Kn. 10. 22, him that was over the *v.*
Vesture. Gen. 41. 42; Ps. 102. 26; Heb. 1. 12.
Vesture, lots cast for Christ's. Mat. 27. 35; John 19. 24. *See* Ps. 22. 18; Rev. 19. 13.

Vex, to harass, torment. Ex. 22. 21; Lev. 19. 33, not *v.* a stranger. R. V. wrong.
Num. 33. 55, those ye let remain shall *v.* you.
2 Sam. 12. 18, how will he *v.* himself?
Job 19. 2, how long will ye *v.* my soul?
Isa. 11. 13, Judah shall not *v.* Ephraim.
Ezek. 32. 9, I will *v.* the hearts of many.
Mat. 15. 22, my daughter is grievously *v.*
2 Pet. 2. 8, *v.* his righteous soul.
See Lev. 18. 18; Jud. 16. 16; Isa. 63. 10; Hab. 2. 7.
Vexation. Eccl. 1. 14; 2. 22; Isa. 9. 1; 28. 19; 65. 14.
Vials full of odours. Rev. 5. 8.
the seven. Rev. 15. 7; 16.
Victory. 2 Sam. 19. 2, *v.* turned to mourning.
1 Chr. 29. 11, thine is the *v.*
Ps. 98. 1, hath gotten him the *v.*
Mat. 12. 20, send forth judgment unto *v.*
1 John 5. 4, this is the *v.*, even our faith.
Victory: over death, Isa. 25. 8; 1 Cor. 15. 54. by faith, 1 John 5. 4.
Victuals. Ex. 12. 39, neither had they prepared *v.*
Jos. 9. 14, the men took of their *v.* R. V. provision.
Neh. 10. 31, bring *v.* on the sabbath.
13. 15, in the day wherein they sold *v.*
Mat. 14. 15; Lu. 9. 12, into villages to buy *v.* R. V. food.
See Gen. 14. 11; Jud. 17. 10; 1 Sam. 22. 10.
View. Jos. 2. 7; 7. 2; 2 Kn. 2. 7; Neh. 2. 13.
Vigilant. 1 Tim. 3. 2; 1 Pet. 5. 8.
Vile. 1 Sam. 3. 13, made themselves *v.* R. V. did bring a curse upon themselves.
Job 18. 3, wherefore are we reputed *v.*? R. V. unclean.
40. 4, I am *v.*, what shall I answer thee? R. V. of small account.
Ps. 15. 4; Isa. 32. 5; Dan. 11. 21, a *v.* person. R. V. a reprobate.
Jer. 15. 19, take the precious from the *v.*
Lam. 1. 11, see, O Lord, for I am become *v.*
Nah. 3. 6, I will make thee *v.*
Rom. 1. 26, gave them up to *v.* affections.
Phil. 3. 21, shall change our *v.* body. R. V. the body of our humiliation.
Jas. 2. 2, a poor man in *v.* raiment.
See 2 Sam. 1. 21. Job 30. 8; Ps. 12. 8; Nah. 1. 14.
Village. Ex. 8. 13; Num. 21. 24; 2 Chr. 28. 18; Mat. 21. 2; Mk. 6. 6; Lu. 24. 13; Acts 8. 25.
Villany. Isa. 32. 6; Jer. 29. 23.
Vine (1) (Gen. 9. 20; 40. 9; Deu. 8. 8). Heb. *Gĕphen*: Gk. *ἄμπελος*: Bot. N. *Vitis vinifera.* Palestine was renowned for the quantity, quality, and productiveness of its vines.
Jud. 13. 14, may not eat any thing that cometh of the *v.*
1 Kn. 4. 25, dwelt every man under his *v.*
2 Kn. 18. 31; Isa. 36. 16, eat every man of his own *v.*
Ps. 80. 8, a *v.* out of Egypt.
128. 3, thy wife as a fruitful *v.*
Isa. 24. 7, the new wine mourneth, the *v.* languisheth.
Hos. 10. 1, Israel is an empty *v.*
Mic. 4. 4, they shall sit every man under his *v.*
Mat. 26. 29; Mk. 14. 25; Lu. 22. 18, this fruit of the *v.*
John 15. 1, I am the true *v.*
(2) (WILD) (2 Kn. 4. 39). Heb. *Gĕphen Sâdeh*: Gk. *ἄμπελος ἐν τῷ ἀγρῷ*. A wild vine bearing a poisonous fruit, a wild gourd. Probably the 'vine of Sodom,' Deu. 32. 32, is the same plant.
Vine. Deu. 8. 8; Gen. 49. 11; S. of S. 2. 15; Jer. 2. 21; Ezek. 15.; 17.; Joel 1. 7; Hos. 10. 1; Hab. 3. 17; Rev. 14. 18.
typical of Christ. John 15.
Vinegar. The Hebrew term *Ḥômĕts* was applied to a beverage consisting usually of wine or strong drink turned sour. By itself it formed a nauseous draught (Ps. 69. 21), and its acid taste passed into a proverb (Prov. 10. 26).

It was drunk by labourers (Ru. 2. 14). Similar to the *Hômets* of the Hebrews was the *acetum* of the Romans, which, under the name of *posca*, was the ordinary drink of the Roman soldiers. (Mat. 27. 48; Mk. 15. 36; John 19. 29, 30).

Vineyard, Noah's. Gen. 9. 20.
of Naboth. 1 Kn. 21.
parables of. Mat. 20. 1; 21. 33; **Mk. 12. 1**; Lu. 20. 9.
laws of. Ex. 22. 5; 23. 11; Lev. 19. 10; 25. 3; Deu. 20. 6; 22. 9; 23. 24; 24. 21.

Vintage. Job 24. 6; Isa. 16. 10; 32. 10; Mic. 7. 1.

Viol (Isa. 14. 11; Am. 5. 23; 6. 5; Isa. 5. 12, R. V. 'lute'). Heb. *Nébel:* Gk. ψαλτήριον, usually translated psaltery. A small portable harp, played with both hands. There were probably several varieties of the *Nebel*.

Violence. Gen. 6. 11, earth was filled with *v.*
Ps. 11. 5, him that loveth *v.*
55. 9, I have seen *v.* in the city.
58. 2, weigh the *v.* of your hands.
72. 14, redeem their soul from *v.*
73. 6, *v.* covereth them as a garment.
Prov. 4. 17, they drink the wine of *v.*
10. 6, *v.* covereth the mouth of the wicked.
Isa. 53. 9, because he had done no *v.*
60. 18, *v.* shall no more be heard.
Ezek. 8. 17; 28. 16, they have filled the land with *v.*
Am. 3. 10, store up *v.* in their palaces.
Hab. 1. 3, *v.* is before me.
Mal. 2. 16, one covereth *v.* with his garment.
Mat. 11. 12, kingdom of heaven suffereth *v.*
Lu. 3. 14, do *v.* to no man.
See Mic. 2. 2; 6. 12; Zep. 1. 9; Heb. 11. 34.

Violent. Ps. 7. 16, his *v.* dealing.
18. 48; 140. 1; Prov. 16. 29, the *v.* man.
See 2 Sam. 22. 49; Eccl. 5. 8; Mat. 11. 12.

Violently. Isa. 22. 18; Mat. 8. 32; Mk. 5. 13.

Viper (Job 20. 16; Isa. 30. 6; 59. 5). Heb. *Eph'eh:* Gk. ἔχιδνα: Zool. S. *Echis arenicola*. T. (sand-viper). A poisonous serpent, of small species, about one foot long; found in sandy districts and under stones by the Dead Sea; quick in movement. The viper which fastened on Paul's hand (Acts 28. 3) was the *Vipera aspis*, common in the Mediterranean Isles.

Virgin. Isa. 23. 12; 47. 1; 62. 5; Jer. 14. 17.

Virgin, Chirst born of one. Mat. 1. 18; Lu. 1. 27.
See Isa. 7. 14.

Virgins, parable of. Mat. 25. 1.

Virtue, efficacy, might. Mk. 5. 30; Lu. 6. 19; 8. 46; Phil. 4. 8; 2 Pet. 1. 5.

Virtues and vices. Prov. 10.–24.

Virtuous. Ru. 3. 11; Prov. 12. 4; 31. 10, 29.

Visage. Isa. 52. 14; Lam. 4. 8; Dan. 3. 19.

Vision. Job 20. 8, as a *v.* of the night.
Prov. 29. 18, where there is no *v.*, people perish.
Isa. 22. 1, the valley of *v.*
28. 7, they err in *v.*
Lam. 2. 9, prophets find no *v.* from the Lord.
Hos. 12. 10, I have multiplied *v.*
Joel 2. 28; Acts 2. 17, young men shall see *v.*
Zec. 13. 4, ashamed every one of his *v.*
Mat. 17. 9, tell the *v.* to no man.
Lu. 24. 23, had seen a *v.* of angels.
Acts 26. 19, not disobedient to heavenly *v.*
See Job 4. 13; Ezek. 8. 3; Mic. 3. 6.

Visions sent by God. Gen. 12. 7; Num. 24. 4; Job 7. 14; Isa. 1. 1; Joel 2. 28; Acts 2. 17; 2 Cor. 12. 1.
of Abram, Gen. 15. Jacob, Gen. 28. 10. Pharaoh, Gen. 41. Micaiah, 1 Kn. 22. 19. Isaiah, Isa. 6. Ezekiel, Ezek. 1.; 10.; 11.; 37.; 40. Nebuchadnezzar, Dan. 4. Daniel, Dan. 7. Zechariah, Zec. 1. Peter, Acts 10. 9. John, Rev. 1.; 4.–22.

Visit. Gen. 50. 24; Ex. 13. 19, God will *v.* you.
Ex. 20. 5; 34. 7; Num. 14. 18; Deu. 5. 9, *v.* the iniquity of the fathers.
32. 34, when I *v.*, I will *v.* their sin upon them.
Ru. 1. 6, how the Lord had *v.* his people.
Job 5. 24, thou shalt *v.* thy habitation.
7. 18, shouldest *v.* him every morning.
Ps. 8. 4; Heb. 2. 6, the son of man, that thou *v.* him.
Ps. 106. 4, *v.* me with thy salvation.
Jer. 5. 9; 9. 9, shall I not *v.* for these things?
29. 10, I will *v.*, and perform my good word.
Ezek. 38. 8, after many days thou shalt be *v.*
Mat. 25. 36, I was sick, and ye *v.* me.
Acts 15. 14, how God did *v.* the Gentiles.
Jas. 1. 27, to *v.* the fatherless and widows.
See Job 31. 14; Lu. 1. 68, 78; 7. 16.

Visitation. Job 10. 12, thy *v.* hath preserved.
Isa. 10. 3; 1 Pet. 2. 12, in the day of *v.*
Jer. 8. 12; 10. 15; 46. 21; 50. 27; Lu. 19. 44, in the time of *v.*
See Num. 16. 29; Jer. 11. 23; Hos. 9. 7.

Vocal music occupies an important place in Scripture, both in religious worship (1 Chr. 6. 32), public rejoicings (1 Sam. 18. 6), and social festivities (Gen. 31. 27; Isa. 5. 1; 24. 9). It is mentioned among the earliest expressions of joy (Ex. 15. 21), and was accompanied by dancing (2 Sam. 6. 16), and clapping of hands, especially in the 'chorus' (Ps. 47. 1). For worship David chose a body of singers (1 Chr. 16. 41); Jehoshaphat appointed a band of singers to praise God in front of his army (2 Chr. 20. 21). After the Captivity we find an equal number of male and female voices (Ez. 2. 65), who sang alternately. They formed a distinguished class, had a separate maintenance (Neh. 11. 23), had cities assigned to them (Neh. 7. 73), and chambers for those in attendance at the temple (Ezek. 40. 44). From the dedication of some Psalms there would seem to have been a written musical notation, but no certain record of it is extant.

Vocation. Eph. 4. 1, worthy of the *v.* R. V. calling.

Voice. Gen. 4. 10, *v.* of thy brother's blood.
27. 22, the *v.* is Jacob's *v.*
Ex. 23. 21, obey his *v.*, provoke him not.
24. 3, all the people answered with one *v.*
32. 18, it is not the *v.* of them that shout.
Deu. 4. 33, did ever people hear *v.* of God and live?
Jos. 6. 10, nor make any noise with thy *v.*
1 Sam. 24. 16; 26. 17, is this thy *v.*?
1 Kn. 19. 12, after the fire, a still small *v.*
2 Kn. 4. 31, there was neither *v.* nor hearing.
Job 3. 7, let no joyful *v.* come therein.
30. 31, my organ into the *v.* of them that weep.
37. 4, a *v.* roareth.
40. 9, canst thou thunder with a *v.* like him?
Ps. 5. 3, my *v.* shalt thou hear in the morning.
31. 22; 86. 6, the *v.* of my supplications.
42. 4, with the *v.* of joy.
95. 7, to day, if ye will hear his *v.*
103. 20, the *v.* of his word.
Prov. 1. 20, wisdom uttereth her *v.* in the streets.
5. 13, not obeyed the *v.* of my teachers.
8. 1, doth not understanding put forth her *v.*?
8. 4, my *v.* is to the sons of man.
Eccl. 5. 3, a fool's *v.* is known.
12. 4, rise up at the *v.* of the bird.
S. of S. 2. 8; 5. 2, the *v.* of my beloved.
2. 12, the *v.* of the turtle is heard.
2. 14, sweet is thy *v.*
Isa. 13. 2, exalt the *v.* unto them.
40. 3; Mat. 3. 3; Mk. 1. 3; Lu. 3. 4, *v.* of him that crieth.
40. 6, the *v.* said, Cry.
48. 20, with a *v.* of singing.
52. 8, with the *v.* together shall they sing.
65. 19, the *v.* of weeping shall be no more heard.
66. 6, a *v.* of noise, a *v.* from the temple.
Jer. 7. 34, the *v.* of mirth, and the *v.* of gladness.
30. 19, the *v.* of them that make merry.
48. 3, a *v.* of crying shall be. R. V. the sound.
Ezek. 23. 42, a *v.* of a multitude at ease.
33. 32, one that hath a pleasant *v.*
43. 2, *v.* like a noise of many waters.
Nah. 2. 7, lead her as with the *v.* of doves.
Mat. 12. 19, neither shall any man hear his *v.*
Lu. 23. 23, the *v.* of them and of the chief priests prevailed.

John 5. 25, the dead shall hear the *v.* of Son of God.
10. 4, the sheep follow, for they know his *v.*
10. 5, they know not the *v.* of strangers.
12. 30, this *v.* came not because of me.
18. 37, every one that is of the truth heareth my *v.*
Acts 12. 14, and when she knew Peter's *v.*
26. 10, I gave my *v.* against them. R. V. vote.
1 Cor. 14. 10, there are so many *v.* in the world.
14. 19, that by my *v.* I might teach others.
Gal. 4. 20, I desire now to change my *v.*
1 Thes. 4. 16, descend with *v.* of archangel.
2 Pet. 2. 16, the dumb ass speaking with man's *v.*
Rev. 3. 20, if any man hear my *v.*
4. 5, out of the throne proceeded *v.*
See Gen. 3. 17; Ps. 58. 5; John 3. 29; Acts 12. 22.

Voice of God proclaims the law. Ex. 19. 19; 20. 1.
its majesty and power. Job 37. 4; 40. 9; Ps. 18. 13; 46. 6; 68. 33; Joel 2. 11.
heard by Elijah. 1 Kn. 19. 12.
by Ezekiel. Ezek. 1. 24; 10. 5.
by Christ, at His baptism, &c. Mat. 3. 17; Mk. 1. 11; Lu. 3. 22; John 12. 28.
by Peter, James, and John, at the transfiguration. Mat. 17. 5; Mk. 9. 7; Lu. 9. 35; 2 Pet. 1. 18.
by Paul. Acts 9. 7.
by John. Rev. 1. 10.

Void. Gen. 1. 2; Jer. 4. 23, without form, and *v.*
Deu. 32. 28, a people *v.* of counsel.
Ps. 89. 39, made *v.* the covenant. R. V. abhorred.
119. 126, they have made *v.* thy law.
Prov. 11. 12, *v.* of wisdom.
Isa. 55. 11, my word shall not return to me *v.*
Jer. 19. 7, make *v.* the counsel of Judah.
Nah. 2. 10, empty, *v.*, and waste.
Acts 24. 16, a conscience *v.* of offence.
See Num. 30. 12; Rom. 3. 31; 4. 14.

Volume. Ps. 40. 7; Heb. 10. 7.

Voluntary. Lev. 1. 3; 7. 16; Ezek. 46. 12; Col. 2. 18.

Vomit. Job 20. 15; Prov. 26. 11; 2 Pet. 2. 22.

Vophsi, vŏph'-sī, 'expansion' (?). Num. 13. 14.

Vow (*n.*). Gen. 28. 20; 31. 13, Jacob vowed a *v.*
Num. 29. 39, these ye shall do beside your *v.*
Deu. 12. 6, thither bring your *v.*
Jud. 11. 30, Jephthah vowed a *v.*, and said.
11. 39, her father did with her according to his *v.*
1 Sam. 1. 21, Elkanah went up to offer his *v.*
Job 22. 27, thou shalt pay thy *v.*
Ps. 22. 25; 66. 13; 116. 14, I will pay my *v.*
50. 14, pay thy *v.* unto the most High.
56. 12, thy *v.* are upon me, O God.
61. 5, for thou hast heard my *v.*
61. 8, that I may daily perform my *v.*
65. 1, to thee shall the *v.* be performed.
Prov. 7. 14, this day have I paid my *v.*
20. 25, after *v.* to make enquiry.
31. 2, the son of my *v.*
Eccl. 5. 4, when thou vowest a *v.*, defer not to pay.
Isa. 19. 21, they shall vow a *v.* unto the Lord.
Jon. 1. 16, feared the Lord, and made *v.*
Acts 18. 18, shorn his head, for he had a *v.*
21. 23, four men which have a *v.* on them.
See 2 Sam. 15. 7; Jer. 44. 25; Nah. 1. 15.

Vow (*v.*). Deu. 23. 22, if forbear to *v.*, no sin.
Ps. 76. 11, *v.*, and pay to the Lord your God.
132. 2, and *v.* to the mighty God.
See Num. 21. 2; Eccl. 5. 5; Jon. 2. 9.

Vows, laws concerning. Lev. 27.; Num. 6. 2; 30.; Deu. 23. 21. *See* Ps. 65. 1; 66. 13; 76. 11; 116. 18; Eccl. 5. 4; Mal. 1. 14.

Voyage, Paul's. Acts 27.; 28. *See* under Paul.

Vulture. (1) (Lev. 11. 14). Heb. *Dâah:* Gk. γύψ: R. V. 'kite.'
(2) (Lev. 11. 18, R. V.). Heb. *Râḥâm:* Gk. ἀετός. A. V. 'gier-eagle' = the Egyptian vulture.
(3) (Lev. 11. 13). R. V. marg. 'Great vulture:' R. V. and A. V. 'eagle.' This is the tawny vulture generally called the griffin (*gyps fulvus*).
Job 28. 7, which the *v.* eye hath not seen. R. V. falcon's.
Isa. 34. 15, there shall the *v.* be. R. V. kites.

Wafers used as offerings. Ex. 29. 2, 23; Lev. 2. 4; 8. 26; Num. 6. 15.

Wag. Jer. 18. 16; Lam. 2. 15; Zep. 2. 15.

Wages are first mentioned in Scripture as paid not in money but in kind by Laban to Jacob (Gen. 29. 15, 20; 30. 28, &c.), and Pharaoh's daughter promises to give the sister of Moses her wages (Ex. 2. 9) for nursing him. In Christ's time a day's wages was one denarius (16 cents), Mat. 20. 2. On the strictness of the Law in requiring daily payment of wages, *see* Lev. 19. 13; Deu. 24. 14, 15.
Gen. 29. 15, what shall thy *w.* be?
30. 28, appoint me thy *w.*
31. 7, changed my *w.* ten times.
Ex. 2. 9, nurse this child, I will give *w.*
Jer. 22. 13, useth neighbour's service without *w.*
Hag. 1. 6, earneth *w.* to put in bag with holes.
Lu. 3. 14, be content with your *w.*
John 4. 36, he that reapeth receiveth *w.*
Rom. 6. 23, the *w.* of sin is death.
2 Pet. 2. 15, the *w.* of unrighteousness.
See Ezek. 29. 18; Mal. 3. 5; 2 Cor. 11. 8; Jas. 5. 4.

Wagons. Gen. 45. 19; Num. 7. 7; Ezek. 23. 24.

Wail. Ezek. 32. 18, *w.* for the multitude.
Am. 5. 16, *w.* shall be in all streets.
Mic. 1. 8, therefore I will *w.* and howl.
Mat. 13. 42, there shall be *w.* and gnashing. R. V. the weeping.
Mk. 5. 38, he seeth them that *w.* greatly.
Rev. 1. 7, all kindreds of the earth shall *w.* R. V. mourn over.
18. 15, the merchants shall stand afar off *w.* R. V. mourning.
See Esth. 4. 3; Jer. 9. 10, 19, 20; Ezek. 7. 11.

Wait. Gen. 49. 18, I have *w.* for thy salvation.
Num. 35. 20; Jer. 9. 8, by laying of *w.*
2 Kn. 6. 33, should I *w.* for the Lord any longer?
Job 14. 14, I will *w.* till my change come.
15. 22, he is *w.* for of the sword.
17. 13, if I *w.*, the grave is my house.
29. 21, to me men *w.*, and kept silence.
29. 23, they *w.* for me as for rain.
30. 26, when I *w.* for light, darkness came.
Ps. 25. 3; 69. 6, let none that *w.* be ashamed.
27. 14; 37. 34; Prov. 20. 22, *w.* on the Lord.
33. 20, our soul *w.* for the Lord.
37. 7, *w.* patiently.
52. 9, I will *w.* on thy name.
62. 1; 130. 6, my soul *w.* upon God.
62. 5, *w.* only on God.
65. 1, praise *w.* for thee in Zion.
69. 3, mine eyes fail while I *w.* for God.
104. 27, these all *w.* upon thee.
106. 13, they *w.* not for counsel.
123. 2, so our eyes *w.* on the Lord.
Prov. 27. 18, he that *w.* on his master.
Isa. 30. 18, the Lord *w.* to be gracious.
40. 31, they that *w.* on the Lord shall renew.
42. 4, the isles shall *w.* for his law.
59. 9, we *w.* for light.
64. 4, prepared for him that *w.* for him.
Lam. 3. 26, good that a man hope and quietly *w.*
Dan. 12. 12, blessed is he that *w.*, and cometh to the days.
Hab. 2. 3, though the vision tarry, *w.* for it.
Zec. 11. 11, poor of the flock that *w.* upon me. R. V. gave heed unto.
Mk. 15. 43, who also *w.* for the kingdom of God. R. V. was looking.
Lu. 2. 25, *w.* for the consolation of Israel. R. V. looking.
12. 36, men that *w.* for their Lord. R. V. looking.
Acts 1. 4, but *w.* for promise of the Father.
Rom. 8. 23, groan, *w.* for the adoption.
8. 25, then do we with patience *w.* for it.
12. 7, let us *w.* on our ministering. R. V. give ourselves to.
1 Cor. 9. 13, they which *w.* at the altar are partakers.
Gal. 5. 5, we *w.* for the hope.

1 Thes. 1. 10, to *w*. for his Son from heaven.
See Num. 3. 10; Neh. 12. 44; Isa. 8. 17.

Waiting upon God. Ps. 27. 14; 37. 34; Prov. 20. 22; Isa. 40. 31; 49. 23; Jer. 14. 22; Lam. 3. 25; Hab. 2. 3; Zep. 3. 8; Lu. 12. 36; Rom. 8. 25; 1 Cor. 1. 7; Gal. 5. 5; 1 Thes. 1. 10; 2 Thes. 3. 5.

Wake. Ps. 139. 18, when I *w*. I am still with thee.
Jer. 51. 39, sleep a perpetual sleep, and not *w*.
Joel 3. 9, prepare war, *w*. up the mighty men. R. V. stir.
Zec. 4. 1, the angel came again, and *w*. me.
1 Thes. 5. 10, whether we *w*. or sleep.
See Ps. 77. 4; 127. 1; S. of S. 5. 2; Isa. 50. 4.

Walk. Gen. 17. 1, *w*. before me, and be perfect.
24. 40, the Lord before whom I *w*.
48. 15, before whom my fathers did *w*.
Ex. 16. 4, whether they will *w*. in my law.
18. 20, the way wherein they must *w*.
Lev. 26. 12, I will *w*. among you.
Deu. 23. 14, God *w*. in midst of the camp.
Jud. 5. 10, speak, ye that *w*. by the way.
2 Sam. 2. 29, Abner and his men *w*. all that night.
Job 18. 8, he *w*. on a snare.
22. 14, he *w*. in the circuit of heaven.
29. 3, when by his light I *w*. through darkness.
Ps. 23. 4, though I *w*. through the valley of the shadow of death.
26. 11, as for me, I will *w*. in mine integrity.
48. 12, *w*. about Zion, and go round about her.
55. 14, we *w*. to house of God in company.
56. 13, that I may *w*. before God in the light of the living.
84. 11, from them that *w*. uprightly.
91. 6, the pestilence that *w*. in darkness.
104. 3, who *w*. upon wings of the wind.
116. 9, I will *w*. before the Lord.
119. 45, I will *w*. at liberty.
138. 7, though I *w*. in the midst of trouble.
Prov. 10. 9; 28. 18, he that *w*. uprightly *w*. surely.
13. 20, he that *w*. with wise men shall be wise.
19. 1; 28. 6, better is the poor that *w*. in integrity.
28. 26, whoso *w*. wisely shall be delivered.
Eccl. 2. 14, the fool *w*. in darkness.
Isa. 2. 5, let us *w*. in the light of the Lord.
9. 2, the people that *w*. in darkness.
20. 3, as my servant hath *w*. naked and barefoot.
30. 21, a voice saying, This is the way, *w*. in it.
35. 9, the redeemed shall *w*. there.
50. 10, that *w*. in darkness, and hath no light.
50. 11, *w*. in the light of your fire.
Jer. 6. 16, ask where is the good way, and *w*. therein.
10. 23, it is not in man that *w*. to direct his steps.
Ezek. 28. 14, hast *w*. in midst of stones of fire.
Dan. 4. 37, those that *w*. in pride.
Hos. 14. 9, the just shall *w*. in them.
Am. 3. 3, can two *w*. together?
Mic. 6. 8, to *w*. humbly with thy God.
Nah. 2. 11, where the lion *w*. [earth.
Zec. 1. 11, we have *w*. to and fro through the
Mal. 3. 14, what profit that we have *w*. mournfully?
Mat. 9. 5; Mk. 2. 9; Lu. 5. 23; John 5. 8, 11, 12; Acts 3. 6, arise, and *w*.
12. 43; Lu. 11. 24, *w*. through dry places. R. V. passeth.
14. 29, he *w*. on the water. [they *w*.
Mk. 16. 12, he appeared to two of them, as
Lu. 13. 33, I must *w*. to day and to morrow.
John 8. 12, shall not *w*. in darkness.
11. 9, if any man *w*. in the day.
Rom. 4. 12, who *w*. in steps of that faith.
6. 4, *w*. in newness of life.
8. 1, who *w*. not after the flesh, but after the Spirit.
2 Cor. 5. 7, we *w*. by faith.
Gal. 6. 16, as many as *w*. according to this rule.
Eph. 2. 2; Col. 3. 7, in time past ye *w*.
2. 10, ordained that we should *w*. in them.
4. 1, *w*. worthy of the vocation.
Eph. 4. 17, that ye *w*. not as other Gentiles.
5. 15, *w*. circumspectly.
Phil. 3. 17, mark them which *w*.
3. 18, many *w*., of whom I told you.
Col. 1. 10; 1 Thes. 2. 12, that ye might *w*. worthy of the Lord.
1 Thes. 4. 1, how ye ought to *w*.
4. 12, ye may *w*. honestly. [orderly.
2 Thes. 3. 6, from every brother that *w*. dis-
1 Pet. 4. 3, when we *w*. in lasciviousness.
5. 8, *w*. about, seeking whom he may devour.
1 John 1. 7, if we *w*. in the light.
2. 6, to *w*., even as he *w*.
See Gal. 5. 16; Eph. 5. 2; Phil. 3. 16.

Walking. Deu. 2. 7, the Lord knoweth thy *w*.
Job 31. 26, the moon *w*. in brightness.
Dan. 3. 25, four men loose, *w*. in the fire.
Mat. 14. 25, Jesus went to them, *w*. on the sea.
Mk. 8. 24, I see men as trees, *w*.
Acts 9. 31, *w*. in the fear of the Lord.
See Isa. 3. 16; 2 Cor. 4. 2; 2 Pet. 3. 3; Jude 16.

Walking WITH GOD. Deu. 5. 33; 28. 9; Jos. 22. 5; 1 Kn. 8. 36; Ps. 1.; 112.; Prov. 2. 7; Isa. 2. 3; 30. 21; Jer. 6. 16; 7. 23; Ezek. 37. 24. of Enoch, Gen. 5. 24. of Noah, Gen. 6. 9.
in faith, love, &c., Rom. 6. 4; 8. 1; 13. 13; 2 Cor. 5. 7; Gal. 5. 16; Eph. 5. 2; Phil. 3. 16; Col. 1. 10; 2. 6; 1 John 1. 6; Rev. 3. 4; 21. 24.

Wall. Gen. 49. 22, branches run over the *w*.
Ex. 14. 22, the waters were a *w*. to them.
Num. 22. 24, a *w*. being on this side, a *w*. on that.
2 Sam. 22. 30; Ps. 18. 29, have I leaped over a *w*.
2 Kn. 20. 2; Isa. 36. 11, turned his face to the *w*.
Ez. 5. 3, who commanded you to make this *w*.?
Neh. 4. 6, so built we the *w*.
Ps. 62. 3, a bowing *w*. shall ye be.
122. 7, peace be within thy *w*.
Prov. 24. 31, the *w*. thereof was broken down.
25. 28, like a city without *w*.
Isa. 26. 1, salvation will God appoint for *w*.
59. 10, we grope for the *w*.
60. 18, thou shalt call thy *w*. Salvation.
Ezek. 8. 7, a hole in the *w*.
Dan. 5. 5, fingers wrote on the *w*. [him.
Am. 5. 19, leaned hand on *w*., and serpent bit
Hab. 2. 11, the stone shall cry out of the *w*.
Acts 23. 3, thou whited *w*.
Eph. 2. 14, the middle *w*. of partition. [14.
See Ezek. 38. 11; Zec. 2. 4; Acts 9. 25; Rev. 21.

Wallow. Jer. 6. 26; 25. 34, *w*. in ashes.
2 Pet. 2. 22, washed, to her *w*. in the mire.
See 2 Sam. 20. 12; Ezek. 27. 30.

Wander. Num. 14. 33, your children shall *w*.
Deu. 27. 18, cursed be he that maketh blind to *w*.
Job 12. 24, he causeth them to *w*.
15. 23, he *w*. abroad for bread.
38. 41, young ravens *w*. for lack of meat.
Ps. 55. 7, then would I *w*. far off.
59. 15, let them *w*. up and down.
119. 10, let me not *w*. from thy commandments.
Prov. 27. 8, as a bird that *w*. from nest.
Isa. 16. 3, bewray not him that *w*.
47. 15, *w*. every one to his quarter.
Jer. 14. 10, thus have they loved to *w*.
Lam. 4. 14, they have *w*. as blind men.
Ezek. 34. 6, my sheep *w*. through mountains.
Am. 4. 8, two cities *w*. to one city to drink.
See Hos. 9. 17; 1 Tim. 5. 13; Heb. 11. 37; Jude 13.

Want (*n*.). Deu. 28. 48, thou shalt serve in *w*.
Jud. 18. 10, a place where there is no *w*.
19. 20, let all thy *w*. lie on me.
Job 24. 8, they embrace the rock for *w*.
31. 19, if I have seen any perish for *w*.
Ps. 34. 9, there is no *w*. to them that fear him.
Am. 4. 6, I have given you *w*. of bread.
Mk. 12. 44, she of her *w*. cast in all.
Lu. 15. 14, he began to be in *w*.
Phil. 2. 25, that ministered to my *w*. R. V. need.
See Prov. 6. 11; Lam. 4. 9; 2 Cor. 8. 14; Phil. 4. 11.

Want (*v*.). Ps. 23. 1, I shall not *w*.
34. 10, shall not *w*. any good thing.
Prov. 9. 4, him that *w*. understanding. R. V. is void of.

THE WAILING WALL, JERUSALEM

Part of the ancient wall enclosing the Temple area, traditionally a place of mourning for Jews lamenting the destruction of the Temple. (*Donald McLeish*)

WATCH-TOWER IN A VINEYARD

Probably very similar to those of Old Testament times. (*L. A. Fereday*)

Prov. 10. 19, in multitude of words there *w.* not sin.
13. 25, the belly of the wicked shall *w.*
Eccl. 6. 2, he *w.* nothing for his soul. R. V. lacketh.
Isa. 34. 16, none shall *w.* her mate.
Jer. 44. 18, we have *w.* all things.
Ezek. 4. 17, that they may *w.* bread and water.
John 2. 3, when they *w.* wine. R. V. the wine failed.
2 Cor. 11. 9, when I *w.*, I was chargeable to no man.
See Eccl. 1. 15; Dan. 5. 27; Tit. 1. 5; Jas. 1. 4.

Wanton. 1 Tim. 5. 11; Jas. 5. 5.

Wantonness condemned. Isa. 3. 16; Rom. 13. 13; 2 Pet. 2. 18.

War (*n.*). Ex. 32. 17, there is a noise of *w.*
Num. 32. 6, shall your brethren go to *w.*
Deu. 24. 5, taken a wife, he shall not go out to *w.*
Jud. 5. 8, then was *w.* in the gates.
1 Chr. 5. 22, many slain, because the *w.* was of God.
Job 10. 17, changes and *w.* are against me. R. V. warfare.
38. 23, reserved against the day of *w.*
Ps. 27. 3, though *w.* should rise against me.
46. 9, he maketh *w.* to cease.
55. 21, *w.* was in his heart.
68. 30, scatter the people that delight in *w.*
Prov. 20. 18, with good advice make *w.*
Eccl. 3. 8, a time of *w.*
8. 8, no discharge in that *w.*
Isa. 2. 4; Mic. 4. 3, nor learn *w.* any more.
Jer. 42. 14, to Egypt, where we shall see no *w.*
Mic. 2. 8, as men averse from *w.*
Mat. 24. 6; Mk. 13. 7; Lu. 21. 9, *w.* and rumours of *w.*
Lu. 14. 31, what king, going to make *w.*?
Jas. 4. 1, from whence come *w.*?
Rev. 12. 7, there was *w.* in heaven.
See Eccl. 9. 18; Ezek. 32. 27; Dan. 7. 21; 9. 26.

War (*v.*). 2 Sam. 22. 35; Ps. 18. 34; 144. 1, teacheth my hands to *w.*
2 Chr. 6. 34, if thy people go to *w.* R. V. battle.
Isa. 41. 12, they that *w.* against thee.
2 Cor. 10. 3, we do not *w.* after the flesh.
1 Tim. 1. 18, *w.* a good warfare.
2 Tim. 2. 4, no man that *w.* entangleth himself. R. V. on service.
Jas. 4. 1, lusts that *w.* in your members.
4. 2, ye fight and *w.*, yet ye have not.
1 Pet. 2. 11, from lusts which *w.* against the soul.
See 1 Kn. 14. 19; Isa. 37. 8; Rom. 7. 23.

War, laws of. Deu. 20.; 23. 9; 24. 5.

Ward, prison (lit., guard). Gen. 40. 3.

Wardrobe. 2 Kn. 22. 14; 2 Chr. 34. 22.

Ware. Lu. 8. 27; Acts 14. 6; 2 Tim. 4. 15.

Warfare. Isa. 40. 2, that her *w.* is accomplished.
2 Cor. 10. 4, weapons of our *w.* are not carnal.
See 1 Sam. 28. 1; 1 Cor. 9. 7; 1 Tim. 1. 18.

Warm. Eccl. 4. 11, how can one be *w.* alone?
Isa. 47. 14, there shall not be a coal to *w.* at.
Hag. 1. 6, ye clothe you, but there is none *w.*
Mk. 14. 54; John 18. 18, Peter *w.* himself.
Jas. 2. 16, be ye *w.* and filled.
See 2 Kn. 4. 34; Job 37. 17; 39. 14; Isa. 44. 15.

Warn. Ezek. 3. 18; Acts 20. 31; 1 Thes. 5. 14.

Warning. 2 Chr. 19. 10; Ezek. 3. 17; 33. 3; 1 Thes. 5. 14; Acts 20. 31; 1 Cor. 4. 14; Col. 1. 28.

Wash. 2 Kn. 5. 10, go, *w.* in Jordan.
5. 12, may I not *w.* in them, and be clean?
Job 9. 30, if I *w.* myself with snow water.
14. 19, thou *w.* away things which grow.
29. 6, when I *w.* my steps with butter.
Ps. 26. 6; 73. 13, I will *w.* my hands in innocency.
51. 2, *w.* me throughly from mine iniquity.
51. 7, *w.* me, and I shall be whiter than snow.
Prov. 30. 12, a generation not *w.*
S. of S. 5. 12, his eyes are *w.* with milk.
Isa. 1. 16, *w.* you, make you clean.
Jer. 2. 22, though thou *w.* thee with nitre.
4. 14, *w.* thy heart.
Ezek. 16. 4, nor wast *w.* in water to supple thee.
Mat. 6. 17, when thou fastest, *w.* thy face.
Mat. 27. 24, took water, and *w.* his hands.
Mk. 7. 3, except they *w.* oft, eat not.
Lu. 7. 38, began to *w.* his feet with tears. R. V. wet.
7. 44, she hath *w.* my feet with her tears. R. V. wetted.
John 9. 7, go, *w.* in the pool of Siloam.
Acts 16. 33, he *w.* their stripes.
22. 16, *w.* away thy sins.
1 Cor. 6. 11, but ye are *w.*
Heb. 10. 22, having our bodies *w.* with pure water.
2 Pet. 2. 22, the sow that was *w.*
Rev. 1. 5, that *w.* us from our sins. R. V. loosed.
7. 14, have *w.* their robes.
See Neh. 4. 23; Heb. 9. 10.

Washing enjoined by the law. Ex. 29. 4; Lev. 6. 27; 13. 54; 14. 8; Deu. 21. 6; 2 Chr. 4. 6.
of the feet, the use of sandals in the East makes the washing of the feet on coming to a feast not only a comfort but a necessity. The water was always poured upon them, and a strainer above the bottom of the dish concealed the fouled water. Gen. 18. 4; 24. 32; 43. 24; 1 Sam. 25. 41; Lu. 7. 38; 1 Tim. 5. 10.
of the hands. Deu. 21. 6; Ps. 26. 6; Mat. 27. 24.
Christ washes His disciples' feet. John 13. 5–14.
superstitious, censured. Mk. 7. 3; Lu. 11. 38.
figuratively. Job 9. 30; Isa. 1. 16; 4. 4; Eph. 5. 26; Tit. 3. 5; Heb. 10. 22.
in the blood of Christ. 1 Cor. 6. 11; Rev. 1. 5; 7. 14.

Waste. Deu. 32. 10; Job 30. 3, in *w.* wilderness.
1 Kn. 17. 14, the barrel of meal shall not *w.*
Ps. 80. 13, the boar out of the wood doth *w.* it. R. V. ravage.
91. 6, nor for the destruction that *w.* at noonday.
Isa. 24. 1, the Lord maketh the earth *w.*
61. 4, they shall build the old *w.*
Joel 1. 10, the field is *w.*, the corn is *w.*
See Prov. 18. 9; Isa. 59. 7; Mat. 26. 8; Mk. 14. 4.

Waste forbidden. John 6. 12.

Watch (*n.*). Ps. 90. 4, as a *w.* in the night.
119. 148, mine eyes prevent the night *w.*
Jer. 51. 12, make the *w.* strong.
Hab. 2. 1, I will stand upon my *w.*
See Mat. 27. 65; Lu. 2. 8.

Watch (*v.*). Gen. 31. 49, the Lord *w.* between me and thee.
Job 14. 16, dost thou not *w.* over my sin?
Ps. 37. 32, the wicked *w.* the righteous.
102. 7, I *w.*, and am as a sparrow.
130. 6, more than they that *w.* for morning. R. V. watchmen.
Isa. 29. 20, all that *w.* for iniquity are cut off.
Jer. 20. 10, my familiars *w.* for my halting.
31. 28, so will I *w.* over them, to build.
44. 27, I will *w.* over them for evil.
Ezek. 7. 6, the end is come, it *w.* for thee. R. V. awaketh against.
Hab. 2. 1, I will *w.* to see what he will say. R. V. look forth.
Mat. 24. 42; 25. 13; Mk. 13. 35; Lu. 21. 36; Acts 20. 31, *w.* therefore.
26. 41; Mk. 13. 33; 14. 38, *w.* and pray.
1 Thes. 5. 6; 1 Pet. 4. 7, let us *w.* and be sober.
Heb. 13. 17, for they *w.* for your souls.

Watches of time. Ex. 14. 24; Jud. 7. 19; Lam. 2. 19; 1 Sam. 11. 11; Mat. 14. 25; Mk. 6. 48. *See also* under Day.

Watchfulness enjoined. Mat. 24. 42; 25. 13; 26. 41; Mk. 13. 35; Lu. 12. 35; 21. 36; 1 Cor. 10. 12; 16. 13; Eph. 6. 18; Col. 4. 2; 1 Thes. 5. 6; 2 Tim. 4. 5; 1 Pet. 4. 7; 5. 8; Rev. 3. 2; 16. 15.

Watchmen, their duty. 2 Sam. 18. 25; 2 Kn. 9. 17; Ps. 127. 1; S. of S. 3. 3; 5. 7; Isa. 21. 5, 11; 52. 8; Jer. 6. 17; 31. 6; Ezek. 3. 17; 33. 7; Hab. 2. 1.
evil, described. Isa. 56. 10.

Watch tower. 2 Chr. 20. 24, Judah came toward the *w.*
Isa. 21. 5, watch in the *w.*

Water (*n.*). Gen. 26. 20, the *w.* is ours.
49. 4, unstable as *w.*
Deu. 8. 7, a land of brooks of *w.*
11. 11, the land drinketh *w.* of rain of heaven.
Jos. 7. 5, their hearts melted, and became as *w.*
2 Sam. 14. 14, as *w.* spilt on the ground.
1 Kn. 13. 22, eat no bread, and drink no *w.*
22. 27; 2 Chr. 18. 26, *w.* of affliction.
2 Kn. 3. 11, who poured *w.* on Elijah's hands.
20. 20, brought *w.* into the city.
Neh. 9. 11, threwest, as a stone into mighty *w.*
Job 8. 11, can the flag grow without *w.*?
14. 9, through the scent of *w.* it will bud.
14. 19, the *w.* wear the stones.
15. 16, who drinketh iniquity like *w.*
22. 7, thou hast not given *w.* to weary to drink.
26. 8, he bindeth up the *w.* in his thick clouds.
38. 30, the *w.* are hid as with a stone.
Ps. 22. 14, I am poured out like *w.*
23. 2, beside the still *w.*
33. 7, he gathereth the *w.* of the sea.
46. 3, though the *w.* roar and be troubled.
63. 1, a dry and thirsty land, where no *w.* is.
73. 10, *w.* of a full cup are wrung out to them.
77. 16, the *w.* saw thee.
79. 3, their blood have they shed like *w.*
124. 4, then the *w.* had overwhelmed us.
148. 4, praise him, ye *w.* above the heavens.
Prov. 5. 15, drink *w.* out of thine own cistern.
9. 17, stolen *w.* are sweet.
20. 5, counsel is like deep *w.*
25. 25, as cold *w.* to a thirsty soul.
27. 19, as in *w.* face answereth to face.
30. 4, who hath bound the *w.* in a garment?
Eccl. 11. 1, cast thy bread upon the *w.*
S. of S. 4. 15; John 7. 38, well of living *w.*
8. 7, many *w.* cannot quench love.
Isa. 1. 22, thy wine is mixed with *w.*
3. 1, take away the whole stay of *w.*
11. 9; Hab. 2. 14, as the *w.* cover the seas.
19. 5, the *w.* shall fail from the sea.
28. 17, *w.* shall overflow the hiding place.
32. 20, blessed are ye that sow beside all *w.*
33. 16, his *w.* shall be sure.
35. 6, in the wilderness shall *w.* break out.
41. 17, when the poor seek *w.*
43. 2, when thou passest through the *w.*
43. 16, a path in the mighty *w.*
43. 20, I give *w.* in the wilderness.
44. 3, I will pour *w.* on him that is thirsty.
55. 1, come ye to the *w.*
57. 20, whose *w.* cast up mire and dirt.
Jer. 2. 13; 17. 13, the fountain of living *w.*
9. 1, Oh that my head were *w.*!
14. 3, their nobles sent little ones to the *w.*
47. 2, behold, *w.* rise up out of the north.
Ezek. 4. 17, that they may want bread and *w.*
7. 17; 21. 7, be weak as *w.*
31. 4, the *w.* made him great.
36. 25, then will I sprinkle clean *w.* upon you.
Am. 8. 11, not famine of bread nor thirst for *w.*
Mat. 3. 11; Mk. 1. 8; Lu. 3. 16; John 1. 26; Acts 1. 5; 11. 16, baptize you with *w.*
10. 42; Mk. 9. 41, whoso giveth a cup of cold *w.*
14. 28, bid me come to thee on the *w.*
27. 24, Pilate took *w.*, and washed.
Lu. 8. 23, ship filled with *w.*
8. 24, and rebuked the raging of the *w*
16. 24, dip the tip of his finger in *w.*
John 3. 5, except a man be born of *w.*
3. 23, there was much *w.* there.
4. 15, give me this *w.*
5. 3, waiting for moving of the *w.*
19. 34, forthwith came out blood and *w.*
Acts 10. 47, can any forbid *w.*?
2 Cor. 11. 26, in perils of *w.*
Eph. 5. 26, cleanse it with washing of *w.*
1 Pet. 3. 20, eight souls were saved by *w.*
2 Pet. 2. 17, wells without *w.*
1 John 5. 6, this is he that came by *w.*
Rev. 22. 17, let him take the *w.* of life freely.
See Ps. 29. 3; Jer. 51. 13; Ezek. 32. 2.

Water (*v.*). Gen. 2. 6, mist that *w.* face of ground.
13. 10, the plain was well *w.*
Deu. 11. 10, *w.* it with thy foot, as a garden.
Ps. 6. 6, I *w.* my couch with tears.
72. 6, as showers that *w.* the earth.
104. 13, he *w.* the hills from his chambers.
Prov. 11. 25, he that *w.*, shall be *w.*
Isa. 16. 9, I will *w.* thee with my tears.
27. 3, I will *w.* it every moment.
55. 10, returneth not, but *w.* the earth.
58. 11; Jer. 31. 12, thou shalt be like a *w.* garden.
Ezek. 32. 6, I will also *w.* with thy blood.
1 Cor. 3. 6, Apollos *w.*, but God gave the increase.
See Ezek. 17. 7; Joel 3. 18.

Water, miracles of. Gen. 21. 19; Ex. 15. 23; 17. 6; Num. 20. 7; 2 Kn. 3. 20.
the trial of jealousy by. Num. 5. 17.
used in baptism. Mat. 3. 11; Acts 8. 36; 10. 47.
Christ walks on. Mat. 14. 25; Mk. 6. 48; John 6. 19.
figuratively mentioned. Ps. 65. 9; Isa. 41. 17; 44. 3; 55. 1; Jer. 2. 13; Ezek. 47.; Zec. 13. 1; John 3. 5; 4. 10; 7. 38; Rev. 7. 17; 21. 6; 22.
of affliction. 1 Kn. 22. 27.

Waters of creation. Gen. 1. 2, 6, 9.
the flood. Gen. 6. 17; 7. 6.
fountain of living. Jer. 2. 13; 17. 13.
living fountains of. Rev. 7. 17.

Wave offering. Ex. 29. 24; Lev. 7. 30; 8. 27; 23. 11, 20; Num. 5. 25; 6. 20.

Wavering. Heb. 10. 23, the profession of our faith without *w.*
Jas. 1. 5, ask in faith, nothing *w.* R. V. doubting.

Waves. Ps. 42. 7, all thy *w.* are gone over me.
65. 7; 89. 9; 107. 29, stilleth noise of *w.*
93. 4, the Lord is mightier than mighty *w.* R. V. breakers.
Isa. 48. 18, thy righteousness as the *w.* of the sea.
Jer. 5. 22, though the *w.* toss.
Zec. 10. 11, shall smite the *w.* in the sea.
Jude 13, raging *w.* of the sea.
See Mat. 8. 24; 14. 24; Mk. 4. 37; Acts 27. 41.

Wax (*n.*). Ps. 22. 14; 68. 2; 97. 5; Mic. 1. 4.

Wax (*v.*), to grow, become. Ex. 22. 24; 32. 10, my wrath shall *w.* hot.
Num. 11. 23, is the Lord's hand *w.* short?
Deu. 8. 4; 29. 5; Neh. 9. 21, raiment *w.* not old.
32. 15, Jeshurun *w.* fat, and kicked.
Ps. 102. 26; Isa. 50. 9; 51. 6; Heb. 1. 11, shall *w.* old as doth a garment.
Mat. 24. 12, the love of many shall *w.* cold.
Lu. 12. 33, bags which *w.* not old.
See Mat. 13. 15; 1 Tim. 5. 11; 2 Tim. 3. 13.

Way. Gen. 6. 12, all flesh had corrupted his *w.*
24. 56, seeing the Lord hath prospered my *w.*
28. 20, if God will keep me in this *w.*
Num. 22. 32, thy *w.* is perverse.
Deu. 8. 6; 26. 17; 28. 9; 30. 16; 1 Kn. 2. 3; Ps. 119. 3; 128. 1; Isa. 42. 24, walk in his *w.*
Jos. 23. 14; 1 Kn. 2. 2, the *w.* of all the earth.
1 Sam. 12. 23, teach you the good and right *w.*
2 Sam. 22. 31; Ps. 18. 30, as for God, his *w.* is perfect.
2 Kn. 7. 15, all the *w.* was full of garments.
2 Chr. 6. 27, when thou hast taught them the good *w.*
Ez. 8. 21, to seek of him a right *w.*
Job 3. 23, to a man whose *w.* is hid.
12. 24; Ps. 107. 40, to wander where there is no *w.*
16. 22, I go the *w.* whence I shall not return.
19. 8, fenced up my *w.*
22. 15, hast thou marked the old *w.*?
23. 10, he knoweth the *w.* that I take.
24. 13, they know not the *w.* of the light.
31. 4, doth not he see my *w.*?
38. 19, where is the *w.* where light dwelleth?
Ps. 1. 6, the Lord knoweth the *w.* of the righteous.
2. 12, lest ye perish from the *w.*
25. 9, the meek will he teach his *w.*

Ps. 27. 11; 86. 11, teach me thy *w*.
36. 4, in a *w*. that is not good.
37. 5, commit thy *w*. unto the Lord.
39. 1, I will take heed to my *w*.
49. 13, this their *w*. is their folly.
67. 2, that thy *w*. may be known.
78. 50, he made a *w*. to his anger. R. V. path for.
95. 10; Heb. 3. 10, they have not known my *w*.
101. 2, behave wisely in a perfect *w*.
119. 5, O that my *w*. were directed.
119. 30, I have chosen the *w*. of truth.
119. 59, I thought on my *w*.
119. 168, all my *w*. are before thee.
139. 24, lead me in the *w*. everlasting.
Prov. 2. 8, he preserveth the *w*. of his saints.
3. 6, in all thy *w*. acknowledge him.
3. 17, her *w*. are *w*. of pleasantness.
5. 21, the *w*. of man are before the Lord.
6. 6, consider her *w*., and be wise.
6. 23; 15. 24; Jer. 21. 8, the *w*. of life.
12. 15, the *w*. of a fool is right in his own eyes.
15. 19, the *w*. of the slothful man.
16. 7, when a man's *w*. please the Lord.
22. 6, train up a child in the *w*.
23. 19, guide thy heart in the *w*.
23. 26, let thine eyes observe my *w*.
26. 13, there is a lion in the *w*.
Eccl. 11. 5, the *w*. of the spirit.
12. 5, fears shall be in the *w*.
Isa. 2. 3; Mic. 4. 2, he will teach us of his *w*.
30. 21, this is the *w*., walk ye in it.
35. 8, and a *w*., called the *w*. of holiness.
40. 27, my *w*. is hid from the Lord.
42. 16, the blind by a *w*. they knew not.
42. 24, they would not walk in his *w*.
45. 13, I will direct all his *w*.
55. 8, neither are your *w*. my *w*.
58. 2, they delight to know my *w*.
Jer. 6. 16, where is the good *w*.?
17. 10; 32. 19, every man according to his *w*.
18. 11, make your *w*. and doings good.
32. 39, I will give them one heart and one *w*.
50. 5, they shall ask the *w*. to Zion. R. V. concerning.
Ezek. 3. 18, to warn the wicked from his *w*.
18. 29, are not my *w*. equal? are not your *w*. unequal?
Joel 2. 7, march every one on his *w*.
Nah. 1. 3, the Lord hath his *w*. in the whirlwind.
Hag. 1. 5, consider your *w*.
Mal. 3. 1, he shall prepare the *w*. before me.
Mat. 7. 13, broad is the *w*. that leadeth.
10. 5, go not into *w*. of Gentiles.
22. 16; Mk. 12. 14; Lu. 20. 21, teachest the *w*. of God.
Mk. 8. 3, they will faint by the *w*.
11. 8; Mat. 21. 8; Lu. 19. 36, spread garments in the *w*.
Lu. 15. 20, when he was yet a great *w*. off. R. V. afar.
19. 4, he was to pass that *w*.
John 10. 1, but climbeth up some other *w*.
14. 4, and the *w*. ye know.
14. 6, I am the *w*., the truth, and the life.
Acts 9. 27, how he had seen the Lord in the *w*.
16. 17, which shew unto us the *w*. of salvation.
18. 26, expounded the *w*. of God more perfectly.
Rom. 3. 12, they are all gone out of the *w*.
11. 33, his *w*. are past finding out.
1 Cor. 10. 13, will make a *w*. to escape.
12. 31, a more excellent *w*.
Col. 2. 14, took handwriting of ordinances out of the *w*.
Heb. 5. 2, compassion on them out of the *w*. R. V. the erring.
9. 8, the *w*. into the holiest.
10. 20, by a new and living *w*.
Jas. 1. 8, unstable in all his *w*.
5. 20, the sinner from error of his *w*.
2 Pet. 2. 2, many shall follow their pernicious *w*. R. V. doings.
2. 15, which have forsaken the right *w*.
2 Pet. 2. 21, better not to have known *w*. of righteousness.
Jude 11, they have gone in the *w*. of Cain.
See Hos. 2. 6; Lu. 10. 31; Rev. 15. 3.

Way (*n*.), the Christian life and doctrine. Acts 9. 2, if he found any of this *w*.
19. 23, no small stir about that *w*.
24. 14, after the *w*. which they call heresy.

Wayfaring. Jud. 19. 17; Isa. 35. 8; Jer. 14. 8.

Waymarks. Jer. 31. 21.

Wayside. 1 Sam. 4. 13; Ps. 140. 5; Mat. 13. 4; Lu. 18. 35.

Weak. Jud. 16. 7, *w*. as other men.
2 Sam. 3. 1, Saul's house waxed *w*. and *w*.
2 Chr. 15. 7, let not your hands be *w*. R. V. slack.
Job 4. 3, thou hast strengthened the *w*. hands.
Ps. 6. 2, I am *w*. R. V. withered away.
Isa. 14. 10, art thou also become *w*. as we?
35. 3, strengthen ye the *w*. hands.
Ezek. 7. 17; 21. 7, shall be *w*. as water.
16. 30, how *w*. is thy heart!
Joel 3. 10, let the *w*. say, I am strong.
Mat. 26. 41; Mk. 14. 38, but the flesh is *w*.
Acts 20. 35, ye ought to support the *w*.
Rom. 4. 19, being not *w*. in faith.
8. 3, for the law was *w*.
1 Cor. 1. 27, *w*. things to confound the mighty.
11. 30, for this cause many are *w*.
2 Cor. 10. 10, his bodily presence is *w*.
11. 29, who is *w*., and I am not *w*.?
12. 10, when I am *w*., then am I strong.
Gal. 4. 9, turn again to *w*. elements.
1 Pet. 3. 7, giving honour to the wife, as *w*. vessel.
See Job 12. 21; Jer. 38. 4.

Weak in the faith. Rom. 14.; 15.; 1 Cor. 8.; 1 Thes. 5. 14; Heb. 12. 12.
Paul's example. 1 Cor. 9. 22.

Weakness. 1 Cor. 1. 25, the *w*. of God.
2. 3, I was with you in *w*.
15. 43, it is sown in *w*., raised in power.
See 2 Cor. 12. 9; 13. 4; Heb. 7. 18; 11. 34.

Wealth. Deu. 8. 18, Lord giveth power to get *w*.
1 Sam. 2. 32, thou shalt see an enemy in all the *w*.
2 Chr. 1. 11, thou hast not asked *w*.
Esth. 10. 3, seeking the *w*. of his people. R. V. good.
Job 21. 13, they spend their days in *w*. R. V. prosperity.
31. 25, if I rejoiced because my *w*. was great.
Ps. 44. 12, dost not increase *w*. by price.
49. 6, they that trust in *w*.
49. 10, wise men die, and leave *w*. to others.
112. 3, *w*. and riches shall be in his house.
Prov. 5. 10, lest strangers be filled with thy *w*. R. V. strength.
10. 15; 18. 11, the rich man's *w*. is his strong city.
13. 11, *w*. gotten by vanity.
19. 4, *w*. maketh many friends.
Acts 19. 25, by this craft we have our *w*.
1 Cor. 10. 24, seek every man another's *w*. R. V. good.
See Deu. 8. 17; Ru. 2. 1; Ez. 9. 12; Zec. 14. 14.

Wealthy. Ps. 66. 12; Jer. 49. 31.

Weaned. 1 Sam. 1. 22; Ps. 131. 2; Isa. 11. 8; 28. 9.

Weapon. Neh. 4. 17, with the other hand held a *w*.
Isa. 13. 5; Jer. 50. 25, the *w*. of his indignation.
54. 17, no *w*. formed against thee shall prosper.
Jer. 22. 7, every one with his *w*.
Ezek. 9. 1, with destroying *w*. in his hand.
2 Cor. 10. 4, the *w*. of our warfare.
See Job 20. 24; Ezek. 39. 9; John 18. 3.

Wear. Job 14. 19, the waters *w*. the stones.
Isa. 4. 1, we will *w*. our own apparel.
Zec. 13. 4, nor shall they *w*. a rough garment.
Mat. 11. 8, that *w*. soft clothing.
See Deu. 22. 5; Esth. 6. 8; Lu. 9. 12; 1 Pet. 3. 3.

Weariness. Eccl. 12. 12; Mal. 1. 13; 2 Cor. 11. 27.

Weary. Gen. 27. 46, I am *w.* of my life.
2 Sam. 23. 10, he smote till his hand was *w.*
Job 3. 17, and the *w.* be at rest.
10. 1, my soul is *w.*
16. 7, now he hath made me *w.*
22. 7, thou hast not given water to the *w.*
Ps. 6. 6, I am *w.* with groaning.
Prov. 3. 11, be not *w.* of the Lord's correction.
25. 17, lest he be *w.* of thee.
Isa. 5. 27, none shall be *w.* among them.
28. 12, cause the *w.* to rest.
32. 2, as the shadow of a great rock in *w.* land.
40. 28, God fainteth not, neither is *w.*
40. 31, they shall run, and not be *w.*
43. 22, thou hast been *w.* of me.
46. 1, a burden to the *w.* beast.
50. 4, a word in season to him that is *w.*
Jer. 6. 11, I am *w.* with holding in.
15. 6, I am *w.* with repenting.
20. 9, I was *w.* with forbearing.
31. 25, I have satiated the *w.* soul.
Gal. 6. 9; 2 Thes. 3. 13, be not *w.* in well doing.
See Jud. 4. 21; Ps. 68. 9; 69. 3; Hab. 2. 13.

Weary (*v.*). Isa. 7. 13, will ye *w.* my God also?
43. 24, thou hast *w.* me.
47. 13, *w.* in the multitude of counsels.
57. 10, *w.* in the greatness of thy way.
Jer. 12. 5, with footmen, and they *w.* thee.
Ezek. 24. 12, she hath *w.* herself with lies.
Mic. 6. 3, wherein have I *w.* thee?
Lu. 18. 5, lest she *w.* me. R. V. wear me out.
John 4. 6, being *w.*, sat thus on the well.
Heb. 12. 3, lest ye be *w.* and faint.
See Eccl. 10. 15; Jer. 4. 31; Mal. 2. 17.

Weasel (Lev. 11. 29). Heb. *Hôled*, glider, or burrower; Gk. γαλῆ. Either a mole-rat or a weasel; probably the latter, for the typical mole genus is believed not to occur in Palestine, while throughout the country are found the weasel and the pole-cat.

Weather. Job 37. 22; Prov. 25. 20; Mat. 16. 2.

Weave. Jud. 16. 13; Isa. 19. 9; 59. 5.

Weaver. Ex. 35. 35; Job 7. 6; Isa. 38. 12.

Web. Jud. 16. 13; Job 8. 14; Isa. 59. 5. [14. 8.

Wedding, parable of. Mat. 22. *See* Lu. 12. 36;

Wedge of gold, lit., 'tongue of gold' (Jos. 7. 21). Before the coinage of money, wedges, bars, or rings of gold and silver were used as money, by weight. Isa. 13. 12.

Weed. Jon. 2. 5. *See* BULRUSH (4) *Sûph.*

Week. Gen. 29. 27, fulfil her *w.*
Jer. 5. 24, the appointed *w.* of harvest.
Dan. 9. 27, in the midst of the *w.*
Mat. 28. 1; Mk. 16. 2, 9; Lu. 24. 1; John 20. 1, 19; Acts 20. 7; 1 Cor. 16. 2, the first day of the *w.*
See Num. 28. 26; Dan. 10. 2; Lu. 18. 12.

Weeks, Feast of. *See* FEASTS.
seventy, prophecy of. Dan. 9. 24.

Weening, imagining. 2 Mac. 5. 21.

Weep. Gen. 43. 30, he sought where to *w.*
1 Sam. 1. 8; John 20. 13, why *w.* thou?
11. 5, what aileth the people that they *w.*?
30. 4, no more power to *w.*
Neh. 8. 9, mourn not, nor *w.*
Job 27. 15, his widows shall not *w.* R. V. make no lamentation.
30. 25, did not I *w.* for him that was in trouble?
Eccl. 3. 4, a time to *w.*
Isa. 15. 2, he is gone up to *w.*
22. 4, I will *w.* bitterly.
30. 19, thou shalt *w.* no more.
Jer. 9. 1, that I might *w.* day and night.
22. 10, *w.* ye not for the dead.
Joel 1. 5, awake, ye drunkards, and *w.*
Mk. 5. 39, why make ye this ado and *w.*?
Lu. 6. 21, blessed are ye that *w.* now.
7. 13; 8. 52; Rev. 5. 5, *w.* not.
23. 28, *w.* not for me, but *w.* for yourselves.
John 11. 31, she goeth to the grave to *w.* there.
Acts 21. 13, what mean ye to *w.*?
Rom. 12. 15, and *w.* with them that *w.*
See John 16. 20; 1 Cor. 7. 30; Jas. 4. 9; 5. 1.

Weeping. 2 Sam. 15. 30, *w.* as they went.
Ez. 3. 13, could not discern noise of joy from *w.*
Job 16. 16, my face is foul with *w.*
Ps. 6. 8, the Lord hath heard the voice of my *w.*
30. 5, *w.* may endure for a night.
102. 9, I have mingled my drink with *w.*
Isa. 65. 19, the voice of *w.* be no more heard.
Jer. 31. 16, refrain thy voice from *w.*
48. 5, continual *w.* shall go up.
Joel 2. 12, turn to me with fasting and *w.*
Mat. 8. 12; 22. 13; 24. 51; 25. 30; Lu. 13. 28, *w.* and gnashing of teeth.
Lu. 7. 38, stood at his feet behind him *w.*
John 11. 33, when Jesus saw her *w.*
20. 11, Mary stood without at sepulchre *w.*
Phil. 3. 18, now tell you even *w.*

Weeping. Num. 25. 6; Ps. 6. 8; 30. 5; Jer. 31. 15; Joel 2. 12; Mal. 2. 13; 2. 18; Mat. 8. 12; 22. 13; Lu. 6. 21; 7. 38; Acts 9. 39; Rom. 12. 15; 1 Cor. 7. 30; Phil. 3. 18; Rev. 18. 15.
for the departed. Gen. 23. 2; 2 Sam. 1. 24; Eccl. 12. 5; Jer. 9. 17; 22. 10; Ezek. 24. 16; Am. 5. 16; Mk. 5. 39; John 11. 35; 20. 13; 1 Thes. 4. 13.
none in heaven. Rev. 21. 4.

Weigh. 2 Sam. 14. 26, *w.* the hair of his head.
Job 6. 2, oh that my grief were *w.*!
31. 6, let me be *w.* in an even balance.
Isa. 26. 7, thou dost *w.* the path of the just. R. V. direct.
40. 12, who hath *w.* the mountains?
Dan. 5. 27, thou art *w.* in the balances.
See Job 28. 25; Prov. 16. 2; Zec. 11. 12.

Weight. Lev. 26. 26, deliver your bread by *w.*
Job 28. 25, to make the *w.* for the winds.
Ezek. 4. 10, thy meat shall be by *w.*
4. 16, they shall eat bread by *w.*
2 Cor. 4. 17, a more exceeding *w.* of glory.
Heb. 12. 1, lay aside every *w.*

Weights. *See* Table, p. 311.

Weights, just, commanded. Lev. 19. 35; Deu. 25. 13; Prov. 11. 1; 16. 11; 20. 10, 23; Ezek. 45. 10; Mic. 6. 10.

Weighty. Prov. 27. 3; Mat. 23. 23; 2 Cor. 10. 10.

Welfare. Neh. 2. 10, to seek *w.* of Israel.
Job 30. 15, my *w.* passeth away.
Ps. 69. 22, which should have been for their *w.* R. V. when they are at peace.
Jer. 38. 4, seeketh not the *w.* of this people.
See Gen. 43. 27; Ex. 18. 7; 1 Chr. 18. 10.

Well (*n.*). Num. 21. 17, spring up, O *w.*
Deu. 6. 11, *w.* which thou diggedst not. R. V. cisterns.
2 Sam. 23. 15; 1 Chr. 11. 17, water of the *w.* of Bethlehem.
Ps. 84. 6, through valley of Baca make it a *w.* R. V. place of springs.
Prov. 5. 15, waters out of thine own *w.*
10. 11, a *w.* of life. R. V. fountain.
S. of S. 4. 15; John 4. 14, *w.* of living waters.
Isa. 12. 3, the *w.* of salvation.
John 4. 6, sat thus on the *w.*
2 Pet. 2. 17, *w.* without water. R. V. springs.
See Gen. 21. 19; 49. 22; 2 Sam. 17. 18.

Well (*adv.*). Gen. 4. 7, if thou doest *w.*
12. 13, *w.* with me for thy sake.
29. 6, is he *w.*? and they said, he is *w.* [thee.
40. 14, think on me when it shall be *w.* with
Ex. 4. 14, I know he can speak *w.*
Num. 11. 18, it was *w.* with us in Egypt.
Deu. 4. 40; 5. 16; 6. 3; 12. 25; 19. 13; 22. 7; Ru. 3. 1; Eph. 6. 3, that it may go *w.* with thee.
1 Sam. 20. 7, if he say thus, it is *w.*
2 Kn. 4. 26, is it *w.* with thee, is it *w.*?
2 Chr. 12. 12, in Judah things went *w.* R. V. good . . . were found.
Ps. 49. 18, when thou doest *w.* to thyself.
Prov. 11. 10, when it goeth *w.* with the righteous.
14. 15, looketh *w.* with the righteous.
30. 29, three things which go *w.* R. V. are stately.
Eccl. 8. 12, it shall be *w.* with them that fear God.

Isa. 3. 10, say to the righteous, it shall be *w.*
Ezek. 33. 32, one that can play *w.*
Jon. 4. 4, doest thou *w.* to be angry?
Mat. 25. 21; Lu. 19. 17, *w.* done.
Mk. 7. 37, he hath done all things *w.*
Lu. 6. 26, when all men speak *w.* of you.
Gal. 5. 7, ye did run *w.*
See Phil. 4. 14; 1 Tim. 3. 5; 5. 17; Tit. 2. 9.

Well of Beth-lehem. 1 Chr. 11. 17, 18.

Wellbeloved. Isa. 5. 1; Mk. 12. 6; 3 John 1.

Wellpleasing. Phil. 4. 18; Col. 3. 20; Heb. 13. 21.

Wells: of Abraham, Gen. 26. 15. Isaac, Gen. 26. 25.
Uzziah, 2 Chr. 26. 10. Jacob, John 4. 6.

Wellspring. Prov. 16. 22; 18. 4.

Went. Gen. 4. 16, Cain *w.* out from the presence.
Deu. 1. 31, in all the way ye *w.*
2 Kn. 5. 26, *w.* not my heart with thee?
Ps. 42. 4, I *w.* with them to the house of God. R. V. led.
106. 32, it *w.* ill with Moses.
Mat. 21. 30, I go, sir, and *w.* not.
Lu. 17. 14, as they *w.* they were cleansed.
18. 10, two men *w.* up into the temple to pray.
See Mat. 11. 7; 20. 1; Lu. 6. 19; John 8. 9.

Wept. 2 Kn. 8. 11, the man of God *w.*
Ez. 10. 1; Neh. 8. 9, the people *w.* very sore.
Neh. 1. 4, I *w.* before God.
Lu. 7. 32, we mourned, and ye have not *w.*
19. 41, beheld the city, and *w.* over it.
John 11. 35, Jesus *w.*
1 Cor. 7. 30, that weep as though they *w.* not.
See 2 Sam. 12. 22; Ps. 69. 10; 137. 1; Rev. 5. 4.

West. Ps. 103. 12; Isa. 43. 5; Mat. 24. 27.

Wet. Job 24. 8; Dan. 4. 15; 5. 21.

Whale. (1) (some *land*-monster: *Dragon*, or *Serpent?*). Ex. 7. 9; Deu. 32. 33; Ps. 91. 13; Jer. 51. 34. Heb. *Tannîn*: Gk. *κῆτος*. The Hebrew word means a 'monster' in animal life. In Gen. 1. 21 'great whale' is generic of *all* monsters moving in the waters. So in Mat. 12. 40 the Greek *κῆτος* means any great sea-monster, as does the Hebrew *Dâg gâdôl* of Jon. 1. 17.

Weights.

							Ordinary Heavy Weight.			Light Weight.		
							Grains.	Pounds.	Oz.	Grains.	Pounds.	Oz.
Gerah, 'grain' = 1/20 shekel							11.2			5.6		
5	Rebah, 'quarter' = ¼ shekel						56			28		
10	2	Bekah, 'half' = ½ shekel					112			56		
20	4	2	Shekel				224.5		½	112		¼
400	80	40	20	Libra, Gk. *Litra*, the Pound of John 12. 3.			5050		Avoir. 11.536			
1000	200	100	50	2½	Mina, Pound of Mat. (silver); Maneh.		11,225	Troy 2 Avoir. 1	8	5612	Troy 1	Avoir. 12
60,000	12,000	6000	3000		60	Talent (silver); Kikkar, 'circle'	673,500	Troy 117 Avoir. 96⅓		336,750	Troy 58 Avoir. 48	5+
						Talent (gold)	758,000	Troy 131 Avoir. 108		379,000	Troy 65 Avoir. 54	5+

NOTE 1. The above table is in accord with the article by A. R. S. Kennedy, D.D., in Hastings' *Bib. Dict.*, and with the weights given in the Tables of Money.

NOTE 2. But there was a great variation in those times as there is now in different countries and at different times in the same country.

Dr. Kennedy makes the Denarius 56 grains.

Harper's *Classical Dictionary* makes it 60 grains, and the Mina and Talent are increased accordingly.

The **Mina** (pound) Heavy Weight Troy = 2 lbs.
" " " " Avoir. = 1½ lbs.
" " Light Weight Troy = 1 lb.
" " " " Avoir. = ¾ lb.
" Silver Roman " " = 1 5/7 lbs.
" " Babylonian " " = 2½ lbs.

NOTE 3. The **Shekel** is the unit of weight.

NOTE 4. The Pound Avoir. = 7000 grains.
The Pound Troy = 5760 grains.

NOTE 5. Pound in John 12. 3; 19. 39 = the Litra = Roman Libra = 5050 grains = 11 ounces, 237½ grains. Pound in Lu. 19. 13 etc. = the Mina.

(2) (some *sea*-monster; *Crocodilus?*). Job 7. 12; Ps. 74. 13; Isa. 27. 1; Ezek. 29. 3; 32. 2. *See* LEVIATHAN.

What. Ex. 16. 15, they wist not *w.* it was.
2 Sam. 16. 10, *w.* have I to do with you?
Ez. 9. 10, *w.* shall we say after this?
Job 7. 17; 15. 14; Ps. 8. 4; 144. 3, *w.* is man?
Isa. 38. 15; John 12. 27, *w.* shall I say?
Hos. 6. 4, *w.* shall I do unto thee?
Mat. 5. 47, *w.* do ye more than others?
Mk. 14. 36, not *w.* I will, but *w.* thou wilt.
John 21. 22, *w.* is that to thee?
See Acts 9. 6; 10. 4; 16. 30; 1 Pet. 1. 11.

Whatsoever. Ps. 1. 3, *w.* he doeth shall prosper.
Eccl. 3. 14, *w.* God doeth shall be for ever.
Mat. 5. 37, *w.* is more than these cometh of evil.
7. 12, *w.* ye would that men should do to you.
20. 4, *w.* is right I will give you.
Phil. 4. 8, *w.* things are true.
See John 15. 16; Rom. 14. 23; 1 Cor. 10. 31.

Wheat (Gen. 30. 14). Heb. *Chittah:* Gk. πυρός: Bot. N. *Triticum compositum*, *Triticum spelta*, *Triticum hybernum*. Wheat was the chief grain of Mesopotamia in Jacob's time; and from that day to this it has continued to be so in Egypt, where the many-eared variety (Gen. 41. 22), depicted on monuments, is still grown.
1 Sam. 12. 17, is it not *w.* harvest to day?
Job 31. 40, let thistles grow instead of *w.*
Ps. 81. 16; 147. 14, the finest of the *w.*
Jer. 12. 13, they have sown *w.*, but reap thorns.
23. 28, what is the chaff to the *w.*?
Mat. 3. 12, gather his *w.* into the garner.
Lu. 22. 31, that he may sift you as *w.*
See John 12. 24; Acts 27. 38; 1 Cor. 15. 37.

Wheat. Ex. 29. 2 (1 Kn. 5. 11; Ezek. 27. 17).
parable concerning. Mat. 13. 25.

Wheel. Ex. 14. 25, took off their chariot *w.*
Jud. 5. 28, why tarry the *w.*?
Ps. 83. 13, make them like a *w.* R. V. the whirling dust.
Prov. 20. 26, a wise king bringeth the *w.* over them. R. V. threshing *w.*
Eccl. 12. 6, or the *w.* broken at the cistern.
Isa. 28. 28, nor break it with the *w.* of his cart.
Nah. 3. 2, the noise of the rattling of the *w.*
See Isa. 5. 28; Jer. 18. 3; 47. 3.

Wheels, vision of. Ezek. 1. 15; 3. 13; 10. 9.

Whelp. 2 Sam. 17. 8; Prov. 17. 12; Hos. 13. 8.

Whelps (lion's), parable of. Ezek. 19.; Nah. 2. 12.

When. 1 Sam. 3. 12, *w.* I begin, I will also. R. V. from the beginning I will.
1 Kn. 8. 30, *w.* thou hearest, forgive.
Ps. 94. 8, *w.* will ye be wise?
Eccl. 8. 7, who can tell him *w.* it shall be? R. V. how.
Mat. 24. 3; Mk. 13. 4; Lu. 21. 7, *w.* shall these things be?
See Deu. 6. 7; John 4. 25; 16. 8; 1 John 2. 28.

Whence. Gen. 42. 7; Jos. 9. 8, *w.* come ye?
Job 10. 21, *w.* I shall not return.
Isa. 51. 1, the rock *w.* ye are hewn.
Jas. 4. 1, from *w.* come wars?
Rev. 7. 13, *w.* came they?
See Mat. 13. 54; John 1. 48; 7. 28; 9. 29.

Where. Gen. 3. 9, *w.* art thou?
Ex. 2. 20; 2 Sam. 9. 4; Job 14. 10, *w.* is he?
Job 9. 24, if not, *w.*, and who is he?
Ps. 42. 3, *w.* is thy God?
Jer. 2. 6, *w.* is the Lord?
Zec. 1. 5, your fathers, *w.* are they?
See Isa. 49. 21; Hos. 1. 10; Lu. 17. 37.

Whereby. Lu. 1. 18, *w.* shall I know this?
Acts 4. 12, none other name *w.* we must be saved. R. V. wherein.
Rom. 8. 15, the spirit of adoption, *w.* we cry.
See Jer. 33. 8; Ezek. 18. 31; 39. 26; Eph. 4. 30.

Wherefore. 2 Sam. 12. 23, *w.* should I fast?
Mat. 14. 31, *w.* didst thou doubt?
26. 50, *w.* art thou come? R. V. do that for which.
See 2 Sam. 16. 10; Mal. 2. 15; Acts 10. 21.

Whereto. Isa. 55. 11; Phil. 3. 16.

Wherewith. Jud. 6. 15, *w.* shall I save Israel?
Ps. 119. 42, so shall I have *w.* to answer. R.V. an.
Mic. 6. 6, *w.* shall I come before the Lord?
See Mat. 5. 13; Mk. 9. 5; John 17. 26; Eph. 2. 4.

Whet. Deu. 32. 41; Ps. 7. 12; 64. 3; Eccl. 10. 10.

Whether. Mat. 21. 31, *w.* of them did the will.
23. 17, *w.* is greater, the gold or the temple?
Rom. 14. 8, *w.* we live or die.
2 Cor. 12. 2, *w.* in the body, or out of the body.
See 1 Kn. 20. 18; Ezek. 2. 5; 3. 11; 1 John 4. 1.

While. 2 Chr. 15. 2, with you, *w.* ye be with him.
Ps. 49. 18, *w.* he lived he blessed his soul.
Isa. 55. 6, *w.* he may be found.
Jer. 15. 9, her sun is gone down *w.* it was yet day.
Lu. 18. 4, he would not for a *w.*
24. 44, *w.* I was yet with you.
John 9. 4, work *w.* it is day.
1 Tim. 5. 6, she is dead *w.* she liveth.
See 1 Sam. 9. 27; 2 Sam. 7. 19; Acts 20. 11.

Whip. 1 Kn. 12. 11; Prov. 26. 3; Nah. 3. 2.

Whirlwinds. 1 Kn. 19. 11; 2 Kn. 2. 1; Job 37. 9; 38. 1; Isa. 66. 15; Jer. 23. 19; Ezek. 1. 4; Nah. 1. 3; Zec. 9. 14.

Whispering. Prov. 16. 28; 26. 20; Rom. 1. 29; 2 Cor. 12. 20. *See* SLANDER, TALEBEARERS.

Whit, a bit, atom. Every whit = wholly; not a whit = not at all. 1 Sam. 3. 18; John 7. 23; 13. 10; 2 Cor. 11. 5.

White. Gen. 49. 12, his teeth shall be *w.* with milk.
Num. 12. 10, leprous, *w.* as snow.
Job 6. 6, is any taste in the *w.* of an egg?
Eccl. 9. 8, let thy garments be always *w.*
S. of S. 5. 10, my beloved is *w.* and ruddy.
Isa. 1. 18, they shall be *w.* as snow.
Mat. 5. 36, thou canst not make one hair *w.* or black.
John 4. 35, *w.* already to harvest.
Rev. 2. 17, a *w.* stone.
3. 4, walk with me in *w.*
See Dan. 11. 35; 12. 10; Mat. 17. 2; 28. 3.

Whited. Mat. 23. 27; Acts 23. 3.

White horse, Rev. 6. 2; 19. 11. cloud, Rev. 14. 14.

Whiter. Ps. 51. 7; Lam. 4. 7.

White raiment, of Christ, at the transfiguration. Mat. 17. 2; Mk. 9. 3; Lu. 9. 29.
of angels. Mat. 28. 3; Mk. 16. 5.
of the redeemed. Rev. 3. 5; 4. 4; 7. 9; 19. 8, 14.

White throne. Rev. 20. 11.

Whither. 2 Kn. 5. 25; S. of S. 6. 1; Heb. 11. 8.

Whole. 2 Sam. 1. 9, my life is yet *w.* in me.
Eccl. 12. 13, this is the *w.* duty of man.
Jer. 19. 11, a vessel that cannot be made *w.*
Ezek. 15. 5, when *w.* it was meet for no work.
Mat. 5. 29, not that thy *w.* body be cast into hell.
9. 12; Mk. 2. 17, the *w.* need not a physician.
13. 33; Lu. 13. 21, till the *w.* was leavened.
16. 26; Mk. 8. 36; Lu. 9. 25, gain the *w.* world.
John 11. 50, expedient that the *w.* nation perish not.
1 Cor. 12. 17, if the *w.* body were an eye.
1 Thes. 5. 23, I pray God your *w.* spirit. R. V. omits.
Jas. 2. 10, keep the *w.* law.
1 John 2. 2, for the sins of the *w.* world.
5. 19, the *w.* world lieth in wickedness.
See Mat. 15. 31; John 5. 6; 7. 23; Acts 9. 34.

Whole, the, need not a physician. Mat. 9. 12; Mk. 2. 17; Lu. 5. 31.
made. Mat. 12. 13; Mk. 3. 5; Lu. 6. 10. *See* MIRACLES.
world, if a man gain, and lose his soul. Mat. 16. 26; Mk. 8. 36; Lu. 9. 25.

Wholesome. Prov. 15. 4; 1 Tim. 6. 3.

Wholly. Job 21. 23, dieth, being *w.* at ease.
Jer. 2. 21, planted thee *w.* a right seed.
46. 28, not *w.* unpunished. R. V. omits.
Acts 17. 16, the city *w.* given to idolatry. R. V. full of.
1 Thes. 5. 23, sanctify you *w.*
1 Tim. 4. 15, give thyself *w.* to them.
See Lev. 19. 9; Deu. 1. 36; Jos. 14. 8.

Whomsoever. Dan. 4. 17, 25, 32, to *w.* he will.
Mat. 11. 27, to *w.* the Son will reveal him.
21. 44; Lu. 20. 18, on *w.* it shall fall.
Lu. 4. 6, to *w.* I will, I give it.
12. 48, to *w.* much is given.
See Gen. 31. 32; Jud. 11. 24; Acts 8. 19.
Whore, vision of the great. Rev. 17.; 18.
Whoredom condemned. Lev. 19. 29; Deu. 22. 21; 23. 17.
spiritual. Ezek. 16.; 23.; Jer. 3.; Hos. 1.; 2. *See* IDOLATRY.
Whoremongers condemned. Eph. 5. 5; 1 Tim. 1. 10; Heb. 13. 4; Rev. 21. 8; 22. 15.
Whose. Gen. 32. 17, *w.* art thou, *w.* are these?
Jer. 44. 28, shall know *w.* words shall stand.
Mat. 22. 20; Mk. 12. 16; Lu. 20. 24, *w.* is this image?
Lu. 12. 20, then *w.* shall these things be?
Acts 27. 23, *w.* I am, and whom I serve.
See 1 Sam. 12. 3; Dan. 5. 23; John 20. 23.
Whosoever. 1 Cor. 11. 27, *w.* shall eat this bread.
Gal. 5. 10, bear his judgment, *w.* he be.
Rev. 22. 17, *w.* will, let him take. R. V. he that.
See Mat. 11. 6; 13. 12; Lu. 8. 18; Rom. 2. 1.
Why. 1 Sam. 2. 23, *w.* do ye such things?
Jer. 8. 14, *w.* do we sit still?
27. 13; Ezek. 18. 31; 33. 11, *w.* will ye die?
Mat. 21. 25; Mk. 11. 31; Lu. 20. 5, *w.* did ye not believe?
Mk. 5. 39, *w.* make ye this ado?
Acts 9. 4; 22. 7; 26. 14, *w.* persecutest thou me?
Rom. 9. 19, *w.* doth he yet find fault?
9. 20, *w.* hast thou made me thus?
See 2 Chr. 25. 16; Lu. 2. 48; John 7. 45; 10. 20.
Wicked. Gen. 18. 23, destroy righteous with *w.*
Deu. 15. 9, a thought in thy *w.* heart. R. V. omits.
1 Sam. 2. 9, the *w.* shall be silent.
Job 3. 17, there the *w.* cease from troubling.
8. 22, dwelling place of the *w.* shall come to nought.
9. 29; 10. 15, if I be *w.*, why labour I in vain? R. V. condemned.
21. 7, wherefore do the *w.* live?
21. 30, the *w.* is reserved to destruction. R. V. evil man.
Ps. 7. 9, let the wickedness of the *w.* come to an end.
7. 11, God is angry with the *w.* R. V. omits.
9. 17, the *w.* shall be turned into hell.
10. 4, the *w.* will not seek God.
11. 2, the *w.* bend their bow.
11. 6, upon the *w.* he shall rain snares.
12. 8, the *w.* walk on every side.
26. 5, I will not sit with the *w.*
34. 21, evil shall slay the *w.*
37. 21, the *w.* borroweth, and payeth not.
37. 32, the *w.* watcheth the righteous.
37. 35, I have seen the *w.* in great power.
58. 3, the *w.* are estranged from the womb.
68. 2, so let the *w.* perish.
94. 3, how long shall the *w.* triumph?
139. 24, see if there be any *w.* way in me.
145. 20, all the *w.* will he destroy.
Prov. 11. 5, the *w.* shall fall by his own wickedness.
14. 32, the *w.* is driven away.
28. 1, the *w.* flee when no man pursueth.
Eccl. 7. 17, be not overmuch *w.*
8. 10, I saw the *w.* buried.
Isa. 13. 11, I will punish the *w.*
53. 9, he made his grave with the *w.*
55. 7, let the *w.* forsake his way.
57. 20, the *w.* are like the troubled sea.
Jer. 17. 9, the heart is desperately *w.* R. V. sick.
Ezek. 3. 18; 33. 8, to warn the *w.*
11. 2, these men give *w.* counsel.
18. 23, have I any pleasure that the *w.* should die?
33. 15, if the *w.* restore the pledge.
Dan. 12. 10, the *w.* shall do wickedly.
Mic. 6. 11, with *w.* balances.
Nah. 1. 3, the Lord will not at all acquit the *w.* R. V. guilty.
Mat. 12. 45; Lu. 11. 26, more *w.* than himself.
13. 49, sever the *w.* from the just.
18. 32; 25. 26; Lu. 19. 22, thou *w.* servant.
Acts 2. 23, and by *w.* hands have crucified and slain. R. V. by hands of lawless men.
1 Cor. 5. 13, put away that *w.* person.
Eph. 6. 16, the fiery darts of the *w.* R. V. evil one.
Col. 1. 21, enemies in your mind by *w.* works. R. V. in your evil.
2 Thes. 2. 8, then shall that *W.* be revealed. R. V. the lawless one.
See Eccl. 9. 2; Isa. 48. 22.
Wicked, their character and doom. Deu. 32. 5; Job 4. 8; 5.; 15.; 18.; 20., 21.; 24.; 27. 13; 30.; 36. 12; Eccl. 8. 10; Isa. 1.; 22.; 28.; 29.; 37. 21; 40. 18; 41. 6; 44. 9; 45. 9; 47.; 57.-59.; 66.; Jer. 2.; Ezek. 5.; 16.; 18.; 23.; Hos. to Mal.; Mat. 5.-7.; 13. 37; 15.; 16.; 21. 33; 25.; John 5. 29; 10.; Rom. 1. 21; 3. 10; 1 Cor. 5. 11; Gal. 5. 19; Eph. 4. 17; 5. 5; Phil. 3. 18; Col. 3. 6; 2 Thes. 2.; 1 Tim. 1. 9; 4.; 6. 9; 2 Tim. 3. 13; Tit. 1. 10; Heb. 6. 4; Jas. 4.; 5.; 1 Pet. 4.; 2 Pet. 2.; 3.; 1 John 2. 18; 4.; Jude; Rev. 9. 20; 14. 8; 18.; 20. 13; 22. 15.
their prosperity not to be envied. Ps. 37. 1; 73.; Prov. 3. 31; 23. 17; 24. 1, 19; Jer. 12.
friendship with, forbidden. Gen. 28. 1; Ex. 23. 32; 34. 12; Num. 16. 26; Deu. 7. 2; 13. 6; Jos. 23. 7; Jud. 2. 2; 2 Chr. 19. 2; Ez. 9. 12; 10. 10; Neh. 9. 2; Ps. 106. 35; Prov. 1. 10; 4. 14; 12. 11; 14. 7; Jer. 2. 25; 51. 6; Rom. 16. 17; 1 Cor. 5. 9; 15. 33; 2 Cor. 6. 14; Eph. 5. 7, 11; Phil. 2. 15; 2 Thes. 3. 6; 1 Tim. 6. 5; 2 Tim. 3. 5; 2 Pet. 3. 17; Rev. 18. 4.
Wickedly. Job 13. 7, will you speak *w.* for God? R. V. unrighteously.
34. 12, God will not do *w.*
Ps. 73. 8; 139. 20, they speak *w.*
Dan. 12. 10, the wicked shall do *w.*
Mal. 4. 1, all that do *w.*
See 2 Chr. 6. 37; 22. 3; Neh. 9. 33; Ps. 106. 6.
Wickedness. Gen. 39. 9, this great *w.*
Jud. 20. 3, how was this *w.*?
1 Sam. 24. 13, *w.* proceedeth from the wicked.
1 Kn. 21. 25, sold himself to work *w.* R. V. do . . . evil.
Job 4. 8, they that sow *w.*, reap the same. R. V. trouble.
22. 5, is not thy *w.* great?
35. 8, thy *w.* may hurt a man.
Ps. 7. 9, let the *w.* of the wicked come to an end.
55. 11, *w.* is in the midst thereof.
55. 15, *w.* is in their dwellings.
58. 2, in heart ye work *w.*
84. 10, the tents of *w.*
Prov. 4. 17, they eat the bread of *w.*
8. 7, *w.* is an abomination to my lips.
11. 5, the wicked shall fall by his own *w.*
13. 6, *w.* overthroweth the sinner.
26. 26, his *w.* shall be shewed.
Eccl. 7. 25, the *w.* of folly.
Isa. 9. 18, *w.* burneth as the fire.
47. 10, thou hast trusted in thy *w.*
Jer. 2. 19, thine own *w.* shall correct thee.
6. 7, she casteth out her *w.*
8. 6, no man repented of his *w.*
44. 9, have you forgot the *w.* of the kings.
Ezek. 3. 19, if he turn not from his *w.*
7. 11, violence is risen up into a rod of *w.*
31. 11, I have driven him out for his *w.*
33. 12, in the day he turneth from his *w.*
Hos. 9. 15, for the *w.* of their doings.
10. 13, ye have plowed *w.*
Mic. 6. 10, are treasures of *w.* in house.
Zec. 5. 8, he said, this is *w.*
Mal. 1. 4, the border of *w.*
3. 15, they that work *w.* are set up.
Mk. 7. 22, out of the heart proceed *w.*
Lu. 11. 39, your inward part is full of *w.*
Rom. 1. 29, being filled with all *w.*
1 Cor. 5. 8, nor with the leaven of *w.*
Eph. 6. 12, spiritual *w.* in high places.

1 John 5. 19, the whole world lieth in *w*. R. V. the evil one.
See Gen. 6. 5; Ps. 94. 23; Prov. 21. 12; Jer. 23. 11.

Wickedness reproductive. Job 4. 8; 20. 1; Prov. 1. 31.

Wide. Ps. 35. 21, they opened their mouth *w.*
104. 25, this great and *w.* sea.
Prov. 21. 9; 25. 24; Jer. 22. 14, a *w.* house.
Mat. 7. 13, *w.* is the gate that leadeth to destruction.
See Deu. 15. 8; Ps. 81. 10; Nah. 3. 13.

Widow, Elijah sustained by one. 1 Kn. 17.
parable of. Lu. 18. 3.
the widow's mite. Mk. 12. 42; Lu. 21. 2.
figurative. Isa. 47. 9; 54. 4; Lam. 1. 1.

Widows to be honoured and relieved. Ex. 22. 22; Deu. 14. 29; 24. 17; 27. 19; Job 29. 13; Isa. 1. 17; Jer. 7. 6; Acts 6. 1; 9. 39; 1 Tim. 5. 3; Jas. 1. 27.
especially under God's protection. Deu. 10. 18; Ps. 68. 5; 146. 9; Prov. 15. 25; Jer. 49. 11.
injurers of widows, condemned. Deu. 27. 19; Ps. 94. 6; Isa. 1. 23; 10. 2; Ezek. 22. 7; Mal. 3. 5; Mat. 23. 14; Mk. 12. 40; Lu. 20. 47.
laws relating to their marriages. Lev. 21. 14; Deu. 25. 5; Ezek. 44. 22; Mk. 12. 19. *See* 1 Cor. 7. 8.

Wife. Prov. 5. 18; Eccl. 9. 9, the *w.* of thy youth.
18. 22, whoso findeth a *w.* findeth a good thing.
19. 14, a prudent *w.* is from the Lord.
Lu. 14. 20, I have married a *w.*
17. 32, remember Lot's *w.*
1 Cor. 7. 14, the unbelieving *w.* is sanctified.
Eph. 5. 23, the husband is the head of the *w.*
Rev. 21. 9, the bride, the Lamb's *w.*
See 1 Tim. 3. 2; 5. 9; Tit. 1. 6; 1 Pet. 3. 7.

Wilderness, the, the Israelites' journeys in. Ex. 14.; Num. 10. 12; 13. 3; 20.; 33.; Deu. 1. 19; 8. 2; 32. 10; Neh. 9. 19; Ps. 78. 40; 95. 8; 107. 4.
Hagar's flight into. Gen. 16. 7.
Elijah's flight into. 1 Kn. 19. 4.
John the Baptist preaches in the wilderness of Judæa. Mat. 3.

Wiles. Num. 25. 18; Eph. 6. 11.

Wilfully. Heb. 10. 26, if we sin *w.*

Will. Mat. 8. 3; Mk. 1. 41; Lu. 5. 13, I *w.*, be thou clean.
18. 14, not the *w.* of your Father.
26. 39, not as I *w.*, but as thou wilt.
Mk. 3. 35, whosoever shall do the *w.* of God.
John 1. 13, born not of the *w.* of the flesh.
4. 34, to do the *w.* of him that sent me.
Acts 21. 14, the *w.* of the Lord be done.
Rom. 7. 18, to *w.* is present with me.
Phil. 2. 13, both to *w.* and to do.
1 Tim. 2. 8, I *w.* that men pray every where. R. V. desire.
Rev. 22. 17, whosoever *w.*, let him take.
See Eph. 1. 11; Heb. 2. 4.

Will of God irresistible. Dan. 4. 17, 35; John 1. 13; Rom. 9. 19; Eph. 1. 5; Jas. 1. 18.
fulfilled by Christ (Ps. 40. 8); Mat. 26. 42; Mk. 14. 36; Lu. 22. 42; John 4. 34; 5. 30; Heb. 10. 7.
how performed. John 7. 17; Eph. 6. 6; Col. 4. 12; 1 Thes. 4. 3; 5. 18; Heb. 13. 21; 1 Pet. 2. 15; 4. 2; 1 John 2. 17; 3. 23.
to be submitted to. Jas. 4. 15. *See* Mat. 6. 10; Acts 21. 14; Rom. 1. 10; 15. 32.
of man. John 1. 13; Rom. 9. 16; Eph. 2. 3; 1 Pet. 4. 3.

Willing. Ex. 35. 5, a *w.* heart.
1 Chr. 28. 9, serve God with a *w.* mind.
29. 5, who is *w.* to consecrate his service?
Ps. 110. 3, *w.* in the day of thy power.
Mat. 26. 41, the spirit is *w.*
2 Cor. 5. 8, *w.* rather to be absent.
8. 12, if there be first a *w.* mind.
1 Tim. 6. 18, *w.* to communicate.
2 Pet. 3. 9, not *w.* that any should perish.
See Lu. 22. 42; John 5. 35; Philem. 14; 1 Pet. 5. 2.

Willow. (1) (Lev. 23. 40; Job 40. 22). Heb. *'Arâbîm;* Gk. ἰτέα: Bot. N. *Salix octandra, Salix Ægyptiaca, Salix Babylonica,* 'weeping willow.'
(2) (Ezek. 17. 5). Heb. *Tzaphtzâphah* (omitted in LXX.). Both words, without doubt, denote the willow, of which many varieties are found in Palestine.

Will worship, a worship of one's choosing. Col. 2. 23.

Wimple, a covering laid in folds over the head, around the chin and neck. Isa. 3. 22. R. V. shawls. Cheyne, 'wrappers;' Delitzsch, 'wrapping cloaks.'

Win. 2 Chr. 32. 1; Prov. 11. 30; Phil. 3. 8.

Wind. Job 6. 26, reprove speeches which are as *w.*
7. 7, remember that my life is *w.*
Prov. 11. 29, he shall inherit *w.*
25. 23, the north *w.* driveth away rain.
30. 4, gathereth the *w.* in his fists.
Eccl. 11. 4, he that observeth the *w.*
Isa. 26. 18, we have brought forth *w.*
27. 8, he stayeth his rough *w.* R. V. blast.
Ezek. 37. 9, prophesy to the *w.*
Hos. 8. 7, they have sown *w.*
Am. 4. 13, he that createth the *w.*
Mat. 11. 7, a reed shaken with the *w.*
John 3. 8, the *w.* bloweth where it listeth.
Eph. 4. 14, carried about with every *w.* of doctrine.
See Acts 2. 2; Jude 12.

Wind, miraculous effects of. Gen. 8. 1; Ex. 15. 10; Num. 11. 31; Ezek. 37. 9; Jon. 1. 4.
rebuked by Christ. Mat. 8. 26.
figuratively mentioned. Job 7. 7; 8. 2; John 3. 8; Jas. 1. 6; 3. 4.

Windows in an Oriental house consisted mainly of apertures for the admission of light and air. They were sometimes partially closed with lattice-work, wooden trellis-work, or curtains. Gen. 7. 11; Jud. 5. 28 (comp. S. of S. 2. 9; Eccl. 12. 3); Jer. 9. 21; Mal. 3. 10.

Wine. Several Hebrew words are translated thus in the Old Testament: (i.) The most general term is *yayin*, connected with the Greek οἶνος and the Latin *vinum* (Gen. 49. 12; Prov. 20. 1; Isa. 5. 11); (ii.) *Tirôsh*, the fruit of the vine, of which the etymological meaning is uncertain, but its intoxicating properties seem clearly indicated in Hos. 4. 11, 'Whoredom and wine (*yayin*) and new wine (*tirôsh*) take away the heart;' (iii.) *'Asis* (S. of S. 8. 2; Joel 1. 5; 3. 18), from a root signifying 'to tread,' indicates *new* wine, the first rich juice or must; (iv.) *Chemer* (Deu. 32. 14), in the Chaldee *chamar* (Ez. 6. 9), seems to point to an unfermented liquid, foaming when freshly poured out; (v.) *Sôbe* is derived from a root meaning to 'soak' or 'drink to excess' (Isa. 1. 22; Hos. 4. 18; Nah. 1. 10). In the New Testament we have (i.) οἶνος, answering to *yayin* as a general term for wine (Mat. 9. 17; John 2. 3; Eph. 5. 18, &c.); (ii.) *Sikera*, a Greek form of the Hebrew *shêcâr*, a generic term applied to all fermented liquors except wine (Lu. 1. 15); (iii.) *Gleukos*, sweet wine (Acts 2. 13). The wine mingled with myrrh given to our Lord was designed to deaden pain (Mk. 15. 23). In connection with the Lord's Supper Jesus never uses the word 'wine,' but always the 'fruit of the vine,' not excluding, but also not requiring, the use of fermented wine.

Wine, made by Noah. Gen. 9. 20.
used by Abram and Melchizedek. Gen. 14. 18.
used in offerings. Ex. 29. 40; Lev. 23. 13; Num. 15. 5.
in the Lord's supper. Mat. 26. 29.
Nazarites not to drink. Num. 6. 3; Jud. 13. 14.
Rechabites abstain from. Jer. 35.
water changed to, by Christ. John 2.
love of. Prov. 21. 17; 23. 20, 30; Hos. 4. 11; Hab. 2. 5; Eph. 5. 18.
its lawful use. Jud. 9. 13; 19. 19; Ps. 104. 15; Prov. 31. 6; Eccl. 10. 19; Eph. 5. 18; 1 Tim. 5. 23.
its abuse. *See* DRUNKENNESS.

Winebibber, an immoderate wine-drinker, drunkard. Mat. 11. 19.
Winefat, wine-vat. Mk. 12. 1.
Winepress. Jud. 6. 11; Neh. 13. 15; Isa. 63. 3; Lam. 1. 15; Mat. 21. 33; Rev. 14. 19; 19. 15.
Wings. Ps. 17. 8; 36. 7; 57. 1; 61. 4; 63. 13; 91. 4, the shadow of thy *w.*
18. 10; 104. 3, on the *w.* of the wind.
55. 6, Oh that I had *w.* like a dove!
139. 9, the *w.* of the morning.
Prov. 23. 5, riches make themselves *w.*
Mal. 4. 2, with healing in his *w.*
See Ezek. 1. 6; Zec. 5. 9; Mat. 23. 37; Lu. 13. 34.
Wink. Job 15. 12; Ps. 35. 19; Prov. 6. 13; 10. 10; Acts 17. 30.
Wink at, to close the eyes to, to avoid noticing. Acts 17. 30.
Winnow. Ru. 3. 2; Isa. 30. 24.
Winter. Gen. 8. 22; S. of S. 2. 11; Mat. 24. 20; Mk. 13. 18.
Wipe. 2 Kn. 21. 13; Isa. 25. 8; Lu. 7. 38; John 13. 5.
Wires. Ex. 39. 3.
Wisdom. Job 4. 21, they die without *w.*
12. 2, *w.* shall die with you.
Prov. 4. 7, *w.* is the principal thing.
16. 16, better to get *w.* than gold.
19. 8, he that getteth *w.* loveth his own soul.
23. 4, cease from thine own *w.*
Eccl. 1. 18, in much *w.* is much grief.
Isa. 10. 13, by my *w.* I have done it.
29. 14, the *w.* of their wise men shall perish.
Jer. 8. 9, they have rejected the word of the Lord; and what *w.* is in them?
Mic. 6. 9, the man of *w.* shall see thy name.
Mat. 11. 19, *w.* is justified of her children.
1 Cor. 1. 17, not with *w.* of words.
1. 24, Christ the *w.* of God.
1. 30, who of God is made unto us *w.*
2. 6, we speak *w.* among them that are perfect.
3. 19, the *w.* of this world is foolishness with God.
2 Cor. 1. 12, not with fleshly *w.*
Col. 1. 9, that ye might be filled with all *w.*
4. 5, walk in *w.* toward them.
Jas. 1. 5, if any lack *w.*
3. 17, the *w.* from above is pure.
Rev. 5. 12, worthy is the Lamb to receive *w.*
13. 18, here is *w.*
See Eccl. 1. 16; Col. 2. 3; 3. 16.
Wisdom given by God. Ex. 31. 3; 1 Kn. 3. 12; 4. 29; 1 Chr. 22. 12; 2 Chr. 1. 10; Ez. 7. 25; Prov. 2. 6; Eccl. 2. 26; Dan. 2. 20; Acts 6. 10; 7. 10; 2 Pet. 3. 15.
its characteristics. Deu. 4. 6; Job 28. 12; Ps. 111. 10; Prov. 1. 2; 9.; 14. 8; 24. 7; 28. 7; Eccl. 2. 13; 7. 19; 9. 13; Jer. 23. 24; Mat. 7. 24; Jas. 3. 13.
to be sought for. Ps. 90. 12; Mat. 10. 16; Rom. 16. 19; Eph. 5. 15; 2 Tim. 3. 15; Jas. 3. 13.
blessings attending it. Prov. 1. 5; 3. 13; 8. 11; 16. 16; 24. 3, 14; Eccl. 7. 11; 9. 13; 12. 11; Mat. 25. 1.
obtained in answer to prayer by Solomon, &c. 1 Kn. 3. 9; 10. 6; Prov. 2. 3; Dan. 2. 21; Jas. 1. 5.
personified. Prov. 1. 20; 8.; 9.
danger of despising. Prov. 1. 24; 2. 12; 3. 21; 5. 12; 8. 36; 9. 12; 10. 21; 11. 12.
apparent in the works of God. Ps. 104. 1, 24; 136. 5; Prov. 3. 19; 6. 6; Jer. 10. 12; Rom. 1. 20; 11. 33.
of Joseph, Gen. 41. 39; 47. 13. Solomon, 1 Kn. 4. 29. Daniel, &c., Ezek. 28. 3; Dan. 1. 17; 5. 14.
worldly, vanity of. Job 5. 13; 11. 12; Prov. 3. 7; Eccl. 2.; Isa. 5. 21; Jer. 8. 9; Zec. 9. 2; Mat. 11. 25; 1 Cor. 1. 17; 2. 4; 3. 19; 2 Cor. 1. 12; Jas. 3. 15.
See Gen. 3. 6.
Wise. Gen. 3. 6, to make one *w.*
Ex. 23. 8, the gift blindeth the *w.* R. V. them that have sight.
Deu. 4. 6, this nation is a *w.* people.
32. 29, O that they were *w.*!
1 Kn. 3. 12, I have given thee a *w.* heart.
Job 9. 4, he is *w.* in heart.
11. 12, vain man would be *w.* R. V. is void of understanding.
22. 2, he that is *w.* may be profitable.
32. 9, great men are not always *w.*
Ps. 2. 10, be *w.* now, O ye kings.
19. 7, making *w.* the simple.
36. 3, he hath left off to be *w.*
94. 8, when will ye be *w.*?
107. 43, whoso is *w.*, and will observe.
Prov. 1. 5, a *w.* man shall attain *w.* counsels.
3. 7, be not *w.* in thine own eyes.
6. 6; 8. 33; 23. 19; 27. 11, be *w.*
9. 12, thou shalt be *w.* for thyself.
11. 30, he that winneth souls is *w.*
16. 21, the *w.* in heart shall be called prudent.
20. 26, a *w.* king scattereth the wicked.
Eccl. 7. 23, I said, I will be *w.*
9. 1, the *w.* are in the hands of God.
12. 11, the words of the *w.* are as goads.
Isa. 19. 11, I am the son of the *w.*
Dan. 12. 3, they that be *w.* shall shine.
Mat. 10. 16, be *w.* as serpents.
11. 25, hid these things from the *w.*
Rom. 1. 14, I am debtor to the *w.*
12. 16, be not *w.* in your own conceits.
1 Cor. 1. 20, where is the *w.*?
4. 10, ye are *w.* in Christ.
2 Tim. 3. 15, *w.* unto salvation.
See Isa. 5. 21; Jer. 4. 22; Mat. 25. 2.
Wise, mode, manner, way. Lev. 19. 17.
Wise men from the east. Mat. 2. *See* MAGI.
Wise woman, David admonished by. 2 Sam. 14.
Wisely. Ps. 58. 5, charmers, charming never so *w.*
101. 2, I will behave myself *w.*
Prov. 16. 20, that handleth a matter *w.* R. V. omits.
See Prov. 21. 12; 28. 26; Eccl. 7. 10; Lu. 16. 8.
Wiser. 1 Kn. 4. 31; Lu. 16. 8; 1 Cor. 1. 25.
Wish. Ps. 73. 7, more than heart could *w.*
Rom. 9. 3, I could *w.* myself accursed.
3 John 2, I *w.* above all things. R. V. pray that [in.
See Job 33. 6; Jon. 4. 8; 2 Cor. 13. 9.
Wist, knew. Mk. 14. 40; Lu. 2. 49.
Wit, to, to know. 2 Cor. 8. 1.
Witch. Ex. 22. 18; Deu. 18. 10, one who uses witchcraft.
Witchcraft. 1 Sam. 15. 23; 2 Kn. 9. 22, the real or pretended use of supernatural power or knowledge gained from spirits.
Witchcraft, forbidden. Ex. 22. 18; Lev. 19. 26, 31; 20. 6, 27; Deu. 18. 10; Mic. 5. 12; Mal. 3. 5; Gal. 5. 20; Rev. 21. 8; 22. 15.
abolished by Josiah. 2 Kn. 23. 24.
practised by Saul, 1 Sam. 28. Manasseh, 2 Kn. 21. 6; 2 Chr. 33. 6. Israelites, 2 Kn. 17. 17. Simon of Samaria, Acts 8. 9. Philippians, Acts 16. 16. Ephesians, Acts 19. 19.
With (Jud. 16. 7). Heb. *Yéther lach:* Gk. νευρὰ ὑγρά. The Anglo-Saxon word *wiðig* denotes a willow, in which sense it occurs in Wycliffe's Bible; whence any supple twig, used for wicker-work. Perhaps as R. V. marg. 'new bow-strings;' or A. V. marg. 'new cords.'
Withal. (1) besides, in addition, likewise. 1 Kn. 19. 1.
(2) with. Job 2. 8.
Withdraw. Job 9. 13; Prov. 25. 17; 2 Thes. 3. 6.
Wither. Ps. 1. 3, his leaf shall not *w.*
37. 2, they shall *w.* as the green herb.
129. 6; Isa. 40. 7; 1 Pet. 1. 24, the grass *w.*
Mat. 21. 19; Mk. 11. 21, the fig tree *w.* away.
Jude 12, trees whose fruit *w.* R. V. without fruit.
See Joel 1. 12; John 15. 6; Jas. 1. 11.
Withered hand of Jeroboam healed. 1 Kn. 13. 6.
hand healed by Christ. Mat. 12. 10; Mk. 3. 1-5; Lu. 6. 6.
Withhold. Ps. 40. 11, *w.* not thy mercies.
84. 11, no good thing will he *w.*
Prov. 3. 27, *w.* not good from them to whom it is due.

Prov. 23. 13, *w.* not correction.
Eccl. 11. 6, *w.* not thy hand.
Jer. 5. 25, your sins have *w.* good things.
See Job 22. 7; 42. 2; Ezek. 18. 16; Joel 1. 13.

Within. Mat. 23. 26, cleanse first what is *w.* R. V. the inside.
Mk. 7. 21, from *w.* proceed evil thoughts.
2 Cor. 7. 5, *w.* were fears.
See Ps. 45. 13; Mat. 3. 9; Lu. 12. 17; 16. 3.

Without. Gen. 24. 31, wherefore standest thou *w.*?
2 Chr. 15. 3, for a long season *w.* the true God.
Prov. 1. 20, wisdom crieth *w.* R. V. aloud in the street.
Isa. 52. 3; 55. 1, *w.* money.
Jer. 33. 10, *w.* man, *w.* beast, *w.* inhabitant.
Hos. 3. 4, Israel *w.* king, *w.* prince, *w.* sacrifice.
2 Cor. 10. 13, things *w.* our measure. R. V. beyond.
Eph. 2. 12, *w.* God in the world. R. V. separate from.
Col. 4. 5; 1 Thes. 4. 12; 1 Tim. 3. 7, them that are *w.*
Heb. 13. 12, Jesus suffered *w.* the gate.
Rev. 22. 15, for *w.* are dogs.
See Prov. 22. 13; Mat. 10. 29; Lu. 11. 40.

Withstand. Eccl. 4. 12, two shall *w.* him.
Acts 11. 17, what was I that I could *w.* God?
Eph. 6. 13, able to *w.* in evil day.
See Num. 22. 32; 2 Chr. 20. 6; Esth. 9. 2.

Witness (*n.*). Gen. 31. 50, God is *w.* betwixt.
Jos. 24. 27, this stone shall be a *w.*
Job 16. 19, my *w.* is in heaven.
Ps. 89. 37, as a faithful *w.* in heaven.
Prov. 14. 5, a faithful *w.* will not lie.
Isa. 55. 4, I have given him for a *w.* to the people.
Jer. 42. 5, the Lord be a true and faithful *w.*
Mat. 24. 14, for a *w.* unto all nations. R. V. testimony.
John 1. 7, the same came for a *w.*
3. 11, ye receive not our *w.*
5. 36, I have greater *w.* than that of John.
Acts 14. 17, he left not himself without *w.*
Rom. 2. 15, conscience also bearing them *w.*
1 John 5. 9, the *w.* of God is greater.
5. 10, hath the *w.* in himself.
See Isa. 43. 10; Lu. 24. 48; Acts 13. 31.

Witness (*v.*). Deu. 4. 26, heaven and earth to *w.*
Isa. 3. 9, countenance doth *w.* against them.
Acts 20. 23, the Holy Ghost *w.* in every city. R. V. testifieth.
Rom. 3. 21, being *w.* by the law and prophets.
1 Tim. 6. 13, before Pilate *w.* a good confession.
See 1 Sam. 12. 3; Mat. 26. 62; 27. 13; Mk. 14. 60.

Witness, God invoked as. Gen. 31. 50; Jud. 11. 10; 1 Sam. 12. 5; Jer. 42. 5; Mic. 1. 2; Rom. 1. 9; 1 Thes. 2. 5.
borne to CHRIST, by the Father. Mat. 3. 16; Lu. 3. 22; John 5. 37; 12. 28; Heb. 2. 4; 1 John 5. 7.
by the Holy Ghost. Mat. 3. 16; Lu. 3. 22; John 1. 33; 15. 26; Acts 5. 32; 20. 23; Heb. 10. 15; 1 John 5. 7.
by the apostles. Acts 1. 8; 2. 32; 4. 33; 5. 32; 10. 41; 22. 15; 26. 16; 1 Pet. 5. 1; Rev. 20. 4.
by the prophets. Acts 10. 43; 1 Pet. 1. 10.
Christ the faithful and true. Rev. 1. 5; 3. 14.
false. Ex. 20. 16; 23. 1; Lev. 19. 11; Deu. 5. 20; 19. 16; Prov. 6. 16, 19; 12. 17; 19. 5, 9, 28; 21. 28; 25. 18; Jer. 7. 9; Zec. 5. 4; Lu. 3. 14.
against Christ. Mat. 26. 60; Mk. 14. 56.

Witnesses, two or three required. Num. 35. 30; Deu. 17. 6; 19. 15; Mat. 18. 16; 2 Cor. 13. 1; 1 Tim. 5. 19.
the two. Rev. 11.

Wits. Ps. 107. 27, are at their *w.* end.

Wittingly, intentionally, knowingly. Gen. 48. 14.

Witty, skilful, clever. Prov. 8. 12, knowledge of *w.* inventions.

Wives, their duties to husbands. Gen. 3. 16; Ex. 20. 14; Rom. 7. 2; 1 Cor. 7. 3; 14. 34; Eph. 5. 22, 33; Tit. 2. 4; 1 Pet. 3. 1.
good. Prov. 12. 4; 18. 22; 19. 14; 31. 10.
Levitical laws concerning. Ex. 21. 3, 22; 22. 16; Num. 5. 12; 30.; Deu. 21. 10, 15; 24. 1; Jer. 3. 1; Mat. 19. 3.
the wife a type of the church. Eph. 5. 23; Rev. 19. 7; 21. 9.

Wizard. *See* WITCHCRAFT. Lev. 20. 27, or that is a *w.*

Woeful. Jer. 17. 16, the *w.* day.

Woes against wickedness, &c. Isa. 5. 8; 10. 1; 29. 15; 31. 1; 45. 9; Jer. 22. 13; Am. 6. 1; Mic. 2. 1; Hab. 2. 6; Zep. 3. 1; Zec. 11. 17; Mat. 26. 24; Lu. 6. 24; Jude 11; Rev. 8. 13; 9. 12; 11. 14.
against unbelief. Mat. 11. 21; 23. 13; Lu. 10. 13; 11. 42.

Woe worth the day! evil be to the day; let the day be accursed. Ezek. 30. 2.

Wolf (Gen. 49. 27; Ezek. 22. 27). Heb. *Zĕēb*: Gk. λύκος. The *Canis lupus* of Syria is larger and of lighter colour than the European species. Its ferocity and night-prowling habits, its frequent attacks on sheep and lambs, are often noticed in the Old and New Testaments. See Ezek. 22. 27; Hab. 1. 8; Jer. 5. 6; Mat. 7. 15; Lu. 10. 3; John 10. 12.

Wolves, figuratively. Zep. 3. 3; Mat. 7. 15; 10. 16; Lu. 10. 3; Acts 20. 29.

Woman. Jud. 9. 54, a *w.* slew him.
Ps. 48. 6; Isa. 13. 8; 21. 3; 26. 17; Jer. 4. 31; 6. 24; 13. 21, 22, 23; 30. 6; 31. 8; 48. 41; 49. 22, 24; 50. 43, pain as of a *w.* in travail.
Prov. 6. 24, to keep thee from the evil *w.*
9. 13, a foolish *w.* is clamorous.
12. 4; 31. 10, a virtuous *w.*
14. 1, every wise *w.* buildeth her house.
21. 9, with a brawling *w.* in wide house.
Eccl. 7. 28, a *w.* among all those have I not found.
Isa. 54. 6, as a *w.* forsaken. R. V. a wife.
Jer. 31. 22, a *w.* shall compass a man.
Mat. 5. 28, whoso looketh on a *w.*
15. 28, O *w.*, great is thy faith.
Mat. 22. 27; Mk. 12. 22; Lu. 20. 32, the *w.* died also.
26. 10, why trouble ye the *w.*?
26. 13, shall this, that this *w.* hath done, be told.
John 2. 4, *w.*, what have I to do with thee?
8. 3, a *w.* taken in adultery.
19. 26, *w.*, behold thy son.
Acts 9. 36, this *w.* was full of good works.
Rom. 1. 27, the natural use of the *w.*
1 Cor. 7. 1, it is good for a man not to touch a *w.*
11. 7, the *w.* is the glory of the man.
Gal. 4. 4, God sent forth his Son, made of a *w.*
1 Tim. 2. 12, I suffer not a *w.* to teach.
2. 14, the *w.* being deceived.
See Isa. 49. 15; Lu. 7. 39; 13. 16; Rev. 12. 1.

Woman, creation and fall of. Gen. 2. 22; 3.
Christ the seed of (Gen. 3. 15); Gal. 4. 4.

Womb. Gen. 49. 25, blessings of the *w.*
1 Sam. 1. 5, the Lord had shut up her *w.*
Ps. 22. 9, took me out of the *w.*
22. 10, cast upon thee from the *w.*
127. 3, the fruit of the *w.* is his reward.
139. 13, thou hast covered me in my mother's *w.*
Eccl. 11. 5, how bones grow in the *w.*
Isa. 44. 2; 49. 5, the Lord formed thee from the *w.*
48. 8, a transgressor from the *w.*
49. 15, compassion on son of her *w.*
Hos. 9. 14, give them miscarrying *w.*
Lu. 1. 42, blessed is the fruit of thy *w.*
11. 27, blessed is the *w.* that bare thee.
23. 29, blessed are the *w.* that never bare.
See Job 3. 11; 24. 20; 31. 15; Prov. 30. 16.

Women. Jud. 5. 24, blessed above *w.*
1 Sam. 18. 7, the *w.* answered one another.
2 Sam. 1. 26, passing the love of *w.*
Ps. 45. 9, among thy honourable *w.*
Prov. 31. 3, give not thy strength to *w.*
Lam. 4. 10, the pitiful *w.* have sodden their children.
Mat. 11. 11; Lu. 7. 28, among them that are born of *w.*
24. 41; Lu. 17. 35, two *w.* grinding at the mill.
Lu. 1. 28, blessed art thou among *w.* R. V. omits.
1 Cor. 14. 34, let your *w.* keep silence.
1 Tim. 2. 9, *w.* adorn themselves.

2 Chr. 31. 21, in every *w.* he began he did it.
34. 12, the men did the *w.* faithfully.
Ez. 5. 8, this *w.* goeth fast on.
6. 7, let the *w.* alone.
Neh. 3. 5, their nobles put not their necks to the *w.*
6. 3, why should the *w.* cease?
6. 16, they perceived this *w.* was of God.
Job 1. 10, thou hast blessed the *w.* of his hands.
10. 3; 14. 15; Ps. 143. 5, the *w.* of thine hands.
34. 11, the *w.* of a man shall he render unto him.
Ps. 8. 3, the *w.* of thy fingers.
19. 1, his handy-*w.*
33. 4, all his *w.* are done in truth.
40. 5; 78. 4; 107. 8; 111. 4; Mat. 7. 22; Acts 2. 11, wonderful *w.*
90. 17, establish thou the *w.* of our hands.
101. 3, I hate the *w.* of them that turn aside.
104. 23, man goeth forth to his *w.*
111. 2, the *w.* of the Lord are great.
141. 4, to practise wicked *w.* R. V. in deeds of.
Prov. 16. 3, commit thy *w.* unto the Lord.
20. 11, whether his *w.* be pure.
24. 12; Mat. 16. 27; 2 Tim. 4. 14, to every man according to his *w.*
31. 31, let her own *w.* praise her.
Eccl. 1. 14, I have seen all the *w.* that are done.
3. 17, there is a time for every *w.*
5. 6, wherefore should God destroy the *w.*?
8. 9, I applied my heart to every *w.*
9. 1, their *w.* are in the hand of God.
9. 7, God now accepteth thy *w.*
9. 10, there is no *w.* in the grave.
12. 14, God shall bring every *w.* into judgment.
Isa. 2. 8; 37. 19; Jer. 1. 16; 10. 3, 9, 15; 51. 18, they worship the *w.* of their own hands.
5. 19, let him hasten his *w.* [whole *w.*
10. 12, when the Lord hath performed his
26. 12, thou hast wrought all our *w.* in us.
28. 21, do his *w.*, his strange *w.*
29. 15, their *w.* are in the dark.
49. 4, my *w.* is with my God. R. V. recompence.
66. 18, I know their *w.* and their thoughts.
Jer. 32. 19, great in counsel, and mighty in *w.*
48. 7, thou hast trusted in thy *w.*
Am. 8. 7, I will never forget any of their *w.*
Hab. 1. 5, I will work a *w.* in your days.
Mat. 23. 3, do not ye after their *w.*
23. 5, all their *w.* they do to be seen of men.
Mk. 6. 5, he could there do no mighty *w.*
John 5. 20, greater *w.* than these.
6. 28, that we might work the *w.* of God.
6. 29, this is the *w.* of God, that ye believe.
7. 21, I have done one *w.*, and ye all marvel.
9. 3, that the *w.* of God should be made manifest.
10. 25, the *w.* I do in my Father's name.
10. 32, for which of those *w.* do ye stone me?
14. 12, the *w.* I do shall he do, and greater *w.*
17. 4, I have finished the *w.*
Acts 5. 38, if this *w.* be of men, it will come to nought.
15. 38, who went not with them to the *w.*
Rom. 3. 27, by what law? of *w.*?
4. 6, imputeth righteousness without *w.*
9. 11, not of *w.*, but of him that calleth.
11. 6, grace, otherwise *w.* is no more *w.* [ness.
13. 12, let us therefore cast off the *w.* of dark-
14. 20, for meat destroy not the *w.* of God.
1 Cor. 3. 13, every man's *w.* shall be made manifest.
9. 1, are not ye my *w.* in the Lord?
Gal. 2. 16, by *w.* of law shall no flesh be justified.
6. 4, let every man prove his own *w.*
Eph. 2. 9, not of *w.*, lest any man should boast.
4. 12, the *w.* of the ministry.
5. 11, the unfruitful *w.* of darkness.
Col. 1. 21, enemies in your mind by wicked *w.*
1 Thes. 5. 13, esteem them in love for their *w.* sake.
2 Thes. 2. 17, in every good word and *w.*
2 Tim. 1. 9; Tit. 3. 5, saved us, not according to our *w.*
2 Tim. 4. 5, do the *w.* of an evangelist.
Tit. 1. 16, in *w.* they deny him.
Heb. 6. 1; 9. 14, from dead *w.*
Jas. 1. 4, let patience have her perfect *w.*
2. 14, if he have not *w.*, can faith save him?
2. 17, faith, if it hath not *w.*, is dead, being alone.
2. 18, shew me thy faith without thy *w.*
2. 21, was not Abraham justified by *w.*?
2. 22, by *w.* was faith made perfect. [up.
2 Pet. 3. 10, earth and *w.* therein shall be burnt
1 John 3. 8, destroy the *w.* of the devil.
Rev. 2. 2, 9, 13, 19; 3. 1, 8, 15, I know thy *w.*
2. 26, he that keepeth my *w.* to the end.
3. 2, I have not found thy *w.* perfect.
14. 13, and their *w.* do follow them.
See Gal. 5. 19; 2 Thes. 1. 11; Rev. 18. 6; 20. 12.

Work (*v.*). 1 Sam. 14. 6, the Lord will *w.* for us.
1 Kn. 21. 20, sold thyself to *w.* evil. R. V. do.
Neh. 4. 6, the people had a mind to *w.*
Job 23. 9, on the left hand, where he doth *w.*
33. 29, all these things *w.* God with man.
Ps. 58. 2, in heart ye *w.* wickedness.
101. 7, he that *w.* deceit.
119. 126, it is time for thee to *w.*
Isa. 43. 13, I will *w.*, and who shall let it?
Mic. 2. 1, woe to them that *w.* evil.
Hag. 2. 4, *w.*, for I am with you.
Mal. 3. 15, they that *w.* wickedness are set up.
Mat. 21. 28, son, go *w.* to day in my vineyard.
Mk. 16. 20, the Lord *w.* with them.
John 5. 17, my Father *w.* hitherto, and I *w.*
6. 28, that we might *w.* the works of God.
6. 30, what dost thou *w.*?
9. 4, the night cometh, when no man can *w.*
Acts 10. 35, he that *w.* righteousness is accepted.
Rom. 4. 15, the law *w.* wrath.
5. 3, tribulation *w.* patience.
8. 28, all things *w.* together for good.
1 Cor. 4. 12, and labour, *w.* with our own hands.
12. 6, it is the same God which *w.* all in all.
2 Cor. 4. 12, death *w.* in us.
4. 17, *w.* for us a far more exceeding weight of glory.
Gal. 5. 6, faith which *w.* by love.
Eph. 1. 11, who *w.* all things after the counsel.
2. 2, the spirit that now *w.*
3. 20, the power that *w.* in us.
4. 28, *w.* with his hands the thing that is good.
Phil. 2. 12, *w.* out your own salvation.
1 Thes. 4. 11, *w.* with your own hands.
2 Thes. 2. 7, the mystery of iniquity doth *w.*
3. 10, if any would not *w.*, neither should he eat.
Jas. 1. 3, the trying of your faith *w.* patience.
See Ezek. 46. 1; Prov. 11. 18; 31. 13; Eccl. 3. 9.

Workman. Hos. 8. 6; Eph. 2. 10; 2 Tim. 2. 15.

Works of God. Job 9.; 37.–41.; Ps. 8.; 19.; 89.; 104.; 111.; 145.; 147.; 148.; Eccl. 8. 17; Jer. 10. 12.
of the law, insufficiency of. Rom. 3. 20; 4. 2; Gal. 3.
good, the evidence of faith, Acts 26. 20; Jas. 2. 14.
necessary, Mat. 5. 16; Acts 9. 36; 2 Cor. 8.; 9.; Eph. 2. 10; Phil. 2. 12; 1 Thes. 4. 11; 2 Thes. 2. 17; 3. 8; Heb. 10. 24; 1 Pet. 2. 12.

World. Job 18. 18, chased out of the *w.*
34. 13, who hath disposed the whole *w.*?
37. 12, on the face of the *w.*
Ps. 17. 14, from men of the *w.*
50. 12, the *w.* is mine.
73. 12, the ungodly, who prosper in the *w.* R. V. being always at ease.
77. 18; 97. 4, lightnings lightened the *w.*
93. 1, the *w.* also is stablished.
Eccl. 3. 11, he hath set the *w.* in their heart.
Isa. 14. 21, nor fill the face of the *w.* with cities.
24. 4, the *w.* languisheth.
34. 1, let the *w.* hear.
Mat. 4. 8; Lu. 4. 5, all the kingdoms of the *w.*
5. 14, the light of the *w.*
13. 22; Mk. 4. 19, the cares of this *w.* choke.
13. 38, the field is the *w.*
13. 40, in the end of the *w.*

Mat. 16. 26; Mk. 8. 36; Lu. 9. 25, gain the whole *w.*
18. 7, woe to the *w.* because of offences.
Mk. 10. 30; Lu. 18. 30; Heb. 2. 5; 6. 5, in the *w.* to come.
Lu. 1. 70; Acts 3. 21, since the *w.* began.
2. 1, all the *w.* should be taxed.
16. 8; 20. 34, children of this *w.*
20. 35, worthy to obtain that *w.*
John 1. 10, he was in the *w.*
1. 29, which taketh away the sin of the *w.*
3. 16, God so loved the *w.*
4. 42; 1 John 4. 14, the Saviour of the *w.*
6. 33, he that giveth life unto the *w.*
7. 4, shew thyself to the *w.*
7. 7, the *w.* cannot hate you.
8. 12; 9. 5, I am the light of the *w.*
12. 19, the whole *w.* is gone after him.
12. 31, now is the judgment of this *w.*
12. 47, not to judge the *w.*, but to save the *w.*
13. 1, depart out of this *w.*
14. 17, whom the *w.* cannot receive.
14. 22, manifest thyself unto us, and not unto the *w.*
14. 27, not as the *w.* giveth, give I unto you.
14. 30, the prince of this *w.* cometh.
15. 18; 1 John 3. 13, if the *w.* hate you.
15. 19, the *w.* would love his own.
16. 33, in the *w.* ye shall have tribulation.
17. 9, I pray not for the *w.*
17. 16, they are not of the *w.*
17. 21, that the *w.* may believe.
21. 25, the *w.* could not contain the books.
Acts 17. 6, turned the *w.* upside down.
Rom. 3. 19, that all the *w.* may become guilty.
12. 2, be not conformed to this *w.*
1 Cor. 1. 20, where is the disputer of this *w.*?
2. 6, the wisdom of this *w.*
7. 31, they that use this *w.* as not abusing it.
2 Cor. 4. 4, the god of this *w.* hath blinded.
Gal. 1. 4, this present evil *w.*
6. 14, the *w.* is crucified unto me.
Eph. 2. 2, according to the course of this *w.*
2. 12, without God in the *w.*
1 Tim. 6. 7, we brought nothing into this *w.*
6. 17, them that are rich in this *w.*
2 Tim. 4. 10, having loved this present *w.*
Heb. 11. 38, of whom the *w.* was not worthy.
Jas. 1. 27, unspotted from the *w.*
3. 6, the tongue is a *w.* of iniquity.
4. 4, the friendship of the *w.*
2 Pet. 2. 5, God spared not the old *w.*
3. 6, the *w.* that then was.
1 John 2. 15, love not the *w.*
3. 1, the *w.* knoweth us not.
5. 19, the whole *w.* lieth in wickedness.
See 2 Sam. 22. 16; 1 Chr. 16. 30; Prov. 8. 26.

World created. Gen. 1.; 2. *See* John 1. 10; Col. 1. 16; Heb. 1. 2.
its corruption. Rom. 5. 12; 8. 22.
conformity to. Rom. 12. 2; Gal. 6. 14; Jas. 1. 27; 4. 4; 1 John 2. 15.

Worldly. Tit. 2. 12; Heb. 9. 1.

Worm. (1) (Isa. 51. 8). Heb. *Sâs:* Gk. σής. The grub of the moth in connection with which it occurs.
(2) (Ex. 16. 20; Job 25. 6; Isa. 14. 11). Heb. *Rimmah:* Gk. σαπρία, σήψις. Larvæ of insects that feed on decayed matter.
(3) (Job 25. 6; Isa. 14. 11). Heb. *Tôlê'ah:* Gk. σκώληξ. The caterpillar eating vines, but used also of the meat fly. In many cases (2) and (3) are used synonymously.
(4) (Earth). Zool. S. *Lumbricus.* T. This is a true worm belonging to the sub-kingdom *Vermes.*
(5) (Canker). *See* LOCUST, *Yelek.*
(6) (Palmer). *See* LOCUST, *Gâzâm.*
(7) (Crimson). *See* COCHINEAL.

Worm. Job 7. 5, my flesh is clothed with *w.*
17. 14, I said to the *w.*, thou art my mother.
19. 26, though *w.* destroy this body. R. V. omits.
Job 21. 26, shall lie down, and *w.* shall cover them.
24. 20, the *w.* shall feed sweetly on him.
25. 6, man, that is a *w.*, etc.
Ps. 22. 6, I am a *w.*, and no man.
Isa. 14. 11, the *w.* is spread under thee.
41. 14, fear not, thou *w.* Jacob.
66. 24; Mk. 9. 44, 46, 48, their *w.* shall not die.
Mic. 7. 17, like *w.* of the earth.
See Jon. 4. 7; Acts 12. 23.

Wormwood (Deu. 29. 18; Jer. 9. 15; 23. 15; Am. 5. 7). Heb. *La'ănah:* Gk. ἄψινθος: Bot. N. *Artemisia Judaica, Artemisia Nilotica, Artemisia absinthium,* &c.

Wormwood, figurative. Deu. 29. 18; Prov. 5. 4; Lam. 3. 15 (Rev. 8. 11).

Worse. Mat. 9. 16; Mk. 2. 21, the rent is made *w.*
12. 45; 27. 64; Lu. 11. 26, last state *w.* than the first.
Mk. 5. 26, nothing bettered, but grew *w.*
John 5. 14, lest a *w.* thing come unto thee.
1 Cor. 11. 17, not for the better, but for the *w.*
1 Tim. 5. 8, he is *w.* than an infidel.
2 Tim. 3. 13, shall wax *w.* and *w.*
2 Pet. 2. 20, the latter end is *w.* with them.
See Jer. 7. 26; 16. 12; Dan. 1. 10; John 2. 10.

Worship. Ps. 95. 6, let us *w.* and bow down.
97. 7, *w.* him, all ye gods.
99. 5, *w.* at his footstool.
Isa. 27. 13, shall *w.* the Lord in the holy mount.
Jer. 44. 19, did we *w.* her without our men?
Zep. 1. 5, them that *w.* the host of heaven.
Mat. 4. 9; Lu. 4. 7, fall down and *w.* me.
15. 9, in vain they do *w.* me.
John 4. 20, our fathers *w.* in this mountain.
4. 22, ye *w.* ye know not what.
12. 20, Greeks came to *w.*
Acts 17. 23, whom ye ignorantly *w.* [serve.
24. 14, so *w.* I the God of my fathers. R. V.
Rom. 1. 25, *w.* the creature more than the Creator.
1 Cor. 14. 25, so falling down he will *w.* God.
See Heb. 1. 6; Rev. 4. 10; 9. 20.

Worship to be given to God alone. Ex. 20. 1; Deu. 5. 7; 6. 13; Mat. 4. 10; Lu. 4. 8; Acts 10. 26; 14. 15; Col. 2. 18; Rev. 19. 10; 22. 8.
mode of. Lev. 10. 3; Eccl. 5.; Joel 2. 16; John 4. 24; 1 Cor. 11.; 14.
enjoined. 2 Kn. 17. 36; 1 Chr. 16. 29; Ps. 29.; 95. 6; 99. 5; 100.

Worth. Job 24. 25; Prov. 10. 20; Ezek. 30. 2.

Worthy. Gen. 32. 10, I am not *w.* of the least.
1 Sam. 26. 16, ye are *w.* to die.
1 Kn. 1. 52, if he shew himself a *w.* man.
Mat. 3. 11, whose shoes I am not *w.* to bear.
8. 8; Lu. 7. 6, I am not *w.* that thou shouldest come.
10. 10, the workman is *w.* of his meat.
10. 37, loveth father or mother more than me is not *w.* of me.
22. 8, they which were bidden were not *w.*
Mk. 1. 7; Lu. 3. 16; John 1. 27, not *w.* to unloose.
Lu. 3. 8, fruits *w.* of repentance.
7. 4, that he was *w.* for whom he should do this.
10. 7; 1 Tim. 5. 18, the labourer is *w.* of his hire.
12. 48, things *w.* of stripes.
15. 19, no more *w.* to be called thy son.
20. 35, *w.* to obtain that world.
Acts 24. 2, very *w.* deeds are done. R. V. evils are corrected.
Rom. 8. 18, not *w.* to be compared with the glory.
Eph. 4. 1; Col. 1. 10; 1 Thes. 2. 12, walk *w.*
Heb. 11. 38, of whom the world was not *w.*
Jas. 2. 7, that *w.* name. R. V. honourable.
Rev. 3. 4, for they are *w.*
See Nah. 2. 5; Rev. 4. 11; 5. 2; 16. 6. [11. 2.

Wot, know. Gen. 21. 26; 39. 8; Ex. 32. 1; Rom.

Would. Num. 22. 29, I *w.* there were a sword.
Ps. 81. 11, Israel *w.* none of me.
Prov. 1. 25, ye *w.* none of my reproof.

Prov. 1. 30, they *w.* none of my counsel.
Dan. 5. 19, whom he *w.* he slew.
Mat. 7. 12; Lu. 6. 31, whatsoever ye *w.* that men.
Mk. 3. 13, and calleth unto him whom he *w.*
Rom. 7. 15, what I *w.*, that do I not.
1 Cor. 7. 7, I *w.* that all men were even as I.
Rev. 3. 15, I *w.* thou wert cold or hot.
See Num. 11. 29; Acts 26. 29; Gal. 5. 17.

Wound (*n.*). Ex. 21. 25, give *w.* for *w.*
Job 34. 6, my *w.* is incurable.
Ps. 147. 3, he bindeth up their *w.*
Prov. 23. 29, who hath *w.* without cause?
27. 6, faithful are the *w.* of a friend.
Isa. 1. 6, but *w.* and bruises.
Jer. 15. 18, why is my *w.* incurable?
30. 17, I will heal thee of thy *w.*
Zec. 13. 6, what are these *w.* in thy hands?
Lu. 10. 34, bound up his *w.*
See Prov. 6. 33; 20. 30; Hos. 5. 13; Rev. 13. 3.

Wound (*v.*). Deu. 32. 39, I *w.*, and I heal.
1 Kn. 22. 34; 2 Chr. 18. 33, carry me out, for I am *w.*
Job 5. 18, he *w.*, and his hands make whole.
Ps. 64. 7, suddenly shall they be *w.*
109. 22, my heart is *w.* within me.
Prov. 7. 26, she hath cast down many *w.*
18. 14, a A. spirit who can bear? R. V. broken.
Isa. 53. 5, he was *w.* for our transgressions.
Jer. 37. 10, there remained but *w.* men.
See Gen. 4. 23; Mk. 12. 4; Lu. 10. 30; Acts 19. 16.

Wrap. Isa. 28. 20; Mic. 7. 3; John 20. 7.

Wrath. Gen. 49. 7, cursed be their *w.*
Deu. 32. 27, were it not I feared the *w.* of the enemy. R. V. provocation.
Job 21. 30; Prov. 11. 4; Zep. 1. 15; Rom. 2. 5; Rev. 6. 17, the day of *w.*
36. 18, because there is *w.*, beware.
Ps. 76. 10, the *w.* of man shall praise thee.
90. 7, by thy *w.* are we troubled.
Prov. 16. 14, *w.* of a king is as messengers of death.
19. 19, a man of great *w.* shall suffer.
27. 3, a fool's *w.* is heavier. R. V. vexation.
27. 4, *w.* is cruel, and anger outrageous.
Eccl. 5. 17, much *w.* with his sickness.
Isa. 13. 9, the day of the Lord cometh with *w.*
54. 8, in a little *w.* I hid my face.
Nah. 1. 2, he reserveth *w.* for his enemies.
Hab. 3. 2, in *w.* remember mercy.
Mat. 3. 7; Lu. 3. 7, from the *w.* to come.
Rom. 2. 5, A. against the day of *w.*
Eph. 6. 4, provoke not your children to *w.*
1 Thes. 5. 9, God hath not appointed us to *w.*
1 Tim. 2. 8, lifting up holy hands, without *w.*
See Rev. 6. 16; 12. 12; 14. 8.

Wrath. Job 5. 2; 19. 29; Ps. 37. 8; Prov. 12. 16; 14. 29; 30. 33; Rom. 12. 19; 13. 5; Gal. 5. 20; Eph. 4. 26; 1 Tim. 2. 8; Jas. 1. 19.
of God. 2 Chr. 28. 11; Job 21. 20; Ps. 106. 23, 32; Prov. 29. 8; Lu. 4. 28; Rom. 2. 5, 8; 9. 22; Rev. 6. 17; 11. 18; 16. 1; 19. 15.

Wrathful. Ps. 69. 24; Prov. 15. 18.

Wreathen work, twisted work. Ex. 28. 14.

Wrest, to pervert. Ex. 23. 2; Deu. 16. 19; Ps. 56. 5; 2 Pet. 3. 16.

Wrestle. Gen. 32. 24; Eph. 6. 12.

Wretched. Num. 11. 15; Rom. 7. 24; Rev. 3. 17.

Wring. Jud. 6. 38; Ps. 75. 8; Prov. 30. 33.

Wrinkle. Job 16. 8; Eph. 5. 27.

Write. Prov. 3. 3; 7. 3, *w.* on table of thy heart.
Isa. 10. 1, *w.* grievousness which they have prescribed.
10. 19, few, that a child may *w.* them.
Jer. 22. 30, *w.* ye this man childless.
31. 33; Heb. 8. 10, I will *w.* it in their hearts.
Hab. 2. 2, *w.* the vision, make it plain.
See Job 13. 26; Ps. 87. 6; Rev. 3. 12.

Writing. Ex. 32. 16; John 5. 47; Col. 2. 14.

Writing of God. Ex. 31. 18; 32. 16; Dan. 5. 5.
on the wall, expounded. Dan. 5.

Writing materials. The common writing materials of the Babylonians consisted of clay, and an instrument of wood, bone, or metal, having a point of three unequal facets, with which to impress the cuneiform characters upon the clay while moist. Such was the writing on the Tel-el-Amarna tablet letters between Jerusalem and Egypt 1500 years before Christ. The writing materials of the Egyptians consisted of papyrus, reeds, ink, and a palette having a hollow for holding the reeds, and a number of circular and oval hollows for holding ink of various colours.

Written. Job 19. 23, Oh that my words were *w.*
Ps. 69. 28, let them not be *w.* with the righteous.
Ezek. 2. 10, roll was *w.* within and without.
Lu. 10. 20, because your names are *w.* in heaven.
John 19. 22, what I have *w.* I have *w.*
1 Cor. 10. 11, *w.* for our admonition.
2 Cor. 3. 2, ye are our epistle *w.* in our hearts.
See Isa. 4. 3; Jer. 17. 1; Rev. 2. 17; 13. 8.

Wrong. Ex. 2. 13, to him that did the *w.*
1 Chr. 12. 17, there is no *w.* in mine hands.
Job 19. 7, I cry out of *w.*, but am not heard.
Jer. 22. 3, do no *w.*
Mat. 20. 13, friend, I do thee no *w.*
1 Cor. 6. 7, why do ye not rather take *w.*?
2 Cor. 12. 13, forgive me this *w.*
Col. 3. 25, he that doeth *w.* shall receive.
Philem. 18, if he hath *w.* thee.
See Prov. 8. 36; Acts 25. 10; 2 Cor. 7. 2.

Wrongfully. Job 21. 27; Ezek. 22. 29; 1 Pet. 2. 19.

Wrote. Dan. 5. 5; John 8. 6; 19. 19; 2 John 5.

Wroth. Gen. 4. 6, why art thou *w.*?
Deu. 1. 34; 3. 26; 9. 19; 2 Sam. 22. 8; 2 Chr. 28. 9; Ps. 18. 7; 78. 21, heard your words, and was *w.*
2 Kn. 5. 11, but Naaman was *w.*, and went away.
Ps. 89. 38, thou hast been *w.* with thine anointed.
Isa. 47. 6, I was *w.* with my people.
54. 9, I have sworn I would not be *w.*
57. 16, neither will I be always *w.*
64. 9, be not *w.* very sore.
Mat. 18. 34, his lord was *w.*, and delivered.
See Num. 16. 22; Isa. 28. 21; Mat. 2. 16.

Wrought. Num. 23. 23, what hath God *w.*!
1 Sam. 6. 6, when God had *w.* wonderfully.
14. 45, Jonathan hath *w.* with God this day.
Neh. 4. 17, with one of his hands *w.* in the work.
6. 16, this work was *w.* of our God.
Job 12. 9, the hand of the Lord hath *w.* this.
36. 23, who can say, thou hast *w.* iniquity?
Ps. 31. 19, hast *w.* for them that trust in thee.
68. 28, strengthen that which thou hast *w.* for us.
139. 15, curiously *w.* in lowest parts of the earth.
Eccl. 2. 11, I looked on all my hands had *w.*
Isa. 26. 12, thou also hast *w.* all our works in us.
41. 4, who hath *w.* and done it?
Jer. 18. 3, he *w.* a work on the wheels.
Ezek. 20. 9, I *w.* for my name's sake.
Dan. 4. 2, the wonders God hath *w.* toward me.
Mat. 20. 12, these last have *w.* but one hour. R. V. spent.
26. 10; Mk. 14. 6, she hath *w.* a good work on me.
John 3. 21, manifest that they are *w.* in God.
Acts 15. 12, what wonders God had *w.*
18. 3, he abode with them, and *w.*
19. 11, *w.* special miracles by hands of Paul.
Rom. 7. 8, *w.* in me all manner of concupiscence.
15. 18, things which Christ hath not *w.*
2 Cor. 5. 5, he that hath *w.* us for the selfsame thing.
7. 11, what carefulness it *w.* in you.
12. 12, the signs of an apostle were *w.*
Gal. 2. 8, he that *w.* effectually in Peter.
Eph. 1. 20, which he *w.* in Christ.
2 Thes. 3. 8, but we *w.* with labour. R. V. working.
Heb. 11. 33, through faith *w.* righteousness.
Jas. 2. 22, faith *w.* with his works.
1 Pet. 4. 3, to have *w.* the will of the Gentiles.
2 John 8, lose not those things we have *w.*
Rev. 19. 20, the false prophet that *w.* miracles.
See Ex. 36. 4; 2 Sam. 18. 13; 1 Kn. 16. 25.

Wrung. Lev. 1. 15; Ps. 73. 10; Isa. 51. 17.

Yarn. 1 Kn. 10. 28; 2 Chr. 1. 16.

Ye. 1 Cor. 6. 11; 2 Cor. 3. 2; Gal. 6. 1.

A WHITED SEPULCHRE

This tomb by the Lake of Galilee illustrates the Gospel phrase. (*L. A. Fereday*)

YOKE AND GOAD

Ploughing with these traditional implements in Palestine. (*L. A. Fereday*)

Yea. Mat. 5. 37; Jas. 5. 12, let your communication be *y.*, *y.*
2 Cor. 1. 17, there should be *y.*, *y.*, and nay, nay.
See 2 Cor. 1. 18; Phil. 3. 8; 2 Tim. 3. 12.
Year. Gen. 1. 14, for seasons, days, and *y.*
47. 9, few and evil have the *y.* of my life been.
Ex. 13. 10, keep this ordinance from *y.* to *y.*
23. 29, I will not drive them out in one *y.*
Lev. 16. 34, make atonement once a *y.*
25. 5, it is a *y.* of rest.
Num. 14. 34, each day for a *y.* shall ye bear.
Deu. 14. 22, thou shalt tithe the increase *y.* by *y.*
15. 9, the *y.* of release is at hand.
26. 12, the third *y.*, which is the *y.* of tithing.
32. 7, consider the *y.* of many generations.
Jud. 11. 40, to lament four days in a *y.*
1 Sam. 2. 19, brought a coat from *y.* to *y.*
7. 16, went from *y.* to *y.* in circuit.
2 Sam. 14. 26, every *y.* he polled it.
1 Kn. 17. 1, there shall not be dew nor rain these [*y.*
2 Chr. 14. 6, the land had rest, no war in those *y.*
Job 10. 5, are thy *y.* as man's days?
15. 20, the number of *y.* is hidden.
16. 22, when a few *y.* are come.
32. 7, multitude of *y.* should teach wisdom.
36. 11, they shall spend their *y.* in pleasures.
36. 26, nor can the number of his *y.* be searched out.
Ps. 31. 10, my *y.* are spent with sighing.
61. 6, prolong his *y.* as many generations.
65. 11, thou crownest the *y.* with thy goodness.
77. 5, the *y.* of ancient times.
77. 10, I will remember the *y.* of the right hand.
78. 33, their *y.* did he consume in trouble.
90. 4, a thousand *y.* in thy sight.
90. 9, we spend our *y.* as a tale that is told.
90. 10, the days of our *y.* are threescore and ten.
102. 24, thy *y.* are throughout all generations.
102. 27, thy *y.* shall have no end.
Prov. 4. 10, the *y.* of thy life shall be many.
5. 9, lest thou give thy *y.* to the cruel.
10. 27, the *y.* of the wicked shall be shortened.
Eccl. 12. 1, nor the *y.* draw nigh.
Isa. 21. 16, according to the *y.* of an hireling.
29. 1, add ye *y.* to *y.*
38. 15, go softly all my *y.*
61. 2; Lu. 4. 19, the acceptable *y.* of the Lord.
63. 4, the *y.* of my redeemed is come.
Jer. 11. 23; 23. 12; 48. 44, the *y.* of their visitation.
17. 8, shall not be careful in *y.* of drought.
28. 16, this *y.* thou shalt die.
51. 46, a rumour shall come in one *y.*
Ezek. 4. 5, I have laid on thee the *y.* of their iniquity.
22. 4, thou art come even unto thy *y.*
38. 8, in latter *y.* thou shalt come.
46. 17, it shall be his to the *y.* of liberty.
Dan. 11. 6, in the end of *y.* they shall join.
Joel 2. 2, to the *y.* of many generations.
Mic. 6. 6, shall I come with calves of a *y.* old?
Hab. 3. 2, revive thy work in the midst of the *y.*
Mal. 3. 4, the offering be pleasant, as in former *y.*
Lu. 13. 8, let it alone this *y.* also.
Gal. 4. 10, ye observe days and *y.*
Rev. 20. 2, Satan bound for a thousand *y.*
See Zec. 14. 16; Jas. 4. 13; Rev. 9. 15.
Year, beginning of, changed. Ex. 12. 1; Lev. 23. 5. *See* MONTHS.
Yearly. 1 Sam. 1. 3; 20. 6; Esth. 9. 21.
Yearn. Gen. 43. 30; 1 Kn. 3. 26.
Yell. Jer. 2. 15; 51. 38.
Yesterday. Job 8. 9; Ps. 90. 4; Heb. 13. 8.
Yet. Gen. 40. 23, *y.* did not the butler remember.
Ex. 10. 7, knowest thou not *y.*?
Deu. 9. 29, *y.* they are thy people.
12. 9, ye are not as *y.* come.
Jud. 7. 4, the people are *y.* too many.
1 Kn. 19. 18, *y.* I have left me.
2 Kn. 13. 23, nor cast them from his presence as [*y.*
Ez. 3. 6, the foundation was not *y.* laid.
Job 1. 16, while he was *y.* speaking.
13. 15, though he slay me, *y.* will I trust in him.
Job 29. 5, when the Almighty was *y.* with me.
Ps. 2. 6, *y.* have I set my king.
Eccl. 4. 3, he which hath not *y.* been.
Isa. 28. 4, while it is *y.* in his hand.
49. 15, *y.* will I not forget.
Jer. 2. 9, I will *y.* plead with you.
23. 21, *y.* they ran.
Ezek. 11. 16, *y.* will I be to them.
36. 37, I will *y.* for this be enquired of. R. V. moreover.
Dan. 11. 35, it is *y.* for a time appointed.
Hos. 7. 9, *y.* he knoweth not. R. V. and.
Am. 6. 10, is there *y.* any with thee?
Jon. 3. 4, *y.* forty days.
Hab. 3. 18, *y.* I will rejoice.
Mat. 15. 17, do not ye *y.* understand? R. V. omits.
19. 20, what lack I *y.*?
24. 6; Mk. 13. 7, the end is not *y.*
Mk. 11. 13, the time of figs was not *y.* R. V. [omits.
Lu. 24. 44, while I was *y.* with you.
John 2. 4; 7. 6; 8. 20, hour is not *y.* come.
11. 25, though dead, *y.* shall he live.
Rom. 5. 6, *y.* without strength.
8. 24, why doth he *y.* hope for? *See* R. V.
1 Cor. 3. 15, *y.* so as by fire.
15. 17, ye are *y.* in your sins.
Gal. 2. 20, *y.* not I, but Christ.
Heb. 4. 15, *y.* without sin.
1 John 3. 2, it doth not *y.* appear.
See Acts 8. 16; Rom. 9. 19; 1 Cor. 3. 3.
Yield. Gen 4. 12, not henceforth *y.* strength.
Lev. 19. 25, that it may *y.* the increase.
26. 4, the land shall *y.* her increase.
Num. 17. 8, the rod *y.* almonds. R. V. bare ripe.
2 Chr. 30. 8, *y.* yourselves to the Lord.
Neh. 9. 37, it *y.* much increase to the kings.
Ps. 67. 6, the earth *y.* her increase.
107. 37, plant vineyards, which may *y.* fruits. R. V. get them.
Prov. 7. 21, she caused him to *y.*
Eccl. 10. 4, *y.* pacifieth great offences.
Hos. 8. 7, if it *y.*, the strangers shall swallow it [up.
Joel 2. 22, the fig tree and vine do *y.* their strength.
Hab. 3. 17, though fields shall *y.* no meat.
Mat. 27. 50, cried again, and *y.* up the ghost.
Acts 23. 21, do not thou *y.* to them.
Rom. 6. 13, neither *y.* ye your members, but *y.* yourselves to God. R. V. present.
6. 16, to whom ye *y.* yourselves servants. R. V. present.
Heb. 12. 11, *y.* the peaceable fruits of righteousness.
See Gen. 1. 29; Isa. 5. 10; Dan. 3. 28.
Yoke. The cross-bar to which draught oxen were fastened by the horns or neck, for drawing carts or plows. The affection known to exist between a pair of oxen yoked together is a fruitful source of illustration, e. g., Paul speaks of his true 'yokefellow' (Phil. 4. 3). *See also* 2 Cor. 6. 14. Christ also uses the yoke as a symbol (Mat. 11. 29, 30).
Gen. 27. 40, thou shalt break his *y.*
Lev. 26. 13, I have broken the bands of your *y.*
Num. 19. 2; 1 Sam. 6. 7, on which never came *y.*
Deu. 28. 48, he shall put a *y.* on thy neck.
1 Kn. 12. 4, thy father made our *y.* grievous.
Isa. 9. 4; 10. 27; 14. 25, thou hast broken the *y.* of his burden.
58. 6, that ye break every *y.*
Jer. 2. 20, of old time I have broken thy *y.*
27. 2; 28. 13, make thee bonds and *y.* R. V. bars.
31. 18, as a bullock unaccustomed to the *y.*
Lam. 3. 27, it is good to bear the *y.* in youth.
Mat. 11. 29, take my *y.* upon you.
11. 30, for my *y.* is easy.
Acts 15. 10, to put a *y.* upon the neck of the dis- [ciples.
2 Cor. 6. 14, not unequally *y.* with unbelievers.
Gal. 5. 1, entangled with the *y.* of bondage.
Phil. 4. 3, I entreat thee also, true *y.*-fellow.
1 Tim. 6. 1, as many servants as are under the *y.*
See Job 1. 3; 42. 12; Lam. 1. 14; Lu. 14. 19.

Yoke of Christ, easy. Mat. 11. 30; 1 John 5. 3.
Yokes, typical. Jer. 27.
Yonder. Gen. 22. 5; Num. 23. 15; Mat. 17. 20.
You. Gen. 48. 21, God shall be with *y*.
Ru. 2. 4, the Lord be with *y*.
1 Chr. 22. 18, is not the Lord with *y*.?
2 Chr. 15. 2, the Lord is with *y*., while ye be with him.
Jer. 18. 6, cannot I do with *y*.
42. 11; Hag. 1. 13; 2. 4, for I am with *y*.
Zec. 8. 23, we will go with *y*., God is with *y*.
Mat. 7. 12; Lu. 6. 21, that men should do to *y*.
28. 20, I am with *y*. alway.
Lu. 10. 16, he that heareth *y*. heareth me.
13. 28, and *y*. yourselves thrust out. R. V. omits.
Acts 13. 46, seeing ye put it from *y*.
Rom. 16. 20; 1 Cor. 16. 23; Phil. 4. 23; Col. 4. 18; 1 Thes. 5. 28; 2 Thes. 3. 18; 2 Tim. 4. 15; Tit. 3. 15; Heb. 13. 25; 2 John 3; Rev. 22. 21, grace be with *y*.
1 Cor. 6. 11, such were some of *y*.
2 Cor. 12. 14, I seek not yours, but *y*.
Eph. 2. 1; Col. 2. 13, *y*. hath he quickened.
Col. 1. 27, Christ in *y*.
4. 9, a brother, who is one of *y*.
1 Thes. 5. 12, know them that are over *y*.
1 John 4. 4, greater is he that is in *y*.
See Hag. 1. 4; Mal. 2. 1; 2 Cor. 8. 13; Phil. 3. 1; 1 Pet. 2. 7.
Young. Ex. 23. 26, there shall nothing cast their *y*.
Lev. 22. 28, ye shall not kill it and her *y*. in one day.
Deu. 22. 6, thou shalt not take the dam with the *y*.
28. 50, which will not shew favour to the *y*.
28. 57, her eyes shall be evil toward her *y*. one.
32. 11, as an eagle fluttereth over her *y*.
1 Chr. 22. 5; 29. 1, Solomon my son is *y*.
2 Chr. 13. 7, when Rehoboam was *y*. and tender.
34. 3, while he was yet *y*., he began to seek God.
Job 38. 41, when his *y*. ones cry to God, they wander.
39. 16, the ostrich is hardened against her *y*.
Ps. 37. 25, I have been *y*., and now am old.
78. 71, from following ewes great with *y*. R. V. that give suck.
84. 3, a nest where she may lay her *y*.
147. 9, he giveth food to the *y*. ravens which cry.
Prov. 30. 17, the *y*. eagles shall eat it.
S. of S. 2. 9; 8. 14, my beloved is like a *y*. hart.
Isa. 11. 7, their *y*. shall lie down together.
40. 11, and gently lead those that are with *y*.
Jer. 31. 12, flow together for *y*. of the flock.
Ezek. 17. 4, cropped off his *y*. twigs.
John 21. 18, when *y*. thou girdedst thyself.
Tit. 2. 4, teach the *y*. women to be sober.
See Gen. 33. 13; Isa. 30. 6; Mk. 7. 25; John 12. 14.
Young, exhortations to. Lev. 19. 32; Prov. 1. 8; Eccl. 12. 1.
Christ's pattern. Lu. 2. 46, 51; Tit. 2. 4; 1 Pet. 5. 5.
Younger. Gen. 25. 23, the elder shall serve the *y*.
Job 30. 1, they that are *y*. have me in derision.
Lu. 22. 26, he that is greatest, let him be as the *y*.
1 Tim. 5. 1, intreat the *y*. men as brethren.
1 Pet. 5. 5, ye *y*., submit yourselves to the elder.
See Gen. 29. 18; Lu. 15. 12; 1 Tim. 5. 2, 11.
Youngest. Gen. 42. 13; Jos. 6. 26; 1 Kn. 16. 34.
Yours. 2 Chr. 20. 15; Lu. 6. 20; 1 Cor. 3. 21.
Youth. Gen. 8. 21, imagination is evil from *y*.
46. 34, about cattle from our *y*. till now.
1 Sam. 17. 33, he a man of war from his *y*.
17. 55, whose son is this *y*.?
2 Sam. 19. 7, evil that befell thee from thy *y*.
1 Kn. 18. 12, I fear the Lord from my *y*.
Job 13. 26, to possess the iniquities of my *y*.
20. 11, his bones are full of the sin of his *y*.
29. 4, as in days of my *y*. R. V. ripeness.
30. 12, on my right hand rise the *y*. R. V. rabble.
33. 25, he shall return to the days of his *y*.
36. 14, hypocrites die in *y*.
Ps. 25. 7, remember not the sins of my *y*.
Ps. 71. 5, thou art my trust from my *y*.
71. 17, thou hast taught me from my *y*.
88. 15, ready to die from my *y*. up.
89. 45, the days of his *y*. hast thou shortened.
103. 5, thy *y*. is renewed like the eagle's.
110. 3, the dew of thy *y*.
127. 4, the children of thy *y*.
129. 1, they have afflicted me from my *y*.
144. 12, as plants grown up in *y*.
Prov. 2. 17, forsaketh the guide of her *y*.
5. 18, rejoice with the wife of thy *y*.
Eccl. 11. 9, rejoice, young man, in thy *y*.
11. 10, childhood and *y*. are vanity. R. V. *y*. and prime of life.
12. 1, remember now thy Creator in days of *y*.
Isa. 47. 12, wherein thou hast laboured from thy *y*.
54. 4, forget the shame of thy *y*.
Jer. 2. 2, the kindness of thy *y*.
3. 4, thou art the guide of my *y*.
22. 21, this hath been thy manner from thy *y*.
31. 19, bear the reproach of my *y*.
32. 30, have done evil before me from their *y*.
48. 11, hath been at ease from his *y*.
Lam. 3. 27, it is good that he bear the yoke in his *y*.
Ezek. 4. 14, soul not polluted from *y*.
16. 22, thou hast not remembered the days of thy *y*.
Hos. 2. 15, she shall sing as in the days of her *y*.
Joel 1. 8, lament for husband of her *y*.
Zec. 13. 5, man taught me to keep cattle from my *y*.
Mat. 19. 20; Mk. 10. 20; Lu. 18. 21, have kept from my *y*.
Acts 26. 4, my manner of life from my *y*.
1 Tim. 4. 12, let no man despise thy *y*.
See Prov. 7. 7; Isa. 40. 30; Jer. 3. 24, 25.
Youthful. 2 Tim. 2. 22, flee *y*. lusts.

Zaanaim, zā-ă-nā'-ĭm, 'wanderings'(?). Jud. 4. 11.
Zaanan, zā'-ă-năn, 'place of flocks.' Mic. 1. 11.
Zaanannim, zā-ă-năn'-nĭm, same as ZAANAIM. Jos. 19. 33.
Zaavan, zā'-ă-văn, 'disturbed'(?). Gen. 36. 27.
Zabad, zā'-băd, 'gift.' (1) 1 Chr. 2. 36. (2) 1 Chr. 11. 41. (3) 2 Chr. 24. 26.
Zabbai, zăb-bā'-ī. Ez. 10. 28.
Zabbud, zăb'-bŭd, 'given.' Ez. 8. 14.
Zabdi, zăb'-dī, 'my gift.' Jos. 7. 1.
Zabdiel, zăb'-dĭ-ĕl, 'my gift is God.' 1 Chr. 27. 2.
Zabud, zā'-bŭd, same as ZABBUD. 1 Kn. 4. 5.
Zabulon, ză-bū'-lon, Greek form of ZEBULUN. Mat. 4. 13.
Zaccai, zăc-cā'-ī, 'pure.' Ez. 2. 9.
Zacchæus, zăc-chæ'-ŭs, Greek form of ZACCAI. Lu. 19. 2.
Zacchur, zăc'-chŭr, 'mindful.' 1 Chr. 4. 26.
Zaccur, zăc'-cŭr, same as preceding. Num. 13. 4.
Zachariah, zăch-ă-rī'-ăh, 'Jehovah has remembered.'
(1) last king of Israel of Jehu's race, as foretold by the word of the Lord; begins to reign. 2 Kn. 14. 29.
smitten by Shallum, who succeeds him. 2 Kn. 15. 10.
(2) father of Abi, Hezekiah's mother. 2 Kn. 18. 2. R. V. Zechariah.
Zacharias, zăch-ă-rī'-ăs, Greek form of preceding.
(1) father of John the Baptist, with Elisabeth his wife, accounted righteous before God. Lu. 1. 6.
is promised a son. Lu. 1. 13.
doubting, is stricken with dumbness. Lu. 1. 18, 22.
his recovery and song. Lu. 1. 64, 68.
(2) son of Barachias, slain between the temple and the altar. Mat. 23. 35; Lu. 11. 51. R. V. Zachariah.
Zacher, zā'-chĕr, 'memorial.' 1 Chr. 8. 31. R. V. Zecher.

Zadok, zā'-dŏk, 'righteous.' (1) priest. 2 Sam. 8. 17; 15. 24; 20. 25.
anoints Solomon king. 1 Kn. 1. 39.
(2) others. 2 Kn. 15. 33; Neh. 3. 4; 13. 13.
Zaham, zā'-hăm, 'loathing.' 2 Chr. 11. 19.
Zair, zā'-ĭr, 'small.' 2 Kn. 8. 21.
Zalaph, zā'-lăph, 'wound' (?). Neh. 3. 30.
Zalmon, zăl'-mŏn, 'shady.' (1) 2 Sam. 23. 28. (2) Jud. 9. 48.
Zalmonah, zăl-mō'-năh, same meaning as preceding. Num. 33. 41.
Zalmunna, zăl-mŭn'-nă, 'shelter denied.' Jud. 8. 5.
Zamzummims, zăm-zŭm'-mĭms, giant race destroyed by the Ammonites. Deu. 2. 20, 21.
Zanoah, ză-nō'-ăh, 'marsh' (?). Jos. 15. 34.
Zaphnath - paaneah, zăph'-năth-pā-ă-nē'-ăh, 'preserver of the age' (?). Gen. 41. 45.
Zaphon, zā'-phŏn, 'north.' Jos. 13. 27.
Zara, zâr'-ă, Greek form of ZARAH. Mat. 1. 3.
Zarah, zâr'-ăh, 'sunrise.' Gen. 38. 30. R. V. Zerah.
Zareah, ză-rē'-ăh, 'hornet.' Neh. 11. 29.
Zareathites, ză-rē'-ă-thītes, inhabitants of Zareah. 1 Chr. 2. 53.
Zared, zâr'-ĕd. Num. 21. 12, a brook, the boundary between Edom and Moab. R. V. Zered.
Zarephath, zăr'-ĕ-phăth, 'workshop for refining metals,' also called Sarepta; Elijah there. 1 Kn. 17. 10. *See* ELIJAH.
Zaretan. zăr'-ĕ-tăn, same as ZARTHAN. Jos. 3. 16.
Zareth-shahar, zâr'-ĕth-shā'-här, 'the splendour of the morning.' Jos. 13. 19.
Zarhites, zär'-hītes, persons descended from Zerah. Num. 26. 13.
Zartanah, zär-tā'-năh. 1 Kn. 4. 12.
Zarthan, zär'-thăn, same as ZARETAN. 1 Kn. 7. 46.
Zatthu, zăt'-thū, same as ZATTU. Neh. 10. 14.
Zattu, zăt'-tū. Ez. 2. 8.
Zavan, zā'-văn, same as ZAAVAN. 1 Chr. 1. 42.
Zaza, zā'-ză. 1 Chr. 2. 33.
Zeal. 2 Sam. 21. 2, sought to slay them in his *z*.
2 Kn. 10. 16, come and see my *z*. for the Lord.
Ps. 69. 9; John 2. 17, the *z*. of thine house.
119. 139, my *z*. hath consumed me.
Isa. 9. 7, the *z*. of the Lord will perform this.
59. 17, clad with *z*. as a cloak.
63. 15, where is thy *z*.?
Ezek. 5. 13, I have spoken it in my *z*.
Rom. 10. 2, they have a *z*. of God.
2 Cor. 9. 2, your *z*. hath provoked many.
Phil. 3. 6, concerning *z*., persecuting the church.
Col. 4. 13, he hath a great *z*. for you.
See 2 Kn. 19. 31; Isa. 37. 32.
Zeal. Rom. 12. 11; 2 Cor. 7. 10, 11; Rev. 3. 19.
of Phinehas. Num. 25. 7, 11; Ps. 106. 30.
of Jehu. 2 Kn. 10. 16.
of the Jews. Acts 21. 20; Rom. 10. 2.
of Paul. Acts 22. 3; Gal. 1. 14; Phil. 3. 6.
Christ an example of. Ps. 69. 9; John 2. 17.
Zealots were the party of political resistance to Herod and the Romans. Their fervent nationalism led them to frequent uprisings. Simon Zelotes, one of the apostles, was probably one of them.
Zealous. Num. 25. 11, he was *z*. for my sake. R. V. jealous.
Acts 21. 20, they are all *z*. of the law.
1 Cor. 14. 12, as ye are *z*. of spiritual gifts.
Tit. 2. 14, *z*. of good works.
Rev. 3. 19, be *z*. therefore, and repent.
Zealous of good works. Gal. 4. 18; Tit. 2. 14; Rev. 3. 19.
Zealously. Gal. 4. 18, *z*. affected.
Zebadiah, zĕb-ă-dī'-ăh, 'Jehovah hath given.' (1) a son of Asahel. 1 Chr. 27. 7.
(2) A Levite teacher. 2 Chr. 17. 8.
(3) others. 1 Chr. 8. 15; 12. 7; 26. 2; 2 Chr. 19. 11; Ez. 8. 8; 10. 20.
Zebah, zē'-băh, 'sacrifice;' and Zalmunna. Jud. 8. 5, 21; Ps. 83. 11.
Zebaim, zĕ-bā'-ĭm, same as ZEBOIM. Ez. 2. 57.
Zebedee, zĕb'-ĕ-dēē, Greek form of ZEBADIAH. Mat. 4. 21; Mk. 1. 20.
Zebina, zĕ-bī'-nă, 'bought.' Ez. 10. 43.
Zeboiim, zĕ-boi'-ĭm, same as ZEBOIM. Gen. 14. 2.
Zeboim, zĕ-bō'-ĭm, 'gazelles.' (1) Gen. 10. 19; 14. 2; Deu. 29. 23; Hos. 11. 8. (2) 1 Sam. 13. 18. (3) Neh. 11. 34.
Zebudah, zĕ-bū'-dăh, 'given.' 2 Kn. 23. 36.
Zebul, zē'-bŭl, 'elevation.' Jud. 9. 28.
Zebulonite, zĕ-bū'-lon-īte, a member of the tribe of Zebulun. Jud. 12. 11.
Zebulun, zĕ-bū'-lŭn, 'elevation.' Gen. 30. 20; 35. 23; 49. 13; Num. 1. 30; 26. 26; Deu. 33. 18; Jos. 19. 10; Jud. 4. 6; 5. 14, 18; 6. 35; 2 Chr. 30. 11, 18; Ps. 68. 27; Ezek. 48. 26; Rev. 7. 8.
Christ preaches in the land of (Isa. 9. 1); Mat. 4. 13.
Zebulunites, zĕ-bū'-lŭn-ītes, a less correct way of spelling ZEBULONITES. Num. 26. 27.
Zechariah, zĕch-ă-rī'-ăh, a better way of spelling ZACHARIAH. (1) son of Jehoiada, stoned in the court of the Lord's house. 2 Chr. 24. 20, 21.
(2) son of Jeberechiah. Isa. 8. 2.
(3) the prophet, his exhortations to repentance, his visions and predictions. Zec. 1.–14.
(4) others. 2 Chr. 26. 5; Ez. 8. 16; Neh. 11. 12.
Zedad, zē'-dăd, 'hunting' (?). Num. 34. 8.
Zedekiah, zĕd-ĕ-kī'-ăh, 'justice of Jehovah.' (1) false prophet. 1 Kn. 22. 11; 2 Chr. 18. 10, 23.
(2) another. Jer. 29. 22.
(3) (Mattaniah), king of Judah. 2 Kn. 24. 17; 25.; 2 Chr. 36. 10, 11; Jer. 37.; 38.; 39.; 52.
Zeeb, zēēb, 'wolf.' Jud. 7. 25.
Zelah, zē'-lăh, 'side.' Jos. 18. 28.
Zelek, zē'-lĕk, 'fissure.' 2 Sam. 23. 37.
Zelophehad, zĕ-lŏph'-ĕ-hăd, 'fracture.' Num. 26. 33.
Zelotes, zĕ-lō'-tēs, Greek equivalent of CANAANÆAN, a zealot. Lu. 6. 15.
Zelzah, zĕl'-zăh, 'shade in the heat.' 1 Sam. 10. 2.
Zemaraim, zĕm-ă-rā'-ĭm, 'two fleeces.' (1) Jos. 18. 22. (2) 2 Chr. 13. 4.
Zemarite, zĕm'-ă-rīte. Gen. 10. 18.
Zemira, zĕ-mī'-ră. 1 Chr. 7. 8.
Zenan, zē'-năn, same as ZAANAN. Jos. 15. 37.
Zenas, zē'-năs, contraction of Zenodorus. Tit. 3. 13.
Zephaniah, zĕph-ă-nī'-ăh, 'Jehovah hid.' (1) priest. 2 Kn. 25. 18; Jer. 29. 25; 37. 3.
(2) prophet. Zep. 1.; 2.; 3.
(3) others. 1 Chr. 6. 36; Zec. 6. 10, 14.
Zephath, zē'-phăth, 'watch-tower' (?). Jud. 1. 17.
Zephathah, zĕph'-ă-thăh. 2 Chr. 14. 10.
Zephi, zē'-phī, same as ZEPHO. 1 Chr. 1. 36.
Zepho, zē'-phō, older form of ZEPHI. Gen. 36. 11.
Zephon, zē'-phŏn, 'a looking out.' Num. 26. 15.
Zephonites, zē'-phŏn-ītes, descendants of Zephon. Num. 26. 15.
Zer, zĕr, 'flint' (?). Jos. 19. 35.
Zerah, zē'-räh, 'dawn.' (1) Gen. 38. 30. (2) 1 Chr. 6. 21, 41. (3) 2 Chr. 14. 9.
Zerahiah, zĕr-ă-hī'-ăh, 'Jehovah hath risen.' 1 Chr. 6. 6.
Zered, zē'-rĕd, same as ZARED. Deu. 2. 13.
Zereda, zĕr'-ĕ-dă, 'cool.' 1 Kn. 11. 26.
Zeredathah, zĕr-ĕ-dā'-thăh *or* zĕr-ĕd'-ă-thăh, same meaning as preceding. 2 Chr. 4. 17.
Zererath, zĕr'-ĕ-răth. Jud. 7. 22.
Zeresh, zē'-rĕsh, 'gold.' Esth. 5. 10.
Zereth, zē'-rĕth, 'gold' (?). 1 Chr. 4. 7.
Zeri, zē'-rī, same as IZRI. 1 Chr. 25. 3.
Zeror, zē'-rôr, 'bundle.' 1 Sam. 9. 1.
Zeruah, zĕ-rū'-ăh, 'leprous.' 1 Kn. 11. 26.
Zerubbabel, zĕ-rŭb'-bă-bĕl, 'begotten in Babylon.' (Zorobabel), prince of Judah. Ez. 2. 2.
restores the worship of God. Ez. 3. 1; Neh. 12 47; Hag. 1. 1, 14; 2. 1; Zec. 4. 6.
Zeruiah, zĕr-ū-ī'-ăh. 1 Sam. 26. 6.
Zetham, zē'-thăm, 'olive' (?). 1 Chr. 23. 8.
Zethan, zē'-thăn, same as ZETHAM. 1 Chr. 7. 10.
Zethar, zē'-thär, 'conqueror' (?). Esth. 1. 10.
Zia, zī'-ă, 'motion.' 1 Chr. 5. 13.

Ziba, zī'-bă, 'planter.' 2 Sam. 9. 2.
Zibeon, zĭb'-ĕ-on, 'dyed.' Gen. 36. 2.
Zibia, zī'-bĭ-ă, 'gazelle' (?). 1 Chr. 8. 9.
Zibiah, zī'-bĭ-ăh, same as Zibia. 2 Kn. 12. 1.
Zichri, zĭch'-rī, 'famous.' 2 Chr. 23. 1; 28.
Ziddim, zĭd'-dĭm, 'sides.' Jos. 19. 35.
Zidkijah, zĭd-kī'-jăh, 'justice of Jehovah.' Neh. 10. 1.
Zidon, zī'-dŏn, 'fishing.' The same as Sidon, one of the chief cities of Phœnicia, on the Mediterranean. Gen. 49. 13; Jos. 11. 8; Jud. 10. 6; 18. 7; 1 Kn. 11. 1; Ez. 3. 7; Lu. 4. 26; Acts 12. 20.
prophecies concerning. Isa. 23.; Jer. 25. 22; 27. 3; 47. 4; Ezek. 27. 8; 28. 21; 32. 30; Joel 3. 4; Zec. 9. 2.
Zidonians, zī-dō'-nĭ-ăns, inhabitants of Zidon. Jud. 10. 12; 18. 7; 1 Kn. 11. 1.
Zif, zĭf, 'blossom' (?). 1 Kn. 6. 1. The second month of the Jewish sacred year = May. *See* Months.
Ziha, zī'-hă, 'drought.' Ez. 2. 43.
Ziim, zī'-ĭm. Isa. 13. 21 (marg.).
Ziklag, zĭk'-lăg. Jos. 15. 31; 1 Sam. 27. 6; 30. 1; 2 Sam. 1. 1; 1 Chr. 12. 1.
Zillah, zĭl'-lăh, 'shade.' Gen. 4. 19.
Zilpah, zĭl'-păh, 'dropping.' Gen. 29. 24.
Zilthai, zĭl'-thāi, 'shady.' 1 Chr. 8. 20.
Zimmah, zĭm'-măh, 'planning.' 1 Chr. 6. 20.
Zimran, zĭm'-răn, 'celebrated' or 'pertaining to an antelope.' Gen. 25. 2.
Zimri, zĭm'-rī, same meaning as Zimran. (1) Num. 25. 14.
(2) same as Zabdi. 1 Chr. 2. 6.
(3) 1 Chr. 8. 36; 9. 42.
(4) 1 Kn. 16. 15.
Zin, zĭn, 'thorn;' wilderness of. Num. 13. 21; Jos. 15. 1.
Zina, zī'-nă, same as Zizah. 1 Chr. 23. 10.
Zion, zī'-on, 'sunny.' (*Sion* in N. T.) One of the hills of Jerusalem, on which David's palace was builded.
(mount). 2 Sam. 5. 7; 1 Kn. 8. 1; Rom. 11. 26; Heb. 12. 22; Rev. 14. 1.
Zior, zī'-ôr, 'smallness.' Jos. 15. 54.
Ziph, zĭph, 'flowing.' 1 Chr. 4. 16.
Ziphah, zī'-phăh, feminine of Ziph. 1 Chr. 4. 16.
Ziphims, zĭph'-ĭms, inhabitants of Ziph. Ps. 54., title.
Ziphion, zĭph'-ĭ-on, same as Zephon. Gen. 46. 16.
Ziphites, zĭph'-ītes, same as Ziphims. 1 Sam. 23. 19.
Ziphron, zĭph'-rŏn. Num. 34. 9.
Zippor, zĭp'-pôr, 'bird.' Num. 22. 2.
Zipporah, zĭp'-pō-răh, fem. of Zippor. Ex. 2. 21; 4. 20.
Zithri, zĭth'-rī, 'protection of Jehovah' (?). Ex. 6. 22.
Ziz, zĭz, 'a flower.' 2 Chr. 20. 16.
Ziza, zī'-ză, 'abundance' (?). 1 Chr. 4. 37.
Zizah, zī'-zăh, 'fulness' (?). 1 Chr. 23. 11.
Zoan, zō'-ăn, 'place of departure.' Num. 13. 22; Ps. 78. 12.
Zoar, zō'-är, 'smallness.' The only one of the five 'Cities of the Plain' which escaped the visitation which destroyed the others. Its site has probably been identified about seven miles to the north-east of the Dead Sea, where ruins have been noted by recent travellers. Gen. 13. 10; 14. 2; 19. 22 (Isa. 15. 5); Deu. 34. 3; Jer. 48. 34.
Zoba, zō'-bă, 'a plantation.' 2 Sam. 10. 6.
Zobah, zō'-băh, same as preceding; kings of, subdued. 1 Sam. 14. 47; 2 Sam. 8. 3; 1 Kn. 11. 23.
Zobebah, zō-bē'-băh, 'walking slowly.' 1 Chr. 4. 8.
Zohar, zō' hăr, 'light.' Gen. 23. 8.
Zoheleth, zō'-hĕ-lĕth, 'serpent stone,' or 'stone of the conduit.' 1 Kn. 1. 9.
Zoheth, zō'-hĕth. 1 Chr. 4. 20.
Zophah, zō'-phăh, 'a cruse' (?). 1 Chr. 7. 35.
Zophai, zō'-phāi, 'honeycomb.' 1 Chr. 6. 26.
Zophar, zō'-phär, 'chatterer.' Job 2. 11; 11.; 20.; 42. 9.
Zophim, zō'-phĭm, 'watchers.' Num. 23. 14.
Zorah, zôr'-ăh, 'a hornet;' city of Samson. Jos. 19. 41; Jud. 13. 2, 25; 16. 31.
Zorathites, zôr'-ă-thītes, people of Zorah. 1 Chr. 4. 2.
Zoreah, zôr'-ĕ-ăh, same as Zorah. Jos. 15. 33.
Zorites, zôr'-ītes, same as Zorathites (?). 1 Chr. 2. 54.
Zorobabel, zō-rŏb'-ă-bĕl, Greek form of Zerubbabel. Mat. 1. 12.
Zuar, zū'-ăr, same as Zoar. Num. 1. 8.
Zuph, zŭph. 1 Sam. 1. 1.
Zur, zur, 'rock.' (1) Num. 25. 15. (2) 1 Chr. 8. 30.
Zuriel, zū'-rĭ-ĕl, 'God is my Rock.' Num. 3. 35.
Zurishaddai, zū-rĭ-shăd'-dāi, 'the Almighty is my Rock.' Num. 1. 6.
Zuzims, zū'-zĭms, 'giants.' Gen. 14. 5.

THE NEW OXFORD BIBLE MAPS

1 Jerusalem in Old Testament times
2 Background of the Exodus
3 The United Monarchy
4 The Background of the New Testament: Rome and the East (including Paul's Journeys)
5 Jerusalem in New Testament times

INDEX TO MAPS

NOTES

NOTES

NOTES

NOTES

NOTES

NOTES

NOTES

NOTES

NOTES

NOTES

NOTES

NOTES

NOTES

NOTES

NOTES

NOTES

NOTES

NOTES

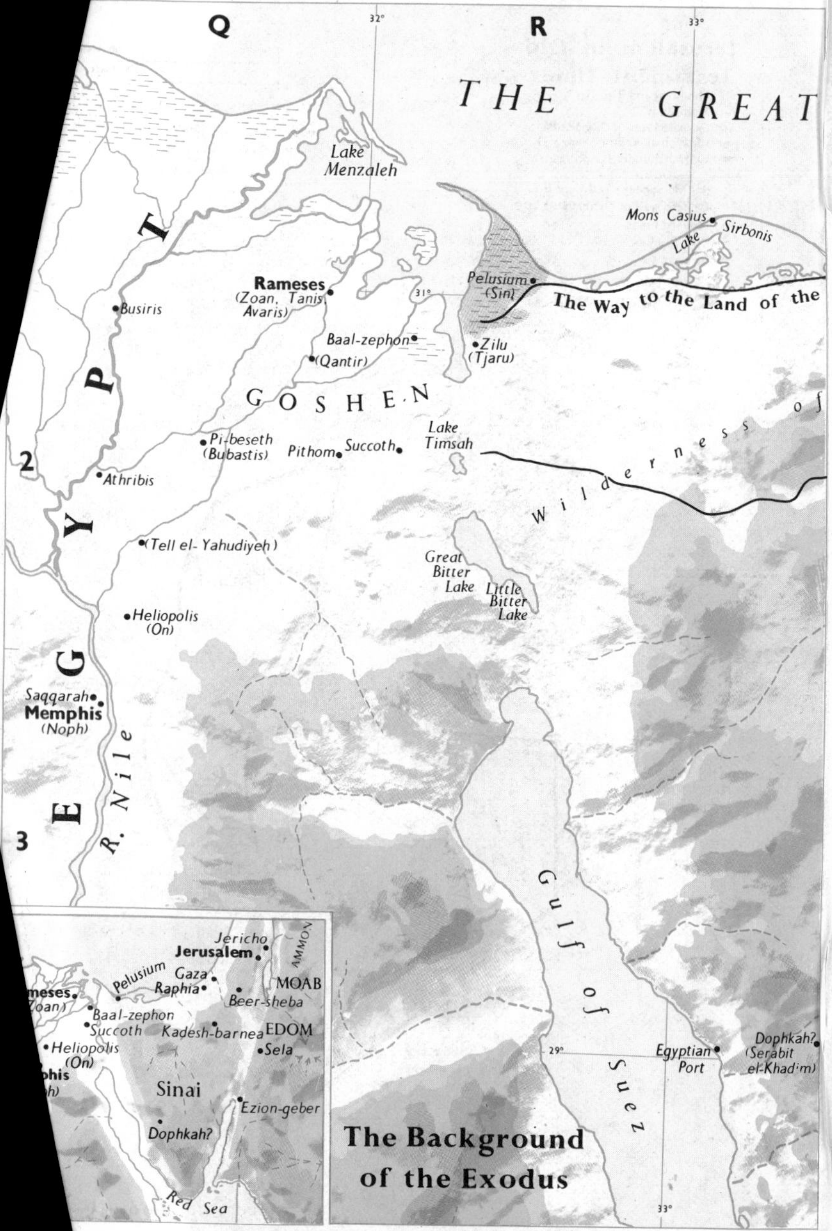

The Background of the Exodus

NOTES

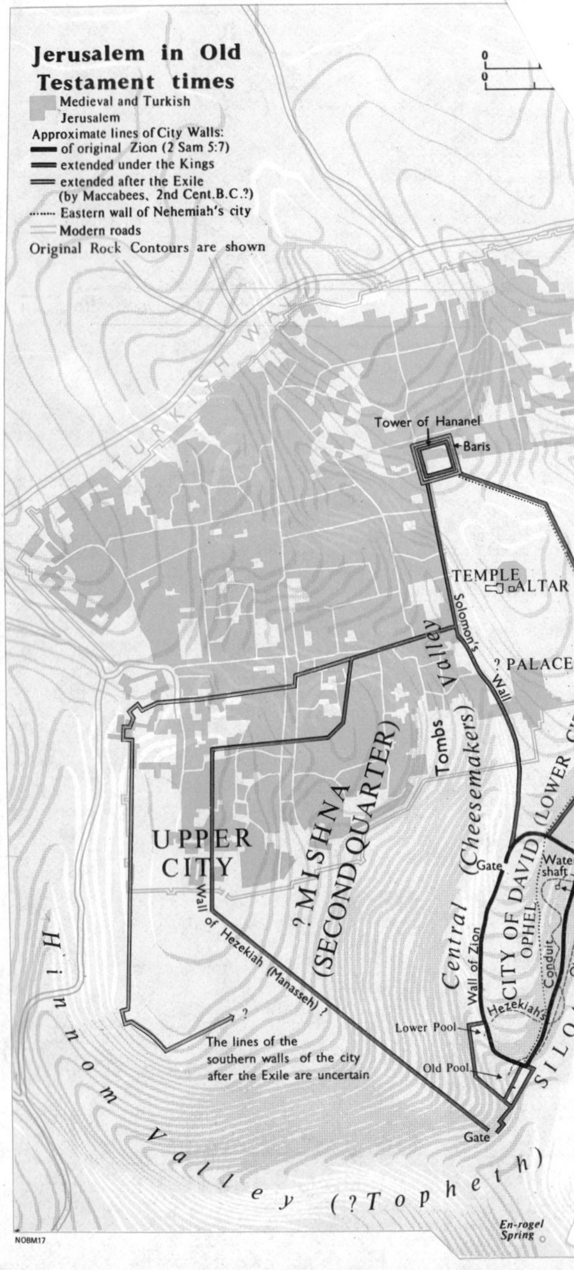
Jerusalem in Old Testament times
Medieval and Turkish Jerusalem
Approximate lines of City Walls:
of original Zion (2 Sam 5:7)
extended under the Kings
extended after the Exile (by Maccabees, 2nd Cent.B.C.?)
Eastern wall of Nehemiah's city
Modern roads
Original Rock Contours are shown
TURKISH WALL
Tower of Hananel
Baris
TEMPLE
ALTAR
Solomon's Wall
? PALACE
Solomon's Wall
(LOWER CITY)
Manasseh's Wall
Tombs
Valley
Central (Cheesemakers)
UPPER CITY
? MISHNA (SECOND QUARTER)
Wall of Hezekiah (Manasseh) ?
Gate
CITY OF DAVID
OPHEL
Water shaft
Gihon Spring
Upper Pool
Old Conduit
Conduit
Hezekiah's
Wall of Zion
Lower Pool
Old Pool
SILOAM
The lines of the southern walls of the city after the Exile are uncertain
Gate
Hinnom Valley (?Topheth)
Kidron Valley
En-rogel Spring
Post-exilic Jewish tombs
Monument of Beni Hezir
Mount of Olives
Pre-exilic Judean tombs
NOBM17

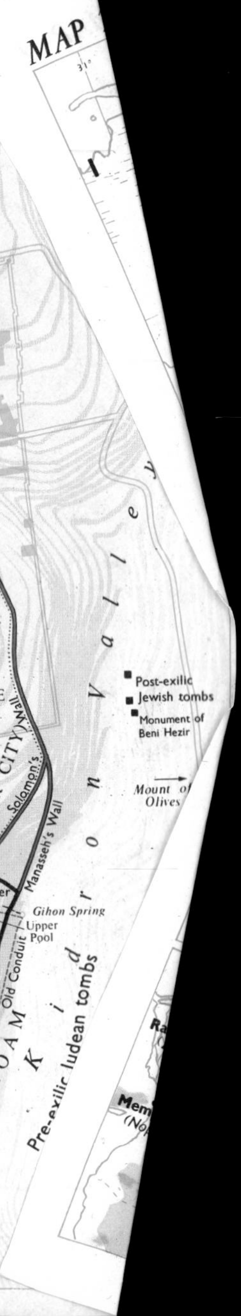
MAP

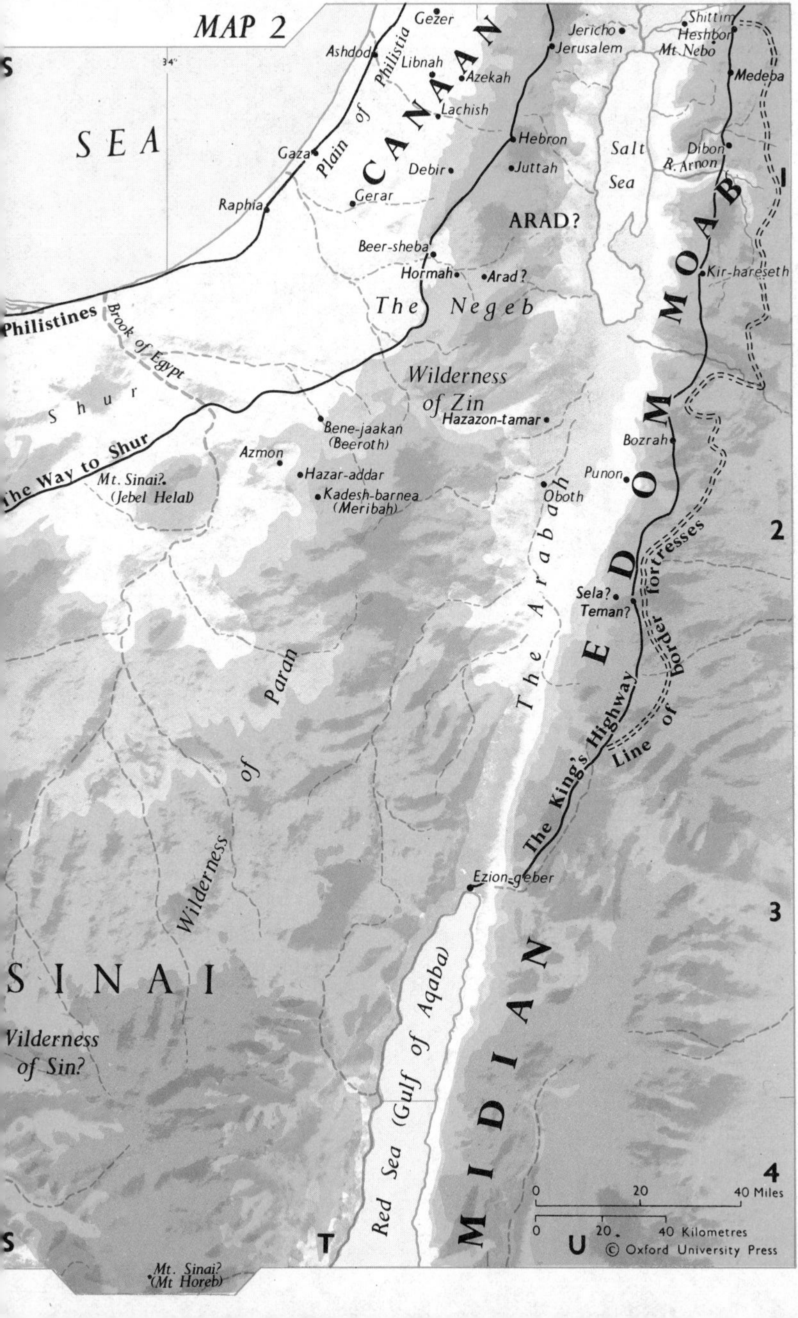
MAP 2
SEA
CANAAN
Plain of Philistia
Gezer
Ashdod
Libnah
Azekah
Lachish
Gaza
Raphia
Gerar
Debir
Hebron
Juttah
Jericho
Jerusalem
Shittim
Heshbon
Mt Nebo
Medeba
Salt Sea
Dibon
R. Arnon
MOAB
ARAD?
Beer-sheba
Hormah
Arad?
Kir-hareseth
The Negeb
Philistines
Brook of Egypt
Shur
The Way to Shur
Wilderness of Zin
Hazazon-tamar
Bene-jaakan (Beeroth)
Azmon
Hazar-addar
Kadesh-barnea (Meribah)
Mt. Sinai? (Jebel Helal)
Bozrah
Punon
Oboth
The Arabah
EDOM
Line of border fortresses
Sela?
Teman?
The King's Highway
Wilderness of Paran
Ezion-geber
SINAI
Wilderness of Sin?
Red Sea (Gulf of Aqaba)
MIDIAN
Mt. Sinai? (Mt Horeb)
34°
2
3
4
S
T
U
0 20 40 Miles
0 20 40 Kilometres
© Oxford University Press

MAP 3

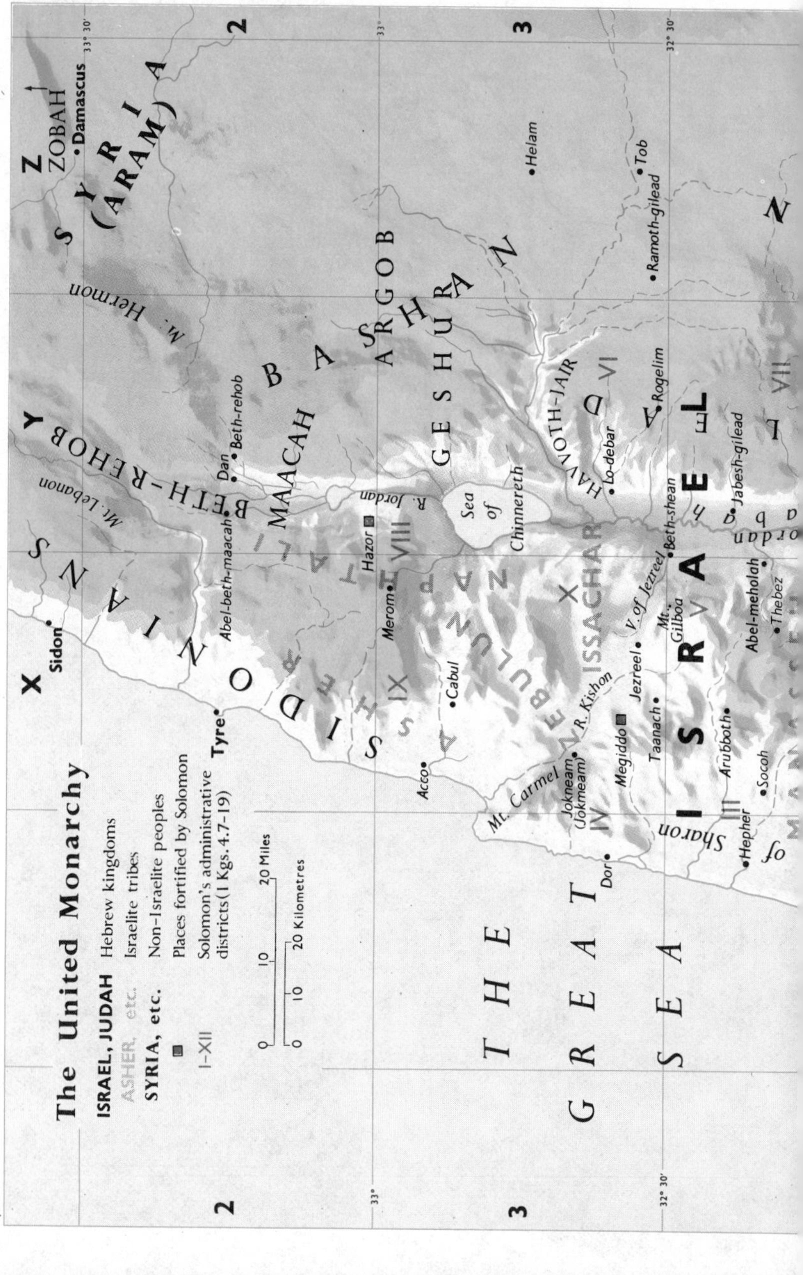

The United Monarchy
ISRAEL, JUDAH Hebrew kingdoms
ASHER, etc. Israelite tribes
SYRIA, etc. Non-Israelite peoples
Places fortified by Solomon
I–XII Solomon's administrative districts (1 Kgs. 4.7–19)
0 10 20 Miles
0 10 20 Kilometres
THE GREAT SEA
SIDONIANS
SYRIA (ARAM)
ZOBAH
Damascus
BETH-REHOB
MAACAH
BASHAN
ARGOB
GESHUR
HAVVOTH-JAIR
ISSACHAR
ZEBULUN
ISRAEL
Sidon
Tyre
Acco
Cabul
Mt. Lebanon
Mt. Hermon
Dan
Beth-rehob
Abel-beth-maacah
Hazor
Merom
R. Jordan
Sea of Chinnereth
Helam
Tob
Ramoth-gilead
Rogelim
Lo-debar
Jabesh-gilead
Beth-shean
V. of Jezreel
Mt. Gilboa
Jezreel
Abel-meholah
Thebez
R. Kishon
Megiddo
Taanach
Jokneam (Jokmeam)
Mt. Carmel
Arubboth
Socoh
Dor
Sharon
Hepher
33° 30′
33°
32° 30′

AMMON
Rabbah
(Rabbath-ammon)
Mahanaim
GI
R. Jabbok
Succoth
Jazer
XII
Heshbon
Medeba
MOAB
Dibon
Aroer
R. Arnon
R. Nahaliel
Kir-hareseth
Brook Zered
EDOM
River
The
Ar
Gilgal
Jericho
Salt Sea
(Sea of the Arabah)
Wilderness of Judah
BENJAMIN
Mt. Ebal
Shechem
Mt. Gerizim
Pirathon
Shiloh
Baal-hazor
Ephraim
EPHRAIM
Bethel
Beeroth
Upper Beth-horon
Geba
XI
Gibeon
Gibeah
Anathoth
Jerusalem
High Place
Kiriath-jearim
Beth-hanan
Lower Beth-horon
Shaalbim
Elon
Zeredah
Gath-rimmon
Plain
Joppa
Gezer
Makaz
Ekron
Sorek
Beth-shemesh
II
Baalath
Bethlehem
Netophah
Tekoa
Giloh
Hebron
Carmel
Arad
Adullam
JUDAH
Debir
Ziklag
Kabzeel
Beer-sheba
Valley of Salt
Tamar
(30° 48'N)
X
Libnah
(Lowland)
The Shephelah
Gath?
Gerar
Ashdod
Ashkelon
Gaza
PHILISTINES
The Negeb
AMALEK
Brook Besor
V
W
X
4
5
6
7
32°
31° 30'
31°
34° 30'
35°
36°
© Oxford University Press

MAP 4

B
C
D
E
3
4
Ariminum
Ancona
Perusia
ITALY
ROME
R. Tiber
Ostia
Antium
Tarracina
Three Taverns
Forum of Appius
(Appii Forum)
Capua
Beneventum
Puteoli
Neapolis
Pompeii
Canusium
Capreae
(Capri)
Paestum
Appian Way
Brundisium
Tarentum
Sybaris
Croton
Panormus
SICILY
Messana
Rhegium
Catana
Syracuse
St. Paul's Bay
Malta
(Melita)
ROMAN EMPIRE
Sea of Adria
Salonae
ILLYRICUM
(DALMATIA)
Sirmium
Singidunum
Viminacium
R. Danube
Oescus
Novae
Istros
Tomi
Odessus
Mesembria
Naissus
MOESIA
Sardica
Scodra
Scupi
Philippopolis
THRACE
Bosphorus
Dyrrhachium
Egnatian Way
Apollonia
MACEDONIA
Philippi
Neapolis
Byzantium
Beroea
Thessalonica
Samothrace
THESSALY
Corcyra
Larissa
Cyzicus
Nicaea
Prusa
Nicopolis
Actium
Troas
(Alexandria)
Assos
Adramyttium
Lesbos
Pergamum
ASIA
Thyatira
Aegean Sea
Corinth
Cenchreae
Athens
Chios
Smyrna
Sardis
Philadelphia
Olympia
ACHAIA
Ephesus
Laodicea
Colossae
Samos
Miletus
Sparta
(Lacedaemon)
Cos
Cnidus
Rhodes
LYCIA
Patara
Myra
CRETE
Phoenix
Lasea
Salmone
Cauda
Fair Havens
Mediterranean Sea
(Mare Internum, Mare Nostrum)
Paul's Journey to Rome
35°
40°
15°
20°
25°
30°
Cyrene
Greater Syrtis
CYRENAICA
AFRICA
LIBYA
Canopus
Alexandria
Naucratis
EGYPT
Oxyrhynchus
Antioch
Iconium
Lystra
Derbe
Attalia
Perga
Antioch
Paphos
Salamis
Paul's 1st Journey
Beroea
Philippi
Neapolis
Thessalonica
Troas
Athens
Cenchreae
Corinth
Ephesus
Antioch
Iconium
Lystra
Derbe
Antioch
Caesarea
Paul's 2nd Journey
Philippi
Troas
Assos
Mitylene
Chios
Ephesus
Corinth
Samos
Miletus
Cos
Rhodes
Patara
Antioch
Tyre
Ptolemais
Caesarea
Jerusalem
Paul's 3rd Journey

The Background of the New Testament

Rome and the East (including St. Paul's Journeys)

MAP 5

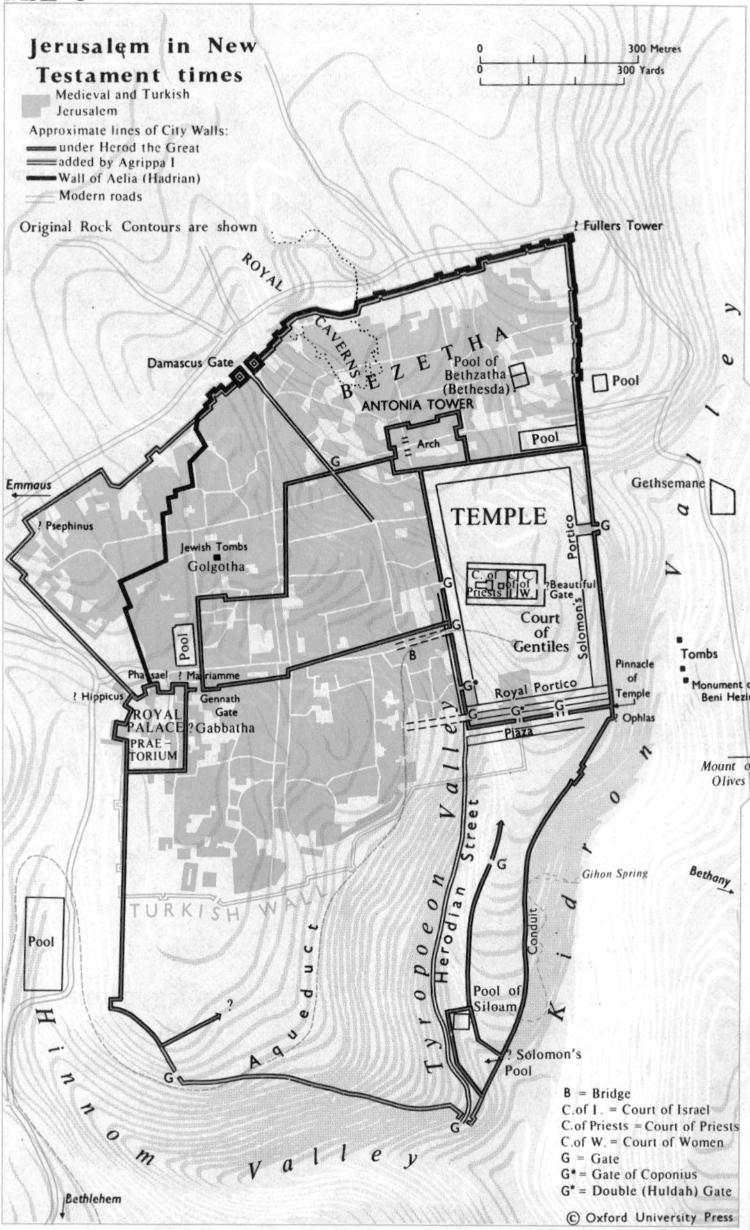
Jerusalem in New Testament times
Medieval and Turkish Jerusalem
Approximate lines of City Walls:
under Herod the Great
added by Agrippa I
Wall of Aelia (Hadrian)
Modern roads
Original Rock Contours are shown
0 300 Metres
0 300 Yards
? Fullers Tower
ROYAL
CAVERNS
BEZETHA
Pool of Bethzatha (Bethesda)
Pool
Damascus Gate
ANTONIA TOWER
Arch
Pool
G
Emmaus
Gethsemane
TEMPLE
Portico
? Psephinus
Jewish Tombs
Golgotha
C. of Priests
C. of I.
C. of W.
?Beautiful Gate
Court of Gentiles
Solomon's
Pool
B
Tombs
Monument of Beni Hezir
Phasael
? Mariamme
? Hippicus
Gennath Gate
ROYAL PALACE
?Gabbatha
PRAETORIUM
Royal Portico
Pinnacle of Temple
? Ophlas
Plaza
Mount of Olives
Tyropoeon Valley
Herodian Street
Kidron Valley
Gihon Spring
Bethany
TURKISH WALL
Aqueduct
Pool
Conduit
Pool of Siloam
?
? Solomon's Pool
Hinnom Valley
B = Bridge
C.of I. = Court of Israel
C.of Priests = Court of Priests
C.of W. = Court of Women
G = Gate
G* = Gate of Coponius
G* = Double (Huldah) Gate
Bethlehem

PRINTED IN ENGLAND BY COOK, HAMMOND & KELL LTD.